BRADF

CROSSWORD
SOLVER'S
POCKET
DICTIONARY

HarperCollins Publishers
Westerhill Road
Bishopbriggs
Glasgow
G64 2QT

Second Edition 2014

© Anne R. Bradford 2008, 2014

Impression 10 9 8 7 6 5 4 3 2 1

The Author hereby asserts her
moral rights to be identified as the
author of this work.

ISBN 978-0-00-753843-0

Collins® is a registered trademark
of HarperCollins Publishers Limited

www.collins.co.uk
www.collinsdictionary.com

A catalogue record for this book is
available from the British Library

Technical support and typesetting
by Thomas Callan

Printed in Great Britain by
Clays Ltd, St Ives plc

Note

MIX
Paper from
responsible sources
FSC
www.fsc.org
FSC® C007454

FSC™ is a non-profit international organisation established to promote
the responsible management of the world's forests. Products carrying the
FSC label are independently certified to assure consumers that they come
from forests that are managed to meet the social, economic and
ecological needs of present and future generations,
and other controlled sources.

Find out more about HarperCollins and the environment at
www.harpercollins.co.uk/green

Author's Preface

Cryptic crosswords are a challenge from the setter to the solver, and it helps to have lateral thinking. Those who enjoy cryptics probably also enjoy riddles and excruciating puns. The word puzzles, particularly acrostics, which were popular even before the advent of the crossword some eighty years ago, were very often in the form of a riddle.

The setter's intent is usually to mislead the solver, so the first step is to try to decide which word or set of words in the clue represent the definition. A verb is often an indicator as to the secondary wordplay, possibly suggesting an anagram or that one part of the solution lies within another. A favourite clue which I encountered many years ago is: *Pineapple rings in syrup (9)*. Here the definition could be either 'pineapple' or 'syrup', but few synonyms for pineapple spring to mind and for the most part they have too few letters. The word 'rings' could be a noun or a verb, and now the penny begins to drop – a word for pineapple surrounds (rings) the word 'in' and eureka! – Grenad-in-e, a syrup.

The *Bradford's Pocket Dictionary* helps, when needed, by giving possible synonyms for nouns, useful for non-cryptic crosswords, too, and also shows when a word may indicate an anagram or some other form of construction. Use it to good effect.

Anne R. Bradford 2014

Solving Crossword Clues

Crossword puzzles tend to be basically 'quick' or 'cryptic'. A 'quick' crossword usually relies on a one- or two-word clue which is a simple definition of the answer required. Many words have different meanings, so that the clue 'ball' could equally well lead to the answer 'sphere', 'orb', or 'dance'. The way to solve 'quick' crosswords is to press on until probable answers begin to interlink, which is a good sign that you are on the right track.

'Cryptic' crosswords are another matter. Here the clue usually consists of a basic definition, given at either the beginning or end of the clue, together with one or more definitions of parts of the answer. Here are some examples taken from all-time favourites recorded over the years:

1. *'Tradesman who bursts into tears'* (**Stationer**)

   Tradesman is a definition of *stationer*. *Bursts* is cleverly used as an indication of an anagram, and *into tears* is an anagram of *stationer*.

2. *'Sunday school tune'* (**Strain**)

   Here *Sunday* is used to define its abbreviation *S*, *school* is a synonym for *train*, and put together they give *strain*, which is a synonym of *tune*.

3. *'Result for everyone when head gets at bottom'* (**Ache**)
   (used as a 'down' clue)

   This is what is known as an '& lit' clue, meaning that the setter has hit on a happy composition which could literally be true. *Everyone* here is a synonym for *each*, move the *head* (first letter) of the word to the *bottom*, and the answer is revealed, the whole clue being the definition of the answer in this case.

4. *'Tin out East'* (**Sen**)

   In this example, *tin*, implying 'money', requires its chemical symbol *Sn* to go *out*(side) *East*, or its abbreviation, *E*, the whole clue being a definition of a currency (*sen*) used in the East.

5. *'Information given to communist in return for sex'* (**Gender**)

   Information can be defined as *gen*; *communist* is almost always *red*, *in return* indicates 'reversed', leading to *gen-der*, a synonym for *sex*.

6. *'Row about no enclosure of this with sardines'* (**Tin-opener**)

   Row is a synonym for *tier*, *about* indicates 'surrounding', *no enclosure* can be *no pen*, leading to *ti-no pen-er*, and another '& lit' clue.

7. *'Cake-sandwiches-meat, at Uncle Sam's party'* (**Clambake**)

   Meat here is *lamb*, *sandwiches* is used as a verb, so we have *C-lamb-ake*, which is a kind of party in America. *Uncle Sam* or *US* is often used to indicate America.

8. *'Initially passionate meeting of boy and girl could result in it'* (**Pregnancy**)

   Initially is usually a sign of a first letter, in this case 'p' for *passionate* + *Reg* (a *boy*) and *Nancy* (a *girl*), and another clever '& lit'.

With 'cryptic' clues the solver needs to try to analyse the parts to see what he or she is looking for – which word or words can be the straight definition, and which refer to the parts or hint at anagrams or other subterfuges. Whilst it would be unrealistic to claim total infallibility, practice has shown that in most crosswords some 90% of the answers are to be found in this work.

Anne R. Bradford

How to Use the Dictionary

This dictionary is the result of over fifty years' analysis of some 300,000 crossword clues, ranging from plain 'quick' crosswords requiring only synonyms to the different level of cryptic puzzles. Therefore the words listed at each entry may be connected to the keyword in various ways, such as:

- a straightforward synonym

- a commonly associated adjective

- an associated or proper noun

- a pun or other devious play on words

Keywords are listed alphabetically; in cases where the heading consists of more than one word, the first of these words is taken to be the keyword, and in cases where the end of a word is bracketed, the material up to the opening bracket is taken to be the keyword. Keywords marked with the symbol ▶ refer the user to other entries where additional information may be found. Keywords marked with the symbol ▷ give leads to anagrams and other ploys used by crossword setters. If the keywords found in the clue do not lead directly to the required answer, the solver should look under words given as cross-references to other entries. These are indicated by the symbol →, with the cross-referenced word shown in capitals.

About the Author

Anne Bradford's love of words began to make itself evident even in her schooldays, when, as Head Girl of her school, she instituted a novel punishment – instead of making rulebreakers write lines, she had them write out pages from a dictionary, on the grounds that this was a more useful exercise. Little did she know this was soon to be her own daily routine!

In time, crosswords became a magnificent obsession for Anne. All lovers of crosswords can understand the irresistible lure of solving them, but Anne's interest went much deeper than most people's, and when she stopped work in 1957 to have her first child, she found herself starting to note down answers to particularly tricky clues as an aid to memory, in case she should come across them again in another puzzle. It was from this simple beginning that this crossword dictionary evolved.

Over the space of 25 years, Anne continued to build on her collection of solutions, analysing every crossword clue as she solved it and adding it to her steadily growing bank of entries. This unique body of material eventually reached such proportions that she had the idea of offering it to her fellow crossword-solvers as a reference book, and since then, the book has gone from strength to strength, providing valuable help to countless cruciverbalists over a number of editions.

Anne Bradford continues to devote time each day to solving crosswords, averaging some 20 a week – both quick and cryptic – and still avidly collects new solutions for her *Crossword Solver's Dictionary* at a rate of around 150 a week, compiling each solution by hand (without the use of a computer!). This latest edition therefore includes much new material, gleaned by a true crossword lover who not only solves crosswords but, as an active member of the Crossword Club, can offer the user an insight into the mind of a cunning crossword compiler.

The Crossword Club

If you are interested in crosswords, you might like to consider joining the Crossword Club. Membership is open to all who enjoy tackling challenging crosswords and who appreciate the finer points of clue-writing and grid-construction. The Club's magazine, Crossword, contains two prize puzzles each month. A sample issue and full details are available on request.

The Crossword Club
Coombe Farm
Awbridge
Romsey, Hants.
SO51 OHN
UK

email: bh@thecrosswordclub.co.uk
website address: www.thecrosswordclub.co.uk

Aa

A, An Ack, Adult, Ae, Alpha, Angstrom, Argon, D, Ein, Her, If, L, One, Per, They

Abandon(ed), Abandonment Abdicate, Abnegate, Abort, Adrift, Aguna(h), Amoral, Apostasy, Back down, Cade, Cancel, Castaway, Chuck, Corrupt, Decommission, Defect, Derelict, → **DESERT**, Desuetude, Dice, Discard, Disown, Dissolute, Disuse, Ditch, Drop, Dump, Elan, Evacuate, Expose, Flagrant, Forhoo(ie), Forhow, Forlend, Forsake, Gomorra, Gretel, Hansel, Immoral, Jack(-in), Jettison, Jilt, Leave, Loose, Louche, Mad, Maroon, Old, Orgiastic, Profligate, Quit, Rakish, Rat, Relinquish, Renounce, Reprobate, Scrap, Shed, Sink, Strand, Vacate, Waive, Wanton, Wild, Yield

Abase Degrade, Demean, Disgrace, Eat crow, Embrute, Grovel, → **HUMBLE**, Kowtow, Lessen

▷ **Abate** *may indicate* a contention

Abate(ment) Allay, Appal, Decrescent, Deduction, Diminish, Lyse, Lysis, Moderate, Reduce, Remit, → **SUBSIDE**

Abbey Abbacy, Ampleforth, Bath, Buckfast, Cloister, Downside, Fonthill, Fountains, Glastonbury, Györ, Je(r)vaulx, Medmenham, Melrose, Minster, Nightmare, Northanger, Priory, Rievaulx, Tintern, Westminster, Whitby, Woburn

Abbot Aelfric, Archimandrite, Brother, Eutyches, Friar

Abbreviate, Abbreviation Abridge, Ampersand, Compendium, Condense, Curtail, → **SHORTEN**, Sigla

Abdicate, Abdication Cede, Disclaim, Disown, Resign

Abdomen Belly, C(o)eliac, Epigastrium, Gaster, Hypochondrium, Opisthosoma, Paunch, Pleon, → **STOMACH**, Tummy, Venter, Ventral

Abduct(ed), Abduction Asport, Enlèvement, Kidnap, Rapt, Ravish, Shanghai, Steal

Abet(tor) Aid, Back, Candle-holder, Second

Abeyance, Abeyant Dormant, Shelved, Sleeping, Store

Abhor(rent) → **DETEST**, → **HATE**, Loathe, Shun

Abide Adhere, Dwell, Inhere, → **LAST**, Lie, Live, Observe, Remain, Stand, Tarry

Ability Acumen, Aptitude, Calibre, Capacity, Cocum, → **COMPETENCE**, Efficacy, ESP, Facility, Faculty, Ingine, Initiative, Instinct, Lights, Potential, Power, Prowess, Savey, Savoir-faire, Savv(e)y, Skill, Talent

Abject Base, Craven, Grovel, Humble, Servile, Slave

Able Ablins, Accomplished, → **ADEPT**, Aiblins, Apt, Capable, → **COMPETENT**, Fere, Fit, Idiot savant, Literate, Proficient, Seaman, Yibbles

Abnormal(ity) Anomalous, Aplasia, Atypical, Autism, → **DEVIANT**, Dysfunction, Ectopic, Erratic, Etypical, Exceptional, Freakish, Hare-lip, Malocclusion, Odd, Peloria, Phenocopy, Preternatural, → **QUEER**, Sport, Teras, Trisome, Unconventional, Unnatural, Varus

Abode Domicile, Dwelling, Habitat, → **HOME**, In(n), Lain, Libken, Limbo, Midgard, Remain, Seat

Abolish, Abolition(ist) Abrogate, Annihilate, Annul, Axe, → **BAN**, D, Delete, Destroy, Eradicate, Erase, Extirpate, John Brown, Nullify, Remove, Repeal, Rescind, Scrap, Tubman, Wilberforce

Abominable, Abominate, Abomination Anathema, Bane, Cursed, → **HATE**, Nefandous, Nefast, Revolting, Snowman, Vile, Yeti

Aboriginal, Aborigine Awakabai, Black-fellow, Boong, Bushman, Devil's Marbles, Dharuk, Dhurga, Dieri, Diyari, Gin, Indigenous, Inuit, Kipper, Lubra, Maori, Mary,

Myall, Negro, Nisga'a, Nyunga(r), Siwash, Vedda(h), Warlpiri, Wemba, Weniba, Wergaia, Wiradhui, Wiradjai, Yagara, Yupik

Abound(ing) Bristle, Copious, Enorm, Flush, Overflow, Rife, Swarm, Teem

About A, Almost, Anent, Around, C, Ca, Cir(c), Circa, Circiter, Concerning, Encompass, Environs, Going, Near, Of, On, Over, Re, Regarding, Soon at

▷ **About** *may indicate* one word around another

Above Abune, Over, Overhead, Overtop, Owre, Sopra, Superior, Supra-, Upon

Abrade, Abrasive Alumina, Carborundum®, Chafe, Emery, Erode, File, Garnet paper, → **GRATE**, Rub, Sand, Scrape

Abreast Afront, Alongside, Au courant, Au fait, Beside, Level, Up

Abridge(ment) Audley, Compress, Condense, Contract, Cut, Digest, Dock, Edit, Epitome, Pot, Shorten, Trim

Abroad Afield, Away, Distant, Elsewhere, Forth, Out, Overseas

▷ **Abroad** *may indicate* an anagram

▷ **Abrupt** *may indicate* a shortened word

Abrupt(ly) Bold, Brusque, Curt, Gruff, Jerky, Offhand, Premorse, Prerupt, Short, Staccato, Terse

Abscond Decamp, Desert, Elope, Escape, Flee, Jump ship, Levant, Run away, Skase, Welch

Absence, Absent(ee), Absent-minded(ness) A, Abs, Abstracted, Away, Distant, Distracted, Distrait, Dreamy, Exeat, Exile, Gone, Hookey, Malingerer, Missing, Mitch, No show, Oblivious, Sabbatical, Scatty, Skip, Truant, Vacuity, Void, Wool-gathering

Absolute(ly) Bang, Complete, Dead, Deep-dyed, Downright, Fairly, Flat, Heartily, Implicit, Ipso facto, Just, Literally, Meer, Mere, Mondo, Nominative, Outright, Plenary, Plumb, Quite, Real, Sheer, Simply, Thorough, Total, Truly, Unadulterated, Unconditional, Unmitigated, Unqualified, Utter, Veritable, Very, Yeah

Absolve, Absolution Assoil, Clear, Exculpate, Excuse, Pardon, Redeem, Shrift, Shrive

Absorb(ed), Absorbent, Absorbing, Absorption Assimilate, Autism, Blot, Consume, Desiccant, Devour, Digest, Dope, Drink, Eat, → **ENGROSS**, Enrapt, Imbibe, Immerse, Ingest, Inhaust, Intent, Merge(r), Occlude, Occupy, Permeable, Porous, Preoccupation, Preoccupied, Rapt, Sorbefacient, Spongy, Subsume, Unputdownable, Yrapt

Abstain(er), Abstemious, Abstention, Abstinence, Abstinent Band of Hope, Celibacy, Chastity, Continent, Desist, Eschew, Fast, Forbear, Forgo, Maigre, Nazarite, Nephalism, Rechab(ite), Refrain, Resist, Sober, Teetotaller, Temperate, TT, Virtue

Abstract(ed), Abstraction Abrege, Abridge, Academic, Appropriate, Brief, Compendium, Deduct, Digest, Discrete, Epitome, Essence, Inconscient, Metaphysical, Musing, Notional, Précis, Preoccupied, Prepossessed, Prescind, Résumé, Reverie, Scatty, Stable, Steal, Subduct, Summary, Tachism

Absurd(ity) Apagoge, Fantastic, Farcical, Folly, Inept, Irrational, Laputan, Ludicrous, Nonsense, Paradox, Preposterous, Ridiculous, Silly, Solecism, Stupid, Toshy

Abundance, Abundant A-gogo, Ample, Aplenty, Bounty, Copious, Corn in Egypt, Cornucopia, Cosmic, Excess, Flood, Flush, Fouth, Fowth, Fruitful, Galore, Lashings, Lavish, Luxuriance, Mickle, Mine, Mint, Muckle, Natural, Oodles, Oodlins, Opulent, Over, Plenitude, Plenteous, → **PLENTIFUL**, Plenty, Pleroma, Plethora, Plurisie, Profusion, Prolific, Relative, Replete, Rich, Rife, Rock and manger, Routh, Rowth, Sonce, Sonse, Store, Stouth and routh, Superabound, Surfeit, Tallents, Teeming, Tons, Uberous

Abuse, Abusive Assail, Becall, Billingsgate, Blackguard, Chemical, Cruelty, Diatribe, Ear-bashing, Flak, Fustilarian, Fustil(l)irian, Hail, Hate mail, Ill-treat, Insolent, Insult, Invective, Jobbery, Limehouse, Malpractice, Maltreat, Miscall, Misuse, Mofo, Molest, Mud, Obloquy, Oppress, Opprobrium, Philippic, Rail, Rampallian, Rate, Rayle, Revile, Satire, Scarab(ee), Scurrilous, Slang, Slate, Sledging, Snash, Solvent, Strap, Tirade, Torture, Verbal, Vilify, Violate, Vituperation, Wosbird

Abut Adjoin, Border, Touch

Academic(ian) A, Della-Cruscan, Don, Erudite, Fellow, Hypothetic(al), Immortals, Literati, Master, Pedantic, PRA, RA, Reader, Rector

Academy, Academic A, Athenaeum, Dollar, Donnish, Forty, Learned, Loretto, Lyceum, Military, Plantilla, RA, St Cyr, Sandhurst, Seminary, Studious, The Shop, West Point

Accelerate, Acceleration, Accelerator Bevatron, Collider, Cyclotron, G, Gal, Grav, Gun, Hasten, Increase, Linac, Linear, Rev, Speed, Stringendo, Supercollider, Synchrotron, Throttle

Accent(ed), Accentuate Acute, Beat, Breve, Brogue, Bur(r), Circumflex, Cut-glass, Doric, Drawl, Enclitic, Enhance, Gammat, Grave, Hacek, Intonation, Kelvinside, Long, Macron, Marcato, Martelé, Mockney, Morningside, Mummerset, Nasal, Orthotone, Oxford, Oxytone, Pitch, Rhotic, Rhythm, Rinforzando, Sforzando, Stress, Tittle, Tone, Twang

Accept(able), Acceptance, Accepted A, Accede, Adequate, Admit, Adopt, Agree, Allow, Alright, Approbate, Bar, Believe, Buy, Can-do, Common, Consent, Cool, Cosher, Decent, Done, Embrace, Going, Grant, Idee recue, Include, Kosher, Meet, Nod, Obey, On, Pocket, Putative, Receive, Resipiscence, Satisfactory, Settle, Stand, Street cred, Suppose, Swallow, Take (on board), Tolerate, U, Valid, Wear, Widespread

Access(ible), Accessibility Avenue, Blue-jacking, Card, Come-at-able, Conditional, Credit, Door, Entrée, →ENTRY, Fit, Gateway, Get-at-able, Ingo, Key, Manhole, Near, Passe-partout, Passkey, Password, Ping, Random, Recourse, Remote, Sequential, Spasm, Telnet, Wayleave

Accessory, Accessories Abettor, Addition, Aide, Ally, Ancillary, Appendage, Appurtenance, Attachment, Attribute, Bandanna, Bells and whistles, Cribellum, Cuff-links, Findings, Staffage, Trappings, Trimming

Accident(al) Adventitious, Arbitrary, Bechance, Blowdown, Blunder, Calamity, →CHANCE, Circumstance, Contingency, Contretemps, Crash, Criticality, Disaster, Double flat, Fall, Fluke, Hap, Hit and run, Inadvertent, Meltdown, Mischance, Mishap, Note, Promiscuous, Random, Rear-ender, Shunt, Smash, Smash-up, Spill, Stramash, Unmeant, Wreck

Acclaim Accolade, Applaud, Brava, Bravo, Cheer, Eclat, Fame, Fanfare, Hail, Kudos, Ovation, Praise, Salute, Zindabad

Acclimatize Attune

Accolade Award, Brace, Dubbing, Honour, Palm, Token

Accommodate, Accommodating, Accommodation Adapt, Almshouse, B and B, Bedsit, Berth, Board, Botel, Bunkhouse, Camp, Chalet, Chambers, Compromise, Crashpad, Flotel, Gaff, Gite, Grace and favour, Homestay, Hostel, Hotel, House, Lend, Loan, Lodge, Lodgement, Minshuku, Motel, →OBLIGE, Parador, Pension, Pliant, Prefab, Quarters, Rapprochement, Recurve, Room, Single-end, Sorehon, Stabling, Stateroom, Steerage, Storage, Tent, Timeshare, Wharepuni

▷ **Accommodating** *may indicate one word inside another*

Accompany(ing), Accompanied (by), Accompaniment, Accompanist Accessory, Alberti, And, Attach, Attend, Chaperone, Chum, Concomitant, Consort, Continuo, Descant, →ESCORT, Fixings, Harmonise, Herewith, Obbligato, Obligate, Obligato, Trimmings, Vamp

Accomplice Abettor, Aide, →ALLY, Bagman, Bonnet, Collaborator, Confederate, Federarie, Federary, Partner, Shill, Stale, Swagsman

Accomplish(ed), Accomplishment Able, →ACHIEVE, Arch, Attain, Clever, Complete, Done, Doss, Effect, Galant, Master, Over, Perform, Polished, Prowess, Put through, Realise, Ripe, Savant

Accord, According(ly), According to After, Agree, Ala, Allow, As per, Attune, Chime, Congree, Consensus, Give, Grant, Harmony, Jibe, Meet, Per, So, Sort, Thus

Accost Abord, Approach, Greet, Hail, Importune, Molest, Solicit, Tackle

Account(s) AC, Appropriation, Audit, Battels, Behalf, Bill, Books, Budget, Cause, Charge, Chequing, Chronicle, Control, Current, Deposit, Discretionary, Enarration,

Expense, Explain, Exposition, ISA, Ledger, Log, Long, Memoir, Narration, Nominal, Procès-verbal, Reason, Recital, Regest, Register, →**REPORT**, Repute, Résumé, Sake, Suspense, Swindlesheet, Tab, Tale, TESSA, Thesis, Version

Accountable Responsible

Accountant Auditor, Bean counter, Bookkeeper, CA, Cost, Liquidator, Reckoner

Accrue Earn, Grow

Accumulate, Accumulation Adsorb, Aggregate, →**AMASS**, Augment, Backlog, Collect, Gather, Hoard, Lodg(e)ment, Oedema, Pile, Pool, Run up, Save, Uplay

Accuracy, Accurate(ly) Bang-on, Cocker, →**CORRECT**, Dead-on, Exact, Fair, Fidelity, Griff, Minute, Precise, Realistic, Right, Spot-on, To scale, True, Unerring, Veracious, Word-perfect

Accusation, Accuse(d) Allege, Arraign, Asperse, Attaint, Bill, Blame, Calumny, Censure, Challenge, Charge, Criminate, Denounce, Dite, Gravamen, Impeach, Incriminate, Indictment, Information, Name, Panel, Plaint, Prosecute, Suspect, Tax, Threap, Threep, Traduce, Wight, Wite, Wyte

Accustom(ed) Acquaint, Attune, Enure, General, Habituate, Harden, Inure, Wont, Woon

Ace(s) Basto, Blackjack, Dinger, →**EXPERT**, Jot, Master, Mega, Mournival, One, Quatorze, Smashing, Spadille, Spadill(i)o, Spot, Tib, Virtuoso, Whizz, Wonderful

Acetylene Ethyne

Ache, Aching Aitch, Die, Hunger, Long, Mulligrubs, Nag, Otalgia, Pain, Sore, Stitch, Stound, Stownd, Work, Yearn, Yen

Achieve(ment) Accomplish, Acquisition, Attain, Big League, Come, Compass, Coup, Cum laude, →**EFFECT**, Enacture, Exploit, Feat, Fulfil, Gain, Hatchment, Masterpiece, Realise, Res gestae, Satisfice, Satisfy, Stroke, Succeed, Threepeat, Triumph, Trock, Troke, Truck

Achilles Heel, Tendon

Acid(ity) Acrimony, Corrosive, Drop, Etchant, Hydroxy, Reaction, Ribosomal, Ribozyme, Sharp, Solvent, Sour, Tart, Vinegar, Vitriol

Acknowledge(ment) Accept, Admit, Agnise, Allow, Answer, Avow, Con, Confess, Grant, Greet, Mea culpa, Nod, Own, Receipt, Recognise, Respect, Righto, Roger, Salute, Ta, Thank you, Touché, Wilco

Acoustic(s) Harmonics, Phenocamptics, Sonics

Acquaint(ance), Acquainted Advise, Cognisant, Enlighten, Familiar, →**INFORM**, Knowledge, Nodding, Notify, Tell, Versed

Acquire, Acquisition, Acquisitive Acquest, Adsorb, Cop, Earn, Ern, Gain, →**GET**, Glom, Irredentist, Land, Learn, Obtain, Procure, Purchase, Rapacity, Secure, Steal, Take-over, Target, Usucap(t)ion

Acquit(tal) Absolve, Assoil, Cleanse, Clear, Exonerate, Free, Loose, Loste, Pardon, Vindicate

Acrid, Acrimony Bitter(ness), Empyreuma, Resentment, Rough, Sour, Surly

Acrobat(s), Acrobatics Equilibrist, Gymnast, Hot dog, Ropedancer, Rope-walker, Splits, Trampoline, Trick cyclist, Tumbler

Across A, Ac, Athwart, Betwixt, O'ed, Opposite, Over, Through

Act(ing), Action, Active, Acts A, Actus reus, Affirmative, Afoot, Antic, Assist, Atonement, Auto, Barnstorm, Barrier, Behave, Business, Camp, Capillary, Caretaker, Case, Caster, Cause, Charade, Class, Conduct, Consolation, COPPA, Deal, Declaratory, →**DEED**, Detinue, Dido, Do, Enabling, Excitement, Exert, Exploit, Factory, Feat, Feign, Forthcoming, Function, Habeas corpus, Homestead, Identic, Impersonate, Impro(visation), Industrial, Juristic, Law, Litigate, Lock-out, Locutionary, Masterstroke, Measure, Method, Mime, Movement, Mutiny, Navigation, Onstage, Overt, Perform(ance), Perlocutionary, Play, Positive, Practice, Pretence, Private, Procedure, Process, Public, Quia timet, Qui tam, Quiver, Reflex, Reform bill, Represent, Rising, Roleplay, Secondary, Septennial, Serve, Settlement, Showdown, Shtick, Sick-out, Simulate, Speech, Sprightly, Suit, Terminer, Test, Theatricise, Transitory, Treat, Truck, Turn, Union, War

Activate Arm, Goad, Spark, Spur, Stur, Styre, Trigger

Active, Activist, Activity A, Agile, Alert, At, Athletic, Brisk, Busy, Cadre, Deedy, DIY, Do(ing), Dynamited, Dynamo, Ecowarrior, Effectual, Energetic, Energic, Erupting, Exercise, Extra-curricular, Floruit, Fluster, Game, Go-go, Goings-on, Hum, Hyper, Leish, Licht, Live, Mobile, Motile, Nimble, Nippy, Ongo, On the go, Op, Operant, Optical, Play, Rambunctious, Residual, Shenanigan, Sideline, Sprightly, Springe, Spry, Sthenic, Stir, Surge, Third house, Vacuum, Voice, Wick, Wimble, Working, Ya(u)ld, Zionist

Actor(s), Actor-like Agent, Alleyn, Artist, Ashe, Barnstormer, Benson, Betterton, Bit player, Burbage, Cast, Character, Company, Diseur, Donat, Gable, Garrick, Gielgud, Guiser, Ham, Hamfatter, Heavy, Histrio(n), Impersonator, Jay, Juve(nile), Kean, Keaton, Luvvie, MacReady, Mime(ster), Mummer, Olivier, O'Toole, Pantomimist, Performer, Player, Playfair, Protagonist, RADA, Roscian, Roscius, Savoyard, Scofield, Sim, Spear-carrier, Stager, Strolling, Super, Theatrical, Thespian, Tragedian, Tree, Tritagonist, Trouper, Understudy, Utility man, Wolfit

Actress Bankhead, Bow, Buffa, Duse, Figurant, Garbo, Harlow, Ingenue, Loren, Pierrette, Siddons, Soubrette, Swanson, Terry, West

Actual(ity), Actually De facto, Entelechy, Literal, Live, Material, Real, Real-life, True, Very

Actuate, Actuator Suppository

Acute Astute, Dire, Fitché, Incisive, →**INTENSE**, Keen, Quick-witted

▶**Ad** *see* **ADVERT(ISE)**

Adage Aphorism, Gnome, Maxim, Motto, Paroemia, Proverb, Saw, Saying, Truism

Adamant Firm, Inexorable, Obdurate, Rigid, Unbending

Add(ed), Addendum, Adder Accrue, Adscititious, Annex, →**APPENDIX**, Attach, Cast, Coopt, Death, Dub, Ech(e), Eik, Eke, Elaborate, Embroider, Enhance, Fortify, Insert, Lace, Reckon, Retrofit, Score, Spike, Sum, Summate, Top up, Tot(e), Total

Addict(ion), Addicted, Addictive Abuser, Acid freak, Acidhead, A colt's tooth, Alcoholic, Blunthead, Buff, Chocoholic, Devotee, Dopehead, Etheromaniac, Fan, Fiend, Freak, Given, Glue-sniffing, Habit-forming, Hophead, Hound, Hype, Jones, Joypopper, Junkie, Mainliner, Mania, Narcotist, Need, Opiate, Opioid, Opium, Pillhead, Pillpopper, Pothead, Shithead, Shooter, Shopaholic, Slave, Snowbird, Space-cadet, Speedfreak, Sybaritism, Theism, User, Wino, Workaholic

Addition(al), Additive Advene, Also, And, Antiknock, Appendage, Carrag(h)anin, Carrageenan, Codicil, Dextran, Encore, Epexegesis, Etc, Extension, →**EXTRA**, Footnote, Increment, Mae, Mo, New, Odd, On, Other, Padding, Plus, PS, Rider, Spare, Suffix, Supplementary, Top-up

Address, Address system Accommodation, →**ATLAS**, Call, Cariad, Chuck, Cousin, Dedication, Delivery, Diatribe, Discourse, Inaugural, IP, Jimmy, Kiddo, Lala, Lecture, Mac, Orate, Past master, Pastoral, Poste-restante, Salute, Sermon, Speech, Squire, Tannoy®, URL, Web, You-all

Adept Able, Adroit, Buff, Dab, Deacon, Don, →**EXPERT**, Fit, Handy, Mahatma, Past master

Adequate Condign, Does, Due, Egal, Equal, Ere-now, Passable, Proper, →**SUFFICIENT**, Tolerable, Valid

Adhere(nt), Adherence, Adhesive Allegiance, Ally, Blutack®, Bond, Burr, Child, Cling, Conform, Dextrin, Disciple, Emplastic, Epoxy, Follower, Glair, Glue, Gum, Jain(a), Loyalist, Mucilage, Nomism, Partisan, Resin, Sectator, Servitor, Stand pat, Sticker, Supporter, Synechia, Votary, Waterglass

Adjacent, Adjoining Bordering, Conterminous, Contiguous, Handy, Neighbouring, Nigh

Adjourn(ment) Abeyance, Delay, →**POSTPONE**, Prorogate, Recess, Rise, Suspend

Adjunct Addition, Aid, Ancillary, Rider

▷**Adjust** *may indicate* an anagram

Adjust(able), Adjustment, Adjuster Accommodate, Adapt, Attune, Coapt, Dress, Ease, Fit, Gang, Gauge, J'adoube, Modify, Modulate, Orientate, Prepare, Primp,

Redo, Reduce, Regulate, Resize, Retrofit, Scantle, Scotopia, Sliding, Suit, Tailor, Temper, Toe-in, Tram, Trim, True, Tune, Tweak

Ad-lib Ex tempore, Improvise, Wing it

Administer, Administration, Administrator Adhibit, Anele, Apply, Arrondissement, Bairiki, Control, Curia, →**DIRECT**, Dispence, Dispense, Executive, Front office, Intendant, Intinction, →**MANAGE**, MBA, Penpusher, Pepys, Regime, Registrar, Run, Secretariat, Steward, Sysop, Trustee

Admirable, Admiration, Admire(d), Admirer Clinker, Clipper, Conquest, Crichton, Esteem, Estimable, →**EXCELLENT**, Fine, Flame, Fureur, Gaze, Gem, Ho, Iconise, Idolater, Laudable, Lionise, Partisan, Rate, Regard, Respect, Ripping, Rocking, Stotter, Toast, Tribute, Venerate, Wonder

Admission, Admit(ting), Admitted, Admittance Accept, Access, Agree, Allow, Avow, Cognovit, Concede, →**CONFESS**, Enter, Entrée, Entry, Estoppel, Give, Grant, Induct, Ingress, Initiate, Intromit, Ordain, Ordination, Owe, Own, Privy, Recognise, Shrift, Take, Tho(ugh), Yield

Admonish, Admonition Caution, Chide, Lecture, Moralise, Rebuke, →**SCOLD**, Tip, Warn

Ado Bother, Bustle, Fuss, Lather

Adolescent Bodgie, Developer, Grower, Halflin, Immature, Juvenile, Neanic, Teenager, Tweenager, Veal, Widgie, Youth

Adopt(ed) Accept, Affiliate, Allonym, Assume, Embrace, Espouse, Father, Foster, Mother

Adoration, Adore(r), Adoring Doat, Dote, Goo-goo, Homage, Love, Pooja(h), Puja, Revere, Venerate, Worship, Zoolater

Adorn(ed), Adornment Aplustre, Attrap, Banderol, Bedeck, Bedight, Begem, Bejewel, Caparison, Clinquant, Deck, Dight, Drape, Embellish, Emblaze, Emblazon, Embroider, Enchase, Equip, Festoon, Flourish, Furnish, Garnish, Grace, Graste, Ornament, Riband, Story, Tattoo, Tatu, Tinsel

Adroit Adept, Clever, Dextrous, Expert, Neat, Skilful

Adulate, Adulation Flatter(y), Praise, →**WORSHIP**

Adult Amadoda, Grown-up, Imago, Man, Mature, Upgrown, X

Advance(d), Advancement A, Abord, Accelerate, Ante, Approach, Ascend, Assert, Better(ment), Breakthrough, Bring on, Charge, Develop, Elevation, Evolué, Extreme, Far, Fast-forward, Fore, Forge, Forward, Further, Get on, Haut(e), Hi-tec(h), Impress, Imprest, Incede, Late, Lend, →**LOAN**, March, Mortgage, Outcome, Overture, Pass, Piaffe, Posit, Postulate, Precocious, Prefer, Prepone, Prest, Process, Progress, →**PROMOTE**, Propose, Propound, Retainer, Ripe, Rise, Sub, Submit, Tiptoe, Top end, Ultramodern, Upfront, Upgang

Advantage(ous) Accrual, Ad, Aid, →**ASSET**, Avail, Batten, Benefit, Bisque, Boot, Bright, Edge, Emolument, Expedient, Exploit, Favour, Fruit, Gain, Grouter, Handicap, Handle, Head-start, Help, Inside (track), Interess, Interest, Lever(age), Mess of pottage, Nonmonetary, Obvention, Odds, One-up, Oneupmanship, Oyster, Percentage, Plus, Privilege, Prize, Pull, Purchase, Salutary, Serviceable, Start, Stead, Strength, Toe-hold, Trump card, Use, Van, Whiphand

Adventure(r), Adventuress, Adventurous Argonaut, Assay, Bandeirante, Buccaneer, Casanova, Conquistador, Dareful, Daring, Emprise, Enterprise, Escapade, Filibuster, Gest, Lark, Mata Hari, Mercenary, Merchant, Picaresque, Picaro, Risk, Routier, Rutter, Swashbuckler, Vamp, Viking, Voyage

Adversary Cope(s)mate, Enemy, Foe, Opponent

Adverse, Adversity Calamity, Cross, Down, Downside, Harrow, Misery, Reversal, Setback, Unfavourable, Woe

Advert(ise), Advertisement, Advertiser, Advertising Above the line, Ad, Allude, Attack, Banner, Bark, Bill, Circular, Classified, Coign(e), Coin, Commercial, Copy, Display, Dodger, Earpiece, Flysheet, Hard sell, Hype, Jingle, Knocking copy, Madison Avenue, Mailshot, Market, Noise, →**NOTICE**, Out, Parade, Personnel, Placard, Playbill, Plug, Proclaim, Promo, Promote, Promulgate, Prospectus, Puff,

Quoin, Refer, Shoutline, Showbill, Skyscraper, Sky-write, Splash, Sponsor, Stunt, Subliminal, Teaser, Throwaway, Tout, Trailer, Trawl, Wrap around

Advice Conseil, Counsel, →**GUIDANCE**, Guideline, Information, Invoice, Opinion, Read, Recommendation, Re(e)de, Reed, Tip (off)

Advise(d), Adviser, Advisable Acquaint, Assessor, Avise(ment), Back-seat driver, Brains trust, CAB, Consultant, Cornerman, Counsel, Enlighten, Expedient, Inform, Instruct, Mentor, Oracle, Peritus, Prudent, Ralph, →**RECOMMEND**, Starets, Staretz, Tutor, Urge, Wise

Advocate(d) Agent, Argue, Attorney, Back, Devil's, Endorse, Exponent, Gospel, Intercede, Lawyer, Move, Paraclete, Peat, Peddle, Pleader, Pragmatist, Preach, Proponent, Silk, Statist, Syndic, Urge

Aeon Hadean, Phanerozoic

Aerial Antenna, Clover leaf, Communal, Dipole, Directional, Dish, Ethereal, Loop, Minidish, Parabolic

Aerodrome →**AIRPORT**, Landing field, Rotor-station

Aerodynamics Slipstream

Aerofoil Spoiler, Trimtab

▶ **Aeroplane** *see* **AIRCRAFT**

Affable, Affability Amiable, Avuncular, Benign, Bonhomie, Cordial, Gracious, Hearty, Suave, Urbane

Affair(s) Amour, Business, Concern, Current, Event, Fight, Fling, Go, Intrigue, Liaison, Matter, Pash, Pidgin, Pi(d)geon, Ploy, Relationship, Res, Romance, Shebang, Subject, Thing

Affect(ed), Affectation, Affection(ate), Affecting Air, Alter, Arty, Breast, Camp, Chi-chi, Concern, Cordial, Crachach, Crazy, Distress, Effete, Endearment, Euphuism, Foppery, Frappant, Grip, Heartstrings, High-sounding, Hit, Ladida, Lovey-dovey, Mimmick, Minnick, Minnock, Mouth-made, Mwah, Phoney, →**POSE**, Poseur, Precieuse, Preciosity, Pretence, Spoilt, Stag(e)y, Storge, Stricken, Strike, Supervene, Susceptible, Sway, Tender, Topophilia, Touched, Touchy-feely, Twee, Unction, Unnatural, Warm, Yah

Affiliate, Affiliation Adopt, Associate, Merge, Unite

Affinity Bro, Kin(ship), Penchant, Rapport, Tie

Affirm(ative), Affirmation Assert, Attest, Avow, Maintain, Positive, Predicate, Profess, Protestation, State, Uh-huh, →**VERIFY**

Afflict(ed), Affliction Aggrieve, Asthma, Cross, Cup, Curse, Dead leg, Disease, Furnace, Harass, Hurt, Lacerate, Lumbago, Molest, Nosology, Palsy, Persecute, Pester, Plague, Scourge, Smit, Sore, →**SORROW**, Stricken, Teen, Tene, Tic, Tine, Tribulation, →**TROUBLE**, Try, Unweal, Visitation, Woe

Affluence, Affluent Abundance, Ease, Fortune, Grey panther, Inflow, Opulence, Upmarket, Wealth

Afford Bear, Manage, Offer, Provide, Run to, Spare

Affront Assault, Defy, Facer, →**INSULT**, →**OFFEND**, Outrage, Scandal, Slight, Slur

Afraid Adrad, Alarmed, Chicken, Fearful, Funk, Nesh, Rad, Regretful, Scared, Timorous, Windy, Yellow

Afresh De novo

Africa(n) Abyssinian, Adamawa, Akan, Algerian, Amakwerekwere, Angolan, Ashanti, Baganda, Bambara, Bantu, Barbary, Barotse, Basotho, Basuto, Bechuana, Beento, Bemba, Beninese, Berber, Biafran, Bintu, Black, Boer, Botswana(n), Bushman, Caffre, Cairene, Carthaginian, Chewa, Chichewa, Ciskei, Congo(l)ese, Cushitic, Dagomba, Damara, Dark continent, Dinka, Duala, Dyula, Efik, Eritrean, Ethiopian, Fang, Fantee, Fanti, Fingo, Flytaal, Fula(h), Gabonese, Galla, Gambian, Ganda, Gazankulu, Grikwa, Griqua, Guinean, Gullah, Hamite, Hausa, Herero, Hottentot, Hutu, Ibibio, Ibo, Igbo, Impi, Ivorian, Kabyle, Kaf(f)ir, Kenyan, Khoikhoi, Khoisan, Kikuyu, Kongo, Lango, Lesotho, Liberian, Libyan, Lowveld, Lozi, Luba, Luo, Maghreb, Maghrib, Malagasy, Malawi, Malian, Malinke, Mande, Mandingo, Mandinka, Masai, Mashona, Matabele, Mende, Moor, Moroccan, Mossi, Mozambican, Mswahili, Munt(u), Mzee, Nama(qua), Namibian, Ndebele, Negrillo, Ngoni, Nguni, Nilot(e), Nubian, Nuer, Numidian,

Nyanja, Oromo, Ovambo, Pedi, Pied noir, Pondo, Qwaqwa, Rastafarian, Rhodesian, Rwandan, Sahelian, San, Senegalese, Shilluk, Shluh, Shona, Somali, Songhai, Songhay, Sotho, Soweto, Sudanese, Susu, Swahili, Swazi, Tanzanian, Temne, Tiv, Togolese, Tonga, Transkei, Transvaal, Tshi, Tsonga, Tswana, Tuareg, Tutsi, Twi, Ugandan, Uhuru, Venda, Voltaic, Waswahili, Watu(t)si, Wolof, X(h)osa, Yoruban, Zairean, Zulu

After(wards) About, At, Behind, Beyond, Eft, Epi-, → **LATER**, On, Past, Post hoc, Rear, Since, Sine, Subsequent, Syne

Afterimage Photogene

▷ **After injury** *may indicate* an anagram

Afterlife Other world, The Great Beyond

Afternoon A, Arvo, Ex-am, PM, Postmeridian, Undern

Afterpiece, Afterthought Addendum, Codicil, Epimetheus, Exode, Footnote, Note, PS, Supplement

Aftertaste T(w)ang

Again Afresh, Agen, Ancora, Anew, Back, Bis, De novo, Ditto, Do, Eft, Eftsoons, Encore, Iterum, More, Moreover, O(v)er, Re-, Recurrence, Reprise, Than, Then

Against A, Anti, Beside, Con, Counter, For, Gainsayer, Into, Nigh, On, One-to-one, Opposing, To, V, Versus

Age(d), Ages, Aging Absolute, Ae, Aeon, Antique, Bronze, Chair-days, Chellean, Cycle, Dark, Date, Discretion, Distress, Eon, Epact, Epoch(a), Era, Eternity, Generation, Golden, Heroic, Ice, Iron, Jurassic, Kalpa, Mature, Mesolithic, Middle, Millennium, Neolithic, New, Paleolithic, Period, Radiometric, Senescence, Senility, Space, Stone, Wrinkly

Ageless Evergreen

Agency, Agent Alkylating, Ambassador, Antistatic, Autolysin, Bailiff, Bargaining, Bicarb(onate), Broker, Bureau, Catalyst, Cat's paw, Chelating, Child support, Commission, Complexone, Confidential, Consul, Consular, Counter, Countryside, Crown, Dating, Defoaming, Developing, Dicumaral, Disclosing, Distributor, Doer, Double, Emissary, Envoy, -er, Escort, Estate, Exciseman, Executant, Executor, Factor, Forwarding, Free, Galactagogue, G-man, Go-between, Good offices, Hand, House, Implement, Indian, Influence, Instrument, Intermediary, Itar Tass, Law, Leavening, Legate, Literary, Magic bullet, Masking, Means, Medium, Melanin, Mercantile, Mitogen, Mole, Moral, Narco, Nerve, Nucleating, OO, Operation, Orange, Oxidizing, Parliamentaire, Parliamentary, Patent, Pathogen, Pawn, Peace corps, Penetration, Pinkerton, Press, Proxy, Realtor, Reducing, Rep(resentative), Reuters, Riot, Road, Runner, Salesman, Secret (service), Shipping, Ship's husband, SIS, Solvent, Soman, Spook, Spy, Stock, Surfactant, Tass, Third party, Ticket, Tiger team, Training, Travel, UNESCO, Virino, Voice, Welfare, Wetting, Wire service

Agenda Business, Order paper, Programme, Remit, Schedule

Aggravate Annoy, Exacerbate, Exasperate, Inflame, Irk, Needle, Nettle, Provoke, Rankle, Try, Vex

Aggression, Aggressive(ly), Aggressor, Aggro Anti-Imperialism, Attack, Ballbreaker, Bare-knuckle, Bellicose, Belligerent, Biffo, Bovver, Bullish, Butch, Defiant, Enemy, Feisty, Foe, Go-getter, Gungho, Hard-hitting, Hawk, Invader, Laddish, Lairy, Macho, Militant, Nasty, On-setter, Pushing, Rambo, Rampant, Sabre-rattling, Shirty, Tooth and nail, Truculent, Wild

Aggrieve(d) Sore

Agile Acrobatic, Deft, Lissom(e), Nifty, Nimble, Quick, Spry, Supple, Swank, Twinkletoes, Wiry

▷ **Agitate** *may indicate* an anagram

Agitate(d), Agitation, Agitator Acathisia, Activist, Ado, Agitprop, Akathisia, Alarm, Boil, Bolshie, Bother, Churn, Commotion, Convulse, Distraught, → **DISTURB**, Ebullient, Emotion, Euoi, Euouae, Evovae, Excite, Extremist, Fan, Ferment, Firebrand, Flap, Fluster, Frenzy, Fuss, Fusspot, Goad, Heat, Hectic, Impatience, Khilafat, Lather, Militant, Overwrought, Perturb, Pother, Protest, Rabble-rouser, Rattle, Restless,

Rouse, Ruffle, Seethed, Shake, Stir(-up), Tailspin, Tempest, Tizzy, Toss, Tremor, Trouble, Turmoil, Twitchy, Twittery, Unrest, Welter, Whisk

Agonise, Agony Ache, Anguish, Ecstasy, Heartache, → PAIN, Torment, Torture

Agree(ing), Agreed, Agreement Accede, Accept, Accord, Acquiescence, Adhere, Agt, Aline, Allow, Amen, Analogy, Assent, Ausgleich, Aye, Camp David, Cartel, Charterparty, Chime, Coincide, Collective, Compact, Comply, Concert, Concord(at), Concur, Condone, Conform, → CONSENT, Consist, Contract, Convention, Correspond, Covenant, Covin, Covyne, Cushty, Deal, Deffo, Embrace, Entente, Equate, Finalise, Gentleman's, Harmony, Homologous, Knock-for-knock, League, Like-minded, Munich, National, Nod, Nudum pactum, Okay, On, Pact(um), Pair, Plant, Plea bargaining, Prenuptial, Procedural, Productivity, Protocol, Recognise, Repo, Repurchase, Right(o), Roger, Sanction, Service, Settlement, Side, Square, Standstill, Substantive, Suit, Sympathy, Synastry, Sync(hronise), Tally, Technology, Trade, Treaty, Trucial, Union, Unison, Unity, Wilco, Wukkas, Yalta, Yea, Yea-say, Yes

Agreeable Amene, Harmonious, Pleasant, Sapid, Sweet, Well-disposed, Willing, Winsome

▷ **Ague(ish)** *may indicate* an anagram

Ahead Anterior, Before, Foreship, Forward, Frontwards, Onward, Precocious, Up

Aid(s), Aide Accessory, ADC, Adjutant, Artificial, Assist, Audiovisual, Audiphone, Decca, → DEPUTY, Galloper, Gift, Grant, Help(line), Key, Legal, Lend-lease, Life-saver, Monitor, Optophone, PA, Relief, Satnav, Seamark, Serve, Sex, Sherpa, Succour, Support, Visual, Zimmer®

AIDS Slim

Ail(ment) Affect, Afflict(ion), Complaint, Croup, Disease, Disorder, Malady, Misorder, Narks, Occupational, Pink-eye, Pip, Sickness, Suffer, TB

Aim Approach, Aspire, Bead, Bend, End, Ettle, Eye, Goal, Hub, Intent, Level, Mark, Mint, Mission, Object, Peg, Plan, Plank, Point, Point blank, Purpose, Quest, Reason, Sake, Seek, Sight(s), Target, Tee, Telos, Train, Try, View, Visie, Vizy, Vizzie

Aimless Drifting, Erratic, Haphazard, Random, Unmotivated

Air(s), Airer, Air-space, Airy Affectation, Ambience, Anthem, Appearance, Arioso, Atmosphere, Attitude, Aura, Bearing, Breath, Ether(eal), Expose, Heat-island, Inflate, Lift, Lullaby, Madrigal, Manner, Melody, Microburst, Mien, Night, Ozone, Parade, Poseur, Screen, Serenade, Shanty, Sinus, Tidal, → TUNE, Ventilate, Wind

Air Chief Marshal Dowding

Aircraft, Airship Aerodyne, Aerostat, Angels, AST, Auster, Autoflare, Autogiro, Autogyro, Aviette, Avion, Biplane, Blimp, Brabazon, Bronco, Camel, Canard, Canberra, Chaser, Chopper, Coleopter, Comet, Concorde, Convertiplane, Corsair, Crate, Cropduster, Cyclogiro, Delta-wing, Dirigible, Dive-bomber, Doodlebug, Drone, Eagle, Enola Gay, Eurofighter, F, Ferret, Fixed-wing, Flivver, Flying fortress, Flying wing, Fokker, Freedom-fighter, Freighter, Galaxy, Glider, Gotha, Gyrodyne, Gyroplane, Hang-glider, Harrier, Hawkeeze, Heinkel, Helicopter, Helo, Hercules, Hunter, Hurricane, Interceptor, Intruder, Jet star, Jumbo, Jump-jet, Kite, Lancaster, Liberator, Lifting-body, Lysander, Messerschmitt, Microjet, Microlight, Microlite, MIG, Mirage, Monoplane, Mosquito, Moth, Multiplane, Nightfighter, Nightfinder, Nimrod, Oerlikon, Orion, Ornithopter, Orthopter, Parasol, Penguin, Phantom, → PLANE, Provider, Prowler, Pusher, Ramjet, Rigid, Rotaplane, Runabout, Scout, Scramjet, Semi-rigid, Skiplane, Skyhawk, Sopwith, Sopwith Camel, Spitfire, SST, Stack, Starfighter, Starlifter, Stealth bomber, STOL, Stratocruiser, Stratotanker, Stuka, Super Sabre, Sweptwing, Swing-wing, Tankbuster, Taube, Taxiplane, Thunderbolt, Thunderchief, Tomcat, Tornado, Torpedo bomber, Towplane, Tracker, Trident, Tri-jet, Triplane, Turbofan, Turbo-jet, Turbo-prop, Turboramjet, Variable geometry, Vessel, Vigilante, Viking, Viscount, Vomit comet, Voodoo, VTOL, War bird, Widebody, Wild weasel, Zeppelin

Aircraftsman, Airman AC, Aeronaut, AR, Bleriot, Co-pilot, Kiwi, LAC, Observer, RAF

Airless Close, Stuffy

Airline, Airway Aeroflot, Anthem, BAC, BEA, Bronchus, Duct, El Al, JAL, Larynx, Lot, Purple, SAS, S(ch)norkel, TWA, Upcast, Vent, Weasand(-pipe), Windpipe

▶**Airman** *see* AIRCRAFTSMAN; FLIER

Airport Chiang Kai Shek, Drome, Entebbe, Faro, Gander, Gatwick, Heliport, Idlewild, John Lennon, Kennedy, La Guardia, Landing strip, Le Bourget, Lod, Luton, Lympne, O'Hare, Orly, Runway, Shannon, Stansted, Stolport, Terminal, Vertiport, Wick

Air-tight Hermetic, Indisputable, Sealed

Ajar Agee

Akin Alike, Cognate, Congener, Kindred, Sib

Alabaster Oriental

Alarm(ed), Alarming Affright, Agitation, Alert, Arouse, Bell, Bleep, Bugaboo, Caution, Dismay, False, Flap, Fricht, Fright, Frit, Ghast, Hairy, Larum, Panic, Perturb, Radio, Rouse, Siren, Smoke, Startle, Tirrit, Tocsin, Unease, Warn, Yike(s)

Alas Ah, Alack, Ay, Eheu, Ha, Haro, Harrow, Io, Lackadaisy, Lackaday, O, Oh, Ohone, O me, Waesucks, Waly, Wel(l)away, Well-a-day, Wellanear, Woe

Alb Sticharion

Albatross Alcatras, Black-footed, Golf, Gooney(-bird), Millstone, Omen, Onus, Quaker-bird

Albion Perfidious

Alchemic, Alchemist, Alchemy Adept, Arch-chimic, Brimstone, Cagliostro, Faust(us), Hermetic(s), Multiplier, Quicksilver, Sal ammoniac, Sorcery, Spagyric, Spagyrist, Witchcraft

Alcohol(ic) Acrolein, Aldehyde, Bibulous, Blue ruin, Booze, Borneol, Catechol, Cetyl, Chaptalise, Cholesterol, Choline, Citronellol, Cresol, Diol, Dipsomaniac, Drinker, Ethal, Ethanol, Ethyl, Farnesol, Firewater, Fusel-oil, Geraniol, Glycerin(e), Grain, Grog, Gut-rot, Hard, Inebriate, Inositol, Isopropyl, Jakey, Lauryl, Linalool, Malt, Mannite, Mannitol, Mercaptan, Mescal, Mescalin(e), Methanol, Meths, Nerol, Phytol, Pisco, Polyol, Potato spirit, Propyl, Pyroligneous, Rotgut, Rubbing, Scrumpy, Sorbitol, Sphingosine, Spirits, Sterol, Taplash, Thiol, Wash, White lightning, Wino, Witblits, Xylitol

Alcove Apse, Bay, Bole, Dinette, Niche, Nook, Recess, Reveal

Ale, Alehouse Audit, Barleybree, Barley-broo, Barley-broth, Beer, Brown, Bummock, CAMRA, Feast, Humming, Humpty-dumpty, Keg, Lager, Lamb's wool, Light, Mild, Morocco, Nappy, Nog, Nogg, October, Porter, Purl, Real, Stout, Swats, Tiddleywink, Tipper, Whitsun, Wort, Yard, Yill

Alert Agog, Amber, Arrect, Astir, Attentive, Aware, Conscious, Gleg, Gogo, Intelligent, Presential, Qui vive, Red, Scramble, Sharp, Sprack, Sprag, Stand-to, Tentie, Up and coming, Vigilant, Volable, Wary, Watchful, Yellow

Alga(e) Anabaena, Blanketweed, Chlorella, Chlorophyte, Conferva, Desmid, Diatom, Dulse, Heterocontae, Isokont, Jelly, Nostoc, Pleuston, Pond scum, Prokaryon, Protococcus, Rhodophyte, Seaweed, Spirogyra, Star-jelly, Stonewort, Ulothrix, Ulotrichales, Valonia, Volvox, Yellow-green, Zooxanthella

Algebra Boolean, Linear, Quadratics

Algonquin Innu, Wampanoag

Alias Aka, Byname, Epithet, Moni(c)ker, Nick(name), Pen-name, Pseudonym

Alibi Excuse, Watertight

Alien(ate), Alienation A-effect, Amortise, Devest, Disaffect, Ecstasy, Erotic, Estrange, ET, Exotic, External, Foreign, Hostile, Little green man, Martian, Metic, Outlandish, Philistine, Repugnant, Strange(r)

Alight Alowe, Avail(e), Avale, Detrain, Disembark, Dismount, Flambe, In, Lambent, Land, Lit, Perch, Pitch, Rest, Settle

Align Arrange, Associate, Collimate, Dress, Juxtapose, Marshal, Orient, Synchronize

▶**Alike** *see* LIKE(NESS)

Alimentary Oesophagus, Pharynx

Alive Alert, Animated, Breathing, Extant, Quick, Teeming

Alkali(ne), Alkaloid Antacid, Apomorphine, Base, Bebeerine, Berberine, Betaine,

Borax, Brak, Brucine, Caffein(e), Capsaicin, Chaconine, Codeine, Colchicine, Curarine, Emetin(e), Ephedrine, Ergotamine, Gelsemin(in)e, Guanidine, Harmalin(e), Harmin(e), Hydrastine, Hyoscine, Hyoscyamine, Ibogaine, Kali, Limewater, Lobeline, Lye, Narceen, Narceine, Nicotine, Papaverine, Physostigmine, Piperine, Potash, Quinine, Reserpine, Rhoeadine, Scopaline, Scopolamine, Soda, Sparteine, Stramonium, Thebaine, Theine, Theobromine, Theophylline, Totaquine, Tropine, Tubocurarine, Veratrin(e), Vinblastine, Vincristine, White, Yohimbine

All A, En bloc, → **ENTIRE**, Entity, Every man Jack, Finis, Omni, Pan, Quite, Sum, → **TOTAL**, Toto, Tutti, Whole

All at once Holus-bolus, Per saltum, Suddenly

Allay Calm, Lessen, Quieten, Soothe

Allegation, Allege(d) Assert, Aver, Claim, Mud, Obtend, Plead, Purport, Represent, Smear, So-called

Allegiance Faith, Foy, Loyalty, Tribalism

Allegory, Allegorical Apologue, Fable, Mystic, Myth, Parable

Alleviate Alleg(g)e, Calm, Mitigate, Mollify, Palliate, → **RELIEVE**, Temper

Alley Aisle, Blind, Bonce, Bowling, Corridor, Ginnel, Lane, Laura, Marble, Passage, Rope-walk, Tin Pan, Vennel, Walk, Wynd

Alliance Agnation, Axis, Bloc, Cartel, Coalition, Combine, Compact, Entente, Federacy, → **LEAGUE**, Marriage, NATO, Syndicate, Union

Alligator Al(l)igarta, Avocado, Caiman, Cayman

Allocate, Allocation Allot, Apportion(ment), Distribute, Earmark, Placement, Ration, Share, Soum, Zone

Allotment, Allowance, Allowed, Allowing Alimony, Allocation, Although, Attendance, Award, Brook, Budget, Bug, Cater, Confess, Discount, Draft, Excuse, Grant, Indulge, Latitude, Let, License, Licit, Mete, Pension, → **PERMIT**, Portion, Prebend, Quota, Ration, Rebate, Sanction, Share(-out), Stipend, Suffer, Though, Tolerance, Viaticum, Whack, Yield

▶ **Allow** *see* **ALLOTMENT**

Allow(ance) Brook, Cap, Field, Fya, Privy purse, Table money

Alloy Albata, Alnico®, Amalgam, Babbitt, Bell-metal, Billon, Brass, Britannia metal, Bronze, Cermet, Chrome(l), Compound, Constantan, Cupronickel, Duralumin®, Dutch leaf, Electron, Electrum, Ferrosilicon, Gunmetal, Invar®, Kamacite, Latten, Magnalium, Magnox, Marmem, Mischmetal, Mix, Monel®, Nicrosilal, Nimonic, Nitinol, Occamy, Oreide, Orichalc, Ormolu, Oroide, Osmiridium, Paktong, Pewter, Pinchbeck, Platinoid, Potin, Shakudo, Shibuichi, Similor, Solder, Speculum, Spelter, Steel, Stellite®, Tambac, Terne, Tombac, Tombak, Tutenag, White metal, Y, Zircal(l)oy, Zircoloy

▷ **Alloy** *may indicate an anagram*

Allright A1, Assuredly, Fit, Hale, Hunky(-dory), OK, Safe, Tickety-boo, Well

All the same Even so, Nath(e)less, Nevertheless

Allude, Allusion Hint, Imply, Innuendo, Mention, Refer, Reference, Suggest

Allure, Alluring Agaçant(e), Charm, Circe, Decoy, Delilah, Glam, Glamour, It, Magnet(ic), SA, Seduce, Seductive, Siren, Tempt, Trap, Trepan, Vamp

Alluvium Carse

Ally, Allied Accomplice, Agnate, Aide, Alley, Alliance, Ami, Backer, Belamy, Co-belligerent, Cognate, Colleague, Dual, Foederatus, German(e), Holy, Marble, Marmoreal, Pal, Partner, Plonker, Related, Taw, Unholy, Unite

Almanac Calendar, Clog, Ephemeris, Morrison, Nostradamus, Whitaker's, Wisden, Zadkiel

Almost Anear, Anigh, Close on, Most, Near(ly), Nigh(ly), Ripe, Une(a)th, Virtually, Well-nigh, Welly

Alms Awmous, Charity, Dole, Handout

Aloft Aheight

Alone Hat, Jack, Lee-lane, Onely, Secco, Separate, Single, Singly, Sola, Solo, Solus, Unaccompanied, Unaided, Unholpen

Along, Alongside Abeam, Aboard, Abreast, Apposed, Beside, By, Parallel

Alpha A, Male

Alphabet ABC, Absey, Augmented Roman, Black-out, Brahmi, Braille, Chalcidian, Christcross, Cyrillic, Deaf, Devanagari, Estrang(h)elo, Finger, Futhark, Futhorc, Futhork, Glagol, Glagolitic, Glossic, Grantha, Hangul, Horn-book, International, IPA, ITA, Kana, Kanji, Katakana, Kufic, Latin, Manual, Nagari, Og(h)am, Pangram, Phonetic, Pinyin, Romaji, Roman, Runic, Signary, Slavonic, Syllabary

Alpine, Alps Australian, Bernese, Cottian, Dinaric, Eiger, Gentian, Graian, Julian, Laburnum, Lepontine, Maritime, Matterhorn, Ortles, Pennine, Rhaetian, Rock plant, Savoy, Southern, Transylvanian, Tyrol, Western

Also Add, And, Eke, Item, Likewise, Moreover, Plus, Too, Und, Withal

Altar, Altar-cloth, Altarpiece Diptych, Dossal, Dossel, Polyptych, Retable, Shrine, Tabula, Triptych

Alter, Alteration Adapt, Adjust, Bushel, Change, Changeover, Chop and change, Convert, Correct, Customise, Evolve, Falsify, Lib, Material, Modify, Modulate, Munge, Mutate, Recast, Revise, Transient, Transmogrify, Transpose, Up-end, Variance, →VARY

▷ **Alter(native)** *may indicate* an anagram

Alternate, Alternating, Alternation, Alternative Aka, Boustrophedon, Bypass, Exchange, Instead, Metagenesis, →OPTION, Or else, Ossia, Other, Rotate, Solidus, Staggered, Stop-go, Systaltic, Tertian, Variant, Vicissitude

▷ **Alternately** *may indicate* every other letter

Although Admitting, Albe(e), All-be, But, Even, Howsomever, Whereas, While

Altitude Elevation, Height, Meridian, Pressure, Rated, Snowline

▷ **Altogether** *may indicate* words to be joined

Altruistic, Altruism Heroic, Humane, Philanthropic, Selfless(ness), Unselfish

Alumnus Graduate, OB

Always Algate(s), Ay(e), Constant, E'er, Eternal, Ever(more), Forever, For keeps, I, Immer, Sempre, Still

Amanuensis Tironian

Amass Accumulate, Assemble, Collect, Gather, Heap, Hoard, Pile, Upheap

Amateur(s) A, AA, Armchair, Beginner, Corinthian, Dabbler, Dilettante, DIY, Hacker, Ham, Inexpert, L, Lay(man), Novice, Prosumer, Tiro, Tyro

Amaze(d), Amazement, Amazing Agape, Astonish, Astound, Awhape, Bewilder, Cor, Criv(v)ens, Dum(b)found, Flabbergast, Gobsmack, Goodnow, Grace, Incredible, Magical, Monumental, O, Open-eyed, Open-mouthed, Perplex, Poleaxe, Pop-eyed, Prodigious, Stagger, Strewth, Stupefaction, Stupendous, Thunderstruck, Unreal, Wow

Ambassador At-large, Diplomat, Elchee, Elchi, Eltchi, Envoy, Extraordinary, Fetial, HE, Internuncio, Ledger, Legate, Leidger, Leiger, Lieger, Minister, Nuncio, Plenipo, Plenipotentiary, Pronuncio

Ambience Atmosphere, Aura, Milieu, Setting

Ambiguous, Ambiguity Amphibology, Cryptic, Delphic, Double, Enigmatic, Epicene, Equivocal, Gnomic, Inexactness, Loophole, Oracular, Weasel words

Ambit Scope

Ambition, Ambitious Adventurer, Aim, Aspiring, Careerism, Drive, Emulate, Go-ahead, Goal, Go-getter, Grail, High-flier, Keen, Office-hunter, Purpose, Pushy, Rome-runner, Thrusting, Type A

Amble Meander, Mosey, Pace, Pootle, Saunter, Single-foot, Stroll

Ambulance, Ambulanceman Badger, Blood-wagon, Meat wagon, Pannier, Van, Yellow-flag, Zambu(c)k

Ambush(ed) Ambuscade, Belay, Bushwhack, Emboscata, Embusque, Forestall, Latitant, Lurch, Perdu(e), Trap, Watch, Waylay

Amen Ammon, Approval, Inshallah, Verify

▷ **Amend** *may indicate* an anagram

Amend(ment) Alter, Change, Correct, Edit, Expiate, Fifth, Protocol, Redress, Reform, Repair, Restore, →REVISE, Satisfy

America(n) A, Algonki(a)n, Algonqu(i)an, Am, Angeleno, Basket Maker, Caddo, Cajun, Canadian, Carib, Chicano, Chickasaw, Chinook, Copperskin, Digger, Doughface, Down-easter, Federalist, Flathead, Fox, Geechee, Gringo, Guyanese, Huron, Interior, Joe, Jonathan, Latino, Miskito, Mission Indian, Mistec, Mixtec, Mound builder, Native, New World, Norteno, Olmec, Paisano, Salish, Stateside, Statesman, Statist, Tar-heel, Tico, Tupi, Uncle Sam, US(A), WASP, Yankee (Doodle), Yanqui

Amethyst Oriental

Amiable, Amicable Friendly, Genial, Gentle, Inquiline, Mungo, Peaceful, Sweet, Warm

Amid(st) Among, Atween, Between, Inter, Twixt

Amine Putrescine, Spermine

Amiss Awry, Ill, Up, Wrong

Ammunition Ammo, Birdshot, Buckshot, Bullets, Chain-shot, Grenade, Round, Shot, Slug, Tracer

Among Amid(st), In, Inter al, Within

Amorous(ly) Erotic, Fervent, Lustful, Nutty, Romantic, Warm

Amount Come, Degree, Dose, Element, Figure, Glob, Gobbet, Handful, Lashings, Levy, Lot, Measure, Nip, Number, Ocean, Offset, Outage, Plethora, Pot(s), Premium, Price, Quantity, Quantum, Shedload, Span, Stint, Sum, Throughput, Volume, Whale, Wheel

Amphibian(s), Amphibious Amb(l)ystoma, Amtrack, Anura, Axolotl, Batrachian, Caecilia, Caecilian, Desman, Eft, Frog, Guana, Hassar, Herpetology, Mermaid, Mudpuppy, Newt, Olm, Ophiomorph, Proteus, Rana, Salamander, Salientia, Seal, Siren, Tadpole, Tree frog, Urodela(n), Urodele, Weasel

Amphitheatre Arena, Bowl, Coliseum, Colosseum, Ring, Stage

Ample, Amplitude Bellyful, Copious, Enough, Generous, Good, Large, Much, Opulent, Profuse, Rich, Roomy, Round, Sawtooth, Spacious, Uberous, Voluminous

Amplifier, Amplify Booster, Double, Eke, Enlarge, Hailer, Laser, Loud hailer, Maser, Megaphone, Push-pull, Solion, Soundboard, Transistor, Treble

Amputate Sever, Transfix

Amulet Charm, Fetish, Pentacle, Talisman, Tiki, Token

Amuse(ment), Amusing(ly) Account, Caution, Disport, Diversion, Divert, Drole, Droll, Entertain, Game, Gas, Glee, Hoke, Hoot, Jocular, Killing, Levity, Light, Occupy, Pleasure, Popjoy, Priceless, Rich, Riot, Scream, Slay, Solace, →**SPORT**, Tickle, Titillate

▶ **An** *see* **A**

Anaesthetic, Anaesthetise(d), Anaesthetist Analgesic, Apgar, Avertin®, Basal, Benzocaine, Bupivacaine, Chloralose, Chloroform, Cocaine, Epidural, Ether, Eucain(e), Freeze, Gas, General, Halothane, Hibernation, Jabber, Ketamine, Lignocaine, Local, Metopryl, Morphia, Novocaine, Number, Opium, Orthocaine, Phenacaine, Phencyclidine, Procaine, Stovaine, Trike, Twilight sleep, Under, Urethan(e)

Analogous, Analogy Akin, Corresponding, Like, Parallel, Similar

Analyse(r), Analysis Alligate, Anagoge, Anatomy, Assess, Blot, Breakdown, Combinatorial, Conformational, Construe, Critique, Dimensional, Discourse, Dissect, Emic, Esda, Eudiometer, Examine, Fourier, Gap, Harmonic, Lexical, Linguistic, Logical, Numerical, Parse, Post-mortem, Process, Qualitative, Quant, Quantitative, Reductionism, Rundown, Sabermetrics, Scan(sion), Semantics, Sift, Spectral, Statistician, →**SWOT**, Systems, Test, Unpick

▷ **Analysis** *may indicate* an anagram

Analyst Alienist, Jung, Lay, Psychiatrist, Quant(ative), Shrink, Trick cyclist

Anarchist, Anarchy Black Bloc(k), Black Hand, Bolshevist, Chaos, Kropotkin, Provo, Rebel, Revolutionary, Trotskyite, Unrule

Anatomy, Anatomist Bones, Cuvier, De Graaf, Dubois, Framework, Henle,

Histology, Hunter, Malpighi, Osteology, Pacini, Prosector, Puccini, Schneider, Spiegel, Topology

Ancestor, Ancestral, Ancestry Adam, Avital, Dawn man, Descent, Extraction, For(e)bear, Gastraea, Hereditary, Humanoid, Kachina, Lin(e)age, Parent, Parentage, Pedigree, Primogenitor, Proband, Profectitious, Progenitor, Propositus, Roots, Sire, Tree

Anchor(age) Atrip, Berth, Bower, Cell, Deadman, Drag, Eremite, Grapnel, Hawse, Hermit, Host, Kedge, Killick, Killock, Laura, Mud-hook, Nail, Ride, Roads(tead), Root, Scapa Flow, Sheet, Spithead, Stock

Ancient Antediluvian, Archaic, Auld-warld, Early, Gonfanoner, Historic, Hoary, Iago, Immemorial, Lights, Neolithic, Ogygian, Old-world, Primeval, Primitive, Pristine, Ur, Veteran

And Als(o), Ampassy, Ampersand, Amperzand, Ampussyand, Besides, Et, Furthermore, 'n', Plus, Und

Anecdote(s) Ana, Exemplum, Story, Tale, Yarn

Anew De integro, De novo

Angel(s) Abdiel, Adramelech, Apollyon, Archangel, Ariel, Arioch, Asmadai, Azrael, Backer, Banker, Beelzebub, Belial, Benefactor, Cake, Cherub, Clare, Deva, Dominion, Dust, Eblis, Fallen, Falls, Gabriel, Guardian, Heavenly host, Hierarchy, Host, Investor, Israfel, Ithuriel, Lucifer, Nurse, Power, Principality, Raphael, Recording, Rimmon, Saint, St, Seraph, Spirit, Throne, Uriel, Uzziel, Virtue, Watcher, Zadkiel, Zephiel

Angelica Archangel

Anger, Angry →**ANNOY**, Apeshit, Bate, Bile, Black, Bristle, Choler(ic), Conniption, Cross, Dander, Displeased, Dudgeon, Enrage, Exasperation, Face, Fired up, Fuff, Fury, Gram, Heat, Het up, Horn-mad, Huff, Incense, Inflame, Infuriate, Iracund, Irascible, Ire, Kippage, Livid, Mad, Monkey, Moody, Nettle, Pique, Provoke, Radge, Rage, Rampant, Ratty, Renfierst, Rile, Roil, Rouse, Sore, Spleen, Steam, Stroppy, Tamping, Tantrum, Tarnation, Teed off, Teen(e), Temper, Tene, Tooshie, Vex, Vies, Warm, Waspish, Waxy, Worked-up, Wound up, Wrath, Wroth, Yond

Angle(d), Angler, Angular, Angles, Angling Acute, Argument, Aspect, Attitude, Axil, Azimuthal, Baiter, Canthus, Cast, Catch, Chiliagon, Coign, Complementary, Conjugate, Contrapposto, Corner, Cos, Critical, Diedral, Diedre, Dihedral, Elbow, Elevation, Ell, Exterior, Facial, Fish, Fish-hook, Fork, Geometry, Gonion, Hade, Hip, Hour, Hyzer, In, Incidence, Interior, L, Laggen, Laggin, Latitude, Loft, Longitude, Mitre, Mung, Negative, Oblique, Obtuse, Parallax, Pediculate, Perigon, Peterman, Phase, Piend, Piscator, Pitch, Pitch-cone, Plane, Polyhedral, Position, Positive, Quoin, Radian, Rake, Re-entrant, Reflex, Right, Rod(ster), Rod(s)man, Round, Salient, Sally, Saltchucker, Sine, Sinical, Slip, Solid, Spherical, Stalling, Steeve, Steradian, Straight, Supplementary, Sweepback, The gentle craft, Trotline, Vertical, Viewpoint, Visual, Walton, Waltonian, Washin, Weather, Wide-gab

Anglican(s) CE-men, Conformist, Episcopal

Angora Goat, Mohair, Rabbit

Angostura Cusparia bark

Anguish(ed) Agony, Distress, Gip, Gyp, Hag-ridden, Heartache, Misery, →**PAIN**, Pang, Sorrow, Throes, →**TORMENT**, Torture, Woe

Animal(s) Acrita, Anoa, Armadillo, Atoc, Bag, Bandog, Barbastel, Beast, Bestial, Brute, Cariacou, Carnal, Chalicothere, Cleanskin, Coati, Creature, Criollo, Critter, Fauna, Felis, Feral, Gerbil, Guanaco, Herd, Huanaco, Ichneumon, Jacchus, Jerboa, Kinkajou, Klipdas, Mammal, Marmoset, Marmot, Menagerie, Moose, Noctule, Oribi, Parazoon, Party, Pet, Political, Protozoa, Pudu, Pygarg, Quadruped, Quagga, Rac(c)oon, Rhesus, Rotifer, Sensual, Sloth, Stud, Tarsier, Teledu, Urson, Waler, Xenurus, Yale, Yapock, Zerda, Zoo

Animate(d), Animation Activate, Actuate, Alive, Arouse, Biophor, Cartoon, Ensoul, Excite, Fire, Frankenstein, Heat, Hot, Inspire, Lit, Live, Morph, Mosso, Perky, Rouse, Spark, Spiritoso, Spritely, Stop-motion, Toon, Verve, Vivacity

Animosity Enmity, Friction, Hostility, Malice, Pique, Rancour

Ankle Coot, Cuit, Cute, Hock, Hucklebone, Knee, Malleolus

Annal(s) Acta, Archives, Chronicles, Register

Annex(e) Acquire, Add, Affiliate, Attach, Codicil, Extension, Lean-to, Subjoin

Annihilate Destroy, Erase, Exterminate, Slay, Unbe

Anniversary Birthday, Feast, Jubilee, Obit, Yahrzeit

Announce(r), Announcement Banns, Bellman, Bill(ing), Blazon, Bulletin, Communiqué, Decree, Disclose, Divulgate, Flash, Gazette, Herald, Hermes, Inform, Intimate, Meld, Name and shame, Newsflash, Post, Preconise, Proclaim, Profess, Promulgate, Pronunciamente, Publish, Release, →**REPORT**, Speaker(ine), State, Tannoy, Trumpet

Annoy(ance), Annoyed, Annoying Aggravate, Aggrieve, Anger, Antagonise, Badger, Bane, Bother, Bug, Bugbear, Chagrin, Choleric, Contrary, Cross, Disturb, Drat, Fash, Fleabite, Frab, Fumed, Gall, Gatvol, Hack off, Hang, Harass, Hatter, Hector, Hip, Hoots, Huff, Hump, Incense, Irk, →**IRRITATE**, Miff, Mischief, Molest, Nag, Nark, Needle, Nettle, Niggle, Noisome, Noy(ance), Peeve, Pesky, Pester, Pipsqueak, Pique, Plague, Provoke, Rankle, Rats, Resentful, Ride, Rile, Roil, Rub, Shirty, Sting, Testy, Tiresome, Tracasserie, Try, Vex

Annual, Annuity Bedder, Book, Consolidated, Contingent, Deferred, Etesian, →**FLOWER**, Half-hardy, Hardy, Immediate, Pension, Perpetuity, →**PLANT**, Rente, Tontine, Yearbook, Yearly

Annul(ment) Abolish, Abrogate, Cashier, Cassation, Dissolution, Invalidate, Irritate, Negate, Repeal, Rescind, Reversal, Revoke, Vacate, Vacatur, Vacuate, →**VOID**

▷ **Anomaly** *may indicate* an anagram

Anon Again, Anew, Erelong, Later, Soon

Anonymous Adespota, Anon, A.N.Other, Faceless, Grey, Impersonal, Nameless, Somebody, Unnamed, Valentine

Answer(ing), Answer(s) Acknowledge, Amoebaean, Ans, Antiphon, Because, Comeback, Crib (sheet), Defence, Dusty, Echo, Key, Lemon, Light, No, Oracle, Rebuttal, Rebutter, Rein, Rejoin(der), Repartee, Reply, Rescript, Respond, Response, Retort, Return, Riposte, Serve, Sol, Solution, Solve, Verdict, Yes

Ant(s), Anthill Amazon, Army, Bull(dog), Carpenter, Colony, Driver, Dulosis, Emmet, Ergataner, Ergates, Ergatogyne, Fire, Formic, Formicary, Myrmecoid, Myrmidon, Nasute, Neuter, Pharaoh, Pismire, Red, Sauba, Slave-maker, Soldier, Termite, Velvet, White, Wood

Ante Bet, Punt, Stake

Ant-eater Aardvark, Banded, Echidna, Edental, Giant, Manis, Numbat, Pangolin, Scaly, S(e)ladang, Spiny, Tamandu, Tamandua, Tapir

Antelope Addax, Blackbuck, Blaubok, Blesbok, Bloubok, Bluebuck, Bongo, Bontebok, Bubal(is), Bushbuck, Chamois, Chikara, Dikdik, Duiker, Duyker, Dzeren, Eland, Elk, Gazelle, Gemsbok, Gerenuk, Gnu, Goa, Goral, Grysbok, Hartbees, Hartebeest, Impala, Inyala, Kaama, Kid, Klipspringer, Kob, Kongoni, Koodoo, Kudu, Lechwe, Madoqua, Nagor, Nilgai, Nilgau, Nyala, Nylghau, Oribi, Oryx, Ourebi, Pale-buck, Pallah, Prongbuck, Pronghorn, Puku, Pygarg, Reebok, Reedbuck, Rhebok, Sable, Saiga, Sasin, Sassaby, Serow, Sitatunga, Situtunga, Steenbok, Steinbock, Stemback, Stembok, Suni, Takin, Thar, Topi, Tragelaph, Tsessebe, Waterbuck, Wildebeest

Antenatal Labour

Antenna Aerial, Dipole, Dish, Feeler, Horn, Rabbit's ears, Sensillum, TVRO

Anterior Anticous, Earlier, Front, Prior

Anteroom Voiding-lobby

Anthem Die Stem, Hymn, Introit, Isodica, Marseillaise, Motet(t), National, Offertory, Psalm, Red Flag, Responsory, Song, Theme, Tract

Anthology Album, Ana, Chrestomathy, Digest, Divan, Florilegium, Garland, Pick, Spicilege

Anti Against, Agin, Averse, Con, Hostile

Anti-abortion Right to life

Anti-bacterial, Antibiotic Aclarubicin, Actinomycin, Allicin, Avoparcin, Bacitracin, Carbenicillin, Cecropin, Cephalosporin, Cipro®, Cloxacillin, Colistin,

Cycloserine, Doxorubicin, Doxycycline, Drug, Erythromycin, Gentamicin, Gramicidin, Griseofulvin, Interferon, Interleukin, Kanamycin, Lincomycin, Macrolide, Magainin, Methicillin, Mitomycin, Neomycin, Nystatin, Opsonin, Oxacillin, Oxytetracycline, Penicillin, Polymyxin, Puromycin, Rifampicin, Rifamycin, Spectinomycin, Streptokinase, Streptomycin, Streptothricin, Terramycin®, Tetracycline, Tyrocidine, Tyrothricin, Virginiamycin

Antibody Agglutinin, Alemtuzumab, Amboceptor, Antitoxin, Blocker, Catuximab, H(a)emolysin, IgA/E/G/M/O, Isoagglutinin, Lysin, Monoclonal, Precipitin, Reagin, Retuximab, Trastuzumab

Antic(s) Caper, Dido, Frolic, Gambado, Hay, Prank, Shenanigan, Stunt

Antichrist The Man of Sin

Anticipate, Anticipation Against, Antedate, Augur, Await, Drool, →**EXPECT**, Forecast, Foresee, Forestall, Foretaste, Forethought, Hope, Intuition, Pre-empt, Preparation, Prevenancy, Prolepsis, Prospect, Type

Anticlimax Bathos, Comedown, Deflation, Disappointment, Letdown

Antidepressant Prozac

Antidote Adder's wort, Alexipharmic, Angelica, Antivenin, Bezoar, Contrayerva, Cure, Emetic, Guaco, Mithridate, Nostrum, Orvietan, Picrotoxin, Remedy, Ribavirin, Senega, Theriac(a), (Venice-)Treacle

Antimonopoly Trust buster

Antinuclear CND

Antipasto Caponata

Antipathy Allergy, Animosity, Aversion, Detest, →**DISLIKE**, Enmity, Intolerance, Repugnance

Antiquated, Antique, Antiquarian Ancient, Archaic, A(u)stringer, Bibelot, Curio, Dryasdust, Egyptian, FAS, Fogram(ite), Fog(e)y, Fossil, Moth-eaten, Old-fangled, Ostreger, Relic

Antiseptic Acriflavine, Carbolic, Cassareep, Creosote, Cresol, Disinfectant, Eupad, Eusol, Formaldehyde, Formalin, Formol, Germicide, Guaiacol, Iodine, Lister, Merbromin, Phenol, Sterile, Thymol, Tutty

Antisocial Hoodie, Hostile, Ishmaelitish, Litterbug, Loner, Misanthropic, Oik, Psychopath

Antithesis Contrary, Converse, Opposite

Antiviral Rebavirin

Antivitamin Pyrithiamine

Anvil Bick-iron, Block, Incus, Stiddie, Stithy

Anxiety, Anxious Angst, Brood, Care(ful), Cark, Concern, Disquiet, Dysthymia, Edgy, Fanteeg, Fantigue, Fantod, Fear, Fraught, Grave, Habdabs, Heebie-jeebies, Hung-up, Hypochondria, Impatient, Inquietude, Itching, Jimjams, Jumpy, Keen, Nerviness, Reck, Restless, Scruple, Separation, Shpilkes, Solicitous, Stewing, Stress, Suspense, Sweat, Tension, Toey, Trepidation, Twitchy, Unease, Unquiet, Upset, Uptight, White-knuckle, Willies, Worriment, Worryguts, Worrywort

Any Arrow, Ary, Some

Anybody, Anyone One, Whoso, You

Anyhow, Anyway Anyroad(s), However, Leastways, Regardless

Anything Aught, Oucht, Ought, Owt, Whatnot

▷ **Anyway** may indicate an anagram

Apart Aloof, Aside, Asunder, Atwain, Beside, Separate

Apartment Atrium, Ben, Condominium, Digs, Duplex, Flat, Insula, Mansion, Paradise, Penthouse, Pied-a-terre, Quarters, Room, Simplex, Solitude, Suite, Unit

Apathetic, Apathy Accidie, Acedia, Incurious, Indifferent, Languid, Lethargic, Listless, Lobotomized, Lukewarm, Mopish, Pococurante, Stoical, Torpid, Unenthusiastic

Ape(-like), Apeman Anthropoid, Barbary, Big-foot, Catarrhine, Copy, Dryopithecine, Gelada, Gibbon, Gorilla, →**IMITATE**, Magot, Mimic, →**MONKEY**, Naked, Orang, Paranthropus, Parrot, Pongid, Pongo, →**PRIMATE**, Proconsul, Simian, Simulate, Troglodyte, Yowie

Apex Acme, Culmen, Gonion, Keystone, Knoll, Knowe, Summit, Vertex

Aphorism Adage, Epigram, Gnome, Pensée, Proverb, Sutra

Aphrodisiac, Aphrodite Cytherean, Erotic, Idalian, Paphian, Philter, Philtre, Spanish fly, Urania, Yohimbine

Apologetic, Apology Ashamed, Excuse, Justifier, Mockery, My bad, Oops, Pardon, Scuse, Sir-reverence

Apostle, Apostolic Cuthbert, → DISCIPLE, Evangelist, Johannine, Jude, Matthew, Pauline, Spoon, Thad(d)eus, Thomas, Twelve

Apothecary Chemist, Dispenser, Druggist, LSA, Pharmacist, Pottingar

Appal(ling) Abysmal, Affear(e), Aghast, Dismay, Egregious, Execrable, Frighten, Horrify, Piacular, Tragic

▷ **Appallingly** *may indicate* an anagram

Apparatus Absorptiometer, Alkalimeter, Appliance, Aqualung, Aspirator, Breeches buoy, Bridgerama, Caisson, Calorimeter, Churn, Clinostat, Codec, Commutator, Condenser, Converter, Convertor, Critical, Cryostat, Decoy, Defibrillator, Desiccator, → DEVICE, Digester, Ebullioscope, Effusiometer, Egg, Electrograph, Electrophorus, Electroscope, Elutriator, Enlarger, Equipment, Gadget, Gasogene, Gazogene, Generator, Giant('s) stride, Gyroscope, Heater, Heliograph, Helioscope, Hemocytometer, Hodoscope, Holophote, Horse, Hydrophone, Hygrostat, Incubator, Inhalator, Injector, Inspirator, Installation, Instrument, Iron lung, Langmuir-trough, Lease-rod, Life-preserver, Loom, Microreader, Mimeograph, Mine-detector, Nephoscope, Nitrometer, Oscillator, Oscillograph, Oxygenator, Pasteuriser, Peat-seeker, Percolator, Phon(o)meter, Photophone, Photostat®, Phytotron, Plate-warmer, Plethysmograph, Plumber's snake, Pommel horse, Potometer, Projector, Proto®, Pulmotor®, Push-pull, Radiator, Radiosonde, Rattlebag, Rattletrap, Rectifier, Replenisher, Resistor, Respirator, Respirometer, Resuscitator, Retort, Rotisserie, Scrubber, Searchlight, Seeder, Semaphore, Set, Skimmer, Slide rest, Smoker, Snake, Sniffer, Snorkel, Snowbox, Soundboard, Spirophore, Starter, Stellarator, Steriliser, Still, Substage, Switchgear, Tackle, Tackling, Talk-you-down, Telecine, Teleprinter, Teleseme, Tellurian, Transformer, Transmitter, Tribometer, Tuner, Ventouse, Wheatstone's bridge, ZETA

Apparel Attire, Besee, → COSTUME, Garb, Raiment, Wardrobe, Wardrop

▷ **Apparent** *may indicate* a hidden word

Apparent(ly) Ap, Clear, Detectable, Manifest, Ostensible, Outward, Overt, Plain, Prima facie, Seeming, Semblance, Visible

Apparition Dream, Eidolon, Fetch, Ghost, → ILLUSION, Phantom, Shade, Spectre, Vision, Visitant, Wraith

Appeal(ing) Ad, Beg, Cachet, Catchpenny, Charisma, Charm, Cri de coeur, Cry, Dreamy, Entreat, Entreaty, Epirrhema, Exhort, Eye-catching, Fetching, Glamorous, Howzat, Invocation, It, Mediagenic, Miserere, O, Oath, Oomph, Plead, SA, Screeve, Sex(iness), Solicit, SOS, Suit, Yummy

Appear(ance) Advent, Air, Arise, Arrival, Aspect, Brow, Colour, Debut, Effeir, Effere, Emerge, Enter, Facade, Feature, Garb, Guise, Hue, Image, Looks, Loom, Manifestation, → MANNER, Mien, Occur, Ostent, Outward, Phenomenon, Physiognomy, Presence, Represent, Rise, Seem, Semblance, Show, Species, Spring, View, Visitation, Vraisemblance, Whistle-stop

Appease(ment) Allay, Atone, Calm, Conciliation, Danegeld, Mitigate, Munichism, Pacify, Placate, Propitiate, Satisfy, Soothe, Sop

Appellant Roe

Append(age) Adjunct, Annex, Antennule, Codpiece, Hanger-on, Lobe, Lug, Pendicle, Postfix, Proboscis, Stipule, Tail, Tentacle, Uvula

Appendix Addendum, Apocrypha, Codicil, Grumbling, Label, Pendant, Pendent, Rider, Schedule, Vermiform

Appetite, Appetitive, Appetise(r), Appetize(r) Amuse-bouche, Amuse-gueule, Antepast, Antipasto, Aperitif, Appestat, Bhagee, Bhajee, Bulimia, Bulimy, Canapé, Concupiscence, Concupy, Crudités, Dim-sum, Entremes(se),

Entremets, Flesh, Hunger, Inner man, Limosis, Malacia, Meze, Nacho, Orectic, Orexis, Passion, Pica, Polyphagia, Relish, Tapa(s), Titillate, Twist, Ventripotent, Whet, Yerd-hunger, Yird-hunger

Applaud, Applause Bravo, →**CHEER**, Clap, Claque, Eclat, Encore, Extol, Olé, Ovation, Praise, Root, Tribute

Apple Alligator, Bad, Baldwin, Balsam, Biffin, Blenheim orange, Bramley, Cashew, Charlotte, Codlin(g), Cooker, Costard, Crab, Custard, Eater, Granny Smith, Greening, Jenneting, John, Jonathan, Kangaroo, Leather-coat, Love, Mammee, Medlar, Nonpareil, Pearmain, Pippin, Pomace, Pome(roy), Pomroy, Pupil, Pyrus, Quarantine, Quarenden, Quar(r)ender, Quarrington, Queening, Redstreak, Reinette, Rennet, Ribston(e), Ripstone, Rotten, Royal gala, Ruddock, Russet, Seek-no-further, Snow, Sops-in-wine, Sturmer (Pippin), Sugar, Sweeting, Thorn, Toffee, Winesap

Application, Applicable, Apply, Appliance(s) Address, Adhibit, Appeal, Appose, Assiduity, Barrage, Blender, Concentration, Devote, Diligence, Dressing, Exercise, Exert, Foment, Germane, Implement, Inlay, Juicer, Lay, Liquidiser, Lotion, Ointment, Pertinent, Petition, Plaster, Poultice, Put, Resort, Rub, Sinapism, Stupe, Talon, Toggle, Truss, →**USE**, White goods

Appoint(ee), Appointment Advowson, Assign, Berth, Co-opt, Date, Delegate, Depute, Designate, Dew, Due, Executor, Induction, Installation, Make, Name, →**NOMINATE**, Nominee, Office, Ordain, Place, Position, Post, Posting, Rendezvous, Room, Set, Tryst

▷ **Appointed** *may indicate* an anagram

Appraise, Appraisal Analyse, →**EVALUATE**, Gauge, Judge, Once-over, Tape, →**VALUE**, Vet

Appreciate, Appreciation Acknowledgement, Cherish, Clap, Comprehensible, Dig, Empathy, Endear, Esteem, Gratefulness, Increase, Phwoar, Prize, Realise, Recognise, Regard, Relish, Rise, Sense, Stock, Taste, Thank you, Treasure, →**VALUE**, Welcome

Apprehend(ing), Apprehension Afears, Alarm, Arrest, Attuent, →**CATCH**, Collar, Fear, Grasp, Insight, Intuit, Perceive, Quailing, See, Suspense, Take, Toey, Trepidation, Uh-oh, Unease, Uptake

Apprehensive Jumpy, Nervous, Uneasy

Apprentice(ship) Article, Cub, Devil, Garzone, Improver, Indent(ure), Jockey, L, Learner, Lehrjahre, Novice, Noviciate, Novitiate, Printer's devil, Pupillage, Trainee, Turnover

Approach(ing), Approachable Abord, Access, Accost, Advance, Anear, Angle, Anigh, Appropinquate, Appulse, Asymptotic, Avenue, Close, Coast, Come, Converge, Cost(e), Draw nigh, Drive, Driveway, Fairway, Feeler, Gate, Imminent, Ingoing, Line, Near, Nie, Open, Overture, Pitch, Procedure, Road, Run-in, Run-up, Stealth, Strategy, Verge, Warm

Appropriate(ly), Appropriateness Abduct, Abstract, Annex, Applicable, Apposite, Apt, Aright, Asport, Assign, Bag, Befitting, Borrow, Collar, Commandeer, Commensurate, Condign, Confiscate, Congruous, Convenient, Due, Element, Eligible, Embezzle, Expedient, Fit, Germane, Good, Happy, Hijack, Hog, Impound, Jump, Just, Meet, Nick, Pertinent, Pilfer, Pocket, Pre-empt, Proper, Propriety, Right, Seise, Seize, Sequester, Sink, Snaffle, Steal, Suit(ed), Swipe, Take, Timely, Trouser, Usurp

Approval, Approve(d), Approbation Accolade, Admire, Adopt, Allow, Amen, Applaud, Assent, Attaboy, Aye, Blessing, Bravo, Brownie points, Change, Clap, Credit, Cushty, Dig, Endorse, Favour, For, Green light, Hear hear, Hubba-hubba, Hurra(h), Imprimatur, Initial, Kitemark, Know, Laud, Nod, Okay, Olé, Orthodox, Pass, Plaudit, Rah, Ratify, Recommend, Right-on, Rubber-stamp, Sanction, Stotter, Thumbs-up, Tick, Tribute, Vivat, Voice, Warm to, Yay, Yes

Approximate(ly), Approximation Almost, Around, Ballpark, Circa, Close, Coarse, Estimate, Guess, Imprecise, Near, Rough and ready, Roughly

Apron Airside, Barm-cloth, Bib, Blacktop, Brat, Bunt, Canvas, Fig-leaf, Napron, Pinafore, Pinny, Placket, Rim, Stage, Tablier, Tier

Apt(ly) Apposite, Appropriate, Apropos, Ben trovato, Capable, Evincive, Fit, Gleg, Happy, Liable, Prone, Suitable, Tends

Aptitude Ability, Bent, Ear, Eye, Faculty, Feel, Flair, Gift, Knack, Nose, Skill, Talent, Taste, Tendency, Touch, Viability

Aquamarine Madagascar

Aquarium Oceanarium

Aqueduct Canal, Channel, Conduit, Hadrome, Xylem

Arab(ian), Arabia, Arabic Abdul, Adnan, Algorism, Ali (Baba), Baathist, Bahraini, Bahrein, Bedouin, Bedu, Druse, Druz(e), Effendi, Fedayee(n), Gamin, Geber, Hani, Hashemite, Hassaniya, Himyarite, Horse, Iraqi, Jawi, Kuwaiti, Lawrence, Moor, Mudlark, Nabat(a)ean, Nas(s)eem, Omani, Omar, PLO, Rag(head), Saba, Sab(a)ean, Saracen, Seleucid, Semitic, Sheikh, Syrian, UAR, Urchin, Yemen(i)

Arbitrary Despotic, Haphazard, Peculiar, Random, Wanton, Whim

Arbitrate, Arbitration, Arbitrator, Arbiter ACAS, Censor, Daysman, Judge, Negotiator, Ombudsman, Pendulum, Prud'homme, Ref(eree), Umpire

Arboreal, Arbour Bower, Dendroid, Pergola, Trellis

Arc Azimuth, Bow, Carbon, →CURVE, Flashover, Fogbow, Foil, Halo, Hance, Haunch, Limb, Octant, Quadrant, Rainbow, Reflex, Trajectory

Arcade Amusement, Burlington, Cloister, Gallery, Loggia, Triforium, Video

Arcane Esoteric, Mystic, Obscure, Occult, Orphism, Recherché, Rune, Secret

Arch(ed), Arching Acute, Admiralty, Alveolar, Arblaster, Arcade, Arcature, Archivolt, Camber, Chief, Counterfort, Crafty, Cross-rib, Ctesiphon, →CUNNING, Curve, Discharging, Eyebrow, Fallen, Flying buttress, Fog-bow, Gothic, Hance, Haunch, Instep, Intrados, Inverted, Keystone, Lancet, Lierne, Limb-girdle, Marble, Neural, Norman, Ogee, Ogive, Opistholomos, Pelvic, Plantar, Pointed, Portal, Proscenium, Recessed, Relieving, Roguish, Roman, Safety, Saucy, Segmental, Shouldered, Skew, Sly, Soffit, Span, Squinch, Stilted, Trajan, Triumphal, Vault

Archaeological, Archaeologist, Archaeology Bell, Carter, Childe, Dater, Dig, Evans, Industrial, Layard, Leakey, Mallowan, Mycenae, Petrie, Pothunter, Qumran, Schliemann, Sutton Hoo, Type-site, Wheeler, Winckelmann, Woolley

Archangel Azrael, Gabriel, Israfeel, Israfel, Israfil, Jerahmeel, Michael, Raguel, Raphael, Sariel, Satan, Uriel, Yellow

Archbishop Anselm, Augustine, Cosmo, Cranmer, Davidson, Dunstan, Ebor, Elector, Hatto, Lambeth, Lanfranc, Lang, Langton, Laud, Metropolitan, Morton, Primate, Scroop, Temple, Trench, Tutu, Whitgift

Archer(y) Acestes, Bow-boy, →BOWMAN, Cupid, Eros, Hood, Petticoat, Philoctetes, Sagittary, Tell, Toxophilite

Archetype Avatar, Model, Pattern

Archimandrite Eutyches

Archimedes Screw

Architect(ure), Architectural Baroque, Bauhaus, Bricolage, Byzantine, Cartouche, Community, Composite, Computer, Corinthian, Data-flow, Decorated style, Domestic, Doric, Early English, Elizabethan, Flamboyant, Georgian, Gothic, Greek Revival, Ionic, Italian, Landscape, Listed, Lombard, Maker, Moorish, Moresque, Mudejar, Naval, Neoclassical, Neo-gothic, Norman, Palladian, Pelasgian, Perpendicular, Picnostyle, Planner, Queen Anne, Romanesque, Saracenic, Saxon, Spandrel, Spandril, Tudor, Tudorbethan, Tuscan, Vitruvian

Archive(s) Morgue, Muniment, PRO, Records, Register

Arctic Estotiland, Frigid, Hyperborean, In(n)uit, Inupiat, Polar, Tundra

Ardent, Ardour Aflame, Aglow, Boil, Broiling, Burning, Enthusiasm, Fervent, Fervid, Fiery, Flagrant, Flaming, Gusto, Heat, Het, →HOT, In, Mettled, Mettlesome, Passion(ate), Perfervid, Rage, Spiritous, Vehement, Warm-blooded, Zealous, Zeloso

Are A, Exist

Area Acre, Aleolar, Apron, Arctogaea, Are, Assisted, Bailiwick, Beat, Belt, Built-up, Catchment, Centare, Centre, Chill-out, Clearing, Conurbation, Courtyard, Craton, Depressed, Dessiatine, Development, Disaster, District, Docklands, Domain,

Downtown, Eruv, Extent, Forecourt, Goal, Grey, Growth, Hectare, Henge, Hide, Hinterland, Hotspot, Input, Landmass, Latitude, Locality, Lodg(e)ment, Metroplex, Milieu, Mofussil, Neogaea, Nidderdale, No-go, No-man's-land, Notogaea, Pale, Parish, Penalty, Place, Plot, Precinct, Province, Purlieu, Quad, Quarter (section), Range, Redevelopment, → **REGION**, Renosterveld, Res(ervation), Reserve, Rest, Restricted, Rule, Sector, Service, Shire, Site, Slurb, Special, Staging, Sterling, Subtopia, Support, Surface, Target, Tartary, Technical, Terra, Terrain, Territory, Theatre, Tract, Tundra, Uptown, Urban, Ure, Weald, White, Wilderness, Work station, Yard, Zone

Arena Battleground, Circus, Cockpit, Dohyo, Field, Maidan, Olympia, → **RING**, Snowdome, Stadium, Tiltyard, Venue

Argue, Argument(ative) Altercation, Argy-bargy, Bandy, Beef, Blue, Cangle, Conflict, Contend, Contest, Contra, Cosmological, Debate, Difference, Dilemma, Ding-dong, Dispute, Dissent, Enthusiasm, Exchange, Expostulate, Fray, Free-for-all, Hysteron proteron, Logic, Mexican standoff, Moot, Object, Patter, Plead, Polylemma, Propound, Pros and cons, Quarrel, Quibble, → **REASON**, Remonstrate, Row, Run-in, Scene, Sequacious, Socratise, Sophistry, Spar, Straw man, Stroppy, Stushie, Summation, Teleological, Third man, Tiff, Transcendental, Verbal, Vociferate, Words

Aria Ballad, Cabaletta, Cantata, Melody, Song

Aris Arse, → **BOTTOM**, Can

Arise Appear, Develop, Emanate, Emerge, Upgo, Wax

Aristocracy, Aristocrat(ic) Blood, Classy, Debrett, Duc, Elite, Gentle, Gentry, Grandee, High-hat, Nob, Noble, Optimate, Passage, Patrician, Toff, Tony, U-men, Upper-crust, Well-born

▷ **Arm** *may indicate* an army regiment, etc.

Arm(ed), Arms Akimbo, Arsenal, Bearing, Brachial, Branch, Bundooks, Canting, Cove, Crest, Cross bow, Embattle, Equip, Escutcheon, Estoc, Fin, Firth, Frith, Gnomon, Halbert, Hatchment, Heel, Heraldic, Inlet, Jib, Krupp, Limb, Loch, Long, Member, Olecranon, Pick-up, Quillon, Radius, Rail, Ramous, Rocker, Rotor, SAA, Secular, Shield, Shotgun, Side, Small, Smooth-bore, Spiral, Tappet, Tentacle, Timer, Tone, Tooled-up, Transept, Tremolo, Ulnar, Water pistol, → **WEAPON**, Whip

Armadillo Dasypod, Dasypus, Fairy, Giant, Pangolin, Peba, Pichiciego, Tatou(ay), Xenurus

Armband Torc, Torque

Armhole Scye

Armless Inermous

Armour(ed), Armoury Ailette, Armet, Barbette, Beaver, Besagew, Bevor, Brasset, Brigandine, Buckler, Byrnie, Camail, Cannon, Casspir, Cataphract, Chaffron, Chain, Chamfrain, Chamfron, Chausses, Corium, Cors(e)let, Couter, Cuirass, Cuish, Cuisse, Culet, Curat, Curiet, Cush, Defence, Fauld, Garderobe, Garniture, Gear, Genouillère, Gorget, Greave, Habergeon, Hauberk, Jack, Jambe, Jambeau, Jazerant, Jesserant, Lamboys, Mail, Mentonnière, Mesail, Mezail, Nasal, Palette, Panoply, Panzer, Pauldron, Petta, Placcat, Placket, Plastron, Poitrel, Poleyn, Pouldron, Rerebrace, Rest, Roundel, Sabaton, Secret, → **SHIELD**, Solleret, Spaudler, Splint, Stand, Tace, Tank, Taslet, Tasse(t), Thorax, Tonlet, Tuille, Vambrace, Vantbrass, Visor, Voider

Army Arrière-ban, BEF, Blue Ribbon, Church, Colours, Confederate, Crowd, Federal, Fyrd, Golden (Horde), Horde, Host, IRA, Junior Service, Land, Landwehr, Legion, Line, Military, Militia, Mobile Command, Multitude, Para-military, Red, SA, Sabaoth, Salvation, SAS, Sena, Service, Soldiers, Squad, Standing, Stratonic, Swarm, TA, Tartan, Terracotta, Territorial, Thin red line, Volunteer, War, Wehrmacht

▷ **Army** *may indicate* having arms

Aroma(tic) Allspice, Aniseed, Aryl, Balmy, Coriander, Fenugreek, Fragrant, Nose, Odorous, Pomander, Spicy, Vanillin, Wintergreen

Around About, Ambient, Circa, Near, Peri-, Skirt, Tour

▷ **Around** *may indicate* one word around another

Arouse, Arousal Alarm, → **EXCITE**, Fan, Fire, Incite, Inflame, Inspire, Must(h), Needle, Provoke, Stimulate, Stole, Suscitate, Urolagnia, Waken, Whet

Arpad ELO

▷ **Arrange** *may indicate* an anagram

Arrange(r), Arrangement Adjust, Array, Attune, Ausgleich, Bandobast, Bank, Bundobust, Concert, Concinnity, Configuration, Coordinate, Design, Display, Dispose, Do, Dress, Echelon, Edit, Engineer, Finger, Fix, Foreordain, Format, Formation, Formwork, Grade, Ikebana, Layout, Lineation, Marshal, Modus vivendi, Neaten, Orchestrate, Orchestration, Ordain, →**ORDER**, Ordonnance, Organise, Pack, Pattern, Perm, Permutation, Plan, Position, Prepare, Prepense, Quincunx, Redactor, Regulate, Run, Rustle up, Schedule, Schema, Scheme, Score, Set, Settle, Sort, Spacing, Stack, Stage-manage, Stereoisomerism, Stow, Straighten, Structure, Style, System, Tabulate, Tactic, Taxis, Tidy, Transcribe, Vertical

Array(ed) Attire, Deck, Herse, Logic, Marshal, Muster

Arrear(s) Aft, Ahint, Backlog, Behind, Debt, Owing

Arrest(ed), Arresting Abort, Alguacil, Alguazil, Ament, Apprehend, Attach, Attract, Blin, Book, Bust, Caption, Capture, Cardiac, Catch, Check, Citizen's, Collar, Detain, False, Forthcoming, Hold, House, Knock, Lag, Lift, Lightning, Nab, Nail, Nick, Nip, Nobble, Pinch, Pull, Restrain, Retard, Riveting, Round-up, Run-in, Salient, Sease, Seize, Snaffle, Snatch, Stasis, Stop, Sus(s)

Arrival, Arrive, Arriving Accede, Advent, Attain, Come, Entrance, Get, Happen, Hit, Inbound, Influx, Johnny-come-lately, Land, Natal, Nativity, Newcomer, Pitch up, Reach, Roll up, Strike

Arrogance, Arrogant Assumption, Bold, Bravado, Bumptious, Cavalier, Cocksure, Cocky, Contemptuous, Disdain, Dogmatic, Effrontery, Haughty, Haut(eur), High, High and mighty, High-handed, High-hat, Hogen-mogen, Hoity-toity, Hubris, Imperious, Jumped up, Lordly, Morgue, Overweening, Presumption, Pretentious, Proud, Proud-stomached, Prussianism, Side, Snobbish, Surquedry, Surquedy, Toploftical, Topping, Uppity, Upstart

Arrow, Arrow-head Acestes, Any, Ary, Bolt, Cloth-yard shaft, Dart, Filter, Flechette, Missile, Pheon, Pointer, Quarrel, Reed, Sagittate, Shaft, Sheaf, Straight

Arsenal Ammo, Armo(u)ry, Depot, Fire-arms, Magazine, Side, Toulon

Arson(ist) Firebug, Pyromania, Torching

▷ **Art** *may indicate* an -est ending

Art(s), Arty, Art movement, Art school, Art style Abstract, Alla prima, Applied, Arte Povera, Bauhaus, Bloomsbury, Bonsai, Britart, Brut, Chiaroscuro, Clair-obscure, Clare-obscure, Click, Clip, Cobra, Collage, Commercial, Conceptual, Constructivism, Contrapposto, Craft, Cubism, Culture vulture, Cunning, Curious, Dada, Daedal(e), Deco, Decorative, Dedal, De Stijl, Die Brucke, Diptych, Divisionism, Enamel(ling), Expressionism, Fauvism, Feat, Fine, Finesse, Flemish, Folk, Futurism, Genre, Graphic, High Renaissance, Humanities, Ikebana, Impressionist, Jugendstil, Kakemono, Kano, Ka pai, Kinetic, Kirigami, Kitsch, Knack, Lacquerware, Land, Liberal, Mandorla, Mannerism, Martial, Masterwork, Mehndi, Minimal, Modern(e), Montage, Motivated, Music, Nabis, Nazarene, Neoclassical, Neo-impressionism, New Wave, Noli-me-tangere, Norwich, Nouveau, Optical, Origami, Orphic Cubism, Orphism, Outsider, Pastiche, Performance, Perigordian, Plastic, Pointillism, Pop, Postimpressionism, Postmodern, Practical, Pre-Raphaelite, Primitive, Psychedelic, Public, Purism, Quadratura, Quadrivium, Relievo, Sienese, →**SKILL**, Social realism, Stained glass, Still-life, Suprematism, Surrealism, Synchronism, Tachism(e), Tactics, Tatum, Tenebrism, Toreutics, Trecento, Triptych, Trivium, Trompe l'oeil, Trouvé, Tsutsumu, Useful, Verism, Virtu, Visual, Vorticism

▷ **Artefact** *may indicate* an anagram

Artery Aorta, Brachial, Carotid, Coronary, Duct, Femoral, Iliac, Innominate, M1, Pulmonary, Route

Artful Cute, Dodger, Foxy, Ingenious, Quirky, Shifty, Sly, Subtle, Tactician, Wily

Article(s) A, An, Apprentice, Clause, Column, Commodity, Cutting, Definite, Feature, Feuilleton, Gadget, Indefinite, Indenture, Item, Leader, Leading, Op-ed, Paper, Part, Piece, Pot-boiler, Shipping, Sidebar, Specify, The, Thing, Thirty-nine, Treatise, Turnover, Ware

Articulation, Articulate(d) Clear, Diarthrosis, Distinct, Eloquent, Enounce, Express, Fluent, Gimmal, Hinged, Intonate, Jointed, Lenis, Limbed, Lisp, Pretty-spoken, Pronounce, Single-tongue, Tipping, Utter, Vertebrae, Voice

Artifice(r), Artificial Bogus, Chouse, Contrived, Davenport-trick, Dodge, Ersatz, Factitious, False, Finesse, Guile, Hoax, In vitro, Logodaedaly, Made, Man-made, Mannered, Opificer, Phoney, Postiche, Pretence, Prosthetic, Pseudo, Reach, Ruse, Sell, Set, Sham, Spurious, Stratagem, → **STRATEGY**, Synthetic, Theatric, → **TRICK**, Unnatural, Wile, Wright

Artillery Battery, Cannon, Cohorn(e), Fougade, Fougasse, Guns, Mortar, Ordnance, Pyroballogy, RA, Rafale, Ramose, Ramus, Train

Artisan Craftsman, Decorator, Joiner, Journeyman, Mechanic, Pioneer, Pioner, Pyoner, Workman

Artist(e), Artistic Aesthetic, Animator, Bohemian, Cartoonist, Colourist, Cubist, Dadaist, Daedal(e), Deccie, Decorator, Enameller, Escape, Etcher, Fine, Foley, Gentle, Gilder, Graffiti, ICA, Illustrator, Impressionist, Landscapist, Limner, Linear, Maestro, Master, Mime, Miniaturist, → **MUSICIAN**, Nabis, Nazarene, Oeuvre, Orphism, → **PAINTER**, Pavement, Paysagist, Perspectivist, Piss, Plein-airist, Pre-Raphaelite, Primitive, Quick-change, RA, Rap, Screever, Sideman, Sien(n)ese, Surrealist, Tachisme, Tagger, Tap dancer, Touch, Trapeze, Trecentist, Virtuose, Virtuoso

Artless Candid, Homespun, Ingenuous, Innocent, Naive, Open, Seely

Art nouveau Jugendstil

As Aesir, Als, Arsenic, Coin, Eg, Forasmuch, Kame, Qua, Ridge, 's, Since, So, Thus, Ut, While

As before Anew, Ditto, Do, Stet

Ascend(ant), Ascent, Ascension Anabasis, Climb, Dominant, Escalate, Gradient, Pull, Ramp, Right, Rise, Sclim, Sklim, Slope, Up, Upgang, Uphill, Uprise, Zoom

Ascertain Determine, Discover, → **ESTABLISH**, Prove

Ascribe Assign, → **ATTRIBUTE**, Blame, Imply, Impute

As good as Equal, Tantamount

Ash(es), Ashen, Ashy Aesc, Aizle, Bone, Breeze, Cinders, Cinereal, Clinker(s), Easle, Embers, Fraxinas, Griseous, Kali, Pallor, Pearl, Pozz(u)olana, Prickly, Rowan, Ruins, Sorb, Stinking, Tephra, Urn, Varec, Volcanic, Wednesday, White, Witchen, Yg(g)drasil(l)

Ashamed Abashed, Embarrassed, Hangdog, Mortified, Repentant, Sheepish, Shent

Ashore Aland, Beached, Grounded, Stranded

Ashram Haven

Asia(n), Asiatic Afghan, Angaraland, Armenian, Balinese, Bengali, Bithynia, Cambodian, Cantonese, Desi, E, Evenki, Ewenki, Gook, Harijan, Harsha, Hun, Hyksos, Indian, Indonesian, Jordanian, Karen(ni), Kazakh, Kirghiz, Korean, Kurd, Kyrgyz, Lao, Lydian, Malay, Medea, Media, Mongol, Naga, Negrito, Nepalese, Pasht(o)um, Pushtu, Samo(y)ed, Shan, Siamese, Sindi, Sogdian, Tamil, Tatar, Tibetan, Turanian, Turk(o)man, Uzbeg, Uzbek, Vietnamese

Aside Apart, By, Despite, Private, Separate, Shelved, Sotto voce

Ask Bed, Beg, Beseech, Bid, Cadge, Charge, Demand, Desire, Enquire, Entreat, Evet, Implore, Intreat, Invite, Lobby, Newt, Petition, Pray, Prithee, Pump, Quiz, Request, Require, Rogation, Seek, Solicit, Speer, Speir, Touch

Askance Asconce, Askew, Oblique, Sideways

Aslant Skew

Asleep Dormant, Dove, Inactive, Napping

As needed Ad hoc

As often as Toties quoties

Aspect Angle, Bearing, Brow, Face, Facet, Facies, Feature, Look, Mien, Nature, Outlook, Perfective, Perspective, Sextile, Side, → **VIEW**, Visage, Vista

Aspen Trembling poplar

Aspersion, Asperse Calumny, Defame, Innuendo, Libel, Slander, Slur, Smear

Asphalt Bitumen, Blacktop, Gilsonite®, Jew's pitch, Pitch, Uinta(h)ite

Asphyxia Apn(o)ea

Aspirant, Aspirate, Aspiration, Aspire Ambition, Breath, Buckeen, Challenger, Desire, Dream, Endeavour, Ettle, Goal, H, Hope(ful), Pretend, Pursue, Rough, Spiritus, Wannabe(e), Would be, Yearn

Assail(ant) Afflict, Assault, Batter, Bego, Belabour, Bepelt, Beset, Bombard, Harry, Impugn, Oppugn, Pillory, Ply, Revile

Assassin(ate), Assassination Attentat, Booth, Brave, Bravo, Brutus, Casca, Cassius, Corday, Cut-throat, Frag, Gunman, Highbinder, Hitman, Killer, Ninja, Oswald, Sword, Sworder, Thuggee, Tyrannicide

Assault ABH, Assail, Assay, Attack, Battery, Bombard, GBH, Hamesucken, Head-butt, Indecent, Invasion, Knee, Maul, Molest, Mug, Push, →RAID, Stoor, Storm, Stour, Stowre

As seen Voetstoots

Assemble(d), Assembly Audience, Ball, Band, Bottom-hole, Chapter, Church, →COLLECTION, Company, Conclave, Congregate, Convention, Convocation, Convoke, Corroboree, Council, Court, Diet, Fit, Folkmote, Forgather, Fuel, Gather(ing), General, Group, House, Jirga, Lekgotla, Levee, Loya jirga, Mass, Meet, →MEETING, Moot, Muster, National, Oireachtas, Panegyry, Parishad, Parliament, Prefabrication, Primary, Quorum, Rally, Rallying-point, Reichstag, Relie, Resort, Riksdag, Roll up, Sanghat, Sejm, Senate, Senedd, Society, Synagogue, Synod, Tribunal, Troop, Turn out, Unlawful, Vidhan Sabha

Assent Accede, Acquiesce, Agree, Amen, Aye, Comply, Concur, Jokol, Nod, Placet, Sanction, Viceregal, Yea, Yield

Assert(ing), Assertion, Assertive Affirm, Allege, Bumptious, Constate, Contend, →DECLARE, Dogmatic, Forceful, Ipse-dixit, →MAINTAIN, Pose, Predicate, Proclaim, Protest, Pushing, Pushy, Swear (blind), Thetical

Assess(ment) Affeer, Appraise, Consider, Critique, Eleven-plus, Estimate, Evaluate, Formative, Gauge, Guesstimate, Inspect, →JUDGE, Levy, Measure, Perspective, Rating, Referee, Report, Risk, Scot and lot, Size up, Stocktake, Summative, Tax, Value, Weigh

Asset(s) Advantage, Capital, Chargeable, Chattel, Current, Fixed, Intangible, Inventory, Liquid, Plant, Property, Resource, Seed corn, Talent, Virtue

Assign(ation), Assignment Allocate, →ALLOT, Apply, Aret, Ascribe, Attentat, Attribute, Award, Date, Dedicate, Detail, Duty, Entrust, Errand, Fix, Give, Grant, Impute, Ordain, Point, Quota, Refer, Sort, Tak(e), Tryst

Assimilate(d) Absorb, Blend, Digest, Esculent, Fuse, Imbibe, Incorporate, Merge, Osmose

Assist(ance), Assistant Acolyte, Adjunct, Adviser, Aid(e), Ally, Alms, Attaché, Au pair, Batman, Busboy, Cad, Collaborate, Counterhand, Dresser, Facilitate, Factotum, Famulus, Gofer, →HAND, Help, Henchman, Legal aid, Matross, Nipper, Number two, Offsider, Omnibus, Proproctor, Reinforce, Relief, Second, Server, Service, Servitor, Sidekick, Sidesman, Stead, Subeditor, Subsidiary, Suffragan, →SUPPORT, Tawny Owl, Usher

Associate(d), Association Accomplice, Affiliate, Alliance, Attach, Bedfellow, Brotherhood, Cartel, Chapel, Club, Combine, Community, Company, Comrade, →CONNECT, Consort(ium), Correlate, Crony, Fellow, Fraternise, Goose club, Guild, Hobnob, Inquiline, Join, League, Liaison, Link, Member, Mix, Partner(ship), Probus, Relate, Ring, Stablemate, Staff, Syndicate, Synonymous, Tenants', Trade, UN(A), Union, Wiener Werkstatte, Word

▷ **Assorted** *may indicate* an anagram

Assuage Allay, Appease, Beet, Calm, Ease, Mease, Mitigate, Mollify, Relieve, Slake, Soften, Soothe

Assume(d), Assuming, Assumption Adopt, Affect, Arrogate, Artificial, Attire, Axiom, Believe, Don, Donné(e), Feign, Hypothesis, Lemma, Occam's Razor, Posit,

Postulate, Preconception, Premise, Premiss, Presuppose, Pretentious, Principle, Putative, Saltus, Say, Suppose, Surmise, Take

▷ **Assumption** *may indicate* 'attire'

Assure(d), Assurance Aplomb, Aver, Avouch, Belief, Calm, →**CERTAIN**, Comfort, Confidence, Confirm, Earnest, Gall, Guarantee, Knowing, Life, Pledge, Poise, Secure, Self-confidence, Term, Warranty

Aster Starwort

Asteroid Ceres, Eros, Hermes, Hygiea, Icarus, Juno, Pallas, Planetoid, Sea-star, Star, Starfish

Astonish(ed), Astonishing, Astonishment, Astound Abash, Admiraunce, Amaze, Banjax, Bewilder, Bowl over, Confound, Corker, Crikey, Daze, Donnert, Dumbstruck, Dum(b)found, Flabbergast, Gobsmack, Open-eyed, Open-mouthed, Phew, Rouse, Shake, Singular, Stagger, Startle, Stupefaction, Stupefy, Stupendous, Surprise, Thunderstruck, Wide-eyed, Wow

Astray Abord, Amiss, Errant, Lost, Will, Wull

Astride Athwart, En cavalier, Spanning, Straddle-back

Astringent Acerbic, Alum, Catechu, Gambi(e)r, Harsh, Kino, Myrobalan, Obstruent, Puckery, Rhatany, Sept-foil, Severe, Sour, Stypsis, Styptic, Tormentil, Witch-hazel

Astrologer, Astrology, Astrological Archgenethliac, Chaldean, Culpeper, Faust, Figure-caster, Genethliac, Lilly, Magus, Midheaven, Moore, Nostradamus, Soothsayer, Starmonger, Zadkiel

Astronaut Aldrin, Cosmonaut, Gagarin, Glenn, Lunarnaut, Spaceman, Spacer

Astronomer, Astronomy, Astronomical Airy, Almagest, Aristarchus, Azimuth, Barnard, Bessel, Bliss, Bradley, Brahe, Callipic, Cassini, Celsius, Christie, Coal sack, Copernicus, Dyson, Eddington, Encke, Eratosthenes, Eudoxus, Flamsteed, Galileo, Gamma-ray, Graham-Smith, Hale, Halley, Herschel, Hertzsprung, Hewish, Hipparchus, Hoyle, Hubble, Huggins, Jeans, Kepler, Lagrange, Laplace, Leverrier, Lockyer, Lovell, Maskelyne, Meton, Moore, Olbers, Omar Khayyam, Oort, Planetesimal, Planetology, Pond, Ptolemy, Quadrivium, Radio, Reber, Rees, Roche, Roemer, Russell, Ryle, Schwarzschild, Seyfert, Sosigenes, Spencer-Jones, Tycho Brahe, Urania, Uranography, Wolfendale, Woolley

Astute Acute, Canny, Crafty, Cunning, Downy, Perspicacious, Shrewd, Subtle, Wide, Wily

As well Additionally, Also, Both, Even, Forby, Too

Asylum Bedlam, Bin, Bughouse, Frithsoken, Funny-farm, Girth, Grith, Haven, Institution, Loony bin, Lunatic, Madhouse, Magdalene, Nuthouse, Political, Rathouse, Refuge, Retreat, Sanctuary, Shelter, Snake-pit

Asymmetric(al) Contrapposto, Lopsided, Skew

At first Erst

Atheist Doubter, Godless, Infidel, Irreligious, Sceptic

Athlete, Athletic(s) Agile, Agonist, Blue, Coe, Discobolus, Field, Gymnast, Hurdler, Jock, Leish, Miler, Milo, Nurmi, Olympian, Owens, Pacemaker, Runner, Sexual, Shamateur, Sportsman, Sprinter, Track, Track and field, Triple jump

Atlas Linguistic, Maps, Range, Silk, Telamon

▷ **At last** *may indicate* a cobbler

Atmosphere Aeropause, Afterdamp, Air, Ambience, Aura, Chemosphere, Climate, Elements, Epedaphic, Ether, Exosphere, F-layer, Geocorona, Ionosphere, Lid, Magnetosphere, Mesophere, Meteorology, Miasma, Mood, Ozone, Stratosphere, Thermosphere, Tropopause, Troposphere, Upper, Vibe(s), Vibrations

Atom(ic), Atoms, Atomism Boson, Chromophore, Dimer, Electron, Excimer, Gram, Ion, Iota, Isobare, Isotone, Isotope, Ligand, Logical, Molecule, Monad, Monovalent, Muonic, Nematic, Nuclide, Particle, Pile, Radionuclide, Side-chain, Species, Steric, Substituent

Atomiser Airbrush, Nebuliser

Atone(ment) Aby(e), Acceptilation, Appease, Assoil, Expiate, Purge, Redeem, Redemption, Yom Kippur

▷ **At random** *may indicate* an anagram

Atrocious, Atrocity Abominable, Brutal, Diabolical, Enorm, Flagitious, Heinous, Horrible, Massacre, Monstrous, Outrage, Piacular, Terrible, Vile

▷ **At sea** *may indicate* an anagram

Attach(ed), Attachment Accessory, Adhesion, Adhibition, Adnate, Adnation, Adscript, Affix, Allonge, Bolt, Bro, Byssus, Covermount, Curtilage, Devotement, Devotion, Distrain, Dobby, Eyehook, Feller, Glue, →**JOIN**, Obconic, Piggyback, Pin, Reticle, Sew, Snell, Stick, Tendon, Tie, Weld

Attack(ing), Attacker Affect, Aggression, Airstrike, Alert, Apoplexy, Assail, Assault, Assiege, Banzai, Batter, Belabour, Beset, Blitz(krieg), Bombard, Bout, Broadside, Calumny, Campaign, Carte, Charge, Clobber, Club, Counteroffensive, Coup de main, Denounce, Depredation, Discomfit, Excoriate, Feint, Fit, Foray, Fork, Forward, Gas, Glass, Happy-slapping, Harry, Hatchet job, Headbutt, Heart, Heckle, Iconoclast, Impingement, Incursion, Inroad, Invade, Inveigh, Knee, Lampoon, Lash out, Let fly, Maraud, Molest, Mug, Offence, Offensive, Onfall, Onrush, Onset, Onslaught, Oppugn, Outflank, Panic, Philippic, Pillage, Pin, Poke, Polemic, Pounce, Pre-emptive, Push, Raid, Rally, Sail, Sandbag, Savage, Second strike, Seizure, Siege, Skitch, Slam, Snipe, Sortie, Storm, Strafe, Straff, Strike, Thrust, Tilt, Vituperate, Wage, Zap

Attain(ment) Accomplish, Arrive, Earn, Fruition, Get, Land, Reach

Attempt Attentat, Bash, Bid, Burl, Crack, Debut, Effort, Egma, Endeavour, Essay, Go, Mint, Nisus, Potshot, Seek, Shot, Shy, Spell baker, Stab, Strive, →**TRY**, Venture, Whack, Whirl

Attend(ance), Attendant Accompany, Acolyte, Aide, Batman, Bearer, Bell-hop, Chaperone, Commissionaire, Courtier, Doula, Dresser, Entourage, Equerry, Escort, Esquire, Footman, Gate(-keeper), G(h)illie, Gilly, Hear, →**HEED**, Janitor, Keeper, →**LISTEN**, Loblolly-boy, Marshal, Note, Orderly, Outrider, Page, Pew-opener, Presence, Respect, Satellite, Second, S(a)ice, Sort, Steward, Syce, Therapeutic, Trainbearer, Trolleydolly, Up at, Valet, Visit, Wait, Watch, Zambuck

Attention, Attentive Achtung, Alert, Assiduity, Care(ful), Court, Coverage, Dutiful, Ear, Gallant, Gaum, Gorm, Hark, Heed, Mind, Note, Notice, Observant, Present, Punctilious, Qui vive, →**REGARD**, Spotlight, Tenty, Thorough, Thought, Uxorious, Voila

Attest Affirm, Certify, Depose, Guarantee, Notarise, Swear, →**WITNESS**

Attic Bee-bird, Garret, Greek, Koine, Loft, Mansard, Muse, Salt, Sky parlour, Solar, Soler, Sollar, Soller, Tallat, Tallet, Tallot

Attire Accoutre, Adorn, Apparel, Clobber, Clothe, Clothing, →**DRESS**, Garb, Habit

Attitude Air, Aspect, Behaviour, Demeanour, Light, →**MANNER**, Mindset, Nimby, Outlook, Pose, Position, Possie, Posture, Propositional, Scalogram, Sense, Song, Spirit, Stance, Tone, Uppity, Viewpoint

Attorney Advocate, Counsellor, DA, Lawyer, Private, Proctor, Prosecutor, Public

Attract(ion), Attractive(ness), Attractor Bait, Beauté du diable, Becoming, Bedworthy, Bewitch, Bonnie, Bonny, Catchy, Charisma, →**CHARM**, Comely, Cute, Dinky, Dish(y), →**DRAW**, Engaging, Entice, Eye-catching, Fascinate, Fetching, Goodly, Great, Heartthrob, Hot, Hot stuff, Hotty, Hunky, Inviting, Jolie laide, Loadstone, Looker, Luscious, Magnet(ism), Pack in, Personable, Pheromone, Photogenic, Picture postcard, Picturesque, Popsy, Pretty, Sexpot, Sideshow, Smasher, Snazzy, Striking, Stunner, Taking, Tasteful, Tasty, Tempt, Toothsome, Tottie, Totty, Triff(ic), Va-va-voom, Winning, Winsome, Zoophilia

Attribute, Attribution Accredit, Allot, Ap(p)anage, Ascribe, Asset, By, Credit, Gift, Impute, Lay, Metonym, Owe, Proprium, Quality, Refer, Resource, Shtick, Strength

Aubergine Brinjal, Brown jolly, Egg-plant, Mad-apple

Auburn Abram, Chestnut, Copper, Vill(age)

Auction(eer) Barter, Bridge, Cant, Dutch, Hammer, Outcry, Outro(o)per, Roup, Sale, Subhastation, Tattersall, Trade sale, Vendue, Warrant sale

Audacious, Audacity Bald-headed, Bold, Brash, Cheek, Chutspah, Chutzpah,

Cool, Der-doing, Devil-may-care, Effrontery, Face, Hardihood, Indiscreet, Insolence, Intrepid, Neck, Nerve, Rash, Sauce

Audible Out loud

Audience, Auditorium Assembly, Court, Durbar, Gate, House, Interview, Pit, Sphendone, Theatre, Tribunal

Audit(or) Accountant, Check, Ear, Examine, Inspect, Listener, Medical, Vet

Auger Miser

Augment(ed) Boost, Eche, Eke, Grow, Ich, Increase, Pad, Supplement, Swell, Tritone

Augury → DIVINATION, Ornithoscopy

Aunt(ie) Agony, Augusta, Beeb, Giddy, Naunt, Sainted, Tia

Aura Aroma, Halo, Mystique, Nimbus, Odour, Vibe(s), Vibrations

Austere, Austerity Astringent, Bleak, Dantean, Dervish, Hard, → HARSH, Moral, Plain, Rigour, Stern, Stoic, Stoor, Strict, Vaudois, Waldensian

Australia(n) A, Alf, Antichthone, Antipodean, .au, Aussie, Balt, Banana-bender, Bananalander, Billjim, Bodgie, Canecutter, Cobber, Coon, Currency, Darwinian, Digger, Gin, Godzone, Gumsucker, Gurindji, Koori, Larrikin, Myall, Norm, Ocker, Ossie, Outbacker, Oz(zie), Pintupi, Roy, Sandgroper, Strine, Sydneysider, Wallaby, Yarra-yabbies

Austrian Cisleithan, Tyrolean

Authentic(ate), Authentication Certify, Des(h)i, Echt, Genuine, Honest, Notarise, Official, Probate, Real, Sign, Simon-pure, Test, True, Validate

▷ **Author** *may refer to* author of puzzle

Author(ess) Anarch, Architect, Auctorial, Hand, Inventor, Me, Parent, Scenarist, Volumist, Wordsmith, → WRITER

Authorise(d), Authorisation Accredit, Clearance, Depute, Empower, Enable, Entitle, Exequatur, Imprimatur, Legal, Legit, → LICENCE, Mandate, Official, OK, Passport, → PERMIT, Plenipotentiary, Sanction, Sign, Stamp, Warrant

Authority, Authoritarian, Authoritative Ascetic, Canon, Charter, Circar, Cocker, Commission, Commune, Crisp, Definitive, Domineering, Dominion, Establishment, Ex cathedra, Expert, Fascist, Free hand, Gravitas, Hegemony, Inquirendo, Jackboot, Leadership, Licence, Light, Local, Magisterial, Mana, Mandate, Mantle, Mastery, Name, Oracle, Permit, PLA, Potency, → POWER, Prefect, Prestige, Pundit, Regime, Remit, Right, Rod, Say-so, Sceptre, Sircar, Sirkar, Source, Supremacy, Supremo, Tyrannous, Unitary, Warrant

Autobiography Memoir

Autochthonous Aboriginal

Autocrat(ic) Absolute, Caesar, Cham, Despot, Neronian, Tenno, Tsar, Tyrant

Automatic, Automaton Android, Aut, Browning, Deskill, Instinctive, Knee-jerk, Machine, Mechanical, Pistol, Reflex, Robot, RUR, Zombi

Auxiliary Adjunct, Adjuvant, Adminicle, Aide, Ancillary, Be, Feldsher, Foederatus, Have, Helper, Ido, Modal

Avail(able) Benefit, Dow, Eligible, Going, Handy, In season, On, On call, On hand, On tap, Open, Out, Pickings, Potluck, → READY, Serve, To hand, Up for grabs, Use, Utilise

Avalanche Deluge, Icefall, Landfall, Landslide, Landslip, Lauwine, Slide, Slip, Snowdrop

Avarice, Avaricious Cupidity, Gimmes, Golddigger, Greed, Money-grubbing, Pleonexia, Predatory, Shylock, Sordid

Avenge(r) Alecta, Eriny(e)s, Eumenides, Goel, Kuraitcha, Megaera, Punish, Redress, Requite, → REVENGE, Tisiphone, Wreak

Avenue Allee, Alley, Approach, Arcade, Channel, Corso, Cradle-walk, Hall, Mall, Passage, Vista, Way, Xyst(us)

Average Adjustment, Av, Batting, Dow Jones, Fair, Mean, Mediocre, Middle-brow, Middling, Moderate, Norm, Par, Run, Soso, Standard

Averse, Aversion, Avert Against, Antipathy, Apositia, Disgust, Distaste,

Hatred, Horror, Opposed, Pet, Phengephobia, Phobic, Photophobia, Risk, Scunner, Sit(i)ophobia

Avert Avoid, → **DEFLECT**, Forfend, Parry, Ward

Aviator Airman, Alcock, Bleriot, Brown, Co-pilot, De Havilland, Earhart, Flier, Hinkler, Icarus, Johnson, Lindbergh, Pilot, Yeager

Avid Athirst, → **EAGER**, Greedy, Keen

Avoid(er), Avoidance Abstain, Ba(u)lk, Boycott, Bypass, Cop-out, Cut, Dodge, Duck, Elude, Escape, Eschew, Evade, Evitate, Evite, Fly, Forbear, Gallio, Hedge, Miss, Obviate, Parry, Prevaricate, Scape, Scutage, Secede, Shelve, Shirk, Shun, Sidestep, Skirt, Skive, Spare, Spurn, Tergiversate, Waive

Avow(ed) Acknowledged, Affirm, Declare, Own, Swear

Await(ed) Abide, Bide, Expect, Godot, Tarry

Awake(ning) Aware, Conscious, Conversion, Fly, Rouse, Vigilant

Award Academy, Accolade, Acquisitive, Addeem, Addoom, Allot, Alpha, Apple, Arbitrament, Aret(t), Bafta, Bar, Bestow, Bursary, Cap, Charter Mark, Clasp, Clio, Compensation, Crown, Degree, Emmy, Exhibition, Genie, Golden handshake, Grammy, Grant, Juno, Lourie, Medal, Meed, Mete, MOBO, Oscar, Palatinate, Palme d'Or, Premium, Present(ation), → **PRIZE**, Rosette, Scholarship, Tony, Trophy, Yuko

Aware(ness) Alert, Aware, Coconscious, Cognisant, Conscious, Conversant, ESP, Est, Hep, Hip, Informed, Knowing, Liminal, Mindshare, Onto, Panaesthesia, Prajna, Presentiment, Samadhi, Scienter, Sensible, Sensile, Sensitive, Sentience, Streetwise, Vigilant, Weet, Wit, Wot

Away Abaxial, Absent, Afield, Apage, Avaunt, By, For-, Forth, Fro(m), Go, Hence, Off, Out, Past

▷ **Away** *may indicate* a word to be omitted

Awe(d) Dread, D(o)ulia, Fear, Intimidate, Loch, Overcome, Popeyed, Regard, Respect, Reverent, Scare, Solemn, Wonderment

Awful(ly) Alas, Appalling, Deare, Dere, Dire, Fearful, Horrendous, Lamentable, Nasty, O so, Piacular, Rotten, Terrible, Third rate

▷ **Awfully** *may indicate* an anagram

Awkward All thumbs, Angular, Blate, Bolshy, Bumpkin, Clumble-fisted, Clumsy, Complicated, Contrary, Corner, Crabby, Cubbish, Cumbersome, Cussed, Dub, Embarrassing, Farouche, Fiddly, Fix, Gangly, Gauche, Gawky, Handless, Howdy-do, Inconvenient, Inelegant, Inept, Kittle-cattle, Knotty, Lanky, Loutish, Lurdan(e), Lurden, Maladdress, Mauther, Mawr, Naff, Nasty, Nonconformist, Ornery, Perverse, Refractory, Slouch, Slummock, So-and-so, Spot, Sticky, Stiff, Stroppy, Stumblebum, Swainish, Ticklish, Uncoordinated, Uncouth, Uneasy, Ungainly, Unhandy, Unwieldy, Wooden, Wry

Awry Agley, Amiss, Askent, Askew, Athwart, Cam, Haywire, Kam(me), Pear-shaped, Wonky

Axe(s) Abolish, Adz(e), Bill, Celt, Chop(per), Cleaver, Gisarme, Gurlet, Halberd, Halbert, Hatchet, Hew, Holing, Ice, Palstaff, Palstave, Partisan, Piolet, Retrench, Sax, Scrub, Sparth(e), Sperthe, Spontoon, Thunderbolt, Tomahawk, Twibill, X, Y, Z

Axeman Bassist, Guitarist, Hendrix

Axe-shaped Securiform

Axiom Adage, Motto, Peano's, Proverb, Saw, Saying

Aye Eer, Ever, Yea, Yes

Bb

B Bachelor, Black, Book, Born, Boron, Bowled, Bravo, Flipside

Babble(r) Blather, Chatter, Gibber, Haver, Lallation, Lurry, Prate, Prattle, Runnel, Tonguester, Tonguework, Twattle, Waffle, Witer

Baboon Ape, Bobbejaan, Chacma, Cynocephalus, Dog-ape, Drill, Gelada, Hamadryas, Mandrill, Sphinx

Baby Bairn, Band-Aid®, Blue, Bub, Bunting, Coddle, Duck, Grand, Infant, Jelly, Litter, Neonate, Nursling, Pamper, Papoose, Preverbal, Sis, Small, Sook, Spoil, Suckling, Tar, Test tube, Tot, Wean

Bachelor BA, Bach, Benedict, Budge, Celibate, En garçon, Knight, Pantagamy, Parti, Single, Stag, Wifeless

Bacillus Comma, Germ, Micrococcus, Tubercle, Virus

Back(er), Backing, Back out, Back up, Backward Abet, Accompany, Addorse, Aft, Again, Ago, Aid, Anticlockwise, Arear, Arrear, Assist, Backare, Bankroll, Buckram, Champion, Chorus, Consent, Cry off, Culet, Defender, Dorsal, Dorse, Dorsum, Dos, Ebb, Empatron, Encourage, Endorse, Fakie, Finance, Frae, Fro, Full, Fund(er), Gaff, Half, Help, Hind, Historic, Incremental, La-la, Late, Notaeum, Notal, Notum, On, Patronise, Pendu, Poop, Pronotum, Punt, Rear(most), Retral, Retro(grade), Retrogress, Retrorse, Retrospective, Return, Rev, Reverse, Ridge, Root, Running, Scenery, Shy, Spinal, Sponsor, Standby, Stern, Sternboard, Sternway, →**SUPPORT**, Sweeper, Syndicate, Tail, Telson, Tergum, Third, Thrae, Three-quarter, Tonneau, Ulu, Uphold, Verso, Vie, Vo, Wager, Watteau

▷ **Back(ing)** *may indicate* a word spelt backwards

Backbone Atlas, Chine, Grit, Guts, Mettle, Spina, Spine

Backchat Lip, Mouth, Sass

Backcloth, Backdrop Cyclorama, Scenery

Backer Angel, Benefactor, Funder, Patron, Punter, Seconder, Sponsor

Backgammon Acey-deucy, Blot, Lurch, Tick-tack, Trick-track, Tric-trac, Verquere

Background Antecedence, Chromakey, Cyclorama, Fond, History, Horizon, Natural, Retrally, Setting, Ulterior

Back problem Kyphosis, Lumbago, Osteoporosis, Scolioma, Scoliosis

Backslide(r), Backsliding Apostate, Lapse, Regress, Relapse, Revert

Bacon Danish, Essayist, Flitch, Francis, Gammon, Lardo(o)n, Pancetta, Pig(meat), Pork, Rasher, Roger, Spec(k), Streaky, Verulam

Bacteria, Bacteriologist, Bacterium Acidophilus, Actinomycete, Aerobe, Bacilli, Bacteriological, Baregin, →**BUG**, Cocci, Culture, Foul-brood, →**GERM**, Hib, Intestinal flora, Koch, Legionella, Listeria, Lysogen, Microbe, Micrococcus, Microphyte, Mother, MRSA, Nitrifying, Nitrite, Nostoc, Operon, Packet, Pasteurella, Pathogen, Peritrich(a), Petri, Pneumococcus, Proteus, Pus, Salmonella, Septic, Serogroup, Serotype, Serum, Spirilla, Spirulina, Spore, Staph, Strep(tococcus), Superbug, Vibrio, Vincent's angina

Bad, Badness Abysmal, Addled, Chronic, Crook, Defective, Diabolic, Drastic, Dud, Duff, Dystopia, Egregious, Execrable, Faulty, Fearful, Fourth-rate, Half-pie, Heinous, Ill (timed), Immoral, Inferior, Injurious, Lither, Lulu, Mal(vu), Naughty, Nefandous, Nefarious, Nice, Off, Ominous, Oncus, Onkus, Parlous, Piacular, Poor, Rank, Reprobate, Ropy, Scampish, Scoundrel, Sinful, Spoiled, The pits, Turpitude, Undesirable, Unspeakable, Useless, Wack, Wick, →**WICKED**

▷ **Bad(ly)** *may indicate* an anagram

Badge Brassard, Brooch, Button, Chevron, Cockade, Cockleshell, Comm, Cordon,

Crest, Eagle, Emblem, Ensign, Epaulet, Episemon, Fáinne, Film, Flash, Garter, Gorget, ID, Insigne, Insignia, Kikumon, Mark, Mon, Numerals, Orange, Pilgrim's sign, Pin, Rondel, Rosette, Scallop, Scallop(-shell), Shield, Shouldermark, → SIGN, Symbol, Tiger, Token, Vernicle, Vine branch, Vine-rod, Wings

Badger → ANNOY, Bait, Bedevil, Beset, Brock, Browbeat, Bug, Bullyrag, Cete, Dassi(e), Ferret, Gray, Grey, → HARASS, Hassle, Hog, Honey, Hound, Nag, Pester, Plague, Provoke, Ratel, Ride, Roil, Sand, Sow, Teledu, Wisconsin

Bad luck Ambs-ace, Ames-ace, Deuce-ace, Hoodoo, Jinx, Jonah, Shame, Voodoo

Bad-tempered Carnaptious, Curmudgeon, Curnaptious, Curst, Grouchy, Grum(py), Irritable, Marabunta, Moody, Patch, Scratchy, Shirty, Splenetic, Stroppy

Baffle(d), Baffling Anan, Balk, Bemuse, Bewilder, Confound, Confuse, Elude, Evade, Floor, Flummox, Foil, Fox, Get, Hush-kit, Mate, Muse, Mystify, Nark, Nonplus, Perplex, Pose, Puzzle, Stump, Throw, Thwart

Bag(gage), Bags Acquire, Air, Alforja, Amaut, Amowt, Bedroll, Besom, Bladder, Blue, Body, Bounty, Bulse, Bum, Buoyancy, Caba(s), Caecum, Capture, Carpet, Carrier, Carryall, Case, Cecum, Clutch, Cly, Cod, Colostomy, Cool(er), Corduroy, Crone, Crumenal, Cyst, Daypack, Dilli, Dilly, Dime, Diplomatic, Ditty, Doggy, Dorothy, Douche, Duffel, Dunnage, → EFFECTS, Emery, Excess, Fanny pack, Flannels, Flotation, Follicle, Game, → GEAR, Gladstone, Goody, Grab, Grip, Gripsack, Grow, Holdall, Ice, Impedimenta, Jelly, Jiffy®, Kill, Knapsack, Ladies' companion, Lavender, Materiel, Meal-poke, Messenger, Minx, Mixed, Money, Monkey, Moon, Mummy, Musette, Musk, Muzzle, Mystery, Nap, Necessaire, Net, Nunny, Organiser, Overnight, Overnighter, Oxford, Packsack, Pantaloons, Plastic, Plus fours, Pochette, Pock(et), Pocketbook, Poke, Politzer's, Poly(thene), Port(manteau), Portmantle, Portmantua, Post, Pot, Pouch, Pounce, Pudding, Punch, Purse, Rake, Red, Reticule, Ridicule, Rucksack, Sabretache, Sac(cule), Sachet, Sack, Saddle, Sag, Satchel, Scent, School, Scrip, Scrotum, Sea, Shopper, Sick, Slattern, Sleeping, Specialty, Sponge, Sporran, Stacks, Sugar, Survival, Tea, Tote, → TRAP, Trews, Trollop, Trouse(r), Tucker (box), Udder, Unmentionables, Valise, Vanity, Viaticals, Waist, Wallet, Water, Weekend, Win, Woolpack, Work, Wrap, Wrapping, Ziplock

Bagpipe Chorus, Cornemuse, Drone, Gaita, Musette, Pibroch, Piffero, Skirl, Sourdeline, Uillean, Zampogna

Bail(er), Bailment Bond, Ladle, Mainpernor, Mainprise, Mutuum, Replevin, Replevy, Scoop

Bailiff Adam, Beagle, Bum, Factor, Grieve, Land-agent, Philistine, Reeve, Steward, Tipstaff, Water

Bait Angleworm, Badger, Berley, Brandling, Burley, Chum, Dap, Decoy, Entice, Gentle, Harass, Incentive, Lobworm, Lug(worm), Lure, Mawk, → RAG, Ragworm, Sandworm, Teagle, Tease, Tempt, Tole, Toll

Bake(r), Baked, Baking Alaska, Batch, Baxter, Coctile, → COOK, Fire, Icer, Kiln-dry, Oven, Pieman, Roast, Scorch, Shir(r)

Bakery Patisserie

Balance(d) Account, Beam, Counterpoise, Countervail, Counterweight, Equate, Equilibrium, Equipoise, Equiponderate, Even, Fixed, Gyroscope, Gyrostat, Horn, Hydrostatic, Isostasy, Launce, Libra, Librate, Meet, Otocyst, Otolith, Pease, Peise, Perch, Peyse, Poise, → REMAINDER, Remnant, Residual, Rest, Scale, Spring, Stability, Stand, Steelyard, Symmetry, Together, → TOTAL, Trial, Trim, Tron(e), Unicycle

Balcony Circle, Gallery, Loggia, Mirador, Moucharaby, Pew, Porch, Sundeck, Tarras, Terrace, Veranda(h)

Bald, Baldness Alopecia, Apterium, Awnless, Barren, Calvities, Coot, Crude, Egghead, Fox-evil, Glabrous, Hairless, Madarosis, Open, Peelgarlic, Pilgarlic(k), Pollard, Psilosis, Slaphead, Smoothpate, Tonsured

Bale Bl, Bundle, Evil, Pack, Truss

Ball(s) Agglomerate, Alley, Ally, Ammo, Aniseed, Beach, Bead, Beamer, Bearings, Bobble, Bolus, Bosey, Bosie, Bouncer, Break, Buckshot, Cap, Cherry, Chinaman, Clew, Clue, Condylar, Cotill(i)on, Cramp, Croquette, Crystal, Cue, Curve, Daisy-cutter,

→**DANCE**, Delivery, Dink, Dollydrop, Doosra, Full-pitch, Full-toss, Fungo, Gazunder, →**GLOBE**, Glomerate, Gobstopper, Googly, Goolies, Gool(e)ys, Grounder, Grub, Grubhunter, Gutta, Gutter, Gutty, Hank, Hop, Hunt, Inswinger, Ivory, Jinglet, Knob, Knur(r), Leather, Leg-break, Leg-cutter, Lob, Long-hop, Marble, Masque(rade), Medicine, Minié, Moth, Nur(r), O, Off-break, Off-spin, Outswinger, Over, Overarm, Parrel truck, Pea, Pellet, Pill, Pompom, Pompon, Prom, Puck, Quenelle, Rissole, Root, Rover, Rundle, Seamer, Sneak, Sphere, Spinner, Strike, Swiss, Tea, Testes, Tice, Time, Witches, Wood, Wrecker's, Wrecking, Yorker, Zorb®

Ballast Kentledge, Makeweight, Stabiliser, Trim, Weight

Ballerina Coryphee, Dancer, Pavlova

Ballet, Ballet movement, Ballet-system Arabesque, Assemblé, Balancé, Ballon, Battement, Bolshoi, Brisé, Cabriole, Cambré, Chainé, Changement, Checkmate, Daphnis and Chloe, Développé, Écarté, Echappé, Enchainement, Entrechat, Firebird, Fouette, Giselle, Jeté, Kirov, Laban, Mayerling, Nutcracker, Pas de basque, Pas de bourrée, Pas de chat, Petit battement, Pirouette, Plastique, Pointe, Port de bras, Relevé, Saut

Ballista Scorpion

Ballistic Wildfire

Balloon(ist) Aeronaut, Aerostat, Airship, Bag, Barrage, Billow, Blimp, Bloat, Dirigible, Distend, Dumont, Enlarge, Fumetto, Hot air, Lead, Montgolfier, Pilot, Rawinsonde, Weather, Zeppelin

Ballot Election, Mulligan, →**POLL**, Referendum, Second, Suffrage, Ticket, Vote

Balm(y) Anetic, Arnica, Balsam, Calamint, Emollient, Fragrant, Garjan, Gilead, Gurjun, Lemon, Lenitive, →**MILD**, Mirbane, Myrbane, Nard, Oil, Opobalsam, Ottar, Redolent, Remedy, Soothe, Spikenard, Tolu, Unguent

Balsam Canada, Copaiba, Copaiva, Nard, Noli-me-tangere, Peruvian, Resin, Spikenard, Tamanu, Tolu(ic), Touch-me-not, Tous-les-mois, Turpentine

Ban(ned) Abolish, Accurse, Anathema, Black(ing), Censor, Curfew, Debar, D-notice, Embargo, Estop, Excommunicate, Forbid, For(e)say, For(e)speak, Gag, Gate, Green, Moratorium, No, Outlaw, Prohibit, Proscribe, Suppress, Taboo, Tabu, Test, Verboten, Veto

Banal Corny, Flat, Hackneyed, Jejune, Mundane, Platitudinous, →**TRITE**, Trivial

Banana(s) Abaca, Hand, Loco, →**MAD**, Musa, Plantain, Split, Top, Zany

Band(ed), Bands Absorption, Alice, Anadem, Anklet, Armlet, Belt, Border, Braid, Brake, Brass, Brassard, Brassart, Caravan, CB, Channel, Chinstrap, Chromosome, Circlet, Citizens', Closet, Cohort, Collar, Collet, Combo, Company, Conduction, Corslet, Coterie, Crape, Crew, Deely boppers, Elastic, ELO, Endorse, Energy, Facia, Falling, Fascia, Ferret, Ferrule, Fess, Filament, Fillet, Fourchette, Fraternity, Frequency, Frieze, Frog, Frontlet, Galloon, Gamelan, →**GANG**, Garage, Garland, Garter, Gasket, Gaskin, Geneva, German, Gird, Girr, Girth, Group, Guard, →**HOOP**, Hope, Iron, Jazz, Jug, Kara, Kitchen, Label, Lytta, Macnamara's, Maniple, Massed, Military, Mourning, Noise, Obi, One-man, Orchestra, Pack, Pass, Patte, Pipe, Plinth, Property, Puttee, Rib, Ribbon, Rim, Ring, Robbers, Round, Rubber, Sash, Scarf, Screed, Sect, Shadow, Sheet, Shoe, Snood, Speckled, Steel, Strake, Strand, Strap, Stratum, String, Stripe, Succinctory, Swath(e), Sweat, Tape, Tendon, Thecla, Thoroughbrace, Tie, Tippet, Tourniquet, Train, Trangle, Tribute, Troop, Troupe, Tumpline, Turm, Tyre, Unite, Valence, Vitrain, Vitta, Wanty, Wedding, Weed, Weeper, Welt, Wings, With(e), Wristlet, Zona, Zone, Zonule

Bandage Bind, Dressing, Fillet, Lint, Living, Pledget, Roller, Sling, Spica, Swaddle, Swathe, T, Tape, Truss, Wadding

Bandit Apache, Bravo, Brigand, Desperado, Outlaw, Pirate, Rapparee, →**ROBBER**, Turpin

Bandstand Kiosk, Stage

Bane Curse, Dioxin, Evil, Harm, Poison

Bang(er) Amorce, Andouillette, Beat, Big, Cap, Chipolata, Clap, Cracker, Crock,

Explode, Firecracker, Flivver, Fringe, Haircut, Heap, Implode, Jalopy, Jammy, Maroon, Pep(p)eroni, Rattletrap, Report, Sausage, Sizzler, Slam, Thrill, → TNT, Wurst

Bangladesh .bd

Bangle Anklet, Armlet, Bracelet, Kara

Banish(ment) Ban, Deport, Depose, Dispel, Exile, Expatriate, Expel, Extradition, Forsay, Maroon, Ostracise, → OUTLAW, Relegate, Rusticate

Bank(ing), Bank on An(n)icut, Asar, Backs, Bar, Bay, Beneficiary, Bet, Bk, Blood, Bluff, Bottle, Brae, Brim, Bund, Camber, Cay, Central, Chesil, Clearing (house), Cloud, Commercial, Cooperative, Data, Depend, Deposit, Dogger, Down, Drawee, Dune, Dyke, Earthwork, Escarp, Fog, Gene, Giro, Glacis, Gradient, Gradin(e), Hack, Hele, Hill(side), Home, Incline, Jodrell, Kaim, Kame, Land, Left, Lender, Levee, Link, Lombard Street, Memory, Merchant, Mound, Nap, National, Needle, Nore, Overslaugh, Oyster, Parapet, Penny, Piggy, Pot, Private, Rake, Ramp, Rampart, Reef, → RELY, Reserve, Retail, Ridge, Rivage, Riverside, Rodham, Row, Sandbar, Savings, Seed, Shallow, Shelf, Side, Slope, Soil, Sperm, Staithe, State, Sunk, Telephone, Terrace, Terreplein, Tier, Trust, Vault, West, World

Banker Agent, Cert(ainty), Financial, Fugger, Gnome, Lombard, Medici, → RIVER, Rothschild, Shroff, Teller

▷ **Banker** *may indicate* a river

▷ **Bankrupt** *may indicate* 'red' around another word

Bankrupt(cy) Break, Broke, Bung, Bust, Cadaver, Carey Street, Chapter-eleven, Crash, Debtor, Deplete, Duck, Dyvour, Fail, Fold, Insolvent, Penniless, Receivership, Ruin, Rump, Scat, Sequestration, Skatt, Smash

Banner Banderol(e), Bandrol, Bannerol, Blue blanket, → FLAG, Gumphion, Labarum, Oriflamme, Sign, Standard, Streamer

Banquet Beanfeast, Dine, Feast, Junket, Nosh-up, Spread

Bantam Dandy-cock, Dandy-hen

Banter Backchat, Badinage, Borak, Borax, Chaff, Dicacity, Dieter, Jest, → JOKE, Persiflage, Picong, Rag, Rally, Repartee, Ribaldry, Roast, Rot, Tease

Baptise(d), Baptism, Baptist Affusion, Amrit, Christen, Clinical, Conditional, Dip, Dipper, Dopper, Dunker, Hypothetical, Illuminati, Immersion, John, Mandaean, Mersion, Palingenesis, Private, Sprinkle, Tinker

Bar(s) Address, Angle-iron, Asymmetric, Axletree, Bail, Ban, Baulk, Beam, Bilboes, Billet, Bistro, Blackball, Blacklist, Block(ade), Bloom, Bolt, Boom, Bottega, Brasserie, Buffet, Bull, Bumper, But, Buvette, → CAGE, Cake, Came, Cantina, Capo, Capstan, Channel, Clasp, Clip joint, Cocktail, Coffee, Colour, Counter, Cramp(on), Cross(head), Crow, Crush, Currency, Dive, Doggery, Double, Draw, Drift, Dumbbell, Efficiency, Espresso, Estaminet, Estop(pel), Except, Exclude, Fern, Fid, Flinders, Fonda, Forbid, Foreclose, Forestall, Fret, Gad, Gastropub, Glazing, Grate, Grid, Grog-shop, Gunshop, Hame, Handrail, Handspike, Heck, → HINDRANCE, Horizontal, Hound, Hyphen, Impediment, Ingot, Inn, Inner, Judder, Juice, Karaoke, Keeper, Kickstand, Knuckleduster, Latch, Let, Lever, Limbo, Line, Lingot, Local, Lock out, Lounge, Macron, Mandrel, Mandril, Measure, Menu, Merchant, Milk, Muesli, Mullion, Nail, Nanaimo, Navigation, Nineteenth hole, No-go, Norman, Obstacle, Omerta, Onely, Outer, Oxygen, Parallel, Perch, Pile, Pinch, Pole, Posada, Prescription, Private, Prohibit, Pub, Public, Rack, Raddle, Rail, Ramrod, Rance, Raw, Reach, Restrict, Rib, Risp, Rod, Roll, Roo, Rung, Saddle, Salad, Saloon, Sand, Sans, Save, Saving, Scroll, Shaft, Shanty, Shet, Shut, Singles, Skewer, Slice, Slot, Snack, Snug, Spacer, Spar, Speakeasy, Spit, Splinter, Sprag, Status, Stave, Stemmer, Stick, Stretcher, Stripe, Strut, Suspend, Sway, Swee, T, Tap(-room), Tapas, Taphouse, Task, Tavern(a), Temple, Tiki, Title, Toll, Tombolo, Tommy, Tool, Torsion, Tow, Trace, Trangle, Transom, Trapeze, Trundle, Type, U-bolt, Vinculum, Wall, Ward, Wet, Whisker, Window, Wine, Wire, Wrecking, Z, Zed

Barb(ed) Bur(r), Fluke, Harl, Herl, → HOOK, Jag(g), Jibe, Pheon, Prickle, Ramus, Tang, Thorn, Vexillum

Barbarian, Barbaric Boor, Fifteen, Foreigner, Goth, Heathen, Hottentot, Hun, Inhuman, Lowbrow, Outlandish, Philistine, Rude, Savage, Tartar, Tatar(ic)

Barbecue Braai(vleis), Chargrill, Cook-out, Flame-grill, Grill, Hangi, Hibachi, Roast, Spit

Barber Epilate, Figaro, Scrape(r), Shaver, Strap, Todd, Tonsor, Trimmer

Bare, Bare-headed Adamic, Aphyllous, Bald, Barren, Blank, Bodkin, Cere, Décolleté, Denude, Hush, Lewd, Marginal, Mere, Moon, → NAKED, Nude, Open, Plain, Scablands, Scant, Sear, Stark, Timber line, Topless, Uncase, Uncover, Unveil

Bareback Godiva

Barely Hardly, Just, Merely, Scarcely, Scrimp

Bargain(ing) Agreement, Bargoon, Barter, Braata, Chaffer, Champerty, → CHEAP, Cheapo, Collective, Compact, Contract, Coup, Deal, Dicker, Distributive, Effort, Find, Go, Haggle, Higgle, Horse-trade, Huckster, Indent, Integrative, Negotiate, Option, → PACT, Plea, Productivity, Scoop, Snip, Steal, Supersaver, Time, Trade, Trock, Troke, Truck, Wanworth, Wheeler-dealing

Barge Birlinn, Bucentaur, Budgero(w), Butty, Casco, Elbow, Gabbard, Gabbart, Galley-foist, Hopper, Intrude, Jostle, Keel, Lighter, Nudge, Obtrude, Pra(a)m, Ram, Scow, → SHIP, Trow, Wherry

▷ **Barge** *may indicate* an anagram

Bark Angostura, Ayelp, Bass, Bast, Bay, Bowwow, Canella, Cascara, Cascara sagrada, Cassia, China, Cinchona, Cinnamon, Cork, Cortex, Honduras, Jamaica, Kina, Kinakina, Liber, Mezereon, Mezereum, Myrica, Parchment, Peel, Pereira, Peruvian, Quebracho, Quest, Quill, Quillai, Quina, Quinquina, Rind, Salian, Sassafras, Scrape, Shag, → SHIP, Skin, Tan, Tap(p)a, Waff, Waugh, Winter's, Woof, Wow, Yaff, Yelp, Yip

Bar-keep(er), Barmaid, Barman, Bartender Advocate, Ale-wife, Barista, Bencher, Curate, Hebe, Luckie, Lucky, Tapster, Underskinker

Barley (water) Awn, Bear, Bere, Bigg, Malt, Pearl, Scotch, Truce

Barn Bank, Byre, Cowshed, Dutch, Grange, Skipper, Tithe

Barnacle Acorn, Cirriped(e), Cypris, Goose(neck), Limpet

Baroque Gothic, Ornate, Rococo

▷ **Baroque** *may indicate* an anagram

Barrack(s), Barracking Asteism, Boo, Cantonment, Casern(e), Cat-call, Garrison, Heckle, Irony, Jeer, Quarters

Barrage Balloon, Fusillade, Heat, Salvo, Shellfire

Barrel Bbl, Bl, Butt, Cade, Capstan, Cascabel, Cask, Clavie, Croze, Cylinder, Drum, Hogshead, Keg, Kibble, Morris-tube, Organ, Pièce, Run(d)let, Tan-vat, Thrall, Tierce, Tun, Vat, Wood

Barren Addle, Arid, Badlands, Blind, Blunt, Clear, Dry, Eild, → EMPTY, Farrow, Hardscrabble, Hi(r)stie, Jejune, Sterile, Unbearing, Waste, Wasteland, Wilderness, Yeld, Yell

Barrier Bail, Barrage, Barricade, Bayle, Block, Boom, Breakwater, Cauld, Checkrail, Cheval de frise, Chicane, Cordon (sanitaire), Crash, Crush, → DAM, Defence, Deterrent, Drawgate, Dyke, Fence, Fraise, Gate, Guard rail, Ha-ha, Handicap, Heat, Hedge, Hurdle, Mach, Obstruct, Pain, Paling, Potential, Rail(-fence), Rampart, Restraint, Revetment, Ring fence, Roadblock, Rope, Screen, Skreen, Sonic, Sound, Spina, Stockade, Thames, Thermal, Tollgate, Trade, Transonic, Traverse, Turnpike, Turnstile, Vapour, → WALL

Barrister Advocate, Attorney, Counsel, Devil, Lawyer, Revising, Rumpole, Serjeant(-at-law), Silk, Templar, Utter

Barrow Applecart, Clyde, Dolly, Handcart, Henge, How, Hurley, Kurgan, Molehill, Mound, Pushcart, Tram, Trolley, Truck, Tumulus

Barter Chaffer, Chop, Dicker, → EXCHANGE, Haggle, Hawk, Niffer, Permutate, Sco(u)rse, Swap, → TRADE, Traffic, Truck

Base Air, Airhead, Alkali, Bag, Bed, Beggarly, Billon, Board, Bottom, Brest, Camp, Choline, Degenerate, Degraded, Dog, Down, E, → ESTABLISH, Floor, Fond, Foot, Foothold, Footstall, Fort Knox, Found, Foundation, Fundus, Harlot, Hydroxide, Ignoble, Ignominious, Imidazole, Infamous, Iniquitous, Install, Knowledge, La Spezia, Leuco, Lewis, → LOW, → MEAN, Nefarious, Nook, Oasis®, Octal, Partite, Patten,

Platform, Plinth, Podium, Predella, Premise, Ptomaine, Purin(e), Raca, Rascally, Ratty, Rests, Ribald, Root, Rude, Scapa Flow, Servile, Shameful, Shand, Sheeny, Snide, Socle, Soda, Sordid, Springing, Staddle, →**STAND**, Station, Substrate, Ten, Tetracid, Torus, Turpitude, Unworthy, Vile

Bash Attempt, Belt, Bonk, Clout, Dint, Go, Hit, Rave, Shot, Slog, Strike, Swat, Swipe

Bashful Awed, Blate, Coy, Diffident, Modest, Retiring, Shamefast, Sheep-faced, Sheepish, →**SHY**

Basic(s), Basically, Basis ABC, Abcee, Alkaline, Aquamanale, Aquamanile, At heart, Brass tacks, Cardinal, Crude, Elemental, →**ESSENTIAL**, Fiducial, Fond, Fundamental, Ground(work), Gut, In essence, Integral, Intrinsic, Logic, Meat and potatoes, Nitty-gritty, No-nonsense, Nuts and bolts, One-horse, Presumption, Primordial, Principle, Protoplasm, Radical, Rudimentary, Spit-and-sawdust, Staple, Substance, Substratum, Underlying, Unsophisticated, Uracil

Basin Artesian, Aspergillum, Aspersorium, Bidet, Bowl, Brazil, Canning, Catch, Chott, Cirque, Corrie, Cwm, Dish, Dock, Great, Lavabo, Laver, Minas, Monteith, Ocean, Okavango, Pan, Park, Piscina, Playa, Porringer, Pudding, Reservoir, Scapa Flow, Sink, Slop(-bowl), Stoop, Stoup, Tank, Tidal, Washhand

Bask Apricate, Revel, Sun, →**WALLOW**

Basket, Basket-work Bass, Bassinet, Bread, Buck, Cabas, Car, Chip, Cob, Coop, Corbeil(le), Corf, Creel, Cresset, Dosser, Fan, Flasket, Frail, Gabian, Goal, Hamper, Hask, Junket, Kipe, Kit, Kite, Leap, Litter, Maund, Mocuck, Moses, Murlain, Murlan, Murlin, Osiery, Pannier, Ped, Petara, Plate, Pottle, Punnet, Rip, Round file, Scull, Scuttle, Seed-lip, Skep, Skull, Trout, Trug, Van, Wagger-pagger(-bagger), Waste(-paper), Wicker(-work), Will(e), Wisket

Basketball Tip-off

Bass Alberti, Ale, Alfie, B, Black, Continuo, Deep, Double, El-a-mi, Fish, Ground, Low, Ostinato, Serran, String

Bassoon Fagotto, Sausage

▷ **Bastard** *may indicate* an anagram

Bat(sman), Bat's wing, Batter, Batting, Batty Ames, Assail, Barbastelle, Baton, Blink, Close, Club, Cosh, Crackers, Crease, Cudgel, Dad, Die Fledermaus, Eyelid, Flittermouse, Fungo, Grace, Hatter, Haywire, Hit, Hobbs, Hook, Horseshoe, In, Ink mouse, Kalong, Knock, Language, Lara, Man, Mastiff, Maul, May, Mormops, Myopic, Nictate, Nictitate, Night, Nightwatchman, Noctilio, Nora, Opener, Paddle, Patagium, Pinch-hit, Pipistrel(le), Poke, Pummel, Rabbit, Racket, Racquet, Ram, Rearmouse, Ruin, Sauch, Scorer, Serotine, Sledge, Spectre, Stick, Stonewall, Striker, Swat, Switch hitter, Tail(ender), Trunnion, Vampire, Viv, Whacky, Willow, Wood

Batch Bake, Bunch, Clutch, Crop, Tranche

Bath(room) Aerotone, Aeson's, Aquae sulis, Bagnio, Bain-marie, Balneotherapy, Banya, Bed, Bidet, Blanket, Blood, Bubble, Caldarium, Cor, Dip, En suite, Epha, Foam, Hammam, Hip, Hummaum, Hummum, Jacuzzi®, Laver, Mik vah, Mud, Mustard, Oil, Piscina, Plunge, Salt, Sauna, Shower, Sitz, Slipper, Soak, Spa, Sponge, Steam, Stew, Stop, Tepidarium, Therm, Tub, Turkish, Tye, Vapour, Whirlpool, Wife

Bathe(r), Bathing Archimedes, Balneotherapy, Bay(e), Beath, Bogey, Bogie, Dip, Dook, Embay, Foment, Immerse, Lave, Lip, Skinny-dip, Souse, Splash, Stupe, →**SWIM**, Tub, →**WASH**

Bathos Anticlimax

Bathrobe Peignoir

Baton Mace, Rod, Sceptre, Staff, Truncheon, Wand

▷ **Bats, Batting** *may indicate* an anagram

Battalion Bn, Corps, Troop

Batter(ed) Bombard, Bruise, Buffet, Decrepit, Pound, Thump

Battery Artillery, Button-cell, Cannonade, Drycell, Field, Heliac, Henhouse, Li(thium)-ion, Masked, Nicad, Nickel cadmium, NIMH, Pra(a)m, Solar, Troop, Voltaic, Waffle

Battle(s), Battleground Action, Affair, Ben, Clash, Cockpit, Combat, →**CONFLICT**, Encounter, Engagement, Field, →**FIGHT**, Fray, Front, Joust, Maiden,

Royal, Running, Sarah, Sciamachy, Skiamachy, Spurs, Stoor, Stour, Stowre, Theatre, Theomachy, Wage, →**WAR**, Wargame

Battle-axe Amazon, Bill, Gorgon, Halberd, Ogress, Sparth(e), Termagant, Termagent, Turmagant, Turmagent

Battlement Barmkin, Crenellate, Merlon, Rampart

Battleship Carrier, Destroyer, Dreadnought, Gunboat, Man-o'-war, Potemkin

Bauble Bagatelle, Gaud, Gewgaw, Trifle

Bawl Bellow, Gollar, Howl, Weep

Bay Ab(o)ukir, Arm, Baffin, Bantry, Bark, Bell, Bengal, Bez, Bight, Biscay, Bonny, Botany, Broken, Byron, Cape Cod, Cardigan, Chesapeake, Classis, Cove, Covelet, Creek, Daphne, Delagoa, Discovery, Dundalk, Dvina, False, Famagusta, Fleet, Frobisher, Fundy, Galway, Gdansk, Georgian, Gibraltar, Glace, Golden, Green, Guanabara, Harbour, Hawke's, Herne, Hervey, Horse, →**HOWL**, Hudson, Inhambane, Inlet, Ise, Islands, James, Jervis, Laura, Laurel, Lobito, Loblolly, Lutzow-Holm, MA, Magdalena, Manila, Massachusetts, Narragansett, Niche, Oleander, Oriel, Pegasus, Pigs, Plymouth, Poverty, Recess, Red, Roan, St Austell, San Pedro, Scene, Shark, Sick, Sligo, Stall, Suvla, Swansea, Tampa, Tasman, Thunder, Tralee, Trincomalee, Ungava, Vae, Vigo, Voe, Vyborg, Waff, Wash, Wick, Yowl

Bazaar Alcaiceria, Emporium, Fair, Fete, Market, Pantechnicon, Sale, Sook, Souk

Beach(head) Anzio, Bondi, Chesil, Coast, Ground, Hard, Lido, Littoral, Machair, Miami, Myrtle, Plage, Sand, Sea-coast, Seashore, Seaside, Shingle, Shore(line), Strand, Waikiki

Beachwear Thong

Beacon Belisha, Brecon, Fanal, Lantern, Lightship, Need-fire, Pharos, Racon, Radar, Radio, Signal

Bead(s), Beaded Adderstone, Aggri, Aggry, Astragal, Baily's, Bauble, Blob, Bugle, Chaplet, Crab's-eyes, Crab-stones, Dewdrop, Drop, Droplet, Gaud, Job's tears, Love, Nurl, Paternoster, Poppet, Poppit, Prayer, Rosary, Sabha, St Cuthbert's, Spacer, Spacer plate, Tear, Wampum(peag), Worry

Beak AMA, Bailie, Bill, Cad, Cere, Coronoid, Gar, JP, Kip(p), Magistrate, Master, Metagnathous, Mittimus, Nasute, Neb, Nose, Pecker, Prow, Ram, Rostellum, Rostrum

Beam(ing) Arbor, Balance, Ba(u)lk, Bar, Binder, Boom, Bowstring, Box, Breastsummer, Broadcast, Bum(p)kin, Cantilever, Carline, Carling, Cathead, Collar, Crossbar, Crosshead, Crosspiece, Deck, Effulge, Electron, Girder, Grin, Hammer, Hatch, I, Irradiate, Joist, Ke(e)lson, Landing, Laser, Lentel, Lintel, Manteltree, Maser, Molecular, Moonlight, Needle, Outrigger, Particle, Pencil, Principal, Proton, Purlin, Putlock, Putlog, Radio, →**RAFTER**, →**RAY**, Rayon, Refulgent, Rident, Ridgepole, Rood, Roof-tree, Sandwich, Scale, Sealed, Searchlight, Shaft, Shine, Shore, Sleeper, Smile, Soffit, Spar, Stanchion, Stemson, Sternpost, Straining, Streamer, Stringer, Stringpiece, Summer, Support, Tailing, Tie, Timber, Transom, Trave, Trimmer, Truss, Universal, Walking, Weigh-bauk, Yard, Yardarm

Bean Abrus, Adsuki, Aduki, Adzuki, Arabica, Berry, Black, Black-eye, Borlotti, Broad, Bush, Butter, Cacao, Calabar, Castor, Cluster, Cocoa, Coffee, Cow-pea, Edamame, Fabaceous, Fava, Flageolet, French, Frijol(e), Garbanzo, Gram, Haricot, Harmala, Head, Horse, Hyacinth, Jack, Jelly, Jequirity, Jumping, Kidney, Lablab, Legume, Lentil, Lima, Locust, Molucca, Moth, Mung, Nelumbo, Nib, Noddle, Ordeal, Pichurim, Pinto, Pulse, Runner, St Ignatius's, Scarlet, Silverskin, Snap, Snuffbox, Soy(a), String, Sugar, Tepary, Tonga, Tonka, Tonquin, Urd, Wax, Winged

Bear(er), Bear lover Abide, Abrooke, Andean, Arctic, Arctophile, Baloo, Balu, Beer, Bigg, Breed, Brook, Brown, Bruin, Brunt, →**CARRY**, Cave, Churl, Cinnamon, Coati-mondi, Coati-mundi, Cub, Demean, Dree, Ean, →**ENDURE**, Engender, Exert, Fur-seal, Gest(e), Gonfalonier, Great, Grizzly, Hack, Ham(m)al, Harbinger, Have, Hod, Hold, Honey, Humf, Hump(h), Jampanee, Jampani, Keb, Kinkajou, Koala, Kodiak, Koolah, Lioncel(le), Lionel, Lug, Mother, Nandi, Nanook, Owe, Paddington, Panda, Pertain, Polar, Pooh, Rac(c)oon, Roller, Rupert, Russia, Sackerson, Seller, Shoulder, Sit, Sloth, Spectacled, Stand, Stay, Stomach, →**SUFFER**, Sun, Sunbear, Sustain,

Targeteer, Teddy, Teem, Thole, Throw, Tolerate, Tote, Transport, Undergo, Upstay, Ursine, Water, Whelp, White, Wield, Withstand, Woolly, Yean, Yield

Beard(ed) Arista, Awn, Balaclava, Barb, Beaver, Charley, Charlie, Confront, Defy, Escort, Face, Five o'clock shadow, Fungus, Goatee, Hair(ie), Hairy, Hear(ie), Imperial, Kesh, Mephistopheles, Newgate frill, Newgate fringe, Outface, Peak, Rivet, Stubble, Tackle, Vandyke, Whiskerando, Whiskery, Ziff

▷ **Bearhug** *may indicate* Teddy or similar around a word

▷ **Bearing** *may indicate* compass points

Bearing(s) Air, Allure, Aspect, Babbitt, Ball, Behaviour, Bush, Carriage, Deportment, Direction, E, Endurance, Gait, Germane, Gest, Gudgeon, Hatchment, Haviour, Heading, →**HERALDIC**, Hugger-mugger, Manner, Martlet, Mascle, Middy, Mien, N, Needle, Nor, Pall, Pheon, Port, Presence, Reference, Relevant, S, Seme(e), Subordinary, Teeming, Tenue, Thrust, W, Yielding

Beast(ly) →**ANIMAL**, Behemoth, Brute, Caliban, Caribou, →**CREATURE**, Dieb, Dragon, Dzeren, Fatstock, Gargoyle, Gayal, Genet, Godzilla, Grampus, Hog, Hy(a)ena, Jumart, Kinkajou, Lion, Mammoth, Marmot, Mastodon, Mhorr, Narwhal, Ogre, Oliphant, Oryx, Panda, Potto, Quagga, Queen's, Rac(c)oon, Rhytina, Rother, Sassaby, Steer, Sumpter, Swinish, Teg, Wart-hog, Yahoo, Yak, Yale, Zizel

Beat(ing), Beaten, Beater(er) Anoint, Arsis, Athrob, Bandy, Bang, Baste, Bastinado, Batter, Battue, Beetle, Belabour, Belt, Bepat, Best, Blatter, Bless, Cadence, Cane, Chastise, Clobber, Club, Clump, Cob, Conquer, Cream, Cuff, Curry, Debel, →**DEFEAT**, Ding, Donder, Dress, Drub, Dunt, Elude, Excel, Fatigue, Faze, Feague, Feeze, Fibbed, Flagellate, Flail, Flam, Float, Flog, Floor, Flush, Fly, Fustigate, Hollow, Horsewhip, Ictus, Jole, Joll, Joule, Jowl, Knock, Knubble, Lace, Laidy, Lambast(e), Larrup, Lash, Lather, Latin, Laveer, Lay, Lick, Lilt, Lounder, Mall, Malleate, Manor, Mell, Mersey, Mullah, Muller, Nubble, Onceover, Outclass, Outdo, Outflank, Outstrip, Outstroke, Palpitate, Pandy, Paradiddle, Pash, Paste, Pip, Ploat, Pommel, Pound, Prat, Pug, Pulsate, Pulsatile, Pulse, Pummel, Pun, Quop, Raddle, Ram, Ratten, Resolve, Retreat, Rhythm, Ribroast, Rope's end, Round, Rout, Ruff(le), Scourge, Slat, Smite, Soak, Sock, Sort, Strike, Swinge, Swingle, Syncopation, Systole, Taber, Tabor, Tact, Tala, Tan, Tattoo, Thesis, Thrash, Thresh, Throb, Thud, Thump, Thwack, Tick, Time, Tired, Top, Torture, Trounce, Tuck, Verberate, Vibrate, Wallop, Wappend, Weary, Welt, Wham, Whip, Whisk, Whitewash, Whup, Wraught, Ybet, Yerk, Yirk

▷ **Beaten-up** *may indicate* an anagram

Beautician Glamoriser

Beautiful, Beautify, Beauty Advantage, Angelic, Astrid, Belle, Bellibone, Bonny, Bright, Camberwell, Charmer, Charming, Colleen, Corker, Dish, Embellish, Enhance, Exquisite, Fair, Fine, Glamour (puss), Glory, Grace, Helen, Houri, Hyperion, Junoesque, Kanta, Lana, Looks, Monism, Ornament, Peri, Picture, Pink, Pride, Pulchritude, Purler, Scenic, Sheen, Smasher(oo), Smicker, Specious, Stunner, Sublime, To kalon

Beaver Beard, Castor, Eager, Grind, Oregon, Rodent, Sewellel

Because (of) As, Forasmuch, Forwhy, Hence, In (that), Inasmuch, Ipso facto, Sens, Since

Beckon Gesture, Nod, Summons, Waft, Wave, Wheft

Become, Becoming Apt, Besort, Decent, Decorous, Enter, Fall, Fit, Flatter, Get, Go, Grow, Happen, Occur, Seemly, Suit, Wax, Worth

Bed(s), Bedding, Bedstead Air, Amenity, Apple-pie, Arroyo, Bacteria, Base, Bassinet, Berth, Border, Bottom, Bottomset, Box, Bundle, Bunk, Caliche, Camp, Capillary, Carrycot, Channel, Charpoy, Cill, Cot(t), Couch(ette), Counterpane, Couvade, Coverlet, Cradle, Crib, Cross, Cul(t)ch, Day, Divan, Doona, Doss, Duvet, Erf, False, Feather, Filter, Fluidized, Flying, Form, Four-poster, Futon, Gault, Greensand, Hammock, Inlay, Kago, Kang, Kingsize, Kip, Knot, Knot garden, Lay(er), Lazy, Lilo®, Litter, Marriage, Mat, Matrix, Mattress, Murphy, Naked, Nap, Nest, Nookie, Oyster, Pad, Paillasse, Pallet, Palliasse, Pan, Parterre, Passage, Patch, Pavement, Pay, Pig, Pit, Plank, Plant, Plot, Procrustean, Puff, Queensize, Quilt, Retire, River, Rollaway, Roost, Rota, Sack, Scalp, Settle, Shakedown, Sill, Sitter, Sleep, Sofa, Standing, Stratum,

Stretcher, Sun, T(h)alweg, Tanning, Test, The downy, Thill, Trough, Truckle, Trundle, Twin, Wadi, Wady, Ware, Water, Wealden, Wedding

Bed-bug B, B flat, Chinch, Flea, Louse, Vermin

Bedchamber, Bedroom Boudoir, Bower, Br, Chamber, Cubicle, Dorm(itory), Dormer, Dorter, Ruelle, Ward

▷ **Bedevilled** *may indicate* an anagram

Bedrock Costean

Bedsit Pad

Bee Afrikanised, Athenia, Bike, Bumble, Carpenter, Cuckoo, Deborah, Debra, Deseret, Dog, Drone, Drumbledor, Dumbledore, Group, Hiver, Honey, Humble, Husking, Killer, King, Lapidary, Leaf-cutter, Mason, Melissa, Pollinator, Queen, Solitary, Spell, Spell-down, Swarm, Trixie, Worker

Beech Hornbeam, Mast, Tree

Beef(y) Aitchbone, Baron, Bleat, Brawny, Bresaola, Bull(y), Bullock, Carp, Carpaccio, Charqui, Chateaubriand, Chuck, Clod, Complain, Corned, Filet mignon, Flank, Groan, Grouch, Grouse, Hough, Jerk, Liebig, Mart, Mice, Moan, Mousepiece, Muscle, Neat, Ox, Pastrami, Peeve, Plate, Porterhouse, Rother, Salt-horse, Sauerbraten, Sey, Shin, Silverside, Sirloin, Stolid, Stroganoff, Topside, Tournedos, Tranche, Undercut, Vaccine, Wagyu

Been Bin

Beer Ale, Alegar, Amber fluid, Amber liquid, Bantu, Barley sandwich, Bitter, Black, Bock, Chaser, Coldie, Draught, Drink, Dry, Entire, Export, Gill, Ginger, Grog, Guest, Heavy, Herb, Home-brew, Kaffir, Keg, Kvass, Lager, Lambic, Lite, Lush, Malt, March, Middy, Mild, Milk stout, Mum, Near, Nog, October, Pils(e)ner, Pint, Pony, Porter, Real, Real ale, Rice, Root, Saki, Scoobs, Sherbet, Six-pack, Skeechan, Small, Spruce, Stingo, Stout, Stubby, Suds, Swankie, Swankie, Swats, Swipes, Switchel, Table, Taplash, Tinnie, Tipper, Tshwala, Tube, Turps, Wallop, Wheat, Zythum

Beet Blite, Chard, Fat-hen, Goosefoot, Mangel(wurzel), Seakale, Silver, Spinach

Beethoven WoO

Beetle Ambrosia, Argos tortoise, Asiatic, Bacon, Bark, Batler, Bee, Blister, Bloody-nosed, Boll weevil, Bug, Bum-clock, Buprestus, Burying, Bustle, Buzzard-clock, Cabinet, Cadelle, Cane, Cantharis, Cardinal, Carpet, Carrion, Chafer, Christmas, Churchyard, Click, Clock, Cockchafer, Cockroach, Coleopterous, Colorado, Darkling, Deathwatch, Devil's coach-horse, Diamond, Diving, Dor(r), Dor-fly, Dumbledore, Dung, Elater, Elmbark, Elytron, Elytrum, Firefly, Flea, Furniture, Glow-worm, Goliath, Gregor, Ground, Hammer, Hangover, Hercules, Hop-flea, Hornbug, Impend, Japanese, Jewel, June, Ladybird, Ladybug, Larder, Leaf, Leather, Longhorned, Mall(et), Maul, May-bug, Minotaur, Oil, Overhang, Pinchbuck, Pine-chafer, Potato, Project, Protrude, Rhinoceros, Roach, Rosechafer, Rove, Saw palmetto, Scarab(ee), Scavenger, Scurry, Sexton, Skelter, Sledge(-hammer), Snapping, Snout, Spanish fly, Spider, Squirr, Stag, Tiger, Tumble-bug, Turnip-flea, Typographer, VW, Water, Weevil, Whirligig, Wireworm, Woodborer

Before(hand) A, Advance, Already, An, Ante, Avant, By, Coram, Earlier, Early, Ere, Erst(while), First, →FORMER, Or (e'er), Parava(u)nt, Pre, Previously, Prior, Pro, Sooner, Till, To, Until, Van, Zeroth

Befriend Assist, Cotton, Fraternise, Support

Beg(gar), Beggarly, Begging Ask, Badgeman, Beseech, Bey, Blighter, Blue-gown, Cadge, Calendar, Crave, →ENTREAT, Exoration, Flagitate, Fleech, Gaberlunzie, Gangrel, Hallan-shaker, Implore, Impoverish, Lackall, Lazar(us), Lazzarone, Limitary, Maund, Mendicant, Montem, Mooch, Mouch, Mump, Niggardly, Panhandle, Pauper, Penniless, →PLEAD, Pled, Pray, Prig, Prog, Rag, Randy, Ruffler, Schnorr(er), Screeve, Scrounge, Shool(e), Skelder, Skell, Solicit, Standpad, Sue, Suppliant, Supplicate, Thig(ger), Toe-rag, Touch, Undo, Uprightman, Whipjack

Begin(ner), Beginning Ab initio, Ab ovo, Alpha, Alphabetarian, Author, B, Black, Cause, Che(e)chako, Clapdash, Commence, Daw, Dawn, Deb, Debut, Embryo, Enter, Exordium, Fall-to, Found, Fountainhead, Genesis, Germ, Go, Greenhorn, Inaugural, Inception, Inchoate, Incipient, Incipit, Initial, Initiate, Intro, Johnny-raw, L, Launch,

Lead, Learn, Learner, Logos, Nascent, Neophyte, Noob, →**NOVICE**, Onset, Ope(n), Ord, →**ORIGIN**, Outbreak, Pose, Prelim(inary), Primer, Rookie, Seed, Set, Shoot, →**START**, Startup, Strike up, Takeoff, Tenderfoot, Threshold, Tiro, To-fall, Yearn

Behave, Behaviour, Behaving Abear, Accepted, Act, Appeasement, Attitude, Carriage, Conduct, Consummatory, Convenance, Decorum, Demean, Do, Effrontery, Etepimeletic, Ethics, Ethology, Form, Freak out, Guise, Horme, Life style, →**MANNER**, Meme, Nature, Netiquette, Noblesse oblige, Obey, Orientation, Practice, Praxeology, Quit, React, Response, Strong meat, Tribalism

Behind(hand) Abaft, Aft(er), Ahind, Ahint, Apoop, Arear, Arere, Arrear, Astern, Backside, Beneath, Bottom, Bum, Buttocks, Can, Croup, Derrière, Fud, Late, Overdue, Prat, →**REAR**, Rump, Slow, Tushie

Being Cratur, Creature, Critter, Ens, Entia, Entity, Esse, Essence, Existence, Human, Man, Metaphysics, Mode, Nature, Omneity, Ontology, →**PERSON**, Saul, Soul, Subsistent, Substance, Wight

Belch Boak, Boke, Brash, Burp, Emit, Eruct, Erupt, Rift, Spew, Toby, Yex

Belgian Flemish, Walloon

Belief, Believe, Believed, Believer, Believing Accredit, Adam and Eve, Bigot, Buy, Capernaite, Catechism, Chiliasm, Conviction, Creationism, Credence, Credit, Creed, Cult, Culture, Deem, Deist, Di(o)physite, Doctrine, Doxy, Dyophysite, Evangelical, Faith, Gnostic, Guess, Heresy, Heterodoxy, Hold, Holist, Idea, Ideology, Idolater, Imagine, Islam, Ism, Latitudinarian, Ludism, Mechanist, Messianic, Methink, Mysticism, Notion, →**OPINION**, Ovist, Pantheism, Pelagianism, Persuasion, Physicism, Pluralism, Postmillenarian, Presumption, Religion, Reputed, Revelationist, S(h)aivism, Second Coming, Secularism, Seeing, Solipsism, Superstition, Supremacist, Swallow, Tenet, Test, Tetratheism, Thanatism, Theist, Theosophy, Think, Threap, Threep, Traducianism, Trinitarian, Triphysite, Trow, Trust, Umma(h), Unitarian, Wear, Ween, Wis(t)

Belittle Cheapen, Decry, Demean, Depreciate, Derogate, Detract, Diminish, Discredit, Disparage, Humble, Slight

Bell(s) Acton, Agogo, Angelus, Ben, Bob, Bow, Bronte, Cachecope, Canterbury, Carillon, Chime, Clanger, Crotal, Curfew, Currer, Daisy, Diving, Division, Ellis, Gong, Grandsire, Jar, Liberty, Low, Lutine, Market, Mass, Muffin, Passing, Pavilion, Peal, Peter, Pinger, Ring, Roar, Sacring, Sanctus, Tailor, Tantony, Tenor, Tent, Tintinnabulum, Toll, Tom, Triple, Tubular, Vair, Vesper, Wind

Bellow(s) Buller, Holla, Holler, Moo, Rant, Rave, Roar, Saul, Thunder, Troat, Tromp(e), Trumpet, Windbag

Belly Abdomen, Alvine, Bag, Beer, Beer-gut, Boep, Bunt, Calipee, Celiac, Coeliac, Gut, Kite, Kyte, Paunch, Pod, →**STOMACH**, Swell, Tum(my), Venter, Wame, Weamb, Wem(b), Womb

Belong, Belonging(s) Appertain, Apply, Appurtenant, Chattels, Effects, Inhere, Intrinsic, Our, Paraphernalia, Pertain, →**PROPERTY**, Relate, Roots, Things, Traps

Beloved Alder-lief(est), Amy, David, Dear, Esme, Inamorata, Joy, Leve, Lief, Loor, Morna, Pet, Popular, Precious

Below Beneath, Inf(erior), Infra, Nether, Sub, Subjacent, Under, Unneath

Belt(ed) Baldric(k), Band, Bandoleer, Bandolier, Baudric(k), Bible, Black, Cartridge, Chastity, Cholera, Clitellum, Clobber, Clock, Commuter, Conveyor, Copper, Cotton, Crios, Equator, Fan, Flog, Galvanic, Garter, Gird(le), Girt, Hydraulic, Inertial, Judoka, Kuiper, Lap, Larrup, Life, Lonsdale, Mitre, Orion's, Orogenic, Polt, Pound, Roller, Roll-on, Safety, Sahel, Sam Browne, Sash, Seat, Speed, Stockbroker, Storm, Strap, Stratosphere, Surcingle, Suspender, Swipe, Taiga, Tawse, Tear, Thump, Tore, Tract, Van Allen, Wampum, Wanty, Webbing, Wing, Zodiac, Zone, Zoster

Bemoan →**LAMENT**, Mourn, Sigh, Wail

Bemuse Infatuate, Stonn(e), Stun, Stupefy, Throw

Bench Banc, Bink, Counter, Court, Cross, Exedra, Form, Knifeboard, Magistrates, Pew, Rout seat, Rusbank, Settle, Siege, Stillage, Thoft, Thwart, Treasury, Trestle

Bend(er), Bending, Bends Angle, Arc, Arch, Articular, Bight, Binge, Bow,

Buck(le), Bust, Camber, Carrick, Chicane, Circumflect, Contort, Corner, Crank(le), Cringe, →CROOK, Crouch, Curl, Curve, Diffraction, Dog-leg, Elbow, Engouled, Epinasty, Es(s), Falcate, Fawn, Flex(ural), Flexion, Flexure, Fold, Geller, Geniculate, Genu, Genuflect, Grecian, Hairpin, Hinge, Hook, Horseshoe, Hunch, Inflect, Jag, Knee(cap), Kneel, Knot, Kowtow, Mould, Nutant, Ox-bow, Pitch, Plash, Plié, Ply, Recline, Reflex, Retorsion, Retortion, Retroflex, Riband, S, Scarp, Souse, Spree, Spring, Stave, Stoop, Swan-neck, Trend, Twist, U, Ups(e)y, Uri, Wale, Warp, →YIELD, Z

▷ **Bendy** *may indicate* an anagram

Beneath Below, Sub, Under, Unworthy

Benefactor Angel, Backer, Barmecide, Carnegie, Donor, Maecenas, →PATRON, Philanthropist, Promoter

Beneficial, Beneficiary, Benefit, Benefice Advantage, →AID, Alms, Ameliorate, Asset, Avail, Behalf, Behoof, Behove, Bespeak, Bonus, Boon, Boot, Charity, Collature, Commendam, Commensal, Devisee, Disablement, Dole, Donee, Endorsee, Enjoy, Enure, FIS, For, Fringe, Grantee, Housing, Incapacity, Incumbent, Inheritor, Injury, Interest, Inure, Invalidity, Legal aid, Living, Manna, Maternity, Ménage, Mileage, Neckverse, Pay, Perk, Perquisite, Plenarty, Plus, Portioner, Postulate, Prebend, Profit, Sake, Salutary, Sanative, Sickness, Sinecure, Spin-off, Stipend, Supplementary, Symbiotic, Trickle down, UB40, Unemployment, Use, Usufruct, Va(u)ntage, Wholesome, Wonderful, Workfare

Benevolence, Benevolent Charitable, Clement, Dobbie, Dobby, Goodwill, Humanitarian, Kind, Liberal, Nis(se), Philanthropy, Pickwickian, Sprite

Bengali Oriya

Benign Affable, Altruistic, Gracious, Innocuous, Kindly, Trinal

Bent Akimbo, Bowed, Brae, Coudé, Courb, Crooked, Curb, Determined, Dorsiflex, Falcate, Fiorin, Flair, Habit, Heath, Inclination, Ingenium, Intent, Inverted, Leant, Out, Peccant, Penchant, Ply, Predisposition, Reclinate, Redtop, Scoliotic, Stooped, Swayed, Talent, Taste, Twisted

▷ **Bent** *may indicate* an anagram

Bequeath, Bequest Bestow, Chantr(e)y, Demise, Endow, Heirloom, →LEAVE, Legacy, Mortification, Pass down, Pittance, Testament, Transmit, Will

Berate(d) Censure, Chastise, Chide, Jaw, Reproach, Scold, Slate, Vilify

Bereave(d), Bereavement Deprive, Loss, Mourning, Orb, Sorrow, Strip, Widow

Berk Clot

Berry Acai, Allspice, Bacca, Blackcurrant, Cubeb, Fruit, Goosegog, Haw, Konini, Miracle, Mistletoe, Pepo, Persian, Pimento, Poke, Pottage, Raccoon, Rhein, Rhine, Sal(l)al, Salmonberry, Slae, Sloe, Sop, Tomatillo

Berserk Amok, Baresark, Frenzy, Gungho, Rage

Berth Anchorage, Bunk, Cabin, Couchette, Dock, Moor, Seat, Space

Beseech Beg, Crave, Entreat, Implore, Invoke, Obsecrate

Beset Amidst, Assail, Assiege, Badger, Bego, Embattled, Environ, Harry, Obsess, Perplex, Scabrid, Siege

Beside(s) Adjacent, Alone, And, At, Au reste, By, Else, Forby(e), Moreover, Next, On, To, Withal

▷ **Besiege** *may indicate* one word around another

Besiege(d) Beset, Best(ed), Blockade, Gherao, Girt, Invest, Obsess, Plague, Poliorcetic, Surround

Besot(ted) Dotard, Infatuate, Intoxicate, Lovesick, Stupefy

Best A1, Ace, All-time, Aristocrat, Beat, Bonzer, Cap, Cat's whiskers, Choice, Conquer, Cream, Creme, Damnedest, Deluxe, Elite, Eximious, Finest, First, Flower, Foremost, Greatest, Highlight, Ideal, Nicest, Optima, Outdo, Outwit, Overcome, Peak, Peerless, Pick, Pink, Plum, Purler, Ream, Sunday, Super, Supreme, The, Tiptop, Top, Topper, Transcend, Vanquish, Wale

Bet(ting), Betting System A cheval, Ante, Antepost, Back, Banco, Banker, Daily double, Double, Flutter, Gaff, Gamble, Go, Hedge, Impone, Lay, Long shot, Martingale, Mise, Note, Pari-mutuel, Parlay, Perfecta, Pip, Place, Pot, Punt,

Quadrella, Quinella, Ring, Risk, Roulette, Saver, Set, Spec, Sport, Stake, Tattersalls, Tatts, Totalisator, Totalise, Tote, Treble, Triella, Trifecta, →**WAGER**, Win, Yankee

Betray(al), Betrayer Abandon, Abuse, Belewe, Bewray, Cornuto, Desert, Disclose, Divulge, Dob, Dobbin, Double-cross, Giveaway, Grass, Judas, Proditor, Renegade, Renege, Rumble, Sell, Sellout, Shop, Sing, Sinon, Split on, Stab, Telltale, Traditor, Traitor, Treachery, Treason, Turncoat

Betroth(ed), Betrothal Affiance, Affy, Assure, Engage, Ensure, Espouse, Fiancé(e), Handfasting, Pledge, Promise, Sponsalia, Subarr(h)ation

Better Abler, Amend, Apter, Bigger, Buck, Cap, Comparative, Fairer, Gambler, Gamester, Imponent, Improve, Meliorate, Mend, Mitigate, Outdo, Outpeer, Outpoint, Piker, Preponderate, Punter, Race-goer, Reform, Score off, Superior, Surpass, Throw, Top, Turfite, Work, Worst

Between Amid, Bet, Betwixt, Inter, Interjacent, Linking, Mesne, Twixt

Beverage Ale, Cocoa, Coffee, Cordial, Cup, →**DRINK**, Nectar, Tea

Bevy Flock, Group, Herd, Host

Beware Cave, Fore, Heed, Look out, Mind, Mistrust, Tut

Bewilder(ed), Bewildering, Bewilderment Amaze, Baffle, Buffalo, Confuse, Consternation, Daze, Distract, Flummox, Mate, Maze, Mind-boggling, Mystify, Obfuscate, Perplex, Stun, Taivert, Tutulbay, Wander, Will, Wull

Beyond Above, Ayont, Besides, Farther, Outwith, Over, Past, Thule, Trans, Ulterior, Ultra

Bezique Royal marriage

Bias(ed) Angle, Bent, Colour, Discriminatory, Forward, Imbalance, One-sided, Partial, Parti pris, Partisan, Penchant, Preconception, Predilection, →**PREJUDICE**, Prepossess, Set, Skew, Slant, Slope, Spin, Tendency, Warp

Bible, Biblical Alcoran, Alkoran, Antilegomena, Apocrypha, ASV, Authority, AV, Avesta, Bamberg, Book, Breeches, Coverdale, Cranmer, Cromwell, Douai, Douay, Family, Gemara, Geneva, Gideon, Good book, Goose, Gospel, Haggada, Helachah, Heptateuch, Hermeneutic, Hexapla, Hexateuch, Itala, Italic, King James (version), Leda, Mazarin(e), Midrash, Missal, Murderer, NT, Omasum, OT, Pentateuch, Peshito, Peshitta, Peshitto, Polyglot, Psalter, Revised Version, RSV, RV, Scriptures, Septuagint, Stomach, Talmud, Tanach, Targum, Taverners, Text, Tyndale, Vinegar, Vulgate, Whig, Wyclif(fe), Zurich

Bicker Argue, Bowl, Brawl, Coggie, Dispute, Tiff, Wrangle

Bicycle, Bike(r) All-terrain, Bee, Bone-shaker, Chopper, Coaster, Crog(gy), Dandy-horse, Draisene, Draisine, Hell's angels, Hobby, Kangaroo, Mixte, Moped, Mount, Mountain, Ordinary, Pedal, Penny-farthing, Raleigh®, Roadster, Rocker, Safety, Scooter, Ski-bob, Solo, Spin, Stationary, Tandem, UCI, Velocipede

Bid(der), Bidding (system) Abundance, Acol, Apply, Blackwood, Call, Canape, Command, Contract, Cue, Declare, Double, Gone, INT, Invite, Misère, Nod, NT, →**OFFER**, Order, Pass, →**PRE-EMPT(IVE)**, Proposal, Puffer, Redouble, Rescue, Summon, Take-out, Take-over, Tell, Tender, Vied

Big Altruistic, Beamy, Bulky, Bumper, Burly, Cob, Enormous, Fat, Ginormous, Gross, →**LARGE**, Loud, Massive, Mighty, Obese, Roomy, Stonker, Strapping, Substantial, Swopper, Thumping, Tidy, Vast, Whacker, Whopper

Bighead Besserwisser, Ego

Bigot(ed) Chauvinist, Dogmatist, Fanatic, Hide-bound, Intolerant, Racialist, Racist, Wowser, Zealot

Bigshot, Bigwig Cheese, Nob, Swell, Titan, Toff, →**VIP**

Bile, Bilious(ness) Cholaemia, Choler, Gall, Icteric, Melancholy, Scholaemia, Venom

Bilge Leak, Pump, Rhubarb, Rot, Waste

Bill(ed), Billy Ac(c), Accommodation, Accompt, Account, Act, Ad, Addition, Allonge, Appropriation, Barnacle, Beak, Becke, Budd, Buffalo, Can, Caress, Carte, Charge, Chit(ty), Cody, Coo, Coronoid, Cross(-bencher), Demand, Dixy, Docket, Double, Due, Egg-tooth, Exactment, Fee, Fin, Finance, Foreign, Gates, Goat, Hybrid, Inland, Invoice, Kaiser, →**LAW**, Lawin(g), Legislation, Liam, Liar, Line-up, List, Measure, Menu, Nail,

Neb, Ness, Nib, →**NOTE**, Notice, Paper, Petition, Platypus, Pork barrel, Portland, Poster, Private, Programme, Pruning, Public, Puffing, Reckoning, Reform, Rostral, Rostrum, Score, Short, Shot, Show, Sickle, Silly, Sparth(e), Sperthe, Spoon, Sticker, Tab, Tenner, Tomium, Trade, Treasury, True, Twin, Victualling, Watch, Willy

Billiards, Billiards player, Billiards stroke Bar, Cueist, Jenny, Lagging, Massé, Pills, Pool, Potter, Pyramids, Short jenny, Snooker, String, Whitechapel

Billow Roil, Roller, Rule, Surge, Swell, Wave

▶**Billy** *see* **BILL(ED)**

Bimbo Twinkle

Bin Bing, Box, Chilly, Container, Crib, Hell, Litter, Loony, Receptacle, Snake-pit, Stall, Throw away, Wagger-pagger, Wheelie, Wheely

Bind(er), Binding Adherent, Adhesive, Alligate, Apprentice, Astrict, Astringent, Bale, Bandage, Bandeau, Bandster, Bias, Boyer, Brail, Burst, Calf, Cement, Cerlox®, Chain, Cinch, Circuit, Clamp, Colligate, Complain, Cord, Cummerbund, Dam, De Vigneaud, Drag, Edge, Embale, Enchain, Engage, Enslave, Enwind, →**FASTEN**, Fetter, Final, Gird, Girdle, Half-leather, Haworth, Hay-wire, Hold, Hole, Hopkins, Incumbent, Indenture, Iron, Keckle, Krebs, Lash(er), Law-calf, Leash, Ligament, Ligature, Mail, Marl, Martin, Meyerhof, Morocco, Muslin, Obi, Obligate, Oblige, Oop, Organdie, Oup, Parpen, Paste grain, Perfect, Pinion, Porter, Raffia, Red Tape, Restrict, Ring, →**ROPE**, Seize, Sheaf, Spiral, Strap, Stringent, Swathe, Tape, Tether, Thirl, Thong, Three-quarter, Tie, Tree-calf, Truss, Twine, Unsewn, Valid, Whip, Withe, Yapp, Yerk, Yoke

Binge, Binging Bat, Beano, Bend(er), Blind, Carouse, Dipsomania, →**DRINK**, Drinking-bout, Engorge, Gorge, Party, Pig out, Riot, Soak, Souse, Spree, Toot, Tout

Bingo Beano, Housey-housey, Lotto, Tombola

Binocular(s) Glasses, Jumelle, OO, Stereoscope

Biographer, Biography Boswell, CV, Hagiography, History, Life, Memoir, Plutarch, Potted, Prosopography, Suetonius, Vita

Biology, Biologist Algology, Berg, Bordet, Carrel, Cladistics, Cohen, Dawkins, Delbruck, Genetics, Haller, Kendrew, Kinsey, Mendel, Molecular, Morphology, Phenetics, Shatten, Stoechiology, Stoich(e)iology, Taxonomy, Transgenics, Weismann

Biped Man, Yahoo

Birch Betula, Birk, Cane, Cow, Flog, Hazel, Kow, Larch, Larrup, Reis, Rice, Rod, Silver, Swish, Twig, Whip, Withe

▷**Bird** *may indicate* a prison sentence

Bird(s) Al(l)erion, Altricial, Bertram, Brood, Damsel, Doll, Early, Flier, Fowl, Gal, →**GIRL**, Grip, Hen, Layer, Left, Limicoline, Nestling, Ornithology, Pecker, Pen, Perching, Poultry, Praecoces, Prison, Quod, Raptor, Rare, Roaster, Sentence, Sis, Skirt, Visitant, Warbler

Bird-watcher Augur, Twitcher

Birth Burden, Congenital, Delivery, Drop, Extraction, Genesis, Geniture, Jataka, Lineage, Multiple, Nativity, Origin, Parage, Parthenogenesis, Parturition, Water, Whelp(ing)

Birthday Anniversary, Genethliac, Prophet's

Birthmark Blemish, Mole, Mother-spot, Naevus, Port wine stain, Stigmata

Birthright Heritage, Mess, Patrimony

Bis Again, Anew

Biscuit Abernethy, Amaretto, Bake, Bath-oliver, Biscotto, Bourbon, Brown George, Butterbake, Charcoal, Cookie, Cracker, Cracknel, Crispbread, Dandyfunk, Digestive, Dunderfunk, Fairing, Flapjack, Florentine, Fly cemetery, Garibaldi, Gingersnap, Hardtack, Jumbal, Kiss, Lavash, Lebkuchen, Macaroon, Marie, Mattress, Nut, Oliver, Osborne, Parkin, Perkin, Petit four, Pig's ear, Poppadom, Poppadum, Pretzel, Puff, Ratafia, Rice, Rusk, Sea, Ship's, Shortbread, Snap, Sweetmeal, Tack, Tan, Teiglach, Tollhouse cookie, Wafer, Zwieback

Bishop(ric) Aaronic, Abba, Aberdeen, Aidan, Ambrose, Apollinaris, Bench, Berkeley, Bp, Cambrensis, Cantuar, Chad, Chorepiscopal, Coadjutor, Coverdale, Cranmer,

Diocesan, Dunelm, Ebor, Ely, Eparch, Episcopate, Eusebian, Exarch, Exon, Golias, Hatto, Henson, Jansen, Latimer, Lord, Magpie, Man, Metropolitan, Missionary, Norvic, Odo, Ordainer, Patriarch, Peter, Petriburg, Piece, Polycarp, Pontiff, Prelate, Priest, Primate, Primus, Proudie, Ridley, Roffen, RR, St Swithin, Sarum, Sleeve, Sodor and Man, Suffragan, The purple, Titular, Tulchan, Weed, Winton, Wrexham

Bison Bonas(s)us, Buffalo, Ox, Wisent

Bit Ate, Baud, Byte, Cantle(t), Chad, Cheesecake, Chip, Coin, Crumb, Curb, Curn, Dash, Degree, Drib, Excerpt, Fraction, Fraise, Haet, Hait, Hate, Ion, Iota, Jaw, Jot, Leptum, Mite, Modicum, Morsel, Mote, Mu, Nit, Ort, Ounce, Pelham, Peni, Penny, → PIECE, Pinch, Port, Rap, Rare, Ratherish, Rowel, Scintilla, Scrap, Section, Shaving, Shiver, Shred, Smattering, Smidgen, Smidgeon, Smidgin, Snaffle, Snatch, Snippet, Soupcon, Spale, Speck(le), Splinter, Spot, Stop, Suspicion, Tad, Tait, Tate, Threepenny, Trace, Unce, Vestige, What, Whit

Bite(r), Biting, Bitten Astringent, Begnaw, Canapé, Caustic, Chelicera, Chew, Cold, Eat, Engouled, Erose, Etch, Gnash, Gnat, Gnaw, Hickey, Hickie, Incisor, Knap, Masticate, Midge, Molar, Mordacious, Mordant, Morsel, Morsure, Nacho, Nibble, Nip(py), Occlude, Pium, Pointed, Premorse, Rabid, Sarcastic, Sharp, Shrewd, Snack, Snap, Tart

Bitter(ness) Absinth, Acerb, Acid, Acrimonious, Ale, Aloe, Angostura, Bile, Caustic, Eager, Edge, Envenomed, Ers, Fell, Gall, Heated, Jaundiced, Keen, Keg, Marah, Maror, Myrrh, Picamar, Pique, Rancorous, Rankle, Resentful, Sarcastic, Sardonic, Snell, Sore, Spleen, Tannin, Tart(aric), Venom, Verjuice, Virulent, Vitriolic, Wersh, Wormwood, Wry

Bizarre Antic, Curious, Eccentric, Exotic, Fantastic, Gonzo, Grotesque, Odd, Offbeat, Off-the-wall, Outlandish, Outré, Pythonesque, Queer, Strange, Surreal, Weird

▷**Bizarre** *may indicate* an anagram

Black(en), Blackness, Black-out Afro-American, Atramental, B, Ban, BB, Bess, Blae, Carbon, Charcoal, Cilla, Coal, Coloured, Coon, Cypress, Darkie, Darky, Death, Debar, Denigrate, Dinge, Dwale, Ebon(y), Eclipse, Ethiop, Evil, Fuzzy-wuzzy, Geechee, Graphite, Grime, Heben, Hole, Ink(y), Ivory, Japan, Jeat, Jet, Jim Crow, Kohl, Malign, Market, Melanic, Melano, Moke, Moor, Muntu, Myall, Negritude, Negro, Niello, Niger, Nigrescent, Nigritude, Obliterate, Obscure, Outage, Oxford, Piceous, Pitch, Platinum, Pongo, Prince, Pudding, Quashee, Raven, Sable, Sambo, Scab, School, Sheep, Sloe, Solvent, Sombre, Soot, Sooterkin, Soul brother, Soul sister, Spade, Spook, Starless, Stygian, Swart(y), Swarth(y), Tar, Thick-lips, Uncle Tom, Weeds

Blackberry Acini, Bramble, Mooch, Mouch

Blackbird Collybird, Crow, Jackdaw, Merl(e), Ousel, Raven

Blackjack Billie, Billy, Cosh, Flag, Sphalerite, Tankard, Truncheon, Vingt(-et)-un

Blackmail(er) Bleed, Chantage, Chout, Exact, Extort, Greenmail, Honey-trap, Ransom, Strike, Vampire

Blackout ARP, Eclipse, Faint, Shallow water, Swoon, Syncope

Black sheep Neer-do-well, Reprobate

Blacksmith Brontes, Burn-the-wind, Farrier, Forger, Harmonious, Plater, Shoer, Vulcan

Blade(s) Acrospire, Andrew Ferrara, Bilbo, Brand, Brown Bill, Cleaver, Co(u)lter, Cutlass, Dandy, Espada, Faible, Foible, Forte, Gleave, Gouge, Guillotine, Hydrofoil, Kris, Lance, Lawnmower, Leaf, Man, Mouldboard, Oar, Paddle, Palmetto, Peel, Propeller, Rachilla, Rapier, Razor, Rip, Rotor, Scalpel, Scimitar, Scull, Skate, Spade-, Spatula, Spatule, Spear, Spoon, Stiletto, Stock, Sweep, → SWORD, Symitar, Toledo, Vane, Vorpal, Wash, Web

Blame(worthy) Accuse, Censure, Condemn, Confound, Culpable, Decry, Dirdam, Dirdum, Fault, Guilt, Incriminate, Inculpate, Odium, Rap, Reproach, Reprove, Stick, Thank, Twit, Wight, Wite, Wyte

Blameless Innocent, Irreproachable, Lily-white

Blanch Bleach, Etiolate, Scaud, Whiten

Bland Anodyne, Insipid, Mild, Neutral, Pigling, Sleek, Smooth, Suave, Tasteless, Unctuous

Blank Burr, Cartridge, Deadpan, Empty, Erase, Flan, Ignore, Lacuna, Mistigris, Planchet, Shot, Space, Tabula rasa, →**VACANT**

Blanket Afghan, All-over, Bluey, Chilkat, Counterpane, Cover, General, Kaross, Mackinaw, Manta, Obscure, Overall, Overlay, Poncho, Quilt, Rug, Saddle, Sarape, Security, Serape, Shabrack, Smog, Space, Stroud, Umbrella, Wagga, Wet, Whittle

Blast(ed), Blasting Blight, Blore, Blow, Bombard, Dang, Darn, Dee, Drat, Dynamite, Explode, Fanfare, Flaming, Flurry, Fo(e)hn, Gale, Grit, Gust, Hell, Pan, Parp, Planet-struck, Pryse, Rats, Ruddy, Scarth, Scath(e), Sere, Shot, Sideration, Skarth, Stormer, Tantara, Toot, Tout, Tromp(e), Trump(et), Volley

Blatant Flagrant, Hard-core, Noticeable, Strident, Unashamed, Vulgar

Blaze(r), Blazing Afire, Beacon, Bonfire, Burn, Cannel, Conflagration, Firestorm, →**FLAME**, Flare, Glare, Jacket, Low(e), Lunt, Palatinate, Race, Ratch, Sati, Star, Sun, Tead(e)

Bleach(er) Agene, Blanch, Chemic, Chloride, Decolorate, Etiolate, Fade, Frost, Keir, Kier, Peroxide, Whiten, Whitster

Bleak Ablet, Bare, Barren, Blay, Bley, Dour, Dreary, Dreich, Gaunt, Midwinter, Raw, Soulless, Wintry

Bleed(er), Bleeding Breakthrough, Cup, Diapedesis, Ecchymosis, Emulge, Epistaxis, Extort, Extravasate, Fleam, Haemorrhage, Leech, Menorrhagia, Menorrh(o)ea, Metrorrhagia, Milk, Purpura, Rhinorrhagia, Root-pressure

Blemish Birthmark, Blot, Blotch, Blur, Botch, Defect, Eyesore, Flaw, Lepra, Mackle, Mark, Milium, Mote, Naevus, Scar, Smirch, Spot, Stain, Sully, Taint, Tash, Verruca, Vice, Wart, Wen

▷ **Blend** *may indicate* an anagram

Blend(ing) Amalgam, Coalesce, Commix, Contemper, Contrapuntal, Counterpoint, Electrum, Fit, Fuse, Go, Harmonize, Hydrate, Interfuse, Interlace, Intermix, Liquidise, Meld, Melt, →**MERGE**, Mingle, Mix, Osmose, Portmanteau, Scumble, Sfumato, Synalepha

Bless(ing), Blessed(ness) Amen, Anoint, Approval, Asset, Beatitude, Benedicite, Benediction, Benison, Benitier, Bensh, Bismillah, Boon, Brachah, Brocho, Charmed, Consecrate, Cup, Damosel, Darshan, Elysium, Ethereal, Felicity, Gesundheit, Gwyneth, Holy (dam), Kiddush, Luck, Macarise, Mercy, Mixed, Sain, Saint, Sanctify, Sanctity, Sneeze, Urbi et orbi, Xenium

Blight Afflict, Ague, American, Apple, Bespot, Blast, Destroy, Early, Eyesore, Late, Rot, →**RUIN**, Rust, Sandy, Shadow, Viticide, Waldersterben, Wither

Blimey Coo, Cor, Crimini, O'Riley, Strewth

Blind(ness), Blind spot Amaurosis, Amblyopia, Artifice, Austrian, Bedazzle, Beesome, Binge, Bisson, Blend, Blotto, Camouflage, Carousal, Cecity, Chi(c)k, Cog, Concealed, Dazzle, Drop serene, Drunk, Eyeless, Feint, Festoon, Flash, Gravel, Hemeralopia, Homer, Hood, Jalousie, Legless, Meropia, Mole, Nyctalopia, Onchocerciasis, Persian, Persiennes, Pew, Pickled, Prestriction, Rash, River, Roller, Scotoma, Seel, Shade, Shutter, Sightless, Snow, Stimie, Stimy, Stymie, Sun, Swear, Teichopsia, Typhlology, Venetian, Visually challenged, Word, Yblent

Blindfold Bandage, Hoodwink, Muffle, Seal, Wimple

Bling Tsatske

Blink, Blinker(s), Blinkered, Blinking Bat, Blinders, Bluff, Broken, Flash, Haw, Idiot, Insular, Nictate, Owl-eyed, Owly, Twink, Wapper, Water, Wink

Bliss(ful) Beatitude, Bouyan, Cheer, Composer, Delight, →**ECSTASY**, Eden, Elysium, Glee, Happy, Heaven, Ignorance, Joy, Married, Millenium, Nirvana, Paradise, Rapture, Sion, Tir-na-nog, Valhalla, Walhalla, Wedded

Blister(ed), Blistering Blab, Blain, Bleb, Bubble, Bullate, Cantharidine, Epispastic, Fever, Herpes, Overgall, Pemphigus, Phlyct(a)ena, Scorching, Tetter, Vesicant, Vesicle

Blitz Attack, Bombard, Onslaught, Raid

Blizzard Buran, Gale, Snowstorm, Whiteout

Bloat(ed), Bloater Buckling, Gross, Puff, Strout, Swell, Tumefy, Two-eyed steak, Yarmouth

Blob Bead, Bioblast, Dollop, Drop, Globule, O, Pick, Spot, Tear

Bloc Alliance, Cabal, Cartel, Party

Block(er), Blockage, Blocked, Blocking Altar, Anvil, Ashlar, →BAR, Barber's, Barricade, Barrier, Battle-axe, Brake, Breeze, Brick, Briquet(te), Building, Bung, Bunt, Capital, Choke, Chunk, Cinder, Cleat, Clint, Clog, Clot, Cloy, Compass, Congest, Constipated, Cylinder, Dado, →DAM, Dead-eye, Debar, Defect, Delete, Dentel, Dentil, Die, Dit, Embolism, Encompass, Erratic, Fiddle, Fipple, Frog, Gypsum, Hack-log, Heart, High-rise, Hunk, Ileus, Impasse, Impede, Impost, Ingot, Input, Insula, Interclude, Interrupt, Investment, Ischaemia, Jam, Licence, Lifestyle, Lingot, Lodgment, Log-jam, Lump, Ministroke, Monkey, Mounting, Nog, Oasis®, Obstacle, →OBSTRUCT, Occlude, Pad, Page, Parry, Pile-up, Planer, Plinth, Pre-empt, Prevent, Ram, Scotch, Seal, Sett, Siege, Stalemate, Stap, Starting, Stenosis, Stimie, Stimy, Stone, Stonewall, Stop, Stumbling, Stymie, Sun, Tamp, Tetrapod, Thwart, Tint, Tower, Tranche, Trig, Triglyph, Truck, Veto, Vibropac®, Wedge, Wig, Writer's

Blockhouse Igloo

Bloke Beggar, Chap, Codger, Cove, Fellow, Gent, Man, Oik

Blond(e) Ash, Bombshell, Cendré, Fair, Goldilocks, Platinised, Platinum, Strawberry, Tallent, Towhead

Blood(y), Blood-letter, Blood-letting A, Ancestry, B, Bally, Blue, Bluggy, Blut, Buck, Butchery, Claret, Clot, Cold, Cruor, Cup, Dutch pink, Ecchymosis, Ensanguine, Epigons, Factor, H(a)emal, Haematoma, Ichor, Introduce, Kin, Knut, Menses, Microcyte, Nut, O, Opsonin, Parentage, Penny dreadful, Persue, Pigeon's, Plasma, Platelet, Properdin, Pup, Purple, Race, Rare, Red, Rh negative, Rh positive, Ruby, Sang, Schistosoma, Serum, Show, Stroma, Thrombin, Toff, Venisection, Welter

Bloodless Anaemic, Isch(a)emic, Wan, White

Blood money Eric

Blood-sucker Anoplura, Asp, Bed bug, Dracula, Flea, Gnat, Ked, Leech, Louse, Mosquito, Parasite, Reduviid, Soucouyant, Sponger, Tick, Vampire(-bat)

Bloodthirsty Tiger

Bloom(er), Blooming Anthesis, Bally, Blossom, Blow, Blush, Boner, Bread, Cobalt, Dew, Dratted, Error, Film, Florence, Florescent, Flourish, Flowery, Flush, Gaffe, Glaucous, Heyday, Knickers, Loaf, Miscalculation, Nickel, Out, Peach, Pruina, Rationals, Reh, Remontant, Rosy, Ruddy, Thrive, Underwear

▷ **Bloomer** *may indicate* a flower

Blossom Blow, Burgeon, Catkin, Develop, Festoon, Flourish, Flower, Marybud, May, Orange, Pip, Springtime

Blot Atomy, Blob, Cartel, Delete, Disgrace, Eyesore, Obscure, Smear, Smudge, Southern, Splodge, Splotch

Blotch(y) Blemish, Giraffe, Monk, Mottle(d), Spot, Stain

Blouse Choli, Garibaldi, Gimp, Guimpe, Middy, Sailor, Shell, Shirtwaist, Smock, Tunic, Waist(er), Windjammer

Blow(er) Bang, Bash, Bat, Bellows, Biff, Billow, Blip, Bloom, Box, Brag, Breeze, Buffet, Bump, Burst, Calamity, Clap, Clat, Claut, Clip, Clout, Clump, Conk, Coup, Cuff, Dad, Daud, Dawd, Dev(v)el, Dint, Dod, Douse, Dowse, Etesian, Exsufflate, Facer, Fan, Fillip, Finisher, Fisticuffs, Fuse, Gale, Grampus, Gust, Hammer, Hander, Haymaker, Hit, Hook, Ictus, Impact, Insufflate, Karate, Kibosh, Knuckle sandwich, KO, Lame, Lander, Left-hander, Lick, Muff, Muzzler, Northerly, Noser, Oner, One-two, Paddywhack, Pash, Peise, Phone, Piledriver, Plague, Plug, Plump(er), Polt, Pow, Puff, Punch, Purler, Raft, Rats, Rattler, Rib-roaster, Roundhouse, Sas(s)arara, Scat, Settler, Short, Sideswipe, Side-winder, Sis(s)erary, Skiff, Skite, Skyte, Slat, Slog, Slug, Snell, Snot, Sock, Sockdolager, Southwester, Spanking, Spat, Spout, Squall, Squander, Squelcher, Stripe, Stroke, Stunning, Sufflate, Supercharger, Swash, Swat, Swinger, Telephone, Thump, Thwack, Tingler, Tootle, Triple whammy, Trump(et), Tuck, Undercut, Upper-cut, Waft, Wallop, Wap, Waste, Welt, Whammy, Whang, Whap, Wheeze, Whiffle, Whirret, Whistle, →WIND, Winder, Wipe

Blow-out Binge, Bloat, Blowhole, Exhale, Feast, Feed, Flat, Fulminate, Lava, Nosh-up, Snuff, Spiracle, → SPREAD

Bludgeon Bulldoze, Bully, Club, Cosh, Cudgel, Sap

▷ **Blue** *may indicate an anagram*

Blue(s), Bluesman Adult, Aqua, Aquamarine, Azure, Azurn, Beard, Berlin, Bice, Bleuâtre, Blow, Bottle, Butterfly, Caesious, Cambridge, Cantab, Celeste, Cerulean, City, Clair de lune, Classic, Cobalt, Copenhagen, Cornflower, Country, Coventry, Cyan, Danish, Danube, Dejected, Dirty, Disconsolate, Doldrums, → DOWN, Duck-egg, Eatanswill, Eggshell, Electric, Erotica, Firmament, Fritter, Gentian, Germander, Glaucous, Glum, Heliotrope, Hump, Indecent, Indigo, Indol(e), Iron, Isatin(e), Lapis lazuli, Lavender, Leadbelly, Lewd, Lionel, Low, Mazarine, Methylene, Midnight, Mope, Morose, Murder, Nattier, Naughty, Navy, Nile, Obscene, Ocean, Off-colour, Oxford, Peacock, Periwinkle, Perse, Petrol, Porn, Powder, Prussian, Rabbi, Racy, Ribald, Riband, Right, Ripe, Robin's egg, Royal, Sad, Sapphire, Saxe, Saxon(y), Scurrilous, → SEA, Shocking, → SKY-TINCTURED, Slate, Smalt(o), Smutty, Sordid, Spirit, Splurge, Squander, Stafford, Steel, Stocking, Teal, Thenard's, Tony, Top shelf, Tory, Trist, True, Turquoise, Ultramarine, Unhappy, Urban, Washing, Watchet, Wedgwood®, Welkin, Woad

Bluebell Blawort, Blewart, Campanula, Harebell

Bluebottle Blawort, Blewart, Blowfly, Blowie, Brommer, Brummer, Cop, Cornflower, Fly, Officer, Policeman

Blueprint Cyanotype, Design, Draft, Drawing, Plan, Recipe

Bluff(ing) Blunt, Cle(e)ve, Cliff, Clift, Crag, Double, Escarpment, Fake, Flannel, Four-flush, Frank, Hal, Headland, Height, Hoodwink, Kidology, Pose, Precipice, Scarp, Steep, Trick

Blunder(er), Blundering Barry (Crocker), Betise, Bévue, Bish, Bloomer, Blooper, Boner, Boob, Bull, Bumble, Bungle, Clanger, Clinker, Cock-up, Crass, Err, Fault, Faux pas, Floater, Flub, Fluff, Gaff(e), Goof, Howler, Inexactitude, Irish, Josser, Malapropism, → MISTAKE, Mumpsimus, Ricket, Slip, Slip up, Solecism, Stumble, Trip

Blunt(ed), Bluntly Abrupt, Alleviate, Bald, Bate, Bayt, Brash, Brusque, Candid, Deaden, Disedge, Downright, Dull, Forthright, Frank, Hebetate, Mole, Morned, Obtund, Obtuse, Outspoken, Pointblank, Rebate, Retund, Retuse, Roundly, Snub, Straight-out, Stubby

Blur(red), Blurring, Blurry Cloud, Confuse, Daze, Fog, Fuzz, Halation, Mackle, Macule, Muzzy, Stump, Tortillon, Unfocussed

Blush(ing) Colour, Cramoisy, Crimson, Erubescent, Erythema, Incarnadine, → REDDEN, Rosy, Rouge, Ruby, Rutilant

Bluster(ing), Blusterer, Blustery Arrogance, Bellow, Blore, Brag, Fanfaronade, Hector, Huff-cap, Rage, Rant, Rodomontade, Roister, Sabre-rattler, Squash, Swagger, Vapour, Wuthering

Boar Barrow, Calydonian, Erymanthian, Hog, Pentheus, Sanglier, Sounder, Tusker

▷ **Board** *may refer to* chess or draughts

Board(s), Boarding Abat-voix, Admiralty, Aquaplane, Baffle, Banker, Barge, Bd, Beaver, Billet, Bristol, Bulletin, Catchment, Centre, Cheese, Chevron, Circuit, Committee, Counter, Cribbage, Dagger, Dam, Dart, Daughter, Deal, Directors, Diving, Draft, Draining, Drawing, Embark, Embus, Emery, Enter, Entrain, Expansion, Fa(s)cia, Fare, Farm out, Featheredge, Fibro, Fibrolite®, Full, Gib(raltar), Groaning, Gunwale, Gutter, Hack, Half, Half-royal, Hawk, Hoarding, Idiot, Instrument, Insulating, Ironing, Kip, Lag, Lap, Leader, Ledger, Lee, Lodge, Magnetic, Malibu, Marketing, Masonite®, Match, Message, Mill, Monkey, Mortar, Moulding, Notch, Notice, Otter, Ouija, Paddle, Palette, Pallet, Panel, Paper, Parochial, Particle, Patch, Pedal, Peg(board), Pension, Planch(ette), Plank, Plug, Ply(wood), Punch, Quango, Ribbon-strip, Roof, Running, Sandwich, Sarking, Scale, Scaleboard, School, Score, Scraper, Scratch, Screen, Sheathing, Shelf, Shifting, Shingle, Shooting, Side-table, Sign, Skim, Skirting, Sleeve, SMART®, Smoke, Snow, Sounding, Splasher, Spring, Stage, Stretcher, Strickle,

Stringboard, Supervisory, Surf, Switch, →**TABLE**, Telegraph, Thatch, Theatre, Trencher, Verge, Wainscot, Wobble, Wokka, Wood chip

Boarder Interne, Pensioner, PG, Roomer

Boarding house Digs, Kip, Lodgings, Pension

Boast(er), Boastful, Boasting Bigmouth, Big-note, Blew, Blow, Blowhard, Bluster, Bobadil, Bounce, Brag, Braggadocio, Bravado, Breeze, Bull, Cock-a-hoop, Crake, Crow, Fanfaronade, Gas, Gascon(nade), Glory, Hot air, Jact(it)ation, Line, Loudmouth, Ostent(atious), Prate, Rodomontade, Scaramouch, Self-glorious, Show-off, Skite, Spread-eagle, Swagger, Swank, Tall, Thrasonic, Vainglory, Vapour, Vaunt, Yelp

Boat(s) Ark, Barge, Bark, Cat, Coaster, Codder, Corvette, Cott, Cruiser, Curragh, Flagship, Flatboat, Fly(ing), Fore-and-after, Goldie, Isis, Keel, Kit, Long, Monkey, Mosquito, Motor, Privateer, PT, Pucan, Sculler, She, →**SHIP**, Smack, Tangle-netter, Tanker, Trek-ox, Vedette, →**VESSEL**, Wager

Boatman Bargee, Charon, Cockswain, Coxswain, George, Gondolier, Harris, Hoveller, Legger, Noah, Phaon, Voyageur, Waterman, Wet-bob

Bob Acres, Beck, Curtsey, Deaner, Dip, Dock, Dop, Duck, Dylan, Eton crop, Float, Hod, Hog, Jerk, Major, Maximus, Minor, Page-boy, Peal, Plain, Plumb, Plummet, Popple, Rob, Royal, S, Shingle, Skeleton, Skip

Bobby Bluebottle, Busy, Copper, Flatfoot, Patrolman, Peeler, Pig, →**POLICEMAN**

Bodgie Aussie, Ted

Body, Bodies, Bodily Administration, Amount, Anatomic, Astral, Barr, Board, Bouk, Buke, Bulk, Cadaver, Cadre, Carcase, Carnal, Caucas, Chapel, Chapter, Chassis, Clay, Cohort, Column, Comet, Committee, Contingent, Corpora, Corpor(e)al, Corps, Corpse, Corpus, Corse, Cytode, Detail, Earth, Elaiosome, Flesh, Frame, Fuselage, Goner, →**GROUP**, Hull, Immune, Inclusion, Kenning, Lich, Lifting, Like, Lithites, →**MASS**, Militia, Mitochondrion, Moit, Mote, Mummy, Nacelle, Nave, Nucleole, Nucleolus, Olivary, Orb, Order, Pack, Personal, Phalanx, Pineal, Plant, Platelet, Platoon, Politic, Posse, Purview, Quango, Relic(t), Remains, Review, Ruck, Satellite, Senate, Shaft, Solid, Soma(tic), Sound-box, Spinar, Spore, Squadron, Square, Staff, Stiff, Strobila, Syndicate, Systemic, Torso, Trunk, Turm, Ulema, Uvula, Vase

▷ **Body** *may indicate* an anagram

Bodyguard Amulet, Beefeater, →**ESCORT**, Gentleman-at-arms, House-carl, Minder, Praetorian, Protector, Retinue, Schutzstaffel, →**SHIELD**, SS, Switzer, Triggerman, Varangian, Yeomen

Boffin Brain, Egghead, Expert

Bog(e)y Boggart, Bug(aboo), Bugbear, Chimera, Colonel, Eagle, Gremlin, Poker, Scarer, Siege, Spectre, Troll

Bog(gy) Allen, Can, Carr, Clabber, Fen, Gents, Glaur, Hag, Lair, Lerna, Lerne, Letch, Loo, Machair, Marish, Marsh, Mire, Moory, Morass, Moss(-flow), Mud, Muskeg, Peat, Petary, Quag, Serbonian, Slack, Slade, Slough, Spew, Spouty, Stodge, Sump, Urinal, Vlei, Washroom, WC, Yarfa, Yarpha

Bogie Trolley

Bohemian Arty, Beatnik, Boho, Calixtin(e), Demi-monde, Gypsy, Hippy

Boil(er), Boiled, Boiling (point) Aleppo, Anthrax, Blain, Botch, Brew, Bubble, C, Coction, Cook, Copper, Cree, Dartre, Decoct, Ebullient, Foam, Furuncle, Gathering, Hen, Herpes, Kettle, Leep, Ligroin, Pimple, Poach, Poule, Rage, Reflux, Samovar, Seethe, Set pot, Simmer, Sod, Sore, Stew, Stye, Tea-kettle, Water tube

Boisterous(ly) Ariot, Gilp(e)y, Gusty, Hoo, Knockabout, Ladette, Noisy, Rambunctious, Randy, Riotous, Rollicking, Rorty, Rough, Rounceval, Splurge, Stormy, Tearer, Termagant, Tomboy, Turbulent, Wild

Bold(ly), Boldness Audacious, Brash, Brass, Bravado, Bravery, Bravura, Brazen, Crust, Daredevil, Dauntless, Defiant, Derring-do, Familiar, Free, Gutsy, Hard-edge, Hardihood, Heroics, High-spirited, Impudent, Intrepid, Malapert, Mature, Minx, Outspoken, Pert, Plucky, Presumptive, Rash, Sassy, Temerity, Unshrinking

Bolt Arrow, Captive, Carriage, Cuphead, Dash, Dead, Do a runner, Eat, Elope, Fasten,

Flee, Gobble, Gollop, Gorge, Gulp, Latch, Levant, Levin, Lightning, Lock, Missile, Pig, Pintle, Ragbolt, Rivet, Roll, Scoff, Slot, Snib, Sperre, Through, Thunder, Toggle, U, Wolf, Wring

Bomb(ed), Bomber, Bombing Atom, Attack, B, Benny, Blast, Blockbuster, Borer, Bunkerbuster, Buzz, Car, Carpet, Cluster, Daisycutter, Deterrent, Doodlebug, Drogue, Egg, Fission, Flop, Flying Fortress, Fusion, Grenade, H, Homicide, Hydrogen, Lancaster, Land-mine, Letter, Liberator, Logic, Mail, Megaton, Mills, Minnie, Mint, Molotov cocktail, Mortar, Nail, Napalm, Necklace, Neutron, Nuclear, Nuke, Packet, Parcel, Petar, Petard, Petrol, Pineapple, Pipe, Plaster, Plastic, Prang, Ransom, Robot, Sex, Shell, Smoke, Stealth, Stick, Stink, Stuka, Suicide, Tactical, Terrorist, Time, Torpedo, V1, Vulcan

Bombard(ment) Attack, Battery, Blitz, Cannonade, Drum-fire, Mortar, Pelt, Shell(fire), Stone, Stonk, Strafe, Straff

Bona fide Echt, Genuine

Bond(s), Bondage, Bonding, Bondsman Adhesive, Affinity, Afrikander, Agent, Baby, Bail, Bearer, Cement, Chain, Chemical, Compact, Connect, Consols, Coordinate, Copula, Corporate, Covalent, Covenant, Daimyo, Dative, Debenture, Deep-discount, Double, Duty, Electrovalent, English, Ernie, Escrow, Esne, Fetter, Fleming, Flemish, Geasa, Gilt, Glue, Granny, Heart, Herringbone, Hydrogen, Hyphen, Income, Investment, Ionic, James, Junk, Knot, Liaise, Ligament, Ligature, Link(age), Long, Manacle, Managed, Metallic, Mortar, Multicentre, Municipal, Nexus, Noose, Obligation, Pair, Peptide, Performance, →**PLEDGE**, Post-obit, Premium, Property, Rapport, Recognisance, Relationship, Revenue, Running, Samurai, Savings, Security, Semipolar, Serf, Servitude, Shackle, Shogun, Single, Singlet, Sinter, Slave, Solder, Stacked, Starr, Superglue, Surety, Thete, Three-per-cent, →**TIE**, Tiger, TIGR, Treasury, Triple, Trivalent, Tusking, Valence, Valency, Vassal, Vinculum, Yearling, Yoke, Zebra

Bone(s), Bony Angular, Atlas, Axis, Busk, Caluarium, Cannon, Capitate, Carpal, Carpus, Cartilage, Catacomb, Centrum, Chine, Chordate, Clavicle, Cly, Coccyx, Coffin, Concha, Coral, Costa, Coxa, Crane, Cranium, Cuboid, Cuneiform, Cuttlefish, Dib, Dice, Diploe, Doctor, Dolos, Endosteal, Femur, Fetter, Fibula, Fillet, Frontal, Funny, Gaunt, Hamate, Haunch, Hause-bane, Horn, Humerus, Hyoid, Ilium, Incus, Interclavicle, Ivory, Kneecap, Knuckle, Lacrimal, Long, Lunate, Luz, Malar, Malleus, Mandible, Marrow, Mastoid, Maxilla, Medulla, Membrane, Metacarpal, Metatarsal, Nasal, Occipital, Orthopaedics, Os, Ossicle, Osteo-, Palatine, Parasphenoid, Parietal, Patella, Pecten, Pectoral, Pedal, Pelvis, Pen, Percoid, Petrous, Phalanx, Ploughshare, Prenasal, Pterygoid, Pubis, Rack, Radiale, Radius, Relic, Rib, Rump-post, Sacrum, Scapula, Sclere, Sepium, Sequestrum, Share, Skeleton, Skull, Spade, Splint, Splinter, Spur, Stapes, →**STEAL**, Sternum, Stifle, Stirrup, T, Talus, Tarsometatarsus, Tarsus, Temporal, Tibia, Tibiotarsus, Tot, Trapezium, True-rib, Turbinate, Tympanic, Ulna, Vertebrae, Whirl, Wish

Bonfire Bale-fire, Beltane, Blaze, Clavie, Pyre

Bonny Blithe, Gay, Merry, Sonsy, Weelfar'd

Bonus Bisque, Bounty, Braata, Bye, Dividend, Hand-out, Lagniappe, No-claim, →**PREMIUM**, Reward, Scrip, Signing, Spin-off, Windfall

Boo Explode

Book(s), Bookish, Bookwork Abcee, Absey, Academic, Album, Appointment, Audio, B, Backlist, Bedside, Bestiary, Bestseller, Black, Block, Blockbuster, Blotter, Blue, Cash, Chick, Classic, Closed, Coffee-table, Diary, Digest, Directory, Diurnal, Eightvo, Engage(ment), Enter, Erudite, Exercise, Folio, Fortune, Good, Gradual, Guide, Hardback, Hymnal, Imprint, Index, Issue, Lectionary, Ledger, Lib, Liber, Literary, Livraison, Manual, Memorandum, Missal, Monograph, Muster, Octavo, Office, Open, Order, Page-turner, Paperback, Pass, Pedantic, Peerage, Phrase, Pica, Plug, Polyglot, Potboiler, Pseudepigrapha, Publication, Puzzle prize, Quarto, Quire, →**RESERVE**, Road, Roman-a-clef, Script, Sealed, Sext, Sexto, Sixmo, Sketch, Softback, Source, Spelling, Spine-chiller, Statute, Studious, Study, Style, Swatch, Symbolical, Table, Tablet, Talking, Tall copy, Te igitur, Text(ual), Thirty-twomo, Thriller, Title, Titule,

Tome, Trade, Transfer, Twelvemo, Twenty-fourmo, Unputdownable, Visiting, Visitor's, Vol(ume), Waste, White, Work, Year

Bookbinder, Bookbinding Fanfare, Grolier, Mutton-thumper, Organdie

Book-case Credenza, Press, Satchel

Bookie(s), Bookmaker Binder, John, Layer, Librettist, Luke, Mark, Matthew, Printer, Ringman, To-bit, Turf accountant

Bookkeeper, Bookkeeping Clerk, Double entry, Librarian, Posting, Recorder, Satchel, Single-entry

Booklet B, Brochure, Folder, Inlay

Boom(ing) Baby, Beam, Boost, Bowsprit, Bump, Gaff, Increase, Jib, Loud, Orotund, Plangent, Prosper, Roar, Sonic, Spar, Thrive, Wishbone

Boon Bene, Benefit, Blessing, Bounty, Cumshaw, Gift, Godsend, Mills, Mitzvah, Prayer, Windfall

Boor(ish) Borel, Bosthoon, Chuffy, Churl, Clodhopper, Crass, Curmudgeon, Goth, Grobian, Hog, Ill-bred, Jack, Keelie, Kern(e), Kernish, Kill-courtesy, Lob, Lout, Lumpen, Lumpkin, Ocker, Peasant, Philistine, Pleb, Trog, Uncouth, Unmannerly, Yahoo, Yob

Boost(er) Adrenalin, Afterburner, Bolster, Eik, Eke, Encourage, Fillip, Help, Hoist, Impetus, Increase, Injection, Invigorate, Lift, Promote, Raise, Reheat, Reinforce, Reinvigorate, Spike, Steal, Step up, Supercharge, Tonic

Boot(s) Addition, Adelaide, Avail, Balmoral, Beetle-crushers, Benefit, Blucher, Bottine, Bovver, Brogan, Brogue, Buskin, Chelsea, Chukka, Cold, Combat, Concern, Cowboy, Denver, Derby, Desert, Dismiss, Field, Finn(e)sko, Finsko, Fire, Galage, Galosh, Gambado, Go-go, Granny, Gum, Heave-ho, Hessian, Hip, Jack, Jemima, Kinky, Lace-up, Last, Mitten, Muchie, Muc(k)luc(k), Pac, Para, Profit, Sabot, →SACK, →SHOE, Shoepac(k), Skivvy, Stogy, Surgical, Tackety, Toe, Tonneau, Tops, Trunk, Ugg, Vibs, Wader, Walking, Warm, Weller, Wellie, Wellington, Welly

Booth Assassin, Crame, Cubicle, Kiosk, Polling, Stall, Stand, Tolsel, Tolsey, Voting

Bootleg(ger) Cooper, Coper, Pirate, Runner

Booty Creach, Creagh, Haul, Loot, Prey, Prize, Spoil(s), Spolia optima, Swag

Booze(r) →DRINK, Inn, Liquor, Spree, Tipple

Bora Rite, Wind

Bordeaux Claret

Border(s), Borderland, Borderline Abut, Adjoin, Apron, Bed, Bind, Bound, Boundary, Brush, Checkpoint, Coast, Cot(t)ise, Dado, Dentelle, →EDGE, Engrail, Fimbria, Frieze, Fringe, Frontier, Furbelow, Head-rig, Hedgerow, Hem, Herbaceous, Impale, Kerb, Limb, Limbate, Limbo, Limes, Limit, Lip, List, March, Marchland, →MARGIN, Mat, Mattoid, Meith, Mete, Mount, Neighbour, Orle, Pand, Pelmet, Perimeter, Purfle, Purlieu, Rand, Rim, Rio Grande, Roadside, Roon, Royne, Rund, Screed, Selvage, Side, Skirt, Splenium, Strand, Strip, Surround, Swage, T(h)alweg, The Marches, Trench, Valance, Valence, →VERGE

▷ **Borders** *may indicate* first and last letters

Bore(d), Boredom, Borer, Boring Aiguille, Airshaft, Anorak, Apathy, Auger, Awl, Beetle, Bind, Bit, Blasé, Broach, Brog, Bromide, Calibre, Cataclysm, Deadly, Drag, →DRILL, Dry, Dullsville, Eagre, Eat, Eger, Elshin, Elsin, Endured, Ennui, Ennuye, Fag, Flat, Foozle, Gim(b)let, Gouge, Gribble, Grind, Had, Heigh-ho, Ho-hum, Irk, Jack, Land, Listless, Longicorn, Longueur, Miser, Mole, Motormouth, Nerd, Nuisance, Pall, Penetrate, Perforate, Pest, Pierce, Pill, Platitude, Probe, Prosaic, Prosy, Punch, Ream(ingbit), Rime, Saddo, Sat, Screw, Severn, Snooze, Snore, Sondage, Spleen, Spod, Spudding-un, Sting, Stob, Tedious, Tedium, Termes, Termite, Thirl, Tire, Trocar, Tunnel, Turn-off, Vapid, →WEARY, Well, Wimble, Windbag, Wonk, Woodworm, Workaday, Worldweary, Yawn

Born B, Free, Great, Nascent, Nat(us), Né(e)

Borneo Kalimantan, Sabahan

Borough Borgo, Close, Pocket, Port, Quarter, Queens, Rotten, Township, Wick

Borrow(ed), Borrowing Adopt, Appropriate, Cadge, Copy, Eclectic, George, Hum, Scunge, Stooze, Straunge, →TAKE, Touch

Boson Gauge, Squark

Boss(ed), Bossy Big White Chief, Blooper, Burr, Cacique, Capo, Cow, Director, Dominate, Domineer, Gadroon, Gaffer, Headman, Honcho, Hump, Inian, Inion, Jewel, Knob, Knop, Knot, Maestro, →MANAGER, Massa, MD, →MISTAKE, Mistress, Netsuke, Noop, Nose-led, Omphalos, Oubaas, Overlord, Overseer, Owner, Padrone, Pellet, Protuberance, Ruler, Run, Stud, Superintendent, Superior, Supervisor, Supremo, Taskmaster, Top banana, Umbo(nate)

Bother(some) Ado, Aggro, Annoy, Brush, Care, Deave, Deeve, Disturb, Drat, Fash, Fluster, Fuss, Get, Harassment, Harry, Hector, Hoot-toot, Incommode, Irritate, Moither, Nag, Nark, Nuisance, Palaver, Perturb, Pest(er), Pickle, Reke, Todo, →TROUBLE, Vex

▷ **Bottle(d)** *may indicate* an anagram or a hidden word

Bottle(s) Ampul(la), Balthasar, Balthazar, Belshazzar, Blackjack, Bravado, Bundle, Carafe, Carboy, Case, Chapine, Cock, Cork, Costrel, Courage, Cruet, Cruse, Cucurbital, Cutter, Dead-man, Decanter, Demijohn, Fearlessness, Feeding, Fiasco, Filette, Flacket, Flagon, Flask, Glass can, Goatskin, Gourd, Grit, Hen, Imperial, Jeroboam, Junk, Klein, Lachrymal, Lagena, Magnum, Matrass, Medicine, Melchior, Methuselah, Mettle, Middy, Nebuchadnezzar, Phial, Pig, Pitcher, Rehoboam, Resource, Retort, Salmanazar, Scent, Siphon, Split, Stubby, Vial, Vinaigret(te), Wad, Water, Water bouget, Winchester, Woulfe

Bottom Anus, Aris, Arse, Ass, Base, Batty, Beauty, Bed, Benthos, Bilge, Booty, Breech, Bum, Butt, Buttocks, Coit, Croup(e), Croupon, Demersal, Derrière, Doup, Dowp, Fanny, Floor, Foot, Foundation, Fud, Fundus, Haunches, Hunkers, Hurdies, Jacksy, Keel(son), Kick, Nadir, Planning, Podex, Posterior, Pottle-deep, Prat, Pyramus, Quark, Rear, Rock, Root, Rump, Seat, Ship, Sill, Sole, Staddle, Tail, Tush, Weaver

Bounce(r), Bouncing, Bouncy Ananias, Ball, Bang, Blague, Bound, Caper, Convention, Dandle, Dap, Dead-cat, Doorman, Dop, Dud, Eject, Evict, Jounce, Kite, Lie, Lilt, Muscleman, Resilient, Ricochet, Spiccato, Spring, Stot, Tale, Tamp, Tigger, Valve, Verve, Vitality, Yorker, Yump

▷ **Bouncing** *may indicate* an anagram

Bound(er), Boundary Adipose, Apprenticed, Articled, Bad, Barrier, Beholden, Border, Bourn(e), Cad, Cavort, Certain, Circumference, Curvet, Decreed, Demarcation, Demarkation, Divide, Duty, End, Engirt, Entrechat, Erub, Eruv, Fence, Finite, Four, Frontier, Galumph, Gambado, Gambol, Girt, Hedge, Heel, Held, Hoarstone, Hops, Hourstone, Interface, Jump, Kangaroo, →LEAP, Limes, Limit, Linch, Lollop, Lope, Mason-Dixon line, Meare, Meer, Mere, Merestone, Mete, Muscle, Obliged, Outedge, Outward, Pale, Parameter, Perimeter, Periphery, Plate, Prance, Precinct, Purlieu, Quickset, Redound, Ring-fence, Roller, Roo, Roped, Rubicon, Scoundrel, Scoup, Side, Sideline, Six(er), Skip, Spang, Spring, Sten(d), Stoit, Sure, T(h)alweg, Tide, Tied, Touchline, Upstart, Vault, Verge, Wallaby

Boundless Illimited, Unlimited

▷ **Bounds** *may indicate* outside letters

Bounty, Bountiful Aid, Bligh, Boon, Christian, Generosity, →GIFT, Goodness, Grant, Head money, Honorarium, Largess(e), Lavish, Queen's

Bouquet Aroma, Attar, Aura, Compliment, Corsage, Fragrancy, Garni, Nose, Nosegay, Odour, Perfume, Plaudit, Posy, Pot pourri, Scent, Spiritual, Spray

Bout Bender, Bust, Contest, Dose, Go, Jag, Match, Spell, Spree, Turn, Venery, Venewe, Venue

Bow(ing), Bower, Bowman Accede, Alcove, Arbour, Arc, Arch, →ARCHER, Arco, Arson, Beck, Bend, Boudoir, Clara, Congé(e), Crescent, Crook, Cupid, →CURVE, Defer, Dicky, Droop, Duck, Eros, Eyes, Fiddle(r), Fiddlestick, Foredeck, Halse, Hawse, Headgear, Honour, Incline, Inswing(er), Jouk, Kneel, Kotow, Lean, Londoner, Loof, Lout, Luff, Nock, Nod, Nutate, Oar, Obeisance, Outswing, Paganini, Pergola, Quarrel, Reverence, Salaam, Seamer, Shelter, Slope, Spiccato, Staccato, Stick, →SUBMIT, Swing, Throw, Tie, Torrent, Tureen, Weather, Yew, Yield

Bowels Entrails, Guts, Innards, Melaena, Viscera

▷ **Bower** *may indicate* using a bow

Bowl(ing), Bowler, Bowl over, Bowls B, Basin, Begging, Bicker, Bodyline, Bool, Bosey, Bouncer, Cage-cup, Calabash, Cap, Carpet, Caup, Chalice, Cheese, Chinaman, Christie, Christy, Cog(g)ie, Concave, Crater, Cup, Derby, → **DISH**, Dismiss, Dome, Doosra, Drake, Dumbfound, Dust, Ecuelle, End, Finger, Goblet, Goldfish, Googly, Grub, Headgear, Hog, Hoop, Inswing(er), Jack, Jeroboam, Jorum, Lavabo, Laver, Leg-spin, Lightweight, Lob, Locke, Monteith, Night, Offbreak, Off-cutter, Old, Outswing, Over-arm, Overpitch, Pace(man), Pan, Pétanque, Pitch, Porringer, Pot-hat, Pottinger, Punch, Raku, Rink, Roll, Roundarm, Seam(er), Skip, Skittle(s), Spare, Spinner, Stadium, Stagger, Super, Swing, Ten-pin, Throw, Tom, Tureen, Underarm, Underhand, Voce, Wassail, Wood, York(er)

Box(ing) Baignoire, Ballot, Bandbox, Bareknuckle, Bento, Bijou, Bimble, Binnacle, Black, Blow, Blue, Bonk, Booth, Bunk, Bush, Caddy, Call, Camera, Canister, Case, Cash, Casket, Chest, Chinese, Christmas, Clog, Coach, Coffer, Coffin, Coffret, Coin, Commentary, Confessional, Cool, Crash, Crate, Cuff, Dabba, Dead-letter, Deed, Dialog(ue), Dispatch, Ditty, Dog, Drawer, Egg, Encase, Enclose, Etui, → **FIGHT**, File, Fist, Fund, Fuse, Fuzz, Gear, Glory, Glove, Go-kart, Grass, Hat, Hay, Hedge, Hive, Honesty, Horse, Humidor, Hutch, Ice, Idiot, Inherce, Inro, Inter, Jewel, Journal, Juke, Junction, Jury, Keister, Kick, Kiosk, Kite, Knevell, Knowledge, Ladle, Letter, Light, Live, Locker, Lodge, Loge, Loose, Lug, Lunch, Match, Message, Mill, Mitre, Mocuck, Money, Musical, Nest(ing), Noble art, Noble science, Omnibus, Orgone, Out, Package, Packing, Paint, Pandora's, Patch, Pattress, Peepshow, Peg, Penalty (area), Petara, Pew, Phylactery, Piggybank, Pill, Pillar, Pitara, Pix, Poor, Post, Powder, Press, Prize fight, Prompt, Protector, Puff, Pugilism, Pyxis, Register, Resonance, Ring, Rope-a-dope, Royal, Safe-deposit, Saggar(d), Sagger, Sand, Savate, Scent, Scrap, Seggar, Sentry, Set-top, Shadow, Shoe, Shooting, Side, Signal, Skinner, Skip(pet), Slipcase, Smudge, Sneeshin-mull, Sneeze, Soap, Solander, Sound, Sound body, → **SPAR**, Spice, Spit, Spring, Squawk, Squeeze, Strong, Stuffing, Swell, Tee, Telephone, Telly, Tick, Tin, Tinder, Tivo, Tool, Touch, Trunk, Tube, Tuck, TV, Urn, Vanity, Vinaigrette, Voice, Weather, Window, Wine, Witness

Boxer Ali, Bantamweight, Bruiser, Bruno, Canine, Carnera, Carpentier, Carthorse, Chinaman, Cooper, Corbett, Crater, Cruiserweight, Darcy, Dempsey, Dog, Eryx, Farr, Featherweight, Flyweight, Foreman, Ham, Heavyweight, Middleweight, Pandora, Pug, Pugil(ist), Rebellion, Rocky, Shadow, Sparrer, Sugar Ray Robinson, Welterweight

▷ **Boy** *may indicate* an abbreviated name

Boy(s) Anchor, Apprentice, Ball, Bevin, Blue-eyed, Bovver, Bub(by), Cabin, Callant, Champagne, Chiel(d), → **CHILD**, Chummy, Cub, Galopin, Garçon, Groom, Grummet, Ha, Jack, Kid, Klonkie, Knave, Lackbeard, → **LAD**, Loblolly, Loon(ie), Minstrel, Nibs, Nipper, Page, Poster, Prentice, Principal, Putto, Rent, Roaring, Rude, Shaver, Ship's, Son, Spalpeen, Sprig, Stripling, Swain, Tad, Ted(dy), Tiger, Toxic, Toy, Urchin, Whipping, → **YOUTH**

Boycott Avoid, Bat, Black, Blacklist, Exclude, Geoff(rey), Hartal, Isolate, Ostracise, Shun

Brace(s), Bracing Accolade, Couple, Crosstree, Gallace, Gallows, Gallus(es), Gird, Hound, Invigorate, Ozone, Pair, Pr, Rear-arch, Rere-arch, Sea air, Skeg, Splint, Stage, Steady, Stiffener, Strut, → **SUPPORT**, Suspenders, Tauten, Tone, Tonic, Two(-hander)

Bracelet Armil(la), Armlet, Bangle, Cuff, Darbies, Handcuff, Manacle, Manilla

Bracken Brake, Fern, Pteridium, Tara

Bracket Ancon, Angle-iron, Bibb, Brace, Cantilever, Console, Corbel, Couple, Cripple, Gusset, Hanger, Misericord(e), Modillion, Mutule, Parenthesis, Potence, Pylon, Rigger, Round, Sconce, Straddle, Strata, Trivet, Truss

Brag(gart), Bragging Birkie, Bluster, Boast, Bobadil, Boister, Braggadocio, Bull, Cockalorum, Crow, Falstaff, Fanfaronade, Gab, Gascon, Hot-air, Loudmouth, Mouth off, Puff, Rodomontader, Skite, Slam, Swagger, Upstart, Vainglorious, Vapour, Vaunt

Braid A(i)glet, Aiguillette, Frog, Galloon, Lacet, Plait, Plat, Rickrack, Ricrac, Scrambled eggs, Seaming-lace, Sennet, Sennit, Sinnet, Soutache, Tress, Trim, Twist, Weave

Brain(box), Brain disease, Brain-power, Brain problem, Brains, Brainstorm, Brainy Appestat, Bean, Boffin, Bright, Cerebellum, Cerebrum, Contravene, Cortex, Crane, Cranium, Dura mater, Encephalon, Fornix, Genius, Gliosis, Gyrus, Harn(s), Head, Headpiece, Hippocampus, Hypothalamus, Inspiration, Insula, Intelligence, IQ, Loaf, Lobe, Mater, Medulla, Mind, Noddle, Noesis, Nous, Peduncle, Pericranium, Pia mater, Pons, Pontile, Quick, Ringleader, Sconce, Sense, Sensorium, Smarty pants, Striatum, Subcortex, Sulcus, Thalamus, Vortex

▷ **Brain(s)** *may indicate* an anagram

Brake, Braking Adiantum, Aerodynamic, Air, Anchors, Bracken, Centrifugal, Curb, Disc, Drag, Drum, Estate car, Fern, Fly, Grove, Hub, Hydraulic, Nemoral, Overrun, Ratchet, Rein, Rim, Shoe, →**SLOW**, Spinney, Sprag, Tara, Thicket, Vacuum

Bramble, Brambly Batology, Blackberry, Boysenberry, Brier, Cloudberry, Rubus, Thorn, Wait-a-bit

Bran Cereal, Chesil, Chisel, Oats, Pollard

Branch(ed), Branches, Branching, Branch office Affiliate, Antler, Arm, BO, Bough, Chapel, Cladode, Cow, Dendron, Dept, Diversify, Diverticulum, Divide, Filiate, Fork, Grain, Jump, Kow, Lateral, Limb, Lobe, Lobus, Loop, Lye, Lylum, Offshoot, Olive, Patulous, Phylloclade, Rachilla, Raguly, Ramate, Ramulus, Reis, Rice, Shroud, Special, Spray(ey), Sprig, Spur, Stirpes, Tributary, Turning, Turn-off, Twig, Wattle, Whip, Yard

Brand Broadsword, Buist, Burn, Cauterise, Chop, Class, Dealer, Denounce, Earmark, Ember, Excalibur, Falchion, Faulchin, Faulchion, Flambeau, Home, Idiograph, Iron, Label, Line, →**MARK**, Marque, Name, Sear, Stigma, Sweard, Sword, Torch, Wipe

Brandy Aguardiente, Applejack, Aqua vitae, Armagnac, Bingo, Calvados, Cape smoke, Cherry bounce, Cognac, Cold without, Dop, Eau de vie, Fine, Fine champagne, Framboise, Grappa, Kirsch, Mampoer, Marc, Mirabelle, Nantes, Nantz, Napoleon, Quetsch, Slivovic(a), Slivovitz, Smoke

Brash Cocky, Flashy, Impudent, Jack-the-lad, Pushy, Rain, Rash, Uppity

Brass(y), Brassware Alpha-beta, Benares, Brazen, Cheek, Corinthian, Cornet, Dinanderie, Effrontery, Face, Front, Harsh, Horn, Horse, Latten, Lip, Lolly, Loot, Lota(h), Loud, Matrix, →**MONEY**, Moola(h), Palimpsest, Pyrites, Sass, Snash, Sopranino, Talus, Top, Trombone, White, Yellow metal

Brassière Gay deceiver

Brat Bairn, Bra(t)chet, Gait(t), Gamin, Get, Imp, Lad, Terror, Urchin

Braun Eva

Bravado, Brave(ry) Amerind, Apache, Bold, Conan, Corragio, Courage, Creek, Dare, Derring-do, Doughty, Dress, Face, Gallant, Game, Gamy, Gutsy, Hardy, Heroism, Indian, Injun, Intrepid, →**LION**, Lion-hearted, Lionly, Manful, Manly, Nannup, Plucky, Prow(ess), Redskin, Russian roulette, Sannup, Stout, Uncas, Valiant, Valour, Wight, Withstand, Yeoman

Bravo Acclaim, Bandit, Bully, Desperado, Euge, Murderer, Olé, Shabash, Spadassin, Villain

Brawl(er) Affray, Bagarre, Bicker, Brabble, Donnybrook, Dust, Dust-up, Fight, Flite, Flyte, Fracas, Fratch, Fray, Melee, Prawl, Punch up, Rammy, Roughhouse, Ruck, Scold, Scuffle, Set-to, Shindig, Slugfest, Stoush, Tar, Wrangle

Brawn Beef, Burliness, Headcheese, He-man, Muscle, Power, Rillettes, Sinew

Bray Cry, Heehaw, Stamp, Vicar, Whinny

Brazen Blatant, Bold, Brassy, Flagrant, Forward, Impudent, Shameless, Unabashed

Breach Assault, Break, Chasm, Cleft, Foul, Gap(e), Great schism, Infraction, Redan, Rift, Rupture, Saltus, Schism, Solecism, Solution, Trespass, Violate

Bread, Bread crumbs Azym(e), Bagel, Baguette, Bannock, Bap, Barmbrack, Barm cake, Batch, Baton, Brewis, Brioche, Brownie, Bun, Cash, Chal(l)ah, Chametz, Chapati, Cheat, Ciabatta, Cob, Coburg, Compone, Corn (pone), Corsned, Croissant, Crostini, Croute, Crouton, Crumpet, Crust, Currency, Damper, Dibs, Dika, Doorstep, Fancy, Flatbread, Focaccia, Fougasse, French (stick), Funds, Garlic, Gluten, Graham, Granary, Grissini, Guarana, Hallah, Horse, Host, Indian, Jannock, Johnny-cake, Kaffir, Lavash,

Laver, Leavened, Loaf, Long tin, Manchet, Maori, Milk loaf, Milk-sop, →MONEY, Monkey, Na(a)n, Pain, Panada, Panary, Pane, Paneity, Panko, Paratha, Pay, Petit pain, Pikelet, Pit(t)a, Pone, Poori, Popover, Poppadom, Poultice, Prozymite, Pumpernickel, Puree, Puri, Quick, Raspings, Ravel, Roll, Rooty, Roti, Round, Rusk, Rye, Sally Lunn, Shewbread, Simnel, Sippet, Smor(re)brod, Soda, Soft-tommy, Sop, Sourdough, Split tin, Staff of life, Standard, Stollen, Stottie, Sugar, Sweet, Tartine, Tea, Tommy, Twist, Wastel, Wrap

Break, Break-down, Break down, Break-in, Break-up, Break up, Broken Adjourn, Analyse, Apn(o)ea, Bait, Breach, Breather, Bust, Caesura, Caesure, Cantle, Career, Cark, Cesure, Chinaman, Chip, Cleave, Coffee, Comb, Comma, Commercial, Comminute, Compost, Compurgatory, Conk, Contravene, Crack, Crock, Crumble, Dash, Debacle, Decompose, Demob, Destroy, Diffract, Disband, Disintegrate, Disperse, Disrupt, Erumpent, Erupt, Exeat, Fast, Fault, Flaw, Four, →FRACTURE, Fragment, Fritter, Frush, Gaffe, Gap, Give, Half-term, Half-time, Harm, Hernia, Hiatus, Holiday, Infringe, Interim, Interlude, Intermission, Interrupt, →INTERVAL, Irrupt, Kark, Knap, Lacuna, Lapse, Layover, Leave, Moratorium, Outage, Parse, Part, Pause, Playtime, Poach, Polarise, Price, Reave, Recess, Relief, Rend, Resolve, Respite, Rest, Rift, Rise, Ruin, Rupture, Saltus, Schism(a), Secede, Service, Shatter, Shear, Shiver, Smash, Snap, Split, Stave, Stop, Stop-over, Stove, Sunder, Take five, Take ten, Tame, Tea-ho, Tear, Tenderise, Time-out, Torn, Transgress, Truce, Twist, Vacation, Violate, Watergate, Weekend

Breakable Brittle, Delicate, Fissile, Fragile, Frail, Friable

Breakdown Abruption, Analyse, Autolysis, Cataclasm, Collapse, Conk, Crack-up, Glitch, Glycolosis, Glycolysis, Histolysis, Lyse, Lysis, Ruin

Breaker Billow, Circuit, Comber, Ice, Roller, Smasher, Surf

Breakfast B, Brunch, Chota-hazri, Continental, Deskfast, Disjune, Kipper, Wedding

Breakthrough Discovery, Quantum leap

Breakwater Groyne, Jetty, Mole, Pier, Tetrapod

Bream Fish, Porgy, Sar(gus), Sea, Silver, Tai, White

Breast(s), Breastbone, Breastwork Bazuma, Boob, Bosom, Brave, Brisket, Bristols, Bust, Chimney, Clean, Counter, Diddy, Duddy, Dug, Garbonza, Gazunga, Heart-spoon, Jubbies, Jugs, Knockers, Norg, Nork, Rampart, Redan, Sangar, Stem, Sternum, Stroke, Sungar, Supreme, Tit, Xiphisternum

Breastplate Armour, Byrnie, Curat, Curiet, Pectoral, Plastron, Rational, Rest, Shield, Thorax, Xiphiplastron

Breath(e), Breathing, Breather Aerobe, Air-sac, Apneusis, Aqualung, Aspirate, Bated, Buteyko method, Exhalation, Expiration, Flatus, Gasp, Gill, H, Halitosis, Hauriant, Inhale, Inspiration, Knee, Lung, Nares, Nostril, Oxygenator, Pant, Plosion, Pneuma, Prana, Pulmo, Rale, Respire, Respite, Rest, Rhonchus, Scuba, Sigh, Smooth, Snorkel, Snotter, Snuffle, Souffle, Spiracle, Spirit, Tachypnoea, Trachea, Vent, Wheeze, Whiff, Whift, Whisper, Whist, Wind, Windpipe

Breathless(ness) Anhelation, Apnoea, Asthma, Dyspnoea, Emphysema, Orthopnoea, Puffed-out, Tachypnoea, Wheezing

Breech(es) Bible, Buckskin, Chaps, Chausses, Flog, Galligaskins, Hose, Jodhpurs, Kneecords, Knickerbockers, Pantaloons, Petticoat, Plushes, Smallclothes, Smalls, Trews, Trouse(rs), Trunk hose, Trusses

Breed(er), Breeding(-place) Bear, Beget, Engender, Eugenics, Fancier, Gentility, Line, Lineage, →MANNERS, Origin, Procreate, Pullulate, Race, Rear, Savoir vivre, Seminary, Sire, Species, Stirpiculture, Stock, Strain, Stud, Tribe

Breeze, Breezy Air, Breath, Brisk, Cakewalk, Catspaw, Chipper, Doctor, Draught, Fresh, Gentle, Gust, Land, Light, Mackerel, Moderate, Pushover, Sea, Slant, Sniffler, Snifter, Strong, Tiff, Zephyr

Brew(ery), Brewer, Brewing Afoot, Ale, Billycan, Boutique, Brose, Browst, Bummock, Contrive, Dictionary, Elixir, Ferment, Infusion, Liquor, Malt, Percolate, Perk, Potion, Scald, Steep, Yeast, Yill, Zymurgy

Bribe(ry) Backhander, Barratry, Barretry, Bonus, Boodle, Bung, Carrot, Dash,

Douceur, Embracery, Get at, Graft, Grease, Hamper, Hush-money, Insult, Kickback, Lubricate, Oil, Palm, Palm-grease, Palm-oil, Payola, Schmear, Slush, Soap, Sop, Square, Straightener, Suborn, Sweeten(er), Tamper, Tempt, Tenderloin, Vail, Vales

Brick(s), Brickwork Adobe, Bat, Bath, Bonder, Bondstone, Boob, Breeze, Bristol, Bullnose, Bur(r), Clanger, Clinker, Closer, Course, Fletton, Gaffe, Gault, Header, Ingot, Klinker, Lateritious, Lego®, Malm, Nog(ging), Opus latericium, Red, Rubber, Soldier, Spawn, Sport, Stalwart, Stretcher, Terra-cotta, Testaceous, Tile, Trojan, Trump

Bride(s) Bartered, Danaides, Ellen, Mail-order, Newlywed, Spouse, War, Wife, Ximena

Bridge(head), Bridge player Acol, Air, Aqueduct, Auction, Australian, Avignon, Ba(u)ck, Bailey, Balance, Barre, Bascule, Bestride, Board, Brig, Brooklyn, Cable-stayed, Cantilever, Capo, Capodastro, Capotasto, Catwalk, Chicago, Chicane, Clapper, Clifton, Contract, Counterpoise, Cross, Cut-throat, Deck, Declarer, Drawbridge, Duplicate, Flying, Flyover, Foot, Four-deal, Gangplank, Gangway, Gantry, Girder, Golden Gate, Hog's back, Humber, Humpback, Humpbacked, Ice, Irish, Jigger, Land, Lattice, Leaf, Lifting, Ligger, Link, London, Menai, Millau, Millennium, Murray, Overpass, Pivot, Pons, Pontifice, Pont levis, Pontoon, Raft, Rainbow, Rialto, Rubber, Severn, Sighs, Skew, Snow, →SPAN, Spanner, Stamford, Straddle, Suspension, Swing, Tay, Temper, Tête-de-pont, Through, Tide over, Transporter, Traversing, Trestle, Truss, Turn, Vertical lift, Viaduct, Waterloo, Weigh, Wheatstone, Wire

Bridle Bit, Branks, Bridoon, Bristle, Browband, Curb, Double, Hackamore, Halter, Headstall, Musrol, Noseband, Rein

Brief(s), Briefing, Briefly, Brevity Acquaint, Advocate, Attorney, Awhile, Bluette, Brachyology, Breviate, Cape, Compact, →CONCISE, Counsel, Curt, Dossier, Ephemeral, Fleeting, Instruct, King's, Laconic, Lawyer, Nearly, Pants, Papal, Pennorth, Pithy, Prime, Scant, →SHORT(EN), Short-term, Short-winded, Sitrep, Sparse, Succinct, Summing, Tanga, Terse, Transient, Undershorts, Undies, Update, Watching

Brigade Anchor Boys, Boys', Corps, Fire, International, Red, Troop

Bright, Brightness Afterglow, Alert, Bertha, Brainbox, Brainy, Breezy, Brilliant, Brisk, Cheery, Chiarezza, Clara, Cla(i)re, Clear, Clever, Cuthbert, Danio, Effulgent, Eileen, Elaine, Ellie, Fair, Floodlit, Florid, Garish, Gay, Glad, Glary, Glow, Hono(u)r, Hubert, Light, Lit, Loud, Lucent, Lucid, Luculent, Luminous, Lustre, Net(t), Nit, Nitid, Radiant, Roarie, Ro(a)ry, Rosy, Scintillating, Sematic, Sharp, Sheeny, Sheer, Shere, Skyre, Smart, Stilb, Sunlit, Sunny, Vive, Vivid, White, Zara

Brilliant, Brilliance Ace, Aine, Blaze, Brainy, Bravura, Bright, Def, Effulgent, Eurian, Flashy, Galaxy, Gay, Gemmy, Gifted, Glitter, Glossy, High flyer, Humdinger, Inspired, Irradiance, Lambent, Leam, Lustre, Mega-, Meteoric, Nitid, Pear, →RADIANT, Refulgent, Resplendent, Shiny, Spangle, Splendid, Splendour, Star, Superb, Virtuoso, →VIVID, Water

Brim Edge, Lip, Rim, Ugly

Brine Muriatic, Ozone, Pickle, Saline, Salt

Bring Afferent, Bear, Carry, Cause, Conduct, Convey, Earn, Evoke, Fet, Fetch, Hatch, Induce, Land, Precipitate, Produce, Wreak

Bring up Breed, Educate, Exhume, Foster, Nurture, Raise, →REAR

Brisk(ly), Briskness Active, Alacrity, Alert, Allegro, Breezy, Busy, Cant, Chipper, Con moto, Crank, Crisp, Crouse, Fresh, Gaillard, Galliard, Jaunty, Kedge, Kedgy, Kidge, Lively, Nippy, Perk, Pert, Rattling, Roaring, Scherzo, Sharp, Smacking, Smart, Snappy, Spanking, Spirited, Sprightly, Vivace, Yare, Zippy

Bristle, Bristling, Bristly Arista, Awn, Barb, Bewhiskered, Birse, Bridle, Chaeta, Flurry, Fraught, Frenulum, Gooseflesh, Hackles, Hair, Hérissé, Horripilation, Seta, Setose, Striga, Strigose, Stubble, Vibraculum, Villus, Whisker

Brit(ish), Briton(s) Anglo, Herring, Iceni, Insular, Isles, Limey, Pict, Pom, Rooinek, Saxon, Silt, Silurian, UK

Britain Alban(y), Albion, Old Dart

Brittle Bruckle, Crackly, Crimp, Crisp, Delicate, Edgy, →FRAGILE, Frush, Redsear, Shivery, Spall, Spalt

▷ **Brittle** *may indicate* an anagram

Broach Approach, Open, Raise, Spit, Suggest, Tap, Widen

Broad(ly) Cheesy, Crumpet, Dame, Doll, Doxy, Drab, Eclectic, General, Generic, Hippy, Largo, Latitudinous, Loose, Outspoken, Ovate, Pro, Roomy, Spatulate, Tart, Thick, Tolerant, Wide, Woman

Broadcast(er), Broadcasting Ad(vertise), Air, Announce, Beam, Breaker, Broadband, CB, Disperse, Disseminate, Emission, Ham, IBA, Monophonic, Multicast, Narrowband, OB, On, Outside, Pirate, Programme, Promulgate, Public address, Put out, Radiate, Radio, Reith, Relay, RTE, Run, → SCATTER, Scattershot, Screen(ed), SECAM, Seed, Sky, Sow, Sperse, Sportscast, Spread, Sprinkle, Stereophonic, Telebridge, Telethon, Transmission, Veejay, Ventilate, Wavelength, Wireless

Brochure Booklet, Leaflet, Pamphlet, Throwaway, Tract

Broke(n) Bankrupt, Boracic, Bust(ed), Duff, Evans, Fritz, Insolvent, Kaput, Puckeroo, Shattered, Skint, Stony, Stove, Strapped

▷ **Broken** *may indicate* an anagram

Broker Agent, Banian, Banyan, Discount, Go-between, Government, Jobber, Mediator, → MERCHANT, Power, Shadchan, Uncle

Bronze, Bronze age Aeneous, Aluminium, Bell, Bras(s), Brown, Corinthian, Gunmetal, Hallstatt(ian), Helladic, Minoan, Mycenean, Ormolu, Phosphor, Schillerspar, Sextans, Talos, Tan, Third, Torso

Brooch Breastpin, Cameo, Clasp, Fibula, Luckenbooth, Ouch, Owche, Pin, Plaque, Preen, Prop, Spang, Sunburst

Brood(y) Clecking, Clock, Clutch, Cogitate, Cour, Cover, Covey, Eye, Eyrie, Hatch, Hover, Incubate, Introspect, Kindle, Litter, Meditate, Mill, Mope, Mull, Nest, Nid, Perch, Pet, → PONDER, Repine, Roost, Sit, Sulk, Team

Brook Babbling, Beck, Branch, Burn, Countenance, Creek, Endure, Ghyll, Gill, Kerith, Kill, Pirl, Purl, Rill(et), River, Rivulet, Runlet, Runnel, Springlet, Stand, Stomach, Stream, Suffer, Thole, Tolerate

Broom Besom, Brush, Butcher's, Cow, Genista, Gorse, Greenweed, Hog, Knee-holly, Kow, Orobranche, Plantagenet, Retama, Spart, Sweeper, Whisk

Brose Atholl, Pease

Broth Bouillon, Bree, Brew(is), Court bouillon, Cullis, Dashi, Kail, Kale, Muslin-kale, Pottage, Ramen, Scotch, Skilly, → SOUP, Stock

Brothel Bagnio, Bawdy-house, Bordel(lo), Cathouse, Corinth, Crib, Den, Honkytonk, Hothouse, Kip, Knocking shop, Leaping-house, Seraglio, Sporting house, Stew

Brother(s), Brotherhood Ally, Bhai, Billie, Billy, Blood, Brethren, Bro, Bud, Comrade, Félibre, Fellow, Fra, Freemason, Grimm, Guild, Lay, Marx, → MONK, Moose, Plymouth, Sib(ling), Theatine, Trappist, Worker

Brought (back) Redux

Brow Crest, Forehead, Glabella, Ridge, Sinciput, Superciliary, Tump-line

Brown(ed) Abram, Adust, Amber, Auburn, Bay, Biscuit, Bisque, Bister, Bistre, Bole, Br, Braise, Brindle, Bronzed, Brunette, Bruno, Burnet, Camel, Capability, Caramel, Caromel, Centennial, Cinnamon, Cook, Coromandel, Drab, Dun, Duncan, Fallow, Filemot, Fulvous, Fusc(ous), Grill, Hazel, Ivor, John, Khaki, Liver, Meadow, Mocha, Mousy, Mulatto, Mushroom, Nut, Philamot, Pygmalion, Rufous, Rugbeian, Russet, Rust, Sallow, Scorch, Sepia, Sienna, Snuff, Soare, Sore, Sorrel, Spadiceous, Tan, Tawny, Tenné, Tenny, Terracotta, Testaceous, Toast, Tom, Umber, Vandyke, Wallflower, Walnut, Wholemeal, Windsor

Brownian movement Agitation, Pedesis

Browse(r) Eland, Graze, Mouch, Pasture, Read, Scan, Stall-read, Surf

Bruise Black eye, Clour, Contund, Contuse, Crush, Damage, Ding, Ecchymosis, Frush, Golp(e), Haematoma, Hurt, Intuse, Livedo, Lividity, Mark, Mouse, Pound, Purpure, Rainbow, Shiner, Ston(n), Stun, Surbate, Vibex

Brush (off), Brushwood Bavin, Brake, Broom, Carbon, Chaparral, Clash, Clothes, Dandy, Dismiss, Dust, Encounter, Fan, Filbert, Filecard, Firth, Fitch, Foxtail, Frith, Grainer, Hag, Hagg, Hair-pencil, Hog, Kiss, Liner, Lip, Loofa(h), Mop, Paint, Pallet,

Pig, Pope's head, Putois, Rebuff, Rice, Rigger, Sable, Scrap, Scrub, Scuff, Shaving, Skim, Striper, Sweep, Tail, Thicket, Touch, Undergrowth

Brutal(ity), Brute Animal, Atrocity, Beast, Bête, Caesar, Caliban, Cruel, Down and dirty, Hun, Iguanodon, Inhuman, Nazi, Nero, Ostrogoth, Pitiless, Quagga, Rottweiler, Roughshod, Ruffian, Thresher-whale, Yahoo

Bubble(s), Bubbly Aeration, Air-bell, Air-lock, Barmy, Bead(ed), Bell, Bleb, Blister, Boil, Buller, Cavitate, Champagne, Cissing, Ebullition, Effervesce, Embolus, Enthuse, Espumoso, Foam, →FROTH, Gassy, Globule, Gurgle, Head, Mantle, Mississippi, Moet, Popple, Rale, Reputation, Roundel, Rowndell, Seed, Seethe, Simmer, Soap, South Sea, Vesicle, Widow

Buck (up) Bongo, Brace, Cheer, Dandy, Deer, Dollar, Elate, Encheer, Hart, Jerk, Leash, Male, Ourebi, Pitch, Pricket, Ram, Rusa, Sore, Sorel(l), Sorrel, Spade, Spay(a)d, Staggard, Stud, Wheel

Bucket(s) Bail, Bale, Clamshell, Ice, Kibble, Ladle, Noria, Pail, Piggin, Rain, Scuttle, Situla, Stoop(e), Stope, Stoup, Tub

Buckle Artois, Bend, Clasp, Contort, Crumple, Deform, Dent, Fasten, Warp

▷ **Buckle** *may indicate* an anagram

▷ **Bucks** *may indicate* an anagram

Bucolic Aeglogue, Eglogue, Idyllic, Pastoral, Rural, Rustic

Bud(ding), Buddy Botoné, Bottony, Bulbil, Burgeon, Cacotopia, Clove, Cobber, Deb, Eye, Gem(ma), Germinate, Hibernaculum, Knosp, Knot, Nascent, Pal, Scion, Serial, Shoot, Sprout, Statoblast, Taste, Turion

Buddha, Buddhism, Buddhist Abhidhamma, Ahimsa, Amitabha, Anata, Anicca, Arhat, Asoka, Bardo, Bodhisattva, Dalai Lama, Gautama, Hinayana, Jain, Jataka, Jodo, Mahatma, Mahayana, Maitreya, Maya, Pali, Pitaka, Pure Land, Sakya-muni, Sila, Sima, Soka Gakkai, Sutra, Tantric, Theravada, Tripitaka, Triratna, Zen(o)

Budge Jee, Move, Stir, Submit

Budgerigar Shell parrakeet, Shell parrot

Budget Allot, Cheap, Estimate, Plan, Programme, Rudder, Save, Shoestring

Buff Altogether, Beige, Birthday suit, Blind man's, Cineaste, Eatanswill, Expert, Fan, Fawn, Maven, Mavin, Nankeen, Natural, Nude, Nut, Polish, →RUB, Streak

Buffalo African, Anoa, Arna, Asiatic, Bison, Bonasus, Bugle, Cap, Cape, Carabao, Ox, Perplex, Takin, Tamarao, Tamarau, Timarau, Water, Zamouse

Buffer Bootblack, Cofferdam, Cutwater, Fender

Buffet Bang, Blow, Box, Counter, Cuff, Fork luncheon, Fork-supper, Hit, Lam, Maltreat, Meal, Perpendicular, Shove, Sideboard, Smorgasborg, Strike, Strook(e)

Bug(s) Ambush, Annoy, Antagonise, Arthropod, Assassin, Bacteria, Beetle, Bishop's mitre, Bunny, Cabbage, Capsid, Chinch, Cimex, Cockchafer, Creepy-crawly, Croton, Damsel, Debris, Demon, Dictograph®, Eavesdrop, E-coli, Error, Exasperate, Get at, Harlequin, Hassle, →INSECT, Irritate, Jitter, June, Kissing, Lace, May, Mealy, Micrococcus, Microphone, Mike, Milkweed, Millennium, Mite, Nark, Pest(er), Rile, Sow, Squash, Tap, Vex, Water-measurer, Wheel, Wiretap

Buggy Beach, Car, Cart, Inside-car, Shay, Tipcart, Trap

Bugle, Bugle call Boots and saddles, Chamade, Clarion, Cornet, Flugelhorn, Hallali, Kent, Last post, Ox, Reveille, Taps, →TRUMPET, Urus

Build, Building(s), Building site, Build-up Accrue, Aggrade, Ar(a)eostyle, Assemble, Barn, Basilica, Big, Boathouse, Bricks and mortar, Capitol, Chapterhouse, Cob, Colosseum, Commons, Construction, Containment, Corncrib, Cot, →CREATE, Cruck, Curia, Days' house, Develop, Dome, Drystone, Duplex, Ectomorph, Edifice, Edify, Endomorph, Erect, Exchange, Fabric, Gatehouse, Hangar, Heapstead, High-rise, Hut, Infill, Insula, Kaaba, Ken, Linhay, Listed, Low-rise, Lyceum, Mesomorph, Minaret, Mosque, Mould, Observatory, Odeon, Odeum, Outhouse, Palace, Palazzo, Pataka, Pavilion, Pentagon, Pentastyle, Phalanx, Physique, Pile, Portakabin®, Premises, Quonset®, Raise, Ribbon, Rotunda, Shippen, Skyscraper, Somatotype, Squat, Stance, Statehouse, Structure, Summerhouse, Suspension,

Synthesis, System, Systyle, Tectonic, Telecottage, Temple, Tenement, Tower, Tower block, Town hall, Whata

▷ **Building** *may indicate* an anagram

Built-up Urban

Bulb Camas(h), Chive, Cive, Corm, Globe, Lamp, Light, Pearl, Scallion, Set, Shallot, Squill

Bulgaria BG

Bulge, Bulging Astrut, Bag, Bias, Biconvex, Bug, Bulbous, Bunchy, Cockle, Entasis, Expand, Exsert, Inion, Prolate, Protrude, Relievo, Rotund, Shoulder, Strout, Strut, →SWELL, Torose, Tumid

Bulk(y) Aggregate, Ample, Big, Body, Bouk, Corpulent, Extent, Gross, Hull, Immensity, Lofty, Massive, Preponderance, Roughage, Scalar, →SIZE, Stout, Vol(ume), Voluminous, Weight

Bull(s), Bullock, Bully(ing) Abuser, Anoa, Apis, Beef, Blarney, Bluster, Bouncer, Bovine, Brag, Brave, Browbeat, Bucko, Centre, Cuttle, Despot, Dragoon, Drawcansir, Englishman, Fancyman, Farnese, Flashman, Flatter, Gold, Gosh, Hapi, Harass, Haze(r), Hector, Hibernicism, Hogwash, Hoodlum, Huff, Intimidate, Investor, Irish(ism), John, Killcow, Lambast, Maltreat, Menace, Mick(e)y, Mistake, Mithraism, Mohock, Neat, Oppressor, Ox, Papal, Pennalism, Piker, Pistol, Placet, Poler, Pussy-whip, Railroad, Rhodian, Roarer, Rot, Ruffian, Sitting, Stag, Strong-arm, Swash-buckler, Taurine, Taurus, Tommy-rot, Tosh, Trash, Tripe, Twaddle, Tyran(ne), Tyrannise, Tyrant, Victimise, Zo(bo)

Bulldoze(r) Coerce, Earthmover, Leveller, Overturn, Raze

Bullet Balata, Ball, Biscayan, Blank, Dumdum, Fusillade, Lead towel, Minié, Minié ball, Missile, Pellet, Plastic, Round, Rubber, Shot, Slug, Tracer

Bulletin All points, Memo, Newscast, Newsletter, Report, Summary

Bull-fight(er), Bull-fighting Banderillero, Banderillo, Corrida, Cuadrilla, Encierro, Escamillo, Faena, Mano a mano, Matador, Picador, Rejoneador, Tauromachy, Toreador, Torero

Bullfinch Monk

Bullshit BS

Bulwark Bastion, Defence, Rampart, Resistor

Bum Ass, Beg, Beggar, Deadbeat, Prat, Scrounge, Sponge, Thumb, Tramp, Vagabond

Bumble Beadle, Bedel(l)

▷ **Bumble** *may indicate* an anagram

Bump(er), Bumps, Bumpy Big, Blow, Bouncer, Bucket, Bustle, Clour, Collide, Dunch, Fender, Hillock, Immense, Inian, Inion, Jo(u)le, Joll, Jolt, Jowl, Keltie, Kelty, Knar, Knock, Mamilla, Mogul, Organ, Phrenology, Reveille, Rouse, Speed, Thump, Uneven

Bumph Loo-roll

Bumpkin Bucolic, Bushwhacker, Clodhopper, Hawbuck, Hayseed, Hick, Jock, Lout, Oaf, Peasant, Put(t), Rube, Rustic, Yokel, Zany

Bun Barmbrack, Bath, Chelsea, Chignon, Chou, Cookie, Hot-cross, Huffkin, Mosbolletjie, Roll, Teacake, Toorie, Wad

Bunch Acinus, Anthology, Bob, Botryoid, Cluster, Fascicle, Finial, Flock, Gang, →GROUP, Hand, Handful, Ilk, Lot, Lump, Panicle, Raceme, Spray, Staphyline, Tassel, Tee, Truss, Tuft, Tussie-mussie

Bundle(d) Axoneme, Bale, Bavin, Bluey, Bottle, Byssus, Desmoid, Dorlach, Drum, Fag(g)ot, Fascicle, Fasciculate, Fascine, Fibre, Fibrovascular, Kemple, Knitch, Lemniscus, Matilda, →PACK(AGE), Parcel, Sack, Sheaf, Shiralee, Shock, Shook, Stela, Stook, Swag, Tie, Top, Trousseau, Truss, Vascular, Wad, Wadge, Wap, Yealm

Bungle(r), Bungled, Bungling Blunder, Blunk, Bodge, Boob, Boss shot, Botch, Bumble, Bummle, Duff, Fluff, Foozle, Foul, Goof, Gum up, Maladroit, Mess, Mis(h)guggle, Muddle, Muff, Mull, Prat, Screw, Spoil, Tinker

Bunk(er), Bunk off, Bunkum Abscond, Absquatulate, Balderdash, Baloney, Berth, Blah, Bolt, Casemate, Claptrap, Clio, Entrap, Guff, Guy, Hazard, History,

Hokum, Hooey, Humbug, Malarky, Moonshine, Rot, Scuttle, Skive, Tommy-rot, Tosh, Trap, Tripe, Truant, Twaddle

Bunting Bird, Cirl, Flag, Fringilline, Ortolan, Pennant, Snow, Streamer, Tanager, Towhee, Yellow-hammer, Yowley

Buoy (up) Bell, Breeches, Can, Dan, Daymark, Dolphin, Float, Marker, Nun, Raft, Reassure, Ring, Seamark, Sonar, Sustain

Buoyant Blithe, Floaty, Resilient

Burden Albatross, Beare, Bob, Cargo, Cark, Chant, Chorus, Cross, Cumber, Drone, Droore, Encumber, Encumbrance, Fa-la, Fardel, Folderol, Fraught, Freight, Gist, Handicap, Hum, Lade, →**LOAD**, Lumber, Millstone, Monkey, Oercome, Onus, Oppress, Payload, Put-upon, Refrain, Rumbelow, Saddle, Servitude, Shanty, Substance, Task, Tax, Tenor, Torch, Trouble, Weight, White man's, Woe, Yoke

Burdensome Irksome, Onerous, Oppressive, Weighty

Bureau Agency, Agitprop, Breakfront, Cominform, Davenport, Desk, Interpol, Kominform, Marriage, →**OFFICE**, Weather

Bureaucracy, Bureaucrat(ic) Bean-counter, CS, Functionary, Impersonal, Jack-in-office, Mandarin, Red tape, Tapist, Technocrat, Wallah

Burgeon(ing) Asprout, Bud, Grow, Sprout

Burgh Burrowstown, Parliamentary, Police, Royal

Burglar(y), Burgle Aggravated, Area-sneak, Break-in, Cat, Crack(sman), Intruder, Peterman, Picklock, Raffles, Robber, Screw, Thief, Yegg

Burial(place) Catacomb, Charnel, Committal, Crypt, Darga(h), Funeral, Golgotha, Grave, Green, Interment, Kurgan, Lair, Last rites, Pyramid, Sepulture, Speos, Tomb, Vault, Vivisepulture, Zoothapsis

Burlesque Caricatura, Caricature, Comedy, Farce, Heroicomical, Hudibrastic(s), Hurlo-thrumbo, Lampoon, Macaronic, Parody, Satire, Skimmington, Skit, Spoof, Travesty

Burma, Burmese Karen(ni), Mon(-Khmer), Myanmar, Naga, Shan

Burn(ed), Burner, Burning, Burnt Ablaze, Adust, Afire, Alow(e), Ardent, Argand, Arson, Ash, Auto-da-fé, Back, Bake, Bats-wing, Beck, Bishop, Blaze, Blister, Blush, Brand, Brent, Brook(let), Bunsen, Caustic, Cauterise, Char, Chark, Chinese, Cinder, Clavie, Coal, Coke, Combust, Conflagration, Cremate, Crucial, Destruct, Effigy, Eilding, Ember, Emboil, Fervid, →**FIRE**, First degree, Fishtail, Flagrant, Flare, Flash, Fresh(et), Gleed, Gut, Holocaust, Ignite, In, Incendiary, Incinerate, Inure, Inust(ion), Itch, Kill, Lean, Live, Lunt, Moorburn, Muirburn, Offering, On, Phlogiston, Pilot, Raster, Rill, Sati, Scald, Scaud, Scorch, Scouther, Scowder, Scowther, Sear, Sienna, Singe, Smart, Smoulder, Stake, Suttee, Swale, Thurible, Torch, Umber, Urent, Ustion, Wick, Ybrent

Burrow(er), Burrowing Dig, Earth, Fossorial, Gopher, Groundhog, Hole, How, Howk, Mine, Mole, Nuzzle, Sett, Terricole, Tunnel, Viscacha, Warren, Wombat, Worm

Bursar(y) Camerlengo, Camerlingo, Coffers, Grant, Purser, Scholarship, Tertiary, Treasurer

Burst(ing), Bursts Blowout, Bout, Brast, Break, Dehisce, Disrupt, Dissilient, Ebullient, Erumpent, Erupt, →**EXPLODE**, Fits and starts, Fly, Gust, Implode, Pop, Salvo, Sforzato, Shatter, Spasm, Spirt, Split, Sprint, Spurt, Stave, Tetterous

Burundi RU

Bury Cover, Eard, Earth, Embowel, Engrave, Enhearse, Entomb, Graff, Graft, Imbed, Inhearse, Inherce, Inhume, Inter, Inurn, Landfill, Repress, Sepulture, Sink, Ye(a)rd, Yird

Bus Aero, Bandwagon, Car, Charabanc, Coach, Crew, Double-decker, Highway, Hondey, Hopper, ISA, Jitney, Mammy-wagon, Purdah, Rattletrap, Single-decker, Tramcar, Trolley, Trunk

Bush(es), Bush-man, Bushy Bitou, Bramble, Brier, Bullace, Busket, Calico, Clump, Cotton, Creosote, Dumose, Firethorn, Greasewood, Hawthorn, Hedge, Hibiscus, Ivy-tod, Jaborandi, Kapok, Kiekie, Mallee, Matagouri, Mulberry, Outback,

Pachysandra, Poinsettia, Poly-poly, President, Prostanthera, Sallee, San, Scrog, Shepherd, Shrub, Sloe, Sloethorn, Sugar, Thicket, Tire, Tod(de), Tumatakuru

Bushel Co(o)mb, Homer, Peck, Weight, Wey

Bushwalker Hoon

Business Affair, Agency, Biz, Bricks and clicks, Brokerage, Bus, Cahoot, Cartel, Cerne, Chaebol(s), Co, Commerce, Company, Concern, Conglomerate, Corporate, Craft, Custom, Dealership, Duty, Enterprise, Ergon, Establishment, Exchange, Fasti, Field, Firm, Funny, Game, Gear, Hong, Industry, Kaizen, Lifestyle, Line, Métier, Monkey, Office, Palaver, Pidgin, Pi(d)geon, Practice, Professional, Racket, Shebang, Shop, Show, To-do, Trade, Traffic, Transaction, Tread, Turnover, Unincorporated, Vocation, Zaibatsu, Zaikai

Businessman Babbitt, City, Dealer, Fat-cat, Realtor, Taipan, Trader, Tycoon

Busk(er) Bodice, Corset, Entertainer, German-band

Bust Beano, Boob, Brast, Break, Chest, Dollarless, Falsies, Herm(a), Kaput, Mamma, Raid, Rupture, Sculp, Shatter(ed), Spree, Statue, Term(inus), To-tear, To-torne, Ups(e)y

▷ **Bust** *may indicate* an anagram

Bustle Ado, Do, Flap, Fuss, Pad, Scurry, →**STIR**, Swarm, To-do, Tournure, Whew

Busy Active, At (it), Deedy, →**DETECTIVE**, Dick, Doing, Eident, Employ, Engaged, Ergate, Eye, Goer, Hectic, Hive, Hot spot, Humming, Manic, Occupied, Operose, Ornate, Prodnose, Stir, Stirabout, Tec, Throng, Worksome

Busybody Bee, Bustler, Meddler, Pantopragmatic, Snooper, Trout, Yenta

But Aber, Algates, Bar, Except, However, Merely, Nay, Only, Save, Sed, Simply, Tun, Without, Yet

Butcher(s), Butchery Cumberland, Decko, Dekko, Eyeful, Flesher, Gander, Ice, Kill, Killcow, Look, Looksee, Mangle, Massacre, Ovicide, Peek, Sever, Shambles, Shochet, Shufti, Slaughter, Slay, Slink

Butler Bedivere, Bread-chipper, Jeeves, RAB, Rhett, Samuel, Servant, Sewer, Sommelier, Steward

Butt (in) Aris, Arse, Ass, Barrel, Buns, Bunt, Clara, Dout, Dowt, Enter, Geck, Glasgow kiss, Goat, Header, Horn, Jesting-stock, Laughing-stock, Mark, Outspeckle, Pantaloon, Pipe, Push, Ram, Roach, Scapegoat, Snipe, Straight man, Stump, Target, Tun, Ups

Butter Adulation, Apple, Beurre, Billy, Blandish, Brandy, Butyric, Cacao, Cocoa, Coconut, Drawn, Flatter, Galam, Garcinia, Ghee, Ghi, Goat, Illipi, Illupi, Kokum, Mahua, Mawha, Mow(r)a, Nutter, Palm, Pat, Peanut, Print, Ram, Rum, Scrape, Shea, Spread

▷ **Butter** *may indicate* a goat or such

Buttercup Crowfoot, Crow-toe, Goldilocks, Ranunculus, Reate, Thalictrum

Butterflies, Butterfly Apollo, Argus, Birdwing, Blue, Brimstone, Brown, Cabbage white, Camberwell beauty, Cardinal, Chequered skipper, Cleopatra, Clouded yellow, Collywobbles, Comma, Common blue, Copper, Dilettante, Eclosion, Elfin, Emperor, Fritillary, Gate-keeper, Grayling, Hair-streak, Heath, Hesperid, Imaginal, Kallima, Large copper, Large white, Leaf, Marbled-white, Meadow brown, Metalmark, Milk-weed, Monarch, Morpho, Mountain ringlet, Nerves, Orange-tip, Owl, Painted lady, Peacock, Pieris, Psyche, Purple emperor, Red admiral, Ringlet, Scotch argus, Silverspot, Skipper, Small white, Snake's head, Speckled wood, Stamper, Stroke, Sulphur, Swallow-tail, Thecla, Thistle, Tiger swallowtail, Tortoiseshell, Two-tailed pasha, Vanessa, Wall brown, White admiral

Buttocks Aristotle, Arse, Ass, Bahookie, Bottom, Buns, Cheeks, Coit, Derrière, Doup, Duff, Fud, Fundament, Gluteus maximus, Heinie, Hinderlan(d)s, Hunkers, Hurdies, Jacksie, Jacksy, Keester, Keister, Nates, Posterior, Prat, Quatch, Quoit, Seat

Button(s) Barrel, Bellboy, Fastener, Frog, Hold, Hot, Knob, Mescal, Mouse, Netsuke, Olivet, Page(boy), Panic, Pause, Press, Snooze, Stud, Switch, Toggle, Toolbar

Buttonhole Accost, Detain, Doorstep, Eye, Flower

Buttress Brace, Counterfort, Pier, Prop, Stay, Support

Butty Chum, Oppo

Buy(ing), Buyer Believe, Bribe, Coemption, Coff, Corner, Customer, Emption, Engross, Monopsonist, Purchase, Redeem, Shop, Shout, Spend, Take, Trade, Treat, Vendee

▷ **Buyer** *may indicate* money

Buzz(er) Bee, Birr, Bombilate, Bombinate, Button, Drone, Fly, Hum, Kazoo, Rumour, Scram, Whirr, Whisper, Zed, Zing, Zoom

Buzzard Bee-kite, Bird, Buteo, Hawk, Honey, Pern, Puttock, Turkey, Vulture

By Alongside, At, Beside, Gin, Gone, In, Near, Neighbouring, Nigh, Of, On, Past, Per, Through, With, X

Bye-bye Adieu, Farewell, Tata

By far Out and away

Bygone Dead, Departed, Past, Yore

Bypass Avoid, Beltway, Circuit, Coronary, → **DETOUR**, Dodge, Evade, Ignore, Omit, Shunt, Skirt

By-product Epiphenomenon, Spill-over, Spin-off

Byre Cowshed, Manger, Stable, Trough

Byte Nybble

By the way Incidentally, Ob(iter)

Byway Alley, Lane, Path

Byword Ayword, Nayword, Phrase, Proverb, Slogan

Cc

C Around, Caught, Celsius, Cent, Centigrade, Charlie, Conservative, San

Cab Boneshaker, Crawler, Drosky, Fiacre, Growler, Hackney, Hansom, Mini, Noddy, Taxi, Vettura

Cabbage(-head), Cabbage soup Black, Bok choy, Borecole, Brassica, Castock, Cauliflower, Chinese (leaf), Chou, Choucroute, Cole, Collard, Crout, Gobi, Kohlrabi, Kraut, Loaf, Loave, Mibuna, Mizuna, Pak-choi, Pamphrey, St Patrick's, Sauerkraut, Savoy, Sea-kale, Thieve, Turnip, Wort

Cabin Berth, Bibby, Bothy, Box, Cabana, Caboose, Camboose, Coach, Cottage, Crannog, Crib, Cuddy, Den, Gondola, Hovel, Hut, Izba, Lodge, Long-house, Room, Roundhouse, Saloon, Shack, Shanty, Signal box, Stateroom

Cabinet Armoire, Bahut, Cabale, Case, Cellaret, Chiffonier, Chill, Closet, Commode, Console, Cupboard, Display, Kitchen, Ministry, Nest, Official family, Repository, Secretaire, Shadow, Shrinal, Unit, Vitrine

Cable(way), Cable-car Arrester, Choucroute, Coax(ial), Extension, Flex, Halser, Hawser, Jump leads, Junk, Kissagram, Landline, Lead, Lead-in, Lifeline, Outhaul, Outhauler, Rope, Shroud, Slatch, Téléférique, →**TELEGRAM**, Telpher(age), Wire

Cackle Cluck, Gaggle, Gas, Haw, Horse laugh, Snicker, Titter

Cactus, Cactus-like Alhagi, Barel, Cereus, Cholla, Christmas, Dildo, Easter, Echino-, Hedgehog, Jointed, Jojoba, Maguey, Mescal, Mistletoe, Nopal, Ocotillo, Ombrophobe, Opuntia, Organ-pipe, Peyote, Pita(ha)ya, Prickly pear, Retama, Saguaro, Schlumbergera, Star, Torch-thistle, Tuna, Xerophytic

Cad Base, Boor, Bounder, Churl, Cocoa, Heel, Oik, Rascal, Rotter, Skunk, Varlet

Cadaver(ous) Body, Corpse, Ghastly, Haggard, Stiff

Cadence Authentic, Beat, Close, Fa-do, Flow, Interrupted, Lilt, Meter, Plagal, Rhythm

Cadet(s) Junior, OTC, Plebe, Recruit, Rookie, Scion, Snooker, Space, Syen, Trainee

Café, Cafeteria Automat, Bistro, Brasserie, Buvette, Canteen, Carvery, Commissary, Diner, Dinette, Donko, Estaminet, Filtré, Greasy spoon, Juke joint, Netcafé, Noshery, Pizzeria, Pull-in, Snackbar, Tearoom, Tea-shop, Transport, Truckstop

Cag(e)y Chary

Cage Bar, Battery, Box, Cavie, Confine, Coop, Corf, Dray, Drey, Enmew, Faraday, Fold, Frame, Grate, Hutch, Mew, Mortsafe, Pen, →**PRISON**, Roll, Trave

Cake Agnus dei, Angel, Baba, Babka, Baklava, Banbury, Bannock, Bara brith, Barm(brack), Battenberg, Bhaji, Biffin, Birthday, Black bun, Brandy snap, Brioche, Brownie, Buckwheat, Bun, Carcake, Cattle, Chapat(t)i, Chillada, Chupati, Chupattie, Chupatty, Clapbread, Clot, Coburg, Cookie, Corn dodger, Cotton, Croquante, Croquette, Cruller, Crumpet, Currant, Dainty, Devil's food, Drizzle, Dundee, Eccles, Eclair, Fancy, Farl(e), Filter, Fish, Flapjack, Frangipane, Frangipani, Fritter, Galette, Gateaux, Genoa, Gingerbread, Girdle, →**HARDEN**, Hockey, Hoe, Idli, Jannock, Johnny, Jumbal, Jumbles, Koeksister, Kruller, Kuchen, Kueh, Lady's finger, Lamington, Lardy, Latke, Layer, Linseed, Macaroon, Madeira, Madeleine, Maid of honour, Marble, Meringue, Millefeuille, Mooncake, Mud, Muffin, Napoleon, Nut, Oatmeal, Oil, Pan, Panettone, Paratha, Parkin, Parliament, Pastry, Pat, Patty, Pavlova, Pepper, Petit four, Pikelet, →**PLASTER**, Pomfret, Pone, Pontefract, Poori, Popover, Potato, Pound, Profiterole, Puff, Puftaloon(a), Puri, Queencake, Ratafia, Ready-mix, Religieuse, Rice, Rock, Rosti, Roti, Rout, Rum baba, Rusk, Sachertorte, Saffron, Sally Lunn, Salt, Sandwich, Savarin, Scone, Seed, Set, Simnel, Singing-hinny, Slab, Slapjack, Soul, Spawn, Spice, Sponge, Stollen, Stottie, Sushi, Swiss roll, Tablet, Tansy,

Tea(bread), Tipsy, Torte, Tortilla, Twelfth, Upside down, Vetkoek, Wad, Wafer, Waffle, Wedding, Wonder, Yeast, Yule log

▷ **Cake** *may indicate* an anagram

Calculate(d), Calculation, Calculator Abacus, Actuary, Comptometer, Compute(r), Cost, Design, Estimate, Extrapolate, Four-function, Log, Number-crunch, Prorate, Quip(p)u, Rate, →**RECKON**, Slide-rule, Sofar, Soroban, Tactical, Tell

Calendar Advent, Agenda, Almanac, Chinese, Diary, Dies fasti, Fasti, Gregorian, Intercalary, Jewish, Journal, Julian, Luach, Menology, Newgate, New Style, Ordo, Perpetual, Planner, Revolutionary, Roman, Sothic

Calf Ass, Bobby, Box, Cf, Deacon, Divinity, Dogie, Dogy, Fatted, Freemartin, Golden, Law, Leg, Mottled, Poddy, Slink, Smooth, Stirk, Sural, Tollie, Tolly, Veal, Vitular

California(n) Fresno, Golden State

Call(ed), Call (for), Calling, Call on, Call up Adhan, Ahoy, Appeal, Arraign, Art, Awaken, Azan, Banco, Bawl, Beck, Behote, Bevy, Bid, Boots and saddles, Bugle, Business, Buzz, Career, Chamade, Cite, Claim, Clang, Clarion, Cleep, Clepe, Close, Cold, Conference, Conscript, Convene, Convoke, Coo, Cooee, Cry, Curtain, Dial, Drift, Dub, Effectual, Entail, Evoke, First post, Game, Go, Hail, Hallali, Halloa, Haro, Heads, Heave-ho, Hech, Hete, Hey, Hight, Ho, Hot(e), Howzat, Huddup, Hurra(h), Invocation, Job, Junk, Last (post), Levy, Line, Local, Look in, Margin, Métier, Misère, Mobilise, Mot, Name, Nap, Need, Nemn, Nempt, Nominate, No trumps, Nuisance, Olé, Page, Peter, Phone, Photo, Pop in, Post, Proo, Pruh, Pursuit, Rechate, Recheat, Retreat, Reveille, Ring, Roll, Rort, Rouse, Route, Sa-sa, See, Sennet, →**SHOUT**, Shut-out, Slam, Slander, Slogan, Soho, Sola, SOS, STD, Style, Subpoena, Summon(s), Tails, Tally ho, Tantivy, Taps, Telephone, Term, Toho, Toll, Trumpet, Trunk, Turn, Tweet, Visit, Vocation, Waken, Wake-up, Whoa-ho-ho, Wo ha ho, Yell, Yo, Yodel, Yodle, Yo-ho(-ho), Yoicks, Yoo-hoo

Caller Fresh, Guest, Herring, Inspector, Muezzin, Rep, Traveller, →**VISITOR**

Callisthenics T'ai chi (ch'uan)

Call off Abort

Calm Abate, Allay, Allege, Appease, Ataraxy, Composed, Cool, Dead-wind, Dispassionate, Doldrums, Easy, Equable, Equanimity, Even, Eye, Flat, Glassy, Halcyon, Level, Loun(d), Lown(d), Lull, Mellow, Mild, Milden, Millpond, Nonchalant, Pacify, Patient, Peaceable, Peaceful, Philosophical, Phlegmatic, Placate, Placid, Quell, Quiet, Raise, Relax(ed), Repose, Restful, Restrained, Sedate, Self-possessed, Seraphic, Serena, Serene, Settle, Sleek, →**SOOTHE**, Steady, Still, Stilly, Subside, Supercool, Tranquil(lise), Unruffled, Windless

Cambric Lawn

Camel, Camel train Arabian, Artiodactyla, Bactrian, Beige, Caisson, Colt, Dromedary, Kafila, Llama, Oont, Sopwith, Tulu

Camelopard Giraffe

Camera, Camera man All-round, Box, Brownie®, Camcorder, Candid, Chambers, Cine, Compact, Digicam, Disc, Dolly, Flash, Gamma, Gatso®, Iconoscope, Image orthicon, Imager, Instant, Kodak®, Lucida, Nannycam, Obscura, Orthicon, Palmcorder, Panoramic, Pantoscope, Periphery, Phone-cam, Pinhole, Point and shoot, Polaroid®, Projectionist, Reflex, Schmidt, SLR, Somascope, Speed, Spycam, Steadicam®, Subminiature, Swing-back, Video

Camouflage Conceal, →**DISGUISE**, Mark, Maskirovka, War-dress

▷ **Camouflaged** *may indicate* an anagram

Camp(er) Affectation, Aldershot, Auschwitz, Banal, Base, Belsen, Bivouac, Boma, Boot, Buchenwald, Caerleon, Cantonment, Castral, Colditz, Concentration, Dachau, David, Death, Depot, D(o)uar, Dumdum, Epicene, Faction, Fat, Flaunt, Gulag, Happy, Health, High, Holiday, Labour, Laer, La(a)ger, Lashkar, Leaguer, Low, Manyat(t)a, Motor, Oflag, Outlie, Peace, Prison, Side, Siwash, Stagey, Stalag, Stative, Summer, Swagman, Tent, Theatrical, Transit, Treblinka, Valley Forge, Work, Zare(e)ba, Zariba, Zereba, Zeriba

Campaign(er) Activist, Agitate, Barnstorm, Battle, Blitz, Blitzkrieg, Canvass, Crusade, Drive, Enterprise, Field, Gallipoli, Hustings, Jihad, Lobby, Mission, Offensive,

Pankhurst, Promotion, Roadshow, Run, Satyagraha, Smear, Stint, Stopes, Strategist, The stump, Venture, Veteran, War, Warray, Warrey, Whistle-stop

Can(s) Able, Aerosol, Billy, Bog, Capable, Churn, Cooler, Dow, Dyke, Gaol, Gents, Headphones, Is able, John, Jug, Karsy, Kazi, Lav(atory), Loo, May, Nick, Pail, Pitcher, Pot, Preserve, → **PRISON**, Privy, Six-pack, Stir, Tin, Tube

Canada, Canadian Abenaki, Acadian, Bella Bella, Bella Coola, Beothuk, Bois-brûlé, .ca, Canuck, Coureur de bois, Dakotan, Dene, Habitans, Heiltsuk, Herring choker, Inuit, Johnny Canuck, Joual, Manitoban, Metis, Quebeccer, Quebecker, Québecois, Salishan, Saulteaux

Canal Alimentary, Ampul, Anal, Birth, Caledonian, Channel, Conduit, Corinth, Cruiseway, Da Yunhe, Duct, Duodenum, Ea, Ear, Enteron, Erie, Foss(e), Gota, Grand (Trunk), Grande Terre, Grand Union, Groove, Gut, Haversian, Houston Ship, Kiel, Klong, Labyrinth, Lode, Manchester Ship, Meatus, Midi, Mittelland, Moscow, Navigation, New York State Barge, Oesophagus, Panama, Pharynx, Pipe, Pound, Regent's, Resin, Rhine-Herne, Ring, Root, Sault Sainte Marie, Scala, Schlemm's, Semi-circular, Ship, Shipway, Soo, Spinal, Stone, Suez, Suo, Urethra, Vagina, Vertebral, Waterway, Welland, Zanja

Canal-boat Barge, Fly-boat, Gondola, Vaporetto

Canary Bird, Grass, Prisoner, Roller, Serin, Singer, Yellow

Cancel(led) Abrogate, Adeem, Annul, Counteract, Countermand, Cross, Delete, Destroy, Erase, Kill, Negate, Nullify, Obliterate, Override, Rained off, Red line, Remit, Repeal, Rescind, Retract, Retrait, Revoke, Scrub, Undo, Unmake, Void, Wipe

Cancer(ian), Cancerous Big C, Carcinoma, Crab, Curse, Hepatoma, Kaposi's sarcoma, Leukaemia, Lymphoma, Marek's disease, Moon child, Oat-cell, Oncogenic, Tropic, Tumour, Wolf

Candid, Candour Albedo, Blunt, Camera, Forthright, Franchise, Frank, Honesty, Ingenuous, Man-to-man, Open, Round, Upfront

Candidate(s) Agrege, Applicant, Aspirant, Contestant, Entrant, Field, Literate, Nomenklatura, Nominee, Office-seeker, Ordinand, Postulant, Running mate, Short list, Slate, Spoiler, Stalking-horse, Testee

Candied, Candy Angelica, Caramel, Cotton, Eryngo, Eye, Glace, Maple, Rock, Snow, Succade, Sucket, Sugar, → **SWEET**

Candle(stick), Candelabra Amandine, Bougie, C(i)erge, Chanukiah, Corpse, Dip, Fetch, Girandole, Hanukiah, Jesse, Lampadary, Light, Menorah, New, Padella, Paschal, Pricket, Roman, Rushlight, Sconce, Serge, Shammash, Shammes, Shortsix, Slut, Sperm, Tace, Tallow, Tallow-dip, Taper, Tea-light, Torchère, Tricerion, Vigil light, Wax

▶**Candy** *see* **CANDIED**

Cane, Caning Arrow, Baculine, Bamboo, Baste, Beat, Birk, Dari, Dhurra, Doura, Dur(r)a, Ferula, Ferule, Goor, Gur, Jambee, Malacca, Narthex, Penang-lawyer, Pointer, Rat(t)an, Rod, Six of the best, Split, Stick, Sugar, Swagger-stick, Swish, Switch, Sword, Swordstick, Tan, Tickler, Vare, Wand, Whangee, Wicker(-work)

Canine Biter, C, Dhole, Dog, Eye-tooth

Cannibal Anthropophagus, Heathen, Long pig, Ogre, Thyestean

Cannon Amusette, Barrage, Basilisk, Bombard, Breechloader, Carom, Carronade, Chaser, Collide, Criterion, Culverin, Drake, Falcon, Gun, Howitzer, Kiss, Long-tom, Monkey, Nursery, Oerlikon, Saker, Stern-chaser, Water, Zamboorak, Zomboruk, Zumbooru(c)k

Canny Careful, Frugal, Prudent, Scot, Shrewd, Slee, Sly, Thrifty, Wice, Wily, Wise

Canoe(ist) Bidarka, Bidarkee, Canader, Canadian, Dugout, Faltboat, Kayak, Monoxylon, Montaria, Oomiack, Paddler, Piragua, Pirogue, Rob Roy, Woodskin

Canon(ise) Austin, Brocard, Camera, Chapter, Chasuble, Code, Crab, Decree, Honorary, Isidorian, → **LAW**, Line, Mathurin(e), Nocturn, Nursery, Pitaka, Polyphony, Prebendary, Premonstrant, Premonstratensian, Regular, Residential, Rota, Round, Rule, Secular, Square, Squier, Squire, Standard, Tenet, Unity, Vice-dean

Canopy Awning, Baldachin, Baldaquin, Chuppah, Ciborium, Dais, Gore, He(a)rse,

Huppah, Majesty, Marquee, Marquise, Parapente, Pavilion, Shamiana(h), State, Tabernacle, Tent, Tester, Veranda(h)

Canticle Benedictus, Nunc dimittis

Canton(ese) Basil, District, Quarter, Tanka

Cantor Haz(z)an

Canvas Awning, Binca®, Burlap, Drab(b)ler, Lug-sail, Mainsail, Maintopsail, Marquee, Oil-cloth, Paint, Raven's-duck, Reef, →**SAIL**, Square-sail, Staysail, Stuns(ai)l, Tent(age), Trysail, Wigan, Woolpack

Canvass(er), Canvassing Agent, Doorstep, Drum, Mainstreeting, Poll, Press flesh, Solicit

▷ **Canvasser** *may indicate* a painter or a camper

Canyon Box, Canada, Coprates, Defile, Grand, Kings, Nal(l)a, Nallah, Ravine

Cap(ped) Abacot, Amorce, Balaclava, Balmoral, Barret, Baseball, Bathing, Bellhop, Bendigo, Ber(r)et, Better, Biggin, Biretta, Black, Blakey, Blue, Blue-bonnet, Bonnet-rouge, Bycoket, Call, Calotte, Calpac(k), Calyptrate, Capeline, Caul, Chaco, Chape, Chapeau, Chaperon, Chapka, Charge, Chechia, Cheese-cutter, Cloth, Cockernony, Coif, College, Coonskin, Cope, Cornet, Cowl, Cradle, Crest, →**CROWN**, Czapka, Davy Crockett, Deerstalker, Dunce's, Dutch, Fatigue, Ferrule, Filler, Flat, Fool's, Forage, Gandhi, Garrison, Gimme, Glengarry, Gorblim(e)y, Grannie, Granny, →**HAT**, Havelock, Hummel bonnet, Hunting, Iceberg, International, Jockey, Juliet, Kalpak, Kepi, Kilmarnock (cowl), Kippa, Kippoth, Kipput, Kiss-me(-quick), Knee, Legal, Liberty, Lid, Maintenance, Mob, Monmouth, Monteer, Montero, Mor(r)ion, Mortar-board, Muffin, Mutch, Newsboy, Night, Old wife, Outdo, Pagri, Patella(r), Percussion, Perplex, Petrol, Phrygian, Pie, Pileus, Pinner, Polar, Puggaree, Quoif, Root, Schapska, Shako, Skullcap, Square, Squirrel-tail, Statute, Stocking, Summit, →**SURPASS**, Taj, Tam(-o'-shanter), Thimble, Thinking, Thrum, Toe, Toorie, Top, Toque, Toy, Trenchard, Trencher, Truck, Tuque, Turk's, Watch, Wishing, Yarmulka, Yarmulke, Zuchetto

Capable, Capability Able, Brown, Capacity, Competent, Deft, Effectual, Efficient, Firepower, Intelligent, Qualified, Skilled, Susceptible, Up to, Viable

Capacitance, Capacity Ability, Aptitude, C, Cab, Calibre, Carrying, Co(o)mb, Competence, Content, Cor, Cubic, Endowment, Full, Function, Legal, Limit, Log, Mneme, Potency, Potential, Power, Qua, Rated, Receipt, Scope, Size, Tonnage, Valence, Vital, Volume

Cape(s) Agulhas, Almuce, Athlete, Beachy Head, Blanc(o), Bon, Burnouse, Byron, C, Calimere Point, Canaveral, Canso, Cardinal, Chelyuskin, Cloak, Cod, Comorin, Delgado, Dezhnev, Domino, Dungeness, East(ern), Fairweather, Faldetta, Fanion, Fanon, Farewell, Fear, Fichu, Finisterre, Flattery, Gallinas Point, Good Hope, Guardafui, Harp, Hatteras, Head(land), Helles, Hoe, Hogh, Hook of Holland, Horn, Inverness, Kennedy, Leeuwin, Lindesnes, Lizard, Mantilla, Mantle, Mant(e)let, Mantua, Matapan, May, Miseno, Moz(z)etta, Muleta, Naze, Ness, Nordkyn, North, Northern, Ortegal, Palatine, Palliser, Parry, Pelerine, Peninsula, Point, Poncho, Race, Ras, Ray, Reinga, Roca, Ruana, Runaway, Sable, St Vincent, Sandy, Scaw, Skagen, Skaw, Sontag, Southwest, Talma, Tippet, Trafalgar, Ushant, Verde, Vert, Waterproof, Western, Wrath, York

Cape of Good Hope Stellenbosch

Capital(s) A1, Assets, Block, Boodle, Bravo, Cap, Chapiter, Chaptrel, Circulating, Doric, Equity, Euge, Excellent, Fixed, Flight, Float, Floating, Fonds, Great, Helix, Human, Initial, Ionic, Lethal, Lulu, Metropolis, Principal, Refugee, Risk, Rustic, Seat, Seed, Share, Social, Splendid, Sport, Stellar, Stock, Super, Topping, UC, Upper case, Venture, Wealth, Working

Capitalise Carpe diem

▷ **Capitalist** *may indicate* a citizen of a capital

▷ **Capless** *may indicate* first letter missing

▷ **Capriccioso** *may indicate* an anagram

Caprice, Capricious Arbitrary, Boutade, Capernoitie, Cap(p)ernoity, Conceit,

Desultory, Eccentric, Erratic, Fancy, Fickle, Fitful, Freak, Humoresk, Humoresque, Irony, Migraine, Mood, Perverse, Quirk, Vagary, Wayward, Whim(sy)

Capsize Keel, Overbalance, Purl, Tip, Turn turtle, Upset, Whemmle, Whomble

▷**Capsized** *may indicate* a word upside down

Capsule Amp(o)ule, Boll, Bowman's, Cachet, Habitat, Nidamentum, Ootheca, Orbiter, Ovisac, Pill, Pyxidium, Spacecraft, Spermatophore, Time, Urn

Captain Ahab, Bligh, Bobadil, Bones, Bossyboots, Brassbound, Capt, Chief, Cid, Commander, Condottiere, Cook, Copper, Cuttle, Flint, Group, Hook, Hornblower, Kettle, Kidd, Leader, Macheath, Master, Nemo, Oates, Old man, Owner, Patroon, Post, Privateer, Protospatharius, Rittmaster, Skip(per), Standish, Subah(dar), Subedar, Swing, Trierarch

Caption Heading, Headline, Inscription, Masthead, Sub-title, Title

Captivate(d), Captivating Beguile, Bewitch, Charm, Enamour, Enthrall, Epris(e), Rapt, Take, Winsome

Captive, Captivity Bonds, Duress, Hostage, POW, Prisoner, Slave, Thrall

Capture Abduct, Annex, Bag, Catch, Collar, Cop, Data, Entrance, Grab, Land, Nail, Net, Prize, Rush, Seize, Snabble, Snaffle, Snare, →**TAKE**

Car Alvis, Astra, Audi, Austin, Auto(matic), Banger, Beemer, Beetle, Berlin, Biza, BL, Bluebird, Bomb, Boneshaker, Brake, Bubble, Buffet, Bugatti, Buick, Bumper, Bus, Cab(riolet), Cadillac, Catafalco, Catafalque, Chariot, Chorrie, Citroen, Classic, Clunker, Coach, Compact, Company, Concept, Convertible, Cortina, Coupé, Courtesy, Crate, Daimler, Diesel, Diner, Dodgem®, Drag(ster), Drophead, Dunger, Elf, Estate, E-type, Fastback, Ferrari, Fiat, Flivver, Ford, Formula, Freight, Friday, Gas guzzler, Ghost, Gondola, Griddle, GT, Gyrocar, Hardtop, Hatchback, Heap, Hearse, Hillman, Horseless carriage, Hot hatch, Hot-rod, Irish, Jaguar, Jalop(p)y, Jamjar, Jammy, Jam sandwich, Jaunting, Jim Crow, Kart, Kit, Knockabout, Lada, Lagonda, Lancia, Landaulet, Landrover, Lift-back, Limo, Limousine, Lincoln, Merc(edes), MG, Mini, Model T, Morgan, Morris, Motor, Muscle, Nacelle, Notchback, Observation, Opel, Pace, Palace, Panda, Parlo(u)r, Patrol, Pimpmobile, Popemobile, Production, Prowl, Pullman, Racer, Ragtop, Railroad, Rattletrap, Restaurant, Roadster, Roller, Rolls (Royce), Rover, RR, Runabout, Runaround, Rust bucket, Saloon, Scout, Sedan, Service, Shooting-brake, Skoda, Sleeper, Sleeping, Soft-top, Speedster, Sports, Squad, Station wagon, Steam, Stock, Stretch-limo, Subcompact, Sunbeam, Supermini, SUV, Tank, Telepherique, Telpher, Three-wheeler, Tin Lizzie, Tonneau, Tourer, Touring, Tram, Triumph, Trolley, Tumble, Turbo, Two-seater, Vehicle, Veteran, Vintage, Voiture, VW, Wheeler, Wheels

Caravan(ner) Caf(f)ila, Convoy, Fleet, Kafila, Motor home, Safari, Trailer, Trailer trash, Winnebago®

Carbohydrate Agar, Agarose, Callose, Carrageenan, Cellulose, Chitin, Dextran, Disaccharide, Glycogen, Heptose, Hexose, Inulin, Ketose, Laminarin, Mannan, Pectin, Pentene, Pentose, Pentylene, Polysaccharide, Saccharide, Sorbitol, Starch, Sucrose, Sugar

Carcase, Carcass Body, Cadaver, Carrion, Corpse, Cutter, Krang, Kreng, Morkin, Mor(t)ling

Card(s), Cardboard, Carding Accelerator, Ace, Affinity, Amex®, Arcana, Baccarat, Basto, Bill, Birthday, Blue Peter, Bower, Business, Calling, Canasta, Cartes, Cash, Caution, Charge, Chicane, Club, Comb, Communion, Community, Compass, Court(esy), Credit, Cue, Dance, Debit, Deck, Deuce, Diamond, Doffer, Donor, Ecarté, Eccentric, Euchre, Expansion, Flaught, Flush, Fourchette, →**GAME**, Goulash, Graphics, Green, Guide, Hand, Heart, Honour, Identity, Idiot, Jack, Jambone, Joker, Kanban, Key, King, Knowing, Loo, Loyalty, Manille, Matador, Meishi, Menu, Mise, Mistigris, Mogul, Mournival, Natural, Notelet, Oddity, Ombre, Pack, Pasteboard, PC, Phone, Picture, Piquet, Placard, Plastic, Playing, Postal, Proximity, Quatorze, Queen, Quiz, Ration, Red, Rippler, Rove, Royal marriage, Score, Scratch, Screwball, Scribble, Singleton, Smart, Soda, Solo, Sound, Spade, Spadille, Squeezer, Store, Strawboard, Sure, Swab, Swipe, Swish, Switch, Swob, Swot, Talon, Tarok, Tarot, Tease(r), Tenace,

Test, Thaumatrope, Ticket, Top-up, Tose, Toze, Trading, Trey, Trump, Two-spot, Valentine, Visiting, Wag, Warrant, Weirdie, Whitechapel, Wild, Wit, Yellow, Zener

Cardigan Ballet-wrap, Jacket, Wampus, Wam(m)us, Woolly

Cardinal Apostolic vicar, Camerlingo, Chief, College, Eight, Eminence, Eminent, Grosbeak, Hat, HE, Hume, Legate, Manning, Mazarin, Medici, Newman, Nine, Number, Pivotal, Polar, Prefect, Prelate, Radical, Red, Red-hat, Richelieu, Sacred college, Seven, Sin, Spellman, Ten, Virtue, Vital, Ximenes

Care(r), Caring Attention, Befriend, Burden, Cark, Caution, Cerne, Cherish, →CONCERN, Cosset, Doula, Grief, Guard, Heed, Intensive, Kaugh, Keep, Kiaugh, Maternal, Mind, Pains, Palliative, Parabolanus, Primary, Reck(e), Reke, Respite, Retch, Shared, Solicitude, →TEND, Tenty, Ward, Worry

Career Course, Hurtle, Life, Line, Profession, Run, Rush, Scorch, Speed, Start, Tear, Vocation

▷ **Career** *may indicate* an anagram

Careful(ly) Canny, Chary, Discreet, Gentle, Hooly, Leery, Meticulous, Mindful, Penny-pinching, Penny-wise, Pernickety, Provident, Prudent, Scrimp, Scrupulous, Softly-softly, Studious, Tentie, Tenty, Thorough, Vigilant, Ware, Wary

Careless(ness), Careless(ly) Anyhow, Casual, Cheery, Debonair, Easy, Free-minded, Gallio, Improvident, Imprudent, Inadvertent, Inattention, Insouciance, Lax, Lighthearted, Négligé, →NEGLIGENT, Nonchalant, Oversight, Raffish, Rash, Remiss, Resigned, Riley, Slam-bang, Slapdash, Slaphappy, Slipshod, Sloppy, Sloven(ly), Slubber, Taupie, Tawpie, Unguarded, Unmindful, Untenty, Unwary

▷ **Carelessly** *may indicate* an anagram

Caress Bill, Coy, Embrace, Feel, Fondle, Kiss, Lallygag, Lollygag, Noursle, Nursle, Pet, Straik, Stroke, Touch

Caretaker Acting, Concierge, Curator, Custodian, Dvornik, Guardian, Janitor, Nightwatchman, Sexton, Shammash, Shammes, Superintendent, Verger, Warden

Careworn Haggard, Lined, Tired, Weary

Cargo Boatload, Bulk, Burden, Fraught, Freight, Lading, Last, →LOAD, Navicert, Payload, Shipment

Caribbean Belonger, Puerto Rican, Soca, Sokah, Spanish Main, Taino, WI

Caricature, Caricaturist Ape, Beerbohm, Burlesque, Caran d'Ache, Cartoon, Cruikshank, Doyle, Farce, Gillray, Mimicry, Rowlandson, Scarfe, Skit, Spy, Toon, Travesty

Carnation Dianthus, Malmaison, Picotee, Pink

Carnival Fair, Festival, Fete, Mardi Gras, Moomba, Rag, Revelry, Surf

Carol(ler) Noel, Sing, Song, Wait, Wassail, Yodel

Carousal, Carouse Bend, Birl(e), Bouse, Bride-ale, Compotation, Drink, Mallemaroking, Mollie, Orge, Orgy, →REVEL, Roist, Screed, Spree, Upsee, Upsey, Upsy, Wassail

Carp(er) Beef, Cavil, Censure, Complain, Crab, Critic, Crucian, Crusian, Gibel, Goldfish, Id(e), Kvetch, Mirror, Mome, Nag, Nibble, Roach, Roundfish, Scold, Twitch, Whine, Yerk, Yirk

Carpenter Beveller, Bush, Cabinet-maker, Carfindo, Chips, Fitter, Joiner, Joseph, Menuisier, Quince, Tenoner, Wright

▷ **Carpenter** *may indicate* an anagram

Carpet(ing) Aubusson, Axminster, Beetle, Berate, Bessarabian, Body, Broadloom, Brussels, Castigate, Chide, Drugget, Durrie, Kali, Kelim, Khilim, Kidderminster, Kilim, Kirman, Lecture, Lino, Mat(ting), Moquette, Persian, Rate, Red, Reprimand, Reproach, Roast, Rug, Runner, Shagpile, Shark, Turkey, Wall-to-wall, What for, Wig, Wilton

Carriage Air, Ar(a)ba, Aroba, Bandy, Barouche, Bearing, Berlin(e), Bier, Brake, Brit(sch)ka, Britska, Britzka, Brougham, Buckboard, Buggy, Cab, Calash, Calèche, Car, Cariole, Caroche, Carriole, Carryall, Cartage, Chaise, Charabanc, Charet, Chariot, Chassis, Chay, Clarence, Coach, Coch, Composite, Conveyance, Coupé, Curricle, Demeanour, Dennet, Deportment, Désobligeante, Diner, Dormeuse, Dormitory-car, Dos-a-dos, Do-si-do, Drag, Dros(h)ky, Ekka, Equipage, Fiacre, Fly, Four-in-hand,

Gait, Gig, Gladstone, Go-cart, Growler, Gun, Haulage, Herdic, Horseless, Howdah, Hurley-hacket, Jampan, Job, Landau(let), Landing, Limber, Mien, Non-smoker, Norimon, Observation-car, Phaeton, Pick-a-back, Pochaise, Pochay, Poise, Port(age), Portance, Postchaise, Posture, Poyse, Pram, Pullman, Purdah, Railcar, Railway, Randem, Rath(a), Remise, Ricksha(w), Rig, Rockaway, Set-up, Shay, Sled, Sleeper, Smoker, Sociable, Spider, Spider phaeton, Stanhope, Sulky, Surrey, Tarantas(s), Taxi, T-cart, Tender, Tenue, Tilbury, Tim-whiskey, Tonga, Trail, Trap, Van, Vetture, Victoria, Voiture, Wagonette, Waterage, Whirligig, Whisk(e)y, Whisky gig

Carrier Aircraft, Airline, Arm, Baldric, Barkis, Barrow, Bomb-ketch, Bulk, Cacolet, Caddy, Cadge, Camel, Coaster, Common, Conveyor, Donkey, Escort, Fomes, Fomites, Frog, Grid, Hamper, Haversack, Hod, Janker, Jill, Majority, Minority, Nosebag, Noyade, Obo, Packhorse, Personnel, Pigeon, Porter, Rucksack, Satchel, Schistosoma, Semantide, Sling, Straddle, Stretcher, Tiffin, Tranter, → **TRAY**, TWA, Vector, Wave

Carrion Cadaver, Carcase, Carcass, Flesh, Ket, Stapelia

Carry(ing), Carry over Asport, Bear, Chair, Convey, Enlevé, Escort, Ferry, Frogmarch, Hawk, Hent, Humf, Hump, Humph, Kurvey, Land, Move, Pack, Pickaback, Port, Reappropriate, Stock, Sustain, Tide over, Tote, → **TRANSPORT**, Trant, Wage, With, Yank

Cart(er) Bandy, Barrow, Bogey, Buck, Cape, Car(r)iole, Chapel, Dandy, Democrat, Democrat wagon, Dog, Dolly, Dray, Egyptologist, Float, Furphy, Gambo, Gill, Golf, Governess, Gurney, Hackery, Jag, Jill, Lead, Mail(-gig), Night, Pie, Pram, Rickshaw, Scot, Scotch, Shandry, T, Tax(ed), Telega, Trolley, Tumbrel, Tumbril, Village, Wag(g)on, Wain, Water, Wheelbarrow, Whitechapel

Cartel Duopoly, Ring, Syndicate, Zaibatsu

Cartilage Chondral, Ensiform, Gristle

Carton Box, Case, Crate, Sydney, Tub

Cartoon(ist) Andy Capp, Animated, Caricature, Comic, Comic strip, Disney, Drawn, Emmet, Garland, Lancaster, Leech, Low, Manga, Mel, Partridge, Popeye, Schulz, Short, Shrek, Spy, Strip, Superman, Tenniel, Tintin, Trog

Cartridge Ball, Blank, Bullet, Cartouche, Crystal, Doppie, Live, Magnetic, Magnum, Rim-free, Shell, Spent

Carve(d), Carver, Carving Abated, Bas relief, Cameo, Chair, Chisel, Cilery, Crocket, Cut, Dismember, Doone, Enchase, Engrave, Entail, Entayle, Fiddlehead, Gibbons, Glyphic, Glyptic, Hew, Incise, Inscribe, Insculp, Intaglio, Netsuke, Nick, Petroglyph, Scrimshaw, Sculp(t), Slice, Tondo, Trophy, Truncheon, Tympanum, Whakairo, Whittle

Cascade Cataract, Fall, Lin(n), Stream, Waterfall

Case(s), Casing Ablative, Accusative, Action, Allative, Altered, Appeal, Aril, Ascus, Assumpsit, Attaché, Basket, Beer, Bere, Bin, Bittacle, Blimp, Box, Brief, Bundwall, Burse, C, Ca, Cabinet, Cachet, Calyx, Canister, Canterbury, Capsule, Cartouch(e), Cartridge, Cask(et), Cause celebre, Cellaret, Chase, Chitin, Chrysalis, Cocoon, Coffin, Comitative, Compact, Crate, Croustade, Crust, Cyst, Dative, Declension, Detinue, Dispatch, Dossier, Dressing, Elytron, Enclose, Ensheath, Ergative, Etui, Etwee, Event, Example, Flan, Flapjack, Flask, Frame, Genitive, Grip, Hanaper, Hard, Hatbox, Hold-all, Housewife, Hull, Humidor, Husk, Illative, Imperial, Index, Indusium, Instance, Kalamdan, Keg, Keister, Locative, Locket, Lorica, Manche, Matter, Mermaid's purse, Mezuzah, Music, Nacelle, Nominative, Non-suit, Nutshell, Objective, Oblique, Ochrea, Ocrea, Outpatient, Packing, Pair, Papeterie, Patient, Pencil, Penner, Phylactery, Plight, Plummer-block, Pod, Port, Portfolio, Possessive, Prima facie, Puparium, Quiver, Recce, Reconnoitre, Red box, Sabretache, Sad, Scabbard, Seashell, Sheath(e), Shell, Situation, Six-pack, Sleeve, Sporocyst, Sporran, Stead, Subjective, Suit, Tantalus, Tea-chest, Telium, Test, Theca, Tichborne, Toolbox, Trial, Trunk, Valise, Vanity bag, Vasculum, Vitrine, Vocative, Volva, Walise, Walking, Wallet, Wardian, Wing, Worst, Writing

Cash Blunt, Bonus, Bounty, Change, Coin, Digital, Dosh, Dot, Float, Funds, Idle money, Imprest, Liquid, Lolly, → **MONEY**, Needful, Ochre, Oof, Pence, Petty, Ready, Realise, Redeem, Rhino, Spondulicks, Stumpy, Tender, Tin, Wampum, Wherewithal

Cashew Hog-plum

Cashier, Cash machine Annul, ATM, Break, Depose, Disbar, Dismiss, Teller, Treasurer

Casino Monte Carlo

Cask(et) Armet, Barrel, Barrico, Bas(i)net, Box, Breaker, Butt, Cade, Casque, Cassette, Drum, Firkin, Galeate, Harness, Heaume, Hogshead, Keg, Leaguer, Octave, Pin, Pipe, Puncheon, Pyxis, Run(d)let, Salade, Sallet, Sarcophagus, Shook, Shrine, Solera, Tierce, Tun

Casserole Diable, Hotpot, Osso bucco, Pot, Salmi, Terrine, Tzimmes

Cassette Cartridge, Tape, Video

Cassock Gown, Soutane

▷ **Cast** *may indicate* an anagram or a piece of a word missing

Cast (down, off, out), Casting Abattu, Actors, Add, Angle, Appearance, Bung, Cire perdue, Dash, Death mask, Die, Discard, Ecdysis, Eject, Emit, Exorcise, Exuviae, Exuvial, Fling, Found, Fusil, Hawk, Heave, Hob, Hue, Hurl, Impression, Ingo(w)es, Keb, Look, Lose, Lost wax, Mew, Mo(u)lt, Moulage, Mould, Plaster(stone), Plastisol®, Players, Print, Put, Reject, Sand, Shed, Shoot, Sling, Slive, Slough, Spoil, Stamp, Stookie, Swarm, Tailstock, →**THROW**, Toss, Tot, Warp, Wax, Ytost

Castaway Adrift, Crusoe, Gunn, Left, Man Friday, Outcast, Robinson, Selkirk, Stranded

▷ **Cast by** *may indicate* surrounded by

Caste Burakumin, Class, Dalit, Group, Harijan, Hova, Kshatriya, Rajput, Rank, Sect, Shudra, Sudra, Untouchable, Varna

Castle(d) Barbara, Bouncy, Broch, C, Casbah, Chateau, Citadel, Fastness, Fort, Kasba(h), Man, Mot(t)e, Move, Palace, Rook, Stronghold, Villa

Castor Muffineer

Casual(ly) Accidental, Adventitious, Airy(-fairy), Blasé, Chance, Chav(ette), Flippant, Grass, Haphazard, Idle, Incidental, Informal, Jaunty, Lackadaisical, Nonchalant, Odd(ment), Odd-jobber, Offhand, Off-the-cuff, Orra, Overly, Passing, Promiscuous, Random, Scratch, Slaphappy, Slipshod, Sporadic, Stray, Temp, Throwaway

Cat Ailuro-, Barf, Boat, Boke, Bush, Catamount, Dandy, Egurgitate, Fat, Felid, Feline, Foss, Gossip, Hipster, Jazzer, Lair, Lash, Mewer, Mog, Native, Neuter, Nib, Painter, Pardal, Practical, Puss, Regurgitate, Scourge, Sick, Spew, Spue, Swinger, Vomit, Whip

Cataclysm Apocalypse

Catalogue(r) Categorise, Dewey, Durchkomponi(e)rt, Index, Inventory, Itemise, K(ochel), List, Litany, Magalog, MARC, Messier, Ragman, Ragment, Raisonné, Record, Register, Star, Table, Tabulate, Thematic

Catalyst Accelerator, Agent, Aldol, Chemical, Enzyme, Erepsin, Influence, Kryptonite, Stereospecific, Unicase, Ziegler

Catapult Ballista, Ging, Launch, Mangon(el), Perrier, Petrary, Propel, Scorpion, Shanghai, Sling, Slingshot, Stone-bow, Tormentum, Trebuchet, Wye, Y

Catastrophe, Catastrophic Calamity, Damoclean, →**DISASTER**, Doom, Epitasis, Fiasco, Meltdown, Ruinous, Tragedy

Catch(y), Caught Air, Apprehend, Arrest, Attract, Bag, Benet, Bone, C, Capture, Chape, Clasp, Cog, Collar, Contract, Cop, Corner, Ct, Deprehend, Detent, Dolly, Engage, Enmesh, Ensnare, Entoil, Entrap, Fang, Field, Fumble, Gaper, Get, Glee(some), Grasp, Had, Hank, Haud, Haul, Hear, Hold, Hook, Inmesh, Keddah, Keight, Kep(pit), Kheda, Kill, Land, Lapse, Lasso, Latch, Lazo, Lime, Lock, Morse, Nab, Nail, Net, Nick, Nim, Nobble, Noose, Overhear, Overhent, Overtake, Parti, Pawl, Rap, Release, Rope, Round, Rub, Safety, Save, Sean, Sear, See(n), Seize, →**SNAG**, Snap, Snare, Snig, →**SONG**, Stop, Surprise, Swindle, Tack, Taen, Take, Tane, Trammel, Trap, Trawl, Trick, Tripwire, Troll, Twenty two, Twig, Understand, Wrestle

Categorise, Category →**CLASS**, Classify, Etic, Genus, Infraclass, Infraorder, Label, Order, Pigeonhole, Range, Stereotype, Taxon, Triage, Type

Cater(er) Acatour, Cellarer, Feed, Manciple, →**PROVIDE**, Serve, Steward, Supply, Victualler, Vivandière

Caterpillar Aweto, Boll worm, Cabbageworm, Cotton-worm, Cutworm, Eruciform, Geometer, Grub, Hop-dog, Hornworm, Inchworm, Larva, Looper, Osmeterium, Palmer, Silkworm, Tent, Webworm, Woolly-bear

Cathedral Amiens, Basilica, Birmingham, Burgos, Chartres, Chester, →**CHURCH**, Cologne, Cortona, Dome, Duomo, Durham, Ely, Evreux, Exeter, Gloucester, Hereford, Hertford, Huesca, Kirkwall, Lateran, Lugo, Minster, Mullingar, Notre Dame, Rheims, Rochester, St Albans, St Davids, St Paul's, Santiago de Compostela, Sens, Teruel, Viseu, Wakefield, Wells, Westminster, Winchester

Catholic Assumptionist, Broad, Christian Socialism, Defenders, Doolan, Ecumenical, Fenian, General, German, Irvingism, Jebusite, Latin, Lazarist, Left-footer, Liberal, Marian, Old, Ostiary, Papalist, Papaprelatist, Papist, Recusant, Redemptionist, Roman, Romish, Salesian, Spike, Taig, Te(a)gue, Teigue, Theatine, Thomist, Tory, Tridentine, Universal, Ursuline, Wide

Cattle(pen) Aberdeen Angus, Africander, Ankole, Aver, Ayrshire, Beefalo, Belgian Blue, Belted Galloway, Black, Brahman, British White, Buffalo, Carabao, Charbray, Charolais, Chillingham, Dexter, Drove, Durham, Fee, Friesian, Friesland, Galloway, Gaur, Gayal, Guernsey, Gyal, Heard, Herd, Hereford, Highland, Holstein (Friesian), Illawarra, Jersey, Kerry, Kine, Kouprey, Kraal, Ky(e), Kyloe, Lairage, Limousin, Lincoln, Longhorn, Luing, Neat, Nout, Nowt, Owsen, Oxen, Piemontese, Rabble, Redpoll, Rother, Santa Gertrudis, Shorthorn, Simment(h)al, Soum, South Devon, Sowm, Steer, Stock, Store, Stot, Sussex, Tamarao, Tamarau, Teeswater, Wagyu, Welsh Black

Caucus Assembly, Cell, Gathering, Race

Caulk Fill, Pay, Pitch, Snooze

Causation, Cause(d), Causes Aetiology, Agent, Bandwagon, Beget, Breed, Bring, Célèbre, Common, Compel, Create, Crusade, Determinant, Due, Effect, Efficient, Encheason, Engender, Entail, Evoke, Expedite, Factor, Final, First, Flag-day, Formal, Gar(re), Generate, Ideal, Induce, Inspire, Lead, Lost, Make, Material, Motive, Movement, Natural, →**OCCASION**, Parent, Pathogen, Probable, Prompt, Provoke, Proximate, Reason, Root, Sake, Secondary, Show, Source, Teleology, Topic, Ultimate, Wreak

Caustic Acid, Acrimonious, Alkaline, Burning, Common, Erodent, Escharotic, Lunar, Moxa, Pungent, Sarcastic, Scathing, Seare, Soda, Tart, Vitriol, Waspish, Withering

Caution, Cautious (person) Achitophel, Admonish, Ahithophel, Alert, Amber, Awarn, Beware, Cagey, Card, Care, Cave, Caveat, Chary, Circumspect, Credence, Cure, Defensive, Deliberate, Discretion, Fabian, Forewarn, Gingerly, Guard(ed), Heedful, Leery, Prudent, Rum, Scream, Skite, Tentative, Timorous, Vigilant, Ware, →**WARN**, Wary, Yellow card

▷ **Cavalier** *may indicate* an anagram

Cave(rn), Caves, Cave-dwelling, Cave in Acherusia, Aladdin's, Altamira, Antar, Antre, Beware, Bone, Capitulate, Cellar, Cheddar, Collapse, Corycian, Den, Domdaniel, Erebus, Fingal's, Fore, Grot(to), Hollow, Jenolan, Lascaux, Look-out, Lupercal, Mammoth, Mind out, Nix, Pot-hole, Proteus, Sepulchre, Spel(a)ean, Speleology, Spelunker, Speos, Tassili, Trophonian, Vault, Waitomo, Ware, Weem, Wookey Hole

Caveman Adullam, Aladdin, Fingal, Neanderthal, Primitive, Troglodyte, Troll

Caviare Beluga, Osietra, Roe, Sevruga, Sturgeon

Cavity Acetabulum, Amygdale, Antrum, Archenteron, Atrial, Atrium, Body, Camera, Celom, Chamber, Cisterna, Coelom(e), Conceptacle, Concha, Countermark, Crater, Crypt, Dent, Druse, Enteron, Follicle, Foss, Gap, Geode, Glenoid, Gloryhole, Hold, Hole, Lacuna, Locule, Mediastinum, Mialoritic, Orbita, Orifice, Pelvis, Pleural, Pocket, Pulp, Sinus, Stomod(a)eum, Tartarus, Tear, Thunderegg, Tympanum, Vacuole, Vein, Ventricle, Vesicle, Vitta, Vomica, Vug, Well

Cayman Islands Tax haven

Cease(fire) Abate, Blin, Cut, Desist, Devall, Die, Disappear, Halt, Ho, Intermit, Lin, Lose, Pass, Refrain, Sessa, →**STOP**, Truce

Cedar(wood) Arolla, Atlas, Barbados, Cryptomeria, Deodar, Incense, Jamaica, Toon

Ceiling Absolute, Barrel, Coffered, Cove, Cupola, Dome, Glass, Lacunar, Laquearia, Limit, Plafond, Roof, Silver, Soffit, Stained glass

Celebrate(d), Celebration, Celebrity Ale, A-list, Beanfeast, Besung, Big name, Bigwig, Binge, B-list, Brat-packer, Carnival, Chant, Commemorate, Distinguished, Do, Emblazon, Encaenia, Epithalamion, Epithalamium, Fame, Feast, Fest(al), Festivity, Fete, Fiesta, First-footing, Gala, Gaudeamus, Gaudy, Glitterati, Glorify, Grog-up, Harvest home, Headliner, Hold, Holiday, Honour, Hoop-la, Jamboree, Jol, Jollifications, Jollities, Jubilee, Keep, Large it, Laud, Legend, Limelight, Lion, Loosing, Lowsening, Maffick, Mardi Gras, Mawlid al-Nabi, Monstre sacre, Name, Noted, Nuptials, Observe, Occasion, Orgy, Panathenaea, Party, Pinata, Praise, Randan, Rave-up, Record, Rejoice, Renown, Repute, Revel, Rite, Roister, Sangeet, Saturnalia, See in, Sex symbol, Shindig, Sing, Spree, Star, Storied, Sung, Tet, Triumph, Wassail, Wet, Whoopee

Celestial Chinese, Cosmic, Divine, Ethereal, Heavenly, Supernal, Uranic

Celibate, Celibacy Bachelor, Chaste, Paterin(e), Rappist, Rappite, Shakers, Single, Spinster

Cell(s), Cellular Battery, Black hole, Bullpen, Cadre, Chamber, Chapel, Crypt, Cubicle, Death, Dungeon, Group, Laura, Lock up, Padded, Peter, →**PRISON**, Safety, Unit

Cellar Basement, Coalhole, Salt, Shaker, Storm, Vault, Vaultage, Vaut

Celt(ic) Breton, Brython, Cornish, Druid, Gadhel, Gael(dom), Goidel, Helvetii, Kelt, La Tène, P, Q, Taffy, Welsh

Cement Araldite®, Asbestos, Blast-furnace, Compo, Concrete, Fix, Flaunch, Glue, Grout, Gunite, Lute, Maltha, Mastic, Mastich, Mortar, Paste, Pointing, Portland, Putty, Rubber, →**STICK**, Trass

Cemetery Aceldama, Arenarium, Arlington, Boneyard, Boot Hill, Campo santo, Catacomb, God's Acre, Golgotha, Graveyard, Musall, Necropolis, Père Lachaise, Saqqara, Urnfield

Censor(ious), Censorship, Censure Accuse, Admonition, AD notice, Airbrush, Animadvert, Appeach, Ban, Banner, Berate, Blame, Blue-pencil, Bowdler, Braid, Cato, Chasten, Comstockery, →**CONDEMN**, Critical, Criticise, Cut, Damn, Dang, Decry, Dispraise, Edit, Excommunicate, Excoriate, Expurgate, Gag, Obloquy, Rap, Rebuke, Repress, Reprimand, Reproach, Reprobate, Reprove, Satirise, Slam, Slate, Suppress, Tax, Tear into, Tirade, Traduce, Wig

Cent(s) Bean, Coin, Ct, Penny, Red, Zack

Central(ly), Centre Active, Amid, Assessment, Attendance, Axis, Broca's, Bunt, Call, Cardinal, Chakra, Civic, Community, Contact, Core, Cost, Crisis, Day, Daycare, Dead, Detention, Detoxification, Deuteron, Deuton, Downtown, Drop-in, Epergne, Eye, Field, Focus, Foyer, Frontal, Garden, Health, Heart, Heritage, Hotbed, Hothouse, Hub, Incident, Inmost, Internal, Interpretive, Juvenile, Juvie, Kernel, Kingpin, Law, Leisure, Lincoln, Live, Main, Mecca, Median, Medulla, Mid(st), Midpoint, Midway, Mission, Music, Nave, Nerve, Nucleus, Omphalus, Pompidou, Profit, Property, Reception, Rehabilitation, Remand, Respiratory, Service, Shopping, Social Education, Storm, Teachers', Trauma, Visitor, Waist, Weather, Youth custody

Central American Mangue, Miskito, Olmec, Otomi, Pueblo, Totomac, Zapotec

▷ **Centre** *may indicate* middle letters

Century Age, C, Era, Magdeburg, Period, Siècle, Ton

Ceramic(s) Arcanist, China, Earthen, Ferrite, Ferronneries, Porcelain, Pottery, Sialon, Syalon®, Tiles

Cereal Amelcorn, Barley, Blé, Bran, Bread-basket, Buckwheat, Bulgar, Bulg(h)ur, Cassava, Corn, Couscous, Emmer, Farina, Gnocchi, Grain, Granola, Hominy, Maize, Mandioc(a), Mandiocca, Manihot, Mani(h)oc, Mealie, Millet, Muesli, Oats, Paddy, Popcorn, Rye(corn), Sago, Samp, Seed, Semolina, Sorghum, Spelt, Tapioca, Tef(f), Triticale, Wheat, Zea

Cerebral Sensoria

Ceremonial, Ceremony Aarti, Amrit, Asperges, Baptism, Barmitzvah, Chado,

Chanoyu, Commemoration, Common Riding, Coronation, Doseh, Durbar, Encaenia, Enthronement, Etiquette, Eucharist, Flypast, Form(al), Formality, Gongyo, Habdalah, Havdalah, Havdoloh, Heraldry, Investiture, Koto(w), Matsuri, Maundy, Mummery, Observance, Occasion, Ordination, Pageantry, Parade, Pomp, Powwow, Protocol, Rite, Rite of passage, Ritual, Sacrament, Sado, Seder, Service, State, Sun dance, Tea, Topping-out, Trooping (the Colour), Unveiling, Usage

Cert(ain), Certainty Absolute, Actual, Assured, Banker, Bound, Cast-iron, Cinch, Cocksure, Confident, Conviction, Convinced, Decided, Definite, Doubtless, Exact, Fact, Fate, Indubitable, Inevitable, Infallible, Lock, Monte, Nap, Needly, One, Positive, Poz, Precise, Racing, Red-hot, Shoo-in, Siccar, Sicker, Snip, Some, Stiff, → SURE, Sure-fire, Truth, Type, Unerring, Yes

Certificate, Certified, Certify Accredit, Affirm, Assure, Attest, Bene decessit, Birth, Bond, Chit, Cocket, Confirm, Credential, Death, Debenture, Depose, Diploma, Docket, Document, End-user, Enseal, Gold, Guarantee, Landscrip, Licence, Lines, Medical, MOT, Notarise, Paper, Patent, Proven, Savings, School, Scrip, Scripophily, Security, Share, Smart-ticket, Stamp note, Stock, Sworn, Talon, Testamur, Testimonial, Treasury, U, Unruly, Voucher, Warrant

Cete(acean) Badger

Chad Dimpled, Swinging

Chafe(r), Chafing Chunter, Fray, Fret, Gall, Harass, Intertrigo, Irritate, Pan, → RUB, Seethe, Worry

Chain(s), Chained Acre's-breadth, Albert, Anklet, Bicycle, Bind, Bond, Bracelet, Bucket, Cable, Catena, Choke, Cistron, Closed, Daisy, Decca, Drive, Dynasty, Engineer's, Esses, Fanfarona, Fetter, Fob, Food, Furlong, Gleipnir, Gunter's, Gyve, Human, Light, Line, Lockaway, Markov, Mayor, Micella(r), Micelle, Noria, Pennine, Pitch, Range, Rode, Roller, Seal, → SERIES, Shackle, Slang, Snow, Span, Sprocket, String, Strobila, Team, Tug, Watch

Chair Balloon-back, Basket, Bath, Bench, Bentwood, Berbice, Bergère, Birthing, Bosun's, Butterfly, Camp, Cane, Captain's, Carver, Club, Cromwellian, Curule, Deck, Dining, Director's, Easy, Elbow, Electric, Estate, Fauteuil, Fiddle-back, Folding, Frithstool, Garden, Gestatorial, Guérite, High, Jampan, Jampanee, Jampani, Ladder-back, Lounger, Love-seat, Lug, Merlin, Morris, Nursing, Pew, Preside, Professorate, Recliner, Rocker, Ruckseat, Rush-bottomed, Sedan, Settee, Steamer, Stool, Straight, Sugan, Swivel, Throne, Wainscot, Wheel, Windsor, Wing

Chairman Convener, Emeritus, Humph, Mao, MC, Pr(a)eses, Prof, Prolocutor, Sheraton, Speaker

Chalcedony Enhydros

Chalk(y) Black, Calcareous, Cauk, Cawk, Crayon, Credit, Cretaceous, Dentin, French, Soapstone, White(n), Whit(en)ing

Challenge(r), Challenging Acock, Assay, Call, Cartel, Champion, Charge, Confront, Contest, Dare, Defy, Dispute, Face, Gage, Gainsay, Gauntlet, Glove, Hazard, Hen(ner), Iconoclasm, Impugn, Insubordinate, Oppugn, Provoke, Query, Question, Recuse, Sconce, Shuttle, Tackle, Taker, Tall order, Tank, Threat, Tongue-twister, Vie, Whynot

Chamber(s) Anteroom, Atrium, Auricle, Bladder, Camarilla, Camera, Casemate, Cavern, Cavitation, Cavity, Cell(a), Chanty, Cloud, Cofferdam, Columbarian, Combustion, Cubicle, Decompression, Dene-hole, Dolmen, Echo, Float, Fogou, Fume, Gas, Gazunder, Hall, Horrors, Hyperbaric, Hypogea, Ionization, Jerry, Jordan, Kiva, Lavatory, Lethal, Locule, Manhole, Manifold, Mattamore, Po(t), Priest('s)-hole, Privy, Roum, Serdab, Silo, Spark, Star, Stateroom, Steam-chest, Swell-box, Synod, Thalamus, Undercroft, Upper, Utricle, Vault, Ventricle, Zeta

Champ(er), Champers Bite, Chafe, Chew, Chomp, Eat, Gnash, Gnaw, Ivories, Mash, Morsure, Munch

Champagne Boy, Bubbly, Charlie, Fizz, Gigglewater, Krug, Mumm, Pop, Sillery, Simkin, Simpkin, Stillery, Troyes, Widow

Champion(s) Ace, Adopt, Ali, Apostle, Artegal, Assert, Back, Belt, Brill(iant), Campeador, Cid, Cock, Defend, Don Quixote, Doucepere, Douzeper, Dymoke,

Endorse, Enoch, Espouse, Gladiator, Gun, Harry, →**HERO**, Herodotus, Horse, Kemp, Kemper(yman), King, Knight, Maintain, Matchless, Messiah, Messias, Neil, Paladin, Palmerin, Peerless, Perseus, Promachos, Proponent, Protagonist, Roland, St Anthony, St David, St Denis, St George, St James, St Patrick, Seven, Spiffing, Spokesman, Star, Support, Title-holder, Tribune, Upholder, Victor, Wardog, →**WINNER**, World-beater, Yokozuna

Chance (upon), Chancy Accident, Adventitious, Aleatory, Aunter, Bet, Break, Buckley's, Cast, Casual, Cavel, Contingent, Dice, Earthly, Even, →**FATE**, Fluke, Fortuitous, Fortuity, Fortune, →**GAMBLE**, Game, Hap, Happenstance, Hobnob, Iffy, Kevel, Light, Look-in, Lot, →**LOTTERY**, Luck, Meet, Mercy, Occasion, Occur, Odds, Opening, Opportunity, Peradventure, Posse, Potluck, Prayer, Probability, Prospect, Random, Rise, Risk, Serendipity, Shot, Slant, Snip, Spec, Stake, Stochastic, Stray, Sweep, Toss-up, Treble, Turn, Tychism, Ventre, Venture, Wager, Wild card

Change(able), Changes, Changing About-face, Adapt, Adjust, Agio, Aleatoric, →**ALTER**, Amendment, Amoeba, Attorn, Backtrack, Barter, Become, Bob-major, Capricious, Cash, Catalysis, Cent, Channel-hop, Chop, Chump, Climacteric, Cline, Commute, Convert, Coppers, Covary, Cut, Denature, Departure, Development, Dissolve, Diversion, Ectopia, Edit, Enallage, Eustatic, Evolution, Exchange, Find, Flighty, Float, Fluctuate, Flux, Grandsire, Guard, Gybe, Histogen, Inflect, Innovate, Instead, Kaleidoscope, Killcrop, Labile, Make-over, Mercurial, Metabolic, Metabolise, Metamorphosis, Metathesise, Mew, Mobile, Modify, Morph, Mutable, Mutation, Ontogeny, Parallax, Paraphrase, Peal, Pejoration, Permute, Prisere, Protean, Quarter, Rat, Realise, Recant, Rectify, Redo, Reform, Refraction, Reshuffle, Rest, Revise, Rework, Sandhi, Sd, Seasonal, Seesaw, Shake-out, Shake-up, Shift, Silver, Small, Substitute, Swap, Swing, Switch, Tolsel, Tolsey, Tolzey, Transfer, Transfiguration, Transform, Transition, Transmute, Transpose, Transubstantial, Triple, Turn (about), Tweak, Uncertain, Upheaval, U-turn, Vagary, Variant, Variation, Vary, Veer, Versatile, Volatile, Volte-face, Weathercock, Wheel, Wow

▷ **Change(d)** *may indicate* an anagram

Channel Access, Airwave, Al Jazeera, Aqueduct, Artery, Beagle, Bed, Billabong, Binaural, Bristol, Canal, Chimb, Chime, Chine, Chute, Conduit, Course, Creek, Culvert, Cut, Cutting, Datagram, Distribution, Ditch, Drain, Duct, Dyke, Ea, Eau, English, Estuary, Euripus, Fairway, Feeder, Floodway, Flume, Foss, Funnel, Furrow, Gat, Gate, Geo, Gio, Glyph, Gully, Gut, Gutter, Head-race, Ingate, Katavothron, Khor, Kill, Kos, Kyle, Lake, La Manche, Lane, Latch, Leat, Lee-lane, Leet, Limber, Major, Meatus, Medium, Minch, Moat, Mozambique, Multiplex, Narrows, North, Offtake, Penstock, Pentland Firth, Pescadores, Pipeline, Qanat, Race, Raceway, Rean, Rebate, Rigol(l), Rigolets, Rivulet, Run, Sea-gate, Seaway, Sewer, Shatt-el-Arab, Shunt, Sinus, Sky, Sloot, Sluice, Sluit, Sny(e), Solent, Solway Firth, Sound, Sow, Spillway, Sprue, Strait, Suez, Sure, Swash, Tailrace, Tideway, Trough, Ureter, Vein, Wasteweir, Watercourse, Waterspout, Yucatan

Chant Anthem, Antiphon, Cantillate, Cantus, Chaunt, Decantate, Euouae, Evovae, Gregorian, Haka, Harambee, Hymn, Incantation, Intone, Introit, Mantra(m), Motet, Pennillion-singing, Proper, Psalm, Sing, Slogan, Te Deum, The Reproaches, Yell

Chaos, Chaotic Abyss, Anarchy, Confusion, Disorder, Fitna, Fractal, Goat fuck, Havoc, Hun-tun, Jumble, Maelstrom, Mayhem, Mess, Muddle, Muss, Shambles, Snafu, Tohu bohu, Turmoil

▷ **Chaotic** *may indicate* an anagram

Chapel Alamo, Bethel, Bethesda, Beulah, Cha(u)ntry, Chevet, Ebenezer, Feretory, Galilee, Lady, Oratory, Proprietary, Sacellum, Sistine

▷ **Chaps** *may indicate* an anagram

Chapter Accidents, C, Canon, Cap, Capitular, Ch, Chap, Cr, Division, Episode, Lodge, Phase, Section, Social, Sura(h), Verse

Character(s) Aesc, Alphabet, Ampersand, Ampussyand, Aura, Backslash, Brand, Calibre, Case, Cipher, Clef, Cliff, Climate, Complexion, Contour, Credit, Digamma, Dramatis personae, Emoticon, Ess, Essence, Eta, Ethos, →**FEATURE**, Fish, Fist,

Form, Grain, Grass, Grit, Hair, Hieroglyphic, Hue, Ideogram, Ideograph, Italic,
Kern, Kind, La(m)bda, Letter, Logogram, Make-up, Mark, Mu, Nagari, →NATURE,
Nu, Ogam, Ogham, Pahlavi, Pantaloon, Part, Pehlevi, Person(a), Personage,
→PERSONALITY, Phonogram, Physiognomy, Protagonist, Psi, Reference,
Reference-mark, Repute, Rho, Role, Rune, Runic, Sampi, San, Sel(f), Sigma, Sirvente,
Slash, Sonancy, Sort, Stamp, Subscript, Superhero, Superscript(ion), Swung dash,
Syllabary, Symbol, Tab, Testimonial, Ton(e), Trait, Uncial, Vav, Vee, Waw, Wen

Characterise(d), Characterism, Characteristic(s) Attribute, Aura, Cast,
Colour, Distinctive, Earmark, Ethos, Example, Facies, Feature, Hair, Hallmark, Has,
Headmark, Idiomatic, Idiosyncrasy, Jizz, Keystroke, Lineament, Mark, Mien, Nature,
Notate, Peculiar, Persona, Point, Property, Quality, Stigma, Strangeness, Streak, Style,
Typical, Vein, Way

Charge(s), Charged, Charger Access, Accusal, Accuse, Aerate, Agist, Allege,
Anion, Annulet, Arraign, Ascribe, Assault, Baton, Battery, Bear, Behest, Blame,
Brassage, Brush, Buckshot, Bum rap, Burden, Care, Carrying, Cathexis, Cellarage,
Commission, Community, Complaint, Congestion, Corkage, Cost, Count, Cover,
Criminate, Damage, Debit, Delate, Delf, Delph, Demurrage, Depth, Depute, Directive,
Dittay, Dockage, Due, Duty, Dynamise, Electric, Electron, Entrust, Entry, Exit,
Expense, Fare, Fee, Fill, Fixed, Flag fall, Fleur-de-lis, Floating, Flock, Freight, Fullage,
Fuse, Fusil, Fuze, Gazump, Giron, Gravamen, Gyron, →HERALDIC, Horse, Hot,
Hypothec, Impeach, Impute, Indict, Inescutcheon, Inform, Instinct, Ion, Isoelectric,
Last, Levy, Lien, Lioncel(le), Lionel, Live, Load, Mandate, Mine, Mount, Nuclear,
Objure, Obtest, Onrush, Onslaught, Onus, Ordinary, Orle, Overhead, Pastoral,
Pervade, Pew-rent, Plaint, Positive, Premium, Prime, Prix fixe, Q, Quayage, Rack-rent,
Rap, Rate, Recrimination, Red-dog, Rent, Report, Reprise, Reverse, Roundel, Run,
→RUSH, Saddle, Service, Specific, Stampede, Steed, Storm, Supplement, Tariff,
Tax(ation), Tear, Terms, Tilt, Toll, →TRAY, Tressure, Trickle, Trust, Tutorage, Upfill,
Vaire, Vairy, Verdoy, Vigorish, Ward, Warhead, Warhorse, Wharfage, Yardage

Charitable, Charity Aid, Alms, Alms-deed, Awmous, Benign, Breadline, Caritas,
Chugger, Dole, Dorcas, Eleemosynary, Good works, Kiwanis, Largesse, Leniency,
Liberal, Lion, Love, Mercy, Oddfellow, Openhanded, Oxfam, Pelican, Philanthropic,
Samaritan, Zakat

Charlock Runch

Charm(er), Charmed, Charming Abracadabra, Abrasax, Abraxas, Agacerie,
Allure, Amulet, Appeal, Aroma, Attraction, Bangle, Beguile, Bewitch, Captivate,
Charisma, Chocolate box, Circe, Comether, Cramp-bone, Cute, Cutie, Debonair,
Delight(ful), Emerods, Enamour, Enchant, Engaging, →ENTRANCE, Fascinate,
Fay, Fetching, Fetish, Grace, Greegree, Gri(s)gris, Hand of glory, Horseshoe, Houri,
Incantation, Juju, Magnetic, Mascot, Mojo, Nice, Obeah, Obi(a), Periapt, Phylactery,
Porte-bonheur, Prince, Pull, Quaint, Quark, Ravish, Siren, Smoothie, Spellbind,
Suave, Sweetness, Taking, Talisman, Telesm, Tiki, Trinket, Unction, Voodoo,
Winsome

▷ **Charming** *may indicate* an anagram

Chart(ed), Charting Abac, Alignment, Bar, Breakeven, Card, Diagram, Eye,
Flip, Flow, Gantt, Graph, Histogram, Horoscope, Hydrography, Isogram, Isopleth,
List, Magna Carta, →MAP, Mappemond, Movement, Nomogram, Plot, Portolano,
Ringelmann, Run, Snellen, Social, Sociogram, Table, Test, Timetable, Waggoner,
Weather

Charta, Charter Book, Covenant, Freedom, Hire, Lease, Let, Novodamus, Rent

Chase(d), Chaser, Chasing Cannock, Chace, Chevy, Chivy, Ciseleur, Ciselure,
Course, Cranbome, Decorate, Drink, Game, Harass, Hound, →HUNT, Inlaid, Jumper,
Oxo, Pursuit, Race, Scorse, Sic(k), Snag, Steeple, Sue, Suit, Wild-goose

Chasm Abyss, Fissure, Gap, Gorge, Gulf, Rent, Schism, Yawn

Chaste, Chastity Aggie, Agnes, Attic, Celibate, Classic, Clean, Continent, Fatima,
Florimell, Ines, Innocent, Modesty, Nessa, Platonic, →PURE, Vestal, Virginal, Virtue

Chat, Chatter(box), Chatterer Babble, Bavardage, Bird, Blab(ber), Blatherskite,
Blether, Campanero, Causerie, Chelp, Chew the fat, Chinwag, Clack, Clishmaclaver,

Confab(ulate), Converse, Cosher, Coze, Crack, Dialogue, Froth, Gab(ble), Gas, Gibble-gabble, Gossip, Gup, Hobnob, Jabber, Jargon, Jaw, Kilfud, Liaise, Madge, Mag(pie), Nashgab, Natter, Patter, Pie, Pourparler, Prate, Prattle, Rabbit, Rabble, Rap, Rattle, Scuttlebutt, Shmoose, Shoot the breeze, Stone, Talk, Talkee-talkee, Tattle, Twattle, Waffle, Whin, Windbag, Witter, Wongi, Yacketyyak, Yad(d)a-yad(d)a-yad(d)a, Yak, Yarn, Yatter, Yellow-breasted, Yoking

Cheap A bon marché, Bargain, Base, Catchpenny, Cheesy, Chintzy, Cut-price, Downmarket, Gimcrack, Giveaway, Knockdown, Low, Off-peak, Poor, Sacrifice, Shoddy, Steerage, Stingy, Tatty, Tawdry, Ticky-tacky, Tinpot, Tinselly, Trashy, Trivial, Twopenny-halfpenny, Undear, Vile

▷ **Cheap** *may indicate* a d- or p- start to a word

Cheat(ers), Cheating Bam, Bamboozle, Beguile, Bilk, Bite(r), Bob, Bonnet, Bubble, Bucket, Bullock, Bunce, Burn, Cabbage, Cardsharp(er), Charlatan, Chiaus, Chicane(ry), Chisel, Chouse, Clip, Cod, Cog(ger), Colt, Con, Cony-catcher, Cozen, Crib, Cross, Cross-bite(r), Cuckold, Cully, Defraud, Delude, Diddle, Dingo, Dish, Do, Doublecross, Double-dealer, Duckshove, Dupe, Escroc, Faitor, Fiddle, Finagle, Fix, Flam, Flanker, Fleece, Fob, Foister, Fox, Fraud, Gaff, Gip, Glasses, Gudgeon, Gum, Gyp, Hoax, Hocus, Hoodwink, Hornswoggle, Horse, Intake, Jockey, Magsman, Mulct, Mump, Nick, Pasteboard, Picaro(on), Poop, Queer, Rib, Rig, Rogue, Rook, Rush, Scam, Screw, Screw over, Sell, Shaft, Sharper, Sharpie, Short-change, Slur, Smouch, Snap, Stack, Stiff, Sting, Swindle, Thimble-rigging, Trepan, Trick(ster), Trim, Twister, Two-time, Welch, Welsh, Wheedle

Check Abort, Arrest, Audit, Ba(u)lk, Bauk, Bill, Block, Bridle, Collate, Compesce, Confirm, Control, Count, Cramp, Cross-index, Curb, Dam, Damp, Detain, Detent, Discovered, Dogs-tooth, Examine, Foil, Forestall, Frustrate, Halt, Hamper, Hobble, Houndstooth, Inhibit, Inspect, Jerk, Jerque, Let, Limit(ation), Mate, Medical, Meter, Monitor, Observe, Overhaul, Parity, Perpetual, Prevent, Rain, Reality, Rebuff, Rebuke, Rein, Repress, Reprime, Repulse, Reread, → **RESTRAIN**, Revoke, Saccade, Screen, Service, Setback, Shepherd's, Shorten, Sit-upon, Sneap, Sneb, Snib, Snub, Sound, Spot, Standard, Std, → **STEM**, Stent, Stint, Stocktake, Stop, Stunt, Suppress, Tab, Tally, Tartan, Tattersall, Test, Thwart, Tick, Trash, Verify, Vet

Cheek(y) Alforja, Audacity, Buccal, Chap, Chit, Chollers, Chutzpah, Crust, Cub, Flippant, Fresh, Gall, Gena(l), Gobby, Gum, Hussy, Jowl, Lip, Malapert, Malar, Masseter, Neck, Nerve, Noma, Pert, Presumption, Quean, Sass, Sauce, Sideburns, Uppity, Wang, Yankie, Zygoma

Cheer(s), Cheerful(ness), Cheering Acclaim, Agrin, Applaud, Arrivederci, Banzai, Barrack, Blithe, Bonnie, Bravo, Bright, Bronx, Bubbly, Buck, Buoy, Cadgy, Canty, Carefree, Cherry, Chin-chin, Chipper, Chirpy, Chirrupy, → **COMFORT**, Crouse, Debonair, Drink, Ease, Elate, Elevate, Encourage, Enliven, Exhilarate, Exuberant, Festive, Genial, Gladden, Happy-go-lucky, Hearten, Hilarity, Holiday, Hooch, Hoorah, Hurra(h), Huzzah, Insouciance, Jocund, Jovial, Kia-ora, L'allegro, Light-hearted, Lightsome, Lively, Meal, Olé, Optimistic, Ovate, Peart, Perky, Please, Praise, Prosit, Rah, Riant, Rivo, Roar, Root, Rosy, Rumbustious, Shout, Sko(a)l, Slainte, Sonsie, Sunny, Ta, Tata, Thanks, Three, Tiger, Tiggerish, Toodle-oo, Up, Upbeat, Warm, Winsome, Yell

Cheese, Cheesy American, Amsterdam, Appenzell, Asiago, Bel Paese, Blue, Blue vein, Boc(c)oncini, Boursin, Brie, Caboc, Caerphilly, Cambazola, Camembert, Cantal, Casein, Caseous, Cheddar, Cheshire, Chessel, Chèvre, Colby, Cottage, Coulommiers, Cream, Crowdie, Curd, Damson, Danish blue, Derby, Dolcelatte, Double Gloucester, Dunlop, Dutch, Edam, Emmental(er), Emmenthal(er), Ermite, Esrom, Ewe, Fet(a), Fontina, Fromage frais, Fynbo, Gloucester, Goat, Gorgonzola, Gouda, Grana Padano, Green, Gruyère, Halloumi, Hard, Havarti, Huntsman, Ilchester, Islay, Jarlsberg®, Junket, Kebbock, Kebbuck, Kenno, Killarney, Lancashire, Leicester, Lemon, Limburg(er), Lymeswold®, Macaroni, Manchego, Mascarpone, Monterey Jack, Mousetrap, Mozzarella, Mu(e)nster, Mycella, Neufchatel, Numero uno, Oka, Orkney, Paneer, Parmesan, Pecorino, Pont l'Eveque, Port Salut, Pot, Provolone, Quark, Raclette, Rarebit, Reblochon, Red Leicester, Rennet, Ricotta, Romano, Roquefort,

Sage Derby, Samso, Sapsago, Skyr, Stilton®, Stone, Stracchino, Swiss, Taleggio, Tilsit, Tofu, Truckle, Vacherin, VIP, Wensleydale, Whey, Yarg

Chef Commis, Escoffier, Oliver, Ramsay

Chemical Acid, Acrolein, Adrenalin®, Alar, Aldehyde, Alkali, Alum(ina), Amide, Avertin, Barilla, Bute, Camphene, Camphor, Carbide, Caseose, Catalyst, Cephalin, Coal tar, Developer, Dopamine, Encephalin, Ethanal, Ethoxy, Ethyl, Fixer, Fluoride, Formyl, Fungicide, Furosemide, Gibbsite, Glutamine, Glycol, Halon, Harmin, Heptane, Hexylene, Histamine, Hormone, Hypo, ICI, Imine, Indican, Inositol, Interleukin, Lewisite, Lipid, Masking-agent, Massicot, Naioxone, Napalm, Naphtha, Natron, Neurotransmitter, Nitre, Nonylphenol, Oestrogen, Olefin, Olein, Oxide, Oxysalt, Paraben, Pentane, Pentene, Pentyl, Peptide, Phenol, Phenyl, Pheromone, Potash, Potassa, Ptomaine, Reagent, Resorcin, Sequestrant, Soup, Stearate, Strontia, Styrene, Sulphide, Terpene, Thio-salt, Toluol, Trimer, Tritide, Weedkiller, Xylol

Chemist Analyst, Apothecary, Dispenser, Druggist, Drugstore, Pharmacist, Pothecary

Chemistry Alchemy, Alchymy, Inorganic, Organic, Physical, Radiation, Spageric, Spagiric, Spagyric, Stinks, Stoecheometry, Stoechiometry

Cheque Blank, Bouncer, Giro, Gregory, Stumer, Tab, Traveller's

Cherry (tree) Amarelle, Amazon, Ball, Barbados, Bigaroon, Bigarreau, Blackheart, Bladder, Cerise, Choke, Cornelian, Gean, Ground, Heart, Jerusalem, Kearton, Kermes, Kermesite, Malpighia, Marasca, Maraschino, May-duke, Maz(z)ard, Merry, Morel(lo), Prunus, Red, Whiteheart

Chervil Cow-parsley

Chessman Bishop, Black, Castle, Cheque, Horse, King, Knight, Pawn, Pin, Queen, Rook, White

Chest(y) Ark, Bahut, Bosom, Box, Breast, Buist, Bunker, Bureau, Bust, Caisson, Cap-case, Case, Cassone, Chapel, Charter, Chiffonier, Coffer, Coffin, Coffret, Commode, Cub, Girnel, Hope, Hutch, Inro, Kist, Larnax, Locker, Lowboy, Medicine, Ottoman, Pectoral, Pereion, Pigeon, Pleural, Ribcage, Safe, Scrine, Scryne, Shrine, Sternum, Tallboy, Tea, Thorax, Toolbox, Treasure, Trunk, Wangun, Wanigan, War

Chestnut Auburn, Badious, Ch, Chincapin, Chinese, Chinkapin, Chinquapin, Cliché, Conker, Favel(l), Hoary, Marron, Marron glacé, Moreton Bay, Roan, Russet, Saligot, Soare, Sorrel, Spanish, Sweet, Water

Chew(ing) Bite, Champ, Chaw, Crunch, Cud, Gnaw, Gum, Manducate, Masticate, Maul, Meditate, Moop, Mou(p), Munch, Ruminate, Siri(h), Spearmint

Chic Dapper, Debonair, Elegant, Heroin, In, Kick, Modish, Posh, Smart, Soigné, Stylish, Swish, Tonish, Trim

Chick(en) Battery, Biddy, Broiler, Cheeper, Chittagong, Chuckie, Clutch, Cochin(-China), Coward, Cowherd, Craven, Drumstick, Eirack, Gutless, Hen, Howtowdie, Kiev, Layer, Marengo, Minorca, Niderling, Pavid, Poltroon, Poot, Pope's nose, Poult, Pout, Prairie, Precocial, Quitter, Roaster, Scaredy-cat, Spatchcock, Spring, Squab, Supreme, Sussex, Timorous, Unheroic, Wimp, Windy, Wishbone, Wyandotte, Yellow

Chief(tain) Ag(h)a, Arch, Ardrigh, Boss, Caboceer, Cacique, Calif, Caliph, Capital, Capitan, Capitayn, Capo, Caradoc, Cazique, Ch, Chagan, Dat(t)o, DG, Dominant, Duke, Emir, First, Foremost, Geronimo, Grand, Haggis, →**HEAD**, Hereward, Jarl, Kaid, Keystone, King, Leader, →**MAIN**, Mass, Mocuddum, Mokaddam, Mugwump, Muqaddam, Nawab, Nizam, Nkosi, Oba, Overlord, Pendragon, Premier, Primal, Prime, Principal, Quanah, Raja(h), Rajpramukh, Rangatira, Ratoo, Ratu, Sachem, Sagamore, Sardar, Sarpanch, Sea-king, Sheikh, Sirdar, Staple, Sudder, Supreme, Tanist, Tank, Taxiarch, Thane, Top

Child(ren), Childhood, Childish Aerie, Alannah, Auf, Babe, Baby, Bach(ch)a, Badger, Bairn, Bambino, Bantling, Boy, Brat, Brood, Butter-print, Ch, Changeling, Cherub, Chick, Chickabiddy, Chit, Collop, Cub, Dream, Duddie weans, Elfin, Eyas, Feral, Foundling, Gangrel, Ge(i)t, Girl, Gyte, Heir, Hurcheon, Imp, Infant, Issue, It, Jailbait, Jejune, Juvenile, Kid, Kiddie(wink), Kiddy, Kidult, Kinder, Lad, Limb, Litter, Littlie, Mamzer, Minion, Minor, Mite, Moppet, Munchkin, Naive, Nipper, Nursling, Offspring, Pantywaist, Papoose, Piccaninny, Pickin, Problem, Progeny, Puerile, Puss,

Putto, Ragamuffin, Rip, Romper, Rug rat, Scion, Seed, Siblings, Smout, Smowt, Sprog, Street arab, Subteen, Ted, Tike, Toddle(r), Tot(tie), Totty, Trot, Tweenie, Tyke, Urchin, Wean, Weanel, Weanling, Weeny-bopper, Whelp, Young, Youngster, Younker, Youth

Chile(an) CH, Mapuche

Chill(er), Chilly Bleak, →COLD, Cool, Cryogen, Frappé, Freeze, Freon®, Frigid, Frosty, Gelid, Ice, Iciness, Laze, Mimi, Oorie, Ourie, Owrie, Parky, Raw, Refrigerate, Rigor, Scare

Chime(s) Bell, Clam, Cymar, Jingle, Peal, Rhime, Semantron, Tink, →TOLL

Chimney (pot), Chimney corner Can, Cow(l), Femerall, Flare stack, Flue, Funnel, Lug, Lum, Smokestack, Stack, Stalk, Tallboy, Tunnel

Chimney-sweep Chummy

China(man), Chinese Ami, Amoy, Bone, Boxer, Bud(dy), Cameoware, Cantonese, Catayan, Cathay, Celestial, Ch, Chelsea, Chow, Coalport, Cochin, Cock, Colleague, Confucius, Crackle, Crockery, Delft, Derby, Dresden, Eggshell, Etrurian, Goss, Hakka, Han, Hizen, Hmong, Imari, Ironstone, Kanji, Kaolin, Kuo-yu, Limoges, Macanese, Manchu, Manchurian, Mandarin, Mangi, Maoist, Mate, Meissen, Middle kingdom, Min, Ming, Minton, Oppo, Pal, Pareoean, Pekingese, Pe-tsai, Pinyin, Porcelain, →POTTERY, Putonghua, Queensware, Quina, Rockingham, Royal Worcester, Rusticware, Semiporcelain, Seric, Sèvres, Shanghai, Sinaean, Sinic, Sino-, Spode®, Sun Yat-sen, Tai-ping, Taoist, Teng, Tocharian, Tungus, Uigur, Wal(l)y, Ware, Wedgwood®, Whiteware, Willow pattern, Willowware, Worcester, Wu, Yao, Yellow peril

▷ **Chip** *may indicate* an anagram

Chip(s) Blitter, Bo(a)st, Carpenter, Counter, Cut, Deep-fried, Fish, Flake, Fragment, Hack, Knap, Micro, Nacho(s), Nick, Pin, Shaving, Silicon, Spale, Spall, Splinter, Tease, Tortilla, Transputer, Virus

Chippendale Chinese

Chirp(y), Chirrup Cheep, Cherup, Chirm, Chirr, Cicada, Peep, Pip, Pipe, Pitter, Stridulate, Trill, Tweet, Twitter

Chisel(ler), Chisel-like Bam, Boaster, Bolster, Bur, Burin, Carve, Cheat, Clip, Drove, Firmer, Gad, Mason, Scalpriform, Scauper, Scorper, Sculpt, Slick, Sting

Chit Docket, Girl, Memo, Note, Voucher

Chivalry, Chivalrous Brave, Bushido, Courtly, Datin, Gallant, Gent, Grandisonian

Chocolate Aero, Brown, Cacao, Carob, Cocoa, Dragee, Ganache, Neapolitan, Noisette, Pinole, Praline, Rolo®, Truffle, Vermicelli

Choice, Choose, Choosy, Chosen Adopt, Anthology, Appoint, Aryan, Cherry-pick, Cull, Dainty, Decide, Druthers, Eclectic, Elect, Elite, Esnecy, Fine, Fork, Free will, Hercules, Hobson's, Leet, Leve, Lief, List, Opt, Option, Or, Ossian, Peach, Peacherino, Peculiar, →PICK, Picking, Plum(p), Precious, Predilect, Prefer, Proairesis, Rare, Recherché, →SELECT, Superb, Try(e), Via media, Volition, Wale

Choir, Choral, Chorister, Chorus Antiphony, Antistrophe, Anvil, Apse, Burden, Chorister, Choryphaeus, Dawn, Decani, Faburden, Fauxbourdon, Group, Hallelujah, Harmony, Hymeneal, Motet, Parabasis, Precentor, Quirister, →REFRAIN, Reprise, Schola cantorum, Serenata, Singing, Strophe, Treble, Triad

Choke(r) Accloy, Block, Clog, Die, Gag, Silence, Smoor, Smore, Smother, Stifle, Stop, Strangle(hold), Strangulate, →THROTTLE, Warp

Choler Irascibility, Yellow bile

Chop, Chops, Chopper(s), Choppy Adze, Air tax, Ax(e), Cakehole, Celt, Charge, Cheek, Chump, Cleave, Côtelette, Cuff, Cutlet, Dice, Fell(er), Flew, Hack, Hash, Helicopter, Hew, Ivory, Karate, Lop, Mince, Mouth, Rotaplane, Rough, Split, Standing, Suey, Teeth, Underhand, Wang

Chord(s) Altered, Arpeggio, Barré, Common, Diameter, Harmony, Intonator, Nerve, Sixth, Triad, Vocal

Chorea Sydenham's

Chow Nosh

Christ Ecce homo, Lamb of God, Logos, Messiah, Paschal Lamb, Saviour, Son (of God), Son of man, X

Christen(ing) Baptise, Launch, Name-day

Christian(ity) Adventist, Albigenses, Antioch, Beghard, Believer, Cathar(ist), Colossian, Coptic, Dior, Donatist, D(o)ukhobor, Ebionite, Fletcher, Galilean, Giaour, Gilbertine, Gnostic, Goy, Holy roller, Homo(i)ousian, Jehovah's Witness, Maronite, Marrano, Melchite, Melkite, Molinism, Monarchian, Monophysite, Moral, Mozarab, Mutineer, Nazarene, Nestorian, Phalange, Pilgrim, Protestant, Quartodeciman, RC, Sabotier, Scientist, SCM, Solifidian, Traditor, Uniat(e), Unitarian, Waldensian, Wesleyan, Xian, Zwinglian

Christmas(time) Beetle, Box, Cactus, Card, Carol, Chrissie, Day, Dec, Island, Nativity, Noel, Nowel(l), Pudding, Stocking, Xmas, Yuletide

Chronicle(r) Anglo-Saxon, Annal, Brut, Calendar, Diary, Froissart, Hall, Historiographer, History, Holinshed, Logographer, Narrative, Paralipomena, Parian, →RECORD, Register, Stow

Church Abbey, Armenian, Auld Licht, Autocephalous, Basilica, Bethel, Bethesda, Brood, Byzantine, →CATHEDRAL, CE, Ch, Chapel, Chevet, Classis, Clergy, Collegiate, Congregational, Coptic, Delubrum, Easter (Orthodox), EC, Ecumenical, Episcopal, Episcopalian, Established, Faith, Fold, Free, High, Institutional, Kirk, Lateran, Low, Lutheran, Maronite, Melchite, Methodist, Minster, Moonie, Moravian, Mormon, Mother, National, Nazarene, Old Light, Oratory, Orthodox, Parish, Peculiar, Prebendal, Presbyterian, Ratana, RC, Reformed, Rome, Schism house, Schism shop, Secession, Shrine, Smyrna, Stave, Steeple, Steeplehouse, Tabernacle, Temple, Title, Titular, Transept, Unification, United Free, Wee Free, Western

Churchgoer, Churchman, Churchwarden Anglican, Azymite, Barnabite, Cameronian, Cantor, Marrowman, Moonie, Pew-opener, Predicant, Predikant, Racovian, Romanist, Ruridecanal, Socinian, Spike, Subchanter, Subdeacon, Succentor, Ubiquitarian, Verger, Vestryman

Church house Deanery

Churl(ish) Ill-natured

Ciao Adieu, Adios, Aloha

Cicerone Guide

CID Sûreté

Cider Drink, Hard, Perry, Scrumpy, Sweet

Cigar(ette), Cigarette cards Beedi(e), Bidi, Biftah, Bifter, Bumper, Burn, Camberwell carrot, Cancer stick, Caporal, Cartophily, Cheroot, Cigarillo, Claro, Coffin nail, Conch, Concha, Corona, Dog-end, Doob, Durry, Fag, Filter-tip, Gasper, Giggle(-stick), Havana, Joint, Locofoco, Long-nine, Loosies, Maduro, Manilla, Number, Panatella, Paper-cigar, Perfecto, Puritano, Reefer, Regalia, Roach, Roll-up, Segar, Smoke, Snout, Splif(f), Stogie, Stog(e)y, Stompie, Tab, Twist, Weed, Whiff, Woodbine, Zol

Cinch Duck soup, Easy, Stroll

Cinema(s) Art house, Big screen, Biograph, Bioscope, Circuit, Drive-in, Films, Fleapit, Flicks, Grindhouse, IMAX®, Megaplex, Movies, Multiplex, Multiscreen, Mutoscope, New Wave, Nickelodeon, Nouvelle Vague, Odeon, Picture palace, Pictures, Plaza, Scope, Theatre, Tivoli

Cinnamon, Cinnamon stone Canella, Cassia (bark), Essonite, Hessonite, Saigon, Spice

Circle Almacantar, Almucantar, Annulet, Antarctic, Arctic, Circassian, Co, Colure, Company, Compass, Corn, Corolla, Coterie, Cromlech, Crop, Cycloid, Cyclolith, Dip, Disc, Dress, Druidical, Eccentric, Ecliptic, Embail, Enclose, Engird, Epicyclic, Equant, Equator, Equinoctial, Euler's, Fairy ring, Family, Fraternity, Full, Galactic, Girdle, Gloriole, Great, Gyrate, Gyre, Halo, Henge, Hoop, Horizon, Hour, Hut, Inner, Inorb, Lap, Longitude, Loop, Magic, Malebolge, Mandala, Meridian, Mohr's, Mural, Nimbus, O, Orb, Orbit, Parhelic, Parquet, Parterre, Penannular, Peristalith, Pitch, Polar, Quality, Red-line, Rigol, →RING, Rondure, Rotate, Roundlet, Seahenge, Sentencing, Set, Setting, Small, Sphere, Stemme, Stone, Stonehenge, Striking, Surround, Tinchel,

Tondino, Traffic, Transit, Tropic, Turning, Umbel, Upper, Vertical, Vicious, Vienna, Virtuous, Volt, Wheel, Whorl

Circuit(-board), Circuitous Ambit, AND, Autodyne, Bridge, Bus, Bypass, Chipset, Closed, Comparator, Daughterboard, Diocese, Discriminator, Dolby®, Equivalent, Eyre, Feedback, Gate, Gyrator, Half-adder, Highway, IC, Integrated, Interface, Lap, Le Mans, Limiter, Live, Logic, Loop, Microchip, Microprocessor, Monza, Motherboard, NAND, NOR, NOT, Open, OR, Perimeter, Phantom, Phase, Printed, Push-pull, Quadripole, Reactance, Ring, Round, Roundure, Rubber-chicken, Scaler, Series, Short, Smoothing, Sound card, Squelch, Stage, Three-phase, Tour, Trunk, Windlass, XNOR, XOR

Circular Annular, Court, Disc(al), Endless, Flysheet, Folder, Leaflet, Mailshot, Orby, Round, Spiral, Unending, Vertical, Wheely

Circulate, Circulation Ambient, Astir, Bandy, Bloodstream, Cyclosis, Disseminate, Flow, Gross, Gyre, Issue, Mingle, Mix, Orbit, Pass, Publish, Report, Revolve, Rotate, Scope, Send round, Spread, Stir, Troll, Utter

▷ **Circulating** *may indicate* an anagram

Circumcise(r), Circumcision Pharaonic, Sandek

Circumference Boundary, Girth, Perimeter, Size

Circumflex Perispomenon

Circumstance(s), Circumstantial Case, Detail, Event, Fact, Formal, →INCIDENT, Mitigating, Precise, Shebang, Situation, Stede

Circus, Circus boy Arena, Big top, Flea, Flying, Hippodrome, Marquee, Maximus, Media, Monty Python, Ring, Three-ring

Cissy Nelly

Cistern Feed-head, Flush-box

Citation, Cite Adduce, Allegation, Instance, Mensh, Mention, Name, Quote, Recall, Reference, Repeat, Sist, Summon

Citizen(s), Citizenship Burgess, Burgher, Civism, Cleruch, Denizen, Dicast, Ephebe, Franchise, Freeman, Jus sanguinis, Jus soli, Kane, Keelie, National, Oppidan, Patrial, People, Proletarian, Propr(a)etor, Quirites, Resident, Roman, Second-class, Senior, Snob, Subject, Trainband, Trierarch, Venireman, Vigilante, Voter

Citrus Acid, Calamondin, Cedrate, Hesperidium, Lemon, Lime, Mandarin, Min(n)eola, Orange, Pomelo, Tangerine, Ugli

City Agra, Astrakhan, Athens, Atlantis, Babylon, Burgh, Cardboard, Carthage, Cosmopolis, Ctesiphon, EC, Empire, Eternal, Forbidden, Gath, Heavenly, Holy, Inner, LA, Leonine, Medina, Megalopolis, Metropolis, Micropolis, Mother, Municipal, Mycenae, Nineveh, NY, Petra, Pompeii, Rhodes, See, Smoke, Sparta, Square mile, Tech, The Big Smoke, Town, Ur, Vatican, Weltstadt

Civil(ian), Civilisation, Civilised, Civility Amenity, Amicable, Christian, Citizen, Civ(vy), Comity, Courtesy, Culture, Fertile crescent, Humane, Indus Valley, Maya, Mufti, Municipal, Nok, Plain clothes, Polite, Politesse, Push-button, Secular, Temporal, Urbane

Claim(s) Allege, Appeal, Arrogate, Assert, Bag, Challenge, Charge, Crave, Darraign(e), Darrain(e), Darrayn, Deraign, Droit, Encumbrance, Exact, Haro, Harrow, Insist, Lien, List, Maintain, Nochel, Plea, Pose, Posit, Postulate, Predicate, Pretence, Pretend, Profess, Pulture, Purport, Puture, Rank, Revendicate, Right, Set-off, Small, Sue, Title

Claimant Irredentist, Petitioner, Pot-waller, Pretender, Prospector, Tichborne, Usurper

Clam Bivalve, Chowder, Cohog, Geoduck, Giant, Gweduc, Hardshell, Littleneck, Mollusc, Mya, Quahang, Quahog, Razor(-shell), Round, Steamer, Tridacna, Venus, Vongole

Clammy Algid, Damp, Dank, Moist, Sticky, Sweaty

Clamp(er) Chuck, Clinch, Denver boot, Fasten, Grip, Haemostat, Holdfast, Jumar, Pinchcock, Potato-pit, Stirrup, Tread, Vice, Wheel

Clan(sman) Brood, Cameron, Campbell, Clique, Gens, Gentile, Group, Horde, Kiltie, Kindred, Name, Ngati, Phratry, Phyle, Sect, Sept, Society, Stewart, Stuart, Tribe

Clap(per), Clapping Applaud, Blow, Castanet, Chop, Crotal, Dose, Jinglet, Peal, Plaudite, Stroke hands, Thunder, Tonant

Clare Nun, Sister

Clarify, Clarified, Clarifier Clear, Despumate, Dilucidate, Explain, Explicate, Fine, Finings, Ghee, Purge, Refine, Render, Simplify, Tease out

Clash(ing) Bang, Clangour, Clank, Claver, Coincide, Collide, Conflict, Dissonant, Friction, Gossip, →IMPACT, Incident, Jar, Loud, Missuit, Riot, Shock, Showdown, Strike, Swash

Clasp(ing) Adpress, Agraffe, Barrette, Brooch, Button, Catch, Chape, Clip, Embrace, Fibula, Grasp, Hasp, Hesp, Hook, Hug, Link, Morse, Ochreate, Ouch, Peace, Press, Slide, Tach(e), Unite

Class(ification), Classify, Classified, Classy Acorn, Arrange, Assort, Bourgeois(ie), Bracket, Brand, Breed, Business, Cabin, Canaille, Caste, →CATEGORY, Chattering, Cheder, Cl, Cladistics, Clan, Clerisy, Clinic, Club, Composite, Course, Criminal, Dalit, Dewey, Digest, Division, Economy, Estate, Evening, Faction, First, Form, Genera, Gentry, Genus, →GRADE, Group, Harvard, Haryan, Heder, Hubble, Ilk, Keep-fit, Kidney, Kohanga reo, League, Lesson, Life, Linn(a)ean, List, Lower, Mammal, Master, Meritocracy, Middle, Night, Number, Nursery, Order, Peasantry, Phenetics, Phylum, Pigeon-hole, Pleb(eian), Posh, Proper, Race, Range, Rank, Rate, Rating, Raypoot, Raypout, Reception, Remove, Ruling, Salariat, Second, Secret, Seminar, Shell, Siege, Social, Sort(ation), Spectral, Sphere, Standard, Steerage, Stratum, Stream, Syntax, Taxonomy, Teach-in, Third, Tony, Tourist, Tribe, Tutorial, →TYPE, U, Universal, Upper, Varna, Water, Working, World, Year

Classic(al), Classics, Classicist Ageless, Ancient, Basic, Derby, Elzevir, Grecian, Greek, Humane, Leger, Literature, Oldie, Pliny, Purist, Roman, Standard, Traditional, Vintage

Clause Acceleration, Adjunct, Apodosis, Article, Complement, Condition, Escalator, Escape, Filioque, Four, Golden parachute, Grandfather, Member, Noun, Novodamus, Object, Poison-pill, Predicator, Protasis, Proviso, Reddendum, Relative, Reservation, Reserve, Rider, Salvo, Sentence, Subject, Subordinate, Sunset, Tenendum, Testatum

Claw Chela, Claut, Cloye, Crab, Dewclaw, Edate, Falcula, Grapple, Griff(e), Hook, Insessorial, Nail, Nipper, Pounce, Scrab, Sere, Talent, Tear, Telson, Unguis

Clay Argil, Blaes, Blaise, Blaize, Blunge, Bole, Boulder, Calm, Cam, Cassius, Caum, Ceramic, Charoset(h), China, Cloam, Clunch, Cob, Earth, Engobe, Fango, Figuline, Fuller's earth, Gault, Glei, Gley, Hardpan, Haroset(h), Illite, Kaolin, Kokowai, Laterite, Lithomarge, Loam, London, Lute, Malm, Marl, Meerschaum, Mire, Mortal, Mud, Oxford, Papa, Pipeclay, Pise, Potter's, Pottery, Pug, Saggar(d), Sagger, Seggar, Slip, Slurry, Terra sigillata, Thill, Till(ite), Varve, Warrant, Warren, Wax

Clean(er), Cleaning, Cleanse Absterge, Ammonia, Besom, Bidet, Blanco, Bleach, Blue flag, Bream, Broom, Careen, Catharise, Catharsis, Chamois leather, Char(e), Chaste, Clear, Cottonbud, Daily, Debride, Depurate, Deterge(nt), Dhobi, Dialysis, Disinfect, Do, Douche, Dredge, Dust(er), Dyson®, Eluant, Emunge, Enema, Epurate, Erase, Ethnic, Evacuant, Evacuate, Expurgate, Fay, Fettle, Fey, Floss, Flush, Full, Grave, Groom, Gut, Heels, Hoover®, House-trained, Hygienic, Immaculate, Innocent, Kosher, Launder, Lave, Linish, Lustrum, Lye, Mouthwash, Mrs Mop(p), Mundify, Net, Nipter, Overhaul, Porge, Prophylaxis, Pull-through, Pumice, Pure, Purgative, Purge, Ramrod, Rebite, Rub, Rump, Sanitize, Scaffie, Scavenge, Scour, Scrub, Shampoo, Shot-blast, Snow-white, Soap, Soogee, Soogie, Soojey, Sponge, Spotless, Square, Squeaky, Squeegee, Squilgee, Sterile, Sujee, Swab, Sweep, Syringe, Uproot, Vac(uum), Valet, →WASH, Whistle, Whiter, Wipe, Zamboni

Clear(ance), Cleared, Clearly Absolve, Acquit, Allow, Aloof, Apparent, Articulate, Assart, Bald, Bell, Berth, Bold, Bore, Brighten, Bus, Clarify, Cloudless, Cogent, Concise, Consomme, Crystal, Daylight, Decode, Definite, Demist, Diaphanous, Dispel, Distinct, Downright, Eidetic, Evacuate, Evident, Exculpate, Exonerate, Explicit, Fair, Flagrant, Gain, Get over, Headroom, Highland, Hyaline, Intelligible, Iron, Laund, Leap, Legible, Limpid, Lucid, Luculent, Manifest, Mop, Neat,

Negotiate, Net(t), Observable, Obvious, Ope(n), Overleap, Overt, Palpable, Patent, Pay, Pellucid, Perspicuous, Plain, Play, Pratique, Predy, Pure, Purge, Quit, Rack, Realise, Reap, Remble, Rid, Ripple, Serene, Sheer, Shere, Silvery, Slum, Specific, Stark, Straight, Strip, Succinct, Sweep, Swidden, Thro(ugh), Thwaite, Transire, Translucent, Transparent, Unblock, Unclog, Uncork(ed), Unequivocal, Unstop, Vault, Vindicate, Vivid, Void, Well, Whiten, Windage, Wipe

Clearing Assart, Glade, Opening, Shire, Slash

Cleft Notch

Clergy(man), Cleric(al) Abbé, Canon, Cantor, Cardinal, Chancellor, Chaplain, Chapter, Circuit rider, Cleric, Clerk, Cloth, Curate, Curé, Deacon, Dean, Ecclesiast(ic), God-botherer, Goliard, Holy Joe, Incumbent, Josser, Levite, Ministerial, Ministry, Minor canon, Non-juror, Non-usager, Notarial, Parson, Pastor, Pontifex, Pontiff, Preacher, Prebendary, Precentor, Prelate, Presbyter, Presenter, Priest, Primate, Prior, Proctor, Rabbi, Rector, Red-hat, Reverend, Rome-runner, Scribal, Secretarial, Secular, Shaveling, Shepherd, Slope, Spin-text, Squarson, Subdeacon, Theologian, Vartabed, Vicar

Clerk(s) Actuary, Articled, Baboo, Babu, Basoche, Circar, Cleric, Cratchit, Cursitor, Enumerator, Limb, Notary, Paper-pusher, Penman, Penpusher, Petty Bag, Poster, Protocolist, Prot(h)onotary, Recorder, St Nicholas's, Scribe, Secretariat, Sircar, Sirkar, Tally, Town, Vestry, Vicar, Writer

Clever(ness) Able, Adroit, Astute, Brainy, Bright, Canny, Cool, Cunning, Cute, Daedal(e), Deft, Genius, Gleg, Habile, Ingenious, Intellectual, Know-all, Natty, Nimblewit, Resourceful, Sage(ness), Shrewd, Skilful, Smart(y), Smarty-pants, Souple, Subtle

Cliché Banality, Boilerplate, Commonplace, Corn, Journalese, Platitude, Saying, Tag

Click(er), Clicking Castanet, Catch, Forge, Implosive, Pawl, Ratch(et), Snick, Succeed, Tchick, Ticktack

Client Account, Customer, End-user, Fat, Gonk, John, Patron, Thin, Trick

Cliff(s) Beachy Head, Bluff, Cleve, Crag, Craig, Escarp, Lorelei, Palisade(s), Precipice, Sca(u)r

Climate Ambience, Atmosphere, Attitude, Continental, Mood, Sun, Temperament, Temperature, Weather

Climax Apex, Apogee, Catastasis, Come, Crescendo, Crest, Crisis, Culminate, Edaphic, End, Head, Height, Heyday, Moment of truth, Orgasm, Payoff, Selling, Top, Zenith

Climb(er), Climbing Aid, Alpinist, Aralia, Aristolochia, Artificial, Ascend, Bignonian, Breast, Briony, Bryony, Clamber, Clematis, Clusia, Cowage, Cowhage, Cowitch, Crampon, Creeper, Cubeb, Cucumber, Dodder, Ers, Heart-pea, Hedera, Ivy, Jamming, Kie-kie, Kudzu, Lawyer, Layback, Liana, Liane, →MOUNT, Pareira, Parvenu, Pea, Peg, Poison oak, Prusik, Rat(t)an, Rhoicissus, Rise, Rope, Scale, Scan, Scandent, Scansores, Sclim, Shin, Shinny, Sklim, Smilax, Social, Speel, Steeplejack, Stegophilist, Sty(e), Swarm, Timbo, Tuft-hunter, Udo, Up(hill), Uprun, Vetch, Vine, Vitaceae, Wistaria, With(y)wind, Zoom

Clinch Attach, Determine, Ensure, Fix, Rivet, Secure, Settle

Cling(er), Clinging Adhere, Bur(r), Cherish, Cleave, Embrace, Hold, Hug, Limpet, Ring, Suctorial, Tendril

Clinic Abortuary, Antenatal, Dispensary, Hospital, Hospitium, Mayo

Clint Limestone

Clip(ped), Clipper, Clipping Alberta, Banana, Barrette, Bicycle, Brash, Bulldog, Butterfly, Cartridge, Chelsea, Clasp, Crocodile, Crop-ear, Crutch, Curt, Curtail, Cut, Cutty Sark, Dag, Dock, Dod, Excerpt, Film, Fleece, Hairslide, Jubilee, Jumar, Krab, Lop, Money, Nail, Outtake, Pace, Paper, Pare, Pedicure, Peg, Prerupt, Prune, Roach, Scissel, Secateur, Shear, Ship, Shore, Shorn, Snip, Spring, Staccato, Tie, Tie-tack, Tinsnips, Toe, Tonsure, Topiarist, Trim, Trot

Clique Cabal, Clan, Club, Coterie, Faction, Four Hundred, Gang, Ring, Set

Cloak(room), Cloaks Aba, Abaya, Abba, Abolla, Amice, Anonymity, Bathroom, Burnous, Capa, Cape, Capote, Caracalla, Cardinal, Cassock, Chasuble, Chimer(e),

Chlamydes, Chlamys, Chuddah, Chuddar, Cocoon, Conceal, Cope, Cover, Disguise, Dissemble, Djellaba(h), Domino, Gabardine, Gaberdine, Gal(l)abea(h), Gal(l)abi(y)a(h), Gal(l)abi(y)eh, Gentlemen, Gents, Hall-robe, Heal, Hele, Himation, Hood, Inverness, Jelab, Jellaba, Joseph, Kaross, Korowai, Manta, Manteau, Manteel, Mantle, Mant(e)let, → MASK, Mousquetaire, Mozetta, Paenula, Paletot, Pallium, Paludamentum, Pelisse, Pilch, Poncho, Rail, Revestry, Rocklay, Rokelay, Roquelaure, Sagum, Sarafan, Scapular, → SCREEN, Shroud, Swathe, Talma, Toga, Vestiary, Vestry, Visite

Clock Alarm, Ammonia, Analogue, Astronomical, Atomic, Beetle, Big Ben, Biological, Blowball, Body, Bracket, Bundy, Caesium, Carriage, Cartel, Clepsydra, Cuckoo, Dandelion, Dutch, Floral, Grandfather, Grandmother, Hit, Knock, Long case, Meter, Paenula, Repeater, Settler's, Solarium, Speaking, Speedo, Strike, Sundial, Taximeter, Tell-tale, Time(r), Wag at the wa', Water

Clog Ball, Block, Clam, Crowd, Dance, Fur, Galosh, Golosh, Hamper, Jam, Lump, Mire, Obstruct, Overshoe, Patten

Close(d), Closing, Closure Adjourn, Agree, Airless, Alongside, Anigh, Atresia, Block, Boon, By, Cadence, Clammy, Clap, Clench, Collapse, Compact, Complete, Concentration, Cone off, Court, Dear, Debar, Dense, Dissolve, → END, Epilogue, Ewest, Eye to eye, Finale, Forby, Gare, Grapple, Handy, Hard, Hard by, Hot, Humid, Imminent, Inbye, Infibulate, Intent, Intimate, Local, Lock, Lucken, Marginal, Mean, Miserly, Muggy, Mure, Narre, Narrow, Near, Nearhand, Neck and neck, Neist, Next, Nie, Niggardly, Nigh, Nip and tuck, Obturate, Occlude, Occlusion, Oppressive, Parochial, Penny-pinching, Placket, Precinct, Reserved, Reticent, Seal, Secret, Serre, Serried, Serry, Shet, Shut(ter), Shutdown, Silly, Slam, Snug, Stap, Sticky, Stifling, Stuffy, Sultry, Tailgate, Temenos, Terminate, Tight(knit), Uproll, Wafer, Wanr, Warm, Yard

Closet Cabinet, Confine, Cubicle, Cupboard, Earth, Locker, Safe, Wardrobe, WC, Zeta

Close-up Detail, Fill, Shut, Stop, Zoom

Clot(ting) Bozo, Clump, Coagulate, Duffer

Clotbuster Heparin

Cloth Aba, Abaya, Abba, Bearing, Bib, Bribe, Carmelite, Clergy, Cloot, Clout, Communion, Corporal(e), → FABRIC, → FELT, Frocking, Frontal, Gremial, G-string, Interfacing, Jharan, Loin, Lungi, Manta, → MATERIAL, Mercery, Meshing, Nap, Napery, Napje, Napkin, Nappie, Neckerchief, Needlework, Netting, Pack, Painted, Pall, Pane, Pilch, Priesthood, Pull-through, Rag, Raiment, Roll, Roon, Runner, Sashing, Scarlet, Serviette, Sheet, Sheeting, Shirting, Shoddy, Stock, Stripe, Stupe, Tapestry, Tea, Throw, Tissue, Toilet, Veronica

Clothe(s), Clothing, Clothed Accoutrements, Ao dai, Apparel, Array, Attire, Baggies, Battledress, Besee, Cape, Casuals, Choli, Cits, Clad, Clericals, Clobber, Combinations, Confection, Coordinates, Costume, Cour, Cover, Croptop, Cruisewear, Culottes, Deck, Diffusion line, Dight, Don, Drag, → DRESS, Duds, Emboss, Endue, Fig leaf, Finery, Foot muff, Frippery, Garb, Garments, Gear, Gere, Get-up, Glad rags, Gymslip, Gyves, Habit, Haute couture, Hejab, Innerwear, Judogi, Jumps, Layette, Leathers, Lederhosen, Long-togs, Mitumba, Muff, Outfit, Pannicle, Pantsuit, Pareu, Pea-coat, Pin-striped, Playsuit, Plus fours, Raiment, Rami, Rigout, Robes, Samfoo, Samfu, Scapulary, Schmutter, Scrubs, Scungies, Shell suit, Shirtwaister, Shroud, Slops, Stomacher, Sundress, Sunsuit, Swaddling, Swathe, Swothling, Tackle, Things, Toggery, Togs, Tracksuit, Trappings, Trews, Trousseau, Tube top, Tweeds, Veiling, Vernicle, Vestiary, Vestiture, Vestment, Wardrobe, Watteau, Weeds, Wetsuit, Workwear, Yclad, Ycled, Y-fronts

Cloud(ing), Clouded, Cloudiness, Cloudy Altocumulus, Altostratus, Benight, Cirrocumulus, Cirrostratus, Cirrus, Coalsack, Coma, Crab Nebula, Cumulonimbus, Cumulus, Dim, Dull, Emission nebula, Fog, Fractocumulus, Fractostratus, Funnel, Goat's hair, Haze, Horsehead Nebula, Infuscate, Magellanic, Mammatus, Mare's tail, Milky, Mist, Mushroom, Nacreous, Nephele, Nephelometer, Nepho-, Nimbostratus, Nimbus, Nubecula, Nubilous, Nuée ardente, Obnubilation, Obscure, Oort, Overcast, Pall, Pother, Protostar, Rack, Roily, Smoor, Stain, Storm, Stratocumulus, Strat(o)us, Thunder(head), Turbid, Virga, War, Water-dog, Weft, Woolpack, Zero-zero

Clove Chive, Eugenia, Garlic, Rose-apple, Split, Yrent

Clover Alfalfa, Alsike, Berseem, Calvary, Cinque, Cow-grass, Hare's-foot, Hop, Hop-trefoil, Japan, Ladino, Lespedeza, Medic(k), Melilot, Owl's, Rabbit-foot, Serradella, Serradilla, Shamrock, Souple, Sucklers, Suckling, Trefoil, Trilobe, Truelove

Clown(ish) Airhead, Antic, Antick, August(e), Boor, Bor(r)el, Buffoon, Carl, Chough, Chuff, Clout-shoe, Coco, →**COMEDIAN**, Comic, Costard, Daff, Feste, Froth, Girner, Gobbo, Goon, Gracioso, Grimaldi, Harlequin, Hob, Jack-pudding, Jester, Joey, Joker, Joskin, Leno, Merry Andrew, Mountebank, Nedda, Nervo, Patch(c)ocke, Peasant, Pickle-herring, Pierrot, Put, Rustic, Slouch, Thalian, Touchstone, Trinculo, Wag, Zany

Club(s), Club-like Adelphi, Airn, Alloa, Almack's, Alpeen, Apex, Army and Navy, Arsenal, Artel, Association, Athen(a)eum, Baffy, Band(y), Basto, Bat, Bath, Beefsteak, Blackjack, Blaster, Bludgeon, Boodles, Bourdon, Brassie, Breakfast, Brook's, Bulger, C, Caman, Card, Carlton, Caterpillar, Cavalry, Chapter, Chartered, Chigiriki, Cleek, Clip-joint, Combine, Compassion, Conservative, Constitutional, Cordeliers, Cosh, Cotton, Country, Crockford's, Cudgel, Devonshire, Disco(theque), Driver, Driving iron, Drones, Fan, Farm team, Fascio, Fellowship, Fleshpot, Garrick, Glee, Golf, Guards, Guild, Hampden, Health, Hell-fire, Hercules', Hetairia, Honky-tonk, Indian, Investment, Iron, Jacobin, Jigger, Job, Jockey, Junior Carlton, Kennel, Kierie, Kiri, Kitcat, Kiwanis, Knobkerrie, Landsdowne, Laughter, League, Leander, Lions, Lofter, Luncheon, Mace, Mallet, Mashie, Maul, Mell, Mere, Meri, Mess, Midiron, Monday, National Liberal, Niblick, Night(stick), Nitery, Oddfellows, Paris, Patu, Polt, Pregnant, Priest, Provident, Pudding, Putter, Putting-cleek, RAC, R & A, Reform, Ring, Rota, Rotarian, Rotary, Savage, Savile, Shillelagh, Slate, Society, Soroptimist, Sorority, Sorosis, Spoon, Spot, Spurs, Strike, Strip, Stunner, Supper, Texas wedge, Thatched House, Tong, Travellers, Trefoil, Truncheon, Trunnion, Union, United Services, Variety, Waddy, Warehouse, Wedge, White's, Wood, Yacht, Youth

Clue 1ac, Across, Anagram, Aradne, Ball, Charade, Clavis, Dabs, Down, →**HINT**, Inkling, Key, Lead, Light, Rebus, Scent, Signpost, Thread, Tip

Clump Cluster, Finial, Knot, Mass, Mot(te), Patch, Plump, Tread, Tuft, Tump, Tussock

▷ **Clumsily** *may indicate an anagram*

Clumsy Artless, Awkward, Bauchle, Bungling, Butterfingers, Calf, Chuckle, Clatch, Clodhopper, Cumbersome, Dub, Dutch, Galoot, Gauche, Gimp, Gink, Ham(-fisted), Heavy-handed, Hulk, Inapt, Inelegant, Inept, Inexpert, Klutz, Lob, Loutish, Lubbard, Lubber, Lumbering, Lummox, Lumpish, Maladdress, Maladroit, Mauther, Mawr, Mawther, Messy, Mor, Nerd, Nurd, Oafish, Overhasty, Palooka, Plonking, Rough, Schlemihl, S(c)hlemiel, Squab, Stot, Stumbledom, Swab, Swob, Two-fisted, Unco, Ungain, Unskilful, Unsubtle, Unwieldy

Clutch(es) Battery, Brood, Chickens, Clasp, Cling, Eggs, Glaum, Grab, →**GRASP**, Gripe, Hold, Nest, Net, Seize, Sitting, Squeeze

Clutter Confusion, Litter, Mess, Rummage

Coach Autodidact, Battlebus, Berlin, Bogie, Bus, Car, Carriage, Chara, Clerestory, Crammer, Diligence, Dilly, Double-decker, Drag, Edifier, Fiacre, Fly, Gig, Griddle car, Hackney, Handler, Landau(let), Microbus, Mourning, Phaeton, Pullman, Railcar, Rattler, Repetiteur, Saloon, Shay, Sleeper, Stage, Surrey, Tally(-ho), Teach(er), Thoroughbrace, Train(er), Transport, Tutor, Voiture

Coal Anthracite, Bituminous, Block, Burgee, Cannel, Char, Cherry, Clinker, Coking, Coom, Crow, Culm, Day, Edge, Eldin, Ember, Fusain, Gathering, Indene, Jud, Knob, Lignite, Open-cast, Parrot, Pea, Purse, Sapropelite, Score, Sea, Slack, Splint, Stone, Surtarbrand, Surturbrand, Vitrain, Wallsend

Coalition Alliance, Bloc, Fusion, Janata, Merger, Tie, Union

Coarse(ness) Base, Bawdy, Blowzy, Bran, Broad, Chav, Common, Crude, Earthy, Fisherman, Foul, Gneissose, Grained, Gross, Ham, Illbred, Indelicate, Low-bred, Plebeian, Rank, Raunchy, Ribald, Rough, Rudas, Rude, Russet, Sackcloth, Schlub, Slob, Sotadic, Vulgar

Coast(al) Barbary, Beach, Cape, Causeway, Coromandel, Costa, Dalmatian, Drift,

Freewheel, Glide, Hard, Heritage, Ivory, Littoral, Longshore, Maritime, Orarian, Riviera, Scrieve, Seaboard, Seafront, Seashore, Seaside, → **SHORE**, Sledge, Strand, Sunshine, Toboggan, Trucial

Coaster Beermat, Drog(h)er, Mat, Ship

Coat(ed), Coating Ab(b)a, Abaya, Achkan, Acton, Admiral, Afghan, Anarak, Anodise, Anorak, Balmacaan, Barathea, Basan, Bathrobe, Belton, Benjamin, Blazer, Bloomed, Box, British warm, Buff, Buff-jerkin, Car, Chesterfield, Cladding, Claw-hammer, Clearcole, Cloak, Clutch, Cocoon, Coolie, Cover, Covert, Creosote, Crust(a), Cutaway, Dip, Doggett's, Drape, Dress, Duffel, Duster, Enamel, Encrust, Envelope, Ermelin, Ermine, Extine, Fearnought, Film, Fleece, Frock, Fur, Gabardine, Galvanise, Gambeson, Glaze, Grego, Ground, Hair, Happi, Ha(c)queton, Impasto, Inverness, Iridise, Jack(et), Jemmy, Jerkin, Jodhpuri, Joseph, Jump, Jupon, Lacquer, Lammie, Lammy, Lanugo, Layer, Laying, Limewash, Loden, Lounge, Mac, Mackinaw, Matinee, Metallise, Mink, Morning, Newmarket, Paint, Paletot, Palla, Paper, Parka, Parkee, Patina(te), Pebbledash, Pelage, Pelisse, Perfuse, Petersham, Pitch, Pla(i)ster, Plate, Polo, Pos(h)teen, Primer, Prince Albert, Raglan, Redingote, Resin, Resist, Riding, Roquelaure, Sable, Sack, Salband, Saque, Sclerotic, Scratch, Seal, Sheepskin, Shellac, Sherwani, Silver, Spencer, Sports, Stadium, Surtout, Swagger, Swallowtail(ed), Tabard, Taglioni, Tail, Tar, Teflon, Tent, Top, Trench, Truss, Trusty, Tunic, Tuxedo, Ulster(ette), Veneer, Verdigris, Warm, Wash, Whitewash, Windjammer, Wool, Wrap-rascal, Zamarra, Zamarro, Zinc

Coax Blandish, Blarney, Cajole, Carn(e)y, Collogue, Cuittle, Entice, Flatter, Lure, Persuade, Wheedle, Whillywha(w)

Cobble(s), Cobbled, Cobbler(s), Cobblestone Bunkum, Clicker, Coggle, Cosier, Cozier, Dessert, Mend, Patch, Pie, Rot, Snob, Soutar, Souter, Sowter, Stone, Sutor, Twaddle, Vamp

Cobweb(by) Arachnoid, Araneous, Gossamer, Snare, Trap

Cochlear Scala

Cock(y), Cockerell Alectryon, Ball, Brash, Capon, Chanticleer, Chaparral, Confident, Erect, Flip, Fowl, France, Fugie, Half, Hay, Henny, Jack-the-lad, Jaunty, Penis, Perk, Roadrunner, Robin, Rooster, Snook, Strut, Sunshine, Swaggering, Tap, Tilt, Turkey, Twaddle, Vain, Valve, Vane, Weather-vane

Cockatoo Bird, Corella, Galah, Major Mitchell, Parrot

Cock crow Skreigh of the day

▷ **Cockle(s)** *may indicate* an anagram

Cockney 'Arriet, 'Arry, Bow, Londoner, Londonese

▷ **Cockney** *may indicate* a missing h

Cocktail Alexander, Aperitif, Atomic, Bellini, Between the sheets, Black Russian, Bloody Mary, Brandy Alexander, Buck's fizz, Bullshot, Bumbo, Calpirinha, Champagne cocktail, Cobbler, Cold duck, Crusta, Daiquiri, Egg-flip, Fruit, Fustian, Gibson, Gimlet, Grasshopper, Harvey Wallbanger, Highball, Horse's neck, Julep, Kir Royale, Mai-Tai, Manhattan, Margarita, Martini®, Mix, Molotov, Moscow mule, Negroni, Old-fashioned, Piña colada, Pink lady, Pisco Sour, Planter's punch, Prawn, Punch, Rickey, Rusty nail, Sangaree, Sangria, Sazerac®, Screwdriver, Sea Breeze, Sherry cobbler, Side-car, Singapore sling, Slammer, Snakebite, Snowball, Sour, Spritzer, Stengah, Stinger, Swizzle, Tequila sunrise, Tom Collins, Twist, Whiskey Sour, White-lady, White Russian

Cocotte Strumpet

Cod Bag, Cape, Coalfish, Fish, Gade, Gadus, Haberdine, Hoax, Keeling, Kid, Lob, Man, Morrhua, Saith, Spoof, Stockfish, Tease, Torsk, Tusk, Whiting

Code, Coding, Codification Access, Alphanumeric, Amalfitan, Area, Bar, Barred, Binary, Brevity, Bushido, Canon, Character, Cheat, Cipher, City, Civil, Clarendon, Codex, Colour, Computing, Condition, Cookie, Country, Cryptogram, Cryptograph, Da Vinci, Dialling, Disciplinary, Dogma, Dress, DX, Easter egg, EBCDIC, Enigma, Error, Escape, Ethics, Etiquette, Fuero, Genetic, Gray, Green Cross, Hammurabic, Highway, Justinian, MAC, Machine, Morse, Napoleon(ic), National, Netiquette, Object, Omerta, Opcode, Penal, PGP, Pindaric, Postal, Price, Protocol, Reflective binary, Rulebook,

Scytale, Sharia, Shulchan Aruch, Signal, Sort, Source, STD, Talmud, Time, Twelve Tables, Zip

Coffee, Coffee beans, Coffee pot Americano, Arabica, Bean, Brazil, Cafetiere, Cappuccino, Decaff, Demi-tasse, Espresso, Expresso, Filter, Frappuccino, Gaelic, Gloria, Granules, Instant, Irish, Java, Latte, Mocha, Peaberry, Percolator, Robusta, Skinny latte, Tan, Triage, Turkish

Coffin Bier, Box, Casket, Hearse, Sarcophagus, Shell

Cog(ged) Contrate, Mitre-wheel, Nog, Pinion, Tooth

Cogent Compelling, Forceful, Good, Sound, Telling

Cohere(nt) Agglutinate, Clear, Cleave, Cling, Logical, Stick

Cohort Colleague, Crony, Soldier

Coil(s), Coiled Bight, Bought, Choke, Choking, Circinate, Clew, Clue, Convolute(d), Convolve, Curl, Current, Fake, Fank, Field, Flemish, Furl, Hank, Helix, Induction, Loop, Mortal, Mosquito, Resistance, Rouleau, Scorpioid, Solenoid, Spark, Spiral, Spiraster, Spire, Tesla, Tickler, Toroid, Twine, Twirl, →**WIND**, Wound, Wreath, Writhe

Coin Base, Bean, Bit, Broad(piece), Cash, Change, Contomiate, Copper, Create, Doctor, Dosh, Dump(s), Fiddler's money, Fiver, Han(d)sel, Imperial, Invent, Lucky piece, Make, Mint, Mintage, →**MONEY**, Neoterise, Numismatic, Nummary, Piece, Plate, Pocket-piece, Proof, Shiner, Slip, Specie, Stamp, Strike, Subsidiary, Sum, Tenner, Token, Unity

Coincide(nt), Coincidence Accident, Chance, Consilience, Conterminous, Fit, Fluke, Overlap, Rabat(to), Simultaneous, Synastry, Synchronise, Tally

Cold(-blooded), Cold(ness) Ague, Algid, Aloof, Apathetic, Arctic, Asperity, Austere, Biting, Bitter, Bleak, Blue, Brr(r), C, Catarrh, Cauld(rife), Chill(y), Colubrine, Common, Coryza, Coy, Dead, Distant, Ectotherm, Emotionless, Fish, Frappé, Frem(d), Fremit, Frigid, Frost(y), Gelid, Glacial, Hiemal, Icy, Impersonal, Jeel, Nippy, Nirlit, Parky, Passionless, Perishing, Poikilotherm(ic), Polar, Psychro-, Remote, Rheumy, Rigor, Rume, Siberia, Snap, Snell, Sour, Starving, Streamer, Subzero, Taters, Unmoved, Weed, Wintry

Collage Cut up, Paste up

Collapse, Collapsing Apoplexy, Breakdown, Burn out, Cave, Conk, Crash, Crumble, Crumple, Debacle, Downfall, Fail(ure), Fall, Flake out, Fold, Founder, Give, Go phut, Implode, Inburst, Landslide, Meltdown, Phut, Purler, Rickety, Rockfall, Rot, Ruin, Scat(ter), Sink, Slump, Snap, Stroke, Subside, Sunstroke, Swoon, Telescope, Tumble, →**TUMBLEDOWN**, Wilt, Zonk

▷**Collapsing** *may indicate* an anagram

Collar(ed) Arrest, Astrakhan, Band, Bermuda, Bertha, Berthe, Bib, Bishop, Blue, Brecham, Buster, Butterfly, Button-down, Buttonhole, Capture, Carcanet, Chevesaile, Choke(r), Clerical, Collet, Dog, Esses, Eton, Falling-band, Flea, Gorget, Grandad, Hame, Head(stall), Holderbat, Horse, Jabot, Jampot, Karenni, Mandarin, Moran, Mousquetaire, Nab, Nail, Neckband, Necklet, Ox-bow, Peter Pan, Piccadell, Piccadillo, Piccadilly, Pikadell, Pink, Polo, Puritan, Rabaline, Rabato, Rebater, Rebato, Revers, Rollneck, Roman, Romance, Ruff, Sailor, Seize, Shawl, Steel, Storm, Tackle, Tappet, Tie-neck, Torque, Turndown, Turtleneck, Vandyke, Whisk, White, Wing, Yoke

Colleague(s) Accomplice, Associate, Bedfellow, Co-host, Confrère, Mate, Mentor, Oppo, Partner, Sociate, Team, Workmate

Collect(ion), Collectable, Collected, Collective(ly), Collectivism, Collector Accrue, Agglomerate, Aggregate, Album, Alms, Amass, Ana, Anthology, Artel, Assemble, Bank, Bow, Budget, Bundle, Burrell, Bygones, Caboodle, Calm, Cap, Clan, Clowder, Compendium, Compile, Congeries, Conglomerate, Covey, Cull, Dossier, Dustman, Earn, Egger, Exaltation, Exordial, Fest, Fetch, Fleet, Gaggle, Garbo, Garner, Gather, Get, Gilbert, Glean, Glossary, Grice, Harvest, Heap, Herd, Hive, Idant, Jingbang, Kit, Kitty, Levy, Library, Magpie, Meal, Meet, Menagerie, Miscellany, Mish-mash, Montem, Munro-bagger, Murmuration, Museum, Muster, Nide, Offertory, Olio, Omnibus, Pack, Paddling, Pile, Plate, Pod, Poor box, Post, Poste restante, Prayer, Quest, Raft, Raise, Rammle, Recheat, Rhapsody, Rouleau, Sangfroid, Scramble, Sedge, Self-possessed, Serene, Set, Shoe, Siege, Skein, Smytrie, Sord, Sottisier, Sounder, Spring, Stand, Team, Toolkit, Tronc, Troop, Ujamaa, Unkindness, Uplift, Watch, Wernher, Whipround, Wisp

▷ **Collection** *may indicate* an anagram

College(s) Academy, All Souls, Ampleforth, Balliol, Brasenose, Business, C, Caius, Campus, CAT, Cheltenham, Clare, Classical, Commercial, Community, Conservatoire, Corpus (Christi), Downing, Dulwich, Electoral, Emmanuel, Eton, Exeter, Foundation, Freshwater, Girton, Grande école, Hall, Heralds', Jail, Keble, King's, Lancing, Linacre, Lincoln, LSE, Lycée, Lyceum, Madras(s)a(h), Madressah, Magdalen(e), Marlborough, Medresseh, Merton, Newnham, Nuffield, Oriel, Pembroke, Poly, Polytechnic, Protonotariat, Queen's, Ruskin, St Johns, Saliens, Selwyn, Seminary, Sixth-form, Somerville, Sorbonne, Staff, Tech(nical), Tertiary, Theologate, Training, Trinity, Tug, UMIST, Up, Village, Wadham, Winchester, Yeshiva(h)

Collide, Collision Afoul, Barge, Bird-strike, Bump, Cannon, Carom(bole), Clash, Conflict, Dash, Elastic, Fender-bender, Foul, Head-on, Hurtle, Impact, Inelastic, Into, Kiss, Meet, Pile-up, Prang, Ram, Smash-up, Strike, Thwack

Colony Acadia, Aden, Burkina Faso, Cape, Cleruchy, Crown, Dependency, Elea, Gibraltar, Halicarnassian, Hongkong, Kaffraria, Nudist, Penal, Plymouth, Presidio, Proprietary, Rookery, Senegal, Settlement, Swarm, Termitarium, Zambia, Zimbabwe

Colossus Eten, Ettin

Colour(ed), Colouring, Colours Achromatic, Bedye, Blanco, Blee, Blush, C, Cap, Chromatic, Chrome, Complementary, Complexion, Crayon, Criant, Cross, Distort, Dye, False, Film, Flag, Florid, Flying, Gouache, Haem, →HUE, Imbue, Ink, Irised, Kalamkari, Leer, Local, Lutein, Metif, Nankeen, Orpiment, Palette, Pantone®, Pastel, Pied, Pigment, Pochoir, Polychrome, Primary, Prism, Prismatic, Process, Queen's, Raddle, Reddle, Regimental, Rinse, Riot, Ruddle, Secondary, Sematic, Shade, Shot, Solid, Spectrum, Stain, Startle, Tertiary, Tie-dye, Tinc(ture), Tinctorial, Tinge, Tint, Tone, Uvea, Wash

▷ **Coloured** *may indicate* an anagram

Colourful Abloom, Brave, Exotic, Flamboyant, Flowery, Gay, Iridescent, Kaleidoscope, Opalescent, Showy, Splashy, Vivid

Colourless Albino, Bleak, Drab, Dull, Faded, Flat, Hyalite, Pallid, Pallor, Wan, White

Colour-spot Gutta

Column(s), Column foot Agony, Anta, Atlantes, Commentary, Corinthian, Correspondence, Cylinder, Decastyle, Diastyle, Distillation, Doric, Editorial, Eustyle, Fifth, File, Flying, Fractionating, Gossip, Hypostyle, Impost, Lat, Lonelyhearts, Monolith, Nelson's, Newel, Notochord, Obelisk, Pericycle, Peripteral, Peristyle, Persian, Personal, Pilaster, →PILLAR, Pilotis, Plume, Prostyle, Pycnostyle, Rouleau, Row, Sheet pile, Spina, Spinal, Spine, Stalactite, Stalagmite, Steering, Stylobate, Systyle, Tabulate, Telamone, Third, Tige, Tore, Torus, Trajan's

Comb(er), Combed, Combing Afro, Alveolate, Beehive, Breaker, Card, Copple, Crest, Curry, Dredge, Fine-tooth, Hackle, Heckle, Hot, Kaim, Kame, Kangha, Kemb, Noils, Pecten, Pectinal, Rake, Rat-tail, Red(d), Ripple(r), Rose, Scribble, Search, Side, Smooth, Tease(l), Toaze, Tose, Toze, Trawl, Tuft, Wave

Combe Hope

Combination, Combine(d), Combining Accrete, Aggregate, Alligate, Ally, Amalgam, Associate, Axis, Bloc, Cartel, Cleave, Clique, Coalesce, Coalition, Concoction, Conflated, Conglomerate, Consolidate, Consortium, Crasis, Fuse, Group, Harvester, Incorporate, Integration, Interfile, Join, Junta, Kartell, League, Meld, Merge(r), Mingle, Mixture, Monogram, Motor cycle, One, Perm(utation), Piece, Pool, Quill, Ring, Solvate, Splice, Syncretize, Synthesis, Terrace, Trivalent, Trona, Unite, Valency, Wed

▷ **Combustible** *may indicate* an anagram

Come, Coming (back), Coming out Accrue, Advent, Anear, Anon, Appear, Approach, Ar(r), Arise, Arrive, Attend, Debouch, Derive, Future, Happen, Iceman, Issue, Millenarian, Orgasm, Parousia, Pass, Pop, Reach, Respond, Second, Via

Come again Eh

Come by Obtain

Comedian Benny, Buffoon, Chaplin, →**CLOWN**, Comic, Durante, Emery, Farceur, Gagman, Goon, Groucho, Hardy, Joe Miller, Joker, Jokesmith, Karno, Keaton, Laurel, Leno, Punster, Quipster, Robey, Scream, Screwball, Stand-up, Starr, Tate, Tati, Wag, Wise, Witcracker, Yell

Comedy Alternative, Blackadder, Com, Custard-pie, Drama, Ealing, Errors, Farce, Humour, Improv(ised), Millamant, Romantic, Romcom, Screwball, Situation, Slapstick, Stand-up, Thalia, Travesty

Comet Chiron, Geminid, Halley's, Kohoutek, Meteor

Come to Cost, Wake(n)

Comfort(able), Comforter, Comforting, Comfy Affluent, Amenity, Analeptic, Balm, Bein, Bildad, Calm, Canny, Cheer, Cherish, Cherry, Cold, Consolation, Console, Convenience, Cose, Cosh, Cosy, Couthie, Couthy, Creature, Crumb, Cushy, Dummy, Dutch, Ease, Easy, Eliphaz, Featherbed, Gemutlich, Heeled, Homely, Homy, Job's, Mumsy, Noah, Reassure, Relaxed, Relief, Relieve, Rosewater, Rug, Scarf, Sinecure, Snug, Solace, Soothe, Succour, Tosh, Trig, Warm, Wealthy, Well, Well-to-do, Zofar, Zophar

Comic(al) Beano, Buff, Buffo(on), Bumpkin, Buster, Chaplin, Clown, →**COMEDIAN**, Dandy, Drag, Droll, Eagle, Facetious, Fields, →**FUNNY**, Gagster, Hardy, Horror, Jester, Knock-about, Laurel, Leno, Mag, Manga, Quizzical, Robey, Stand up, Strip, Tati, Trial, Wag, Zany

Command(eer), Commanding, Commandment(s) Behest, Bid, Categorical imperative, Charge, Coerce, Control, Decalogue, Direct, Direction, Dominate, Easy, Edict, Fiat, Fiaunt, Fighter, Firman, Grip, Haw, Hest, Hijack, Imperious, Injunction, Instruction, Jussive, Magisterial, Mandate, Mastery, Mitzvah, →**ORDER**, Peremptory, Precept, Press, Query language, Requisition, Rule, Seize, Ukase, Warn, Warrant, Will, Wish, Writ

Commander Ag(h)a, Agamemnon, Ameer, Barleycorn, Bey, Bloke, Blucher, Boss, Brennus, Brig, Caliph, Centurion, Cid, Decurion, Dreyfus, Emir, Emperor, Encomendero, Field cornet, Generalissimo, Hetman, Hipparch, Imperator, Killadar, Kitchener, Leader, Manager, Marshal, Master, Meer, Moore, Officer, Overlord, Pendragon, Polemarch, Pr(a)efect, Raglan, Shogun, Sirdar, Supreme, Taxiarch, Trierarch, Warlord

Commemorate, Commemoration Encaenia, Epitaph, Eulogy, Keep, Memorial, Month's mind, Monument, Plaque, Remember, Saint's day, Trophy, Year's mind

Comment(ary), Commentator Analyst, Animadvert, Annotate, Comm, Coryphaeus, Coverage, Critic, Descant, Discuss, Editorial, Essay, Exegete, Explain, Exposition, Expound, Fair, Footnote, Gemara, Gloss(ographer), Glosser, Hakam, Kibitz, Margin, Marginalia, Midrash(im), Note, Obiter dictum, Observation, Par, Platitude, Play-by-play, Postil, Remark, Rider, Scholiast, Scholion, Scholium, Sidenote, Voice-over

Commerce, Commercial Ad, Adland, Barter, Business, Cabotage, Jingle, Marketable, Mercantile, Mercenary, Merchant, Retail, Shoppy, Simony, Trade, Traffic, Wholesale

Commissar People's, Political

Commission(er), Commissioned Agio, Audit, Bonus, Boundary, Brevet, Brokage, Brokerage, Charge, Charity, Competition, Contango, Countryside, Delegation, Depute, ECE, Employ, Engage, Envoy, Errand, Factor, Gosplan, High, Husbandage, Job, Kickback, Magistrate, Mandate, Office(r), Official, Ombudsman, Order, Oyer and terminer, Percentage, Perpetration, Place, Poundage, Rake-off, Roskill, Shroffage, Task, Task force, Trust

Commit(tal), Committed, Commitment Allegiance, Aret(t), Consign, Contract, Decision, Dedication, Delegate, Devotion, Devout, Do, Engage, Entrust, Enure, Paid up, Perpetrate, Pledge, Position, Rubicon

Committee ACRE, Audit, Board, Body, Collegium, Commission, Commune, Council,

Delegacy, Group, Hanging, Joint, Junta, Politburo, Presidium, Propaganda, Riding, Samiti, Select, Standing, Steering, Syndicate, Table, Think tank, Vigilance, Watch, Ways and means

Common(ly), Commoner, Commons Alike, Average, Cad, Conventional, Diet, Dirt, Ealing, Eatables, Enclosure, Endemic, Epicene, Everyday, Familiar, Fare, Folk, General, Green, Gutterblood, House, Law, Lay, Low, Mark, Mere, MP, Mutual, Naff, Non-U, Normal, People, Pleb, Plebe(i)an, Prevalent, Prole, Public, Related, Rife, Roturier, Ryfe, Scran, Sense, Shared, Stock, Stray, Tarty, The mob, Tie, Trite, Tritical, Tuft, Two-a-penny, Tye, Use, → USUAL, Vile, Vul(gar), Vulgo, Vulgus, Widespread, Wimbledon, Working-class

Commonsense Gumption, Nous, Savoir-faire, Smeddum, Wit

Communal, Commune Agapemone, Collective, Com, Meditate, Mir, Phalanstery, Public, Talk, Township

Communicate, Communication Ampex, Anastomosis, Announce, Appui, Baud, Bluetooth, Boyau, Braille, Cable, Cellnet, Channelling, Citizen's band, Conversation, Convey, Cybernetic, E-mail, Expansive, Exude, Impart, Infobahn, Inform, Infrastructure, Intelsat, Internet, Liaison, Lifeline, Memoranda, Message, Multichannel, Multimedia, Note, Oracy, Paralanguage, Prestel®, Proxemics, Put across, Reach, Reportage, Revelation, Road, Semiotics, Signal, Sitrep, Syncom, Talkback, Tannoy®, Telecom, Telepathy, Telephony, Teletex, Telex, Telstar, Tieline, Transmit, Utraquist, Webmail, Word of mouth

Communism, Communist Apparat(chik), Aspheterism, Bolshevist, Brook Farm, Castroism, Com, Comecon, Cominform, Comintern, Commo, Comsomol, Deviationist, Engels, Essene, Fourier, Fraction, Khmer Rouge, Komsomol, Leninite, Maoist, Marxist, Menshevist, Nomenklatura, Perfectionist, Pinko, Politburo, Red (Guard), Revisionism, Second World, Soviet, Spartacist, Tanky, Titoist, Trot, Vietcong, Vietminh

Communities, Community Agapemone, Alterne, Ashram, Association, Biome, Body, Brotherhood, Clachan, Climax, Closed, Coenobitism, Coenobium, Colonia, Colony, Consocies, District, EC, Ecosystem, EEC, Enclave, Etat, European, Faith, Frat(e)ry, Gated, Hamlet, Kahal, Kibbutz, Mesarch, Mir, Neighbourhood, Pantisocracy, People, Phalanx, Phyle, Preceptory, Public, Pueblo, Republic, Sarvodaya, Seral, Sere, Settlement, Shtetl, Sisterhood, Sociation, Society, Speech, Street, Town, Tribe, Ujamaa, Ummah, Village, Virtual, Zupa

Commute(r) Change, Convert, Reduce, Shuttle, Standee, Straphanger, Travel

Compact Agreement, Cement, Concise, Conglobe, Covenant, Covin, Coyne, Dense, Entente, Fast, Firm, Flapjack, Hard, Knit, League, Match, Neat, Pledge, Powder, Solid, Tamp, Terse, Tight, Treaty, Well-knit

Companion(able) Achates, Arm candy, Associate, Attender, Barnacle, Bedfellow, Bonhomie, Brolga, Bud(dy), Butty, CH, China, Comate, Compeer, Compotator, Comrade, Consort, Contubernal, Crony, Cupman, Duenna, Ephesian, Escort, Feare, Felibre, → FELLOW, Fere, Franion, Furked, Handbook, Man Friday, Mate, Native, Oliver, Pal, Pard, Pheer(e), Pot, Roland, Shadow, Sidekick, Stablemate, Thane, Thegn, Vade-mecum, Wag, Walker

Company, Companies Actors, Along, Artel, Ass, Assembly, Band, Bank, Battalion, Bevy, Brigade, → BUSINESS, Bv, Cahoot, Cartel, Cast, Cavalcade, Chartered, CIA, Circle, City, Close, Club, Co, Conger, Consort, Cordwainers, Core, Corporation, Corps, Coy, Crew, Crowd, Crue, Decury, Dotcom, East India, Enterprise, Entourage, Faction, Finance, Fire, → FIRM, Flock, Free, Gang, Garrison, Ging, Guild, Haberdashers, Heap, Holding, Hudson's Bay, ICI, Inc, Indie, In-house, Intercourse, Investment, Joint-stock, Limited, Listed, Livery, Management, Maniple, Muster, Order, Organisation, Parent, Plc, Present, Pride, Private, Public, Public limited, Push, Quoted, Rep(ertory), Room, SA, Sedge, Set, Set out, Shell, Siege, Sort, SpA, Stationers', Stock, Subsidiary, Syndicate, Table, Team, Touring, Troop, Troupe, Trust, Twa, Two(some), Visitor, White, Yfere

Compare(d), Comparison Analogy, Beside, Bracket, Collate, Confront, Contrast, Correspond, Cp, Equate, Liken, Match, Odious, Parallel, Relation, Simile, Weigh

Compartment Bay, Booth, Box, Cab, Carriage, Casemate, Cell, Chamber, Cockpit, Cubbyhole, Cubicle, Dog box, Glove, Locellate, Locker, Loculament, Loculus, Panel, Partition, Pigeonhole, Pocket, Room(ette), Severy, Smoker, Stall, Till, Trunk, Wind chest

Compass Ambit, Area, Beam, Bounds, Bow, Dividers, Extent, Gamut, Goniometer, Gyro, Gyroscope, Infold, Magnetic, Needle, Orbit, Pencil, Perimeter, → RANGE, Reach, Rhumb, Room, Scale, Trammel

Compassion(ate) Aroha, Clemency, Commiseration, Empathy, Goodwill, Heart, Humane, Kuan Yin, Kwan Yin, Loving kindness, Mercy, Pity, Remorse, Samaritan, Sympathy, Ubuntu

Compel(ling), Compelled, Compulsion, Compulsive, Compulsory Addiction, Coact, Coerce, Cogent, Command, Constrain, Dragoon, Duress, Enforce, Extort, Fain, → FORCE, Force majeure, Gar, Make, Mandatory, Obligate, Oblige, Pathological, Steamroller, Strongarm, Tyrannise, Urge, Walk Spanish

Compensate, Compensation Amend(s), Balance, Boot, Bote, Comp, Counterbalance, Counterpoise, Damages, Demurrage, Guerdon, Indemnity, Offset, Payment, Recoup, Redeem, Redress, Reparation, Reprisal, Requital, Restitution, Restore, Retaliation, Salvage, Satisfaction, Solatium, Wergild, X-factor

Compete Contend, Dog eat dog, Enter, Match, Play, Rival, Run, Vie

Competence, Competent Ability, Able, Adequate, Can, Capable, Capacity, Dab, Dow, Efficient, Fit, Proficient, Responsible, Sui juris, Worthy

Competition, Competitive, Competitor Agonist, Battle, Bee, Biathlon, Buckjumping, Checks and balances, Concours, Contender, Contention, Contest, Cook off, Cup, Dog eat dog, Drive, Entrant, Event, Field, Finals, Gamesman, Grand prix, Gymkhana, Head over heels, Heptathlon, Iron woman, Jump off, Keen, Match, Monopolistic, Olympiad, Open, Opponent, Outsider, Pairs, Panellist, Pentathlon, Player, Pools, Premiership, Puissance, Race, Rally, Rat race, Repechage, Rival(ise), Rodeo, Run, Runner-up, Show-jumping, Slam, Spelldown, Stableford, Starter, Tenson, Test, Three-day event, Tiger, Tournament, Tourney, Track meet, Trial, Triallist, Wap(p)enshaw, Wild card

Compile(r), Compilation Anthology, Arrange, Collect, Cross, Doxographer, Edit, Prepare, Synthesis, Zadkiel

Complain(t), Complainer Adenoids, Affection, Affliction, Alas, Alopecia, Anaemia, Angina, Arthritis, Asthma, Barrack, Beef, Bellyache, Bitch, Bleat, BSE, Carp, Charge, Chorea, Colic, Crab, Cramp, Criticise, Diatribe, Disorder, Dropsy, Epidemic, Ergot, Exanthema, Girn, Gout, Gravamen, Grievance, Gripe, Groan, Grouch, Grouse, Growl, Grudge, Grumble, Grutch, Harangue, Hives, Hone, Hypochondria, Ileitis, → ILLNESS, Jeremiad, Lament, Lumbago, Lupus, Malady, Mange, Mean(e), Mein, Mene, Moan, Morphew, Mump(s), Murmur, Nag, Natter, Neuralgia, Pertussis, Plica, Poor-mouth, Protest, Pyelitis, Rail, Remonstrate, Repine, Report, Rhinitis, Rickets, Sapego, Sciatica, Scold, Sequacious, Sigh, Silicosis, Squawk, Staggers, Thrush, Tic, Tinea, Upset, Whimper, Whine, Whinge, Yammer, Yaup, Yawp

▷ **Complement** *may indicate* a hidden word

Complete(d), Completely, Completion Absolute, Accomplish, All, Altogether, Arrant, Attain, Clean, Congenital, Consummate, Crashing, Crown, Dead, Do, Downright, End, Entire, Finalise, Finish, Flat, Foregone, Fruition, Fulfil, Full, Full-blown, Head over heels, Hollow, Incept, Integral, In toto, Neck and crop, One, Out, Out and out, Perfect, Plenary, Plum, Prolative, Pure, Quite, Rank, Root and branch, Rounded, Self-contained, Sheer, Spang, Sum, Teetotal, Thorough(going), Total, Unbroken, Uncensored, Uncut, Unequivocal, Unmitigated, Utter, Whole (hog), Wrap

Complex(ity) Abstruse, Advanced, Compound, Daedal, Difficult, Electra, Hard, Inferiority, Intricate, Intrince, Involute, Knot, Manifold, MHC, Military-industrial, Mixed, Multinucleate, Nest, Network, Obsession, Oedipus, Overwrought, Paranoid, Phaedra, Plexiform, Ramification, Subtle, Superiority, Syndrome, System, Tangle, Web

Complexion Aspect, Blee, Hue, Leer, Permatan, Temper, Tint, View

Compliance, Compliant, Comply Abet, Agree, Amenable, Assent, Conform, Deference, Hand-in-glove, Obedience, Obey, Observe, Sequacious, Surrender, Wilco

Complicate(d), Complication Bewilder, Complex, Deep, Elaborate, Embroil, Implex, Intricate, Involution, Involve, Inweave, Node, Nodus, Perplex, Ramification, Rigmarole, Tangle, Tirlie-wirlie

▷ **Complicated** *may indicate an anagram*

Compliment(s), Complimentary Backhanded, Baisemain, Bouquet, Congratulate, Devoirs, Douceur, Encomium, Esteemed, Flatter, Flummery, Freebie, Glowing, Greetings, Praise, Soap, Tribute

Compose(d), Composure Aplomb, Arrange, Calm, Consist, Cool, →**CREATE**, Equable, Equanimity, Equilibrium, Even, Face, Improvise, Indite, Level-headed, Lull, Notate, Patience, Pen, Phlegm, Placid, Poise, Produce, Reconcile, Sangfroid, Sedate, Serenity, Settle, Soothe, Tranquil

Composer Contrapunt(al)ist, Inventor, Maker, Melodist, Minimalist, Musician, Musicker, Serialist, Songsmith, Symphonist, Triadist, Tunesmith, Writer

▷ **Composing** *may indicate an anagram*

Composition, Compositor Aleatory, Beaumontage, Capriccio, Caprice, Cob, Concerto, Concertstuck, Concetto, Creation, Dite, Essay, Etude, Fantasia, Inditement, Ingredient, Literature, Loam, Met, Montage, Morceau, Nonet(te), Nonetto, Opus, Oratorio, Organum, Pastiche, Piece, Poem, Polyphony, Polyrhythm, Port, Printer, Quartette, Raga, Repoussage, Rhapsody, Setting, Ship, Sing, Smoot, Smout, Sonata, Sonatina, Structure, Study, Symphony, Synthesis, Terracotta, Texture, Toccata, Treatise, Trio, Typesetter, Work

▷ **Compound(ed)** *may indicate an anagram*

Compound (stop), Compound word Addition, Aggravate, Amalgam, Anti-inflammatory, Anti-knock, Blend, →**CAMP**, Composite, Constitute, Cpd, Derivative, Mix, Multiply, Synthesise, Tatpurusha, Type

Comprehend, Comprehensive All-in, Broad-brush, Catch-all, Catholic, Compass, Compendious, Contain, Exhaustive, Fathom, Follow, General, Global, Grand, Grasp, Include, Indepth, Ken, Large, Omnibus, Overall, Panoptic, Panoramic, Perceive, School, Sweeping, Thoroughgoing, Tumble, →**UNDERSTAND**, Wide

Compress(ed), Compression, Compressor Astrict, Axial-flow, Bale, Coarctate, Contract, Pump, Shoehorn, Solidify, Squeeze, Stupe, Thlipsis

Compromise, Compromising Avoision, Brule, Commit, Concession, Endanger, Fudge, Golden mean, Halfway house, Honeytrap, Involve, Middleground, Modus vivendi, Negotiate, Settlement, Time-server, Trade off, Via media

Computation, Compute(r) Analog(ue), Apple (Mac)®, Calcular, Desknote, Desktop, Digital, Eniac, Fifth generation, Front-end, Host, IALI, Laptop, Mainframe, Micro, Multiuser, Network, Number-cruncher, Palmtop, Personal, Proxy server, Reckon, TALISMAN, Voice response, WIMP

Computer hardware, Computer memory Busbar, Chip, Dataglove®, Docking station, DRAM, EAROM, EPROM, Floptical, IDE, Modem, Neurochip, Pentium®, Platform, Plug'n'play, Processor, PROM, RAM, ROM, Router, Tower, Track(er)ball

Computer language ADA, ALGOL, APL, ASCII, Assembly, AWK, Basic, C, COBOL, COL, Computerese, CORAL, Fortran, High-level, ICL, Java®, Java script®, LISP, LOGO, Low-level, OCCAM, PASCAL, PROLOG, Python, Scratchpad, Scripting, Small-talk, SNOBOL, SQL, Visual Basic, Weblish

Computer network, Computer systems ARPANET, BIOS, Cambridge ring, ERNIE, Evernet, Executive, Extranet, Fileserver, Freenet, HOLMES, Hypermedia, Internet, Intranet, JANET, LAN, MIDI, Multipoint, Neural, Stand-alone, TALISMAN, Tally, TAURUS, Telnet, Token ring, Unix, Usenet, VAN, WAN, Web, Wide-area, WIMP

Computer programs, Computer software Abandonware, Acrobat, ActiveX, Address harvester, Adware, Agent, App(let), Application, Assembler, Auto-responder, Bot, Browse, CADMAT, Cancelbot, Careware, Case, Casemix, Chatbot, Checksum,

Choiceboard, Client, Closed-loop, Columbus, Courseware, CU See Me, Datel®, Debugger, Demo, Device-driver, Diagnostic, Dictionary, Disassembler, Emacs, Enterprise, ERP, Est, Extreme, Facemail, Flash, Formatter, Free-to-air, Freeware, Groupware, HAL, Hard card, Heuristic, ITunes®, Linker, Loader, Logic bomb, Macro, Mail-merge, Malware, Mmorpg, Module, Neural net, Object, OCR, Plug-in, Powerpoint, Relocator, Ripper, Rootkit, Screensaver, Servlet, Shareware, Shell, Shopping agent, Shovelware, Spam killer, Spellchecker, Spider, Spreadsheet, Spyware, Stiffware, TELNET, Text editor, Translator, Trialware, Utility, Vaccine, Vaporware, Virus, Warez, Web browser, Webcast, Web crawler, Wiki, Windows®, Word processor, Worm

Computer terms Address bus, Alert box, Authoring, Autosave, Backslash, Bank-switching, Bitmap, Blog(ging), Blogroll, Bookmark, Boot, Boot-virus, Bot army, Breakpoint, Broadband, Calculate, Calculus, Cascade, Chatroom, Choke route, Clickstream, Client-server, Cobweb site, Coder, Cold boot, Conf, Core(dump), Counter, Cron, Cuspy, Cyber(netics), Cybercafe, Cyberslacking, Dataglove, Defrag(ment), Dial-up, DIF, Disk drive, Domain name, Dotcom, Earcon, Enqueue, Estimate, FAT, Figure, Flash ROM, Floptical, GIGO, Greybarland, Half-adder, Hardwire, Hashing, Hotlist, Hypertext, Inbox, Inputter, Integrator, Interface, IT, Joypad, Kludge, Linear, List serv, Logic, Measure, Meatspace, Memory stick, Moblog, Motherboard, Mouseover, Mouse potato, Mung, Non-volatile, Notwork, Numlock, Nybble, Nyetwork, Object, On-line, Outbox, Package, Packet sniffer, Pageview, Patch, Path name, Peer-to-peer, Pel, Permalink, Pharming, Phishing, Phreak, Pixel, Plug and play, Podcast, Podcatcher, Point and click, Poke, Popunder, Pop-up, Pseudocode, Pseudorandom, Public-key, Pushdown, Reader farm, README file, Read-out, Realtime, Reboot, Reckoner, Report program, Rogue dialler, Rogue site, Rootserver, Screensaver, Screen turtle, Scriptkiddie, Search engine, Serial port, Server farm, Shared logic, Shell, Shovelware, Sim, Smart, Smurfing, Soft return, Source, Spigot, Spim, Splog, Spreadsheet, Sprite, Style sheet, Superserver, Systems, Telecottage, Time slice, Toggle, Token ring, Triple, Turnkey, Turtle graphics, Unicode, Username, Utility program, Vaccine, Vlog, Vodcast, Voice response, Voxel, Wave file, Webbie, WebBoard, Webfarm, Wideband, Wi-fi, Wiki, WIMAX, Wordwrap, WORM, Wysiwyg, Yottabyte, Zettabyte, Zmodem

Computer user(s) Alpha geek, Brain, Cast(er), Chiphead, Cyberpunk, Cybersurfer, Digerati, Hacker, Liveware, Nethead, Netizen, Nettie, Onliner, Pumpking, Surfer, Tiger team, Troll, Webhead, White hat

Con(man) Against, Anti, Bunco, Defraudment, Diddle, Dupe, Gyp, Inveigle, Jacob, Learn, Peruse, Pretence, Read, Scam, Scan, Steer, Sucker, Swindle

Concede, Concession Acknowledge, Admit, Allow, Appeasement, Carta, Charter, Compromise, Confess, Favour, Forfeit, Franchise, Grant, Munich, Ou, Ow, Owe, Own, Privilege, Sop, Synchoresis, Yield

Conceit(ed) Bumptious, Caprice, Carriwitchet, Cocky, Concetto, Crank, Crotchet, Device, Dicty, Egoist, Egomania, Fancy, Fastuous, Fop, Fume, Hauteur, Idea, Notion, Podsnappery, Popinjay, Prig, Princock, Princox, Puppyism, Quiblin, Side, Snotty, Stuck-up, Swellhead, Swollenhead, Toffee-nose, Vain(glory), Wind

Conceive, Conceivable Beget, Create, Credible, Imagine, Possible, Surmise

Concentrate(d), Concentration Aim, Apozem, Application, Bunch, Centre, Collect, Condense, Dephlegmate, Distil, Elliptical, Essence, Extract, Focalise, Focus, Geographical, Intense, Listen, Major, Mantra, Mass, Molality, Molarity, Potted, Reduce, Rivet, Samadhi, Strong, Titrate, Titre, Undivided

Concern(ed), Concerning About, Affair, After, Ail, Altruism, Anent, As to, Bother, Business, Care, Cerne, Company, Disturb, Dot com, Firm, Going, Heed, House, Humanitarian, In re, Intéressé, Interest, Into, Lookout, → **MATTER**, Mell, Misease, Over, Part, Pidgin, Pigeon, Re, Reck, Regard, Reke, Relevant, Respect, Retch, Shake, Solicitude, Touch, Trouble, Versant, Wirra, Worry

▷ **Concerned** *may indicate* an anagram

Concert (place) Agreement, Ballad, Benefit, Chamber, Charivari, Cooperation, Device, Dutch, Gig, Hootanannie, Hootananny, Hootenanny, Hootnannie, Hootnanny,

Odeon, Odeum, Pop, Prom(enade), Recital, Singsong, Smoker, Smoking, Subscription, Symphony, The Proms, Together, Unison, Unity, Wit

Concierge Housekeeper, Porter

Concise Compact, Curt, Laconic, Short, Succinct, Telegraphic, Terse, Tight

Conclude(d), Conclusion, Conclusive Achieve, A fortiori, Afterword, Amen, Binding, Button-up, Cease, Clinch, Close, Complete, Consectary, Dead, Decide, Deduce, Demise, Diagnosis, →END, End-all, Endwise, Envoi, Epilogue, Explicit, Finding, Fine, Finis, →FINISH, Foregone, Gather, Illation, Infer, Lastly, Limit, Non sequitur, Omega, Over, Peroration, Point, Postlude, Punchline, Reason, Resolve, Settle, Showdown, Summary, Terminate, Upshot, Uptie

Concrete, Concretion Actual, Aggregate, Beton, Bezoar, Breeze, Cake, Calculus, Caprolite, Clot, Dogger, Gunite, Hard, Laitance, Mass, Minkstone, No-fines, Pile-cap, Positive, Real, Reify, Siporex, Solid, Tangible, Tremie, Vacuum

Condemn(ation) Abominate, Beknave, Blame, Blast, Cast, Censor, Censure, Convict, Damn, Decry, Denounce, Deprecate, Doom, Judge, Kest, Obelise, Proscribe, Reprove, Sentence, Theta, Upbraid

Condense(d), Condenser Abbreviate, Abridge, Capacitator, Compress, Contract, Distil, Encapsulate, Epitomise, Liebig, Précis, Rectifier, Reduce, Shorten, Shrink, Summarise, Surface

Condescend(ing) De haut en bas, Deign, Patronise, Snobbish, Stoop, Superior, Vouchsafe

Condiment Caraway, Catsup, Cayenne, Chutney, Flavour, Kava, Ketchup, Mustard, Pepper, Relish, Salt, Sambal, Sauce, Spice, Tracklement, Turmeric, Vinegar, Zedoary

Condition(al), Conditioning Autism, Case, Cense, Cinchonism, Circ(s), Circumstance, Classical, Congenital, Connote, Contingent, Disease, Disomy, Dropsy, Experimental, Feather, Fettle, Finite, Going, Hammertoe, Health, Hood, Hunk, If, Kelter, Kernicterus, Kilter, Latah, Necessary, Nick, Order, Pass, Pavlovian, Plight, Pliskie, Ply, Point, Position, Predicament, Premise, Premiss, Prepare, Prerequisite, Presupposition, Protasis, Provisory, Repair, Reservation, Reserve, Rider, Ropes, Sine qua non, Sis, Spina bifida, Standing, State (of play), Status quo, Sted, Stipulation, String, Sufficient, Term, Tid, Tox(a)emia, Trim, Trisomy, Understanding, Unless, Vir(a)emia, White finger

Condom(s) Cap, Gumboot, Johnny, Letter, Prophylactic, Rubber, Rubber goods, Safe, Sheath

Conduct(or), Conductress Abbado, Accompany, Administer, Anode, Ansermet, Arm, Arrester, Barenboim, Bearing, Behaviour, Bohm, Boult, Bus-bar, Cad, Clippie, Coil, Comport, Demean(our), Deportment, Direct, Drive, Editor, Electrode, Escort, Fetch, Guide, Hallé, Ignitron, Klemperer, Lark, Lead, Liber, Lightning, Mackerras, Maestro, Mantovani, Mho, Microchip, Nerve, Officiate, Ormandy, Outer, Ozawa, Parts, →PILOT, Previn, Prosecute, Psychagogue, Rattle, Safe, Sargent, Scudaller, Scudler, Silicon, Solicit, Solti, Stokowski, Strauss, Szell, Tao, Thermal, Thermistor, Thyristor, Toscanini, Transact, →USHER, Walter, Wire, Wood

▷ **Conducting** may indicate an '-ic' ending

Conduit Aqueduct, Canal, Carrier, Channel, Duct, Main, Pipe, Tube, Wireway

Cone(s), Conical, Cone-shaped Alluvial, Cappie, Conoidal, Egmont, Ellipse, Fir, Monticule, Moxa, Pastille, Peeoy, Pineal, Pingo, Pioy(e), Pottle, Puy, Pyramid, Pyrometric, Shatter, Spire, Storm, Strobilus, Taper, Tee, Traffic, Volcanic, Windsock

Confederal, Confederacy, Confederate, Confederation Accessory, Alliance, Ally, Association, Body, Bund, Bunkosteerer, Cover, Creek, F(o)edarie, Gueux, Illinois, League, Partner, Union

Confer(ence) Bestow, Cf, Collogue, Colloqium, Colloquy, Congress, Council, Diet, Do, Dub, Fest, Forum, Grant, Huddle, Imparlance, Indaba, Intercommune, Lambeth, Meeting, Munich, Negotiate, Palaver, Parley, Pawaw, Pear, Potsdam, Pourparler, Powwow, Press, Pugwash, Quadrant, Seminar, Settle, Summit, Symposium, Synod, →TALK, Vouchsafe, Yalta

Confess(ion), Confessor Acknowledge, Admit, Agnise, Avowal, Concede,

Confiteor, Cough up, Declare, Disclose, Edward, Helvetic, Own, Recant, Shema, Shrift, Shriver, Sing, Tetrapolitan, Verbal, Whittle

Confide(nce), Confident(ial), Confidant Aplomb, Aside, Assertive, Assured, Authoritative, Bedpost, Belief, Bottle, Bouncy, Brash, Can do, Certitude, Chutzpah, Cocksure, Cocky, Cred, Crouse, Entre nous, Entrust, Extravert, Extrovert, Faith, Favourite, Fearless, Feisty, Gatepost, Hardy, Hope, Hubris, Hush-hush, Intimate, Morale, Nerve, Pack, Positive, Private, Privy, QT, Sanguine, Secret, Secure, Self-assured, Self-possessed, Self-trust, Suavity, Sub rosa, Sure, Sure-footed, Tell, Together, Trust, Unbosom, Under the rose, Vaulting

Confine(d), Confines, Confinement Ambit, Bail, Bale, Cage, CB, Chain, Closet, Constrain, Contain, Coop, Cramp, Crib, Detain, Emmew, Encase, Enclose, Endemic, Enmew, Ensheath, Gate, Gender-moon, Immanacle, Immew, Immure, Impound, →**IMPRISON**, Incommunicado, Inertial, Inhoop, Intern, Limit, Local, Mail, March, Mew, Mure, Narrow, Pen, Pent, Pinion, Poky, Quarantine, Restrict, Rules, Solitary, Trammel

Confirm(ed), Confirmation Addict, Approve, Assure, Attest, Bear (out), Certify, Chris(o)m, Christen, Chronic, Clinch, Corroborate, Dyed-in-the-wool, Endorse, Homologate, Ink in, Obsign, Official, OK, Qualify, Ratify, Reassure, Sacrament, Sanction, Seal, Strengthen, Substantiate, Ten-four, Tie, Validate, Vouch

Conflict(ing) Agon, Antinomy, Armageddon, At odds, Battle, Boilover, Camp, Casus belli, Clash, Contend, Contravene, Controversy, Disharmony, Diverge, Encounter, Feud, Fray, Inconsistent, Internecine, Jar, Lists, Mêlée, Muss, Off-key, Oppose, Psychomachia, Rift, Strife, →**STRUGGLE**, Tergiversate, War

Conform(ist), Conformity Accord, Adjust, Comply, Conservative, Consistence, Correspond, Normalise, Obey, Procrustean, Propriety, Quadrate, Standardize, Stereotype(d), Suit, Time-server, Trimmer, Yield

▷ **Confound** *may indicate an anagram*

Confound(ed) Abash, Amaze, Astound, Awhape, Baffle, Bewilder, Blamed, Blasted, Blest, Bumbaze, Contradict, Darn, Dismay, Drat, Dumbfound, Elude, Floor, Jigger, Mate, Murrain, Nonplus, Perishing, Perplex, Rabbit, Spif(f)licate, Stump, Throw

Confront(ation) Appose, Beard, Breast, Brush, Cross, Eyeball, Face, Face down, Head-to-head, Incident, Mau-Mau, Meet, Militance, Nose, Oppose, Outface, Showdown, Smackdown, Tackle, Toe-to-toe, War

Confuse(d), Confusedly, Confusion Addle, Adrift, Anarchy, Astonishment, At sea, Babel, Baffle, Bedevil, Befog, Befuddle, Bemuse, Bewilder, Blur, Burble, Bustle, Callaloo, Chaos, Cloud, Clutter, Complicate, Consternation, Debacle, Desorienté, Didder, Disarray, Disconcert, Disorient, Distract, Dither, Dizzy, Dudder, Dust, Dwaal, Embrangle, Embroglio, Embroil, Entanglement, Farrago, Flap, Flummox, Flurry, Fluster, Fog, Fox, Fubar, Fuddle, Gaggle, Galley-west, Garble, Guddle, Hash, Havoc, Hazy, Hirdy-girdy, Huddle, Hugger-mugger, Hurly-burly, Hurry-skurry, Imbrangle, Imbroglio, Inchoate, Incoherent, →**IN CONFUSION**, Indistinct, Litter, Lost, Lurry, Maelstrom, Maffled, Maving, Mayhem, Maze, Melange, Melee, Mess, Mingle, Mish-mash, Misorder, Mither, Mixter-maxter, Mixtie-maxtie, Mizzle, Moider, Moither, Moonstruck, →**MUDDLE**, Mudge, Muss(e), Muzzy, Obfuscate, Overset, Pellmell, Perplex, Pi(e), Pose, Puzzle head, Ravel, Razzle-dazzle, Razzmatazz, Rout, Rummage, Snafu, Spaced out, Spin, Stump, Stupefy, Surprise, Swivet, Tangle, Tapsalteerie, Throw, Topsy-turvy, Toss, Turbulence, Turmoil, Tzimmes, Upside down, Welter, Whomble, Woolly, Woozy

▷ **Confuse(d)** *may indicate an anagram*

Conger Sea-eel

Congratulate, Congratulation Applaud, Felicitate, Laud, Mazeltov, Preen, Salute

Congregate, Congregation(alist) Assembly, Barnabite, Body, Brownist, Class, Community, Conclave, Ecclesia, Flock, Fold, Gathering, Host, Laity, Oratory, Propaganda, Synagogue

Congress(man) Assembly, Capitol, Conclave, Council, Eisteddfod, Intercourse, Legislature, Rally, Senator, Solon, Synod, Vienna

Conjunction Alligation, Ampersand, And, Combination, Consort, Coordinating, Inferior, Subordinating, Superior, Synod, Syzygy, Together, Union, Unition

Conk Nose

Connect(ed), Connection, Connector Accolade, Adaptor, Affiliate, Affinity, Agnate, Anastomosis, And, Associate, Attach, Band, Bind, Bridge, Bridle, Cable, Chiasm, Clientele, Cognate, Coherent, Colligate, Conjugate, Correlate, Couple, Cross-link, Delta, DIN, Dovetail, Downlink, Drawbar, Earth, Fishplate, Fistula, Interlink, Interlock, Interrelation, Join, Jumper, Kinship, Liaison, Lifeline, Link, Linkup, Marry, Merge, Neck, Network, Nexus, On, Online, Pons, Raphe, Rapport, Relate, Relative, Respect, Sentence, Shank, Splice, S-R, Tendon, Through, Tie, Tie-in, Union, Yoke, Zygon

Connive, Connivance Abet, Cahoots, Collude, Condone, Conspire, Lenocinium, Plot

Connoisseur Aesthete, Barista, Cognoscente, Epicure, Expert, Fancier, Gourmet, Judge, Oenophil(e)

Conquer(or), Conquering, Conquest Alexander, Beat, Conquistador, Cortes, Crush, Debel, Defeat, Genghis Khan, Hereward, →**MASTER**, Moor, Norman, Ostrogoth, Overcome, Overpower, Overrun, Pizarro, Saladin, Subjugate, Tame, Tamerlane, Vanquish, Victor, Vincent, Win

Conscience, Conscientious Casuistic, Heart, Inwit, Morals, Painstaking, Pang, Remorse, Scruple(s), Scrupulous, Sense, Superego, Syneidesis, Synteresis, Thorough, Twinge

Conscious(ness) Awake, Aware, Black, Deliberate, Limen, Sensible, Sentient, Witting

Consent Accord, Affo(o)rd, Agree, Approbate, Comply, Concur, Grant, Informed, Permit, Ratify, Submit, Una voce, Volens, Yes-but, Yield

Consequence, Consequent(ial), Consequently Aftermath, Consectaneous, Corollary, Effect, End, Implication, Importance, Issue, Karma, Knock-on, Moment, Outcome, Out-turn, Ramification, Repercussion, →**RESULT**, Sequel, Thence, Thereat, Thus

Conservative Blimpish, Blue, C, Cautious, Diehard, Disraeli, Fabian, Hard-hat, Hunker, New Right, Old guard, Old School, Rearguard, Right(-wing), Square, Thrifty, Tory, True blue, Unionist, Verkrampte, Young Fogey

Conserve, Conservation(ist) Comfiture, Husband(ry), Jam, Jelly, Maintain, Maintenance, NT, Protect, Save

Consider(able), Considerate, Consideration Ad referendum, Animadvert, Attention, Avizandum, By-end, Case, Cogitate, Contemplate, Count, Courtesy, Debate, Deem, Deliberate, Entertain, Envisage, Factor, Fair, Feel, Gay, Gey, Heed, Importance, Inasmuch, Judge, Kind, Many, Materially, Measure, Meditate, Muse, Pay, Perpend, Poise, Ponder, Pretty, Pro and con, Rate, Reck, Reckon, Reflect, Regard, Respect, Scruple, See, Sensitive, Several, Solicitous, Song, Speculate, Steem, Study, Substantial, Think, Tidy, Vast, View, Ween, Weigh

Consign(ment) Allot, Award, Batch, Bequeath, Delegate, Deliver, Entrust, Lading, Ship, Shipment, Transfer

Consist(ent), Consistency Changeless, Coherent, Comprise, Concordant, Enduring, Liaison, Rely, Sound, Steady, Texture

Consolation, Console Ancon, Appease, Balm, Cheer, Comfort, Games, Panel, Play, Reassure, Relief, Solace, Station

Conspicuous Arresting, Blatant, Bold, Clear, Eminent, Glaring, Kenspeck(le), Landmark, Light, Manifest, Patent, Radiant, Salient, Shining, Showy, Signal, Striking

Conspiracy, Conspirator, Conspire, Conspiring Brutus, Cabal, Cartel, Casca, Cassius, Catiline, Cato St, Cinna, Collaborate, Colleague, Collogue, Collude, Complot, Connive, Covin, Covyne, Guy, In cahoots, Intrigue, Oates, Omerta, →**PLOT**, Practisant, Ring, Scheme

Constable High, Hog, Lord High, Petty, →**POLICEMAN**, Uniformed

Constancy, Constant Abiding, Boltzmann, C, Changeless, Chronic, Coefficient,

Cosmic, Cosmological, Decay, Devotion, Dielectric, Diffusion, Dilys, Dirac, Eccentricity, Equilibrium, Eternal, Faith, Firm, Fixed, Fundamental, G, Gas, Gravitational, H, Honesty, Hubble's, K, Lambert, Leal(ty), Logical, Loyal, Magnetic, Nonstop, Often, Parameter, Pi, Planck's, Pole star, Rate, Regular, Relentless, Resolute, Sad, Solar, Staunch, Steadfast, Steady, Time, True, Unceasing, Unfailing, Uniform, Usual

Constellation Andromeda, Antlia, Apus, Aquarius, Aquila, Ara, Argo, Aries, Auriga, Bootes, Caelum, Camelopardalis, Camelopardus, Canes Venatici, Canis Major, Canis Minor, Carina, Cassiopeia, Centaurus, Cepheus, Cetus, Cham(a)eleon, Circinus, Columba, Coma Berenices, Coma Cluster, Corvus, Crater, Cygnus, Cynosure, Delphinus, Delta, Dolphin, Dorado, Draco, Equuleus, Eridanus, Fornax, Galaxy, Gemini, Great Bear, Gru(i)s, Hercules, Horologium, Hydra, Hydrus, Indus, Lacerta, Leo, Leo Minor, Lepus, Libra, Little Bear, Little Dipper, Lupus, Lynx, Lyra, Mensa, Microscopium, Monoceros, Musca, Norma, Octans, Ophiuchus, Orion, Pavo, Pegasus, Perseus, Phoenix, Pictor, Piscis Austrinus, → **PLANET**, Puppis, Pyxis, Reticulum, Sagitta, Sagittarius, Scorpius, Sculptor, Scutum, Serpens, Sextans, Southern Cross, Spica, → **STAR**, Telescopium, The Rule, Triangulum (Australe), Tucana, Twins, Unicorn, Vela, Vilpecula, Virgin, Virgo, Volans, Vulpecula, Wag(g)oner, Whale, Zodiacal

Constituency, Constituent Borough, Component, Element, Part, Seat, Staple, Ultimate, Voter

▷ **Constituents** *may indicate* an anagram

Constitute, Constitution(al) Appoint, Character, Charter, Clarendon, Compose, Comprise, Congenital, Creature, Establishment, Form, Fuero, Health, Physique, Policy, Polity, Seat, State, Stroll, Synthesis

Constrain(ed), Constraint Bind, Bondage, Coerce, Confine, Coop, Curb, Duress(e), Force, Hard, Localise, Oblige, Pressure, Repress, Stenosis, Taboo, Tie

Constrict(ed), Constriction Bottleneck, Cage, Choke, Coarctate, Contract, Cramp, Hour-glass, Impede, Isthmus, Limit, Narrow, Phimosis, Squeeze, Stegnosis, Stenosis, Strangle, Thlipsis, Tighten, Venturi

Construct(ion), Constructor, Constructive Build, Cast, Compile, Engineer, Erect, Fabricate, Facture, Fashion, Form, Frame, Make, Manufacture, Meccano, Partners, Seabee, Stressed-skin, Tectonic, Weave

Consult(ant), Consultation Avisement, Confer, Deliberate, Discuss, Imparl, Peritus, See, Sexpert, Shark watcher, Surgery

Consume(r), Consumption, Consumptive Bolt, Burn, Caterpillar®, Conspicuous, Decay, Devour, Diner, Eat, End-user, Engross, Exhaust, Expend, Feed, Glutton, Hectic, Mainline, Scoff, Spend, Swallow, TB, Use, Waste, Wear

Contact Abut, Address, Contingence, Electrode, Eye, Fax, Hook-up, Lens, Liaise, Liaison, Meet, Outreach, Radio, Reach, Shoe, → **TOUCH**

Contagious, Contagion Infection, Noxious, Poison, Taint, Variola, Viral

Contain(er) Amphora, Ampulla, Aquafer, Aquifer, Ashcan, Barrel, Basket, Bass, Beaker, Bidon, Billy(-can), Bin, Boat, Bottle, Box, Brazier, Buddle, Bunker, Butt, Butter-boat, Cachepot, Can, Canakin, Canikin, Canister, Cannikin, Cantharus, Capsule, Carafe, Carboy, Carry, Carton, Case, Cask, Cassette, Censer, Chase, Chest, Chilly bin, Churn, Clip, Coffer, Comprise, Coolamon, Crate, Crater, Crucible, Cup, Cupel, Cuvette, Decanter, Dracone, Dredger, Encircle, Enclose, Encompass, Enseam, Esky®, Feretory, Flagon, Flask, Flat, Gabion, Galliport, Gourd, Growler, → **HOLD**, House, Humidor, Igloo, Include, Incubator, Intray, Jar, Jeroboam, Jerrican, Jerrycan, Jug, Keg, Kirbeh, Leaguer, Lekythos, Locker, Magnox, Melting-pot, Monkey, Monstrance, Mould, Muffineer, Nosebag, Olpe, Ostensorium, Out-tray, Pail, Percolator, Pinata, Piscina, Pitcher, Pithos, Pod, Pottle, Punnet, Pyxis, Receptacle, Reliquary, Repository, Restrain, Sac(k), Safe, Saggar, Scyphus, Shaker, Situla, Skin, Skip, Snaptin, Solander, Spittoon, Stamnos, Stillage, Tank, Tantalus, Terrarium, Tinaja, Trough, Tub, Tun, Tupperware®, Urn, Valise, Vase, Vessel, Vinaigrette, Wardian case, Wineskin, Woolpack, Workbag

Contaminate(d), Contamination Corrupt, Defile, Flyblown, Impure, Infect, Moit, Mysophobia, Soil, Spike, Stain, Tarnish

Contemporary AD, Coetaneous, Concomitant, Current, Equal, Fellow, Modern, Modish, Present, Verism

Contempt(ible), Contemptuous Abject, Ageism, Aha, Arsehole, Bah, BEF, Blithering, Cheap, Contumely, Crud, Crumb, Crummy, Cullion, Cur, Cynical, Derision, Diddy, Dis(s), Disdain, Dismissive, Disparaging, Disrespect, Dog-bolt, Dusty, Fico, Fig, Figo, Git, Ignominious, Jive-ass, Lousy, Low, Mean, Measly, Misprision, Och, Paltry, Pelting, Pfui, Phooey, Pipsqueak, Pish, Poof, Poxy, Pshaw, Rats, Razoo, Scabby, Scarab, Scofflaw, →**SCORN**, Scumbag, Scurvy, Sdeign, Sexism, Shabby, Shitface, Shithead, Sneer, Sneeze, Sniffy, Snook, Snooty, Snot, Snotty, Soldier, Sorry, Sprat, Squirt, Squit, Supercilious, Toad, Toerag, Tossy, Turd, Tush, Weed, Wretched

Contend(er) Allege, Candidate, Claim, Clash, Compete, Cope, Debate, Dispute, Fight, Grapple, Oppose, Rival, Stickle, →**STRIVE**, Struggle, Submit, Tussle, →**VIE**, Wrestle

Content(ed) Apaid, Apay, Appay, Blissful, Happy, Inside, Please, Raza, Reza, Satisfy, Subject matter, Volume

▷ **Content** *may indicate* a hidden word

Contention, Contentious Argument, Bellicose, Cantankerous, Case, Combat, Competitive, Logomachy, Perverse, Polemical, Rivalry, Strife, Struggle, Sturt

Contest(ant) Agon, Battle (royal), Beauty, Beetle drive, Biathlon, Bout, Catchweight, Challenge, Championship, Combat, Competition, Concours, Darraign, Decathlon, Defend, Deraign, Dogfight, Duathlon, Duel(lo), Entrant, Eurovision, Event, Examinee, Finalist, Free-for-all, Fronde, Handicap, Heptathlon, Kemp, Kriegspiel, Lampadephoria, Match, Matchplay, Olympiad, Pancratium, Par, Paralympics, Pentathlon, Pingle, Play-off, Prizer, Race (meeting), Rat race, Rival, Roadeo, Rodeo, Scrap, Scrum, Set-to, Skirmish, Slam, Slugfest, Strife, Struggle, Tenson, Tetrathlon, Tournament, Triathlon, Tug-of-war, Vie, War, With

Continent(al) Abstinent, Asia, Atlantis, Austere, Chaste, Epeirogeny, Euro, Gallic, Gondwanaland, Greek, Landmass, Laurasia, Lemuria, Mainland, Moderate, NA, Pang(a)ea, Shelf, Teetotal, Temperate, Walloon

Continual(ly), Continuous Adjoining, At a stretch, Away, Ceaseless, Chronic, Connected, Eer, Endlong, Eternal, Eterne, Ever, Forever, Frequent, Incessant, On(going), Unbroken, Unceasing

Continue, Continuation, Continuing, Continuity Abye, Duration, Dure, During, Enduring, Enjamb(e)ment, Hold, Keep, Last, Link, Onward, Perpetuate, Persevere, Persist, Proceed, Prolong, Push on, Resume, Sequel, Sequence, Stand, Subsist, Survive, Sustain, Tenor

▷ **Continuously** *may indicate* previous words to be linked

Contraception, Contraceptive Billings method, Cap, Coil, Condom, Depo-Provera®, Diaphragm, Etonogestrol, IU(C)D, Legonorgestrel, Lippes loop, Loop, Minipill, Oral, Pessary, Pill, Precautions, Prophylactic, Sheath, Spermicide, Vimule®

Contract(ion), Contractor Abbreviate, Abridge, Affreightment, Agreement, Astringency, Bargain, Biceps, Binding, Bridge, Builder, Catch, Champerty, Charter (party), Clench, Clonus, Concordat, Condense, Constringe, Contrahent, Convulsion, Covenant, Cramp, Curtail(ment), Debt, Develop, Dwindle, Engage, Entrepreneur, Escrow, Extrasystole, Fibrillation, Forward, Gainsay, Gooseflesh, Guarantee, Hire, Incur, Indenture, Jerk, Knit, Labour, Lease, Lessen, Levator, Make, Mandate, Miosis, Myosis, Narrow, Outsource, Party, Privilege, Promise, Pucker, Purse, Restriction, Shrink, Shrivel, Sign, Slam, Slim, Social, Spasm, Specialty, Squinch, Stenosis, Stipulation, Straddle, Supplier, Swap, Sweetheart, Synaloepha, Systole, Telescope, Tender, Tetanise, Tetanus, Tic, Tighten, Tittle, Tonicity, Tontine, Treaty, Triceps, Trigger-finger, Trismus cynicus, Undertaker, Wrinkle, Yellow-dog, Z

▷ **Contract** *may indicate* a bridge call, e.g. 1S, 1C, 1D

Contradict(ion), Contradictory Ambivalent, Antilogy, Antinomy, Bull, Contrary,

Counter, Dementi, Deny, Disaffirm, Disprove, Dissent, Negate, Oxymoron, Paradox, Sot, Stultify, Sublate, Threap, Threep, Traverse

Contralto Clara Butt

Contraption Contrivance, Scorpion

Contrapuntal Fugue

Contrarily, Contrary Adverse, A rebours, Arsy-versy, But, Captious, Converse, Counter, Crosscurrent, Froward, Hostile, Inverse, Mary, Opposite, Oppugnant, Ornery, Perverse, Rebuttal, Retrograde, Wayward, Withershins

Contrast Chiaroscuro, Clash, Compare, Differ, Foil, Relief

Contribute, Contribution Abet, Add, Assist, Conduce, Donate, Dub, Furnish, Go, Help, Input, Mite, Offering, Share, Sub, Subscribe, Whack

▷ **Contributing to** *may indicate* a hidden word

Contrivance, Contrive(r), Contrived Art, Artificial, Cam, Chicaner, Contraption, Cook, Deckle, Deus ex machina, Device, Devise, Dodge, Engine, Engineer, Finesse, Frame, Gadget, Gimmick, Gin, Hatch, Hokey, Intrigue, Invention, Machinate, Manage, Manoeuvre, Page, Plan, Plot, Procure, Rest, Rowlock, Scheme, Secure, Shift, Stage, Trump, Wangle, Weave

Control(ler), Controllable, Controlled Ada, Aircon, Appestat, Autopilot, Big Brother, Birth, Boss, Boundary layer, Bridle, Cabotage, Camshaft, Chair, Check, Choke(hold), Christmas tree, Contain, Corner, Corset, Curb, Cybernetics, Damage, Descendeur, Dirigible, Dirigism(e), Dominate, Dominion, Driving seat, Duopsony, Dynamic, Elevon, Etatiste, Fader, Fast-forward, Fet(ch), Finger, Flood, Fly-by-wire, Gain, Gar, George, Gerent, Govern, Ground, Gubernation, Hae, Harness, Have, Heck, Helm, Hog, Influence, Influx, Inhibitor, Interchange, Joystick, Keypad, Knee-swell, Lead, Lever, Limit, Line, → **MANAGE**, Martinet, Mastery, Moderate, Mouse, Nipple, Noise, Nozzled, Numerical, Operate, Override, Pilot, Placebo, Police, Population, Possess, Power, Preside, Price, Process, Puppeteer, Quality, Radio, Referee, Regulate, Regulo®, Rein, Remote, Rent, Repress, Restrain, Restrict, Rheostat, Ride, Ripple, Rule, Run, School, Servo, Slide(r), Snail, Solion, Spoiler, Stage-manage, Steady, Steer, Stop, Stranglehold, Stringent, Subdue, Subject, Subjugate, Supervise, Suzerain, Svengali, Sway, Switch, Takeover, Tame, Temperate, Thermostat, Throttle, Tie, Tiller, Tone, Traction, Umpire, Upper hand, Valve, Weld, Wield, Zapper

Controversial, Controversy Argument, Contention, Debate, Dispute, Emotive, Eristic(al), Furore, Heretical, Hot potato, Troll

▷ **Contuse** *may indicate* an anagram

Convenience, Convenient Behoof, Cosy, Easy, Eft, Ethe, Expedient, Facility, Gain, Gents, Handsome, → **HANDY**, Hend, Lav, Leisure, Near, Opportune, Pat, Privy, Public, Suitable, Toilet, Use, Well

Convent Abbatial, Cloister, Fratry, Friary, House, Motherhouse, Nunnery, Port-royal, Priory, Retreat

Convention(al) Academic, Accepted, Babbitt, Blackwood, Bourgeois, Caucus, Code, Conclave, Conformity, → **CUSTOMARY**, Diet, Done, Formal, Geneva, Habitude, Hidebound, Iconic, Lame, Lingua franca, Mainstream, Meeting, Middlebrow, Middle-of-the-road, More, National, Nomic, Orthodox, Ossified, Pompier, Proper, Propriety, Readymade, Schengen, Staid, Starchy, Stereotyped, Stock, Straight, Stylebook, Synod, The thing, Uptight, Usage, Warsaw

Conversation(alist), Converse, Conversant Abreast, Antithesis, Antitype, Board, Buck, Cackle, Causerie, Chat, Chitchat, Colloquy, Commune, Convo, Crack, Crossfire, Deipnosophist, Dialogue, Discourse, Eutrapelia, Eutrapely, Exchange, Facemail, Hobnob, Interlocution, In tune with, Jaw-jaw, Natter, Opposite, Palaver, Parley, Rap, Rhubarb, Shop, Shoptalk, Sidebar, Small talk, Socialise, → **TALK**, Transpose, Trialogue, Wongi, Word

Conversion, Converter, Convert(ible) Adapt, Alter, Assimilate, Bessemer, Cabriolet, Cash, Catalytic, Catechumen, Change, Commutate, Commute, Cyanise, Damascene, Diagenesis, Disciple, Encash, Evangelize, Exchange, Expropriate, Fixation, Ismalise, Landau, Liquid(ate), Marrano, Metamorphosis, Metanoia, Missionary, Neophyte, Noviciate, Novitiate, Persuade, Proselyte, Put, Ragtop, Realise,

Rebirth, Reclamation, Recycle, Revamp, Romanise, Sheik(h), Soft-top, Souper, Tablet, Transduce, Transmute, Try, Vert

▷ **Conversion, Converted** *may indicate* an anagram

Convey(ance) Assign, BS, Carousel, Carry, Carrycot, Cart, Charter, Coach, Conduct, Cycle, Deed, Deliver, Eloi(g)n, Enfeoffment, Esloyne, Exeme, Grant, Guide, Lease, Litter, Lorry, Mailcar(t), Pirogue, Re-lease, Sac, Sled, Soc, Tip, Title deed, Tote, Tram, Transfer, Transit, Transmit, Transport, Trolley, Vehicle

Convict(ion) Attaint, Belief, Botany Bay, Bushranger, Canary, Certitude, Cockatoo, Cogence, Crawler, Credo, Creed, Crime, Criminal, Demon, Dogma, Emancipist, Faith, Felon, Forçat, Gaolbird, Government man, Jailbird, Lag, Magwitch, → **PERSUASION**, Plerophory, Previous, Prisoner, Record, Ring, Trusty, Vehemence, Yardbird

Convince(d), Convincing Assure, Certain, Cogent, Credible, Doubtless, Luculent, Persuade, Plausible, Satisfy, Sold, Sure

Convulse, Convulsion(s), Convulsive Agitate, Clonic, Clonus, Commotion, Disturb, DT, Eclampsia, → **FIT**, Galvanic, Paroxysm, Spasm, Throe, Tic

▷ **Cook** *may indicate* an anagram

Cook(s), Cooker(y), Cooking Aga®, Babbler, Babbling brook, Bake, Balti, Beeton, Benghazi, Bhindi, Bouche, Braise, Broil, Cacciatore, Calabash, Captain, Charbroil, Chargrill, Chef, Coction, Coddle, Concoct, Cordon bleu, Creole, Cuisine, Cuisinier, Delia, Devil, Do, Doctor, Dumple, Easy over, Edit, En papillote, Escoffier, Explorer, Fake, Falsify, Fiddle, Fireless, Fix, Flambé, Forge, Fricassee, Fry, Fudge, Fusion, Gastronomy, Gratinate, Greasy, Griddle, Grill, Haute cuisine, Haybox, Hibachi, Jackaroo, Kiln, Lyonnaise, Marengo, Marinière, Meunière, Microwave, Mount, Poach, Prepare, Pressure, Range, Ring, Roast, Roger, Sauté, Short-order, Silver, Sous-chef, Spit, Steam, Stew, Stir-fry, Stove, Tandoori, Tire, Toast

Cool(er), Coolant, Cooling, Coolness Ace, Aloof, Aplomb, Calm, Can, Chill, Chokey, Collected, Composed, Cryogen, Cryostat, Defervescence, Dignified, Dispassionate, Distant, Esky®, Fan, Frappé, Fridge, Frigid, Frosty, Gaol, Goglet, Hip, Ice(box), Imperturbable, In, Jail, Jug, Keel, Lubricating oil, Maraging, Nervy, Nonchalant, Offish, Phlegm, Poise, Prison, Quad, Quod, Refresh, Reserved, Sangfroid, Serene, Shady, Skeigh, Splat, Stir, Super-duper, Sweat, Temper(ate), Thou(sand), Unruffled

Coop Cage, Cavie, Confine, Gaol, Hutch, Mew, Pen, Rip

Cooperate, Cooperation, Cooperative Ally, Artel, Bipartisan, Collaborate, Combine, Conspire, Contribute, Coop, Credit union, Liaise, Pitch in, Tame, Teamwork, Together

Coordinate(s), Coordinated, Coordination Abscissa, Abscisse, Agile, Arrange, Cartesian, Del, Ensemble, Harmony, Nabla, Orchestrate, Ordonnance, Peer, Polar, Synergy, Tight, Twistor, Waypoint, X, Y, Z

Cop(s) Bag, Bull, Catch, Copper, Dick, Flic, Keystone, Peeler, Peon, → **POLICEMAN**

Cope Chlamys, Deal, Face, Fare, Handle, → **MANAGE**, Mantle, Meet, Negotiate, Pallium, Poncho

Copy(ing), Copier, Copyist, Copywriter Adman, Aemule, Ape, Apograph, Association, Autotype, Calk, Calque, Carbon, Clerk, Clone, Counterpart, Crib, Cyclostyle, Diazo, Ditto, Dyeline, Echo, Echopraxia, Ectype, Edition, Eidograph, Electro, Emulate, Engross, Estreat, Example, Facsimile, Fair, Fax, Flimsy, Forge, → **IMITATE**, Issue, Knockoff, Manifold, Manuscript, Match, Me-tooer, Microdot, Milline, Mimeograph®, Mimic, Mirror, MS, Ozalid, Pantograph, Parrot, Photostat®, Plagiarism, Read-out, Repeat, Replica, Reprint, Repro, Reproduce, Rip, Roneo®, Scanner, Scribe, Script, Scrivener, Sedulous, Simulate, Skim, Soft, Spit, Stat, Stencil, Stuff, Tall, Telefax, Tenor, Tenure, Trace, Transcribe, Transume, Transumpt, Vidimus, Xerox®

Coral (reef) Alcyonaria, Aldabra, Atoll, Brain, Gorgonia(n), Laccadives, Madrepore, Millepore, Organ-pipe, Pink, Reef, Sea fan, Sea ginger, Sea-pen, Sea whip, Staghorn, Zoothome

Cord, Cord-like Aiguillette, Band, Bedford, Bind, Boondoggle, Cat-gut, Chenille, Communication, Creance, Cybernaculum, Drawstring, Elephant, Flex, Fourragère,

Cordon | 96

Funicle, Gasket, Heddle, Laniard, Lanyard, Ligature, Line, Moreen, Myelon, Nerve,
Net, Ocnus, Picture, Piping, Quipo, Quipu, Rep(s), Restiform, Rip, Rope, Sash, Sennit,
Service, Sinew, Sinnet, Spermatic, Spinal, → **STRING**, Tendon, Tie, Tieback, Twine,
Twitch, Umbilical, Vocal

Cordon Band, Beltcourse, Picket, Ring, Surround

Core Barysphere, Calandria, Campana, Centre, Essence, Filament, Heart, Hub,
Magnetic, Nife, Plerome, Quintessence, Runt

Corfu Corfiot(e)

Cork(ed), Corker Balsa, Bouché, Bung, Float(er), Humdinger, Oner, Periderm,
Phellem, Phellogen, Plug, Seal, Shive, Stopper, Suber(ate)

Corkscrew Bore, Opening, Spiral, Twine

Cormorant Duiker, Duyker, Scart(h), Shag, Skart(h)

Corn(y) Bajr(a), Banal, Blé, Callus, Cereal, Cob, Dolly, Durra, Emmer, Epha, Flint,
Gait, Graddan, Grain, Grist, Hokey, Icker, Indian, Kaffir, Kanga pirau, Mabela, Maize,
Mealie, Muid, Nubbin, Pickle, Pinole, Posho, Rabi, Shock, Stitch, Straw, Tail ends,
Thrave, Trite, Zea

Corner Amen, Angle, Bend, Canthus, Cantle, Canton, Chamfer, Cranny, Dangerous,
Diêdre, Elbow, Entrap, Hog, Hole, Hospital, Long, Lug, Monopoly, NE, Niche, Nook,
NW, Predicament, Quoin, SE, Speakers', Spot, SW, Tack, Tattenham, Trap, Tree,
Vertex

Coronation Enthronement

Corporation Belly, Body, Breadbasket, Commune, Company, Conglomerate, Guild,
Kite, Kyte, Paunch, Pot(-belly), Public service, Stomach, Swag-belly, Tum, Wame,
Wem

Corps Body, C, Crew, Diplomatic, Marine, Peace, RAC, RE, REME, Unit

Corpse(s) Blob, Body, Cadaver, Carcass, Carrion, Deader, Dust, Goner, Like, Mort,
Quarry, Relic, Remains, Stiff, Zombi(e)

Corral Kraal, OK

Correct(ive), Correcting, Correctly, Correctness, Correction, Corrector
About east, Accepted, Accurate, Alexander, Align, Amend, Aright, Bodkin, Castigate,
Chasten, Chastise, Check, Cheese, Decorous, Diorthortic, Edit, Emend, Epanorthosis,
Ethical, Exact, Fair, Fix, Grammatical, Legit, Mend, Orthopaedic, Preterition, Probity,
Proofread, Proper, Propriety, Punctilious, Punish, Rebuke, Rectify, Red pencil,
Redress, Remedial, Reprove, Revise, Right(en), Scold, Spinning-house, Spot-on,
Straighten, Sumpsimus, Tickety-boo, Tippex®, Trew, True, Twink, U, Yep, Yes

▷ **Corrected** *may indicate* an anagram

Correspond(ence), Correspondent, Corresponding Accord, Agree,
Analogy, Assonance, Coincident, Communicate, Congruence, Counterpart,
Cynghanedd, Epistolist, Equate, Eye-rhyme, Fit, Homolog(ue), Identical, Isomorph,
Lobby, Match, On all fours, One-one, One to one, Par, Parallel, Parity, Penpal,
Post(bag), Relate, Symmetry, Sync, Tally, Veridical, Write

Corridor Air, Aisle, Gallery, Greenway, Lobby, Passage, Penthouse

Corrode(d), Corrosion, Corrosive Acid, Acid rain, Brinelling, Burn, Canker,
Decay, Eat, Erode, Etch, Fret, Gnaw, Hydrazine, Mordant, → **ROT**, Rubiginous, Rust,
Waste

Corrupt(er), Corrupting, Corruption Abuse, Adulterate, Bastardise, Bent,
Canker, Cesspit, Debase, Debauch, Decadent, Defile, Degenerate, Depravity,
Dissolute, Dry rot, Emancipate, Embrace(o)r, Embrasor, Empoison, Enseam, Etch,
Evil, Fester, Gangrene, Graft(er), Immoral, Impaired, Impure, Infect, Inquinate,
Jobbery, Leprosy, Malversation, Nefarious, Obelus, Payola, Perverse, Poison, Pollute,
Power, Putrefaction, Putrid, Rakery, Ret(t), Rigged, Rot, Scrofulous, Seduce, Sepsis,
Septic, Sleaze, Sodom, Sophisticate, Spoil, Suborn, Taint, Tammany, Twist, Ulcered,
Venal, Vice, Vitiate

Cosmetic Aloe vera, Beautifier, Blusher, Bronzer, Chapstick, Conditioner, Detangler,
Eye-black, Eyeliner, Eye-shadow, Face-pack, Foundation, Fucus, Highlighter,
Kohl, Lightener, Liner, Lip gloss, Lip liner, Lipstick, Lotion, Maquillage, Mascara,

Moisturizer, Mousse, Mudpack, Nail polish, Paint, Panstick, Pearl-powder, Pearl-white, Powder, Q-tip, Reface, Rouge, Talcum, Toner

Cosmos, Cosmic Globe, Heaven, Infinite, Mundane, Nature, Universe, World

Cost(s), Costly Be, Bomb, Carriage, Charge, Current, Damage, Disadvantage, Earth, Escuage, Estimate, Exes, →**EXPENSE**, Fetched, Hire, Historic(al), Loss, Marginal, Outlay, Overhead, Precious, Price, Quotation, Rate, Rent, Running, Sacrifice, Standard, Storage, Sumptuous, Tab, Toll, Unit, Upkeep, Usurious

Costume(s) Apparel, Attire, Camagnole, Cossie, Dress, Ensemble, Get-up, Gi(e), Guise, Judogi, Livery, Maillot, Motley, Nebris, Polonaise, Rig, Ruana, Surcoat, Tanga, Trollopee, Tutu, Uniform, Wardrobe

Cosy Cosh, Gemutlich, Intime, Snug

Cottage(r) Bach, Batch, Bordar, Bothie, Bothy, Bower, Box, Bungalow, Cabin, Cape Cod, Chalet, Cot, Crib, Dacha, Hut, Lodge, Mailer, Thatched

Cotton Absorbent, Agree, AL, Alabama, Balbriggan, Batiste, Batting, Calico, Candlewick, Ceiba, Chambray, Chino, Chintz, Collodion, Coutil(le), Cretonne, Denim, Dho(o)ti, Dimity, Ducks, Fustian, Galatea, Gossypine, Gossypium, Humhum, Ihram, Jaconet, Lawn, Lea, Lille, Lint, Lisle, Longcloth, Madras, Manchester, Marcella, Muslin, Nainsook, Nankeen, Nankin, Percale, Pongee, Sateen, Sea-island, Seersucker, Silesia, Stranded, Surat, T-cloth, Thread, Twig, Upland, Velveteen

Couch Bed, Davenport, Daybed, Express, Grass, Lurk, Palanquin, Palkee, Palki, Quick, Recamier, Sedan, Settee, Sofa, Studio, Triclinium, Vis-à-vis, Word

Cough(ing) Bark, Chin, Croup, Expectorate, Hack, Harrumph, Hawk, Hem, Hoast, Kink, Rale, Tisick, Tussis, Ugh, Whooping

Council (meeting), Councillor, Counsel(lor) Achitophel, Admonish, Admonitor, Advice, Advocate, Ahithophel, Alderman, Alfred, Aread, Assembly, Attorney, Aulic, Board, Body, Boule, Bundesrat, Burgess, Cabal, Cabinet, Casemate, Committee, Consistory, Corporation, County, Cr, Decurion, Devil, Divan, Douma, Duma, Ecofin, Egeria, Europe, Exhort, General, Greenbag, Hebdomadal, Indaba, Induna, Info, Jirga, Junta, Kabele, Kebele, Kite, Landst(h)ing, Lateran, Leader, Legislative, Majlis, Mentor, Nestor, Nicene, Panchayat, Parish, Powwow, Privy, Provincial, Rede, Reichsrat, Runanga, Samaritan, Sanhedrim, Sanhedrin, Security, Senate, Shura, Sobranje, Sobranye, Soviet, States, Syndicate, Synod, Thing, Tradeboard, Trent, Tridentine, Trullan, Unitary, Volost, Whitley, Witan, Witenagemot, Works, Zila, Zila parishad, Zillah

Count(ed), Counter(balance), Counting Abacus, Add, Algoriam, Anti, Aristo, Balance, Bar, Basie, Buck, Buffet, Calculate, Calorie, Cavour, Census, Check, Chip, Compute, Coost, Crystal, Cuisenaire rods, Desk, Disc, Dracula, Dump, Earl, Enumerate, Fish, Geiger, Geiger-Muller, Graf(in), Grave, Itemise, Jet(t)on, Landgrave, Margrave, Matter, Meet, Merel(l), Meril, Milton work, Number, Numerate, Obviate, Olivia, Oppose, Outtell, Palatine, Palsgrave, Paris, Pollen, Presume, Rebut, →**RECKON**, Refute, Rejoinder, Rely, Resist, Retaliate, Retort, Rhinegrave, Scaler, Scintillation, Score, Shopboard, Sperm, Squail, Statistician, Stop, Sum, Table, Tally, Tell, Tiddleywink, Tolstoy, Ugolino, Weigh, Zeppelin

Counterfeit(er) Bastard, Belie, Bogus, Boodle, Brum, Coiner, Doctor, Duffer, Dummy, Fain, Fantasm, Fayne, Flash, Forge, Fraudster, Imitant, Paperhanger, Phantasm, Phoney, Pseudo, Queer, Rap, Schlenter, Sham, Shan(d), Simular, Simulate, Skim, Slang, Slip, Smasher, Snide, Spurious

Counties, County Co, Comital, Comitatus, District, Hundred, Metropolitan, Palatine, Parish, Seat, Shire, Six

Countless Infinite, Innumerable, Myriad, Umpteen, Unending, Untold

Country(side), Countrified Annam, Arcadia, Bangladesh, Bolivia, Boondocks, Bucolic, Champaign, Clime, Colchis, Edom, Enchorial, Farmland, Fatherland, Jordan, Karoo, Karroo, →**LAND**, Lea, Lee, Mongolia, Motherland, Nation, Nature, Parish, Paysage, People, Province, Rangeland, Realm, Region, Republic, Rural, Rustic, Satellite, Scythia, Soil, State, The sticks, Tundra, Veld, Venezuela, Weald, Wold, Yemen

Coup Blow, Deal, KO, Move, Putsch, Scoop, Stroke, Treason

Coup d'etat Putsch

Couple(r), Coupling Acoustic, Ally, Attach, Band, Brace, Bracket, Connect, Duet, Duo, Dyad, Enlink, Fishplate, Gemini, Geminy, Hitch, Interlock, Item, →JOIN, Marry, Mate, Meng(e), Ment, Ming, Pair, Pr, Relate, Shackle, Tenace, Tie, Tirasse, Turnbuckle, Tway, Union, Unite, Universal, Voltaic, Wed, Yoke

Coupon(s) Ration, Ticket, Voucher

Courage(ous) Balls, Ballsy, Bottle, Bravado, Bravery, Bulldog, Daring, Derring-do, Dutch, Fortitude, Gallantry, Game, Gimp, Grit, Gumption, Guts, Hardy, Heart, Heroism, Indomitable, Lion-heart, Macho, Manful, Mettle, Moral, Moxie, Nerve, Pluck, Rum, Spirit, Spunk, Stalwart, Steel, Stomach, Valiant, Valour, Wight

Course(s) Afters, Aim, Aintree, Antipasto, Appetiser, Arroyo, Ascot, Assault, Atlantic, Back straight, Bearing, Beat, Canal, Career, Channel, Chantilly, Chase, Circuit, Civics, Consommé, Conversion, Correspondence, Crash, Current, Curriculum, Cursus, Damp(-proof), Dessert, Diadrom, Dish, Dromic, Easting, Entrée, Fish, →FOOD, Foundation, Going, Goodwood, Greats, Gut, Heat, Hippodrome, Induction, Lacing, Lane, Lap, Layer, Leat, Leet, Line, Lingfield, Links, Longchamp, Meal, Meat, Mess, Mizzen, Newbury, Newmarket, Nine-hole, Northing, Nulla, Obstacle, →OF COURSE, Orbit, Orthodromic, Period, Policy, PPE, Practicum, Procedure, Process, Programme, Progress, Pursue, Race, →RACETRACK, Raik, Ravioli, Refresher, Regimen, Rhumb, Ride, Ring, Rink, Road, Rota, Route, Routine, Run, Rut, Sandown, Sandwich, Semester, Series, Slalom, Soup, Southing, Starter, Stearage, Steerage, Step(s), Straight, Stratum, Streak, Stream, Stretch, String, Syllabus, Tack, Tanride, Tenor, Track, Trade, Trail, Troon, Way, Westing

Court(ier), Courtship, Courtyard Ad(vantage), Address, Admiralty, Appellate, Arbitration, Arches, Atrium, Attention, Audience, Audiencia, Aula, Banc, Bar, Basecourt, Bench, Beth Din, Bishop's, Boondock, Caerleon, Camelot, Canoodle, Caravanserai, Cassation, Centre, Chancery, Chase, Clay, Cloister-garth, Commercial, Commissary, Commission, Conscience, Conservancy, Consistory, County, Criminal, Crown, CS, Ct, Curia, Curia Regis, Curtilage, Date, Dedans, Deuce, Diplock, District, Divisional, Doctor's Commons, Domestic, Duchy, Durbar, Dusty Feet, En tout cas, Eyre, Faculties, Federal, Fehm(gericht), Fiars, Fifteen, Forensic, Forest, Forum, Fronton, Galleria, Garth, Go steady, Grass, Guildenstern, Halimot(e), Hampton, Hard, High, High Commission, Hof, Holy See, Hustings, Inferior, Innyadr, Intermediate, Invite, Jack, Judicatory, Justice, Juvenile, Kacheri, Kangaroo, Keys, King, King's Bench, Kirk Session, Knave, Law, Leet, Lobby, Lyon, Magistrate's, Majlis, Marshalsea, Mash, Moot, Old Bailey, Open, Osric, Palace, Parvis, Patio, Peristyle, Petty Sessions, Philander, Piepowder, Police, Porte, Prerogative, Presbytery, Prize, Probate, Provincial, Provost, Quad, Quarter Sessions, Queen, Queen's Bench, Racket, Request, Retinue, Romance, Rosenkrantz, Royal, St James's, Sanhedrin, Scottishland, See, Service, Session, Sheriff, Shire-moot, Small-claims, Spoon, Stannary, Star Chamber, Sudder, Sue, Suitor, Superior, Supreme, Swanimote, Sweetheart, Synod, Thane, Thegn, Traffic, Trial, Tribunal, Vehm, Vestibulum, Walk out, Ward, Wardmote, Wench, Woo, World, Wow, Yard, Youth

Courteous, Courtesy Affable, Agreement, Bow, Comity, Devoir, Etiquette, Fair, Genteel, Gentilesse, Gentility, Gracious, Hend, Polite, Politesse, Refined, Strain, Urbanity, Well-mannered

Courtly Aulic, Chivalrous, Cringing, Dignified, Flattering, Refined

Courtyard Area, Atrium, Close, Cortile, Marae, Patio, Quad

Cousin(s) Bette, Cater, Country, Coz, Cross, First, German, Kin, Kissing, Parallel, Robin, Second, Skater

Couthy Bien, Nice

Cover(ed), Covering Adventitia, Air, A l'abri, Amnion, Antependium, Antimacassar, Apron, Aril, Armour, Attire, Awning, Barb, Bard(s), Bark, Bathrobe, Bedspread, Bestrew, Bind, Blanket, Bodice, Bonnet, Brood, Bubblewrap, Bury, Cache-sex, Camouflage, Canopy, Cap, Caparison, Cape, Capsule, Cartonnage, Casing, Casque, Catch-all, Caul, Ceil, Ciborium, Cladding, Clapboard, Cleithral, Clithral,

Coat, Cocoon, Coleorhiza, Conceal, Cope, Copyright, Cosy, Cot, Counterpane, Cour, Covert, Cowl, Crust, Curtain, Deadlight, Debruised, Deck, Deputise, Dividend, Dome, Drape(t), Dripstone, Duchesse, Dusting, Dust-sheet, Duvet, Eiderdown, Encase, Endue, Enguard, Enlace, Ensheathe, Enshroud, Envelop(e), Enwrap, Exoderm(is), Exoskeleton, Extra, Eyelid, Face, Falx, Fanfare, Felting, Fielder, Figleaf, Fingerstall, First-day, Flashing, Flown, Fother, Front, Gaiter, Gambado, Glove, Gobo, Grolier, Ground, Groundsheet, Hap, Harl, Hat, Hatch, Havelock, Heal, Heel, Hejab, Hele, Hell, Helmet, Hide, Hijab, Hood, Housing, Hubcap, Immerse, Incase, Include, Indument, Indusium, Inmask, Insulate, Insurance, Insure, Jacket, Lag, Lambrequin, Lay, Leap, Leep, Legging, Legwarmer, Lid, Ligger, Liner, Loose, Manche, Mantle, Mask, Mat, Metal, Mort-cloth, Mount, Muffle, Mulch, Mulch, Overlap, Overlay, Overnet, Overwrap, Pad, Palampore, Palempore, Pall, Pand, Panoply, Parcel, Partlet, Pasties, Patch, Patent, Pavilion, Pebbledash, Pelmet, Periderm, Perigone, Pillow sham, Plaster, Plate, Pleura, Point, Pseudonym, Pullover, Quilt, Radome, Redingote, Regolith, Riza, Robe, Roof, Roughcast, Rug, Run, Sally, Screen, Serviette, Setting, Sheath, Sheet, Shell, Shelter, Shield, Shower, Shrink-wrap, Shroud, Shuck, Skin, Slipcase, Smokescreen, Solleret, Span, Spat, Splashback, Stand-by, Stifle, Stomacher, Strew, Strow, Superfrontal, Superimpose, Swathe, Tampian, Tampion, Tapadera, Tapis, Tarp(aulin), Teacosy, Tectorial, Tectum, Tegmen, Tegument, Tent, Test(a), Tester, Thatch, Thimble, Thumbstall, Tick(ing), Tidy, Tile, Tilt, Tonneau, Top, Trapper, Trench, Trip, Turtleback, Twill, Twilt, Umbrella, Up, Upholster, Valance, Veale, Veil, Vele, Veneer, Ventail, Vert, Vesperal, Vest, Vestiture, Visor, Volva, Wainscot, Warrant, Waterdeck, Whelm, Whemmle, Whitewash, Whomble, Whommle, Whummle, Wrap, Wrappage, Wrapper, Wreathe, Yapp, Yashmak

Covet(ed), Covetous Avaricious, Crave, Desiderata, Desire, Eager, Envy, Greedy, Hanker, Yearn

Cow(s) Adaw, Alderney, Amate, Appal, Awe, Belted Galloway, Boss(y), Bovine, Browbeat, Cash, Cattle, Charolais, Colly, Crummy, Dant(on), Daunt, Dexter, Dsomo, Dun, Friesian, Galloway, Gally, Goujal, Guernsey, Hawkey, Hawkie, Heifer, Hereford, Intimidate, Jersey, Kouprey, Kyloe, Lea(h), Mart, Milch, Milker, Mog(gie), Moggy, Mooly, Muley, Mulley, Neat, Oppress, Overawe, Redpoll, Red Sindhi, Rother(-beast), Runt, Sacred, Santa Gertrudis, Scare, Simmental, Slattern, Steer, Step on, Stirk, Subact, Subjugate, Teeswater, Threaten, Unnerve, Vaccine, Zebu, Z(h)o

Coward(ice), Cowardly Bessus, Cat, Chicken, Cocoa, Craven, Cuthbert, Dastard, Dingo, Dunghill, Fraidy-cat, Fugie, Funk, Gutless, Hen, Hilding, Lily-livered, Mangy, Meacock, Nesh, Niddering, Nidderling, Nidering, Niderling, Niding, Nithing, Noel, Panty-waist, Poltroon, Pusillanimous, Recreant, Scaramouch(e), Scaredy cat, Sganarelle, Sissy, Slag, Sook, Viliaco, Viliago, Villagio, Villiago, Weak-spirited, White feather, Yellow, Yellow-belly

Cowboy, Cowgirl Buckaroo, Gaucho, Inexpert, Io, Jerrybuilder, Leger, Llanero, Neatherd, Puncher, Ranchero, Ritter, Roper, Shoddy, Vaquero, Waddy, Wrangler

Cowpat Dung, Tath

Coy Arch, Coquettish, Mim, Modest, Nice, Shamefast, →**SHY**, Skittish

▷**Crab** *may indicate an anagram*

Crab(by), Crablike Apple, Attercop, Boston, Cancer, Cancroid, Cantankerous, Capernoity, Cock, Coconut, Daddy, Decapoda, Diogenes, Dog, Ethercap, Ettercap, Fiddler, Ghost, Grouch, Hard-shell, Hermit, Horseman, Horseshoe, King, Land, Limulus, Mantis, Mitten, Nebula, Ochidore, Oyster, Pagurian, Partan, Perverse, Podite, Roast, Robber, Rock, Saucepan-fish, Scrawl, Sentinel, Sidle, Soft-shell, Soldier, Spider, Std, Stone, Velvet-fiddler, Xiphosura, Zoea

Crack(ed), Cracker(s), Cracking Ace, Ad-lib, Admirable, Bananas, Beaut, Biscuit, Bonbon, Break, Cat, Catalytic, Chap, Chasm, Chat, Chink, Chip, Chop, Clap, Cleave, Cleft, Cloff, Confab, Cranny, Craquelure, Craqueture, Craze, Cream, Crepitate, Crevasse, Crevice, Crispbread, Dawn, Decipher, Decode, Def, Doom, Dunt, Elite, Fab, Fatiscent, Fent, Firework, First-rate, Fisgig, Fissure, Fizgig, Flaw, Flip-flop, Fracture, Gem, Go, Graham, Grike, Gryke, Gully, Hairline, Hit, Insane, Jibe, Joint, Leak, Liar,

Little-endian, Lulu, Matzo, Mot, Moulin, Oner, Peterman, Pleasantry, Pore, Praise, Prawn, Quip, Rap, Report, Rhagades, Rictus, Rift, Rille, Rima, Rime, Rimous, Rive, Rock, Saltine, Seam, Shatter, Snap, Soda, Solve, Split, Spring, Squib, Sulcus, Top, Try, Waterloo, Wind shake, Yegg

Cradle Bassinet, Berceau, Book rest, Cat's, Cot, Crib, Cunabula, Hammock, Knife, Nestle, Rocker

Craft(y) Aerostat, Arch, Art, Aviette, Barbola, Batik, Boat, Canal boat, Cautel, Cunning, Disingenuous, Finesse, Fly, Guile, Hydroplane, Ice-breaker, Insidious, Knack, Kontiki, Landing, Loopy, Machiavellian, Mister, Mystery, Oomiack, Pedalo, Powerboat, Reynard, Saic, Shallop, Ship, Shuttle, →**SKILL**, Slee, Sleeveen, Slim, Slippy, Sly, Slyboots, Sneaky, State, Subdolous, Subtil(e), Subtle, Suttle, Tender, Trade, Triphibian, Umiak, Underhand, Versute, →**VESSEL**, Wile, Workmanship

Craftsman AB, Artificer, Artisan, Artist, Chippy, Coppersmith, Cutler, Ebonist, Fabergé, Finisher, Gondolier, Guild, Hand, Joiner, Journeyman, Mason, Mechanic, Morris, Opificer, Potter, Tinsmith, Wainwright, Wright

Craig Ailsa

Cram(mer) Bag, Bone up, Candle-waster, Cluster, Craig, Fill, Gag, Gavage, Mug up, Neck, Pang, Prime, Revise, Rugged, Scar(p), Spur, Stap, Stodge, Stow, Swat, Tuck

Cramp(ed) Agraffe, Charleyhorse, Claudication, Confine, Constrict, Crick, Hamper, Hamstring, Incommodious, Musician's, Myalgia, Narrow, Pinch, Poky, Potbound, Restrict, Rigor, Sardines, Scrivener's palsy, Squeeze, Stunt, Tenesmus, Tetany, Writer's

Crane, Crane-driver Adjutant-bird, Australian, Cherry picker, Container, Davit, Demoiselle, Derrick, Dogman, Gantry, Herd, Heron, Hooper, Ichabod, Jenny, Jib, Jigger, Native companion, Numidian, Rail, Sandhill, Sarus, Sedge, Seriema, Shears, Sheer, Siege, Stork, Stretch, Whooper, Winch

Cranium Harnpan

Crap Feculence

Crash Accident, Bingle, Collapse, Ditch, Dush, Fail, Fall, Fragor, Frush, Intrude, Linen, Nosedive, Plough into, Prang, Rack, Ram, Rote, Shock, Shunt, Slam, Smash, South Sea Bubble, Thunderclap, Topple, Wham, Wrap

▷ **Crashes** *may indicate* an anagram

Crate Banger, Biplane, Box, Case, Ceroon, Crib, Hamper, Jalopy, Langrenus, Petavius, Purbach, Tube

Crave, Craving Appetent, Appetite, Aspire, Beg, Beseech, Covet, Desire, Entreat, Hanker, Hunger, Itch, Libido, Long, Lust, Malacia, Methomania, Orexis, Pica, Polyphagia, Sitomania, The munchies, Thirst, Yearn, Yen

Crayfish Astacology, Gilgie, Jilgie, Marron, Yabbie, Yabby

Crayon Chalk, Colour, Conté®, Pastel, Pencil

Craze(d), Crazy Absurd, Ape, Apeshit, Avid, Barmy, Bats, Batty, Berserk, Bonkers, Break, Cornflake, Crack(ers), Crackpot, Cult, Daffy, Dement, Derange, Dingbats, Dippy, Distraught, Doiled, Doilt, Doolally, Doolally tap, Dottle, Dotty, Fad, Flaky, Flaw, Folie, Frantic, Furious, Furore, Furshlugginer, Gaga, Geld, Gonzo, Gyte, Haywire, Headbanger, Insane, Loco, Loony, Loopy, Lunatic, Madden, Maenad(ic), Mania, Manic, Mattoid, Meshug(g)a, Moonstruck, Nuts, Out to lunch, Porangi, Potty, Psycho(path), Rage, Rave, Round the bend, Round the twist, Scatty, Screwball, Skivie, Stunt, Thing, Troppo, Typomania, Unhinge, Wacko, W(h)acky, Wet, Whim, Wowf, Zany

▷ **Crazy** *may indicate* an anagram

Creak(y) Cry, Grate, Grind, Rheumatic, Scraich, Scraigh, Scroop, Seam, Squeak

Cream(y) Barrier, Bavarian, Best, Chantilly, Cherry-pick, Cleansing, Cold, Crème fraîche, Devonshire, Double, Elite, Foundation, Frangipane, Glacier, Heavy, Lanolin, Liniment, Lotion, Mousse, Off-white, Ointment, Opal, Paragon, Pastry, Pick, Ream, Rich, Salad, Single, Skim, Vanishing

Crease Bowling, Crinkle, Crumple, →**FOLD**, Goal, Lirk, Pitch, Pleat, Popping, Ridge, Ruck(le), Ruga, Rugose, Wreathe, Wrinkle

Create, Creation, Creative Brainstorm, Build, Cause, Coin, Compose, Craft,

Devise, Dreamtime, Engender, Establish, Fabricate, Forgetive, Form, Found, Generate, Genesis, Godhead, Hexa(h)emeron, Ideate, →INVENT, Kittle, Knit, Omnific, Oratorio, Originate, Produce, Promethean, Shape, Synthesis, Universe

Creature Animal, Ankole, Basilisk, Beast, Being, Bigfoot, Chevrotain, Cratur, Critter, Crittur, Indri, Man, Moner(on), Nekton, Sasquatch, Sphinx, Whiskey, Wight, Zoon

Credibility, Credible, Credit(or), Credits Ascribe, Attribute, Belief, Billboard, Brownie points, Byline, Carbon, Catholic, Crawl, Easy terms, Esteem, Extended, Family, Ghetto, Honour, HP, Kite, Kudos, LC, Lender, Mense, On the nod, Post-war, Probable, Reliable, Renown, Repute, Revolving, Shylock, Social, Strap, Tally, Tax, Tick, Title, Trust, Weight, Youth

Creep(er), Creeping, Creeps, Creepy Ai, Aseismic, Cleavers, Crawl, Eery, Function, Grew, Grovel, Grue, Heebie-jeebies, Heeby-jeebies, Herpetic, Inch, Insect, Ivy, Nerd, Nuthatch, Periwinkle, Pussyfoot, Repent, Reptant, Sarmentous, Sidle, Silverweed, Sittine, Skulk, Slink, Snake, Sobole(s), Steal, Toad, Truckle, Vine, Virginia, Willies

Crepe Blini, Blintz(e), Canton, Pancake

Crescent Barchan(e), Bark(h)an, Fertile, Lune(tte), Lunulate, Lunule, Meniscus, Moon, Red, Sickle, Waxing

Crest(ed) Acme, Brow, Chine, Cimier, Cockscomb, Comb, Copple, Crista, Height, Kirimon, Knap, Mon, Peak, Pileate, Pinnacle, Plume, Ridge, Rig, Summit, Tappit, Tee, →TOP, Wreath

Crevice Chine, Cranny, Fissure, Interstice, Ravine, Vallecula

Crew Boasted, Company, Complement, Co-pilot, Core, Deckhand, Eight, Four, Ground, Lot, Manners, Men, Oars, Sailors, Salts, Seamen, Ship men, Team, Teme

Crib Cheat, Cot, Cowhouse, Cradle, Cratch, Filch, Horse, →KEY, Manger, Pony, Purloin, Putz, Shack, Stall, Steal, Trot

Crikey Argh, Gosh

Crime Attentat, Barratry, Bias, Caper, Car jack, Chantage, Chaud-mellé, Computer, Corpus delicti, Ecocide, Embracery, Fact, Felony, Fraud, GBH, Graft, Heist, Iniquity, Insider trading, Malefaction, Mayhem, Misdeed, Misdemeanour, →OFFENCE, Organised, Ovicide, Peccadillo, Perjury, Pilferage, Public wrong, Rap, Rape, Rebellion, →SIN, Stranger, Theft, Tort, Transgression, Treason, Villa(i)ny, White-collar, Wrong

Criminal Accessory, Arsonist, Bandit, Bent, Bigamist, Bushranger, Chain gang, Chummy, Con, Cosa Nostra, Counterfeiter, Crack-rope, →CROOK, Culpable, Culprit, Delinquent, Desperado, Escroc, Fagin, Felon, Flagitious, Forensic, Gangster, Goombah, Hard men, Heavy, Heinous, Highbinder, Hitman, Hood(lum), Jailbird, Ladrone, Lag, Larcener, Lifer, Looter, Lowlife, Maf(f)ia, Malefactor, Maleficent, Malfeasant, Mens rea, Miscreant, Mob(ster), Molester, Ndrangheta, Nefarious, Nefast, Offender, Outlaw, Peculator, Pentito, Perp(etrator), Peterman, Prohibited, Racketeer, Ram raider, Receiver, Recidivist, Reprehensible, Rustler, Safe blower, Sinner, Snakehead, Thug, Triad, Triggerman, Underworld, Villain, Wicked, Wire, Yakuza, Yardie, Yegg

▷ **Criminal** *may indicate* an anagram

Criminologist Lombroso

Cringe, Cringing Cower, Creep, Crouch, Cultural, Fawn, Grovel, Recoil, Shrink, Sneaksby, Sycophantic, Truckle

Cripple(d) Damage, Disable, Game, Hamstring, Handicap, Injure, →LAME, Lameter, Lamiter, Maim, Paralyse, Polio, Scotch, Spoil

Crisis Acme, Crunch, Drama, Emergency, Exigency, Fastigium, Fit, Flap, Head, Identity, Make or break, Panic, Pass, Shake-out, Solution, Suez, Test, Turn

Crisp(ness) Brisk, Clear, Crimp, Crunchy, Fire-edge, Fresh, Sharp, Short, Succinct, Terse

Critic(al), Criticise, Criticism Acute, Agate, Agee, Armchair, Arnold, Attack, Backbite, Badmouth, Barrack, Berate, Bird, Blame, Boileau, Boo, Brickbat, Bucket, Captious, Carp, Castigate, Cavil, Censor(ious), →CENSURE, Clobber, Comment, Condemn, Connoisseur, Crab, →CRUCIAL, Crunch, Dangle, Decisive, Denigrate, Denounce, Deprecate, Desperate, Diatribe, Do down, Earful, Exacting, Excoriate,

Exegesis, Fastidious, Fateful, Flak, Flay, Fulminous, Hammer, Harrumph, Higher, Important, Impugn, Inge, Inveigh, Judge, Judgemental, Knife-edge, Knock(er), Lambast, Lash, Leavis, Life and death, Literary, Lower, Masora(h), Mas(s)orete, Nag, Nasute, Nibble, Nice, Niggle, Nitpicker, Obloquy, Overseer, Pan, Pater, Peck, Puff, Pundit, Quibble, Rap, Rebuke, Reprehend, Reproach, Review(er), Rip, Roast, Ruskin, Scalp, Scarify, Scathe, Scorn, Second guess, Serious, Severe, Sharp-tongued, Shaw, Sideswipe, Slag, Slam, Slashing, Slate, Sneer, Snipe, Spray, Stick, Stricture, Strop, Swipe, Tense, Textual, Thersitic, Threap, Tipping-point, Touch and go, Trash, Upbraid, Urgent, Vet, Vitriol, Vivisect, Watershed

Croak(er) Creak, Crow, Die, Grumble, Gutturalise, Perish, Sciaena

Crockery Ceramics, China, Dishes, Earthenware, Service, Ware

▷ **Crocks** *may indicate* an anagram

Crocodile Cayman, File, Garial, Gavial, Gharial, Gotcha lizard, Line, Mugger, River-dragon, Saltie, Saltwater, Sebek, Teleosaur(ian)

Croft Bareland, Pightle

Crook(ed), Crookedness Adunc, Ajee, Asymmetric, Awry, Bad, Bend, Bow, Cam, Camsheugh, Camsho(ch), Cock-eyed, Criminal, Cromb, Crome, Crosier, Crummack, Crummock, Crump, Curve, Dishonest, Elbow, Fraud, Heister, Hook, Ill, Indirect, Kam(me), Kebbie, Lituus, Malpractitioner, Obliquity, Shank, Sheep-hook, Shyster, Sick, Skew(whiff), Slick(er), Staff, Swindler, Thraward, Thrawart, Thrawn, Twister, Wonky, Wrong'un, Wry, Yeggman

▷ **Crooked** *may indicate* an anagram

Crop(ped), Cropping, Crops, Crop up Basset, Browse, Cash, Catch, Cereal, Clip, Craw, Cut, Distress, Dock, Emblements, Emerge, Epilate, Eton, Foison, Forage, → **HAIRCUT**, Harvest, Hog, Ladino, Lop, Not(t), Plant, Poll, Produce, Prune, Rawn, Riding, Rod, Root, Scythe, Shear, Shingle, Sithe, Standing, Stow, Strip, Succession, Top, Truncate

▷ **Cross** *may indicate* an anagram

Cross(ing), Crossbred Angry, Ankh, Ansate, Archiepiscopal, Banbury, Bandog, Basta(a)rd, Baster, Beefalo, Bestride, Boton(n)e, Brent, Bridge, Bristling, Buddhist, Burden, Calvary, Cancel, Cantankerous, Canterbury, Capital, Capuchin, Cat(t)alo, Cattabus, Celtic, Channel, Charing, Chi, Chiasm(a), Choleric, Clover-leaf, Compital, Constantine, Crosslet, Crosswalk, Crotchety, Crucifix, Crux, Cut, Decussate, Demi-wolf, Dihybrid, Double, Dso(mo), Dzobo, Eleanor, Encolpion, Faun, Fiery, Fitché, Fleury, Foil, Footbridge, Ford, Frabbit, Fractious, Frampold, Franzy, Funnel, Fylfot, Geneva, George, Grade, Greek, Hinny, Holy rood, Hybrid, Ill, Imp, Indignant, Interbreed, Intersect, Intervein, Iona, Iracund, Irascible, Irate, Irked, Iron, Jersian, Jerusalem, Jomo, Jumart, King's, Kiss, Ladino, Latin, Level, Liger, Lorraine, Lurcher, Maltese, Mameluco, Market, Mermaid, Military, Misfortune, Mix, Moline, Mongrel, Mule, Narky, Nattery, Node, Norman, Northern, Nuisance, Oblique, Obverse, Ordinary, Orthodox, Overpass, Overthwart, Papal, Patonce, Patriarchal, Pattée, Pectoral, Pedestrian, Pelican, Percolin, Plus, Pommé, Potence, Potent, Preaching, Puffin, Quadrate, Railway, Ratty, Reciprocal, Red, Roman, Rood, Rose, Rosy, Rouen, Rouge, Rubicon, Sain, St Andrew's, St Anthony's, St George's, St Patrick's, St Peter's, Saltier, Saltire, Sambo, Satyr, Shirty, Sign, Snappy, Southern, Span, Splenetic, Strid, Svastika, Swastika, T, Tangelo, Tau, Tayberry, Ten, Testy, Thraw, Thwart, Tiglon, Tigon, Times, Toucan, Transit, Transom, Transverse, Traverse, Tree, Unknown, Urdé, Vexed, Vext, Victoria, → **VOTE**, Weeping, Whippet, Wholphin, Wry, X, Zebra(ss), Zhomo, Z(h)o, Zobu

Cross-examination, Cross-examine Elenctic, Grill, Interrogate, Question, Targe

Crossword Cryptic, Grid, Puzzle, Quickie

Crouch Bend, Cringe, Falcade, Fancy, Lordosis, Ruck, Set, Squat, Squinch

Crow Big-note, Bluster, Boast, Brag, Carrion, Chewet, Chough, Corbie, Corvus, Crake, Currawong, Daw, Gab, Gloat, Gorcrow, Hooded, Hoodie, Huia, Jackdaw, Jim(my), Murder, Raven, Rook, Scald, Skite, Squawk, Swagger, Vaunt

Crowd(ed) Abound, Army, Bike, Boodle, Bumper, Bunch, Byke, Caboodle, Clutter,

Concourse, Congest(ed), Cram, Crush, Crwth, Dedans, Dense, Doughnut, Drove, Fill, Flock, Galere, Gang, Gate, Gathering, Herd, Horde, →HOST, Huddle, Hustle, Jam, Jam-packed, Lot, Many, Meinie, Mein(e)y, Menyie, Mob, Mong, Multitude, Ochlo-, Pack, Pang, Populace, Press, Rabble, Raft, Ragtag, Ram, Ratpack, Ring, Ruck, Scrooge, Scrouge, Scrowdge, Scrum, Serr(é), Shoal, Shove, Slew, Slue, Squash, Squeeze, Stuff, Swarm, Swell, Thick, Thrang, Three, Throng, Trinity, Varletry

Crown Acme, Apex, Bays, Bull, Camp, Cantle, Cap, Capernoity, Cidaris, Civic, Coma, Corona, Cr, Diadem, Ecu, Engarland, Enthrone, Fillet, Garland, Gloria, Haku, Head, Headdress, Instal, Iron, Ivy, Krantz, Laurel, Monarch, Mural, Naval, Nole, Noll, Northern, Noul(e), Nowl, Olive, Ore, Ovation, Pate, Peak, Pediment, Pschent, Sconce, Stephen's, Taj, Thick'un, Tiar(a), →TOP, Triple, Triumphal, Trophy, Vallary, Vertex

Crucial Acute, Critical, Essential, Key, Paramount, Pivotal, Vital, Watershed

Crud Red snow

Crude(ness) Bald, Brash, Brute, Coarse, Earthy, Halfbaked, Immature, Incondite, No tech, Primitive, Raunch, Raw, Rough, Rough and ready, Rough-hewn, Rough-wrought, Tutty, Uncouth, Unrefined, Vulgar, Yahoo

▷**Cruel** *may indicate an anagram*

Cruel(ty) Barbarous, Bloody, Brutal, Cut-throat, Dastardly, De Sade, Draconian, Fell, Fiendish, Flinty, Hard, Heartless, Immane, Inhuman(e), Machiavellian, Neronic, Pitiless, Raw, Remorseless, Stern, Tiger, Tormentor, Tyranny, Unmerciful, Vicious, Wanton

Cruise(r) Busk, Cabin, Coast, Nuke, Orientation, Prowl, Sail, Sashay, Ship, Tom, Travel, Trip, Voyager

Crumb(le), Crumbly, Crumbs Coo, Cor, Decay, Disintegrate, Ee, Fragment, Friable, Golly, Law, Leavings, Moulder, Mull, Murl, Nesh, Nirl, Ort, Panko, Particle, Ped, Pulverise, Raspings, Rot

Crunch(y) Abdominal, Acid test, Chew, Craunch, Crisp, Gnash, Grind, Munch, Occlude, Scranch

Crush(ed), Crusher, Crushing Acis, Anaconda, Annihilate, Beetle, Bow, Breakback, Champ, Comminute, Conquer, Contuse, Cranch, Crunch, Defeat, Destroy, Graunch, Grind, Hug, Humble, Jam, Knapper, Levigate, Litholapaxy, Mangle, Mash, Mill, Molar, Mortify, Nib, Oppress, Overcome, Overwhelm, Pash, Policeman, Pound, Press, Pulp, Pulverise, Quash, Quell, Ruin, Schwarmerei, Scotch, Scrum, Scrumple, Scrunch, Smash, Squabash, Squash, Squeeze, Squelch, Squish, Stamp, Stave, Steam-roll, Stove, Stramp, Suppress, Telescope, Trample, Tread, Vanquish

Crusoe Robinson, Selkirk

Crust(y) Argol, Beeswing, Cake, Coating, Coffin, Continental, Cover, Crabby, Craton, Fur, Gratin, Heel, Horst, Ice fern, Kissing, Kraton, Lithosphere, Orogen, Osteocolla, Pie, Reh, Rind, Rine, Sal, Salband, Scab, Scale, Shell, Sial, Sima, Sinter, Surly, Tartar, Teachie, Tectonics, Terrane, Tetchy, Upper, Wine-stone

Crustacea(n) Amphipod, Barnacle, Cirriped, Copepod, Crab, Crayfish, Cyclops, Cyprid, Cypris, Daphnia, Decapod(a), Entomostraca, Fishlouse, Foot-jaw, Gribble, Isopod, Krill, Limulus, Lobster, Marine borer, Maron, Nauplius, Nephrops, Ostracoda, Prawn, Red seed, Sand-hopper, Sand-skipper, Scampi, Shrimp, Slater, Squilla, Woodlouse

Cry(ing) Aha, Alalagmus, Alew, Baa, Banzai, Bark, Battle, Bawl, Bay, Bell, Bemoan, Bill, Blat, Bleat, Bleb, Blub(ber), Boo, Boohoo, Boom, Bray, Bump, Caramba, Caw, Cheer, Chevy, Chirm, Chivy, Clang, Cooee, Crake, Croak, Crow, Dire, Euoi, Eureka, Evoe, Evoke, Exclaim, Eye-water, Fall, Field-holler, Gardyloo, Gathering, Geronimo, Gowl, Greet, Halloo, Harambee, Haro, Harrow, Havoc, Heigh, Hemitrope, Herald, Hinny, Hoicks, Holler, Honk, Hoo, Hoop, Hosanna, Hout(s)-tout(s), Howl, Humph, Io, Kaw, Low, Mewl, Miaou, Miau(l), Miserere, Mourn, Night-shriek, Nix, O(c)hone, Oi, Olé, Ow, Pugh, Rabbito(h), Rallying, Rivo, Sab, Scape, Scream, Screech, Sell, Sese(y), Sessa, →SHOUT, Shriek, Slogan, Snivel, Snotter, Sob, Soho, Sola, Squall, Squawk, Street, Sursum corda, Tally-ho, Tantivy, Umph, Vagitus, View-halloo, Vivat, Vociferate, Wail, War, War whoop, Watchword, Waterworks, Waul, Wawl, Weep, Westward ho, Whammo, Whee(ple), Whimper, Whine, Whinny, Whoa, Whoop,

Winge, Wolf, Yammer, Yawl, Yelp, Yicker, Yikker, Yip, Yippee, Yodel, Yo-heave-ho, Yo-ho-ho, Yoick, Yoop, Yowl

Crypt(ic) Catacomb, Cavern, Chamber, Crowde, Encoded, Enigmatic, Esoteric, Favissa, Grotto, Hidden, Obscure, Occult, Secret, Sepulchre, Short, Steganographic, Tomb, Unclear, Undercroft, Vault

Cryptaesthesia ESP

Crystal(s), Crystal-gazer, Crystalline, Crystallise Allotriomorphic, Baccara(t), Beryl, Candy, Clear, Cleveite, Copperas, Coumarin, Cumarin, Cut-glass, Dendrite, Druse, Enantiomorph, Epitaxy, Form, Geode, Glass, Hemitrope, Ice-stone, Jarosite, Lase, Lead, Liquid, Love-arrow, Macle, Melamine, Needle, Nematic, Nicol, Orthogonal, Pellucid, Penninite, Pericline, Phenocryst, Piezo, Pinacoid, Pinakoid, Prism, Pseudomorph, Purin(e), Quartz, R(h)aphide, R(h)aphis, Rhinestone, Rock, Rotenone, Rubicelle, Scryer, Shoot, Silica, Skatole, Skryer, Snowflake, Sorbitol, Spar, Spherulite, Table, Tina, Tolan(e), Trichite, Triclinic, Trilling, Wafer, Watch-glass, Xenocryst, Yag

Cub(s) Baby, Kit, Lionet, Novice, Pup, Sic, Whelp, Youth

Cuba C

Cubicle Alcove, Booth, Carrel(l), Stall

Cuckoo Ament, Ani, April fool, Bird, Chaparral cock, Dotty, Gouk, Gowk, Inquiline, Insane, Koekoea, Koel, → **MAD**, Mental, Piet-my-vrou, Rabid, Stupid

▷ **Cuckoo** *may indicate* an anagram

Cuddle, Cuddly Canoodle, Caress, Clinch, Embrace, Fondle, Hug, Inarm, Nooky, Smooch, Smuggle, Snog, Snuggle, Zaftig

Cue Billiard, Cannonade, Catchword, Feed, Half-butt, Hint, Mace, → **PROMPT**, Reminder, Rod, Sign, Signal, Wink

Cuisine Balti, Cookery, Food, Menu, Nouvelle

Cult Cabiri, Cargo, Creed, Flower power, New Age, Sect, Snake, Voodoo, Worship

Cultivate(d), Cultivation, Cultivator Agronomy, Arty, Breed, Civilise, Developed, Dig, Dress, Farm, Garden, Genteel, Grow, Hoe, Hydroponics, Improve, Labour, Plough, Polytunnel, Pursue, Raise, Reclaim, Refine, Sative, Sophisticated, Tame, Tasteful, Till, Tilth, Wainage, Woo, Work

Culture(d), Cultural Abbevillean, Acheulean, Acheulian, Agar, Art(y), Aurignacian, Azilian, Bacterian, Bel esprit, Brahmin, Broth, Canteen, Capsian, Civil(isation), Clactonian, Club, Compensation, Dependency, Enterprise, Ethnic, Experiment, Explant, Fine arts, Folsom, Gel, Gravettian, Grecian, Halafian, Hallstatt, Hip-hop, Humanism, Intelligentsia, Kultur(kreis), La Tène, Learning, Levallois, Madelenian, Magdalenian, Meristem, Monolayer, Mousterian, New Age, Polish, Polite, Refinement, Solutrean, Sophisticated, Strepyan, Tissue

Cunning Arch, Art, Artifice, Astute, Cautel, Craft(y), Deceit, Deep, Devious, Down, Finesse, Foxy, Guile, Insidious, Leary, Leery, Machiavellian, Quaint, Skill, Slee(kit), Sleight, Slim, Sly(boots), Smart, Sneaky, Stratagem, Subtle, Vulpine, Wheeze, Wile, Wily

▷ **Cup** *may indicate* a bra size

Cup(s), Cupped Aecidium, America's, Beaker, Bledisloe, Calcutta, Calix, Calyculus, Cantharus, Ca(u)p, Chalice, Claret, Communion, Cotyle, Cruse, Cupule, Cyathus, Cylix, Davis, Demitasse, Dish, Dop, European, Eyebath, FA, Fairs, Final, Fingan, Finjan, Glenoid, Goblet, Grace, Gripe's egg, Hanap, Horn, Kylix, Loving, Melbourne, Merry, Monstrance, Moustache, Mug, Noggin, Nut, Optic, Pannikin, Paper, Planchet, Plate, Pot, Procoelous, Quaich, Quaigh, Rhyton, Rider, Ryder, Sangrado, Scyphus, Sippy, Stirrup, Suction, Tantalus, Tass(ie), Tastevin, Tazza, Tea-dish, Tig, Tot, → **TROPHY**, Tyg, UEFA, Volva, World

Cupboard Airing, Almery, Almirah, A(u)mbry, Armoire, Beauf(f)et, Cabinet, Chiffonier, Chiff(o)robe, Closet, Coolgardie safe, Court, Credenza, Dresser, Encoignure, Locker, Press

Cupid Amoretto, Amorino, Archer, Blind, Bow-boy, Cherub, Dan, Eros, Love, Putto

Curator Aquarist

Curb Bit, Brake, Bridle, Check, Clamp, Coaming, Dam, Edge, Puteal, Rein, Restrain, Restringe, Rim, Snub

▷ **Cure** *may indicate* an anagram

Cure(d), Curative Amend, Antidote, Antirachitic, Bloater, Cold turkey, Dry-salt, Euphrasy, Faith, Fix, Flue, Ginseng, Heal, Heal-all, Heat treatment, Hobday, Jadeite, Jerk, Kipper, Magic bullet, Medicinal, Nostrum, Panacea, Park-leaves, → **PRESERVE**, Recover, Recower, Reest, Relief, Remede, Remedy, Re(i)st, Restore, Salt, Salve, Save, Serum, Smoke, Smoke-dry, Snakeroot, Tan, → **TREATMENT**, Tutsan

Curfew Bell, Gate, Prohibit, Proscribe

Curio, Curiosity, Curious Agog, Bibelot, Bric a brac, Ferly, Freak, Inquisitive, Interesting, Meddlesome, Nos(e)y, Objet d'art, Objet de vertu, Odd, Peculiar, Prurience, Quaint, Rarity, Rum, Spectacle, → **STRANGE**, Wondering

▷ **Curious(ly)** *may indicate* an anagram

Curl(s), Curler, Curling, Curly Ailes de pigeon, Bonspiel, Cirrus, Coil, Crimp, Crimple, Crinkle, Crisp, Crocket, Earlock, Eddy, Favourite, Frisette, Friz(z), Frizzle, Heart-breaker, Hog, Inwick, Kiss, Leaf, Loop, Love-lock, Outwick, Perm, Pin, Quiff, Repenter, Ringlet, Roll, Roulette, Shaving, Spiral, Spit, Tress, Twiddle, → **TWIST**, Undée, Wave, Wind

Currant Berry, Raisin, Rizard, Rizzar(t), Rizzer

Currency Cash, Circulation, → **COIN**, Coinage, Decimal, Euro(sterling), Finance, Jiao, Kip, Koruna, Managed, Monetary, → **MONEY**, Prevalence

▷ **Currency** *may indicate* a river

Current Abroad, AC, Actual, Alternating, Amp(ere), Amperage, California, Canary, Contemporaneous, Cromwell, Dark, DC, Direct, Draught, Drift, Dynamo, Ebbtide, Electric, El Nino, Emission, Equatorial, Euripus, Existent, Faradic, Flow, Foucault, Galvanic(al), Going, Headstream, Hot button, Humboldt, I, Immediate, Inst, Intermittent, In vogue, Japan, Kuroshio, Labrador, Live, Maelstrom, Millrace, Modern, Newsy, Now, Ongoing, Present, Present day, Prevalent, Race, Rapid, Rife, Rip, Roost, Running, Ryfe, Stream, Thames, Thermal, Thermionic, Tide, Topical, Torrent, Turbidity, Underset, Undertow, Up-to-date

Curry Bhuna, Brush, Comb, Cuittle, Dhansak, Fawn, Groom, Ingratiate, Korma, Ruby (Murray), Skater, Spice, Tan, Turmeric, Vindaloo

Curse Abuse, Anathema, Badmouth, Ban, Bane, Beshrew, Blast, Chide, Dam(me), Damn, Dee, Drat, Ecod, Egad, Evil, Excommunicate, Execrate, Heck, Hex, Hoodoo, Imprecate, Jinx, Malediction, Malgre, Malison, Maranatha, Mau(l)gré, Mockers, Moz(z), Mozzle, Nine (of diamonds), Oath, Paterson's, Pize, Plague, Rant, Rats, Scourge, Snails, Spell, Swear, Tarnation, Upbraid, Vengeance, Vituperate, Wanion, Weary, Winze, Wo(e)

Curtain(s), Curtain raiser, Curtain-rod Air, Arras, Backdrop, Bamboo, Café, Canopy, Casement, Caudle, Cloth, Death, Demise, Drape, Drop, Dropcloth, Dropscene, Fatal, Hanging, Iron, Lever de rideau, Louvre, Net, Pall, Portière, Purdah, Rag, Safety, Scene, Screen, Scrim, Swag, Tab, Tableau, Tormentor, Tringle, Vail, Valance, Veil, Vitrage

Curtsey Bob, Bow, Dip, Dop, Honour

Curve(d), Curvaceous, Curvature, Curving, Curvy Aduncate, Arc, Arch, Archivolt, Assurgent, Axoid, Bend, Bezier, Bow, Brachistochrone, Camber, Catacaustic, Catenary, Caustic, Chordee, Cissoid, Conchoid, Contrapposto, Crescent, Cycloid, Demand, Dowager's hump, Ellipse, Entasis, Epinastic, Ess, Evolute, Exponential, Extrados, Felloe, Felly, Freezing point, Geodesic, Gooseneck, Growth, Hance, Harmonogram, Helix, Hodograph, Hyperbola, Inswing, Intrados, Invected, Isochor, J, Jordan, Laffer, Learning, Lemniscate, Limacon, Linkage, Lissajous figure, Lituus, Lordosis, Loxodrome, Meniscus, Nowy, Ogee, Parabola, Pothook, Rhumb, RIAA, Roach, Rondure, Rotundate, Scolioma, Scoliosis, Sheer, Sigmoid flexure, Sinuate, Sonsie, Spiral, Spiric, Strophoid, Supply, Swayback, Tie, Trajectory, Trisectrix, Trochoid, Twist, Witch (of Agnesi)

Cushion(s) Air, Allege, Bank, Beanbag, Bolster, Buffer, Bustle, Hassock, → **PAD**, Pillow, Pouf(fe), Pulvinus, Soften, Squab, Tyre, Upholster, Whoopee

Custodial, Custodian, Custody Care, Claviger, Curator, Guard, Hold,

Incarceration, Janitor, Keeping, Protective, Retention, Sacrist, Steward, Trust, Ward, Wardship

Custom(ised), Customs (officer), Customs house, Customary Agriology, Chophouse, Coast-waiters, Cocket, Consuetude, Conventional, Couvade, De règle, Douane, Exciseman, Familiar, Fashion, Folklore, → **HABIT**, Lore, Manner, Montem, Mores, Nomic, Obsequy, Octroi, Ordinary, Perfunctory, Practice, Praxis, Protocol, Relic, Rite, Routine, Rule, Set, Sororate, Sunna, Tax, Thew, Tidesman, Time-honoured, Tradition, Trait, Unwritten, Usance, Used, Usual, Won, Wont, Woon, Zollverein

Customer(s) Client, Cove, End user, Footfall, Gate, Patron, Prospect, Punter, Purchaser, Shillaber, Shopper, Smooth, Trade, Trick, Vendee

▷ **Cut** *may indicate* an anagram

Cut(ter), Cutdown, Cutting Abate, Abbreviate, Abjoint, Ablate, Abridge, Abscond, Acute, Adeem, Adze, Aftermath, Ali Baba, Amputate, Apocopate, Axe, Bang, Bisect, Bit, Bite, Bowdlerise, Boycott, Brilliant, Broach, Caesarean, Caique, Canal, Cantle, Caper, Carver, Castrate, Caustic, Censor, Chap, Cheese, Chisel, Chopper, Circumscribe, Cleaver, Clinker-built, Clip, Colter, Commission, Concise, Coulter, Coupé, Crew, Crop, Cruel, Cube, Curtail, Deadhead, Decrease, Dicer, Die, Discide, Discount, Disengage, Dismember, Dissect, Division, Divorce, Dock, Dod, Edge, Edit, Embankment, Engraver, Entail, Epistolary, Epitomise, Escalope, Eschew, Etch, Excalibur, Excide, Excise, Exscind, Exsect, Exude, Fashion, Fell, Filet mignon, Fillet, Flench, Flense, Flinch, Flymo®, Form, Framp, Froe, Frow, Garb, Gash, Grater, Graven, Gride, Groove, Gryde, Hack, Hairdo, Handsaw, Hew(er), Ignore, Incision, Incisor, Indent, Insult, Intersect, Jigsaw, Joint, Junk, Kerf, Kern, Kirn, Lacerate, Lance, Leat, Lesion, Limit, Lin, Lop, Math, Medaillon, Medallion, Microtome, Milling, Minimise, Mohel, Mortice, Mortise, Mower, Nick, Not, Notch, Nott, Occlude, Omit, Open, Operate, Oxyacetylene, Padsaw, Pare, Pink, Plant, Pliers, Ploughshare, Poll, Pollard, Pone, Power, Precisive, Proin, Quota, Race, Rake off, Rase, Razee, Razor, Reap, Rebate, Reduction, Re-enter, Resect, Retrench, Revenue, Ring, Ripsaw, Roach, Rose, Rout, Saddle, Sarcastic, Saw(n), Saw-tooth, Scaloppine, Scarf, Scathing, Scion, Scission, Scissor, Score, Scrap, Sculpt, Scye, Scythe, Secant, Secateurs, Sect, Sever, Sey, Share (out), Shaver, Shears, Shingle, Ship, Shive, Shorn, Short, Shred, Shun, Sickle, Side, Sirloin, Skip, Slane, Slash, Slice(r), Slip, Slit, Sloop, Sned, Snee, Snib, Snick, Snip, Snippet, Snub, Spade, Spin, Spud, Stall, Steak, Stencil, Stir, Stramazon, Style, Surgeon, Tailor(ess), Tap, Tart, Tenderloin, Tomial, Tonsure, Tooth, Topside, Transect, Trash, Trench, Trenchant, Trepan, Trim, Truant, Truncate, Urchin, Vivisection, Whang, Whittle

▷ **Cutback** *may indicate* a reversed word

Cute Ankle, Perspicacious, Pert, Pretty, Taking

Cutlery Canteen, Eating irons, Flatware, Fork, Knife, Service, Setting, Silver, Spoon, Spork, Sunbeam, Tableware, Trifid

Cyborg Replicant

Cycle, Cyclist, Cycling Anicca, Arthurian, Bike, Biorhythm, Biospheric, Born-Haber, Business, Cal(l)ippic, Calvin, Carbon, Carnot, Cell, Circadian, Citric acid, Closed, Daisy, Eon, Era, Fairy, Frequency, Heterogony, Indiction, Keirin, Ko, Krebs, Life, Lytic, Madison, Metonic, Natural, Oestrus, Operating, Orb, Otto, Pedal, Peloton, Period, Product life, Repulp, Revolution, Ride, Roadman, Roadster, Rota, Round, Samsara, Saros, Scorch, Series, Sheng, Solar, Song, Sonnet, Sothic, Spin, TCA, Trike, Turn, UCI, Vicious, Water, Wheeler, Wheelman, Wu

Cyclone Storm, Tornado, Tropical, Typhoon, Willy-willy

Cylinder, Cylindrical Air, Capstan, Clave, Column, Dandy-roll, Drum, Licker-in, Magic, Nanotube, Pipe, Roll, Rotor, Siphonostele, Slave, Spool, Steal, Stele, Swift, Terete, Torose, Treadmill, Tube, Vascular

Cyst Atheroma, Bag, Blister, Chalazion, Dermoid, Hydatid, Impost(h)ume, Meibomian, Ranula, Sac, Vesicle, Wen

Cytogenesis Amoebic

Czar Despot, Nicholas

Dd

Dab(s) Bit, Daub, Fish, Flounder, Lemon, Pat, Print, Ringer, Smear, Smooth, Spot, Stupe, Whorl

Dad(dy) Blow, Dev(v)el, Father, Generator, Hit, Male, Pa(pa), Pater, Polt, Pop, Slam, Sugar, Thump

Daffodil Asphodel, Jonquil, Lent-lily, Narcissus

Daft Absurd, Crazy, Potty, Ridiculous, Silly, Simple, Stupid

Dagga Cape, Red, True

Dagger(s) An(e)lace, Ataghan, Baselard, Bayonet, Bodkin, Crease, Creese, Da(h), Diesis, Dirk, Double, Dudgeon, Hanger, Han(d)jar, Jambiya(h), Katar, Kindjahl, Kirpan, Kreese, Kris, Lath, Misericord(e), Obelisk, Obelus, Poi(g)nado, Poniard, Puncheon, Sgian-dubh, Shank, Skean, Skene(-occle), Stiletto, Whiniard, Whinyard, W(h)inger, Yatag(h)an, Yuc(c)a

Daily Adays, Broadsheet, Char(lady), Circadian, Cleaner, Diurnal, Domestic, Guardian, Help, Journal, Mail, Mirror, Mrs Mopp, Paper, Per diem, Quotidian, Rag, Regular, Scotsman, Sun, Tabloid

Dainty, Daintiness Cate(s), Cute, Delicacy, Dinky, Elegant, Elfin, Entremesse, Entremets, Exquisite, Genty, Junket, Lickerish, Liquorish, Mignon(ne), Minikin, →**MORSEL**, Neat, Nice, Particular, Petite, Precious, Prettyism, Pussy, Sunket, Twee

Dairy Creamery, Days' house, Loan, Parlour, Springhouse

Daisy African, Aster, Bell, Boneset, Felicia, Gerbera, Gowan, Groundsel, Hardheads, Hen and chickens, Livingstone, Michaelmas, Ox-eye, Ragweed, Saw-wort, Shasta, Transvaal

Dale(s) Dell, Dene, Diarist, Dingle, Glen, Nidder, Ribbles, Swale, Vale, Valley, Wensley, Wharfe

Dalmatian Spotted dog

Dam An(n)icut, Arch, Aswan, Aswan High, Bar, Barrage, Barrier, Block, Boulder, Bund, Cabora Bassa, Cauld, Check, Dental, Grand Coulee, Grande Dixence, Gravity, Hoover, Kariba, Kielder, Ma, Mangla, Mater, Obstacle, Obstruct, Pen, Sennar, Stank, →**STEM**, Sudd, Tank, Three Gorges, Turkey nest, Volta River, Weir, Yangtze

Damage(d), Damages, Damaging Accidental, Appair, Bane, Banjax, Bloody, Blunk, Bruise, Buckle, Charge, Contuse, Cost, Cripple, Dent, Desecrate, Detriment, Devastate, Devastavit, Discredit, Distress, Estrepe, Expense, Fault, Flea-bite, Harm, Havoc, Hedonic, Hit, Hole, Hurt, Impair, Injury, Lesion, Loss, Mar, Mayhem, Moth-eaten, Nobble, Opgefok, Pair(e), Prang, Price, Reparation, Retree, Ruin, Sabotage, Scaith, Scath(e), Scotch, Scratch, Skaith, Smirch, Solatium, →**SPOIL**, Tangle, Tear, Tigger, Toll, Value, Vandalise, Violate, Wear and tear, Wing, Wound, Wreak, Wreck, Write off

▷ **Damage(d)** *may indicate* an anagram

Dame Crone, Dowager, Edna (Everage), Gammer, Lady, Matron, Nature, Naunt, Partlet, Peacherino, Sis, Title(d), Trot, Woman

Damn(ation), Damned Accurst, Attack, Blame, Blast, Blinking, Condemn, Curse, Cuss, D, Darn, Dee, Doggone, Drat, Execrate, Faust, Heck, Hell, Hoot, Jigger, Malgre, Perdition, Predoom, Sink, Swear, Very

Damp(en), Damping, Dampness Aslake, Black, Blunt, Check, Clam(my), Dank, Dewy, Fousty, Humid(ity), Mesarch, Moch, Moist(ure), Muggy, Raw, Retund, Rheumy, Rising, Roric, Soggy, Sordo, Sultry, Unaired, →**WET**

Dance(r), Dancing Alma(in), Astaire, Baladin(e), Balanchine, Ballabile, Ballant, Ballerina, Ballroom, Baryshnikov, Bayadère, Bob, Body-popping, Caper, Ceili(dh),

Chorus-girl, Comprimario, Contredanse, Corp de ballet, Corybant, Coryphee, Dervish, De Valois, Diaghilev, Dinner, Dolin, Exotic, Figurant, Figure, Fooling, Foot, Foot-it, Gandy, Gigolo, Groove, Hetaera, Hetaira, Hoofer, Isadora Duncan, Kick-up, Knees-up, Leap, Maenad, Majorette, Markova, Modern, Nautch-girl, Night, Nijinsky, Nod, Nureyev, Oberek, Old-time, Orchesis, Partner, Pavlova, Peeler, Petipa, Pierette, Prom(enade), Pyrrhic, Rambert, Raver, Reindeer, Ring, St Vitus, Salome, Saltant, Saltatorious, Shearer, Skank, Skipper, Slammer, Spring, Step, Strut, Table, Tea, Terpsichore, Thé dansant, Tread, Trip(pant), Vogue(ing), Whirl, Wire-walker

Dance hall Disco, Juke-joint, Palais

▷ **Dancing** *may indicate an anagram*

Danger(ous) Apperil, Breakneck, Crisis, Critical, Dic(e)y, Dire, Emprise, Fear, Hairy, Hazard, Hearie, Hero, Hot, Hotspot, Insecure, Jeopardy, Lethal, Menace, Mine, Minefield, Nettle, Nocuous, Parlous, Pitfall, Plight, Precarious, Quicksand, Risk, Rock, Serious, Severe, Sicko, Snag, Tight, Tight spot, Trap, Treacherous, Ugly

Dangle A(i)glet, Aiguillette, Critic, Flourish, Hang, Loll, Swing

Dank Clammy, Damp, Humid, Moist, Wet, Wormy

Dare, Dare-devil, Daring Adventure, Audacious, Aweless, Bold, Brave, Bravura, Challenge, Courage, Dan, Da(u)nton, Defy, Durst, Emprise, Face, Gallant, Gallus, Groundbreaking, Hardihood, Hazard, Hen, Prowess, Racy, Risk, Swashbuckler, Taunt, Venture

Dark(en), Darkie, Darkness Aphelia, Aphotic, Apophis, Black(out), Blind, Byronic, Caliginous, Cimmerian, Cloud, Colly, Crepuscular, Depth, Dim, Dingy, Dirk(e), Dusky, Eclipse, Egyptian, Erebus, Evil, Gloom, Glum, Grim, Inky, Inumbrate, Jet, Kieran, Low-key, Mare, Maria, Melanous, Mulatto, Murk(y), Negro, Night, Obfuscate, Obnubilation, Obscure, Obsidian, Ominous, Ousel, Ouzel, Overcast, Pall, Phaeic, Pitch-black, Pit-mirk, Rooky, Sable, Sad, Secret, Shades, Shady, Shuttered, Sinister, Solein, Sombre, Sooty, Sphacelate, Sullen, Sunless, Swarthy, Tar, Tenebrose, Tenebr(i)ous, Unfair, Unlit, Wog, Woosel, Yellowboy, Yellowgirl

Darling Acushla, Alannah, Asthore, Beloved, Charlie, Cher, Chéri(e), Chick-a-biddy, Chick-a-diddle, Chuck-a-diddle, Dear, Dilling, Do(a)ting-piece, Duck(s), Favourite, Grace, Honey, Idol, Jarta, Jo(e), Lal, Love, Luv, Mavourneen, Mavournin, Minikin, Minion, Oarswoman, Own, Peat, Pet, Poppet, Precious, Squeeze, Sugar, Sweetheart, Sweeting, Yarta, Yarto

Dart(s), Darter Abaris, Arrow, Banderilla, Beetle, Dace, Dash, Deadener, Dodge, Fleat, Fléchette, Flirt, Flit, Harpoon, Javelin, Launch, Leap, Lunger, Pheon, Scoot, Shanghai, Skrim, Speck, Spiculum, Strike, Thrust, Wheech

Dash(ing), Dashed Backhander, Bally, Blade, Blight, Blow, Bribe, Buck, Charge, Collide, Cut, Dad, Dah, Damn, Dapper, Dart(le), Daud, Dawd, Debonair, Ding, Dod, Elan, Em (rule), En (rule), Flair, Fly, Go-ahead, Hang, Hurl, → **HURRY**, Hustle, Hyphen, Impetuous, Jabble, Jaw, Jigger, Lace, Leg it, Line, Minus, Modicum, Morse, Natty, Nip, Panache, Pebble, Race, Raffish, Rakish, Ramp, Rash, Rule, Run, Rush, Sally, Scamp(er), Scapa, Scarper, Scart, Scoot, Scrattle, Scurry, Scuttle, Shatter, Showy, Skitter, Soupçon, Souse, Spang, Speed, Splash, Splatter, Sprint, Strack, Streak, Stroke, → **STYLE**, Swashbuckling, Swung, Throw, Tinge, Touch, Treacherous, Ugly

Data(base), Datum Archie, Evidence, Factoid, Facts, Fiche, File, Floating-point, Garbage, Gen, Hard copy, Info, Input, IT, Material, Matrix, Newlyn, News, Ordnance, Read-out, Statistic, Table, Triple

Date(d), Dates, Dating AD, Age, AH, Almanac, Appointment, Blind, Boyfriend, Calendar, Carbon, Carbon-14, Computer, Court, Deadline, Engagement, Epoch, Equinox, Era, Escort, Exergue, Expiry, Fission-track, Fixture, Gig, Girlfriend, Ides, Julian, Meet, Outmoded, Passé, Past, Radio-carbon, Rubidium-strontium, See, System, Target, Ult(imo), Uranium-lead

Daunt Adaw, Amate, Awe, Deter, Dishearten, Intimidate, Overawe, Quail, Stun, Stupefy, Subdue

Dawdle(r) Dally, Draggle, Drawl, Idle, → **LOITER**, Malinger, Potter, Shirk, Slowcoach, Snail, Troke, Truck

Dawn(ing) Aurora, Cockcrow, Daw, Daybreak, Day-peep, Dayspring, Enlightenment,

Eoan, Eos, False, French, Light, Morning, Morrow, Occur, Prime, Sparrowfart, Spring, Start, Sunrise, Sun up

Day(s) Account, Ahemeral, All Fools', All Hallows', All Saints', All Souls', Anniversary, Annunciation, Anzac, April Fool's, Arbor, Armistice, Ascension, Australia, Bad hair, Baker, Banian, Banyan, Barnaby, Bastille, Borrowing, Box, Boxing, Broad, Calendar, Calends, Calpa, Canada, Canicular, Childermas, Civil, Columbus, Commonwealth, Contango, Continental, Continuation, D, Daft, Date, Decoration, Degree, Derby, Der Tag, Dismal, Distaff, Dog, Dominion, Double, Dress down, Dressed, Duvet, Early, Ember, Empire, Epact, Fast, Fasti, Father's, Feast, Ferial, Field, Fiesta, Flag, Fri, Gang, Gaudy, Glory, Groundhog, Guy Fawkes', Halcyon, Hey, High, Hogmanay, Holocaust, Holy, Holy Innocents', Holy-rood, Hundred, Ides, Inauguration, Independence, Intercalary, Judgment, Juridical, Kalends, Kalpa, Labo(u)r, Lady, Lammas, Last, Law(ful), Lay, Leap, Mardi, Market, May, Memorial, Michaelmas, Midsummer, Mon, Morrow, Mother's, Muck-up, Mufti, Mumping, Name, Ne'erday, New Year's, Nones, Oak-apple, Octave, Off, Open, Orangeman's, Pancake, Paper, Pay, Poppy, Post, Pound, Present, Press(ed), Primrose, Pulvering, Quarter, Rag, Rainy, Red-letter, Remembrance, Rent, Rest, Robin, Rock, Rogation, Rood(-mas), Rosh Chodesh, Sabbath, St John's, Saint's, St Swithin's, St Thomas's, St Valentine's, Salad, Sansculotterie, Sat, Scambling, Settling, Sexagesima, Show, Sidereal, Snow, Solar, Solstice, Speech, Sports, Station, Sun, Supply, Tag, Term, Thanksgiving, Thurs, Ticket, Time, Transfer, Trial, Triduum, Tues, Twelfth, Utas, Valentine's, Varnishing, VE, Vernissage, Veterans', Victoria, Visiting, VJ, Wash, Wed, Wedding, Working

Daydream(er), Daydreaming Brown study, Castle(s) in the air, Dwam, Dwaum, Fancy, Imagine, Muse, Reverie, Rêveur, Walter Mitty, Woolgathering

Daze(d) Amaze, Bemuse, Confuse, Dwaal, Gally, Muddle, Muzzy, Petrify, Reeling, →**STUN**, Stupefy, Stupor, Trance

Dazzle(d), Dazzler, Dazzling Bewilder, Blend, Blind, Bobby, Eclipse, Foudroyant, Glare, Larking glass, Meteoric, Outshine, Radiance, Resplendent, Splendour, Yblent

Dead(en) Abrupt, Accurate, Alamort, Asgard, Asleep, Bang, Blunt, Bung, Cert, Cold, Complete, D, Deceased, Defunct, Dodo, Doggo, Expired, Extinct, Flatliner, Gone(r), Inert, Infarct, Late, Lifeless, Muffle, Mute, Napoo, Numb, Obsolete, Obtund, Ringer, Sequestrum, She'ol, Smother, Stillborn, True, Under hatches, Utter, Waned

Dead end, Deadlock Cut-off, Dilemma, Impasse, Logjam, Stalemate, Stoppage

Deadline Date, Epitaph, Limit

Deadly Baleful, Dull, Fell, Funest, Internecine, →**LETHAL**, Malign, Mortal, Pestilent, Thanatoid, Unerring, Venomous

Deal(er), Dealership, Dealing(s), Deal with Address, Agent, Agreement, Allot(ment), Arb, Arbitrageur, Bargain, Biz, Breadhead, Brinjarry, Broker, Bulk, Business, Cambist, Candyman, Chandler, Chapman, Clocker, Commerce, Connection, Cope, Coup, Cover, Croupier, Dispense, Distributor, Do, Dole, East, Eggler, Exchange, Fir, Franchise, Fripper, Front-running, Goulash, Hack, Hand(le), Help, Inflict, Insider, Interbroker, Jiggery-pokery, Jobber, Lashing, Lay on, Lay out, Loads, Lot, Manage, Mercer, Merchandise, Merchant, Mickle, Middleman, Monger, Mort, Negotiate, New, North, Operator, Package, Pine, Plain, Post, Productivity, Pusher, Raft, Raw, Red, Sale, Serve, Side, Sight, Simoniac, Slanger, Sort, South, Spicer, Square, Stapler, Stockist, Stockjobber, Takeover, Tape, Timber, Totter, Tout(er), →**TRADE**, Traffic, Traffick, Transaction, Treat, Truck, West, Wheeler, White, Wholesaler, Wield, Woolstapler, Yarborough, Yardie

Dear(er), Dearest, Dear me Ay, Bach, Beloved, Cara, Caro, Cher(e), Cherie, Chuckie, Darling, Duck(s), Expensive, High, Honey(bun), Joy, Lamb, Leve, Lief, Lieve, Loor, Love, Machree, Mouse, My, Pet, Soote, Steep, Sugar, Sweet, Sweeting, Toots(ie), Unreasonable, Up

Death(ly) Abraham's bosom, Bane, Bargaist, Barg(h)est, Black, Carnage, Cataplexis, Charnel, Commorientes, Curtains, Cypress, Demise, Deodand, Departure, Dormition, End, Eschatology, Euthanasia, Exit, Extinction, Fatality, Fey, Funeral, Gangrene, Grim Reaper, Hallal, Infarction, Jordan, King of Terrors, Lethee, Leveller, Loss, Mortality, Necrosis, Nemesis, Night, Obit, Passing, Quietus, Reaper, Sati, Sergeant, SIDS,

Small-back, Strae, Sudden, Suttee, Terminal, Thanatism, Thanatology, Thanatopsis, Thanatos, Yama

Deathless(ness) Athanasy, Eternal, Eterne, Immortal, Struldberg, Timeless, Undying

Debag Dack, Unbreech

Debase(d) Adulterate, Allay, Bemean, Corrupt, Demean, Depreciate, Dialectician, Dirty, Grotesque, Hedge, Lower, Pervert, Traduce, Vitiate

Debate(r) Adjournment, Argue, Casuist, Combat, Contention, Contest, Deliberate, Dialectic, Discept, Discourse, Discuss(ion), →DISPUTE, Flyte, Forensics, Moot, Paving, Polemics, Reason, Teach-in, Warsle, Wrangle, Wrestle

Debrief Wash up, Wind up

Debris Bahada, Bajada, Detritus, Eluvium, Flotsam, Jetsam, Moraine, Moslings, Pyroclastics, Refuse, Ruins, Shrapnel, Tel, Tephra, Waste, Wreckage

▷ **Debris** *may indicate* an anagram

Debt(or) Abbey-laird, Alsatia, Arrears, Arrestee, Bankrupt, Bonded, Dr, Due, Floating, Funded, Insolvent, IOU, Liability, Moratoria, National, Obligation, Oxygen, Poultice, Public, Queer Street, Score, Senior, Subordinated, Tick, Tie, Unfunded

Debt-collector Bailiff, Forfaiter, Remembrancer

Decadence, Decadent Babylonian, Decaying, Degeneration, Dissolute, Effete, Fin-de-siècle, Libertine

▷ **Decapitated** *may indicate* first letter removed

Decay(ed), Decaying Alpha, Appair, Beta, Biodegrade, Blet, Canker, Caries, Caseation, Crumble, Decadent, Declension, Decline, Decompose, Decrepit, Dieback, Disintegrate, Doat, Doddard, Doddered, Dote, Dricksie, Druxy, Dry rot, Ebb, Fail, F(o)etid, Forfair, Gamma, Gangrene, Heart-rot, Impair, Moulder, Pair(e), Plaque, Ptomaine, Putrefy, Ret, Rot, Rust, Saprogenic, Sap-rot, Seedy, Sepsis, Spoil, Tabes, Thoron, Time-worn, Wet-rot

Decease(d) Death, Decedent, Demise, Die, Stiff

Deceit(ful), Deceive(r) Abuse, Ananias, Artifice, Bamboozle, Befool, Bitten, Blag, Blind, Bluff, →CHEAT, Chicane, Chouse, Cozen, Cuckold, Defraud, Deke (out), Delude, Diddle, Dissemble, Double-cross, Double-dealing, Dupe, Duplicity, False(r), Fast-talk, Fiddle, Fineer, Flam, Fool, Four-flusher, Fox, Fraud, Gag, Guile, Gull, Hoax, Hoodwink, Humbug, Hype, Hypocritical, Imposition, Inveigle, Invention, Jacob, Kid, Lead on, Liar, Mamaguy, Misinform, Mislead, Patter, Perfidy, Poop, Poupe, Pretence, Prevaricate, Punic, Rig, Ruse, Sell, Sham, Sinon, Spruce, Stratagem, Swindle, Swizzle, Take in, Trick, Trump, Two-time, Weasel, Wile

Decency, Decent Chaste, Decorum, Fitting, Godly, Healsome, Honest, Kind, Mensch, Modest, Moral, Salubrious, Seemly, Sporting, Wholesome, Wise-like

Deception, Deceptive Abusion, Artifice, Bluff, Catchpenny, Catchy, Cheat, Chicanery, Codology, →DECEIT, Disguise, Dupe, Duplicity, Elusive, Eyewash, Fallacious, False, Feigned, Fineer, Flam, Fraud, Fubbery, Gag, Gammon, Guile, Gullery, Have-on, Hocus-pocus, Hokey-pokey, Hum, Hunt-the-gowks, Hype, Ignes-fatui, Ignis-fatuus, Illusion, Insidious, Jiggery-pokery, Kidology, Lie, Mamaguy, Moodies, Phantasmal, Runaround, Ruse, Sciolism, Sell, Sleight, Smoke and mirrors, Specious, Sting, The moodies, Thimblerig, →TRICK, Trompe l'oeil, Two-timing, Underhand

Decide(r), Decided, Decisive Addeem, Adjudge, Agree, Ar(r)e(e)de, Ballot, Barrage, Bottom-line, Call, Cast, Clinch, Conclude, Conclusive, →DECISION, Deem, Definite, Determine, Distinct, Effectual, Fatal, Firm, Fix, Foregone, Jump-off, Mediate, Opt, Parti, Predestination, Pronounced, Rescript, Resolute, →RESOLVE, Result, Rule, Run-off, See, Settle, Split, Sure, Tiebreaker, Try

▷ **Decipher(ed)** *may indicate* an 'o' removed

Decipher(ing) Cryptanalysis, Decode, Decrypt, Descramble, Discover, Interpret

Decision Arbitrium, Arrêt, Bottom line, Crossroads, Crunch, Crux, Decree, Fatwa, Fetwa, Firman, Judg(e)ment, Parti, Placit(um), Referendum, Resolution, Resolve, Responsa, Ruling, Sentence, Split, Verdict

Decisive Climactic, Clincher, Critical, Crux, Definite, Final, Pivotal

Deck Adonise, Adorn, Angled, Array, Attrap, Bejewel, Boat, Canted, Cards, Clad, Daiker, Daub, Decorate, Dizen, Embellish, Equip, Flight, Focsle, Forecastle, Garland, Hang, Helideck, Hurricane, Lower, Mess, Orlop, Pack, Pedestrian, Platform, Poop, Prim, Promenade, Quarter, Sun, Tape, Upper, Void, Weather

Declare, Declaration, Declaim, Decree Absolute, A(r)e(e)de, Affidavit, Affirm, Air, Allege, Announce, Aread, Assert, Asseverate, Aver, Avow, Balfour, Bann(s), Bayyan, Breda, Dictum, Diktat, Doom, Edict, Emit, Enact, Fatwa(h), Fiat, Firman, Go, Grace, Harangue, Indiction, Insist, Interlocutory, Irade, Law, Mandate, Manifesto, Meld, Mou(th), Nisi, Noncupate, Novel(la), Nullity, Orate, Ordain, Order, Ordinance, Parlando, Petition of Right, Pontificate, Present, Proclaim, Profess, Promulgate, Pronounce, Protest, Publish, Rant, Read, Recite, Rescript, Resolve, Restatement, Rights, Rule, Ruling, SC, Sed, Senatus consultum, Signify, Speak, Spout, State, Swear, Testament-dative, Testify, Testimony, UDI, Ukase, Ultimatum, Unilateral, Vie, Voice, Vouch, Will, Word

▷ **Declaring** *may indicate* a word beginning 'Im'

Decline, Declination, Declining Age, Ail, Atrophy, Catabasis, Comedown, Decadent, Degeneration, Degringoler, Deny, Descend, Deteriorate, Devall, Die, Diminish, Dip, Dissent, Downhill, Downtrend, Downturn, Droop, Drop, Dwindle, Ebb, Escarpment, Fade, Fall, Flag, Forbear, Lapse, Magnetic, Opt out, Paracme, Pejoration, Peter, Plummet, Quail, Recede, Recession, Reflow, Refuse, Retrogression, Rot, Ruin, Rust, Sag, Senile, Set, Sink, Slide, Slump, Slumpflation, Stoop, Tumble, Twilight, Wane, Welke, Withdraw, Wither

Decorate(d), Decoration, Decorative Adorn, Aiguilette, Angelica, Attrap, Award, Bard, Bargeboard, Baroque, Bauble, Beaux-arts, Bedizen, Bells and whistles, Bordure, Braid, Breastpin, Brooch, Cartouche, Centrepiece, Chain, Champlevé, Chinoiserie, Christingle, Cinquefoil, Cloissoné, Coffer, Crocket, Croix de guerre, Daiker, Decoupage, Dentelle, Dentil, Diamante, Doodad, Doodah, Do over, Dragée, Emblazon, Emboss, Embrave, Enrich, Epaulet, Epergne, Etch, Fancy, Festoon, Filigree, Finery, Finial, Fleuron, Floriated, Fob, Frieze, Frill, Frog, Frost, Furbish, Garniture, Gaud, Gilt, Glitter, Goffer, Gradino, Grotesque, Guilloche, Ice, Illuminate, Impearl, Inlay, Intarsia, Intarsio, Interior, Jabot, Jari, Knotwork, Leglet, Linen-fold, Marquetry, MC, Medal(lion), Moulding, Oath, OBE, Openwork, Order, →**ORNAMENT**, Ornate, Orphrey, Overglaze, Ovolo, Paint, Paper, Parament, Photomural, Pokerwork, Polychromy, Prettify, Prink, Purfle, Rag-rolling, Rangoli, Repoussé, Ribbon, Rich, Ric(k)-rac(k), Ruche, Scallop, Scrimshaw, Set-off, Sgraffito, Soutache, Spangle, Staffage, Stomacher, Strapwork, Stucco, Tailpiece, Tart up, Tattoo, TD, Titivate, Tool, Topiary, Tracery, Trim, Vergeboard, Wallpaper, Wirework, Zari

Decoy Allure, Bait, Bonnet, Button, Call-bird, Coach, Crimp, Entice, Lure, Piper, Roper, Ruse, Shill, Stale, Stalking-horse, Stall, Stool-pigeon, Tame cheater, Tice, Tole, Toll, Trap, Trepan

Decrease Cut back, Decrew, Diminish, Dwindle, Iron, Lessen, Press, Ramp down, Reduce, Rollback, Step-down, Subside, Wane, Wanze

Decree →**DECLARE**

Decrepit Dilapidated, Doddery, Doitit, Failing, Feeble, Frail, Moth-eaten, Spavined, Tumbledown, Warby, Weak

Decriminalise Launder

Dedicate(d), Dedication Corban, Determination, Devote, Dinah, Endoss, Hallow, Inscribe, Oblate, Pious, Sacred, Single-minded, Votive, Work ethic

Deduce, Deduction, Deductive A priori, Assume, Conclude, Consectary, Corollary, Derive, Discount, Gather, Illation, Infer(ence), Natural, Reason, Rebate, Recoup, Reprise, Stoppage, Surmise, Syllogism

Deed(s) Achievement, Act(ion), Atweel, Backbond, Back letter, Charta, Charter, Defeasance, Derring-do, Escrol(l), Escrow, Exploit, Fact(um), Indeed, Indenture, Manoeuvre, Mitzvah, Muniments, Settlement, Specialty, Starr, →**TITLE**, Work

Deep(en), Deeply Abstruse, Bass(o), Brine, Briny, Enhance, Excavate, Grum, Gulf,

Hadal, Intense, Low, Mindanao, Mysterious, →**OCEAN**, Profound, Re-enter, Rich, Sea, Sonorous, Sunk(en), Throaty, Upsee, Ups(e)y

Deer(-like) Axis, Bambi, Barasing(h)a, Barking, Brocket, Buck, Cariacou, Carjacou, Cervine, Chevrotain, Chital, Doe, Elaphine, Elk, Fallow, Gazelle, Hart, Irish elk, Jumping, Moose, Mouse, Mule, Muntjac, Muntjak, Musk, Père David's, Pricket, Pudu, Red, Rein, Roe, Rusa, Sambar, Sambur, Selenodont, Sika, Sorel(l), Spade, Spay(d), Spayad, Spitter, Spottie, Stag(gard), Tragule, Ungulate, Virginia, Wapiti

▷ **Defaced** *may indicate* first letter missing

Defame, Defamatory, Defamation Abase, Blacken, Calumny, Cloud, Denigrate, Detract, Dishonour, Impugn, In rixa, Libel, Mud, Mudslinging, Obloquy, Sclaunder, Scurrilous, Slander, Smear, Stigmatise, Traduce, Vilify

Default(er) Absentee, Bilk, Dando, Delinquent, Flit, Levant, Neglect, Omission, Waddle, Welsh

Defeat(ed), Defeatist Beat, Best, Bowed, Caning, Capot, Cast, Codille, Conquer, Counteract, Cream, Debel, Defeasance, Demolish, Destroy, Discomfit, Dish, Ditch, Donkey-lick, Drub, Fatalist, Floor, Foil, Foyle, Hammer, Hiding, Kippered, Laipse, Lick, Loss, Lurch, Marmelize, Master, Mate, Moral, Negative, Out, Outclass, Outdo, Outfox, Outgeneral, Outgun, Outplay, Outvote, Outwit, →**OVERCOME**, Overmarch, Overpower, Overreach, Overthrow, Overwhelm, Pip, Plaster, Pulverise, Quitter, Rebuff, Reverse, Rout, Rubicon, Scupper, Set, Shellacking, Sisera, Skunk, Squabash, Stump, Tank, Thrash, Thwart, Toast, Tonk, Trounce, Undo, Vanquish, War, Waterloo, Whap, Whip, Whitewash, Whop, Whup, Wipe-out, Worst

Defect(ion), Defective, Defector Abandon, Amateur, Apostasy, Bug, Coma, Crawling, Deficient, Desert, Failing, Faulty, Flaw, Frenkel, Halt, Hamartia, Hiatus, Kink, Low, Manky, Mass, Mote, Natural, Renegade, Renegate, Ridgel, Ridgil, Rig, Rogue, Runagate, Shortcoming, Spina bifida, Stammer, Substandard, Terrace, Treason, Trick, Want, Wanting, Weakness

Defence, Defend(er), Defensible, Defensive Abat(t)is, Alexander, Alibi, Antibody, Antidote, Antigenic, Antihistamine, Apologia, Arm, Back, Bailey, Barbican, Barmkin, Barricade, Bastion, Battery, Battlement, Berm, Bridgehead, Bulwark, Calt(h)rop, CD, Champion, Civil, Curtain, Demibastion, Ditch, Embrasure, Estacade, Goalie, Hedgehog, Herisson, Hold, Immunity, J(i)u-jitsu, Justify, Kaim, Keeper, Kraal, Laager, Laer, Libero, Maginot-minded, Maintain, Martello tower, Moat, Motte and bailey, Muniment, Outwork, Palisade, Parapet, Pentagon, Protect, Rampart, Redan, Redoubt, Refute, Resist, Ringwall, Sangar, Seawall, →**SHELTER**, Shield(wall), Stonewall, Strategic, Support, Tenail(le), Testudo, Tower, Trench, Trou-de-loup, Uphold, Vallation, Vallum, Vindicate, Wall, Warran(t)

Defenceless Helpless, Inerm, Naked, Sitting duck, Vulnerable

Defendant Accused, Apologist, Respondent, Richard Roe

Defer(ence), Deferential, Deferring Bow, Curtsey, Delay, Dutiful, Homage, Moratory, Morigerous, Obeisant, Pace, Polite, Postpone, Procrastinate, Protocol, Respect, Roll over, Shelve, Stay, Submit, Suspend, Waive, Yield

Defiance, Defiant, Defy Acock, Bite the thumb, Bold, Brave, Cock a snook, Dare, Daring, Disregard, Do or die, Flaunt, Insubordinate, Outbrave, Outdare, Rebellion, Recalcitrant, Recusant, Scab, Stubborn, Titanism, Truculent, Unruly, Yahboo

Deficiency, Deficient Absence, Acapnia, ADA, Anaemia, Anoxia, Aplasia, Beriberi, Defect, Failing, Hypinosis, Inadequate, Incomplete, Lack, Scant, Scarcity, SCID, Shortage, Spanaemia, Want

▷ **Deficient** *may indicate* an anagram

Deficit Anaplerotic, Arrears, Defective, Ischemia, Loss, Poor, Shortfall

Define(d), Definition, Definitive Classic, Clear-cut, Decide, Demarcate, Determine, Diorism, Distinct, Explain, Fix, Limit, Parameter, Set, Sharp, Specific, Tangible, Term

Definite(ly) Categorically, Classic, Clear, Concrete, Deffo, Emphatic, Firm, Hard, Indeed, Positive, Precise, Sans-appel, Specific, Sure, Yes

Deflate Burst, Collapse, Flatten, Lower, Prick, Squeeze

Deflect(or), Deflection Avert, Back-scatter, Bend, Detour, Diverge, Divert, Glance, Holophote, Otter, Paravane, Refract, Snick, Swerve, Throw, Trochotron, Veer, Windage

Deform(ed), Deformity Anamorphosis, Blemish, Boutonniere, Contracture, Crooked, Disfigure, Distort, Gammy, Hammer-toe, Harelip, Miscreated, Misfeature, Mishapt, Mutilate, Polt-foot, Stenosed, Talipes, Valgus, Warp

▷ **Deformed** *may indicate an anagram*

Defraud Bilk, Cheat, Cozen, Gyp, Lurch, Mulct, Skin, Sting, Swindle, Trick

Degrade, Degradation Abase, Cheapen, Culvertage, Debase, Demission, Demote, Diminish, Disennoble, Humble, Imbase, Imbrute, Lessen, Lower, →**SHAME**, Sink, Waterloo

Degree(s) Aegrotat, As, Attila (the Hun), Azimuthal, BA, Baccalaureate, BCom, BD, B es S, C, Class, D, Doctoral, Double first, Engler, Extent, External, F, First, Forbidden, Foundation, Geoff (Hurst), German, Gradation, Grade, Grece, Gree(s), Greece, Gre(e)se, Grice, Griece, Grize, Incept, Incidence, K, Lambeth, Latitude, Letters, Level, Licentiate, Longitude, MA, Measure, Mediant, Nuance, Order, Ordinary, Pass, Peg, PhD, Pin, Poll, Rate, Reaumur, Remove, Second, Stage, Status, Step, Submediant, Subtonic, Supertonic, Third, Water

Deject(ed), Dejection Abase, Abattu, Alamort, Amort, Chap-fallen, Crab, Crestfallen, Despondent, Dismay, Dispirited, Downcast, Gloomy, Hangdog, Humble, Low, Melancholy, Spiritless, Wae

Delaware DE(L)

Delay(ed), Delaying Adjourn(ment), Ambage, Avizandum, Backlog, Behindhand, Check, Cunctator, Dawdle, Defer, Demurrage, Detention, Dilatory, Fabian, Filibuster, Forsloe, For(e)slow, Frist, Hangfire, Hesitate, Hinder, Hitch, Hold up, Hysteresis, Impede, Laches, Lag, Late, Laten, Let, Linger, Mora(torium), Obstruct, Pause, Procrastinate, Prolong, Prorogue, Remanet, Reprieve, Respite, Retard, Rollover, Setback, Slippage, Sloth, Slow, →**STALL**, Stand-over, Stay, Stonewall, Suspend, Temporise, Wait

Delegate, Delegation Agent, Amphictyon, Apostolic, Appoint, Assign, Commissary, Decentralise, Depute, Devolution, Mission, Nuncio, Offload, Representative, Secondary, Transfer, Vicarial, Walking

Delete Adeem, Annul, Cancel, Cut, Erase, Expunge, Purge, Rase, Scratch, Scrub, Strike

Deliberate(ly), Deliberation Adagio, Calculated, Consider, Debate, Intentional, Meditate, Moderate, Muse, On purpose, Overt, Plonking, Pointedly, Ponder, Prepensely, Purposely, Ruminate, Studied, Thought, Voulu, Weigh, Witting

Delicacy, Delicate Airy-fairy, Beccafico, Canape, Cate, Caviare, Dainty, Difficult, Discreet, Dorty, Ectomorph, Eggshell, Elfin, Ethereal, Fastidious, Filigree, Fine, Finespun, Finesse, Flimsy, Fragile, →**FRAIL**, Friand, Gentle, Goody, Gossamer, Guga, Hothouse, Inconie, Incony, Lac(e)y, Ladylike, Light, Lobster, Nesh, Nicety, Niminy-piminy, Oyster, Pastel, Reedy, Roe, Sensitive, Soft(ly-softly), Subtle(ty), Sunket, Tactful, Taste, Tender, Tenuous, Ticklish, Tidbit, Titbit, Trotter, Truffle, Wispy

Delicatessen Charcuterie

Delicious Ambrosia, Delectable, Exquisite, Fragrant, Goloptious, Goluptious, Gorgeous, Lekker, Lip-smacking, Mor(e)ish, Mouthwatering, Savoury, Scrummy, Scrumptious, Tasty, Toothsome, Yummy, Yum-yum

▷ **Delight** *may indicate* 'darken'

Delight(ed), Delightful Bewitch, Bliss, Charm, Chuff, Coo, Delice, Dreamy, Edna, Elated, Enamour, Enjoyable, Enrapture, Exhilarate, Exuberant, Felicity, Fetching, Frabjous, Gas, Glad, Glee, Gratify, Honey, Joy, Lap up, Overjoy, Please, Pleasure, Precious, →**RAPTURE**, Regale, Rejoice, Revel, Scrummy, Super, Sweet, Taking, Turkish, Whacko, Whee, Whoopee, Yippee, Yum-yum

Delinquent Bodgie, Criminal, Halbstarker, Hoody, Negligent, Offender, Ted

Delirious, Delirium Deranged, DT, Fever, Frenetic, Frenzy, Insanity, Mania, Phrenetic, Phrenitis, Spaced out, Spazz, Wild

Deliver(ance), Delivered, Deliverer, Delivery(man) Accouchement, Air-lift, Bailment, Ball, Birth, Born, Bowl, Caesarean, Consign, Convey, Courier, Deal, Doosra, Escape, Give, Googly, Lead, Liberate, Mail drop, Orate, Over, Pronounce, Receipt, Recorded, Redeem, Refer, Release, Relieve, Render, Rendition, →RESCUE, Rid, Round(sman), Salvation, Save, Say, Seamer, Sell, Shipment, Soliloquy, Speak, Special, Tice, Transfer, Underarm, Underhand, Ventouse extraction, Wide, Yorker

Dell Dale, Dargle, Dene, Dimble, Dingle, Dingl(e)y, Glen, Valley

Delude, Delusion Bilk, Cheat, Deceive, Fallacy, Fool, Hoax, Megalomania, →MISLEAD, Trick, Zoanthropy

Delve Burrow, Dig, Excavate, Exhume, Explore, Probe, Search

Demand(ing) Appetite, Ball-buster, Call, Claim, Cry, Derived, Dun, Exact, Exigent, Fastidious, Final, Heavy, Hest, →INSIST, Market, Necessitate, Need, Order, Postulate, Pressure, Request, Requisition, Rigorous, Rush, Sale, Severe, Stern, Stipulate, Stringent, Summon, Tax, Ultimatum, Want

Demean(ing) Comport, Debase, Degrade, Lower, Maltreat

Dement(ed) Crazy, Frenetic, Hysterical, Insane, Mad, Possessed

Demo March, Parade, Protest, Rally, Sit-in

Democracy, Democrat, Democratic D, Liberal, Locofoco, Menshevik, Montagnard, People's, Popular, Republic, Sansculotte, Social, Tammany

Demolish, Demolition Bulldoze, Devastate, Devour, Floor, KO, Level, Rack, Smash, Tear down, Wreck

▶**Demon** see DEVIL(ISH)

Demonstrate, Demonstration, Demonstrator Agitate, Barrack, Dharma, Display, Endeictic, Évènement, Evince, Explain, Maffick, Manifest, March, Morcha, Ostensive, Peterloo, Portray, Proof, Protest, Prove, Provo, →SHOW, Sit-in, Touchy-feely, Verify, Vigil

Demoralise, Demoralisation Bewilder, Corrupt, Depths, Destroy, Dishearten, Shatter, Unman, Weaken

Demos, Demotic Greek

Demote, Demotion Comedown, Degrade, Disbench, Embace, Embase, Reduce, Relegate, Stellenbosch

Demotic Enchorial

Demure Coy, Mim, Modest, Prenzie, Primsie, Sedate, Shy

Den Dive, Domdaniel, Earth, Hell, Hide-away, Holt, Home, Lair, Lie, Lodge, Room, Shebeen, Spieler, Study, Sty, Wurley

Denial, Deny, Denier Abnegate, Antinomian, Aspheterism, Bar, Belie, Contradict, Controvert, Démenti, Disavow, Disenfranchise, Disown, Forswear, Nay, Negate, Nick, Nihilism, Protest, Refuse, Refute, Renague, Renay, Reneg(e), Renegue, Reney, Renig, Renounce, Reny, Repudiate, Sublate, Withhold

Denote Import, Indicate, Mean, Signify

Denounce, Denunciation Ban, Commination, Condemn, Criticise, Decry, Diatribe, Fulminate, Hatchet job, Hereticate, Proclaim, Proscribe, Shop, Stigmatise, Thunder, Upbraid

Dense, Density B, Buoyant, Charge, Compact, Critical, D, Firm, Intense, Opaque, Packing, Rank, Relative, Single, Solid, Spissitude, Tesla, Thick, Woofy

Dent(ed) Batter, Dancette, Depress, Dimple, Dinge, Dint, Nock, Punctate, Punt, V

Dental (problem), Dentist(ry) DDS, Extractor, Kindhart, LDS, Malocclusion, Odontic, Paedodontics, Periodontic, Toothy

Denude Strip

▶**Deny** see DENIAL

Depart(ed), Departing, Departure Abscond, Absquatulate, Apage, Bunk, D, Dead, Decamp, Decession, Defunct, Demise, Die, Digress, Divergence, Egress, Exception, Exit, Exodus, Flight, French leave, →GO, Imshi, Late, Leave, Lucky, Moonlight flit, Outbound, Remue, Send-off, Vacate, Vade, Vamoose, Walkout

Department Achaea, Ain, Aisne, Allier, Alpes de Provence, Alpes-Maritimes, Angers, Arcadia, Ardeche, Ardennes, Argo, Arrondissement, Arta, Attica, Aube, Aude, Belfort, Bell-chamber, Branch, Bureau, Calvados, Cantal, Charente-Maritime, Cher, Cleansing, Commissariat, Cote d'Or, Cotes d'Armor, Cotes du Nord, Creuse, Deme, Deuxième Bureau, Deux-Sevres, Division, Domain, Dordogne, Essonne, Extramural, Faculty, Finistere, FO, Foggy Bottom, Gard, Gironde, Greencloth, Guadeloupe, Gulag, Hanaper, Hautes-Pyrenees, Helpdesk, Inspectorate, Isere, Jura, Loire, Loiret, Lot, Lot-et-Garonne, Marne, Martinique, Ministry, Nome, Nomos, Office, Oise, Ordnance, Orne, Portfolio, Province, Puy de Dôme, Region, Savoie, Secretariat(e), Section, Somme, Sphere, State, Treasury, Tuscany, Unit, Var, Vienne, Wardrobe, Yonne

Depend(ant), Dependence, Dependency, Dependent Addicted, Child, Client, Colony, Conditional, Contingent, Count, Dangle, E, Fief, Habit, Hang, Hinge, Icicle, Lean, Lie, Lippen, Minion, Pensioner, Relier, Rely, Retainer, Sponge, Stalactite, Statistical, Subject, Subordinate, Trust, Turn on, Vassal, Virgin Islands

Dependable Reliable, Reliant, Rock, Safe, Secure, Solid, Sound, Staunch, Sure, →TRUSTWORTHY

▷ **Deploy(ment)** *may indicate* an anagram

Deport(ation), Deportment Address, Air, Banish, →BEARING, Carriage, Demeanour, Mien, Renvoi, Renvoy, Repatriation

Depose, Deposition Affirm, Banish, Dethrone(ment), Displace, Dispossess, Hoard, Overthrow, Pieta, Testify

Deposit(s), Depository Aeolian, Alluvial, Alluvium, Aquifer, Arcus, Argol, Arles, Atheroma, Bank, Bathybius, Bergmehl, Calc-sinter, Calc-tuff, Caliche, Cave-earth, Coral, Crag, Crystolith, Delta, Depone, Diatomite, Diluvium, Dust, Evaporite, Fan, File, Firn, Fort Knox, Fur, Glacial, Gyttja, Hoard, Illuvium, Kieselguhr, Land, Laterite, Lay, Lay away, Lay-by, Laydown, Lead tree, Limescale, Lodge(ment), Loess, Löss, Measure, Natron, Outwatch, Park, Pay in, Phosphorite, Placer, Plank, Plaque, Put, Repose, Residuum, Saburra, Salamander, Sandbank, Saprolite, Saturn's tree, Scale, Sea dust, →SEDIMENT, Silt, Sinter, Sludge, Soot, Speleothem, Stockwork, Storeroom, Stratum, Surety, Tartar, Terramara, Terramare, Tophus, Tripoli, Turbidite

Depot Barracoon, Base, Camp, Depository, Etape, Station, Terminus, Treasure-city, Warehouse

Deprave(d), Depravity Bestial, Cachexia, Cachexy, Caligulism, →CORRUPT, Dissolute, Evil, Immoral, Low, Outrage, Rotten, Sodom, Turpitude, Ugly, Unholy, Vice, Vicious, Vile

Depress(ed), Depressing, Depression Agitated, Alamort, Amort, Black dog, Blight, Blue devils, Blues, Cafard, Canada, Canyon, Chill, Col, Combe, Couch, Crab, Crush, Cyclone, Dampen, Deject, Dell, Demission, Dene, Dent, Despair, Dip, Dismal, Dispirit, Ditch, Drear, Drere, Dumpish, Exanimate, Flatten, Foss(ula), Fossa, Glen, Gloom, Ha-ha, Hammer, Heart-spoon, Hilar, Hilum, Hilus, Hollow, Howe, Hyp, Hypothymia, Indentation, Joes, Kettle, Kick(-up), Lacuna, Leaden, Low(ness), Low-spirited, Megrims, Moping, Morose, Neck, Pit, Postnatal, Postpartum, Prostrate, Punt, Recession, Re-entrant, Retuse, Sad, Saddle, Sag, Salt-cellar, Salt-pan, Sink, Sinkhole, Sinus, Slot, →SLUMP, Soakaway, Spiritless, Sump, Swag, Swale, Trench, Trough, Vale, Valley, Wallow

Deprivation, Deprive(d) Amerce, Bereft, Deny, Disenfranchise, Disfrock, Disseise, Disseize, Expropriate, Geld, Ghetto, Have-not, Hunger, Reduce, Remove, Rob, Sensory, Starve, Strip, Withhold

Depth F, Fathom, Gravity, Intensity, Isobath, Pit, Profundity

Deputise, Deputy Act, Agent, Aide, Assistant, Commis(sary), Delegate, Legate, Lieutenant, Locum, Loot, Number two, Pro-chancellor, Proxy, Represent, Secondary, Sidekick, Standby, Sub, Subchanter, Substitute, Succentor, Surmistress, Surrogate, Tanaiste, Vicar, Vice, Viceregent, Vidame

Derange(d), Derangement Craze, Détraqué, Disturb, Insane, Loopy, Manic, Trophesy, Troppo, Unhinge, Unsettle

Derelict Abandoned, →**DECREPIT**, Deserted, Negligent, Outcast, Ramshackle, Tramp

Deride, Derision, Derisive Contempt, Gup, Guy, Hiss, Hoot, Jeer, Mock, Nominal, Pigs, Raspberry, →**RIDICULE**, Sardonic, Scoff, Scorn, Sneer, Snifty, Snort, Ya(h)boo (sucks), Yah

Derive, Derivation, Derivative Amine, Ancestry, Apiol, Creosote, Deduce, Descend, Extract, Get, Kinone, Of, Offshoot, Origin, Pedigree, Picoline, Secondary, Taurine, Tyramine

Descend(ant), Descent Ancestry, Avail, Avale, Bathos, Blood, Cadency, Catabasis, Chute, Cion, Decline, Degenerate, Dégringoler, Derive, Dismount, Dive, Drop, Epigon, Extraction, Heir, Heraclid, Offspring, Pedigree, Posterity, Progeny, Prone, Purler, Rappel, Said, Say(y)id, Scarp, Scion, Seed, Shelve, Sien(t), Sink, Spearside, Stock, Syen, Vest, Volplane

Describe, Describing, Description, Descriptive Blurb, Define, Delineate, Depict, Designate, Draw, Epithet, Exposition, Expound, Graphic, Job, Label, Narrate, Outline, Paint, Portray, Rapportage, Recount, Relate, Report, Sea-letter, Semantic, Signalment, Sketch, Specification, Synopsis, Term, Trace, Vignette, Write-up

▷ **Describing** *may indicate* 'around'

Desecrate, Desecration Abuse, Defile, Dishallow, Profane, Sacrilege, Unhallow

▷ **Desecrated** *may indicate* an anagram

Desert(er), Deserted, Deserts Abandon, Absquatulate, Apostasy, Arabian, Arid, Arunta, Atacama, AWOL, Badland, Barren, Bug, Bunk, D, Defect, Desolate, Dissident, Due, Empty, Eremic, Factious, Fail, Foresay, Forhoo, Forhow, Forlorn, Forsake, Forsay, Gibson, Gila, Gobi, Great Basin, Great Sandy, Great Victoria, Heterodox, Kalahari, Karma, Libyan, Lurch, Merit, Mojave, Nafud, Namib, Negev, Nubian, Ogaden, Painted, Patagonian, Pindan, Rat, Refus(e)nik, Reg, →**RENEGADE**, Reward, Run, Sahara(n), Sands, Secede, Sertao, Simpson, Sinai, Sonoran, Sturt, Syrian, Tergiversate, Turncoat, Void, Wadi, Waste(land), Wild, Worthiness

Deserve(d) Condign, Earn, →**MERIT**, Rate, Well-earned, Worthy

Design(er) Adam, Aim, Amies, Arabesque, Architect(ure), Argyle, Armani, Ashley, Batik, Between-subjects, Broider, Cable stitch, Calligram(me), Cardin, Cartoon, Chop, Cloisonné, Courreges, Couturier, Create, Cul de lampe, Damascene, Decor, Deep, Depict, Devise, Dévoré, Dior, Draft, Embroidery, End, Engine(r), Engineer, Erté, Etch, Fashion, Flanch, Format, Former, Hepplewhite, Hitech, Iconic, Imagineer, Impresa, Imprese, Inlay, Intend(ment), Intent(ion), Interior, Layout, Le Corbusier, Limit-state, Linocut, Logo, Marquetry, Matched pairs, Mean, Meander, Mehndi, Modiste, Monogram, Morris, Mosaic, Motif, Multifoil, Nailhead, Nissen, Paisley, →**PLAN**, Plot, Propose, Pyrography, Quant, Ruse, Schema, Scheme, Schiaparelli, Seal, Sheraton, Sketch, Sopwith, Spatterwork, Specification, Sprig, Stencil, Stubble, Tatow, Tattoo, Tatu, Think, Tooling, Townscape, Trigram, Vignette, Watermark, Weiner, Werkstalte, Whittle, Within-subjects

Desirable, Desire, Desirous Ambition, Aphrodisia, Appetite, Aspire, Avid, Best, Cama, Conation, Concupiscence, Covet, Crave, Cupidity, Des, Dreamboat, Earn, Eligible, Epithymetic, Fancy, Gasp, Greed, Hanker, Hope, Hots, Hunger, Itch, Kama(deva), Le(t)ch, Libido, List, Long, Luscious, Lust, Mania, Notion, Nymphomania, Orectic, Owlcar, Pica, Plum, Reak, Reck, Request, Residence, Salt, Slaver, Spiffing, Streetcar, Thirst, Urge, Velleity, Vote, Wanderlust, Want, Whim, Will, Wish, Yearn, Yen

Desk Almemar, Ambo, Bonheur-du-jour, Bureau, Carrel(l), Cash, Check-in, Cheveret, City, Copy, Davenport, Desse, Devonport, E(s)critoire, Enquiry, Faldstool, Lectern, Lettern, Litany, Pay, Pedestal, Prie-dieu, Pulpit, Reading, Roll-top, Scrutoire, Secretaire, Vargueno, Writing

Desolate, Desolation Bare, Barren, Desert, Devastate, Disconsolate, Forlorn, Gaunt, Gousty, Moonscape, Waste, Woebegone

Despair, Desperate, Desperation Acharne, Dan, De profundis, Despond,

Dire, Extreme, Frantic, Gagging, Giant, Gloom, Hairless, Headlong, Hopelessness, Reckless, Unhopeful, Urgent, Wanhope

▶**Despatch** *see* DISPATCH

Despise(d) Condemn, Conspire, Contemn, Forhow, Futz, Hate, Ignore, Scorn, Spurn, Vilify, Vilipend

Despite For, Malgré, Notwithstanding, Pace, Though, Venom

Despot(ism) Autarchy, Autocrat, Bonaparte, Caesar, Darius, Dictator, Little Hitler, Martinet, Napoleon, Nero, Satrap, Stratocrat, Tsar, Tyrant, Tzar

Dessert Afters, Baked Alaska, Baklava, Banana split, Bavarian cream, Bavarois, Blancmange, Bombe, Cannoli, Charlotte, Charlotte russe, Cheesecake, Clafoutis, Cobbler, Compote, Coupe, Cranachan, Cream, Crème brulée, Crème caramel, Crepe Suzette, Dulce de leche, Entremets, Eve's pudding, Floating Island, Flummery, Fool, Granita, Junket, Kissel, Knickerbocker glory, Kulfi, Marquise, Mousse, Mud pie, Nesselrode, Pannacotta, Parfait, Pashka, Pavlova, Peach Melba, →PUDDING, Rasmalai, Roulade, Sabayon, Sawine, Semifreddo, Shoofly pie, Split, Spumone, Strudel, Sundae, Syllabub, Tart, Tarte tatin, Tartufo, Tiramisu, Tortoni, Trifle, Vacherin, Whip, Zabaglione

Destine(d), Destination Born, Design, End, Fate, Foredoom, Goal, Gole, Home, Intend, Joss, Port, Purpose, Vector, Weird

Destiny Doom, →FATE, Karma, Kismet, Lot, Manifest, Moira, Portion, Yang, Yin

Destress Anneal

Destroy(er) Annihilate, Apollyon, Atomise, Blight, Bulldoze, Can, Crush, D, Decimate, Deface, Delete, Demolish, Demyelinate, Denature, Destruct, Dish, Dismember, Dissolve, Eat, Efface, End, Eradicate, Erase, Exterminate, Extirpate, Fordo, Graunch, Harry, Iconoclast, Incinerate, Invalidate, →KILL, KO, Locust, Murder, Obliterate, Overkill, Perish, Predator, Pulverize, Q-ship, Ravage, Raze, Ruin, Saboteur, Sack, Scuttle, Slash, Smash, Spif(f)licate, Sterilize, Stew-can, Stonker, Stultify, Subvert, Undo, Uproot, Vandal, Vitiate, Waste, Whelm, Wreck, Zap

Destruction, Destructive Adverse, Bane, Can, Catabolism, Collapse, Deathblow, Deleterious, Devastation, Doom, Downfall, Ecocide, End, Götterdämmerung, Grave, Havoc, Holocaust, Hunnish, Iconoclasm, Insidious, Internecine, Kali, Lethal, Loss, Maelstrom, Maleficent, Moorburn, Nihilistic, Pernicious, Pestilential, Pogrom, Rack, Ragnarok, Ravage, Ruination, Sabotage, Stroy, Wrack, Wreckage

Detach(ed), Detachment Abeigh, Abstract, Alienate, Aloof, Apart, Body, Calve, Clinical, Cut, Detail, Discrete, Dispassionate, Distinct, Isolate, Loose, Outlying, Outpost, Patrol, Separate, Sever, Staccato, Stoic, Unfasten, Unhinge, Unit

Detail(s), Detailed Annotate, Circumstances, Dock, Elaborate, Embroider, Expatiate, Explicit, Exploded, Expound, Instance, →ITEM, Itemise, Minutiae, Nicety, Nuts and bolts, Particular(ise), Pedantry, Point, Recite, Recount, Relate, Respect, Send, Spec, Special, Specific, Specification, Technicality, Touch

▷**Detailed** *may indicate* last letter missing

Detain(ee), Detention (centre) Arrest, Buttonhole, Collar, Custody, Delay, Demurrage, Detinue, Gate, Glasshouse, Hinder, Intern, Juvie, Keep, POW, Retard, Sin bin, Stay, →WITHHOLD

Detect(or), Detective Agent, Arsène, Asdic, Bloodhound, Brown, Bucket, Busy, Catch, Chan, CID, Cuff, Det, Dick, Discover, Divine, Doodlebug, Dupin, Espy, Eye, Fed, Find, Flambeau, Flic, Fortune, French, Geigercounter, Geophone, G-man, Gumshoe, Hanaud, Hercule, Holmes, Interpol, Investigator, Jack, Lecoq, Lupin, Maigret, Methanometer, Minitrack®, Morse, Nail, Nose, Peeper, PI, Pinkerton, Plant, Poirot, Private, Private eye, Prodnose, Radar, Reagent, Retinula, Rumble, Scent, Scerne, Sense, Sensor, Shadow, Shamus, Sherlock, Sleuth-hound, Sofar, Solver, Sonar, Sonobuoy, Spot, Tabaret, Take, Tec, Thorndyke, Toff, Trace, Trent, Vance, Wimsey, Yard(man)

Deter(rent) Block, Check, Daunt, Dehort, Delay, Disincentive, Dissuade, Prevent, Restrain, Turn-off, Ultimate

Detergent Clean(s)er, Non-ionizing, Solvent, Surfactant, Syndet, Tepol, Whitener

Deteriorate, Deterioration Decadence, Degenerate, Derogate, Pejoration, Relapse, Rust, Worsen

▷ **Deterioration** *may indicate* an anagram

▷ **Determination** *may indicate* 'last letter'

Determine(d), Determination All-out, Appoint, Arbitrament, Ardent, Ascertain, Assign, Assoil, Bent, Causal, Condition, Dead-set, →**DECIDE**, Define, Dictate, Doctrinaire, Dogged, Do-or-die, Dour, Drive, Earnest, Fix, Govern, Granite, Grim, Grit(ty), Headstrong, Hell-bent, Indomitable, Influence, Intent, Ironclad, Judgement, Law, Liquidate, Orient, Out, Point, Pre-ordain, Purpose, Quantify, →**RESOLUTE**, Resolve, Rigwiddie, Rigwoodie, Self-will, Set, Settle, Set upon, Shape, Soum, Sowm, Stalwart, Steely, Tenacious, Type, Valiant, Weigh

Detest(able), Detested Abhor, Anathema, Despise, Execrable, Execrate, Hate, Loathsome, Pestful, Vile

Detonate, Detonator Blast, Explode, Fire, Fuse, Fuze, Ignite, Kindle, Plunger, Primer, Saucisse, Saucisson, Spring, Tetryl, Trip-wire

Detour Bypass, Deviate, Divert

Detract Belittle, Decry, Diminish, Discount, Disparage

Detroit Motown

Devalue Cheapen, Debase, Impair, Reduce, Undermine

Devastate, Devastation Demolish, Destroy, Gut, Overwhelm, Ravage, Sack, Waste, Wrack

▷ **Develop** *may indicate* an anagram

Develop(er), Developed, Developing, Development Advance, Age, Agile, Apotheosis, Breed, Build, Cutting edge, Dark room, Educe, Elaborate, Enlarge, Escalate, Evolve, Expand, Expatriate, Fulminant, Germinate, Gestate, Grow, Hatch, Hothouse, Hypo, Imago, Improve, Incubate, Larva, Mature, Metamorphose, Metol, Morphosis, Mushroom, Nascent, Nurture, Offshoot, Ongoing, Pathogeny, Pullulate, Pupa, Pyro, Quinol, Ribbon, Ripe(n), Sarvodaya, Sensorimeter, Separate, Shape, Soup, Sprawl, Subtopia, Technography, Unfold, Upgrow

Deviant, Deviate, Deviation Aberrance, Abnormal, Anomaly, Brisure, Deflect, Deflexure, Depart, Derogate, Detour, Digress, Discrepant, Diverge, Divert, Drift, Error, Kurtosis, Pervert, Quartile, Sheer, Solecism, Sport, Stray, Swerve, →**TURN**, Valgus, Varus, Veer, Wander, Wend

Device Allegory, →**APPARATUS**, Appliance, Artifice, Bush, Contraption, Contrivance, Dodge, Emblem, Expedient, Gadget, Gimmick, Gismo, Gubbins, Instrument, Logo, Mnemonic, Motto, Plan, Pointing, Ruse, Safeguard, →**STRATAGEM**, Subterfuge, Tactic, Tag, Thing, Tool, Trademark, Trick, Wile

Devil(ish), Demon Abaddon, Afrit, Apollyon, Asmodeus, Auld Hornie, Beelzebub, Belial, Buckra, Cacodemon, Cartesian, Clootie, Cloots, Deev, Deil, Demon, Deuce, Diable, Diabolic, Dickens, Div, Drudge, Eblis, Familiar, Fiend, Ghoul, Hornie, Iblis, Imp, Incubus, Infernal, Knave, Lucifer, Mahoun(d), Man of Sin, Mephisto(pheles), Mischief, Nick, Nickie-ben, Old Nick, Ragman, Rahu, Ralph, Satan, Satyr, Scratch, Succubine, Succubus, Tasmanian, Tempter, Wicked, Worricow

Devious Braide, Cunning, Deep, Eel(y), Erroneous, Evasive, Heel, Implex, Indirect, Scheming, Shifty, Sly, Sneaky, Stealthy, Subtle, Tortuous, Tricky

Devise(d) Arrange, Coin, Comment, Concoct, Contrive, Decoct, Hit-on, Imagine, Invenit, Invent, Plan, Plot

Devolution West Lothian question

Devote(e), Devotion(al), Devoted Addiction, Aficionado, Âme damnée, Angelus, Attached, Bhakti, Buff, Bunny, Commitment, Consecrate, Corban, Dedicate, Employ, Enthusiast, Fan, Fervid, Fetishism, Fidelity, Fiend, Grebo, Holy, Hound, Loyalty, Mariolate, Novena, Nut, Partisan, Passion, Pious, Puja, Religioso, Sacred, Saivite, Savoyard, Sivaite, Solemn, Sworn, True, Voteen, Zealous

▷ **Devour** *may indicate* one word inside another

Devour(ing) Consume, Eat, Engorge, Engulf, Manducate, Moth-eat, Scarf, Scoff, Snarf, →**SWALLOW**

Devout Holy, Pious, Religiose, Reverent, Sant, Sincere, Solemn

Dew(y) Bloom, Gory, Moist, Mountain, Rime, Roral, Roric, Rorid, Roscid, Serene, Tranter

Diagnose, Diagnosis, Diagnostic Amniocentesis, Findings, Identify, Iridology, Pulse, Radionics, Scan, Scintigraphy, X-ray

Diagonal(ly) Bias, Cater(-corner), Counter, Oblique, Principal, Slant, Solidus, Speed, Twill

Diagram Argand, Butterfly, Chart, Chromaticity, Cladogram, Compass rose, Decision tree, Drawing, Feynman, Figure, Graph, Graphics, Grid, Map, Phase, Plan, Plat, Scatter, Schema, Schematic, Scintigram, Stemma, Stereogram, Topo, Tree, Venn

Dial(ling) Card, Face, Mug, Phiz, Phone, Ring, Speed, STD, Visage

Dialect Acadian, Accent, Amoy, Anglican, Burr, Castilian, Damara, Eldin, Epic, Erse, Eye, Franconian, Gascon, Geordie, Hassaniya, Idiom, Ionic, Isogloss, Jargon, Jockney, Ladin, Lallans, Landsmaal, Langue d'oui, Ledden, Lingo, Low German, Min, Norman, Norn, Occitan, Old Icelandic, Old North French, Parsee, Parsi, Patavinity, Patois, Pedi, Picard, Prakrit, Rhaeto-Romance, Rhotic, Rock English, Romans(c)h, Ruthenian, Salish, Savoyard, Scouse, Taal, Tadzhik, Ta(d)jik, Talky-talky, Tongue, Tuscan, Tyrolese, Umbrian, Vaudois, Walloon, West Saxon, Yenglish, Yinglish

Dialogue Colloquy, Conversation, Critias, Discussion, Exchange, Lazzo, Pastourelle, Speech, Stichomythia, Talk, Upspeak

Diameter Breadth, Calibre, Gauge, Width

Diamond(s), Diamond-shaped Adamant, Black, Boart, Brilliant, Bristol, Carbon, Carbonado, Cullinan, D, DE, Delaware, Eustace, False, Florentine, Hope, Ice, Isomer, Jim, Koh-i-Noor, Lasque, Lattice, Lozenge, Paragon, Pick, Pitch, Pitt, Reef, Rhinestone, Rhomb, Rock, Rose-cut, Rosser, Rough, Sancy, Solitaire, Spark, Sparklers, Squarial, Suit

Diary, Diarist Adrian Mole, Blogger, Burney, Chronicle, Dale, Day-book, Evelyn, Frank, Hickey, Journal, Journal intime, Kilvert, Log, Nobody, Noctuary, Pepys, Personal organiser, Planner, Pooter, Record

Dibble(r) Marsupial, Theria

Dice(r), Dicey Aleatory, Astragals, Bale, Bones, Chop, Craps, Cube, Dodgy, Fulham, Fullams, Fullans, Gourd(s), Hash, Highman, Jeff, Novum, Shoot, Smalto, Snake-eyes, Tallmen

▷ **Dick** *may indicate* a dictionary

▷ **Dicky** *may indicate* an anagram

Dictate, Dictator(ial) Amin, Autocrat, Caesar, Castro, Cham, Command, Czar, Decree, Demagogue, Despot, Duce, Franco, Fu(e)hrer, Gaddafi, Gauleiter, Hitler, Impose, Indite, Lenin, Mussolini, Ordain, Peremptory, Peron, Pol Pot, Salazar, Shogun, Stalin, Tell, Tito, Totalitarian, Trujillo, Tsar, Tyrant, Tzar

Dictionary Alveary, Calepin, Chambers, Etymologicon, Fowler, Gazetteer, Glossary, Gradus, Hobson-Jobson, Idioticon, Johnson's, Larousse, Lexicon, Lexis, OED, Onomasticon, Thesaurus, Webster, Wordbook

Die(d), Dying Ache, Buy the farm, Cark, Choke, Conk out, Crater, Croak, Cube, D, Decadent, Desire, End, Evanish, Exit, Expire, Fade, Fail, Forfair, Fulham, Fulhan, Fullam, Go, Hallmark, Hang, Highman, Hop, Hop the twig, Infarct, Kark, Long, Morendo, Moribund, Ob(iit), Orb, Pass, Perdendosi, Perish, Peter, Pop off, Pop one's clogs, Slip the cable, Snuff, Solidum, Sphacelation, Stagheaded, Stamp, Sterve, Succumb, Suffer, Swage, Swelt, Terminal, Tine, Touch, Wane

Diesel Red

Diet(er), Dieting Assembly, Atkins, Augsburg, Bant(ing), Council, Dail, Eat, Fare, Feed, Hay, Intake, Landtag, Lent, Macrobiotic, Parliament, Reduce, Regimen, Reichstag, Short commons, Slim, Solid, Sprat, Staple, Strict, Tynwald, Vegan, Vegetarian, Weightwatcher, Worms, Yo-yo

Differ(ence), Differing, Different(ly) Afresh, Allo, Alterity, Barney, Change, Cline, Contrast, Contretemps, Deviant, Diesis, Disagree, Discord, Discrepant, Disparate, Dispute, Dissent, Distinct, Diverge, Diverse, Else, Elsewise, Epact, Exotic,

Gulf, Heterodox, Nuance, Omnifarious, Other, Othergates, Otherguess, Otherness, Otherwise, Poles apart, Quantum, Separate, Several, Special, Tiff, Unlike, Variform, Various, Vary

Difficult(y), Difficult person Abstruseness, Ado, Aporia, Arduous, Augean, Badass, Balky, Ballbuster, Bitter, Block, Bolshie, Bother, Cantankerous, Catch, Choosy, Complex, Complication, Corner, Cough drop, Crisis, Crotchety, Deep, Delphic, Depth, Dysphagia, Embarrassment, Extreme, Fiddly, Formidable, Gnomic, Gordian, →HARD, Hassle, Hazard, Hiccough, Hiccup, Hobble, Hole, Hoor, Hump, Ill, Impasse, Indocile, Inscrutable, Intractable, Intransigent, Jam, Kink, Kittle, Knot, Lob's pound, Lurch, Mulish, Net, Nodus, Obstacle, Parlous, Pig, Pitfall, Plight, Predicament, Quandary, Queer St, Recalcitrant, Rough, Rub, Scabrous, Scrape, Scrub, Setaceous, Shlep, Snag, Soup, Steep, Stey, Stick, Sticky, Stiff, Stinker, Strait, Stubborn, Stymie, Swine, Tall order, Testing, Thorny, Ticklish, Tight spot, Tough, Trial, Tricky, Troublous, Trying, Une(a)th, Uphill, Via dolorosa, Woe

Diffuse, Diffusion Disperse, Disseminate, Endosmosis, Exude, Osmosis, Permeate, Pervade, Radiate, Run, Sperse, Spread

Dig(s), Digger, Digging, Dig up Antipodean, Australian, Backhoe, Barb, Beadle, Bed(e)ral, Billet, Bot, Burrow, Costean, Delve, Deracinate, Enjoy, Excavate, Flea-bag, Flophouse, Fork, Fossorial, Gaulter, Get, Gibe, Gird, Graft, Graip, Grub, Hoe, Howk, Into, Jab, Kip, Lair, Like, Lodgings, Luxor, Mine, Navvy, Nervy, Nudge, Pad, Pioneer, Probe, Prod, Raddleman, Resurrect, Root(le), Ruddleman, Sap, See, Sneer, Spade, Spit, Spud, Star-nose, Taunt, Till, Tonnell, Trench, Tunnel, Undermine, Unearth

Digest(ible), Digestion, Digestive Abridgement, Absorb, Abstract, Aperçu, Archenteron, Assimilate, Beeda, Codify, Concoct, Endue, Epitome, Eupepsia, Eupepsy, Fletcherism, Gastric, Indew, Indue, Light, Pandect, Pem(m)ican, Pepsin(e), Peptic, Précis, Salt-cat, Steatolysis, →SUMMARY

Dignified, Dignify August, Elevate, Ennoble, Exalt, Grace, Handsome, Honour, Imposing, Lordly, Maestoso, Majestic, Manly, Proud, Stately, Statuesque

Dignity Aplomb, Bearing, Cathedra, Decorum, Face, Glory, Grandeur, Gravitas, High horse, Majesty, Nobility, Poise, Presence, Scarf

Digress(ion) Deviate, Diverge, Ecbole, Episode, Excurse, Excursus, Maunder, Vagary, Veer, Wander

Dilate, Dilation, Dilatation Amplify, Develop, Diastole, Ecstasis, Enlarge, Expand, Increase, Mydriasis, Sinus, Tent, Varix

Dilemma Casuistry, Choice, Cleft(stick), Dulcarnon, Fix, Horn, Jam, Predicament, Quandary, Why-not

Diligence, Diligent Active, Application, Assiduous, Coach, Conscience, Eident, Hard-working, Industry, Intent, Painstaking, Sedulous, Studious

Dilute(d), Dilution Adulterate, Allay, Deglaze, Delay, Diluent, Lavage, Qualify, Simpson, Thin, Water, Weaken, Wishy-washy

Dim(ness), Dimming, Dimwit(ted) Becloud, Blear, Blur, Brownout, Caligo, Clueless, Crepuscular, Dense, Dusk, Eclipse, Fade, Faint, Feint, Fozy, Gormless, Ill-lit, Indefinable, Indistinct, Mist, Nebulous, Ninny, Obscure, Overcast, Owl, Pale, Purblind, Shadow, Unsmart

Dimension(s) Area, Breadth, Extent, Height, Length, Linear, Measure, New, Scantling, Size, Space, Third, Volume, Width

Dimer Cystine

Diminish(ed), Diminishing, Diminuendo, Diminution, Diminutive Abatement, Assuage, Baby, Calando, Contract, Cot(t)ise, Deactivate, Decline, Decrease, Détente, Detract, Disparage, Dissipate, Dwarf, Dwindle, Erode, Fourth, Hypocorism(a), Lessen, Lilliputian, Minify, Minus, Mitigate, Petite, Pigmy, Ritardando, Scarp, Small, Stultify, Subside, Taper, Toy, Trangle, Wane, Whittle

Dingy Crummy, Dark, Dirty, Drear, Dun, Fleapit, Fusc(ous), Grimy, Isabel(la), Isabelline, Lurid, Oorie, Ourie, Owrie, Shabby, Smoky

Dining-room Cafeteria, Cenacle, Commons, Frater, Hall, Langar, Mess hall, Refectory, Restaurant, Triclinium

Dinky Twee

Dinner Banquet, Collation, Feast, Hall, Kail, Kale, Meal, Prandial, Repast

Dinner jacket Penguin suit

Dinosaur Aepyornis, Allosaurus, Archosaur, Atlantosaurus, Baryonyx, Brachiosaurus, Brontosaurus, Ceratosaurus, Ceteosaurus, Compsognathus, Diplodocus, Galeopithecus, Hadrosaur, Ichthyosaur(us), Iguanodon, Megalosaur, Microraptor, Odontornithes, Pachycephalosaur, Perissodactyl, Plesiosaur, Pliosaur, Prehistoric, Pterodactyl, Pterosaur, Pythonomorpha, Raptor, Rhynchocephalian, Sauropod, Sauropterygian, Smilodon, Square, Stegosaur, Teleosaurus, Titanosaurus, Triceratops, Tyrannosaurus

Diocese Bishopric, District, Eparchate, Eparchy, See

Dip(per), Dippy Baptise, Basin, Bathe, Bob, Brantub, Dabble, Dap, Dean, Dib, Diver, Dop, Duck, Dunk, Fatuous, Foveola, Geosyncline, Guacomole, Houmous, H(o)ummus, Humus, Immerge, Immerse, Intinction, Ladle, Lucky, Ousel, Ouzel, Paddle, Plough, Rinse, Rollercoaster, Salute, Sheep-wash, Star, Submerge, Tzatziki, Ursa

Diploma Bac, Charter, Parchment, Qualification, Scroll, Sheepskin

Diplomacy, Diplomat(ic) Alternat, Ambassador, Attaché, Career, CD, Chargé d'affaires, Consul, DA, Dean, Discretion, Doyen, El(t)chi, Emissary, Envoy, Fanariot, Fetial, Finesse, Gunboat, Legation, Lei(d)ger, Metternich, Phanariot, Suave, → **TACT**

▷ **Dippy** *may indicate a bather*

Dire Dreadful, Fatal, Fell, Grim, Hateful, Ominous, Urgent

Direct(or), Directed, Directly Ad hominem, Administer, Advert, Aim, Airt, Air-to-air, Auteur, Beeline, Board, Boss, Cann, Cast, Chairperson, Channel, Charge, Chorus-master, Command, Compere, Con(n), Conduct, Control, Cox, Dead, Due, Dunstable road, Enjoin, Explicit, Fair, Fellini, First-hand, Forthright, Frontal, Guide, Helm, Immediate, Impresario, Instruct, Kapellmeister, Lead, Manager, Navigate, Outright, Oversee, Pilot, Play, Point-blank, Ready, Refer, Régisseur, Rudder, Send, Set, Signpost, Slap-bang, Stear, → **STEER**, Straight, Teach, Telic, Tell, Train, Vector

Direction Aim, Airt, Arrow, Astern, Bearings, Course, Cross-reference, E, End-on, Guidance, Guide, Heading, Keblah, L, Line, N, Orders, Orientation, Passim, Quarter, R, Recipe, Route, Rubric, S, Sanction, Send, Sense, Side, Slap, Tacet, Tack, Tenor, Thataway, Trend, W, Way

Directory Crockford, Data, Debrett, Encyclop(a)edia, Folder, French, Kelly, List, Red book, Register, Root, Search, Web

Dirge Ballant, Coronach, Dirige, Epicedium, Knell, Monody, Requiem, Song, Threnody

Dirigible Airship, Balloon, Blimp, Zeppelin

Dirk Dagger, Skean, Whinger, Whiniard, Whinyard

Dirt(y) Augean, Bed(r)aggled, Begrime, Bemoil, Chatty, Clag, Clarty, Colly, Contaminate, Coom, Crock, Crud, Defile, Distain, Draggle, Dung, Dust, Earth, Filth, Foul, Gore, Grime, Grubby, Grufted, Grungy, Impure, Manky, Moit, Mote, Muck, Obscene, Ordure, Pay, Pick, Ray, Scandal, Scody, Sculdudd(e)ry, Scum, Scuttlebutt, Scuzzy, Skulduddery, Slattery, Smirch, Smut(ch), Soil, Sordor, Squalid, Squalor, Stain, Sully, Trash, Unclean, Unwashed, Yucky, Yukky

Disability, Disable(d) Cripple, Crock, Gimp, Handicapped, Hors de combat, Kayo, Lame, Maim, Paralyse, Scotch, Supercrip, Wreck

Disabuse Unteach

Disadvantage Detriment, Disamenity, Drawback, Flipside, Handicap, Mischief, Out, Penalise, Penalty, Prejudice, Supercherie, Upstage, Wrongfoot, Zugswang

Disaffected Malcontent

Disagree(ing), Disagreeable, Disagreement Altercation, Argue, Argy-bargy, Bad, Clash, Conflict, Contest, Debate, Differ, Discrepant, Dispute, Dissent, Dissonant, Evil, Fiddlesticks, Friction, Heterodoxy, Pace, Rift, Troll, Uh-uh, Vary

Disappear(ing) Cook, Dispel, Evanesce, Evanish, Evaporate, Fade, Kook, Latescent, Melt, Occult, Pass, Skedaddle, Slope, → **VANISH**

Disappoint(ment), Disappointed, Disappointing Anticlimax, Balk, Baulk, Chagrin, Comedown, Crestfallen, Delude, Disgruntle, Fizzer, Frustrate, Gutted,

Heartsick, Lemon, Letdown, Mislippen, Off, Regret, Sell, Setback, Shucks, Sick, Suck-in, Sucks, Swiz(zle), Thwart, Tsk, Underwhelm

Disapproval, Disapprove(d) Ach, Animadvert, Boo, Catcall, Censure, Condemn, Deplore, Deprecate, Fie, Frown, Harrumph, Hiss, Mal vu, Napoo, Object, Pejorative, Po-faced, Pshaw, Raspberry, Reject, Reproach, Reprobate, Squint, Tush, Tut, Umph, Veto, Whiss

Disarm(ament), Disarming Bluff, Defuse, Demobilise, Nuclear, Winsome

Disarray Disorder, Mess, Rifle, Tash, Undress

Disaster, Disastrous Accident, Adversity, Apocalypse, Bale, Calamity, Cataclysm(ic), Catastrophe, Crash, Crisis, Debacle, Dire, Doom, Evil, Fatal, Fiasco, Flop, Impostor, Meltdown, Mishap, Pitfall, Providence, Quake, Rout, Ruin, Shipwreck, Titanic, Tragedy, Wipeout

Disbelief, Disbelieve(r) Acosmism, Anythingarian, Atheism, Cor, Doubt, Incredulity, Mistrust, Nothingarianism, Occamist, Pfui, Phew, Phooey, Puh-lease, Puh-leeze, Question, Sceptic, Stroll on, Voetsak

Disc, Disk Accretion, Bursting, Button, CD, Cheese, Clay pigeon, Compact, Coulter, Counter, Diaphragm, Dogtag, EP, Epiphragm, Fla(w)n, Flexible, Floppy, Frisbee®, Gold, Gong, Granum, Grindstone, Hard, Hard card, Harrow, Impeller, Intervertebral, Laser, LP, Magnetic, Mono, O, Optic(al), Parking, Paten, Patin, Planchet, Plate, Platinum, Platter, Puck, RAID, RAM, Rayleigh, Record, Reflector, Rosette, Roundel, Rowel, Rundle, Sealed unit, Silver, Slipped, Slug, Stereo, Sun, Swash plate, System, Tax, Thylacoid, Token, Video, Wafer, Wharve, Whorl, Winchester, Wink, WORM, Zip®

Discard(ed) Abandon, Crib, Dele, Jettison, Kill, Leave, Obsolete, Off, Offload, Oust, Outtake, → **REJECT**, Scrap, Shuck, Slough, Sluff, Supersede, Throw over

Discern(ing), Discernment Acumen, Acute, Clear-eyed, Descry, Detect, Discrimination, Flair, Insight, Perceive, Percipient, Perspicacity, Quick-sighted, Realise, Sapient, Scry, See, Skry, → **TASTE**, Tell, Wate

Discharge Absolve, Acquit, Arc, Assoil, Blow off, Boot, Brush, Cashier, Catarrh, Conditional, Corona, Corposant, Deliver, Demob, Depose, Disembogue, Disgorge, Dishono(u)rable, Dismiss, Disruptive, Dump, Efflux, Effusion, Egest, Ejaculate, Eject, Emission, Emit, Enfilade, Evacuate, Excrete, Execute, Exemption, Expulsion, Exude, Fire, Flashover, Flower, Flux, Free, Fusillade, Glow, Honourable, Issue, Jaculatory, Lava, Lay off, Leak, Let off, Liberate, Loose, Maturate, Menses, Muster out, Mute, Offload, Oust, Pass, Pay, Perform, Period, Pour, Purulence, Pus, Pyorrhoea, Quietus, Redeem, Release, Rheum, Run, Sack, Salvo, Sanies, Secretion, Seepage, Show, Shrive, Snarler, Spark, Spill(age), Static, Suppurate, Teem, Unload, Unloose, Vent, Void, Water

Disciple(s) Adherent, Apostle, Babi, Catechumen, Chela, Dorcas, Follower, John, Judas, Luke, Mark, Matthew, Peter, Simon, Son, Student, Thomist, Votary

Disciplinarian, Discipline(d) Apollonian, Ascesis, Chasten, Chastise, Constrain, Correct, Despot, Drill, Exercise, Feng shui, Inure, Judo, Martinet, Mathesis, Penal, Punish, Ramrod, Regimentation, Regulate, School, Science, Spartan, Stickler, Subject, Train, Tutor

Disclaim(er) Deny, Disown, No(t)chel, Recant, Renounce, → **REPUDIATE**, Voetstoots

Disclose, Disclosure Apocalypse, Confess, Divulge, Expose, Impart, Leak, Manifest, Propale, → **PUBLISH**, Report, Reveal, Spill, Tell, Unheal, Unhele, Unrip, Unveil

Discomfort(ed) Ache, All-overish, Angst, Dysphoria, Gyp, Heartburn, Pain, Unease

▷ **Disconcert(ed)** *may indicate an anagram*

Disconcert(ing) Abash, Astound, Confuse, Disturb, Embarrass, Faze, Feeze, Flurry, Nonplus, Phase, Pheese, Pheeze, Phese, Put off, → **RATTLE**, Shatter, Startle, Tease, Throw, Unnerve, Upset, Wrong-foot

Disconnect(ed) Asynartete, Decouple, Detach, Disassociate, Disjointed, Off-line, Segregate, Sever, Staccato, Trip, Uncouple, Undo, Ungear, Unplug

Discontent(ed) Disquiet, Dissatisfied, Repined, Sour

Discord(ant) Absonant, Ajar, Charivari, Conflict, Din, Dispute, Eris, Faction, Hoarse, Jangle, Jar(ring), Raucous, Ruction, Strife

▷ **Discord(ant)** *may indicate* an anagram

Discount Agio, Cashback, Deduct, Disregard, Forfaiting, Invalidate, Quantity, →**REBATE**, Trade

Discourage(ment) Caution, Chill, Dampen, Dash, Daunt, Deject, Demoralise, Deter, Dishearten, Disincentive, Dismay, Dispirit, Dissuade, Enervate, Frustrate, Intimidate, Opposition, Stifle

Discourse Address, Argument, Colloquy, Conversation, Descant, Diatribe, Dissertate, Eulogy, Expound, Homily, Lecture, Lucubrate, Orate, Philippic, Preach, Recount, Relate, Rigmarole, Sermon

Discover(y), Discoverer Amundsen, Anagnorisis, Ascertain, Betray, Breakthrough, Columbus, Cook, Descry, Detect, Determine, Discern, Discure, Esery, Eureka, →**FIND**, Heureka, Heuristic, Hit on, Learn, Locate, Manifest, Moresby, Protegé, Rumble, Serendip, Serendipity, Spy, Tasman, Trace, Trouvaille, Unearth, Unhale, Unmask, Unveil

▷ **Discovered in** *may indicate* an anagram or a hidden word

Discredit(able) Debunk, Decry, Disbelieve, Disgrace, Explode, Infamy, Scandal, Slur, Unworthy

Discreet, Discretion Cautious, Circumspect, Finesse, Freedom, Judicious, Option, Polite, Politic, Prudence, Prudent, Trait, Unobtrusive, Wise

Discrepancy Difference, Gap, Lack, Shortfall, Variance

Discriminate, Discriminating, Discrimination Ag(e)ism, Colour bar, Diacritic, Differentiate, Discern, Distinguish, Elitism, Fastidious, Handism, Invidious, Lookism, Nasute, Racism, Rankism, Reverse, Secern, Segregate, Select, Sexism, Siz(e)ism, Speciesism, Subtle, Taste

Discuss(ed), Discussion Agitate, Air, Bat around, Canvass, Commune, Confer(ence), Consult, Corridor work, Debate, Deliberate, Dialectic, Dialog(ue), Dicker, Disquisition, Emparl, Examine, Gabfest, Handle, Heart-to-heart, Hob and nob, Imparl, Interlocution, Issue, Kick-about, Korero, Moot, Negotiation, Over, Palaver, Parley, Pourparler, Prolegomenon, Quodlibet, Rap, Re, Symposium, Talk, Talkathon, Talkboard, Tapis, Treatment, Trialogue, Words

Disdain(ful) Belittle, Contempt, Coy, Deride, Despise, Geck, Poof, Pooh-pooh, Pugh, Puh, Rats, Sassy, Scoffer, →**SCORN**, Scout, Sneering, Sniffy, Spurn, Stuffy, Supercilious

Disease(d) Affection, Ailment, Bug, Communicable, Comorbid, Complaint, Deficiency, Defluxion, Epidemic, Fever, Infection, Malady, Notifiable, Occupational, Rot, Scourge, Sickness

▷ **Diseased** *may indicate* an anagram

Disengage(d), Disengagement Clear, Detach, Divorce, Liberate, Loosen, Neutral, Release, Untie

▷ **Disfigured** *may indicate* an anagram

Disgrace, Disgraceful Atimy, Attaint, Baffle, Blot, Contempt, Contumely, Degrade, Discredit, Dishonour, Dog-house, Ignoble, Ignominious, Ignominy, Indign, Indignity, Infamous, Infamy, Mean, Notorious, Obloquy, Opprobrium, Pity, Reprehensible, Scandal, Scandalous, Shame, Shameful, Shend, Slur, Soil, Stain, Stigma, Turpitude, Yshend

▷ **Disgruntled** *may indicate* an anagram

Disguise(d) Alias, Blessing, Camouflage, Cloak, Colour, Conceal, Cover, Covert, Dissemble, Hide, Hood, Incog(nito), Mantle, Mask, Masquerade, Obscure, Peruke, Pretence, Pseudonym, Ring, Stalking-horse, Travesty, Veil, Vele, Veneer, Visagiste, Vizard

▷ **Disguised** *may indicate* an anagram

Disgust(ing) Ach-y-fi, Ad nauseam, Aversion, Aw, Bah, Cloy, Discomfort, Execrable, Faugh, Fie, Foh, Fulsome, Grisly, Grody, Icky, Irk, Loathsome, Manky, Nauseous, Noisome, Obscene, Odium, Oughly, Ouglie, Pah, Pho(h), Pish, Repel, Repugnant,

Repulse, → **REVOLT**, Revulsion, Scomfish, Scumfish, Scunner, Scuzz, → **SICKEN**, Sir-reverence, Slimeball, Slimy, Squalid, Turn off, Tush, Ugh, Ugly, Ugsome, Vile, Yech, Yu(c)k

Dish(y) Adonis, Allot, Apollo, Ashet, Basin, Belle, Bowl, Chafing, Charger, Cocotte, Compotier, Concoction, Cook-up, Cutie, Dent, Diable, Dreamboat, Epergne, Flasket, Grail, Kitchen, Laggen, Laggin, Lanx, Luggie, Pan, Pannikin, Paten, Patera, Patin(e), Petri, Plate, Platter, Porringer, Ramekin, Ramequin, Receptacle, Rechauffé, Remove, Sangraal, Sangrail, Sangreal, Satellite, Saucer, Scorifier, Scupper, Serve, Service, Side (order), Smasher, Special, Stunner, Watchglass

Dishevel(led) Bedraggled, Blowsy, Blowzy, Daggy, Mess, Rumpled, Scraggly, Touse, Tousle, Touzle, Towse, Tumble, Uncombed, Unkempt, Untidy, Windswept

Dishonest(y) Bent, Crooked, Cross, Dodgy, False, Fraud, Graft, Hooky, Hot, Knavery, Light-fingered, Malpractice, Malversation, Maverick, Rort, Shonky, Sleazy, Snide, Stink, Twister, Underhand, Venal, Wrong'un

Dishonour Abatement, Defile, Disgrace, Disparage, Ignom(in)y, Indignity, Seduce, → **SHAME**, Violate, Wrong

Disinfect(ant) Acriflavin(e), Carbolic, Carvacrol, Cineol(e), Cleanse, Dip, Eucalyptole, Formalin, Fuchsine, Fumigate, Lysol®, Orcein, Phenol, Purify, Sheep-dip, Sheep-wash, Terebene

Disjoint(ed) Bitty, Dismember, Incoherent, Rambling, Scrappy

Disjunction Exclusive, Inclusive

▶ **Disk** *see* **DISC**

Dislike(d) Abhor, Allergy, Animosity, Animus, Antipathy, Aversion, Bete noire, Derry, Disesteem, Displeasure, Distaste, Gross out, Hate, Lump, Mind, Resent, Ug(h)

Dislocate, Dislocation Break, Diastasis, Displace, Fault, Luxate, Slip, Subluxate

Dislodge Budge, Displace, Expel, Oust, Rear, Uproot

Disloyal(ty) Blue, False, Recreant, Treason, Unfaithful, Untrue

Dismal Black, Bleak, Blue, Cheerless, Dark, Dowie, Drack, Dreary, Funereal, → **GLOOMY**, Grey, Morne, Obital, Sepulchral, Sombre, Sullen, Trist(e), Wae, Woebegone, Wormy

Dismantle(d), Dismantling Derig, Divest, Get-out, Sheer-hulk, Strike, Strip, Unrig

Dismay(ed) Aghast, Alarm, Amate, Appal, Confound, Consternation, Coo, Criv(v)ens, Daunt, Dispirit, Dread, Ha, Hah, Horrify, Lordy, Lumme, Qualms, Strewth, Uh-oh

Dismember Quarter

Dismiss(al), Dismissive Airy, Annul, Ax, Boot, Bounce, Bowl(er), Brush off, Bum's rush, Can, Cancel, Cashier, Catch, Chuck, Congé, Daff, Discard, Discharge, Dooced, Expulsion, Fire, Forget, Golden bowler, Heave-ho, Lay off, License, Marching orders, Mitten, Och, Pink-slip, Prorogue, Push, Recall, Reform, Reject, Remove, Road, Sack, Scout, Send, Shoo, Shrug off, Skittle out, Spit, Stump, Suka wena, Via, Walking papers, Wicket, York

Disobedience, Disobedient, Disobey Contumacy, Defy, Flout, Insubordination, Rebel, Sit-in, Unruly, Wayward

▷ **Disorder(ed)** *may indicate an anagram*

Disorder(ly), Disordered Affective, Ague, Ailment, Anarchy, Ariot, Asthma, Ataxia, Betumbler, Catatonia, Chaos, Clutter, Collywobbles, Conduct, Confuse, Consumption, Contracture, Conversion, Defuse, Derange, Deray, Diabetes, Dishevel, DT's, Dyslexia, Dystrophy, Echolalia, Entropy, Farrago, Folie a deux, Greensickness, Grippe, Haemophilia, Heartburn, Huntington's chorea, Hypallage, Inordinate, Irregular, Mare's nest, ME, Mess, Misrule, Mistemper, → **MUDDLE**, Muss(y), Neurosis, Oncus, Onkus, Overset, Pandemonium, Para-, Phenylketonuria, Priapus, Psychomatic, Psychoneurosis, Psychopathic, Psychosis, Rile, Rumple, SAD, Schizothymia, Seborrh(o)ea, Shell-shock, Slovenly, Snafu, Thalass(a)emia, Thought, Tousle, Turmoil, Unhinge, Unruly, Upheaval, Upset, Virilism

Disorientation Jet lag

Disparate Motley

Dispatch Bowl, Celerity, Consign, Destroy, Dismiss, Epistle, Expede, Expedite, Express, Gazette, Kibosh, Kill, Letter, Message, Missive, Note, Post, Pronto, Remit, Report, →SEND, Shank, Ship, Slaughter, Slay, Special

Dispensation, Dispense(r), Dispense with Absolve, Administer, Ax(e), Cashpoint, Chemist, Chop, Container, Distribute, Dose, Dropper, Exempt, Fountain, Handout, Hole in the wall, Indult, Optic, Pour, Scrap, Siphon, Soda fountain, Spinneret, Vendor

Displace(ment), Displaced Antevert, Blueshift, Chandler's wobble, Depose, Dethrone, Disturb, Ectopia, Ectopy, Fault, Heterotopia, Load, Luxate, Move, Oust, Proptosis, Ptosis, Reffo, Stir, Subluxation, Unsettle, Uproot, Upthrow, Valgus, Varus

Display, Display ground Air, Array, Blaze, Blazon, Brandish, Bravura, Depict, Eclat, Epideictic, Etalage, Evidence, Evince, Exhibition, Exposition, Express, Extend, Extravaganza, Exude, Fireworks, Flash, Flaunt, Float, Gala, Gondola, Hang, Head-down, Head-up, Heroics, Iconic, Lay out, LCD, LED, Lek, Liquid crystal, Manifest, Motorcade, Mount, Muster, Ostentation, Outlay, Overdress, Pageant, Parade, Paraf(f)le, Peepshow, Pixel, Pomp, Present(ation), Propale, Pyrotechnics, Rode, Rodeo, Roll-out, Scene, Scroll, Set piece, Shaw, →SHOW, Showcase, Sight, Spectacle, Splash, Splurge, Sport, Spree, State, Stunt, Tableau, Tattoo, Tournament, Turn out, Up, Vaunt, Wear, Window dressing

Displease(d), Displeasure Anger, Dischuffed, Humph, Irritate, Provoke, Umbrage

Dispose(d), Disposal, Disposition Arrange, Bestow, Bin, Cast, Despatch, Dump, Eighty-six, Kybosh, Lay(-out), Mood, Prone, Riddance, Sale, Sell, Service, Settle, Spirit, Stagger, Throwaway

▷ **Disposed, Disposition** *may indicate* an anagram

Disposition Affectation, Attitude, Bent, Bias, Humour, Inclination, Kidney, Lie, Nature, Penchant, Propensity, Talent, Temper(ament), Trim

Disprove, Disproof, Disproval Debunk, Discredit, Invalidate, Negate, Rebut, Redargue, Reductio ad absurdum, Refel, Refute

Dispute(d), Disputant Argue, Argy-bargy, At odds, Barney, Brangle, Cangle, Case, Chaffer, Chorizont(ist), Contend, Contest, Contretemps, Controversy, Debate, Demarcation, Deny, Differ, Discept, Discuss, Eristic, Feud, Fracas, Fray, Haggle, Kilfud-yoking, Lock-out, Loggerheads, Militate, Ob and soller, Odds, Oppugn, Plea, Polemic, Pro-and-con, Quarrel, →QUESTION, Rag, Resist, Slanging-match, Spar, Spat, Stickle, Stoush, Threap(it), Threep(it), Tiff, Tissue, Tug-of-love, Variance, Wrangle

Disqualify Debar, Incapacitate, Recuse, Reject, Unfit

Disregard(ed) Anomie, Anomy, Contempt, Disfavour, Flout, Forget, Ignore, Neglect, Oblivion, Omit, Overlook, Oversee, Pass, Pretermit, Slight, Spare, Violate, Waive

Disreputable, Disrepute Base, Black sheep, Bowsie, Disgrace, Grubby, Ken, Louche, Low, Lowlife, Notorious, Raffish, Ragamuffin, Reprobate, Rip, Scuzz(ball), Scuzzbag, Scuzzbucket, Seamy, Seamy side, Shady, Shameful, Shy, Shyster, Sleazy

Disrespect(ful) Contempt, Discourtesy, Impiety, Impolite, Irreverent, Levity, Profane, Slight, Uncivil, Violate

Disrupt(ion) Breach, Cataclasm, Dislocate, Disorder, Distract, Hamper, Hiatus, Interrupt, Jetlag, Mayhem, Perturb, Quonk, Ruffle, Screw, Upheaval

▷ **Disruption** *may indicate* an anagram

Dissatisfaction Displeasure, Distaste, Humph, Umph

Dissent(er), Dissension, Dissenting Contend, Differ, Disagree, Discord, Dissident, Divisiveness, Faction, Flak, Heretic, Holmes, Jain, Leveller, Lollard, Maverick, Noes, Non-CE, Non-con(formist), Occasional conformist, Old Believer, Pantile, Protest, Raskolnik, Recusant, Remonstrant, Sectary, Splinter group, →STRIFE, Vary

Dissertation Essay, Excursus, Lecture, Paper, Thesis, Treatise

Dissidence →DESERTER, Schism

Dissipate(d) Debauch, Decadent, Diffuse, Disperse, Dissolute, Gay, Revel, Scatter, Shatter, Squander, Waste

▷ **Dissipated** *may indicate* an anagram

Dissolute Decadent, Degenerate, Hell, Lax, Libertine, Licentious, Loose, Rake-helly, Rakish, Rip, Roué

▷ **Dissolute** *may indicate* an anagram

Dissolve Deliquesce, Digest, Disband, Disunite, Lap, Liquesce, Melt, Terminate, Thaw

Distance Absciss(a), Afield, Apothem, Breadth, Coss, Declination, Eloi(g)n, Elongation, Farness, Focal, Foot, Headreach, Height, Ice, Intercalumniation, Interval, Klick, Kos(s), Latitude, League, Length, Long-haul, Maintenance, Mean, Middle, Mileage, Ordinate, Parasang, Parsec, Range, Reserve, Rod, Skip, Span, Spitting, Stade, Striking, Way, Yojan

Distant Aloof, Chilly, Cold, Far, Frosty, Icy, Long, Offish, Outremer, Remote, Tele-, Timbuctoo, Timbuktu, Unfriendly, Yonder

Distaste(ful) Dégoût, Gory, Grimace, Repellent, Repugnant, Ropy, Scunner, Unpalatable, Unpleasant, Unsavoury

Distil(late), Distillation, Distiller, Distilling Alcohol, Alembic, Anthracine, Azeotrope, Brew, Cohobate, Condense, Destructive, Drip, Ethanol, Fractional, Naphtha, Pelican, Pyrene, Pyroligneous, Rosin, Turps, Vacuum, Vapour

▷ **Distillation** *may indicate* an anagram

Distinct(ive) Apparent, Characteristic, Clear, Different, Discrete, Evident, Grand, Idiosyncratic, Individual, Peculiar, Plain, Separate, Several, Signal, → **SPECIAL**, Stylistic, Trenchant, Vivid

Distinction Beaut(y), Blue, Cachet, Credit, Diacritic, Difference, Dignity, Diorism, Disparity, Division, Eclat, Eminence, Honour, Lustre, Mark, Mystique, Nicety, Note, Nuance, OM, Prominence, Quiddity, Rank, Renown, Speciality, Style, Title

Distinguish(ed), Distinguishing Classify, Contrast, Demarcate, Denote, Diacritic, Different(iate), Discern, Discriminate, Divide, Elevate, Eminent, Eximious, Mark, Nameworthy, Notable, Perceive, Pick out, Prestigious, Prominent, Rare, Renowned, Scerne, Secern, Special, Tell

▷ **Distort(ed)** *may indicate* an anagram

Distort(ion), Distorted Anamorphosis, Bend, Bias, Caricature, Colour, Contort, Deface, Deform, Dent, Fudge, Harmonic, Helium speech, Jaundiced, Mangle, Misshapen, Pervert, Rubato, Skew, Stretch, Shorn, Straiten, Thraw, Time-warp, Twist, → **WARP**, Wow, Wrest, Wring, Writhe, Wry

Distract(ed), Distraction Absent, Agitate, Amuse, Avocation, Bewilder, Divert, Éperdu, Forhaile, Frenetic, Lost, Madden, Mental, Nepenthe, Perplex, Scatty, Upstage

▷ **Distract(ed)** *may indicate* an anagram

Distress(ed), Distressing Afflict, Aggrieve, Agony, Ail, Alack, Alopecia, Anger, Anguish, Antique, Crise, Distraint, Dolour, Exigence, Extremity, Gnaw, Grieve, Harass, Harrow, Hurt, Ill, → **IN DISTRESS**, Irk, Misease, Misfortune, Need, Oppress, Pain, Poignant, Prey, Privation, Sad, Shorn, Sore, SOS, Straiten, Suffering, Tole, Torment, Tragic, Traumatic, → **TROUBLE**, Une(a)th, Unstrung, Upset, Wound

Distribute(d), Distribution, Distributor Allocate, Allot, Binomial, Busbar, Carve, Chi-square, Colportage, Deal, Deliver(y), Deploy, Dish, Dispense, Dispose, Dissemination, Geographical, Issue, Ladle out, Lie, Lot, Mete, Out, Pattern, Poisson, Prorate, Renter, Repartition, Send out, Serve, Strew

▷ **Distributed** *may indicate* an anagram

District Alsatia, Amhara, Arcadia, Ards, Area, Attica, Bail(l)iwick, Banat, Banate, Bannat, Barrio, Belt, Canton, Cantred, Circar, Classis, Community, Congressional, Diocese, Encomienda, End, Exurb, Falernian, Federal, Fitzrovia, Gau, Ghetto, Hundred, Land, Lathe, Liberty, Locality, Loin, Manor, Metropolitan, Nasik, → **NEIGHBOURHOOD**, Oblast, Pachalic, Pale, Pargana, Parish(en), Paroch, Pashalik, Patch, Peak, Pergunnah, Precinct, Province, Quarter, Quartier, Rape, → **REGION**, Reserve, Ride, Riding, Ruhr, Sanjak, Section, Sheading, Sircar, Sirkar,

Soc, Soke(n), Stake, Stannary, Suburb, Sucken, Talooka, Taluk, Tenderloin, Township, Urban, Venue, Vicinage, Walk, Wapentake, Way, Zila, Zillah, Zone

Disturb(ance), Disturbed, Disturbing Ado, Aerate, Affray, Aggrieve, Agitate, Atmospherics, Autism, Betoss, Brabble, Brainstorm, Brash, Brawl, Broil, Carfuffle, Collieshangie, Concuss, Delirium, Dementia, Derange, Desecrate, Disquiet, Dust, Feeze, Firestorm, Fray, Fret, Harass, Hoopla, Incident, Incommode, Infest, Interference, Interrupt, Intrude, Jee, Kerfuffle, Kick-up, Kurfuffle, Macabre, Muss, Neurosis, Outbreak, Prabble, Ramp, Riot, Ripple, Romage, Rook, Roughhouse, Rouse, Ruckus, Ruction, Ruffle, Rumpus, Shake, Shindig, Shindy, Shook-up, Stashie, Static, Steer, Stir, Sturt, Tremor, Troppo, Trouble, Turbulent, Turmoil, Unquiet, Unrest, Unsettle, Upheaval, Uproot, → UPSET, Vex, Whistler

▷ **Disturb(ed)** *may indicate* an anagram

Ditch Abolish, Barathron, Barathrum, Channel, Chuck, Cunette, Delf, Delph, Dike, Discard, Donga, Drainage, Drop, Dyke, Euripus, Foss(e), Graft, Grip, Gully, Ha(w)-ha(w), Jettison, Khor, Level, Lode, Moat, Nal(l)a(h), Nulla(h), Rean, Reen, Rhine, Rid, Sea, Sheuch, Sheugh, Sike, Sloot, Sluit, Spruit, Stank, Sunk-fence, Syke, Trench

Dive, Diver(s), Diving Armstand, Backflip, Belly-flop, Crash, Dart, Den, Didapper, Duck, Embergoose, File, Flop, Free-fall, Frogman, Full-gainer, Gainer, Grebe, Guillemot, Half-gainer, Header, Honkytonk, Jackknife, Joint, Ken, Loom, Loon, Lungie, Merganser, Nitery, Nose, Pass, Pearl, Pickpocket, Pike, Plong(e), Plummet, Plunge, Plutocrat, Pochard, Poker, Power, Puffin, Saturation, Sawbill, Scoter, Scuba, Skin, Snake-bird, Sound, Speakeasy, Stage, Step-to, Stoop, Submerge, Swallow, Swan, Swoop, Tailspin, Urinant, Urinator, Zoom

Diverge(nce) Branch, Deviate, Spread, Swerve, Variant, Veer

Divers(e), Diversify Alter, Branch out, Dapple, Different, Interlard, Intersperse, Manifold, Many, Motley, Multifarious, Separate, Sundry, Variegate, Various, Vary

Diversion, Divert(ing) Amuse, Avocation, Beguile, Cone, Deflect, Detour, Disport, Dissuade, Distract, Entertain, Game, Hare, Hijack, Hive off, Hobby, Interlude, Pastime, Pleasure, Prolepsis, Ramp, Red-herring, Refract, Reroute, Ruse, Shunt, Sideshow, Sidetrack, Siphon, Smokescreen, Sport, Stalking-horse, Steer, Stratagem, Sublimation, Sway, Switch, Syphon, Tickle, Upstage, Yaw

▷ **Diverting** *may indicate* an anagram

Divide(d), Divider, Division Abkhazia, Adzharia, Apportion, Balkanise, Band, Bifurcate, Bipartite, Bisect, Branch, Cantle, Chancery, Cleave, Cleft, Comminute, Commot(e), Continental, Counter-pale, Cut, Deal, Demerge, Dimidiate, Estrange, Fork, Great, Indent, Parcel, Part, Partite, Party wall, Pentomic, Plebs, Polarise, Potantial, Ramify, Rend, Rift, Sectionalise, Separate, Sever, Share, → SPLIT, Stanza, Sunder, Transect, Tribalism, Trisect, Twixt, Utgard, Voltage, Watershed, Zone

Dividend Bonus, Div, Interim, Into, Numerator, Share

Divine, Divine presence, Divinity Acoemeti, Aitu, Ambrose, Atman, Avatar, Beatific, Blessed, Celestial, Clergyman, Conjecture, Curate, DD, Deduce, Deity, Douse, Dowse, Ecclesiastic, Empyreal, Forecast, Foretell, Fuller, → GOD, → GODDESS, Godhead, Godlike, Guess, Hallowed, Hariolate, Heavenly, Holy, Hulse, Immortal, Inge, Isiac, Mantic, Numen, Olympian, Pontiff, Predestinate, Predict, Presage, Priest, Prophesy, RE, Rector, RI, Rimmon, Scry, Sense, Seraphic, Shechinah, Shekinah, Spae, Supernal, Theandric, Theanthropic, Theologise, Theology, Triune

Division, Divisible Arcana, Arm, Arrondissement, Banat(e), Bar, Branch, Caesura, Canto, Canton, Cantred, Cantref, Caste, Category, Chapter, Classification, Cleft, Cloison, Clove, Commune, Compartment, Corps, County, Crevasse, Curia, Department, Dichotomy, Disagreement, Disunity, Div, Fork, Fragmentation, Glires, Grisons, Gulf, Hapu, Hedge, Hide, Holland, Hotchpot, Hundred, Inning, Lathe, Leet, Legion, List, Lobe, Mannion, Maturation, Nome, Oblast, Over, Part, Partition, Period, Pipe, Pitaka, Platoon, Polarisation, Presidency, Province, Quartering, Quotition, Rape, Region, Reservation, Riding, Schism, Section, Sector, Segment, Sept(ate), Sever, Share, Shed, Shire, Stage, Stake, Subheading, Suborder, Tahsil, Theme, Trichotomy, Trio, Troop, Unit, Wapentake, Ward

Divorce(d) Alienate, Diffarreation, Dissolve, Disunion, Div, Estrange, Get(t), Part, Put away, Separate, Sequester, →**SUNDER**, Talak, Talaq

Divulge Confess, Disclose, Expose, Publish, Reveal, Split, Tell, Unveil, Utter

Dizziness, Dizzy Beaconsfield, Ben, Capricious, Dinic, Disraeli, Giddy, Giglot, Lightheaded, Mirligoes, Scotodinia, Scotomania, Swimming, Vertiginous, →**VERTIGO**, Woozy

▷ **Do** *may indicate an anagram*

Do(es), Doing Accomplish, Achieve, Act, Anent, Barbecue, Bash, Beano, Blow-out, Char, Cheat, Chisel, Cod, Con, Cozen, Deed, Dich, Diddle, Dish, Div, Doth, Dupe, Effectuate, Enact, Execute, Fare, Fleece, Function, Fuss, Gull, Handiwork, Hoax, Imitate, Measure up, Mill, Occasion, Perform, Perpetrate, Provide, Rip off, Same, Serve, Settle, Shindig, Spif(f)licate, Suffice, Swindle, Thrash, Thrive, Tonic, Up to, Ut

Dobbie Elf, Fairy

Dock(er), Docked, Docks Abridge, Barber, Basin, Bistort, Bob, Camber, Canaigre, Clip, Crop, Curta(i)l, Cut, Deduct, De-tail, Dry, Floating, Grapetree, Knotweed, Lay-up, Longshoreman, Lop, Lumper, Marina, Monk's rhubarb, Moor, Off-end, Pare, Patience, Pen, Pier, Quay, Rhubarb, Rumex, Rump, Seagull, Shorten, Snakeweed, Sorrel, Sourock, Stevedore, Tilbury, Watersider, Wet, Wharf, Yard

▷ **Doctor(ed)** *may indicate an anagram*

Doctor(s) Alter, Arnold, Barefoot, Barnardo, Bleeder, BMA, Bones, Breeze, Bright, Brighton, Brown, Caius, Castrate, Clinician, Cook, Crocus, Cup(per), Cure(r), Dale, Diagnose, Dr, Erasmus, Extern(e), Fake, Falsify, Family, Faustus, Fell, Fiddle, Finlay, Flying, Foster, Fu manchu, Galen, GP, Healer, Homeopath, Houseman, Hyde, Intern, Internist, Jekyll, Jenner, Johnson, Kildare, Lace, Leach, Leech, Linacre, Load, Locum, Luke, Manette, Manipulate, Massage, MB, MD, Medicate, Medico, Mganga, Minister, Misrepresent, MO, MOH, Molla(h), Moreau, Mulla(h), Myologist, Neuter, No, Ollamh, Ollav, Paediatrician, Panel, Pangloss, Paracelsus, Paramedic, Pedro, PhD, Physician, Pill(s), Practitioner, Quack, Quacksalver, Rabbi, RAMC, Registrar, Resident, Rig, Rorschach, Salk, Saw, Sawbones, School, Script, Seraphic, Seuss, Slammer, Slop, Spay, Spin, Surgeon, Syn, Thorne, Treat, Vet, Water, Watson, Who, Wind, Witch

Doctrine Adamitism, Adoptionism, Archology, Blairism, Cab(b)ala, Cacodoxy, Calvanism, Catastrophism, Chiliasm, Credo, Creed, Diabology, Ditheism, Divine right, Dogma, Doxie, Doxy, Dualism, Dysteleology, Encratism, Eschatology, Esotery, Evangel, Febronianism, Federalism, Gnosticism, Gospel, Henotheism, Hesychasm, Holism, Idealism, Illuminism, Immaterialism, Immersionism, Indeterminism, Islam, Ism, Jansenism, Lore, Machtpolitik, Malthusian, Materialism, Modalism, Monadism, Monothel(et)ism, Monroe, Neomonianism, Panentheism, Pantheism, Pelagianism, Physiocracy, Pluralism, Pragmatism, Premillennialism, Preterition, Probabilism, Psilanthropism, Quietism, Real presence, Reformism, Scotism, Secularism, Sheria, Shibboleth, Solidism, Soteriology, Subjectivism, Substantialism, Syndicalism, Synergism, System, Theory, Thomism, Transubstantiation, Trialism, Tridentine, Universalism

Document(s), Documentary Blog, Brevet, Bumph, Carta, Certificate, Charge sheet, Charter, Chop, Contract, Conveyance, Copy, Covenant, Daftar, Deed, Diploma, Docket, Doco, Dompass, Dossier, Elegit, Escrow, Fieri Facias, Fly-on-the-wall, Form, Holograph, Latitat, Logbook, Mandamus, Papers, Permit, Policy, Production, Pro forma, Ragman, Ragment, Roll, Roul(e), Screed, Scroll, Sea brief, Voucher, Waybill, Weblog, Webpage, Writ

Dodge, Dodgy Artful, Avoid, Column, Elude, Evade, Evasion, Evite, Jink, Jook, Jouk, Malinger, Racket, Ruse, Scam, Shirk, Sidestep, Skip, Slalom, Slinter, Tip, Trick, Twist, Urchin, Weave, Welsh, Wheeze, Wire, Wrinkle

Dog(s), Doglike Assistance, Attack, Bowwow, Canes, Canidae, Canine, Cynic, Feet, Hearing, Hot, Huntaway, Isle, Kennel, Native, Pursue, Ranger, Ratter, Shadow, Sleuthhound, Sniffer, Stalk, Strong-eye, Tag, Tail, Therapy, Top, Toto, Tracker, Trail, Truffle, Tumbler, Water dog, Working

Dogma(tic) Assertive, Belief, Bigotry, Conviction, Creed, Doctrinal, En têté, Ewe, Ideology, Opinionative, Pedagogic, Peremptory, Pontifical, Positive

Dole Alms, Batta, B(u)roo, Give, Grief, Maundy, Mete, Payment, Pittance, Ration, →**SHARE**, Tichborne, Vail, Vales

Doleful Sombre

Doll(y) Barbie®, Bimbo, Bobblehead, Common, Corn, Crumpet, Dress, Dutch, Ewe, Golliwog, Kachina, Kewpie®, Maiden, Marionette, Matryoshka, Maumet, Mommet, Moppet, Mummet, Ookpik®, Ornament, Parton, Pean, Peen, Peggy, Pein, Pene, Poppet, Puppet, Ragdoll, Russian, Sindy®, Sis(ter), Sitter, Tearsheet, Toy, Trolley, Varden, Washboard

Dollar(s) Balboa, Boliviano, Buck, Cob, Euro, Fin, Greenback, Iron man, Peso, Piastre, Pink, S, Sand, Sawbuck, Sawhorse, Scrip, Smacker, Spin, Wheel

▷ **Dolly** *may indicate* an anagram

Dolly Varden Hat

Dolphin Amazon, Arion, Beluga, Bottlenose, Cetacean, Coryphene, Delphinus, Grampus, Lampuka, Lampuki, Mahi-mahi, Meer-swine, Porpess(e), Risso's, River, Sea-pig

DOM Lewdsby

Dome(-shaped) Bubble, Cap, Cupola, Dagoba, Geodesic, Head, Imperial, Louvre, Millennium, Onion, Periclinal, Rotunda, Stupa, Tee, Tholobate, Tholos, Tholus, Tope, Vault

Domestic(ate) Char, Cinderella, Cleaner, Dom, Esne, Familiar, Homebody, Home-keeping, Homely, House, Housetrain, Humanise, Interior, Internal, Intestine, Maid, Menial, →**SERVANT**, Swadeshi, Tame, Woman

Dominate, Dominance, Dominant, Domination Alpha, Ascendancy, Baasskap, Bethrall, Boss, Clou, Coerce, Control, Enslave, Henpeck, Maisterdome, Master, Mesmerise, Momism, Monopolise, O(v)ergang, Overmaster, Override, Overshadow, Power, Preponderant, Preside, Rule, Soh, →**SUBDUE**, Subjugate, Top dog, Tower

Dominion Dom, Empire, Khanate, NZ, Realm, Reame, Reign, →**RULE**, Supremacy, Sway, Territory

Domino(es) Card, Fats, Mask, Matador

Don Academic, Address, Assume, Caballero, Endue, Fellow, Garb, Giovanni, Grandee, Indew, Juan, Lecturer, Prof, Quixote, Reader, Señor, Spaniard, Tutor, Wear

Donate, Donation Aid, Bestow, Contribution, Gift, Give

Done Achieved, Complete, Crisp, Ended, Executed, Had, Over, Spitcher, Tired, Weary

Donkey Ass, Burro, Cardophagus, Cuddie, Cuddy, Dapple, Dick(e)y, Eeyore, Engine, Funnel, Fussock, Genet(te), Ignoramus, Jackass, Jacket, Jennet, Jenny, Jerusalem pony, Kulan, Modestine, Moke, Mule, Neddy, Onager, Stupid, Years

Donor Benefactor, Bestower, Settlor

Doofer Thingumabob

Doom(ed) Condemned, Date, Destine, Destiny, →**FATE**, Fay, Fey, Fie, Goner, Ill-omened, Ill-starred, Lot, Predestine, Preordain, Ragnarok, Ruined, Sentence, Spitcher, Star-crossed, Weird

Door(s), Doorstep, Doorway Aperture, Communicating, Drecksill, Dutch, Elephant, Entry, Exit, Fire, Folding, Front, Gull-wing, Haik, Hake, Hatch, Heck, Ingress, Jib, Lintel, Louver, Louvre, Muntin, Oak, Open, Overhead, Patio, Portal, Postern, Revolving, Rory, Screen, Sliding, Stable, Stage, Storm, Street, Swing, Tailgate, Trap, Up and over, Vomitory, Wicket, Yett

Doorkeeper, Doorman Bouncer, Commissionaire, Concierge, Guardian, Janitor, Nab, Ostiary, Porter, Tiler, Tyler, Usher

Dope Acid, Amulet, Bang, Coke, Crack, →**DRUG**, Facts, Fuss, Gen, Goose, Info, Narcotic, Nitwit, Nobble, Rutin, Sedate, →**STUPID PERSON**

Doppelganger Double, Look-alike, Ringer

Dormer Luthern

Dormitory Barrack, Bunkhouse, Dorter, Dortour, Hall, Hostel, Quarters

Dosage, Dose Absorbed, Administer, Aperient, Cascara, Draught, Drug, Fix, Kilogray, Lethal, →MEASURE, Permissible, Physic, Posology, Potion, Powder, Standing off

Dot(s), Dotted, Dotty Absurd, Bullet (point), Criblé, Dieresis, Dit, Dower, Dowry, Engrailed, Leader, Lentiginous, Limp, Micro, Occult, Or, Particle, Pinpoint, Pixel, →POINT, Pointillé, Polka, Precise, Punctuate, Punctulate, Punctum, Schwa, Semé(e), Set, Speck, Spot, Sprinkle, Stigme, Stipple, Stud, Tap, Tittle, Trema, Umlaut

Dote, Dotage, Doting, Dotard Adore, Anile, Anility, Cocker, Dobbie, Idolise, Imbecile, Pet, Prize, Senile, Spoon(e)y, Tendre, Twichild

Double(s) Amphibious, Ancipital, Bi-, Bifold, Binate, Counterpart, Crease, Dimeric, Doppel-ganger, Dual, Duo, Duple(x), Duplicate, Equivocal, Fetch, Fold, Foursome, Geminate, Gimp, Image, Ingeminate, Ka, Look-alike, Loop, Martingale, Pair, Parlay, Polyseme, Reflex, Replica, Ringer, Run, Similitude, Spit, Stuntman, Trot, Turnback, Twae, →TWIN, Two(fold), Two-ply

Doubt(s), Doubter, Doubtful Agnostic, Ambiguous, Aporia, Askance, But, Debatable, Discredit, Distrust, Dubiety, Dubitate, Erm, Hesitate, Hum, Iffy, Incertitude, Misgiving, Mistrust, Or, Precarious, Qualm, Query, →QUESTION, Rack, Scepsis, Sceptic, Scruple, Second thoughts, Shady, Shy, Sic, Skepsis, Sus, Suspect, Suss, Thomas, Thos, Umph, Uncertain, Unsure, Waver

Dough(y) Boodle, Cake, Calzone, Cash, Duff, Gnocchi, Hush-puppy, Knish, Loot, Magma, Masa, Money, Paste, Pop(p)adum, Ready, Sad, Spondulicks

Doughnut Bagel, Cruller, Fried cake, Knish, Sinker, Torus

Dour Glum, Hard, Mirthless, Morose, Reest, Reist, Sinister, Sullen, Taciturn

Douse Dip, Drench, Extinguish, Snuff, Splash

Dove Collared, Columbine, Culver, Cushat, Diamond, Doo, Ground, Ice-bird, Mourning, Pacifist, →PIGEON, Ring, Rock, Stock, Turtle

Dowdy Frumpish, Mopsy, Mums(e)y, Plain Jane, Shabby, Sloppy, Slovenly

Down(s), Downbeat, Downsize, Downward, Downy A bas, Abase, Abattu, Alow, Amort, Bank, Below, Blue, Cast, Catabasis, Chapfallen, Comous, Cottony, Crouch, Darling, Dejected, Descent, Disconsolate, Dowl(e), Drink, Epsom, Feather, Fledge, Floccus, Flue, Fluff, Fly, Fuzz, Glum, Goonhilly, Ground, Hair, Hill, Humble, Humiliate, Lanate, Lanugo, Latitant, Losing, Low, Lower, Miserable, Moxa, Nap, Neck, North Wessex, Oose, Ooze, Owing, Pappus, Pennae, Pile, Plumage, Quark, Quash, Repress, Scuttle, Sebum, Sussex, Thesis, Thistle, Tomentum, Under, Vail, Watership, Wretched

Downcast Abject, Chapfallen, Dejected, Despondent, Disconsolate, Dumpish, Hopeless, Melancholy, Woebegone

Downfall, Downpour Brash, Cataract, Collapse, Deluge, Fate, Flood, Hail, Onding, Overthrow, Plash, Rain, Rainstorm, Ruin, Shower, Thunder-plump, Torrent, Undoing, Waterspout

Downmarket Naff

Downright Absolute, Arrant, Bluff, Candid, Clear, Complete, Flat, Plumb, Plump, Pure, Rank, Sheer, Stark, Utter

Downstream Tail

Downturn Recession, Slump

Downwind Leeward

Dowry Dot, Dower, Lobola, Lobolo, Merchet, Portion, Settlement, Tocher

Doze Ca(u)lk, Catnap, Dove(r), Nap, Nod, Semi-coma, Sleep, Slip, Slumber

Drab Cloth, Dell, Dingy, Dowdy, Dreary, Dull, Dun, Ecru, Hussy, Isabel(line), Lifeless, Livor, Olive, Prosaic, Pussel, Quaker-colour, Rig, Road, Scarlet woman, Slattern, Sloven, Strumpet, Subfusc, Tart, Taupe, Trull, Wanton, Whore

Draft Bank, Bill, Cheque, Draw, Ebauche, Essay, Landsturm, Minute, MS, Outline, Paste up, Plan, Press, Protocol, Rough, Scheme, Scroll, Scrowle, →SKETCH

Drag Car, Clothing, Drail, Dredge, Drogue, Elicit, Eonism, Epicene, Extort, Gender-bender, Hale, Hang, Harl, →HAUL, Keelhaul, La Rue, Lug, Nuisance, Puff, Pull, Rash, Sag, Schlep, Shockstall, Shoe, Skidpan, Sled, Snake, Snig, Sweep, Toke,

Tote, Tow, Trail, Trailing vortex, Train, Travail, Travois, Trawl, Treck, Trek, Tug, Tump

Dragon Aroid, Basilisk, Bel, Bellemère, Chaperon(e), Chindit, Draco, Drake, Komodo, Kung-kung, Ladon, Lindworm, Opinicus, Python, Rouge, Serpent, Wantley, Wivern, Worm, Wyvern, Yacht

Drain(ed), Drainage, Draining, Drainpipe Bleed, Brain, Buzz, Can(n)ula, Catchment, Catchwater, Channel, Cloaca, Condie, Culvert, Cundy, Cunette, Delf, Delph, Dewater, Ditch, Dry, Ea(u), →**EMPTY**, Emulge(nt), Exhaust, Fleet, Grating, Grip, Gully, Gutter, Ketavothron, Kotabothron, Lade, Leach, Leech, Limber, Lose, Lymphatic, Milk, Nalla(h), Pump, Rack, Rone, Sanitation, Sap, Scalpins, Scupper, Seton, Sew(er), Sheuch, Sheugh, Shore, Silver, Siver, Sluice, Sluse, Small-trap, Soakaway, Sough, Spend, Stank, Suck, Sump, Sure, Syver, Tile, Trench, Trocar, Unwater, Ureter, U-trap

Drainpipe(s) Downspout, →**TROUSERS**

Dram Drink, Drop, Portion, Snifter, Tickler, Tiff, Tot, Wet

Drama(tic), Drama school Azione, Charade, Comedy, Costume, Epic, Eumenides, Farce, Heroic, Histrionic, Kabuki, Kathakali, Kitchen sink, Legit, Legitimate, Mask, Masque, Mime, Moralities, Music, No, Nogaku, Noh, Oresteia, Piece, Play, RADA, Sangeet, Scenic, Sensational, Singspiel, Soap, Spinto, Stagy, Striking, Sudser, Tetralogy, Theatric, The Birds, Thespian, Tragedy, Unities, Wagnerian, Wild

Drape(ry) Adorn, Coverlet, Coverlid, Curtain, Festoon, Fold, Hang, Lambrequin, Swag, Swathe, Valance, Veil, Vest

▷ **Draught** *may refer to* fishing

Draught(s), Draughtsman(ship) Aloetic, Apozem, Breeze, Dam, Dams, Design, Dose, Drench, Drink, Fish, Gulp, Gust, Haal, Hippocrene, King, Line, Men, Nightcap, Outline, Plan, Potation, Potion, Pull, Quaff, Sketch, Sleeping, Slug, Swig, Tracer, Veronal, Waft, Waucht

▷ **Draw** *may indicate* something to smoke

Draw (off), Drawer(s), Drawing, Drawn Adduct, Allure, Attract, Blueprint, Bottom, Cartoon, Charcoal, Cityscape, Cock, Crayon, Dead-heat, Delineate, Dentistry, Derivation, Describe, Detail, Diagram, Doodle, Dr, Draft, Drag, Dress, Educe, Elevation, Elicit, Elongate, Entice, Equalise, Escribe, Evaginate, Extract, Fet(ch), Freehand, Fusain, Gather, Gaunt, Glorybox, Goalless, Graphics, Gut, Haggard, Hale, Halve, Haul, Identikit, Indraft, Induce, Indue, Inhale, Isometric, Lead, Lengthen, Limn, Line, Longbow, Lots, Lottery, Mechanical, Monotint, No-score, Orthograph, Pantalet(te)s, Panty, Pastel(list), Pen and ink, Perpetual check, Petroglyph, Profile, Protract, Pull, RA, Rack, Raffle, Realize, Reel, Remark, Scenography, Scent, Seductive, Sepia, Sesquipedalian, Shottle, Shuttle, Silverpoint, Siphon, Sketch, Slub, Snig, Spin, Stalemate, Stretch, Study, Stumps, Sweepstake, Syphon, Tap, Taut, Technical, Tempera, Tempt, Tenniel, Tie, Till, Toke, Tole, Tombola, Top, Tose, Tow(age), Toze, Trace, Traction, Trice, Troll, Tug, Unsheathe, Uplift, Visual, Wash, Working

▷ **Drawn** *may indicate* an anagram

Dread(ed), Dreadful Angst, Anxiety, Awe, Awful, Chronic, Dearn, Dern, Dire, Fear, Formidable, Funk, Ghastly, Horrendous, →**HORROR**, Nosophobia, Penny, Redoubt, Sorry, Terrible, Thing, Tragic, Unholy, Willies

Dream(er), Dream home, Dream state, Dreamy Aisling, Alchera, Alcheringa, American, Aspire, Desire, Drowsy, Dwa(u)m, Fantast, Fantasy, Faraway, Idealise, Illusion, Imagine, Languor, Mare, Mirth, Moon, Morpheus, Muse, Nightmare, On(e)iric, Pensive, Phantom, Pipe, Rêveur, Romantic, Somniate, Stargazer, Surreal, Sweven, Trance, Trauma, Vague, Vision, Walter Mitty, Wet, Wool-gathering

Dreary Bleak, Desolate, Dismal, Doleful, Dreich, Dull, Gloom, Gousty, Gray, Grey, Oorie, Ourie, Owrie, Sad

Dress(ing), Dressed Adjust, Adorn, Align, Apparel, Array, Attire, Attrap, Bandage, Boast, Clad, →**CLOTHING**, Comb, Compost, Compress, Curry, Deck, Deshabille, Dink, Don, Dub, Dubbin, Enrobe, Fertiliser, French, Garnish, Gauze, Girt, Gussy up,

→**HABIT**, Italian, Jaconet, Ketchup, Line, Lint, Marie Rose, Mayonnaise, Mulch, Oil, Pad, Patch, Plaster, Pledget, Pomade, Potash, Poultice, Prank, Preen, Prepare, Rational, Rehearsal, Rémoulade, Rig, Salad, Salad cream, Sartorial, Sauce, Sterile, Tartare, Taw, Thousand Island, Tiff, Tire, Toilet, Treat, Trick, Trim, Vinaigrette, Wear, Wig, Window

▷ **Dressed up, Dressing** *may indicate* an anagram

Dresser Adze, Almery, Bureau, Chest, Couturier, Deuddarn, Dior, Lair, Lowboy, Sideboard, Transvestite, Tridarn, Welsh

Dribble Drip, Drivel, Drop, Slaver, Slop, Trickle

Drift(ing), Drifter Becalmed, Continental, Crab, Cruise, Current, Digress, Drumlin, Float, Flow, Heap, Impulse, Maunder, Nomad, North Atlantic, Plankton, Purport, Rorke, Slide, Tendence, Tendency, →**TENOR**, Tramp, Waft, Wander

Drill(ing) Archimedean, Auger, Bore, Burr, Close order, Educate, Exercise, Form, Hammer, Jackhammer, Jerks, Monkey, Pack, PE, Pierce, Pneumatic, PT, Reamer, Ridge, Rock, Rope, Seeder, Sow, Square-bashing, Teach, Train, Twill, Twist, Usage, Wildcat

Drink(er), Drunk(enness) AA, Absorb, Alky, A pip out, Bacchian, Bender, Beverage, Bev(v)y, Bibber, Binge, Bladdered, Blind, Blitzed, Bloat, Blootered, Blotto, Bombed, Boose, Booze, Borachio, Bosky, Bottled, Bouse, Bowsey, Bowsie, Bracer, Brahms and Liszt, Brew, Bucket, Bumper, Capernoitie, Cap(p)ernoity, Carafe, Carousal, Cat-lap, Chaser, Chota peg, Corked, Cot case, Crapulous, Crocked, Cuppa, Cut, Demitasse, Dipsomaniac, Discombobulated, Double, Down, Drain, Draught, Drop, Ebriate, Elixir, Energy, Entire, Eye-opener, Feni, Feny, Finger, Flush, Fou, Fuddled, Full, Gnat's piss, Grog, Half-cut, Half-seas-over, Happy, Heavy wet, High, Hobnob, Hogshead, Hooker, Hophead, Imbibe, In-cups, Indulge, Inked, In liquor, Intemperate, Irrigate, Jag, Jakey, Jar, Kaylied, Lager lout, Langered, Lap, Legless, Lethean, →**LIQUOR**, Lit, Loaded, Lord, Lower, Lush(y), Maggoty, Maudlin, Mellow, Merry, Moon-eyed, Mops and brooms, Mortal, Mug, Mullered, Neck, Nog(gin), Obfuscated, Ocean, Oiled, On, One, Overshot, Paid, Paint, Paralytic, Partake, Particular, Pickled, Pick-me-up, Pie-eyed, Pint(a), Piss-artist, Pissed, Pisshead, Pisspot, Piss-up, Pixil(l)ated, Pledge, Potion, Primed, Quaff, Quencher, Quickie, Rat-arsed, Ratted, Rolling, Rotten, Rummer, St Martin's evil, Screamer, Screwed, Sea, Shebeen, Shotover, Sink, Sip(ple), Skinned, Slake, Slewed, Sloshed, Slug, Slurp, Smashed, Snort, Soak, Soused, Sponge, Squiffy, Stewed, Stimulant, Stinko, Stoned, Stukkend, Sucker, Suckle, Suiplap, Sup, Swacked, Swallow, Swig, Swill, Tank, Tanked up, Tape, Tiddl(e)y, Tiff, Tight, Tincture, Tipple, Tipsy, Tope, Toss, Tot, Two-pot, Under the weather, Up the pole, Usual, Wash, Wat, Well away, Well-oiled, Wet, Winebag, Wine bibber, Wino, Wish-wash, Woozy, Wrecked, Zonked

Drip Bore, Dribble, Drop, Gloop, Gutter, IV, Leak, Milksop, Seep, Splatter, Stillicide, Trickle, Wimp

Drive(r), Driving, Drive out AA, Actuate, Ambition, Automatic, Backseat, Banish, Battue, Beetle, Belt, Ca', Cabby, Campaign, Carman, Charioteer, Chauffeur, Coachee, Coachy, Coact, Coerce, Crankshaft, Crew, Crowd, Disk, Dislodge, Dr, Drover, Drum, Dynamic, Economy, Eject, Emboss, Energy, Enforce, Engine, Exorcise, Faze, Ferret, Fire, Flash, Fluid, Force, Four-wheel, Front-wheel, Fuel, Goad, Hack, Hammer, Haste, Heard, Helmsman, Herd, Hie, Hish, Hiss, Hoon, Hoosh, Hot-rod, Hoy, Hunt, Hurl, Hydrostatic, Impel, Impetus, Impinge, Impulse, Instinct, Jehu, Jockey, Juggernaut, Key(ring), Lash, Libido, Lunge, Mahout, Make, Mall, M(a)cGuffin, Micro, Motor, Motorman, Muleteer, Offensive, Peg, Penetrate, Piston, Pocket, Power, P-plater, Propel, Push, Put, Quill, RAC, Rack, Rally(e), Ram, Rear-wheel, Rebut, Ride, Road, Roadhog, Run, Sales, Scorch, Screw, Scud, Senna, Sex, Shepherd, Shoo, Shover, Spank, Spin, Spur, Start, Steer, Stroke, Sunday, Sweep, Swift, Task-master, Teamster, Tee, Test, Testosterone, Thrust, Thumb, Toad, Toe and heel, Tool, Tootle, Trot, Trucker, Truckie, Truckman, Turn, Twoccer, Two-stroke, Urge, Urgence, USB, Wagoner, Warp, Wood, Wreak, Zest

Drivel Balderdash, Blether(skate), Drip, Drool, Humbug, Nonsense, Pap, Rot, Salivate, Slabber, Slaver

Drizzle Drow, Haze, Mist, Mizzle, Roke, Scotch mist, Scouther, Scowther, Serein, Skiffle, Smir(r), Smur, Spit

Droop(y), Drooping Cernuous, Decline, Epinasty, Flag, Languish, Lill, Limp, Lob, Loll, Lop, Nutate, Oorie, Ourie, Owrie, Peak, Pendulous, Ptosis, Slink, Slouch, Slump, Weeping, Welk(e), Wilt, Wither

Drop(s), Dropping Acid, Airlift, Apraxia, Bag, Bead, Beres, Blob, Cadence, Calve, Cascade, Cast, Chocolate, Cowpat, Dap, Decrease, Delayed, Descent, Deselect, Dew, Dink, Dip, Downturn, Drappie, Drib(let), Ean, Ease, Ebb, Escarp(ment), Fall, Floor, Flop, Fruit, Fumet, Gallows, Glob(ule), Gout(te), Guano, Gutta, Guttate, Ha-ha, Instil, Knockout, Land, Lapse, Minim, Modicum, Muff, Mute, Omit, Pilot, Plap, Plonk, Plop, Plummet, Plump, Plunge, Plunk, Precept, Precipice, (Prince) Rupert's, Rain, Scat, Scrap, Shed, Sip, Skat, Slurry, Spat, Spill, Splash, Spraint, Stilliform, Tass, Taste, Tear, Thud, Trapdoor, Turd, Virga, Wrist

Drop-out Beatnik, Hippie, Hippy

Drought Dearth, Drouth, Lack, Thirst

Drove(r) Band, Crowd, Flock, Herd, Host, Masses, Mob, Overlander, Puncher

Drown(ed), Drowning Drook, Drouk, Engulf, Inundate, Noyade, Overcome, Sorrows, Submerge

Drudge(ry) Boswell, Devil, Dogsbody, Fag, Grind, Hack, Hackwork, Jackal, Johnson, Menial, Plod, Scrub, Slave(y), Snake, Spadework, Stooge, Sweat, Thraldom, Toil, Trauchle, Treadmill

Drug(ged) Anorectic, Antabuse®, Antarthritic, Anti-depressant, Antimetabolite, Antipyrine, Bag, Base, Blow, Blue devil, Bolus, Bomber, Boo, Chalybeate, Clofibrate, Clot buster, Contraceptive, Corrigent, Custom, Dadah, Deck, Depot, Designer, Dope, Downer, Elixir, Fantasy, Fertility, Fig, Gateway, Gear, Generic, Hallucinogen, Hard, High, Hocus, Hypnotic, Indinavir, Joint, Lifestyle, Line, Load, Mainline, Medicine, Mercurial, Mind-expanding, Miracle, Modified release, Monged, Nervine, Nobble, Nootropic, Obstruent, Opiate, Orphan, Painkiller, Paregoric, Parenteral, Pharmaceutics, Pharmacology, Pharmacopoeia, Poison, Prophylactic, Psychedelic, Psychodelic, Purgative, Sedate, Sedative, Shit, Shot, Skin-pop, Smart, Snort, Soft, Spike, Stimulant, Street name, Stupefy, Styptic, Substance, Sudorific, Suppressant, Toot, Tout, Truth, Upper, Vasoconstrictor, Vasodilator, Vermifuge, Weed, White stuff, Wonder

Drum(mer), Drumming, Drumbeat Arête, Atabal, Barrel, Bass, Beatbox, Bodhran, Bongo, Brake, Carousel, Chamade, Conga, Cylinder, Cymograph, Daiko, Dash-wheel, Devil's tattoo, Dhol, Dr, Drub, Ear, Flam, Kettle, Kymograph, Lambeg, Mridamgam, Mridang(a), Mridangam, Myringa, Naker, Pan, Percussion, Rappel, Rataplan, Reel, Rep, Ridge, Rigger, Ringo, Roll, Ruff, Ruffle, Salesman, Side, Snare, Steel, Tabla, Tabour, Tabret, Taiko, Tambour, Tambourin(e), Tam-tam, Tap, Tattoo, Tenor, Thrum, Timbal, Timp(ano), Tom-tom, Touk, Traps, Traveller, Tuck, Tymbal, Tympanist, Tympano, Whim, Work

▷ **Drunken** *may indicate an anagram*

Dry(ing), Drier, Dryness Air, Anhydrous, Arefaction, Arefy, Arid, Blot, Bone, Brut, Corpse, Crine, Dehydrate, Desiccate, Detox, Drain, Droll, Dull, Eild, Evaporate, Exsiccator, Firlot, Fork, Harmattan, Hasky, Hi(r)stie, Humidor, Jejune, Jerk, Khor, Kiln, Mummify, Oast, →**PARCH**, Prosaic, Reast, Rehab, Reist, Rizzar, Rizzer, Rizzor, Scarious, Sciroc, Scorch, Sear, Season, Sec(co), Seco, Sere, Shrivel, Siccative, Silical gel, Siroc(co), Sober, Sponge, Squeegee, Squeeze, Steme, Stove, Ted, Thirsty, Thristy, Toasted, Torrefy, Torrid, Towel, Tribble, Trocken, TT, Tumbler, Unwatery, Watertight, Welt, Wilt, Win(n), Windrow, Wipe, Wither, Wizened, Wry, Xeransis, Xerasia, Xero(sis), Xeroderma, Xerophthalmia, Xerostomia

Dual Double, Twin, Twofold

Dubious Arguable, Backscratching, Doubtful, Elliptic, Equivocal, Fishy, Fly-by-night,

Hesitant, Iffy, Improbable, Left-handed, Questionable, Scepsis, Sceptical, Sesey, Sessa, →**SHADY**, Suspect, Unclear, Unlikely

▷**Dubious** *may indicate* an anagram

Duck(ling), Ducked Amphibian, Avoid, Aylesbury, Bald-pate, Bargander, Bathe, Bergander, Blob, Blue, Bob, Bombay, Bufflehead, Bum(m)alo, Burrow, Butterball, Canard, Canvasback, Dead, Dearie, Decoy, Dip, Dodge, Dodo, Douse, Drook, Drouk, Dunk(er), Eider, Elude, Enew, Escape, Evade, Ferruginous, Flapper, Gadwall, Garganey, Garrot, Golden-eye, Goosander, Greenhead, Hareld, Harlequin, Heads, Herald, Immerse, Jook, Jouk, King-pair, Long-tailed, Mallard, Mandarin, Muscovy, Musk, Nil, O, Oldsquaw, Paddling, Pair of spectacles, Palmated, Paradise, Pekin(g), Pintail, Plunge, Pochard, Poker, Putangitangi, Ring-bill, Ruddy, Runner, Rush, St Cuthbert's, Scaup, Scoter, Sheld(d)uck, Shieldrake, Shirk, Shovel(l)er, Shun, Sitting, Smeath, Smee(th), Smew, Sord, Souse, Sowse, Spatula, Sprigtail, Surf(scoter), Teal, Team, Tufted, Tunker, Velvet scoter, Whio, Whistling, Whitewing, Widgeon, Wigeon, Wild, Wood, Zero

Duct Bile, Canal(iculus), Channel, Conduit, Epididymus, Fistula, Gland, Lachrymal, Laticifer, Mesonephric, Pancreatic, Passage, Pipe, Tear, Thoracic, Tube, Ureter, Vas deferens, Wolffian

Due(s) Accrued, Adequate, Annates, Arrearage, Claim, Debt, Deserts, Expected, Fit(ment), Forinsec, Geld, Heriot, Inheritance, Just, Lot, Mature, Needful, Offerings, Offload, Owing, Reddendo, Rent, Right, →**SUITABLE**, Thereanent, Toll, Tribute, Worthy

Dug-out Canoe, Shelter, Trench, Trough

Duke(dom) Albany, Alva, Chandos, Clarence, D, Duc, Ellington, Fist, Iron, Milan, Orsino, Peer, Prospero, Rohan, Wellington

Dull(ard), Dullness Anodyne, Anorak, Bald, Banal, Barren, Besot, Bland, Blear, Blockish, Blunt, Boeotian, Boring, Cloudy, Colourless, Commonplace, Dead (and alive), Deadhead, Dense, Dim, Dinge, Dingy, Ditchwater, Doldrums, Dowf, Dowie, Drab, Drear, Dreich, Dry, Dunce, Faded, Flat, Fozy, Gray, Grey, Heavy, Hebetate, Himbo, Ho-hum, Humdrum, Illustrious, Insipid, Jejune, Lacklustre, Lifeless, Log(y), Lowlight, Mat(t), Matte, Monotonous, Mopish, Mull, Mundane, Obtund, Obtuse, Opacity, Opiate, Ordinary, Overcast, Owlish, Pall, Pedestrian, Perstringe, Plodder, Podunk, Prosaic, Prose, Prosy, Rebate, Rust, Saddo, Slow, Solein, Sopite, Staid, Stick, Stodger, Stodgy, Stolid, Stuffy, Stultify, →**STUPID**, Sunless, Tame, Tarnish, Tedious, Ticky-tacky, Toneless, Torpor, Treadmill, Trite, Tubby, Unimaginative, Unresponsive, Vapid, Wonk, Wooden, Zoid

Dumb(ness) Alalia, Aphonic, Blonde, Crambo, Hobbididance, Inarticulate, Mute, Mutism, Shtum, Silent, Stumm, Stupid, Thunderstruck

Dummy Clot, Comforter, Copy, Effigy, Lummox, Mannequin, Mock-up, Model, Pacifier, Table, Waxwork

Dump(ing), Dumps Abandon, Blue, Core, Dispirited, Doldrums, Empty, Eyesore, Hole, Jettison, Jilt, Junk, Laystall, Offload, Scrap, Screen, Shoot, Store(house), Tip, Toom, Unlade, Unload

Dumpling Clootie, Dim sum, Dough(boy), Gnocchi, Gyoza, Knaidel, Knish, Norfolk, Perogi, Pi(e)rogi, Quenelle, Suet, Won ton

Dune Areg, Bar, Barchan(e), Bark(h)an, Erg, Sandbank, Seif, Star, Whaleback

Dungeon Bastille, Cell, Confine, Donjon, Durance

Dupe Catspaw, Chiaus, Chouse, Cony, Cull(y), Delude, Easy game, Easy mark, Easy meat, Geck, Gull, Hoax, Hoodwink, Mug, Pawn, Pigeon, Plover, Sitter, Soft mark, Sucker, Swindle, →**TRICK**, Victim

Durable Enduring, Eternal, Eterne, Hardy, Lasting, Permanent, Stout, Tough

Duration Extent, Limit, Period, Span, Timescale

Duress Coercion, Pressure, Restraint

During Amid, Dia-, For, In, Live, Over, Throughout, While, Whilst

Dusk(y) Dark, Dewfall, Dun, Eve, Eventide, Gloaming, Gloom, Half-light, Owl-light, Phaeic, Twilight, Umbrose

Dust(y) Arid, Ash, Bo(a)rt, Calima, Clean, Coom, Cosmic, Derris, Devil, Dicht, Duff,

Earth, Fuss, Gold, Khak(i), Lemel, Limail, Limit, Lo(e)ss, Miller, Nebula, Pollen, Pother, Pouder, Poudre, Powder, Pozz(u)olana, Pudder, Rouge, Sea, Seed, Shaitan, Slack, Springfield, Stour, Talc, Timescale, Volcanic, Wipe

▷ **Dusted** *may indicate* an anagram

Duster Cloth, Feather, Talcum, Torchon

Dutch(man), Dutchwoman Batavian, Boor, Butterbox, Cape, Courage, D(u), Double, Elm, Erasmus, Fri(e)sian, Frow, German, Kitchen, Knickerbocker, Missis, Missus, Mynheer, Patron, Sooterkin, Taal, Vrouw, Wife

Dutiful, Duty Active, Ahimsa, Allegiance, Attentive, Average, Blench, Bond, Charge, Corvee, Countervailing, Customs, Death, Debt, Deontology, Detail, Devoir, Docile, Drow, Due, Duplicand, End, Estate, Excise, Export, Fatigue, Feu, Filial, Function, Heriot, Homage, Import, Imposition, Impost, Incumbent, Lastage, Legacy, Likin, Mission, Mistery, Mystery, Obedient, Obligation, Octroi, Office, Onus, Pia, Picket, Pious, Point, Preferential, Prisage, Probate, Rota, Sentry-go, Shift, Stamp, Stillicide, Stint, Succession, Tariff, → **TASK**, Tax, Toll, Transit, Trap, Trow, Watch, Zabeta

Dwarf(ism) Achondroplasia, Agate, Alberich, Andvari, Ateleiosis, Bashful, Belittle, Bes, Black, Bonsai, Brown, Doc, Dopey, Droich, Drow, Durgan, Elf, Gnome, Grumpy, Happy, Hobbit, Homuncule, Hop o' my thumb, Knurl, Laurin, Leetle, Little man, Man(n)ikin, → **MIDGET**, Mime, Minikin, Minim, Nanism, Nectabanus, Ni(e)belung, Nurl, Outshine, Overshadow, Pacolet, Pigmy, Pygmy, Red, Regin, Ront, Rumpelstiltskin, Runt, Skrimp, Sleepy, Sneezy, → **STUNT**, Tiddler, Titch, Tokoloshe, Tom Thumb, Toy, Troll, Trow, White

Dwindle Decline, Diminish, Fade, Lessen, Peter, Shrink, Wane

Dye(ing), Dyestuff, Dye-seller Alkanet, Anil, Anthracene, Anthraquinone, Archil, Aweto, Azo(benzine), Bat(t)ik, Benzidine, Camwood, Canthaxanthin, Carthamine, Catechin, Chay(a), Chica, Choy, Cinnabar, Cobalt, Cochineal, Colour, Congo, Coomassie blue, Corkir, Crocein, Crotal, Crottle, Cudbear, Dinitrobenzene, Direct, Embrue, Engrain, Envermeil, Eosin, Flavin(e), Fuchsin(e), Fustet, Fustic, Fustoc, Gambi(e)r, Grain, Henna, Hue, Ice colours, Ikat, Imbrue, Imbue, Incarnadine, Indamine, Indican, Indigo, Indigotin, Indirubin, Indoxyl, Indulin(e), Ingrain, Kamala, Kermes, Kohl, Korkir, Lightfast, Madder, Magenta, Mauvein(e), Mauvin(e), Myrobalan, Nigrosin(e), Orcein, Orchel(la), Orchil, Para-red, Phenolphthalein, Phthalein, → **PIGMENT**, Ponceau, Primuline, Puccoon, Purple, Purpurin, Pyronine, Quercitron, Quinoline, Raddle, Resorcinol, Rhodamine, Rosanilin(e), Safranin(e), Salter, Shaya, → **STAIN**, Stilbene, Stone-rag, Stone-raw, Sumac(h), Sunfast, Tannin, Tartrazine, Tie-dye, Tinct, Tint, Tropaeolin, Trypan blue, Turmeric, Turnsole, Ultramarine, Valonia, Vat, Wald, Weld, Woad, Woald, Wold, Xanthium, Xylidine

▶ **Dying** *see* **DIE(D)**

Dyke Aboideau, Aboiteau, Bund, Devil's, Ditch, Gall, Offa's, Ring, Sea-wall

Dynamic(s) Ballistics, Ball of fire, Driving, Energetic, Forceful, High-powered, Kinetics, Potent

Dynamite Blast, Explode, Gelignite, Giant powder, TNT, Trotyl

Dynasty Abbasid(e), Angevin, Bourbon, Capetian, Carolingian, Chen, Chin(g), Ch'ing, Chou, Era, Fatimid, Frankish, Habsburg, Han, Hanoverian, Hapsburg, Holkar, Honan, House(hold), Hyksos, Khan, Manchu, Maurya, Merovingian, Ming, Omayyad, Osman, Pahlavi, Plantagenet, Ptolemy, Qajar, Q'in(g), Rameses, Romanov, Rule, Safavid, Saga, Sassanid, Seleucid, Seljuk, Shang, Song, Sui, Sung, Tai-ping, Tang, Tudor, Umayyad, Wei, Yi, Yuan, Zhou

Dysfunction Kernicterus

Ee

E Boat, East, Echo, Energy, English, Spain

Each All, Apiece, A pop, Ea, → EVERY, Ilka, Per (capita), Respective, Severally

Eager(ly) Agog, Antsy, Ardent, Avid, Beaver, Bore, Bright-eyed, Dying, Earnest, Enthusiastic, Fain, Fervent, Fervid, Fidge, Frack, Game, Greedy, Gung-ho, Hot, Intent, → KEEN, Perfervid, Prone, Race, Raring, Rath(e), Ready, Roost, Sharp-set, Sore, Spoiling, Thirsty, Toey, Wishing, Yare, Zealous

Eagle Al(l)erion, Altair, American, Aquila, Bald, Bateleur, Berghaan, Eddy, Ensign, Erne, Ethon, Gier, Golden, Harpy, Legal, Lettern, Ossifrage

Ear(drum), Ear problem Ant(i)helix, Attention, Audience, Auricle, Cauliflower, Cochlea, Concha, Deafness, External, Glue, Hearing, Inner, Jenkins, Listen, Lug, Otalgia, Otalgy, Otic, Otocyst, Parotic, Pinna, Presby(a)c(o)usis, Souse, Spikelet, Stapes, Tragus, Utricle

Earlier, Early Above, Ago, Ahead, AM, Auld, Betimes, Cockcrow, Daybreak, Ex, Germinal, Incipient, Matin, Precocious, Precursor, Prehistoric, Premature, Premie, Prevernal, Previous, Primeur, Primeval, Primordial, Prior, Rear, Rough, Rudimentary, Small hours, Soon, Timely, Tim(e)ous

▷ **Early** *may indicate* belonging to an earl

▷ **Early stages of** *may indicate* first one or two letters of the words following

Earmark Allocate, Bag, Book, Characteristic, Flag, → RESERVE, Tag, Target, Ticket

Earn(er), Earning(s) Achieve, Addle, Breadwinner, Curdle, Deserve, Ern, Gain, Make, Merit, Pay packet, Reap, Rennet, Runnet, Win, Yearn

Earnest(ly) Agood, Ardent, Arle(s)(-penny), Devout, Fervent, Imprest, Intent, Promise, Serious, Sincere, Token, Wistly, Zealous

Earring Drop, Ear bob, Hoop, Keeper, Pendant, Sleeper, Snap, Stud

Earth(y), Earthling Antichthon, Art, Barbados, Bury, Capricorn, Carnal, Clay, Cloam, Clod, Cologne, Den, Dirt, Drey, Dust, Eard, Epigene, Foxhole, Friable, Fuller's, Gaea, Gaia, Gault, Ge, Globe, Green, Ground, Heavy, Horst, Kadi, Lair, Loam, Malm, Mankind, Mantle, Mools, Mould, Mouls, Papa, Pise, Planet, Podsol, Racy, Rare, Raunchy, Red, Samian, Seat, Sett, Sod, → SOIL, Surcharge, Taurus, Telluric, Tellus, Terra, Terrain, Terramara, Terran, Terrene, Topsoil, Virgo, Ye(a)rd, Yird

Earthquake Aftershock, Aseismic, Bradyseism, Mercalli, Richter, Seism, Shake, Shock, Temblor, Trembler

Ease, Easing, Easygoing Alleviate, Carefree, Clear, Clover, Comfort, Content, Defuse, Deregulate, Détente, Easy-osy, Facility, Genial, Hands down, Informal, Lax, Mellow, Mid(dy), Mitigate, Otiosity, Palliate, Peace, Quiet, Relieve, Reposal, Repose, Soothe

East(erly), Eastward Anglia, Asia, Chevet, E, Eassel, Eassil, Eothen, Eurus, Far, Levant, Morning-land, Orient, Ost, Sunrise

Easter Festival, Island, Pace, Pasch(al), Pasque

East German Ossi

Easy, Easily ABC, Cakewalk, Carefree, Cinch, Comfy, Cushy, Doddle, Doss, Duck soup, Facile, Free, Gift, Glib, Gravy train, Jammy, Kid's stuff, Lax, Light, Natural, No-brainer, Picnic, Pie, Plain sailing, Pushover, Romp, Scoosh, Simple, Skoosh, Snap, Snotty, Soft, Spoon fed, Tolerant, Turkey shoot, Walk-over, Yare

▷ **Easy** *may indicate* an anagram

Easy-care Non-iron

Eat(able), Eater, Eating Bite, Bolt, Break bread, Chop, Consume, Corrode, Cram, Devour, Dig in, Dine, Edible, Erode, Esculent, Etch, Fare, Feast, → FEED, Fret, Gnaw,

Go, Gobble, Gourmand, Gourmet, Graze, Grub, Have, Hoe into, Hog, Hyperorexia, Mess, Muckamuck, Munch, Nosh, Nutritive, Omnivore, Partake, Phagomania, Refect, Scoff, Snack, Stuff, Sup, Swallow, Take, Taste, Trencherman, Tuck away, Tuck into, Twist

Eating problem Anorexia, Bulimia, Cachexia

Eavesdrop(per) Detectophone, Earwig, Listen, Overhear, Snoop, Tap

Ebb(ing) Abate, Decline, Recede, Sink

Ebonite Hard rubber

Eccentric Abnormal, Antic, Atypical, Cam, Card, Character, Crackpot, Crank, Curious, Dag, Deviant, Dingbat, Ditsy, Ditzy, E, Farouche, Fay, Fey, Fie, Freak, Geek, Gonzo, Iffish, Irregular, Kinky, Kook(y), Madcap, Mattoid, Monstre sacré, Nutcase, Odd(ball), Offbeat, Off-centre, Original, Outré, → PECULIAR, Pixil(l)ated, Queer, Quirky, Quiz, Rake, Raky, Recondite, Rum, Scatty, Screwball, Screwy, Spac(e)y, Wack(y), W(h)acko, Way-out, Weird(o), Weirdie

▷ **Eccentric** *may indicate* an anagram

Ecclesiast(es), Ecclesiasticus, Ecclesiastical Abbé, Clergyman, Clerical, Lector, Secular, Sir(ach), Theologian, The Preacher, Vatican

Echinoderm Asteroidea, Basket-star, Brittle-star, Comatulid, Crinoid, Ophiurid, Sea-egg, Sea-lily, Sea-urchin, Starfish

Echo, Echoing, Echo-sounder Angel, Answer, Ditto, E, Fathometer®, Imitate, Iterate, Phonocamptic, Rebound, Repeat, Repercussion, Reply, Resemble, Resonant, Respeak, Reverb(erate), Ring, Rote, Sonar

Eclipse Annular, Block, Cloud, Deliquium, Excel, Hide, Lunar, Obscure, Occultation, Outmatch, Outshine, Outweigh, Overshadow, Penumbra, Rahu, Solar, Total, Transcend, Upstage

Eco-friendly Biodegradable

Ecology Bionomics

Economise Budget, Conserve, Eke, Finance, Husband, Pinch, Retrench, Scrimp, Skimp, Spare, Whip the cat

Economy, Economic(al), Economics Agronomy, Autarky, Black, Brevity, Careful, Chrematistics, Cliometrics, Conversation, Cut, Domestic, Frugal, Hidden, Home, Informal, LSE, Market, Mitumba, Neat, Parsimony, Provident, Pusser's logic, Retrenchment, Shadow, Shoestring, Sparing, Stumpflation, Thrift

Ecstasy, Ecstatic Bliss, Delight, Dove, E, Exultant, Joy, Lyrical, Pythic, Rapture, Sent, Trance, Transport

Edda Elder, Prose, Younger

Eden Bliss, Fall, Heaven, Paradise, PM, Utopia

Edge, Edging, Edgy Advantage, Arris, Bleeding, Border, Bordure, Brim, Brink, Brittle, Brown, Burr, Chamfer, Chimb, Chime, Chine, Coaming, Costa, Creston, Cutting, Dag, Deckle, Ease, End, Flange, Flounce, Frill, Fringe, Frontier, Furbelow, Gunnel, Gunwale, Hem, Hone, Inch, Inside, Kerb, Knife, Leading, Leech, Limb(ate), Limbus, Limit, Lip, List, Lute, Marge(nt), Margin, Neckline, Nosing, Orle, Outside, Parapet, Periphery, Picot, Pikadell, Piping, Rand, Reeding, Rim, Rund, Rymme, Selvage, Selvedge, Side, Sidle, Skirt, Strand, Surbed, Tense, Tomium, Trailing, Trim, Tyre, Uptight, Verge, Wear, Whet

▶ **Edible** *see* EATABLE

Edict(s) Ban, Bull, Clementines, Decree, Decretal, Extravagantes, Fatwa, Interim, Irade, Nantes, Notice, Order, Pragmatic, Proclamation, Pronouncement, Sext, Ukase

Edit(or), Editorial Abridge, Amend, Article, City, Cut, Dele, Desk, Dramaturg(e), Ed, Emend, Expurgate, Footsteps, Garble, Leader, Manipulate, Overseer, Recense, Redact, Revise, Seaman, Tweak

▷ **Edited** *may indicate* an anagram

Edith Sitwell

Edition Aldine, Ed, Extra, Facsimile, Hexapla(r), Issue, Limited, Number, Omnibus, Variorum, Version

Educate(d) Academic, Baboo, Babu, Enlighten, Evolué, Informed, Instruct, Learned,

Lettered, Noursle, Nousell, Nousle, Nurture, Nuzzle, Polymath, Preppy, Progressive, Scholarly, School, →**TEACH**, Train, Yuppie

Education(alist) Adult, Basic, B.Ed, Classical, D.Ed, Didactics, Estyn, Heurism, Learning, Literate, Mainstream, Montessori, Pedagogue, Pestalozzi, Piarist, Primary, Schooling, Special, Teacher, Tertiary, Upbringing

Edward Confessor, Ed, Elder, Lear, Longshanks, Martyr, Ned, Ted

Eel Conger, Electric, Elver, Hagfish, Lamprey, Launce, Moray, Olm, Salt, Sand(ling), Snake

Efface Cancel, Delete, Dislimn, →**ERASE**, Expunge, Obliterate

Effect(s), Effective(ness), Effectual Achieve, Acting, Alienation, Auger, Bags, Belongings, Binaural, Bit, Bite, Border edge, Bystander, Causal, Coastline, Competent, Consequence, Do, Domino, Doppler, Edge, Efficacious, Electro-optical, Enact, End, Estate, Execute, Fet, Functional, Fungibles, Gangbuster, Gear, General, Goods, Greenhouse, Hall, Hangover, Home, Impact, Implement(al), Impression, Influence, Knock-on, Magneto-optical, Militate, Moire, Mutual, Neat, Net, Nisi, Operant, Outcome, Personal, Phi, Position, Potent, Practical, Promulgate, Punchy, Reaction, Redound, Repercussion, →**RESULT**, Ripple, Shadow, Shore, Side, Slash-dot, Sound, Special, Spectrum, Spin-off, Stage, Striking, Subsidiary, Tableau, Telling, Upshot, Viable, Virtual, Well, Work

Effervescence, Effervescent Bubbling, Ebullient, Fizz

▷ **Effervescent** *may indicate* an anagram

Efficiency, Efficient Able, Businesslike, Capable, Competent, Despatch, Ecological, Ergonomics, High-powered, Productivity, Smart, Spectral luminous, Streamlined, Strong

Effigy Buddha, Figure, Guy, Idol, Image, Statua, Statue

Effluence, Effluent, Effluvia Air, Aura, Billabong, Discharge, Fume, Gas, Halitus, Miasma, Odour, Outflow, Outrush

Effort Achievement, All-out, Attempt, Best, Conatus, Concerted, Damnedest, Drive, Endeavour, Essay, Exertion, Fit, Frame, Hardscrabble, Herculean, Labour, Molimen, Nisus, Pull, Rally, Shy, Spurt, Stab, Strain, Struggle, Team, →**TRY**, Work, Yo

Effrontery Audacity, Brass, Cheek, Face, Gall, Neck, Nerve, Temerity

Effuse, Effusion, Effusive Emanate, Exuberant, Exude, Gush, Lyric, Ode, Outburst, Prattle, Rhapsody, Screed, Spill

Eg As, Example

Egg(s), Egg on Abet, Addled, Benedict, Berry, Blow, Bomb, Caviar(e), Cavier, Chalaza, Cheer, Cleidoic, Clutch, Cockney, Collop, Coral, Curate's, Darning, Easter, Edge, Encourage, Fabergé, Fetus, Flyblow, Foetus, Free-range, Glair(e), Goad, Goog, Graine, Hoy, Incite, Instigate, Isolecithal, Layings, Mine, Nit, Oocyte, Oophoron, Ova, Ovum, Pasch, Prairie oyster, Press, Prod, Raun, Roe, Rumble-tumble, Scotch, Seed, Setting, Spat, Spawn, Spur(ne), Tar(re), Tooth, Tread(le), Urge, Yelk, Yolk

Egg-case Eggshell, Pod

Egghead Brainbox, Don, Highbrow, Intellectual, Mensa, Pedant

Eggnog Flip

Ego(ism), Egoist, Egotist(ical) Che, Conceit, I, Narcissism, Not-I, Pride, Self, Self-seeker, Solipsism, Tin god, Vanity

Egret Snowy

Egypt(ian), Egyptologist Arab, Cairene, Carter, Cheops, Chephren, Cleopatra, Copt(ic), ET, Goshen, Imhotep, Nasser, Nefertiti, Nilote, Nitrian, Old Kingdom, Osiris, Ptolemy, Rameses, Syene, Wafd

Eight(h), Eighth day Acht, Byte, Crew, Cube, Nundine, Oars, Octa, Octad, Octal, Octastrophic, Octave, Octet, Octonary, Octuor, Ogdoad, Okta, Ottava, Ure, Utas

Either Also, Both, O(u)ther, Such

Ejaculate Blurt, Discharge, Emit, Exclaim

Eject Belch, Bounce, Defenestrate, Disgorge, Dismiss, Emit, Erupt, Evict, Expel, Oust, Propel, Spew, Spit, Spue, Turf out, Vent, Void

Eke Augment, Eche, Enlarge, Husband, Supplement

Elaborate Creation, Detail, Develop, Enlarge, Fancy, Flesh out, Florid, Intricate, Magnificent, Opulent, Ornate, Spectacular

Elan Dash, Drive, Esprit, →FLAIR, Gusto, Lotus, Spirit, Style, Vigour

Elastic(ity) Adaptable, Buoyant, Dopplerite, Elater, Flexible, Give, Resilient, Rubber, Scrunchie, Scrunchy, Spandex®, Springy, Stretchy, Tone, Tonus

Elastomer Adiprene®

Elate(d), Elation Cheer, Euphoric, Exalt, Exhilarate, Gladden, Hault, High, Lift, Rapture, Ruff(e), Uplift

Elbow, Elbow tip Akimbo, Ancon, Angle, Bender, Cubital, Hustle, Joint, Jolt, Jostle, Kimbo, Noop, Nudge, Olecranon, Tennis

El Cid Diaz

Elder(ly), Eldest Ainé(e), Ancestor, Ancient, Bourtree, Chief, Classis, Coffin dodger, Eigne, Geriatric, Greying, Guru, Kaumatua, OAP, Presbyter, →SENIOR, Sire, Susanna, Wallwort

Elect(ed), Election(eer), Elective, Elector(al) Ballot, Choice, Choose, Chosen, Co-opt, Eatanswill, Elite, Gerrymander, Hustings, In, Israelite, Khaki, Opt, Optional, Pick, PR, Predetermine, Primary, Psephology, Rectorial, Return, Select, Stump

Electricity Galvanism, Grid, HT, Inductance, Juice, Power, Static, Utility

Electrify Astonish, Galvanise, Startle, Stir, Thrill

Elegance, Elegant Artistic, Bijou, Chic, Classy, Concinnity, Dainty, Daynt, Debonair, Dressy, Fancy, Finesse, Gainly, Galant, Grace, Luxurious, Neat, Polished, Refined, Ritzy, →SMART, Soigné(e), Style, Svelte, Swish, Tall, Urbane

Element(s), Elementary Abcee, Abecedarian, Absey, Barebones, Detail, →ESSENCE, Essential, Factor, Feature, Fuel, Heating, Hot-plate, Ideal, Identity, Insertion, Logical, M(a)cGuffin, Milieu, Non-metal, Peltier, Pixel, Primary, Principle, Rare earth, Rudimental, Sieve, Simple, Simplex, Strand, Superheavy, Trace(r), Tramp, Transition, Transuranic, Weather

Elephant(ine) African, Indian, Jumbo, Mammoth, Mastodon, Oliphant, Pachyderm, Rogue, Stegodon, Tusker, White

Elevate(d), Elevation, Elevator Agger, Attitude, Bank, Cheer, Eminence, Ennoble, Glabella, Haute, Heighten, Hoist, Jack, Lift, Pitch, Promote, →RAISE, Random, Relievo, Ridge, Rise, Sublimate, Up(lift)

Eleven Elf, Legs, O, Side, Team, XI

Eligible Available, Catch, Fit, Nubile, Parti, Qualified, Worthy

Eliminate, Elimination Cull, Cure, Deep-six, Delete, Discard, Exclude, Execute, Extirpate, Knock out, Liquidate, Omit, Preclude, Purge, Rid, Zap

Elite Bèst, Choice, Crachach, Crack, →CREAM, Crème, Egalitarian, Elect, Flower, Meritocracy, Ton, Top drawer, Twelve pitch, U, Zaibatsu

Elm Rock, Slippery, Wich, Wych

Elongate Extend, Lengthen, Protract, Stretch

Eloquence, Eloquent Articulate, Demosthenic, Facundity, Fluent, Honey-tongued, Oracy, Rhetoric, Speaking, Vocal

Else(where) Absent, Alibi, Aliunde, Et al, Other

Elude, Elusion, Elusive Avoid, Dodge, Eel, Escape, →EVADE, Evasive, Foil, Intangible, Jink, Pimpernel, Sliddery, Slippy, Subt(i)le, Will o' the wisp

Emaciated, Emaciation Atrophy, Erasmus, Gaunt, Haggard, Lean, Skeleton, Skinny, Sweeny, Tabid, Thin, Wanthriven, Wasted

Email Flame, Spam, Spim

Emancipate(d), Emancipation Catholic, Deliver, Forisfamiliate, Free, →LIBERATE, Manumission, Uhuru

Embankment Bund, Causeway, Dam, Dyke, Earthwork, Levee, Mattress, Mound, Rampart, Remblai, Stopbank

Embargo →BAN, Blockade, Boycott, Edict, Restraint

Embark Begin, Board, Enter, Inship, Launch, Sail

Embarrass(ed), Embarrassing, Embarrassment Abash, Awkward, Besti, Buttock-clenching, Colour, Cringe-making, Cringe-worthy, Disconcert,

Discountenance, Encumber, Mess, Plethora, Pose, Predicament, Scundered, Scunnered, Shame, Sheepish, Squirming, Straitened, Tongue-tied, Whoopsie

▷ **Embarrassed** *may indicate* an anagram

Embassy Chancery, Consulate, Embassade, Legation, Mission

Embellish(ed), Embellishment Adorn, Beautify, Bedeck, Curlicue, Deck, Decór(ate), Embroider, Enrich, Fioritura, Garnish, Garniture, Melisma(ta), →**ORNAMENT**, Ornate, Overwrought, Prank, Prettify, Story, Twist

Ember(s) Ash, Cinder, Clinker, Gleed

Emblem(atic) Badge, Bear, Colophon, Daffodil, Device, Figure, Hammer and sickle, Ichthys, Impresa, Insignia, Kikumon, Leek, Lis, Maple leaf, Oak, Pip, Rose, Roundel, Shamrock, Sign, Spear-thistle, →**SYMBOL**, Tau-cross, Thistle, Token, Totem(ic), Triskelion, Wheel

Emboss(ed) Adorn, Chase, Cloqué, Engrave, Pounce

Embrace(d) Accolade, Arm, Bear hug, Canoodle, Clasp, Clinch, Clip, Coll, Complect, Comprise, Cuddle, Embosom, Encircle, Enclasp, Enclose, Enfold, Envelop, Espouse, Fold, Grab, Hug, Include, Inlace, Kiss, Lasso, Neck, Overarch, Press, Snog, Snug(gle), Twine, Welcome, Wrap

▷ **Embraces, Embracing** *may indicate* a hidden word

Embroider(y) Add, Appliqué, Arpillera, Braid, Brede, Colour, Couching, Crewellery, Crewel-work, Cross-stitch, Cutwork, Embellish, Exaggerate, Fag(g)oting, Fancywork, Featherstitch, Gros point, Handiwork, Lace(t), Laid work, Needlepoint, Needlework, Orfray, Ornament, Orphrey, Orris, Petit point, Pinwork, Purl, Queen-stitch, Sampler, Sew, Smocking, Spider-wheel, Stitch, Stitchery, Stumpwork, Tent, Zari

Embryo(nic), Embryologist Archenteron, Blastocyst, Blastospore, Blastula, Fo(e)tus, Gastrula, Germ, Mesoblast, Origin, Rudiment, Undeveloped, Wolff

Emend Adjust, Alter, Edit, Reform

Emerge(ncy), Emerging Anadyomene, Arise, Craunch, Crise, Crisis, Crunch, Debouch, Emanate, Erupt, Exigency, Flashpoint, Hard-shoulder, Issue, Last-ditch, Need, Outcrop, Pinch, SOS, Spare, Spring, Stand-by, Strait

▷ **Emerge from** *may indicate* an anagram or a hidden word

Eminence, Eminent Altitude, Cardinal, Distinguished, Grand, Height, Hill, Hywel, Illustrious, Light, Lion, Lofty, Luminary, Noble, →**NOTABLE**, Prominence, Red hat, Renown, Repute, Stature, Tor, →**VIP**

Emirate Abu Dhabi, Dubai, Qatar, Sharjah

Emission, Emit Discharge, Emanate, Give, Issue, Radiate, Utter, Vent

Emolument Income, Perk, Remuneration, Salary, Stipend, Tip, Wages

Emotion(s), Emotional Anger, Anoesis, Breast, Cathartic, Chord, Ecstasy, Excitable, Feeling, Flare up, Freak-out, Gushing, Gut-wrenching, Hate, Heartstrings, Hippocampus, Histrionics, Hoo, Hysteria, Intense, Joy, Limbic, Maenad, Nympholepsy, Passion, Poignant, Reins, Rhapsodic, Roar, Sensibility, Sensitive, Sentiment, Spirit, Stormy, Theopathy, Transport, Weepy, Wigged out

Empathy Rapport, Rapprochement, Sympathy

Emperor Agramant(e), Akbar, Akihito, Antoninus, Augustus, Aurelian, Babur, Bao Dai, Barbarossa, Bonaparte, Caesar, Caligula, Caracalla, Charlemagne, Claudius, Commodus, Concerto, Constantine, Diocletian, Domitian, Ferdinand, Flavian, Gaius, Galba, Genghis Khan, Gratian, Great Mogul, Hadrian, Haile Selassie, Heraclius, Hirohito, HRE, Imp, Inca, Jimmu, Justinian, Kaiser, Keasar, Kesar, King, Manuel I Comnenus, Maximilian, Meiji, Menelik, Mikado, Ming, Mogul, Montezuma, Mpret, Napoleon, Negus, Nero, Nerva, Otho, Otto, Penguin, Peter the Great, Purple, Pu-yi, Rex, Rosco, Ruler, Severus, Shah Jahan, Shang, Sovereign, Sultan, Tenno, Theodore, Theodosius, Tiberius, Titus, Trajan, Tsar, Valens, Valentinian, Valerian, Vespasian, Vitellius

Emphasis(e), Emphasize, Emphatic Accent, Birr, Bold, Dramatise, Ek se, Forcible, Foreground, Forzando, Forzato, Hendiadys, Highlight, Italic, Marcato, Point up, Positive, Resounding, Risoluto, Sforzando, Sforzato, Underline, Underscore, Vehement

Empire Assyria, British, Byzantine, Domain, Empery, French, Kingdom, Latin, Ottoman, Realm, Reich, Roman

Employ(ment) Bestow, Business, Calling, Engage, Hire, Occupy, Pay, Post, Practice, Pursuit, Retain, Use, Using, Utilise, Vocation

Employee(s) Barista, Casual, Clock-watcher, Factotum, Hand, Help, Minion, Payroll, Personnel, Salariat, Servant, Staff, Staffer, Worker, Workforce, Workpeople

Employer Baas, Boss, Master, Padrone, Taskmaster, User

▷ **Employs** *may indicate* an anagram

Empress Eugenie, Josephine, Matilda, Messalina, Sultana, Tsarina, VIR

Empty Addle, Bare, Barren, Blank, Buzz, Clear, Deplete, Deserted, Devoid, Disembowel, Drain, Exhaust, Expel, Forsaken, Futile, Gut, Hent, Hollow, Inane, Jejune, Lave, Meaningless, Null, Pump, Shallow, Teem, Toom, Tum(e), Unfurnished, Uninhabited, Unoccupied, Vacant, Vacate, Vacuous, Vain, →**VOID**

▷ **Empty** *may indicate* an 'o' in the word or an anagram

Empty-headed Vain

Emulate Ape, Copy, Envy, Equal, Imitate, Match

Enable Authorise, Capacitate, Empower, Permit, Potentiate, Qualify, Sanction

Enamel(led), Enamel work Aumail, Champlevé, Cloisonné, Della-robbia, Dentine, Fabergé, Ganoin(e), Lacquer, Mottled, Nail, Polish, Porcelain, Schwarzlot, Shippo, Smalto, Stoved, Vitreous

Encampment Bivouac, Castrametation, Douar, Dowar, Duar, Laager, Laer, Settlement

Encase(d), Encasement Box, Crate, Emboîtement, Encapsulate, Enclose, Obtect, Sheathe

Enchant(ing), Enchanted, Enchantment Captivate, Charm, Delight, Gramary(e), Incantation, Magic, Necromancy, Rapt, Sirenize, Sorcery, Spellbind, Thrill

Enchanter, Enchantress Archimage, Archimago, Armida, Circe, Comus, Faerie, Fairy, Houri, Lorelei, Magician, Medea, Mermaid, Prospero, Reim-kennar, Sorcerer, Vivien, Witch

Encircle(d), Encirclement Besiege, Enclose, Encompass, Enlace, Entrold, Gird, Hoop, Inorb, Introld, Orbit, Pale, Ring, Siege, Stemme, →**SURROUND**

Enclose(d), Enclosing, Enclosure Bawn, Beset, Boma, Box, Bullring, Cage, Carol, Carrel, Case, Circumscribe, Common, Compound, Corral, Court, Embale, Embower, Enceinte, Enchase, Encircle, Enclave, Engirt, Enhearse, Enlock, Enshrine, Fence, Fold, Garth, Haining, Haw, Hem, Henge, Hope, Impound, In, Incapsulate, Inchase, Inlock, Insert, Interclude, Lairage, Obvolute, Paddock, Pale, Parrock, Peel, Pele, Pen(t), Pin, Pinfold, Playpen, Plenum, Pocket, Radome, Rail, Rath, Recluse, Ree(d), Ring, Run, Saleyard, Seal, Sekos, Sept, Seraglio, Serail, Several, Sin bin, Steeld, Stell, Stive, Stockade, Sty, →**SURROUND**, Tatt(ersall)s, Terrarium, Tine, Vibarium, Ward, Wrap, Yard, Zareba

Encompass Bathe, Begird, Beset, Environ, Include, Surround

Encounter Battle, Brush, Close, Combat, Contend, Cope, Experience, Face, Hit, Incur, Interview, →**MEET**, Rencontre, Ruffle, Skirmish

Encourage(ment), Encouraging Abet, Acco(u)rage, Alley-oop, Attaboy, Barrack, Bolster, Boost, Buck, Cheer, Chivy, Cohortative, Come-on, Commend, Dangle, Egg, Embolden, Exhort, Fillip, Fire, Fortify, Foster, Fuel, Gee, Hearten, Heigh, Help, Heuristic, Hortatory, Incite, Inspire, Invite, Lift, Nourish, Nurture, Pat, Patronise, Pep talk, Prod, Promote, Push, Reassure, Root, Seed, Spur, Stimulate, Support, Tally-ho, Uplift, Urge, Yay, Yo, Yoicks

Encroach(ment) Eat out, Impinge, Infringe, Intrude, Invade, Overlap, Overstep, Poach, Trespass, Usurp

Encumber, Encumbrance Accloy, Burden, Clog, Dead weight, Deadwood, Dependent, →**HANDICAP**, Impede, Load, Obstruct, Saddle

End(ing) Abolish, Abort, Abut, Aim, Ambition, Amen, Anus, Arse, Big, Bitter, Bourn(e), Butt, Cease, Cessation, Cesser, Climax, Close, Closure, Cloture, Coda, Conclude, Crust, Culminate, Curtain, Curtains, Cut off, Dead, Death, Decease,

Denouement, Desinence, Destroy, Determine, Dissolve, Domino, Effect, Envoi, Envoy, Epilogue, Exigent, Expire, Explicit, Extremity, Fade, Fatal, Fattrels, Feminine, Fin, Final(e), Fine, Finis, →**FINISH**, Finite, Gable, Grave, Heel, Ice, Ish, Izzard, Izzet, Kill, Kybosh, Lapse, Last, Let up, Limit, Little, Loose, Masculine, Mill, Nirvana, No side, Ort, Out, Outrance, Outro, Period, Peter, Pine, Point, Purpose, Quench, Receiving, Remnant, Rescind, Result, Roach, Round off, Runback, Scotch, Scrag, Shank, Slaughter, Sopite, Split, Sticky, Stub, Surcease, Swansong, Tag, Tail, Tailpiece, Telic, Telos, Term, Terminal, Terminate, Terminus, Thrum, Tip, Toe, Top, Ultimate, Up, Upshot, Utterance, West, Z

Endeavour Aim, Attempt, Effort, Enterprise, Essay, Strain, Strive, Struggle, Try, Venture

Endless Aeonian, Continuous, Ecaudate, Eternal, Eterne, Infinite, Interminable, Perpetual, Undated

▷ **Endlessly** *may indicate* a last letter missing

Endorse(ment) Adopt, Affirm, Approve, Assurance, Back, Certify, Confirmation, Docket, Initial, Okay, Oke, Ratify, Rubber stamp, Sanction, Second, Sign, →**SUPPORT**, Underwrite, Visa

Endow(ment) Assign, Bequeath, Bestow, Bless, Cha(u)ntry, Dotation, Enrich, Foundation, Gift, Leave, Patrimony, Vest

Endurance, Endure(d), Enduring Abide, Bear, Bide, Brook, Dree, Dure, Face, Fortitude, Granite, Have, Hold, →**LAST**, Livelong, Lump, Marathon, Patience, Perseverance, Persist, Pluck, Ride, Stamina, Stand, Stay, Stomach, Stout, Substantial, Sustain, Swallow, Thole, Timeless, Tolerance, Undergo, Wear, Weather

Enemy Adversary, Antagonist, Boer, Devil, Fifth column, Foe(n), Fone, Opponent, Public, Time

Energetic, Energise, Energy Active, Amp, Animation, Arduous, Barnstorming, Binding, Bond, Brisk, Cathexis, Chakra, Chi, Dash, Doer, Drive, Dynamic, Dynamo, E, Enthalpy, Entropy, EV, Fermi, Fireball, Force, Fructan, Fusion, Gism, Go, Go ahead, Hartree, Horme, Hustle, Hyper, Input, Instress, Internal, Isotonic, →**JET**, Jism, Jissom, Joie de vivre, Joule, Kerma, Kinetic, Kundalini, Libido, Life, Luminous, Magnon, Moxie, Nuclear, Orgone, Pep, Phonon, Pithy, Potency, Potential, →**POWER**, Powerhouse, QI, Quantum, Quasar, Rad, Radiant, Radiatory, Rydberg, S(h)akti, Sappy, Second-wind, Solar, Steam, Trans-uranic, Verve, Vigour, Vim, Vital, Vivo, Wave, Whammo, Whirlwind, Zealous, Zero point, Zing, Zip

Enervate Exhaust

Enforce(ment) Administer, Coerce, Control, Exact, Implement, Impose

Engage(d), Engagement, Engaging Absorb, Accept, Adorable, Appointment, Attach, Bespoken, Betrothal, Bind, Book, Busy, Contract, Date, Embark, Employ, Engross, Enlist, Enmesh, Enter, Fiance(e), Fight, Gear, Gig, Hire, Hold, In gear, Interest, Interlock, Lock, Mesh, Met, Occupy, Pledge, Promise, Prosecute, Rapt, Reserve, Residency, Sapid, Skirmish, Sponsal, Sponsion, Spousal, Trip, Wage, Winsome

▷ **Engagement** *may indicate* a battle

Engine, Engine part Air, Analytical, Atmospheric, Banker, Banking, Beam, Bricole, Carburettor, Catapult, Compound, Dashpot, Diesel, Dividing, Donkey, Dynamo, Fan-jet, Fire, Four-cycle, Gas, Humdinger, ICE, Internal combustion, Ion, Iron horse, Jet, Lean-burn, Light, Little-end, Loco(motive), Machine, Mangonel, Mogul, →**MOTOR**, Nacelle, Oil, Orbital, Otto, Outboard, Overhead valve, Petrol, Pilot, Plasma, Podded, Pony, Puffer, Pug, Pulp, Pulsejet, Push-pull, Radial, Ramjet, Reaction, Reciprocating, Retrorocket, Rocket, Rose, Rotary, Scramjet, Search, Side-valve, Sleeve valve, Stationary, Steam, Sustainer, Tank, Testudo, Thermometer, Thruster, Top-end, Traction, Turbine, Turbofan, Turbojet, Turboprop, Turbo-ram-jet, Two-stroke, V, Vernier, V-type, Wankel, Water, Wildcat, Winding

▷ **Engineer** *may indicate* an anagram

Engineer(ing), Engineer(s) Aeronautical, AEU, Arrange, Badge, Chartered, Concurrent, Contrive, Greaser, Human, Interactive, Knowledge, Liability, Manhattan District, Manoeuvre, Marine, Mastermind, Operator, Organise, Paper, Planner,

Repairman, Reverse, Sales, Sanitary, Sapper, Scheme, Software, Sound, Stage, Usability, Wangle

England Albany, Albion, Blighty, John Bull, Merrie

English(man) Ang(le), Anglican, Brit, Bro talk, Canajan, E, Ebonics, Eng, Estuary, Gringo, Hiberno, John Bull, King's, Limey, Middle, Modern, Morningside, New Zealand, Nigerian, Norman, Officialese, Old, Oxford, Pidgin, Plain, Pom(my), Pommie, Pongo, Queen's, Rosbif, Sassenach, Saxon, Scotic, Scottish, Seaspeak, Shopkeeper, Singlish, Southron, Southroun, Spanglish, Standard, Wardour Street, Whingeing Pom, World

Engrave(r), Engraving Aquatint, Blake, Bury, Carve, Cerotype, Chalcography, Chase, Cut, Dry-point, Durer, Enchase, Etch, Glyptic, Glyptograph, Heliogravure, Hogarth, Impress, Inchase, Inciser, Inscribe, Intagliate, Lapidary, Mezzotint, Niello, Photoglyphic, Photogravure, Plate, Scrimshandy, Scrimshaw, Steel, Stillet, Stipple, Stylet, Stylography, Toreutics, Xylographer

Engross(ed) Absorb, Engage, Enwrap, Immerse, Inwrap, Monopolise, →**OCCUPY**, Preoccupy, Prepossess, Rapt, Rivet, Sink, Writ large

Enhance(r) Add, Augment, Better, Catalyst, Embellish, Exalt, Heighten, Improve, Intensify, Supplement

Enigma(tic) Charade, Conundrum, Dilemma, Gioconda, Gnomic, Mystery, Oracle, Poser, Problem, →**PUZZLE**, Quandary, Question, Rebus, Recondite, Riddle, Secret, Sphinxlike, Teaser

Enjoy(able), Enjoyment Apolaustic, Appreciate, Ball, Brook, Delectation, Fruition, Glee, Groove, Gusto, Have, High jinks, Lap up, Lekker, Like, Own, Palate, Pleasing, Possess, Relish, Ripping, Sair, Savour, Stonking, Taste, Wallow

Enlarge(ment), Enlarger Accrue, Acromegaly, Add, Aneurism, Aneurysm, Augment, Blow-up, Diagraph, Dilate, Exostosis, Expand, Expatiate, Explain, Increase, →**MAGNIFY**, Pan, Piece, Ream, Rebore, Sensationalize, Spavin, Swell, Telescope, Tumefy, Varicosity, Zoom

Enlighten(ed), Enlightenment Aufklarung, Awareness, Disabuse, Edify, Educate, Explain, Illumine, Instruct, Liberal, Luce, Nirvana, Relume, Revelation

Enlist Attest, Conscript, Draft, Engage, Enrol, Induct, Join, Levy, Prest, Recruit, Rope in, Roster, Sign on, Volunteer

Enliven(ed) Animate, Arouse, Brighten, Cheer, Comfort, Exhilarate, Ginger, Invigorate, Juice, Merry, Pep, Refresh, Warm

Enmity Animosity, Aversion, Bad blood, Hatred, Malice, Nee(d)le, Rancour

Ennoble(ment) Dub, Elevate, Exalt, Honour, Raise

Enormous Colossal, Exorbitant, Gargantuan, Giant, Gigantic, Googol, Hellacious, Huge, Humongous, Humungous, →**IMMENSE**, Jumbo, Mammoth, Mega, Vast, Walloper, Walloping

Enough Adequate, →**AMPLE**, Anow, Basta, Belay, Enow, Fill, Geyan, Nuff, Pax, Plenty, Qs, Sate, Satis, Sese, Sessa, Suffice, Sufficient, Via

Enquire, Enquiring, Enquiry Ask, Case, Check, Curious, Eh, Inquire, Organon, Public, Request, Research, Scan, See, Trial

Enrage(d) Bemad, →**INCENSE**, Inflame, Infuriate, Irate, Livid, Madden, Wild

Enrich Adorn, Endow, Enhance, Fortify, Fructify, Oxygenate

Enrol(ment) Attest, Conscribe, Conscript, Empanel, Enlist, Enter, Incept, →**JOIN**, List, Matriculate, Muster, Register

Ensign Ancient, Badge, Banner, Duster, Ens, →**FLAG**, Gonfalon, Officer, Pennon, Red, White

Enslave(ment) Bondage, Captivate, Chain, Yoke

Ensnare Illaqueate, →**TRAP**

Ensue, Ensuing Et sequens, Follow, Result, Succeed, Transpire

Ensure Check

Entangle(ment) Amour, Ball, Elf, Embroil, Encumber, Ensnarl, Entrail, Fankle, Implicate, →**KNOT**, Liaison, Mat, Ravel, Retiarius, Trammel

Enter, Entry Admit, Broach, Come, Enrol, Field, Infiltrate, Ingo, Insert, Intromit,

Invade, Item, Key in, Lodge, Log, Penetrate, Pierce, Post, Record, Slate, Submit, Table, Wild card

Enterprise, Enterprising Adventure, Ambition, Aunter, Dash, Emprise, Forlorn hope, Free, Goey, Go-getter, Gumption, Indie, Industry, Initiative, Plan, Private, Project, Public, Push, Spirit, Stunt, Venture

Entertain(er), Entertaining, Entertainment Acrobat, Afterpiece, All-dayer, All-nighter, Amphitryon, Amuse, Apres ski, Balladeer, Ballet, Barnum, Beguile, Bread and circuses, Bright lights, Burlesque, Busk, Cabaret, Carnival, Cater, Charade, Cheer, Circus, Comedian, Comic, Concert (party), Conjure, Consider, Cottabus, Crack, Craic, Cuddy, Distract, Divert, Divertissement, ENSA, Extravaganza, Fete (champetre), Fleshpots, Floorshow, Foy, Friendly lead, Fun, Gaff, Gala, Gas, Gaudy, Geisha, Gig, Harbour, Harlequin, Have, Hospitality, Host(ess), Impresario, Impressionist, Infotainment, Interest, Interlude, Intermezzo, Jester, Juggler, Karaoke, Kidult, Kursaal, Lap-dancer, Lauder, Leg-show, Levee, Liberace, Light, Masque, Melodrama, Mind candy, Minstrel, Movieoke, Musical, Music hall, Olio, Opera, Palladium, Panto, Pap, Party, Peepshow, Performer, Piece, Pierrot, Play, Pop singer, Reception, Recreation, Regale, Review, Revue, Rice, Ridotto, Rinky-dink, Roadshow, Rodeo, Rush, Serenade, Showbiz, Showgirl, Sideshow, Simulcast, Singer, Sitcom, Slapstick, Snake-charmer, Soirée, Son et lumière, Street theatre, Striptease, Table, Tamasha, Tattoo, Treat, Tumbler, Tummler, Variety, Vaudeville, Ventriloquist

Enthuse, Enthusiasm, Enthusiast(ic) Ardour, Buff, Bug, Cat, Cheerleader, Devotee, Ebullience, Ecstatic, Empresse, Energy, Fervid, Fiend, Fire, Flame, Freak, Furor(e), Geek, Get-up-and-go, Gung-ho, Gusto, Hearty, Hype, Into, Keen, Lyrical, Mad, Mane, Mania, Motivated, Muso, Oomph, Outpour, Overboard, Passion, Perfervid, Petrolhead, Rah-rah, Raring, Rave, Relish, Rhapsodise, Sold, Spirit, Verve, Warmth, Whacko, Whole-hearted, Young gun, Zealot, Zest

Entice(ment), Enticing Allure, Angle, Cajole, Carrot, Dangle, Decoy, Draw, Lure, Persuade, Seductive, →TEMPT, Tole, Toll, Trap, Trepan

Entire(ly), Entirety Absolute, All, Complete, Genuine, Intact, Integral, In toto, Lot, Purely, Root and branch, Systemic, Thorough, Total, →WHOLE

Entity Being, Body, Existence, Holon, Tao, Tensor, Thing, Transfinite

Entrail(s) Bowels, Giblets, Gralloch, Guts, Ha(r)slet, Humbles, Lights, Numbles, Offal, Tripe, Umbles, Viscera

Entrance(d), Entrant, Entry Access, Adit, Admission, Anteroom, Arch, Atrium, Attract, Avernus, Bewitch, Charm, Closehead, Contestant, Door, Doorstop, Double, Eye, Fascinate, Foyer, Gate, Ghat, Hypnotise, In-door, Infare, Inflow, Ingate, Ingress, Inlet, Jaws, Mesmerise, Mouth, Pend, Porch, Porogamy, Portal, Postern, Propylaeum, Propylon, Reception, Record, Registration, Single, Spellbound, Starter, Stem, Stoa, Stoma, Stulm, Throat

Entreat(y) Appeal, Ask, Beg, Beseech, Flagitate, Impetrate, Orison, Petition, Plead, Pray, Precatory, Prevail, Prig, Rogation, Solicit, Sue, Supplicate

Entrepreneur Branson, Businessman, E-tailer, Wheeler-dealer, Yettie

Entropy S

▶ **Entry** *see* **ENTRANCE(D)**

Entwine Complect, Impleach, Intervolve, Lace, Twist, Weave

Enumerate, Enumeration Catalogue, Count, List, Tell

Envelop(e) Corolla, Corona, Cover(ing), Enclose, Enshroud, Entire, Flight, Flown cover, Invest, Involucre, Muffle, Nuclear, Perianth, Sachet, Serosa, Shroud, Skin, Smother, Surround, Swathe, Wrap

Environment(s), Environmental(ist) ACRE, Ambience, Cyberspace, Entourage, Green(ie), Habitat, Milieu, SEPA, Setting, Sphere, Surroundings

Envoy Agent, Diplomat, Hermes, Legate, Plenipo(tentiary)

Epaulette Swab

Epic Aeneid, Ben Hur, Beowulf, Calliope, Colossal, Dunciad, Edda, Epopee, Gilgamesh, Homeric, Iliad, Kalevala, Lusiad(s), Mahabharata, Nibelungenlied, Odyssey, Ramayana, Saga

Epicure(an) Apicius, Connoisseur, Gastronome, Glutton, →GOURMAND, Gourmet, Hedonist, Sybarite

Epidemic Enzootic, Outbreak, Pandemic, Pestilence, Plague, Prevalent, Rampant, Rife

Epilogue Appendix, Coda, End, Postlude, Postscript

Epiphany Twelfthtide

Episode(s), Episodic Bipolar, Chapter, Incident, Microsleep, Page, Picaresque, Scene, Serial

Epistle(s) Catholic, Dispatch, General, Lesson, Letter, Missive, Pastoral

Epitome, Epitomise Abridge, Abstract, Avowal, Digest, Image, Model, Summary, Typify

Epoch Age, Era, Holocene, Miocene, Oligocene, Palaeocene, Period, Pleistocene, Pl(e)iocene

Equable, Equably Calm, Just, Placid, Smooth, Tranquil

Equal(ly), Equality, Equal quantities Across the board, Alike, All square, As, Balanced, Commensurate, Compeer, Co-partner, Egal(ity), Emulate, Equinox, Equiparate, Equity, Even, Even-steven, Ex aequo, Feer, Fe(a)re, Fiere, Fifty-fifty, For, Identical, Identity, Is, Iso-, Isocracy, Level, Level-pegging, Make, Match, Par, Parage, Parametric, Peregal, Rise, Rival, →SO, Square

Equate, Equation(s) Arrhenius, Balance, Chemical, Defective, Differential, Dirac, Identity, Nernst, Parametric, Quadratic, Reduce, Relate, Simultaneous

Equestrian Dressage, Eventer, Turfite

Equilibrium Balance, Composure, Homeostasis, Instable, Isostasy, Poise, Stasis, Tautomerism

Equine Hinny

Equip(ment), Equipage Accoutrement, Accustrement, Adorn, Apparatus, Apparel, Appliance, Array, Attire, Carriage, Clobber, Clothe, Deck, Dight, Expertise, →FURNISH, Gear, Get-up, Graith, Hand-me-up, Hardware, Headset, Hi-tech, Incubator, iPod®, Kit, Lie-detector, Material, Matériel, Monitor, Muniments, Outfit, Pile-driver, Plant, Receiver, Refit, Retinue, Rig, Sonobuoy, Stapler, Stereo, Stock, Stuff, Tabulator, Tack(le), Tool, Turn-out, Vision-mixer, Webcam

Equitable Fair, Just

Equivalence, Equivalent Akin, Amounting to, Correspondent, Dose, Equal, Same, Tantamount, Version

Equivocate Flannel, Lie, Palter, Prevaricate, Quibble, Tergiversate, Weasel

Era Age, Archaean, C(a)enozoic, Christian, Common, Cretaceous, Decade, Dynasty, Ediocaron, Epoch, Hadean, Hegira, Hej(i)ra, Hijra, Jurassic, Lias, Mesozoic, Period, Precambrian, Proterozoic, Torridonian

Eradicate, Erase Abolish, Delete, Demolish, Destroy, Dislimn, Efface, Expunge, Exterminate, Extirp, Obliterate, Purge, Root, Scratch, Strike out, Uproot

Eratosthenes Sieve

Erect(ion), Erector Boner, Build, Construct(ion), Elevate, Hard-on, Perpendicular, Priapism, Prick, Rear, Upend, Upright, Vertical

Ergo Argal, Hence, Therefore

Erode, Erosion Corrasion, Degrade, Denude, Destroy, Deteriorate, Detrition, Etch, Fret, Hush, Wash, Wear, Yardang

Eros, Erotic(a) Amatory, Amorino, Amorous, Aphrodisiac, Carnal, Cupid, Lascivious, Philtre, Prurient, Salacious, Steamy

Err(or) Aliasing, Anachronism, Bish, Blip, Blooper, Blunder, Boner, Boob(oo), Bug, Clanger, Comedy, Corrigendum, Execution, Fat-finger, Fault, Fluff, Glaring, Heresy, Hickey, Human, Inaccuracy, Inherited, K'thibh, Lapse, Lapsus, Literal, Misgo, Misprint, Misprise, Misprize, Misstep, →MISTAKE, Out, Parachronism, Probable, Recoverable, Rounding, Rove, Runtime, Sampling, Semantic, Sin, Slip, Slip-up, Solecism, Standard, Stray, Trip, Truncation, Type I, Type II, Typo, Typographical, Unforced

Errand Ance, Chore, Commission, Message, Mission, Once, Sleeveless, Task, Yince

Erratic Haywire, Planetary, Spasmodic, Temperamental, Vagary, Vagrant, Wayward, Whimsical

Erroneous False, Inaccurate, Mistaken, Non-sequitur

Erudite, Erudition Academic, Learned, Well-bred, Wisdom

Erupt(ion), Erupture Belch, Brash, Burst, Eject, Emit, →**EXPLODE**, Fumarole, Hives, Lichen, Mal(l)ander, Mallender, Outbreak, Outburst, Papilla, Plinian, Pustule, Rash

Escape(e), Escapade, Escapist Abscond, Adventure, Avoid, Bale out, Bolt, Bolthole, Breakout, Caper, Close call, Eject, Elope, Elude, Elusion, Esc, Eschewal, Evade, Exit, Fire, Flee, Flight, Fredaine, Frolic, Fugacity, Gaolbreak, Get-out, Hole, Hoot, Houdini, Houdini act, Hout, Lam, Lark, Leakage, Leg-it, Let-off, Levant, Lifeline, Loop(-hole), Meuse, Mews, Miss, Muse, Narrow, Near thing, Outlet, Prank, Refuge, Runaway, Scarper, Seep(age), Shave, Slip, Splore, Squeak, Vent, Walter Mitty

Escort Accompany, Arm candy, Attend, Beard, Bodyguard, Bring, Chaperone, Comitatus, Conduct, Convoy, Cortège, Corvette, Date, Destroyer, Entourage, Frigate, Gallant, Gigolo, Guard, Guide, Lead, Outrider, Protector, Retinue, See, Squire, Take, Tend, Usher, Walker

Esoteric Abstruse, Orphic, Rarefied, Recondite, Secret

Especial(ly) Chiefly, Esp, Espec, Outstanding, Particular

Espionage Industrial, Spying, Surveillance

Esprit Insight, Spirit, Understanding, Wit

Essay(s) Article, Attempt, Critique, Disquisition, Dissertation, Endeavour, Paper, Sketch, Stab, Study, Thesis, Tractate, Treatise, Try

Essayist Addison, Bacon, Columnist, Elia, Ellis, Emerson, Hazlitt, Holmes, Hunt, Huxley, Lamb, Locke, Montaigne, Pater, Prolusion, Ruskin, Scribe, Steele, Tzara, →**WRITER**

Essence Alma, Atman, Attar, Aura, Being, Core, Crux, Element, Entia, Esse, Extract, Fizzen, Flavouring, Flower, Foison, Gist, Heart, Hom(e)ousian, Inbeing, Inscape, Kernel, Marrow, Mauri, Mirbane, Myrbane, Nub, Nutshell, Ottar, Otto, Perfume, Per-se, Pith, Quiddity, Ratafia, Saul, Soul, Substance, Sum, Ylang-ylang

Essential(ly) Arabin, At heart, Basic, Central, Crucial, Entia, Formal, Fundamental, Imperative, In, Indispensable, Inherent, In se, Integral, Intrinsic, Kernel, Key, Lifeblood, Linch-pin, Marrow, Material, Mun, Must, Necessary, Need, Nitty-gritty, Nuts and bolts, Part-parcel, Per-se, Prana, Prerequisite, Quintessence, Radical, Requisite, Sine qua non, Soul, Vital, Whatness

Essex Roseland

Establish(ed) Abide, Anchor, Ascertain, Base, Bred-in-the-bone, Build, Chronic, Create, Deep-seated, Deploy, Embed, Enact, Endemic, Ensconce, Entrench, Erect, Evidence, Fix, →**FOUND**, Haft, Honoured, Imbed, Ingrain, Instal(l), Instate, Instil, Institute, Inveterate, Ordain, Pitch, Pre-set, Prove, Radicate, Raise, Redintegrate, Root(ed), Secure, Set, Stable, Standing, State, Stell, Substantiate, Trad, Trite, Valorise, Verify

Establishment Building, Business, CE, Church, Co, Concern, Creation, Hacienda, Household, Instauration, Institution, Lodge, Proving ground, Salon, School, Seat, Succursal, System, Traditional

Estate, Estate-holder Allod(ium), Alod, Assets, Campus, Car, Commons, Dais, Demesne, Domain, Dominant, Dowry, Est, Estancia, Fazenda, Fee-simple, Fee-tail, Fen, First, Fourth, General, Hacienda, Hagh, Haugh, Having, Hay, Housing, Industrial, Jointure, Land-living, Latifundium, Legitim, Life, Manor, Messuage, Odal, Patrimony, Pen, Personal(ity), Plantation, Press, Princedom, →**PROPERTY**, Real, Runrig, Situation, Spiritual, Standing, Talooka, Taluk(a), Temporal, Termer, Termor, Thanage, Trading, Udal

Esteem(ed), Estimable Account, Admiration, Appreciation, Count, Credited, Have, Honour, Izzat, Los, Precious, Prestige, Price, Pride, Prize, Rate, →**REGARD**, Respect, Revere, Store, Value, Venerate, Wonder, Worthy

▶**Estimable** *see* **ESTEEM(ED)**

Estimate, Estimation Appraise, Assess, Calculate, Carat, Conceit, Cost, Esteem, Extrapolation, Forecast, Gauge, Guess(timate), Opinion, Projection, Quotation, Rate, Rating, Reckon, Regard, Sight, Value, Weigh

Etch(ing) Aquafortis, Aquatint(a), Bite, →**ENGRAVE**, Incise, Inscribe

Eternal(ly), Eternity Aeonian, Ageless, All-time, Amarantine, Endless, Everlasting, Evermore, Eviternal, Ewigkeit, Forever, Immortal, Infinity, Never-ending, Perdurable, Perpetual, Sempiternal, Tarnal, Timeless, Triangle

Ether Atmosphere, Ch'i, Gas, Sky, Yang, Yin

Ethereal Airy, Delicate, Fragile, Heavenly, Nymph

Ethic(al), Ethics Deontics, Ideals, Marcionite, Moral, Principles, Situation

Ethiopia(n) African, Amharic, Asmara, Cushitic, Falasha, Geez, Kabele, Kebele, Ogaden

Etiquette Code, Conduct, Decorum, →**MANNERS**, Propriety, Protocol, Ps and Qs, Punctilious

Eucalyptus Blackbutt, Bloodwood, Cadaga, Cadagi, Coolabah, Gum-tree, Ironbark, Mallee, Marri, Morrell, Red gum, Sallee, Sally, Stringybark, Tallow wood, Tewart, Tooart, Tuart, Wandoo, White gum, Woolly butt

Euchre Jambone

Eunuch Ridg(e)ling, Rig

Euphonic Huge

Euphoria, Euphoric Buzz, Cock-a-hoop, Elation, High, Jubilation, Nirvana, Rapture, Rush

Europe(an) Andorran, Balt, Bohunk, Bosnian, Catalan, Community, Continent, Croat, E, Esth, Estonian, Faringee, Faringhi, Feringhee, Fleming, Hungarian, Hunky, Icelander, Japhetic, Lapp, Lett, Lithuanian, Magyar, Palagi, Polack, Ruthene, Ruthenian, Serb, Slavonian, Slovak, Slovene, Topi-wallah, Transleithan, Tyrolean, Vlach, Yugoslav

Evacuate, Evacuation Dunkirk, Excrete, Expel, Getter, Medevac, Movement, Planuria, Planury, Retreat, Scramble, Stercorate, Stool, Vent, Void, Withdraw

Evade, Evasion, Evasive Ambages, Avoid, Circumvent, Cop-out, Coy, Dodge, Duck, Elude, Escape, Fence, Fudge, Hedge, Jink, Loophole, Parry, Prevaricate, Quibble, Quillet, Quirk, Salvo, Scrimshank, Shifty, Shirk, Shuffling, Sidestep, Skive, Skrimshank, Stall, Subterfuge, Tergiversate, Waive, Weasel, Whiffler

Evaluate, Evaluation Appraise, Assess, Estimate, Gauge, Measure, Ponder, Rate, Review, Waid(e), Weigh

Evangelical, Evangelist(ical) Buchman, Clappy-doo, Converter, Crusader, Fisher, Godsquad, Gospeller, Graham, Happy-clappy, Hot gospeller, Jansen, Jesus freak, John, Luke, Marist, Mark, Matthew, Missioner, Moody, Morisonian, Peculiar, Preacher, Propagandist, Revivalist, Salvo, Sim(eonite), Stundist, Wild

Evaporate, Evaporation Condense, Dehydrate, Desorb, Disappear, Exhale, Steam, Steme, Ullage, Vaporise

Eve(ning) Nightfall, Postmeridian, Soirée, Subfusk, Sunset, Tib(b)s, Twilight, Vesperal, Vespertinal, Vigil, Watch night, Yester

Even(ly), Evenness Aid, Albe(e), Albeit, All, Average, Balanced, Clean, Drawn, Dusk, Een, Ene, Equable, Equal, Erev, Fair, Fair play, Flush, Iron, Level, Meet, Pair, Par, Plain, Plane, Plateau, Quits, Rib, Smooth, Square, Standardise, Temperate, Tie(d), Toss-up, Uniform, Yet

Even-handed Ambidextrous

Event(ing) Bash, Case, Circumstance, Cross-country, Discus, Dressage, Encaenia, Episode, Fest, Field, Fiesta, Function, Gymkhana, Happening, Heat, Incident, Landmark, Leg, Liquidity, Media, Meeting, Milestone, Occasion, Occurrence, Ongoing, Outcome, Pass, Rag-day, Regatta, Result, Show-jumping, Soirée, Three-ring circus, Time trial, Track

Eventual(ity), Eventually Case, Contingent, Finally, Future, In time, Later, Nd, Ultimate

Ever Always, Ay(e), Constantly, Eternal, Eviternity

Evergreen Abies, Ageless, Arbutus, Cembra, Cypress, Gaultheria, Golden lie, Holly, Ivy, Myrtle, Olearia, Periwinkle, Pinaster, Privet, Thuja, Thuya, Washington, Winterberry

Everlasting Cat's ear, Changeless, Enduring, Eternal, Immortal, Immortelle, Perdurable, Recurrent, Tarnal

Every(one), Everything All, A'thing, Catch-all, Complete, Each, Et al, Ilk(a), Sub chiz, Sum, The full monty, The works, Tout, Tout le monde, Universal, Varsal

Everyday Informal, Mundane, Natural, Ordinary, Plain, Routine

Everywhere Ambient, Omnipresent, Passim, Rife, Throughout, Ubique, Ubiquity, World

Evidence, Evident Adminicle, Apparent, Argument, Axiomatic, Circumstantial, Clear, Compurgation, Confessed, Credentials, Deposition, Direct, Distinct, DNA, Document, Empirical, Exemplar, Flagrant, Hearsay, Indicate, Internal, King's, Manifest, Marked, Material, Naked, Obvious, Overt, Plain, Premise, Prima facie, Probable, Proof, Queen's, Record, Sign, Smoking gun, State's, Surrebuttal, Testimony, Understandable

Evil Ahriman, Alastor, Amiss, Bad, Badmash, Bale, Beelzebub, Budmash, Corrupt, Curse, Depraved, Eale, Falling, Guilty, Harm, Hydra, Ill, Iniquity, Loki, Malefic, Malign, Mare, Mischief, Monstrous, Nasty, Necessary, Night, Perfidious, Rakshas(a), Satanic, Shrewd, Sin, Theodicy, Turpitude, Vice, Villainy, Wicked

Evince Disclose, Exhibit, Indicate, Show

▷ **Evolution** *may indicate* an anagram

Evolution(ary) Convergent, Countermarch, Development, Growth, Holism, Lamarck, Lysenkoism, Moner(on), Phylogeny, Turning

Evolve Speciate

Ex Former, Late, Quondam, Ten

Exacerbate Aggravate, Embitter, Exasperate, Inflame, Irritate, Needle

Exact(ing), Exactitude, Exactly Accurate, Authentic, Bang on, Careful, Dead, Definite, Due, Elicit, Estreat, Even, Exigent, Extort, Fine, Formal, It, Jump, Literal, Literatim, Mathematical, Meticulous, Nice(ty), On the nail, Pat, Point-device, → **PRECISE**, Require, Slap-bang, Spang, Specific, Spot-on, Strict, T, Verbatim

Exaggerate(d), Exaggeration Agonistic, Amplify, Boast, Brag, Camp, Colour, Distend, Dramatise, → **EMBROIDER**, Exalted, Goliathise, Hype, Hyperbole, Inflate, Magnify, Overdo, Overegg, Overpaint, Overpitch, Overplay, Overrate, Overstate, Overstretch, Over-the-top, Play up, Shoot a line, Stretch, Theatrical, Writ large

Exalt(ed), Exaltation Attitudes, Deify, Dignify, Elation, Enhance, Ennoble, Ensky, Enthrone, Erect, Extol, Glorify, High, Jubilance, Larks, Lofty, → **PRAISE**, Raise, Rapture, Sublime

Exam(ination), Examine, Examinee, Examiner A-level, Alnage, Analyse, Analyst, Assess, Audit, Autopsy, Baccalauréat, Biopsy, Case, Check-out, Check-up, Collate, Comb, Common Entrance, Concours, Consideration, Cross-question, CSE, Deposal, Depose, Disquisition, Dissect, Edexcel, Eleven plus, Entrance, Explore, Eyeball, Finals, GCE, GCSE, Going-over, Grade(s), Great-go, Greats, Gulf, Hearing, Higher, Inspect, Inter, Interrogate, Interview, Introspection, Jury, Laparoscopy, Local, Look, Mark, Matriculation, Medical, Mocks, Moderator, Mods, Mug, O-level, Once-over, Oral, Ordeal, Overhaul, Palp(ate), Paper, Peruse, Physical, Post-mortem, Prelims, Probe, Professional, Pry, Psychoanalyse, Pump, → **QUESTION**, Quiz, Ransack, Recce, Reconnaissance, Resit, Review, Sayer, Scan, Schools, Scope, Screen, Scrutineer, Scrutinise, Search, Seek, Sift, Sit, Smalls, Study, Survey, Sus(s), Test, Trial, Tripos, Try, Vet, Viva, Vivisection

Example Byword, Epitome, Erotema, Foretaste, → **FOR EXAMPLE**, Illustration, Instance, Lead, Lesson, Model, Monument, Paradigm, Paragon, → **PATTERN**, Praxis, Precedent, Prototype, Quintessence, Say, Shining, Showpiece, Specimen, Standard, Touchstone, Type, Typify

Excavate, Excavation, Excavator Burrow, Catacomb, Crater, Delf, Delph,

→**DIG**, Dike, Ditch(er), Dredge, Drift, Graft, Heuch, Heush, Hollow, JCB, Mine, Pioneer, Pioner, Power shovel, Quarry, Shaft, Sink, Sondage, Spade, Stope, Well

Excel(lence), Excellency, Excellent A1, Ace, Admirable, Awesome, Bangin(g), Bang on, Beat, Beaut, Beezer, Better, Blinder, Bodacious, Boffo, Bonzer, Booshit, Boss, Bravo, Brill, Bully, Capital, Champion, Cheese, Choice, Class(y), Classical, Cool, Corking, Crack, Crackajack, Crackerjack, Crucial, Cushty, Daisy, Def, Dic(k)ty, Dilly, Dominate, Doozy, Dope, Elegant, Excelsior, Exemplary, Eximious, Exo, Fab, Fabulous, Fantastic, First rate, Five-star, Goodly, Goodness, Great, HE, Hellacious, High, Humdinger, Hunky(-dory), Inimitable, Jake, Jammy, Kiff, Knockout, Laudable, Matchless, Mean, Mega-, Merit, Neat, Noble, Nonesuch, Olé, Out and outer, Outdo, Outstanding, Outstrip, Overdo, Overpeer, Paragon, Peachy, Peerless, Perfection, Prime, Pure, Quality, Rad, Rare, Rattling, Ring, Rinsin', Ripping, Ripsnorter, Shagtastic, →**SHINE**, Sick-dog, Sik, Slammin(g), Socko, Sound, Spanking, Spiffing, Stellar, Stonking, Stupendous, Sublime, Superb, Super-duper, Superior, Supernal, Supreme, Surpass, Swell, Terrific, Tip-top, Top flight, Top-hole, Topnotch, Topping, Tops, Virtue, Virtuoso, Wal(l)y, War, Way-out, Whizzo, Whizzy, Wicked, Worth

Exceptional Abnormal, Anomaly, Doozy, Egregious, Especial, Extraordinary, Extreme, Inimitable, Rare, Ripsnorter, Singular, Spanking, Special, Super, Unco(mmon), Unusual, Zinger

Excess(ive), Excessively All-fired, Almighty, Basinful, Binge, De trop, Epact, Exaggeration, Exorbitant, Extortionate, Extravagant, Flood, Fulsome, Glut, Hard, Inordinate, Lake, →**LAVISH**, Mountain, Needless, Nimiety, OD, Old, OTT, Outrage, Over, Overage, Overblown, Overcome, Overdose, Overkill, Overmuch, Overspill, Over-the-top, Owercome, Plethora, Preponderance, Profuse, Salt, Satiety, Spate, Spilth, Staw, Steep, Superabundant, Superfluity, Surplus, Surfeit, Surplus, Terrific, Thundering, Too, Troppo, Ultra, Undue, Unequal, Woundily

Exchange Baltic, Bandy, Banter, Barter, Bourse, Cambist, Cash, Catallactic, Change, Chop, Commodity, Commute, Confab, Contango, Convert, Cope, Corn, Ding-dong, Employment, Enallage, Excambion, Foreign, Global, Inosculate, Intercooler, Interplay, Ion, Labour, Logroll, →**MARKET**, Mart, Needle, Niffer, Paraphrase, PBX, Post, Quid pro quo, Rally, Rate, RE, Recourse, Redeem, Rialto, Royal, Scorse, Scourse, Sister-chromated, Stock, Swap, Switch, Swop, Telephone, Tolsel, Tolsey, Tolzey, →**TRADE**, Traffic, Transfusion, Transpose, Trophallaxis, Truck

▷**Excite(d)** *may indicate an anagram*

Excite(ment), Excitable, Excitability, Excited, Exciting Ablaze, Abuzz, Aerate, Aflutter, Agog, Amove, Amp, Animate, Apeshit, Aphrodisiac, Arouse, Athrill, Atwitter, Awaken, Brouhaha, Buck-fever, Climactic, Combustible, Commotion, Delirium, Dither, Electrify, Emove, Enthuse, Erethism, Eventful, Feisty, Fever, Fire, Flap, Frantic, Frenzy, Frisson, Furore, Fuss, Galvanise, Gas, Headiness, Heat, Hectic, Het, Hey-go-mad, Highly-strung, Hilarity, Hobson-Jobson, Hoopla, Hothead, Hyped, Hyper, Hypomania, Hysterical, Impel, Incite, Inebriate, Inflame, Intoxicate, Jimjams, Kick, Kindle, Liven, Maenad, Mania, Metastable, Must, Nappy, Neurotic, Oestrus, On fire, Orgasm, Overheat, Overwrought, Panic, Passion, Pride, Provoke, Racy, Radge, Red-hot, Rile, Roil, Ruff(e), Rut, Salutation, Send, Shivering, Spin, Splash, Spur, Startle, Stimulate, Stir(e), Suscitate, Suspense, Swashbuckling, Tense, Tetanoid, Tetany, Tew, Thrill, Tickle, Titillate, Turn-on, Twitter, Upraise, Waken, Whee, Whoopee, Work up, Yahoo, Yerk, Yippee, Yirk, Yoicks

Exclaim, Exclamation (mark) Ahem, Arrah, Aue, Begorra, Bliksem, Blurt, Bo, Ceas(e), Crikey, Criv(v)ens, Dammit, Ecphonesis, Eina, Eish, Ejaculate, Eureka, Expletive, Fen(s), Good-now, Haith, Heigh-ho, Hem, Hosanna, Inshallah, Interjection, Moryah, Omigod, Oof, Oops, Phew, Pish, Pow, Protest, Pshaw, Push, Uh-oh, Uh-uh, Unberufen, Whoops, Wirra, Yay, Yeehaw, Yippee, Yo-ho-ho, Yummy, Zounds

Exclave Cabinda

Exclude, Excluding, Exclusion Ban, Banish, Bar, Berufsverbot, Block, Competitive, Corner, Debar, Disbar, Eliminate, Ex, Except, Excommunicate, Ice out, Omit, Ostracise, Proscribe, Rule out, Upmarket

Excursion Airing, Cruise, Dart, Digression, Jaunt, Junket, Outing, Pleasure-trip, Railtour, Road, Sally, Sashay, Sortie, Tour, Trip

Excuse, Excusable Absolve, Alibi, Amnesty, Condone, Cop-out, Evasion, Exempt, Exonerate, Explain, Forgive, Gold brick, Hook, Let off, Mitigate, Occasion, Out, Overlook, Palliate, → **PARDON**, Plea, Pretext, Release, Venial, Viable, Whitewash

Execute(d), Executioner, Executive, Executor Accomplish, Administrate, Behead, Discharge, Finish, Fry, Gar(r)otte, Guardian, Hang, Headsman, Implement, Ketch, Kill, Koko, Literary, Lynch, Management, Martyr, Monsieur de Paris, Noyade, Official, Perform, Perpetrate, Pierrepoint, Politburo, Top, Tower Hill, Trustee

Exempt(ion) Dispensation, Exclude, Free, Immune, Impunity, Indemnity, Indulgence, Quarter, Spare, Tyburn ticket

▷ **Exercise(d)** *may indicate an anagram*

Exercise(s) Aerobics, Apply, Bench press, Burpee, Buteyko method, Cal(l)isthenics, Callanetics®, Chi kung, Chin-up, Circuit training, Cloze, Constitutional, Dancercise, Drill, Employ, Enure, Eurhythmics, Exert, Falun dafa, Falun gong, Fartlek, Five-finger, Floor, Gradus, Hatha yoga, Inure, Isometrics, Kata, Keepy-uppy, Lat spread, Lesson, Limber, Medau, Op, Operation, PE, Ply, Plyometrics, Practice, Practise, Preacher curl, Press-up, Prolusion, PT, Pull-up, Push-up, Qigong, Sadhana, Shintaido, Sit-up, Solfege, Solfeggi(o), Step (aerobics), Tae-Bo®, Tai chi (ch'uan), Thema, Theme, Thesis, Train, Trunk curl, Use, Warm-down, Warm-up, Wield, Work, Work-out, Xyst(us), Yogalates, Yomp

Exert(ion) Conatus, → **EFFORT**, Exercise, Labour, Operate, Strain, Strive, Struggle, Trouble, Wield

Exhaust(ed), Exhausting, Exhaustion, Exhaustive All-in, Backbreaking, Beaten, Beggar, Burn, Burn-out, Bushed, Clapped-out, Collapse, Consume, Deadbeat, Debility, Deplete, Detailed, Dissipate, Done, Drain, Effete, Emission, Empty, End, Enervate, Euchred, Fatigue, Flue, Fordo, Frazzle, Gruelling, Heat, Heatstroke, Jet-lagged, Jet-stream, Jiggered, Knacker, Mate, Milk, Out, Overtax, Peter, Play out, Poop, Powfagged, Prostrate, Puckerood, Rag, Ramfeezle, Rundown, Sap, Shatter, Shot, Shotten, Spend, Spent, Stonkered, Tailpipe, Tax, Tire, Use, Used up, Washed-up, Wasted, Waygone, → **WEARY**, Wind, Worn, Zonked

Exhibition (centre), Exhibit(ing), Exhibitionist, Exhibitioner Aquashow, Bench, Circus, Concours, Demo, Demonstrate, Demy, Diorama, Discover, Display, ENC, Endeictic, Evince, Expo, Expose, Extrovert, Fair, Hang, Indicate, Installation, Lady Godiva, NEC, Olympia, Pageant, Panopticon, Parade, Present, Retrospective, Rodeo, Salon, Scene, Show(piece), Show-off, Showplace, Sideshow, Stand, Viewing, Waxworks, Zoo

Exigency, Exigent Demanding, Emergency, Pressing, Taxing, Urgent, Vital

Exile Adam, Babylon, Ban, Banish, Deport, Deportee, Eject, Emigré, Eve, Expatriate, Exul, Galut(h), Ostracise, Outlaw, Relegate, Tax, Wretch

Exist(ence), Existing Be(ing), Corporeity, Dwell, Enhypostasia, Entelechy, Esse, Extant, Haecceity, Identity, Inbeing, Inherent, Life, Lifespan, Live, Ontology, Perseity, Solipsism, Status quo, Substantial, Ubiety

Exit Débouché, Door, Egress, Emergency, Exhaust, Gate, Leave, Outgate, Outlet, Swansong, Vent, Vomitory

Exodus Book, Departure, Flight, Hegira, Hejira, Passover

Exorbitant Excessive, Expensive, Slug, Steep, Tall, Undue

Exotic Alien, Chinoiserie, Ethnic, Foreign, Outlandish, Strange

Expand(able), Expanse, Expansion Amplify, Boom, Bulking, Develop, Diastole, Dilate, Distend, Ectasis, Elaborate, → **ENLARGE**, Escalate, Grow, Increase, Magnify, Ocean, Outstretch, Snowball, Sprawl, Spread, Stretch, Swell, Tensile, Vastitude, Wax, Wire-draw

Expatiate Amplify, Descant, Dwell, Enlarge, Perorate

Expect(ant), Expectation, Expected, Expecting Agog, Anticipate, Ask, Await, Due, Foresee, Gravid, Hope, Imminent, Lippen, Look, Natural, On cue,

Par, Pip, Predict, Pregnant, Presume, Probable, Prognosis, Prospect, Require, →SUPPOSE, Tendance, Think, Thought, Usual, Ween

Expedient Advisable, Artifice, Contrivance, Dodge, Fend, Make-do, Makeshift, Measure, Politic, Resort, Resource, Salvo, Shift, Stopgap, Suitable, Wise

Expedite, Expedition, Expeditious Advance, Alacrity, Anabasis, Celerity, Crusade, Dispatch, Excursion, Field trip, Hasten, Hurry, Kon-Tiki, Mission, Pilgrimage, Post-haste, Rapidity, Safari, Speed, Trek, Trip, Turn out, Voyage, Warpath

Expel Amove, Deport, Dispossess, Egest, Evacuate, Evict, Excommunicate, Excrete, Exile, Exorcize, Hoof, Oust, Out(cast), Spit, Turn forth, Void

Expend(iture) Budget, Consume, Cost, Dues, Oncost, Outgo(ing), Outlay, Poll, Squander, Tithe, Toll, Use

Expense(s) Boodle, Charge, Cost, Exes, Fee, Housekeeping, Law, Oncost, Outgoing, Outlay, Overhead, Price, Sumptuary

Expensive Chargeful, Costly, Dear, Executive, Ruinous, Salt, Steep, Top dollar, Upmarket, Valuable

Experience(d) Accomplished, A posteriori, Assay, Blasé, Come up, Discovery, Empiric, Encounter, Expert, →FEEL, Felt, Foretaste, Freak-out, Gust, Hands-on, Hard way, Have, Incur, Know, Learn, Live, Mature, Meet, Mneme, Old hand, Pass, Plumb, Seasoned, See, Senior, Sense, Sensory, Spin, Stager, Stand, Street-smart, Streetwise, Taste, Transference, Trial, Trip, Trocinium, Try, Undergo, Versed, Veteran, Work, Worldly wise

Experiment(al) Attempt, Aufgabe, Avant-garde, Ballon d'assai, Empirical, Essay, Gedanken, →JET, Michelson-Morley, Peirastic, Pilot, Sample, Shy, Single-blind, Taste, Tentative, →TRIAL, Trial balloon, Try, Venture

Expert(ise) Able, Accomplished, Ace, Adept, Adroit, Arch, Astacologist, Au fait, Authority, Boffin, Buff, Cambist, Cocker, Cognoscente, Competent, Connoisseur, Crack, Dab(ster), Dab hand, Dan, Deft, Demon, Diagnostician, Digerati, Don, Egghead, Fancier, Fundi, Gourmet, Gun, Hotshot, Karateka, Know-all, Know-how, Learned, Luminary, Maestro, Masterly, Mastery, Maven, Mavin, Meister, Nark, Old hand, Oner, Oneyer, Oneyre, Oracle, Peritus, Practised, Pro, Proficient, Pundit, Ringer, Rubrician, Savvy, Science, Skill(y), Sly, Specialist, Techie, Technique, Technocrat, Technofreak, Technophile, Tipster, Ulema, Used, Whizz, Wireman, Wisard, W(h)iz, Wizard, Wonk

Expire(d), Expiry Blow, Collapse, Croak, →DIE, End, Exhale, Go, Invalid, Ish, Lapse, Neese, Pant, →PERISH, Sneeze, Terminate

Explain(able), Explanation Account, Annotate, Aperçu, Appendix, Clarify, Conster, Construe, Decline, Define, Describe, Eclaircissement, Elucidate, Epexegesis, Expose, Expound, Extenuate, Gloss, Glossary, Gloze, Justify, Outline, Parabolize, Salve, Solve, Tell, Upknit, Why

Explanation, Explanatory Apology, Commentary, Exegesis, Exegetic, Exposition, Farse, Gloss, Gloze, Hypothesis, Key, Note, Preface, Reading, Rigmarole, Solution, Theory

Expletive Arrah, Darn, Exclamation, Oath, Ruddy, Sapperment

Explicit Clean-cut, Clear(-cut), Definite, Express, Frank, Graphic, Outspoken, →PRECISE, Specific, Unequivocal

Explode, Explosion, Explosive Agene, Airburst, Amatol, Ammonal, Aquafortis, Backfire, Bang(er), Bangalore torpedo, Big bang, Blast, Blow-out, Booby-trap, Burst, C4, Cap, Cheddite, Chug, Controlled, Cordite, Cramp, Crump, Cyclonite, Debunk, Demolitions, Depth bomb, Detonate, Dualin, Dunnite, Dust, Erupt, Euchlorine, Fiery, Fireball, Firecracker, Firedamp, Firework, Flip, Fulminant, Fulminate, Gasohol, Gelatine, Gelignite, Glottal stop, Grenade, Guncotton, Gunpaper, Gunpowder, HE, Initiator, Jelly, Landmine, Low, Megaton, Melinite, Mine, Nail-bomb, Napalm, Nitre, Nitro(glycerine), Nitrobenzene, Nitrocotton, Outburst, Payload, Petar(d), Petre, Phreatic, Plastic, Plastique, Pop, Pow, Propellant, Roburite, SAM, Saucisse, Semtex®, Sheet, Shrapnel, Snake, Squib, TATP, Tetryl, Thermite, Thunderflash, Tinderbox, TNT, Tonite, Trinitrobenzene, Trotyl, Volatile, Volcanic, Warhead, Xyloidin(e)

Explore(r), Exploration Bandeirante, Chart, Discover, Dredge, Examine, Feel,

Investigate, Map, Navigator, Pathfinder, Pioneer, Potholer, Probe, Research, Scout, Search, Spaceship, Voyageur

▷ **Explosive** *may indicate* an anagram

Exponent Advocate, Example, Index, Interpreter, Logarithm

Expose(d), Exposure Adamic, Air, Anagogic, Bare, Bleak, Blot, Blow, Burn, Crucify, Debag, Debunk, Denude, Desert, Disclose, Double, Endanger, En prise, Exhibit, Flashing, Glareal, Indecent, Insolate, Liable, Moon, Nail, Nude, Object, Open, Out, Over, Paramo, Propale, Reveal, Showdown, Snapshot, Starkers, Streak, Strip, Subject, Sun, Time, Uncover, Unmask, Unrip, Unshroud, Windburn, Windswept

Expound(er) Discourse, Discuss, Exegete, Explain, Open, Prelict, Red, Scribe, Ulema

Express(ed), Expression, Expressionism, Expressive Abstract, Air, APT, Arrah, Aspect, Breathe, Cacophemism, Circumbendibus, Cliché, Colloquialism, Conceive, Concetto, Couch, Countenance, Crumbs, Declare, Denote, Eloquent, Embodiment, Epithet, Estafette, Explicit, Face, Fargo, Flying Scotsman, Formulate, Function, Godspeed, Good-luck, Gotcha, Gup, Hang-dog, Hech, Heck, Hell's bells, Idiom, Isit, Limited, Locution, Lyrical, Manifest, Metonym, Mien, Mot (juste), Neologism, Non-stop, Orient, Paraphrase, Phrase, Pleonasm, Pony, Precise, Pronouncement, Pronto, Put, Quep, Rapid, Register, Say(ne), Shade, Show, Soulful, → **SPEAK**, State, Strain, Succus, Sumpsimus, Taxeme, Term, Token, Tone, Topos, Trope, Utterance, Vent, → **VOICE**

Expressionless Blank, Deadpan, Glassy, Impassive, Inscrutable, Po(ker)-faced, Vacant, Wooden

Expulsion Abjection, Discharge, Eccrisis, Ejection, Eviction, Exile, Pride's Purge, Removal, Sacking, Synaeresis

Extempore, Extemporise(d) Ad lib, Autoschediasm, Improvise, Pong

Extend(ed), Extension Aggrandise, Aspread, Augment, Cremaster, Dendrite, Draw, Drop-leaf, Ecarté, Eke, Elapse, Elongate, Enlarge, Escalate, Expand, Exsert, Extrapolation, Fermata, Grow, Increase, Lanai, Leaf, Length, Long, Long-range, Long-stay, Long-term, Offer, Outgrowth, Overbite, Overlap, Pong, Porrect, Proffer, Prolong, Propagate, Protract, Reach, Renew, Retrochoir, Span, Spread, Steso, → **STRETCH**, Substantial, Vert, Widen

Extensive, Extent Acre, Ambit, Area, Capacious, Catch-all, Compass, Comprehensive, Degree, Distance, Far-reaching, Large, Length, Limit, Outspread, Panoramic, Range, Reach, Scale, Scope, Size, Spacious, Sweeping, Wholesale, Wide, Widespread

Exterior Aspect, Crust, Derm, Exoteric, Facade, Outer, → **OUTSIDE**, Shell, Surface, Veneer

External Exoteric, Exterior, Extraneous, Foreign, Outer

Extinguish Douse, Dout, Dowse, Extirpate, Obscure, Quash, Quell, Quench, Slake, Slo(c)ken, Snuff, Stifle, Suppress

Extra Accessory, Additament, Addition(al), Additive, Adjunct, And, Annexe, Attachment, Bisque, Bonus, By(e), Codicil, Debauchery, Encore, Etcetera, Frill, Further, Gash, Lagniappe, Left-over, Leg bye, Make-weight, Mo, More, Nimiety, No ball, Odd, Optional, Out, Over, Perk, Plus, Plusage, Reserve, Ripieno, → **SPARE**, Spilth, Staffage, Sundry, Super, Superadd, Supernumerary, Supplementary, Suppletive, Surplus, Top up, Trop, Undue, Walking-gentleman, Walking-lady, Wide, Woundy

Extract(ion), Extractor Bleed, Breeding, Catechu, Clip, Corkscrew, Decoction, Descent, Distil, Draw, Educe, Elicit, Essence, Excerpt, Extort, Gist, Gobbet, Insulin, Liebig, Malta, Parentage, Passage, Pick, Piece, Prize, Pry, Quintessence, Quotation, Render, Smelt, Snippet, Soundbite, Succus, Suck, Summary, Tap, Tincture, Trie, Try, Vanilla, Vegemite®, Winkle, Worm, Wring

Extraordinary Amazing, Egregious, Humdinger, Important, Non(e)such, Phenomenal, Preternatural, Rare, Signal, Singular, Sorter, Startling, Strange, Unusual

Extrasensory Clairaudience, Clairvoyance, → **ESP**

Extra time Lean

Extravagance, Extravagant, Extravaganza Bizarre, Dissipation, Elaborate,

Enthusiasm, Excessive, Fancy, Feerie, Flamboyant, Heroic, High-flown, High roller, Hyperbole, Immoderate, Lavish, Luxury, Outré, Prodigal, Profuse, Rampant, Reckless, Riotise, Splash, Splurge, Squander, Sumptuous, Superfluous, Waste

▷ **Extreme** *may indicate* a first or last letter

Extreme(s), Extremely, Extremist, Extremity Acute, All-fired, Almighty, Butt, Desperate, Die-hard, Drastic, Edge, Exceptional, Farthermost, Gross, In spades, →**INTENSE**, Major, Maximum, Mega-, Merveilleux, Militant, Minimum, National Front, Opposite, OTT, Over the top, Parlous, Pretty, Radical, Remote, Solstice, Sublime, Tendency, Terminal, The last cast, Tip, Too, Tremendous, Ultimate, Ultra, Utmost, Utter(ance), →**VERY**, Violent, Vitally, Wing

Exuberance, Exuberant Brio, Copious, Ebullient, Effusive, Feisty, Flamboyant, Gleeful, Gusto, Hearty, Joie de vivre, Lavish, Mad, Overflowing, Profuse, Rumbustious, Skippy, Streamered

Exult(ant) Crow, Elated, →**GLOAT**, Glorify, Jubilant, Paeonic, Rejoice, Tripudiate, Triumphant, Whoop

Eye(d), Eyes, Eye-ball, Eyeful, Eye movement, Eyepiece Aperture, Evil, Glass, Goggles, Iris, Jack, Keek, Klieg, Lamp, Lazy, Lens, Magic, Mincepie, Mind's, Naked, →**OBSERVE**, Ocellar, Ogle, Optic, Orb, Peeper, PI, Pupil, Regard, Retina, Roving, Saccade, Saucer, Sheep's, Sight, Spy, Stemma, Uvea, Watch, Weather, Windows

Eyesore Blot, Carbuncle, Disfigurement, Sty(e)

Eye trouble Amblyopia, Ametropia, Anirida, Aniseikonia, Anisomatropia, Asthenopia, Astigmatism, Cataract, Ceratitis, Coloboma, Detached retina, Diplopia, Ectropion, Ectropium, Entropion, Exophthalmus, Glaucoma, Hemeralopia, Hemi(an)op(s)ia, Hypermetropia, Iritis, Keratitis, Leucoma, Lippitude, Micropsia, Miosis, Mydriasis, Myosis, Nebula, Nyctalopia, Nystagmus, Presbyopia, Proptosis, Ptosis, Retinitis, Scotoma(ta), Stigmatism, Strabismus, Synechia, Teichopsia, Thylose, Thylosis, Trachoma, Tritanopia, Tylosis, Wall-eye, Xeroma, Xerophthalmia

Ff

F Fahrenheit, Fellow, Feminine, Fluorine, Following, Force, Foxtrot

Fable(s) Aesop, Allegory, Apologue, Exemplum, Fiction, Hitopadesa, La Fontaine, Legend, Lie, Marchen, Milesian, Myth, Panchatantra, Parable, Romance, Tale

Fabric Acetate, →CLOTH, Dévoré, Evenweave, Framework, Interfacing, Interlining, Orlon®, Plissé, Ripstop, Spandex, Stretch-knit, Textile, Velour

Fabricate, Fabrication Artefact, Concoct, Construct, Contrive, Cook, Fake, Figment, Forge, →INVENT, Lie, Make up, Porky, Trump, Weave, Web

Fabulous (beast), Fabulous place Chimera, Cockatrice, Eldorado, Fictitious, Fung, Gear, Incredible, Jabberwock(y), Legendary, Magic, Manticore, Merman, Mythical, Orc, Phoenix, Roc, Romantic, Sphinx, Unicorn, Unreal, Wyvern

Face, Facing Abide, Affront, Ashlar, Ashler, Aspect, Audacity, Bide, Bold, Brave, Brazen, Caboched, Caboshed, Cheek, Chiv(v)y, Cliff, Coal, Confront, Countenance, Culet, Dalle, Dare, Dartle, Deadpan, Dial, Eek, Elevation, Encounter, Facade, Fat, Favour, Features, Fineer, Fortune, →FRONT, Gardant, Girn, Gonium, Grid, Groof, Groue, Grouf, Grufe, Gurn, Hatchet, Head-on, Jib, Kisser, Light, Lining, Look, Lore, Mascaron, Meet, Metope, Moe, Mug, Mush, Obverse, Oppose, Opposite, Outstare, Outward, Pan, Paper tiger, Pavilion, Phisnomy, Phiz(og), Physiognomy, Poker, Puss, Revet, Revetment, Roughcast, Rud, Rybat, Side, Snoot, Socle, Straight, Stucco, Tallow, Three-quarter, Type, Veneer, Vis(age), Visnomy, Wall, Withstand, Zocco(lo)

Facetious Frivolous, Jocose, Jocular, Waggish, Witty

Facile Able, Adept, Complaisant, Ductile, Easy, Fluent, Glib

Facilitate, Facilities, Facility Amenity, Assist, Benefit, Capability, Committed, →EASE, Expedite, Fluency, Gift, ISO, Knack, Lavatory, Loo, Provision, Skill

Fact(s), Factual Actual, Brass tacks, Case, Correct, Data, Datum, Detail, Eo ipso, French, Gospel, In esse, Info, Information, Literal, Mainor, Material, Nay, Poop, Really, Stat, Statistics, Truism, Truth, Veridical, Yes

Faction Bloc, Cabal, Camp, Caucus, Clique, Contingent, Group(let), Junto, Party, Schism, Sect, Tendency, Wing

Factor(s) Agent, Aliquot, Broker, Cause, Chill, Clotting, Coagulation, Co-efficient, Common, Divisor, Edaphic, Element, F, Feedback, Feel-bad, Feel-good, Fertility, Growth, House, Imponderabilia, Institorial, Intrinsic, Judicial, Load, Modulus, Multiple, Power, Pull, Q, Quality, Reflection, Representative, Rh, Rhesus, Risk, Safety, Sex, Steward, Transfer, Unit, Utilization, Wind chill, X

Factory Ashery, Bakery, Brickworks, Cannery, Etruria, Gasworks, Glassworks, Hacienda, Ironworks, Maquiladora, Mill, Plant, Refinery, Sawmill, Shot tower, Steelworks, Sugarhouse, Sweatshop, Tanyard, Tinworks, Wireworks, Works, Workshop

Faculty Aptitude, Arts, Capacity, Department, Ear, Ease, Indult, Knack, Lavatory, Loo, Moral, Power, School, Sense, Speech, →TALENT, Teachers, Uni(versity), Wits

Fad(dish) Crank, Craze, Cult, Fashion, Foible, Ismy, Thing, Vogue, Whim

Fade(d), Fading Blanch, Die, Diminuendo, Dinge, Disperse, Elapsion, Etiolate, Evanescent, Fall, Filemot, Lessen, Mancando, Miffy, Pale, Passé, Perdendo(si), Peter, Smorzando, Smorzato, Stonewashed, Vade, Vanish, Wallow, Wilt, Wither

Fag(ging) Chore, Cigarette, Drag, Drudge, Fatigue, Gasper, Homosexual, Menial, Quean, Reefer, Snout, Tire, Toil, Weary

Fail(ing), Failure Achalasia, Ademption, Anile, Anuria, Awry, Backfire, Blemish, Blow, Bomb, Bummer, Burst-up, Cark, Chicken, →COLLAPSE, Common-mode,

Conk, Crack up, Crash, Cropper, Debacle, Decline, Defalcation, Default, Defeat, Defect, Demerit, Demise, Die, Dog, Down the tubes, Dry, Dud, Fatigue, Fault, Feal, Fiasco, Fink out, Flame out, Flivver, Flop, Flow, Flunk, Fold, Founder, Frost, Glitch, Goner, Go phut, Gutser, Impotent, Infraction, Isn't, Lapse, Lemon, Lose, Lossage, Malfunction, Manqué, Meltdown, Mis-, Miscarry, Misfire, Misprision, Miss, Muff, Nerd, No-hoper, No-no, No-show, Omission, Omit, Outage, Oversight, Pip, Plough, Plow, Pluck, Pratfall, Reciprocity, Refer, Refusal, Respiratory, Shambles, Short(coming), Short circuit, Shortfall, Sink, Slippage, Smash, Spin, Stumer, Tank, Turkey, Vice, Wash-out, Waterloo, Weakness, White elephant, Wipeout

Faint(ness) Black-out, Conk, Darkle, Dim, Dizzy, Dwalm, Fade, Giddy, Lassitude, Pale, Stanck, Swarf, Swarve, Swelt, Swerf, Swerve, Swoon, Swound, Syncope, Unclear, Wan, Whitish

Fair Aefauld, Aefwld, A(e)fald, Barnet, Bartholomew, Bazaar, Beauteous, Belle, Blond, Bon(n)ie, Bonny, Brigg, Clement, Decent, Donnybrook, Eirian, Equal, Equitable, Evenhanded, Exhibition, Fancy, Feeing-market, →FESTIVAL, Fête, Fine, Fiona, Funfair, Gaff, Gay, Gey, Goose, Gwyn, Hiring, Honest, Hopping, Isle, Isold(e), →JUST, Kermess, Kermis, Kirmess, Light, Market, Mart, Mediocre, Mela, Mop, Nundinal, Objective, OK, Paddington, Passable, Play, Pro rata, Rosamond, Sabrina, So-so, Sportsmanlike, Square, Statute, Straight, Tavistock, Tidy, Tolerable, Tow-headed, Trade, Tryst, Unbias(s)ed, Vanity, Wake, Widdicombe, Xanthe

Fairly Clearly, Enough, Evenly, Midway, Moderately, Pari passu, Pretty, Properly, Quite, Ratherish, So-so

Fairy, Fairies Banshee, Befana, Brownie, Cobweb, Dobbie, Dobby, Elf(in), Fay, Gloriana, Good neighbour, Hob, Hop o' my thumb, Leprechaun, Lilian, Mab, Morgane(tta), Morgan le Fay, Moth, Mustardseed, Nis, Oberon, Peri, Pigwidgin, Pigwiggen, Pisky, Pixie, Pouf, Puck, Punce, Queen Mab, Sandman, Spirit, Sprite, Sugar-plum, Tink(erbell), Titania, Tooth, Urchin-shows

Faith(ful) Accurate, Achates, Belief, Constant, Creed, Cupboard, Devoted, Doctrine, Faix, Fay, Feal, Fegs, Fideism, Fiducial, Haith, Implicit, Islam, Lay, Liege, Loyal, Pantheism, Plerophory, Puritanism, Quaker, Reliance, Religion, Shema, Solifidian, Staunch, Strict, Troth, →TRUE, True-blue, Trust, Truth, Umma(h), Vera

Fake(d), Faker, Faking Bodgie, Bogus, Charlatan, Cod, Copy, Counterfeit, Duff(er), Ersatz, False, Fold, Forgery, Fraud, Fudge, Imitation, Imposter, Impostor, Paste, Phoney, Pirate(d), Postiche, Pretend, Pseudo, Sham, Spurious, Straw man, Toy, Trucage, Trumped up, Truquage, Truqueur, Unreal

Falcon Cast, Gentle, Hawk, Hobby, Kestrel, Lanner(et), Merlin, Nankeen kestrel, Nyas, Peregrine, Prairie, Saker, Sakeret, Sparrow-hawk, Stallion, Staniel, Stannel, Stanyel, Stone, Tassel-gentle, Tassell-gent, Tercel-gentle

Fall(s), Fallen, Falling, Fall out Abate, Accrue, Alopecia, Angel, Anticlimax, Arches, Astart, Autumn, Boyoma, Cadence, Caducous, Cascade, Cataract, Chute, Collapse, Crash, Cropper, Cross press, Declension, Decrease, Degenerate, Descent, Dip, Domino effect, Douse, Downswing, Dowse, →DROP, Ebb, Firn, Flop, Flump, Folding press, Free, Grabble, Gutser, Gutzer, Horseshoe, Idaho, Iguaçu, Incidence, Kabalega, Kaieteur, Keel over, Lag, Landslide, Lapse, Lin(n), Montmorency, Mtarazi, Niagara, Oct(ober), Overbalance, Owen, Perish, Plonk, Plummet, Plump, Plunge, Precipitance, Prolapse, Ptosis, Purl(er), Rain, Reaction, Relapse, Ruin, Season, Sheet, Sin, Sleet, Slide, Slip, Snow, Spill, Sutherland, Swallow, Tailor, Takakkau, Topple, Toss, Trip, Tugela, Tumble, Victoria, Voluntary, Wipeout, Yosemite

Fallacious, Fallacy Elench(us), Error, Idolon, Idolum, Illogical, Illusion, Pathetic, Sophism, Unsound

▷ **Falling** *may indicate* an anagram or a word backwards

False, Falsify, Falsification, Falsehood Adulterate, Assumed, Bastard, Bodgie, Bogus, Braide, Bricking, Bum, Calumny, Canard, Cavil, Charlatan, Cook, Counterfeit, Deceitful, Disloyal, Dissemble, Doctor, Façade, Fake, Feigned, Fiddle, Forge, Illusory, Knave, Lying, Meretricious, Misconception, Mock, Mooncalf, Mooncall, Myth, Obreption, Perjury, Pinchbeck, Postiche, Pretence, Pseudo, Refute,

Roorback, Sham, Specious, Spoof, Spurious, Strumpet, Treacherous, Trumped-up, Two-faced, Untrue

Fame, Famous A-list, All-star, Bruit, Cause célèbre, Celebrity, Distinguished, Eminent, Five, Glitterati, Gloire, Glory, Greatness, History, Humour, Illustrious, Known, Kudos, Legendary, Luminary, Luminous, Megastar, Mononym, Name, Noted, Notorious, Prestige, Reclamé, Renown, Repute, Robert, Rumour, Splendent, Spotlight, Spur, Stardom, Word

Familiar(ise), Familiarity Accustom, Acquaint, Assuefaction, Au fait, Auld, Chummy, Comrade, Consuetude, Conversant, Couth, Crony, Dear, Demon, Easy, Free, Fresh, Friend, Habitual, Homely, Homey, Incubus, Intimate, Known, Liberty, Maty, Old, Old-hat, Privy, Python, Streetwise, Used, Versant, Versed, Warhorse

Family Ainga, Ancestry, Bairn-team, Blood, Breed, Clan, Class, Cognate, Consanguine, County, Descent, Dynasty, Extended, Eye, Hapsburg, House(hold), Issue, Kin, Kind, Kindred, Line, Mafia, Medici, Name, Nuclear, Orange, People, Phratry, Progeny, Quiverful, Race, Roots, Sept, Sib(b), Sibship, Single-parent, Stem, Stirps, Storge, Strain, Sub-order, Syndyasmian, Taffy, Talbot, Totem, Tribe

Famine Dearth, Lack, Scarcity

▷ **Famished** *may indicate an 'o' in the middle of a word*

▷ **Fan** *may indicate an anagram*

Fan(s), Fan-like Adherent, Admirer, Aficionado, Alligator, Alluvial, Arouse, Bajada, Barmy-army, B-boy, Blow, Cat, Clapper, Claque, Colmar, Cone, Cool, Cuscus, Devotee, Diadrom, Dryer, Ducted, Enthusiast, Extractor, Fiend, Flabellum, Following, Goth, Grebo, Groupie, Groupy, Headbanger, Hepcat, Khuskhus, Muso, Outspread, Partisan, Popette, Propellor, Public, Punka(h), Rhipidate, Ringsider, Rooter, Sail, Spread, Supporter, Tail, Tartan army, Tifosi, Trekkie, Ventilate, Votary, Voteen, Washingtonia, Wing, Winnow, Zealot, Zelant

Fanatic(al) Bigot, Boatie, Devotee, Energumen, Enthusiastic, Extremist, Fiend, Frenetic, Glutton, Mad, Maniac, Nut, Partisan, Phrenetic, Picard, Rabid, Santon, Ultra, Workaholic, Wowser, Zealot

Fancy, Fancies, Fanciful Caprice, Chim(a)era, Conceit, Concetto, Crotchet, Daydream, Dream, Dudish, Elaborate, Fangle, Fantasy, Fit, Flam, Florid, Flowery, Frilly, Frothy, Guess, Hallo, Idea(te), Idolon, →**IMAGINE**, Inclination, I say, Itch, Lacy, Liking, Maggot, Maya, Mind, My, Nap, Notion, Opine, Ornamental, Ornate, Petit four, Picture, Pipe dream, Predilection, Preference, Reverie, Rococo, Suppose, Thought, Unreal, Urge, Vagary, Visionary, Ween, Whigmaleerie, Whigmaleery, Whim(sy), Woolgather

▷ **Fancy** *may indicate an anagram*

Fanfare Flourish, Sennet, Show, Tantara, Trump, Tucket

Fantasist, Fantasy, Fantastic Absurd, Amazing, Antic, Bizarre, Brilliant, Caprice, Centaur, Chimera, Cloud-cuckoo land, Cockaigne, Cockayne, Escapism, Fab, Fanciful, First class, Grotesque, Hallucination, Idola, Illusion, Kickshaw(s), Lucio, Make believe, Mega, Myth, Outré, Phantasmagoria, Pipe-dream, Queer, Reverie, Romance, Schizoid, Transcendent, Unreal, Untrue, →**WHIM**, Whimsical, Wild, Wishful thinking, Wuxia

Far Apogean, Away, Distal, Distant, Eloi(g)n, Extreme, Outlying, Remote, Thether, Thither

Fare Apex, Charge, Cheer, Commons, Do, Eat, →**FOOD**, Go, Passage, Passage money, Passenger, Rate, Saver, Table, Traveller

Farewell Adieu, Adios, Aloha, Apopemptic, Bye, Cheerio, Departure, Godspeed, →**GOODBYE**, Leave, Prosper, Sayonara, Send off, So long, Toodle-oo, Toodle-pip, Totsiens, Vale, Valediction

Farm(ing), Farmhouse Agronomy, Arable, Bender, Bowery, Cold Comfort, Collective, Croft, Cultivate, Dairy, Deep-litter, Emmerdale, Estancia, Extensive, Factory, Fat, Fish(ery), Funny, Geoponical, Grange, Hacienda, Health, Home, Homestead, Husbandry, Intensive, Kibbutz, Kolkhoz, Land, Ley, Loaf, Location, Mains, Mas, Mixed, No-tillage, Onstead, Orley, Oyster, Pen, Poultry, Ranch, Render,

Rent, Set-aside, Sewage, Shamba, Smallholding, Sovkhoz, Station, Stead(ing), Sted(d), Stedde, Steed, Stock, Subsistence, Tank, Till, Toon, Toun, Town, Trout, Wick, Wind

Farmer Boer, Campesino, Carl, Cockatoo, Cocky, Collins Street, Colon, Crofter, Estanciero, Gebur, George, Giles, Hick, Husbandman, Macdonald, Metayer, Nester, NFU, Peasant, Pitt Street, Publican, Rancher, Reaper, Ryot, Share-cropper, Sodbuster, Squatter, Tax, Tenant, Tiller, Whiteboy, Yeoman, Zeminda(r)

Farmhand Cadet, Churl, Cottar, Cotter, Cottier, Cowman, Ditcher, Hand, He(a)rdsman, Hind, Land girl, Orraman, Peon, Ploughman, Redneck, Rouseabout, Roustabout, Shearer, Sheepo, Stockman, Swineherd, Thresher

▶**Farmhouse** *see* **FARM(ING)**

Faroe Islands FO

Farthing Brass, F, Fadge, Har(r)ington, Mite, Q, Quadragesimal, Rag

Fascinate(d), Fascinating, Fascinator Allure, Attract, Bewitch, →**CHARM**, Dare, Enchant, Engross, Enrapt, Enthral(l), Fetching, Inthral, Into, Intrigue, Jolie laide, Kill, Mesmeric, Rivet, Sexy, Siren, Witch

Fascist Blackshirt, Blue shirt, Brownshirt, Dictator, Falange, Falangist, Iron Guard, Lictor, Nazi, Neo-Nazi, NF, Phalangist, Rexist, Sinarchist, Sinarquist

Fashion(able), Fashioned, Fashion house Aguise, À la (mode), Alta moda, Armani, Bristol, Build, Chic, Construct, Convention, Cool, Corinthian, Craze, Create, Cult, Custom, Cut, Design, Directoire, Du jour, Elegant, Entail, Fabricate, Fad, Feat, Feign, Fly, Forge, Form, Garb, Genteel, Go, Hew, Hip, In, Invent, Kitsch, Look, →**MAKE**, Manière, Manners, Method, Mode, Mondain(e), Mould, Newgate, Pink, Prada, Preppy, Rage, Rate, Sc, Shape, Smart, Smith, Snappy, Snazzy, Stile, Stylar, Style, Swish, Tailor, Ton, Ton(e)y, →**TREND(Y)**, Turn, Twig, Vogue, Waif, Way, Wear, Wise, With-it, Work, Wrought

Fast(ing), Faster Abstain, Apace, Ashura, Breakneck, Brisk, Citigrade, Clappers, Clem, Clinging, Daring, Double-quick, Elaphine, Express, Fizzer, Fleet, Hypersonic, Immobile, Lent, Lightning, Loyal, Maigre, Meteoric, Moharram, Muharram, Muharrem, Pac(e)y, Posthaste, Presto, Promiscuous, Pronto, Quadragesimal, Quick, Raffish, Raking, Ramadan, Ramadhan, Rash, Rathe, Sehri, Spanking, Speedy, Stretta, Stretto, Stuck, Supersonic, Sure, Swift, Tachyon, Thick, Tisha b'Av, Whistle-stop, Xerophagy, Yarer, Yom Kippur

Fasten(er), Fastening Anchor, Attach, Bar, Belay, Belt, Bind, Bolt, Buckle, Button, Chain, Clamp, Clasp, Click, Clinch, Clip, Cramp, Cufflink, Dead-eye, Diamond-hitch, Dome, Espagnolette, Eye-bolt, Frog, Gammon, Hasp, Hesp, Hitch, Hook, Infibulation, Lace, Latch, Lock, Moor, Morse, Nail, Netsuke, Nip, Nut, Padlock, Parral, Patent, Pectoral, Pin, Preen, Press stud, Reeve, Rivet, Rope, Rove, Safety pin, Screw, Seal, →**SECURE**, Sew up, Shut, Spar, Sprig, Staple, Steek, Stitch, Strap, Suspender, Swift(er), Tach(e), Tag, Tape, Tassel, Tether, Thong, Tintack, Toggle, Twist-tie, U-bolt, Velcro®, Wedge, Zip

Fastness Bastille

Fat(s), Fatted, Fatten, Fatty Adipic, Bard, Batten, Battle, Blubber, Butter, Calf, Calipash, Chubby, Corpulent, Curd, Deutoplasm, Dripping, Embonpoint, Endomorph, Ester, Flab, Flesh, Frank, Grease, Gross, Lanolin, Lard, Lard-ass, Love handles, Margarine, Mart, Moti, Motu, Obese, Oil, Olein, Oleomargarine, Olestra, Plump, Podgy, Polyunsaturated, Portly, Pudgy, Puppy, Rich, Rolypoly, Rotund, Saturated, Seam(e), Shortening, Stearic, Steatosis, Suet, Tallow, Tomalley, Trans, Tub, Unsaturated, Well-padded

Fatal(ism), Fatality, Fate(s), Fated, Fateful Apnoea, Atropos, Cavel, Chance, Clotho, Deadly, Death, Decuma, Destiny, Doom, End, Fay, Fell, Joss, Karma, Kismet, Lachesis, Lethal, Lethiferous, Loss, Lot, Meant, Moera(e), Moira, Morta, Mortal, Mortiferous, Nemesis, Nona, Norn(a), Parca, Pernicious, Portion, Predestination, Skuld, Urd, Verdande, Waterloo, Weird

Father(s), Fatherly Abba, Abbot, Abuna, Adopt, Agnation, Apostolic, Bapu, Begetter, Breadwinner, Brown, City, Conscript, Curé, Da, Dad, Engender, Founding, Fr, Generator, Genitor, Getter, Governor, Male, NASCAR dad, Pa, Padre, Papa, Pappy,

Parent, Pater(nal), Paterfamilias, Patriarch, Patroclinic, Père, Pop(pa), Popper, Priest, Rev, Seraphic, Sire, Stud, Thames, Tiber, William

Fathom Delve, Depth, Dig, F, Plumb, Plummet, Understand

Fatigue(d) Battle, Bonk, Compassion, Exhaust, Fag, Jade, Jet lag, ME, Neurasthenia, Overdo, Overwatch, Swinked, Time-zone, Tire, Weariness, Weary

Fault(y), Fault-finding Arraign, Bad, Beam, Blame(worthy), Blunder, Bug, Cacology, Captious, Carp, Compound, Culpa, Culpable, Defect, Demerit, Dip, Dip-slip, Drop-out, Dud, Duff, →**ERROR**, Failing, Flaw, Foot, Frailty, Gall, Glitch, Gravity, Henpeck, Hitch, Impeach, Imperfect, Knock, Literal, Massif, →**MISTAKE**, Mortal sin, Nag, Nibble, Niggle, Nit-pick, Oblique, Oblique-slip, Out, Outcrop, Overthrust, Pan, Para, Peccadillo, Pre-echo, Quibble, Rate, Reprehend, Rift, Rupes Recta, San Andreas, Sclaff, Set-off, Short, Slip, Snag, Step, Strike, Strike-slip, Technical, Thrust, Trap, Trough, Underthrust, Upbraid, Vice

Faux pas Blunder, Boner, Gaffe, Leglen-girth, Solecism

Favour(able), Favoured, Favourite Advance, Advantage(ous), Aggrace, Agraste, Alder-liefest, Anne, Approval, Auspicious, Aye, Back, Befriend, Behalf, Benign, Bless, Boon, Bribe, Cert, Chosen, Cockade, Condescend, Conducive, Countenance, Curry, Darling, Ewe lamb, Ex gratia, Fancy, Favonian, Grace, Gracioso, Graste, Gratify, Gree, Hackle, Hot, In, Indulge, Kickback, Minion, Nod, Odour, Optimal, Particular, Peat, Persona grata, Pet, Pettle, Popular, →**PREFER**, Promising, Propitious, Resemble, Rib(b)and, Roseate, Rose-knot, Rosette, Side, Smile, Toast, Token, White boy, White-headed

Fawn(er), Fawning Adulate, Bambi, Beige, Blandish, Brown-nose, Camel, Crawl, Creep, Cringe, Deer, Ecru, Elaine, Flatter, Fleech, Footlick, Grovel, Ko(w)tow, Lickspittle, Obsequious, Servile, Slavish, Smarm, Smoo(d)ge, Subservient, Sycophant, Tasar, Toady, Truckle, Tussah, Tusseh, Tusser, Tussore

Fax Replica

Faze Unnerve

Fear Angst, Apprehension, Astra(po)phobia, Awe, Bathophobia, Bugbear, Claustrophobia, Cold sweat, Crap, Cyberphobia, Dismay, Doubt, Drad, Dread, Dromophobia, Ecophobia, Foreboding, Fright, Funk, Genophobia, Hang-up, Horripilation, Horror, Kenophobia, Monophobia, Mysophobia, Nostopathy, Nyctophobia, Ochlophobia, Panic, Redoubt, Revere, Taphephobia, Taphophobia, Terror, Trepidation, Willies

Fearful Afraid, Cowardly, Dire, Horrific, Nervous, Pavid, Rad, Redoubtable, Timorous, Tremulous, Windy

Fearless Bold, Brave, Courageous, Daring, Gallant, Impavid, Intrepid, Proud, Unafraid

Feast(s) Adonia, Agape, Assumption, Banquet, Barmecide, Beano, Belshazzar's, Blow-out, Candlemas, Carousal, Celebration, Convive, Dine, Do, Double, Eat, Encaenia, Epiphany, Epulation, Festival, Fleshpots, Fool's, Gaudeamus, Gaudy, Hakari, Hallowmas, Heortology, Hockey, Hogmanay, Holy Innocents, Id-al-Adha, Id-al-Fitr, Immaculate Conception, Ingathering, Isodia, Junket, Kai-kai, Lady Day, Lamb-ale, Lammas, Luau, Martinmas, Michaelmas, Movable, Noel, Passover, Pentecost, Pesach, Pig, Potlatch, Purim, Regale, Repast, Revel, Roodmas, Seder, Shindig, Spread, Succoth, Sukkot(h), Tabernacles, Trumpets, Tuck-in, Wayzgoose, Weeks, Yule, Zagmuk

Feat Achievement, Deed, Effort, Exploit, Gambado, Stunt, Trick

Feather(s), Feathered, Feather-star Aigrette, Alula, Barbicel, Boa, Braccate, Cock, Contour, Covert, Crinoid, Crissum, Down, Duster, Egret, Filoplume, Fledged, Fletch, Flight, Gemmule, Hackle, Harl, Hatchel, Herl, Lure, Macaroni, Oar, Ostrich, Pen(na), Pin, Pinna, Pith, Plumage, Plume, Plumule, Prince's, Pteryla, Ptilosis, Rectrix, Remex, Remiges, Rocket-tail, Saddle-hackle, Scapular, Scapus, Semiplume, Sickle, Standard, Stipa, Swansdown, Tail covert, Tectrix, Tertial, Tippet, Vibrissa, White, Wing covert

Feather-pate Man-milliner

Feature(s) Amenity, Appurtenance, Article, Aspect, Attribute, Brow, Character, Chin,

Depict, Eye, Eyebrow, Face, Facet, Figure, Fronton, Hallmark, Highlight, Item, Jizz, Landmark, Lineament, Neotery, Nose, Nucleus, Overfold, Phiz(og), Physiognomy, Signature, Snoot, Spandrel, Star, Temple, Topography, Touch, Trait, Underlip

Fed Agent, G-man

Federal, Federation Alliance, Axis, Bund, Commonwealth, Interstate, League, Solidarity, Statal, Union

Fee(s) Base, Bench, Capitation, Charge, Conditional, Consideration, Consultation, Corkage, Corporation, Dues, Duty, Emolument, Entrance, Entry, Faldage, Fine, Great, Hire, Honorarium, Kill, Mortuary, Mouter, Multure, Obvention, Pay, Pierage, Premium, Ransom, Refresher, Retainer, Sub, Transfer, Tribute

Feeble Banal, Characterless, Daidling, Debile, Decrepit, Droob, Effete, Feckless, Flabby, Flaccid, Footling, Fragile, Geld, Ineffective, Infirm, Jessie, Limp, Mimsy, Namby-pamby, Pale, Puny, Rickety, Sickly, Silly, Slender, Slight, Soppy, Tailor, Tame, Thin, Tootle, Unmanly, Wallydrag, Wallydraigle, Washy, Wastrel, Weak, Weak-kneed, Weak-minded, Weed, Weedy, Wersh, Wet, Wimpish, Worn

Feed(er), Feeding Battle, Bib, Browse, Cake, Cater, Cibation, Clover, Diet, Dine, Drip, →EAT, Fatten, Fire, Fishmeal, Fodder, Food, Gavage, Graze, Hay, Input, Intravenous, Line, Lunch, Meal, Nourish, Nurse, Paid, Pecten, Provender, Refect, Repast, Sate, Soil, Stoke, Stooge, Storer, Stover, Stuff, Suckle, Sustain, Tire, Tractor, Wean

Feel(ingly), Feeling(s) Aesthesia, Affetuoso, Algesis, Angst, Animus, À tâtons, Atmosphere, Compassion, Darshan, →EMOTION, Empathy, Empfindung, Euphoria, →EXPERIENCE, Fellow, Finger, Flaw, Frisk, Grope, Groundswell, Handle, Hard, Heart, Heartstrings, Hunch, Intuit, Knock, Know, Palp(ate), Passible, Passion, Pity, Premonition, Presentiment, Probe, Realise, Sensate, Sensation, →SENSE, Sensitive, Sentiency, Sentiment, Spirit, Sprachgefühl, Tactual, Tingle, Touch, Turn, Undercurrent, Vehemence, Vibes, Zeal

▶**Feet** see FOOT(ING)

Feign Act, Affect, Assume, Colour, Fake, Malinger, Mime, Mock, →PRETEND, Sham, Simulate

Fel(d)spar Adularia, Albite, Anorthite, Bytownite, Gneiss, Hyalophane, Labradorite, Moonstone, Orthoclase, Peristerite, Petuntse, Petuntze, Plagioclase, Sanidine, Saussurite, Sun-stone

▶**Feline** see CAT

Fell Axe, Chop, Cruel, Cut down, Deadly, Dire, Dread, Fierce, Floor, Hew, Hide, Hill, Inhuman, Knock-down, KO, Lethal, Lit, Log, Moor, Pelt, Poleaxe, Ruthless, Sca, Shap, Skittle

Fellow(s), Fellowship Academic, Associate, Bawcock, Birkie, Bloke, Bo, Bro, Bucko, Buffer, Callan(t), Carlot, Cat, Chal, Chap(pie), Chi, China, Chum, Co, Cock, Cod(ger), Collaborator, Co-mate, Communion, Companion, Comrade, Confrère, Cove, Cully, Cuss, Dandy, Dean, Dog, Don, Dude, Equal, F, Fogey, Fop, Gadgie, Gadje, Gaudgie, Gauje, Gink, Guy, Joe, Joker, Josser, Lad, Like, M, Mall, Man, Match, Mate, Member, Mister, Mun, Odd, Partner, Peer, Professor, Rival, Sister, Skate, Sociate, Society, Sodality, Stablemate, Swab, Teaching, Twin, Waghalter, Wallah

Felt Baize, Bat(t), Drugget, Knew, Met, Numdah, Numnah, Pannose, Roofing, Sensed, Tactile, Underlay, Velour

▷**Female, Feminine** *may indicate* an -ess ending

Female (bodies), Feminine, Feminist Anima, Bint, Bit, Dame, Distaff, Doe, F, Fair sex, Filly, Girl(y), Greer, Harem, Hen, Her, Kermes, Lady, Libber, Maiden, Pen, Petticoated, Pistillate, Riot girl, Sakti, Shakti, She, Sheila, Shidder, Soft, Spindle, Thelytoky, -trix, →WOMAN, Womens' libber, Yin

Fence(r), Fencing (position) Appel, Bar, Barrier, Botte, Carte, Deer, Dogleg, Electric, Enclose, Épée, Fight, Flanconade, Foils, Fraise, Haha, Hay, Hedge, Hurdle, Iaido, Imbroccata, Kendo, Kittle, Line, Link, Mensur, Netting, Obstacle, Oxer, Pale, Paling, Palisade, Passado, Pen, Picket, Quart(e), Quinte, Rabbit-proof, Raddle, Rail, Rasper, Receiver, Reset, Ring, Scrimure, Seconde, Sepiment, Sept(um), Septime,

Singlestick, Sixte, Snake, Stacket, Stockade, Stramac, Stramazon, Sunk, Swordplay, Tac-au-tac, Trellis, Virginia, Wattle, Wear, Weir, Wire, Zigzag

Fend(er), Fend off Buffer, Bumper, Cowcatcher, Curb, Mudguard, Parry, Provide, Resist, Skid, Stiff-arm, Ward, Wing

Fennel Finnochio, Finoc(c)hio, Florence, Herb, Love-in-a-mist, Narthex, Ragged lady

Ferment(ation) Barm, Brew, Enzym(e), Leaven, Mowburn, Protease, Ptyalin, Seethe, Solera, Stum, Trypsin, Turn, Vinify, Working, Ye(a)st, Zyme, Zymosis, Zymotic, Zymurgy

Fern Acrogenous, Adder's-tongue, Adiantum, Archegonial, Asparagus, Aspidium, Asplenium, Azolla, Barometz, Beech, Bird's nest, Bladder, Bracken, Brake, Buckler, Ceterach, Cinnamon, Cryptogam, Cyathea, Cycad, Dicksonia, Elkhorn, Filicales, Filices, Filmy, Grape, Hard, Hart's-tongue, Holly, Isoetes, Maidenhair, Man, Mangemange, Marsh, Marsilea, Marsilia, Meadow, Miha, Moonwort, Mosquito, Mulewort, Nardoo, Nephrolepis, Northern, Ophioglossum, Osmunda, Para, Parsley, Peppergrass, Pepperwort, Pillwort, Polypody, Ponga, Pteridology, Pteris, Punga, Rachilla, Rockbrake, Royal, Rusty-back, Scale, Schizaea, Scolopendrium, Silver, Soft tree, Spleenwort, Staghorn, Sweet, Sword, Tara, Tree, Venus's hair, Whisk, Woodsia

Ferry(man) Charon, Convey, Flying bridge, Harper's, Hovercraft, Passage, Plier, Roll-on, RORO, Sea-cat, Sealink, Shuttle, Traject, Tranect

Fertile, Fertility (symbol), Fertilisation Arable, Ashtoreth, Battle, Cleistogamy, Fat, Fecund, Fruitful, Green, Linga, Priapus, Productive, Prolific, Rhiannon, Rich, Uberous

Fertilise(r), Fertilisation Ammonia, Auxin, Bee, Bone-ash, Bone-earth, Bone-meal, Caliche, Caprify, Compost, Fishmeal, Guano, Heterosis, Humogen, Humus, In-vitro, IVF, Kainite, Krilium®, Manure, Marl, Night soil, Nitrate, Nitre, Pearl-ash, Phallus, Phosphate, Pollen, Potash, Seaware, Self, Sham, Side dressing, Stamen, Superfetation, Superphosphate, Tankage, Top dressing

Fervent, Fervid, Fervour Ardent, Burning, Earnest, Heat, Hot, Hwyl, Intense, Into, Keen, Passionate, White-hot, Zeal, Zeloso

Festival, Festive, Festivity Anniversary, Beano, Carnival, Celebration, Commemoration, Convivial, En fête, →**FAIR**, Feast, Feis, Fête, Gaff, Gaudy, High day, →**HOLIDAY**, Lemural, Play, Revel, Semi-double, Wake

Fête Bazaar, Champêtre, Entertain, →**FESTIVITY**, Gala, Honour, Tattoo

Fetish(ist) Charm, Compulsion, Idol, Ju-ju, Obeah, Obi(a), Talisman, Totem, Voodoo

Fetter Anklet, Basil, Bilboes, Chain, Gyve, Hamshackle, Hopple, Iron, Leg-iron, Manacle, Shackle

Feu Tenure

Feud Affray, Clash, Dissidence, Feoff, Fief, Quarrel, Strife

Fever(ish) Ague, Biliary, Brain, Cabin, Camp, Childbed, Dandy, Dengue, Enteric, Febrile, Ferment, Frenetic, Glandular, Heatstroke, Hectic, Jungle, Kissing disease, Malaria, Marsh, Milk, Parrot, Passion, Phrenitis, Pyretic, Rheumatic, Scarlatina, Scarlet, Ship, Splenic, Spring, Stage, Sunstroke, Swine, Trench, Typhoid, Valley, Weed, Yellow(jack)

Few(er) Handful, Infrequent, →**LESS**, Limited, Scarce, Some, Wheen

Fiancé(e) Betrothed, Intended, Promised

Fiasco Bomb, Debacle, Disaster, Failure, Flask, Flop, Lash-up, Wash-out

Fibre, Fibrous Abaca, Acrilan®, Acrylic, Aramid, Arghan, Backbone, Bass, Bast, Buaze, Bwazi, Cantala, Coir, Constitution, Corpus Callosum, Cotton, Courtelle®, Cuscus, Desmosome, Dralon®, Elastane, Filament, Filasse, Flax, Funicle, Giant, Glass, Gore-Tex®, Hair, Harl, Hemp, Henequen, Henequin, Herl, Istle, Ixtle, Jipyapa, Jute, Kapok, Kenaf, Kevlar®, Kittul, Maguey, Monkey-grass, Monofil, Monomode, Moorva, Moral, Murva, Natural, Noil(s), Nylon, Oakum, Orlon®, Peduncle, Piassaba, Piassava, Pine-wool, Pita, Pons, Pontine, Pulu, Raffia, Ramee, Rami, Ramie, Rayon, Rhea, Roughage, Shoddy, Sinew, Sisal, Slub(b), Spherulite, Staple, Stepped-index, Strick, Sunn-hemp, Tampico, Tencel®, Toquilla, Tow, Towy, Viver, Watap, Whisker, Wood pulp

Fickle(ness) Capricious, Change, False, Flibbertigibbet, Inconsistent, Inconstant, Kittle, Light, Mutable, Protean, Shifty, Varying, Volatile, Wind-changing

Fiction(al), Fictitious Airport, Bogus, Chick-lit, Cyberpunk, Fable, Fabrication, Myth, Pap, Phoney, Pulp, Romance, Science, Sex and shopping, Speculative, Splatterpunk, →STORY, Sword and sorcery, Transgressive, Whole cloth

Fiddle(r), Fiddling, Fiddlestring Amati, Bow, Calling-crab, Cello, Cheat, Crab, Cremona, Croud, Crouth, Crowd, Crwth, Do, Fidget, Fix, Gju, Ground, Gu(e), Gut-scraper, Jerrymander, Kit, Launder, Nero, Peculate, Petty, Potter, Racket, Rebec(k), Rig, Rote, Sarangi, Saw, Sawah, Scam, Scrape, Scrapegut, Second, Sharp practice, Short change, Spiel, Strad, Sultana, →TAMPER, Tinker, Trifle, Tweedle(-dee), Twiddle, Viola, →VIOLIN, Wangle

Fiddle-faddle Nipperty-tipperty

Fidget(y) Fantad, Fanteeg, Fantigue, Fantod, Fike, Fuss, Fyke, Hirsle, Hotch, Impatient, Jimjams, Jittery, Niggle, Restive, Trifle, Twiddle, Twitch, Uneasy

▷ **Field** *may indicate* cricket

Field(er), Fielding, Fields(man) Aalu, Aaru, Abroad, Aceldama, Aerodrome, Area, Arena, Arish, Arpent, Arrish, Baseman, Bocage, Campestral, Campestrian, Catch, Champ(s), Chief, Close, Colour, Coulomb, Cover, Cover-point, Diamond, Domain, Electric, Electromagnetic, Electrostatic, Elysian, Entry, Extra cover, Fid, Fine leg, Flodden, Flying, Force, Forte, Fylde, Glebe, Gracie, Gravitational, Grid(iron), Gull(e)y, Hop-yard, Ice, Keep wicket, Killing, Land, Landing, Lare, Lay, Lea(-rig), Leg slip, Ley, Line, Long leg, Long-off, Long-on, Longstop, Lords, Magnetic, Mead(ow), Mid-off, Mid-on, Mid-wicket, Mine, Oil, Padang, Paddock, Paddy, Parrock, Pasture, Peloton, Pitch, Playing, Point, Potter's, Province, Quintessence, Realm, Reame, Runners, Salting, Sawah, Scarecrow, Scope, Scout, Shamba, Short leg, Short stop, Silly, Slip, Sphere, Square leg, Stage, Stray, Stubble, Territory, Third man, Tract, Unified, Vector, Visual, W.C., World

Field marshal Allenby, Bulow, French, Haig, Ironside, Kesselring, Kitchener, Montgomery, Roberts, Robertson, Rommel, Slim, Wavell

Fiend Barbason, Buff, Demon, →DEVIL, Enthusiast, Flibbertigibbet, Frateretto, Hellhound, Hellion, Hobbididance, Mahn, Modo, Obidicut, Smulkin, Succubus

Fierce(ly) Amain, Billyo, Breem, Breme, Cruel, Draconic, Dragon, Grim, Hard-fought, Lorcan, Ogreish, Rampant, Renfierst, →SAVAGE, Severe, Tigrish, Violent, Wild, Wood, Wrathy, Wud

Fiery Abednego, Ardent, Argand, Aries, Con fuoco, Dry, Eithna, Fervent, Hot, Hotspur, Idris, Igneous, Impassioned, Leo, Mettlesome, Phlogiston, Piri-piri, Sagittarius, Salamander, Zealous

Fiesta Festival, Fête, Gala, Holiday

Fifth Column, Diapente, Hemiol(i)a, Nones, Quentin, Quint(ile), Sesqualtera

Fig Bania, Banyan, Benjamin-tree, Caprifig, Fico, Figo, Footra, Fouter, Foutra, Foutre, Hottentot, Moreton Bay, Sycamore, Sycomium, Sycomore, Trifle

Fight(er), Fighting Achilles, Action, Affray, Aikido, Alpino, Altercate, Arms, Bandy, Bare-knuckle, Barney, →BATTLE, Bicker, Biffo, Blue, Bout, Box, Brave, Brawl, Bruiser, Bush-whack, Camp, Campaign, Chetnik, Chindit, Combat, Compete, Conflict, Contest, Contra, Crusader, Defender, Digladiation, Ding-dong, Dog, Dreadnought, Duel, Ecowarrior, Encounter, Engagement, Extremes, F, Faction, Fence, Fisticuffs, Fray, Freedom, Free-for-all, Fund, Gamecock, Garibaldi, Gladiator, Grap(p)le, Green beret, Grudge, Guerilla, Gunslinger, Gurkha, Handicuffs, Hurricane, J(o)ust, Karate, Kendo, Kite, Lapith, Maquis, Marine, Med(d)le, Medley, Mêlée, Mercenary, MIG, Mill, Night, Partisan, Pellmell, Pillow, PLO, Press, Pugilist, Pugnacity, Punch up, Rapparee, Rejoneo, Repugn, Resist, Ring, Rough and tumble, Ruck, Ruction, Rumble, Run-in, Running, Savate, Scold, Scrap, Scrape, Scrimmage, Scuffle, Set-to, Shadow, Shine, Shoot-out, Skirmish, Slam, Slugger, Soldier, Spar, Spat, Spitfire, Squabble, Stealth, Straight, Strife, Struggle, Sumo, Swordsman, Tar, Tatar, Tilt, Toreador, Tussle, Ultimate, Umbrella, War(-dog), War-horse, War-man, Warplane, Warrior, Wrestle

Figure(d), Figures, Figurine, Figurative Action, Allegoric, Arabic, Aumail,

Bas-relief, Body, Build, Cartouche, Caryatid, Cast, Cinque, Cipher, Cone, Cube, Cypher, Decahedron, Digit, Ecorché, Effigy, Eight, Ellipse, Enneagon, Equiangular, →**FORM**, Fret, Fusil, Gammadion, Giosphinx, Girth, Graph, Hour-glass, Icon, Idol, Ikon, Image, Insect, Intaglio, Integer, Lay, Manaia, Mandala, Monogram, Motif, Nonagon, Number, Numeral, Numerator, Numeric, Octagon, Octahedron, Ornate, Outline, Ovoid, Parallelepiped, Parallelogram, Pentacle, Polygon, Polyhedron, Prism, Puppet, Pyramid, Reckon, Repetend, Sector, See, →**SHAPE**, Simplex, Stat(istic)s, Statue(tte), Stick, Tableau, Telamon, Tetragon, Tetrahedron, Torus, Triangle, Trigon, Triskelion, Trisoctahedron, Tropology, Undecagon, Waxwork

Figure of speech Abscission, Allegory, Analogy, Antimask, Antimasque, Antimetabole, Antithesis, Antonomasia, Assonance, Asyndeton, Catachresis, Cataphora, Chiasmus, Deixis, Diallage, Ellipsis, Euphemism, Hypallage, Hyperbaton, Hyperbole, Hysteron proteron, Irony, Litotes, Meiosis, Metalepsis, Metaphor, Metonymy, Oxymoron, Paral(e)ipsis, Prolepsis, Prosopopoeia, Siddhuism, Simile, Syllepsis, Synecdoche, Taxeme, Tmesis, Trope, Zeugma

Filament Barbule, Byssus, Cirrus, Fibre, Fimbria, Floss, Gossamer, Hair, Hormogonium, Hypha, Mycor(r)hiza, Myofibril, Paraphysis, Protonema, →**THREAD**

File, Filing(s) Abrade, Archive, Bastard, Batch, Binary, Binder, Box, Burr, Circular, Clyfaker, Coffle, Croc(odile), Crosscut, Data set, Dead-smooth, Disc, Disk, Dossier, Download, Enter, Floatcut, Folder, Generation, In-box, Index, Indian, Lemel, Lever-arch, Limail, Line, Nail, Out-box, Packed, Pickpocket, Pigeon-hole, Podcast, Pollute, Quannet, Rank, Rasp, Rat-tail, README, Riffler, Risp, Rolodex®, Row, Scalprum, Scratch, Signature, Single, String, Swap, Swarf, Text, Tickler, TIF(F)

Filibuster Freebooter, Hinder, Obstruct, Pirate, Run on, Stonewall

Fill(ing), Filler Anaplerosis, Balaam, Banoffee, Banoffi, Beaumontag(u)e, Beaumontique, Billow, Bloat, Brick-nog, Brim, Bump, Centre, Charge, Cram, Ganache, Gather, Gorge, Heart, Imbue, Implete, Impregn(ate), Inlay, Jampack, Line, Load, Mastic, Mincemeat, Nagging, Occupy, Pabulous, Packing, Permeate, Plug, Replenish, Repletive, Salpicon, Sate, Satisfy, Sealant, Shim, Slush, Stack, Stock, Stocking, Stopgap, Stopping, →**STUFF**, Tales, Tampon, Teem, Ullage

Fillet(s) Anadem, Annulet, Band, Bandeau, Bandelet, Bone, Cloisonné, Flaunching, Fret, Goujons, Grenadine, Headband, Infula, Label, Lemniscus, List(el), Mitre, Moulding, Reglet, Regula, Ribbon, Rollmop, Slice, Snood, Sphendone, Stria, Striga, Taeniate, Tape, Teniate, Tournedos, Vitta

Film(s), Filmmaker, Filmy, Filming Acetate, Animatronics, Anime, Biopic, Blockbuster, Bollywood, Buddy, Cartoon, Caul, Cel, Chopsocky, Cine, Cinerama®, Cliffhanger, Cling, Clip, Colour, Deepie, Dew, Diorama, Docudrama, Documentary, Dramedy, Dust, Epic, ET, Exposure, Fantasia, Feature, Featurette, Fiche, Flick, Floaty, Footage, Genevieve, Gigi, Gossamer, Hammer, Haze, Hollywood, Horror, Ident, Jaws, Kell, Lacquer, Lamella, Layer, Limelight, Loid, Machinima, Mask, Membrane, Microfiche, Mist, Monochrome, Montage, Mylar®, Newsreel, Noir, Oater, Outtake, Ozacling®, Panchromatic, Pathé, Patina, Pellicle, Photo, Plaque, Prequel, Projection, Psycho, Quickie, Reel, Release, Rockumentary, Rush, Scale, Scenario, Screen, Scum, Sepmag, Short, Shot, Silent, Skin, Skin flick, Slashfest, Slick, Slo-mo, Snuff, Spaghetti western, Splatter, Star Wars, Studio, Super 8, Suspensor, Sword and sandal, Take, Talkie, Tear-jerker, Technothriller, Toon, Trailer, Two-shot, Ultrafiche, Ultra-rapid, Vertigo, Vicenzi, Video, Videogram, Video-nasty, Wardour St, Web, Weepie, Weepy, Western, Wuxia

Filmgoer Cineaste

Filter(ing) Bo(u)lt, Clarify, Dialysis, High-pass, Leach, Percolate, Perk, Polarizing, Refine, Seep, Sieve, Sile, Skylight, Strain

Filth(y) Addle, Augean, Bilge, Bogging, Colluvies, Crock, Crud, Defile, Dirt, Dung, Foul, Grime, Hard core, Litter, Lucre, Mire, Muck, Obscene, Pythogenic, Refuse, Slime, Smut(ch), Soil, Squalor, Stercoral, Yuck

Final(e), Finalise, Finally Absolute, Apogee, At last, Closing, Coda, Conclusive, Cup, Decider, Denouement, End, End-all, Epilogue, Eventual, Exam, Extreme, Grand, Last, Last gap, Net(t), Peremptory, Sew up, Swansong, Terminal, Ultimate, Utter

Finance, Financial, Financier Ad crumenam, Angel, Back, Banian, Banker, Bankroll, Banyan, Bay Street, Cambism, Chrematistic, City (man), Exchequer, Fiscal, Forfaiting, Gnome, Grubstake, Monetary, Moneyman, Patronise, Revenue, Sponsor, Subsidise, Treasurer, Underwrite, Wall Street

Finch Bird, Brambling, Bunting, Canary, Charm, Chewink, Conirostral, Crossbill, Darwin's, Fringillid, Linnet, Marsh-robin, Peter, Serin, Siskin, Spink, Twite

Find(er), Finding Ascertain, Come across, Detect, Dig up, Direction, Discover(y), Get, Gobind, Govind, Hit, Inquest, →LOCATE, Meet, Minitrack®, Provide, Rake up, Rarity, Rumble, Trace, Track down, Trouvaille, Unearth, Verdict

Fine, Fine words A1, Admirable, Amerce(ment), Arts, Assess, Beau(t), Bender, Boss, Brandy, Brave, Braw, Bully, Buttock-mail, Champion, Cobweb(by), Dainty, Dandy, Dry, End, Eriach, Eric(k), Estreat, F, Fair, Famous, Forfeit, Godly, Good(ly), Gossamer, Gradely, Grand, Hair, Hairline, Handsome, Heriot, Hunkydory, Idle, Immense, Issue, Keen, Log, Mulct, Nice, Nifty, Niminy-piminy, Noble, OK, Oke, Okey-doke(y), →PENALTY, Precise, Pretty, Pure, Relief, Righto, Safe, Sconce, Scratch, Sheer, Sicker, Slender, Smart, Spanking, Subtle, Summery, Super, Sure, Tax, Ticket(t)y-boo, Tiptop, Topping, Transmission, Wally, Waly, Well, Wispy

Finery Braws, Fallal, Frills, Frippery, Gaudery, Ornament, Trinket, Wally, Warpaint

Finger(s), Fingernail Annular, Dactyl, Digit, Fork, Handle, Idle worms, Index, Lunula, Medius, Name, Nip, Piggy, Pinky, Pointer, Prepollex, Pusher, Ring(man), Shop, Talaunt, Talon, Tot, Trigger, White

Fingerprint(ing) Arch, Dabs, Dactylogram, Genetic, Loop, Whorl

Finish(ed), Finishing (touch) Arch, Blanket, Calendar, Close, Coating, Coda, Complete, →CONCLUDE, Crown, Dénouement, Die, Dish, Do, Dope, Dress, Eggshell, →END, Epilog(ue), Epiphenomena, Exact, Fine, Full, Gloss, Grandstand, Ice, Intonaco, Kibosh, Lacquer, Log off, Mat(t), Mirror, Neat, Outgo, Outwork, Pebbledash, Peg out, Perfect, Photo, Picking, Polish off, Refine, Ripe, Round, Satin, Settle, Shellac, Shot, Spitcher, Surface, Terminate, Through, Top out, Up (tie), Varnish, Veneer, Washed-up, Wau(l)k, Wind-up, Wrap

Finland, Finn(ish) Esth, Esthonian, Huck(leberry), Karelian, Mickey, Mordvin, Suomic, Udmurt, Votyak

Fire(side), Firing Accend, Agni, Aidan, Aiden, Animate, Anneal, Ardour, Arouse, Arson, Atar, Awaken, Axe, Bake, Bale, Barbecue, Barrage, Beacon, Behram, Biscuit, Blaze, Boot, Brand, Brazier, Brush, Burn, Bush, Cashier, Central, Chassé, Conflagration, Corposant, Counterbattery, Covering, Delope, Discharge, Dismiss, Élan, Electric, Element, Embolden, Ena, Energy, Enfilade, Enkindle, Enthuse, Flak, Flame, Friendly, Furnace, Glost, Greek, Gun, Hearth, Heater, Hob, Ignite, Inferno, Ingle, Inspire, Kentish, Kiln, Kindle, Launch, Let off, Light, Liquid, Lowe, Oust, Pop, Prime, Prometheus, Pull, Pyre, Quick, Radiator, Rake, Rapid, Red, Red cock, Sack, St Anthony's, St Elmo's, Scorch, Shell, Shoot, Smudge, Spark, Spirit, Spunk, Stoke, Stove, Strafe, Torch, Tracer, Trial, Trigger, Wake, Watch, Wisp, Zeal, Zip

▶ **Firearm** see GUN(FIRE)

Fire-break Epaulement, Greenstrip

Firedamp Blower

Fireplace Chiminea, Chimney, Grate, Hearth, Hob, Ingle, Loop-hole, Range

Fireproof Abednego, Asbestos, Incombustible, Inflammable, Meshach, Salamander, Shadrach, Uralite

Firewood Billet, Faggot, Knitch, Tinder

Firework(s) Banger, Bengal-light, Bunger, Catherine wheel, Cherry bomb, Cracker, Devil, Feu d'artifice, Firedrake, Fisgig, Fizgig, Fountain, Gerbe, Girandole, Golden rain, Indian fire, Iron sand, Jumping jack, Maroon, Pastille, Peeoy, Petard, Pinwheel, Pioy(e), Pyrotechnics, Realgar, Rocket, Roman candle, Serpent, Set piece, Skyrocket, Slap-bang, Sparkler, Squib, Tantrum, Throwdown, Tourbill(i)on, Volcano, Waterloo cracker, Wheel, Whizzbang

Firm, Firmness Adamant, Agency, Al dente, Binding, Business, Collected, Compact, Company, Concern, Concrete, Consistency, Constant, Crisp, Decided, Definite,

Determined, Duro, Establishment, Faithful, Fast, Fixed, Hard, House, Inc, Insistent, Loyal, Marginal, Oaky, Obdurate, Obstinate, Persistent, →RESOLUTE, Sclerotal, Secure, Set, Siccar, Sicker, →SOLID, Sound, Stable, Stalwart, Staunch, Steady, Ste(a)dfast, Steely, Steeve, Stern, Stieve, Stiff, Strict, Sturdy, Tight, Tough, Unflinching, Unshakeable, Well-knit

First 1st, Ab initio, Alpha, Arch, Archetype, Best, Calends, Champion, Chief, Earliest, Eldest, E(a)rst, Foremost, Former, Front, Head, I, Ideal, Imprimis, Initial, Kalends, Led, Maiden, No 1, One, Opener, Or, Original, Pioneer, Pole, Premier, Première, Prima, Primal, Prime, Primo, Primordial, Principal, Prototype, Rudimentary, Senior, Starters, Top, Victor, Yama

First class, First rate A1, Crack, Plump, Prime, Pukka, Slap up, Super-duper, Supreme, Tiptop, Top(notch)

First man Adam, Ask, Premier, President, Yama

▶**First rate** see FIRST CLASS

First woman Embla, Eve, Pandora, Premier

Firth Dornoch, Estuary, Forth, Inlet, Moray, Tay

Fish(ing) Angle, Bob, Cast, Catch, Chowder, Coarse, Counter, Cran, Creel, Deep-sea, Dib, Dredge, Dry-fly, Episcate, Fly, Flying, Fry, Gefilte, Gefulte, Goujons, Guddle, Halieutics, Haul, Hen, Ledger, Mess, Net, Odd, Offshore, Oily, Otterboard, Overnet, Piscary, Piscine, Poisson, Roe, Runner, Sacred, Sashimi, Shoal, Skitter, Sleeper, Snigger, Sniggle, Spin, Spot, Surfcasting, Surimi, Trawl, Troll, Trotline, Tub, White

Fish and chips Greasies

Fisher(man) Ahab, Andrew, Angler, Black cat, Caper, Heron, Herringer, High-liner, Liner, Pedro, Peter (grimes), Piscator, Rodster, Sharesman, Walton

▶**Fisherwoman** see FISH-SELLER

Fish-seller, Fisherwoman Fishwife, Molly Malone, Ripp(i)er, Shawley, Shawlie

Fissure Chasm, Cleft, Crack, Crevasse, Crevice, Gap, Grike, Gryke, Lode, Rent, Rift, Sand-crack, Scam, Vallecula, Vein, Zygon

Fist Clench, Dukes, Hand, Iron, Join-hand, Mailed, Neaf(f)e, Neif, Neive, Nief, Nieve, Pud, Punch, Thump, Writing

Fit(s), Fitful, Fitter, Fitting(s), Fitness Able, Access, Adapt, Ague, Align, Aline, Apoplexy, Appointment, Appropriate, Apropos, Apt, A salti, Bayonet, Beseemly, Bout, Canto, Capable, Competent, Condign, Congruous, Convulsion, Decent, Decorous, Dod, Dove-tail, Due, Eligible, Ensconce, Epilepsy, Equip, Expedient, Fairing, Fiddle, Form, Furnishing, Gee, Germane, Gusty, Hale, Handsome, Hang, Health, Hissy, Huff, Hysterics, In-form, Jactitation, Jag, Just, Like, Lune, Mate, Meet, Mood, Nest, Opportune, Paroxysm, Pertinent, Pet, Prepared, →PROPER, Ready, Rig, Rightful, Rind, Ripe, Roadworthy, Rynd, Seemly, Seizure, Serving, Set, Sit, Sliding, Slot, Snit, Sort, Sound, Spasm, Spell, Start, Suit(able), Tailor, Tantrum, Tenoner, Throe, Tide, Tref(a), Treif, Trim, Turn, Up to, Well, Worthy, Wrath

▷**Fit(ting)** *may indicate* a 't'

Fitzwilliam Darcy

Five(s), Fiver Cinque, Flim, Mashie, Pallone, Pedro, Pentad, Quinary, Quincunx, Quintet, Sextan, Towns, V

Five hundred D, Monkey

Fix(ation), Fixed, Fixer, Fixative Affeer, Anchor, Appoint, →ARRANGE, Assess, Assign, Attach, Bind, Brand, Cement, Clamp, Clew, Clue, Constant, Cure, Decide, Destine, Determine, Do, Embed, Engrain, Establish, Fast, Fasten, Fiddle, Firm, Fit, Freeze, Hard and fast, Hold, Immutable, Impasse, Imprint, Ingrain, Iron on, Jag, Jam, Locate, Lodge, Mend, Nail, Name, Narcotic, Nitrogen, Nobble, Odd-job man, Orientate, Peen, Peg, Persistent, Pin, Place, Point, Repair, Resolute, Rig, Rigid, Rivet, Rut, Screw, Seat, Seize, Set, Settle, Shoo, Skewer, Splice, Square, Stable, Staple, Steady, Step, Stereotype, Swig, Swing, Tie, Toe, Unchangeable, Weld

Fixture Attachment, Away, Event, Home, Match, Permanence, Unit

Fizz(ed), Fizzy Bubbles, Buck's, Effervesce, Gas, Hiss, Pop, Sherbet, Sod, Soda

Flab(by) Flaccid, Lank, Lax, Limp, Pendulous, Saggy, Tubby

Flabbergast(ed) Amaze, Astound, Floor, Thunderstruck

Flag(gy), Flags Acorus, Ancient, Ashlar, Banderol, Banner, Black, Blue Peter, Bunting, Burgee, Chequered, Colour(s), Decline, Droop, Duster, Ensign, Fail, Faint, Falter, Fane, Fanion, Gladdon, Gonfalon, Hail, Hoist, House, Iris, Jack, Jade, Jolly Roger, Kerbstone, Languish, Lis, Maple leaf, Old Glory, Orris, Pave(ment), Paviour, Pennant, Pennon, Peter, Pin, Rag, Rainbow, Red, Red Duster, Red Ensign, Repeater, Royal standard, Sag, Semaphore, Sett, Sink, Slab(stone), Slack, Stand, Standard, Stars and Bars, Stars and Stripes, Streamer, Substitute, Sweet, Tire, Tricolour, Union (Jack), Vane, Waft, Weaken, Whiff, Whift, White (ensign), Wilt, Wither

Flagon Bottle, Carafe, Ewer, Jug, Pitcher, Stoop, Stoup, Vessel

Flagrant Blatant, Egregious, Glaring, Heinous, Patent, Rank, Wanton

Flag-waving Jingoism

Flail Beat, Drub, Swingle, Threshel

Flair Art, Bent, Élan, Gift, Instinct, Knack, Nose, Panache, Style, →**TALENT**

Flake Chip, Flame, Flaught, Flaw, Floccule, Flocculus, Fragment, Peel, Scale, Smut, Snow, Spark

Flamboyant Baroque, Brilliant, Florid, Garish, Grandiose, Jazzy, Loud, Ornate, Ostentatious, Paz(z)azz, Piz(z)azz, Pzazz, Showoff, Swash-buckler

Flame, Flaming Ardent, Blaze, Fire, Flake, Flambé, Flammule, Flareback, Glow, Kindle, Leman, Lover, Lowe, Oxyacetylene, Reducing, Sweetheart

Flank(s) Accompany, Anta, Flange, Flitch, Ilia, Lisk, Loin, Side, Spur

Flannel Blather, Canton, Cloth, Flatter, Soft-soap, Waffle, Washrag, Zephyr

Flap(ped), Flapper, Flapping Ado, Aileron, Alar, Alarm(ist), Bate, Beat, Bird, Bobbysoxer, Bustle, Chit, Dither, Earcap, Elevon, Epiglottis, Flag, Flaught, Flutter, Fly, Fuss, Giglet, Hover, →**IN A FLAP**, Labrum, Lapel, Loma, Luff, Lug, Omentum, Panic, Spin, Spoiler, State, Tab, Tag, Tailboard, Tailgate, Tiswas, To-do, Tongue, Wave, Whisk

Flare(d), Flares, Flare up Bell, Bell-bottoms, Fishtail, Flame, Flanch, Flaunch, Godet, Magnesium, Scene, Signal, Skymarker, Spread, Spunk, Ver(e)y, Widen

Flash(y), Flasher, Flashpoint Bling, Bluette, Brainstorm, Brash, Emicant, Exposure, Flare, Flaught, Fulgid, Garish, Gaudy, Gleam, Glent, Glint, Glisten, Glitzy, Instant, Lairy, Levin, Lightning, Loud, Mo, Moment, Raffish, Ribbon, Roary, Scintillation, Second, Sequin, Showboater, Showy, Snazzy, Spark, Sparkle, Sport, Streak, Strobe, Swank(e)y, Tick, Trice, Tulip, Twinkle, Vivid, Wink, Wire

▷ **Flashing** *may indicate* an anagram

Flask(-shaped) Ampulla, Aryballos, Bottle, Canteen, Carafe, Cask, Coffin, Costrel, Cucurbit, Dewar, Erlenmeyer, Fiasco, Flacket, Flacon, Florence, Goatskin, Hip, Lekythos, Livery pot, Matrass, Mick(e)(y), Moon, Pycnidium, Reform, Retort, Thermos®, Vacuum, Vial

Flat(s), Flatness, Flatten(ed), Flattener Adobe, Alkali, Amaze, Ancipital, Apartment, Bachelor, Bald, Banal, Beat, Bed-sit, Blow-out, Bulldoze, Callow, Cape, Compress, Condominium, Cottage, Court, Dead, Demolish, Double, Dress, Dry, Dull, Even, Feeble, Flew, Floor, Flue, Fool, Gaff, Garden, Granny, High-rise, Home-unit, Horizontal, Insipid, Ironed, Jacent, Key, KO, Law, Lay, Level, Lifeless, Llano, Lodge, Maderised, Marsh, Monotonous, Mud, Nitwit, Obcompressed, Oblate, Ownership, Pad, Pancake, Pedestrian, Penthouse, Pied-à-terre, Plain, Plane, Plap, Plat, Plateau, Platitude, Press, Prone, Prostrate, Recumbent, Rooms, Salt, Scenery, Service, Smooth, Spread-edged, Squash, Studio, Tableland, Tame, Tasteless, Tenement, True, Uniform, Unsensational, Vapid, Walk-up

Flatter(er), Flattering, Flattery Adulate, Beslaver, Blandish, Blarney, Bootlick, Butter, Cajole, Candied, Carn(e)y, Claw(back), Complimentary, Court-dresser, Damocles, Fawn, Flannel, Flummery, Foot-licker, Fulsome, Grease, Honey, Imitation, Lip-salve, Moody, Palp, Poodle-faker, Puffery, Sawder, Smarm, Soap, Soother, Spaniel, Stroke, Sugar, Sweet talk, Sycophant, Taffy, Toady, Treacle, Unction, Wheedle

Flatulence, Flatulent Belch, Borborygmus, Burp, Carminative, Colic, Gas, Tympanites, Ventose, Wind, Wind dropsy

Flaunt Brandish, Flourish, Gibe, Parade, Skyre, Sport, Strout, Strut, Wave

Flavour(ed), Flavouring, Flavoursome Absinth(e), Alecost, Amaracus, Anethole, Angostura, Anise, Aniseed, Aroma, Bergamot, Bold, Borage, Bouquet garni, Clove, Coriander, Cumin, Dill, Essence, Eucalyptol, Fenugreek, Flor, Garni, Marinate, Mint, Orgeat, Quark, Race, Ratafia, Relish, Sair, Sapor, Sassafras, Season, Spearmint, Tack, Tang, Tarragon, →**TASTE**, Tincture, Twang, Umami, Vanilla, Yummy

Flaw Blemish, Brack, Bug, Chip, Crack, Defect, Fallacy, →**FAULT**, Gall, Hamartia, Imperfection, Infirmity, Kink, Lophole, Nick, Rima, Spot, Stain, Taint, Tear, Thief, Windshake

Flax(en) Aleseed, Blonde, Codilla, Harakeke, Harden, Hards, Herden, Herl, Hurden, Line, Linseed, Lint, Linum, Mill-mountain, Poi, Tow

Flea Aphaniptera, Chigger, Chigoe, Chigre, Daphnid, Hopper, Itch-mite, Lop, Pulex, Sand, Water

Flee(ing) Abscond, Bolt, Decamp, Escape, Eschew, Fly, Fugacity, Lam, Loup, Run, Scapa, Scarper, Scram

Fleece, Fleecy Bilk, Bleed, Coat, Despoil, Flocculent, Golden, Lambskin, Lanose, Nubia, Pash(i)m, Pashmina, Plo(a)t, Pluck, Rifte, Ring, Rob, Rook, Shave, Shear, Sheepskin, Skin, Skirtings, →**SWINDLE**, Toison

Fleet(ing) Armada, Brief, Camilla, Caravan, Convoy, Ephemeral, Evanescent, Fast, Flit, Flota, Flotilla, Fugacious, Fugitive, Glimpse, Hasty, Hollow, Lightfoot, Navy, Pacy, Passing, Prison, Spry, Street, Swift, Transient, Velocipede, Volatile

Flemish Flamingant

Flesh(y) Beefy, Body, Carneous, Carrion, Corporeal, Corpulent, Creatic, Digastric, Finish, Gum, Hypersarcoma, Joint, Jowl, Ket, Longpig, Love handles, Lush, Meat, Mole, Mons, Muffin top, Muscle, Mutton, Pulp, Quick, Sarcous, Spare tyre, Succulent, Tissue, Wattle

Flex(ible), Flexibility Adaptable, Bend(y), Elastic, Genu, Leeway, Limber, Lissom(e), Lithe, Pliant, Rubbery, Squeezy, Tensile, Tonus, Tractile, Versatile, Wieldy, Willing, Willowy, Wiry

▷ **Flexible, Flexuous** *may indicate* an anagram

Flick(er), Flicks Bioscope, Cinema, Fillip, Film, Flip, Flirt, Flutter, Glimmer, Gutter, Movie, Movy, Riffle, Snap, Snow, Spark, Switch, Talkie, Twinkle, Waver, Wink, Zap

Flier Airman, Alcock, Amy, Aviator, →**BIRD**, Blimp, Brown, Crow, Daedalus, Erk, Fur, George, Gotha, Handout, Icarus, Insert, Leaflet, Lindbergh, Pilot, RAF, Scotsman, Spec, Speedy

Flight(y), Flight path Air corridor, Backfisch, Birdbrain, Bolt, Bubble-headed, Capricious, Charter, Contact, Dart, Dash, Departure, Escalier, Escape, Exaltation, Exodus, Fast, Fickle, Flapper, Flaught, Flibbertigibbet, Flip, Flock, Flyby, Fly-past, Free, Fugue, Getaway, Giddy, Grece, Grese, Gris(e), Guy, Hegira, Hejira, Hejra, Hellicat, Hijra, Lam, Loup-the-dyke, Mercy, Milk-run, Mission, Open-jaw, Pair, Proving, Redeye, R(a)iser, Rode, Ro(a)ding, Rout, Runaway, Skein, Sortie, Stairs, Stayre, Steps, Swarm, Test, Top, Tower, Trap, Vol(age), Volageous, Volatile, Volley, Whisky-frisky, Wing

▷ **Flighty** *may indicate* an anagram

Flimsy Finespun, Fragile, Gimcrack, Gossamer, Jimcrack, Paper thin, Sleazy, Sleezy, Tenuous, Thin, Weak, Wispy

Flinch Blench, Cringe, Funk, Quail, Recoil, Shrink, Shudder, Start, Wince

Fling Affair, Dance, Flounce, Heave, Highland, Hurl, Lance, Pitch, Shy, Slat, Slug, Slump, Spanghew, Spree, Throw, →**TOSS**

Flint Chert, Firestone, Granite, Hag-stone, Hornstone, Microlith, Mischmetal, Pirate, Rock, Silex, Silica, Stone, Touchstone, Tranchet

Flip(pant), Flippancy, Flipping Airy, Bally, Brash, Cocky, Facetious, Flick, Frivolous, Impudent, Jerk, Nog, Overturn, Persiflage, Pert, Purl, Ruddy, Sassy, Saucy, Toss, Turn, Upend

Flirt(ation), Flirtatious, Flirting Bill, Buaya, Carve, Chippy, Cockteaser, Come-hither, Come-on, Coquet(te), Dalliance, Demivierge, Fizgig, Footsie, Gallivant,

Heart-breaker, Kittenish, Mash, Minx, Neck, Philander(er), Pickeer, Prick-teaser, Prink, Rig, Spark, Toy, Trifle, Vamp, Wow

Float(er), Floating, Flotation Balsa, Bob, Bubble, Buoy, Caisson, Camel, Carley, Clanger, Drift, Fleet, Flotsam, Flutterboard, Froth, Fucus, Jetsam, Jetson, Levitate, Lifebuoy, Milk, Natant, Neuston, Oropesa, Outrigger, Paddle, Planula, Pontoon, Pram, Quill, Raft, Ride, Sail, Skim, Sponson, Stick, Trimmer, Vacillate, Waft, Waggler, Waterwings, Weightless

Flock(s) Assemble, Bevy, Charm, Chirm, Company, Congregation, Dopping, Drove, Flight, Fold, Forgather, Gaggle, Gather, Gregatim, Herd, Mob, Paddling, Rally, Rout, School, Sedge, Sord, Spring, Trip, Tuft, Vulgar, Walk, Wing, Wisp, Wool

Flog(ger), Flogging Beat, Birch, Breech, Cane, Cat, Clobber, Exert, Flay, Hawk, Hide, Knout, Lace, Lambast, Larrup, Lash, Lather, Lick, Orbilius, Rope's end, Scourge, Sell, Strap, Tat, Taw, →**THRASH**, Thwack, Tout, Vapulate, Welt, Whip, Whipping-cheer

Flood(ed) Avalanche, Bore, Cataclysm, Deluge, Deucalion's, Diluvium, Dump, Eger, Flash, Freshet, Gush, Inundate, Irrigate, Noachic, Ogygian deluge, Outpouring, Overflow, Overswell, Overwhelm, Pour, Rage, Smurf, Spate, Speat, Suffuse, Swamp, Tide, Undam, Washland

Floor(ing) Area, Astonish, Astound, Baffle, Barbecue, Beat, Bemuse, Benthos, Chess, Deck(ing), Dev(v)el, Down, Entresol, Étage, Fell, Flags(tone), Flatten, Flight, Gravel, Ground, Kayo, KO, Mezzanine, Mould loft, Paralimnion, Parquet, Pelvic, Piano nobile, Pit, Planch, Platform, Puncheon, Screed, Shop, Siege, Sole, Stage, Stagger, Story, Stump, Terrazzo, Tessella, Tessera, Thill, Throw, Trading, Woodblock

Flop Belly-landing, Bomb, Collapse, Dud, Failure, Fizzer, Fosbury, Lollop, Mare's-nest, Misgo, Phut, Plump, Purler, Washout, Whap, Whitewash

Florid Baroque, Coloratura, Cultism, Flamboyant, Fresh, Gongorism, High, Red, Rococo, Rubicund, Ruddy, Taffeta

Florin Scotchman

Florist Spry

Flotsam Detritus, Driftwood, Flotage, Waift, Waveson, Weft

Flounce Falbala, Frill, Furbelow, Huff, Prance, Ruffle, Sashay, Toss

Flounder Blunder, Fluke, Reel, Sandsucker, Slosh, Struggle, Stumble, Tolter, Toss, Wallop, Wallow

Flour Buckwheat, Cassava, Couscous(ou), Cribble, Crible, Farina, Graham, Gram, Kouskous, Meal, Middlings, Pinole, Powder, Red-dog, Rice, Strong, Wheatmeal, Wholegrain, Wholemeal, Wholewheat

Flourish(ed), Flourishing Blague, Bless, Bloom, Blossom, Boast, Brandish, Bravura, Burgeon, Cadenza, Epiphonema, Fanfare, Fiorita, Fl, Flare, Florescent, Green, Grow, Kicking, Lush, Melisma, Mort, Palmy, Paraph, Pert, Prosper, Rubric, Scroll, Swash, Tantara, Thrive, Tucket, Veronica, Vigorous, Wampish, Wave, Welfare

Flow(ing) Abound, Afflux, Cantabile, Cantilena, Cash, Circumference, Current, Cursive, Cusec, Data, Distil, Ebb, Emanate, Estrang(h)elo, Fleet, Fluent, Fluid, Flush, Flux, Freeform, Gush, Issue, Knickpoint, Lahar, Laminar, Liquid, Loose-bodied, Nappe, Nickpoint, Obsequent, Onrush, Ooze, Popple, Pour, Purl, Rail(e), Rayle, Rill, Rin, Run, Rush, Scapa, Seamless, Seep, Seton, Setter, Slur, Spate, Stream, Streamline, Teem, Tidal, Torrent

▷ **Flower** *may indicate* a river

Flower (part), Flowering, Flowers, Flower bed Best, Bloom, Bloosme, Blossom, Composite, Cream, Develop, Disc, Efflorescence, Elite, Fiori, Inflorescence, Parterre, Plant, Pre-vernal, Prime, Quatrefeuille, Quatrefoil, →**RIVER**, Rogation, Serotine, Spray, Stalked, Thyrse, Trefoil, Verdoy, Vernal, Wreath

Flu Bird, Fujian, Gastric, →**INFLUENZA**, ME, Wog

Fluctuate(r), Fluctuation Ambivalence, Balance, Seasonal, Seiche, Trimmer, Unsteady, Vacillate, Vary, Waver, Yo-yo

Flue Chimney, Duct, Funnel, Pipe, Recuperator, Tewel, Uptake, Vent

Fluent(ly) Eloquent, Facile, Flowing, Glib, Liquid, Oracy, Verbose, Voluble

Fluff(y) Bungle, Candyfloss, Dowl(e), Down, Dust, Dust bunny, Feathery, Fleecy, Flocculent, Floss, Flue, Fug, Fuzz, Girl, Lint, Muff, Noil, Oose, Ooze, Plot, Thistledown

Fluid Aldehyde, Amniotic, Anasarca, Ascites, Bile, Broo, Chyle, Cisterna, Colostrum, Condy's, Correcting, Dewdrop, Enema, Erf, Fixative, Fl, Glycerin, Humour, Juice, →LIQUID, Lymph, Mucus, Oedema, Perilymph, Plasma, Pus, Sap, Serum, Shifting, Succus, Synovia, Transudate, Vitreum, Vril, Water

▷ **Fluid** *may indicate an anagram*

Fluke Accident, Anchor, Chance, Fan, Flounder, Ga(u)nch, Grapnel, Killock, Liver, Lobe, Redia, Scratch, Spud, Upcast

Flummery BS, Pudding

Flush(ed) Affluent, Beat, Even, Ferret, Florid, Flow, Gild, Hectic, Hot, Level, Red, Rolling, Rose, Royal, Rud, Scour, Sluice, Spaniel, Start, Straight, Sypher, Thrill, Tierce, Vigour, Wash, Well-heeled

Fluster(ed) Befuddle, Confuse, Disconcert, Faze, Flap, Jittery, Pudder, Rattle, Shake

Flute (player) Bellows-mender, Bohm, Channel, Claribel(la), Crimp, English, Fife, Fipple, Flageolet, Glass, Glyph, Groove, Marsyas, Nose, Ocarina, Piccolo, Pipe, Poogye(e), Quena, Shakuhachi, Sulcus, Thisbe, Tibia, Toot, Transverse, Whistle, Wineglass, Zuf(f)olo

Flutter Bat, Bet, Fan, Fibrillate, Flacker, Flaffer, Flaught, Flichter, Flicker, Flitter, Fly, →GAMBLE, Hover, Palpitate, Pitapat, Play, Pulse, Sensation, Twitter, Waft, Winnow

Fly(ing), Flies Abscond, Agaric, Airborne, Alder, Alert, Antlion, Arch, Assassin, Astute, Aviation, Awake, Aware, A-wing, Baker, Bedstead, Bee, Black, Blister, Blowfly, Blue-arsed, Bluebottle, Bolt, Bot, Breese, Breeze, Brize, Brommer, Bulb, Bush, Cab, Caddis, Canny, Carriage, Carrot, Cecidomyia, Chalcid, Cheesehopper, Cheese skipper, Cleg, Cluster, Cock-a-bondy, Crane, Cuckoo, →CUNNING, Damsel, Dash, Decamp, Deer, Diptera, Dobson, Doctor, Dolphin, Doodlebug, Dragon, Drake, Drone, Drosophila, Dry, Dung, Dutchman, Escape, Face, Fiacre, Flee, Flesh, Flit, Fox, Frit, Fruit, Gad, Glide, Glossina, Gnat, Goutfly, Grannom, Greenbottle, Greenhead, Hackle, Hairy Mary, Harl, Harvest, Hedge-hop, Herl, Hessian, Homoptera, Hop, Horn, Horse, Hover, Hurtle, Ichneumon, Instrument, Jenny-spinner, Jock Scott, Lace-wing, Lamp, Lantern, Laputan, March brown, Midge, Mosquito, Mossie, Moth, Motuca, Murragh, Musca, Mutuca, Namu, Needle, New Forest, Nymph, Onion, Opening, Ox-warble, Palmer, Para, Pilot, Pium, Plecopteran, Pomace, Rapid, Robber, Sacrifice, Saucer, Sciaridae, Scorpion, Scotsman, Screwworm, Scud, Sedge, Sheep ked, Silverhorn, Simulium, Smart, Smother, Snake, Snipe, Soar, Spanish, Speed, Spinner, Stable, Stream, Syrphidae, Tabanid, Tachina, Tail, Tear, Thrips, Tipula, Trichopteran, Tsetse, Tube, Turkey brown, Turnip, Vamoose, Vinegar, Volatic, Volitate, Warble, Watchet, Water, Welshman's button, Wet, Wheat, Wide-awake, Willow, Wily, Wing, Yellow Sally, Yogic, Zebub, Zimb, Zipper, Zoom

Fly-catcher Attercop, Clamatorial, Cobweb, Darlingtonia, Dionaea, King-bird, Phoebe, Spider, Tanrec, Tentacle, Tyrant, Yellowhead

Flyover Overpass

Foam(ing) Aerogel, Barm, Bubble, Froth, Head, Lather, Mousse, Oasis®, Polystyrene, Ream, Scum, Seethe, Spindrift, Spooming, Spume, Sud(s), Surf, Yeast, Yest

Focal, Focus Centre, Centrepiece, Clou, Concentrate, Converge, Fix, Hinge, Hub, Narrow, Nub, Pinpoint, Point, Real, Spotlight, Train, Zoom

Fodder Alfalfa, Browsing, Buckwheat, Cannon, Clover, Eatage, Ensilage, Foon, Forage, Gama-grass, Grama, Guar, Hay, Lucerne, Mangle, Mangold, Oats, Pasture, Provender, Rye-grass, Sainfoin, Silage, Stover, Straw, Ti-tree, Vetch, Yarran

Foe Anti, Arch, Contender, →ENEMY, Opponent, Rival

Fog Aerosol, Brume, Cloud, Damp, Fret, Haar, Miasm(a), Mist, Murk, Obscure, Pea-soup(er), Roke, Sea-fret, Sea-haar, Smog, Smoke, Soup, Thick, Vapour, Yorkshire

Foil(ed) Ba(u)lk, Chaff, Cross, Dupe, Epée, Fleuret(te), Frustrate, Gold leaf, Lametta, Leaf, Offset, Paillon, Pip, Scotch, Silver, Stime, Stooge, Stump, Stymie, Sword, Thwart, Tinsel, Touché

Fold(er), Folding, Folded, Folds Close, Collapse, Concertina, Corrugate, Crease, Crimp, Crinkle, Fan, Fourchette, Frill, Furl, Gather, Geanticline, Inflexure, Intussuscept, Jacket, Jack-knife, Mantle, Mitre, Monocline, Nappe, Pintuck, →PLEAT, Ply, Pound, Ruck(le), Sheep-pen, Syncline, Tuck, Wrap

Foliage Coma, Finial, Frond, Frondescence, Greenery, Leafage, Leaves

Follow(er), Following Acolyte, Acolyth, Adhere, Admirer, After, Agree, Amoret, Anthony, Attend(ant), Believer, Chase, Clientele, Consequence, Copy, Dangle, Disciple, Dog, Echo, Ensew, Ensue, Entourage, Epigon(e), Equipage, F, Fan, Groupie, Heel(er), Henchman, Hereon, Hunt, Imitate, Jacob, Man, Merry men, Mimic, Minion, Muggletonian, Myrmidon, Neist, Next, Obey, Pan, Post, Pursue, Rake, Road, Run, Satellite, School, Sectary, Secundum, Seewing, Segue, Sequel, Seriation, Shadow, Sheep, Sidekick, S(h)ivaite, Stag, Stalk, Stear, Steer, Subsequent, Succeed, Sue, Suivez, Supervene, Tag, Tail, Tantony, Trace, Track, Trail, Train, Use, Vocation, Votary

▷ **Follower** *may indicate B*

Folly Absurd, Antic, Bêtise, Idiocy, Idiotcy, Imprudence, Lunacy, Madness, Mistake, Moria, Stupidity, Unwisdom, Vanity

Fond(ness) Amatory, Ardour, Attachment, Dote, Keen, Loving, Partial, Tender, Tendre

Fondle Canoodle, Caress, Dandle, Grope, Hug, Nurse, Pet, Snuggle, Stroke

Food Aliment, Ambrosia, Bento, Board, Broth, Bully, Burger, Bush-tucker, Carry-out, Cate, Cereal, Cheer, Cheese, Chop, Chow, Collation, Comestible, Commons, Cook-chill, Course, Cud, →DISH, Doner kebab, Eatage, Eats, Famine, Fare, Fodder, Forage, Formula, Fuel, Giffengood, Grub, Gruel, Hamburger, Keep, Makan, Maki, Manna, Meat (loaf), Nosh, Nourishment, Obento, Opsonium, Ort, Pasta, Pasture, Provand, Provender, Provision, Pu(l)ture, Real, Refreshment, Risotto, Roughage, Samosa, Schri, Scoff, Scran, Scroggin, Skran, Snack, Soft meat, Square meal, Staple, Stir fry, Stodge, Table, Tack, Takeaway, Tempeh, Tex-Mex, Trimmings, Tripe, Tsamba, Tuck(er), Viand, Victuals, Vivres, Waffle

Fool(hardy), Foolish(ness) April, Asinico, Asinine, Berk, Blithering, Booby, Bottom, Buffoon, Chump, Clot, Clown, Cockeyed, Coney, Coof, Coxcomb, Cuif, Delude, Desipience, Dilly, Divvy, Doat, Doilt, Dote, Dummy, Dunce, Dweeb, Flannel(led), Folly, Gaby, Gaga, Git, Goat, Goon, Goose, Gubbins, Gull, Halfwit, Have, Haverel, Hoax, Idiotic, Imbecile, Inane, Insensate, Jest, Jester, Joke, Kid, Lark, Madcap, Misguide, Mislead, Moron, Muggins, Nerk, Ni(n)compoop, Ninny, Noodle, Nose-led, Nut, Pea-brained, Prat, Senseless, S(c)hmo, Simpleton, Soft, Sot, Stultify, →STUPID, Sweet, Trifle, Turkey, Yap, Zany

Fool's gold Mundic, Pyrites

Foot(ing), Footwork, Feet Anap(a)est, Athlete's, Base, Board, Choliamb, Choreus, Choriamb, Club, Dactyl, Dance, Dipody, Flat, Ft, Hoof, Iamb(us), Infantry, Pad, Paeon, Paw, Pedal, Penthemimer, Pettitoes, Podiatry, Podium, Shanks's pony, Splay, Standing, Tarsus, Terms, Tootsie, Tread, Trench, Trochee, Trotter, Ungula

Football(er) American, Association, Back, Banyana-banyana, Barbarian, Ba'spiel, Best, Camp, Centre, Double header, Fantasy, FIFA, Flanker(back), Futsal, Gaelic, Gazza, Goalie, Gridder, Half, Hooker, Keeper, Kicker, Libero, Linebacker, Lineman, Lock, Midfield, Moore, National code, Nickelback, Pack, Pele, Pigskin, Ranger, RU, Rugby, Rugger, Rules, Safety, Soccer(oos), Sport, Striker, Superbowl, Sweeper, Table, Total, Touch(back), Wing

Foothills Submontane

Footling Trivial

Footman Attendant, Flunkey, Hiker, Lackey, Ped(estrian), Pompey, Valet de chambre, Yellowplush

Footpath, Footway Banquette, Catwalk, Clapper, Track

Footprint Carbon, Electronic, Ichnite, Ichnolite, Ornithichnite, Pad, Prick, Pug, Seal, Slot, Trace, Track, Vestige

Footwear Gumboot, Jackboot, →SHOE, Slipper, Sock, Spats, Stocking

Fop(pish) Apery, Barbermonger, Beau, Buck, Cat, Coxcomb, Dandy, Dude, Exquisite,

Fallal, Fantastico, Finical, La-di-da, Macaroni, Monarcho, Muscadin, Petit maître, Popinjay, Skipjack, Toff

For Ayes, Because, Concerning, Cos, Pro, Since, To

Forage Alfalfa, Fodder, Graze, Greenfeed, Lucern(e), Pickeer, Prog, Raid, Rummage, Sainfoin, Search

Forbear(ance), Forbearing Abstain, Clement, Endure, Indulgent, Lenience, Lineage, Longanimity, Mercy, Overgo, Pardon, Parent, Patient, Quarter, **→REFRAIN**, Suffer, Tolerant, Withhold

Forbid(den), Forbidding Ban, Bar, City, Denied, Don't, Dour, Enjoin, For(e)speak, Gaunt, Grim, Haram, Hostile, Loury, NL, Prohibit, Proscribe, Sinister, Stern, Taboo, Tabu, Tapu, Tref(a), Verboten, Veto

Force(d), Forceful, Forces, Forcible, Forcing Agency, Army, Assertive, Back emf, Bludgeon, Body, Brigade, Bring, Brunt, Bulldoze, Capillary, Centrifugal, Coerce, Coercive, Commando, Compel, Constrain, Cops, Cram, Detachment, Domineer, Dragoon, Drive, Duress(e), Edge, Electromotive, Emphatic, Energetic, Exact, Exchange, Expeditionary, Fifth, Fire brigade, Foot-pound, Foot-ton, Foss, Frogmarch, Full-line, Gendarmerie, Gravitational, Great Attractor, High-powered, Host, Hunter-killer, Impetus, Impose, Impress, Impulsion, Inertial, Interpol, Juggernaut, Kinetic, Kundalini, Labour, Land, Landsturm, Landwehr, Legion, Leverage, Life, Lift, Live load, Magnetomotive, Make, Manpower, Market, Met, Muscle, Nature-god, Oblige, Od, Old Contemptibles, Orotund, Personnel, Physical, Plastic, Police, Polis, Posse, Potent, Pound, Power, Press(gang), Pressure, Prise, Psyche, Psychic, Pull, Punchy, Pushy, Railroad, Ram, Rape, Ravish, Reave, Red Army, Require, SAS, Shoehorn, Spent, Squad, Squeeze, Steam(roller), Steem, Stick, Stiction, Sting and ling, Strength, Strong-arm, Subject, Sword, TA, Task, Teeth, Territorial, The Bill, The Great Attractor, Thrust, Torque, Tractive, Troops, Upthrust, Vehement, Vigorous, Vim, Violence, Vis visa, Vital, Vociferous, Weak, Wedge, Wrench, Wrest, Wring, Zap

▷ **Force(d)** *may indicate* an anagram

▶ **Forebear** *see* **FORBEAR(ANCE)**

Foreboding Anxiety, Augury, Cloudage, Croak, Feeling, Freet, Hoodoo, **→OMEN**, Ominous, Premonition, Presage, Presentient, Presentiment, Sinister, Zoomantic

Forecast(er), Forecasting Augury, Auspice, Divine, Extrapolation, Glass, Horoscope, Long-range, Metcast, Metman, Omen, Perm, Precurse, Predicate, Predict, Presage, Prescience, Prevision, Prognosis, Prognosticate, Projection, Prophesy, Quant, Rainbird, Scry, Shipping, Skry, Soothsay, Spae, Tip, Weather

Foreground Repoussage, Repoussoir

Forehead Brow, Front(let), Frontal, Glabella(r), Nasion, Sincipitum, Temple

▷ **Foreign** *may indicate* an anagram

Foreign(er) Adventitious, Alien, Arab, Auslander, Barbarian, Easterling, Eleanor, Ethnic, Étranger, Exclave, Exotic, External, Extraneous, Extrinsic, Forane, Forinsecal, Forren, Fraim, Fremit, Gaijin, German, Gringo, Gweilo, Malihini, Metic, Moit, Mote, Outlander, Outside, Oversea, Peregrine, Remote, **→STRANGE**, Stranger, Taipan, Tramontane, Uitlander, Unfamiliar, Wog

Foreign Office FO, Quai d'Orsay

Foreknowledge Prescience

Foreman Baas, Boss, Bosun, Chancellor, Clicker, Gaffer, Ganger, Manager, Overseer, Steward, Straw boss, Superintendent, Tool pusher, Topsman, Walla(h)

Foremost First, Front, Leading, Primary, Prime, Salient, Supreme, Upfront, Van

▷ **Foremost** *may indicate* first letters of words following

Forerunner Augury, Harbinger, Herald, Messenger, Omen, Pioneer, Precurrer, Precursor, Trailer, Vaunt-courier

Foreshadow Adumbrate, Augur, Bode, Forebode, Hint, Portend, Pre-echo, Prefigure, Presage, Type

Foresight Ganesa, Prescience, Prophecy, Prospect, Providence, Prudence, Taish, Vision

Forest(ry), Forested Arden, Ardennes, Argonne, Ashdown, Black, Bohemian, Brush, Bush, Caatinga, Charnwood, Chase, Cloud, Cranborne Chase, Dean, Deer,

Elfin, Epping, Firth, Gallery, Gapo, Glade, Greenwood, Igapo, Jungle, Katyn, Monte, Nandi, Nemoral, New, Nottingham, Savernake, Selva, Sherwood, Taiga, Teutoburg, Urman, Virgin, Wealden, → **WOOD**, Woodland

Forestall Anticipate, Head-off, Obviate, Pip, Pre-empt, Prevent, Queer, Scoop

Foretaste Antepast, Antipasto, Appetiser, Avant-goût, Pregustation, Prelibation, Sample, Trailer

Foretell(ing), Forewarn Augur, Bode, Caution, Divine, Fatidic, Forecast, Portend, Predict, Premonish, Presage, Previse, Prognosticate, Prophecy, Soothsay, Spae, Weird

Forethought Anticipation, Caution, Prometheus, Provision, Prudence

Forever All-time, Always, Amber, Ay(e), Constant, Eternal, Evermore, Keeps

▶ **Forewarn** *see* FORETELL(ING)

Foreword Introduction, Preamble, Preface, Proem, Prologue

For example Eg, Say, Vg, ZB

Forfeit(ed) Confiscated, Deodand, Fine, Forgo, → **PENALTY**, Phillepina, Phillepine, Philop(o)ena, Relinquish, Rue-bargain, Sconce

Forge(d), Forger(y) Blacksmith, Copy, Counterfeisance, Counterfeit, Drop(-hammer), Dud, Fabricate, Fake, Falsify, Fashion, Foundry, Hammer, Heater, Horseshoe, Ireland, Ironsmith, Lauder, Mint, Nailery, Paper-hanger, Pigott, Progress, Rivet head, Smith(y), Smithery, Spurious, Stiddie, Stiff, Stithy, Stumer, Tilt, Trucage, Truquage, Utter, Valley, Vermeer, Vulcan, Weld

Forget(ful), Forget-me-not, Forgetting Amnesia, Dry, Fluff, Infonesia, Lethe, Lotus, Myosotis, Neglect, Oblivious, Omit, Overlook, Senior moment, Unlearn, Wipe

Forgive(ness), Forgiving Absolution, Amnesty, Clement, Condone, Divine, Excuse, Lenity, Merciful, Overlook, Pardon, Placable, Remission, Remittal, Tolerant

Forgo(ne) Abstain, Expected, Refrain, Renounce, Waive

For instance As

Fork(ed), Fork out Bifurcate, Biramous, Branch, Caudine, Cleft, Crotch, Divaricate, Forficate, Fourchette, Grain, Graip, Morton's, Osmeterium, Pastry, Pay, Pickle, Prong, Runcible, Slave, Tine, Toaster, Toasting, Tormenter, Tormentor, Trident, Trifid, Tuner, Tuning, Y

▷ **Form** *may indicate* a hare's bed

Form(s) Allotropic, Alumni, Bench, Bumf, Cast, Ceremonial, Charterparty, Class, Clipped, Constitute, Coupon, Create, Document, Draw up, Dress, Experience, Fashion, Feature, Fig, → **FIGURE**, Formula, Frame, Free, Game, Generate, Gestalt, Hare, Idea, Image, Inscape, Keto, Lexicalise, Life, Logical, Mode, Mood, Morph(ic), Morphology, Mould, Order, Originate, P45, Penitent, Physique, Protocol, Questionnaire, Redia, Remove, Rite, Ritual, Schedule, Shape, Shell, Sonata, Song, Stage, Stamp, State, Stem, Stereotype, Structure, Style, Symmetry, Talon, Ternary, Version

Formal, Formality Amylum, Black tie, Ceremony, Conventional, Dry, Exact, Fit, Ice, Literal, Methodic, Official, Pedantic, Pedantry, Perfunctory, Pomp, Precise, Prim, Protocol, Punctilio, Reserved, Routine, Set, Starch, Starched, Stiff, Stiff-necked, Stodgy, Stuffed shirt, Tails

Formation Battalion, Brown, Catenaccio, Configuration, Diapyesis, Echelon, Eocene, Fours, Growth, Layout, Line, Manufacture, Origin, Pattern, Phalanx, Potence, Prophase, Reticular, Riss, Series, Serried, Shotgun, Testudo, Wedge

▷ **Former** *may indicate* something that forms

Former(ly) Ance, Auld, Before, Ci-devant, Earlier, Ere-now, Erst(while), Ex, Late, Maker, Matrix, Old(en), Once, One-time, Past, Previous, Prior, Pristine, Quondam, Sometime, Then, Umquhile, Umwhile, Whilom, Yesterday

Formidable Alarming, Armipotent, Battleaxe, Fearful, Forbidding, Gorgon, Powerful, Redoubtable, Shrewd, Stoor, Stour, Stowre, Sture, Tiger

▷ **Form of, Forming** *may indicate* an anagram

Formula(te) Define, Devise, Doctrine, Empirical, Equation, Frame, Graphic, Incantation, Invent, Kekule, Lurry, Molecular, Paternoster, Prescription, Protocol, Prunes and prisms, Reduction, Rite, Ritual, Stirling's, Structural

For now Interim, Meanwhile

For sure Pukka

Fort(ification), Fortress Abatis, Acropolis, Alamo, Bastel-house, Bastide, Bastille, Battlement, Berchtesgaden, Blockhouse, Burg, Casbah, Castle, Citadel, Counterscarp, Earthwork, Fastness, Fieldwork, Garrison, Gatehouse, Haven, Hill, Kasba(h), Keep, La(a)ger, Legnaga, Line, Mantua, Moat, Pa(h), Peel, Peschiera, Przernysl, Rampart, Ravelin, Redan, Redoubt, Salient, Stavropol, Stockade, Stronghold, Ticonderoga, Tower, Tower of London, Vallum, Verona

Forthright(ness) Blunt, Candid, Direct, Four-square, Frank, Glasnost, Outspoken, Prompt, Vocal

Fortify Arm, Augment, Brace, Casemate, Embattle, Lace, Munify, Soup up, Steel, →**STRENGTHEN**

Fortitude Endurance, Grit, Guts, Mettle, Patience, Pluck, →**STAMINA**

Fortune, Fortunate, Fortuitous Auspicious, Blessed, Blest, Bomb, Chance, Coincident, Godsend, Happy, Killing, →**LUCKY**, Madoc, Opportune, Pile, Providential, Sonce, Tyche, Up, Well, Well off

Fortune teller, Fortune-telling Auspicious, Bonanza, Bumby, Cartomancy, Chaldee, Cha(u)nce, Chiromancy, Destiny, Dukkeripen, Fame, Fate, Felicity, Forecast, Genethliac, Geomancy, Hap, Hydromancy, I Ching, Lot, Luck, Mint, Motser, Motza, Oracle, Packet, Palmist, Peripety, Pile, Prescience, Pyromancy, Sibyl, Soothsayer, Sortilege, Spaewife, Success, Taroc, Tarok, Tarot, Tyche, Wealth, Windfall

Forum Arena, Assembly, Debate, Platform, Synod, Tribunal

Forward (looking), Forward(s) Accede, Advanced, Ahead, Along, Arch, Assertive, Assuming, Avanti, Bright, Cheeky, Early, Flanker, Forrad, Forrit, Forth, Fresh, Future, Hasten, Hooker, Immodest, Impudent, Insolent, Lock, Malapert, Minx, Number eight, On(wards), Pack, Pert, Petulant, Porrect, Precocious, Prescient, →**PROGRESS**, Promote, Prop, Readdress, Redirect, Saucy, Scrum, Send, Stem, Striker, To(ward), Van, Wing

Fossil(ised), Fossils Amber, Ammonite, Baculite, Belemnite, Blastoid(ea), Calamite, Ceratodus, Chondrite, Conodont, Cordaites, Creodont, Crinite, Derived, Dolichosauria, Encrinite, Eohippus, Eozoon, Eurypterus, Exuviae, Fogy, Goniatite, Graptolite, Hippurite, Hominid, Ichnite, Ichnolite, Ichnology, Ichthyodurolite, Ichthyolite, Index, Kenyapithecus, Lingulella, Mosasauros, Nummulite, Olenellus, Olenus, Orthoceras, Osteolepis, Ostracoderm, Petrifaction, Phytolite, Plesiosaur, Pliohippus, Pliosaur, Pterygotus, Pythonomorph, Relics, Reliquiae, Remanié, Sigillaria, Sinanthropus, Snakestone, Stigmaria, Stromatolite, Taphonomy, Tentaculite, Thunderegg, Titanotherium, Trace, Trilobite, Uintatherium, Wood-opal, Zinganthropus, Zone, Zoolite

Foster (child, mother), Fostering Adopt, Cherish, Da(u)lt, Develop, Feed, Fornent, Further, Harbour, Incubation, Metapelet, Metaplot, Nourish, Nourse(l), Noursle, Nousell, Nurse, Nurture, Nuzzle, →**REAR**

Foul, Foul-smelling Base, Bastardise, Bedung, Beray, Besmirch, Besmutch, Bewray, Bungle, Dreggy, Drevill, Dunghole, Enseam, Evil, Feculent, Gross, Hassle, Hing, In-off, Mephitic, Mud, Noisome, Olid, Osmeterium, Paw(paw), Personal, Professional, Putid, Putrid, →**RANK**, Reekie, Reeky, Rotten, Sewage, Soiled, Squalid, Stagnant, Stain, Stapelia, Technical, Unclean, Unfair, Vilde, Vile, Violation, Virose

▷ **Foul** *may indicate* an anagram

Found(ation), Foundations Base, Basis, Bedrock, Cribwork, Establishment, Fond, Footing, Girdle, Grillage, Ground, Grounding, Groundwork, Hard-core, Infrastructure, Initiate, Institution, Matrix, Mattress, Pile, Pitching, Roadbed, Rockefeller, Scholarship, Stays, Subjacent, Substrata, Substructure, Trackbed, Underlie, Underlinen

Found (in) Among, Base, Bed, Bottom, Build, Cast, Emong, Endow, →**ESTABLISH**, Eureka, Institute, Introduce, Met, Occur, Plant, Recovered, Rest, Stablish, Start, Table

▷ **Foundations** *may indicate* last letters

Founder Author, Bell, Crumple, Fail, Inventor, Iron-master, Miscarry, Oecist, Oekist, Patriarch, Perish, Progenitor, Settle, Sink, Stumble

Fountain Acadine, Aganippe, Bubbler, Castalian, Cause, Conduit, Drinking, Fauwara,

Forts, Gerbe, Head, Hippocrene, Jet, Pant, Pirene, Salmacis, Scuttlebutt, Soda, Spring, Trevi, Well-spring, Youth

Four(times), Foursome, Four-yearly Cater, Georges, Horsemen, IV, Mess, Mournival, Penteteric, Quartet, Quaternary, Quaternion, Reel, Tessara, Tessera, Tetrad, Tetralogy, Tiddy, Warp

Fourth Deltaic, Estate, Fardel, Farl(e), Forpet, Forpit, July, Martlet, Quartet, Quaternary, Quintan, Sesquitertia, Tritone

Fowl Barnyard, Biddy, Boiler, Brahma, Brissle-cock, Burrow-duck, Capon, Chicken, Chittagong, Cob, Cock, Coot, Duck, Ember, Gallinaceous, Gallinule, Game, Guinea, Hamburg(h), →HEN, Houdan, Jungle, Knob, Kora, Leghorn, Moorhen, Papageno, Partridge, Pheasant, Pintado, Poultry, Quail, Rooster, Rumkin, Rumpy, Scrub, Solan, Spatchcock, Spitchcock, Sultan, Sussex, Teal, Turkey, Wyandotte

Fox(y) Alopecoid, Arctic, Baffle, Bat-eared, Bewilder, Blue, Charley, Charlie, Corsac, Crafty, Cunning, Desert, Fennec, Floor, Fool, Friend, Fur, Grey, Kit, Lowrie(-tod), Outwit, Pug, Puzzle, Quaker, Red, Reynard, Rommel, Russel, Silver, Skulk, →SLY, Stump, Swift, Tod, Uffa, Uneatable, Vixen, White, Zerda, Zoril(le), Zorro

Foxtrot Dance, F

Fracas Brawl, Dispute, Mêlée, Prawle, Riot, Rumpus, Shindig, Uproar

Fraction Complex, Decimal, Improper, Ligroin, Mantissa, Mixed, Mole, Part, Piece, Proper, Scrap, Simple, Some, Tithe, Vulgar

Fracture Break, Colles, Comminuted, Complicated, Compound, Crack, Fatigue, Fault, Fissure, Gap, Greenstick, Hairline, Impacted, Incomplete, Oblique, Pathological, Platy, Pott's, Rupture, Shear, Simple, Spiral, Splintery, Split, Stress, Transverse

Fragile Brittle, Crisp, Delicate, Flimsy, Frail, Frangible, Nesh, Slender, Tender, Vulnerable, Weak

Fragment(s) Agglomerate, Atom, Bit, Bla(u)d, Brash, Breccia, Brockage, Brockram, Cantlet, Clastic, Crumb, Disjecta membra, End, Flinder, Fritter, Frust, Graile, Lapilli, Mammock, Morceau, Morsel, Ort, →PARTICLE, Piece, Piecemeal, Potshard, Potsherd, Relic, Rift, Rubble, Scrap, Segment, Shard, Shatter, Sheave, Shiver, Shrapnel, Skerrick, Sliver, Smithereens, Smithers, Snatch, Splinter

▷ **Fragment of** *may indicate* a hidden word

Fragrance, Fragrant Aromatic, Attar, Balsam, Bouquet, Conima, Nosy, Odiferous, Odour, Olent, →PERFUME, Pot-pourri, Redolent, →SCENT, Sent, Spicy, Suaveolent

Frail Brittle, Creaky, Delicate, Feeble, Flimsy, →FRAGILE, Puny, Rushen, Slight, Slimsy, Tottery, Weak

Frame(work) A, Angle, Bier, Body, Build, Bustle, Cage, Case, Casement, Casing, Chassis, Coaming, Cold, Cradle, Dutchwife, Fabric, Falsework, Fender, Fit-up, Form, Gantry, Haik, Hake, Hovel, Incriminate, Lattice, Louvre, Monture, Pack, Pergola, Pumphead, Punchboard, Quilting, Rack, Reading, Roof rack, Scaffold, Screen, Setting, Skeleton, Spider, Stand, Stern, Stitch up, →STRUCTURE, Swift, Tabouret, Timeline, Zimmer®

Franchise Charter, Concession, Contract, Liberty, Pot-wall(op)er, Privilege, Right, Suffrage, Vote, Warrant

Frank(ish) Bluff, Blunt, →CANDID, Direct, Easy, Four square, Free, Free-spoken, Guileless, Honest, Ingenuous, Man-to-man, Merovingian, Natural, Open, Outspoken, Postage, Postmark, Raw, Ripuarian, Salian, Sincere, Squareshooter, Stamp, Straight, Sty, Upfront

Frantic Demoniac, Deranged, Distraught, Drissy, Frenzied, Hectic, Mad, Overwrought, Phrenetic, Rabid, Violent, Whirl(ing)

▷ **Frantic** *may indicate* an anagram

Fraternise, Fraternity Affiliate, Brotherhood, Burschenschaft, Consort, Elk, Fellowship, Lodge, Mingle, Moose, Order, Shriner, Sodality

Fraud(ulent) Barratry, Bobol, Bogus, Bubble, Chain-letter, Charlatan, Cheat, Chisel, Collusion, Covin, Cronk, Deceit, Diddle, Do, Fineer, Grift, Gyp, Humbug, Hypocrite, →IMPOSTOR, Imposture, Jiggery-pokery, Jobbery, Kite, Liar, Peculator, Phishing, Phon(e)y, Piltdown, Pious, Pseud(o), Put-up, Quack, Ringer, Rip-off, Roguery, Rort,

Salami technique, Scam, Shoulder surfing, South Sea Bubble, Stellionate, Sting, Stumer, Supercherie, Swindle, Swiz(z), Swizzle, Tartuffe, Trick, Vishing, Wire

Fray(ed) Bagarre, Brawl, Contest, Feaze, Frazzle, Fret, Fridge, Ravel, Riot, Scrimmage, Wigs on the green

Frazzle Wear down

Freak(ish) Bizarre, Cantrip, Caprice, Chimera, Control, Deviant, Geek, Lusus naturae, Sport, Teras, Vagary, Weirdo, Whim, Whimsy

▷ **Free** *may indicate* an anagram

Free(d), Freely Abstrict, Acquit, Assoil, At large, Buckshee, Candid, Canny, Church, Clear, Complimentary, Cuffo, Dead-head, Deliver, Deregulate, Detach, Devoid, Disburden, Disburthen, Disembarrass, Disembroil, Disengage, Disentangle, Eleutherian, Emancipate, Enfranchise, Enlarge, Excuse, Exeem, Exeme, Exempt, Exonerate, Extricate, Familiar, Footloose, Frank, French, Gratis, House, Idle, Immune, Indemnify, Independent, Kick, Large, Lavish, Lax, Leisure, Let, Liberate, Loose, Manumit, Open, Parole, Pro bono, Pure, Quit(e), Range, Ransom, Redeem, →**RELEASE**, Relieve, Requiteless, Rescue, Reskew, Rick, Rid, Sciolto, Scot, Solute, Spare, Spring, Stald, Stall, Trade, Unbowed, Unlace, Unlock, Unloosen, Unmew, Unmuzzle, Unshackle, Unsnarl, Unstick, Untangle, Untie, Untwist, Vacant, Verse, Voluntary

Freedom Abandon, Autonomy, Breadth, Carte blanche, Eleutherian, Exemption, Fear, Fling, Four, Immunity, Impunity, Independence, Latitude, Leeway, Leisure, Liberty, Licence, Play, Releasement, Speech, Uhuru, UNITA, Want, Wiggle room, Worship

Freehold(er) Enfeoff, Franklin, Frank tenement, Seisin, Udal(ler), Yeoman

▷ **Freely** *may indicate* an anagram

Freemason(ry), Freemason's son Craft, Lewis, Lodge, Moose, Templar

Freeze(s), Freezer, Freezing Alcarrazo, Arctic, Benumb, Congeal, Cool, Cryogenic, Eutectic, Freon®, Frost, Geal, Harden, Ice, Ice cold, Lyophilize, Nip, Numb, Paralyse, Regelate, Riss, Stiffen

Freight(liner) Cargo, Carriage, Fraught, Goods, Goods train, Load

French(man), Frenchwoman Alain, Alsatian, Anton, Basque, Breton, Crapaud, Creole, Dawn, Emil(e), Frog(-eater), Gallic(e), Gaston, Gaul, Gombo, Grisette, Gumbo, Homme, Huguenot, Joual, M, Mamselle, Marianne, Midi, Mounseer, Neo-Latin, Norman, Parleyvoo, René, Rhemish, Savoyard, Yves

Frenzied, Frenzy Amok, Berserk, Corybantic, Deliration, Delirium, Demoniac, Enrage, Enrapt, Euhoe, Euoi, Evoe, Fever, Fit, Fury, Hectic, Hysteric, Lune, Maenad, Mania, Must, Nympholepsy, Oestrus, Phrenetic, Rage, Tantrum

Frequency, Frequent(er), Frequently Attend, Audio, Channel, Common, Constant, Familiar, Formant, FR, Fresnel, Habitué, Hang-out, Haunt, Hertz, High, Incidence, Kilocycle, L-band, Low, Megahertz, Mode, Often, Passband, Penetrance, Pulsatance, Radio, Recurrent, Spectrum, Superhigh, Terahertz, Thick, Waveband

Fresh(en), Freshness Anew, Aurorean, Brash, Caller, Chilly, Clean, Crisp, Deodorise, Dewy, Entire, Evergreen, Fire-new, Forward, Green, Hot, Insolent, Live(ly), Maiden, Nas(s)eem, New, Novel, Quick, Rebite, Recent, Roral, Roric, Rorid, Smart, Span-new, Spic(k), Sweet, Tangy, Uncured, Verdure, Vernal, Virent, Virescent

Fret(ful) Chafe, Filigree, Fray, Gnaw, Grate, Grecque, Haze, Impatient, Irritate, Key, Mist, Ornament, Peevish, Repine, Rile, Ripple, Roil, Rub, Tetchy, Tracery, Whittle, Worry

Friar(s) Augustinian, Austin, Bacon, Barefoot, Black, Bonaventura, Bonaventure, Brother, Bungay, Capuchin, Carmelite, Conventual, Cordelier, Crutched, Curtal, Dervish, Dominican, Fra(ter), Franciscan, Frate, Jacobin, Laurence, Limiter, Lymiter, Minim, Minorite, →**MONK**, Observant, Observantine, Preaching, Predicant, Recollect, Recollet, Rush, Tuck, White

Fricative Rill

Friction Attrition, Conflict, Detrition, Dissent, Drag, Massage, Rift, Rub, Stridulation, Tribology, Tripsis, Wear, Windblast, Xerotripsis

Friend(ly), Friends Ally, Alter ego, Ami(cable), Amigo, Bach, Benign, Bosom, Bra, Bro, Bru, Bud(dy), China, Chommie, Chum, Cobber, Companion, Comrade,

Confidant, Cordial, Cotton, Couthy, Crony, Damon, Ehoa, Familiar, Folksy, Gossip, Homeboy, Intimate, Kidgie, Lover, Mate, McKenzie, Mutual, Next, Oppo, Pal, Pen, Playmate, Quaker, Sidekick, Sociable, Sport, Steady, Thawing, Thick, Type B, User, Well-disposed, Yaar

Friendliness, Friendship Amity, Bonhomie, Camaraderie, Contesseration, Entente, Platonic, Rapprochement, Sodality

Fright(en), Frightened, Frightening, Frightful Afear, Affear(e), Agrise, Agrize, Agryze, Alarm, Aroint, Aroynt, Ashake, Chilling, Cow, Da(u)nt, Dare, Deter, Eek, Eerie, Eery, Faceache, Fear(some), Flay, Fleg, Fleme, Fley, Flush, Gallow, Gally, Ghast, Gliff, Glift, Grim, Grisly, Hairy, Horrid, Horrific, Intimidate, Ordeal, Panic, Petrify, Scar, Scarre, Scaur, Schrecklich, Sight, Skear, Skeer, Skrik, Spook, Stage, Startle, Terrible, Terrify, Terror, Tirrit, Unco, Unman, Windy

Frill(y) Armil, Armilla, Bavolet, Falbala, Flounce, Furbelow, Jabot, Lingerie, Newgate, Ornament, Papillote, Ruche, Ruff(le), Shirt, Tucker, Valance

▷ **Frilly** *may indicate* an anagram

Fringe(s), Fringed Bang, Border, Bullion, Celtic, Ciliated, Ciliolate, Edge, Fall, Fimbria, Frisette, Laciniate, Loma, Lunatic, Macramé, Macrami, Newgate, Pelmet, Peripheral, Robin, Ruff, Run, Thrum, Toupee, Toupit, Tzitzit(h), Valance, Verge, Zizith

Frisk(y) Caper, Cavort, Curvet, Fisk, Flimp, Frolic, Gambol, Search, Skip, Wanton

Fritter Batter, Beignet, Dribble, Dwindle, Fragment, Fribble, Pakora, Potter, Puf(f)taloon, Squander, Waste, Wonder

Frivolity, Frivolous Butterfly, Empty(-headed), Etourdi(e), Facetious, Featherbrain, Flighty, Flippant, Frippet, Frothy, Futile, Giddy, Idle, Inane, Levity, Light, Lightweight, Moth, Persiflage, Playboy, Skittish, Trifling, Trivial

Frog Anoura, Anura, Arrow poison, Batrachia(n), Braid, Breton, Bullfrog, Cape nightingale, Depression, Fourchette, Frenchman, Frush, Goliath, Hairy, Hyla, Leopard, Marsupial, Mounseer, Nic, Nototrema, Paddock, Paradoxical, Peeper, Pelobatid, Platanna, Puddock, Puttock, Rana, Ranidae, Spring peeper, Tree, Wood, Xenopus

Frolic(some) Bender, Bust(er), Cabriole, Caper, Disport, Escapade, → **FRISK(Y)**, Fun, Galravage, Galravitch, Gambol, Gammock, Gil(l)ravage, How's your father, Jink, Kittenish, Lark, Play, Prank, Rag, Rand, Rant, Rig, Romp, Scamper, Skylark, Splore, Sport, Spree, Stooshie, Tittup, Wanton

From A, Against, Ex, For, Frae, Off, Thrae

Front(al), Frontman Antependium, Anterior, Bow, Brass, Brow, Cold, Cover, Dead, Dickey, Dicky, Esplanade, Façade, Face, Fore(head), Forecourt, Fore end, Foreground, Groof, Grouf, Grufe, Head, Home, Insolence, Metope, National, Newscaster, Nose, Occluded, Paravant, People's, Plastron, Polar, Popular, Pose, Preface, Presenter, Pro, Prom, Prow, Rhodesian, Sector, Sinciput, Stationary, Tabula, Temerity, Van, Vaward, Ventral, Warm, Western

Frost(ing), Frosty, Frostbite Air, Alcorza, Black, Chill, Cranreuch, Cryo-, Freon®, Frigid, Frore(n), Frorne, Glacé, Ground, Hoar, Hore, Ice, Icing, Jack, Mat, Rime, Silver, Trench foot, White

Froth(y) Barm, Bubble, Chiffon, Despumate, Foam, Frogspit, Gas, Head, Lather, Nappy, Off-scum, Ream, Saponin, Scum, Seethe, Shallow, Spoom, Spoon, Spume, Sud, Toadspit, Yeasty, Yest

Frugal Meagre, Parsimonious, Provident, Prudent, Scant, Skimpy, Spare, Spartan, Thrifty

Fruit(ing), Fruit tree, Fruity Accessory, Achaenocarp, Achene, Akene, Allocarpy, Apothecium, Autocarp, Bacciform, Catapult, Cedrate, Coccus, Compot(e), Confect, Conserve, Cremocarp, Crop, Dessert, Drupe, Eater, Encarpus, Etaerio, First, Follicle, Forbidden, Fritter, Harvest, Issue, Multiple, Orchard, Poof, Primeur, Primitiae, Product(ion), Pseudocarp, Regma(ta), Replum, Result, Return, Rich, Ripe, Schizocarp, Seed, Silicle, Siliqua, Silique, Soft, Sorosis, Stoneless, Succade, Sweetie, Sweety, Syconium, Syncarp, Utricle, Valve, Wall, Xylocarp, Yield

Fruitcake Dundee, Madman, Nutter

Fruitful(ness) Calathus, Ephraim, Fat, Fecund, Feracious, Fertile, Productive, Prolific, Teeming, Uberty, Worthwhile

Frustrate(d), Frustration Baffle, Ba(u)lk, Beat, Blight, Bugger, Check, Cheesed off, Confound, Countermine, Dash, Discomfit, Dish, Disillusionment, Foil, Hogtie, Outwit, Scotch, Spike, Stymie, Thwart

Fry, Fried Blot, Brit, Fricassee, Fritter, Frizzle, Parr, Sauté, Skirl-in-the-pan, Small, Spawn, Whippersnapper, Whitebait

Fuddle(d) Drunk, Fluster, Fuzzle, Maudlin, Ta(i)vert, Tosticated, Woozy

▷ **Fuddle(d)** *may indicate* an anagram

Fudge Cook, Doctor, Dodge, Drivel, Evade, Fiddlesticks, Nonsense, Rot, Stop-press, Sweet(meat)

Fuel Anthracite, Argol, Astatki, Avgas, Benzine, Benzol, Biodiesel, Biogas, Borane, Briquet(te), Brown coal, Bunker, Butane, Candle-coal, Cannel, Coal, Coalite®, Coke, Derv, Diesel, Eilding, Eldin(g), Faggot, Feed, Fire(wood), Fossil, Gasahol, Gasohol, Gasoline, Hexamine, Hydrazine, Hydyne, Ignite, Jud, Kerosene, Kerosine, Kindling, Knitch, Lead-free, Lignite, Lox, Mox, Napalm, Naphtha, Nuclear, Oilgas, Outage, Paraffin, Peat, Propane, Propellant, Smudge, Sterno®, Stoke, SURF, Synfuel, Tan balls, Triptane, Yealdon

Fugitive Absconder, Ephemeral, Escapee, Fleeting, Hideaway, Lot, Outlaw, Refugee, Runagate, Runaway, Runner, Transient, Vagabond

Fulfil(ment) Accomplish, Complete, Consummate, Fruition, Honour, Meet, Pass, Realise, →**SATISFY**, Steed

Full(est), Fullness, Fully Abrim, Ample, Arrant, Bouffant, Capacity, Chock-a-block, Chocker, Complete, Copious, Embonpoint, Engorged, Entire, Fairly, Fat, Fed, Fou, Frontal, German, High, Hoatching, Hotch, Mill, Orotund, Plein, Plenary, Plenitude, Pleroma, Plethora, Plump, Replete, Rich, Rotund, Sated, Satiated, Thorough, Torose, Torous, Toss, Turgid, Turgor, Ullage, Uncut, Up, Wau(l)k, Whole hog, Wholly

Full-bodied Amoroso

Full-grown Seeded

Fulminate, Fulmination Detonate, Explode, Levin, Lightning, Rail, Renounce, Thunder

Fumble Blunder, Faff, Grope, Misfield, Muff

Fume(s) Bluster, Gas, Halitus, Incense, Nidor, Rage, Reech, Reek, Settle, Smoke, Stum, Vapours

Fun(ny), Funny bone Amusing, Antic, Boat, Buffo, Caper, Clownery, Comedy, Comic(al), Crack, Craic, Delight, Droll, Frolic, Gammock, Gas, Gig, Giocoso, Glaik, Guy, Hilarity, Humerus, Humorous, Hysterical, Ironic, Jest, Jouisance, Jouysaunce, Killing, Lark, Pleasure, Priceless, Rag, Rib-tickling, Rich, Rummy, Scream, Sidesplitting, Skylark, Slap and tickle, Sport, Suspect, Weird(o), Wisecrack, Wit, Yell

Function(al), Functioning, Functions Act, Antilog, Arccos, Arcsin(e), Arctan, Assignment, Behave, Bodily, Business, Ceremony, Circular, Cosec, Cosh, Cot(h), Cotangent, Dance, Discriminant, Do, Dynamic, Exponential, Gibbs, Hamilton(ian), Helmholtz, Hyperbolic, Integral, Integrand, Inverse, Job, Logarithm, →**OPERATE**, Periodic, Practicable, Quadric, Quantical, Quartic, Reception, Role, Run, Sec(h), Sensation, Service, Sin(e), Sinh, Ste(a)d, Step, Surjection, Tan(h), Tangent, Tick, Tool bar, Truth, Up and running, Use, Wave, Wingding, →**WORK**

Functionary Official

Fund(ing), Fund raiser, Fundraising, Funds -(a)thon, Bank, Bankroll, Barrel, Capital, Chest, Consolidated, Emendals, Endow, Evergreen, Finance, Fisc, Fisk, Focus, Gap, Gild, Green, Hedge, Imprest, Index, Jackpot, Kitty, Maestro®, Managed, Mutual, Nest-egg, Pension, Pool, Pork-barrel, Prebend, Private, Public, Purse, Rest, Revolving, Roll-up, Sinking, Slush, Social, Sou-sou, Stabilisation, Stock, Store, Subsidise, Sustentation, Susu, Telethon, -thon, Tracker, Treasury, Trust, Vulture, Wage(s), War chest, Wherewithal

Fundamental(ist) Basic(s), Bedrock, Cardinal, Essence, Grass-roots, Hamas, Integral, Nitty-gritty, Organic, Prime, Principle, Radical, Rudimentary, Taleban, Ultimate

Funeral, Funereal Charnel, Cortege, Dismal, Exequy, Feral, Interment, Obit, Obital, Obsequy, Sad-coloured, Solemn, Tangi

Fungicide Benomyl, Biphenyl, Bordeaux mixture, Captan, Diphenyl, Ferbam, Menadione, Pentachlorophenol, Resveratrol, Thiram, Zineb

Fungoid, Fungus Endophyte, Pest

Funnel Buchner, Chimney, Choana, Flue, Hopper, Infundibulum, Smokestack, Stack, Stovepipe, Tun-dish, Tunnel

Fur(ry) Astrakhan, Astrex, Atoc, Beaver(skin), Boa, Broadtail, Budge, Calabre, Caracul, Castor, Chinchilla, Civet, Coati, Cony-wool, Coonskin, Crimmer, Deposit, Ermelin, Ermine, Fitchew, Flix, Flue, Fun, Galyac, Galyak, Genet, Genette, Kolinsky, Krimmer, Lettice, Marten, Minever, Miniver, Mink, Mouton, Musquash, Ocelot, Otter, Palatine, Pane, Pashm, Pean, Pekan, Rac(c)oon, Roskyn, Sable, Sealskin, Sea-otter, Stole, Stone-marten, Tincture, Tippet, Vair(e), Victorine, Wolverine, Zibeline, Zorino

Furl Clew up, Fold, Roll, Stow, Wrap

Furnace Arc, Athanor, Blast, Bloomery, Bosh, Breeze, Calcar, Cockle, Cremator, Cupola, Destructor, Devil, Finery, Firebox, Forge, Gas, Glory-hole, Incinerator, Kiln, Lear, Lehr, Lime-kiln, Oast, Oon, Oven, Producer, Reverberatory, Scaldino, Stokehold, Stokehole

Furnish(ing) Appoint, Array, Deck, Decorate, Endow, Endue, Equip, Feed, Fledge, Gird, Lend, Nourish, Produce, Provision, Purvey, Soft, Stock, Suit, Supply, Tabaret, Upholster

Furniture, Furniture designer Armoire, Biedermeier, Bombe, Chattels, Chippendale, Encoignure, Escritoire, Flatpack, Fyfe, Hallstand, Hatstand, Hepplewhite, Highboy, Insight, Lowboy, Lumber, Moveable, Screen, Sheraton, Sideboard, Sticks, Stoutherie, Tire, Unit, Whatnot

Furrow(ed) Crease, Feer, Feerin(g), Furr, Groove, Gutter, Plough, Pucker, Rabbet, Ridge, Rill(e), Rugose, Rut, Stria, Sulcus, Vallecula, Wrinkle

Further(est), Furthermore, Furthest Additional, Advance, Again, Aid, Also, Apolune, Besides, Deeper, Else, Expedite, Extend, Extra, Extreme, Fresh, Infra, Longer, Mo(e), Mow, Onwards, Other, Promote, Serve, Speed, Then, To boot

Furtive(ly) Clandestine, Covert, Cunning, Secret, Shifty, Sly, Sneaky, Stealthy, Stowlins

Fury, Furies, Furious Acharné, Agitato, Alecto, → ANGER, Apoplexy, Atropos, Avenger, Eriny(e)s, Eumenides, Exasperation, Frantic, Frenzied, Furor, Hairless, Hot, Incandescent, Incensed, → IRE, Livid, Maenad, Manic, Megaera, Paddy, Rabid, Rage, Red, Ripsnorter, Savage, Tisiphone, Virago, Wood, Wrath, Yond

Fuse(d), Fusion Anchylosis, Ankylosis, Arthrodesis, Blend, Coalesce, Cohere, Colliquate, Conflate, Converge, Encaustic, Endosmosis, Flow, Flux, Igniter, Integrate, Knit, Match, Melt, Merge, Merit, Nuclear, Plasmogamy, Portfire, Proximity, Rigelation, Run, Sacralization, Saucisse, Saucisson, Slow-match, Solder, Symphytic, Syncretism, Syngamy, Tokamak, Unite, Weld

Fuss(y) Ado, Agitation, Anile, Ballyho, Bobsie-die, Bother, Br(o)uhaha, Bustle, Carfuffle, Carry on, Chichi, Coil, Commotion, Complain, Cosset, Create, Cu(r)fuffle, Dust, Elaborate, Faddy, Faff, Fantod, Fiddle-faddle, Finical, Finikin, Futz, Hairsplitter, Hoohah, Hoopla, Mither, Mother, Niggle, Nit-pick, Noise, Old-womanish, Overnice, Palaver, Particular, Pedantic, Perjink, Pernickety, Picky, Pother, Precise, Prejink, Primp, Prissy, Pudder, Racket, Raise cain, Razzmatazz, Rout, Song, Song and dance, Spoffish, Spoffy, Spruce, Stashie, Stickler, → STIR, Stishie, Stooshie, Stushie, Tamasha, To-do, Tracasserie

Futile Empty, Feckless, Idle, Inept, No-go, Nugatory, Null, Otiose, Pointless, Sleeveless, Stultified, Trivial, → VAIN

Future(s), Futurist Again, Avenir, Be-all, By and by, Coming, Demain, Hence, Horoscope, Later, Long-range, Offing, Ovist, Prospect, To-be, To come, Tomorrow, Vista

Gg

Gad(about), Gadzooks Gallivant, Lud, Rover, Sbuddikins, Sdeath, Traipse, Trape(s), Viretot

Gadget Adaptor, Appliance, Artifice, Device, Dingbat, Dingus, Doodad, Doodah, Doofer, Doohickey, Gismo, Gizmo, Gubbins, Hickey, Jiggumbob, Jimjam, Notion, Possum, Toy, Utility, Widget

Gag Brank, Choke, Estoppel, Joke, Pong, Prank, Silence(r), Smother, Wheeze, Wisecrack

Gain(s), Gained Acquire, Appreciate, Attain, Avail, Boot, Bunce, Carry, Catch, Chevisance, Clean-up, Derive, Earn, Edge, Fruit, →**GET**, Good, Gravy, Ill-gotten, Land, Lucre, Obtain, Plus, Profit, Purchase, Rake-off, Reap, Thrift, Unremittable, Use, Velvet, Wan, Win, Windfall, Winnings

Gait Bearing, Canter, →**CHILD**, Pace, Piaffer, Rack, Trot, Volt(e)

Galaxy, Galaxies Blazar, Elliptical, Heaven, Irregular, Local group, Magellanic cloud, Milky Way, Radio, Regular, Seyfert, Spiral, Stars

Gale(s) Backfielder, Near, Peal, Ripsnorter, Sea turn, Snorter, Squall, Storm, Strong, Tempest, Winder

Gallant(ry) Admirer, Amorist, Beau, Blade, Buck, Cavalier, Chevalier, Cicisbeo, Courtliness, Lover, Prow, Romeo, Sigisbeo, Spark, Valiance

Gallery Accademia, Amphitheatre, Arcade, Balcony, Belvedere, Burrell (Collection), Catacomb, Cupola, Gods, Hayward, Hermitage, Loft, Loggia, Louvre, Mine, Minstrel, National, Picture, Prado, Press, Rogues', Scaffolding, Shooting, Singing, Strangers', Tate, Traverse, Uffizi, Veranda(h), Whispering

Galley Bireme, Bucentaur, Caboose, Drake, Galliot, Kitchen, Lymphad, Penteconter, Proof

Gallows Dule-tree, Gibbet, Nub, Stifler, Tree, Tyburn, Tyburn-tree, Woodie

Galvanometer Tangent

Gambia WAG

Gambit Manoeuvre, Ploy, Stratagem

Gamble(r), Gambling(-house), Gambling place Amber, Back, Bet, Bouillotte, Casino, Chance, Dice(-play), Double or quits, Flutter, Hell, Lotto, Mise, Pari-mutuel, Parlay, Piker, Policy, Punt(er), Raffle, Risk, Roulette, Spec, Speculate, Speculator, Sweep(stake), Throw(ster), Tinhorn, Tombola, Tontine, Two-up, →**WAGER**, Wheeze

Game (birds) Bag, Covey, Fowl, Grouse, Guan, Hare, Meat, Partridge, Pheasant, Prairie chicken, Ptarmigan, Quail, →**QUARRY**, Rype(r), Snipe, Spatchcock, Venery, Wildfowl, Woodcock

Game(s) Away, Caper, Circensian, Closed, Commonwealth, Computer, Console, Decider, Easy, Electronic, Elis, Exhibition, Fair, Frame, Gallant, Gammy, Ground, Gutsy, High-jinks, Highland, Home, Intrepid, Isthmian, Jeu, →**LAME**, Match, Middle, Mind, MUD, Needle, Nemean, Numbers, Olympic, On, Open, Panel, Paralympic, Parlour, Perfect, Platform, Play, Plaything, Preference, Pythian, Raffle, Ready, Road, Role-playing, Round, Rubber, Saving, Scholar's, Secular, Sport, Square, Strategy, String, Table, Test, Tie-break, Tournament, Video, Vie, Waiting, Willing

Gamete Ootid

Gamin(e) Hoyden

Gang Baader-Meinhof, Band(itti), Bevy, Bikers, Bing, Canaille, Chain, Coffle, Core, Crew, Crue, Elk, Go, Group, Hell's Angels, Horde, Massive, Mob, Nest, Outfit, Pack,

Posse, Press, Push, Ratpack, Rent-a-mob, Ring, Shearing, Tribulation, Troop, Tsotsi, Yardie

Gangster Bandit, Capone, Crook, Goodfella, Hatchet-man, Highbinder, Home boy, Homey, Homie, Hood, Mafioso, Ochlocrat, Skinhead, Skollie, Skolly, Yakuza, Yardie

▶**Gaol(er)** *see* **JAILER**

Gap Breach, Chasm, Chink, Credibility, Cumberland, Day, Embrasure, F-hole, Flaw, Fontanel(le), Generation, Hair-space, Hiatus, Hole, Interlude, Interstice, Lacunae, Leap, Loophole, Node of Ranvier, Opening, Outage, Pass, Rest, Rift, Shard, Sherd, Slap, →**SPACE**, Spark, Spread, Street, Synapse, Vacancy, Vent, Window

Garb Apparel, Costume, Gear, Gere, Guise, Ihram, Invest, Leotard, Raiment, Toilet, Uniform

Garbage Bunkum, Junk, Refuse, Rubbish, Trash

▷**Garble** *may indicate* an anagram

Garcon Waiter

Garden(ing), Gardens Arboretum, Arbour, Area, Babylon(ian), Bear, Beer, Botanic, Container, Cottage, Covent, Dig, Eden, Floriculture, Gethsemane, Hanging, Herb(ar), Hesperides, Hoe, Horticulture, Italian, Japanese, Kew, Kitchen, Knot, Landscape, Lyceum, Market, Orchard, Orchat, Paradise, Parterre, Physic, Plantie-cruive, Pleasance, Plot, Potager, Rockery, Roof, Rosarium, Stourhead, Tea, Topiary, Truck-farm, Tuileries, Vauxhall, Walled, Window, Winter, Zoological

Gardener Adam, Capability Brown, Hoer, Hoy, Jekyll, Landscape, Mary, Nurseryman

Garibaldi Biscuit, Blouse, Red Shirt

Garland Anadem, Anthology, Chaplet, Coronal, Crants, Festoon, Lei, Stemma, Toran(a), Vallar(y), Wreath

Garment →**DRESS**, Habit, Vestment, Vesture

Garnish Adorn, Attach, Cress, Crouton, Decorate, Engild, Gremolata, Lard, Parsley, Sippet, Staffage

Garotte(r) Thug(gee), Ugly man

Gas(sy) Blah(-blah), Blather, Blether, Blow off, Bottle(d), Chat, Emanation, Flatulence, Gabnash, Jaw, Meteorism, Prate, →**TALK**, Waffle, →**WIND**, Yackety-yak

Gash Incise, Rift, Rip, Score, Scotch, →**SLASH**

Gasket Seal

Gasp(ing) Anhelation, Apn(o)ea, Breath, Chink, Exhale, Kink, Oh, Pant, Puff, Singult, Sob

Gast(e)ropod Ataata, Cowrie, Cowry, Doris, Euthyneura, Glaucus, Harp-shell, Helmet-shell, Limpet, Mollusc, Money cowry, Murex, Nerita, Nerite, Nudibranch, Opisthobranch, Ormer, Pennywinkle, Periwinkle, Purpura, Sea-ear, Sea-hare, Slug, Snail, Spindle-shell, Streptoneura, Stromb, Top shell, Unicorn, Whelk, Winkle

Gate(s), Gateway Alley, Bill, Brandenburg, Caisson, Corpse, Crowd, Decuman, Entry, Erpingham, Golden, Head, Iron, Kissing, Lych, Menin, Moon, NOR, Payment, Pearly, Port, Portal, Portcullis, Postern, Propylaeum, Propylon, Pylon, Sallyport, Silver, Starting, Toran(a), Torii, Traitor's, Turnstile, Vimana, Wicket, Yate, Yet(t)

Gateau Black Forest

▷**Gateshead** *may indicate* 'g'

Gather(ed), Gatherer, Gathering Accrue, AGM, Amass, Army, Assemble, Bee, Braemar, Clambake, Cluster, Collate, →**COLLECT**, Colloquium, Concentration, Concourse, Conglomerate, Congregate, Conventicle, Conversazione, Corral, Corroboree, Crop, Crowd, Cull, Derive, Eve, Fest, Frill, Function, Gabfest, Galaxy, Get together, Glean, Glomerate, Hangi, Harvest, Hear, Hive, Hootenanny, Hotchpot, Hui, Hunter, Husking, In, Infer, Jamboree, Kommers, Learn, Lek, Lirk, Love-in, Meinie, Menyie, Multitude, Pleat, Plica, Plissé, Pluck, Pucker, Purse, Raft, Raising-bee, Rake, Rally, Rave, Reap, Reef, Reunion, Round-up, Rout, Ruche, Ruck, Ruff(le), Salon, Scrump, Sheave, Shindig, Shir(r), Shoal, Shovel, Singsong, Social, Spree, Suppurate, Swapmeet, Take, Tuck, Vindemiate, Vintage, Wappensc(h)aw, Witches' sabbath

Gauche Awkward, Clumsy, Farouche, Graceless, Tactless

Gaudy Classy, Criant, Fantoosh, Flash, Garish, Glitz(y), Meretricious, Tacky, Tawdry, Tinsel

Gauge Alidad(e), Anemometer, →ASSESS, Block, Bourdon, Broad, Calibre, Denier, Depth, Estimate, Etalon, Evaluate, Feeler, Judge, Loading, Manometer, Marigraph, Measure, Meter, Narrow, Nilometer, Oil, Ombrometer, Oncometer, Pressure, Rate, Scantle, Size, Standard, Steam, Strain, Tape, Tonometer, Tram, Tread, Udometer

Gaunt Cadaverous, Haggard, Lancaster, Lean, Peaked, Randletree, Ranneltree, Rannletree, Rantletree, Rawbone, →THIN, Wasted

Gauze, Gauzy Dandy-roll, Gas mantle, Gossamer, Illusion, Muslin, Sheer, Tiffany

Gear(ing), Gearbox Alighting, Angel, Apparatus, Arrester, Attire, Bags, Bevel, Capital, Clobber, Dérailleur, Differential, Draw, Duds, Engrenage, Epicyclic, Fab, Finery, Granny, G-suit, Harness, Helical, Herringbone, High, Hypoid, Idle wheel, Involute, Kit, Landing, Lay-shaft, Low, Mesh, Mess, Mitre, Neutral, Notchy, Overdrive, Planetary, Ratio, Reduction, Reverse, Rig, Riot, Rudder, Running, Spur, Steering, Stickshift, Straight, Sun and planet, Switch, Synchromesh, →TACKLE, Timing, Tiptronic®, Top, Trim, Tumbler, Valve, Variable, Worm(-wheel)

Geek Creep, Nerd, Nurd, Uncool

Geld(ing) Castrate, Lib, Neuter, Sort, Spado

Gem Intaglio, →JEWEL, →STONE

Gemma Bud, Knosp

Gene(tics) Allel(e), Allelomorph, Anticodon, Codominant, Codon, Control, Creation, Disomic, Dysbindin, Episome, Exon, Factor, Genome, Hereditary, Heterogamy, Homeobox, Homeotic, Intron, Mendel, Muton, Operon, Orthologue, Paralogue, Plasmon, Promoter, Proteome, Reporter, Reverse, Selfish, STR, Suppressor, Synteny, Terminator, Testcross

Genealogist, Genealogy Armory, Cadency, Family, Heraldry, Line, Pedigree, Seannachie, Seannachy, Sennachie, Whakapapa

General(ly) At large, Broad, Common, Communal, Current, Eclectic, Ecumenical, Election, Five-star, Gen, Inspector, In the main, In the mass, Main, Omnify, Overall, Overhead, Prevailing, Public, Rife, Rough, Strategist, Sweeping, Tactician, →UNIVERSAL, Usual, Vague, Wide

Generate, Generation, Generator Abiogenetic, Age, Beat, Beget, Breeder, Charger, Cottonwool, Create, Dynamo, Epigon, Father, Fuel-cell, House, Kipp, Loin, Lost, Magneto, Me, Olds, Sire, Spawn, Stallion, Stonewall, Turbine, Van de Graaff, Yield

Generosity, Generous Ample, Bounty, Charitable, Expansive, Free-handed, Handsome, Kind, Largess(e), →LAVISH, Liberal, Magnanimous, Munificent, Noble(-minded), Open, Open-handed, Open-hearted, Philanthropic, Plump, Profuse, Round, Sporting, Tidy

Genesis Episome

▶**Genetic** *see* GENE(TICS)

Genial(ity) Affable, Amiable, Benign, Bluff, Bonhomie, Convivial, Cordial, Expansive, Human, Mellow

Genitive Ethical

Genius Agathodaimon, Daemon, Einstein, Engine, Flash, Ingine, Inspiration, Ka, Mastermind, Michaelangelo, Numen, Prodigy

Genome Prophage

Genre Splatterpunk, Tragedy, Variety

Gentle(ness) Amenable, Amenage, Bland, Clement, Delicate, Gradual, Grub, Kind, Lamb, Light, Linda, Lynda, Maggot, Mansuete, Mansuetude, Mild, Soft, Sordamente, Tame, Tender

Gentry County, Landed, Quality, Squir(e)age

Genuflexion Bend, Curts(e)y, Knee, Kowtow, Salaam

Genuine Authentic, Bona-fide, Dinkum, Dinky-di, Echt, Entire, Fair dinkum, Frank, Heartfelt, Intrinsic, Jonnock, Kosher, Legit(imate), Nain, Pucka, Pukka, Pure, Pusser, →REAL, Real McCoy, Right, Simon-pure, Sincere, Square, Sterling, True, Unfeigned, Unsophisticated, Veritable

Germ(s) Bacteria, Bug, Klebsiella, Seed, Sperm, Spirilla, Staph(ylococcus), Strep, Virus, Wog, Zyme

German(y), Germanic Angle, Anglo-Saxon, Bavarian, Berliner, Boche, Denglish, Franconian, Frank, Fritz, G, Goth, Habsburg, Hans, Hapsburg, Herr, Hun, Jerry, Jute, Kaiser, Kraut, Ludwig, Pennsylvania, Prussian, Rolf, Salic, Saxon, Squarehead, Teuton(ic), Visigoth, Volsungs, Wolfgang

Gesticulate, Gesticulation, Gesture(s) Air quotes, Beck(on), Ch(e)ironomy, Fig, Mannerism, Mime, Motion, Nod, Pass, Salaam, Salute, → **SIGN**, Signal, Token, Wink

Get(ting), Get back, Get off, Get(ting) by, Get(ting) on, Get out Acquire, Advance, Aggravate, Annoy, Attain, Become, Becoming, Brat, Bring, Capture, Click, Come by, Cop, Cope, Debark, Derive, Draw, Escape, Fathom, Fet(ch), Fette, Gain, Gee, Land, Learn, Make, Manage, Milk, Net, Niggle, Noy, → **OBTAIN**, Pass, Peeve, Procure, Progress, Reach, Realise, Recure, Rile, Roil, Secure, See, Shift, Sire, Twig, Understand, Win

▷ **Getting** *may indicate* an anagram

Getting better Convalescing, Improving, Lysis

Ghana .gh

Ghastly Charnel, Gash, Grim, Gruesome, Hideous, Lurid, Macabre, Pallid, Spectral, Welladay, White

Ghost(ly) Acheri, Apparition, Apport, Banquo, Caddy, Chthonic, Duende, Duppy, Eerie, Eery, Fantasm, Fetch, Gytrash, Haunt, Hint, Jumbie, Jumby, Larva(e), Lemur, Malmag, Masca, No'canny, Paraclete, Pepper's, Phantasm(agoria), Phantom, Poe, Revenant, Sampford, Shade, Shadow, Spectre, Spectrology, → **SPIRIT**, Spook, Trace, Truepenny, Umbra, Unearthly, Vision, Visitant, Waff, Wraith

Giant(ess) Alcyoneus, Alifanfaron, Anak, Antaeus, Archiloro, Argus, Ascapart, Balan, Balor, Bellerus, Blunderbore, Bran, Briareus, Brobdingnagian, Cacus, Colbrand, Colbronde, Colossus, Coltys, Cormoran, Cottus, Cyclop(e)s, Despair, Drow, Enceladus, Ephialtes, Eten, Ettin, Ferragus, Gabbara, Galligantus, Gargantua, Géant, Gefion, Geirred, Gigantic, Gog, Goliath, Great, Grim, Harapha, Heimdal(l), Hrungnir, Hymir, Idris, Jotun(n), Jumbo, Krasir, Large, Lestrigon, Leviathan, Magog, Mammoth, Mimir, Monster, Oak, Og, Ogre, Orion, Otus, Pallas, Pantagruel, Patagonian, Polyphemus, Pope, Red, Rounceval, Skrymir, Slaygood, Talos, Talus, Thrym, Titan, Tityus, Tregeagle, Triton, Troll, Tryphoeus, Typhon, Urizen, Utgard, Ymir, Yowie

Gibberish Claptrap, Double Dutch, Drivel, Greek, Jargon, Mumbo-jumbo

Gibe Barb, Brocard, Chaff, Fleer, Glike, Jeer, Jibe, Quip, Shy, Slant, Wisecrack

Gift(s), Gifted Ability, Alms, Aptitude, Bef(f)ana, Bequest, Blessing, Blest, Bonbon, Bonsel(l)a, Boon, Bounty, Charism(a), Congiary, Corban, Covermount, Cumshaw, Dash, Deodate, → **DONATION**, Etrenne, Fairing, Fidecommissum, Flair, Foy, Free, Freebie, Frumentation, Gab, Garnish, Give, Godsend, Goody-bag, Grant, Handout, Han(d)sel, Hogmanay, Indian, Knack, Koha, Kula, Lagniappe, Largesse, Legacy, Manna, Ne'erday, Nuzzer, Offering, Parting, Potlatch, → **PRESENT**, Presentation, Prezzie, Propine, Reward, Sop, Talent, Tongues, Tribute, Windfall

Gigantic Atlantean, Briarean, Colossal, Goliath, → **HUGE**, Immense, Mammoth, Rounceval, Titan

Giggle, Giggling Cackle, Fou rire, Ha, Ha-ha, He-he, Simper, Snicker, Snigger, Tehee, Titter

Gild(ed), Gilding Checklaton, Embellish, Enhance, Inaurate, Ormolu, S(c)hecklaton, Vermeil

Gill(s) Beard, Branchia, Cart, Ctenidium, Dibranchiate, Jill, Noggin, Spiracle, Trematic

Gimmick Doodad, Doodah, Hype, Novelty, Ploy, Ruse, Stunt

Gin Bathtub, Blue ruin, Geneva, Genever, Hollands, Illaqueable, Juniper, Lubra, Max, Noose, Old Tom, Ruin, Schiedam, Schnapp(s), Sloe, Snare, Springe, Square-face, Toil, Trap, Trepan, Twankay

Gingerbread D(o)um-palm, Lebkuchen, Parkin, Parliament(-cake)

▶ **Gipsy** *see* **GYPSY**

Girder Beam, Binder, Box, I-beam, Loincloth, Spar

Girdle Baldric, Cestus, Chastity, Cincture, Cingulum, Corset, Equator, Hippolyte, Hoop, Mitre, Panty, Ring, Sash, Surcingle, Surround

▷ **Girl** *may indicate* a female name

Girl(s) Backfisch, Ball, Bimbo, Bint, Bird, Bit, Bobby-dazzler, Bohemian, Bondmaid, Broad, Burd, Call, Charlie, Chick, Chit, Chorus, Coed, Colleen, Crumpet, Cutey, Cutie, Deb, Demoiselle, Dish, Doll, Dollybird, Essex, Filly, Flapper, Flower, Fluff, Fraulein, Frippet, Gaiety, Gal, Geisha, Gibson, Giselle, Good-time, Gouge, Grisette, Hen, Hoiden, Hoyden, Hussy, It, Judy, Kimmer, Ladette, Land, Lass(ock), Maid(en), May, Miss(y), Moppet, Muchacha, Nymph(et), Nymphette, Peach, Peacherino, Popsy, Poster, Puss, Quean, Queyn, Riot, Señorita, Sheila, Shi(c)ksa, Sis(s), Tabby, Teenybopper, Tootsie, Totty, Trull, Vi, Wench

Gist Drift, Essence, Kernel, →**NUB**, Pith, Substance

Give(r), Give up, Giving Abandon, Abstain, Accede, Accord, Administer, Afford, Award, Bend, Bestow, Buckle, Cede, Confiscate, Consign, Contribute, Dative, Dispense, Dole, →**DONATE**, Duck, Elasticity, Enable, Endow, Forswear, Gie, Hand, Impart, Indian, Jack, Largition, Present, Provide, Render, Resign, Sacrifice, Sag, Spring, Stop, Tip, Vacate, Yeve, Yield

Give out Belch, Bestow, Dispense, Emit, Exude, Peter

Glace Candied

Glacier Aletsch, Crevasse, Drumline, Fox, Franz-Josef, Iceberg, Ice-cap, Icefall, Moraine, Moulin, Muir, Riss, Serac, Stoss, Stoss and lee, Tasman

Glad(ly), Gladden, Gladness Cheer, Fain, →**HAPPY**, Lettice, Lief, Willing

Glamour, Glamorise, Glamorous Charm, Glitter(ati), Glitz, Halo, It, Prestige, SA, Sex up, Spell, Swanky, Tinseltown

Glance Allusion, Blink, Browse, Copper-head, Coup d'oeil, Dekko, Glad eye, Glimpse, Lustre, Oeillade, Once-over, Peek, →**PEEP**, Ray, Ricochet, Scan, Sheep's eyes, Shufti, Shufty, Side, Silver, Skellie, Skelly, Slant, Snick, Squint, Squiz, Tip, Vision, Waff

Gland(s) Adenoid, Adrenal, Apocrine, Bartholin's, Bulbourethral, Clitellum, Colleterial, Conarium, Cowper's, Crypt, Dart-sac, Digestive, Eccrine, Endocrine, Epiphysis, Exocrine, Goitre, Green, Holocrine, Hypophysis, Ink-sac, Lachrymal, Lacrimal, Liver, Lymph, Mammary, Melbomian, Musk-sac, Nectary, Oil, Osmeterium, Ovary, Pancreas, Paranephros, Parathyroid, Parotid, Parotis, Pineal, Pituitary, Pope's eye, Prostate, Prothoracic, Racemose, Salivary, Salt, Scent, Sebaceous, Sericterium, Silk, Suprarenal, Sweat, Tarsel, Testicle, Testis, Third eye, Thymus, Thyroid, Tonsil, Uropygial, Vesicle, Vulvovaginal

Glare, Glaring Astare, Blare, Blaze, Dazzle, Egregious, Flagrant, Garish, Gleam, Glower, Gross, Holophotal, Iceblink, Lour, Low(e), Shine, Vivid, Whally

Glass(es), Glassware, Glassy Amen, Ampul(la), Aneroid, Avanturine, Aventurine, Aviator, Baccara(t), Balloon, Barometer, Bell, Bifocals, Bin(ocular)s, Borosilicate, Bottle, Brimmer, Bumper, Burmese, Burning, Calcedonio, Case, Cheval, Claude Lorraine, Cloche, Cocktail, Cooler, Copita, Cordial, Coupe, Cover, Crookes, Crown, Crystal, Cullet, Cupping, Cut, Dark, Delmonico, Dildo, Diminishing, Eden, Euphon, Favrile, Fibre, Field, Flint, Float, Flute, Foam, Frigger, Frit, Fulgurite, Gauge, Glare, Goblet, Goggles, Granny, Green, Ground, Hand, Handblown, Highball, Horn-rims, Humpen, Hyaline, Iceland agate, Jar, Jena, Jigger, Keltie, Kelty, Lace, Lacy, Lalique, Laminated, Lanthanum, Larking, Latticinio, Lead, Lead crystal, Lens, Liqueur, Liquid, Log, Lorgnette, Loupe, Lozen(ge), Lunette, Magma, Magnifying, Metal, Mica, Middy, Milk, Millefiori, Minimizing, Mirror, Moldavite, Monocle, Mousseline, Multiplying, Murr(h)ine, Muscovy, Musical, Nitreous, Object, Obsidian, One-way, Opal(ine), Opera, Optical, Ovonic, Pane, Parison, Paste, Pearlite, Pebble, Peeper, Pele, Pele's hair, Perlite, Perspective, Pier, Pince-nez, Pinhole, Pitchstone, Plate, Pocket, Pon(e)y, Pressed, Prism, Prospective, Prunt, Psyche, Pyrex®, Quarrel-pane, Quarry, Quartz, Reducing, Roemer, Ruby, Rummer, Safety, Schmelz, Schooner, Seam, Seidel, Shard, Sheet, Silex, Silica, Sleever, Slide, Sliver, Smalt(o), Snifter, Soluble, Specs, →**SPECTACLES**, Spun, Stained, Stein, Stem, Stemware,

Stone, Storm, Strass, Straw, Sun, Supernaculum, Tachilite, Tachylite, Tachylyte, Tektite, Telescope, Tiffany, Tiring, Toilet, Trifocals, Triplex®, Tumbler, Uranium, Varifocals, Venetian, Venice, Vernal, Vita, Vitrail, Vitreous, Vitreous silica, Vitrescent, Vitro-di-trina, Volcanic, Watch, Water, Waterford, Weather, Window (pane), Wine, Wire, Yard of ale

Glass-house Conservatory, Orangery

Gleam(ing) Aglow, Blink, Flash, Glint, Glitter, Gloss, Leme, Light, Lustre, Ray, Relucent, Sheen, Shimmer, →**SHINE**

Glee Delight, Exuberance, Hysterics, Joy, Madrigal, Mirth, Song

Glide(r), Glideaway, Gliding Aquaplane, Aviette, Chassé, Coast, Elapse, Float, Illapse, Lapse, Luge, Microlight, Monoplane, Parascend, Portamento, Sail, Sailplane, Sashay, Scorrendo, Scrieve, Skate, Ski, Skim, Skite, Skyte, Sleek, Slide, Slip, Swim, Volplane

Glimpse Aperçu, Flash, Glance, Gledge, Glisk, Peep, Stime, Styme, Waff, Whiff

Glint Flash, Shimmer, →**SPARKLE**, Trace, Twinkle

Glisten(ing) Ganoid, Glint, Sheen, Shimmer, →**SHINE**, Sparkle

Glitter(ing) Asterism, Clinquant, Garish, Gemmeous, Paillon, Scintillate, Sequin, Spang(le), Sparkle, Tinsel

Gloat(ing) Crow, Drool, Enjoy, Exult, Schadenfreude

Globe, Globule Ball, Bead, Celestial, Drop, Earth, Orb, Pearl, Planet, Shot, Sphear, Sphere, Terrestrial, World

Gloom(y) Atrabilious, Blues, Cheerless, Cimmerian, Cloud, Crepuscular, Damp, Dark, →**DESPAIR**, Dingy, Disconsolate, Dismal, Dool(e), Drab, Drear, Drumly, Dump(s), Dyspeptic, Funereal, Glum, Grey, Grim, Louring, Lowery, Mirk, Misery, Mopish, Morbid, Morne, Morose, Murk, Obscurity, Overcast, Sable, Sad, Saturnine, Sepulchral, Shadow, Solemn, →**SOMBRE**, Sourpuss, Stygian, Subfusc, Tenebrious, Tenebrose, Tenebrous, Wan

Glorification, Glorify Aggrandise, Apotheosis, Avatar, Bless, →**EXALT**, Halo, Laud, Lionise, Praise, Radiance, Roose, Splendour

Glorious, Gloria, Glory Chorale, Grand, Halo, Hosanna, Ichabod, Kudos, Lustre, Magnificent, Nimbus, Sublime

Gloss(y) Enamel, Gild, Glacé, Interpret, Japan, Lip, Lustre, Mag, Patina, →**POLISH**, Postillate, Sheen, Sleek, Sleekit, Slick, Slide, Slur, Veneer, Whitewash

Glove Boxing, Cestus, Dannock, Gage, Gauntlet, Kid, Mitten, Oven, Rubber, Velvet

Glow(er), Glowing, Glowworm Aflame, Aura, Bloom, Burn, Candescence, Emanate, Fire, Flush, Foxfire, Gleam, Glimmer, Halation, Incandescence, Lambent, Lamp-fly, Luculent, Luminesce, Lustre, Phosphorescence, Radiant, Ruddy, Rutilant, Shine, Sullen, Translucent, →**WARMTH**

Glue(y) Araldite®, Bee, Cement, Colloidal, Epoxy, Fish, Gelatin(e), Gunk, Hot-melt, Ichthyocolla, Isinglass, Paste, Propolis, Rice, Size, Solvent, Spetch, Uhu®

Glum Dour, Livery, Lugubrious, Moody, Morose, Ron, Sombre

Glut Choke, Gorge, Plethora, Sate, Satiate, Saturate, Surfeit

Glutton(ous), Gluttony Bellygod, Carcajou, Cormorant, Edacity, Feaster, Free-liver, Gannet, Gorb, Gourmand, Gulosity, Gutsy, Hog, Lurcher, Pig, Ratel, Scoffer, Sin, Trencherman, Trimalchio, Wolverine

Gnat Culex, Culicidae, Midge, Mosquito

Gnaw(ing) Corrode, Erode, Fret, Lagomorph, Rodent

Gnome Adage, Bank-man, Chad, Cobalt, Epigram, Europe, Financier, Garden, Hobbit, Kobold, Maxim, Motto, Proverb, Saw, Sprite, Zurich

Go, Going (after, ahead, back, for, off, on, through, up, etc) Advance, Afoot, Anabasis, Animation, Ascent, Assail, Attempt, Attend, Bash, Bing, Bout, Brio, Choof, Clamber, Comb, Continuance, Deal, Depart, Die, Do, Energy, Fare, Function, Gae, Gang, Gaun, Gee, Green, Hamba, Hark, Heavy, Hence, Hie, Hup, Imshi, Imshy, Ish, Kick, →**LEAVE**, March, Match, Move, Off, OK, Path, Pee, Pep, Perpetual, Ply, Quit, Raik, Repair, Resort, Resume, Run, Scat, Scram, Segue, Shoo, Shot, Skedaddle, Snick-up, Sour, Spank, Spell, Square, Stab, Success, Transitory, Trine, Try, Turn,

Vamo(o)se, Vanish, Verve, Via, Viable, Vim, Wend, Work, Yead, Yede, Yeed, Zap, Zest, Zing, Zip

Goad Ankus, Brod, Gad, Incite, →**NEEDLE**, Prod, Provoke, Spur, Stimulate, Stimulus, Taunt

Goal(posts) Ambition, Basket, Bourn(e), Cage, Destination, Dream, Drop, End, Field, Grail, Mark, Mission, Net, Own, Score, Silver, Target, Ultima Thule

Goalless Idle

Goat(-like) Angora, Billy, Bucardo, Buck, Caprine, Cashmere, Cilician, Hircine, Ibex, Kashmir, Kid, Markhor, Nan(ny), Roue, Ruminant

Gobble Bolt, Devour, Gorge, Gulp, Scarf, Slubber, Wolf

Go-between Broker, Factor, Intermediate, Link, Mediate, Middleman, Pandarus, Pander, Shuttle

Goblin Banshee, Bargaist, Barg(h)est, Bodach, Bogey, Bogle, Bogy, Bucca, Bull-beggar, Croquemitaine, Empusa, Erl-king, Genie, Gnome, Gremlin, Knocker, Kobold, Lob-lie-by-the-fire, Lubberfiend, Lutin, Nis(se), Phooka, Phynnodderree, Pooka, Pouke, Puca, Puck, Pug, Red-cap, Red-cowl, Shellycoat, Troll, Trow

Gobstopper Everlasting

God(s) Amen, Ancient of Days, Deus, Di, Divine, First Cause, Gallery, Gracious, Inner Light, Light, Maker, Od(d), Principle, Shechina, Soul, Supreme Being, Tin, Trinity, Truth, Unknown, Vanir, Water

Goddess(es) Divine, Muse, Sea nymph

Godless Agnostic, Atheistic, Atheous, Impious, Profane

Go-go Alert

▷ **Going wrong** *may indicate* an anagram

Gold(en) Age, Amber, Apple, Ass, Au, Auriel, Auriferous, Auriol, Aurum, Bough, Bull, Bullion, Bull's eye, California, Chryselephantine, Doubloon, Dutch, Eagle, Electron, Electrum, Emerods, Fairy, Filigree, Fleece, Fool's, Gate, Gilden, Handshake, Hind, Horde, Horn, Ingot, Kolar, Leaf, Lingot, Moidore, Mosaic, Muck, Nugget, Oaker, Obang, Ochre, Ophir, Or, Oreide, Ormolu, Oroide, Pistole, Placer, Pyrites, Red, Reef, Rolled, Silence, Sol, Standard, Stubborn, Taelbar, Talmi, Thrimsa, Tolosa, Treasury, Wash-up, White, Xanthe, Yellow

Gold-digger Forty-niner, Prospector

Golfer Alliss, Braid, Cotton, Faldo, Hogan, Lyle, Pivoter, Rees, Roundsman, Seve, Snead, Teer, Texas scramble, Tiger Woods, Trevino, Wolstenholme, Yipper

Goliath Giant

Gone Ago, Dead, Defunct, Deid, Napoo, Out, Past, Ygo(e), Yod

▷ **Gone off** *may indicate* an anagram

Good(ness), Goody-goody Agatha, Agathodaimon, Altruism, Angelic, Ascertained, Bad, Bein, Benefit, Blesses, Bon, Bonzer, Bosker, Bounty, Braw, Brod, Budgeree, Canny, Castor, Civil, Classy, Clinker, Common, Coo, Cool, Crack(ing), Credit, Crikey, Dab, Dandy, Def, Divine, Dow, Enid, Estimable, Fancy that, Fantabulous, Finger lickin', First-class, G, Gear, Giffen, Glenda, Gold, Gosh, Guid, Hooray, Humdinger, Lekker, Lois, Lor, Ma foi, Mega, Merchandise, Moral, Neat, Nobility, Pi, Plum, Prime, Proper, Pucka, Pukka, Purler, Rattling, Rectitude, Riddance, Right(eous), Rum, St, Sake, Salutary, Samaritan, Sanctity, Slap-up, Smashing, Spiffing, Splendid, Suitable, Super, Taut, Tollol, Topping, Valid, Virtue, Virtuous, Weal, Welfare, Whacko, Wholesome, Worthy

Goodbye Addio, Adieu, Adios, Aloha, Arrivederci, Cheerio, Cheers, Ciao, Farewell, Haere ra, Hamba kahle, Later, Sayonara, See-you, So long, Tata, Toodle-oo, Toodle-pip, Vale

Goods Brown, Cargo, Commodities, Consumer, Disposable, Durable, Durables, Fancy, Flotsam, Freight, Gear, Hardware, Line, Luxury, Piece, Products, Property, Schlock, Soft, Wares, White

Goodwill Amity, Bonhom(m)ie, Favour, Gree

Goofy Simple-minded

Goop Ooze

Goose, Geese Anserine, Barnacle, Bernicle, Blue, Brent, Canada, Cape Barren,

Colonial, Daftie, Ember, Gaggle, Gander, Gannet, Golden, Greylag, Grope, Harvest, Hawaiian, Idiot, Juggins, MacFarlane's, Magpie, Michaelmas, Mother, Nana, Nene, Pink-footed, Pygmy, Quink, Roger, Saddleback, Silly, Simpleton, Skein, Snow, Solan, Strasbourg, Stubble, → STUPID PERSON, Swan, Team, Wav(e)y, Wawa, Wedge, Whitehead

Goosefoot Allgood, Amarantaceae, Beet, Blite, Fat-hen, Mercury, Orache, Saltbush

Gorge(s) Abyss, Barranca, Barranco, Canyon, Carnarvon, Chasm, Cheddar, Cleft, Couloir, Cram, Defile, Donga, Flume, Gap, Ghyll, Glut, Grand Canyon, Gulch, Ironbridge, Katherine, Khor, Kloof, Lin(n), Nala, Nalla(h), Nulla(h), Olduvai, Overeat, Pass, Pig, Ravine, Staw, → STUFF, Throat, Tire, Tums, Valley, Valley of the Kings, Yosemite

Gorgeous Dreamboat, Grand, Splendid, Superb

Gorilla Heavy, → MONKEY, Silverback

Gosh Begad, Begorra, Blimey, Cor, Crumbs, Ecod, Gadzooks, Gee, Golly, Gracious, Gum, Lor, My, Odsbobs, Odso, Really, Shucks

Gossip Ana(s), Aunt, Backbite, Cackle, Cat, Causerie, Chat, Chin, Chitchat, Clash, Clash-me-clavers, Claver, Cleck, Clish-clash, Clishmaclaver, Confab, Cosher, Crack, Dirt, Flibbertigibbet, Furphy, Gab(nash), Gabfest, Gas, Gash, Hearsay, Jaw, Loose-tongued, Maundrel, Moccasin telegraph, Natter, Newsmonger, Noise, Pal, Prattle, Prose, Quidnunc, Rumour(monger), Scandal(monger), Schmooze, Scuttlebutt, Shmoose, Shmooze, Talk(er), Tattle, Tattletale, Tittle(-tattle), Twattle, Whisper, Yak, Yatter

Gourmand, Gourmet Aesthete, Apicius, Chowhound, → EPICURE, Free-liver, Gastronome, Gastrosopher, Lickerish, Table, Trencherman, Ventripotent

Govern(or), Government Administer, Alderman, Andocracy, Archology, Aristocracy, Autarchy, Autocrat, Autonomy, Bashaw, Bencher, Bureaucracy, Cabinet, Caciquism, Caliphate, Caretaker, Cassio, Coalition, Command, Condominium, Congress, Constitution, Despotocracy, Diarchy, Dinarchy, Domain, Dominate, Duarchy, Dulocracy, Dyarchy, Ecclesiarchy, Eminent domain, Federal, G, Gerontocracy, Gov, Gubernator, Guv, Gynarchy, Hagiarchy, Hagiocracy, Helm, Heptarchy, Hierocracy, Inspector, Isocracy, Kakistocracy, Kawanatanga, Kremlin, Legate, Matriarchy, Monarchy, Monocracy, Nomocracy, Ochlocracy, Oligarchy, Patriarchism, Petticoat, Plutocracy, Polyarchy, Power, Raj, Regency, Regime(n), Regulator, Reign, Republican, → RULE, Senate, Stear, Steer, Stratocracy, Subah(dar), Sway, Technocracy, Thalassocracy, Thalattocracy, Thearchy, Theocracy, Third Republic, Timocracy, Triarchy, Vaivode, Vichyssois(e), Voivode, Whitehall, Woiwode

Governess Duenna, Eyre, Fraulein, Griffin, Mademoiselle, Prism, Vicereine

Grab Accost, Annexe, Areach, Bag, Clutch, Cly, Collar, Glaum, Grapnel, Hold, Holt, Nab, Rap, Reach, Seise, Seize, Snaffle, Swipe

Grace(s), Graceful Aglaia, Amazing, Amnesty, Anna, Beauty, Become, Benediction, Ben(t)sh, Blessing, Charis(ma), Charites, Charity, Cooperating, Darling, Dr, Elegance, Eloquent, Euphrosyne, Fluent, Gainly, Genteel, Genty, Godliness, Handsome, Honour, Mense, Mercy, Mordent, Omnium, Ornament, Plastique, Polish, Prayer, Sacrament, Spirituelle, Streamlined, Style, Svelte, Thalia, Thanks, Thanksgiving, Tuesday, Willowy

Grace note Nachschlag

Gracious Benign, By George, Charismatic, Generous, Good, Handsome, Hend, Mamma mia, Merciful, Polite

Grade, Gradient Alpha, Analyse, Angle, Assort, Beta, Bubs, Class(ify), Conservation, Dan, Degree, Delta, Echelon, Gamma, Gon, Gride, Hierarchy, Inclination, Kyu, Lapse, Measure, Order, Ordinary, Rank, Reserve, Score, Seed, Slope, Stage, Standard, Status, Thermocline, Tier

Graduate, Graduation Alumnus, BA, Bachelor, Calibrate, Capping, Incept, Laureateship, Licentiate, LlB, MA, Master, Nuance, Optime, Ovate

Graft Anaplasty, Autoplasty, Boodle, Bribery, Bud, Cion, Cluster, Dishonesty, Dub,

Enarch, Enrace, Heteroplasty, Imp, Implant, Inarch, Inoculate, Payola, Pomato, Racket, Scion, Shoot, Sien(t), Slip, Syen, Transplant, Ympe

Grain(y) Bajra, Bajree, Bajri, Barley(corn), Bear, Bere, Boll, Bran, Cereal, Corn, Couscous, Crop, Curn, Curn(e)y, Cuscus, D(o)urra, Dye, Extine, Floor, Frumentation, Gr, Graddan, Granule, Grit(s), Groats, Grout, Grumose, Intine, Kaoliang, Knaveship, Malt, Mashlam, Mashlin, Mashloch, Mashlum, Maslin, Mealie, Millet, Milo, Minim, Mongcorn, Oats, Pickle, Pinole, Pollen, Polynology, Popcorn, Proso, Psyllium, Puckle, Quinoa, Rabi, Raggee, Raggy, Ragi, Rhy, Rye, Sand, Scruple, Seed, Semsem, Sorghum, Tef(f), Tola, Touch, Wheat, Wholemeal

Grand(eur), Grandiose Big, Canyon, Epical, Flugel, G, Gorgeous, Guignol, High-faluting, Hotel, Imposing, La(h)-di-da(h), Lordly, Magnificent, Majestic, Noble, Overblown, Palatial, Piano(forte), Pompous, Regal, Splendid, Stately, Stoor, Stour, Stowre, Sture, Sublime, Swell, Tour

Granite Aberdeen, Chinastone, Greisen, Luxul(l)ianite, Luxulyanite, NH, Pegmatite, Protogine

Grant(ed) Accord, Aid, Allot, Allow, Award, Benefaction, Bestow, Block, Bounty, Bursary, Carta, Cary, Cede, Charta, Charter, Concession, →**CONFER**, Cy, Datum, Endow, Enfranchise, Exhibition, Feoff, Hugh, Lend, Let, License, Munich, Patent, President, Scholarship, Send, Sop, Subsidy, Subvention, Supply, Ulysses, Ure, Vouchsafe, Yeven, Yield

Grape(s) Aligoté, Botros, Botryoid, Bullace, Cabernet, Cabernet Sauvignon, Carmenère, Catawba, Cépage, Chardonnay, Chenin blanc, Colombard, Concord, Cot, Delaware, Fox, Gamay, Garnacha, Gewurztraminer, Haanepoot, Hamburg(h), Hanepoot, Honeypot, Hyacinth, Lambrusco, Malbec, Malmsey, Malvasia, Malvesie, Malvoisie, Marsanne, Merlot, Montepulciano, Muscadel, Muscadine, Muscat(el), Nebbiolo, Noble rot, Pinot, Pinotage, Primitivo, Racemose, Raisin, Rape, Riesling, Sangiovese, Sauvignon, Scuppernong, Sémillon, Sercial, Shiraz, Sour, Sultana, Sweet-water, Sylvaner, Syrah, Tokay, Uva, Verdelho, Véronique, Vino, Vognier, Zinfandel

Grape-grower Vigneron, Vine-dresser

Graph, Graphic(s) Bar, Chart, Clip art, Computer, Contour, Diagram, Histogram, Ogive, Picturesque, Pie (chart), Plot, Profile, Raster, Sine curve, Sonogram, Table, Turtle, Vivid, Waveform, Waveshape

Grapple Clinch, Close, Hook, Lock, Struggle, Wrestle

Grasp(ing) Apprehend, Catch, Clat, Claut, Claw, Clench, →**CLUTCH**, Compass, Comprehend, Fathom, Get, Go-getting, Grab, Grapple, Greedy, Grip(e), Hend, Hold, Hug, Knowledge, Prehend, Prehensile, Raptorial, Realise, Rumble, Seize, Sense, Snap, Snatch, Twig, Uptak(e)

Grass(land), Grass roots, Grassy Agrostology, Alang, Alfa(lfa), Arrow, Avena, Bahia, Bamboo, Bang, Barbed wire, Barley, Barnyard, Beard, Bennet, Bent, Bermuda, Bhang, Blade, Blady, Blue(-eyed), Blue moor, Bristle, Brome-grass, Bromus, Buffalo, Buffel, Bunch, Bush, Campo, Canary, Cane, Canna, Cannach, Carpet, Cat's tail, Cheat, Chess, China, Citronella, Cleavers, Clivers, Clover, Cochlearia, Cocksfoot, Cockspur, Cogon, Cord, Cortaderia, Cotton, Couch, Cow, Crab, Culm, Cuscus, Cutty, Dactylis, Danthonia, Dari, Darnel, Deergrass, Dhur(r)a, Diss, Divot, Dogstail, Dog's tooth, Dogwheat, Doob, Doura, Dura, Durra, Eddish, Eel, Eelwrack, Elephant, Emmer, Ers, Esparto, Feather, Fescue, Finger, Fiorin, Flinders, Floating, Flote, Fog, Foggage, Foxtail, Gage, Gama-grass, Ganja, Gardener's garters, Glume, Glumella, Goose, Grama, Gramineae, Green(sward), Hair, Halfa, Harestail, Hashish, Hassock, Haulm, Hay, Haycock, Heath(er), Hemp, Herbage, High veld, Holy, Indian corn, →**INFORM**, Jawar(i), Job's tears, Johnson, Jowar(i), Kangaroo, Kans, Kentucky blue, Khuskhus, Kikuyu, Knoll, Knot, Lalang, Laund, Lawn, Lay, Lea, Lemon, Locusta, Lolium, Lop, Lucern(e), Lyme, Mabela, Machair, Maize, Manna, Marram, Marrum, Mary Jane, Mat, Materass, Matweed, Mead, Meadow(-fescue), Meadow foxtail, Mealies, Melic, Melick, Millet, Milo, Miscanthus, Monkey, Moor, Moss-crop, Nark, Nassella tussock, Nature strip, Negro-corn, Nit, Nose, Nut, Oat, Orange, Orchard, Oryza, Painted, Palet, Pamir, Pampas, Panic, Paspalum, Pasturage, Peach, Pennisetum, Pepper, Persicaria,

Phleum, Pilcorn, Plume, Poa, Porcupine, Pot, Purple moor, Puszta, Quack, Quaking, Quick, Quitch, Ramee, Rami(e), Rat, Rat on, Redtop, Reed, Rescue, Rhodes, Rib, Ribbon, Rice, Rips, Roosa, Rotgrass, Rough, Rumble(r), Rusa, Rush, Rye(-brome), Sacaton, Sago, Salt, Sand, Savanna(h), Saw, Scorpion, Scraw, Scurvy, Scutch, Sea-reed, Sedge, Seg, Sesame, Shave, Sheep's fescue, Shop, Sing, Sinsemilla, Sisal, Sneak(er), Snitch, Snout, Snow, Sorghum, Sour-gourd, Sourveld, Spanish, Spear, Spelt, Spike, Spinifex, Splay, Split, Squeal, Squirrel-tail, Squitch, Stag, Star(r), Stipa, Stool-pigeon, Storm, Sudan, Sugar, Sward, Swath(e), Sword, Tape, Taramea, Tath, Tea, Tef(f), Tell, Teosinte, Timothy, Toad, Toetoe, Toitoi, Triticale, Triticum, True-love, Tuffet, Turf, Tussac, Tussock, Twitch, Veld(t), Vernal, Vetiver, Viper's, Whangee, Wheat, Wheatgrass, Whistleblower, Whitlow, Wild oat, Windlestraw, Wire, Witch, Wood melick, Worm, Yard, Yellow-eyed, Yorkshire fog, Zizania, Zostera, Zoysia

Grasshopper Cicada, Cricket, Katydid, Locust, Reeler, Short-horned

Grate(r), Grating Abrade, Burr, Cancelli, Chafe, Chain, Chirk, Crepitus, Diffraction, Erosure, →**FRET**, Graticule, Grid, Grill, Guichet, Guttural, Hack, Haik, Hake, Harsh, Hearth, Heck, Hoarse, Ingle, Iron, Jar, Nag, Portcullis, Rasp, Risp, Rub, Ruling, Scrannel, →**SCRAPE**, Scrat, Scroop, Shred, Siver, Strident, Syver

Gratin Tian

Gratuitous, Gratuity Baksheesh, Beer-money, Bonsella, Bonus, Bounty, Cumshaw, Dash, Free, Glove-money, Gratis, Lagn(i)appe, Mag(g)s, Tip

Grave(yard) Accent, Arlington, Barrow, Bass, Bier, Burial, Charnel, Chase, Critical, Darga, Demure, Dust, God's acre, Heavy, Heinous, Important, Ingroove, Kistvaen, Kurgan, Mool, Mould, Mound, Passage, Pit, Sad, Saturnine, Serious, Sober, Solemn, Sombre, Speos, Staid, Stern, Tomb, Watery

Gravel(ly) Calculus, Channel, Glareous, Grail(e), Grit, Hard, Hoggin(g), Murram, Nonplus, Shingle

Gravity Barycentric, G, Geotaxis, Geotropism, Magnitude, Mascon, Specific, Weight

▶**Gray** *see* **GREYING**

Grease, Greasy Bribe, Creesh, Dope, Dubbing, Elaeolite, Elbow, Enlard, Enseam, Glit, Lanolin, Lard, Oil, Ointment, Pinguid, Saim, Seam(e), Shearer, Sheep-shearer, Smarm, Smear, Suint, Unctuous

Greater, Greatest, Great(ly), Greats Alfred, Ali, A majori, Astronomical, Brilliant, Bully, Capital, Classical, Colossus, Cosmic, Enorm(ous), Ever so, Excellent, Extreme, Fantastic, Gargantuan, Gatsby, Gran(d), Gt, Guns, Hellova, Helluva, Immense, Immortal, Important, Intense, Large, Lion, Macro, Magic, Magnus, Main, Major, Massive, Mega, Mickle, Modern, Much, Muckle, No end, OS, Preponderant, Profound, Rousing, Splendiferous, Stupendous, Sublime, Super, Superb, Superduper, Swingeing, Tall, Thrice, Titan(ic), Top notch, Tremendous, Unco, Untold, Utmost, Vast, Voluminous, Wide, Zenith

Greed(y) Avarice, Avid, Bulimia, Bulimy, Cupidity, Edacious, Esurient, Gannet, Gare, Grabby, Grip(ple), Gulosity, Guts(e)y, Insatiable, Killcrop, Lickerish, Liquorish, Mercenary, Money-grubbing, Piggery, Pleonexia, Rapacity, Selfish, Shark's manners, Solan, Voracity, Wolfish

Greek(s) Achaean, Achaian, Achilles, Aeolic, Agamemnon, Ajax, Ancient, Aonian, Arcadia, Archimedes, Argive, Aristides, Athenian, Attic, Boeotian, Byzantine, Cadmean, Cleruch, Corinthian, Cretan, Delphian, Demotic, Demotike, Ding, Diomedes, Dorian, Doric, Elea, Eoka, Eolic, Epaminondas, Ephebe, Epirus, Euclid, Evzone, Fanariot, Gr, Helladic, Hellene, Hellenic, Hesychast, Homer, Hoplite, Ionian, Isocrates, Italiot(e), Javan, Katharev(o)usa, Klepht, Koine, Lapith, Late, Leonidas, Linear B, Locrian, Lucian, Lysander, Macedonia, Medieval, Milesian, Momus, Nestor, Nike, Nostos, Orestes, Paestum, Patroclus, Pelasgic, Pelopid, Perseus, Phanariot, Pythagoras, Romaic, Samiot, Seminole, Spartacus, Spartan, Stagirite, Strabo, Sybarite, Tean, Teian, Theban, Thersites, Theseus, Thessal(on)ian, Thracian, Timon, Typto, Uniat, Xenophon, Zorba

Green(ery) Apple, Bleaching, Bottle, Callow, Celadon, Cerulein, Chartreuse, Chlorophyll, Chrome, Common, Copper, Crown, Eau de nil, Eco-, Ecofriendly, Ecologic, Econut, Emerald, Emerande, Envious, Environmentalist, Erin, Fingers,

Foliage, Forest, Fuchsin, Fundie, Fundy, Glaucous, Goddess, Gretna, Immature, Inexpert, Jade, L, Lawn, Leafage, Lime, Lincoln, Loden, Lovat, Moss, Naive, New, Nile, Olive, Pea, Peridot, Pistachio, Putting, Raw, Realo, Reseda, Rifle, Rink, Sage, Sap, Scheele's, Seasick, Shaw, Sludge, Sward, Teal, Tender, Tiro, Tyro, Unfledged, Uninitiated, Unripe, Unsophisticated, Untrained, Uranite, Verdant, Verdigris, Verdure, Vert, Vir(id)escent, Viridian, Yearn

Greenland(er) Inuit

Greens Broccoli, Cabbage, Calabrese, Castor, Sprout, Vegetable(s)

Greet, Greeting(s) Accost, Air-kiss, Aloha, Banzai, Benedicite, Bid, Bonsoir, Ciao, Den, G'day, Glad hand, Gorillagram, Hail, Hallo, Handshake, Heil, Herald, Hi, High-five, Hiya, How, Howsit, Jambo, Kia ora, Kiss, Respects, Salaam, Salue, Salute, Salve, Save you, Shalom, Shalom aleichem, Sorry, Tena koe, Tena korua, Tena koutou, Wave, Weep, →**WELCOME**, Wellmet, Wotcha, Wotcher, Yo

▶**Gremlin** *see* **GOBLIN**

Grenadine(s) Bequia, Canouan, Mustique, Union Island

Grey(ing), Gray, Greybeard Argent, Ashen, Ashy, Battleship, C(a)esius, Charcoal, Cinereous, Clair de lune, Dapple, Dorian, Dove, Drab, Earl, Glaucous, Gloomy, Gr, Gridelin, Grise, Grisy, Grizzled, Gunmetal, Hoary, Hore, Iron, Leaden, Lipizzaner, Lloyd, Mouse-coloured, Oldster, Pearl, Putty, Slaty, Steel

Greyhound Grew, Lapdog, Longtail, Ocean, Saluki, Sapling, Whippet

Grid(dle), Gridiron Bar, Barbecue, Brandreth, Cattle, Dot matrix, Grate, Graticule, Grating, Lattice, Network, Reseau, Reticle, Roo-bar, Schema, Tava(h), Tawa, Windscale

Grief, Grievance, Grieve, Grievous Axe, Bemoan, Bitter, Complaint, Condole, Cry, Dear(e), Deere, Distress, Dole, Dolour, Eyedrop, Gram(e), Gravamen, Grudge, Heartbreak, Hone, Illy, Io, →**MISERY**, Monody, Noyous, O(c)hone, Overset, Pain, Pathetic, Plaint, Plangent, Rue, Sorrow, Tears, Teen, Tene, Tragic, Wayment, Weeping, Woe, Wrong

Grill(er), Grilling Braai, Brander, Broil, Carbonado, Crisp, Cross-examine, Devil, Gridiron, Inquisition, Interrogate, Kebab, Mixed, Pump, Question, Rack, Reja, Yakimona

Grim Austere, Dire, Dour, Forbidding, Gaunt, Glum, Gurly, Hard, Reaper, Stern

▷**Grim** *may indicate* an anagram

Grimace Face, Girn, Moe, Mop, Moue, Mouth, Mow, Murgeon, Pout, Wince

Grime(s), Grimy Colly, Coom, Dirt, Grunge, Peter, Reechie, Reechy, Soil, Sweep, Tash

Grin Fleer, Girn, Risus, Simper, Smirk, Sneer

Grind(er), Grinding Bray, Bruxism, Chew, Crunch, →**CRUSH**, Droil, Drudgery, Gnash, Grate, Graunch, Grit, Kern, Kibble, Labour, Levigate, Mano, Mill, Mince, Molar, Muller, Offhand, Pug, Pulpstone, Pulverise, Slog, Stamp, Triturate

Grip(ping), Gripper Absorb, Arm lock, Ascendeur, Bite, Chuck, Clam, Clamp, Cleat, Clip, Clutch, Craple, Dog, Embrace, Engrasp, Enthral, Get, Grapple, →**GRASP**, Haft, Hairpin, Handhold, Headlock, Hend, Hold, Hug, Interesting, Jaw, Kirby®, Lewis, Obsess, Pincer, Pinion, Prehensile, Purchase, Raven, Rhine, Sally, Sipe, Strain, Streigne, Thrill, Traction, Valise, Vice, Walise, Wrestle

Gripe(s) Colic, Complain, Ditch, Grasp, Griffin, Ileus, Pain, Tormina, Whine

Grit(s), Gritty Blinding, Clench, Gnash, Granular, Grate, Guts, Mattress, Millstone, Pennant, Pluck, Resolution, Sabulose, Sand, Shingle, Swarf, Toughness

Gritty Tacky, Ugly

Groin Gnarr, Inguinal, Lisk

▷**Groom** *may indicate* an anagram

Groove(d), Grooves, Groovy Bezel, Canal, Cannelure, Chamfer, Channel, Chase, Clevis, Cool, Coulisse, Croze, Dièdre, Exarate, Fissure, Flute, Fuller, Furr, Furrow, Glyph, Gouge, Hill and dale, Kerf, Key-seat, Keyway, Nock, Oche, Pod, Quirk, Rabbet, Race(way), Raggle, Rare, Rebate, Rif(f)le, Rifling, Rigol(l), Rout, →**RUT**, Scrobe, Scrobiculate, Sipe, Slot, Sulcus, Throat, Track, Trough, Vallecula

Grope(r) A tatons, Feel, Fumble, Grabble, Hapuka, Ripe, Scrabble

Gross All-up, Coarse, Coarse-grained, Complete, Crass, Dense, Earthy, Flagrant, Frankish, Giant, Gr, Material, Obese, Obscene, Outsize, Overweight, Pre-tax, Rank, Ribald, Rough, Stupid, Whole

▷ **Gross** *may indicate* an anagram

Grotesque Antic, Bizarre, Fantastic, Fright, Gargoyle, Macaroni, Magot, Outlandish, Rabelaisian, Rococo

Grotty Tacky, Ugly

▷ **Ground** *may indicate* an anagram

Ground(ed), Grounds Acreage, Arena, Astroturf, A terre, Basis, Bottom, Breeding, Campus, Cause, Common, Criterion, Crushed, Deck, Dregs, Eard, Earth, Epig(a)eal, Epig(a)ean, Epigene, Epig(a)eous, Etching, Footing, Forbidden, Grated, Grist, Grouts, Happy hunting, Headingley, Home, Justification, Lees, Leeway, Lek, Lords, Lot, Marl, Meadow, Mealed, Motive, Occasion, Oval, Parade, Pitch, Plat, Plot, Policy, Proving, Quad, → REASON, Rec(reation), Réseau, Ring, Sandlot, Sediment, Slade, Soil, Solum, Stadium, Strand, Terra, Terrain, Tiltyard, Tract, Turf, Udal, Venue, Waste(land), Yard, Yird

Ground-breaker Pioneer

Group(ie), Grouping Affinity, Al Fatah, Bananarama, Band, Batch, Battle, Beatles, Bee, Bevy, Bloc(k), Board, Body, Break-out, Bunch, Camp, Cartel, Category, Cell, Choir, Circle, Clan, Class(is), Clique, Clump, Cluster, Clutch, Coachload, Colony, Commune, Community, Complex, Confraternity, Conglomerate, Congregation, Consort(ium), Constellation, Contingent, Coterie, Crew, Decile, Dectet, Department, Detachment, Drove, Ensemble, Faction, Family, Fauna, Fleet, Flora, Follower, Functional, Gaggle, Generation, Genotype, Genus, Guild, Herd, Household, In-crowd, Interest, Keiretsu, Knob, League, Led Zeppelin, Lichfield, Linkage, Local, Lot, Lumpenproletariat, Minority, Minyan, Network, Oasis, Order, Outfit, Panel, Party, Peer, Phalanx, Platoon, PLO, Plump, Posse, Powerbase, Retinue, Ring, Salon, School, Sector, Seminar, Senate, Series, Set, Several, Shoal, Society, Sort, Species, Squad(ron), Stick, Subclass, Subfamily, Sub-order, Subset, Subspecies, Symbol, Syndicate, Synectics, Syntagm, System, Team, The few, Topological, Tribe, Trio, Troika, Troop, Troupe, Umbrella, Undecimole, Unit, Usenet®, Vertical, Wing

Grouse Bellyache, Blackcock, Bleat, Caper(caillie), Capercailzie, Covey, Game, Gorcock, Greyhen, Gripe, Growl, Grumble, Hazel-hen, Heath-cock, Heathfowl, Heath-hen, Jeremiad, Kvetch, Moan, Moorcock, Moorfowl, Moor-pout, Muir-poot, Muir-pout, Mutter, Natter, Peeve, Pintail, Prairie chicken, Prairie-hen, Ptarmigan, Red game, Resent, Rype(r), Snarl, Spruce, Squawk, Twelfth, Wheenge, Willow, W(h)inge

Grout Cement, Lees

Grove Academy, Arboretum, Bosk, Bosquet, Copse, Glade, Hurst, Lyceum, Nemoral, Orchard, Orchat, Silva, Tope

Grow(ing), Grow out, Growth Accrete, Accrue, Acromegaly, Adenoma, Aggrandisement, Angioma, Apophysis, Arborescence, Auxesis, Bedeguar, Boom, Braird, Breer, Burgeon, Carcinoma, Car(b)uncle, Chancre, Cholelith, Chondroma, Compensatory, Condyloma, Corn, Crescendo, Crop, Culture, Cyst, Down, Ectopia, Edema, Ellagic, Enate, Enchondroma, Enlarge, Epiboly, Epinasty, Epitaxy, Excrescence, Exostosis, Expansion, Fibroid, Flor, Flourish, Flush, Gain, Gall, Germinate, Get, Glareal, Goitre, Hepatocele, Hummie, Hyperostosis, Hypertrophy, Hyponasty, Increase, Involucrum, Keloidal, Knur(r), Lichen, Lipoma, Monopodial, Moss, Mushroom, Myoma, Neoplasia, Nur(r), Oak-nut, Oedema, Oncology, Osselet, Osteoma, Pharming, Polyp, Polypus, Proleg, Proliferate, Rampant, Scirrhus, Scopa, Septal, Snowball, Spavin, → SPROUT, Stand, Stipule, Sympodial, Tariff, Thigmotropism, Thrive, Trichome, → TUMOUR, Tylosis, Vegetable, Wart, Wax, Weed, Witches'-broom, Wox, Zeatin

▷ **Grow(n)** *may indicate* an anagram

Growl(er), Growling Fremescent, Gnar, Groin, Grr, Gurl, Iceberg, Knar, Roar(e), Roin, Royne, Snar(l)

Groyne Breakwater

Grub(by) Assart, Bardie, Bardy, Caddis, Caterpillar, Cheer, Chow, Chrysalis, Deracinate, Dig, Eats, Fare, Fodder, →**FOOD**, Gentle, Groo-groo, Gru-gru, Larva, Leatherjacket, Maggot, Mawk, Mess, Nosh, Palmerworm, Peck, Pupa, Root(le), Rout, Rowt, Sap, Slave, Stub, Tired, Wireworm, Witchetty, Worm

Gruesome Ghastly, Grisly, Grooly, Horror, Macaberesque, Macabre, →**MORBID**, Sick

Grumble Beef, Bellyache, Bitch, Bleat, Chunter, Croak, Girn, Gripe, Grizzle, Groin, Growl, Moan, Mump, Murmur, Mutter, Nark, Natter, Repine, Rumble, Whinge, Yammer

Grump(y) Attercop, Bearish, Cross, Curmudgeon, Ettercap, Grouchy, Moody, Ogre(ish), Sore-headed, Surly, Testy

Grunt Groin, Grumph, Humph, Oink, Pigfish, Ugh, Wheugh

Guarantee(d) Accredit, Assure, Avouch, Certify, Collateral, Ensure, Fail-safe, Gage, Hallmark, Insure, Mainprise, Money-back, Pignerate, Pignorate, →**PLEDGE**, Plight, Promise, Seal, Secure, Sponsion, Surety, Underwrite, →**VOUCHSAFE**, Warn, Warrandice, Warrant(y)

Guard(ed), Guards Advance, Apron, Beefeaters, Blues, Bouncer, Centinel(l), Centry, Chamfrain, Colour, Conductor, Cordon, Crinoline, Custodian, Defend, Duenna, Escort, Fender, Gaoler, Gateman, Gauntlet, Hedge, Home, Horse, Insure, Irish, Iron, Jailer, Keep, Life, Look out, Mask, Militia, Muzzle, National, Nightwatch(man), Noncommital, Old, Palace, Patrol, Picket, Point, Policeman, →**PROTECT**, Provost, Rail, Ride, Roof, Scots, Screw, Secure, Security, Sentinel, Sentry, Shadow, Shield, Shin, Shopping, Shotgun, Splashback, Splashboard, Splasher, SS, Switzer, Turnkey, Vambrace, Vigilante, Visor, Ward, Warder, Watch (and ward), Watchdog, Watchman, Wire, Yeoman

Guardian(ship) Agathodaimon, Altair, Argus, Caretaker, Chaperone, Curator, Custodian, Custos, Dragon, Gemini, Granthi, Hafiz, Janus, Julius, Miminger, Patron, Protector, Templar, Trustee, Tutelage, Tutelar(y), Tutor, Warder, Watchdog, Xerxes

Guatemala(n) Mam

Guer(r)illa Bushwhacker, Chetnik, Comitadji, Contra, ETA, Fedayee, Gook, Haiduk, Heyduck, Irregular, Khmer Rouge, Komitaji, Maquis, Mujahadeen, Mujahedeen, Mujahed(d)in, Mujahideen, Partisan, Phalanx, Red Brigade, Tamil Tiger, Terrorist, Tupamaro, Urban, Viet Cong, Zapata, Zapatista

Guess Aim, Aread, Arede, Arreede, Assume, Augur, Conjecture, Divine, Educated, Estimate, Harp, Hazard, Hunch, Imagine, Infer, Inspired, Level, Mor(r)a, Mull, Psych out, Reckon, Shot, Speculate, Stab, Suppose, Surmise, Theorise, Venture

Guest(s) Caller, Company, Invitee, Parasite, Paying, PG, Symbion(t), Symphile, Synoecete, Visitant, →**VISITOR**, Xenial

Guidance, Guide, Guiding, Guideline Advice, Aunt, Baedeker, Bradshaw, Cicerone, Clue, Command, Conduct, Counsel, Courier, Cox, Cybrary, Director(y), Engineer, →**ESCORT**, Homing, Index, Inspire, Itinerary, Key, Landmark, Mahatma, Manoeuvre, Map, Mark, Mentor, Michelin, Missile, Model, Navigate, Nose, Pilot, Pointer, Providence, Rainbow, Ranger, Reference, Rudder, Sea Ranger, Shepherd, Sign, Sixer, Standard, Steer, Target, Template, Terminal, Train, Usher(ette), Waymark

Guild Artel, Basoche, Company, Gyeld, Hanse, Hoastman, League, Society, Tong, Union

Guillotine Closure, Decapitate, Louisiette, Maiden, Marianne

Guilt(y) Affluenza, Angst, Blame, Cognovit, Flagitious, Hangdog, Nocent, Peccavi, Remorse, Wicked

Guitar(ist) Acoustic, Axe(man), Bass, Bottleneck, Cithern, Cittern, Dobro®, Fender®, Fretman, Gittern, Hawaiian, Humbucker, Lute, Plankspanker, Samisen, Sancho, Sanko, Shamisen, Sitar, Spanish, Steel, Uke, Ukulele

Gulf Aden, Anadyr, Aqaba, Bay, Bothnia, California, Cambay, Campeche, Carpentaria, Chasm, Chihli, Darien, Exmouth, Finland, Fonseca, G, Hauraki, Honduras, Iskenderun, Isthmus, Izmit, Lepanto, Lingayen, Lions, Mannar, Martaban, Maw,

Mexico, Ob, Oman, Patras, Persian, Pozzuoli, Queen Maud, Rapallo, Riga, St Lawrence, St Vincent, Salerno, Salonika, Saronic, Saros, Sidra, Spencer, Taranto, Thailand, Tonkin, Trieste, Tunis, Venice

Gull(s) Bamboozle, Bonxie, Cheat, Cob(b), Cod, Cozen, Cull(y), Dupe, Fool, Geck, Glaucous, Haglet, Hoodwink, Hum, Laridae, Larus, Lie to, Maw, Mew, Pickmaw, Pigeon, Queer, Ring-billed, Rook, Scaury, Scourie, Scowrie, Sea-cob, Sea-mew, Sell, Simp, Skua, Sucker, Tern, Tystie, Xema

Gullet Crop, Enterate, Maw, Throat, Weasand-pipe

Gully Couloir, Donga, Fielder, Geo, Gio, Goe, Grough, Gulch, Infielder, Pit, Rake, Ravine, Sloot, Sluit, Wadi

Gulp Bolt, Draught, Gollop, Quaff, Slug, Sob, →SWALLOW, Swipe, Wolf

Gum (tree) Acacia, Acajou, Acaroid, Agar, Algin, Angico, Arabic, Arabin, Arar, Arctic, Asafoetida, Bablah, Balata, Balm, Bandoline, Bdellium, Benjamin, Benzoin, Bloodwood, Boot, Bubble, Cerasin, Chicle, Chuddy, Chutty, Coolabah, Courbaril, Dextrin(e), Dragon's-blood, Ee-by, Eucalyptus, Frankincense, Galbanum, Gamboge, Gingival, →GLUE, Goat's-thorn, Gosh, Guar, Ironbark, Juniper, Karri, Kauri, Lac, La(b)danum, Lentisk, Mastic(h), Mucilage, Myrrh, Nicotine, Olibanum, Opopanax, Oshac, River red, Sagapenum, Sarcocolla, Scribbly, Size, Sleep, Spearmint, Spirit, Sterculia, Stringybark, Sugar, Tacamahac, Tragacanth, Tupelo, Xanthan

Gun(fire), Guns, Gunfight Amusette, Archibald, Archie, Arquebus, Automatic, Barker, Baton, Bazooka, Beanbag, Beretta, Big Bertha, Biscayan, Blunderbuss, Bofors, Bombard, Breech(-loader), Bren, Broadside, Brown Bess, Browning, Bulldog, Bullpup, Bundook, Burp, Caliver, Cannonade, Carbine, Carronade, Cement, Chokebore, Chopper, Coehorn, Colt®, Dag, Derringer, Electron, Elephant, Escopette, Falcon(et), Field, Fieldpiece, Firearm, Fire lock, Flame, Flash, Flintlock, Four-pounder, Fowler, Fowlingpiece, Full-bore, Garand, Gas, Gat(ling), Gingal(l), Grease, HA, Hackbut, Half-cock, Harquebus, Heater, Hired, Howitzer, Jezail, Jingal, Kalashnikov, Lewis, Long Tom, Luger®, Machine, Magazine, Magnum, Maroon, Martini-Henry®, Matchlock, Mauser®, Maxim, Metal, Minnie, Minute, Mitrailleuse, Mons Meg, Mortar, Musket(oon), Muzzle-loader, Nail, Needle, Neutron, Noonday, Oerlikon, Ordnance, Over and under, Owen, Paderero, Paterero, Ped(e)rero, Pelican, Perrier, Petronel, Piece, Pistol(et), Pompom, Pump (action), Punt, Purdey®, Quaker, Radar, Ray, Repeater, Rev, Revolver, Riot, Rod, Roscoe, Saker, Sarbacane, Saturday night special, Scatter, Self-cocker, Shooter, Shooting iron, Shoot-out, Sidearm, Siege, Smoothbore, Snapha(u)nce, Spear, Speed, Spray, Squirt, Staple, Starting, Sten, Sterculia, Sterling, Stern-cannon, Stern-chaser, Stun, Swivel, Taser®, Tea, Thirty eight, Thompson, Three-pounder, Tier, Time, Tire, Tommy, Tool, Tupelo, Turret, Uzi, Walther, Wesson, Wheel-lock, Young, Zip

Gunner, Gunner's assistant Arquebusier, Arsenal, Artillerist, Cannoneer, Cannonier, Culverineer, Gr, Matross, RA

Gunpowder Charcoal, Saucisse, Saucisson

Gurgle Burble, Clunk, Gollar, Goller, Guggle, Ruckle, Squelch

Gush(er), Gushing Blether, Effusive, →FLOOD, Flow, Fountain, Jet, Outpour, Rail, Regurgitate, Scaturient, Spirt, Spout, Spurt, Surge, Too-too

Gust Blast, Blore, Flaught, Flaw, Flurry, Puff, Sar, Squall, Waff

Gut(s), Gutty Abdomen, Archenteron, Balls, Beer, Bowel(s), Chitterlings, Cloaca, Disembowel, Draw, Duodenum, Enteral, Enteron, Entrails, Fore, Gill, Hind, Ileum, Insides, Kyle, Mesenteron, Mid, Omental, Omentum, Remake, Sack, Sand, Snell, Stamina, Staying-power, Strip, Thairm, Tripe, Ventriculus, Viscera

Gutta-percha Jelutong, Pontianac, Pontianak

Gutter(ing) Channel, Conduit, Cullis, Grip, Gully, Kennel, Rhone, Rigol(l), Roan, Rone, Runlet, Runnel, Sough, Spout, Strand, Swale, Swayl, Sweal

Guy Backstay, Bo, Burgess, Buster, Cat, Chaff, Clewline, Decamp, Deride, Dude, Effigy, Fall, Fawkes, Fellow, Gink, Josh, Mainstay, Mannering, Parody, Rag, Rib, Ridicule, Rope, Scarecrow, Stay, Taunt, Tease, Vang, Wise

Gym(nasium), Gymnast(ic) Acrobat, Akhara, Arena, Dojo, Exercise, Jungle, Lyceum, Palaestra, PE, PT, Real, Rhythmic, Sokol, Tumbler

Gypsum Alabaster, Gesso, Plaster, Satin spar, Satin-stone, Selenite

Gypsy, Gipsy Bohemian, Cagot, Caird, Caqueux, Chai, Chal, Chi, Collibert, Egyptian, Esmeralda, Faw, Gipsen, Gitano, Hayraddin, Lavengro, Meg, Pikey, Rom(any), Rye, Scholar, Siwash, Tinker, Traveller, Travelling folk, Tsigane, Tzigane, Tzigany, Vagabond, Vlach, Walach, Wanderer, Zigan, Zigeuner, Zincala, Zincalo, Zingaro

Gyrate Revolve, Rotate, → **SPIN**, Twirl

Hh

H Ache, Aitch, Aspirate, Height, Hospital, Hotel, Hydrant, Hydrogen, Zygal

Habit(s), Habitual, Habituate, Habitué Accustom, Addiction, Apparel, Assuetude, Bent, Chronic, Clothes, Coat, Consuetude, Cowl, Custom, Dress, Ephod, Frequenter, Garb, Hand-me-down, Inure, Inveterate, Motley, Mufti, Nature, Outfit, Practice, Quirk, Raiment, Regular, Riding, Robe, Routine, Scapular, Schema, Season, Second nature, Set, Soutane, Suit, Surplice, Toge, Trait, Trick, Usual, Way, Won, Wont

Habitable, Habitat(ion) Element, Environment, Haunt, Home, Locality, Pueblo, Refugium, Station, Tel

Hack(er), Hacking Blackhat, Chip, Chop, Cough, Cut, Cypherpunk, Drudge, Garble, Gash, Ghost, Grub-Street, Hag, Hash, Hedge-writer, Heel, Hew, Horse, Mangle, Mutilate, Nag, Nerd, Notch, Pad, Paper-strainer, Penny-a-liner, Phreak, Pick, Plater, Pot-boiler, Rosinante, Script kiddie, Slash, Spurn, Tadpole, Taper, Tap into, Tiger team, Tussis, Unseam, Warchalking

Hackney(ed) Banal, Cab, Cliché, Corny, Percoct, Stale, Threadbare, Tired, Trite, Twice-told, Worn

Haddock Arbroath smokie, Finnan, Whitefish

Hades Dis, Hell, Orcus, Pit, Tartarus

Haemoglobin Chelate, Hb

Hag(-like) Anile, Beldame, Besom, Carlin(e), Crone, Harpy, Harridan, Hell-cat, Hex, Moss, Rudas, Runnion, Sibyl, Trot, Witch

Haggard Drawn, →**GAUNT**, Pale, Rider

Haggle Argue, Badger, →**BARGAIN**, Barter, Chaffer, Dicker, Horse-trade, Niffer, Palter, Prig

Hail(er) Acclaim, Ahoy, Ave, Bull-horn, Cheer, Fusillade, Graupel, Greet, Gunfire, Hi, Ho, Megaphone, Salue, Salute, Shower, Signal, Skoal, Skol, Sola, Stentor, Storm, What ho, Whoa-ho-ho

Hair(y), Haircut, Hairlike, Hair problem/condition, Hair style Afro, Backcomb, Bang, Barnet, Beard, Bob, Bouffant, Braid, Bristle, Bun, Bunches, Bush, Capillary, Chignon, Coiffure, Combings, Comose, Cowlick, Crew-cut, Crinigerous, DA, Dicey, Dreadlocks, Excrement, Eyelash, Fibril, Fringe, Fur, Goatee, Lock, Mane, Mohawk, Mohican, Mop, Mophead, Pageboy, Peekabo(o), Perm(anent), Pigtail, Pincurl, Plait, Plica Polonica, Pompadour, Ponytail, Prison crop, Rug, Rush, Scaldhead, Sericeous, Shingle, Shock, Sideburns, Switch, Tache, Thatch, Tonsure, Toorie, Topknot, Tour(ie), Tress, Trichosis, Ulotrichous, Updo, Whisker, Wig, Wiglet

Hairdresser Barber, Coiffeur, Comb, Crimper, Friseur, Marcel, Salon, Stylist, Trichologist

Hairless Bald, Callow, Glabrate, Glabrous, Irate

Hairline Brow, Nape

Hairpiece Merkin, Strand, Toupee, →**WIG**

Halcyon Calm, Kingfisher, Mild

Half, Halved Bifid, Demi, Dimidiate, Divide, Hemi, Moiety, Semi, Share, Split, Stand-off, Term

Half-dead Alamort

Half-time Midhour

Half-wit Changeling, Mome, Simpleton, →**STUPID**

Hall Anteroom, Assembly, Atrium, Auditorium, Aula, Bachelor's, Basilica, Bingo, Carnegie, Chamber, Citadel, City, Concert, Dance, Divinity, Dotheboys, Festival,

Foyer, Guild, Hostel, Ivied, Judgement, Liberty, Lobby, Music, Odeon, Palais, Passage, Rideau, Salle, Saloon, Study, Tammany, Town, Trullen, Vestibule, Wildfell

Halloween Guiser

Hallucinate, Hallucinating, Hallucination, Hallucinogen Autoscopy, Fantasy, Freak, Illusion, Image, Mirage, Negative, Psychedelic, Psychotic

Halo Antheolion, Areola, Aura, Aureola, Corona, Gloria, Gloriole, Mandorla, Nimbus, Rim, Vesica

Halt(er) Abort, Arrest, Block, Brake, Bridle, Cavesson, Cease, Cesse, Check, End, Full stop, Game, Hackamore, Heave-to, Hilch, Lame(d), Limp, Noose, Prorogue, Rope, Stall, Standstill, →**STOP**, Stopover, Toho, Whoa, Widdy

Ham(s) Amateur, Barnstormer, Flitch, Gammon, Haunch, Hock, Hoke, Hough, Hunker, Jambon, Jay, Mutton, Nates, Overact, Overplay, Parma, Pigmeat, Prat, Prosciutto, Serrano, Spe(c)k, Tiro, Westphalian, York

Hamburger Sloppy joe

Hamlet(s) Aldea, Auburn, Cigar, Dane, Dorp, Hero, Kraal, Stead, Thorp(e), Tower, Vill(age), Wick

Hammer(ed), Hammerhead, Hammering Atmospheric, Ballpeen, Ballpein, Beetle, Bully, Bush, Celt, Claw, Dolly, Flatten, Fuller, Gavel, Hack, Incuse, Kevel, Knap, Madge, Mall(et), Malleate, Martel, Maul, Mjol(l)nir, Nevel, Ossicle, Pane, Pean, Peen, Pein, Pene, Percussion, Percussor, Piledriver, Plessor, Plexor, Rawhide, Rout, Shingle, Sledge, Strike, Tenderizer, Tilt, Trip, Trounce, Umbre, Water

▷ **Hammered** *may indicate* an anagram

▷ **Hammy** *may indicate* an anagram

Hamper Basket, Cabin, Cramp, Cumber, Delay, Encumber, Entrammel, Hamstring, Handicap, Hobble, Hog-tie, Impede, Obstruct, Pad, Pannier, Restrict, Rub, Shackle, Tangle, Trammel, Tuck

Hand(s), Hand over, Hand down, Hand-like, Handwriting Applause, Assist(ance), Bananas, Bequeath, Charge, Clap(ping), Club, Clutch, Copperplate, Court, Crabbed, Crew, Cursive, Dab, Deal, Deck, Deliver, Devolve, Dukes, Dummy, Extradition, Fin, Fist, Flipper, Flush, Free, Full (house), Glad, Graphology, Half-text, Help, Helping, Hidden, Impart, L, Laydown, Loof, Man, Manual, Mitt(en), Mutton-fist, Operative, Pad, Palaeography, Part, Pass, Paw, Post, Pud, R, Running, Script, Secretary, Signature, Span, Straight, Text, Uncial, Upper, Whip, Worker

Handbag Caba(s), Grip, Indispensable, Pochette, Purse, Reticule, Valise

Handbook Baedeker, Companion, Enchiridion, Guide, Manual, Vade-mecum

Handcuff(s) Bracelet, Darbies, Irons, Manacle, Mittens, Nippers, Shackle, Snaps

Handicap Burden, Disable, Encumber, Half-one, Hamper, Impede, Impost, Lame, Liability, →**OBSTACLE**, Off, Restrict, Scratch, Weigh(t), Welter-race

Handkerchief, Hanky Bandan(n)a, Clout, Curch, Kleenex®, Napkin, Nose-rag, Orarium, Tissue, Wipe(r)

Handle(d), Handler Ansate, Bail, Bale, Bitstock, Brake, Broomstick, Cope, Crank, Dead man's, Deal, Doorknob, Dudgeon, Ear, Feel, Field, Finger, Forename, Gaum, Gorm, Grip, Gunstock, Haft, Helve, Hilt, Hold, Knob, Knub, Lug, →**MANAGE**, Manipulate, Manubrium, Maul, Name, Nib, Palp, Paw, Pistol-grip, Pommel, Port-crayon, Process, Roadie, Rounce, Shaft, Snath(e), Snead, Sneath, Sned, Staff, Staghorn, Stale, Starting, Steal(e), Steel, Steil, Stele, Stilt, Stock, Sweep, Tiller, Title, To-name, Touch, Treat, Use, Whipstock, Wield, Winder, With(e)

Hand-out Alms, Charity, Dole, Gift, Issue, Release, Sample

Handsome Adonis, Apollo, Attractive, Bonny, Brave, Comely, Dishy, Featuous, Fine, Gracious, Kenneth, Liberal, Lush, Resplendent, Seemly

▶ **Handwriting** *see* **HAND(S)**

Handy(man) Accessible, Close, Convenient, Deft, Dext(e)rous, Digit, Factotum, Gemmy, Get-at-able, Jack(-of-all-trades), Jemmy, Near, Nigh, Palmate, Palmist, Ready, Skilful, Spartan, Useful

Hang, Hanger, Hanging(s) Append, Arras, Aweigh, Chick, Chik, Curtain, Dangle, Darn, Depend, Dewitt, Dorser, Dossal, Dossel, Dosser, Drape, Droop, Execute, Exhibit, Frontal, Gobelin, Hinge, Hoove, Hove(r), Icicle, Kakemono, Kilt,

Lobed, Loll, Lop, Lynch, Mooch, Noose, Nub, Oudenarde, Pend(ant), Sag, Scenery, Scrag, Set, Sit, Sling, String up, Suspend, Suspercollate, Swag, Swing, Tapestry, Tapet, Tapis, The rope, Toran(a)

Hanger-on Bur, Lackey, Leech, Limpet, Liripoop, Parasite, Satellite, Sycophant, Tassel, Toady

Hangman, Hangmen Bull, Calcraft, Dennis, Derrick, Executor, Gregory, Ketch, Lockman, Marwood, Nubbing-cove, Pierrepoint, Topsman

Hangover Canopy, Cornice, Crapulence, Drape, DT's, Executer, Head, Hot coppers, Katzenjammer, Mistletoe, Relic, Tester, Valance

Hanker(ing) Desire, Envy, Hunger, Itch, Long, Yearn, Yen

Haphazard Anyhow, Casual, Chance, Higgledy-piggledy, Promiscuous, →RANDOM, Rough and tumble, Scattershot, Slapdash, Willy-nilly

Happen(ing), Happen to Afoot, Are, Be, Befall, Befortune, Betide, Come, Crop up, Event(uate), Fall-out, →OCCUR, Pan, Pass, Prove, Thing, Tide, Transpire, Worth

Happiness, Happy Apposite, Ave, Beatific, Beatitude, Blessed, Bliss, Bonny, Carefree, Cheery, Chirpy, Chuffed, Cloud nine, Cock-a-hoop, Dwarf, Ecstatic, Elated, Eud(a)emony, Felicity, Felix, Fortunate, Glad(some), Gleeful, Golden, Goshen, Gruntled, Halcyon, Half-cut, Hedonism, High-feather, Inebriated, Jovial, Joy, Jubilant, Kvell, Larry, Light-hearted, Mellow, Merry, Opportune, Radiant, Rapture, Sandboy, Seal, Seel, Sele, Serene, Slap, Sunny, Tipsy, Trigger, Warrior

Happy medium Juste milieu

Harangue Declaim, Diatribe, Laisse, Lecture, Oration, Perorate, Philippic, Sermon, Speech, Spruik, Tirade

Harass(ed) Afflict, Annoy, Badger, Bait, Beleaguer, Beset, Bother, Chivvy, Distract, Dun, Gall, Hassle, Heckle, Hector, Henpeck, Hound, Importune, Irritate, Molest, Nettle, Overdo, Persecute, Pester, Pingle, Plague, Press, Sekuhara, Stalk, Tailgate, Vex

Harbour(ed) Anchorage, Basin, Brest, Cherish, Deep water, Dock, Entertain, Heard, Herd, Hide, Incubate, Kaipara, Macquarie, Marina, Mulberry, Nurse, Pearl, PLA, Port, Quay, Reset, Seaport, →SHELTER, Waitemata, Waterfront

Hard(en), Hardened, Hardness Abstruse, Adamant(ine), Austere, Billy-o, Bony, Brittle, Bronze, Cake, Calcify, Callous, Cast-iron, Crusty, Difficult, Dour, Ebonite, Emery, Endure, Enure, Exacting, Fiery, Firm, Flint(y), Geal, Granite, Gruelling, H, Hawkish, HH, Horny, Inure, Inveterate, Iron(y), Knotty, Metallic, Mohs, Murder, Nails, Obdurate, Osseous, Ossify, Permafrost, Petrify, Raw, Rugged, Ruthless, Scirrhus, Set, Severe, Solid, Sore, Steel(y), Steep, Stern, Sticky, Stiff, Stoic, Stony, Strongly, Teak, Temper, Temporary, Tough, Uneasy, Unyielding, Wooden

Hardboard Masonite®

Hardship Affliction, Austerity, Grief, Mill, Mishap, Ordeal, Penance, Privation, Rigour, Trial, Trouble

Hardy Brave, Gritty, Manful, Oliver, Ollie, Rugged, Sturdy, Thomas

Hare Arctic, Belgian, Doe, Down, Electric, Jugged, Jumping, Leporine, Malkin, Mouse, Piping, Scut, Snowshoe

Harebell Blawort

Harm(ed), Harmful Aggrieve, Bane, Blight, Damage, Deleterious, Dere, Detriment, Discredit, Evil, Hurt, Inimical, Injury, Insidious, Maim, Maleficent, Malignant, Maltreat, Mischief, Noisome, Noxious, Pernicious, Sinister, Spoil, Wroken, Wrong

Harmless Benign, Canny, Drudge, Informidable, Innocent, Innocuous, Innoxious, Inoffensive

Harmonious, Harmonise, Harmonist, Harmony Accord, Agree(ment), Alan, Allan, Allen, Alternation, Assort, Atone, Attune, Balanced, Barbershop, Blend, Chord, Community, Concent, Concentus, Concert, Concinnity, Concord, Congruous, Consonant, Consort, Correspondence, Counterpoint, Descant, Diapason, Diatessaron, Doo-wop, Euphony, Eur(h)ythmy, Faburden, Feng-shui, Jibe, Keeping, Melody, Musical, Overblow, Overtone, Rapport, Salve, Solidarity, Suit, Symmetry, Sympathy, Sync, Thorough-bass, Tone, Tune, Unanimity, Unison

Harness(maker) Breeching, Bricole, Bridle, Cinch, D-ring, Equipage, Frenum,

Gear, Gere, Girth, Hitch, Inspan, Lorimer, Loriner, Pad-tree, Partnership, Tack(le), Throat-stop, Tie, Trace, Trappings, Yoke

Harp(sichord) Aeolian, Cembalo, Clairschach, Clarsach, Clavier, Drone, Dwell, Irish, Jew's, Kora, Lyre, Nebel, Trigon, Triple, Virginal, Welsh, Zither

Harridan Hag, Harpy, Shrew, Termagant, Xantippe, Zantippe, Zentippe

Harris Boatman, Cloth, Island, Isle, Rolf

Harry Aggravate, Badger, Bother, Champion, Chase, Chivvy, Coppernose, Dog, Dragoon, Flash, Fret, Hal, Harass, Hassle, Hector, Herry, Houdini, Hound, Lauder, Lime, Maraud, Molest, Nag, Pester, Plague, Rag, Ravage, Reave, Reive, Rieve, Rile, Tate, Tchick, Torment

▷ **Harry** *may indicate* an anagram

Harsh(ness) Acerbic, Asperity, Austere, Barbaric, Brassy, Coarse, Cruel, Desolate, Discordant, Draconian, Glary, Grating, Gravelly, Grim, Gruff, Guttural, Hard, Hoarse, Inclement, Oppressive, Raucid, Raucle, Raucous, Raw, Rigour, Risp, Rude, Ruthless, Scabrid, Scrannel, Screechy, → **SEVERE**, Sharp, Spartan, Stark, Stern, Stoor, Stour, Stowre, Strict, Strident

Hart Deer, Spade, Spay, Spay(a)d, Venison

Harvest(er), Harvest home Combine, Crop, Cull, Fruit, → **GATHER**, Hairst, Hawkey, Hay(sel), Hockey, Horkey, In(ning), Ingather, Kirn, Lease, Nutting, Pick, Produce, Rabi, Random, Reap, Seed-time, Shock, Spatlese, Spider, Tattie-howking, Thresh, Vendage, Vendange

Hash(ish) Benj, Bungle, Charas, Discuss, Garble, Garboil, Hachis, Lobscouse, Mince, Pi(e), Ragout

▷ **Hashed** *may indicate* an anagram

Haste(n), Hastening, Hastily, Hasty Amain, Cursory, Despatch, Elan, Express, Festinately, Fly, Hare, Headlong, Hie, Hotfoot, → **HURRY**, Impetuous, Precipitant, Race, Ramstam, Rash, Run, Rush, Scuttle, Speed, Spur, Stringendo, Sudden, Tear, Tilt, Whistle-stop

Hat Broad-brim, Bronx, → **CAP**, Cocked, Crush, Hard, → **HEADDRESS**, Head-rig, Lid, Lum, Nab, Red, Silk, Straw, Tit(fer)

Hatch(ment), Hatching Achievement, Altricial, Booby, Breed, Brew, Brood, Cleck, Clutch, Companion, Concoct, Cover, Devise, Eclosion, Emerge, Escape, Incubate, Serving, Set, Trap-door

▷ **Hatching** *may indicate* an anagram

Hate(d), Hateful, Hatred Abhor, Abominable, Abominate, Animus, Antipathetic, Aversion, Bugbear, Detest, Enmity, Haterent, Loathe, Misogyny, Odium, Pet, Phobia, Racism, Resent, Sacred, Spite, Toad, Ug(h), Vitriol

Hatless Bareheaded, Unbeavered

Hat-trick Threepeat

Haughty, Haughtiness Aloof, Aristocratic, Arrogant, Disdainful, Dorty, Fastuous, High, Hogen-mogen, Hoity-toity, Hye, Imperious, Lofty, Morgue, Paughty, → **PROUD**, Scornful, Sniffy, Stiff-necked, Toffee-nosed, Upstage

Haul(age), Haulier Bag, Bouse, Bowse, Brail, Carry, Cart, Catch, Drag, Heave, Hove, Kedge, Long, Loot, Plunder, Pull, Rug, Sally, Scoop, Snake, Snig, Touse, Touze, Tow(se), Towze, Transporter, Winch, Yank

Haunt(s) Catchy, Den, Dive, Frequent, Ghost, Hang-out, Honky-tonk, Houf(f), Howff(f), Obsess, Purlieu, Resort, Spot

Havana Cigar

Have, Having Bear, Ha(e), Han, Hoax, Hold, Hoodwink, Know, Of, → **OWN**, Possess, Sell, With

Haven Asylum, Harbour, Hithe, Hythe, Oasis, Port, Refuge, Refugium, Retreat, Safe, Sekos, Shelter, Tax

Havoc Desolation, Devastation, Hell, Ravage, Waste

▷ **Havoc** *may indicate* an anagram

Hawk(er), Hawkish Accipitrine, Auceps, Austringer, Badger, Bastard, Buzzard, Caracara, Cast, Cheapjack, Cooper's, Cry, Eagle, Elanet, Eyas, Falcon, Gerfalcon, Goshawk, Haggard, Hardliner, Harrier, Hobby, Keelie, Kestrel, Kight, Kite,

Lammergeier, Lanner(et), Marsh, Merlin, Monger, Musket, Night, Nyas, Osprey, Ossifrage, Passage(r), Pearly, Peddle, Pedlar, Peregrine, Privet, Ringtail, Sell, Slab, Soar(e), Sorage, Sore(-eagle), Sparrow, Spiv, Staniel, Stone, Tallyman, Tarsal, Tarsel(l), Tassel, Tercel(et), Tiercel, Tote, Tout, Trant(er), Warlike

Hawthorn Albespine, Albespyne, May(flower), Quickset, Quickthorn

Hay(cock), Hey, Haybox Antic, Bale, Cock, Contra-dance, Fodder, Goaf, Hi, Kemple, Math, Mow, Norwegian nest, Norwegian oven, Pleach, Salt, Stack, Straw, Truss, Windrow

Hazard(ous) Bet, Breakneck, Bunker, Chance, Danger, Dare, Die, Dye, Game, Gremlin, Guess, Hero, Ice, Imperil, In-off, Jeopardy, Losing, Main, Minefield, Mist, Moral, Nice, Niffer, Occupational, Perdu(e), Peril, Pitfall, Play, Pothole, Queasy, →**RISK**, Risque, Stake, Trap, Venture, Vigia, Wage, Winning

Haze, Hazy Blear, Cloud, Filmy, Fog, →**MIST**, Mock, Muzzy, Nebulous, Smog, Tease

▷**Haze** *may indicate* an anagram

▷**Head** *may indicate* the first letter of a word

Head(s), Heading, Headman, Head shaped, Heady Apex, Beachy, Bean, Behead, Bill, Block, Bonce, Boss, Bound, Brain, Brow, But(t), Cabbage, Cape, Capo, Captain, Caudillo, Cauliflower, Chief, Chump, Coarb, Coconut, Coma, Comarb, Commander, Conk, Cop, Coppin, Costard, Crest, Crisis, Crown, Crumpet, Crust, Dateline, Dean, Director, Dome, Each, Ear, Figure, Flamborough, Foam, Froth, Hoe, Huff-cap, Inion, Jowl, Keyword, Knob, Knowledge-box, Lead(er), Lemma, Lid, Lizard, Loaf, Loo, Lore, Manager, Mayor, Maz(z)ard, Morne, Mull, Nab, Nana, Napper, Ness, Nob, Noddle, Noggin, Noll, Noup, Nowl, Nut, Obverse, Occiput, Onion, Panorama, Pate, Pater(familias), Patriarch, Point, Poll, Pow, Prefect, President, Principal, Promontory, Provost, Ras, Ream, Rector, Scalp, Sconce, Short, Sinciput, Skull, Source, Squeers, Stad(t)holder, Strapline, Subject, Superior, Talking, Tete, Throne, Tight, Tintagel, Tip, Title, Toilet, Top, Topic

Headbanger Grebo, Nutcase

Head cover, Headdress Aigrette, Alice band, Ampyx, Balaclava, Bandeau, Bas(i)net, Bonnet, Burnous(e), Busby, Calotte, Caul, Chaplet, Circlet, Comb, Commode, Cor(o)net, Cowl, Coxcomb, Crownet, Curch, Diadem, Doek, Dopatta, Dupatta, Fascinator, Feather bonnet, Fontange, Hat(tock), Helm(et), Joncanoe, Juliet cap, Kaffiyeh, Kell, Kerchief, Kuffiyeh, Kufiah, Kufiya(h), Madras, Mantilla, Mitre, Mobcap, Modius, Mortarboard, Nubia, Periwig, Pill-box, Plug-hat, Porrenger, Porringer, Quoif, Romal, Rumal, Sakkos, Skullcap, Sphendone, Taj, Tarbush, Tiara, Tire-vallant, Topi, Tower, Tulban, Turban, War bonnet, Wig, Wimple, Wreath

Headland Bill, Cape, Foreland, Head-rig, Hoe, Hogh, Land's End, Morro, Naze, Ness, Noup, Point, Ras, Ross, Scaw, Skaw

Headline Banner, Caption, Frown, Scare-head, Screamer, Splash, Strapline, Streamer, Title

Headlong Breakneck, Helter-skelter, Pell-mell, Plummet, Precipitate, Ramstam, Reckless, Steep, Sudden, Tantivy, Tearaway

▶**Headman** *see* **HEAD(S)**

Headphone(s) Cans, Earpiece, Walkman®

Headquarters Base, Command, Command post, Depot, Guardhouse, Pentagon, Praetorium, Station, Torshavn, Valley Forge

▷**Heads** *may indicate* a lavatory

Headsman Executioner

Headstrong Obstinate, Rash, Stubborn, Unruly, Wayward

Headway Advancement, Headroom, Progress

Heal(ing) Absent, Aesculapian, Ayurveda, Balsam, Chiropractic, Cicatrise, Cleanse, Curative, Cure, Distant, Esculapian, G(u)arish, Hele, Knit, Mend, Naturopathy, Olosis, Osteopathy, Recuperation, Restore, Sain, Salve, Sanative, Sanitary, Styptic, Therapeutic, Time

Healer Althea, Asa, Doctor, Homeopath, Naturopath, Osteopath, Sangoma, Shaman, Time

Health(y) Aglow, Bracing, Cheerio, Chin-chin, Constitution, Cosy, Doer,

Environmental, Fat-free, Fit(ness), Flourishing, Gesundheit, Hail, Hale, Hartie-hale, Heart, Holism, Kia-ora, L'chaim, Lustique, Lusty, Medicaid, Medicare, Piert, Pink, Prosit, Public, Robust, Ruddy, Salubrious, Sane, Slainte, Sound, Toast, Tope, Valentine, Valetudinarian, Vigour, Welfare, Well, WHO, Wholesome

Heap(ed), Heaps Acervate, Agglomerate, Amass, Bing, Bulk, Car, Clamp, Cock, Compost, Congeries, Cumulus, Drift, Hog, Jalopy, Lot, Molehill, Pile, Rick(le), Ruck, Scads, Scrap, Shell, Slag, Stash, Toorie

Hear(ing), Hearing problem Acoustic, Attend, Audience, Audile, Avizandum, Captain's mast, Catch, Clairaudience, Dirdum, Ear, Glue ear, Harken, Learn, List(en), Oyer, Oyez, Panel, Pick up, Session, Subpoena, Tin ear, Tinnitus

▷ **Hear(say)** *may indicate* a word sounding like one given

Hearsay Account, Gossip, Report, Rumour, Second-hand, Surmise

Heart(en), Heartily, Hearty, Heart-shaped AB, Agood, Auricle, Backslapping, Beater, Bleeding, Bluff, Bosom, Bradycardia, Buoy, Cant, Cardiac, Centre, Cheer, Cockles, Columella, Cordate, Cordial, Core, Courage, Crossed, Daddock, Embolden, Encourage, Essence, Fatty, Floating, Gist, H, Hale, Herz, Hub, Inmost, Jarta, Kernel, Lepid, Lonely, Lusty, Memoriter, Mesial, Mid(st), Middle, Nub, Nucleus, Obcordate, Pericardium, Pith, Purple, Reassure, Robust, Root, Sacred, Sailor, Seafarer, Seaman, Sinoatrial, Staunch, Tachycardia, Tar, Ticker, Yarta, Yarto

Hearth Cupel, Finery, Fireside, Home, Ingle

Heartless Callous, Cored, Cruel, Inhumane, Three-suited

Heart-throb Valentino

Heat(ed), Heater, Heating Anneal, Ardour, Arousal, Atomic, Background, Bainite, Barrage, Blood, Brazier, Calcine, Calescence, Caloric, Calorifier, Central, Chafe, Convector, Dead, Decay, Dielectric, Dudgeon, Element, Eliminator, Estrus, Etna, Excite, Fan, Ferment, Fever, Fire, Fluster, Fug, Furnace, Gat, Gun, Het, Hyperthermia, Hypocaust, Immersion, Incalescence, Induction, J, Kettle, Kindle, Latent, Lust, Mowburn, Normalise, Oestrus, Panel, Passion, Prelim, Prickly, Q, Quartz, Radiant, Radiator, Red, Render, Rut, Salt, Scald, Sizzle, Smelt, Solar, Space, Specific, Spice, Stew, Storage, Stove, Swelter, Temperature, Thermotics, Tind, Tine, Torrefy, Total, Underfloor, Warming-pan, Warmth, White, Zip®

Heathen(s) Ethnic, Gentile, Godless, Idolator, Infidel, Litholatrous, Pagan, Pa(i)nim, Paynim, Philistine, Primitive, Profane

▷ **Heating** *may indicate* an anagram

▷ **Heave** *may indicate* 'discard'

Heave(d), Heaving Cast, Emesis, Fling, Heeze, Hoise, Hoist, Hump, Hurl, Popple, Retch, Shy, Sigh, Vomit

Heaven(s), Heavenly Air, Aloft, Ama, Ambrosial, Arcady, Asgard, Bliss, Celestial, Celia, Divine, Ecstasy, Elysian, Elysium, Empyrean, Ethereal, Fiddler's Green, Firmament, Hereafter, Himmel, Hog, Holy, Hookey Walker, Lift, Mackerel, New Jerusalem, Olympus, Paradise, Pole, Seventh, Shangri-la, Sion, Sky, Sublime, Supernal, Svarga, Swarga, Swerga, Tir na n'Og, Uranian, Utopia, Welkin, Zion

Heavy(weight), Heavily, Heaviness Ali, Bodyguard, Bouncer, Dutch, Elephantine, Embonpoint, Endomorph, Gorilla, Grave, Hefty, Last, Leaden, Onerous, Osmium, Pesante, Ponderous, Roughneck, Sad, Scelerate, Stodgy, Stout, Torrential, Upsee, Ups(e)y, Weighty, Wicked

Heckle Badger, Gibe, Harass, Jeer, Needle, Spruik

Hedge, Hedging Box, Bullfinch, Enclosure, Equivocate, Evade, Haw, Hay, Lay off, Meuse, Mews, Muse, Pleach, Prevaricate, Privet, Pussyfoot, Quickset, Raddle, Sepiment, Shield, Stall, Stonewall, Temporise, Thicket

Hedgehog Gymnure, Hérisson, Tenrec, Tiggywinkle, Urchin

Hedge-hop Fly low

Heed(ed), Heedful Attend, Cavendo tutus, Gaum, Gorm, Listen, →MIND, Notice, Obey, Observe, Rear, Reck, Regard(ant), Respect, Rought, Tent, Tinker's cuss

Heedless Blithe, Careless, Inattentive, Incautious, Rash, Scapegrace, Scatterbrain

Heel Cad, Calcaneum, Cant, Careen, Cuban, Dogbolt, Foot, French, Kitten, List, Louse, Parliament, Rat, Rogue, Seel, Spike, Stacked, Stiletto, Tilt, Wedge, Wedgie

Height(en), Heights Abraham, Altitude, Cairngorm, Ceiling, Dimension, Elevation, Embroider, Eminence, Enhance, Golan, H, Hill, Hypsometry, Level, Might, Mount, Peak, Procerity, Roof, Stature, Stud, Sum, →**SUMMIT**, Tallness, Tor

Heir Alienee, Claimant, Coparcener, Dauphin, Devisee, Eigne, Institute, Intitule, Legatee, Parcener, Scion, Sprig, Successor, Tanist

▷ **Held by** *may indicate a hidden word*

Hell(ish) Abaddon, Ades, Agony, Amenthes, Annw(yf)n, Avernus, Below, Blazes, Bottomless pit, Chthonic, Dis, Erebus, Furnace, Gehenna, Hades, Heck, Inferno, Malebolge, Naraka, Netherworld, Orcus, Pandemonium, Perditious, Pit, Sheol, Stygian, Tartar(ean), Tartarus, Tophet, Torment

Hellenic Dorian

Hello, Hallo, Hullo Aloha, Chin-chin, Ciao, Dumela, Hi, Ho(a), Hoh, Howdy, Howzit, Wotcha, Wotcher, Yoo-hoo

Helmet Armet, Balaclava, Basinet, Bearskin, Beaver, Brain bucket, Burganet, Burgonet, Cask, Casque, Comb, Crash, Galea, Gas, Heaume, Knapscal, Knapscull, Knapskull, Montero, Mor(r)ion, Nasal, Pickelhaube, Pith, Plumed, Pot, Salade, Sal(l)et, Shako, Skid-lid, Tin hat, Topee, Topi

Help(er), Helping, Helpful Abet, Accomplice, Adjuvant, Advantage, Aid(ance), Aidant, Aide, Alexis, Alleviate, Ally, →**ASSIST**, Avail, Back, Befriend, Benefit, Bestead, Boon, Brownie, Char(woman), Coadjutor, Collaborate, Complice, Daily, Dollop, Dose, Ezra, Forward, Further(some), Go, Hand, Handyman, Hint, Hyphen, Instrumental, Intercede, Kind, Leg-up, Maid, Mayday, Obliging, Ophelia, Order, Patronage, Pitch in, Quantity, Ration, Recourse, Relieve, Samaritan, Servant, Serve, Slice, SOS, Stead, Sted, Subserve, Subvention, Succour, Taste, Therapeutic, Use

Helpless(ness) Anomie, Downa-do, Feeble, High and dry, Impotent, Incapable, Paralytic, Prostrate

Hen(s) Ancona, Andalusian, Australorp, Biddy, Buff Orpington, Chock, Clocker, Cochin, Deep litter, Dorking, Eirack, Fowl, Houdan, Langshan, Layer, Leghorn, Mother, Orpington, Partlet, Pertelote, Plymouth Rock, Poulard, Poultry, Pullet, Ree(ve), Rhode Island red, Sitter, Spanish fowl, Speckled, Sultan, Tappit, Welsummer, Wyandotte

Hence Apage, Avaunt, Ergo, Go, Hinc, Scram, So, Therefore, Thus

Hen-party Kitchen tea

Herald(ic), Heraldry Crier, Hermes, Messenger

Herb(aceous), Herbs Garnish, Maror, Simple, Suffruticose, Weed

Herbalist Simplist

Herbarium Hortus siccus

Herbicide Agent Orange, Atrazine, Defoliant, Diquat, Glufosinate, Picloram, Simazine

Herd(er), Herding, Herdsman Band, Buffalo, Byreman, Corral, Cowpuncher, Drive, Drover, Flock, Gang, Meinie, Mein(e)y, Menyie, Mob, Pod, Rabble, Raggle-taggle, Round-up, Shepherd, Tail, Vaquero, Wrangling

Here Adsum, Hi, Hic, Hither, Kilroy, Local, Now, Oy, Present

Hereafter Eternity, Other world

Hereditary, Heredity Ancestry, Blood, Breeding, Codon, Eugenics, Genetics, Id(ant), Idioplasm, Inborn, Mendelism, Panagenesis

▷ **Herein** *may indicate a hidden word*

Heresy, Heretic(al) Agnoitae, Albi, Albigensian, Apostasy, Arian, Arius, Bogomil, Bugger, Cathar, Docete, Dulcinist, Encratite, Eudoxian, Giaour, Gnosticism, Heresearch, Heterodoxy, Lollard, Montanism, Nestorian, Non-believer, Nonconformist, Origen, Patarin(e), Pelagius, Phrygian, Racovian, Rebel, Unitarian, Zendik

Hermaphrodite Androgynous, Bi-, Gynandromorph, Monochinous, Monoecious, Prot(er)andry, Protogyny

Hermit(age), Hermit-like Anchoret, Anchorite, Ascetic, Ashram(a), Augustinian, Austin, Cell, Cloister, Crab, Eremite, Grandmontine, Hieronymite, Loner, Marabout,

Monk, Museum, Nitrian, Pagurid, Peter, Recluse, Retreat, Sannyasi, Solitary, Troglodyte

Hero(es), Heroic Asgard, Brave, Champ(ion), Couplet, Derring-do, Eidola, Epic, Eponym, Folk, God, Goody, Great, Ideal, Idol, Lion, Noble, Olitory, Priestess, Principal, Resolute, Tragic, Valiant, VC, White knight

Heroine Andromeda, Ariadne, Candida, Cleopatra, Darling, Demigoddess, Eurydice, Hedda, Imogen, Isolde, Judith, Juliet, Leda, Leonora, Lulu, Manon, Mimi, Nana, Norma, Pamela, Star, Tess, Tosca, Una

Herring Bloater, Brisling, Caller, Glasgow magistrate, Kipper, Red, Rollmop, Sild, Silt

Hesitant, Hesitate, Hesitation Balance, Boggle, Cunctation, Delay, Demur, Dicker, Dither, Doubtful, Dwell, Erm, Falter, Halting, Haver, Haw, Mammer, Mealy-mouthed, →PAUSE, Qualm, Scruple, Shillyshally, Shrink, Stagger, Stammer, Stutter, Swither, Tarrow, Teeter, Tentative, Think twice, Um, Um and ah, Ur, Vacillate, Wait, Waver

Hew(er) Ax, Chop, Cut, Gideon, Hack, Sever

▶ **Hey** *see* HAY(COCK)

Hiatus Caesura, Gap, Hernia, Interregnum, Lacuna, Lull

Hibernal, Hibernate, Hibernating Estivate, Hiemal, Latitant, Sleep, Winter

Hiccup Blip, Glitch, Hitch, Singultus, Snag, Spasm, Yex

Hidden Buried, Cabalistic, Covert, Cryptic, Delitescent, De(a)rn, Doggo, Healed, Hooded, Latent, Obscure, Occult, Pentimento, Recondite, Screened, Secret, Shuttered, Sly, Ulterior, Unseen, Veiled, Wrapped

▷ **Hidden** *may indicate a concealed word*

Hide, Hiding (place) Abscond, Babiche, Basan, Befog, Bield(y), Blind, Box-calf, Burrow, Bury, Butt, Cache, Camouflage, Cane, Ceroon, Coat, Coonskin, Cootch, Cordwain, Couch, Cour, Crop, Curtain, Cwtch, Dea(r)n, Deerskin, Derm, Doggo, Earth, Eclipse, Encave, Ensconce, Enshroud, Envelop, Epidermis, Fell, Flaught, Flay, Fur, Gloss over, Harbour, Heal, Heel, Hele, Hell, Hole-up, Hoodwink, Incave, Inter, Kip, Kipskin, Lair, Leather, Mai-mai, Mask, Mew, Mobble, Morocco, Nebris, →OBSCURE, Paper over, Parfleche, Pell, Pelt, Plank, Plant, Priest's hole, Repress, Robe, Saffian, Screen, Secrete, Shadow, Shellac(k), Shroud, Skin, Spetch, Squirrel, Stash, Strap-oil, Tappice, Thong, Thrashing, Trove, Veil, Wallop, Whang, Wrap

Hideous(ness) Deform(ed), Enormity, Gash, Ghastly, Grotesque, Horrible, Monstrous, Odious, Ugly, Ugsome

Hi-fi, High-fidelity Ambisonics®, Ghetto blaster

▷ **High** *may indicate an anagram*

High(er), Highly, Highness Alt(a), Altesse, Alteza, Altissimo, Apogee, Atop, Brent, Climax, Culminant, Doped, Drugged, E-la, Elation, Elevated, Eminent, Euphoria, Exalted, Excelsior, Exhilarated, Five, Frequency, Gamy, Haut(e), Intoxicated, Jinks, Lofty, Mind-blowing, Orthian, Prime, Rancid, Ripe, School, Senior, Sent, Shrill, So, Steep, Stenchy, Stoned, Stratospheric, String-out, Strong, Superior, Swollen, Tall, Tension, Tipsy, Top-lofty, Topmost, Treble, Turned on, Ultrasonic, Up(per), Very, Wired, Zonked

Highbrow Brain, Egghead, Intelligentsia, Long-hair, Third programme

Highest Best, Climax, Culminant, Ne plus ultra, Supreme

Highland(er), Highlands Black Forest, Blue-bonnet, Blue-cap, Cameron, Cat(h)eran, Down, Dun(n)iewassal, Duniwassal, Gael, Gaelic, Irish Scot, Kiltie, Plaid(man), Redshank, Riff, Scot, Seaforth, Shire, Teuchter

▶ **High-pitched** *see* HIGH(ER)

Highway Alaska, Alcan, Autobahn, Autopista, Autostrada, Bus, Camino Real, Flyover, Freeway, Information, Interstate, King's, Motorway, Overpass, Parkway, Pass, Thoroughfare, Tightrope, Tollway, Watling St

Highwayman, Highway robber(y) Bandit, Bandolero, Duval, Footpad, Gilderoy, Jack Sheppard, Latrocinium, MacHeath, Scamp, Skyjacker, Toby, Turpin

Hike(r) Backpack, Bushbash, Bushwalk, Raise, Rambler, Ramp, Rise, Traipse, Tramp, Trape(s), Up(raise)

Hill(ock), Hills, Hillside Ant, Antidine, Arafar, Areopagus, Aventine, Barrow,

Beacon, Ben, Bent, Berg, Beverly, Blackdown, Bluff, Brae, Brew, Broken, Bunker, Butte, Caelian, Calvary, Capitol(ine), Cheviots, Chiltern, Chin, Cleve, Coast, Cone, Coolin, Coteau, Crag-and-tail, Crest, Cuillin, Damon, Djebel, Drumlin, Dun(e), Eminence, Esquiline, Fell, Gebel, Golan Heights, Golgotha, Gradient, Grampians, Hammock, Height, Helvellyn, Highgate, Horst, How, Howe, Hummock, Incline, Inselberg, Janiculum, Jebel, Kip(p), Knap, Knoll, Knot, Kopφje), Koppie, Lammermuir, Lavender, Law, Loma, Low, Ludgate, Majubar, Malvern, Mamelon, Man, Marilyn, Mendip, Merrick, Mesa, Monadnock, Monticule, Morro, Mound, Mount Lofty Ranges, Nab, Nanatak, North Downs, Otway Ranges, Palatine, Pap, Pennines, Pike, Pingo, Pnyx, Quantocks, Quirinal, Rand, Range, Saddleback, Scaur, Silbury, Sion, Steep, Stoss, Strawberry, Tara, Tel(l), Toft, Toot, Tor, Toss, Tump, Tweedsmuir, Vatican, Viminal, Wolds, Wrekin, Zion

Hilt Basket, Coquille, Haft, Handle, Hasp, Shaft

Hind(er), Hindering, Hindrance, Hindsight Back, Bar, Block, Check, Counteract, Cramp, Crimp, Cumber, Debar, →DELAY, Deter, Encumber, Hamper, Handicap, Harass, Holdback, Imbar, Impeach, Impede, Inconvenience, Inhibit, Obstacle, Porlock, Posterior, Preclusion, Rear, Rein, Remora, Retard, Retrospect, Rump, Rumple, Set back, Shackle, Slow, Stunt, Stymie, Taigle, Thwart, Trammel

Hind(most) Back, Deer, Lag, Rear, Starn, Stern

Hindi, Hindu(ism) Arya Samaj, Babu, Bania(n), Banyan, Brahman, Brahmin, Dalit, Gentoo, Gurkha, Harijan, Jain(a), Kshatriya, Maharishi, Pundit, Rajpoot, Rajput, Rama, Sad(d)hu, Saiva, S(h)akta, Saktas, Sankhya, Shaiva, Sheik(h), Shiv Sena, Shudra, Sudra, Swami, Trimurti, Untouchable, Urdu, Vais(h)ya, Varna, Vedanta, Vedism

Hinge(d) Butt, Cardinal, Cross-garnet, Garnet, Gemel, Gimmer, Gullwing, Joint, Knee, Piano, Pivot

▷ **Hinge(s)** *may indicate* a word reversal

Hint Allude, Clew, Clue, Cue, Echo, Element, Gleam, Hunch, Imply, Inkle, Inkling, Innuendo, Insinuate, Intimate, Key, Mint, Nod, Nuance, Office, Overtone, Pointer, Preview, Ray, Reminder, Scintilla, Shadow, Soupçon, →SUGGEST, Tang, Tip, Touch, Trace, Trick, Wind, Wink, Wisp, Word, Wrinkle

▷ **Hint** *may indicate* a first letter

Hip(pie), Hippy, Hips Cafard, Cheer, Coxa(l), Drop-out, Huck(le), Hucklebone, Hunkers, Ilium, Informed, Ischium, Pubis, Sciatic

Hire(d), Hiring Affreightment, Charter, Engage, Fee, Freightage, Job, Lease, Merc(enary), Never-never, Rent, Shape-up, Ticca, Wage

▷ **His** *may indicate* greetings

Hispanic Latino

Hiss(ing) Boo, Fizzle, Goose, Hish, Sibilant, Siffle, Sizzle, Static, Swish

Historian Acton, Antiquary, Archivist, Arrian, Asellio, Bede, Biographer, Bryant, Buckle, Camden, Carlyle, Chronicler, Du Bois, Etain, Eusebius, Froude, Gibbon, Gildas, Green, Griot, Herodotus, Knickerbocker, Livy, Macaulay, Oman, Pliny, Plutarch, Ponsonby, Procopius, Read, Renan, Roper, Sallust, Starkey, Strabo, Strachey, Suetonius, Tacitus, Taylor, Thiers, Thucydides, Toynbee, Trevelyan, Wells, Xenophon

History, Historic(al) Account, Age, Anamnesis, Annal, Bunk, Case, Chronicle, Clio, Diachronic, Epoch(a), Epoch-making, Ere-now, Ever, Heritage, Legend, Life, Mesolithic, Natural, Ontogeny, Past, Record, Story

Hit Bang, Bash, Baste, Bat, Bean, Belt, Bepat, Blip, Blockbuster, Bloop, Blow, Bludgeon, Boast, Bolo, Bonk, Bunt, Catch, Chip, Clip, Clobber, Clock, Clout, Club, Collide, Cuff, Dot, Flail, Flick, Flip, Foul, Fourpenny-one, Fungo, Fustigate, Get, Hay, Head-butt, Home(-thrust), Ice-man, Impact, Knock, Lam, Lob, Magpie, Mug, Pandy, Paste, Pepper, Pistol-whip, Polt, Prang, Punto dritto, Ram, Roundhouse, Sacrifice, Score, Sensation, Six, Skier, Sky, Slam, Slap, Slosh, Smash(eroo), Smit(e), Sock, Spank, Spike, Stoush, Straik, Stricken, Strike, Strook, Struck, →SUCCESS, Swat, Switch, Thwack, Time-thrust, Tip, Tonk, Touché, Twat, Undercut, Venewe, Venue, Volley, Wallop, Whack, Wham, Wing, Ythundered, Zap, Zonk

Hitch(ed) Catch, Cat's paw, Contretemps, Edge, Espouse, Harness, Hike, Hirsle,

Hoi(c)k, Hotch, Jerk, Kink, Lorry-hop, Rub, Setback, Sheepshank, Sheet bend, Shrug, Snag, Technical, Thumb

Hitman Gun

HIV Viral load

Hoard(ing) Accumulate, Amass, Bill, Cache, Coffer, Eke, Heap, Hog, Hoord, Husband, Hutch, Mucker, Plant, Pose, Save, Sciurine, Snudge, Squirrel, Stash, Stock, Stockpile, Store, Treasure

Hoarse(ness) Croupy, Frog, Grating, Gruff, Husky, Raucous, Roar(er), Roopit, Roopy, Roup, Throaty

Hoax Bam, Canard, Cod, Do, Doff, Fub, Fun, Gag, Gammon, Gowk, Gull, Have on, Hum, Huntie-gowk, Kid, Leg-pull, Piltdown, Quiz, Sell, Sham, Skit, Spoof, String, Stuff, → **TRICK**

Hob Ceramic, Cooktop, Ferret, Goblin, Lout

Hobble, Hobbling Enfetter, Game, Hamshackle, Hilch, Hitch, Lame, Limp, Pastern, Picket, Shackle, Spancel, Stagger, Tether

Hobby Avocation, Fad, Falcon, Interest, Pastance, Predator, Pursuit, Recreation, Scrimshaw

Hock Cambrel, Dip, Gambrel, Gambril, Gammon, Ham, Heel, Hough, Hypothecate, Pawn, Pledge, Rhenish, Wine

Hoe Claut, Draw, Dutch, Grub, Grubbing, Jembe, Nab, Pecker, Rake, Weed

Hog Babiroussa, Babirussa, Boar, Glutton, Guttle, Peccary, Pig, Porker, Puck, Road, Shoat, Shott, Whole

Hoist Boom, Bouse, Bunk-up, Crane, Davit, Derrick, Garnet, Gin, Heft, Hills, Jack, Lewis, Lift, Raise, Shearlegs, Shears, Sheerlegs, Sheers, Sway, Teagle, Trice, Whip-and-derry, Wince, Winch, Windas, Windlass

Hold(er), Holding, Hold back, out, up, etc Absorb, Allege, Alow, Anchor, Apply, Argue, Belay, Believe, Boston crab, Caesura, Canister, Cease, Cement, Cinch, Clamp, Clasp, Cling, Clip, Clutch, Contain, Cresset, Defer, Delay, Detain, Display, Document, Dog, Embrace, Engage, Engross, Er, Farm, Fast, Fistful, Frog, Full nelson, Garter, → **GRASP**, Grip, Half-nelson, Hammerlock, Handle, Have, Headlock, Heft, Heist, Hinder, Hitch, Ho(a), Hoh, Hoy, Hug, Impedance, Impede, Impediment, In chancery, Incumbent, Inhibit, Intern, Keep, Keepnet, Lease, Maintain, Nef, Nelson, Nurse, Oasis, Obstacle, Occupant, Own, Port, Proffer, Purchase, Rack, Reach, Reserve, Restrain, Retain, Rivet, Rob, Save, Scissors, Shelve, Shore, Sleeve, Sostenuto, Stand, Stock, Suspend, Take, Tenancy, Tenement, Tenure, Toehold, Tripod, Trivet, Wait, → **WRESTLING**, Wristlock, Zarf

Hole(s), Holed, Holey Ace, Albatross, Antrum, Beam, Birdie, Black, Bogey, Bolt, Burrow, Cat, Cave, Cavity, Cissing, Coal, Coalsack, Collapsar, Crater, Cubby, Cup, Dell, Den, Dene, Dog-leg, Dormie, Dormy, Dreamhole, Dry, Dugout, Eagle, Earth, Eye(let), Finger, Foramen, Funk, Gap, Geat, Glory, Gutta, Hag(g), Hideout, Kettle, Knot, Lill, Limber, Loop, Loup, Maar, Moulin, Nineteenth, Oillet, → **OPENING**, Orifice, Ozone, Perforate, Pierce, Pigeon, Pinprick, Pit, Pocket, Pore, Port, Pot, Potato, Priest's, Punctuate, Puncture, Rabbet, Rivet, Scupper, Scuttle, Sinus, Situation, Slot, Snag, Snow, Soakaway, Socket, Sound, Spandrel, Spider, Starting, Stead, Stew, Stop, Stove, Swallow, Tear, Thumb, Tight spot, Touch, Trema, Vent, Voided, Watering, Weep(er), Well, White, Wookey

Holiday(s), Holiday maker Away, Bank, Benjo, Break, Camper, Carnival, Childermas, Days of Awe, Ferial, Festa(l), → **FESTIVAL**, Fête, Fiesta, Fly-drive, Furlough, Gala, Half(term), High, Kwanzaa, Laik, Leasure, Leave, Leisure, Long, Minibreak, Outing, Pace, Packaged, Pink-eye, Playtime, Recess, Repose, Rest, Roman, Schoolie, Seaside, Shabuoth, Shavuot, Stay, Sunday, Trip, → **VACATION**, Villeggiatura, Wake(s), Whitsun

Hollow(ed) Aeolipile, Alveary, Antar, Antre, Armpit, Boss, Bowl, Cave(rn), Cavity, Chasm, Cirque, Comb(e), Concave, Coomb, Crater, Cup(mark), Dean, Dell, Delve, Den(e), Dent, Dimple, Dingle, Dip, Dish(ing), Empty, Groove, Grot(to), Hole, How, Howe, Igloo, Incavo, Insincere, Intaglio, Keck(sy), Kettle(hole), Kex, Lap, Mortise,

Niche, Orbita, Pan, Philtrum, Pit, Punt, Rut, Scoop, Sinus, Sleepy, Slot, Slough, Socket, Trough, Vacuous, Vesicle

Holy(man), Holiness Adytum, Alliance, Ariadne, Blessed, → DIVINE, Godly, Grail, Halidom, Hallowed, Helga, Hery, Khalif, Loch, Mountain, Olga, Orders, Pious, Sacred, Sacrosanct, Sad(d)hu, Saintly, Sanctitude, Sannyasi(n), Santon, Sekos, Sepulchre, Shrine, Starets, Staretz, SV, Tirthankara, War

Holy books, Holy writing Adigranth, Atharvaveda, Bible, Gemara, Granth, Hadith, Hagiographa, Koran, Mishnah, NT, OT, Pia, Purana, Rigveda, Sama-Veda, → SCRIPTURE, Shaster, Shastra, Smriti, Sura(h), Tanach, Writ

Holy building, Holy city, Holy place Chapel, Church, Kaaba, Mashhad, Mecca, Medina, Meshed, Najaf, Penetralia, Sanctum, Station, Synagogue, Temenos, Temple

Homage Bow, Cense, Honour, Kneel, Obeisance, Tribute

Home(land), Homeward Abode, Apartment, Base, Blighty, Bro, Broken, Burrow, Cheshire, Chez, Clinic, Community, Convalescent, Domal, Domicile, Earth, Eventide, Family, Fireside, Flat, Funeral, Gaff, Goal, Habitat, Harvest, Heame, Hearth, Heme, Hospice, House, In, Lair, Libken, Lockwood, Lodge, Maisonette, Mental, Mobile, Montacute, Motor, Nest, Nursing, Old sod, Orphanage, Pad, Penny-gaff, Pied à terre, Pile, Pit dwelling, Plas Newydd, Remand, Res(idence), Rest, Starter, Stately, Tepee, Turangawaewae, Up-along, Villa, Warren

Homespun Cracker-barrel, Plain, Raploch, Russet, Simple

Homicidal, Homicide Chance-medley, Killing, Manslaughter

Homily Lecture, Pi, Postil, Prone, Sermon

▷ **Homing** may indicate coming back

Homogram, Homograph Abac, Heteronym

Honest(y), Honestly Aboveboard, Afauld, Afawld, Amin, Candour, Clean, Genuine, Incorruptible, Injun, Jake, Jannock, Jonnock, Legitimate, Lunaria, Lunary, Mensch, Open-faced, Penny, Probity, Realtie, Rectitude, Reputable, Righteous, Round, Sincere, Soothfast, Square, Squareshooter, Straight, Straight-out, Trojan, → TRUE, Truepenny, Upright, Upstanding

Honey Comb, Flattery, Hybla(ean), Hymettus, Mel, Melliferous, Nectar, Peach, Popsy-wopsy, Sis, Sugar, Sweetheart, Sweetie (pie), Virgin, Wild

Honeydew Mildew

Honeysuckle Lonicera, Twinflower, Woodbind, Woodbine

Hong Kong .hk

Honour(able), Honorary, Honoured, Honorific, Honours A, Accolade, Ace, Adward, Birthday, Blue, Bow, CBE, Commemorate, Credit, Crown, Curtsey, Dan, Elate, Emeritus, Ennoble, → ESTEEM, Ethic, Face-card, Fame, Fête, Gloire, Glory, Grace, Greats, Homage, Insignia, Invest, J, Jack, K, King, Knave, Knight, Kudos, Laudation, Laureate, Laurels, MBE, Mensch, Mention, OBE, Optime, Pundonor, Q, Queen, Regius, Remember, Repute, Respect, Revere, Reward, Salute, Straight, Ten, Tenace, Titular, Tripos, Venerate, White, Worship, Wranglers

Hood(ed) Almuce, Amaut, Amice, Amowt, Apache, Balaclava, Bashlik, Biggin, Blindfold, Calash, Calèche, Calyptra, Capeline, Capuccio, Capuche, Chaperon(e), Coif, Cope, Cowl, Cucullate(d), Faldetta, Fume, Gangster, Jacobin, Kennel, Liripipe, Liripoop, Mantle, Mazarine, Nithsdale, Pixie, Robin, Rowdy, Snood, Trot-cosey, Trot-cozy, Visor

Hook(ed), Hooker, Hooks Addict, Adunc, Aduncous, Arrester, Barb(icel), Barbule, Becket, Butcher's, Cant(dog), Catch, Chape, Claw, Cleek, Clip, Clove, Cocotte, Corvus, Crampon, Cromb, Crome, Crook, Crotchet, Cup, Drail, Duck, Fish, Floozy, Gaff, Grap(p)le, Grapnel, Grappling, Gripple, Hamate, Hamose, Hamulus, Heel, Hitch, Inveigle, Kype, Meat, Picture, Pot, Prostitute, Snare, Snell, Sniggle, Tala(u)nt, Tenaculum, Tenter, Tie, Trip, Uncus, Wanton

Hooligan Apache, Bogan, Casual, Desperado, Droog, Goonda, Hobbledehoy, Hoon, Keelie, Larrikin, Lout, Ned, Rough(neck), Ruffian, Skollie, Skolly, Tearaway, Ted, Tityre-tu, Tough, Tsotsi, Vandal, Yahoo, Yob(bo)

Hoop(s) Bail, Band, Circle, Farthingale, Garth, Gird, Girr, Hula®, O, Pannier,
→ RING, Sleeper, Tire, Trochus, Trundle

Hoot(er) Deride, Honk, Madge, Nose, Owl, Riot, Screech-owl, Siren, Ululate

Hop(per) An(o)ura, Ball, Bin, Cuscus, Dance, Flight, Jeté, Jump, Kangaroo, Leap, Lilt,
Long, Opium, Pogo, Roo, Saltate, Scotch, Skip, Tremié, Vine

Hope(ful) Anticipate, Aspirant, Combe, Comer, Contender, Daydream, Desire,
Dream, Esperance, Evelyn, Expectancy, Forlorn, Gleam, Inshallah, Pipe-dream,
Promising, Roseate, Rosy, Sanguine, Trust, Valley, Wannabe, White, Wish

Hopeless(ness), Hopeless quest Abattu, Anomie, Anomy, Black, Buckley's
chance, Dead duck, Despair, Despondent, Forlorn, Gloom, Goner, Non-starter, Perdu,
Pessimist

Hophead Drinker, Lush, Sot

Horizon A, Apparent, Artificial, Event, Scope, Sea-line, Sensible, Skyline, Visible

Horn(s), Horny Acoustic, Advancer, Amalthea, Antenna(e), Baleen, Basset, Beeper,
Bez, Brass, Buck, Bugle, Bur(r), Cape, Ceratoid, Cor, Cornet, Cornett, Cornopean,
Cornu(a), Cornucopia, Cromorna, Cromorne, Cusp, Dilemma, English, Flugel-horn,
French, Frog, Gemshorn, Golden, Gore, Hooter, Hunting, Ivory, Keratin, Klaxon, Lur,
Morsing, Mot, Oliphant, Parp, Periostracum, Plenty, Post, Powder, Pryse, Saddle,
Shofar, Shophor, Spongin, Tenderling, Trey, Trez, Trumpet, Tusk, Vulcan's badge,
Waldhorn

Hornblende Syntagmatite

Hornet Stinger

Horrible, Horror Appalling, Aw(e)some, Beastly, Brat, Creepy, Dire, Distaste,
Dread(ful), Execrable, Gashful, Ghastly, Grand Guignol, Grisly, Grooly, Gruesome,
Grysie, Hideous, Minging, Nightmare, Odious, Panic, Rascal, Shock, Stupefaction,
Terror, Ugh

Horrid, Horrific, Horrify(ing) Agrise, Appal, Dire, Dismay, Dreadful, Frightful,
Ghastly, Gothic, Grim, Grisly, H, Loathy, Odious, Spine-chilling, Spiteful, Ugly

Hors d'oeuvres Antipasto, Canapé, Carpaccio, Ceviche, Hoummos, Houmus,
Hummus, Mez(z)e, Pâté, Smorgasbord, Starter, Zak(o)uski

Horse Airer, Bidet, Bloodstock, Carriage, Cut, Cutting, Dark, Doer, Dray, Drier,
Drug, Equine, Form, H, High, Hobby, Iron, Knight, Kt, Light, Lot, Maiden, Malt,
Non-starter, Outsider, Pack, Pantomime, Plug, Ride, Rocking, Sawbuck, Scag, Screen,
Selling-plater, Sense, Stalking, Standard-bred, Starter, Stayer, Steeplechaser, Stiff,
Stock, Teaser, Trestle, Vanner, Vaulting, White, Willing, Wooden

Horse complaint, Horse disease, Horse problem, Horse trouble
Blood spavin, Bogspavin, Bot(t)s, Broken wind, Canker, Capel(l)et, Cratches, Curb,
Dourine, Drepance, Equinia, Eweneck, Farcin, Farcy, Fives, Frush, Glanders, Gourdy,
Grape, Grass-sickness, Head staggers, Heaves, Hippiatric, Malander, Megrims, Moon
Blindness, Mooneye, N(a)gana, Parrot mouth, Poll-evil, Quartercrack, Quitter, Quittor,
Ringbone, Roaring, Sallenders, Sand crack, Scratches, Seedy-toe, Shaft, Spavie,
Spavin, Springhalt, Staggers, Strangles, Stringhalt, Surra, Sween(e)y, Thorough-pin,
Thrush, Tread, Vives, Weed, Weid, Whistling, Windgall, Wire-heel, Yellows

Horseman Ataman, Caballero, Cavalry, Centaur, Conquest, Cossack, Cowboy, Death,
Dragman, Famine, Farrier, Hobbler, Hussar, Knight, Lancer, Nessus, Ostler, Parthian,
Picador, Pricker, Quadrille, Revere, → RIDER, Slaughter, Spahi, Stradiot, Tracer,
Wrangler

Horseplay Caper, Polo, Rag, Rant, Romp

Horseshoe(-shaped) Henge, Hippocrepian, King-crab, Lophophorate, Lunette,
Manilla, Oxbow, Plate

Hose Chausses, Fishnet, Galligaskins, Gaskins, Lisle, Netherstock(ing), Nylons, Panty,
Sock, Stockings, Tights, Trunk, Tube

Hospice, Hospital Ambulance, Asylum, Barts, Base, Bedlam, Booby hatch,
Bughouse, Clinic, Cottage, Day, Dressing station, ENT, Field, Foundation,
Guest-house, Guys, H, Home, Hospice, Hôtel dieu, Imaret, Infirmary, Isolation,
Karitane, Lazaretto, Leprosarium, Leprosery, Lock, Loony bin, MASH, Mental,

Nosocomial, Nuthouse, Nuttery, Pest-house, Polyclinic, Rathouse, San, Scutari, Sick bay, Spital, Spittle, Teaching, Trauma centre, UCH

Hospitable, Hospitality Cadgy, Convivial, Corporate, Entertainment, Euxine, Kidgie, Lucullan, Open house, Philoxenia, Social, Xenial

Host(s), Hostess Alternate, Amphitryon, Army, Barmecide, Bunny girl, Chatelaine, Compere, Crowd, Definitive, Emcee, Entertainer, Geisha, Hirsel, Hotelier, Innkeeper, Inviter, Laban, Landlady, Landlord, Legend, Legion, Licensee, Lion-hunter, Lot, Mass, Mavin, MC, Number, Presenter, Publican, Quickly, Speakerine, Swarm, Taverner, Throng, Torrent, Trimalchio, Wafer

Hostile, Hostility Adverse, Aggressive, Alien, Anger, Animus, Anti, Arms, Aversion, Bellicose, Bitter, Currish, Diatribe, Feud, Forbidding, Hating, Icy, Ill, Ill-will, Inimical, Inveterate, Oppugnant, Pugnacity, Unfriendly, Virulent, Vitriolic, War

Hot(spot), Hot (tempered) Aboil, Ardent, Big, Blistering, Breem, Breme, Cajun, Calid, Candent, Dog days, Enthusiastic, Erotic(al), Facula, Fervid, Feverish, Fiery, Fuggy, Gospeller, Het, In, Incandescent, Irascible, Latest, Live, Mafted, Mirchi, Mustard, Nightclub, Pepper, Piping, Potato, Quick, Randy, Red, Roaster, Scalding, Scorcher, Sexpot, Sexy, Sizzling, Spicy, Spitfire, Steamy, Stewy, Stifling, Stolen, Sultry, Sweaty, Sweltering, Sweltry, Tabasco®, Thermidor, Torrid, Toustie, Tropical, Zealful

Hotchpotch Bricolage, Farrago, Mish-mash, Powsowdy, Welter

Hotel, Hotelkeeper Bo(a)tel, Boutique, Commercial, Flophouse, Gasthaus, Gasthof, H, Hilton, Hydro, Inn, Internet, Military, Motel, Parador, Pension, Posada, Ritz, Roadhouse, Savoy, Tavern, Telco, Waldorf, Watergate

Hothead(ed) Impetuous, Rash, Spitfire, Volcano

Hot-house Conservatory, Forcing-house, Nursery, Orangery, Vinery

Hotshot Whiz

Hotspot Bricolage, Farrago, Mish-mash, Powsowdy, Welter

Hound(s) Afghan, Badger, Basset, Beagle, Bellman, Brach, Cad, Canine, Cry, →**DOG**, Entry, Gaze, Harass, Harrier, Hen-harrier, Javel, Kennet, Lyam, Lym(e), Mute, Otter, Pack, Persecute, Pursue, Rache, Ranter, Reporter, Saluki, Talbot, True, Tufter

Hour(s) Canonical, Complin(e), Daylight, Elders', Flexitime, H, Happy, Holy, Hr, Literacy, None(s), Office, Orthros, Peak, Prime, Rush, Sext, Small, Terce, Tide, Time, Undern, Unsocial, Vespers, Visiting, Witching, Zero

Hourglass Meniscoid

House(s), Housing, Household(er) Abode, Accepting, Adobe, Aerie, Aery, Astrology, Audience, Auditorium, Billet, Bingo, Black, Brick veneer, Broiler, Clan, Coffee, Cottage (orné), Counting, Country, Crankcase, Death, Discount, Disorderly, Domestic, Domicile, Drostdy, Dynasty, Establishment, Eyrie, Finance, Firm, Forcing, Fraternity, Free, Gambling, Government, Grace and favour, Habitation, Hall, Hearth, Homestead, Ice, Infill, Inner, Issuing, Joss, Lodge, Lofted, Loose, Lot(t)o, Malting, Meiney, Ménage, Menyie, Mobility, Monastery, Nacelle, Node, Open(-plan), Outer, Picts, Picture, Pilot, Pleasure, Pole, Post, Prefab, Printing, Public, Radome, Ranch, Register, Residence, Rooming, Root, Rough, Sacrament, Saltbox, School, Sheltered, Show, Social, Software, Spec-built, Sporting, State, Station, Steeple, Storey, Succession, Tea, Tenement, Third, Treasure, Tree, Trust, Try, Upby, Vaulting, Villa(-home), Wash, Watch, Weather, Weigh, Wheel, Work, Zodiac

Housemate Co-tenant

Housing Case, Crankcase, Shabrack, Shelter, Slum, Tenement

Hovel Cru(i)ve, Den, Pigsty, Shack, Shanty

Hovercraft Air-car

However Although, As, But, Even-so, Leastwise, Sed, Still, Though, Yet

Howl(er) Banshee, Bawl, Bay, Bloop, Clanger, Hue, Mycetes, Slip up, Ululate, War whoop, Wow, Yawl, Yowl

Hub Boss, Boston, Centre, Focus, Hob, Nave, Nucleus, Pivot, Tee

Hubbub Charivari, Chirm, Coil, Din, Level-coil, Palaver, Racket, Row, Stir

Huckster Hawker, Kidd(i)er, Pedlar

Huddle Cringe, Gather, Hunch, Ruck, Shrink

Hue Chrome, Colour, Dye, Outcry, Proscription, Steven, Tincture, Tinge, Umbrage, Utis

Huff Dudgeon, Hector, Pant, Pet, Pique, Strunt, Umbrage, Vex

Huge (number) Astronomical, Brobdingnag, Colossal, Enorm(ous), Gargantuan, Giant, →**GIGANTIC**, Gillion, Ginormous, Humongous, Humungous, Immane, Immense, Leviathan, Lulu, Mega-, Milliard, Monumental, Octillion, Socking, Stupendous, Thumping, Titanian, Tremendous, Voluminous, Whacking

Hull Bottom, Framework, Husk, Inboard, Monocoque, Pod, Sheal, Sheel, Shell, Shiel, Shill

▶ **Hullo** *see* **HELLO**

Hum(ming) BO, Bombilate, Bombinate, Bum, Buzz, Chirm, Chirr, Drone, Eident, Lilt, Moan, Murmur, Nos(e)y, Odorate, Odorous, Pong, Rank, Reek, Sough, Sowf(f), Sowth, Stench, Stink, Stir, Whir(r), Zing

Human(e), Humanist, Humanity Anthropoid, Anthropology, Bang, Colet, Earthling, Earthman, Erasmus, Incarnate, Kindness, Mandom, Meatbot, Merciful, Mortal, Philanthropic, Species, Sympathy, Ubuntu

Humble Abase, Abash, Afflict, Baseborn, Chasten, Conquer, Cow, Degrade, Demean, Demiss(ly), Lower, Lowly, Mean, Mean-born, →**MEEK**, Modest, Morigerate, Obscure, Poor, Rude, Small, Truckle

Humbug Berley, Blague, Blarney, Burley, Claptrap, Con, Delude, Eyewash, Flam, Flummery, Fraud, Fudge, Gaff, Gammon, Gas, Guff, Gum, Hoax, Hoodwink, Hookey-walker, Kibosh, Liar, Maw-worm, Nonsense, Prig, Shenanigan, Tosh, Wind

Humdrum Banal, Boredom, Bourgeois, Monotonous, Mundane, Ordinary, Prosaic, Routine, Tedious

Humiliate(d), Humiliation, Humility Abase(ment), Abash, Baseness, Comedown, Degrade, Disbench, Eating crow, Fast, Indignity, Laughing stock, Lose face, Lowlihead, Mortify, Put-down, →**SHAME**, Skeleton, Take-down, Wither

Humorist Cartoonist, Comedian, Jester, Leacock, Lear, Punster, Thurber, Twain, Wodehouse

Humour, Humorous Aqueous, Bile, Blood, Caprice, Cardinal, Chaff, Choler, Coax, Cocker, Coddle, Cosher, Cuiter, Cuittle, Daut, Dawt, Droll, Dry, Facetious, Fun, Gallows, Ichor, Indulge, Irony, Jocose, Jocular, Juice, Kidney, Lavatorial, Levity, Light, Melancholy, →**MOOD**, Observe, One-liner, Pamper, Phlegm, Pun, Pythonesque, Ribaldry, Salt, Serum, Sick, Temper, Trim, Vein, Vitreous, Vitreum, Wetness, Whim, Whimsy, Wit

Hump(ed), Humping Boy, Bulge, Dorts, Dowager's, Gibbose, Gibbous, Hog, Huff, Hummock, Hunch, Pip, Ramp, Sex, Sleeping policeman, Tussock

▶ **Humpback** *see* **HUNCH(ED)**

Humus Compost, Leafmould, Moder, Mor, Mull

Hunch(ed), Hunchback Camel, Chum, Crookback, Hump, Intuition, Kyphosis, Premonition, Quasimodo, Roundback, Squat, Urchin

Hundred(s), Hundredth Burnham, C, Cantred, Cantref, Cent, Centum, Century, Chiltern, Commot, Desborough, Host, Northstead, Shire, Stoke, Tiyin, Ton, Tyiyn, Wapentake

Hundred thousand C

Hungarian, Hungary Bohunk, Csardas, Magyar, Nagy, Szekely, Tzigane, Ugric, Vogul

Hunger (strike), Hungry Appestat, Appetite, Bulimia, Bulimy, Clem, →**CRAVE**, Desire, Edacity, Empty, Esurient, Famine, Famish, Fast, Hanker, Hunter, Insatiate, Itch, Orectic, Pant, Peckish, Pine, Pyne, Rapacious, Raven, Ravin, Sharp-set, Starve, Unfed, Unfuelled, Yaup, Yearn

▷ **Hungry** *may indicate* an 'o' in another word

Hunker Squat

Hunt(er), Hunting, Huntress, Huntsman Bushman, Chasseur, Dog, Drag(net), Gun, Hound, Kennet, Letterbox, Lurcher, Nimrod, Poacher, Predator,

Pursue, Quest, Quorn, Ride, Run, San, Scavenge(r), Scout, →**SEARCH**, Seek, Stalk, Ticker, Trap, Venerer, →**WATCH**, Whipper-in, Woodman, Yager

Hunting-call Rechate, Recheat, Tally-ho, View-halloo

Hurdle(r) Barrier, Doll, Fence, Flake, Gate, Hemery, Obstacle, Raddle, Sticks, Wattle

Hurl(ing) Camogie, Cast, Dash, →**FLING**, Heave, Put(t), Sling, Throw, →**TOSS**

Hurry Belt, Bustle, Chivvy, Chop-chop, Dart, Dash, Drive, Expedite, Festinate, Fisk, Frisk, Gad, Gallop, Giddap, Giddup, Giddy-up, Hadaway, Hare, Haste, Hie, Hightail, Induce, Mosey, Post-haste, Press, Push, Race, Railroad, →**RUSH**, Scamper, Scoot, Scramble, Scur(ry), Scutter, Scuttle, Skelter, Skurry, Spank, Speed, Streak, Tear, Whirr

Hurt(ful) Abuse, Ache, Aggrieve, Ake, Bruise, Damage, De(a)re, Detriment, Disservice, Harm, Harrow, Hit, →**INJURE**, Lesion, Maim, Nocent, Nocuous, Noisome, Noxious, Noyous, Offend, Pain, Pang, Prick(le), Scaith, Sting, Trauma, Wring

Husband(ry), Husbands Add, Baron, Betty, Breadwinner, Consort, Darby, Ear, Eche, Economy, Eke, Ere, Farm, Gander(-mooner), Georgic, Goodman, Groom, H, Hoddy-doddy, Hodmandod, Hubby, Ideal, Lord and master, Man, Manage, Mate, Partner, Polyandry, Reserve, Retrench, Save, Scrape, Scrimp, Spouse, Squirrel, →**STORE**, Tillage

Husk(s), Husky Acerose, Bran, Draff, Eskimo, Hoarse, Hull, Malemute, Seed, Sheal, Shiel, Shuck

Hustle(r) Fast talk, Frogmarch, Jostle, Pro, Push, Railroad, Shoulder, Shove, Skelp

Hut(s) Banda, Booth, Bothie, Bothy, Bustee, Cabin, Chalet, Choltry, Gunyah, Hogan, Humpy, Igloo, Mia-mia, Nissen, Pondok(kie), Quonset®, Rancheria, Rancho, Rondavel, Shack, Shanty, Sheal(ing), Shebang, Shed, Shiel(ing), Skeo, Skio, Succah, Sukkah, Tilt, Tolsel, Tolsey, Tolzey, Wan(n)igan, Wigwam, Wi(c)kiup, Wil(t)ja, Wurley

Hybrid Bigener, Bois-brûlé, Cama, Catalo, Centaur, Chamois, Chichi, Citrange, Cross, Dso, Funnel, Geep, Graft, Incross, Interbred, Jomo, Jumart, Lurcher, Mameluco, Mermaid, Merman, Metif, Métis, Mongrel, Mule, Mutation, Noisette, Onocentaur, Ox(s)lip, Percolin, Plumcot, Pomato, Ringed, Single-cross, Tangelo, Tiglon, Tigon, Topaz, Ugli, Werewolf, Zedonk, Zho(mo)

▷ **Hybrid** *may indicate an anagram*

Hydrocarbon Acetylene, Aldrin, Alkane, Alkene, Alkyl, Alkyne, Amylene, Arene, Asphaltite, Benzene, Butadiene, Butane, Butene, Camphane, Camphene, Carotene, Cetane, Cubane, Cumene, Cyclohexane, Cyclopropane, Decane, Diene, Dioxin, Diphenyl, Ethane, Ethylene, Gutta, Halon, Hatchettite, Heavy oil, Heptane, Hexane, Hexene, Hexyl(ene), Indene, Isobutane, Isoprene, Ligroin, Limonene, Mesitylene, Methane, Naphtha, Naphthalene, Naphthalin(e), Nonane, Octane, Olefin(e), Paraffin, Pentane, Pentene, Pentylene, Phenanthrene, Phene, Picene, Pinene, Polyene, Propane, Pyrene, Pyridine, Pyrimidine, Retene, Squalene, Stilbene, Styrene, Terpene, Toluene, Triptane, Wax, Xylene, Xylol

Hydrogen Deut(er)on, Diplon, Ethene, H, Heavy, Protium, Tritium

Hydroid Sea-fir

Hydrolysis Saponification

Hydrometer Salinometer

Hyena Aard-wolf, Earthwolf, Nandi bear, Strand-wolf, Tiger-wolf

Hymn(s) Amazing Grace, Anthem, Benedictine, Bhajan, Canticle, Carol, Cathisma, Choral(e), Coronach, Dies Irae, Dithyramb, Doxology, Epithalamia, Gloria, Hallel, Introit(us), Ithyphallic, Lay, Magnificat, Mantra, Marseillaise, Nunc Dimittis, Ode, P(a)ean, Psalm, Psalmody, Recessional, Rigveda, Sanctus, Sequence, Stabat Mater, Sticheron, Tantum Ergo, Te Deum, Trisagion, Troparion, Veda

Hymnographer, Hymnologist David, Faber, Heber, Moody, Neale, Parry, Sankey, Watts

Hype(d) Aflutter, Ballyhoo

Hyperbola Rectangular

Hypnosis, Hypnotise, Hypnotic, Hypnotism, Hypnotist Braidism,

Chloral, Codeine, Entrance, Fluence, Magnetic, Magnetise, Mesmerism, Psychognosis, Svengali

Hypocrisy, Hypocrite, Hypocritical Archimago, Bigot, Byends, Cant, Carper, Chadband, Creeping Jesus, Deceit, Dissembler, Dissimulating, False-faced, Heep, Holy Willie, Humbug, Mucker, Nitouche, Pecksniff, Pharisaic, Pharisee, Piety, Plaster saint, Prig, Sepulchre, Tartuf(f)e, Two-faced, Whited sepulchre

Hypothesis, Hypothetical Avogadro, Biophor, Conditional, Gaia, Gluon, Graviton, Micella, Suppositious, Theory, Virtual, Whorf

Hysteria, Hysteric(al) Conniption, Crazy, Delirium, Frenzy, Meemie, Mother

Ii

I A, Ch, Cham, Che, Dotted, Ego, Ich, Indeed, India, Iodine, Italy, J, Je, Me, Myself, Self, Yours truly

Iambus Scazon

Iberian Celtiberian

Ice(d), Ice-cream, Icing, Icy A la mode, Alcorza, Anchor, Arctic, Ballicatter, Banana split, Berg, Black, Brainstorm, Brash, Camphor, Cassata, Coconut, Cone, Cool, Cornet, Coupe, Cream, Crystal, Diamonds, Drift, Dry, Field, Floe, Frappé, Frazil, Freeze, Frigid, Frore, Frosting, Frosty, Gelato, Gelid, Gems, Glacé, Glacial, Glacier, Glare, Glaze, Glib, Granita, Graupel, Ground, Hailstone, Hok(e)y-pok(e)y, Intention, Kitty-benders, Knickerbocker glory, Kulfi, Lolly, Marzipan, Neapolitan, Neve, Oaky, Pack, Pancake, Pingo, Polar, Popsicle®, Rime, Rink, Rivière, Ross, Royal, Sconce, Serac, Shelf, Sherbet, Slay, Slider, Slob, Sludge, Slush, Sorbet, Spumone, Spumoni, Stream, Sugar, Sundae, Theme, Tickly-benders, Topping, Tortoni, Tutti-frutti, Verglas, Wafer, Water, Wintry

Iceberg Calf, Floe, Growler

▶**Ice-cream** see ICE(D)

ID PIN

Idea(s) Archetype, Brainstorm, Brainwave, Clou, Clue, Conceit, Concept, Fancy, Figment, Germ, Hunch, Idée fixe, Idolum, Image, Inkling, Inspiration, Intention, Interpretation, Light, Meme, →NOTION, Obsession, Plan, Plank, Rationale, Recept, Theme, Theory, Thought, Zeitgeist

Ideal(ise) A1, Abstract, At best, Dream, Eden, Erewhon, Goal, Halo, Hero, Model, Monist, Mr Right, Nirvana, Notional, Paragon, Pattern, →PERFECT, Prince Charming, Role-model, Rose, Siddhi, Sidha, Sublimate, Utopian, Vision

Identical Alike, Clone, Congruent, Indistinguishable, One, Same, Selfsame, Verbatim

Identification, Identify Codeword, Cookie, Credentials, Designate, Diagnosis, Differentiate, Discern, Document, Dog-tag, Earmark, E-fit, Empathy, Espy, Finger(print), ID, Identikit®, Label, Mark, Monomark, Name, Name-tape, Password, Photofit®, Pin, Pinpoint, Place, Point up, Recognise, Registration, Reg(g)o, Specify, Spot, Swan-upping, Verify

Identity Alias, Appearance, Corporate, Credentials, Equalness, Likeness, Mistaken, Numerical, Oneness, Personal, Qualitative, Seity, Self, Selfhood

Idiom Argot, Cant, Dialect, Expression, Jargon, Language, Pahlavi, Parlance, Pehlevi, Persism, Scotticism, Slavism, Syri(a)cism, Syrism

Idiot(ic), Idiocy Airhead, Congenital, Dingbat, Dipstick, Dolt, Dumbo, Eejit, Fatuity, Fool, Goose, Half-wit, Headbanger, Imbecile, Inane, Maniac, Moron, Nana, Natural, Nerk, Nidget, Noncom, Numpty, Oaf, Ouph(e), Stupe, →STUPID, Tony, Twit, Village, Whacko, Zany

Idle(ness), Idler Beachcomber, Bum, Couch potato, Deadbeat, Dilly-dally, Drone, Eric, Farnarkel, Fester, Flaneur, Frivolous, Gold brick, Groundless, Indolent, Inert, Lackadaisical, Layabout, Laze, Lazy, Lead-swinger, Lie, Lig, Loaf, Loll, Lollop, Lounge, Mooch, Potato, Ride, Scapegrace, Shiftless, Skive, Slob, Sloth, Sluggard, Spiv, Stock-still, Stooge, Sweirt, Tarry, Tick over, Trifle, Truant, Twiddle, Unoccupied, Vacuity, Vain, Vegetate, Waste, Whip the cat, Workshy

Idol(ise) Adore, Adulate, Baal(im), Baphomet, Bel, Crush, Eikon, E(i)luned, Fetich(e), Fetish, God, Hero, Icon, Image, Joss, Juggernaut, Lion, Mammet, Manito, Manitou, Matinee, Maumet, Mawmet, Molech, Moloch, Mommet, Mumbo-jumbo, Pagoda, Swami, Teraph(im), Termagant, Vision, Wood, Worship

Idyll(ic) Arcady, Eclogue, Eden, Paradise, Pastoral, Peneian

Igneous Pyrogenic

Ignite, Ignition Coil, Flare, Kindle, Lightning, Spark, Spontaneous, Starter

Ignominious, Ignominy Base, Dishonour, Fiasco, Humiliation, Infamous, Scandal, →SHAME

Ignorance, Ignorant 404, Agnoiology, Analphabet, Anan, Artless, Benighted, Blind, Clueless, Darkness, Green, Hick, Illiterate, Inerudite, Ingram, Ingrum, Inscient, Irony, Know-nothing, Lewd, Lumpen, Misken, Nescience, Night, Oblivious, Oik, Philistine, Purblind, Red-neck, Unaware, Uneducated, Unlessoned, Unlettered, Unread, Unschooled, Untold, Unversed, Unwist

Ignore(d) Alienate, Ba(u)lk, Blink, Bypass, Connive, Cut, Discount, Disregard, Forget, Leave, Neglect, Omit, Overlook, Overslaugh, Pass, Pass up, Scrub round, Slight, Snub, Tune out, Unheeded

Iguana Chuckwalla

Iliad Homeric

Ill(ness) Adverse, All-overish, Bad, Bilious, Cronk, Disorder, Evil, Gout, Grotty, Income, Indisposed, Labyrinthitis, Misorder, Off-colour, Poorly, Queer, Ropy, Rough, SARS, Schistosomiasis, Scrofula, Sea-sick, →SICK, Strongylosis, Strung out, Unpropitious, Unweal, Unwell, Valetudinarian, Vomito, Wog, Wrong

▷ **Ill** *may indicate* an anagram

Ill-adjusted Sad sack

Ill-bred Carl, Churlish, Plebeian, Uncouth, Unmannerly

▷ **Ill-composed** *may indicate* an anagram

Ill-disposed Baleful

Illegal, Illicit Adulterine, Black, Bootleg, Breach, Contraband, Furtive, Ill-gotten, Malfeasance, Misbegotten, Pirated, Shonky, Unlawful, Wrong(ous)

Illegitimate Baseborn, Bastard, By-blow, Come-o'-will, Fitz, Irregular, Natural, Scarp, Slink, Spurious, Unlawful

Ill-fated Inauspicious

Ill-feeling, Ill-humour Bad blood, Bile, Complaint, Curt, Dudgeon, Glum, Hate, Miff, Peevish, Pique, Rheum(atic)

▶ **Illicit** *see* **ILLEGAL**

Ill-mannered, Ill-natured, Ill-tempered Attercop, Coarse, Crabby, Crotchety, Curst, Ethercap, Ettercap, Gnarly, Goop, Gurrier, Guttersnipe, Huffy, Stingy, Sullen, Surly, Ugly, Unkind

Illness Aids, Ailment, Attack, Autism, Brucellosis, Chill, Complaint, Croup, Diabetes, Disease, DS, Dwalm, Dwaum, Dyscrasia, Eale, Eclampsia, Grippe, Hangover, Hypochondria, Malady, ME, SAD, Scarlatina, Sickness, Toxaemia, Urosis, Weed, Weid, Wog

Ill-sighted Owl, Purblind

▶ **Ill-tempered** *see* **ILL-MANNERED**

Ill-treat Harm, Hurt, Shaft

Illuminate(d), Illumination, Illuminating Ambient, Aperçu, Brighten, Bright-field, Clarify, Cul-de-lampe, Daylight, Decorate, Enlighten, Floodlit, Lamplight, Langley, Light, Limbourg, Limelight, Limn, Miniate, Moonlight, Nernst, Phot, Pixel, Radiate, Rushlight, Starlight

Illusion(ary), Illusionist, Illusory, Illusive Air, Apparition, Barmecide, Chimera, Deception, Escher, Fallacy, Fancy, Fantasy, Fata morgana, Hallucination, Ignis-fatuus, Indian rope trick, Mare's-nest, Maya, Mirage, Optical, Phantasmal, Phantom, Size-weight, Specious, Transcendental, Will o'the wisp

Illustrate(d), Illustration, Illustrator Artwork, Attwell, Bleed, Case, Centrefold, Collotype, Demonstrate, Dore, Drawing, Eg, Elucidate, Epitomise, Exemplify, Explain, Figure, Frontispiece, Grangerize, Graphic, Half-tone, Heath Robinson, Hors texte, Illume, Illumin(at)e, Instance, Instantiate, Keyline, Limner, Plate, Rockwell, Show, Sidelight, Spotlight, Tenniel, Vignette, Visual, Woodcut

Ill-will Animosity, Enmity, Grudge, Hostility, Malice, Mau(l)gre, Spite

Image(s), Imaging Atman, Blip, Brand, Corporate, Discus, Effigy, Eidetic, Eidolon, Eikon, Emotion, Favicon, Fine-grain, Graphic, Graven, Hologram, Icon, Iconograph, Ident, Idol, Invultuation, Joss, Latent, Likeness, Matte, Mirror, Morph, Murti, Paraselene, Persona, Photogram, Photograph, Pic(ture), Pieta, Pixel(l)ated, Pixil(l)ated, Poetic, Profile, Public, Radionuclide, Real, Recept, Reflectogram, Reflectograph, Representation, Scintigram, Search, Shrine, Simulacrum, Sonogram, Species, Spectrum, Spitting, Split, Stereotype, Symbol, Teraph(im), Thermal, Thermogram, Thumbnail, Tiki, Totem, Vectograph, Venogram, Video, Virtual, Waxwork

Imagine(d), Imaginary (land), Imagination, Imaginative Assume, Bandywallop, Believe, Bullamakanka, Cloud-cuckoo-land, Conceive, Conjure, Create, Cyborg, Dystopia, Envisage, Erewhon, Faery, Faine, Fancy, Feign, Fictional, Fictitious, Fictor, Figment, Figure, Hallucinate, Hobbit, Ideate, Invent, Moral, Narnia, Never-never-land, Notional, Otherworldly, Oz, Picture, Poetical, Prefigure, Propose, Recapture, Replicant, Scotch mist, →**SUPPOSE**, Surmise, Think, Tulpa, Visualise, Whangam, Wonderland

Imam Ismail

▷ **Imbecile** *may indicate* an anagram

Imbibe Absorb, Drink, Lap, Quaff, Suck, Swallow

Imitate, Imitation, Imitator Act, Ape, Burlesque, Caricature, Clone, Copy(cat), Counterfeit, Crib, Dud, Echo, Echopraxia, Emulate, Epigon(e), Ersatz, Facsimile, Fake, False, Faux, Hit off, Marinist, Me-too, Mime, Mimesis, Mimetic, Mimic(ry), Mini-me, Mockery, Monkey, Onomatopoeia, Parody, Parrot, Paste, Paste grain, Pastiche, Pinchbeck, Potichomania, Repro, Rhinestone, Rip-off, Sham, Simulate, Stumer, Take-off, Travesty

Immaculate Conception, Flawless, Lily-white, Perfect, Pristine, Spotless, Virgin

▷ **Immature** *may indicate* a word not completed

Immature(ly), Immaturity Adolescent, Beardless, Callow, Childish, Crude, Embryo, Ergate(s), Green, Inchoate, Larval, Neotenic, Nymph, Puberal, Pupa, Raw, Rudimentary, Sophomoric, Tender, Unbaked, Underage, Unformed, Unripe, Young

Immediate(ly) Anon, At once, Direct, First-time, Forthwith, Imminent, Incontinent, Instantaneous, Lickety-split, Near, Next, →**NOW**, Now-now, On the knocker, Outright, Posthaste, Present, Pronto, Right-off, Short-term, Slapbang, Spontaneous, Stat, Statim, Straight, Straight off, Sudden, Then

Immense Astronomical, Brobdingnag, Cosmic, Enormous, →**GIGANTIC**, Huge, Vast

Immerse Baptise, Demerge, Demerse, Drench, Emplonge, Enew, Engage, Plunge, Soak, Steep, Submerge

Immobility, Immobile, Immobilise(r) Akinesia, Cataplexy, Catatonia, Hamstring, Hog-tie, Inertia, Pinion, Rigidity, Taser, Tether

Immodest(y) Brash, Brazen, Forward, Impudicity, Indelicate, Unchaste

Immoral(ity) Corrupt, Degenerate, Dissolute, Evil, Lax, Libertine, Licentious, Nefarious, Peccable, Reprobate, Scarlet, Sleazebag, Sleazeball, Sleazy, Turpitude, Unchaste, Unclean, Unholy, Unsavoury, Vice, Vicious, Wanton

Immortal(ity) Agelong, Amarant(h), Amritattva, Athanasy, →**DIVINE**, Endless, Enoch, Eternal, Famous, Godlike, Memory, Sin, Struldbrug, Timeless, Undying

Immune, Immunisation, Immunise(r), Immunity Acquired, Active, Amboceptor, Anamnestic, Anergy, Antiserum, Bar, Cree, Diplomatic, Dispensation, Free, Humoral, Inoculate, Klendusic, Natural, Non-specific, Passive, Pasteurism, Pax, Premunition, Properdin, Serum, Tachyphylaxis, Vaccine

Imp(ish) Devilet, Elf, Flibbertigibbet, Gamin(e), Gremlin, Hobgoblin, Limb, Lincoln, Litherly, Monkey, Nickum, Nis(se), Puck, Rascal, Spright, Sprite

Impact Astrobleme, Bearing, Bump, Chase, Clash, Collision, Feeze, Glance, Head-on, High, Impinge, Imprint, Jar, Jolt, Pack, Percuss, Pow, Slam, Souse, Strike home, Wham, Whammo

Impartial(ity) Candid, Detached, Disinterest, Dispassionate, Equitable, Equity, Even-handed, Fair, Just, Neutral, Unbiased

Impasse, Impassable Deadlock, Dilemma, Invious, Jam, Log jam, Mexican standoff, Snooker, Stalemate, Zugzwang

Impatience, Impatient Chafing, Chut, Dysphoria, Dysthesia, Eager, Fiddle-de-dee, Fiddlesticks, Fidgety, Fretful, Hasty, Hoot(s), Irritable, Och, Peevish, Peremptory, Petulant, Pish, Pshaw, Restless, Tilly-fally, Till(e)y-vall(e)y, Tut

Impedance, Impede, Impediment Burr, Clog, Dam, Encumber, Halt, Hamper, Hamstring, Handicap, →**HINDER**, Hog-tie, Let, Log, Obstacle, Obstruct, Reactance, Rub, Shackle, Snag, Speed bump, Stammer, Tongue-tie, Trammel, Veto, Z

Imperative Dire, Hypothetical, Jussive, Mood, Need-be, Pressing, Vital

Imperfect(ion) Aplasia, Aplastic, Blotch, Defect, Deficient, Faulty, Flawed, Half-pie, Kink, Lame, Poor, Rough, Second

Imperial(ist), Imperious Beard, Commanding, Dictatorial, Flag-waver, Haughty, Lordly, Majestic, Masterful, Mint, Peremptory, Regal, Rhodes, Royal

Imperishable Eternal, Immarcescible, Immortal, Indestructible

Impersonal Abstract, Cold, Detached, Inhuman, Institutional

Impersonate(d), Impersonation, Impersonator Amphitryon, Ape, As, Drag queen, Echo, Imitate, Imposter, Impostor, Impression, Mimic, Pose

Impertinence, Impertinent Backchat, Crust, Flip(pant), Fresh, Impudent, Irrelevant, Rude, Sass, Sauce

Impetuous, Impetuosity Birr, Brash, Bullheaded, Élan, Harum-scarum, →**HASTY**, Headstrong, Heady, Hothead, Impulsive, Rash, Rees, Rhys, Tearaway, Vehement, Violent

Impetus Birr, Drift, Drive, Incentive, Momentum, Propulsion, Slancio

Implacable Deadly

Implant(ation) AID, Cochlear, Embed, Engraft, Enrace, Enroot, Graft, Inset, Instil, Silicone, Sow

Implement Agent, Apply, Backscratcher, Biffer, Curette, Do, Flail, Fork, Grater, Grubber, Hacksaw, Harrow, Hayfork, Mezzaluna, Mop, Muller, Neolith, Pin, Pitchfork, Plectrum, Plough, Pruning-bill, Rest, Ricker, Ripple, Scuffler, Seed drill, Snuffer, Spatula, Spork, Squeegee, Sucket fork, Sucket spoon, Tongs, →**TOOL**, Toothpick, Tribrach, Utensil, Wheelbrace

Implicate, Implication Accuse, Concern, Connotation, Embroil, Incriminate, Innuendo, →**INVOLVE**, Overtone

Imply, Implied Hint, Insinuate, Intimate, Involve, Predicate, Signify, →**SUGGEST**, Tacit, Unstated, Unwritten

Importance, Important (person) Account, Big, Big cheese, Big pot, Big wheel, Billing, Calibre, Cardinal, Central, Cheese, Cob, Coming, Consequence, Considerable, Core, Cornerstone, Count, Critical, Crucial, Crux, Earth-shaking, Earth-shattering, Ego-trip, Eminent, Epochal, Flagship, Grave, Gravitas, Gravity, Greatness, Heavy, High, High-profile, His nibs, Historic, Honcho, Hotshot, Huzoor, Key, Keystone, Leading, Life and death, Macher, Magnitude, Main, Major, Material, Matters, Megastar, Mighty, Milestone, Moment(ous), Nabob, Nawab, Nib, Note, Numero uno, Obbligato, Outbalance, Overriding, Paramount, Personage, Pivotal, Pot, Preponderate, Prime, Principal, Red-carpet, Red-letter, Salient, Seminal, Senior, Serious, Signal, Significant, Something, Special, Stature, Status, Stress, Substantive, Tuft, Urgent, VIP, Visiting fireman, Vital, Weight, Weighty, Worth

Importune, Importunate Beg, Coax, Flagitate, Press(ing), Prig, Solicit, Urgent

Impose(r), Imposing, Imposition Allocate, Assess, August, Burden, Charge, Diktat, Dread, Enforce, Enjoin, Epic, Fine, Flam, Foist, Fraud, Grand(iose), Handsome, Hidage, Homeric, Hum, Impot, Inflict, Kid, Lay, Levy, Lumber, Majestic, Noble, Obtrude, Penance, Pensum, Pole, Scot, Sponge, Statuesque, Stonehand, Sublime, Titan, Try-on, Whillywhaw

Impossible Can't, Hopeless, Inconceivable, Incorrigible, Insoluble, Insurmountable, Irreparable, No-no, Unacceptable

Imposter, Impostor Bunyip, Charlatan, Disaster, →**FAKE**, Fraud, Idol, Phantasm, Pretender, Ringer, Sham, Triumph, Warbeck

Impotent Barren, Helpless, Spado, Sterile, Weak

Impoverish(ed) Bankrupt, Bare, Beggar, Exhaust, Needy, Poor, Straiten

Impractical Absurd, Academic, Blue-sky, Chim(a)era, Idealist, Laputan, Non-starter, Not on, Other-worldly, Quixotic, Theoretic, Useless

Imprecise Approximate, Inaccurate, Indeterminate, Intangible, Loose, Nebulous, Rough, Sloppy, Vague

Impregnable, Impregnate Conceive, Embalm, Imbue, Inexpugnable, Inseminate, Milt, Permeate, Watertight

Impress(ive), Impression(able) Appearance, Astonish, Awe(struck), Class act, Description, Effect, Engrain, Etch, Feel(ing), Glorious, Greeking, Idea, Imitation, Imposing, Imprint, Indent, Majestic, Mould, Name-drop, Pliable, Powerful, Press(gang), Print, Prodigious, Proof, Register, Resplendent, Stamp, Strike, Stunning, Take, Type, Watermark, Whale, Woodcut

Imprison(ment) Cage, Cape, Confine, Constrain, Custody, Durance, Emmew, Gherao, Immure, Incarcerate, Inside, Intern, Jail, Lock-up, Quad, Quod, Stretch, Time

Impromptu Ad lib(itum), Extempore, Improvised, Offhand, Pong, Spontaneous, Sudden, Unrehearsed

Improper, Impropriety Abnormal, Blue, Demirep, False, Indecent, Indecorum, Naughty, Outré, Prurient, Solecism, Undue, Unmeet, Unseemly, Untoward

▷ **Improperly** *may indicate* an anagram

Improve(ment), Improver, Improving Advance, Ameliorate, Beat, Benefit, Bete, Better, Boost, Break, Buck, Cap, Chasten, Conditioner, Convalesce, Détente, Didactic, Ease, Edify, Embellish, Embroider, Emend, Enhance, Enrich, Eugenic, Euthenics, File, Gentrify, Kaizen, Meliorate, Mend, Modernise, Potentiate, Promote, Rally, Refine, Reform, Resipiscence, Retouch, Revamp, Slim, Surpass, Tart, Tatt, Titivate, Top, Touch-up, Turn round, Upswing, Uptrend, Upturn

Improvise(d), Improvisation Ad hoc, Adlib, Break, Busk it, Devise, Extemporise, Gorgia, Invent, Jury-rig, Knock-up, Lash-up, Noodle, On the fly, Pong, Ride, Scratch, Sodain, Sudden, Tweedle, Vamp, Wing it

Impudence, Impudent Audacious, Backchat, Bardy, Bold, Brash, Brassy, Brazen, Cheeky, Cool, Crust, Effrontery, Forward, Gall, Gallus, Hussy, Impertinent, Insolent, Jackanapes, Jack-sauce, Lip, Malapert, Neck, →**NERVE**, Pert, Sass(y), Sauce, Saucebox, Saucy, Skipjack, Slack-jaw, Temerity, Whippersnapper, Yankie

Impulse, Impulsive Acte gratuit, Beat, Compelling, Conatus, Dictate, Drive, Efferent, Foolhardy, Headlong, Horme, Ideopraxist, Impetus, Instigation, →**INSTINCT**, Madcap, Nisus, Precipitant, Premature, Premotion, Send, Signal, Snap, Spontaneous, Tearaway, Tendency, Thrust, Tic, Urge, Whim

Impure, Impurity Adulterated, Contaminated, Donor, Faints, Feints, Indecent, Lees, Lewd, Regulus, Scum, Unchaste, Unclean

In A, Amid, Amidst, At, Batting, Chic, Current, Hip, Home, Hostel, I', Indium, Inn, Intil, Occupying, Pop(ular), Pub, Trendy, Within

Inaccurate Distorted, Erroneous, Faulty, Imprecise, Inexact, Misquote, Out, Overestimate, Rough, Slipshod

Inactive, Inaction, Inactivity Acedia, Anestrum, Anoestrus, Cabbage, Comatose, Dead, Dormant, Extinct, Fallow, Hibernate, Idle, Inert, Languor, Lotus-eater, Masterly, Moratorium, Passive, Quiescent, Racemic, Recess, Rusty, Sluggish, Stagnation, Stasis, Torpid, Vacancy, Veg(etate)

Inadequate Derisory, Feeble, Hopeless, Inapt, Inferior, Joke, Measly, Pathetic, Poor, Ropy, Slight, Thin, Unable, Unequal

▷ **In a flap** *may indicate* an anagram

Inane Empty, Fatuous, Foolish, Imbecile, Silly, Vacant

Inappropriate Amiss, Incongrous, Infelicitous, Malapropos, Off-key, Out of place, Pretentious, Unapt, Unbecoming, Undue, Unmeet, Unsuitable, Untoward

Inattentive, Inattention Absent, Asleep, Careless, Deaf, Distrait, Dwaal, Dwa(l)m, Dwaum, Heedless, Loose, Slack, Unheeding, Unobservant

Inaugurate Han(d)sel, Initiate, Install, Introduce, Swear in

Inauspicious Adverse, Ominous, Sinister

▷ **In a whirl** *may indicate* an anagram

▷ **In a word** *may indicate* two clue words linked to form one

Inborn, Inbred Inherent, Innate, Native, Selfed, Sib

Inca Quechua, Quichua

Incandescent Alight, Bright, Brilliant, Excited, Radiant

Incantation Chant, Charm, Magic, Mantra, Spell

Incapacitate Paralyse

Incarcerate Intern

Incendiary Arsonist, Firebug, Fire-lighter, Napalm, Thermite

Incense(d), Incenser Anger, Aroma, Elemi, Enfelon, Enrage, Homage, Hot, →**INFLAME**, Joss-stick, Mosquito coil, Navicula, Onycha, Outrage, Pastil(le), Provoke, Stacte, Thurible, Thus, Vex, Wrathful

Incentive Carrot, Feather-bed, Fillip, Impetus, Inducement, Motive, Spur, Stimulus

Inch(es) Ait, Edge, Isle(t), Miner's, Sidle, Uncial

Incident(al) Affair, Baur, Bawr, Carry-on, Case, Chance, Circumstance, Episode, Event, Facultative, Negligible, Occasion, Occurrent, Page, Peripheral, Scene

Incinerate, Incinerator Burn, Combust, Cremate

Incise, Incision, Incisive(ness) Bite, Cut, Edge, Engrave, Episiotomy, Mordant, Phlebotomy, Pleurotomy, Rhizotamy, Slit, Surgical, Thoracotomy, Tracheotomy, Trenchant

Incite(ment) Abet, Agitate, Drive, Egg, Fillip, Goad, Hortative, Hoy, Impassion, Inflame, Instigate, Kindle, Motivate, Onsetting, Prod, Prompt, Provoke, Put, Rouse, Sa sa, Sedition, Set, Sic(k), Sool, →**SPUR**, Stimulus, Sting, Suborn, Suggest, Tar, Urge

Incline(d), Inclination Acclivity, Angle, Aslant, Aslope, Atilt, Bank, Batter, Bent, Bevel, Bias, Bow, Camber, Clinamen, Cock, Crossfall, Declivity, Dip, Disposed, Drift, Enclitic, Escarpment, Glacis, →**GRADIENT**, Grain, Habitus, Hade, Heel, Hill, Italic, Kant, Kip, Lean, Liable, Liking, List, Maw, Minded, Nod, On, Partial, Peck, Penchant, Proclivity, Prone, Propensity, Rake, Ramp, Ready, Rollway, Set, Shelve, Slant, →**SLOPE**, Steep, Steeve, Stomach, Supine, Sway, Tend, Tilt, Tip, Trend, Upgrade, Uptilt, Velleity, Verge, Weathering, Will

Include(d), Inclusion, Inclusive Add, All-told, Bracket, Compass, Comprise, Connotate, Contain, Cover, Embody, Embrace, Enclose, Involve, Short-list, Social, Therein

Incognito Anonymous, Disguised, Faceless, Secret, Unnamed, Unobserved

Income Annuity, Discretionary, Disposable, Dividend, Earned, Entry, Living, Meal-ticket, Milch cow, Notional, Penny-rent, Prebend, Primitiae, Proceeds, Rent(al), Rent-roll, Returns, Revenue, Salary, Stipend, Take, Unearned, Wages

Incomeless E

Incomparable Par excellence, Supreme, Unequalled, Unique, Unmatched

Incompatible, Incompatibility Clashing, Contradictory, Dyspathy, Inconsistent, Mismatched, Unsuited

Incompetent(ly) Blind Freddie, Bungler, Deadhead, Helpless, Hopeless, Ill, Inefficient, Inept, Not for nuts, Palooka, Shlepper, Shower, Slouch, Unable, Unfit, Useless

Incomplete Cagmag, Catalectic, Deficient, Inchoate, Lacking, Partial, Pendent, Rough, Sketchy, Unfinished

▷ **In confusion** *may indicate* an anagram

Incongruous, Incongruity Absurd, Discordant, Irish, Ironic, Sharawadgi, Sharawaggi, Solecism

Inconsequential Light

Inconsiderate Asocial, High-handed, Light-minded, Petty, Presumptuous, Roughshod, Thoughtless, Unkind, Unthinking

Inconsistency, Inconsistent Alien, Anacoluthon, Anomaly, Contradictory, Discrepant, Oxymoronic, Paradoxical, Patchy, Variance

Inconvenience, Inconvenient Awkward, Bother(some), Discommode, Fleabite, Incommodious, Inopportune, Put out, →TROUBLE, Ungain(ly)

Incorporate(d), Incorporation Absorb, Embody, Hard wire, Inc, Inorb, Integrate, Introgression, Introject, Join, Merge, Subsume

Incorrect Catachresis, False, Improper, Naughty

Incorruptible Honest, Immortal, Pure, Sea-green

Increase(s), Increasing Accelerando, Accelerate, Accession, Accretion, Accrew, Accrue, Add, Additur, Aggrandise, Amplify, Amp up, Appreciate, Approve, Augment, Auxetic, Bolster, Boost, Build up, Bulge, Burgeon, Charge, Crank up, Crescendo, Crescent, Crescive, Deepen, Dilate, Double, Ech(e), Eech, Eik, Eke, Enhance, Enlarge, Escalate, →EXPAND, Explosion, Extend, Gain, Greaten, →GROW, Heighten, Hike, Ich, Increment, Interbreed, Jack, Jack up, Joseph, Lift, Magnify, Mark up, Mount, Multiply, Plus, Proliferate, Prolong, Propagate, Ramp up, Redshift, Reflation, Regrate, Resurgence, Rise, Snowball, Speed up, Supercharger, Surge, Swell, Thrive, Up, Upsize, Upswell, Upswing, Wax, Write up

Incredible Amazing, Astonishing, Cockamamie, Extraordinary, Fantastic, Steep, Stey, Tall, Unreal

Incredulity, Incredulous As if, Distrust, Sceptic, Suspicion, Thunderstruck

Incriminate Accuse, Implicate, Inculpate, Stitch up

Incumbent Lying, Obligatory, Occupier, Official, Resident

Incursion Foray, Inroad, Invasion, Raid, Razzia

Indecent Bare, Blue, Free, Immodest, Immoral, Improper, Lewd, Obscene, Racy, Scurril(e), Uncomely, Unnatural, Unproper, Unseem(ly)

Indecision, Indecisive Demur, Dithery, Doubt, Hamlet, Hesitation, Hung jury, Shilly-shally, Suspense, Swither, Weakkneed, Wishy-washy

Indecorous Graceless, Immodest, Outré, Unbecoming, Unseemly

Indefinable Je ne sais quoi

Indefinite(ly) A, An, Any, Evermore, Hazy, Nth, Some, Undecided, Vague

Indelicate Broad, Coarse, Improper, Sultry, Vulgar, Warm

Indent(ed), Indentation Apprentice, Contract, Crenellate, Dancetty, Dimple, Impress, Niche, Notch, Order, Prophet's thumbmarks, Subentire

Independence, Independent Apart, Autocephalous, Autogenous, Autonomy, Crossbencher, Detached, Extraneous, Free(dom), Free-lance, Freethinker, I, Individual, Liberty, Mana motuhake, Maverick, Mugwump, Perseity, Self-contained, Self-sufficient, Separate, Separatist, Swaraj, Udal, UDI, Uhuru, Viscosity

Indestructible Enduring, Impenetrable, Inextirpable

Index Alidad(e), All-Ordinaries, Catalogue, Cephalic, Colour, Cranial, Cross, DAX, Dial, Dow Jones, Exponent, Facial, Finger, Fist, Fog, Footsie, Forefinger, Gazetteer, Glycaemic, Hang Seng, Kwic, Margin, Misery, Mitotic, Nasal, Nikkei, Power, Price, Refractive, →REGISTER, Rotary, Share, Stroke, Table, Therapeutic, Thumb, TPI, UV, Verborum, Zonal

India(n) Adivisi, Assamese, Ayah, Baboo, Babu, Bharat(i), Canarese, Chin, Dard, Dravidian, East, File, Gandhi, Goanese, Gond(wanaland), Gujarati, Harijan, Harsha, Hindu, .in, Ink, Jain, Jat, Jemadar, Kanarese, Kannada, Khalsa, Kisan, Kolarian, Kshatriyas, Lepcha, Maratha, Ma(h)ratta, Maya, Mazhbi, Mishmi, Mission, Mofussil, Mogul, Munda, Munshi, Nagari, Nair, Nasik, Nation, Nayar, Ocean, Oriya, Pali, Parsee, Parsi, Pathan, Peshwa, Poppadom, Prakrit, Punjabi, Red, Redskin, Sanskrit, Sepoy, Shri, Sikh, Sind(h), Sowar, Summer, Swadeshi, Taino, Tamil, Telegu, Treaty, Vakeel, Vakil, West, Ynd

Indiana, Indianian Hoosier

Indicate, Indication, Indicative, Indicator Adumbrate, Allude, Argue, Barcode, Bespeak, Betoken, Cite, Clue, Convey, Cursor, →DENOTE, Design, Designate, Desine, Dial, Dial gauge, Endeixis, Evidence, Evince, Gesture, Gnomon, Hint, Litmus, Manifest, Mean, Mood, Nod, Notation, Pinpoint, Plan-position, Point,

Portend, Proof, Ray, Register, Remarque, Representative, Reveal, →**SIGN**, Signify, Specify, Speedo, Symptom, Tip, Token, Trace, Trait, Winker

Indifference, Indifferent Adiaphoron, Aloof, Apathetic, Apathy, Blasé, Blithe, Callous, Cavalier, Cold, Cool(th), Dead, Deaf, Detached, Disdain, Easy-osy, Empty, Fico, Incurious, Insouciant, Jack easy, Lax, Lukewarm, Mediocre, Neutral, Nonchalant, Perfunctory, Phlegm, Pococurante, Sangfroid, So-so, Stoical, Supercilious, Supine, Tepid, Thick-skinned, Unconcerned

Indignant, Indignation Anger, Annoyed, Bridling, Incensed, Irate, Outrage, Resentful, Steamed up, Umbrage, Wrathful

Indigo Anil, Blue, Bunting, Carmine, Indole, Isatin(e), Wild

Indirect Aside, Back-handed, By(e), Circumlocution, Devious, Implicit, Mediate, Oblique, Remote, Roundabout, Second-hand, Sidelong, Subtle, Vicarious, Zig-zag

Indiscreet, Indiscretion Folly, Gaffe, Imprudence, Indelicate, Injudicious, Loose cannon, Rash, Unguarded

Indiscriminate Haphazard, Random, Scattershot, Sweeping, Wholesale

Indispensable Basic, Essential, King-pin, Linch-pin, Necessary, Requisite, Vital

Indispose(d), Indisposition Adverse, Disincline, Ill, Incapacitate, Reluctant, Sick, Unwell

Indistinct Ambiguous, Bleary, Blur, Bumble, Bummle, Faint, Filmy, Fuzzy, Grainy, Hazy, Misty, Mumbling, Mush-mouthed, Nebulous, Neutral, Nondescript, Pale, Sfumato, Slurred, Smudged, →**VAGUE**

Indistinguishable Nondescript

▷ **In distress** *may indicate* an anagram

Indite Compose, Pen, Write

Individual(ist), Individuality Apiece, Being, Discrete, Exclusive, Free spirit, Gemma, Haecceity, Identity, Ka, Libertarian, Loner, Man, Man-jack, Morph, One-to-one, Own, Particular, Person, Poll, Respective, Seity, Separate, Single, Singular, Solo, Soul, Special, Unit, Zoon

Indolence, Indolent Bone idle, Fainéance, Inactive, Languid, Lazy, Lentor, Otiose, Purposeless, Shiftless, Sloth, Sluggish, Supine

Indomitable Brave, Dauntless, Invincible

Indubitably Certainly, Certes, Manifestly, Surely

Induce(ment) Bribe, Carrot, Cause, Coax, Draw, Encourage, Evoke, Get, Inveigle, Lead, Motivate, →**PERSUADE**, Prevail, Suasion, Suborn, Tempt

Induct(ion), Inductance Epagoge, Henry, Inaugurate, Initiate, Install, L, Logic, Mutual, Ordain, Prelude, Remanence

Indulge(nce), Indulgent Absolution, Aristippus, Binge, Coddle, Cosset, Dissipation, Drink, Favour, Gratify, Humour, Lie-in, Luxuriate, Oblige, Orgy, Pamper, Pander, Pardon, Partake, Permissive, Pet, Pettle, Pig-out, Please, Plenary, →**SATISFY**, Splurge, Spoil, Spoonfeed, Spree, Surfeit, Sybarite, Tolerant, Venery, Voluptuous, Wallow

Industrial, Industrious, Industry Appliance, Application, Basic, Business, Busy, Cottage, Deedy, Diligence, Eident, Energetic, Growth, Heavy, Heritage, Labour, Legwork, Millicent, Ocnus, Process, Ruhr, Service, Technical, Technics, Tertiary, Tourism, Zaibatsu

▶ **Inebriate** *see* **INTOXICATE(D)**

Ineffective, Ineffectual Chinless wonder, Clumsy, Deadhead, Drippy, Droob, Dud, Empty, Eunuch, Fainéant, Feeble, Fruitless, Futile, Idle, Ill, Impotent, Lame, Mickey Mouse, Neuter, Neutralised, Otiose, Powerless, Resty, Sterile, Stumbledown, Toothless, →**USELESS**, Void, Weak, Wet, Wimp

Inefficient Clumsy, Incompetent, Lame, Shiftless, Slack, Slouch

Inept Absurd, Amateurish, Anorak, Farouche, Fumbler, Galoot, Loser, Maladjusted, Nerd, Otaku, Plonker, Sad sack, Schlimazel, Schmo, Unskilled, Wet

Inert(ia) Catatonia, Comatose, Dead, Dull, Excipient, Inactive, Krypton, Languid, Leaden, Mollusc, Motionless, Neon, Oblomovism, Potato, Rigor, Sluggish, Stagnant, Stagnation, Thowless, Torpid

Inescapable Act of God

Inevitable, Inevitably Automatic, Certain, Fateful, Inescapable, Inexorable, Infallible, Necessary, Needs, Perforce, TINA, Unavoidable

Inexact(itude) Cretism, Incorrect, Terminological, Wrong

Inexhaustible Infinite, Tireless

Inexpedient Impolitic, Imprudent, Unwise

Inexpensive Bargain, Cheap, Dirt-cheap, Economic

Inexperience(d), Inexpert Amateur, Awkward, Callow, Colt, Crude, Fledgling, Fresh, →GREEN, Ham, Ingénue, Jejune, Put(t), Raw, Rookie, Rude, Tender, Unseasoned, Unversed, Waister, Wide-eyed, Youthful

Inexplicable Magical, Mysterious, Paranormal, Unaccountable

In fact Insooth

Infamous, Infamy Base, Ignominious, Notorious, Opprobrium, Shameful, Villainy

Infant, Infancy Babe, Baby, Innocent, Lamb, Minor, Nurseling, Oral, Rug rat, The cradle

▷ **Infantry** *may refer to* babies

Infantry(man) Buff, Foot, Grunt, Jaeger, Phalanx, Pultan, Pulto(o)n, Pultun, →SOLDIER, Tercio, Turco, Twenty, Voetganger

Infatuate(d), Infatuating, Infatuation Assot, Besot, Crush, Enamoured, Engou(e)ment, Entêté, Epris, Fanatic, Foolish, Lovesick, Mash, →OBSESSION, Pash, Rave, Turn

Infect(ed), Infecting, Infection, Infectious Adenoviral, Angina, Anthrax, Babesiasis, Babesiosis, Canker, Carrier, Catching, Catchy, Cholera, Communicable, Contagious, Contaminate, Corrupt, Cowpox, Cryptococcosis, Cryptosporidiosis, Dermatophytosis, Diseased, E-coli, Fester, Gonorrhoea, Herpes, Impetigo, Listeria, Lockjaw, Mycetoma, Opportunistic, Overrun, Poison, Polio(myelitis), →POLLUTE, Pyoderma, Rife, Ringworm, Roup, Salmonella, SARS, Scabies, Secondary, Septic, Shingles, Strep throat, Strongyloidiasis, Taint, Taking, Tetanus, Thrush, Tinea, Toxoplasmosis, Transfection, Typhoid, Typhus, Varroa, Vincent's angina, Viral pneumonia, Virulent, Whitlow, Zoonosis

▷ **Infer** *may indicate* 'fer' around another word

Infer(ence), Inferred Conclude, Deduce, Divine, Educe, Extrapolate, Generalise, Guess, Illation, Imply, Judge, Surmise

Inferior Base, Bodgier, Cheap-jack, Cheesy, Coarse, Crummy, Degenerate, Dog, Epigon, Ersatz, Gimcrack, Grody, Grub-Street, Impair, Indifferent, Infra, Jerkwater, Less, Lo-fi, Lower, Low-grade, Mediocre, Minor, Naff, Nether, One-horse, Ornery, Paravail, Petty, Poor, Rop(e)y, Schlock, Second, Second-best, Shilpit, Shlock, Shoddy, Shonky, Slopwork, Sprew, Sprue, Subjacent, Subordinate, Substandard, Surat, Tatty, Tinpot, Trashy, Underdog, Underneath, Untermensch, Waste, Worse

Infest(ed), Infestation Beset, Blight, Dog, Hoatching, Overrun, →PLAGUE, Swamp, Swarm, Taeniasis, Torment, Trypanosomiasis

Infidel Atheist, Caffre, Heathen, Heretic, Kafir, Miscreant, Pagan, Saracen

Infiltrate(d), Infiltrator Encroach, Enter, Fifth columnist, Gatecrash, Instil, Intrude, Mole, Pervade, Trojan horse

Infirm Decrepit, Doddery, Feeble, Frail, Lame, Shaky, Sick

▷ **Infirm** *may indicate* 'co' around another word

Inflame(d), Inflammable, Inflammation Afire, Anger, →AROUSE, Bloodshot, Enamoured, Enchafe, Enfire, Enkindle, Fever, Fire, Gleet, Ignite, Incense, Infection, Ire, Kindle, Methane, Napalm, Naphtha, →RED, Stimulate, Swelling, Touchwood

Inflate(d), Inflation Aerate, Aggrandise, Bloat, Bombastic, Bracket-creep, Demand-pull, Dilate, Distend, Distent, Increase, Pneumatic, Pompous, Pump, Raise, Remonetise, RPI, Spiral, Stagnation, Swell, Wage-push

Inflexible, Inflexibility Adamant(ine), Byzantine, Doctrinaire, Hard-ass, Hard-liner, Iron, Obstinate, Ossified, Ramrod, Relentless, Resolute, Rigid, Rigour, Set, Staid, Stubborn

Inflict(ion) Force, Give, Impose, Subject, Trouble, Visit, Wreak

Inflorescence Bostryx, Catkin, Ci(n)cinnus, Drepanium, Glomerule, Panicle, Pleiochasium, Raceme, R(h)achis, Umbel

Influence(d), Influential Act, Affect, After, Amenable, Backstairs, Brainwash, Catalyse, Charm, Clamour, Clout, Colour, Credit, Determine, Dominant, Drag, Earwig, Eclectic, Embracery, Éminence grise, Factor, Force, Govern, Guide, Hold, Impact, Impinge, Impress, Incubus, Inspire, Interfere, Lead, Leverage, Lobby, Mastery, Militate, Mogul, Mould, Nobble, Octopus, Operation, Outreach, Panjandrum, Power, Preponderant, Pressure, Prestige, →**PULL**, Push, Reach, Rust, Say, Securocrat, Seminal, Significant, Star, Star-blasting, Stimulus, Suggest, Svengali, Sway, Swing, Telegony, Thrall, Undue, Weigh with, Will, Work, Wull

Influenza Asian, Equine, Flu, Gastric, Grippe, Lurgi, Spanish, Wog, Yuppie

Influx Inbreak

Infold(ing) Invagination

Inform(ation), Informant, Informed, Informer Acquaint, Advise, Agitprop, Apprise, Au fait, Aware, Beagle, Bit, Blow, Burst, Callboard, Canary, Ceefax®, Clype, Contact, Datum, Deep throat, Delate, Dicker, Dob(ber), Dobber-in, Dope, Education, Facts, Feedback, Fink, Fisgig, Fiz(z)gig, Gen, Genome, Good oil, Grapevine, Grass, Griff, Gunsel, Hep, Immersive, Input, Inside, Instruct, Izvesti(y)a, Light, Lowdown, Media, Metadata, Microdot, Moiser, Nark, Nepit, Nit, Nose, Occasion, Peach, Pem(m)ican, Pentito, Poop, Prestel®, Prime, Promoter, Propaganda, Prospectus, Rat, Read-out, Report, Revelation, Rheme, Rumble, Shelf, Shop, Sidelight, Sing, Sneak, Snitch, Squeak, Squeal, Stag, Stoolie, Stool-pigeon, Supergrass, Sycophant, Tell, Throughput, Tidings, Tip-off, Up, Whistle(-blower), Wire, Witting

Informal Casual, Intimate, Irregular, Outgoing, Rough and ready, Unofficial

Infuriate Anger, Bemad, Bepester, Enrage, Exasperate, Incense, Madden, Pester, Provoke

Ingenious, Ingenuity Acumen, Adept, Adroit, Art, Artificial, Clever, Cunning, Cute, Inventive, Natty, Neat, Resourceful, Smart, Subtle, Trick(s)y, Wit

Ingenuous Artless, Candid, Green, Innocent, Naive, Open, Transparent

Ingle Bardash, Hearth, Nook

Ingot Bar, Billet, Bullion, Lingot, Sycee, Wedge

Ingratiate, Ingratiating Bootlick, Butter, Court, Flatter, Greasy, Oily, Pick-thank, Smarm(y)

Ingredient(s) Additive, Admixture, Asafoetida, Basis, Content, Element, Factor, Formula, Makings, Mincemeat, Staple

Inhabit(ant), Inhabitants Affect, Children, Denizen, Dweller, Inholder, Inmate, Live, Native, Occupant, People, Populate, Population, Populous, Resident, Towny

Inhale(r), Inhalation Aspirate, Breath(e), Draw, Gas, Inspire, Intal, Sniff, Snort, Snuff, Take, Toot, Tout

Inherit(ance), Inherited, Inheritor Accede, Birthright, Congenital, Esnecy, Gene, Genom, Heirloom, Heritage, Inborn, Legacy, Legitim, Meek, Patrimony, Portion, Succeed

Inhibit(ing), Inhibition, Inhibitor ACE, Antihistamine, Anuria, Captopril, Chalone, Chalonic, Deter, Donepezil, Enalapril, Etanercept, Feedback, Finasteride, Forbid, Hang-up, Protease, Restrain, Retard, Retroactive, Stunt, Suppress, Tightass

Initial Acronym, First, Letter, Monogram, Paraph, Prelim(inary), Primary, Rubric

▷ **Initially** *may indicate* first letters

Initiate(d), Initiating, Initiation, Initiative Begin, Bejesuit, Blood, Bora, Bring, Ceremony, Debut, Enter, Enterprise, Epopt, Esoteric, Gumption, Induct, Instigate, Instruct, →**LAUNCH**, Neophyte, Nous, Onset, Proactive, Spark, →**START**

Inject(or), Injection Antiserum, Bang, Blast, Bolus, Booster, Collagen, Direct, Enema, Epidural, Epipen®, Fuel, Hypo, Immit, Implant, Innerve, Inoculation, Instil, Introduce, Jab, Jack up, Jag, Lidocaine, Mainline, Pop, Reheat, Serum, Shoot, Shoot up, Skin-pop, Solid, Spike, Syringe, Transfuse, Venipuncture

Injunction Command, Embargo, Freezing, Mandate, Mareva, Quia timet, Writ

Injure(d), Injury, Injurious, Injustice ABH, Abuse, Accloy, Aggrieve, Bale, Barotrauma, Bled, Bruise, Casualty, Contrecoup, Contuse, Damage, De(a)re, Disservice, Frostbite, Gash, GBH, Harm, → HURT, Ill-turn, Impair, Industrial, Iniquity, Lesion, Malign, Mar, Mayhem, Mistreat, Mutilate, Needlestick, Nobble, Nocuous, Non-accidental, Noxal, Nuisance, Occupational, Oppression, Outrage, Packet, Paire, Prejudice, Rifle, RSI, Scaith, Scald, Scath(e), Scotch, Shend, Sore, Sprain, Tene, Tort, Trauma, Umbrage, Whiplash, Wound, Wrong

▶ **Injury** see AFTER INJURY

Ink(y) Black, Copying, Cyan, Indian, Invisible, Marking, Monk, Printing, Sepia, Stained, Toner

Inlaid, Inlay(er) Boulle, Buhl, Clear, Compurgation, Crustae, Damascene, Emblemata, Empaestic, Enamel, Enchase, Incrust, Intarsia, Intarsio, Marquetrie, Marquetry, Piqué, Set, Tarsia, Unsuspecting, Veneer

Inlet Arm, Bay, Cook, Cove, Creek, Entry, Fiord, Firth, Fjord, Fleet, Flow, Geo, Gio,
· Golden Horn, Gulf, Gusset, Hope, Infall, Jervis Bay, Loch, Port Phillip Bay, Puget Sound, Rio de la Plata, Sogne Fjord, Strait, Sullom Voe, Table Bay, The Wash

▷ **Inlet** may indicate 'let' around another word

▷ **Inn** may refer to the law

Inn(s), Innkeeper Albergo, Alehouse, Auberge, Barnard's, Boniface, Caravanserai, Coaching, Gray's, Halfway-house, Host(ry), Hostelry, Hotel(ier), House, Imaret, In, Inner Temple, Khan, Kneipe, Ladin(ity), Law, Licensee, Lincoln's, Lodging, Luckie, Lucky, Maypole, Middle Temple, Padrone, Parador, Patron, Porterhouse, Posada, Posthouse, Pothouse, Publican, Roadhouse, Ryokan, Serai, Stabler, Tabard, Tavern(er), Victualler

Innards Entrails, Giblets, Gizzard, Guts, Harigals, Harslet, Haslet, Omasa, Rein, Viscera

▶ **Innkeeper** see INN(S)

Innocent Absolved, Angelic, Arcadian, Babe, Blameless, Canny, Chaste, Cherub, Childlike, Clean, Clear, Compurgation, Dewy-eyed, Doddypoll, Dodipoll, Dove, Encyclical, Green, Guileless, Idyllic, Ingenue, Lamb, Lily-white, Maiden, Naive, Opsimath, Pope, → PURE, Sackless, St, Seely, Simple, Unsuspecting, White

Innu Naskapi

Inoperative Futile, Nugatory, Silent, Void

Inordinate Excessive, Irregular, Undue

▷ **Inordinately** may indicate an anagram

In place of For, Qua, Vice, With

Inquest Debriefing, Hearing, Inquiry, Investigation

Inquire, Inquiring, Inquiry Ask, Demand, Investigation, Nose, Organon, Probe, Public, Query, Question, See, Speer, Speir

Inquisition, Inquisitive, Inquisitor Curious, Interrogation, Meddlesome, Nosy, Prying, Rubberneck, Snooper, Stickybeak, Torquemada

▷ **In revolt, In revolution** may indicate an anagram

Insane, Insanity Absurd, Batty, Berserk, Crazy, Dementia, Deranged, Loco, Looniness, Mad, Manic, Mental, Paranoia, Pellagra, Psycho, Schizo, Troppo

Inscribe(d), Inscription Chisel, Colophon, Dedicate, Emblazon, Endoss, Engrave, Enter, Epigraph, Epitaph, Graffiti, Hic jacet, Hierograph, Lapidary, Legend, Lettering, Ogham, Writ

Insect(s) Entomic, Nonentity, Non-person, Stridulator, Wax

Insectivore Agouta, Desman, Donaea, Drongo, Drosera, Hedgehog, Jacamar, Nepenthaceae, Tanrec, Tenrec(idae), Tupaia, Venus flytrap, Zalambdodont

Insecure Infirm, → LOOSE, Needy, Precarious, Shaky, Unsafe, Unstable, Unsteady, Vulnerable

Insensible Iron-witted

Insert(ed), Insertion, Inset Anaptyxis, Cue, Empiecement, Enchase, Enter, Entry, Epenthesis, Foist, Fudge, Godet, Gore, Graft, Gusset, Immit, Imp, Implant,

Inchase, Inject, Inlay, Input, Interject, Interpolate, Interpose, Intersperse, Introduce, Intromit, Intubate, Mitre, Pin, Punctuate, Sandwich

Inside(r) Content, Core, Entrails, Gaol, Giblets, Heart, Indoors, Interior, Internal, Interne, Inward, Inwith, Mole, Tum, →**WITHIN**

Insignia Armour, Arms, Badger, Charge, Chevron, Mark, Order, Regalia, Ribbon, Roundel, Tab

Insignificant (person) Bobkes, Bubkis, Bupkes, Bupkis, Chickenfeed, Dandiprat, Fico, Fiddling, Flea-bite, Fractional, Gnat, Inconsiderable, Insect, Jerkwater, Mickey Mouse, Minimus, Miniscule, Minnow, Nebbich, Nobody, Nominal, Nondescript, Nonentity, Non-event, One-eyed, Peanuts, Petit, Petty, Pipsqueak, Pissant, Quat, Rabbit, Scoot, Scout, Scrub, Shrimp, Slight, Small potatoes, Small-time, Squirt, Squit, Tenuous, Trifling, Trivial, Two-bit, Unimportant, Venial, Warb, Whiffet, Whippersnapper, Wind

Insincere, Insincerity Affected, Artificial, Barmecide, Cant, Double, Double-faced, Duplicity, Empty, Factitious, Faithless, False, Forced, Glib, Greenwash, Hollow, Janus-faced, Lip service, Mealy-mouthed, Meretricious, Mouth-made, Pseudo, Shallow, Synthetic, Tongue-in-cheek, Two-faced, Unnatural

Insipid Banal, Blab, Bland, Fade, Flat, Insulse, Jejune, Lash, Mawkish, Milk and water, Shilpit, Spiritless, Tame, Tasteless, Vapid, Weak, Wearish

Insist(ent) Adamant, Assert, Demand, Dogmatic, Exact, Press, Stickler, →**STIPULATE**, Stress, Swear, Threap, Threep, Urge

Insolence, Insolent Audacity, Bardy, Brassy, Cheek, Contumely, Cub, Effrontery, Gum, Hectoring, Hubris, Hybris, Impudence, Lip, Rude, Snash, Stroppy, Wanton

Insolvent Bankrupt, Broke, Destitute, Penniless

Inspect(ion), Inspector Ale-conner, Alnage(r), Auditor, Comb, Conner, Cook's tour, Examine, Exarch, Government, Investigator, Jerque, Keeker, Look over, Maigret, Muster, Once-over, Peep, Perlustrate, Proveditor, Rag-fair, Recce, Review, School, Scrutinise, Searcher, Supervisor, Survey, Test, Vet, Vidimus, Visitation

Inspire(d), Inspiration, Inspiring Actuate, Aerate, Afflatus, Aganippe, Animate, Brainstorm, Brainwave, Breath(e), Castalian, Draw, Elate, Exalt, Fire, Flash, Geist, Hearten, Hunch, Hwyl, Idea, Illuminate, Imbue, Impress, Impulse, Induce, Inflatus, Infuse, Inhale, Motivate, Move, Muse, Pegasus, Plenary, Prompt, Prophetic, Satori, Sniff(le), Stimulus, Stoke, Taghairm, Theopneust(y), Uplift, Vatic

Install(ation) Elect, Enchase, Enthrone, Inaugurate, Induction, Infrastructure, Insert, Invest, Put (in)

Instalment Call, Episode, Fascicle, Heft, Livraison, Never-never, Part, Serial, Tranche

Instance, Instant As, Case, Example, Flash, Jiffy, Moment, Present, Say, Shake, Spur, Tick, Trice, Twinkling, Urgent

Instead (of) Deputy, For, Lieu, Locum, Vice

Instigate, Instigating Arouse, Foment, Impel, Incite, Proactive, Prompt, Spur

Instinct(ive) Automatic, Conation, Flair, Gut, Herd, Id, Impulse, Inbred, Innate, Intuition, Knee-jerk, Life, Nature, Nose, Prim(a)eval, Reflex, Second nature, Talent, Tendency, Visceral

Institute, Institution Academy, Activate, Asylum, Bank, Begin, Bring, Charity, College, Collegiate, Create, Erect, Found(ation), Halls of ivy, I, Inaugurate, Mechanics, MORI, Organise, Orphanage, Poorhouse, Raise, Redbrick, Retract, Retrait(e), Retreat, Smithsonian, Start, Technical, University, Varsity, WI, Women's, Workhouse

Instruct(ed), Instruction, Instructor Advice, Algorithm, Apprenticeship, Brief, Catechism, Chautauquan, Clinic, Coach, Course, Didactic, Direct(ive), Document, Edify, Educate, Ground(ing), Guide, How-to, Inform, Lesson, Maharishi, Manual, Master class, Notify, Order, Patch, Pedagogue, Precept, RE, Recipe, RI, Rubric, Sensei, Statement, Swami, →**TEACH**, Train, Tutelage, Tutorial, Up

Instrument(al) Ablative, Act, Agent, Helpful, Mean(s), Measure, →**MUSICAL INSTRUMENT**, Negotiable, →**RESPONSIBLE**, →**TOOL**, →**UTENSIL**, Weapon

Insubordinate Contumacious, Faction, Mutinous, Rebel, Refractory

Insubstantial Airy, Brief, Flimsy, Frothy, Illusory, Jackstraw, Scotch mist, Slender, Slight, Syllabub, Thin, Wispy, Ye(a)sty

Insult(ing) Abuse, Affront, Aspersion, Barb, Becall, Contumely, Cut, Derogatory, Dyslogistic, Effrontery, Embarrass, Facer, Fig, Lese-majesty, Mud, Mud-pie, Offend, Opprobrious, Scurrilous, Skit, Slagging, Sledge, Slight, Slur, Snub, Trample, Trauma, Uncomplimentary, Verbal, Wazzock, Yenta, Yente

Insure(r), Insurance Abandonee, Accident, Comprehensive, Cover, Death futures, Endowment, Fire, Group, Guarantee, Hedge, Indemnity, Knock-for-knock, Life, Lloyds, Medibank, Medicaid, Medicare, Mutual, National, Policy, Public liability, Reversion, Safety net, Security, Third party, Tontine, Travel, Underwrite

Insurgent, Insurrection Cade, Mutiny, Outbreak, Rebel, Revolt, Sedition, Terrorist, Uprising

▷ **Insurgent** *may indicate* 'reversed'

Intact Complete, Entire, Inviolate, Unused, Whole

Integrate(d), Integration Amalgamate, Assimilate, Combine, Coordinate, Fuse, Harmonious, Mainstream, Merge, Postural, Synergism, Vertical

Integrity Honesty, Principle, Rectitude, Strength, Uprightness, Whole, Worth

Intellect, Intellectual(s) Academic, Aptitude, Belligerati, Brain (box), Cerebral, Chattering class, Cultural, Dianoetic, Egghead, Eggmass, Far-out, Genius, Grey matter, Highbrow, Intelligent, Intelligentsia, -ist, Learned, Literati, Luminary, Mastermind, Mental(ity), Mind, Noesis, Noetic, Noology, Nous, Pointy-headed, Profound, Reason, Sublime, Titan

Intelligence, Intelligent Advice, Artificial, Boss, Brainiac, Brains, Bright, CIA, Discerning, Dope, Eggmass, Emotional, Esprit, G, Grey matter, GRU, Guile, Humint, Info, Ingenious, IQ, Knowledgeable, Machiavellian, Machine, MI, Mossad, Mother wit, News, Pate, Perspicacity, Pointy-headed, Rational, Sconce, Sense, Sharp(-witted), Shrewd, Smart, Spetsnaz, Spetznaz, Tidings, Wit

Intend(ed), Intending Allot, Contemplate, Deliberate, Design, Destine, Ettle, Fiancé(e), Going, →MEAN, Meditate, Planned, Propose, Purpose, Think

Intense, Intensify, Intensity Acute, Aggravate, Ardent, Compound, Crash, Crescendo, Deep, Earnest, Earthquake, Emotional, Enhance, Escalate, Excess, Extreme, Fervent, Hot up, Keen, Luminous, Might, Profound, Radiant, Redouble, Saturation, Sharpen, Strong, Towering, Vehement, Vivid, Warmth

Intent, Intention(al) À dessein, Aim, Animus, Deliberate, Design, Dole, Earmark, Earnest, Ettle, Hellbent, Manifesto, Mens rea, Mind, Prepense, Purpose, Rapt, Resolute, Set, Special, Studious, Systematic, Thought, Wilful, Witting, Yrapt

Interaction Enantiodromia, Solvation, Synergy

Intercede, Intercession Mediate, Negotiate, Plead, Prayer

Intercom Entryphone®

Interdict Ban, Forbid, Prohibit, Taboo

Interest(ed), Interesting Amusive, APR, Attention, Behalf, Benefit, Care, Clou, Compound, Concern, Contango, Controlling, Coupon, Dividend, Double-bubble, Ear-grabbing, Engage, Engross, Enthusiasm, Fad, Fascinate, Fee-simple, Fee-tail, Grab, Hot, Human, Import, Income, Insurable, Int(o), Intrigue, Juicy, Landed, Life, Line, Negative, Part, Partisan, Percentage, Public, Readable, Rente, Respect, Revenue, Reversion, Riba, Riding, Scene, Sepid, Share, Side, Sideline, Simple, Spice, Stake, Tasty, Tickle, Topical, Usage, Usance, Use, Usure, Usury, Vested, Vig(orish), Warm

Interface Centronics, Spigot

Interfere(r), Interference Atmospherics, Busybody, Clutter, Disrupt, Disturb, Hamper, Hinder, Hiss, Intrude, Mar, Molest, Noise, Nose, Officious, Pry, Shash, Shot noise, Static, Tamper, Teratogen

Interim Break, Meanwhile, Temporary

Interior Backblocks, Cyclorama, Domestic, Innards, Innate, Inner, Inside, Outback, Plain, Up-country, Vitals

Interject(ion) Ahem, Begorra(h), Chime-in, Doh, Duh, Haith, Hoo-oo, Interpolate, Lackaday, Lumme, Nation, Sese(y), Sessa, 'Sheart, 'Slid, Tarnation, Tush

Interlace Mingle, Weave, Wreathe

Interloper Cowan, Gate-crasher, Intruder, Trespasser

Interlude Antimask, Antimasque, Divertimento, Entr'acte, Interruption, Kyogen, Lunch-hour, Meantime, Pause, Verset

Intermediary, Intermediate, Intermediatory Agent, Bardo, Between, Bytownite, Comprador(e), Contact man, Go-between, In-between, Instar, Mean, Medial, Mesne, Mezzanine, Middleman, Middle-of-the-road, Negotiant, Transitional

Intermission Apyrexia, Break, Interval, Pause, Recess

Intermittent Broken, Fitful, Periodic, Random, Spasmic, Spasmodic, Sporadic

Intermix, Intermingle Lace, Melting pot

Intern(e) Confine, Doctor, Impound, Restrict, Trainee

Internal Domestic, Inner, Internecine, Inward, Within

International Cap, Cosmopolitan, Fourth, Lion, Second, Trotskyist, UN, Universal

Interpret(er) Aread, Ar(r)e(e)de, Conster, Construe, Decipher, Decode, Dragoman, Exegete, Explain, Exponent, Expositor, Expound, Glossator, Hermeneutist, Jehovist, Linguistic, Linkster, Medium, Moralise, Oneiroscopist, Polyglot, Prophet, Rabbi, Rationalise, Read, Rede, Reed(e), Render, Represent, Spokesman, Subjectivity, Textualist, →TRANSLATE, Ulema

Interpretation Anagoge, Anagogy, Analysis, Cabbala(h), Construction, Copenhagen, Dittology, Eisegesis, Exegesis, Exegete, Gematria, Gloss(ary), Gospel, Halacha(h), Halakah, Hermeneutics, Kabbala(h), Midrash, Oneirocriticism, Portray, Reading, Rede, Rendition, Targum, Translation, Zohar

Interrogate, Interrogation Catechism, Corkscrew, Cross-question, Debrief(ing), Enquire, Examine, Grill, Inquisitor, Pump, →QUESTION, Quiz

Interrupt(ion), Interrupter Ahem, Blip, Break, Butt, Chequer, Chip in, Cut in, Disturb, Entr'acte, Heckle, Hiatus, Intercept, Interfere, Interject, Interlard, Interpellate, Interim, Interpolate, Interpose, Interregnum, Intrusion, Pause, Portage, Punctuate, Rheotome, Stop, Suspend, Tmesis

Intersect(ion), Intersecting Carfax, Carfox, Chiasm(a), Clover-leaf, Compital, Cross, Crunode, Cut, Decussate, Divide, Groin, Metacentre, Node, Orthocentre, Quadrivium, Trace

Intersperse Dot, Interlard, Interpose, Scatter, Sprinkle

Intertwine Braid, Knit, Lace, Plait, Splice, Twist, Wreathe, Writhe

Interval Between, Break, Breather, Class, Closed, Comma, Confidence, Diesis, Distance, Duodecimo, Entr'acte, Fifth, Gap, Half-time, Harmonic, Hiatus, Hourly, Imperfect, Interim, Interlude, Interregnum, Interruption, Interspace, Interstice, Leap, Limma, Lucid, Lull, Meantime, Meanwhile, Melodic, Minor third, Ninth, Octave, Open, Ottava, Parenthesis, Pycnon, QT, Respite, Rest, Schisma, Semitone, Seventh, Sixth, Space, Span, Spell, Third, Thirteenth, Time lag, Twelfth, Wait

Intervene, Intervening, Intervention Agency, Arbitrate, Expromission, Hypothetical, Interfere, Interjacent, Interrupt, Intromit, Mediate, Mesne, Step in, Theurgy, Up

Interview Audience, Audition, Conference, Debriefing, Examine, Hearing, Oral, Press conference, See, Vox pop

Interweave, Interwoven, Interwove Complect, Entwine, Interlace, Monogram, Plait, Plash, Pleach, Raddle, Splice, Wreathed

Intestinal, Intestine(s) Bowel, Chit(ter)lings, Derma, Duodenum, Enteric, Entrails, Guts, Harigals, Innards, Jejunum, Kishke, Large, Mesenteron, Omenta, Rectum, Small, Splanchnic, Thairm, Tripes, Viscera

In the club Gravid, Pregnant, Up the spout

Intimacy, Intimate(ly) Achates, À deux, Boon, Bosom, Close, Communion, Confidante, Connote, Familiar, Far ben, Friend, Hint, Inmost, Innuendo, Intrigue, Nearness, Opine, Pack, Private, Signal, Special, Thick, Throng, Warm, Well

Intimidate, Intimidating Browbeat, Bulldoze, Bully, Cow, Daunt, Dragon, Hector, Menace, Overawe, Psych, Scare, Threaten, Unnerve

Intolerant, Intolerable Allergic, Bigotry, Egregious, Excessive, Illiberal, Impatient, Impossible, Insupportable, Ombrophobe, Redneck, Self-righteous

Intone, Intonation Cadence

Intoxicate(d), Intoxicant, Intoxicating, Intoxication Bhang, Crink, Half-cut, Krunk, La-la land, Methystic, Narcotise, Nitrogen narcosis, Potent, Rapture of the deep, Shroom, Swacked, The narks, Zonked

Intractable Disobedient, Kittle, Mulish, Obdurate, Perverse, Surly, Unruly, Wilful

Intransigent Adamant, Inflexible, Rigid, Uncompromising

Intravenous IV

Intrepid(ity) Aweless, Bold, Bottle, Brave, Dauntless, Doughty, Fearless, Firm, →**RESOLUTE**, Stout, Unafraid, Undaunted, Valiant

Intricate Complex, Crinkum-crankum, Daedal(ian), Daedale, Dedal, Gordian, Intrince, Involute, Knotty, Parquetry, Pernickety, Tricky, Vitruvian

Intrigue(r), Intriguing Affaire, Artifice, Brigue, Cabal, Camarilla, Cloak and dagger, Collogue, Conspiracy, Fascinate, Hotbed, Ignatian, Interest, Jesuit, Jobbery, Liaison, Machinate, Plot, Politic, Rat, →**SCHEME**, Stairwork, Strategy, Traffic, Trinketer, Web

▷ **Intrinsically** *may indicate* something within a word

Introduce(r), Introduction, Introductory Acquaint, Alap, Anacrusis, Code name, Curtain-raiser, Debut, Emcee, Enseam, Entrée, Exordial, Foreword, Immit, Import, Induct, Initiate, Inject, Insert, Instil(l), Institutes, Intercalate, Interpolate, Introit, Isagogic, Lead-in, Lead up, Opening, Plant, Preamble, Preface, Preliminary, Prelude, Prelusory, Preparatory, Present, Proem, Prolegomena, Prolegomenon, Prolog, Prologue, Prooemium, Proponent, Referral, Start, Usher

▷ **Introduction** *may indicate* a first letter

▷ **In trouble** *may indicate* an anagram

Intrude(r), Intrusion, Intrusive Abate, Aggress, Annoy, Bother, Burglar, Derby dog, →**ENCROACH**, Gatecrash, Inroad, Interloper, Invade, Lopolith, Meddle, Nosey, Personal, Porlocking, Presume, Raid, Sorn, Trespass

In truth En verite

Intuition, Intuitive Belief, ESP, Hunch, Insight, Instinct, Noumenon, Premonition, Seat-of-the-pants, Telepathy

Inturn(ing) Trichiasis

▷ **In two words** *may indicate* a word to be split

Inundate, Inundation Engulf, Flood, Overflow, Overwhelm, Submerge, Swamp

Inure Acclimatise, Accustom, Harden, Season, Steel

Invade(r), Invasion Angle, Attack, Attila, Dane, Descent, Encroach, Goth, Hacker, Hengist, Horsa, Hun, Incursion, Infest, Inroad, Intruder, Jute, Lombard, Martian, Norman, Norsemen, Occupation, Ostrogoth, Overrun, Permeate, Raid, Trespass, Vandal, Viking

In vain No go

Invalid(ate), Invalidation Bad, Bogus, Bunbury, Cancel, Chronic, Clinic, Defunct, Diriment, Erroneous, Expired, False, Inauthentic, Inform, Inoperative, Irritate, Lapsed, Nugatory, Null, Nullify, Overturn, Quash, Refute, Shut-in, Terminate, Vitiate, Void

Invaluable Essential, Excellent, Precious, Useful

Invariable, Invariably Always, Constant, Eternal, Habitual, Perpetual, Steady, Uniform

Invective Abuse, Billingsgate, Diatribe, Philippic, Reproach, Ribaldry, Tirade

Inveigle Charm, Coax, Entice, Persuade, Subtrude

Invent(ion), Inventive Adroit, Babe, Baby, Brainchild, Chimera, Coin, Concept, Contrive, Cook up, →**CREATE**, Creed, Daedal, Design, Device, Dream up, Embroider, Excogitate, Fabricate, Fain, Fantasia, Feign, Fiction, Figment, Imaginary, Improvise, Independent, Ingenuity, Make up, Mint, Myth, Originate, Patent, Plateau, Pretence, Resourceful, Synectics, Whittle, Wit

Inventor Artificer, Author, Coiner, Creator, Engineer, Idea-hamster, Mint-master, Patentee

Inventory Account, Index, Itemise, List, Register, Stock, Terrier

Inverse, Inversion, Invert(ed) Arch, Back to front, Capsize, Chiasmus, Entropion, Entropium, Lid, Opposite, Overset, Reciprocal, Retrograde, Reverse, Turn, Upset, Upside down

Invertebrate Acanthocephalan, Annelida, Anthozoan, Arthropod, Brachiopod, Chaetognath, Crinoid, Ctenophore, Decapod, Echinoderm, Echinoid, Entoprocta, Euripterid, Feather star, Gast(e)ropod, Globigerina, Holothurian, Hydrozoan, Lobopod, Mollusc, Nacre, Onychophoran, Parazoan, Pauropod, Peritrich, Platyhelminth, Polyp, Poriferan, Protostome, Rotifer, Roundworm, Scyphozoan, Sea-cucumber, Sea-lily, →SHELLFISH, Slug, Spineless, Sponge, Spoonworm, Starfish, Tardigrade, Trepang, Trochelminth, Trochophore, Water bear, Worm, Zoophyte

▷ **Invest** *may indicate* one word surrounding another

Invest(or), Investment Ambient, Angel, Beleaguer, Besiege, Bet, Blockade, Blue-chip, Bond, Bottom-fisher, Capitalist, Clothe, Contrarian, Dignify, Dub, Embark, Enclothe, Endow, Enrobe, Ethical, Financier, Flutter, Gilt, Girt, Gross, Holding, Infeft, Install, Inward, On, Pannicle, Parlay, Place, Portfolio, Put, Retiracy, Ring, Robe, Saver, Share, Siege, Sink, Smart money, Spec, Speculation, Stag, Stake, Stock, Tessa, Tie up, Trochophore, Trojan War, Trust, Trustee, Venture

Investigate, Investigator, Investigation Analyse, Audit, Canvass, Case, CID, Delve, DI, Enquire, Examine, Explore, Fact-find, Fed, Fieldwork, Going over, Gumshoe, Hunt, Inquest, Inquirendo, Inquiry, Inquisition, McCarthyism, Nose, Organon, Organum, Probe, Prodnose, Pry, Quester, Rapporteur, Research, Scan, Scrutinise, Search, Sleuth, Snoop, Study, Suss, Tec, Test, T-man, Track, Try, Zetetic

Inveterate Chronic, Dyed-in-the-wool, Habitual, Hardened

Invidious Harmful, Hostile, Malign

Invigorate, Invigorating, Invigoration Analeptic, Animate, Brace, Brisk, Cheer, Crispy, Elixir, Energise, Enliven, Fortify, Insinew, Pep, Refresh, Renew, Stimulate, Tonic, Vital

Invincible Almighty, Brave, Stalwart, Valiant

Invisible Blind, Hidden, Imageless, Infra-red, Secret, Tusche, Unseen

Invite, Invitation, Inviting Ask, Attract, Bid, Call, Card, Overture, →REQUEST, Solicit, Stiffie, Summons, Tempt, Woo

Invocation, Invoke Appeal, Begorra, Call, Conjure, Curse, Entreat, Epiclesis, Solicit, White rabbits

Invoice Account, Bill, Itemise, Manifest, Pro forma

Involve(d), Involvement Active, Close knit, Commitment, Complicate, Complicit, Concern, Deep, Embroil, Engage, Enlace, Entail, Entangle, Envelop, Imbroglio, Immerse, →IMPLICATE, Include, Intricate, Knee-deep, Meet, Necessitate, Tangle, Tortuous, Tricksy

▷ **Involved** *may indicate* an anagram

Inward(s) Afferent, Homefelt, Introrse, Mental, Private, Varus, Within

Iolanthe Peri

Iota Atom, Jot, Subscript, Whit

IOU Cedula, Market, PN, Vowels

Iran(ian) Babist, Kurd, Mede, Pahlavi, Parsee, Pehlevi, Persic

Irascible Choleric, Crusty, Fiery, Grouchy, Peevish, Quick-tempered, Snappy, Tetchy

Irate Angry, Cross, Infuriated, Wrathful

Ire Anger, Cholera, Fury, Rage, Wrath

Irenic Peaceful

Iridescence, Iridescent Chatoyant, Opaline, Reflet, Shimmering, Shot, Water-gall

Iris Areola, Eye, Flag, Fleur-de-lis, Florence, Gladdon, Gladioli, Ixia, Lily, Lis, Orris, Rainbow, Sedge, Seg, Sunbow, Triandria, Uvea, Water flag

Irish(man) Bark, Bog-trotter, Boy, Bucko, Celt(ic), Clan-na-gael, Declan, Defender, Dermot, Dubliner, Eamon(n), Eirann, Eoin, Erse, Fenian, Gaeltacht, Goidel,

Greek, Hibernian, Jackeen, Keltic, Kern(e), Mick(e)(y), Milesian, Mulligan, Ogamic, Orange(man), Ostmen, Paddy(-whack), Partholon, Pat(rick), Rapparee, Redshank, Reilly, Riley, Rory, Sean, Shoneen, Teague, Ultonian

Iron(s), Ironstone, Ironwork(s) Airn, Alpha, Angle, Beta, Bloom, Branding, Carron, Cast, Cautery, Chains, Chalybeate, Chancellor, Channel, Climbing, Coquimbite, Corrugated, Cramp(on), Crimp, Cross, Curling, Curtain, Delta, Derringer, Dogger, Dogs, Driving, Eagle-stone, Even, Fayalite, Fe, Ferredoxin, Ferrite, Fetter, Fiddley, Flip-dog, Galvanised, Gamma, Gem, Golfclub, Goose, Grappling, Grim, Grozing, →GUN, Gyve, Horse, Ingot, Italian, Kamacite, Laterite, Lily, Lofty, Long, Maiden, Malleable, Marcasite, Mars, Martensite, Mashie, Mashy, Merchant, Meteoric, Mitis (metal), Pea, Pig, Pinking, →PRESS, Pro-metal, Rabble, Rations, Rod, Sad, Scrap, Shooting, Short, Smoother, Soft, Soldering, Spathic, Specular, Speeler, Spiegeleisen, Steam, Stirrup, Stretching, Strong, Taconite, Taggers, Terne, Tin terne, Toggle, Tow, Turfing, Wafer, Waffle, Wear, Wedge, White, Wrought

Ironic, Irony Antiphrasis, Asteism, Dramatic, Meiosis, Metal, Ridicule, Sarcasm, Satire, Socratic, Tongue-in-cheek, Tragic, Trope, Wry

▶ **Ironwork(s)** *see* IRON(S)

Irrational Absurd, Brute, Delirious, Doolally, Foolish, Illogical, Squirrelly, Superstitious, Surd, Wild, Zany

▷ **Irregular** *may indicate* an anagram

Irregular(ity) Abnormal, Anomaly, A salti, Asymmetric, Bashi-bazouk, Blotchy, Carlylean, Casual, Crazy, Eccentric, Ectopic, Episodic, Erratic, Evection, Fitful, Flawed, Formless, Glitch, Guerilla, Heteroclitic, Incondite, Inordinate, Intermittent, Jitter, Kink, Occasional, Orthotone, Para-military, Partisan, Patchy, Random, Rough, Scalene, Scraggy, Sebundy, Solecism, Sporadic, Strange, TA, Uneven, Unorthodox, Unsteady, Variable, Wayward, Zigzag

Irrelevant Digression, Gratuitous, Immaterial, Inapplicable, Inconsequent, Inept, Pointless, Ungermane

Irreproachable Blameless, Spotless, Stainless

Irresistible Almighty, Endearing, Inevitable, Mesmeric, Overwhelming

Irresolute, Irresolution Doubtful, Hesitant, Timid, Unsure, Wavery

Irresponsible Capricious, Feckless, Flighty, Free spirit, Gallio, Reckless, Skittish, Slap-happy, Strawen, Trigger-happy, Wanton, Wildcat

Irreverent Disrespectful, Godless, Impious, Profane

Irrigate, Irrigation Colonic, Drip, Enema, Flood, Water

Irritable, Irritability, Irritant, Irritate(d), Irritation Acerbate, Anger, Annoy, Bête noire, Bile, Blister, Bother, Bug, Chafe, Chauff, Chippy, Chocker, Choleric, Crabbit, Crabby, Cross-grained, Crosspatch, Crotchety, Crusty, Dod, Dyspeptic, Eat, Eczema, Edgy, Emboil, Enchafe, Erethism, Ewk, Exasperate, Eyestrain, Fantod, Feverish, Fiery, Fleabite, Frabbit, Fractious, Fraught, Fretful, Gall, Get (to), Gnat, Goad, Grate, Gravel, Hasty, Heck, Hoots, Humpy, Impatience, Intertrigo, Irk, Itch, Jangle, Livery, Mardy, Narky, Needle, Nerk, Nettle, Niggly, Ornery, Peckish, Peevish, Peppery, Pesky, Pestilent(ial), Pet, Petulance, Pinprick, Pique, Prickly, Provoke, Rag'd, Ragde, Rankle, Rasp, Rattle, Ratty, Rile, Riley, Roil, Rub, Ruffle, Savin(e), Scratchy, Shirty, Snappy, Snit, Snitchy, Sore, Splenetic, Sting, Tease, Techy, Testy, Tetchy, Thorn, Tickle, Tiresome, Toey, Touchy, Uptight, →VEX, Waxy, Windburn

▷ **Irritated** *may indicate* an anagram

Islam(ic) Crescent, Druse, Druz(e), Kurd(ish), Pillars, Salafism, Sanusi, Senus(si), Sheriat, Shia(h), Shiite, Wah(h)abi

Island, Isle(t) Ait, Archipelago, Atoll, Cay, Char, Desert, Eyot, Floating, Heat, Holm, I, Inch, Is, Key, Lagoon, Motu, Refuge, Traffic

Isn't Aint, Nis, Nys

Isolate(d) Alienate, Ancress, Backwater, Cut off, Desolate, Enclave, Enisle, Exclude, Incommunicado, Inisle, In vacuo, Island, Lone, Lonely, Maroon, Outlying, Pocket, Quarantine, Sea-girt, Seclude, Secret, Segregate, Separate, Sequester, Sequestration, Set apart, Six-finger country, Solitary, Sporadic, Stray

Isopod Gribble

Isotope | 226

Isotope Actinon, Cobalt-60, Deuterium, Muonium, Protium, Radiothorium, Strontium-90, Thoron, Tritium

Issue(s) Bonus, Capitalization, Children, Come, Crux, Debouch, Denouement, Derive, Disclose, Dispense, Edition, Effluence, Egress, Emerge, Emit, Escape, Exit, Exodus, Family, Feigned, Fiduciary, Flotation, Fungible, General, Government, Gush, Handout, Immaterial, Ish, Litter, Material, Matter, Mise, Number, Offspring, Outcome, Outflow, Part, Privatization, Proof, Publish, Release, Result, Rights, Sally, Scion, Scrip, Seed, Side, Son, Spawn, Special, Spring, Stream, Subject, Topic, Turn, Utter

Isthmus Darien, Karelian, Kra, Neck, Panama, Suez

It A, Chic, Hep, Hip, Id, Italian, Oomph, SA, Same, Sex appeal, 't, Vermouth

Italian, Italy Alpini, Ausonian, Bolognese, Calabrian, Chian, Dago, Ding, Este, Etnean, Etrurian, Etruscan, Eyeti(e), Eytie, Faliscan, Florentine, Genoese, Ghibelline, Guelf, Guelph, Hesperia, Irredentist, It, Latian, Latin, Lombard, Medici, Milanese, Moro, Oscan, Paduan, Patarin(e), Roman, Sabine, Samnite, Sicel, Sienese, Signor(i), Sikel, Spag, Tuscan, Umbrian, Venetian, Vermouth, Volscian, Wop

Itch(ing), Itchiness Annoy, Burn, Cacoethes, Dhobi, Heat rash, Hives, Prickle, Prickly heat, Prurience, Prurigo, Pruritis, Psora, Scabies, Scrapie, Seven-year, Swimmer's, Tickle, →URGE, Yen

Item(ise) Also, Article, Bulletin, Couple, Detail, Entry, Equipment, Flash, Line, List, Note, Number, Pair, Piece, Point, Spot, Talking point, Too, Topic, Twosome, Unit

Itinerant, Itinerary Ambulant, Didakai, Didakei, Did(d)icoy, Dusty Feet, Gipsy, Gypsy, Journey, Log, Pedlar, Peripatetic, Pie-powder, Roadman, Roamer, Romany, Rootless, Route, Stroller, Traveller, Vagrom, Wayfarer

Ivory (tower) Bone, Chryselephantine, Dentine, Distant, Eburnean, Impractical, Incisor, Key, Solitude, Teeth, Tusk, Vegetable

Ivy Ale-hoof, Aralia, Boston, Bush, Climber, Creeper, Grape, Hedera, Helix, Japanese, Poison, Rhoicissus, Shield, Sweetheart, Weeping

Izzard Z

Jj

Jab(ber) Chatter, Foin, Gabble, Immunise, Immunologist, Inject, Jaw, Jook, Nudge, Peck, Poke, Prattle, Prod, Proke, Punch, Puncture, Sook, Sputter, Stab, Venepuncture, Yak

Jack(s) AB, Apple, Ass, Ball, Boot, Bowl(s), Boy, Cade, Card, Cheap, Coatcard, Crevalle, Deckhand, Dibs(tones), Five stones, Flag, Frost, Giant-killer, Hoist, Honour, Horner, Hydraulic, Idle, J, Jock, Jumping, Ketch, Kitty, Knave, Lazy, London, Loord, Lout, Lumber, Maker, Mark, Matlow, Mistress, Nob, Noddy, Pilot, Point, Pot, Pur, Rabbit, Raise, Rating, Ripper, Roasting, Robinson, Russell, Sailor, Salt, Screw, Seafarer, Seaman, Sprat, Spring-heeled, Springtail, Steeple, Sticker, Straw, Tar, Tee, Tradesman, Turnspit, Union, Uplift, Wood, Yellow

Jacket Acton, Afghanistan, Air, Amauti(k), Anorak, Atigi, Baju, Bania(n), Banyan, Barbour®, Basque, Battle, Bed, Biker, Blazer, Blouse, Blouson, Body-warmer, Bolero, Bomber, Brigandine, Bumfreezer, Bush, Cagoul(e), Camisole, Cardigan, Carmagnole, Casing, →**COAT**, Combat, Cover, Dinner, Dolman, Donkey, Drape, Dressing, Dressing-sack, Duffel coat, Duffle coat, Dust-cover, Dustwrapper, Duvet, Fearnought, Flak, Fleece, Gambeson, Gendarme, Grego, Habergeon, Hacking, Half-kirtle, Ha(c)queton, Hug-me-tight, Jerkin, Jupon, Kagool, Life, Life preserver, Lumber, Mackinaw, Mae West, Mandarin, Mao, Matinée, Mess, Monkey, Nehru, Newmarket, Norfolk, Parka, Pea, Pilot, Polka, Potato, Pyjama, Reefer, Roundabout, Sackcoat, Safari, Shell, Shooting, Shortgown, Simar(re), Slip-cover, Smoking, Spencer, Sports, Steam, Strait, Sweatshirt, Tabard, Tailcoat, Toreador, Tunic, Tux(edo), Tweed, Vareuse, Waistcoat, Wampus, Wam(m)us, Water, Waxed, Windbreaker®, Windcheater, Windjammer, Wrapper, Zouave

Jackknife Dive, Fold, Jockteleg, Pike

Jacob Epstein, Ladder, Sheep

Jade(d) Axe-stone, Cayuse, Cloy, Crock, Exhaust, Fatigue, Greenstone, Hack, Hag, Horse, Hussy, Limmer, Minx, Nag, Nephrite, Sate, Screw, Slut, Stale, Tired, Trite, Weary, Yu(-stone)

Jaeger Skua

Jag(ged) Barbed, Cart, Drinking, Erose, Gimp, Hackly, Injection, Laciniate, Ragde, Ragged, Serrate, Snag, Spree, Spur, Tooth

Jaguar Car, Caracal, Cat, E-type, Ounce, Tiger

Jail(er) Adam, Alcatraz, Bastille, Bedford, Bin, Can, Clink, Cooler, Gaol, Hoosegow, Imprison, Incarcerate, Jug, Keeper, Limbo, Lockup, Marshalsea, Newgate, Nick, Pen, Pokey, Porridge, →**PRISON**, Screw, Shop, Strangeways, Turnkey, Warder

Jailbird Con, Lag, Lifer, Trusty

Jalopy Banger, Boneshaker, Buggy, Car, Crate, Heap, Stock-car

Jam(my) Block, Choke, Clog, Confiture, Crowd, Crush, Cushy, Damson, Dilemma, Extra, Fix, Gridlock, Hold-up, Hole, How d'ye do, Improvise, Jeelie, Jeely, Lock, Log, Pack, Paper, Plight, →**PREDICAMENT**, Preserve, Press, Quince, Rat run, Rush hour, Seize, Snarl-up, Spot, Squeeze, Standstill, Stick, Tailback, Traffic, Vice, Vise, Wedge

Jamb Doorpost, Durn, Sconcheon, Scontion, Scuncheon, Upright

Jane Austen, Calamity, Eyre, Seymour, Shore, Sian

Jangle Clank, Clapperclaw, Clash, Rattle, Wrangle

Japan(ese), Japanese drama Ainu, Burakumin, Daimio, Eta, Finish, Geisha, Genro, Gloss, Gook, Haiku, Heian, Hondo, Honshu, Issei, Japlish, Kabuki, Kami, Kana, Kirimon, Lacquer, Mandarin, Mikado, Mousmé, Mousmee, Nihon, Nip,

Jar(ring) | 228

Nippon, Nisei, No(h), Resin, Sansei, Satsuma, Shinto, Shogun, Taisho, Togo, Tycoon, Yamato, Yellow peril

Jar(ring) Albarello, Amphora, Bell, Canopus, Churr, Clash, Crock, Cruet, Din, Dolium, Enrough, Gallipot, Gas, Grate, Greybeard, Gride, Grind, Gryde, Humidor, Hydria, →**JOLT**, Kalpis, Kang, Kilner®, Leyden, Mason, Monkey, Off-key, Olla, Pint, Pithos, Pot(iche), Rasp, Rock, Screwtop, Shake, Shelta, Shock, Stamnos, Start, Stave, Stean, Steen, Stein, Tankard, Terrarium, Tinaja, Turn, Vessel, Water-monkey

Jargon Argot, Baragouin, Beach-la-mar, Buzzword, Cant, Chinese, Chinook, Cyberspeak, Eurobabble, Eurospeak, Geekspeak, Gobbledegook, Gobbledygook, Jive, Kennick, Legalese, Lingo, Lingoa geral, Lingua franca, Mumbo-jumbo, Netspeak, Newspeak, Parlance, Patois, Patter, Shelta, Shoptalk, →**SLANG**, Sociologese, Technospeak, Vernacular

Jargoon Chinook

Jaundice(d) Cholestasis, Cynical, Icterus, Prejudiced, Sallow, Yellow

Jaunt Journey, Outing, Sally, Stroll, Swan, Trip

Jaunty Airy, Akimbo, Chipper, Debonair, Perky, Rakish

▷ **Jaunty** may indicate an anagram

Javelin Dart, Gavelock, Harpoon, Jereed, Jerid, Pile, Pilum, Spear

Jaw(s), Jawbone Blab, Chaft, Chap, Chat, Chaw, Cheek, Chide, Chin, Confab, Entry, Gills, Glass, Gnathite, Gonion, Jabber, Jobe, Kype, Lantern, Mandible, Maxilla, Mesial, Muzzle, Mylohyoid, Natter, Opisthognathous, Overbite, Overshot, Phossy, Pi, Premaxillary, Prognathous, Ramus, Shark, Stylet, Underhung, Undershot, Wapper-jaw, Ya(c)kety-Ya(c)k

Jazz(er), Jazzman Acid, Afro-Cuban, Barber, Barrelhouse, Bebop, Blues, Boogie, Boogie-woogie, Bop, Cat, Coleman, Cool, Dixieland, Enliven, Free, Funky, Gig, Gutbucket, High life, Hipster, Jam, Jive, Kansas City, Latin, Lick, Mainstream, Modern, New Wave, Nouvelle Vague, Progressive, Ragtime, Riff, Scat, Skiffle, Slap base, Stomp, Stride, Swinger, Tailgate, Trad, Traditional

Jealous(y) Envious, Green(-eyed), Grudging, Zelotypia

Jeer(ing) Barrack, Belittle, Birl, Boo, Burl, Digs, Fleer, Flout, Frump, Gird, Heckle, Hoot, Jape, Jibe, →**MOCK**, Rail, Razz, Ridicule, Scoff, Sneer, Taunt

Jehovah God, Lord, Yahve(h), Yahwe(h)

Jelly Agar(-agar), Aspic, Brawn, Calf's foot, Chaudfroid, Comb, Cranberry, →**EXPLOSIVE**, Flummery, Gel, Isinglass, Jam, K-Y®, Liquid paraffin, Meat, Medusa, Mineral, Mould, Napalm, Petrolatum, Petroleum, Royal, Sterno®, Vaseline®

▷ **Jelly** may indicate an anagram

Jellyfish Aurelia, Box, Cnidaria, Hydrozoa, Medusa, Nettlefish, Physalia, Portuguese man-of-war, Sea-blubber, Sea-nettle, Sea-wasp

Jenny Ass, Lind, Mule, Spinner, Spinster, Wren

Jeopardise, Jeopardy Danger, Expose, Hazard, Peril, Risk

Jerk(y), Jerkily, Jerking, Jerks Aerobics, A salti, Bob, Braid, Cant, Diddle, Ebrillade, Flirt, Flounce, Gym(nastics), Hike, Hitch, Hoi(c)k, Idiot, Jigger, Jut, Kant, PE, Peck, Physical, Saccade, Shove, Shrug, Spasm, Start, Surge, Switch, Sydenham's chorea, Tic, Toss(en), Tweak, →**TWITCH**, Wrench, Yank

Jerry, Jerry-built Boche, Flimsy, Fritz, Hun, Kraut, Lego, Mouse, Po(t), Slop-built

Jersey(s) Bailiwick, Cow, Football, Frock, Gansey, Guernsey, Kine, Lily, Maillot, Polo, Potato, Roll-neck, Singlet, →**SWEATER**, Sweatshirt, V-neck, Yellow, Zephyr

Jest(er), Jesting Badinage, Barm, Buffoon, Clown, Cod, Comic, Droll, Gleek, Humorist, Jape, Joculator, Joker, Josh, Miller, Mot, Motley, Patch, Quip, Raillery, Ribaldry, Ribaudry, Rigoletto, Sport, Toy, Wag, Waggery, Wit, Yorick

Jesus →**CHRIST**, Emmanuel, IHS, INRI, Jabers, Lord

Jet, Jet lag Airbus®, Aircraft, Beadblast, Black, Burner, Chirt, Douche, Executive, Fountain, Geat, Harrier, Jumbo, Plane, Pump, Sable, Sandblast, Sloe, Soffione, Spirt, Spout, Spray, Spurt, Squirt, Stream, Time-zone disease, Time-zone fatigue, Turbine, Turbo, Vapour

Jettison Discard, Dump, Flotsam, Jetsam, Lagan, Ligan

Jew(ish), Jews Ashkenazi, Chas(s)id, Diaspora, Essene, Falasha, Has(s)id,

Haskala(h), Hebrew, Hellenist, Hemerobaptist, Kahal, Karaite, Kike, Ladino, Levite, Lubavitch, Maccabee, Mitnag(g)ed, Nicodemus, Pharisee, Sadducee, Semite, Sephardim, Shemite, Shtetl, Tobit, Wandering, Yid(dish)

Jeweller(y), Jewel(s) Agate, Aigrette, Almandine, Artwear, Beryl, Bijouterie, Bling(-bling), Brilliant, Cameo, Chrysoprase, Cloisonné, Coral, Cornelian, Costume, Crown, Diamond, Earbob, Ear-drop, Emerald, Ewe-lamb, Fabergé, Fashion, Ferron(n)ière, Finery, Garnet, →**GEM**, Girandole, Gracchi, Jade, Junk, Lherzolite, Locket, Marcasite, Navette, Olivine, Opal, Parure, Paste, Pavé, Pearl, Pendant, Peridot, Rivière, Rock, Rubin(e), Ruby, Sapphire, Sard, Scarab, Smaragd, Solitaire, Stone, Sunburst, Taonga, Tiara, Tiffany, Tom, Tomfoolery, Topaz, Torc, Treasure, Trinket

Jib Ba(u)lk, Boggle, Face, Foresail, Genoa, Milk, Reest, Resist, Sideswipe, Stay-sail

Jibe Barb, Bob, Correspond, Crack, Fling, Gleek, →**JEER**, Mock, Sarcasm, Slant, Taunt

Jig(gle) Bob, Bounce, Dance, Fling, Frisk, Hornpipe, Jog, Juggle

Jilt(ed) Discard, Lorn, Reject, Shed, Throw-over

Jingle(r) Clerihew, Clink, Ditty, Doggerel, Rhyme, Tambourine, Tinkle

Jinx Curse, Hex, Jonah, Kibosh, Spoil, Voodoo, Whammy

Jitter(s), Jittery Coggly, DT, Fidgets, Funk, Jumpy, Nervous, Willies

▷ **Jitter(s)** *may indicate* an anagram

▷ **Job** *may indicate* the biblical character

Job(bing), Jobs Appointment, Assignment, Berth, Career, Chore, Comforter, Crib, Darg, Desk, Duty, Earner, Errand, Gig, Gut, Homer, Inside, Métier, Mission, Occupation, Oratorio, Paint, Parergon, Patient, Pensum, Plum, Position, Post, Problem, Put-up, Sinecure, Spot, Steady, →**TASK**, Ticket, Trotter, Truck, Undertaking, Work

Jockey Carr, Cheat, Diddle, Eddery, Horseman, Jostle, Jump, Lester, Manoeuvre, Mouse, Piggott, Rider, Steve, Swindle, Trick, Video, Vie, Winter

▷ **Jockey** *may indicate* an anagram

Jocose, Jocular, Jocund Cheerful, Debonair, Facete, Facetious, Jesting, Lepid, Scurril(e), Waggish

Joe(y), Joseph Addison, Dogsbody, GI, Kangaroo, Pal, Roo, Sloppy, Stalin, Surface, Trey

Jog(ger), Joggle, Jog-trot Arouse, Canter, Dunch, Dunsh, Heich-how, Heigh-ho, Hod, Jiggle, Jolt, Jostle, Mnemonic, Mosey, Nudge, Prompt, Ranke, Refresh, Remind, Run, Shake, Shog, Tickle, Trot, Whig

Johannesburg Jozi

Johnny-come-lately Upstart

Join(er), Joined, Joining Accompany, Add, Affix, Alligate, Amalgamate, Annex, Associate, Attach, Bond, Brad, Cabinet-maker, Club, Cold-well, Combine, Confluent, Conglutinate, Conjunct, Connect, Cope, →**COUPLE**, Dovetail, Engraft, Enlist, Enrol, Enter, Entrant, Entrist, Fay, Fuse, Glue, Graft, Include, Inosculate, Interconnect, Link, Marry, Meet, Member, Merge, Mix, Pin, Push fit, Rabbet, Regelation, Rivet, Seam, Sew, Solder, Splice, Staple, Stick, Tack-weld, Tenon, Toenail, Together, Unite, Wed, Weld, Wire, Yoke

Joint(ed) Ankle, Bar, Butt, Capillary, Carpus, Chine, Clip, Co, Cogging, Collar, Colonial goose, Compression, Conjunction, Coursing, Cuit, Cup and ball, Cut, Dive, Dovetail, Drumstick, Elbow, Entrecôte, False, First, Fish, Genu, Haunch, Heel, Hinge, Hip, Hough, Housing, Huck, J, Joggle, Jolly, Junction, Knee, Knuckle, Loin, Marijuana, Meat, Mitre, Mortise, Mutton, Phalange, Phalanx, Pin, Push-fit, Rabbet, Rack, Reefer, Ribroast, Roast, Saddle, Scarf, Seam, Second, Shoulder, Silverside, Sirloin, Soaker, Splice, Stifle, Straight, Strip, Synchondrosis, Syndesmosis, T, Tarsus, T-bone, Temperomandibular, Tenon, Together, Toggle, Tongue and groove, Topside, Trochite, Undercut, Union, Universal, Water, Wedging, Weld, Wrist

Joist Bar, Beam, Dormant, Ground plate, Groundsill, I-beam, Rib, Sleeper, Solive, String

Joke(r), Joke-book, Joking Banter, Bar, Baur, Bawr, Boff, Booby-trap, Card, Chaff, Chestnut, →**CLOWN**, Cod, Comedian, Comic, Crack, Cut-up, Facete,

Farceur, Farceuse, Fool, Fun, Funster, Gab, Gag, Glike, Guy, Have-on, Hazer, Hoax, Hum, Humorist, In fun, Jape, Jest, Jig, Jocular, Josh, Knock-knock, Lark, Legpull, Merry-andrew, Merryman, One-liner, Practical, Prank(ster), Pun, Punchline, Quip, Rag, Rib-tickler, Rot, Sally, Scherzo, Sick, Skylark, Squib, Standing, Throwaway, Tongue-in-cheek, Wag, Wheeze, Wild, Wisecrack, Wit

Jollity, Jolly, Jollification 'Arryish, Bally, Beano, Bright, Cheerful, Convivial, Cordial, Do, Festive, Galoot, Gaucie, Gaucy, Gawcy, Gawsy, Gay, Hilarious, Jocose, Jovial, Marine, Mirth, Rag, Revel, RM, Roger, Sandboy, Sight, Tar, Trip, Very

Jolt(ing) Bump, Jar, Jig-a jig, Jog(gle), Jostle, Jounce, Jumble, Shake, Shog, Start

▶**Joseph** *see* **JOE(Y)**

Josh Chaff, Kid, Rib, Tease

Jostle Barge, Bump, Compete, Elbow, Hustle, Jockey, Push, Shoulder, Throng

Journal Band(e), Blog, Chronicle, Daily, Daybook, Diary, E-zine, Gazette, Hansard, Lancet, Log, Mag, Organ, Paper, Periodical, Pictorial, Punch, Rag, Record, Reuter, Trade, Waste book, Webzine

Journalism, Journalist Cheque-book, Columnist, Commentariat, Contributor, Diarist, Ed, Fleet St, Freelance, (GA) Sala, Gazetteer, Gonzo, Hack, Hackery, Hackette, Interviewer, Investigative, Keyhole, Leader-writer, Lobby, Marat, Muckraker, Newshound, Newsman, Northcliffe, NUJ, Penny-a-liner, Pepys, Press(man), Reporter, Reviewer, Scribe, Sob sister, Stead, Stringer, Wireman, →**WRITER**, Yellow

Journey Bummel, Circuit, Cruise, Errand, Expedition, Eyre, Foray, Hadj, Jaunce, Jaunse, Jaunt, Lift, Long haul, Mush, Odyssey, Passage, Peregrination, Periegesis, Ply, Raik, Rake, Red-eye, Ride, Round trip, Run, Sabbath-day's, Sentimental, Soup run, Step, Swag, Tour, Travel, Trek, Trip, Voyage, Walkabout

Journeyman Artisan, Commuter, Craftsman, Sterne, Trekker, Yeoman

Joust Pas d'armes, Tilt, Tiltyard, Tournament, Tourney

Jovial Bacchic, Boon, Convivial, Cordial, Festive, Genial, Jolly

Joy(ful), Joyous Ah, Blithe, Charmian, Cheer, →**DELIGHT**, Dream, Ecstasy, Elation, Exulting, Fain, Felicity, Festal, Frabjous, Glad, Glee, Gloat, Groove, Hah, Hey, Jubilant, Nirvana, Rapture, Schadenfreude, Sele, Tra-la, Transport, Treat, Yahoo, Yay, Yippee

Joyrider Twoccer

Jubilant, Jubilation, Jubilee Celebration, Cock-a-hoop, Diamond, Ecstatic, Elated, Holiday, Joy, Triumphant

Judas Double-crosser, Traitor, Tree

Judder Put-put, Shake, Vibrate

Judge(ment), Judges Absolute, Adjudicator, Arbiter, Assess, Assize, Award, Believe, Calculate, Chancellor, Chief Justice, Connoisseur, Consider, Coroner, Court, Critic(ise), Dayan, Decide, Dempster, Dies irae, Dies non, Estimate, Evaluate, Faisal, Gauge, Guess, Hearing, Honour, Interlocutor, J, Justice, Kadi, Line, Lord Chief Justice, Opinion, Provisional, Puisne, Ragnarok, Reckon(ing), Recorder, Ref(eree), Regard, Second guess, Sentence, Sheriff, Sizer, Sober, Solomon, Suppose, Think, Touch, Try, Umpire, Verdict, Ween, Wig, Wine-taster, Wisdom, Worship

Judicious Critical, Discreet, Politic, Rational, Sage, Sensible, Shrewd, Sound

Jug(s) Amphora, Aquamanale, Aquamanile, Bird, Blackjack, Can, Cooler, Cream(er), Crock, Ewer, Flagon, Gaol, Gotch, Pitcher, Pound, Pourer, Pourie, →**PRISON**, Quad, Quod, Sauceboat, Shop, Slammer, Stir, Toby

Juice, Juicy Aloe vera, Bacca, Cassareep, Cassaripe, Cremor, Current, Fluid, Fruity, Gastric, Hypocist, Ichor, La(b)danum, Laser, Latex, Lush, Must, Oil, Pancreatic, Perry, Petrol, Ptisan, Rare, Sap, Snake, Soma, Spanish, Stum, Succulent, Succ(o)us, Thridace, Vril, Zest

Juliet J

Jumble Cast offs, Chaos, Conglomeration, Farrago, Garble, Hodge-podge, Huddle, Jabble, Lumber, Mass, Medley, Mingle-mangle, Mish-mash, Mixter-maxter, Mixture, Pasticcio, Pastiche, Praiseach, Raffle, Ragbag, Scramble, Shuffle, Wuzzle

▷**Jumbled** *may indicate* an anagram

Jumbo Aircraft, Colossal, Elephant, Jet, Large-scale, Mammoth, OS, Plane, Vast

Jump(er), Jumping, Jumpy Aran, Assemble, Axel, Base, Batterie, Bean, Boomer, Bound, Bungee, Bungy, Bunny-hop, Caper, Capriole, Cicada, Cicata, Crew-neck, Cricket, Croupade, Daffy, Desultory, Entrechat, Euro, Eventer, Flea, Fosbury flop, Frog, Gansey, Gazump, Gelande(sprung), Grasshopper, Guernsey, Halma, Helicopter, High, Hurdle, Impala, Itchy, Jersey, Joey, Jolly, Kangaroo, Katydid, Kickflip, Knight, Lammie, Lammy, Leap(frog), Lep, Long, Lope, Lutz, Nervous, Nervy, Ollie, Para, Parachute, Pig, Pogo, Polo-neck, Pounce, Prance, Prank, Pronking, Puissance, Quantum, Quersprung, Rap, Roo, Salchow, Saltatory, Saltigrade, Saltus, Scissors, Scoup, Scowp, Shy, Skip, Skipjack, Skydiver, →**SPRING**, Star, Start, Steeplechaser, Straddle, Sweater, Toe(-loop), Trampoline, Triple, Turtle-neck, Vau(l)t, V-neck, Water, Western roll

Junction Abutment, Alloyed, Box, Bregma, Carfax, Circus, Clapham, Clover-leaf, Connection, Crewe, Crossroads, Intersection, Joint, Josephson, Knitting, Meeting, Node, Point, Raphe, Rhaphe, Roundabout, Spaghetti, Stage, Suture, T, Turn off, Union

Jungle Asphalt, Blackboard, Boondocks, Bush, Concrete, Forest, Maze

Junior Cadet, Dogsbody, Filius, Fils, Gofer, Office, Petty, Scion, Second fiddle, Sub(ordinate), Underling, Younger

▷**Junk** *may indicate* an anagram

Junk(ie), Junkshop Addict, Bric-à-brac, Jettison, Litter, Lorcha, Lumber, Refuse, Schmeck, Ship, Shmek, Spam, Tatt, Trash, Tripe, User

Junket(ing) Beano, Creel, Custard, Feast, Picnic, Rennet, Spree

Juno Lucina, Moneta

Jurisdiction Authority, Bailiwick, Domain, Pashalic, Pashalik, Province, Soke(n), Sucken, Verge

Juror(s), Jury Array, Assize, Blue-ribbon, Dicast, Grand, Hung, Inquest, Judges, Man, Mickleton, Old Fury, Pais, Panel, Panellist, Party, Petit, Petty, Sail, Special, Strike, Tales, Talesman, Tribunal, Venire, Venireman, Venue

Just(ice) Adeel, Adil, Alcalde, All, Aristides, Astraea, Balanced, Barely, By a nose, Condign, Cupar, Deserved, E(v)en, Equal, Equity, Fair, Fair-minded, Forensic, Honest, Impartial, J, Jasper, Jeddart, Jethart, Jurat, Kangaroo, Mere(ly), Moral, Natural, Nemesis, Newly, Nice, Only, Palm-tree, Piso, Poetic, Precisely, Provost, Puisne, Pure and simple, Quorum, Recent, Restorative, Right(ful), Righteous, Rightness, Rough, Shallow, Silence, Simply, Solely, Sommer, Street, Themis, Tilt, Upright

Justifiable, Justification, Justify Apology, Autotelic, Avenge, Aver, Avowry, Clear, Darraign(e), Darrain(e), Darrayn, Defend, Deraign, Deserve, Excusable, Explain, Grounds, Pay off, Raison d'etre, Rationale, Reason, Vindicate, Warrant

Jut Beetle, Bulge, Overhang, Project, Protrude, Sail

Juvenile Childish, Pupa, Teenage(r), Yonkers, Young, Younkers, Youth

Kk

K Kelvin, Kilo, King, Kirkpatrick

Kangaroo Bettong, Boodie-rat, Boomer, Boongary, Bounder, Cus-cus, Diprotodont, Euro, Forester, Joey, Macropodidae, Nototherium, Old man, Potoroo, Rat, Steamer, Tree, Troop, Wallaby, Wallaroo

Karate (costume) Gi(e), Kung Fu, Shotokan, Wushu

Karma Destiny, Fate, Predestination

Kebab Cevapcici, Gyro, Satay, Sate, Shashli(c)k, Souvlakia

Keel Bilge, Bottom, Carina, Centreboard, Cheesecutter, Daggerboard, Even, Faint, False, Fin, List, Overturn, Skeg(g), Sliding

Keen(ness), Keener Acid, Acuity, Acute, Agog, Ardent, Argute, Aspiring, Astute, Athirst, Avid, Aygre, Bemoan, Bewail, Breem, Breme, Cheap, Coronach, Cutting, Dash, Devotee, Dirge, Eager, Elegy, Enthusiastic, Fanatical, Fell, Game, Greet, Grieve, Hone, Hot, Howl, Into, Itching, Lament, Mourn, Mustard, Mute, Narrow, Ochone, Ohone, Overfond, Partial, Peachy, Perceant, Persant, Pie, Raring, Razor, Ready, Red-hot, Rhapsodic, Sharp, Shrewd, Shrill, Snell, Thirsting, Threnodic, Thrillant, Trenchant, Ululate, Wail, Whet, Zeal(ous)

Keep(er), Keeping, Kept Ames, Armature, Austringer, Castellan, Castle, Celebrate, Chatelain(e), Citadel, Conceal, Conserve, Curator, Custodian, Custody, Custos, Depositary, Depository, Detain, Donjon, Escot, Fastness, Finder, Fort, Gaoler, Goalie, Guardian, Harbour, Have, Hoard, →**HOLD**, Maintain, Nab, Net, Observe, On ice, Ostreger, Own, Park, Pickle, Preserve, Retain, Safe, Safeguard, Save, Stay, Stet, Stock, Store, Stow, Stronghold, Stumper, Support, Sustain, Tower, Warden, Withhold

Keepsake Memento, Relic, Souvenir, Token

Keep up Float

Keg(s) Barrel, Cask, Ks, Tub, Tun, Vat

Kelp Varec

Kennel(s) Guard, Home, House, Shelter

Kerb Edge, Gutter, Roadside

Kernel Copra, Core, Grain, Nucleus, Pistachio, Praline, Prawlin

Kestrel Bird, Hawk, Keelie, Stallion, Staniel, Stannel

Kettle Boiler, Caldron, Cauldron, Dixie, Dixy, Drum, Fanny, Pot, Turpin

Keuper Trias

Key(s), Keyhole A, Ait, Ash, Atoll, B, Backspace, C, Cardinal, Cay, Claver, Clue, Command, Cryptographer, D, Del(ete), E, Essential, F, Flat, Function, G, Grecque, Ignition, Important, Inch, Index, Isle(t), Ivory, Largo, Linchpin, Major, Minor, Note, Opener, Shift, Signature, Skeleton, Subdominant, Swipecard, USB, West, Yale®

Keyboard, Keypad Azerty, Console, Digitorium, Dvorak, Manual, Martenot, Numeric(al), Piano, Pianola®, Qwerty, Spinet

Kibbutz Collective

Kick(ing) Abandon, Back-heel, Banana, Bicycle, Boot, Buzz, Corner, Dribble, Drop, Fling, Flutter, Fly, Free, Frog, Garryowen, Goal, Grub, Hack, Heel, High, Hitch, Hoof, Lash, Nutmeg, Pause, Penalty, Pile, Place, Punce, Punt, Recalcitrate, Recoil, Recoyle, Renounce, Savate, Scissors, Shin, Sixpence, Speculator, Spot, Spur, Spurn, Squib, Stab, Tanner, Tap, Thrill, Toe, Up and under, Vigour, Volley, Wince, Yerk, Zip

Kid(s) Arab, Bamboozle, Befool, Billy, Brood, Chaff, Cheverel, Cheveril, Chevrette, Child, Chit, Con, Delude, Fox, Giles, Goat, Hoax, Hocus, Hoodwink, Hum, Joke, Josh, Leather, Mag, Minor, Misguide, Nappe, Nipper, Offspring, Pretend, Rag, Rib, Small fry, Spoof, Sprig, Suede, Sundance, →**TEASE**, Tot, Trick, Whiz(z), Wiz

Kidnap(per) Abduct, Captor, Hijack, Plagium, Snatch, Spirit, Steal

Kildare Dr

Kill(ed), Killer, Killing Asp, Assassin, Axeman, Bag, Behead, Booth, Bump off, Butcher, Carnage, Category, Choke, Coup de grâce, Croak, Crucify, Cull, Deep six, Despatch, Destroy, Do in, Electrocute, Eradicate, Euthanasia, Execute, Exhibition, Exterminate, Fallen, Garotte, Gun(man), Handsel, Hatchet man, Hilarious, Homicide, Honour, Humane, Ice, Infanticide, Jugulate, Knacker, Knock off, Liquidate, Lynch, Mactation, Mercy, Misdo, Mortify, Murder, Necklace, Penalty, Pesticide, Pick off, Predator, Put down, Quell, Sacrifice, Serial, Shoot up, Slaughter, Slay(er), Slew, Smite, Spike, Strangle, Take out, Thagi, Thug(gee), Top, Toreador, Total, Vandal, Veto, Waste, Written off, Zap

Kilt Drape, Filabeg, Fustanella, Plaid, Tartan

Kin(ship), Kin(sman) Ally, Family, Kith, Like, Nearest, Phratry, Relation

Kind(ly) Akin, Amiable, Avuncular, Benefic, Benevolent, Benign, Boon, Breed, Brood, Brotherly, Category, Class, Clement, Considerate, Doucely, Favourable, Gender, Generic, Generous, Genre, Gentle, Genus, Good, Gracious, Human, Humane, Ilk, Indulgent, Kidney, Kin, Lenient, Manner, Merciful, Modal, Nature, Sisterly, Species, Strain, Strene, Thoughtful, Trine, Type, Understanding, Variety, Well-disposed, Ylke

Kindle, Kindling Accend, Fire, Ignite, Incense, Incite, Inflame, Kitten, →**LIGHT**, Litter, Lunt, Spark, Stimulate, Teend, Tind, Tine

King(s), Kingly Ard-ri(gh), Butcher, Cobra, Csar, English, ER, Evil, Face card, Highness, Hyksos, Kong, Ksar, Majesty, Monarch, Negus, Pearly, Peishwa(h), Penguin, Peshwa, Pharaoh, Philosopher, Potentate, R, Raja, Ransom, Reigner, Rex, Rial, Roi, Royalet, Ryal, Sailor, Seven, Shah, Shepherd, Shilling, Sophy, Sovereign, Stork, Tsar, Tzar

Kingdom, Kingship An(n)am, Animal, Aragon, Arles, Armenia, Ashanti, Assyria, Austrasia, Babylonia, Barataria, Belgium, Bhutan, Bohemia, Brandenburg, Brunel, Buganda, Burgundy, Dahomey, Darfur, Denmark, Dominion, Edom, Elam, Fife, Galicia, He(d)jaz, Heptarchy, Hijaz, Jordan, Kongo, Latin, Lydia, Lyonnesse, Macedon(ia), Media, Mercia, Meroe, Mineral, Moab, Murcia, Naples, Navarre, Nepal, Noricum, Nubia, Numidia, Parthia, Phyla, Pontic, Protista, Pruce, Rayne, Realm, Reich, Reign, Royalty, Sardinia, Saul, Siam, Sphere, Sweyn, Throne, Tonga, Ulster, Vegetable, Wessex, Westphalia, World

Kink(y) Bent, Buckle, Crapy, Enmeshed, Flaw, Gasp, Knurl, Null, Nurl, Odd, Perm, Perverted, Quirk, SM, Twist, Wavy

▷ **Kink(y)** *may indicate* an anagram

Kiosk Booth, Call-box

Kip(per) At, Cure, Dosser, Doze, Limey, Nap, →**SLEEPER**, Smoke, →**TIE**

Kish Rubbish, Scum, Tat

Kiss(er), Kissing Air, Baisemain, Buss, Butterfly, Caress, Contrecoup, Cross, French, Graze, Lip, Mwah, Neck, Osculate, Pax(-board), Pax-brede, Peck, Pet, Plonker, Pree, Salue, Salute, Smack(er), Smooch, Smouch, Snog, Spoon, Suck face, Thimble, Tonsil hockey, Tonsil tennis, Trap, X, Yap

Kitchen Caboose, Chuck-wagon, Cookhouse, Cuisine, Dinette, Galley, Percussion, Scullery, Soup

Kitsch Naff

Kitty Ante, Cat, Fisher, Float, Fund, Jackpot, Pool, Pot, Puss, Tronc

Knack Art, Faculty, Flair, Forte, Gift, Hang, Instinct, →**TALENT**, Trick

Knead Massage, Mould, Pug, Pummel, Work

Knee-jerk Unthinking

Kneel(er) Defer, Genuflect, Hassock, Kowtow, Truckle

Knicker(bockers), Knickers Bloomers, Culottes, Directoire, Irving, Panties, Plus-fours, Rational dress, Shorts, Trousers

Knick-knack Bagatelle, Bibelot, Bric-à-brac, Gewgaw, Pretty(-pretty), Quip, Smytrie, Toy, Trangam, Trifle, Victoriana

Knife Anelace, Athame, Barlow, Barong, Bistoury, Blade, Boline, Bolo, Bolster, Bowie,

Bread, Bush, Butterfly, Canelle, Carver, Carving, Case, Catling, Chakra, Chiv, Clasp, Cleaver, Couteau, Cradle, Cuttle, Cutto(e), Da(h), Dagger, Dirk, Fleam, Flick, Fruit, Gamma, Gulley, Gully, Hay, Hunting, Jockteleg, Kard, Keratome, Kukri, Lance(t), Machete, Matchet, Moon, Oyster, Palette, Panga, Paper, Parang, Paring, Peeler, Pen, Pigsticker, Pocket, Putty, Scalpel, Scalping, Sgian-dhu, Sgian-dubh, Sheath, Shiv, Simi, Skean-dhu, Slash, Snee, Snickersnee, Spade, Stab, Stanley, Steak, Sticker, Stiletto, Swiss army, Switchblade, Table, Toothpick, Tranchet, Trench

Knight(hood) Accolon, Aguecheek, Alphagus, Artegal, Banneret, Bayard, Bedivere, Black, Bliant, Bors, Britomart, Caballero, Calidore, Cambel, Caradoc, Carpet, Cavalier, Chevalier, Companion, Crusader, Douceper, Douzeper, Dub, Equites, Errant, Galahad, Gallant, Gareth, Garter, Gawain, Giltspurs, Gladys, Guyon, Hospitaller, Jedi, Kay, KB, KBE, KG, Lamorack, La(u)ncelot, Launfal, Lionel, Lochinvar, Lohengrin, Maecenas, Malta, Mark, Medjidie, Melius, Modred, N, Noble, Orlando, Paladin, Palmerin, Palomides, Papal, Paper, Parsifal, Perceforest, Perceval, Percival, Pharamond, Pinel, Red Cross, Ritter, Samurai, Sir, Tannhauser, Templar, Teutonic, Tor, Trencher, Tristan, Tristram, Valvassor, Vavasour, White

Knit(ting), Knitter, Knitwear Cardigan, Contract, Crochet, Entwine, Hosiery, Intarsia, Intertwine, Jersey, Jumper, Marry, Mesh, Porosis, Pullover, Purl, Seam, Set, Stockinet, Sweater, Tricoteuse, Weave, Woolly, Wrinkle

Knob(by) Berry, Boll, Boss, Botoné, Bottony, Bouton, Bur(r), Cam, Caput, Cascabel, Croche, Handle, Hill, Inion, Knur(r), Mouse, Mousing, Node, Noop, Pellet, Pommel, Protuberance, Pulvinar, Snib, Snub, Snuff, Stud, Torose, Trochanter, Tuber, Tuner, Wildfowl

Knock(er), Knocked, Knock(ed) down, (off, out), Knockout Bang, Beaut, Biff, Blow, Bonk, Bump, Ca(a), Chap, Chloroform, Clash, Clour, Collide, Con, Criticise, Dad, Daud, Dawd, Degrade, Denigrate, Dent, Deride, Dev(v)el, Ding, Dinnyhauser, Dod, Etherise, Eyeful, Floor, Grace-stroke, →**HIT**, Innings, KD, King-hit, Knap, KO, Lowse, Lowsit, Mickey Finn, Pan, Pink, Quietus, Rap, Rat-tat, Semi-final, Skittle, Socko, Spat, Steal, Stop, Stoun, Strike, Stun(ner), Sucker punch, Tap, Technical, Thump, Tonk, Wow

Knot(ted), Knotty Apollo, Baff, Band, Bend, Bind, Blackwall hitch, Bow, Bowline, Bur(r), Burl, Carrick-bend, Cat's paw, Clinch, Clove hitch, Cluster, Crochet, Diamond hitch, Englishman's, Entangle, Figure of eight, Fisherman's (bend), Flat, French, Geniculate, Gnar, Gordian, Granny, Half-hitch, Harness hitch, Hawser-bend, Herculean, Hitch, Interlace, Knag, Knap, Knar, Knob, Knur(r), Loop, Love(r's), Macramé, Macrami, Magnus hitch, Marriage-favour, Matthew Walker, Mouse, Nirl, Node, Nowed, Nub, Nur(r), Overhand, Peppercorn, Picot, Porter's, Problem, Prusik, Quipu, Reef, Rolling hitch, Root, Rosette, Running, Seizing, Sheepshank, Sheetbend, Shoulder, Shroud, Sleave, Slip, Slub, Spurr(e)y, Square, Stevedore's, Surgeon's, Sword, Tangle, Tat, Thumb, Tie, Timberhitch, Torose, Truelove, True lover's, Tubercle, Turk's head, Virgin, Wale, Wall, Weaver's (hitch), Windsor, Witch

Know(how), Knowing(ly), Knowledge(able), Known Acquaintance, Au fait, Autodidactic, Aware, Cognition, Compleat, Comprehend, Cred, Epistemics, Erudite, Experience, Expertise, Famous, Fly, Gnosis, Gnostic, Have, Hep, Hip, Info, Information, Insight, Intentional, Intuition, Jnana, Ken, Kith, Kydst, Lare, Light, Lore, Mindful, Omniscience, On, Pansophy, Party, Polymath, Positivism, Privity, Realise, Recherché, →**RECOGNISE**, Resound, Sapient, Savvy, Science, Scilicet, Sciolism, Sciosophy, Shrewd, Smartarse, Smattering, Suss, Technology, Telegnosis, Understand(ing), Up, Versed, Wat(e), Weet(e), Well-informed, Well-read, Wis(dom), Wise(acre), Wist, Wit, Wonk, Wost, Wot

Ku Klux Klan Nightrider

Ll

L Latitude, League, Learner, Left, Length, Liberal, Lima, Litre, Long, Luxembourg, Pound

Label Band, Book-plate, Brand, Care, Designer, Docket, File, Indie, Mark, Name tag, Own, Seal, Sticker, Style, Tab, Tag, Tally, Ticket, Trace

Laboratory Lab, Language, Skunkworks, Skylab, Space-lab, Studio, Workshop

Labour(er), Laboured, Laborious Agonise, Arduous, Begar, Birth, Bohunk, Carl, Casual, Childbirth, Chore, Churl, Confinement, Coolie, Cooly, Corvée, Cottager, Cottar, Culchie, Dataller, Dwell, Effort, Emotional, Farmhand, Gandy-dancer, Ganger, Gibeonite, Grecian, Grind, Grunt, Hard, Hercules, Hod carrier, Hodge, Ida, Job, Journeyman, Kanaka, Katorga, Leaden, Manpower, Moil, Navvy, New, Okie, Operose, Pain, Peon, Pioneer, Prole, Redneck, Roll, Roustabout, Rouster, Seagull, Serf, Sisyphean, Slave, Stertorous, Stint, Strive, Sudra, Sweated, Task, Tedious, →**TOIL(S)**, Toss, Travail, Uphill, Vineyard, Wetback, →**WORK(ER)**, Workforce, Workmen

Laburnum Golden chain

Labyrinth Daedalus, Maze, Mizmaze, Warren, Web

▷ **Labyrinthine** *may indicate* an anagram

Lace, Lacy Alençon, Babiche, Beat, Blonde, Bobbin, Bone, Bourdon, Brussels, Chantilly, Cluny, Colbertine, Dash, Dentelle, Duchesse, Embraid, Entwine, Filet, Galloon, Guipure, Honiton, Inweave, Irish, Jabot, Lash, Macramé, Malines, Mechlin, Mignonette, Mode, Net, Orris, Pearlin, Picot, Pillow, Point, Queen Anne's, Reseau, Reticella, Ricrac, Rosaline, Seaming, Shoestring, Shoe-tie, Spiderwork, Spike, Stay, Tat(ting), Tawdry, Thrash, Thread, Tie, Torchon, Trim, Troll(e)y, Truss, Tucker, Valenciennes, Venise, Weave, Welt, Window-bar

Lack(ing), Lacks Absence, Ab(o)ulia, Aplasia, Bereft, Catalexis, Dearth, Decadent, Famine, Gap, Ha'n't, Manqué, Meagre, Minus, →**NEED**, Paucity, Poor, Poverty, Privation, Remiss, Sans, Shortage, Shortfall, Shy, Void, Want

Lackey Boots, Flunkey, Moth, Page, Poodle, Underling

Lacquer Coromandel, Enamel, Japan, Shellac, →**VARNISH**

Lad Boy(o), Bucko, Callan(t), Chiel(d), Child, Geit, Gyte, Knight, Loonie, Master, Nipper, Shaver, Stableman, Stripling, Tad, Whipper-snapper

Ladder(y) Accommodation, Bucket, Companion, Companionway, Etrier, Extension, Jack, Jacob's, Pompier, Potence, Rope, Run, Salmon, Scalado, Scalar, Scaling, Step, Stie, Sty, Stye, Trap, Turntable

▶ **Lade** *see* **LOAD(ED)**

Ladle Bail, Dipper, Divider, Scoop, Toddy

Lady, Ladies Baroness, Bevy, Bountiful, Burd, Dame, Dark, Don(n)a, Duenna, Female, Frau, Frow, Gemma, Godiva, Hen, Khanum, Lavatory, Leading, Loo, Luck, Maam, Madam(e), Martha, Memsahib, Nicotine, Peeress, Powder room, Señ(h)ora, Signora, Slate, Tea, WC, Windermere

▷ **Lady** *may indicate* an '-ess' ending

▷ **Ladybird** *may indicate* a female of a bird family

Laevorotatory L, Left

Lair Couch, Den, Earth, Haunt, Hideaway, Holt, Kennel, Lodge, Warren

Lake(s) Alkali, Basin, Bayou, Carmine, Crater, Crimson, L, Lacustrine, Lagoon, Lagune, Limnology, →**LOCH**, Lochan, Lode, Lough, Madder, Meer, Mere, Natron, Nyanza, Ox-bow, Poets, Pool, Pothole, Red, Reservoir, Salt, Shott, Tank, Tarn, Vlei, Zee

Lamb(skin) Baa, Barometz, Beaver, Budge, Bummer, Cade, Canterbury, Caracul,

Cosset, Ean(ling), Elia, Fell, Innocent, Keb, Larry, Noisette, Paschal, Persian, Poddy, Rack, Shearling, Target, Yean(ling)

Lame(ness) Accloy, Claude, Cripple, Crock, Game, Gammy, Gimp(y), Halt, Hamstring, Hirple, Hors de combat, Maim, Main, Spavined, Springhalt, Stringhalt, Useless, Weak

Lament(able), Lamentation, Lamenter Bemoan, Bewail, Beweep, Boo-hoo, Complain, Croon, Cry, Deplore, Dirge, Dumka, Elegy, Funest, Jeremiad, Jeremiah, Keen, Meane, Mein, Mene, Moon, Mourn, Ochone, Paltry, Piteous, Plaint, Repine, Sorry, Threne, Threnody, Ululate, →WAIL, Wel(l)away, Welladay, Yammer

Lamina(te), Laminated Film, Flake, Folium, Formica®, Lamella, Layer, Plate, Scale, Table, Tabular, Veneer

Lamp(s) Aladdin's, Aldis, Anglepoise, Arc-light, Argand, Blow, Bowat, Bowet, Buat, Cru(i)sie, Crusy, Davy, Daylight, Discharge, Diya, Eye, Eyne, Flame, Fluorescent, Fog, Gas, Geordie, Glow, Head, Hurricane, Incandescent, Induction, Kudlik, Lampion, Lantern, Lava, Lucigen, Mercury vapour, Miner's, Moderator, Neon, Nernst, Nightlight, Padella, Pendant, Photoflood, Pilot, Platinum, Quartz, Reading, Riding, Safety, Sanctuary, Scamper, Searchlight, Signal, Sodium, Sodium-vapour, Spirit, Standard, Street, Stride, Striplight, Strobe, Stroboscope, Sun, Tail, Tantalum, Tiffany, Tilley, Torch, Torchier(e), Tungsten, Uplight(er), Veilleuse, Xenon

Lampblack Soot

Lampoon Caricature, Parody, Pasquil, Pasquin(ade), Satire, Skit, Squib

Lance Dart, Harpoon, Impale, Morne, Pesade, Pike, Prisade, Prisado, Rejôn, Spear, Speisade, Thermic

Land(s), Landed Acreage, Alight, Alluvion, Bag, Beach, Brownfield, Byrd, Corridor, Country, Croft, Crown, Curtilage, Debatable, Demain, Demesne, Disbark, Disembark, Ditch, Dock, Earth, Enderby, Estate, Fallow, Farren, Farthingland, Fee, Feod, Feoff, Feud, Fief, Freeboard, Gair, Glebe, Gore, Graham, Greenfield, Ground, Hide, Holding, Holm, Holy, Horst, Ind, Innings, Isthmus, Kingdom, La-la, Lea, Leal, Ley, Light, Link, Maidan, Manor, Marginal, Marie Byrd, Mesnalty, Moose pasture, Mortmain, Nation, Net, Never-never, Nod, No man's, Odal, Onshore, Oxgang, Oxgate, Pakahi, Palmer, Panhandle, Parcel, Pasture, Peneplain, Peneplane, Peninsula, Piste, Plot, Point, Polder, Premises, Private, Promised, Property, Public, Purlieu, Queen Maud, Real estate, Realm, Realty, Reservation, Run, Runrig, Rupert's, Seigniory, Set-aside, Settle, Several, Smallholding, Soil, Spit, Splash down, Tack, Tenement, Terra(e), Terra-firma, Terrain, Territory, Tie, Touchdown, Udal, Unship, Ure, Van Diemen's, Veld(t), Victoria, Waste, Wilkes

Landing (craft, stair, system) Autoflare, Duck, Forced, Gha(u)t, Halfpace, LEM, Module, Pancake, Pier, Quay, Quayside, Roman candle, Soft, Solar, Sol(l)er, Sollar, Splashdown, Three-point, Touchdown, Undercarriage

Landless Dispossessed

Landlord, Land owner Absentee, Balt, Boniface, Copyholder, Fiar, Franklin, Herself, Host, Innkeeper, Junker, Laird, Lessor, Letter, Patron, Proprietor, Publican, Rachman, Rentier, Squatter, Squattocracy, Squire

Landscape Karst, Paysage, Picture, Saikei, Scene, Stoss and lee

Landslide, Landfall Avalanche, Earthfall, Éboulement, Lahar, Scree

Lane Alley, Bikeway, Boreen, Bus, Corridor, Crawler, Drury, Express, Fast, Fetter, Gut, La, Loan, Lois, Loke, Lovers', Memory, Middle, Mincing, Nearside, Offside, Passage, Passing, Petticoat, Pudding, Ruelle, Sea-road, Twitten, Twitting, Vennel, Wynd

Language(s) Argot, Armoric, Artificial, Assembly, Auxiliary, Basic, Body, Cant, Centum, Clinic, Community, Comparative, Computer, →COMPUTER LANGUAGE, Demotic, Descriptive, Dialect, Estem, Georgian, Gothic, Heritage, High-level, Humanities, Idioglossia, Idiom, Inclusive, Jargon, Legalese, Lingo, Lingua franca, Macaronic, Median, Meta-, Mobspeak, Neutral, Newspeak, Object, Parlance, Patois, Penutian, PERL, Pidgin, Plain, Pragmatics, Procedural, Programming, Prose, Rabbinic, Register, Rhetoric, Satem, Semitic, Sign, Slanguage, →SPEECH, Strong, Style, Symbolic, Target, Technobabble, Telegraphese, Tone, →TONGUE, Tropology, Tushery, Verbiage, Vernacular, Vocabulary, Wawa, Words, World

Languid, Languish Die, Divine, Droop, Feeble, Flagging, Listless, Lukewarm, Lydia, Melancholy, Quail, Torpid, Wilt

Langur Simpai, Wanderoo

Lanky Beanpole, Gangly, Gawky, Lean(y), Spindleshanks, Windlestraw

Lantern Aristotle's, Bowat, Bowet, Buat, Bull's eye, Chinese, Dark(e)y, Epidiascope, Episcope, Glim, Jaw, Lanthorn, Magic, Sconce, Stereopticon, Storm

Lap Drink, Gremial, Leg, Lick, Lip, Luxury, Override, Pace, Sypher

▷ **Lapdog** *may indicate* 'greyhound'

Lapse Drop, Error, Expire, Fa', Fall, Nod, Sliding, Trip

Large(ness), Largest Ample, Astronomical, Big, Boomer, Bulky, Bumper, Buster, Colossus, Commodious, Considerable, Decuman, Enormous, Epical, Extensive, Gargantuan, →**GIGANTIC**, Ginormous, Gog, Great, Grit, Gross, Handsome, Hefty, Helluva, Huge, Hulking, Humdinger, Humongous, Humungous, Kingsize, L, Labour intensive, Lg, Lunker, Macrocephaly, Magog, Man-sized, Massive, Maximin, Maximum, Outsize, Plethora, Prodigious, Rounceval, Rouncival, Scrouger, Skookum, Slew, Slue, Snorter, Sollicker, Spacious, Spanking, Stonker, Stout, Swingeing, Tidy, Titanic, Vast, Voluminous, Well-endowed, Whopping

Largess Alms, Charity, Frumentation

Lark Adventure, Aunter, Caper, Dido, Dunstable, Exaltation, Fool, Gammock, Giggle, Guy, Laverock, Mud, Pipit, Prank, Spree

Larva Amphibiotic, Amphiblastule, Army-worm, Axolotl, Bagworm, Bipinnaria, Bloodworm, Bookworm, Bot(t), Budworm, Caddice, Caddis(-worm), Cankerworm, Caterpillar, Chigger, Chigoe, Corn borer, Corn earworm, Cysticercoid, Doodlebug, Glass-crab, Grub, Jigger, Jointworm, Leather-jacket, Maggot, Mealworm, Measle, Microfilaria, Muckworm, Mudeye, Naiad, Nauplius, Neoteny, Ox-bot, Planula, Pluteus, Polypod, Shade, Silkworm, Spat, Tadpole, Warble, Wireworm, Witchetty, Woodworm, Xylophage, Zoea

Lascivious(ness) Crude, Drooling, Goaty, Horny, Lewd, Lubric, Paphian, Raunch(y), Satyric, Sotadic, Tentigo

Laser Argon

Lash(ed), Lashing(s) Cat, Cilium, Firk, Flagellum, Flog, Frap, Gammon, Gripe, Knout, Mastigophora, Mousing, Oodles, Oup, Quirt, Riem, Rope's end, Scourge, Secure, Sjambok, Stripe, Swinge, Tether, Thong, Trice, Whang, →**WHIP**, Wire

Lass(ie) Colleen, Damsel, Maid, Quean, Queyn, Quin(i)e

Lasso Lariat, Lazo, Reata, Rope

Last(ing) Abide, Abye, Aft(er)most, →**AT LAST**, Boot-tree, Bottom, Cargo, Chronic, Dernier, Dure, Dying, Eleventh, Endmost, Endurance, Endure, Extend, Extreme, →**FINAL**, Hinder, Hindmost, Hold out, In extremis, Latest, Latter, Linger, Live, Load, Long-life, Model, Nightcap, Outstay, Perdure, Permanent, Perpetuate, Persist, Rearmost, Spin, Stable, Stamina, Stand, Stay, Supper, Survive, Swan-song, Thiller, Thule, Tree, Trump, Ult(imate), Ultima, Ultimo, Utmost, Wear, Weight, Whipper-in, Z

Last word(s) Amen, Envoi, Farewell, Ultimatum, Zythum

Latch Bar, Clicket, Clink, Espagnolette, Lock, Sneck, Thumb, Tirling-pin

Late(r), Latest After(wards), Afterthought, Anon, Behindhand, Chit-chat, Dead, Delayed, Ex, Former, Gen, Infra, Lag, Lamented, New(s), Overdue, Owl-car, Past, PM, Recent, Serotine, Sine, Slow, Stop-press, Syne, Tardive, Tardy, Trendy, Umquhile, Update

Latent Concealed, Delitescent, Dormant, Maieutic, Potential

Lateral Askant, Edgeways, Sideways

Lathe Capstan, Mandrel, Mandril, Turret

Lather Flap, Foam, Froth, Sapples, Suds, Tan

Latin(ist) Biblical, Classical, Criollo, Dago, Dog, Erasmus, Eyeti, Greaseball, High, Humanity, Italiot, L, Late, Law, Low, Medieval, Mexican, Middle, Modern, Neapolitan, New, Pig, Quarter, Rogues', Romanic, Romish, Scattermouch, Silver, Spic, Thieves', Uruguayan, Vulgar, Wop

Latitude Breadth, Celestial, Free hand, Horse, L, Leeway, Liberty, Licence, Meridian, Parallel, Play, Roaring forties, Scope, Tropic, Width, Wiggle room

Latrine Ablutions, Benchhole, Bog, Cloaca, Furphy, Garderobe, Loo, Privy, Rear

Lattice Bravais, Cancelli, Clathrate, Crystal, Espalier, Grille, Matrix, Pergola, Red, Treillage, Treille, Trellis

Laugh(ing), Laughable, Laughter Belly, Boff, Cachinnate, Cackle, Canned, Chortle, Chuckle, Cod, Corpse, Democritus, Deride, Derision, Fit, Fou rire, Gas, Gelastic, Giggle, Goster, Guffaw, Ha, He-he, Ho-ho, Homeric, Hoot, Horse, Hout, Howl, Irrision, Isaac, Jackass, Lauch, Leuch, Levity, Mock, Nicker, Peal, Present, Riancy, Riant, Rich, Rident, Ridicule, Risus, Scream, Snigger, Snirt(le), Snort, Tehee, Titter, Yo(c)k

Launch(ing), Launch pad Begin, Blast-off, Catapult, Chuck, Debut, Fire, Float, Hurl, Initiate, Lift-off, Pioneer, Presentation, Release, Rolling, Send, Shipway, Shot, Slipway, →**TOSS**, Unstock, Upsend, VTO

Launder, Laund(e)rette, Laundress, Laundry Bagwash, Blanchisseuse, Clean, Coin-op, Lav, Linen, Steamie, Tramp, Transfer, Wash(ery), Washhouse, Whites

Laurel(s) Aucuba, Bay, Camphor, Daphne, Kalmia, Kudos, Pichurim, Sassafras, Spicebush, Spurge, Stan, Sweet-bay

Lava Aa, Bomb, Coulée, Cysticercus, Dacite, Lahar, Lapilli, Magma, Mud, Nuée ardente, Pahoehoe, Palagonite, Pitchstone, Pumice, Pyroclast, Scoria, Tephra, Toadstone

Lavatory Ajax, Bogger, Brasco, Can, Carsey, Carzey, Cludgie, Comfort station, Convenience, Cottage, Dike, Draught, Dunnakin, Dunny, Dyke, Earth closet, Elsan®, Facilities, Forica, Furphey, Gents, Heads, Jakes, Jane, John, Kars(e)y, Karzy, K(h)azi, Kleinhuisie, Kybo, Ladies, Lat(rine), Loo, Necessary, Netty, Office, Outhouse, Pissoir, Portaloo®, Privy, Rear(s), Reredorter, Shithouse, Shouse, Siege, Smallest room, Superloo, Throne, Thunderbox, Toilet, Toot, Tout, Urinal, Washroom, WC

Lavish Barmecidal, Copious, Excessive, Extravagant, Exuberant, Flush, Free, Fulsome, Generous, Lucullan, Lush, Palatial, Prodigal, Shower, Sumptuous, Wanton, Waste

Law(ful), Laws Act, Agrarian, Anti-trust, Ass, Association, Avogadro's, Bar, Barratry, →**BILL**, Biogenetic, Blue-sky, Bonar, Bourlaw, Boyle's, Bragg's, Brewster's, Brocard, Byelaw, Byrlaw, Cain, Canon, Capitulary, Case, Chancery, Charles's, Civil, Code, Common, Constitution, Corn, Coulomb's, Criminal, Cupar, Curie's, Cy pres, Dalton's, Dead-letter, Decree, Decretum, De Morgan's, Dharma, Dictate, Digest, Din, Distributive, Dry, Edict, Einstein's, Enact, Excise, Fiqh, Forensic, Forest, Fundamental, Game, Gas, Graham's, Gresham's, Grimm's, Grotian, Halal, Halifax, Henry's, Hess's, Homestead, Hooke's, Hubble's, Hudud, Hume's, International, Irade, Iure, Joule's, Jura, Jure, Jus, Kain, Kepler's, Kirchhoff's, Labour, Land, Lay, Legal, Leibniz's, Lemon, Lenz's, Licit, Lien, Liquor, Lor(d), Losh, Lydford, Lynch, Magdeburg, Mariotte's, Martial, May, Megan's, Mendel's, Mercantile, Military, Moral, Mosaic, Murphy's, Natural, Newton's, Nomistic, Octave, Ohm's, Oral, Ordinance, Parity, Parkinson's, Pass, Penal, Periodic, Planck's, Plebiscite, Poor, Principle, Private, Public, Rape shield, Regulation, Rhodian, Roman, Rubric, Rule, Salic, Salique, Scout, Sharia(h), Sheria(t), Shield, Shulchan Aruch, Snell's, Sod's, Stefan's, Stokes, Sumptuary, Sunna, Sus(s), Sword, Table, Talmud, Tenet, The (long) robe, Thorah, Thorndike's, Torah, Tort, Tradition, Twelve Tables, Ulema, Unwritten, Use, Valid, Verner's, Vigilante, Written

Lawmaker, Lawman, Lawyer Alfaqui, Att(orney), AV, Avocat, Avvogadore, Barrack room, Barrister, Bencher, BL, Bluebottle, Bramble, Bush, Cadi, Coke, Counsel, DA, Decemvir, Deemster, Defence, Dempster, Doge, Draco, Eagle(t), Enactor, Fiscal, Greenbag, Grotius, Hammurabi, Jurisconsult, Jurist, Juvenal, Legist, Mooktar, Moses, MP, Mufti, Mukhtar, Nomothete, Notary, Penang, Pettifoggers, Rabbi, Shirra, Shyster, Silk, Solicitor, Spenlow, Stratopause, Talmudist, Templar, Writer

Lawn Cambric, Cloth, Grass, Green, Linen, Ruche, Sward, Turf

Lawsuit Case, Cause, Plea, Trover

▶**Lawyer(s), Lawman** *see* **LAWMAKER**

▷**Lax** *may indicate* an anagram

Lax(ity) Freedom, Inexact, Laissez-aller, Latitude, Lenience, Loose, Remiss, →**SLACK**, Wide

Lay(ing), Layman, Laic, Laid, Laity Air, Antepost, Aria, Ballad, Bed, Bet, Blow, Chant, Christian Brothers, Ditty, Drop, Earthly, Egg, Embed, Fit, Impose, Lied, Lodge, Man, Minstrel, Oat, Oblate, Ode, Outsider, Oviparous, Oviposit, Parabolanus, Pose, Secular, Set, Sirvente, →**SONG**, Songsmith, Sypher, Temporalty, Tertiary, Tribal, Untrained, Wager, Warp

Layer(s) Abscission, Aeuron(e), Ancona, Appleton, Battery, Bed, Boundary, Cake, Caliche, Cambium, Canopy, Chromosphere, Cladding, Coating, Crust, D, Depletion, E, Ectoplasm, Ectosarc, Ekman, Epiblast, Epilimnion, Epitaxial, Epitheca, Epithelium, Erathem, E-region, Exine, Exocarp, F, Film, Flake, Friction, Ganoin, Germ, Gossan, Gozzan, Granum, Ground, Heaviside, →**HEN**, Herb, Hypotheca, Intima, Inversion, Kennelly(-Heaviside), Kerf, Lamella, Lamina, Lap, Leghorn, Lenticle, Lie, Malpighian, Media, Miocene, Ozone, Palisade, Pan, Patina, Paviour, Photosphere, Ply, Retina, Reversing, Rind, Scale, Scattering, Sclerite, Screed, Shrub, Skim, Skin, Skiver, Sliver, Spathic, Stratify, Stratopause, Stratum, Substratum, Tabular, Tapetum, Tier, Tremie, Trophoblast, Trophoderm, Uvea, Varve, Vein, Velamen, Veneer

Lay-off Dismiss, Hedge, Redundance, Suspend

Lay-out Ante, Design, Expend, Fell, Format, Map, Mise, Pattern, Spend, Straucht, Straught, Streak, Streek, Stretch

Laze, Laziness, Lazy (person), Lazybones Bed-presser, Bone idle, Bummer, Cabbage, Couch potato, Faineant, Grunge, Hallian, Hallion, Hallyon, Indolent, Inert, Lackadaisical, Laesie, Languid, Layabout, Lie-abed, Lig(ger), Lime, Lither, Loaf, Lotus-eater, Lusk, Shiftless, Sleepyhead, Sloth, Slouch, Slug(-a-bed), Sluggard, Susan, Sweer, Sweir, Timeserver, Veg, Workshy

▷**Lazily** *may indicate* an anagram

Lead(er), Leading, Leadership Ag(h)a, Ahead, Akela, Amakosi, Arch, Article, Atabeg, Atabek, Ayatollah, Bab, Bellwether, Black, Bluey, Bodhisattva, Bonaparte, Brand, Cable, Cade, Calif, Caliph, Came, Capitano, Capo, Captain, Castro, Caudillo, Centre, Cheer, Chief, Chieftain, Chin, China white, CO, Codder, Concert-master, Condottiere, Conducive, Conduct, Corporal, Coryphaeus, Coryphee, Czar, Dalai Lama, De Gaulle, Demagogue, Dictator, Dominant, Drail, Duce, Dux, Editorial, Escort, Ethnarch, Extension, Figurehead, First, Flake-white, Floor, Foreman, Foremost, Frontrunner, Fu(e)hrer, Gaffer, Gandhi, Garibaldi, General, Gerent, Go, Graphite, Guide(r), Halter, Hand, Headman, Headmost, Headnote, Hegemony, Hero, Hetman, Hiawatha, Hierarch, Honcho, Idi, Imam, Imaum, Induna, Ink(h)osi, Inveigle, Jason, Jeune premier(e), Jump, Juve(nile), King, Ksar, Leam, Livid, Loss, Lost, Lyam, Lym(e), Mahatma, Mahdi, Main, Market, Marshal, Massicot, Mayor, Meer, Mehdi, Minium, Mir, No 1, Nomarch, Nose, Numero uno, Open, Pacemaker, Pacesetter, Padishah, Panchen Lama, Patriarch, Pb, Petain, Pilot, Pioneer, Pit, Plummet, PM, Pointer, Precede, Precentor, Premier(e), President, Price, Primo, Rangitara, Ratoo, Rebbe, Rebecca, Red, Role, Ruler, Sachem, Sagamore, Saturn, Saturn's tree, Scotlandite, Scout, Scudler, Senior, Shaper, Sharif, Sheik(h), Sixer, Skipper, Skudler, Soaker, Soul, Sounding, Spearhead, Stalin, Staple, Star, Start, Sultan, Supremo, Taoiseach, Tetraethyl, Top banana, Top dog, Trail(blazer), Tribune, Tsar, Up, Usher, Vaivode, Van(guard), Va(u)nt, Vaunt-courier, Voivode, Waivode, Wali, Warlord, White, Whitechapel, Wulfenite, Yeltsin, Youth

▷**Lead(s), Leaders** *may indicate* first letters of words

Leaf(y), Leaves Acanthus, Acrospire, Amphigastrium, Amplexicaul, Ascidia, At(t)ap, Baccy, Betel, Blade, Bract, Carpel, Cataphyll, Cladode, Compound, Consent, Corolla, Costate, Cotyledon, Crocket, Drop, Duff, Fig, Finial, Foil, Foliage, Foliar, Folio(se), Folium, Frond, Frondose, Glume, Gold, Green, Holiday, Induviae, Jugum, K(h)at, Lattice, Lilypad, Lobe, Lobulus, Megaphyll, Microphyll, Needle, Nervate, Out, P, Pad, Page, Paper, Phyllid, Phyllode, Phyllome, Pot, Qat, Repair, Riffle, Rosula,

Salad, Scale, Sclerophyll, Secede, Sepal, Sheet, Siri(h), Skim, Skip, Spathe, Stipule, Succubus, Tea, Tobacco, TTL, Valve, Vert, Withdraw

Leaflet At(t)ap, Bill, Bracteole, Circular, Dodger, Fly-sheet, Foliolose, Handbill, Hand-out, Pinna, Pinnula, Prophyll, Stipel, → **TRACT**

League Alliance, Amphictyony, Band, Bund, Compact, Decapolis, Delian, Denominal, Entente, Federation, Gueux, Guild, Hanse(atic), Holy, Ivy, L, Land, Little, Major, Muslim, Parasang, Primrose, Redheaded, Rugby, Solemn, Super, Union, Zollverein, Zupa

Leak(y) Bilge, Drip, Escape, Extravasate, Gizzen, Holed, Holey, Ooze, Pee, Porous, Run, Seepage, Sype, Trickle, Wee, Weep

Lean(ing) Abut, Aslope, Barren, Batter, Bend, Careen, Carneous, Carnose, Griskin, Heel, Hike out, → **INCLINE**, Lie, Lig(ge), List, Minceur, Partiality, Propend, Rake, Rawboned, Rely, Rest, Scraggy, Scrawny, Skinny, Spare, Stoop, Taste, Tend, Thin, Tilt, Tip, Walty, Wiry

Leap(ing), Leapt Assemblé, Bound, Brisé, Cabriole, Caper, Capriole, Cavort, Clear, Croupade, Curvet, Echappé, Entrechat, Falcade, Fishdive, Flying, Frisk, Gambade, Gambado, Gambol, Jeté, Jump, Loup, Luppen, Over, Pounce, Pronk, Quantum, Sally, Salto, Somersa(u)lt, Somerset, → **SPRING**, Transilient, Vault, Volte

Learn(ed), Learner Associative, Beginner, Blended, Blue, Bluestocking, Chela, Classical, Con, Culture, Discipline, Discover, Distance, Doctor, Don, Erudite, Erudition, Gather, Get, Glean, Hear, Insight, Instrumental, Kond, L, Lear(e), Leir, Lere, Lifelong, Literate, Literati, Literato, Lore, Lucubrate, Master, Memorise, Mirza, Mug up, → **NOVICE**, Opsimath(y), Pandit, Programmed, Pundit, Pupil, Rep, Rookie, Savant, Scan, Scholar(ship), See, Sleep, Starter, Student, → **STUDY**, Tiro, Trainee, Tutee, Tyro, Visile, Wise, Wit

Lease(-holder) Charter, Farm, Feu, Gavel, Hire, Let, Long, Novated, → **RENT**, Set(t), Subtack, Tack, Tacksman

Leash Lead, Lyam, Lym(e), Slip, Three, Trash, Triplet

Leather(s), Leather-worker, Leathery Aqualeather, Artificial, Bouilli, Bouilly, Box-calf, Brail, Buckskin, Buff, Cabretta, Calf, Capeskin, Chammy, Chamois, Chaps, Checklaton, Cheverel, Chevrette, Chrome, Cordovan, Cordwain, Corium, Counter, Cowhide, Crispin, Crocodile, Cuir(-bouilli), Currier, Deacon, Deerskin, Diphthera, Doeskin, Dogskin, Durant, Fair, Foxing, Goatskin, Grain, Hide, Hog-skin, Horsehide, Japanned, Kid, Kip(-skin), Labretta, Lacquered, Lamp, Levant, Marocain, Maroquin, Mocha, Morocco, Mountain, Nap(p)a, Neat, Nubuck®, Oak, Ooze, Oxhide, Paste-grain, Patent, Pigskin, Plate, Rand, Rawhide, Rexine®, Riem(pie), Roan, Rock, Rough-out, Russet, Russia, Saffian, Shagreen, Shammy, Sharkskin, Shecklaton, Sheepskin, Shoe, Skiver, Slinkskin, Snakeskin, Spetch, Split, Spruce, Spur, Spur-whang, Stirrup, Strand, Strap, Strop, Suede, Tan, Taw, Thong, Upper, Wallop, Wash, Waxed, White, Whitleather, Yuft

Leave(r), Leaving(s), Leave off Abandon, Abiturient, Abscond, Absit, Absquatulate, Acquittal, Adieu, Annual, Avoid, Bequeath, Betake, Blessing, Blow, Broken meats, Bug, Compassionate, Congé, Congee, Days off, Decamp, Depart, Desert, Devisal, Devise, Ditch, Evacuate, Except, Exeat, Exit, Exodus, Extrude, Forego, Forgo, Forsake, French, Furlough, Gardening, Garlandage, Get out, → **GO**, Inspan, Ish, Legate, Licence, Log off, Maroon, Mass, Mizzle, Omit, Orts, Pace, Parental, Park, Part, → **PERMISSION**, Permit, → **QUIT**, Residue, Resign, Sabbatical, Scapa, Scat, Scram, Shore, Sick(ie), Skedaddle, Skidoo®, Strand, Vacate, Vade, Vamo(o)se

Leaven Barm, Ferment, Yeast

Lecher(ous), Lechery Gate, Goaty, Lascivious, Libertine, Lickerish, Lustful, Profligate, Rake, Randy, Roué, Salaciousness, Satirisk, Satyr, Silen, Wolf

Lecture(r), Lectures, Lecturing Address, Aristotelian, Creed, Curtain, Dissert(ator), Docent, Don, Earful, Erasmus, Expound, Harangue, Homily, Hulsean, Jaw, Jawbation, Jobe, L, Lantern, Lector, Orate, Prelect, Prone, Rate, Read(er), Rede, Reith, Roasting, Rubber chicken circuit, Sententious, → **SERMON**, Spout, Take to task, Talk, Teacher, Teach-in, Tongue-lashing, Wigging, Yaff

Ledge Altar, Berm, Buttery-bar, Channel, Fillet, Linch, Miserere, Misericord(e), Nut, Rake, Scarcement, Settle, Subsellium

Ledger Book, General, Purchase, Register

Left (hand), Left-handed, Left-hander, Left-winger Abandoned, Avoided, Balance, Bolshy, Corrie-fisted, Fellow traveller, Forsaken, Haw, Hie, High, L, Laeotropic, Laevorotation, Larboard, Links, Loony, Lorn, Militant, Near, Other, Over, Pink, Pinko, Port, Quit, Rad, Red (Brigade), Relic, Residuum, Resigned, Secondo, Sinister, Soc(ialist), Southpaw, Split, Thin, Titoism, Trot, Unused, Verso, Vo, Went, West, Wind, Yet

Leg(s), Leggings, Leggy, Leg-wear Antigropelo(e)s, Bandy, Barbados, Bow, Breeches, Cabriole, Cannon, Chaparajos, Chaparejos, Chaps, Crural, Crus, Cuisse, Cush, Dib, Drumstick, Fine, Gaiter, Galligaskins, Gam(b), Gamash, Gambado, Garter, Gaskin, Gigot, Gramash, Gramosh, Haunch, Jamb, Jambeaux, Limb, Long, Member, Milk, Myriapod, Oleo, On(side), Peg, Peraeopod, Periopod, Peroneal, Pestle, Pin, Podite, Proleg, Puttees, Pylon, Relay, Section, Shanks, Shanks's pony, Shaps, Shin, Short, Spats, Spatterdash, Spindleshanks, Square, Stage, Start up, Stifle, Stump, Thigh, Tights, White

Legacy Bequest, Dowry, Entail, Heirloom

Legal(ism), Legally, Legitimate Above board, Bencher, Decriminalised, De regle, Forensic, Halacha, Halaka(h), Halakha, Lawful, Licit, Nomism, Scienter

Legato Slur

▷ **Legend** *may indicate* leg-end e.g. foot, talus

Legend(ary) Arthurian, Caption, Edda, Fable, Folklore, Hadith, Motto, Myth, Saga, Story, Urban, Yowie

Legible Clear, Lucid, Plain

Legion(ary), Legionnaire Alauda, Army, British, Cohort, Countless, Deserter, Foreign, Geste, Honour, →**HOST**, Maniple, Many, Throng, Zillions

Legislate, Legislation, Legislator, Legislature Assemblyman, Congress, Decemvir, Decree, Delegated, MP, Nomothete, Oireachtas, →**PARLIAMENT**, Persian, Senator, Supreme soviet, Thesmothete

Legume, Leguminous Bean, Guar, Lentil, Lomentum, Pea, Peanut, Pod, Pulse

Leicester Sheep

Leisure(ly) Adagio, Bytime, Ease, Liberty, Moderato, Off day, Otium, Respite, Rest, Vacation

Lemming Morkin

Lemon Answer, Cedrate, Citron, Citrus, Dud, Twist, Yellow

Lemonade Pop

Lemur Angwantibo, Aye-aye, Babacoote, Bush-baby, Colugo, Cynocephalus, Galago, Half-ape, Indri(s), Loris, Macaco, Malmag, Mongoose, →**MONKEY**, Nagapie, Potto, Ringtail, Sifaka, Tana, Tarsier

Lend(er) Advance, Library, Loan, Prest, Sub, Vaunce

Length(y), Lengthen(ing), Lengthwise Archine, Arsheen, Arshin(e), Aune, Cable, Chain, Cubit, Distance, Eke, Ell, →**ELONGATE**, Endways, Ennage, Epenthetic, Expand, Extensive, Foot, Footage, Furlong, Inch, Ley, Mile, Nail, Passus, Perch, Piece, Plethron, Pole, Prolix, Prolong, Protract, Reach, Remen, Rigmarole, Rod, Rope, Slow, Span, Stadium, Toise, Vara, Verbose, Yard

Lenient, Leniency Clement, Exurable, Lax, Mild, Permissive, Soft line, Tolerant

Lens Achromatic, Acoustic, Anamorphic, Anastigmat, Bifocal, Bull's eye, Contact, Corneal, Crookes, Crown, Crystalline, Dielectric, Diopter, Dioptre, Diverging, Electron, Eye, Eyeglass, Eye-piece, Field, Fish-eye, Gas-permeable, Gravitational, Hard, Lentil, Macro, Magnetic, Metallic, Mirror, Object(ive), Optic, Pantoscope, Soft, Stanhope, Sunglass, Telephoto, Toric, Trifocal, Wide-angle, Zoom

Leopard Catamountain, Clouded, Cougar, Jaguar, Leap, Libbard, Oceloid, Ounce, Panther, Pard, Snow, Spots, Tiger

Lesbian Boi, Bull dyke, Crunchie, Diesel, Dike, Dyke, Homophile, Lipstick, Sapphist, Tribade

Lese-majesty Treason

Lesion Cut, Gash, Scar, Serpiginous, Sore, Wheal, Whelk

Less(en), Lesser, Lessening Abate, Alaiment, Bate, Comedown, Contract, Deaden, Decline, Deplete, Derogate, Dilute, →**DWINDLE**, Extenuate, Fewer, Junior, Littler, Meno, Minus, Play down, Reduce, Relax, Remission, Sen, Shrink, Subordinate, Subsidiary, Tail, Under

Lesson Class, Example, Lear(e), Lection, Leir, Lere, Liripipe, Masterclass, Moral, Object, Period, Sermon, Tutorial

Let (go, off, out), Letting Allow, Cap, Charter, Conacre, Displode, Divulge, Enable, Entitle, Explode, Hire, Impediment, Indulge, Leak, Lease, Litten, Loot(en), Luit(en), Lutten, Obstacle, Obstruct, →**PERMIT**, Rent, Reprieve, Sett, Unhand, Warrant

Lethal Deadly, Fatal, Fell, Mortal

Lethargic, Lethargy Accidie, Apathy, Coma, Drowsy, Ennui, Hebetude, Inactive, Inertia, Lassitude, Listless, Logy, Passive, Sleepy, Sluggish, Stagnant, Stupor, Supine, Torpid, Turgid, Weariness

Letter(s) Ache, Aerogram, Aesc, Airgraph, Aleph, Alif, Alpha, Aspirate, Bayer, Begging, Beta, Beth, Block, Breve, Canine, Capital, Capon, Chain, Cheth, Chi, Chitty, Circular, Col, Collins, Consonant, Covering, Cue, Cuneiform, Dead, Dear John, Delta, Digamma, Digraph, Dispatch, Dominical, Edh, Ef(f), Emma, Encyclical, Ep(isemon), Epistle, Epsilon, Eta, Eth, Fan, Favour, Form, French, Gamma, Gimel, He, Heth, Hieratic, Initial, Iota, Izzard, Jerusalem, Kaph, Kappa, Koppa, Labda, Lambda, Lamed(h), Landlady, Landlord, Lessee, Lessor, Literal, Love, Mail, Mail-shot, Majuscule, Mem, Memo, Message, Missive, Monogram, Mu, Nasal, Night, Note, Notelet, Nu, Nun, Og(h)am, Omega, Omicron, Open, Ou, Pacifical, Paragoge, Pastoral, Patent, Pe(h), Phi, Pi, Plosive, Poison-pen, Polyphone, Postbag, Psi, Pythagorean, Qof, Rho, Rhyme, Rom, Runestave, Sad(h)e, Samian, Sampi, San, Scarlet, Screed, Screeve, Screwtape, Script, See, Shin, Ship, Sigma, Sign, Signal, Sin, Sort, Stiff, Swash, Tau, Tav, Taw, Teth, Theta, Thorn, Toc, Typo, Uncial, Upsilon, Vau, Vav, Versal, Vowel, Waw, Wen, Xi, Yod(h), Yogh, Ypsilon, Zed, Zeta

Lettuce Batavia, Chicon, Corn-salad, Cos, Iceberg, Lactuca, Lamb's, Lollo rosso, Mache, Radicchio, Romaine, Salad, Sea, Thridace

Level(ler) A, Abney, Abreast, Aclinic, Aim, Bargaining, Base, Break even, Champaign, Confidence, Countersink, Degree, Dumpy, Echelon, Equal, →**EVEN**, Extent, Eye, Flat, Flush, Grade, Horizontal, Impurity, Infill, Meet, O, Par, Plane, Plat(eau), Point, Race, Rank, Rase, Raze, Savanna, Spirit, Split, Springing, →**SQUARE**, Status, Stor(e)y, Stratum, Strew, Strickle, Summit, Tear-down, Tier, Trophic, Water, Wye

Lever(age) Backfall, Bell-crank, Brake, Cock, Crampon, Crowbar, Dues, Gear, Handspike, Jaw, Jemmy, Joystick, Key, Knee-stop, Landsturm, Pawl, Peav(e)y, Pedal, Pinch, Prise, Prize, Pry, Purchase, Stick, Sweep, Swipe, Tappet, Throttle, Tiller, Treadle, Treddle, Tremolo arm, Trigger, Tumbler, Typebar, Whipstaff

Levy Impose, Imposition, Leave, Militia, Octroi, Raise, Scutage, Stent, Talliate, Tax, Tithe

Lewd(ness) Bawd(r)y, Blue, Cyprian, Debauchee, Impure, Libidinous, Lubricity, Obscene, Priapism, Prurient, Raunchy, Silen(us), Tentigo, Unclean

Lexicographer, Lexicon Compiler, Craigie, Drudge, Etymologist, Florio, Fowler, Grove, Johnson(ian), Larousse, Liddell, Murray, OED, Thesaurus, Vocabulist, Webster, Words-man

Liability, Liable Anme, Apt, Debt, Incur, Limited, Open, Prone, Subject, Susceptible, White elephant

Liaison Affair, Contact, Link

Libel(lous) Blasphemous, Defamatory, Malign, Sclaunder, Slander, Smear, Sully, Vilify

Liberal(ity) Abundant, Adullamites, Ample, Besant, Bounteous, Bountiful, Breadth, Bright, Broad, Catholic, Enlightened, Free(hander), Free-hearted, →**GENEROUS**, Giver, Grey, Grimond, Handsome, Indulgent, L, Largesse, Latitudinarian, Lavish,

Limousine, Munificent, Octobrist, Open, Permissive, →**PROFUSE**, Rad(ical), Samuelite, Simonite, Spender, Steel, Tolerant, Trivium, Unstinted, Verlig, Verligte, Whig

Liberate(d), Liberation, Liberator Bolivar, Deliver, Dissimure, Emancipate, Fatah, →**FREE**, Gay, Inkatha, Intolerant, Messiah, Nick, PLO, Release, Risorgimento, Save, Steal, Sucre, Unfetter, UNITA, Women's

Liberty Bail, Discretion, Franchise, Freedom, Hall, Latitude, Licence, Mill, Sauce

Libra L

Library, Librarian Bibliothecary, BL, Bodleian, Bookmobile, British, Chartered, Copyright, Cottonian, Dewey, Genomic, Harleian, Laurentian, Lending, Mazarin, Public, Radcliffe, Reference, Rental, Tauchnitz

Licence, License Abandon, Allow, Authorisation, Carnet, Charter, Dispensation, Driving, Enable, Exequatur, Fling, Franchise, Free(dom), Gale, Import, Imprimatur, Indult, →**LATITUDE**, Let, Marriage, Occasional, Passport, →**PERMIT**, Poetic, Pratique, Provisional, Road-fund, Rope, Slang, Special, Table, Ticket of leave

Lichen Apothecia, Archil, Corkir, Crotal, Crottle, Epiphyte, Epiphytic, Graphis, Korkir, Lecanora, Litmus, Moss, Oakmoss, Orchel, Orchil(la), Orcine, Orseille, Parella, Parelle, Roccella, Rock tripe, Soredium, Stone-rag, Stone-raw, Tree-moss, Usnea, Wartwort

Lick(ing) Bat, Beat, Deer, Felch, Lambent, Lap, Leather, Rate, Salt, Slake, Speed, Whip

Lid Cover, Hat, Kid, Maximum, Opercula, Screwtop, Twist-off

Lie(s), Liar, Lying Abed, Accubation, Accumbent, Ananias, Bam, Bare-faced, Bask, Billy, Bounce(r), Braide, Cau(l)ker, Cellier, Clipe, Clype, Concoction, Contour, Couch(ant), Cracker, Cram(mer), Cretism, Cumbent, Deception, Decubitous, Decumbent, Direct, Doggo, Fable, Fals(e), Falsehood, Falsify, Falsity, Fib, Fiction, Figment, Flam, Gag, Gonk, Hori, Incumbent, Invention, Inveracity, Kip, Lair, Leasing, Lee(ar), Lig(ge), Lurk, Mythomania, Nestle, Obreption, Oner, Perjury, Plumper, Porky (pie), Procumbent, Prone, Prostrate, Pseudologia, Recline, Recumbent, Repent, Repose, Reptant, Ride, Romance(r), Sham, Sleep, Strapper, Stretcher, Supine, Swinger, Tale, Tappice, Tar(r)adiddle, Thumper, Tissue, Try, Untruth, Whacker, Whid, White, Whopper, Yanker

Lieutenant Flag, Loot, Lt, No 1, Sub(altern)

Life Age, Animation, Being, Bio, Biog(raphy), Breath, Brio, Chaim, Clerihew, Energy, Esse, Eva, Eve, Existence, Good, Heart, Memoir, Mortal coil, Nellie, Nelly, Night, Non-fiction, Plasma, Public, Quick, Riley, Span, Spirit, Still, Subsistence, Time, Vita, Vitality, Zoe

Lifeless(ness) Abiosis, Algidity, Amort, Arid, Azoic, Barren, Cauldrife, →**DEAD**, Dull, Flat, Inanimate, Inert, Key-cold, Log, Mineral, Possum, Sterile, Stonen, Wooden

Lift(ed), Lifter, Lifting Araise, Arayse, Arsis, Attollent, Bone, Cable-car, Camel, Chair, Cly, Copy, Crane, Davit, Dead, Dumb waiter, Elate, Elevator, Enhance, Extol, Filch, Fillip, Heave, Heeze, Heezie, Heft(e), Heist, Hitch, Hoise, Hoist, Hove, Jack, Jigger, Kleptomania, Leaven, Lefte, Lever, Lewis, Nab, Nap, Nim, Otis®, Paternoster, Pilfer, Pulley, →**RAISE**, Ride, Rotor, Scoop, Service, Shearlegs, Ski, Sky, Snatch, Sneak, Spout, Steal, Surface, T-bar, Thumb, Topping, Up, Winch, Windlass

▷ **Light** *may indicate* an anagram

Light(en), Lighting, Lighter, Lights Aerate, Afterglow, Airglow, Airy, Albedo, Ale, Alow, Alpenglow, Amber, Ancient, Ans(wer), Arc, Aurora, Back-up, Barge, Batement, Beacon, Beam, Behgal, Beshine, Bezel, Birlinn, Black, Bleach, Blond(e), Brake, Breezy, Bulb, Calcium, Candle, Canstick, Casco, Casement, Chiaroscuro, Cierge, Clue, Courtesy, Day, Dewali, Diffused, Direct, Diwali, Dormer, Drop, Eddystone, Electrolier, Ethereal, Fairy, Fall, Fan, Fantastic, Fastnet, Feathery, Fetch-candle, Fill, Filter, Fire, First, Fixed, Flambeau, Flame, Flare, Flicker, Flimsy, Flippant, Flit(t), Floating, Flood, Fluorescent, Fog (lamp), Frothy, Fuffy, Gas-poker, Glare, Gleam, Glim(mer), Glow, Gossamer, Green, Guiding, Halation, Hazard, Head, House, Idiot, Ignite, Illum(in)e, Incandescence, Indirect, Induction, Inner, Irradiate, Junior, Keel, Key, Kindle, Kiran, Klieg, Lamp, Lampion, Land, Lantern, Lanthorn,

Laser, Leading, LED, Leerie, Levigate, Lime, Link, Linstock, Loadstar, Lodestar, Lucarne, Lucigen, Luminaire, Lumine, Luminescence, Luminous, Lunt, Lustre, Lux, Mandorla, Match, Menorah, Mercurial, Mithra(s), Moon, Naphtha, Navigate, Navigation, Neon, New, Nit, Northern, Obstruction, Od(yl), Optics, Pale, Pane, Parhelion, Pavement, Pennyweight, Phosphorescence, Phot(ic), Photon, Photosphere, Pilot, Pipe, Polar, Pontoon, Portable, Pra(a)m, Range, Rear, Red, Reflex, Relieve, Rembrandt, Reversing, Riding, Robot, Rocket, Running, Rush, Safe(ty), Scoop, Sea-dog, Sea fire, Search, Shine, Shy, Solid-state, Southern, Southern-vigil, Spill, Spot, Spry, Steaming, Strip, Strobe, Stroboscope, Subtle, Sun, Sunshine, Svelte, Tail, Tally, Taper, Taps, Tead, Threshold, Tind, Tine, Torch, Torchère, Touchpaper, Track, Traffic, Trivial, Ultraviolet, Unchaste, Unoppressive, UV, Ver(e)y, Vesica, Vesta, Vigil, Watch, Wax, Welsbach burner, White, → **WINDOW**, Winker, Zippo, Zodiacal

Light-headed Captious, Dizzy, Kicksin

Light-hearted Gay

Lighthouse Beacon, Caisson, Eddystone, Fanal, Fastnet, Phare, Pharos, Signal

Lightning Ball, Bolt, Catequil, Éclair, Enfouldered, Forked, Fulmination, Levin, Sheet, Thunderbolt, Wildfire, Zigzag

Like(ness), Liking À la, Analogon, As, Assimilate, Attachment, Broo, Care, Corpse, Dig, Duplicate, Effigy, Eg, Egal(ly), Enjoy, Equal, Fancy, Fellow, Guise, Lich, Palate, Parallel, Peas, Penchant, -philus, Please, Predilection, Resemblance, Semblant, Shine, Similar, Simile, Simulacrum, Smaak, Sort, Speaking, Taste, Tiki, Uniformity

Likely, Likelihood Apt, Fair, Liable, Odds-on, On, Plausible, Possible, Probable, Probit, Prone, Prospective

Lily African, Agapanthus, Aloe, Amaryllis, Annunciation, Arum, Asphodel, Aspidistra, Belladonna, Calla, Camas(h), Camass, Canada, Candock, Chincherinchee, Colchicum, Colocasia, Convallaria, Corn, Crinum, Dale, Day, Easter, Elaine, Endogen, Fawn, Fleur de lys, Fritillary, Funkia, Galtonia, Haemanthus, Hellebore, Hemerocallis, Herb-Paris, Jacobean, Jacob's, Kniphofia, Laguna, Lent, Leopard, Lote, Lotus, Madonna, Martagon, Nelumbo, Nenuphar, Nerine, Nuphar, Nymphaea, Padma, Phormium, Plantain, Quamash, Regal, Sarsa, Scilla, Sego, Skunk cabbage, Smilax, Solomon's seal, Spider, Star of Bethlehem, Stone, Sword, Tiger, Trillium, Tritoma, Tuberose, Turk's cap, Victoria, Water, Water maize, Yucca, Zephyr

Limb Arm, Bough, Branch, Crural, Exapod, Flipper, Forearm, Hindleg, Imp, Leg, Leg-end, Member, Proleg, Ramus, Scion, Shin, Spald, Spall, Spaul(d), Wing

Lime Bass(wood), Beton, Calc, Calcicolous, Caustic, Lind(en), Malm, Mortar, Slaked, Soda, Teil, Tilia, Trap, Viscum, Whitewash

▷ **Limit** *may indicate* 'surrounding'

Limit(ation), Limited, Limiting Ambit, Asymptote, Bind, Border, Bound, Bourn(e), Brink, Cap, Cash, Ceiling, Circumscribe, Climax, Compass, Confine, Constrict, Curb, Deadline, Define, Demark, Determine, Earshot, Eddington, Edge, Edition, End, Entail, Esoteric, → **EXTENT**, Extreme, Finite, Fraenum, Frontier, Gate, Goal, Hourlong, Impound, Insular, Limes, Line, Lite, Lynchet, March, Maximum, Mete, Minimum, Nth, Outedge, Pale, Parameter, Perimeter, Periphery, Predetermine, Qualify, Range, Rate-cap, Ration, Reservation, Restrict, Rim, Roof, Scant, Shoestring, Sky, Somedeal, Somedele, Speed, Stint, String, Tail(lie), Tailye, Term(inus), Tether, Three-mile, Threshold, Thule, Tie, Time, Tramline, Tropic, Twelve-mile, Utmost, Utter, Verge

Limp Claudication, Dot, Droopy, Flabby, Flaccid, Flaggy, Flimsy, Floppy, Gimp, Hamble, Hobble, Hop, Lifeless, Spancel, Tangle, Wilting

Line(d), Lines, Lining Abreast, Agate, Agonic, Allan, → **ANCESTRY**, Anent, Angle, Apothem, Arew, Assembly, Attention, Axis, Bakerloo, Bar, Barcode, Baton, Battle, Baulk, Becket, Bikini, Bluebell, Bob, Body, Bombast, Bottom, Boundary, BR, Brail, Branch, Bread, Building, Bush, By, Canal, Carriage, Casing, Cathetus, Ceil, Cento, Ceriph, Chord, Ciel, Clew, Club, Coach, Colour, Column, Command, Contour, Cord(on), Course, Crease, Credit, Crib, Crocodile, Crowfoot, Crow's feet, Cunard, Curve, Cushion, Dancette, Danger, Date, Datum, Dead-ball, Decidua, Delay, Descent, DEW, Diagonal, Diameter, Diffusion, Distaff, Dochmiachal, Dotted, Downhaul,

Dress, Dynasty, Earing, El, E-la-mi, Encase, End, Equator, Equinoctial, Equinox, Faint, Fall(s), Fathom, Fault, Feint, Fess(e), Fettle, File, Finishing, Firing, Firn, Fixed, Flex, Flight, Frame, Front, Frontier, Frost, Furr(ow), Geotherm, Germ, Gimp, Giron, Goal, Graph, Grass, Green, Gridiron, Gymp, Gyron, Hachure, Halyard, Hard, Hatching, Hawser, Header, Hemistich, Heptameter, Hexameter, High-watermark, Hockey, Hot, House, Impot, Inbounds, Inbred, Incase, Inhaul(er), Insole, Intima, Isallobar, Isobar, Isobath, Isochron(e), Isoclinic, Isoclude, Isogloss, Isogonal, Isogonic, Isogram, Isohel, Isohyet, Isomagnetic, Isometric, Isonome, Isophote, Isopiestic, Isopyenal, Isotherm, Kill, Knittle, L, Land, Lane, Lansker, Lap, Lariat, Lateral, Latitude, Lead, Leash, Le(d)ger, Length, Ley, Lie, Ling, LMS, Load, Log, Longitude, Lossy, Loxodrome, Lubber, Lugger, Lye, Macron, Maginot, Main, Mainsheet, Mark, Marriage, Mason-Dixon, Median, Meridian, Mesal, Metropolitan, Monorail, Nacre, Naman, Noose, Norsel, Northern, Number, Oche, Octastichon, Ode, Oder-Neisse, Og(h)am, Omentum, Onedin, Ordinate, Orphan, Orthostichy, Painter, Panty, Parallel, Parameter, Parastichy, Party, Paternoster, Path, Penalty, Pencil, Phalanx, Picket, Pinstripe, Plasterboard, Pleuron, Plimsoll, Plumb, Poetastery, Polar, Police, Policy, Popping-crease, Poverty, Power, Princess, Product(ion), Profession, Punch, Pure, Queue, Race, Radial, Radius, Rail, Rank, Raster, Ratlin(e), Ratling, Rattlin, Ray, Receiving, Red, Reticle, Retinue, Rew, Rhumb, Ripcord, Rope, Route, Row, Rule, Ry, Scazon, Score, Scotch, Scratch, Scrimmage, Script, Secant, Seperatrix, Serif, Seriph, Service, Set, Shielded, Shore, Shout, Shroud, Siding, Siegfried, Sight, Silver, Six-yard, Slur, Snow, Soft, Solidus, Sounding, Specialty, Spectral, Spider, Spilling, Spring, Spunyarn, Squall, SR, Staff, Stance, Stanza, Starting, Static, Stave, Stean, Steen, Stein, Stem, Stich(os), Stock, Story, Strain, Strap, Streak, Strene, Striate, String, Stripe, Stuff, Subject, Swap, Symphysis, Tag, Tailback, Talweg, Tangent, Teagle, Tea lead, Terminator, Tetrameter, Thalweg, Thin blue, Thin red, Thread, Throwaway, Tidemark, Tie, Tier, Tiercet, Timber, Touch, Trade, Transmission, Transoceanic, Transversal, Tree, Trimeter, Tropic, Trot, Trunk, Try, Tudor, Twenty-five, Twenty-two, Upstroke, Variety, Verse, Virgule, Wad, Wallace's, Washing, Water(shed), White, Widow, Wire, World, Wrinkle, Z, Zag, Zip

Linen Amice, Amis, Barb, Bed, Byssus, Cambric, Crash, Damask, Dornick, Dowlas, Duck, Ecru, Harn, Lawn, Line, Lint, Napery, Percale, Seersucker, Sendal, Silesia, Snow, Table, Toile, Undies

Liner Artist, Bin-bag, RMS, Rule(r), Ship, Sleeve, Steamer, Steen, Titanic

Linger(ing) Dawdle, Dwell, Hang, Hove(r), Lag, Loaf, →**LOITER**, Straggle, Taigle, Tarry, Tie

Linguist(ic), Linguistics Clitic, Comparative, Descriptive, Glottic, Onomastics, Philological, Phonemics, Polyglot, Pragmatics, Semantics, Stylistics, Taxeme

Link(ed), Linking, Links Associate, Between, Bond, Bridge, Chain, Cleek, Close knit, Colligate, Concatenation, Connect, Copula, Couple, Course, Cuff, Desmid, Drag, Draw-gear, Ess, Flambeau, Golf (course), Hookup, Hotline, Incatenation, Index, Interconnect, Interface, Internet, Interrelation, Intertwine, Karabiner, Krab, Liaise, Machair, Missing, Modem, Nexus, On-line, Pons, Preposition, Reciprocal, Relate, Ring, Tead(e), Terrestrial, →**TIE**, Tie-in, Tie-line, Torch, Unite, Wormhole, Yoke

Lion(ess) Androcles, Aphid, Aslan, Chindit, Elsa, Glitterati, Hero, Leo, Maned, Nemean, Opinicus, Personage, Pride, Simba

Lip(py), Lips Cheek, Cupid's bow, Fat, Fipple, Flews, Helmet, Jib, Labellum, Labial, Labiate, Labret, Labrum, Ligula, Muffle, Philtrum, →**RIM**, Rubies, Sass, Sauce, Slack-jaw, Spout, Submentum

Lipase Steapsin

Lipid Ganglioside, Inositol, Sphingarine

Liqueur, Liquor Bree, Brew, Broo, Broth, Creature, Elixir, Fumet, Hard stuff, Hooch, Lap, Mother, Ooze, Pot, Potation, Stock, Stuff, Vat

Liquid(ate), Liquidity, Liquids, Liquefaction Acetal, Amortise, Annihilate, Apprize, Aqua-regia, Bittern, Bouillon, Bromine, Cash, Court-bouillon, Creosol, Decoction, Dope, Eluate, Erase, Ethanol, Ether, Eucalyptol, Fluid, Fural, Furfural, Guaiacol, Indisputable, Ink, Isoprene, Jaw, Lye, Mess, Minim, Nebula, Pipe, Potion,

Protoplasm, PSL, Ptisan, Quinoline, Semen, Serum, Smectic, Solution, Solvent, Syrup, Thinner, Titre, Triptane, Tuberculin, Ullage, Washing-up, Whey, Wind up

▷ **List** *may indicate* 'listen'

List(s), Listing A, Active, Agenda, Antibarbarus, Appendix, Army, Atilt, B, Barocco, Barrace, Bead-roll, Bibliography, Border, British, Canon, Cant, Catalog(ue), Categorise, Catalog, Cause, Check, Choice, Civil, Class, Compile, Credits, Danger, Debrett, Docket, Empanel, Entry, Enumerate, Front, Glossary, Hark, Hearken, Heel, Hit, Hit-parade, Honours, Index, Indian, Interdiction, Inventory, Itemise, Laundry, Lean, Leet, Line-up, Linked, Litany, Lloyds, Mailing, Manifest, Menu, Navy, Notitia, Official, Panel, Paradigm, Party, Price, Prize, Register, Repertoire, Reserved, Retired, Roin, Roll, Roon, Roster, Rota, Rund, Schedule, Script, Short, Sick, Slate, Slope, Strip, Syllabary, Syllabus (of Errors), Table, Tariff, Tick, Ticket, Tilt, Timetable, Tip, To-do, Transfer, Union, Waiting, Waybill, White, Wine, Wish

Listen(er) Attend, Auditor, Auscultate, Bug, Ear, Eavesdropper, Gobemouche, Hark, →**HEED**, List, Lithe, Lug, Monitor, Oyez, Simon, Tune-in, Wire-tap

▷ **Listen to** *may indicate* a word sounding like another

Lister Plough, Surgeon

Listless(ness) Abulia, Accidie, Acedia, Apathetic, Atony, Dawney, Indolent, Lackadaisical, Languor, Mooning, Mope, Mopus, Sloth, Thowless, Torpor, Upsitting, Waff

▷ **Lit** *may indicate* an anagram

Literary Academic, Bas bleu, Booksie, Erudite, Lettered

Literature Agitprop, Belles lettres, Comparative, Corpus, Fiction, Gongorism, Hagiology, Midrash, Musar, Page, Picaresque, Prose, Responsa, Samizdat, Sci-fi, Sturm und Drang, Wisdom

Litter Bed, Brancard, Brood, Cacolet, Cat, Cubs, Debris, Deep, Doolie, Emu-bob, Farrow, Jampan, Kago, Kajawah, Kindle, Mahmal, Nest, Norimon, Palankeen, Palanquin, Palkee, Palki, Pup, →**REFUSE**, Scrap, Sedan, Stretcher, Team, Whelp

Little Beans, Brief, Chota, Curn, Diddy, Dorrit, Drib, Drop, Fewtrils, Fraction, Haet, Hait, Hate, Ickle, Insect, Iota, John, Jot, Leet, Lilliputian, Limited, Lite, Lyte, Means, Mini, Miniscule, Minnow, Minuscule, →**MINUTE**, Modicum, Morceau, Nell, Paltry, Paucity, Paul, Petite, Pink, Scant, Scut, Shade, Shoestring, Short, Shred, Shrimp, Slight, Sma', →**SMALL**, Smattering, Smidge(o)n, Smidgin, Smout, Smowt, Some, Soupçon, Spot, Tad, Teensy(-weensy), Tich, Tiddly, Tine, Titch, Touch, Tyne, Vestige, Wee, Weedy, Whit, Women

Littoral Coast(al)

Live(d), Livelihood, Living, Liveliness, Lively, Lives Active, Alert, Allegro, Animated, Animato, Animato, Are, AV, Awake, Be, Bouncy, Breezy, Brio, Brisk, Cant(y), Cheery, Chipper, Chirpy, Cohabit, Con moto, Con spirito, Crouse, Dash, Durante vita, Dynamic, Ebullient, Entrain, Exist, Extant, Exuberant, Feisty, Frisky, Gamy, Gay, Giocoso, Hang-out, Hard, High jinks, Hijinks, Is, Jazz, Kedge, Lad, Lead, Mercurial, Merry, Mouvementé, Outgo, Pacey, Peart, Pep, Piert, Quicksilver, Rackety, Racy, Reside, Rousing, Salt, Saut, Scherzo, Skittish, Smacking, Spanking, Sparky, Spiritoso, Spirituel(le), Sprack, Sprightly, Spry, Spunky, Swinging, Thrive, Unrecorded, Up tempo, Vibrant, Vital, Vitality, Vive, →**VOLATILE**, Wick, Zappy, Zingy, Zippy, Zoe

▶ **Livelihood** *see* LIVED

Living Advowson, Benefice, Biont, Bread, Canonry, Crust, Glebe, Inquiline, Lodging, Quick, Resident, Simony, Subsistence, Symbiotic, Vicarage, Vital

Lizard Abas, Agama, American chameleon, Amphisbaena, Anguis, Anole, Basilisk, Bearded, Blindworm, Blue-tongued, Brontosaurus, Chameleon, Chuckwalla, Dinosaur, Draco, Dragon, Eft, Evet, Frilled, Galliwasp, Gecko(ne), Gila, Gila monster, Glass snake, Goanna, Guana, Hatteria, Hellbender, Horned, Iguana, Jew, Kabaragoya, Komodo (dragon), Lacerta, Legua(a)n, Lounge, Malayan monitor, Mastigure, Menopome, Mokomoko, Moloch, Monitor, Mosasaur(us), Newt, Ngarara, Perentie, Perenty, Reptile, Rock, Sand, Sauria, Scincoid, Seps, Skink, Slow-worm, Snake, Sphenodon, Stellio(n), Sungazer, Swift, Tegu(exin), Teiid, Tokay, Tuatara, Tuatera, Varan, Wall, Whiptail, Worm, Worral, Worrel, Zandoli

Load(ed), Loader, Loading, Loads Accommodation, Affluent, Back-end, Ballast, Base, Biased, Boot-strap, Boozy, Burden, Cargo, Charge, Cobblers, Dead weight, Disc, Dope, Drunk, Dummy, Fardel, Fother, Frau(gh)tage, Freight, Front-end, Fulham, Full, Gestant, Glyc(a)emic, Heap, Input, Jag, Lade, Lard, Last, Live, Onus, Pack, Packet, Pay, Peak, Power, Prime, Raft, Rich, Scads, Seam, Shipment, Shoal, Some, Span, Super, Surcharge, →**TIGHT**, Tipsy, Tod, Traction, Ultimate, Useful, Wealthy, Weight, Wharfinger, Wing

Loaf(er), Loaves Baguette, Bannock, Barmbrack, Baton, Beachbum, Beachcomber, Bloomer, Bludge, Bonce, Boule, Bread, Brick, Bum, Bu(r)ster, Cad, Cob, Coburg, Cottage, Currant, Farmhouse, Hawm, Head, Hoe-cake, Idle, Layabout, →**LAZE**, Long tin, Lusk, Manchet, Meat, Miche, Milk, Mooch, Mouch, Pan(h)agia, Plain, Roll, Roti, Shewbread, Showbread, Slosh, Split tin, Stollen, Stotty, Sugar, Tin, Vantage, Yob

Loan(s) Advance, Balloon, Benevolence, Bottomry, Bridging, Call, Consolidation, Debenture, Demand, Imprest, Lane, Mutuum, Omnium, Out, Prest, Respondentia, Roll-over, Start-up, Student, Sub, Top-up

Loathe, Loathing, Loathsome Abhor(rent), Abominate, Carrion, Detest, Execrate, Hate, Keck, Nauseate, Odious, Reptilian, Scunner, Ug(h)

Lobby Demo, Entry, Foyer, Gun, Hall, Press, Urge

Lobster Cock, Crawfish, Crayfish, Crustacean, Decapoda, Langouste, Macrura, Norway, Pereion, Pot, Scampo, Spiny, Squat, Thermidor, Tomalley

▷**Local** *may indicate* a dialect word

Local(ity) Area, Bro, Close, Des(h)i, Endemic, Home, Inn, Landlord, Native, Near, Nearby, Neighbourhood, Number, Parochial, Pub, Regional, Resident, Tavern, Topical, Vernacular, Vicinal

Locate(d), Location Address, Connect, Echo, Emplacement, Find, Fix, Lay, Milieu, Pinpoint, Place, Placement, Plant, Put, Recess, Sat, Set-up, Site, Situate, Situation, Sofar, Spot, Theatre, Trace, Ubiety, Website, Where(abouts), Workplace, Zone

Loch, Lough Ashie, Awe, Derg, Earn, Eil, Erne, Etive, Fine, Gare, Garten, Glen Lyon, Holy, Hourn, Katrine, →**LAKE**, Larne, Leven, Linnhe, Lomond, Long, Moidart, Morar, More, Na Keal, Neagh, Ness, Rannoch, Ryan, Sea, Shiel, Strangford, Tay, Torridon

Lock(ing), Locker, Locks, Lock up Bar, Barnet, Bolt, Canal, Central, Chain, Chubb®, Clap-sill, Clinch, Combination, Cowlick, Curlicue, Davy Jones, Deadbolt, Detent, Drop, Fastener, Fermentation, Foretop, Gate, Haffet, Haffit, Handcuff, Hasp, Hold, Intern, Key, Latch, Lazaretto, Man, Mane, Mortise, Percussion, Prison, Quiff, Ragbolt, Rim, Ringlet, Safety, Sasse, Scalp, Scissors, →**SECURE**, Sluice, Snap, Spring, Staircase, Sta(u)nch, Stock, Strand, Tag, Talon, Tetanus, Time, Trap, Tress, Tuft, Tumbler, Vapour, Villus, Ward, Wheel, Wrestle, Yale®

Locomotive Banker, Bogie, Bul(l)gine, Engine, Iron horse, Mobile, Mogul, Rocket, Steamer, Train

Locust, Locust tree Acacia, Anime, Carob, Cicada, Hopper, Nymph, Robinia, Seventeen-year, Voetganger

Lodge(r) Billet, Board(er), Box, Cosher, Deposit, Dig, Doss, Encamp, Entertain, Freemason, Grange, Grove, Guest, Harbour, Host, Hunting, Inmate, Inquiline, Layer, Lie, Masonic, Nest, Orange, Parasite, PG, Porter's, Put up, Quarter, Rancho, Resident, Room(er), Stay, Storehouse, Stow, Tenant, Tepee, Wigwam

Lodging(s) Abode, B and B, Chummage, Dharms(h)ala, Diggings, Digs, Dosshouse, Ferm, Grange, Grove, Hospitium, Hostel, Inquiline, Kip, Minshuku, Pad, Pension, Pied-à-terre, Quarters, Resiant, Rooms, Singleen, Sponging-house, Spunging-house, YHA

Loft(iness), Lofty Aerial, Airy, Arrogant, Attic, Celsitude, Chip, Exalted, Garret, Garryowen, Grand, Haymow, High, Jube, Lordly, Magniloquent, Noble, Organ, Rarefied, Rigging, Rood, Roost, Sky(ish), Sublime, Tallat, Tallet, Tallot

Log(ging) Billet, Black box, Cabin, Chock, Deadhead, Diarise, Diary, Enter, Hack, Key(stroke), Mantissa, Nap(i)erian, Neper, Patent, Poling, →**RECORD**, Stock, Tachograph, Yule

Logic(al) Alethic, Analytical, Aristotelian, Boolean, Chop, Cogent, Deontic,

Dialectic(s), Digital, Doxastic, Elench(us), Epistemics, Hardhead(ed), Modal, Organon, Ramism, Ratiocinate, Rational(e), Reason, Sane, Sequacious, Shared, Sorites, Syllogism, Symbolic, Trivium, Vienna circle

Loiter(ing) Dally, Dare, Dawdle, Dilatory, Dilly-dally, Idle, Lag, Lallygag, Leng, Lime, →**LINGER**, Loaf, Lollygag, Mike, Mooch, Mouch, Potter, Saunter, Scamp, Suss, Taigle, Tarry

London(er) 'Arry, Big Smoke, Cockaigne, Cockney, Co(c)kayne, East-ender, Flat-cap, Jack, Port, Roseland, Smoke, Town, Troynovant, Wen

Lone(r), Lonely Bereft, Isolated, Recluse, Remote, Rogue, Saddo, Secluded, Sole, Solitary, Unked, Unket, Unkid

Long(er), Longing, Longs Ache, Aitch, Ake, Appetent, Aspire, Brame, Covet, Desire, Die, Earn, Erne, Eternal, Far, Greed, Green, Grein, →**HANKER**, Huey, Hunger, Island, Itch, L, Lanky, Large, Lengthy, Longa, Lust, Macron, Miss, More, Nostalgia, Option, Pant, Parsec, →**PINE**, Prolix, Side, Sigh, Tall, Thirst, Trews, Wearisome, Weary, Wish, Wist, Yearn, Yen

Longitude Celestial, Meridian

Longshoreman Hobbler, Hoveller, Wharfinger

Long-sighted(ness) Hypermetropia

Loo Ajax, Bog, Can, Chapel, Dike, Game, Gents, Jakes, John, Latrine, Privy, Toilet

Loofah Towel gourd

Look(s), Look at After-eye, Air, Aspect, Await, Behold, Belgard, Bonne-mine, Browse, Busk, Butcher's, Butcher's hook, Case, Clock, Close-up, Crane, Daggers, Decko, Deek, Dekko, Ecce, Ecco, Expression, Eye, Eye-glance, Face, Facies, Gander, Gawp, Gaze, Geek, Glad-eye, Glance, Glare, Gleam, Gledge, Glimpse, Glom, Glower, Goggle, Good, Grin, Hallo, Hangdog, Hey, Hippocratic, Iliad, Inspect, Keek, La, Leer, Lo, Mien, New, Ogle, Old-fashioned, Peek, Peep, Prospect, Ray, Recce, Refer, →**REGARD**, Scan, Scrutinise, Search, See, Seek, Shade, Sheep's eyes, Shufti, Shufty, Spy, Squint, Squiz, Stare, Survey, Toot, V, Vista, Wet

Look-out (man) Cockatoo, Crow's nest, Huer, Mirador, Nit, Pas op, Picket, Prospect, Sangar, Sentry, Spotter, Sungar, Tentie, Toot(er), Watch, Watchtower

▷ **Look silly** *may indicate* an anagram

Loom Beamer, Dobby, Emerge, Impend, Jacquard, Lathe, Lease-rod, Menace, Picker, Temple, Threaten, Tower

Loon(y) Airhead, Nutter

Loop(ed), Loophole, Loopy Becket, Bight, Billabong, Bouclé, Carriage, Chink, Closed, Coil, Eyelet, Eyesplice, Fake, Feedback, Frog, Frontlet, Grom(m)et, Grummet, Hank, Heddle-eye, Henle's, Hysteresis, Infinite, Kink, Knop, Lasket, Local, Lug, Noose, Oillet, Parral, Parrel, Pearl(-edge), Picot, Purl, Squiggle, Staple, Stirrup, Swag, Terry, Toe, Twist

Loose(n), Loose woman Absolve, Abstrict, Adrift, Afloat, Anonyma, Baggage, Bail, Besom, Bike, Bunter, Chippie, Chippy, Clatch, Cocotte, Demi-mondaine, Demirep, Desultory, Dissolute, Dissolve, Doxy, Draggletail, Dratchell, Drazel, Ease, Emit, Flabby, Flipperty-flopperty, Flirt-gill, Floosie, Floozie, Floozy, Floppy, Franion, Free, Gangling, Gay, Geisha, Hussy, Insecure, Jade, Jay, Jezebel, Lax, Limp, Loast, Loon, Loste, Mob, Mort, Painted, Pinnace, Profligate, Promiscuous, Quail, Ramp, →**RELAX**, Sandy, Scrubber, Slag, Slapper, Slipshod, Slut, Streel, Strumpet, Tart, Tramp, Trull, Unhasp, Unhitch, Unlace, Unlash, Unleash, Unpin, Unreined, Unscrew, Unstuck, Untie, Vague, Wappend, Whore

Loot Boodle, Booty, Cragh, Creach, Foray, Haul, Mainour, Peel, Pluck, →**PLUNDER**, Ransack, Rape, Reave, Reif, Rieve, Rob, Sack, Smug, Spoils, Spoliate, Stouth(e)rie, Swag, Treasure, Waif

Lop Behead, Clip, Clop, Curtail, Detruncate, Droop, Shroud, Sned, Trash

Lord(s), Lordship, Lordly Adonai, Ahura Mazda, Anaxandron, Arrogant, Boss, Byron, Cardigan, Cripes, Dieu, Domineer, Dominical, Drug, Duc, Earl, Elgin, Gad, Gilded Chamber, God, Haw-haw, Herr, Idris, Imperious, Jim, Justice, Kami, Kitchener, Land, Landgrave, Law, Ld, Liege, Lonsdale, Losh, Lud, MCC, Meneer, Misrule,

Mynheer, Naik, Oda Nobunaga, Omrah, Ordinary, Ormazd, Ormuzd, Palsgrave, Peer, Seigneur, Seignior, Shaftesbury, Sire, Spiritual, Taverner, Temporal, Tuan, Ullin

Lore Cab(b)ala, Edda, Lair, Lare, Riem, Upanis(h)ad

Lorry Artic(ulated), Camion, Carrier, Crummy, Double-bottom, Drag, Drawbar outfit, Dropsided, Flatbed, Juggernaut, Low-loader, Rig, Tipper, Tonner, →TRUCK, Wagon

Lose(r) Also-ran, Decrease, Drop, Elude, Forfeit, Leese, Misère, Mislay, Misplace, Nowhere, Spread, Tank, Throw, Tine(r), Tyne, Underdog, Unsuccessful, Waste, Weeper

Loss, Lost Angel's share, Anosmia, Aphesis, Aphonia, Apocope, Apraxia, Astray, Attainder, Boohai, Chord, Cost, Dead, Decrease, Depreciation, Detriment, Disadvantage, Elision, Extinction, Foredamned, Forfeited, Forgotten, Forlorn, Gone, Hurtful, Lore, Lorn, Lurch, Missing, Omission, Outage, Pentimento, Perdition, Perdu, Perished, Preoccupied, Privation, Psilosis, Tine, Tinsel, Tint, Toll, Traik, Tribes, Tyne(d), Ullage, Unredeemed, Wastage, Wasted, Will, Wull

▷ **Lost** *may indicate* an anagram or an obsolete word

Lot(s) Abundant, Amount, Aret(t), Badly, Batch, Boatload, Bomb, Caboodle, Cavel, Chance, Deal, Dole, Doom, Due, →FATE, Fortune, Hantle, Hap, Heaps, Horde, Host, Item, Job, Kevel, Kismet, Lank, Lashings, Legion, Loads, Loadsa, Luck, Manifold, Many, Mass, Moh, Moira, Mony, Mort, Myriad, Oceans, Omnibus, Oodles, Oodlins, Pack, Parcel, Plenitude, Plenty, Portion, Power, Purim, Raft, Scads, Set, Sight, Slather, Slew, Slue, Sortilege, Stack, Sum, Tall order, Tons, Vole, Wagonload, Weird

Lothario Lady-killer, Libertine, Rake, Womaniser

Lotion After-shave, Blackwash, Calamine, Collyrium, Cream, Emollient, Humectant, Suntan, Unguent, Wash

Lottery, Lotto Bingo, Cavel, Draw, Gamble, Pakapoo, Pools, Punchboard, Raffle, Rollover, Scratchcard, Sweepstake, Tombola

Louche Rip

Loud(ness), Loudly Bel, Big, Blaring, Booming, Brassy, Decibel, Ear-splitting, F, FF, Flashy, Forte, Fracas, Full-mouthed, Garish, Gaudy, Glaring, Hammerklavier, High(pitched), Lumpkin, Noisy, Orotund, Plangent, Raucous, Roarie, Siren, Sone, Stentor(ian), Strident, Tarty, Vocal, Vociferous, Vulgar

Loudspeaker Action, Boanerges, Bullhorn, Hailer, Megaphone, PA, Squawk box, Stentor, Subwoofer, Tannoy®, Tweeter, Woofer

Lounge(r) Daiker, Da(c)ker, Departure, Doze, Executive, Hawm, Idle, Laze, Lie, Lizard, Loaf, Loll, Lollop, Parlour, Settee, Slouch, Sun, Sunbed, Transit, Transitive

Louse (up), Lousy, Lice Acrawl, Argulus, Bolix, Bollocks, Chat, Chicken, Cootie, Crab, Crummy, Head, Isopod(a), Kutu, Mallophaga, Nit, Oniscus, Pedicular, Phthiriasis, Psocid, Psocoptera, Psylla, Pubic, Slater, Snot, Sowbug, Sucking, Vermin

Lout Auf, Clod(hopper), Coof, Cuif, Galere, Hallian, Hallion, Hallyon, Hick, Hob, Hobbledehoy, Hooligan, Hoon, Jack, Jake, Keelie, Lager, Larrikin, Lob(lolly), Loord, Lubber, Lumpkin, Lycra, Oaf, Oik, Rube, Swad, Tout, Yahoo, Yob(bo)

Louvre Shutter

Love(d), Lovable, Lover Abelard, Admire, Adore, Adulator, Affection, Agape, Alma, Amabel, Amanda, Amant, Amateur, Ami(e), Amoret, Amoroso, Amour, Angharad, Antony, Ardour, Ariadne, Aroha, Aucassin, Beau, Bidie-in, Blob, Calf, Care, Casanova, Chamberer, Cicisbeo, Concubine, Coquet, Court, Courtly, Cupboard, Cupid, Dear, Dotard, Dote, Doxy, Duck(s), Ducky, Dulcinea, Eloper, Emotion, Enamorado, Eros, Esme, Fan(boy), Flame, Frauendienst, Free, Gal(l)ant, Goose-egg, Hon(ey), Idolise, Inamorata, Inamorato, Iseult, Isolde, Item, Jo, Lad, Lancelot, Leander, Leman, Like, Lochinvar, Loe, Loo, Lurve, Man, Nada, Nihility, Nil, Nothing, Nought, Nut, O, Pairs, Paramour, Pash, Passion, Pet, Philander, Philtre, Platonic, Precious, Protestant, Psychodelic, Puppy, Revere, Rhanja, Romance, Romeo, Spark, Spooner, Stale, Storge, Suitor, Swain, Thisbe, Toyboy, Treasure, Tristan, Troilus, True, Turtle(-dove), Valentine, Venus, Virtu, Woman, Zeal, Zero

Lovely Adorable, Belle, Cute, Dishy, Dreamy, Fair, Gorgeous, Nasty, Super

Love-making Kama Sutra, Sex, Snog

Low(est), Low-born, Low-cut, Lower(ing), Low-key Abase, Abate,

Low country Abysmal, Amort, Area, Avail(e), Avale, B, Basal, Base(-born), Bass(o), Beneath, Blue, Canaille, Cartoonist, Cheap, Church, Cocktail, Condescend, Contralto, Couch, Cow, Crestfallen, Croon, Crude, Darken, Debase, Declass, Décolleté, Deepen, Degrade, Demean, Demit, Demote, Depress, Despicable, Devalue, Dim, Dip, Dispirited, Doldrums, Drawdown, Drop, Early, Embase, Flat, Foot, Frown, Gazunder, Glare, Guernsey, Gurly, Gutterblood, Hedge(-hopping), Hidalgo, Humble, Ignoble, Imbase, Inferior, Jersey, Laigh, Lallan, Law, Mass, Mean(born), Menial, Moo, Mopus, Morose, Nadir, Net, Nether, Nett, Non-U, Ornery, Ostinato, Paravail, Plebeianise, Profound, Prole, Relegate, Ribald, Rock-bottom, Sad, Scoundrel, Scowl, Secondo, Shabby, Short, Soft, Stoop, Subordinate, Sudra, Sunken, Undermost, Unobtrusive, Vail, Vulgar, Weak, Wretched

Low country Flanders

▷ **Lower** *may refer to* cattle

Lowry LS

Loyal(ty) Adherence, Allegiant, Brand, Brick, Dependable, Diehard, Faithful, Fast, Fealty, Fidelity, Firm, Gungho, Leal, Liegedom, Patriotic, Pia, Stalwart, Staunch, Tribalism, Troth, → TRUE, Trusty

Lozenge Cachou, Catechu, Coughdrop, Fusil, Jujube, Mascle, Pastille, Pill, Rhomb, Rustre, Tablet, Troche, Voided

Lubricant, Lubricate, Lubrication Carap-oil, Coolant, Derv, Fluid, Force-feed, Grease, Oil, Petrolatum, Sebum, Unguent, Vaseline®, Wool-oil

Lucid Bright, Clear, Perspicuous, Sane

Lucifer Devil, Match, Proud, Satan, Venus

Luck(y) Amulet, Auspicious, Beginner's, Bonanza, Break, Caduac, Canny, Cess, Chance, Charmed, Chaunce, Daikoku, Dip, Fat, Fate, Fluke, → FORTUNE, Godsend, Hap, Heather, Hit, Jam(my), Jim, Joss, Lady, Lot, Mascot, Mercy, Mozzle, Prosit, Providential, Pudding-bag, Purple passage, Purple patch, Seal, Seel, Sele, Serendipity, Sess, Sonsie, Sonsy, Spawny, Star(s), Streak, Success, Talisman, Tinny, Tough, Turn-up, White rabbits, Windfall, Worse

Lucrative Earner

Ludicrous Absurd, Bathetic, Bathos, Crackpot, Farcical, Fiasco, Inane, Irish, Jest, Laughable, Risible

Luggage Bags, Carryon, Cases, Dunnage, Excess, Grip, Hand, Kit, Petara, Samsonite®, Suiter, Traps, Trunk

Lull, Lullaby Berceuse, Calm, Cradlesong, Hushaby, Respite, Rock, Sitzkreig, Soothe, Sopite

Lumbar Hip

Lumber(ing) Clump, Galumph, Jumble, Pawn, Ponderous, Raffle, Saddle, Scamble, Timber

Luminance, Luminous, Luminosity, Luminescence Aglow, Arc, Candela, Dayglo, Glow, Hero, Ignis-fatuus, L, Light, Meteor, Nit, Phosphorescent, Scintillon, Sea-dog, Wildfire, Will o' the wisp

Lummox Galoot

Lump(ectomy), Lump(s), Lump(y) Aggregate, Bolus, Bubo, Bud, Bulge, Bur(r), Caruncle, Chuck, Chunk, Clat, Claut, Clod, Clot, Cob, Combine, Da(u)d, Dallop, Dollop, Enhydros, Epulis, Flocculate, Ganglion, Geode, Gnarl, Gob(bet), Goiter, Goitre, Goop, Grape, Grip, Grumose, Hunch, Hunk, Inium, Knarl, Knob, Knub, Knur(r), Knurl, Lob, Lunch, Malleolus, Mass, Moss-litter, Mote, Mott, Myxoma, Neuroma, Nibble, Nirl, Node, Nodule, Nodulus, Nub(bin), Nubble, Nugget, Nur(r), Nurl, Osteophyte, Plook, Plouk, Quinsy, Raguly, Sarcoma, Scybalum, Sitfast, Slub, Strophiole, Tragus, Tuber(cle), Tumour, Tylectomy, Wart, Wodge

Lunacy, Lunatic Bedlam, Dementia, Demonomania, Folly, Insanity, Mad(ness), Madman, Maniac, Nutter, Psychosis

▷ **Lunatic** *may indicate* an anagram

Lunch(time) Bait, Box, Crib, Dejeune, Déjeuner, Fork, L, Liquid, Nacket, Nuncheon, Packed, Piece, Ploughman, Pm, Tiff(in), Working

Lung(s) Alveoli, Bellows, Book, Coalminer's, Farmer's, Iron, Lights, Pulmo, Pulmonary, Soul

Lunge Breenge, Breinge, Dive, Stab, Thrust, Venue

Lurch Reel, Slew, Stoit, Stumble, Swee, Toss

Lure Bait, Bribe, Carrot, Decoy, Entice, Horn, Inveigle, Jig, Judas, Plug, Roper, Spinner, Spoon, Squid, Stale, Temptation, Tice, Tole, Toll, Train, Trepan

Lurgi Illness

Lurk(ing) Dare, Latitant, Skulk, Slink, Snoke, Snook, Snowk

Lush Alcoholic, Alkie, Alky, Dipso(maniac), Drunk, Fertile, Green, Juicy, Lydian, Soak, Sot, Succulent, Toper, Tosspot, Verdant

Lust(ful), Lusty Cama, Concupiscence, Corflambo, Desire, Eros, Frack, Greed, Kama, Lech(ery), Lewd, Megalomania, Obidicut, Prurience, Radge, Randy, Rank, Raunchy, Salacious, Venereous

Lustre, Lustrous Brilliance, Census, Chatoyant, Galena, Gaum, Gilt, Gloss, Gorm, Inaurate, Lead-glance, Lovelight, Pearlescent, Pearly, Pentad, Reflet, Satiny, Schiller, Water

Lute, Lutist Amphion, Chitarrone, Cither, Dichord, Orpharion, Pandora, Pandore, Pipa, Theorbo, Vielle

Luxuriant, Luxuriate, Luxurious, Luxury (lover) Apician, Bask, Clover, Cockaigne, Cockayne, Comfort, Copious, Delicate, Deluxe, Dolce vita, Extravagant, Exuberant, Fleshpots, Lavish, Lucullan, Lush, Mollitious, Ornate, Palatial, Pie, Plush(y), Posh, Rank, →**RICH**, Ritzy, Sumptuous, Sybarite, Wallow

▶**Lying** *see* **LIE(S)**

Lyre Box, Cithern, Harp, Psaltery, Testudo, Trigon

Lyric(s), Lyrical, Lyricist, Lyrist Awdl, Cavalier, Dit(t), Epode, Gilbert, Hammerstein, Melic, Ode, Orphean, Paean, Pean, Poem, Rhapsodic, Song, Spinto, Words

Mm

M Married, Member, Metre, Mike, Mile, Thousand

Macabre Gothic, Grotesque, Morbid, Sick

Machete Bolo

Machiavellian Savvy

Machine(ry) Apparat(us), Appliance, Bathing, → **DEVICE**, Facsimile, Fax, Fruit, Infernal, Instrument, Life-support, Party, Plant, Propaganda, Rowing, Sausage, Sewing, Slot, Spin, Tape, Teaching, Time, Vending, Virtual, War, Washing, Weighing

Mackintosh Burberry®, Mac, Mino, Oilskin, Slicker, Waterproof

Mad(den), Madman, Madness Angry, Balmy, Bananas, Barking, Barmy, Bedlam, Besotted, Bonkers, Crackbrained, Crackpot, Crazy, Cuckoo, Cupcake, Delirious, Dement, Détraqué, Distract, Dotty, Enrage, Fay, Fey, Folie, Folly, Frantic, Frenetic(al), Fruitcake, Furioso, Fury, Gelt, Gyte, Harpic, Hatter, Idiotic, Insane, Insanie, Insanity, Into, Irate, Ireful, Irritate, Kook, Livid, Loco, Lunatic, Lycanthropy, Madbrained, Maenad, Mango, Mania, Mental, Meshug(g)a, Metric, Midsummer, Moonstruck, Mullah, Nuts, Porangi, Psycho, Rabid, Raving, Redwood, Redwud, Scatty, Screwy, Short-witted, Starkers, Tonto, Touched, Troppo, Unhinged, Wood, Wowf, Wrath, Wud, Xenomania, Yond, Zany

▷ **Mad(den)** *may indicate* an anagram

Made (up) Synthesized

Madeira Cake

▷ **Madly** *may indicate* an anagram

Madonna Lady, Lily, Mary, Pietà, Virgin

Madras Chennai

Mafia, Mafioso Camorra, Capo, Cosa Nostra, Godfather, Goombah, Mob, Ndrangheta, Omerta, Padrone, Pentito, Sicilian

Magazine Arsenal, Clip, Colliers, Cornhill, Cosmopolitan, Digizine, Economist, E-zine, Field, Girlie, Glossy, Granta, House organ, Ladmag, Lady, Lancet, Life, Listener, Magnet, New Yorker, Organ, Paper, Part work, Periodical, Pictorial, Playboy, Powder, Private Eye, Pulp, Punch, She, Slick, Spectator, Store, Strand, Tatler, Time, Vogue, Warehouse, Weekly, Yoof, Zine

Magic(al), Magician, Magic square Alchemy, Art, Black, Charm, Conjury, Diablerie, Diablery, Druid, Enchanting, Fabulous, Faust, Fetish, Genie, Goetic, Goety, Gramary(e), Houdini, Illusionist, Incantation, Makuto, Math, Medea, Medicine man, Merlin, Mojo, Moly, Morgan le Fay, Necromancer, Powwow, Prospero, Rhombus, Sorcery, Spell, Speller, Supernatural, Talisman, Voodoo, Warlock, White, Wizard

Magistracy, Magistrate Aedile, Amman, Amtman, Archon, Avoyer, Bailie, Bailiff, Bailli(e), Beak, Bench, Boma, Burgess, Burgomaster, Cadi, Censor, Consul, Corregidor, Curule, Decemvirate, Demiurge, Doge(ate), Edile, Effendi, Ephor, Field cornet, Finer, Foud, Gonfalonier, JP, Judiciary, Jurat, Justice, Kotwal, Landamman(n), Landdrost, Maire, Mayor, Mittimus, Novus homo, Pilate, Podesta, Portreeve, Pr(a)efect, Pr(a)etor, Prior, Proconsul, Propraetor, Provost, Qadi, Quaestor, Recorder, Reeve, Shereef, Sherif, Stad(t)holder, Stipendiary, Syndic, Tribune, Worship

Magnate Baron, Beaverbrook, Bigwig, Industrialist, Mogul, Tycoon, VIP

Magnet(ic), Magnetism Animal, Artificial, Attraction, Bar, Charisma, Field, Gauss, Horseshoe, Induction, It, Loadstone, Lodestone, Maxwell, Od, Oersted, Oomph, Permanent, Personal, Polar, Pole, Pole piece, Poloidal, Pull, Remanence, Retentivity, Slug, Solenoid, Terrella, Terrestrial, Tesla, Tole, Weber

Magnificence, Magnificent Fine, Gorgeous, Grandeur, Imperial, Laurentian, Lordly, Noble, Pride, Regal, Royal, Splendid, State, Sumptuous, Superb

Magnifier, Magnify(ing) Aggrandise, Augment, Binocle, →ENLARGE, Exaggerate, Increase, Loupe, Microscope, Praise, Teinoscope, Telescope

Magnolia An(n)ona, Beaver-tree, Champac, Champak, Mississippi, Sweet bay, Umbrella-tree, Yulan

Magpie Bell, Bird, Bishop, Chatterer, Hoarder, Madge, Mag, Margaret, Outer, Pica, Piet, Pyat, Pyet, Pyot

Maid(en) Abigail, Aia, Amah, Biddy, Bonibell, Bonne, Bonnibell, Burd, Chamber, Chloe, Clothes-horse, Dam(o)sel, Debut, Dell, Dey, Dresser, First, Girl, Guillotine, Ignis-fatuus, Imago, Inaugural, Io, Iras, Iron, Lorelei, M, Marian, May, Miss, Nerissa, Nymph, Opening, Over, Pucelle, Racehourse, Rhian, Rhine, Skivvy, Soubrette, Stillroom, Suivante, Table, Thestylis, Tirewoman, Tweeny, Valkyrie, Virgin, Wench

Mail Air, →ARMOUR, Byrnie, Cataphract, Chain, Da(w)k, E(lectronic), Express, Fan, Gusset, Habergeon, Hate, Hauberk, Helm, Junk, Letter, Media, Panoply, Pony express, Post, Ring, Send, Snail, Spam, Surface, Tuille(tte), Voice

Mailbag Pouch

Main(s) Brine, Briny, Bulk, →CENTRAL, Chief, Cockfight, Conduit, Essential, Foremost, Gala, Generally, Grid, Gross, Head, →KEY, Lead(ing), Palmary, Predominant, Prime, Principal, Ring, →SEA, Sheer, Spanish, Staple, Water

Maintain(er), Maintenance Alimony, Allege, Ap(p)anage, Argue, Assert, Aver, Avouch, Avow, Claim, Contend, Continue, Defend, Escot, Insist, Lengthman, Preserve, Run, Serve, Service, Sustain, Upbear, Uphold, Upkeep

Maize Corn, Hominy, Indian, Mealie, Milo, Polenta, Popcorn, Samp

Majestic, Majesty August, Britannic, Dignity, Eagle, Grandeur, Imperial, Maestoso, Olympian, Regal, Royal, SM, Sovereign, Stately, Sublime, Tuanku

Major (domo) Drum, →IMPORTANT, Momentous, PM, Read, Seneschal, Senior, Sergeant, Star, Trumpet, Wig

Majority Absolute, Age, Body, Eighteen, Landslide, Latchkey, Maturity, Moral, Most, Preponderance, Relative, Silent, Working

▷ **Make** *may indicate* an anagram

Make(r), Make do, Making Amass, Brand, Build, Cause, Clear, Coerce, Coin, Compel, Compulse, Concoct, Creant, Create, Devise, Earn, Execute, Fabricate, Factive, Fashion, Faute de mieux, Fet(t), Forge, Form, Gar(re), God, Halfpenny, Increate, Mail(e), Manage, Marque, Meg, Prepare, Production, Reach, Render, Shape, Sort, Turn

Make believe Fantasy, Fictitious, Pretend, Pseudo

Makeover Redo

Make up, Make-up artist Ad lib, Compensate, Compose, Concealer, Constitution, Cosmetics, Gaud, Gawd, Gene, Genotype, Identikit®, Kohl, Liner, Lipstick, Maquillage, Mascara, Metabolism, Orchel, Paint, Pancake, Panstick, Powder, Prime, Reconcile, Rouge, Slap, Tidivate, Titivate, Toiletry, White-face

Male Alpha, Arrhenotoky, Buck, Bull, Dog, Ephebe, Ephebus, Gent, Hob, John Doe, Macho, Mansize, Masculine, Patroclinous, Ram, Rogue, Spear(side), Stag, Stamened, Telamon, Tom, Worthiest of the blood

Malfunction Glitch, Hiccup

Malice, Malicious Bitchy, Catty, Cruel, Despiteous, Envy, Malevolent, Malign, Mudslinger, Narquois, Schadenfreude, Serpent, Snide, Spite, Spleen, Venom, Viperish, Virulent

Malign(ant), Malignity Asperse, Backbite, Baleful, Bespatter, Defame, Denigrate, Evil, Gall, Harm, Hate-rent, Hatred, Libel, Sinister, Slander, Spiteful, Swart(h)y, Toxin, Traduce, Vicious, Vilify, Vilipend, Viperous, Virulent

Malleable Clay, Ductile, Fictile, Pliable

▷ **Malleable** *may indicate* an anagram

Mallet Beetle, Club, Gavel, Hammer, Mace, Maul, Stick, Tenderizer

Mammal Animal, Primate

Mammoth Epic, Gigantic, Huge, Jumbo, Mastodon, Whopping, Woolly

Man(kind), Manly, Manliness Adam, Advance, Andrew, Ask(r), Belt, Best, Betty, Bimana(l), Biped, Bloke, Bo, Boxgrove, Boy, Boyo, Bozo, Cad, Cairn, Calf, Castle, Cat, Chal, Chap, Checker, Chequer, Chiel, Cockey, Cod, Contact, Continuity, Crew, Cro-Magnon, Cuffin, Cully, Dog, Don, Draught, Dude, Emmanuel, Essex, Everyman, Family, Fancy, Fella, Feller, Fellow, Folsom, Friday, Front, G, Gayomart, Geezer, Gent, Gingerbread, Grimaldi, Guy, He, Heidelberg, Himbo, Hombre, Hominid, Homme, Homo, Homo sapiens, Inner, IOM, Iron, Isle, It, Jack, Java, Joe (Bloggs), Joe Blow, Joe Sixpack, Joe Soap, John(nie), John Doe, Josser, Limit, Link, Lollipop, M, Mac, Male, Medicine, Microcosm, Mister, Mon, Mondeo, Mr, Muffin, Mun, Neanderthal, Numbers, Nutcracker, Oreopithecus, Organisation, Ou, Paleolithic, Party, Pawn, Peking, Person, Piece, Piltdown, Pin, Pithecanthropus, Property, Raff, Ray, Remittance, Renaissance, Resurrection, Rhodesian, Right-hand, Rook, Sandwich, Servant, Servitor, Ship, Sinanthropus, Sodor, Soldier, Solo, Spear, Staff, Stag, Standover, Straw, Terran, Third, Thursday, Trinil, Twelfth, Tyke, Type, Utility, Valet, Vir(ile), Vitality, White van, Wight

Manage(r), Manageable, Management, Managing Administer, Amildar, Attain, Aumil, Behave, Board, Boss, Chief, Conduct, Contrive, Control, Cope, Crisis, Darogha, Direct, Docile, Eke, Exec(utive), Fare, Find, Govern, Grieve, Handle, Honcho, IC, Impresario, Intendant, Logistical, MacReady, Maître d('hotel), Make do, Manipulate, Manoeuvre, Proctor, Procurator, Régisseur, Rig, Roadie, →RUN, Scrape, Shift, Steward, Strategy, Subsist, Succeed, Suit, Superintend, Supervisor, Sysop, Tawie, Tractable, Treatment, Trustee, Wangle, Webmaster, Wield(y), Yare

Mandala Kalachakra

Mandate Authority, Decree, Fiat, Order

Mandela Madiba, Nelson

Mange, Mangy Sarcoptic, Scabby

Mangle Agrise, Butcher, Distort, Garble, Hack, Hackle, Haggle, Mammock, Wring(er)

▷ **Mangle** *may indicate* an anagram

Mania Cacoethes, Craze, Frenzy, Lunacy, Paranoia, Passion, Rage

Manifesto Communist, Plank, Platform, Policy, Pronunciamento

Manipulate, Manipulative, Manipulator, Manipulation Bend, Chiropractor, Control, Cook, Demagogic, Diddle, Fashion, Finesse, Gerrymander, Handle, Hellerwork, Jerrymander, Juggle, Logodaedalus, Massage, Master-slave, McTimoney chiropractic, Milk, Osteopath, Ply, Rig, Spin, Svengali, Swing, Tong, Tweeze, Use, Wangle

▷ **Manipulate** *may indicate* an anagram

Manner(ism), Mannerly, Manners Accent, Airs, À la, Appearance, Attitude, Bedside, Behaved, Behaviour, Bon ton, Breeding, Carriage, Conduct, Couth, Crew, Custom, Deportment, Ethos, Etiquette, Farand, Farrand, Farrant, Guise, Habit, How, Mien, Mode, Mood, Morality, Mores, Of, Ostent, Panache, Politesse, Presence, Presentation, P's & Q's, Quirk, Rate, Rhetoric, Sort, Style, Thew(s), Thewe(s), Trick, Urbanity, Way, Wise

▷ **Manoeuvre** *may indicate* an anagram

Manoeuvre(s) Alley-oop, Campaign, Castle, Démarche, Ebrillade, Engineer, Exercise, Faena, Fianchetto, Fork, Gambit, Grey mail, Heimlich, Hot-dog, Jink(s), Jockey, Loop, Manipulate, Op(eration), Pesade, Ploy, Pull out, Ruse, Short cut, Skewer, Steer, Stickhandle, Tactic, Takeover, Telemark, Use, U-turn, Valsalva, Wheel(ie), Whipstall, Wile, Wingover, Zigzag

Manor (house) Area, Demain, Demesne, Estate, Hall, Schloss, Vill(a)

Mansion Broadlands, Burghley House, Casa, Castle Howard, Chatworth House, Cliveden, Knole, Luton Hoo, Mentmore, Penshurst Place, Pile, Queen's House, Seat, Stourhead, Stowe, Waddesdon Manor, Woburn Abbey

Mantle Asthenosphere, Authority, Burnous(e), Capote, Caracalla, Cloak, Dolman, Elijah, Gas, Lithosphere, Pall, Pallium, Paludament, Pelisse, Rochet, Shawl, Sima, Toga, Tunic, Vakas, Veil

Manual Blue collar, Bradshaw, Cambist, Console, Enchiridion, Guide, Hand, Handbook, How-to, Portolan(o), Positif

Manure Compost, Dressing, Dung, →FERTILISER, Guano, Hen-pen, Lime, Muck, Sha(i)rn, Tath

Manuscript(s) Codex, Codicology, Folio, Hand, Holograph, Longhand, MS, Opisthograph, Palimpsest, Papyrus, Parchment, Script, Scroll, Scrowl(e), Slush-pile, Uncial, Vellum

▷ **Manx** *may indicate* a last letter missing

Many C, CD, Countless, Crew(e), D, Hantle, Herd, Horde, Host, L, Lot, M, Manifold, Mony, Multi(tude), Myriad, Numerous, Oodles, Power, Scad, Sight, Slew, Stacks, Tons, Umpteen, Untold

▷ **Many** *may indicate* the use of a Roman numeral letter

Map(s), Mapping Atlas, A-Z, Bijection, Card, Cartogram, Chart, Chorography, Choropleth, Cognitive, Contour, Face, Genetic, Image, Inset, Key, Loxodromic, Mappemond, OS, Plan(isphere), Plat, Plot, Portolano, Relief, Sea-card, Sea-chart, Site, Star, Topography, Weather

Maple Acer, Bird's-eye, Box elder, Japanese, Mazer, Norway, Plane, Sugar, Sycamore, Syrup

Map-maker Cartographer, OS, Speed

Marble(s), Marbling Agate, All(e)y, Arch, Bonce, Bonduc, Bool, Boondoggle, Bowl, Calcite, Chequer, Devil's, Dump, Elgin, Forest, Humite, Knicker, Languedoc, Marl, Marmoreal, Mosaic, Mottle, Nero-antico, Nicker, Onychite, Ophicalcite, Paragon, Parian, Petworth, Plonker, Plunker, Purbeck, Rance, Ringer, Ring-taw, Sanity, Scagliola, Taw, Tolley, Variegate, Verd antique, Wits

▷ **March** *may indicate* 'Little Women' character, Amy, Beth, Jo, Meg

March(ing), Marcher Abut, Adjoin, Advance, Anabasis, Border(er), Borderland, Boundary, Colonel Bogey, Dead, Defile, Demo(nstration), Étape, File, Footslog, Forced, Freedom, Fringe, Galumph, Go, Goosestep, Grand, Hunger, Ides, Jarrow, Lide, Limes, Lockstep, Meare, Music, →PARADE, Paso doble, Progress, Protest, Quick, Route, Saint, Slow time, Step, Strunt, Strut, Tramp, Trio, Tromp, Troop, Wedding, Yomp

Mardi Gras J'ouvert

Marge, Margin(al) Andean, Annotate, Bank, Border, Borderline, Brim, Brink, Constructive, Convergent, Curb, Edge, Gross, Hair's breadth, Lean, Limit, Littoral, Neck, Nose, Profit, Rand, Repand, →RIM, Selvedge, Sideline, Spread, Tail, Term

Marijuana Alfalfa, Bhang, Camberwell carrot, Dagga, Gage, Ganja, Grass, Greens, Hay, Hemp, Herb, J, Jimson weed, Jive, Joint, Kaif, Kef, Kif, Leaf, Lid, Locoweed, Mary-Jane, Pot, Roach, Rope, Shit, Sinsemilla, Splay, Spliff, Tea, Toke, Weed

Marinade Chermoula, Escabeche

Mariner AB, Ancient, MN, RM, Sailor, Salt, Seafarer, Tar

Mark(ing), Marked, Marks, Marker Accent, Aesc, Annotate, Anoint, Antony, Apostrophe, Asterisk, Astrobleme, Badge, Banker, Bethumb, Birth, Blaze, Blot, Blotch, Brand, Bruise, Bull, Buoy, Butt, Cachet, Calibrate, Caract, Caret, Caste, CE, Cedilla, Chatter, Chequer, Cicatrix, Class, Clout, Colon, Comma, Coronis, Crease, Criss-cross, Cross(let), Cup (and ring), Dash, Denote, Dent, Diacritic, Diaeresis, Dieresis, Distinction, Ditto, DM, Dot, Duckfoot quote, Dupe, Emblem, Enseam, Ensign, Enstamp, Exclamation, Expression, Feer, Flash, Fleck, Fox(ing), Freckle, Genetic, Glyph, Gospel, Grade, Guillemet, Gybe, Hacek, Haemangioma, Hair-line, Hash, Hatch, Heed, Hickey, High water, Hoofprint, Hyphen, Impress(ion), Imprint, Indicium, Ink, Inscribe, Insignia, Interrogation, Keel, Kite, Kumkum, Lentigo, Line, Ling, Livedo, Logo, Lovebite, Low water, M, Macron, Matchmark, MB, Medical, Merk, Mint, Minute, Mottle, NB, Nick, Nota bene, Notal, Note, Notice, Obelisk, Observe, Oche, Paginate, Paragraph, Paraph, Peg, Period, Pilcrow, Pin, Pit, Plage, Pling, Pock, Point(ille), Popinjay, Port wine, Post, Presa, Printer's, Proof, Punctuation, Question, Quotation, Record, Reference, Register, Regulo, Remarque, Rillmark, Ripple, Roundel, Sanction, Scar, Scorch, Score(r), Scratch, Section, See, Service, Shadow, Shelf, Shilling, Shoal, Sigil, Sign(ature), Smit, Smut, Smutch, Soft touch, Speck, Splodge, Splotch,

Spot, Stain, Stamp, Stencil, Stigma(ta), Strawberry, Stress, Stretch, Stroke, Sucker, Swan-upping, Symbol, Tag, Target, Tarnish, Tatow, Tattoo, Tee, Theta, Thread, Tick, Tide, Tika, Tikka, Tilak, Tilde, Tittle, Token, Touchmark, Trace, Track, Trema, Trout, Tug(h)ra, Twain, Umlaut, Ure, Victim, Wand, Warchalking, Watch, Weal, Welt, Whelk

Market(ing), Market day, Market place Advergaming, Agora, Alcaiceria, Available, Baltic, Bazaar, Bear, Billingsgate, Black, Black stump, Borgo, Bull, Buyers', Capital, Captive, Cattle, Change, Chowk, Cinema, Circular, Cluster, Commodity, Common, Covent Garden, Demo, Denet, Direct, Discount, Dragon, EC, Emerging, Emporium, Errand, Exchange, Exhibition, Fair, Farmers', Feeing, Flea, Forum, Forward, Free, Grey, Growth, Insert, Internal, Kerb, Lloyds, Main, Mandi, Mart, Mass, Meat, Mercat, Money, Niche, Nundine, Obigosony, Oligopoly, Open, Order-driven, Outlet, Overt, Pamphlet, Perfect, Piazza, Poster, Press, Publicity, Radio, Reach, Relationship, Rialto, Sale, Sellers', Servqual, Share, Shop, Single, Social, Societal, Sook, Souk, Spot, Stance, Staple, Stock, Stock Exchange, Tattersall's, TECHMARK®, Terminal, Test, Third, Tiger, Trade, Tron, Tryst, USP, Vent, Viral, Wall Street, Yard sale

Market garden Truck-farm

Maroon Brown, Castaway, Enisle, Firework, Inisle, Isolate, Strand

Marriage, Marry, Married →ALLIANCE, Ally, Amate, Arranged, Bed, Beenah, Bigamy, Bridal, Buckle, Cleek(it), Coemption, Combine, Commuter, Companionate, Confarreation, Conjugal, Connubial, Couple, Digamy, Endogamy, Espousal, Espouse, Exogamy, Feme covert, Forsooth, Fuse, Gandharva, Genial, Hetaerism, Hetairism, Hitch, Hymen(eal), Indeed, Join, Jugal, Ketubah, Knit, Knot, Lavender, Levirate, M, Match, Mating, Matrilocal, Matrimony, Matron, Memsahib, Mésalliance, Ming, Missis, Missus, Monandry, Monogamy, Morganatic, Nikah, Noose, Nuptial, Pair, Pantagamy, Pardie, Polygamy, Punalua, Quotha, Sacrament, Sannup, Shidduch, Splice, Tie, Tie the knot, Troggs, Troth, Umfazi, →UNION, Unite, W, Wed, Wedding, Wedlock, Wive

Marrow Courgette, Friend, Gist, Kamokamo, Medulla, Myeloid, Pith, Pumpkin, Spinal, Squash, Vegetable

Marsh(y) Bayou, Bog, Chott, Corcass, Emys, Everglades, Fen(land), Hackney, Maremma, Merse, Mire, Morass, Ngaio, Paludal, Palustrine, Plashy, Pontine, Pripet, Quagmire, Rann of Kutch, Romney, Salina, Salt, Shott, Slade, Slough, Sog, Spew, Spue, Swale, Swamp, Taiga, Terai, Vlei, Wetlands

Marshal Arrange, Array, Commander, Earp, Foch, French, Hickok, MacMahon, Muster, Neil, Ney, Order, Pétain, Provost, Shepherd, Sky, Steward, Tedder, Usher, Vauban

Marsupial Bandicoot, Bilby, Cuscus, Dasyure, Dibbler, Didelphia, Diprotodon(t), Dunnart, Euro, Honey mouse, Honey possum, Kangaroo, Koala, Macropod, Metatheria, Notoryctes, Nototherium, Numbat, Opossum, Pademelon, Pad(d)ymelon, Petaurist, Phalanger, Pig-rat, Polyprodont, Possum, Potoroo, Pouched mouse, Pygmy glider, Quokka, Quoll, Roo, Tammar, Tasmanian devil, Theria, Thylacine, Tuan, Wallaby, Wambenger, Wombat, Yapo(c)k

Martensite Sorbite

Martial (arts) Bellicose, Budo, Capoeira, Capuera, Chopsocky, Dojo, Iai-do, Judo, Ju-jitsu, Karate, Kata, Kendo, Krav Maga, Kumite, Kung fu, Militant, Ninjitsu, Ninjutsu, Sensei, Shintaido, Tae Bo®, Tae kwon do, T'ai chi (chuan), Warlike, Wushu

Martyr(dom), Martyrs Alban, Alphege, Campion, Colosseum, Cranmer, Donatist, Justin, Lara, Latimer, MM, Passional, Persecute, Ridley, Sebastian, Shaheed, Shahid, Stephen, Suffer, Tolpuddle, Wishart

Marvel(lous) Brilliant, Épatant, Fab, Fantabulous, Marl, Miracle, Mirific, Phenomenon, Prodigious, Selcouth, Superb, Super-duper, Terrific, Wonder

Marx(ism), Marxist Aspheterism, Chico, Comintern, Commie, Groucho, Gummo, Harpo, Karl, Lenin, Mao, Menshevik

Mary Bloody, Celeste, Contrary, Madonna, Magdalene, Moll, Morison, Tum(my), Typhoid, Virgin

Mascot Charm, Four-leaf clover, Telesm, Token

Masculine, Masculinity He, He-man, Linga(m), M, Machismo, Macho, Male, Manly, Virile, Yang

Mash(er) Beau, Beetle, Brew, Lady-killer, Pap, Pestle, Pound, Puree, Sour, Squash

Mask(ed) Bird cage, Camouflage, Cloak, Cokuloris, Death, Disguise, Dissemble, Domino, Face pack, False face, Front, Gas, Hide, Larvated, Life, Loo, Loup, Mascaron, Matte, Oxygen, Persona, Respirator, Screen, Semblance, Shadow, Ski, Stalking-horse, Stocking, Stop out, Template, Visor, Vizard

Mass(es) Aggregate, Agnus Dei, Anniversary, Atomic, Banket, Bezoar, Bike, Blob, Body, Bulk, Cake, Canon, Chaos, Clot, Compound, Congeries, Conglomeration, Consecration, Core, Crith, Critical, Crowd, Demos, Density, Dozens, Flake, Floc, Flysch, Folk, Geepound, Gramme, Gravitational, Great, Herd, High, Horde, Hulk, Inertial, Isobare, Jud, Kermesse, Kermis, Kilo(gram), Kirmess, Low, Lump, M, Magma, Majority, Missa, Missa solemnis, Mob, Month's mind, Mop, Nelson, Nest, Phalanx, Pile, Plebs, Plumb, Pontifical, Populace, Proper, Raft, Red, Requiem, Rest, Ruck, Salamon, Salmon, Scrum, Sea, Serac, Service, Shock, Sicilian, Size, Slub, Slug, Solar, Solemn, Solid, Stack, Stroma, Sursum Corda, Te Igitur, Tektite, Trental, Vesper, Vigil, Volume, Wad, Weight, Welter

Massacre Amritsar, Battue, Beziers, Blood-bath, Butcher, Carnage, Glencoe, Havock, Kanpur, Lidice, Manchester, Peterloo, Pogrom, Purge, Scullabogue, Scupper, September, Sicilian vespers, Slaughter, Slay, Trounce

Massage, Masseur An mo, Cardiac, Chafer, Chavutti thirumal, Do-in, Effleurage, →**KNEAD**, Malax, Manipulate, Palp, Petrissage, Physio, Reiki, Rolf(ing), Rubber, Shampoo, Shiatsu, Swedish, Tapotement, Thai, Tripsis, Tui na

Massif Makalu

Massive Big, Bull, Colossal, Gang, Heavy, Herculean, Huge, Monolithic, Monumental, Ponderous, Strong, Titan

Mast(ed), Masthead Acorn, Crosstree, Foreyard, Hounds, Jigger, Jury, Mizzen, Pannage, Pole, Racahout, Royal, Ship-rigged, Spar, Top-gallant

Master(ly), Mastery Artful, Baalebos, Baas, Beak, Beat, Boss, Buddha, Bwana, Careers, Checkmate, Choir, Chorus, Conquer, Control, Dan, Dominate, Dominie, Employer, Enslave, Exarch, Expert, Genius, Gov, Grand, Grip, Harbour, Herr, Himself, International, Learn, Lord, MA, Maestro, Magistral, Mas(s), Massa, Maulana, Mes(s), Nkosi, Old, Ollamh, Ollav, Oner, Oppress, Original, Overcome, Overlord, Overpower, Overseer, Passed, Past, Pedant, Question, Rabboni, Schoolman, Seed, Seigneur, Seignior, Signorino, Sir(e), Skipper, →**SUBDUE**, Subjugate, Superate, Surmount, Swami, Tame, Task, Teach, Thakin, Towkay, Tuan, Usher, Vanquish, Virtuoso

Mastersinger Sachs

Mastic Sealant

Mat(ted), Matting Bast, Capillary, Coaster, Doily, Dojo, Doyley, Dutch mattress, Felt, Inlace, Pad, Paunch, Plat, Rug, Rush, Surf, →**TANGLE**, Tat(ami), Tatty, Taut, Tautit, Tawt, Tomentose, Web, Welcome, Zarf

Match(ed) Agree, Alliance, Amate, Balance, Besort, Bonspiel, Bout, Carousel, Compare, Compeer, Congreve, Consolation, Contest, Cope, Correlate, Correspond, Counterpane, Cup tie, Doubles, Emulate, Engagement, Equal(ise), Equate, Even, Exhibition, Fellow, Fit, Fixture, Four-ball, Foursome, Friction, Friendly, Fusee, Fuzee, Game, Go, Greensome, Grudge, International, Joust, Light, Locofoco, Love, Lucifer, Main, Marrow, Marry, Meet, Mouse, Needle, Pair(s), Paragon, Parallel, Parti, Pit, Play-off, Prizefight, Promethean, Quick, Replica, Reproduce, Return, Rival, Road game, Roland, Rubber, Safety, Semifinal, Sevens, Shield, Shoo-in, Shooting, Shouting, Singles, Slanging, Slow, Slugfest, Spunk, Striker, Suit, Sync(h), →**TALLY**, Team, Test, Texas scramble, Tie, Twin, Twosome, Union, Venue, Vesta, Vesuvian, Wedding

Mate, Mating Achates, Adam, Amigo, Amplexus, Assistant, Assortative, Bedfellow, Bo, Breed, Buddy, Buffer, Butty, Chess, China, Chum, Cobber, Comrade, Consort, Crony, Cully, Digger, Eve, Feare, Feer, Fellow, Fere, Fiere, Fool's, Helper, Husband, Inbreed, Maik, Make, Marrow, Marry, Match, Mister, Mucker, Nickar, Oldster, Oppo,

→**PAIR**, Pal, Pangamy, Paragon, Partner, Pheer(e), Pirrauru, Scholar's, Serve, Sex, Skaines, Smothered, Soul, Sport, →**SPOUSE**, Tea, Tup, Wack, Wife, Wus(s)

Material(ism) Agitprop, Appropriate, Apt, →**CLOTH**, Compo, Composite, Copy, Corporeal, Data, Documentation, Earthling, Earthly, →**FABRIC**, Factual, Fallout, Fertile, Fuel, Germane, Historical, Hylic, Illusion, Infill, Leading, Matter, Pertinent, Physical, Positive, Raw, Real, Reify, Relevant, Repertoire, Substance, Tangible, Thingy, Worldly

Mathematician Optime, Statistician, Wrangler

Mathematics, Mathematical, Maths Algebra, Arithmetic, Arsmetrick, Calculus, Combinatorics, Exact science, Geometry, Haversine, Logarithms, Mechanics, Numbers, Trig

Matter Affair, Alluvium, Bioblast, Biogen, Body, Business, Concern, Condensed, Consequence, Count, Dark, Degenerate, Empyema, Epithelium, Front, Gear, Gluon, Go, Grey, Hyle, Ichor, Impost(h)ume, Issue, Mass, Material, Molecule, Multiverse, Phlegm, Pith, Plasma, Point, Positron, Premise, Protoplasm, Pulp, Pus, Quark, Reading, Reck, Reke, Scum, Shebang, Signify, Solid, Sputum, Stereome, Stuff, Subject, →**SUBSTANCE**, Theme, Thing, Topic, Tousle, Touzle, Vinyl, White, Ylem

Matter of fact Pragmatic

Mattress Bed(ding), Biscuit, Foam, Futon, Lilo®, Pallet, Pa(i)lliasse, Tick

Mature, Maturity Adult, Age, Auld, Blossom, Bold, Concoct, Develop, Fully-fledged, Grow (up), Mellow, Metaplasis, Puberty, Ripe(n), Rounded, Seasoned, Upgrow(n)

Maul Hammer, Manhandle, Paw, Rough, Savage, Tear

Max Ernst

Maximum All-out, Full, Highest, Most, Peak, Utmost

May Blossom, Can, Hawthorn, Merry, Might, Month, Mote(n), Quickthorn, Shall, Whitethorn

Maybe Happen, Mebbe, Perchance, Perhaps, Possibly

▷ **May become** *may indicate* an anagram

Mayor Alcaide, Burgomaster, Casterbridge, Charter, Councilman, Portreeve, Provost, Syndic, Whittington, Worship

Maze Honeycomb, Labyrinth, Meander, Network, Theseus, Warren, Wilderness

MC Compere, Host, Ringmaster

Mead(ow) Flood, Grass(land), Haugh, Inch, Ing, Lea(se), Ley, Meath(e), →**PASTURE**, Runnymede, Saeter, Salting, Water

Meagre Arid, Bar, Bare, Exiguous, Measly, Mingy, Paltry, Pittance, Scant, Scrannel, Scranny, Scrawny, Skimpy, Skinny, Spare, Stingy, Thin

Meal(s), Mealie, Mealy Allseed, Banquet, Barbecue, Barium, Beanfeast, Blow-out, Board, Breakfast, Brunch, Buffet, Carry out, Cassava, Cereal, Chilled, Cholent, Chota-hazri, Collation, Corn, Cornflour, Cottoncake, Cottonseed, Cou-cou, Cribble, Dejeune(r), Deskfast, Dinner, Drammock, Ear, Ervalenta, Fare, Farina, Feast, Flour, Food, Glacier, Grits, Grout, Hangi, High tea, Iftar, Indian, Italian, Kai, Lock, Lunch, Mandioc, Mandioc(c)a, Mani(h)oc, Matzo, Melder, Meltith, Mensal, Mess, Morning, Mush, No-cake, Nosh, Nuncheon, Obento, Ordinary, Picnic, Piece, Plate, Poi, Polenta, Porridge, Prandial, Prix fixe, Rac(c)ahout, Refection, Repast, Revalenta, Rijst(t)afel, Salep, Scambling, Scoff, Seder, Sehri, Smorgasbord, Snack, Sohur, Spread, Square, Suhur, Supper, Table d'hôte, Takeaway, Tea, Thali, Tiffin, Tightener, Tousy tea, Twalhours, Undern

Mean(ing), Meant Aim, Arithmetic(al), Average, Base, Betoken, Bowsie, Caitiff, Cheap, Connotation, Curmudgeon, Definition, Denotate, Denote, Design, Dirty, Drift, Essence, Ettle, Feck, Footy, Foul, Geometric(al), Gist, Golden, Hang, Harmonic, Humble, Hunks, Ignoble, Illiberal, Imply, Import, Inferior, Insect, Intend, Intermediate, Kunjoos, Lexical, Low(down), Mang(e)y, Marrow, Medium, Mesquin, Message, Method, Mid, Miserly, Narrow, Near, Norm, Nothing, One-horse, Ornery, Paltry, Par, Penny-pinching, Petty, Piker, Pinch-penny, Pith, Point, Purport, →**PURPOSE**, Quadratic, Ratfink, Revenue, Ribald, Roinish, Roynish, Scall, Scrub,

Scurvy, Semanteme, Semantic(s), Sememe, Sense, Shabby, Signify, Slight, Slink, Small, Sneaky, Snoep, Snot, Sordid, Sparing, Spell, Stingy, Stink(ard), Stinty, Substance, Symbol, Thin, Threepenny, Tight-lipped, Tightwad, Two-bit, Value, Vile, Whoreson

Means Agency, Dint, Income, Instrumental, Media, Method, Mode, Opulence, Organ, Private, Resources, Staple, Substance, Tactics, Visible, Ways

Measure(d), Measuring, Measure(ment) By(e)law, Calibre, Centile, Circular, Crackdown, Customise, → DANCE, → DIMENSION, Distance, Dose, Dry, → GAUGE, Gavotte, Gross, Imperial, → INSTRUMENT, Limit, Linear, Liter, Litre, Meed, Metage, Moratorium, Of, Offset, Precaution, Prophylactic, Quickstep, Ration, Remen, Sanction, Share, Short, → SIZE, Sound, Standard, Statute, Step, Stichometry, Strike, Struck, Survey, Tachymetry, Token, Triangulate, → UNIT, Wine

Meat(s) Bacon, Bard, Beef, Beefsteak, Biltong, Brawn, Brisket, Brown, Burger, Cabob, Carbonado, Carrion, Charcuterie, Chop, Collop, Confit, Croquette, Cut, Dark, Devon, Dog-roll, Easy, Edgebone, Entrecôte, Escalope, Essence, Fanny Adams, Fatback, Fleishig, Fleishik, Flesh, Flitch, Force, Galantine, Gigot, Gobbet, Gosht, Griskin, Ham, Haslet, Jerky, Joint, Junk, Kabab, Kabob, Kebab, Kebob, Lamb, Loin, Luncheon, Mart, Medaillon, Medallion, Mince, Mutton, Noisette, Offal, Olive, Oyster, Pastrami, Paupiette, Pem(m)ican, Piccata, Pith, Pope's eye, Pork, Processed, Prosciutto, Rack, Red, Rillettes, Roast, Saddle, Sasatie, Satay, Scaloppino, Schnitzel, Scran, Scrapple, Sey, Shank, Shashlik, Shishkebab, Short ribs, Side, Sirloin, Sosatie, Spam®, Spare rib, Spatchcock, Spaul(d), Steak, Strong, Tenderloin, Tiring, Tongue, Variety, Veal, Venison, Vifda, Virgate, Vivda, White, Wiener schnitzel, Wurst

▷ **Mechanic(al)** *may indicate* characters from 'A Midsummer Night's Dream'

Mechanic(s) Apron-man, Artificer, Artisan, Banausic, Barodynamics, Card, Celestial, Classical, Dynamics, Engineer, Fitter, Fundi, Hand, Journeyman, Kinematics, Kinesiology, Kinetics, Operative, Statics, Technician

Mechanical, Mechanism Action, Apparatus, Auto, Autodestruct, Banausic, Clockwork, Dérailleur, Escapement, Foul-safe, Gimmal, Gust-lock, Instrument, Machinery, Movement, Organical, Pulley, Pushback, Rackwork, Regulator, Robotic, Servo, Synchroflash, Traveller, Trippet, Works

Medal(lion)(s) Award, Bar, Bronze, Croix de guerre, Decoration, Dickin, DSM, GC, George, Gold, Gong, Gorget, MM, Numismatic, Pan(h)agia, Purple Heart, Putty, Roundel, Silver, Touchpiece, VC, Vernicle

Mediate, Mediator ACAS, Arbitrate, Intercede, Interpose, Intervene, Liaison, Muti, Referee, Stickler, Thirdsman, Trouble-shooter

Medical, Medicine (chest), Medicament, Medication Aesculapian, Algology, Aloetic, Alternative, Amulet, Anodyne, Antacid, Antibiotic, Antidote, Antisepsis, Antiseptic, Arnica, Arrowroot, Aurum potabile, Aviation, Bariatrics, Bi, Bismuth, Blister, Charm, Chinese, Chiropody, Chlorodyne, Clinician, Complementary, Cordial, Corpsman, Cubeb, Curative, Defensive, Demulcent, Diapente, Discutient, Doctor's stuff, Dose, Draught, Drops, → DRUG, Dutch drops, Eardrop, Electuary, Elixir, Emetic, Empirics, Enema, Excipient, Expectorant, Fall-rank, Febrifuge, Folk, Forensic, Fringe, Functional, Galen, Galenism, Gelcap, Genitourinary, Gripe water®, Gutta, Haematinic, Haematology, Herb, Herbal, Holistic, Hom(o)eopathy, Iatric(al), Indian, Industrial, Inhalant, Inro, Internal, Iodine, Iron, Ko cycle, Lariam®, Laxative, L-dopa, Leechcraft, Legal, Loblolly, Lotion, Magnesia, Maqui, Menthol, Microbubbles, Mishmi, Mixture, Moxar, Muti, Natural, Naturopathy, Nephritic, Nephrology, Nervine, Neurology, Nosology, Nostrum, Nuclear, Nux vomica, Ob-gyn, Occupational, Officinal, Oncology, Oporice, Orthopoedics, Osteopath, Palliative, Panacea, Paregoric, Patent, Pathology, Pectoral, P(a)ediatrics, Pharmacy, Phlegmagogue, Physic, Physical, Pill, Placebo, Polypill, Potion, Poultice, Preparation, Preventive, Prosthetics, Psionic, Psychiatry, Ptisan, Purgative, Quin(quin)a, Quinine, Radiology, Reborant, Red Crescent, Red Cross, Relaxative, → REMEDY, Salve, Sanative, Sebesten, Senna, Serology, Simple, Snake-oil, Space, Specific, Sports, Steel, Stomachic, Stomatology, Stupe, Suppository, Synergast, Syrup, Tablet, Tar-water, Therapeutics, Thimerosal, TIM, Tisane, Tocology, Tonic, Totaquine, Trade, Traditional Chinese, Treatment, Trichology, Troche, Valerian, Veronal, Veterinary, Virology

Medieval Archaic, Feudal, Gothic, Med, Old, Trecento

Meditate, Meditation, Meditator, Meditative Brood, Chew, Cogitate, Contemplate, Falun gong, Fifteen o's, Insight, Muse, Mystic, Ponder, Reflect, Reverie, Revery, Ruminate, Samadhi, Tantric, Transcendental, Vipassana, Weigh, Yogic flying, Zazen

Medium (A)ether, Agency, Air, Average, Channel, Clairvoyant, Contrast, Culture, Dispersive, Earth, Element, Ether, Even, Fire, Happy, Home, Intermediary, Interstellar, M, Magilp, Mean, Megilp, Midsize, Midway, Milieu, Oils, Organ, Ouija, Planchette, Press, Radio, Regular, Shaman, Spiritist, Spiritualist, Television, Telly, TV, Vehicle, Water

Medley Charivari, Collection, Gallimaufry, Individual, Jumble, Macedoine, Melange, Mishmash, Mix, Pastiche, Patchwork, Pi(e), Pot-pourri, Quodlibet, Ragbag, Salad, Salmagundi, Series

▷ **Medley** *may indicate* an anagram

Meek Docile, Griselda, Humble, Milquetoast, Patient, Sheepy, Tame

Meerkat Suricate

Meet(ing), Meeting place Abide, Abutment, AGM, Appointment, Apropos, Ascot, Assemblage, Assemble, Assembly, Assignation, Audience, Baraza, Bosberaad, Briefing, Camporee, Caucus, Chapterhouse, Chautauqua, Clash, Commissure, Conclave, Concourse, Concur, Confluence, Confrontation, Congress, Connivance, Conseil d'etat, Consistory, Consultation, Contact, Conterminous, Convene, Convent(icle), Convention, Converge, Conversazione, Convocation, Correspond, Cybercafé, Defray, Demo, EGM, Encounter, Ends, Experience, Face, Find, Fit, For(e)gather, Forum, Fulfil, Gemot, General, Giron, Gorsedd, Greeting, Guild, Gyeld, Gymkhana, Gyron, Hall, Howf(f), Hunt, Hustings, Imbizo, Indaba, Infall, Interface, Interview, Join, Junction, Kgotla, Korero, Lekgotla, Liaise, Marae, Moot, Mother's, Obviate, Occlusion, Occur, Oppose, Overflow, Partenariat, Pay, Plenary, Plenum, Pnyx, Pow-wow, Prayer, Prosper, Quadrivial, Quaker, Quorate, Quorum, Race, Races, Rally(ing point), Rencontre, Rencounter, Rendezvous, Reunion, Sabbat(h), Satisfy, Séance, See, Seminar, Session, Sit, Social, Sports, Suitable, Summit, Swap, Symposium, Synastry, Synaxis, Synod, Tackle, Talkfest, Talk-in, Talking-shop, Think-in, Town, Track, Tryst, Venery, Venue, Vestry, Wapinshaw, Wardmote, Wharenui, Wharepuni, Workshop

Mellow Age, Genial, Mature, Ripe, Smooth

Melody, Melodious Air, Arioso, Cabaletta, Canorous, Cantabile, Cantilena, Cantus, Cavatina, Chant, Chopsticks, Conductus, Counterpoint, Descant, Dulcet, Euphonic, Fading, Musical, Orphean, Part-song, Plainsong, Ranz-des-vaches, Strain, Sweet, Theme, Tunable, → **TUNE(S)**

Melon(like) Cantaloupe(e), Cas(s)aba, Charentais, Galia, Gourd, Honeydew, Mango, Musk, Nar(r)as, Ogen, Pepo, Persian, Rock

Melt(ed), Melting Ablate, Colliquate, → **DISSOLVE**, Eutectic, Eutexia, Flux, Found, Fuse, Fusil(e), Liquescent, Liquid, Run, Smectic, Syntexis, Thaw, Touch

Member Adherent, Arm, Branch, Bro(ther), Charter, Chin, Confrère, Cornice, Crossbeam, Crypto, Direction, Felibre, Fellow, Forearm, Forelimb, Gremial, Harpin(g)s, Insider, Leg, Limb, Longeron, M, MBE, Montant, MP, Organ, Part, Partisan, Peer, Politicaster, Politician, Private, Tie

Membrane, Membranous Amnion, Arachnoid, Axilemma, Bilayer, Caul, Chorioallantois, Chorion, Choroid (plexus), Chromoplast, Conjunctiva, Cornea, Decidua, Dissepiment, Dura (mater), Eardrum, Endocardium, Endometrium, Endosteum, Ependyma, Exine, Extine, Fell, Film, Foetal, Frenulum, Haw, Head, Hyaloid, Hymen, Indusium, Intima, Intine, Involucre, Kell, Mater, Mediastinum, Meninx, Mesentery, Mucosa, Mucous, Neurolemma, Nictitating, Nuclear, Parchment, Patagium, Pellicle, Pericardium, Pericarp, Perichondrium, Pericranium, Periost(eum), Periton(a)eum, Pia mater, Plasma, Plasmalemma, Pleura, Putamen, Rim, Sarcolemma, Scarious, Schneiderian, Sclera, Serosa, Serous, Synovial, Tela, Third eyelid, Tissue, Tonoplast, Trophoblast, Tunic, Tympan(ic), Vacuolar, Velum, Vitelline, Web

Memento, Memoir Keepsake, Locket, Relic, Remembrancer, Souvenir, Token, Trophy

Memo(randum) Bordereau, Cahier, Chit, IOU, Jot, Jurat, Minute, Note, Notepad, →REMINDER, Slip

Memorable, Memorise, Memory Associative, ATLAS, Bubble, Cache, Catchy, Collective, →COMPUTER MEMORY, Con, Core, DRAM, Dynamic, Echoic, Engram(ma), Extended, Flash (bulb), Folk, Get, Highlight, Historic, Hypermnesia, Iconic, Immortal, Immunological, Learn, Living, Long-term, Main, Mainstore, Memoriter, Mind, Mneme, Mnemonic, Mnemosyne, Non-volatile, Noosphere, Notable, Pelmanism, Photographic, Race, Read-write, Recall, Recollection, Recovered, Red-letter day, →REMEMBER, Retention, Retrospection, ROM, Ro(a)te, Samskara, Screen, Semantic, Short-term, SIMM, Souvenir, Sovenance, Static, Study, Video, Virtual, Volatile, Word, Working

Memorial Albert, Altar tomb, Cenotaph, Cromlech, Ebenezer, Gravestone, Hatchment, Marker, Martyr's, Monument, Mount Rushmore, Obelisk, Plaque, Relic, Relique, Statue, Tomb, Trophy, Wreath

Menace, Menacing Danger, Dennis, Endanger, Foreboding, Intimidate, Jeopardise, Minatory, Ominous, Peril, Pest, Scowl, Sinister, Threat(en)

Mend Beet, Bete, Bushel, Cobble, Correct, Cure, Darn, Fix, Heal, Improved, Mackle, Patch, Piece, Recover, Remedy, →REPAIR, Set, Sew, Solder, Trouble-shoot

Menial Drudge, Drug, Eta, Fag, Flunkey, Lackey, Lowly, Scullion, Servile, Toady, Underling, Wood-and-water joey

▷ **Mental** *may indicate* the chin

Mention(ed) Advert, Allusion, Bename, Benempt, Broach, Bynempt, Citation, Hint, Honourable, Instance, Name(-check), Notice, Quote, Refer, Same, Speech, State, Suggest, Touch

Menu Card, Carte, Carte du jour, Cascading, Fare, List, Option, Table d'hôte, Tariff

Mercenary Arnaout, Condottiere, Freelance, Greedy, Hack, Hessian, Hired gun, Hireling, Landsknecht, Legionnaire, Pindaree, Pindari, Rutter, Sordid, Spoilsman, Swiss Guard, Switzer, Venal, Warmonger, Wildgeese

Merchandise Cargo, Goods, Line, Produce, Ware(s)

Merchant(man) Abbas, Abudah, Antonio, Argosy, Broker, Bun(n)ia, Burgher, Chandler, Chap, Commission, Crare, Crayer, Dealer, Factor, Flota, Gossip, Hoastman, Importer, Jobber, Magnate, Marcantant, Mercer, Monger, Négociant, Pedlar, Polo, Provision, Retailer, Seller, Shipper, Speed, Squeegee, Stapler, Trader, Vintner, Wholesaler

Merciful, Mercy Amnesty, Charity, Clement, Compassionate, Corporal, Grace, Humane, Kind, Kyrie, Lenient, Lenity, Miserere, Misericord(e), Pacable, Pity, Quarter, Ruth, Sparing, Spiritual

Merciless Cruel, Hard, Hard-hearted, Inclement, Pitiless

Mere(ly) Allenarly, Bare, Common, Lake, Pond, Pool, Poor, Pure, Sheer, Tarn, Ullswater, Very

Merge(r), Merging Amalgamate, Blend, Coalesce, Coalise, Composite, Conflate, Consolidate, Die, Elide, Fusion, Incorporate, Interflow, Interpenetrate, Liquesce, Meld, Melt, Mingle, Symphysis, Syncretism, Synergy, Unify, Unite

Merit(ed) CL, Condign, Deserve, Due, Earn, Found, Meed, Rate, Virtue, Worth(iness)

Mesmer(ise) Hypnotise

Mess(y), Mess up Anteroom, Balls-up, Bedraggled, Boob, Boss, Botch, Canteen, Caudle, Chaos, Clamper, Clutter, Cock-up, Dining-room, Dog's dinner, Failure, Farrago, Fiasco, Flub, Garboil, Glop, G(l)oop, Gory, Guddle, Gunge, Gunk, Gun-room, Hash, Horlicks, Hotch-potch, Hugger-mugger, Imbroglio, Lash-up, Louse, Mash, Meal, Mismanage, Mix, Mixter-maxter, Modge, Muck, Muddle, Muff, Mullock, Muss, Mux, Pi(e), Piss-up, Plight, Pollute, Pottage, Screw-up, Scungy, Shambles, Shambolic, Shemozzle, Sight, Slaister, Smudge, Snafu, Soss, Sty, Sully, Tousle, Trifle, Untidy, Wardroom, Whoopsie, Yuck(y)

Message(s), Messaging Aerogram, Bull, Bulletin, Cable, Caption, Contraplex, Dépêche, Despatch, Dispatch, Epistle, Errand, Flame, Inscription, Kissagram, Kissogram, Letter, Marconigram, Missive, News, Note, Pager, Ping, Posting, Postscript, Radiogram, Radio telegraph, Read-out, Rumour, Signal, Slogan, SOS, Subtext, Telco, Telegram, Telepheme, Telephone, Teletype®, Telex, Tidings, Toothing, Tweet, Valentine, Voice mail, Wire, →**WORD**

Messenger Angel, Angela, Apostle, Azrael, Beadle, Caddie, Caddy, Carrier pigeon, Chaprassi, Chuprassy, Corbie, Courier, Culver, Despatch-rider, Emissary, Envoy, Gaga, Gillie whitefoot, Hatta, Herald, Hermes, Internuncio, Iris, Ladas, Mercury, Nuncio, Peon, Post, Pursuivant, Runner, Send, Seraph, Valet de place

Messiah Christ, Emmanuel, Immanuel, Mahdi, Mashiach, Prince of peace, Saviour, Shiloh, Son of man, Southcott

Metal(s), Metallic, Metalware, Metalwork Aeneous, Antifriction, Base, Death, Expanded, Filler, Fine, Fusible, Heavy, Hot, Jangling, Leaf, Mercuric, Mineral, Noble, Nonferrous, Ore, Perfect, Planchet, Precious, Prince's, Road, Scrap, Sheet(-iron), Sprue, Stannic, Thrash, Tramp, Transition, Type, White, Yellow

Metallurgy Powder

▷ **Metamorphosing** *may indicate* an anagram

Metaphor Conceit, Figure, Image, Kenning, Mixed, Symbol, Trope, Tropical

Meteor(ic), Meteorite Achondrite, Aerolite, Aerosiderite, Bolide, Chondrite, Comet, Drake, Fireball, Geminid, Iron, Leonid, Perseid, Siderite, Siderolite, Star(dust), Stony(-iron)

Method(ology), Methodical Art, Billings, Formal, Formula, Gram's, How, Kumon, Line, Manner, Mode, Modus, Modus operandi, Monte Carlo, Montessori, Neat, Orderly, Organised, Organon, Organum, Painstaking, Phonic, Plan, Ploy, Procedure, Process, Stanislavski, Systematic, Tactics, Technique, Way, Withdrawal

Meths White Lady

Metre, Metrical Alexandrine, Amphibrach, Amphimacer, Anapaest, Antispast, Arsis, Ballad, Cadence, Choliamb, Choree, Choriamb, Common, Dipody, Galliambic, Iambic, Ithyphallic, Long, M, Penthemimer, Prosody, Pyrrhic, Rhythm, Sapphic, Scansion, Scazon, Semeion, Service, Short, Spondee, Strophe, Tribrach, Tripody, Trochee

Metrosexual Epicene

Michael Mick(e)y

Microbiologist Fleming, Salk

Microphone Bug, Crystal, Directional, Mike, Phonic Ear®, Radio, Throat

Microwave Nuke

Mid(st) Amongst

Midday Meridian, N, Noon

Middle, Middling, Midpoint Active, Ariston metron, Basion, Centre, Core, Crown, Enteron, Epitasis, Eye, Girth, Heart, Innermost, Internal, Loins, Median, Mediocre, Meridian, Meseraic, Mesial, Mesne, Meso, Midriff, Moderate, Nasion, Noon, Passive, Turn, Twixt, Undistributed, Via media, Wa(i)st

Middle European Magyar

Middleman Broker, Comprador(e), Diaphragm, Interlocutor, Intermediary, Jobber, Median, Navel, Regrater, Regrator

Midget Dwarf, Homunculus, Lilliputian, Pygmy, Shrimp

Midlander Brummie

▶ **Midst** *see* **MID(ST)**

Midsummer Solstice

Mid-Westerner Indianan

Midwinter Solstice

Might(iness), Mighty Force, Main, Maud, Mote, Nibs, Oak, Potence, →**POWER**, Prowess, Puissant, Should, Strength

Migrate, Migration, Migratory Colonise, Diapedesis, Diaspora, Drift, Eelfare, Exodus, Fleet, Run, Tre(c)k

Mild(ly) Balmy, Benign, Bland, Clement, Euphemism, Genial, Gentle, Lenient, Litotes, Mansuete, Meek, →**MODERATE**, Pacific, Patient, Pussycat, Sarcenet, Sars(e)net, Temperate

Mile(r), Miles Admiralty, Coss, Coverdale, Food, Geographical, Hour, Irish, Knot, Kos, League, Li, Mi, Milliary, Nautical, Passenger, Roman, Royal, Scots, Sea, Soldier, Square, Standish, Statute, Swedish, Train

Militancy, Militant, Military Activist, Aggressive, Battailous, Black Power, Commando, Fortinbras, Hawkish, Hezbollah, Hizbollah, Hizbullah, Hostile, Ireton, Janjaweed, Janjawid, Junta, Kshatriya, Landsturm, Landwehr, Leftist, Logistics, Lumper, Mameluke, Martial, Presidio, Soldatesque, Stratocracy, Tactical, War machine, War paint, West Point

Militia(-man) Band, Guard, Milice, Minuteman, Peshmerga, Reserve, Trainband, Yeomanry

Milk(er), Milky Acidophilus, Beestings, Bland, Bleed, Bonny-clabber, Bristol, Butter, Casein, Certified, Churn, Colostrum, Condensed, Creamer, Crud, Curd, Dairy, Emulge, Evaporated, Exploit, Galactic, Glacier, Goat's, Homogenised, Jib, Kefir, Kephir, K(o)umiss, Lactation, Lacteal, Latex, Maas, Madafu, Madzoon, Magnesia, Mamma, Matzoon, Mess, Moo-juice, Opaline, Pigeon's, Pinta, Posset, Rice, Sap, Shedder, Skim(med), Soya, Squeeze, Strip(pings), Stroke, Suckle, Town, UHT, Use, Whig, Yaourt, Yogh(o)urt

Mill(ing), Mills Aswarm, Ball, Barker's, Boxing, Coffee, Crazing, Economist, Flour, Gang, Gastric, Gig, Grind(er), Hayley, Kibble, Knurl, Lumber, Malt, Mano, Melder, Molar, Nurl, Oil, Paper, Pepper, Plunge-cut, Post, Powder, Press, Pug, Pulp, Quartz, Quern, Reave, Rob, Rolling, Rumour, Satanic, Scutcher, Smock, Spinning, Stamp, Stamping, Strip, Sucken, Sugar, Surge, Thou, Tide, Tower, Tuck, Water, Wool(len), Works

Milliner Hatter, Modiste

Mime, Mimic(ry) Ape, Batesian, Copycat, Echo, Farce, Imitate, Impersonate, Marceau, Mina, Mock, Mullerian, Mummer, Sturnine, Take-off

Mind(er) Aide, Beware, Bodyguard, Brain, Gaum, Genius, Grasshopper, Handler, Head, →**HEED**, Herd, Id, Intellect, Mentality, Month's, Nous, Open, Psyche, Psychogenic, Resent, Sensorium, Tabula rasa, Tend, Thinker, View, Wit, Woundwort, Year's

Mine, Mining Acoustic, Antenna, Appalachia, Biomining, Bomb, Bonanza, Bord and pillar, Bottom, Bouquet, Burrow, Camouflet, Chemical, Claymore, Colliery, Contact, Creeping, Dane-hole, Data, Dig(gings), Drifting, Egg, Eldorado, Excavate, Explosive, Fiery, Floating, Flooder, Fougasse, Fougade, Fougasse, Gallery, Gob, Golconda, Gold, Gopher, Grass, Homing, Land, Limpet, Magnetic, Microbiological, Naked-light, Nostromo, Open-cast, Open-cut, Ophir, Pit, Placer, Pressure, Prospect, Rising, Sap, Set(t), Show, Sonic, Stannary, Stope, Strike, Strip, Undercut, Wheal, Win, Workings

Miner, Mine-worker, Mine-working Bevin boy, Butty-gang, Collier, Corporal, Cutter, Digger, Faceworker, Forty-niner, Geordie, Leaf, Molly Maguire, Noisy, NUM, Oncost(man), Pitman, Shot-firer, Stall, Tippler, Tributer, Tunneler, UDM

Mineral(s) Accessory, Index, Ore, Owre

Mineralogy, Mineralogist Haüy, Heuland, Miller-Smithson, Oryctology

Mingle, Mingling Blend, Commix, Consort, Interfuse, Mell, Merge, →**MIX**, Participate, Socialise, Theocrasy, Unite

Minimise, Minimum (range) Bare, Downplay, Fewest, Floor, Gloze, Least, Neap, Pittance, Scant, Shoestring, Stime, Styme, Threshold, Undervalue

▷ **Minimum of** *may indicate* the first letter

Minister Ambassador, Attend, Buckle-beggar, Chancellor, Chaplain, Cleric, Coarb, Commissar, Deacon, Dewan, Diplomat, Divine, Dominee, Dominie, D(i)wan, Envoy, Mas(s)john, Mes(s)john, Moderator, Nurse, Officiant, Ordinand, Ordinee, Padre, Parson, Peshwa, Preacher, Predikant, Presbyter, Priest, Rector, Richelieu, Secretary, Seraskier, →**SERVE**, Stick, Stickit, Tanaiste, Tend, Visier, Vizier

Ministry Defence, Department, Dept, DoE, MOD, MOT, Orders, Service, Treasury

▷ **Ministry** *may indicate* some government department

Minor(ity) Child, Comprimario, Ethnic, Faction, Few, Fractional, Incidental, Infant, Junior, Less(er), Marginal, Minutia, Nonage, One-horse, Peripheral, Petty, Pupillage, Signed, Slight, Sub(sidiary), Trivial, Ward, Weeny

Mint Aim, Bugle-weed, Bull's eye, Catnip, Coin, Ettle, Fortune, Herb, Horse, Humbug, Labiate, Monarda, Monetise, Nep, New, Penny-royal, Pepper, Pile, Polo®, Poly, Rock, Selfheal, Spear, Stamp, Stone, Strike, Unused, Utter, Water

Minus Less, Nonplus

Minute(s), Minutiae Acta, Alto, Degree, Detailed, Diatom, Entry, Infinitesimal, Little, Mere, Micron, Mo, Mu, Nano-, New York, Resume, Small, Teen(t)sy, Teeny, Tine, Tiny, Trivia, Tyne, Wee

Miracle(s), Miraculous, Miracle worker Cana, Marvel, Merel(l), Meril, Morris, Mystery, Mythism, Phenomenon, Saluter, Thaumatology, Thaumaturgic, Theurgy, Wonder

Mirror(s), Mirrored Alasnam, Antidazzle, Busybody, Cambuscan, Catoptric, Cheval, Claude Lorraine glass, Coelostat, Conde, Conjugate, Dare, Driving, Enantiomorph, Glass, Image, Imitate, Keeking-glass, Lao, Magnetic, Merlin, One-way, Pierglass, Primary, Psyche, Rearview, → **REFLECT**, Reynard, Sign, Specular, Speculum, Stone, Tiring-glass, Two-way, Vulcan, Wing

▷ **Misalliance** *may indicate* an anagram

Miscellaneous, Miscellany Ana, Assortment, Chow, Collectanea, Diverse, Etceteras, Job lot, Misc, Odds and ends, Odds and sods, Olio, Omnium-gatherum, Pie, Potpourri, Raft, Ragbag, Sundry, Varia, Variety, Various

Mischance Misfare

Mischief(-maker), Mischievous Ate, Bale, Bane, Cantrip, Cloots, Devilment, Diablerie, Dido, Disservice, Gallus, Gremlin, Hanky-panky, Harm, Hellery, Hellion, Hob, Imp, Injury, Jinks, Larky, Larrikin, Limb, Make-bate, Malicho, Mallecho, Monkeyshines, Nickum, Owl-spiegle, Pestilent, Pickle, Prank, Puckish, Rascal, Scally(wag), Scamp, Scapegrace, Shenanigans, Spalpeen, Spriteful, Tricksy, Varmint, Wag, Wicked

Misconception Delusion, Idol(on), Idolum, Mirage, Misunderstanding

▷ **Misdelivered** *may indicate* an anagram

Miser(ly) Carl, Cheapskate, Cheese-parer, Close, Curmudgeon, Flay-flint, Gare, Grasping, Harpagon, Hunks, Marner, Meanie, Mingy, Muckworm, Niggard, Nipcheese, Nipfarthing, Pennyfather, Pinch-commons, Puckfist, Runt, Save-all, Scrape-good, Scrape-penny, Screw, Scrimping, Scrooge, Shylock, Skinflint, Snudge, Storer, Tightwad, Timon

Miserable, Misery, Miserably Abject, Bale, Cut up, Distress, Dole, Face-ache, Forlorn, Gloom, Grief, Heartache, Hell, Joyless, Killjoy, Lousy, Mean, Measly, Perdition, Sorry, Sourpuss, Tragic, Triste, → **UNHAPPY**, Wet blanket, Woe(begone), Wretched

Misfortune Accident, Affliction, Bale, Calamity, Curse, Disaster, Distress, Dole, Hex, Ill, Ill-luck, Kicker, Reverse, Rewth, Ruth, Wroath

▷ **Misguided** *may indicate* an anagram

Misheard Mondegreen

Misinformation Bum steer

Misjudge Misween, Overrate

Mislead(ing) Blind, Con, Cover-up, Deceive, Delude, Dupe, Equivocate, Fallacious, False, Gag, Half-truth, Red herring, Runaround, Snow job

▷ **Misled** *may indicate* an anagram

Mismanage Blunder, Bungle, Muddle

Misprint Error, Literal, Literal error, Slip, Typo

Misrepresent(ation) Abuse, Belie, Calumny, Caricature, Colour, Distort, Falsify, Garble, Lie, Slander, Traduce, Travesty

▷ **Miss** *may refer to* Missouri

Miss(ing) Abord, Air, Astray, Avoid, Colleen, Desiderate, Dodge, Drib, Err(or), Fail, Forego, Gal, → **GIRL**, Kumari, Lack, Lass, Link, Lose, Mademoiselle, Maid, Maiden,

Mile, Muff(et), Neglect, Negligence, Omit, Otis, Overlook, Señorita, Skip, Spinster, Unmeet, Wanting

Missile Air-to-air, ALCM, Ammo, Anti-ballistic, Arrow, Artillery, Atlas, Ball, Ballistic, Beam Rider, Blue streak, Bolas, Bolt, Bomb, Boomerang, Brickbat, Bullet, Condor, Cruise, Dart, Death star, Dingbat, Doodlebug, Dum-dum, Exocet®, Falcon, Fléchette, Genie, Grenade, Guided, HARM, Harpoon, Hawk, Hellfire, Hound Dog, ICBM, Interceptor, Jired, Kiley, Kyley, Kylie, Lance, Mace, MARV, Maverick, Minuteman, MIRV, Missive, Mx, Onion, Patriot, Pellet, Pershing, Phoenix, Polaris, Poseidon, Qual, Quarrel, Rocket, SAM, Scud, Sea Skimmer, Sergeant, Shell, Shillelagh, Shot, Shrike, Side-winder, Smart bomb, Snowball, Sparrow, Spartan, Spear, Sprint, SSM, Standard Arm, Standoff, Styx, Subroc, Surface to air, Surface to surface, Talos, Tartar, Terrier, Thor, Titan, Tomahawk, Torpedo, Tracer, Trident, UAM, Warhead

Mission(ary) Aidan, Alamo, Antioch, Apostle, Assignment, Barnabas, Bethel, Boniface, Caravan, Charge, Columba, Cuthbert, Cyril, Delegation, Embassage, Embassy, Errand, Evangelist, Happy-clappy, Iona, Legation, Livingstone, LMS, Message, Missiology, NASA, Neurolab, Op, Paul, Pr(a)efect, Quest, Reclaimer, Silas, Task, Vocation

Mist(y) Aerosol, Australian, Blur, Brume, Cloud, Dew, Drow, Fog, Fret, Haar, Haze, Hoar, Miasma, Moch, Nebular, Niflheim, Rack, Roke, Scotch, Sfumato, Smir(r), Smog, Smur, Spotted, Vapour, Veil

Mistake(n) Aberration, Barry (Crocker), Bish, Bloomer, Blooper, Blue, Blunder, Boner, Boob, Booboo, Boss, Botch, Bull, Category, Clanger, Clinker, Confound, Deluded, Domino, Erratum, Error, Fault, Floater, Flub, Fluff, Folly, Gaffe, Goof, Hash, Horlicks, Howler, Identity, Incorrect, Lapse, Malapropism, Misprision, Miss, Muff, Mutual, Nod, Off-beam, Oops, Oversight, Own goal, Plonker, Pratfall, Ricket, Screw-up, → SLIP, Slip-up, Solecism, Stumer, Trip, Typo, Wrongdoing

▷ **Mistake(n)** *may indicate* an anagram

Mistress Amie, Aspasia, Canary-bird, Chatelaine, Concubine, Courtesan, Goodwife, Herself, Hussif, Inamorata, Instructress, Kept woman, Lady, Leman, Maintenon, Montespan, Mrs, Natural, Paramour, Querida, Stepney, Teacher, Wardrobe, Wife

Mistrust(ful) Doubt, Gaingiving, Suspect, Suspicion

Misunderstand(ing) Disagreement, Discord, Generation gap, Mistake

Misuse Abuse, Defalcate, Malappropriate, Malapropism, Maltreat, Perversion, Torment

Mix(ed), Mixer, Mixture, Mix-up Allay, Alloy, Amalgam, Ambivalent, Associate, Assortment, Attemper, Balderdash, Bigener, Bittersweet, Bland, Blend, Blunge, Bombay, Bordeaux, Brew, Carburet, Card, Caudle, Chichi, Chow, Cocktail, Co-meddle, Compo, Compound, Conché, Conglomerate, Consort, Cross, Cut, Disperse, Diversity, Dolly, Drammock, Embroil, Emulsion, Eutectic, Farrago, Fold-in, Freezing, Friar's balsam, Garble, Grill, Griqua, Half-breed, Heather, Hobnob, Hodge-podge, Hotchpotch, Hybrid, Imbroglio, Immingle, Interlace, Intermingle, Isomorphous, Jumble, Lace, Lard, Lignin, Linctus, Load, Macedoine, Marketing, Matissé, Meddle, Medley, Melange, Mell, Meng(e), Ment, Mess, Mestizo, Métis, Ming(le), Miscellaneous, Miscellany, Mishmash, Mong, Motley, Muddle, Muss(e), Neapolitan, Octaroon, Octoroon, Olio, Olla, Pi(e), Potin, Pousowdie, Powsowdy, Praiseach, Preparation, Promiscuous, Raggle-taggle, Ragtag, Salad, Scramble, Shuffle, Soda, Spatula, Stew, Stir, Temper, Through-other, Tonic, Trail, Vision, Witches' brew, Yblent

▷ **Mixed** *may indicate* an anagram

Mixed marriage Miscegenation

Moan(ing) Beef, Bewail, Bleat, Groan, Grouse, Grumble, Hone, Keen, → LAMENT, Meane, Plangent, Sigh, Snivel, Sough, Wail, W(h)inge

Mob(ster) Army, Assail, Canaille, Crew, Crowd, Flash, Gang, Herd, Hoi-polloi, Hoodlum, Horde, Lynch, Many-headed beast, Ochlocrat, Press, Rabble, Rabble rout, Raft, Ragtag, Riff-raff, Rout, Scar-face

Mobile, Mobilise, Mobility Agile, Donna, Fluid, Intergenerational, Movable, Plastic, Rally, Social, Thin, Upward(ly), Vagile, Vertical

Mock(ery), Mocking Ape, Banter, Catcall, Chaff, Chyack, Cod, Cynical, Deride, Derisory, Dor, Ersatz, False, Farce, Fleer, Flout, Gab, Geck, Gibe, Guy, Imitation, Ironise, Irony, Irrisory, →JEER, Jibe, Lampoon, Mimic, Narquois, Paste, Pillorise, Piss-taking, Rail(lery), Ridicule, Sacrilege, Sardonic, Satirise, Scorn, Scout, Send up, Serve, Sham, Simulate, Slag, Sneer, Snide, Sport, Tease, Travesty, Twit, Wry

Mode Authentic, Church, Convention, Fashion, Form, Hyperdorian, Hypo(dorian), Hypolydian, Insert, Manner, Rate, Step, Style, Ton

Model(ler), Modelling Archetype, Bozzetto, Cast, Copy, Cutaway, Demonstration, Diorama, Doll, Dress-form, Dummy, Ecorché, Effigy, Epitome, Example, Exemplar, Exemplary, Fashionist, Fictor, Figure, Figurine, Icon, Ideal, Image, Instar, Jig, Last, Lay-figure, Layman, Madame Tussaud, Manakin, Manikin, Mannequin, Maquette, Mark, Matchstick, Mirror, Mock-up, Moulage, →MOULD, Norm, Original, Orrery, Papier-mâché, Parade, Paradigm, Paragon, Pattern, Phelloplastic, Pilot, Plasticine, Plastilina, Play-Doh®, Pose(r), Posture-maker, Precedent, Prototype, Replica, Role, Scale, Schema, Sedulous, Sitter, Specimen, Standard, Superwaif, T, Tellurion, Template, Templet, Terrella, Toy, Type, Typify, Waif, Waxwork

▷ **Model(s)** *may indicate an anagram*

Moderate(ly), Moderation Abate, Allay, Alleviate, Attemper, Average, Ca'canny, Centre, Chasten, Continent, Decent, Diminish, Discretion, Ease, Gentle, Girondist, Ho(a), Lessen, Lukewarm, Measure, Medium, Menshevik, Mezzo, Middling, Mild, Mitigate, Muscadin, OK, Politique, Realo, Reason(able), Restraint, RR, Slake, So-so, Sparing, Temper(ate), Tolerant, Tone, Via media, Wet

Modern(ise) AD, Aggiornamento, Contemporary, Fresh, Latter(-day), Milly, Neonomian, Neoterical, →NEW, New-fangled, Present-day, Progressive, Recent, Space age, State-of-the-art, Swinger, Trendy, Update

Modest(y) Aidos, Blaise, Chaste, Coy, Decent, Demure, Fair, Humble, Humility, Ladylike, Low-key, Lowly, Maidenly, Mim, Mussorgsky, Propriety, Prudish, Pudency, Pudicity, Pure, Reserved, Reticent, Shame, Shamefaced, Shy, Simple, Unpretending, Unpretentious, Verecund

Modifiable, Modification, Modified, Modifier, Modify Adapt, Adjust, Alter, Backpedal, Change, Enhance, Extenuate, Genetically, H, Hotrod, Leaven, Plastic, Qualify, Restyle, Retrofit, Soup, Streamline, Temper, Top, Trim, Vary

Moist(en), Moisture Baste, Bedew, Damp, Dank, De(a)w, Dewy, Humect, Imbue, Latch, Love-in-a-mist, Madefy, Mesarch, Mesic, Nigella, Precipitation, Soggy, Sponge, Wet

▷ **Moither** *may indicate an anagram*

Molecule, Molecular Acceptor, Achiral, Aptameter, Atom, Buckyball, Carbene, Cavitand, Chimera, Chiral, Chromophore, Closed chain, Cobalamin, Codon, Coenzyme, Cofactor, Dimer, DNA, Enantiomorph, Footballene, Fullerene, Gram, Hapten, Iota, Isomer, Kinin, Kisspeptin, Ligand, Long-chain, Metabolite, Metameric, Monomer, Nanotube, Peptide, Polymer, Polysaccharide, Quark, Replicon, Semantide, Stereoisomer, Synthon, Triatonic, Trimer, Uridine

Mollusc(s) Bivalve, Malacology, Opisthobranch, →SHELLFISH, Tectibranch, Univalve

Moment(s), Momentous Aha, Bit, Blonde, Eureka, Eventful, Flash(point), Gliffing, Import, Instant, Jiffy, →MINUTE, Mo, Nonce, Point, Pun(c)to, Sagging, Sands, Sec, Senior, Shake, Stound, Stownd, Tick, Time, Trice, Twinkling, Two-ticks, Weighty, Wink

Momentum Angular, Impetus, L, Speed, Steam, Thrust

Monarch(y) Absolute, Autocrat, Butterfly, Caesar, Crown, Dual, Emperor, HM, Karling, King, Kuwait, Netherlands, Norway, Potentate, Queen, Raine, Realm, Reign, Ruler, Saudi Arabia, Swaziland, Sweden, Tonga, Tsar

Monastery, Monastic Abbey, Abthane, Celibate, Charterhouse, Chartreuse, Cloister, Community, Gompa, Holy, Hospice, Iona, Lamaserai, Lamasery, Laura, Monkish, Oblate, Priory, Sangha, Secluded, Tashi, Vihara, Wat

Money, Monetary Ackers, Akkas, Allowance, Annat, Ante, Appearance, Archer,

Assignat, Banco, Batta, Blood, Blue, Blunt, Boodle, Bottle, Brass, Bread, Bread and honey, Broad, Bull's eye, Bunce, Cabbage, Capital, Cash, Caution, Century, Change, Chink, Circulating medium, Cob, Cock, → COIN, Collateral, Confetti, Conscience, Crackle, Cranborne, Crinkly, Crust, Currency, Danger, Dib(s), Dingbat, Dollar, Dosh, Dough, Dump, Dust, Earnest, Easy, Escrow, Even, Fat, Fee, Fiat, Finance, Float, Folding, Fonds, Found, Fund, Funny, Gate, Gelt, Gilt, Godiva, Gold, Grand, Grant, Gravy, Greens, Gross, Hard, Head, Heavy sugar, Hello, Hoot, Hot, Housekeeping, Hush, Idle, Ingots, Investment, Jack, Kale, Kembla, Key, Knife, L, Legal tender, Lolly, Loot, Lucre, M, Mammon, Maundy, Mazuma, Means, Mint, Monkey, Monopoly, Moola(h), Narrow, Near, Necessary, Needful, Nest-egg, Note, Nugger, Numismatic, Nummary, Oaker, Ocher, Ochre, Offertory, Oof, Option, Outlay, P, Packet, Paper, Passage, Pavarotti, Payroll, Peanuts, Pecuniary, Pelf, Petrodollar, Pin, Pine-tree, Pink, Pittance, Plastic, Plum, Pocket, Pony, Posh, Press, Prize, Proceeds, Profit, Protection, Purse, Push, Quid, Ration, Ready, Reap silver, Rebate, Remuneration, Resources, Revenue, Rhino, Ring, Risk, Rogue, Rowdy, Salt(s), Score, Scratch, Scrip, Seed, Shekels, Shell, Shin-plaster, Ship, Short, Siller, Silly, Silver, Sinews of war, Slush, Smart, Soap, Soft, Spending, Spondulicks, Stake, Sterling, Stipend, Stuff, Subsidy, Subsistence, Sugar, Sum, Surety, Table, Take, Takings, Tea, Tender, Tin, Toea, Token, Tranche, Treaty, Tribute, Turnover, Viaticum, Wad, Wealth, Windfall, Wonga

Monitor(ing) Dataveillance, Detect, Goanna, Iguana, Komodo dragon, Lizard, Observe, Oversee, Prefect, Preview, Record, Regulator, Ship, Sniffer, Sphygmophone, Surveillance, Tag, Track, Warship, Watchdog, Worral, Worrel

Monk(s) Bodhidharma, Bro, Brother, Frere, General, Order, Provincial, Thelonious, Votary

Monkey Anger, Ape, Aye-aye, Baboon, Bandar, Bobbejaan, Bonnet, Bushbaby, Capuchin, Catar(r)hine, Cebidae, Cebus, Chacma, Coaita, Colobus, Cynomolgus, Diana, Douc, Douroucouli, Drill, Durukuli, Entellus, Galago, Gelada, Gibbon, Gorilla, Grease, Green, Grison, Grivet, Guenon, Guereza, Hanuman, Hoolock, Howler, Hylobates, Imp, Indri, Jacchus, Jackey, Jocko, Kippage, Kipunji, Langur, Leaf, Lemur, Loris, Macaco, Macaque, Magot, Malmag, Mandrill, Mangabey, Marmoset, Meddle, Meerkat, Mico, Midas, Mona, Mycetes, Nala, Nasalis, New World, Old World, Orang-utang, Ouakari, Ouistiti, Phalanger, Platyrrhine, Pongo, Powder, Proboscis, Pug, Puzzle, Rage, Ram, Rapscallion, Rascal, Rhesus, Sago(u)in, Saguin, Sai(miri), Sajou, Saki, Sapajou, Satan, Scamp, Semnopithecus, Siamang, Sifaka, Silen(us), Silverback, Simian, Simpai, Slender loris, Spider, Squirrel, Talapoin, Tamarin, Tamper, Tana, Tarsier, Tee-tee, Titi, Toque, Trip-hammer, Troop, Tup, Uakari, Urchin, Vervet, Wanderoo, White-eyelid, Wistiti, Wou-wou, Wow-wow, Wrath, Zati

Monologue Dramatic, Patter, Rap, Recitation, Soliloquy, Speech

Monopolise, Monopoly Absolute, Appalto, Bloc, Cartel, Coemption, Corner, Engross, Octroi, Régie, Trust

Monorail Aerobus

Monosyllable Proclitic

▷ **Monsoon** *may indicate* weekend Mon soon

Monster, Monstrous Alecto, Asmodeus, Bandersnatch, Behemoth, Bunyip, Caliban, Cerberus, Cete, Charybdis, Chichevache, Chim(a)era, Cockatrice, Colossal, Cyclops, Dalek, Deform, Dinoceras, Div, Dragon, Echidna, Enormous, Erebus, Erl-king, Eten, Ettin, Fiend, Fire-drake, Frankenstein, Freak, Geryon, Ghost, Giant, Gila, Goblin, Godzilla, Golem, Gorgon, Green-eyed, Grendel, Harpy, Hippocampus, Hippogriff, Hippogryph, Huge, Hydra, Jabberwock, Kraken, Lamia, Leviathan, Mastodon, Medusa, Minotaur, Moloch, Mooncalf, Nessie, Nicker, Nightmare, Ogre, Ogr(e)ish, Opinicus, Orc, Outrageous, Pongo, Prodigy, Sasquatch, Satyral, Scylla, Shadow, Simorg, Simurg(h), Siren, Skull, Snark, Spectre, Sphinx, Spook, Stegodon, Stegosaur, Succubus, Taniwha, Teras, Teratism, Teratoid, Triceratops, Triffid, Troll, Typhoeus, Typhon, Unnatural, Vampire, Vast, Wasserman, Wendego, Wendigo, Wer(e)wolf, Wyvern, Yowie, Ziffius

Monstrance Ostensory

Month(ly) Ab, Abib, Adar, April, Asadha, Asvina, August, Bhadrapada, Brumaire, Bul, Caitra, Cheshvan, Chislev, December, Dhu-al-Hijjah, Dhu-al-Qadah, Elul, February, Floréal, Frimaire, Fructidor, Gander, Germinal, Hes(h)van, Iy(y)ar, January, July, Jumada, June, Jyaistha, Karttika, Kisleu, Kislev, Lide, Lunar, Magha, March, Margasirsa, May, Messidor, Mo, Moharram, Moon, Muharram, Muharrem, Nisan, Nivôse, November, October, Periodical, Phalguna, Pluviôse, Prairial, Rabi(a), Rajab, Ramadan, Safar, Saphar, S(h)ebat, September, Sha(a)ban, Shawwal, Sivan, Solar, Tammuz, Tebeth, Thermidor, Tishri, Tisri, Vaisakha, Veadar, Vendémiaire, Ventôse

Monument Ancient, Arch, Archive, Cairn, Cenotaph, Column, Cromlech, Cross, Dolmen, Eugubine, Henge, Megalith, Memorial, Menhir, National, Pantheon, Pyramid, Stele(ne), Stone, Stonehenge, Stupa, Talayot, Tombstone, Trilith, Trilithon, Urn

Mood(y) Active, Anger, Atmosphere, Attitude, Capricious, Dudgeon, Emoticon, Enallage, Fit, Foulie, Glum, Grammar, Humour, Hump, Imperative, Infinitive, Miff, Morale, Optative, Passive, Peat, Pet, Revivalist, Sankey, Spleen, Strop, Subjunctive, Sulky, Temper, Temperamental, Tid, Tone, Tune, Vein, Vinegar, Whim

Moon(light), Moony Aah, Adrastea, Alignak, Amalthea, Aningan, Apogee, Artemis, Astarte, Blue, Callisto, Calypso, Chandra, Cheese, Cynthia, Diana, Epact, Europa, Eye, Flit, Full, Gander, Ganymede, Gibbous, Glimmer, Grimaldi, Harvest, Hecate, Hunter's, Hyperion, Iapetus, Inconstant, Io, Juliet, Leda, Lucina, Luna(r), Mani, Mascon, McFarlane's Buat, Midsummer, Mock, Month, Mooch, Mope, New, Nimbus, Nocturne, Octant, Oliver, Orb, Paddy's lantern, Paraselene, Paschal, Pasiphaë, Phobos, Phoebe, Plenilune, Proteus, Raker, Rear-view, Satellite, Selene, Set, Shepherd, Shot, Sickle, Sideline, Silvery, Sonata, Stargaze, Stone, Syzygy, Thebe, Thoth, Titan, Triton, Umbriel, Wander

Moon god Thoth, Trismegistus

Mop(ping) Dwile, Flibbertigibbet, Girn, Glib, Malkin, Shag, Squeegee, Squilgee, Swab, Swob, Thatch, →**WIPE**

Moral(ity), Morals Apologue, Deontic, Ethic(al), Ethos, Everyman, Fable, Gnomic, High-minded, Integrity, Laxity, Message, Parable, Precept, Principled, Probity, Puritanic, Righteous, Tag, Upright, Virtuous

Morale Ego, Mood, Spirit, Zeal

Morbid(ity) Anasarca, Ascites, Cachaemia, Dropsy, Ectopia, Ghoul(ish), Gruesome, Pathological, Plethora, Prurient, Religiose, Sick, Sombre, Unhealthy

More Additional, Else, Extra, Increase, Intense, Less, Mae, Merrier, Mo(e), Over, Piu, Plus, Rather, Seconds, Stump, Utopia

Morning Ack-emma, Am, Antemeridian, Dawn, Daybreak, Early, Levée, Matin(al), Morrow

Morose Acid, Boody, Churlish, Cynical, Gloomy, Glum, Grum, Moody, Sour-eyed, Sullen, Surly

Morsel Bit, Bite, Bouche, Canape, Crumb, Dainty, Morceau, Ort, Scrap, Sippet, Sop, Tidbit, Titbit

Mortal(ity) Averr(h)oism, Being, Deathly, →**FATAL**, Grave, Human, Lethal, Yama

Mortgage(e) Balloon, Bond, Cap and collar, Cedula, Debt, Dip, Encumbrance, Endowment, Hypothecator, Loan, Pledge, Repayment, Reverse, Wadset(t)

Mortuary Deadhouse

Mosaic Buhl, Cosmati, Impave, Inlay, Intarsia, Musive, Pietra dura, Screen, Terrazzo, Tessella(te), Tessera

▶ **Moslem** see **MUSLIM**

Mosque Dome of the Rock, El Aqsa, Jami, Masjid, Medina, Musjid

Moss(y) Acrogen, Agate, Bryology, Bur(r), Carrag(h)een, Ceylon, Club, Fairy, Fog, Fontinalis, Hag(g), Hypnum, Iceland, Irish, Lecanoram, Lichen, Litmus, Long, Lycopod, Marsh, Musci, Muscoid, Parella, Peat, Polytrichum, Protonema, Reindeer, Rose, Scale, Selaginella, Spanish, Sphagnum, Staghorn, Usnea, Wolf's claw

Most(ly) Basically, Largest, Major, Maxi(mum), Optimum

Mother Abbess, Bearer, Church, Cognate, Cosset, Courage, Dam(e), Den, Dregs, Ean, Earth, Eoan, Eve, Generatrix, Genetrix, Goose, Hubbard, Lees, Ma, Machree, Mam(a),

Mamma, Mater, Matroclinic, Maya, Minnie, Mollycoddle, Mom, Multipara, Mum, Mummy, Native, Nature, Nourish, Parent, Parity, Pourer, Progenitress, Reverend, Shipton, Slime, Superior, Surrogate, Theotokos, Venter, Wit

▷ **Mother** *may indicate* a lepidopterist; moth-er

Mother-in-law Naomi

Motion Angular, Blocking, Composite, Contrary, Direct, Diurnal, Early day, Fast, Free-fall, Gesture, Harmonic, Impulse, Kepler, Kinematics, Kinetic, Kipp, Link, Move, Oblique, Offer, Parallactic, Parallel, Peculiar, Perpetual, PL, Precession, Proper, Proposal, Rack and pinion, Rider, Sewel, Similar, Slow, Spasm, Wave

Motionless Doggo, Frozen, Immobile, Inert, Quiescent, Stagnant, Stasis, Still, Stock-still

Motive, Motivate, Motivation Actuate, Cause, Drive, Ideal, Impel, Incentive, Intention, Mainspring, Mobile, Object, →**PURPOSE**, Reason, Spur, Ulterior

Motor(boat) Auto, Benz, Car, Dynamo, →Engine, Hot rod, Hydroplane, Inboard, Induction, Jato, Linear, Mini, Outboard, Paint job, Rocket, Scooter, Series-wound, Supermini, Sustainer, Thruster, Turbine, Turbo, Vaporetto

Motorway Autobahn, Autopista, Autoput, Autoroute, Autostrada, Expressway, M(1), Orbital, Superhighway

Motto Device, Epigraph, Excelsior, Gnome, Impresa, Imprese, Impress(e), Legend, Maxim, Mot, Poesy, Posy, Saw, Slogan

Mould(ed), Moulder, Mouldable, Moulding, Mouldy Accolade, Architrave, Archivolt, Astragal, Baguette, Bandelet, Beading, Bend, Black, Bread, Briquet(te), Cabling, Casement, Cast(ing), Chain, Chessel, Chill, Cold, Cornice, Coving, Cyma, Dancette, Dariole, Die, Dripstone, Echinus, Egg and dart, Flong, →FORM, Foughty, Fungus, Fust, Gadroon, Geat, Godroon, Gorgerin, Hood-mould, Hore, Humus, Injection, Matrix, Mildew, Model, Mool, Mucedinous, Mucid, Must, Mycetozoan, Necking, Noble rot, Ogee, Ovolo, Palmette, Papier-mâché, Penicillin, Phycomycete, Pig, Plasm(a), Plaster, Plastic, Plastisol, Plat, Prototype, Prunt, Reglet, Rib, Rot, Rust, Sandbox, Scotia, Shape, Smut, Soil, Spindle, Stringcourse, Tailor, Talon, Template, Templet, Timbale, Tondino, Torus, Water table

Mound Agger, Bank, Barp, Barrow, Berm, Cahokia, Cone, Dike, Dun, Embankment, Heap, Hog, Knoll, Kurgan, Mogul, Monticule, Mote, Motte, Orb, Pile, Pingo, Pome, Rampart, Rampire, Tuffet

Mount(ed), Mounting, Mountain (peak), Mountains Air, →**ALPINE**, Ascend, Back, Barp, Ben, Berg, Board, Breast, Butter, Chain, Charger, →**CLIMB**, Colt, Cordillera, Cradle, Dew, Display, Djebel, Dolly, Eminence, Escalade, Frame, Hinge, Horse, Inselberg, Jebel, Massif, Monture, Mt, Nunatak, Orography, Orology, Passe-partout, Peak, Pike, Pile, Pin, Pownie, Quad, →**RANGE**, Ride, Saddlehorse, Saddle up, Scalado, Scale, Sclim, Set, Soar, Stage, Stie, Strideways, Tel, Tier, Topo, Tor, Turret, Upgo, Volcano

Mountaineer(ing) Aaron, Abseil, Alpinist, Arnaut, Climber, Hunt, Sherpa, Smythe, Upleader

Mourn(er), Mournful, Mourning Adonia, Black, Cypress, Dirge, Dole, Elegiac, Grieve, Grone, Hatchment, Keen, Lament, Mute, Niobe, Omer, Ovel, Plangent, Saulie, Shivah, Shloshim, Sorrow, Tangi, Threnetic, Threnodial, Weeds, Weep, Willow

Mouse(like), Mousy Black eye, Bus, Church, Deer, Dormouse, Dun(nart), Flitter, Harvest, Honey, Icon, Jerry, Jumping, Kangaroo, Meadow, Mechanical, Mickey, Minnie, Muridae, Murine, Optical, Pocket, Rodent, Shiner, Shrew, Vermin, Waltzer

Mousetrap Samson's post

Mouth(piece) Aboral, Bazoo, Brag, Buccal, Cakehole, Chapper, Check, Crater, Debouchure, Delta, Embouchure, Estuary, Fauces, Fipple, Gab, Gam, Gills, Gob, Gub, Gum, Hard, Horn, Kisser, Labret, Laughing gear, Lawyer, Lip, Manubrium, Maw, Neb, Orifex, Orifice, Os, Oscule, Ostium, Outfall, Peristome, Port, Potato trap, Speaker, Spokesman, Spout, Stoma, Swazzle, Swozzle, Teat, Trap, Uvula

Mouth-watering Sialogogue

Move(d), Mover, Movable, Moving Act, Actuate, Affect, Andante, Astir, Aswarm, Budge, Career, Carry, Castle, Catapult, Chattel, Claw off, Coast,

Counter-measure, Coup, Decant, Démarche, Deploy, Displace, Disturb, Ease, Eddy, Edge, Evoke, Extrapose, False, Fidget, Flit, Flounce, Fluctuate, Forge, Fork, Frogmarch, Gambit, Gee, Go, Give and go, Gravitate, Haulier, Hustle, Inch, Inspire, Instigate, Jee, Jink, Jump, Kedge, Kinetic, Knight's progress, Link, Lunge, March, Mill, Mobile, Mosey, Motivate, Motor, Nip, Opening, Outwin, Overcome, Pan, People, Poignant, Prime, Proceed, Progress, Progressional, Prompt, Propel, Propose, Qui(t)ch, Quicken, Quinche, Rearrange, Redeploy, Relocate, Remuage, Retrocede, Roll, Rollaway, Rouse, Roust, Sashay, Scoot, Scramble, Scroll, Scurry, Scuttle, Sealed, Sell, Shift, Shog, Shoo, Shunt, Sidle, Skelp, Skitter, Slide, Soulful, Spank, Steal, Steer, Step, Stir, Styre, Surf, Swarm, Sway, Swish, Tack, Tactic, Taxi, Teleport, Touch, Transfer, Translate, Translocate, Transplant, Transport, Travel, Troll, Trundle, Turn, Unstep, Up, Up sticks, Vacillate, Vagile, Veronica, Vire, Volt(e), Waft, Wag, Wapper, Whirry, Whish, Whisk, Whiz, Whoosh, Wuther, Yank, Zoom, Zwischenzug

Movement(s) Action, Akathisia, Allegro, Allemande, Almain, Andantino, Antic, Antistrophe, Arts and crafts, Bandwagon, Buchmanism, Cadence, Capoeira, Cell, Charismatic, Chartism, Course, Crusade, Dadaism, Diaspora, Diastole, Ecumenical, Enlightenment, Eoka, Epeirogeny, Eurhythmics, Expressionism, Faction, Feint, Fianchetto, Fris(ka), Gait, Geneva, Gesture, Groundswell, Heliotaxis, Hip-hop, Honde, Imagism, Indraught, Intermezzo, Jor, Kata, Kinematics, Kinesis, Kin(a)esthetic, Kinetic, Kipp, Larghetto, Largo, Lassu, Ligne, Logistics, Maltese cross, Manoeuvre, Men's, Migration, Motion, Mudra, Nastic, Naturalism, Naziism, Neofascism, Neorealism, New Age, New Urbanism, New Wave, Nihilism, Official, Operation, Orchesis, Overspill, Oxford, Oxford Group, Panislamism, Pan-Slavism, Pantalon, Parallax, Pase, Passade, Passage, Photokinesis, Photonasty, Piaffer, Pincer, Plastique, Play, Populist, Port de bras, Poule, Poulette, Procession, Progress, Provisional, Punk, Puseyism, Reconstructionism, Reformation, Regression, REM, Renaissance, Resistance, Revivalism, Ribbonism, Risorgimento, Romantic, Rondo, Scherzo, Scissors, Seismic, Sinn Fein, Spuddle, Stir(e), Subsidence, Swadeshi, Swing, Symbolist, Tamil Tigers, Tantrism, Taphrogenesis, Taxis, Tectonic, Telekinesis, Thermotaxis, Thigmotaxis, Tic, Tide, Trend, Ultramontanism, UNITA, Verismo, Veronica, Wave, Wheel, White flight, Women's, Zionism

Mow(er), Mowing Aftermath, Cut, Grimace, Lattermath, Math, Rawing, Rawn, Reap, Rowan, Rowen, Rowing, Scytheman, Shear, Sickle, Strimmer®, Tass, Trim

MP Backbencher, Commoner, Gendarme, Knight of the Shire, Member, Oncer, Provost, Redcap, Retread, Snowdrop, Stannator, Statist, TD

Mrs Brown VR

Mrs Simpson Marge, Wallis

Much Abundant, Ever so, Far, Glut, Great, Lots, Mickle, Rotten, Scad, Sore, Viel

Muck (up), Mucky Bungle, Dirt, Dung, Grime, Island, Lady, Leep, Manure, Midden, Mire, Rot, Slush, Soil, Sordid, Spoil, Stercoral

Mud(dy) Adobe, Clabber, Clart, Clay, Cutcha, Dirt, Drilling, Dubs, Fango, Glaur, Glob, Gutter, Kacha, Lahar, Lairy, Limous, Lumicolous, Moya, Mudge, Ooze, Peloid, Pise, Poach, Red, Riley, Roily, Salse, Silt, Slab, Slake, Sleech, Slime, Slob, Slobland, Slough, Sludge, Slur(ry), Slush, Slutch, Tocky, Trouble, Turbid, Volcanic

Muddle(d) Befog, Bemuse, Botch, Cock up, Confuse, Disorder, Embrangle, Fluster, Gump, Higgledy-piggledy, Jumble, Mash, Mêlée, Mess, Mess up, Mix, Mull, Pickle, Puddle, Screw up, Shemozzle, Stupefy, Tangle, Ta(i)vert, Tiert

▷ **Muddled** *may indicate* an anagram

Muffle(d), Muffler Baffle, Damp, Deaden, Envelop, Hollow, Mob(b)le, Mute, Scarf, Silencer, Sourdine, Stifle

Mug(ger), Muggy Assault, Attack, Bash, Beaker, Bock, Can, Club, Con, Croc(odile), Cup, Dial, Do over, Dupe, Enghalskrug, Face, Fool, Footpad, Gob, Humid, Idiot, Latron, Learn, Mou, Noggin, Pan, Pot, Puss, Rob, Roll, Sandbag, Sap, Sconce, Simpleton, Steamer, Stein, Sucker, Swot, Tankard, Tax, Thief, Thug(gee), Tinnie, Tinny, Toby, Trap, Ugly, Visage, Yap

Mule, Mulish Ass, Bab(o)uche, Barren, Donkey, Funnel, Hemionus, Hybrid, Mocassin, Moccasin, Moyl(e), Muffin, Muil, Obdurate, Rake, Shoe, Slipper, Sumpter

Multiple, Multiplication, Multiplied, Multiplier, Multiply Augment, Breed, Chorisis, Common, Double, Elixir, →**INCREASE**, Manifold, Modulus, Populate, Product, Proliferate, Propagate, Raise, Severalfold

Multitude Army, Crowd, Hirsel, Horde, Host, Legion, Populace, Shoal, Sight, Throng, Zillion

Mumble Grumble, Moop, Moup, Mouth, Mump, Mushmouth, Mutter, Royne, Slur

Munch Champ, Chew, Chomp, Expressionist, Moop, Moup, Scranch

Mundane Banal, Common, Earthly, Nondescript, Ordinary, Prosaic, Quotidian, Routine, Secular, Trite, Workaday, Worldly

Mungo Park

Munition(s) Arms, Arsenal, Artillery, Matériel, Ordnance

Murder(er), Murderess, Murderous Abort, Aram, Assassin, Blue, Bluebeard, Bravo, Burke, Butcher, Butler, Cain, Cathedral, Crackhalter, Crippen, Crows, Cutthroat, Danaid(e)s, Do in, Eliminate, End, Filicide, First degree, Fratricide, Genocide, Hare, Hatchet man, Hitman, Homicide, Hyde, Internecine, →**KILL**, Liquidate, Locusta, Made man, Man-queller, Massacre, Matricide, Modo, Mullah, Muller, Parricide, Patricide, Poison, Red, Regicide, Removal, Ripper, Ritual, Ritz, Rub out, Second degree, Sikes, Slaughter, Slay, Stiff, Strangle(r), Sweeney Todd, Take out, Thagi, Throttle, Thug(gee), Ugly man, Vaticide, Whodun(n)it

Murk(y) Black, Dirk(e), Gloom, Obscure, Rookish, Stygian

Muscle, Muscleman, Muscular Abductor, Abs, Accelerator, Accessorius, Adductor, Agonist, Anconeus, Aristotle's lantern, Aryepiglottic, Arytaenoid, Athletic, Attollens, Azygous, Beef(y), Beefcake, Biceps, Bowr, Brachialus, Brawn, Buccinator, Buff, Cardiac, Ciliary, Clout, Complexus, Corrugator, Creature, Cremaster, Delt(oid), Depressor, Diaphragm, Digastric, Dilat(at)or, Duvaricator, Écorché, Effector, Elevator, Erecter, Erector, Evertor, Extensor, Eye-string, Flexor, Force, Gastrocnemius, Gemellus, Glute, Glut(a)eus, Gluteus maximus, Gracilis, Hamstring, Heavy, Hiacus, Hunky, Iliacus, Intrinsic, Involuntary, Kreatine, Lat, Latissimus dorsi, Laxator, Levator, Lumbricalis, Masseter, Mesomorph, Might, Motor, Mouse, Myalgia, Mylohyoid, Myology, Myotome, Myotonia, Nasalis, Obicularis, Oblique, Occlusor, Omohyoid, Opponent, Orbicularis, Pathos, Pec(s), Pectoral, Perforans, Perforatus, Peroneus, Plantaris, Platysma, Popliteus, →**POWER**, Pronator, Protractor, Psoas, Pylorus, Quad(riceps), Quadratus, Rambo, Rectus, Retractor, Rhomboid, Rhomboideus, Ripped, Risorius, Rotator cuff, Sarcolemma, Sarcous, Sartorius, Scalene, Scalenus, Serratus, Sinew, Six-pack, Smooth, Soleus, Sphincter, Spinalis, Splenial, Sthenic, Striated, Striped, Supinator, Suspensory, Temporal, Tenaculum, Tendon, Tensor, Teres, Thenar, Thew, Tibialis, Toned, Tonus, Trapezius, Triceps, Vastus, Voluntary, Xiphihumeralis, Zygomatic

Muse(s), Muse's home, Musing Aglaia, Aonia(n), Attic, Calliope, Clio, Cogitate, Consider, Dream, Erato, Euphrosyne, Euterpe, Goddess, Helicon, Inspiration, IX, Laura, Melpomene, Nine, Nonet, Pensée, Pierides, Poly(hy)mnia, Ponder, →**REFLECT**, Ruminate, Study, Teian, Terpsichore, Thalia, Tragic, Urania, Wonder

Museum Ashmolean, BM, British, Fitzwilliam, Gallery, Guggenheim, Hermitage, Kelvingrove, Louvre, Metropolitan, National Gallery, Parnassus, Prado, Repository, Smithsonian, Tate, Te papa Tongarewa, Uffizi, VA, V and A

Mushroom Aecidium, Aedium, Agaric, Ascomycetes, Blewits, Burgeon, Button, Cep, Champignon, Darning, Destroying angel, Enoki, Escalate, Expand, Field, Fly agaric, →**FUNGUS**, Girolle, Grisette, Gyromitra, Honey fungus, Horse, Hypha(l), Ink-cap, Liberty cap, Magic, Matsutake, Meadow, Morel, Oyster, Parasol, Penny-bun, Porcino, Reishi, Russula, Sacred, Scotch bonnet, Shaggy cap, Shaggymane, Shiitake, Shroom, Sickener, Spread, Start-up, Straw, Truffle, Upstart, Velvet shank, Waxcap

Music Absolute, A-side, B-side, Classical, Colour, Electro, Indeterminate, Lesson, Light, Lounge, Medieval, Minstrelsy, Mood, Morceau, →**MUSICAL INSTRUMENTS**, Passage work, Phase, Piece, Popular, Programme, Quotation, Recital, Score, Sound, Table, Tremolando

Musical Annie, Arcadian, Azione, Brigadoon, Canorous, Carousel, Cats, Chess,

Euphonic, Evergreen, Evita, Gigi, Grease, Hair, Half a Sixpence, Harmonious, Kabuki, Kismet, Lyric, Mame, Melodic, My Fair Lady, Oliver, →**OPERA**, Operetta, Oratorio, Orphean, Revue, Showboat, South Pacific, West Side Story

Musician(s), Musicologist Accompanist, Arion, Arist, Armstrong, Bassist, Boy band, Brain, Buononcini, Carmichael, Casals, Chanter, Combo, →**COMPOSER**, Conductor, Crowder, Ensemble, Executant, Flautist, Gate, Group, Grove, Guslar, Handel, Jazzer, Jazzman, Joplin, Keyboardist, Klezmer, Labelmate, Lyrist, Maestro, Mahler, Mariachi, Menuhin, Minstrel, Muso, Orphean, Percussionist, Pianist, Pied Piper, Rapper, Reed(s)man, Répétiteur, Rubinstein, Satchmo, Schonberg, Sideman, Spohr, String, Tortelier, Trouvère, Violinist, Waits

Musket Brown Bess, Caliver, Carabine, Eyas, Flintlock, Fusil, Gingal(l), Hawk, Jingal, Nyas, Queen's-arm, Weapon

Muslim (ritual), Moslem Alaouite, Ali, Almohad(e), Balochi, Baluchi, Berber, Caliph, Dato, Dervish, Fatimid, Ghazi, Hadji, Hafiz, Hajji, Hamas, Hizbollah, Hizbullah, Iranian, Islamic, Ismaili, Karmathian, Khotbah, Khotbeh, Khutbah, Mahometan, Mawlawi, Meivievi, Mog(h)ul, Moor, Morisco, Moro, Muezzin, Mufti, Mughal, Mus(s)ulman, Mutazilite, Nawab, Paynim, Pomak, Said, Saracen, Say(y)id, Senus(s)i, Shafiite, Shia(h), Shiite, Sofi, Sonnite, Sufi, Sulu, Sunna, Sunni(te), Turk, Wahabee, Wahabi(te), Whirling Dervish

Mussolini Benini, Il Duce

▷ **Must** *may indicate* an anagram

Must(y) Amok, Essential, Foughty, Fousty, Froughy, Frowsty, Frowy, Funky, Fust, Gotta, Man, Maun(na), Mote, Mould, Mucid, Mun, Need(s)-be, Shall, Should, Stum, Vinew, Wine

Mustard Black, Brown, Charlock, Cress, English, Erysimum, French, Garlic, Gas, Nitrogen, Praiseach, Quinacrine, Runch, Sarepta, Sauce-alone, Senvy, Treacle, Wall, White, Wild, Wintercress

Musteline Atoc, Atok, Skunk

▷ **Mutation** *may indicate* an anagram

Mute(d) Deaden, Dumb, Noiseless, Saulie, Silent, Sorda, Sordino, Sordo, Sourdine, Stifle, Stop

Mutilate(d), Mutilation Castrate, Concise, Deface, Dismember, Distort, Garble, Hamble, Injure, Maim, Mangle, Mayhem, Obtruncate, Riglin, Tear

▷ **Mutilate(d)** *may indicate* an anagram

Mutineer, Mutiny Bounty, Caine, Curragh, Indian, Insurrection, Jhansi, Nore, Pandy, →**REVOLT**, Rising, Sepoy

Mutter(ing) Chunter, Fremescent, Maunder, Mumble, Mump, Murmur, Mussitate, Rhubarb, Roin, Royne, Rumble, Sotto voce, Witter

Muzzle Decorticate, Gag, Jaw, Mouth, Restrain, Snout

Mysterious, Mystery Abdabs, Abdals, Acroamatic, Arcane, Arcanum, Cabbala, Closed book, Craft, Creepy, Cryptic, Dark, Deep, Delphic, Eleusinian, Enigma(tic), Esoteric, G(u)ild, Grocer, Incarnation, Inscrutable, Miracle, Mystagogue, Numinous, Occult, Original sin, Orphic, Penetralia, Recondite, Riddle, Sacrament, →**SECRET**, Shady, Telestic, Trinity, UFO, Uncanny, Unearthly, Unexplained, Whodunit

▷ **Mysterious(ly)** *may indicate* an anagram

Mystic (word), Mystical Abraxas, Agnostic, Cab(e)iri, Eckhart, Epopt, Fakir, Familist, Gnostic, Hesychast, Mahatma, New Age, Occultist, Rasputin, Secret, Seer, Sofi, Sufi, Swami, Theosophy, Transcendental

Mystify Baffle, Bamboozle, Bewilder, Metagrabolise, Metagrobolise, Perplex, Puzzle

Myth(ology), Mythological, Mythical (beast) Allegory, Atlantis, Behemoth, Bunyip, Centaur, Cockatrice, Dragon, Dreamtime, Euhemerism, Fable, Fantasy, Fictitious, Folklore, Garuda, Geryon, Griffin, Hippocampus, Impundulu, Kelpie, Kylin, Legend, Leviathan, Lore, Lyonnesse, Otnit, Pantheon, Pegasus, Phoenix, Sasquatch, Sea horse, Sea serpent, Selkie, Solar, Speewah, Sphinx, Sun, Tarand, Therianthropic, Thunderbird, Tokoloshe, Tragelaph, Unicorn, Urban, Wivern, Wyvern, Yale, Yeti

Nn

N Name, Nitrogen, Noon, North, November

Nadir Bottom, Depths, Dregs, Minimum

Nag(ging) Badger, Bidet, Brimstone, Callet, Cap, Captious, Complain, Fret, Fuss, Harangue, Harp, Henpeck, Horse, Jade, Jaw, Keffel, Peck, Pester, Pick on, Plague, Rosinante, Rouncy, →SCOLD, Tit, Yaff

Nail(ed) Brad, Brod, Catch, Clinker, Clout, Fasten, Frost, Hob, Horse, Keratin, Onyx, Pin, Rivet, Seize, Sisera, Sixpenny, Sparable, Sparrow-bill, Spick, Spike, Sprig, Staple, Stub, Stud, Tack(et), Talon, Tenterhook, Thumb, Tingle, Toe, Unguis

Naive(té) Artless, Dewy-eyed, Green(horn), Guileless, Ingenuous, Innocence, Open, Simplistic, Starry-eyed, Trusting, Unsophisticated, Wide-eyed

Naked(ness) Adamical, Artless, Bare, Blunt, Buff, Clear, Cuerpo, Defenceless, Encuerpo, Exposed, Gymno-, Nature, Nuddy, Nude, Querpo, Raw, Scud, Simple, Stark(ers), Uncovered

Name(d), Names Agnomen, Alias, Anonym, Appellation, Appoint, Attribute, Baptise, Byline, Call, Celeb(rity), Christen, Cite, Cleep, Clepe, Cognomen, Day, Designate, Dinges, Dingus, Dit, Domain, Dub, Entitle, Epithet, Eponym, Exonym, Family, First, Font, Generic, Given, Handle, Hete, Hight, Identify, Identity, Label, Maiden, Marque, Masthead, Mention, Metronymic, Middle, Moni(c)ker, Mud, N, Nap, Nemn, Nempt, Nom, Nomen(clature), Noun, Patronymic, Pennant, Personage, Pet, Place, Praenomen, Proper, Proprietary, Pseudonym, Quote, Red(d), Repute, Sign, Signature, Sir, Specify, Stage, Street, Subdomain, Substantive, Tag, Tautonym, Term, →TITLE, Titule, Trade, Trivial

Namibian Herero

Nap(py) Bonaparte, Diaper, Doze, Drowse, Fluff, Frieze(d), Fuzz, Game, Kip, Moze, Nod, Oose, Ooze, Oozy, Put(t), Shag, Siesta, →SLEEP, Slumber, Snooze, Tease, Teasel, Teaze, Terry, Tipsy, Tuft

Napkin Cloth, Diaper, Doily, Sanitary, Serviette

▷ **Napoleon** *may indicate* a pig

Narcotic Ava, B(h)ang, Benj, Charas, Churrus, Coca, Codeine, Dagga, Datura, Dope, →DRUG, Heroin, Hop, Kava, Laudanum, Mandrake, Marijuana, Meconium, Methadone, Morphia, Narceen, Narceine, Nicotine, Opiate, Opium, Pituri, Sedative, Tobacco

Narrate, Narration, Narrative, Narrator Allegory, Anecdote, Cantata, Describe, Diegesis, Fable, History, Ishmael, Periplus, Plot, Raconteur, Récit, Recite, Recount, Saga, Sagaman, Scheherazade, Splatterpunk, Story, Tell, Thanatography

Narrow(ing), Narrow-minded Alf, Babbitt, Bigoted, Borné, Bottleneck, Constringe, Cramp, Ensiform, Grundy(ism), Hairline, Hidebound, Illiberal, Insular, Kyle, Limited, Meagre, Nary, One-idea'd, Parochial, Phimosis, Pinch, Pinch-point, Prudish, Puritan, Scant, Shrink, Slender, Slit, Specialise, Squeak, Stenosed, Strait, Straiten, Strait-laced, Strict, Suburban, Verkramp, Wafer-thin, Waist

Nastiness, Nasty Disagreeable, Drevill, Filth, Fink, Ghastly, Lemon, Lo(a)th, Malign(ant), Noisome, Noxious, Obscene, Odious, Offensive, Ogreish, Ribby, Scummy, Sif, Sordid, Unholy, Vile, Virose

Nation(s), National(ist), Nationalism Anthem, Baathist, Broederbond, Casement, Chetnik, Country, Cuban, Debt, De Valera, Eta, Federal, Folk, Grand, Hindutva, Indian, IRA, Jingoist, Kuomintang, Land, Malcolm X, Mexican, Oman, Pamyat, Parnell, Patriot, →PEOPLE, Polonia, Race, Risorgimento, Scottish, Shiv

Sena, Subject, Swadeshi, Timor-Leste, Tonga, Tribespeople, Turk, United, Vanuatu, Vatican City, Wafd, Yemini, Young Ireland, Young Turk, Zionist

Native(s) Abo(rigin), Aborigine, African, Amerind, Annamese, Arab, Ascian, Australian, Autochthon, Aztec, Basuto, Belonging, Bengali, Boy, Cairene, Carib, Carioca, Chaldean, Citizen, Colchester, Conch, Creole, Criollo, Domestic, Dyak, Edo, Enchorial, Eskimo, Fleming, Genuine, Habitual, Inborn, Indigene, Indigenous, Inhabitant, Intuitive, Kaffir, Libyan, Local, Malay, Maori, Mary, Micronesian, Moroccan, Norwegian, Oyster, Polack, Portuguese, Son, Spaniard, Te(i)an, Thai, Tibetan, Uzbeg, Uzbek, Whitstable, Yugoslav

Natural(ly), Naturalise(d), Naturalism Altogether, Artless, Ass, Easy, Endenizen, Genuine, Green, Gut, Homely, Idiot, Illegitimate, Inborn, Inbred, Indigenous, Ingenerate, Inherent, Innate, Instinctive, Moron, Native, Nidget, Nitwit, Nude, Ordinary, Organic, Prat, Real, Sincere, True, Untaught

Nature Adam, Character, Disposition, Esse(nce), Ethos, Hypostasis, Inbeing, Inscape, Manhood, Mould, Quintessence, Root, Second, SN, Temperament

Naught Cypher, Failure, Nil, Nothing, Zero

Naughty Bad, Girly, Improper, Indecorous, Light, Marietta, Offender, Rascal, Remiss, Spright, Sprite, Wayward

Nausea, Nauseous Disgust, Fulsome, Malaise, Queasy, Sickness, Squeamish, Wamble, Wambly

Nave Aisle, Apse, Centre, Hub, Modiolus, Nef

Navigate, Navigator Albuquerque, Baffin, Bering, Bougainville, Cabot, Cartier, Columbus, Control, Cook, Da Gama, Davis, Dias, Direct, Drake, Franklin, Frobisher, Gilbert, Hartog, Haul, Henry, Hudson, Keel, Magellan, Navvy, Orienteer, Pilot, Raleigh, Sail, Star-read, →STEER, Weddell

Navy, Naval AB, Armada, Blue, Fleet, French, Maritime, Merchant, N, Red, RN, Wavy, White squadron, Wren

Near(er), Nearest, Nearby, Nearly, Nearness About, Adjacent, All-but, Almost, Anigh, Approach, Approximate, Beside, By, Close, Cy pres, Degree, Even, Ewest, Feckly, Forby, Gain, Handy, Hither, Imminent, Inby(e), Mean, Miserly, Most, Narre, Neist, Next, Nie, Niggardly, Nigh, Oncoming, Outby, Propinquity, Proximity, Short-range, Stingy, Thereabout(s), To, Upon, Warm, Well-nigh

Neat(ly), Neatness Bandbox, Cattle, Clean-cut, Clever, Dainty, Dapper, Deft, Dink(y), Doddy, Donsie, Elegant, Feat(e)ous, Featuous, Gayal, Genty, Gyal, Intact, Jemmy, Jimpy, Nett, Nifty, Ninepence, Orderly, Ox(en), Perjink, Preppy, Pretty, Rother, Saola, Shipshape, Short(horn), Smug, Snod, Spick and span, Spruce, Straight, →TIDY, Trig, Trim, Uncluttered, Unwatered, Well-groomed

Necessary, Necessarily Bog, Cash, De rigueur, →ESSENTIAL, Estovers, Imperative, Important, Indispensable, Intrinsic, Loo, Money, Moolah, Needful, Ought, Perforce, Requisite, Vital, Wherewithal

Necessitate, Necessity Ananke, Compel, Constrain, Cost, Emergency, Entail, Exigent, Fate, Indigence, Logical, Mathematical, Moral, Must, Natural, Need, Need-be, Oblige, Perforce, Require, Requisite, Staple

Neck(ed) Bottle, Brass, Canoodle, Cervical, Cervix, Channel, Col, Crag, Craig, Crew, Crop, Embrace, Gall, Gorgerin, Halse, Hause, Hawse, Inarm, Inclip, Isthmus, Kiss, Mash, Nape, Pet, Polo, Rubber, Scrag, Scruff, Smooch, Snog, Strait, Swan, Swire, Theorbo, Torticollis, Trachelate, Vee, Volcanic

▷ **Necking** *may indicate* one word around another

Necklace Afro-chain, Anodyne, Bib, Chain, Choker, Collar, Corals, Pearls, Rope, Sautoir, String, Torc, Torque

Neckline Boat, Collar, Cowl, Crew, Décolletage, Plunging, Scoop, Sweetheart, Turtle, Vee

Neckwear Ascot, Barcelona, Boa, Bow, Collar, Cravat, Fur, Steenkirk, Stock, Tie

Nectar Ambrosia, Amrita, Honey, Mead

Need(ed), Needy Call, Demand, Desiderata, Egence, Egency, Exigency, Gap, Gerundive, Impecunious, Indigent, →LACK, Mister, Prerequisite, Pressing, PRN, Require, Special, Strait, Strapped, Want

Needle(s) Acerose, Acicular, Aciform, Acupuncture, Anger, Between, Bodkin, Cleopatra's, Darner, Darning, Dip, Dipping, Dry-point, Electric, Etching, Goad, Gramophone, Hagedorn, Hype, Hypodermic, Ice, Icicle, Inoculate, Knitting, Leucotome, Magnetic, Miff, Monolith, Neeld, Neele, Netting, Obelisk, Packing, Pine, Pinnacle, Pique, Pointer, Prick, R(h)aphis, Sew, Sharp, Spanish, Spicule, Spike, Spine, Spud, Stylus, Tattoo, Tease, Thorn, Wire

Needlework Applique, Baste, Crewel, Embroidery, Gros point, Lacet, Mola, Patchwork, Piqué, Rivière, Sampler, Tapestry, Tattoo, White-seam

Negation, Negative Anion, Apophatic, Cathode, Denial, Downside, Enantiosis, Infinitant, Ne, No, Non, Nope, Nullify, Photograph, Refusal, Resinous, Unresponsive, Veto, Yin

Neglect(ed), Neglectful, Negligence, Negligent Careless, Casual, Cinderella, Cuff, Default, Dereliction, Disregard, Disuse, Failure, Forget, Forlorn, For(e)slack, G-devant, Heedless, Inattention, Incivism, Laches, Malpractice, Misprision, Omission, Oversight, Pass, Pass-up, Rack and ruin, Scamp, Shirk, Slight, Slipshod, Undone, Unilateral, Unnoticed

▷ **Neglected** *may indicate* an anagram

Negligee Déshabillé, Manteau, Mob, Nightgown, Robe

Negotiate, Negotiator Arbitrate, Arrange, Bargain, Barter, Clear, Confer, Deal, Diplomat, Intercede, Interdeal, Intermediary, Liaise, Manoeuvre, Mediator, Parley, Petition, Talk, Trade, Transact, Treat(y), Tret, Weather

Neigh Bray, Hinny, Nicker, Whicker, Whinny

Neighbour(ly), Neighbouring, Neighbours Abut(ter), Alongside, Amicable, Bor, Border, But, Friendly, Joneses, Nearby, Next-door

Neighbourhood(s) Acorn®, Area, Community, District, Environs, Locality, Precinct, Vicinage, Vicinity

Nerve(s), Nervous(ness), Nervure, Nerve centre, Nervy Abdabs, Accessory, Acoustic, Afferent, Aflutter, Afraid, Alveolar, Antsy, Auditory, Autonomic, Axon, Baroreceptor, Bottle, Bouton, Brass neck, Buccal, Butterflies, Chord, Chutzpah, Collywobbles, Column, Commissure, Cones, Courage, Cranial, Cyton, Dendron, Depressor, Edgy, Effector, Efferent, Electrotonus, Epicritic, Excitor, Facial, Fearful, Fidgety, Gall, Ganglion, Glossopharyngeal, Grit, Guts, Habdabs, Heart-string, High, Highly-strung, Hyp, Impudence, Jitters, Jittery, Jumpy, Median, Mid-rib, Motor, Moxie, Myelon, Nappy, Neck, Neurological, Nidus, Oculomotor, Olfactory, On edge, Optic, Pavid, Perikaryon, Pons, Proprioceptor, Protopathic, Rad, Radial, Receptor, Restiform, Restless, Sacral, Sangfroid, Sass, Sauce, Sciatic, Screaming abdabs, Sensory, Shaky, Solar plexus, Somatic, Splanchnic, Spunk, Stage fright, Steel, Strung-up, Sympathetic, Synapse, Tense, Timorous, Tizzy, Toey, Tongue-tied, Trembler, Tremulous, Trigeminal, Trochlear, Twitchy, Ulnar, Uptight, Vagus, Vapours, Vasodilator, Vestibular, Vestibulocochlear, Wandering, Willies, Windy, Wired, Wittery, Yips

▷ **Nervously** *may indicate* an anagram

Nest Aerie, Aery, Aiery, Ayrie, Bike, Bink, Brood, Byke, Cabinet, Cage, Caliology, Clutch, Dray, Drey, Eyrie, Eyry, Guns, Hive, Lodge, Nid, Nide, Nidify, Nidus, Sett, Termitarium, Turkey, Wurley

Nestle Burrow, Cose, Cuddle, Nuzzle, Rest, Snug(gle)

Net(ting), Nets, Network(ing), Networker Bamboo, BR, Bunt, Bus, Butterfly, Cast, Casting, Catch, Caul, Clap, Clear, Co-ax(ial), Cobweb, **→COMPUTER NETWORK**, Craquelure, Crinoline, Criss-cross, Crossover, Diane, Drift, Earn, Eel-set, Enmesh, Equaliser, Fetch, File server, Filet, Final, Fish, Fisherman, Flew, Flue, Fret, Fyke, Gain, Gill, **→GRID**, Hammock, Honeycomb, Hose, Insect, Kiddle, Lace, LAN, Land, Landing, Lattice, Leap, Line, Linin, Mains, Mattress, Maze, Mist, Mosquito, Mycelium, Nerve, Neural, Neuropil, Old boys', PCN, Plexus, Portal system, Pound, Pout, Purse-seine, Quadripole, Reseau, Rete, Retiary, Reticle, Reticulate, Reticulum, Ring, Safety, Sagene, Scoop, Screen, Sean, Seine, Senior, Set(t), Shark,

Skype®, Snood, Speed, Stake, Symplast, System, Tangle, Tela, Telex, Tissue, Toil, Torpedo, Trammel, Trap, Trawl, Trepan, Tulle, Tunnel, Wire

Nettle(rash) Anger, Annoy, Day, Dead, Hemp, Hives, Horse, Irritate, Labiate, Nark, Ongaonga, Pellitory, Pique, Ramee, Rami, Ramie, Rhea, Rile, Ruffle, Sting, Urtica(ceae), Urticaria

Neuter Castrate, Gib, Impartial, Neutral, Sexless, Spay

Neutral(ise) Alkalify, Buffer zone, Counteract, Degauss, Grey, Impartial, Inactive, Schwa, Sheva, Shiva, Unbiased

Never(more) As if, Nary, Nathemo(re), No more

Never mind Nix my dolly

Nevertheless Algate, All the same, Anyhow, But, Howbeit, However, Still, Yet

▷ **New** *may indicate* an anagram

New(s), Newborn, News agency Avant garde, Bulletin, Communique, Copy, Coranto, Dope, Euphobia, Evangel, Flash, Forest, Fresh, Fudge, Gen, Green, Griff, Info(rmation), Initiate, Innovation, Intake, Intelligence, Item, Kerygma, Latest, Mint, Modern, N, Novel, Oil(s), Original, PA, Paragraph, Pastures, Pristine, Propaganda, Raw, Recent, Report, Reuter, Scoop, Sidebar, Snippet, Span, Splash, Stranger, Tass, Teletext®, Tidings, Ultramodern, Unco, Update, Word, Young

Newcomer Dog, Freshman, Griffin, Immigrant, Jackaroo, Jackeroo, Jillaroo, Johnny-come-lately, L, Learner, Newbie, Novice, Parvenu, Pilgrim, Settler, Tenderfoot, Upstart

New Orleans Big easy

Newsman, News-reader Announcer, Editor, Journalist, Legman, Press, Reporter, Sub, Sysop

Newspaper Beast, Big Issue, Blat(t), Broadsheet, Compact, Courier, Daily, Express, Fanzine, Feuilleton, Freesheet, Gazette, Guardian, Heavy, Herald, Intelligencer, Izvestia, Journal, Jupiter, Le Monde, Mercury, National, Organ, Patent inside, Patent outside, Post, Pravda, Press, Print, Rag, Red-top, Scotsman, Sheet, Spoiler, Squeak, Sun, Tabloid, Today, Yellow Press

Newsworthy Topical

Newt(s) Ask(er), Eft, Evet, Swift, Triton, Urodela

New Zealand(er) Aotearoa, Diggers, Enzed, Kiwi, Maori, Moriori, .nz, Pakeha, Pig Island, Ronz(er), Shagroon

Next Adjacent, Adjoining, After, Alongside, Beside, By, Following, Immediate, Later, Nearest, Neighbour, Neist, Proximate, Proximo, Sine, Subsequent, Syne, Then, Thereafter

Nib(s) Cocoa, J, Pen, Point, Tip

Nibble Bite, Brouse, Browse, Byte, Canapé, Crop, Eat, Gnaw, Knap(ple), Moop, Moup, Munch, Nag, Nepit, Nosh, Peck, Pick, Snack

Niblick Wedge

Nice(ly), Nicety Accurate, Amene, Appealing, Dainty, Fastidious, Fine, Finical, Genteel, Lepid, Ninepence, Pat, Pleasant, Precise, Quaint, Rare, Refined, Subtil(e), Subtle, Sweet, T, To a t

Niche Alcove, Almehrahb, Almery, Ambry, Apse, Aumbry, Awmrie, Awmry, Columbarium, Cranny, Exedra, Fenestella, Mihrab, Recess, Slot

Nick(ed) Appropriate, Arrest, Bin, Blag, Can, Chip, Cly, Colin, Copshop, Crib, Cut, Denay, Dent, Deny, → **DEVIL**, Erose, Groove, Hoosegow, Kitty, Knock, Nab, Nap, Nim, Nock, Notch, Pinch, Pocket, Pook, Pouk, Prison, Run in, Scratch, Serrate, Sneak, → **STEAL**, Steek, Swan-upping, Swipe, Thieve, Wirricow, Worricow, Worrycow

Nickname Alias, Byname, Byword, Cognomen, Monicker, So(u)briquet

Niger RN

Night(s), Nightfall Acronical, Acronychal, Arabian, Burns, Darkling, Darkmans, First, Gaudy, Guest, Guy Fawkes, Hen, Leila, Nacht, Nicka-nan, Nutcrack, Nyx, Opening, School, Sleepover, Stag, Twelfth, Twilight, Walpurgis, Watch, White

Night-cap Biggin, Cocoa, Nip, Pirnie, Sundowner

Nightingale Bulbul, Florence, Frog, Jugger, Lind, Philomel, Philomena, Scutari, Swedish, Watch

Nightmare, Nightmarish Cacod(a)emon, Ephialtes, Incubus, Kafkaesque, Oneirodynia, Phantasmagoria

Nightshade Atropin(e), Belladonna, Bittersweet, Circaea, Dwale, Henbane, Morel, Solanum

Nil Nothing, Nought, Zero

Nimble(ness), Nimbly Active, →AGILE, Alert, Deft, Deliver, Fleet, Legerity, Light, Light-footed, Lissom(e), Lithe, Quiver, Sciolto, Springe, Spry, Supple, Sure-footed, Swack, Wan(d)le, Wannel, Wight, Ya(u)ld

Nip(per), Nippers Bite, Brat, Check, Chela, Chill, Claw, Cutpurse, Dip, Dram, Foil, Gook, Jack Frost, Jap, Lad, Lop, Nep, Nirl, Outsiders, Peck, Pickpocket, Pincers, Pinch, Pook, Scotch, Sneap, Susan, Tad, Talon, Taste, Tot, Tweak, Urchin, Vice, Vise

Nipple Dug, Mastoid, Pap, Teat

Nit-picking Carping, Pedantry, Quibble

No Aikona, Denial, Na(e), Nah, Naw, Negative, Nix, Nope, Nyet, O, Refusal

Nob(by) Grandee, Parage, Prince, Swell, Toff

▷ **Nobbled** *may indicate* an anagram

Noble(man), Noblewoman, Nobility, Nobly Adela, Adele, Adeline, Aneurin, Aristocrat, Atheling, Baron(et), Baroness, Baronet(ess), Baronne, Bart, Blue blood, Boyar, Brave, Bt, Burgrave, Childe, Contessa, Count, County, Cousin, Daimio, Datuk, Dauphine, Dom, Don, Doucepere, Douzeper(s), Duc, Duke, Duniwassal, Earl, Empress, Eorl, Ethel, Eupatrid, Fine, Galahad, Gent, Glorious, Graf, Grandee, Grandeur, Great, Heroic, Hidalgo, Highborn, Illustrious, Infant, Jarl, Junker, King, Landgrave, Lofty, Lord, Maestoso, Magnate, Magnificent, Magnifico, Manly, Margrave, Marquis, Mona, Nair, Nawab, Nayar, Palatine, Patrician, Patrick, Peer, Rank, Ritter, Rose, Seigneur, Seignior, Sheik(h), Stately, Sublime, Thane, Thegn, Titled, Toiseach, Toisech, Vavasour, Vicomte, Vidame, Viscount, Waldgrave

Noble gas(es) Argon, Helium, Krypton, Neon, Radon, Xenon

Nobody Diarist, Gnatling, Jack-straw, Nebbish, Nemo, None, Nonentity, Nyaff, Pipsqueak, Pooter, Quat, Schlepp, Scoot, Shlep, Zero

Nod(ding) Agree, Assent, Beck(on), Bob, Browse, Catnap, Cernuous, Dip, Doze, Drowsy, Mandarin, Nutant, Somnolent

Node, Nodular, Nodule Boss, Enhydros, Geode, Knot, Lump, Lymph, Milium, Pea-iron, Ranvier, Septarium, Swelling, Thorn, Tophus

No go Anergia

Noise, Noisy Ambient, Babel, Bedlam, Big, Blare, Blat(t), Bleep, Blip, Blue murder, Bobbery, Boing, Boink, Bray, Bruit, Cangle, Charm, Cheep, Chellup, Clam, Clamant, Clamour, Clangour, Clash, Clatter, Clitter, Clutter, Coil, Crackle, Creak, Deen, Din, Dirdum, Discord, Euphonia, Euphony, F, Flicker, Fuss, Hewgh, Howlround, Hubbub, Hue, Hullabaloo, Hum, Hurly-burly, Knocking, Loud, Mush, Obstreperous, Phut, Ping, Pink, Plangent, Quonk, Racket, Raucous, Report, Risp, Roar, Roarie, Roary, Robustious, Rorie, Rort, Rory, Row(dow-dow), Rowdedow, Rowdy(dow)(dy), Rucous, Rumble, Schottky, Schottky-Utis, Scream, Screech, Shindig, Shindy, Shot, Shreek, Shreik, Shriech, Shriek, Slosh, Solar, Sone, Sonorous, Sound, Stridor, Surface, Thermal, Thunder, Tinnitus, Top, Trumpet, Tumult, →UPROAR, VIP, Visual, Vociferous, Whinny, White, Whoomph, Zoom

Nomad(ic) Bedawin, Bedu, Bed(o)uin, Berber, Chal, Drifter, Edom(ite), Errant, Fula(h), Gypsy, Hottentot, Hyksos, Kurd, Kyrgyz, Lapp, Rom, Rootless, Rover, Saracen, Sarmatian, Strayer, Tsigane, Tsigany, Tuareg, Vagabond, Vagrant, Wanderer, Zigan

No man's land Tom Tiddler's ground

Nomenclature Term

Nominate, Nomination Appoint, Baptism, Designate, Elect, Postulate, Present, →PROPOSE, Slate, Specify, Term

Non-Aboriginal Wudjula

Non-attachment Limbo

Non-attribute Ens

Nonchalance, Nonchalant Blasé, Casual, Cool, Debonair, Insouciant, Jaunty, Poco

Non-Christian New-age, Saracen

Non-conductor Insulator

Non-conformist, Non-conformity Beatnik, Bohemian, Chapel, Deviant, Dissent(er), Dissident, Drop-out, Ebenezer, Enfant terrible, Heresiarch, Heretic, Maverick, Odd-ball, Outlaw, Pantile, Patarine, Rebel, Recusant, Renegade, Renegate, Sectarian, Wesleyan

Non-directional Scalar

Non-drip Thixotropic

None Nada, Nary, Nil, Nought, Zero

Nonentity Cipher, Nebbich, Nebbish(er), Nebish, Nobody, Pipsqueak, Quat

▷**Nonetheless** *may indicate* an 'o' to be omitted

Non-existent Unbeing, Virtual

Non-orthodox Progressive

Nonsense Absurdity, Amphigory, Balderdash, Baloney, Bilge, Bizzo, Blague, Blah, Blarney, Blat(her), Blatherskite, Blether, Bollocks, Boloney, Borax, Bosh, Bs, Bull, Bulldust, Bullshit, Bull's wool, Buncombe, Bunk, Bunkum, Clamjamfr(a)y, Clamjamphrie, Claptrap, Cobblers, Cock, Cockamamie, Cod, Codswallop, Crap, Crapola, Drivel, Dust, Eyewash, Faddle, Fandangle, Fiddlededee, Fiddle-faddle, Fiddlesticks, Flannel, Flim-flam, Footling, Fudge, Gaff, Gammon, Gas and gaiters, Get away, Gibberish, Gobbledygook, Guff, Gum, Hanky-panky, Haver, Hogwash, Hokum, Hooey, Hoop-la, Horsefeathers, Humbug, Jabberwocky, Jazz, Jive, Kibosh, Kidstakes, Malark(e)y, Moonshine, Mouthwash, Mumbo-jumbo, My eye, Phooey, Piffle, Pshaw, Pulp, Ratbaggery, Rats, Rawmaish, Rhubarb, Rigmarole, Rot, Rubbish, Scat, Shenanigans, Shit(e), Squit, Stuff, Taradiddle, Tom(foolery), Tommy-rot, Tosh, Trash, Tripe, Tush, Twaddle, Unreason, Waffle

Non-specialist User-friendly

Non-standard Anomalous

Non-starter No-no

Non-transferable Adiabatic

Non-Unionist Freerider

Noodle(s) Capellini, Crispy, Daw, Fool, Head, Laksa, Lokshen, Manicotti, Mee, Moony, Ninny, Pasta, Sammy, Simpleton

Nook Alcove, Angle, Corner, Cranny, Niche, Recess, Rookery

Noose Fank, Halter, Hempen caudle, Lanyard, Loop, Necktie, Rebecca, Rope, Rope's end, Snare, Twitch

▶**Nor** *see* NOT

Norm Canon, Criterion, Rule, Standard

Normal Average, Everyday, Natural, Norm, Ordinary, Par, Perpendicular, Regular, Standard, Straightforward, Usu(al)

North(ern), Northerner Arctic, Boreal, Cispontine, Copperhead, Dalesman, Doughface, Eskimo, Hyperborean, Magnetic, N, Norland, Runic, Scotia, Sea, Septentrion, True, Up

North American (Indian) Injun, Papoose, Red(skin), Scalper, Totemist, Tribe

Northern Ireland NI, Six Counties

North star Tyrian cynosure

Nose, Nosy A(d)jutage, Aquiline, Beak, Bergerac, Boko, Bouquet, Breather, Conk, Copper, Cromwell, Curious, Desman, Droop, Fink, Gnomon, Grass, Grecian, Honker, Hooknose, Hooter, Index, Informer, Meddle, Muffle, Muzzle, Nark, Neb, Nozzle, Nuzzle, Proboscis, Prying, Pug, Red, Rhinal, Roman, Schnozzle, Shove, Smelly, Sneb, Sniff, Snoot, Snout, Snub, Squeal, Stag, Stickybeak, Toffee

Nostalgia Longing, Memory lane, Oldie, Retrophilia, Wistfulness, Yearning

Not, Nor Aikona, Dis-, Na(e), Narrow A, Ne, Neither, Never, No, Pas, Polled, Taint

Notable, Notability Conspicuous, Dignitary, Distinguished, Eminent, Especial, Landmark, Large, Lion, Memorable, Personage, Signal, Striking, Unco, VIP, Worthy

▷ **Not allowed** *may indicate* a word to be omitted

Not at all Au contraire

Notation(al) Benesh, Entry, Formalism, Infix, Memo, Polish, Positional, Postfix, Scientific

Notch(ed) Crena(l), Crenel, Cut, Dent, Erode, Erose, Gain, Gap, Gimp, Indent, Insection, Jag, Kerf, Mush, Nick, Nock, Raffle, Serrate, Serrulation, Sinus, Snick, Tally, Vandyke

Note(s), Notebook, Noted A, Accidental, Advance, Advice, Apostil(le), Apparatus, Arpeggio, Auxiliary, B, Bill(et), Bradbury, Bread and butter letter, Breve, C, Cedula, Chit(ty), Chord, Cob, Comment, Conceit, Continental, Cover, Credit, Crotchet, Currency, D, Debit, Delivery, Demand, Dig, Dispatch, Do(h), Dominant, Double-dotted, E, E-la, F, Fa(h), False, Fame, Fiver, Five-spot, Flat, Flim, G, Gamut, Gloss(ary), Gold, Grace, Greenback, Gruppetto, Heed, Hypate, Identic, Index rerum, IOU, Iron man, Item(ise), Jot(tings), Jug(-jug), Key, Kudos, La, Large, Leading, Letter, Line(r), Log, Long, Longa, Lower mordent, Marginalia, Mark, Masora(h), Masoretic, Me, Mediant, Melisma, Melody, Memo(randum), Mese, Message, Mi, Minim, Minute, Missive, →MONEY, Mordent, Music, Muzak®, Natural, NB, Nete, Neum(e), Oblong, Observe, Octave, Oncer, On record, Open, Ostmark, Outline, Passing, Postal, Post-it®, Pound, Promissory, Prompt, Protocol, PS, Quarter, Quaver, Rag-money, Re, Reciting, Record, Remark, Renown, Request, Right, Root, Scholion, Scotch catch, Scotch snap, Semibreve, Semiquaver, Semitone, Sensible, Septimole, Sextolet, Sharp, Shoulder, Si, Sick, Sixteenth, Sixty-fourth, Sleeve, Smacker, Snuff-paper, So(h), Sol, Some, Stem, Strike, Subdominant, Submediant, Subtonic, Supertonic, Te, Ten(ner), Third, Thirty-second, Tierce, Tonic, Treasury, Treble, Two-spot, Ut, Verbal, Wad, Whole, Wolf, Wood

▷ **Notes** *may indicate* the use of letters A-G

Noteworthy Eminent, Extraordinary, Memorable, Particular, Signal, Special

Nothing, Nought Buckshee, Bugger-all, Cipher, Damn-all, Devoid, Diddlysquat, Emptiness, FA, Gratis, Jack, Love, Nada, Naught, Nihil, Niks-nie, Nil, Nix(-nie), Noumenon, Nowt, Nuffin, O, Ought, Rap, Rien, Small beer, Sweet FA, Void, Z, Zero, Zilch, Zip(po)

Notice(able) Ad(vertisement), Advance, Advice, Affiche, Apprise, Attention, Avis(o), Banns, Bill, Blurb, Bold, Bulletin, Caveat, Circular, Clock, Cognisance, Crit, D, DA, Descry, Detect, Discern, Dismissal, Enforcement, Evident, Gaum, Get, Gorm, Handbill, →HEED, Intimation, Marked, Mensh, Mention, NB, No(t)chel, Obit, Observe, Oyez, Perceptible, Placard, Plaque, Playbill, Poster, Press, Proclamation, Prominent, Pronounced, →REMARK, Review, See, Short, Si quis, Spot, Spy, Sticker, Tent, Warning, Whip

Notify, Notification Acquaint, Advise, Apprise, Aviso, Awarn, Inform, Payslip, →TELL

Notion(al) Conceit, Crotchet, Fancy, Hunch, Idea, Idolum, Inkling, Opinion, Reverie, Vapour, Whim

Notoriety, Notorious Arrant, Byword, Crying, Egregious, Esclandre, Fame, Flagrant, Infamous, Infamy, Legendary, Proverbial, Réclame, Repute

▶ **Nought** *see* NOTHING

Noumenon Thing-in-itself

Noun Agent, Agentive, Aptote, Collective, Common, Concrete, Count, Gerund, Mass, N, Proper, Seg(h)olate, Substantive, Tetraptote, Verbal, Vocative

Nourish(ing), Nourishment Aliment, Cherish, Cultivate, Feed, Ingesta, Manna, Meat, Nurse, Nurture, Nutrient, Promote, Repast, Replenish, Sustenance, Trophic

▷ **Novel** *may indicate* an anagram

Novel(ty) Aga-saga, Airport, Bonkbuster, Book, Campus, Change, Clarissa, Different, Dime, Dissimilar, Epistolary, Erewhon, Fad, Fiction, Fresh, Gimmick, Gothic, Graphic, Historical, Horror, Idiot, Innovation, →NEW, Newfangled, Novation, Original, Outside, Page-turner, Paperback, Penny dreadful, Picaresque, Pot-boiler, Primeur, Pulp, River, Roman-à-clef, Romance, Roman fleuve, Saga, Scoop, Sex and shopping,

She, Shilling-dreadful, Shilling-shocker, Terror, Thesis, Ulysses, Unusual, Weepie, Whodun(n)it, Yellowback

▶**Novelist** *see* **WRITER**

November N, Nov

Novice Acolyte, Apprentice, Beginner, Chela, Colt, Cub, Green(horn), Griffin, Jackaroo, Jillaroo, Kyu, L, Learner, Neophyte, New chum, Noob, Patzer, Postulant, Prentice, Rabbit, Rookie, Tenderfoot

Now(adays) AD, Alate, Anymore, Current, Here, Immediate, Instantaneously, Instanter, Interim, Nonce, Nunc, Present, Pro tem, This

No-win Dead heat

Nozzle Aerospike, A(d)jutage, Fishtail, Nose, Nose-piece, Rose, Spout, Stroup, Syringe, Tewel, Tuyere, Tweer, Twier, Twire, Twyer(e)

Nuance Gradation, Nicety, Overtone, Shade

Nub Crux, Gist, Knob, Lump, Point

Nuclear, Nucl(e)ide, Nucleus Cadre, Calandria, Centre, Core, Crux, Daughter, Deuteron, Eukaryon, Euratom, Heartlet, Hub, Isomer, Isotone, Karyon, Kernel, Linin, Mesic, Mesonic, Mushroom, Nuke, Organelle, Pith, Prokaryon, Recoil, Triton

▷**Nucleus** *may indicate* the heart of a word

Nude, Nudism, Nudist, Nudity Adamite, Altogether, Aphylly, Bare, Buff, Eve, Exposed, Gymnosophy, →**NAKED**, Nuddy, Scud, Stark, Stripped, Undress

Nudge Dunch, Dunsh, Elbow, Jostle, Knee, Poke, Prod

Nuisance Bore, Bot, Bugbear, Chiz(z), Drag, Impediment, Inconvenience, Mischief, Pest, Plague, Public, Terror, Trial

Null(ification), Nullify Abate, Cancel, Counteract, Defeasance, Destroy, Diriment, Disarm, Invalid(ate), Negate, Neutralise, Overturn, Recant, Terminate, Undo, Veto, Void

Numb(ness) Asleep, Blunt, Dead(en), Stun, Stupor, Torpefy, Torpescent, Torpid

▷**Number** *may indicate* a drug

Number(s) Abundant, Access(ion), Air, Algebraic, Algorithm, Aliquant, Aliquot, Amiable, Amicable, Anaesthetic, Analgesic, Antilog, Army, Atomic, Babylonian, Binary, Box, Calculate, Cardinal, Cetane, Chromosome, Class, Cocaine, Coefficient, Cofactor, Complex, Composite, Concrete, Constant, Coordination, Count, Cyclic, Decillion, Deficient, Deficit, Diapason, Digit, DIN, Drove, E, Edition, Epidural, Ether, Eucaine, Ex-directory, F, Feck, Figurate, Figure, Folio, Folksong, Fraction, Friendly, Frost(bite), Gas, Gobar, Golden, Googol, Handful, Hash(mark), Hemlock, Host, Hyperreal, Imaginary, Include, Incomposite, Index, Integer, Irrational, Isotopic, Item, Lac, Lakh, Legion(s), Lepton, Livraison, Local, Mach, Magazine, Magic, Mantissa, Mass, Melodic, Milliard, Minyan, Mixed, Mort, Muckle, Multiple, Multiplex, Multiplicity, Multitude, Myriadth, Natural, Neutron, No(s), Nonillion, Nth, Nuclear, Num, Numerator, Numerical, Octane, Octillion, Opiate, Opium, Opposite, Opus, Ordinal, OT, Paginate, Par, Paucal, Peck, Perfect, Pile, PIN, Plural, Polygonal, Prime, Procaine, Production, Proton, Quantum, Quorum, Quota, Quotient, Random, Rational, Real, Reckon, Registration, Regulo®, Root, Scads, Serial, Show-stopper, Sight, Slew, Slue, Some, Square, Strangeness, Strength, Summand, Surd, T, Tale, Telephone, Tell, Thr(e)ave, Totient, Totitive, Transcendental, Troop, Turn-out, Umpteen, Umpty, Urethan(e), Verse, Wave, Whole, Wrong

Numeral(s) Arabic, Chapter, Figure, Ghubar, Gobar, Integer, Number, Roman, Sheep-scoring

Nun Basilian, Beguine, Bhikkhuni, Clare, Cloistress, Cluniac, Conceptionist, Dame, Deaconess, Gilbertine, Minim, Minoress, Mother Superior, Outsister, Pigeon, Poor Clare, Religeuse, Salesian, Sister, Sister of Mercy, Top, Trappistine, Vestal, Visitant, Vowess, Zelator, Zelatrice, Zelatrix

▷**Nun** *may indicate* a biblical character, father of Joshua

Nurse(ry), Nursing Aia, Alice, Amah, Angel, Ant, Ayah, Barrier, Bonne, Caledonia, Candy-striper, Care(r), Cavell, Charge, Cherish, Consultant, Cradle, Crèche, Day, Deborah, District, Dry, EN, Flo(rence), Foster, Gamp, Glumdalclitch, Harbour, Health visitor, Karitane, Mammy, Midwife, Minister, Mother, Mrs Gamp, Nan(n)a, Nanny,

Night, Nightingale, Norland, Nourice, Nourish, Parabolanus, Phytotron, Playroom, Playschool, Plunket, Practical, Probationer, RN, School, Scrub, Seminary, SEN, Sister, Staff, Suckle, Tend, VAD, Visiting, Wet

Nursery(man) Conservatory, Crèche, Garden, Hothouse, Rhyme, Seedsman, Slope

▷**Nursing** *may indicate* one word within another

Nut *may refer to* Egyptian god, father of Osiris

Nut(s), Nutcase, Nutshell, Nutter, Nut tree, Nutty Acajou, Acorn, Almond, Amygdalus, Aphorism, Arachis, Areca, Arnut, Babassu, Barcelona, Barking, Barmy, Bats, Beech-mast, Bertholletia, Betel, Bonce, Brazil, Briefly, Buffalo, Butterfly, Butternut, Cashew, Castle, Chock, Coal, Cob, Coco-de-mer, Coffee, Cohune, Coke, Cola, Conker, Coquilla, Coquina, Core, Cranium, Crank, Cream, Cuckoo, Dukka(h), En, Filberd, Filbert, Frog, Gelt, Gilbert, Gland, Glans, Goober, Goober-pea, Gum, Hard, Hazel, Head, Helmet, Hickory, Illipe, Ivory, Kachang puteh, Kernel, Kola, Kooky, Lichee, Li(t)chi, Litchi, Loaf, Lug, Lunatic, Lychee, Macadamia, Macahuba, Macaw-palm, Macoya, Manic, Marking, Mast, Mockernut, Monkey, Noisette, Noodle, Oak, Oil, Pakan, Palmyra, Para, Pate, Pecan, Pekan, Philippina, Philippine, Philopoena, Physic, Pili, Pine, Pin(y)on, Pistachio, Poison, Praline, Prawlin, Quandang, Quantong, Queensland, Rhus, Sapucaia, Sassafras, Scrotum, Shell, Skull, Slack, Sleeve, Stuffing, Supari, Testicles, Thumb, Tiger, Tough, Walnut, Weirdo, Wing, Zany, Zealot

Nutcracker Cosh

Nutrient, Nutriment, Nutrition Betacarotene, Eutrophy, Food, Ingesta, Protein, Sitology, Sustenance, Trace element, Trophic, Vitamin

▷**Nuts** *may indicate* an anagram

Nymph(et) Aegina, Aegle, Amalthea, Arethusa, Callisto, Calypso, Camenae, Carme, Clytie, Constant, Cymodoce, Daphne, Doris, Dryad, Echo, Egeria, Eurydice, Galatea, Hamadryad, Hesperides, Houri, Hyades, Ida, Insect, Larva, Liberty, Lolita, Maelid, Maia, Maiden, Mermaid, Naiad, Nereid, Oceanid, Oenone, Oread, Pupa, Rusalka, Sabrina, Satyra, Scylla, Siren, Sylph, Syrinx, Tessa, Tethys, Thetis, Water, Wood

Oo

O Blob, Duck, Nought, Omega, Omicron, Oscar, Oxygen, Spangle, Tan, Zero

Oar(s), Oarsmen Blade, Ctene, Eight, Galley slave, Leander, Organ, Paddle, Propel, Rower, Scull, Spoon, Sweep

Oat(meal), Oats Ait, Athole brose, Avena, Brome-grass, Fodder, Grain, Grits, Groats, Gruel, Haver, Loblolly, Parritch, Pilcorn, Pipe, Porridge, Quaker®, Rolled, Wild

Oath Affidavit, Begorrah, Blast, Blimey, Bribery, Burgess, Curse, Damn, Dang, Dash, Demme, Doggone, Drat, Ecod, Egad, Expletive, God-so, Halidom, Hell, Hippocratic, Igad, Imprecation, Jabers, Jesus, Keech, Lumme, Lummy, Nouns, Oons, Promise, Rats, Sacrament, Sal(a)mon, 'sbodikins, Sbud(dikins), Sheart, Shoot, 'slife, 'slight, Snails, Sonties, Strewth, Stygian, Swear, Tarnation, Tennis-court, Voir dire, Vow, Zbud

Obedient, Obedience, Obey Biddable, Bridlewise, Comply, Dutiful, Follow, Good, Hear, Mindful, Obsequious, Observe, Obtemper, Perform, Pliant, Servant, Yielding

Obese, Obesity Bariatrics, Corpulent, Fat, Stout

▷ **Object** *may indicate* a grammatical variant

Object(s), Objection(able), Objective(ness), Objector Ah, Aim, Ambition, Argue, Artefact, Article, Artifact, Bar, Beef, But, Case, Cavil, Challenge, Clinical, Cognate, Complain(t), Conchy, Conscientious, Cow, Demur, Detached, Direct, Dissent, Doodah, End, Exception, Fetish, Found, Fuss, →**GOAL**, Her, Him, Ifs and buts, Impersonal, Improper, Indifferent, Indirect, Intensional, Intention, It, Item, Jib, Lion, Loathe, Mind, Moral, Near-earth, Niggle, Nitpick, Non-ego, Non-partisan, Noumenon, Ob, Obnoxious, Offensive, Oppose, Outness, Percept, Perspective, Plan, Plot, Point, Protest, Proximate, Quasi-stellar, Question, Quibble, Quiddity, Rank, Rebarbative, Recuse, Refuse, Relation, Resist, Retained, Sake, Scruple, Sex, Subject, Sublime, Target, Thing, Transitive, Tut, Ultimate, Unbiased, Virtu, Wart

Objet d'art Curio

Oblige, Obliging, Obligation, Obligatory Accommodate, Affable, Behold, Binding, Burden, Charge, Coerce, Compel, Complaisant, Compliant, Contract, Corvée, Debt, De rigueur, Duty, Easy, Encumbent, Force, Giri, Gratify, Impel, Incumbent, IOU, Mandatory, Must, Necessitate, Novation, Obruk, Obstriction, Peremptory, Promise, Responsibility, Sonties, Synallagmatic, Tie, Wattle

▷ **Oblique** *may indicate* an anagram

Oblique(ly) Askance, Askew, Awry, Cross, Diagonal, Perverse, Separatrix, Skew, Skewwhiff, Slanting, Solidus, Squint, Virgule

Oblivion, Oblivious Forgetful, Lethe, Limbo, Nirvana, Obscurity, Unaware

Obloquy Opprobrium

Obnoxious Eyesore, Foul, Horrid, Offensive, Pestilent, Repugnant, Unpleasant, Wart

Oboe Piffero

Obscene(ly), Obscenity Bawdy, Blue, Fescennine, Filth, Gross, Hard-core, Indecent, Lewd, Lubricious, Paw(paw), Porn(o), Profane, Raunchy, Ribald, Salacious, Scatology, Smut, Vulgar

Obscure, Obscurity Abstruse, Anheires, Becloud, Befog, Blear, Blend, Blot out, Blur, Break, Cloud, Cobweb, Conceal, Cover, Cryptic, Darken, Deep, Dim, Disguise, Eclipse, Elliptic, Encrypt, Engloom, Envelop, Esoteric, Filmy, Fog, Hermetic, Hide, Indistinct, Jude, Mantle, Mist, Murk, Nebular, Night, Nubecula, Obfuscate, Obnubilate, Opaque, Oracular, Overcloud, Overshade, Overshadow, Recherché, Recondite, Shadowy, Tenebrific, Twilit, Unclear, Unobvious, →**VAGUE**, Veil, Vele, Wrap

▷ **Obscure(d)** *may indicate* an anagram

Observance, Observant, Observation Adherence, Alert, Attention, Comment, Custom, Empirical, Espial, Experience, Eyeful, Holy, Honour, Hour-angle, Lectisternium, →**NOTICE**, Obiter dicta, Perceptive, Percipient, Practice, Quip, Ready-eyed, Recce, Remark, Right, Rite, Ritual, Use, Vising

Observe(d), Observer Behold, Bystander, Celebrate, Commentator, Detect, Espy, Eye, Heed, Keep, Mark, NB, Note, Notice, Obey, Onlooker, Optic, Pharisee, Regard(er), Remark, Rite, Scry, See, Seer, Sight, Spectator, Spial, Spot, Spy, Study, Take, Twig, View, Voyeur, Watch, Witness

Obsess(ed), Obsession, Obsessive Anal, Anorak, Besot, Bug, Complex, Craze, Dominate, Fetish, Fixation, Hang-up, Haunt, Hobbyhorse, Hooked, Idée fixe, Infatuation, Mania, Monomania, Necrophilia, Nerd, Neurotic, One-track, Preoccupy, Smitten, Thing, Wonk

Obsidian Pe(a)rlite

Obsolete, Obsolescence, Obsolescent Abandoned, Antique, Archaic, Dated, Dead, Defunct, Disused, Extinct, Latescent, Obs, Outdated, Outworn, Passé

Obstacle Barrage, Barrier, Boyg, Cheval de frise, Chicane, Dam, Drag, Dragon's teeth, Drawback, Gate, Handicap, Hazard, Hindrance, Hitch, Hurdle, Node, Oxer, Remora, Rock, Sandbank, Snag, Stimie, Stumbling-block, Stymie

Obstinacy, Obstinate Asinine, Bigoted, Bitter-ender, Buckie, Bullheaded, Bullish, Contrarian, Contumacious, Cussed, Dour, Froward, Headstrong, High-stomached, Inflexible, Intractable, Intransigent, Mule, Persistent, Perverse, Pervicacious, Piggish, Pig-headed, Recalcitrant, Refractory, Restive, Rusty, Self-will, Stiff(-necked), Strure, Stubborn, Wilful

Obstruct(ion) Bar, Barricade, Barrier, Block, Bottleneck, Caltrop, Chicane, Clog, Crab, Cross, Cumber, Dam, Embolus, Fil(l)ibuster, Gridlock, Hamper, Hand-off, Hedge, Hinder, Hurdle, Ileus, Impede, Let, Obstacle, Occlude, Sab(otage), Sandbag, Snarl-up, Snooker, Stall, Stap, Stonewall, Stop, Stymie, Sudd, Thwart, Trammel, Trump

Obtain Achieve, Acquire, Buy, Cop, Derive, Exist, Gain, Get, Land, Pan, Prevail, Procure, Realise, Secure, Succeed, Wangle, Win

Obvious Apparent, Axiom, Bald, Blatant, Brobdingnag, Clear, Distinct, Evident, Flagrant, Frank, Inescapable, Kenspeck(le), Manifest, Marked, Needless, Open(ness), Open and shut, Overt, Palpable, Patent, Pikestaff, Plain, Pronounced, Salient, Self-evident, Staring, Stark, Transparent, Truism, Visible

Occasion Call, Cause, Ceremony, Do, Encheason, Engender, Event, Fête, Field day, Nonce, →**OPPORTUNITY**, Reason, Ride, Tide, Time, Treat, Whet

Occasional(ly) At times, Casual, Chance, Daimen, Ever and anon, Intermittent, Irregular, Motive, Orra, Periodic, Scattered, Sometimes, Sporadic, While

Occupant, Occupation, Occupy(ing) Absorb, Activity, Avocation, Beset, Business, Busy, Career, Denizen, Dwell, Embusy, Employ, Engage, Engross, Hold, In, Incumbent, Indwell, Inhabitant, Inmate, Invade, Involve, Line, Man, Métier, Overrun, People, Profession, Pursuit, Residency, Resident, Runrig, Sideline, Squat, Stay, Tenancy, Tenant, Tenure, Thrift, Trade, Upon, Use, Vocation, Walk of life

Occur(rence) Arise, Be, Betide, Betime, Case, Event, Fall, Happen, Incident, Instance, Outbreak, Outcrop, Pass, Phenomenon

Ocean(ic), Oceania Abundance, Abyssal, Antarctic, Arctic, Atlantic, Blue, Deep, German, Hadal, Herring-pond, High seas, Indian, Melanesia, Micronesia, Pacific, Panthalassa, Pelagic, Polynesia, Pond, Sea(way), Southern, Thalassic, Waves, Western

Octopus Cephalopod, Devilfish, Polyact, Scuttle, Squid

Odd (person), Oddity Abnormal, Anomaly, Bizarre, Card, Cure, Curio, Droll, Eccentric, Eery, Erratic, Fishy, Freaky, Gink, Gonzo, Impair, Imparity, Jimjam, Offbeat, Original, Orra, Outré, Paradox, Parity, Peculiar, Queer, Quirky, Quiz, Random, Rare, Remote, Rum, Screwball, Singular, Spooky, →**STRANGE**, Unequal, Uneven, Unmatched, Unpaired, Unusual, Weird, Whims(e)y, Zany

▷ **Odd(s)** *may indicate* an anagram or the odd letters in words

Oddfellow OF

Odds, Oddments Bits, Carpet, Chance, Gubbins, Handicap, Line, Price, SP, Tails, Variance

Ode Awdl, Dit, Epicede, Epicedium, Epinicion, Epinikion, Genethliacon, Horatian, Hymn, Lay, Lyric, Monody, Paeon, Pindaric, Poem, Sapphic, Song, Stasimon, Threne, Threnody, Verse

Odium, Odious Comparison, Disestimation, Disgrace, Foul, Hatred, Heinous, Invidious, Repellent, Repugnant, Stigma

Odorous, Odour Air, Aroma, BO, Flavour, Funk, Hum, Opopanax, Perfume, Quality, Redolence, Sanctity, Scent, Smell, Stench, Waff, Waft

▷**Of** *may indicate an anagram*

Of course Certainly, Natch, Yes

Off Absent, Agee, Ajee, Away, Discount, Distance, Far, From, High, Inexact, Licence, Odd, Rancid, Reasty, Reesty, Relâche, Start

▷**Off** *may indicate an anagram*

▷**Off-colour** *may indicate an anagram*

Offence Attack, Crime, Delict, Delinquency, Distaste, Fault, Huff, Hurt, Indictable, Lapse, Lese majesty, Miff, Misdemeanour, Misprision, Odium, Outrage, Peccadillo, Pip, Pique, Piracy, Praemunire, Regrate, Sedition, →**SIN**, Summary, Trespass, Umbrage, Violation

Offend(ed), Offender Affront, Anger, Annoy, Bridles, Criminal, Culprit, Default, Delinquent, Disoblige, Displease, Distaste, Hip, Huff, Hurt, Hyp, Infringe, Inveigh, Miffy, Miscreant, Nettle, Nonce, Nuisance, Peeve, Perp, Provoke, Serial, Sin(ner), Sledge, Sting, Stray, Twoccer, Umbrage, Violate, Wrongdoer

Offensive(ness) Affront, Aggressive, Alien, Attack, Bombardment, Campaign, Charm, Cruel, Derisatory, Derogatory, Dysphemism, Embracery, Euphemism, Execrable, Eyesore, Foul, Gobby, Indecent, Indelicate, Inroad, Insulting, Invidious, Nasty, Noisome, Obnoxious, Obscene, Odious, Peccant, Personal, Push, Putrid, Rank, Repugnant, →**RUDE**, Scandalous, Scurrilous, Sortie, Storm, Ugly, Unbecoming, Unsavoury, War

Offer(ing) Alms, Altarage, Anaphora, Approach, Bargain, Bid, Bode, Bouchée, Cadeau, Corban, Deodate, Dolly, Epanophora, Extend, Ex voto, Gift, Give, Godfather, Heave, Hold, Inferiae, Introduce, Invitation, Libation, Oblation, Overture, Peace, Peddle, Plead, Pose, Potla(t)ch, Present, Propine, →**PROPOSE**, Propound, Sacrifice, Shewbread, Shore, Special, S(h)raddha, Stamp, Stand, Submit, Suggestion, Tender, Utter, Volunteer, Votive, Wave, Xenium

Offhand Airy, Banana, Brevi manu, Brusque, Casual, Cavalier, Currente calamo, Curt, Extempore, Impromptu, Indifferent, Snappy

Office(s) Abbacy, Agency, Booking, Box, Branch, Broo, Bucket shop, Bureau, Buroo, Chair, Chancery, Circumlocution, Clerical, Colonial, Commonwealth, Complin(e), Consulate, Crown, Cube farm, Cutcher(r)y, Dead-letter, Deanery, Decemvirate, Den, Divine, Dogate, Drostdy, Employment, Evensong, Foreign, Front, Function, Holy, Home, Job, Land, Last, Lav(atory), Left luggage, Lieutenancy, Little, Little hours, Loan, Lost property, Mayoralty, Met(eorological), Ministry, Mistery, Nocturn, Nones, Obit, Oval, Palatinate, Papacy, Patent, Patriarchate, Penitentiary, Personnel, Petty Bag, Pipe, Place, Plum, Portfolio, Position, Post, Prefecture, Prelacy, Press, Prime, Printing, Record, Regency, Register, Registry, Rite, Satrapy, Scottish, Secretarial, Secretariat, See, Sinecure, Situation, Sorting, Stamp, Stationery, Sultanate, Tariff, Terce, Ticket, Tierce, Tol(l)booth, Vespers, Vicary, War

Officer(s) Branch, Compliance, Counter-round, Customs, Duty, Engineer, Executive, First, Flag, Flying, Gal(l)ant, Gazetted, Group, Incumbent, Liaison, Non-commissioned, Nursing, Orderly, Peace, Petty, PO, Police, Presiding, Press, Prison, Probation, Radio, Relieving, Returning, Rodent, Safety, Scene-of-crime, Staff, Treasurer, Wardroom, Warrant, Watch

Office-worker Clerk, Peon, Temp, Typist

Official(s), Officiate, Officious Aga, Agent, Aleconner, Amban, Amtman, Apparatchik, Atabeg, Atabek, Attaché, Authorised, Beadle(dom), Borough-reeve,

Bossy, Bumble, Bureaucrat, Catchpole, Censor, Chamberlain, Chancellor, Commissar, Commissioner, Consul, Convenor, Coroner, Count, Count palatine, Dean, Dignitary, Diplomat, Dockmaster, Dogberry, Ephor, Equerry, Escheater, Eurocrat, Executive, Factotum, →**FORMAL**, Fourth, Functionary, Gauleiter, Governor, Gymnasiarch, Handicapper, Hayward, Hazzan, Incumbent, Inspector, Intendant, Jack-in-office, Jobsworth, Keeper, Landdrost, Lictor, Line judge, Linesman, Macer, Mandarin, Marplot, Marshal, Mayor, MC, Meddlesome, Mirza, Mueddin, Muezzin, Notary, Notary public, Ombudsman, Palatine, Panjandrum, Paymaster, Placeman, Plenipotentiary, Polemarch, Pontificate, Poohbah, Postmaster, Postulator, Praefect, Pragmatic, Prefect, Proconsul, Proctor, Procurator, Prog, Proveditor, Provedor(e), Providor, Provost, Purveyor, Reeve, Ref(eree), Régisseur, Registrar, Remembrancer, Sachem, Scrutineer, Secretary, Shammash, Shammes, Sherpa, Souldan, Spoffish, Stadtholder, Staff, Standard, Steward, Subdean, Suit, Summoner, Surveyor, Timekeeper, Tipstaff, Touch judge, Tribune, Trier, Trior, Triumvir, Turncock, Valid, Valuer General, Verderer, Verger, Vicar-general, Viscount, Vizier, Walla(h), Whip, Yamen, Yeoman

Offset Balance, Cancel, Compensate, Counter(act), Counterbalance

Offspring Boy, Brood, Burd, Chick, Children, Daughter, Descendant, Family, Fruit, Fry, Get, Girl, Heir, Litter, Procreation, Product, Progeny, Seed, Sient, Son, Spawn

Off-the-cuff Improv(isation)

Off-white Cream, Ecru

Often Frequent, Habitual, Repeated

▷ **Often** *may indicate* 'of ten'

Oil(s), Oily, Oil producer Anele, Anoint, Balm, Black gold, Bribe, Crude, Derv, Diesel, Drying, Essence, Essential, Ethereal, Fatty, Fish, Fixed, Frying, Fuel, Good, Grease, Hair, Heavy, Joint, Lamp, Lipid, Long, Lube, Lubricant, Macaw-tree, Midnight, Mineral, Monounsaturated, Multigrade, Oint, Oleaginous, Polyunsaturated, Pomade, Residual, Seed, Short, Sleek, Slick, Smalmy, Smarmy, Smeary, Sweet, Topped crude, Unction, Zest

Ointment Balm, Basilicon, Boracic, Boric, Cerate, Collyrium, Cream, Liniment, Lipsalve, Nard, Pomade, Pomatum, Rub, Salve, Spikenard, Tiger balm®, Unction, Unguent, Vaseline®, Zinc

OK Agree(d), Approve, Authorise, Clearance, Copacetic, Copesettic, Go-head, Green light, Hunky-dory, Initial, Kosher, Mooi, No sweat, Respectable, Right(o), Roger, Sanction, Sound, U, Vet

Old(er), Oldie Ae(t), Aged, Aine(e), Ancient, Antique, Auld, Bean, Decrepit, Dutch, Earlier, Elderly, Fogram, Former, Gaffer, Geriatric, Glory, Golden, Gray, Grey, Hills, Hoary, Immemorial, Major, Mature, Methusaleh, Moore, Nestor, Nick, O, OAP, Obsolete, Off, Ogygian, One-time, Outworn, Palae-, Passé, Primeval, Ripe, Rugose, Sen(escent), Senile, Senior, Shot, Signeur, Stager, Stale, Trite, Venerable, Veteran, Victorian(a), Worn

Old-fashioned Aging, Ancient, Antediluvian, Arch(aic), Arriéré, Back number, Bygone, Corn(y), Dated, Dodo, Dowdy, Fogey, Fuddy-duddy, Fusty, Hidebound, Medieval, No tech, Obsolete, Ogygian, Outmoded, Outre, Outworn, Passé, Podunk, Primeval, Quaint, Relic, Retro, Rinky-dink, Schmaltzy, Shot, Square, Steam, Stick-in-the-mud, Traditional, Uncool, Victorian, Vintage

Old man, Old woman Anile, Aunty, Bodach, Buda, Budi, Burd, Cailleach, Carlin(e), Codger, Crinkly, Crow, Crumbly, Faggot, Fantad, Fantod, Fogey, Fogramite, Fogy, Fussy, Gammer, Geezer, Gramps, Grannam, Greybeard, Greyhen, Husband, Kangaroo, Koro, Kuia, Luckie, Lucky, Matriarch, Methuselah, Mort, Mzee, OAP, Oom, Pantaloon, Patriarch, Presbyte, Roo, Southernwood, Tripod, Trout, Whitebeard, Wife, Wight, Woopie, Wrinkly

Oleander Nerium, Rhododaphne

Ombudsman Trouble shooter

Omelette Crêpe, Foo yong, Foo yung, Frittata, Fu yung, Pancake, Spanish, Tortilla

Omen Abodement, Absit, Augury, Auspice, Foreboding, Forewarning, Freet, Freit, Portent, Presage, Prodrome, Sign, Token, Warning

Ominous Alarming, Baleful, Bodeful, Dire, Dour, Forbidding, Grim, Inauspicious, Menacing, Oracular, Portentous, Sinister, Threatening

Omission, Omit Aph(a)eresis, Apocope, Apospory, Apostrophe, Caret, Disregard, Drop, Elide, Elision, Ellipse, Ellipsis, Failure, Haplography, Haplology, Lipography, Loophole, Miss, Neglect, Nonfeasance, Non-user, Oversight, Paral(e)ipomenon, Pass, Pretermit, Senza, Skip

▷**On** *may indicate* an anagram

On (it) Aboard, About, Agreed, An, An't, At, Atop, By, Game, Half-cut, In, Leg, O', Of, Oiled, Over, Pon, Re, Tipsy, Up(on), Viable

▷**On board** *may indicate* chess, draughts, or 'SS' around another word

Once(r) Ance, As was, Bradbury, Earst, Erst(while), Ever, Ex, Fore, Former, Jadis, Oner, Onst, Secular, Sole, Sometime, Whilom

One(self) A, Ace, Ae, Alike, An(e), Any, Body, Chosen, Eeny, Ego, Ein, I, Individual, Integer, Me, Monad, Per se, Person, Single(ton), Singular, Solo, Tane, Un, Unify, Unit(y), Unitary, United, We, Yin, You

One o'clock 1 am, NNE

Ongoing Continual

Onion(s) Allium, Bengi, Bonce, Bulb, Chibol, Chive, Cibol, Cive, Eschalot, Head, Ingan, Jibbons, Leek, Lyonnaise, Moly, Pate, Pearl, Ramp, Ramson, Rocambole, Ropes, Scallion, Scilla, Shal(l)ot, Spanish, Spring, Squill, Sybo(e), Sybow

Onlooker Beholder, Bystander, Kibitzer, Observer, Rubberneck, Spectator, Witness

Only Allenarly, Anerly, But, Except, Just, Meer, Merely, Nobbut, Seul, Singly, Sole, Sommer, Unique

On the way Agate

On this side Cis

Onward Advance, Ahead, Away, Forth, Forward, Progress

Ooze, Oozy Drip, Exhale, Exude, Gleet, Globigerena, Ichorous, Mud, Percolate, Pteropod(a), Radiolarian, Seep, Sew, Sipe, Slime, Slob, Spew, Spue, Sweat, Uliginose, Uliginous

Opaque, Opacity Dense, Dull, Leucoma, Milky, Obscure, Obtuse, Onycha, Onyx, Roil, Thick, Turbid

Open(er), Opening, Openness Adit, Aedicule, Agape, Airhole, Ajar, Antithesis, Anus, Apert(ure), Apparent, Apse, Armhole, Autopsy, Bald, Bare, Bat, Bay, Begin, Bole, Breach, Break, Broach, Buttonhole, Candid, Cardia, Cavity, Chance, Chasm, Chink, Clear, Crevasse, Crowbar, Dehisce, Deploy, Door(way), Dup, Embrasure, Exordium, Expansive, Explicit, Eyelet, Fair, Fenestra, Fissure, Fistula, Flue, Fontanel(le), Foramen, Frank, Free, Free-for-all, Gambit, Gap, Gaping, Gat, Gate, Give, Glasnost, Glottis, Hagioscope, Hatch, Hatchback, Hatchway, Hiatus, Hilus, →HOLE, Inaugural, Intake, Interstice, Intro, Key, Lacy, Lance, Lead, Loid, Loophole, Loose, Manhole, Meatus, Mofette, Mouth, Naked, Nare, Oillet, Orifice, Os, Oscule, Osculum, Ostiole, Ostium, Overt, Overture, Pandora, Patent, Peephole, Pert, Pervious, Pick(lock), Placket, Plughole, Pop, Pore, Port(age), Porta, Porthole, Preliminary, Premiere, Prise, Pro-am, Public, Pylorus, Relaxed, Rent, Ring-pull, Room, Scuttle, Sesame, Sicilian, Sincere, Slit, Slot, Spare, Spirant, Squint, Start, Stokehole, Stoma, Stulm, Syrinx, Thereout, Thirl, Touchhole, Transparent, Trapdoor, Trema, Trou, Truthful, Unbar, Unbolt, Unbutton, Uncope, Uncork, Undo, Unfurl, Unhasp, Unlatch, Unreserved, Unscrew, Unstop, Unsubtle, Untie, Unzip, Upfront, Vent, Vulnerable, Wide, Window, Yawning

Opera(tic), Opera house, Operetta Aida, Ariadne, Ballad, Boris Godunov, Bouffe, Burletta, Comic, Die Flédermaus, Don Carlos, Don Giovanni, ENO, Ernani, Falstaff, Faust, Fedora, Fidelio, Glyndebourne, Grand, Hansel and Gretel, Horse, Idomeneo, Iolanthe, I Puritani, Kirov, La Bohème, La Donna e Mobile, La Scala, Light, Lohengrin, Lulu, Magic Flute, Met, Musical, Nabucco, Norma, Oater, Oberon, Onegin, Orfeo, Otello, Pag, Parsifal, Pastorale, Patience, Peter Grimes, Pinafore, Rigoletto, Ring, Ruddigore, Rusalka, Salome, Savoy, Seria, Simon Boccanegra, Singspiel, Soap, Space, Sudsen, Tell, The Met, Threepenny, Tosca, Turandot, Verismo, Work, Zarzuela

Operate, Operation(s), Operative Act(ion), Activate, Actuate, Agent, Artisan, Attuition, Barbarossa, Bypass, Caesarean, Campaign, Combined, Conduct, Couching, Current, Desert Storm, Detective, Doffer, Exercise, Function, Game, Hobday, Holding, Hysterectomy, Jejunostomy, Keystroke, Laparotomy, Leucotomy, Liposuction, Lithotomy, Lithotripsy, Lobotomy, Logical, Manipulate, Mechanic, Mules, Nip and tuck, Nose job, Oner, Overlord, Plastic, Practice, Rhytidectomy, Run, Sealion, Shirodkar's, Sortie, Splenectomy, Sting, Strabotomy, Surgery, Titration, Unit, Ure, Valid, Wertheim, Work

Operator Agent, Conductor, Dealer, Manipulator, Nabla, Sawbones, Sparks, Surgeon, Sysop, System

Opiate, Opium Buprenorphine, Dope, Drug, Hop, Laudanum, Meconin, Meconite, Morphine, Narcotic, Paregoric, Religion, Soporific, Thebaine .

Opinion, Opinionative Attitude, Belief, Bet, Bias, Conjecture, Consensus, Cri, Deem, Diagnosis, Dictum, Dogma, Doxy, Editorial, Entêté, Esteem, Fatwa(h), Feeling, Guess, Heresy, Impression, Judgement, Mind, Mumpsimus, Pious, Prejudice, Private, Public, Pulse, Say, Second, Sense, Sentence, Sentiment, SO, Stand, Syndrome, Take, Tenet, Thought, Utterance, View, Viewpoint, Voice, Vote

Opponent(s) Adversary, Antagonist, Anti, Denier, E-N, Enemy, E-S, Foe, Gainsayer, Mitnaged, N-E, N-W, S-E, Straw-man, S-W, Tiger, W-N, W-S

Opportune, Opportunist, Opportunity Appropriate, Apropos, Break, Buccaneer, Carpetbagger, → **CHANCE**, Day, Equal, Facility, Favourable, Ganef, Ganev, Ganof, Godsend, Go-go, Golden, Gonif, Gonof, Heaven-sent, Occasion, Opening, Pat, Photo, Providential, Room, Scope, Seal, Seel, Sele, Snatcher, Sneak thief, Tabula rasa, Tide, Timely, Timous, Vantage, Well-timed, Window

Oppose(d), Opposer, Opposing, Opposite, Opposition Against, Agin, Anti, Antipathy, Antipodes, Antiscian, Antithesis, Antithetic, Antitype, Antonym, Argue, At, Au contraire, Averse, Battle, Beard, Black, Breast, Collision, Colluctation, Combat, Confront, Contradict, Contrary, Converse, Counter(part), Diametric, Dissent, Dissident, Distance, E contrario, Face, Foreanent, Fornen(s)t, Hinder, Hostile, Impugn, Inimical, Inverse, Ironic, Meet, Militate, Noes, Object, Obscurant, Overthwart, Polar, Reactance, Reaction, Recalcitrate, Reluct, Repugn, Resist, Retroact, Reverse, Rival, Shadow, Subtend, Syzygy, Teeth, Terr, Thereagainst, They, Thwart, Toe to toe, Toto caelo, Traverse, V, Versus, Vice versa, Vis-à-vis, Withstand

Oppress(ion), Oppressive Airless, Bind, Burden, Close, Crush, Dead hand, Despotic, Holy cruel, Incubus, Jackboot, Laden, Onerous, Overbear, Overpower, Persecute, Ride, Snool, Stifling, Sultry, Totalitarian, Tyrannise

Opt, Option(al) Alternative, Call, → **CHOICE**, Choose, Decide, Default, Double zero, Elect, Facultative, Fine, Menu, Naked, Omissible, Pick, Plump, Put, Select, Soft, Swap(tion), Voluntary, Votive, Wale, Zero(-zero)

Optimism, Optimist(ic) Chiliast, Elated, Expectant, Hopeful, Micawber, Morale, Pangloss, Pollyanna, Rosy, Sanguine, Starry-eyed, Upbeat

Or Au, Either, Ere, Gold, Ossia, Otherwise, Sol

Orange Agent, An(n)atta, An(n)atto, Arnotto, Aurora, Bergamot, Bigarade, Blenheim, Blood, Blossom, Chica, Clockwork, Croceate, Flame, Flamingo, Fulvous, Genip(ap), Jaffa, Kamala, Kamela, Kamila, Karaka, Mandarin, Methyl, Mock, Naartje, Nacarat, Nartjie, Navel, Ochre, Osage, Petit grain, Pig, Roucou, Ruta, Satsuma, Seville, Shaddock, Tangerine, Tenné, Ugli®, Ulsterman

Orate, Oration Address, Eloge, Elogium, Elogy, Eulogy, Harangue, Panegyric, Speech

Oratorio, Orator(y) Boanerges, Brompton, Brougham, Cantata, Cicero, Creation, Demagogue, Demosthenes, Diction, Elijah, Hwyl, Isocrates, Morin, Nestor, Prevaricator, Proseucha, Proseuche, Rant, Rhetor, Samson, Spellbinder, Stump, Tub-thumper, Windbag

Orbit(al) Apolune, Apse, Apsis, Circuit, Dump, Eccentric, Ellipse, Eye, Lunar, Path, Revolution, Stationary, Subshell

Orchestra(te), Orchestration Ensemble, Gamelan, Hallé, Instrumentation, LPO, LSO, Ripieno, Score, Sinfonietta, Symphony

Orchid Adam and Eve, Adder's mouth, Arethusa, Bee, Bird's nest, Bog, Burnt-tip, Calanthe, Calypso, Cattleya, Coralroot, Coral wort, Cymbidium, Disa, Epidendrum, Fly, Fragrant, Frog, Helleborine, Hyacinth, Lady, Lady's slipper, Lady's tresses, Lizard, Man, Marsh, Military, Miltonia, Monkey, Musk, Naked lady, Odontoglossum, Oncidium, Phalaenopsis, Puttyroot, Salep, Slipper, Snakemouth, Swamp pink, Swan, Twayblade, Vanda, Vanilla

Ordain Arrange, Command, Decree, Destine, Enact, Induct, Japan, Priest

Ordeal Corsned, Disaster, Preeve, Test, →**TRIAL**

Order(ed), Orderly, Orders Adjust, Administration, Affiliation, Alphabetical, Anton Piller, Apollonian, Apple-pie, Arrange, Array, ASBO, Attachment, Attendant, Attention, Attic, Augustine, Avast, Bade, Banker's, Bankruptcy, Bath, Batman, Battalia, Bed, Behest, Benedictine, Bernardine, Bespoke, Bid, Book, Boss, Call, Camaldolite, Canon, Category, Caveat, CB, Charter, Cheque, Chit, Class, Coherent, Command(ment), Committal, Compensation, Composite, Cosmo, Court, Decorum, Decree, Demand, Dictate, Diktat, Direct(ion), Directive, Dispone, Dominican, Doric, DSO, Edict, Embargo, Enclosed, Enjoin, En règle, Errand, Established, Establishment, Eviction, Exclusion, Fiat, Fiaunt, Firing, Firman, Form(ation), Franciscan, Fraternity, Freemason, Full, Gagging, Garnishee, Garter, Gilbertine, Ginkgo, Good, Grade, Group, Habeas corpus, Hest, Holy, Hospitaller, Indent, Injunction, Instruct, Interdict, Ionic, Irade, Khalsa, Kilter, Knights Hospitallers, Kosmos, Language, Large, Lexical, Loblolly boy, Loblolly man, Loose, Mail, Major, Mandamus, Mandate, Marching, Marist, Market, Marshal, Masonic, Merit, Methodical, Minor, Monastic, Money, Monitor, Moose, Natural, Neatness, Nunnery, OBE, Oddfellows, Official, OM, Open, Orange, Ord, Ordain, Organic, Organised, Pecking, Plot, Possession, Postal, Precedence, Precept, Premonstrant, Prescribe, Preservation, Prioritise, Provisional, Rank, Receiving, Reception, Règle, Regular, Religious, Requisition, Restraining, Return, Right, Rule, Ruly, Sailing, Sarvodaya, Sealed, Search, Sequence, Seraphic, Series, Settle, Shipshape, Short, Side, Standing, Starter's, State, Statutory, Stop(-loss), Straight, Subpoena, Summons, Supervision, System, Tabulate, Tall, Taxis, Tell, Templar, Teutonic, Third, Thistle, Tidy, Trim, Ukase, Uniformity, Warison, Warrant, Word, Working, Writ

▷ **Ordering** *may indicate* an anagram

Ordinary Average, Banal, Bog standard, Canton, Chevron, Comely, Common (or garden), Commonplace, Cot(t)ise, Everyday, Everyman, Exoteric, Fess(e), Flanch, Flange, Folksy, Grassroots, Hackneyed, Humdrum, Mass, Mediocre, Middling, Mundane, →**NORMAL**, O, OR, Pedestrian, Plain, Prosy, Pub, Rank and file, Routine, Ruck, Run-of-the-mill, Saltier, Saltire, Scarp, Simple, So-so, Tressure, Trite, Trivial, Undistinguished, Unexceptional, Uninspired, Usual, Vanilla, Workaday, Your

Ore Alga, Babingtonite, Bauxite, Bornite, Braunite, Calamine, Calaverite, Cerusite, Chalcocite, Chalcopyrite, Chloanthite, Coffinite, Coin, Copper, Crocoite, Dry-bone, Element, Enargite, Galenite, Glance, Haematite, Hedyphane, Horseflesh, Ilmenite, Iridosmine, Ironstone, Limonite, Magnetite, Mat, Melaconite, Middlings, Mineral, Minestone, Morass, Niobite, Oligist, Owre, Peacock, Pencil, Phacolite, Pitchblende, Proustite, Psilomelane, Pyrargyrite, Pyromorphite, Realgar, Ruby silver, Schlich, Seaweed, Slug, Smaltite, Sphalerite, Stephanite, Stilpnosiderite, Stockwork, Stream-tin, Taconite, Tailing, Tenorite, Tetrahedrite, Tin, Wad(d)

Organ(s), Organic Adjustor, Adnexa, American, Antimere, Appendix, Archegonium, Barrel, Biogenic, Biotic, Bursa, Calliope, Carbon, Carpel, Carpogonium, Cercus, Chamber, Chemoreceptor, Choir, Chord, Claspers, Clave, Colour, Conch(a), Console, Corti's, Cribellum, Ctene, Ear, Echo, Electric, Electronic, Electroreceptor, Emunctory, End, Epinastic, Essential, Exteroceptor, Eyeball, Feeler, Fin, Flabellum, Fundus, Gametangium, Gill, Glairin, Gonad, Hammond®, Hand, Hapteron, Harmonica, Harmonium, Haustorium, House, Hydathode, Hydraulos, Imine, Isomere, Kerogen, Kidney, Lien, Light, Liver, Lung-book, Lyriform, Mag(azine),

Means, Mechanoreceptor, Media, Medulla, Melodion, Ministry, Modiolus, Nasal, Natural, Nectary, Nematocyst, Nephridium, Newspaper, Olfactory, Oogonia, Ovary, Ovipositor, Ovotestis, Palp, Pancreas, Parapodium, Part, Pedal, Photogen, Photophore, Photoreceptor, Physharmonics, Pipe, Pipeless, Placenta, Plastid, Portative, Positive, Procarp, Prothallus, Pudenda, Pulmones, Purtenance, Radula, Receptor, Recit, Reed, Regal, Relict, Rhizoid, Sang, Saprobe, Scent, Sense, Sensillum, Serinette, Serra, Siphon, Spinneret, Spleen, Sporangium, Sporocarp, Sporophore, Stamen, Steam, Swell, Syrinx, Systaltic, Tentacle, Theatre, Theca, Thymus, Tongue, Tonsil, Tool, Trichocyst, Tympanum, Uterus, Vegetative, Velum, Verset, Viscera, Viscus, Vitals, Voice, Voluntary, Wing, Womb, Wurlitzer®

Organelle Peroxisome

Organise(d), Organisation, Organiser Activate, Administer, Agency, Aggregator, Amnesty, Anatomy, Apparat, →ARRANGE, Association, Body, Brigade, Broederbond, Caucus, Class(ify), Codify, Collect, Comecon, Company, Constitution, Coordinate, Design, Direct, Edifice, Embody, Entrepreneur, Eoka, Fascio, Fatah, Firm, Group, Guild, Hierarchy, Impresario, Infrastructure, Jaycee, Krewe, Ku Klux Klan, Logistics, Machine, Mafia, Marshal, Mastermind, Mobilise, Movement, NATO, Octopus, Opus Dei, Orchestrate, Outfit, Personal, PLO, Promotor, Quango, Rally, Red Crescent, Red Cross, Regiment, Resistance, Rosicrucian, Run, Setup, Sharpbender, Social, Soroptimist, Sort, Stage, Stage manage, Stahlhelm, Steward, Sysop, System, Tidy, Together, UN, UNESCO, Viet Minh

▷ **Organise(d)** *may indicate* an anagram

Organism(s) Aerobe, Agamic, Alga, Archaea, Asymmetron, Auxotroph, Being, Biometric, Biont, Biotic, Cell, Chimeric, Ciliate, Clade, Coral, Detritivore, Diplont, Ecad, Endosymbiont, Entity, Eozoon, Epibenthos, Epizoon, Eurytherm, Extremophile, Germ, Hemiparasite, Incross, Infauna, Infusoria(n), Lichen, Medusa, Meiosis, Metamale, Microaerophile, Microbe, Moneron, Nekton, Neuston, Osmoconformer, Pathogen, Periphyton, Phenetics, Ph(a)enology, Plankton, Pleuston, Poikilotherm, Prokaryote, Protist, Protista, Protozoan, Saprobe, Saprotroph, Schizomycete, Seaslater, Sea spider, Sea squirt, Streptococcus, Symbion(t), Teratogen, Thermophile, Trypanosome, Volvox, Vorticella, Zoarium

Orgasm Climax, Come

Orgy Bacchanalia(n), Binge, Bust, Carousal, Dionysian, Feast, Revel, Saturnalia, Spree, Wassail

Orient(al) Adjust, Annamite, Attune, Chinoiserie, Dawn, Dayak, E, East(ern), Fu Manchu, Hindu, Laotian, Levant, Leyton, Malay, Mongol, Mongolian, Shan, Sunrise, Tatar, Thai, Tibetan, Turk(o)man

Orientation Tropism

Origin(al), Originate, Originating Abiogenesis, Abo, Adam, Arise, As per, Beginning, Big bang, Birth, Come, Cradle, Creation, Derive, Editio princeps, Elemental, Emanate, Epicentre, Etymon, Extraction, First, Firsthand, Focus, Found, Generic, Genesis, Genetical, Germ, Grow, Hatch, Incunabula, Ingenious, Innovate, Invent, Master, Mother, Nascence, Natality, New, Novel, Ord, Parentage, Precedent, Primal, Primary, Primigenial, Primordial, Pristine, Promethean, Protoplast, Prototype, Provenance, Provenience, Rise, Root, Seed, Seminal, Source, Spring, Start, Unborrowed, Ur, Urtext, Ylem, Zoism

Orion Alnilam, Alnitak, Ballatrix, Betelgeuse, Hatsya, Lambda, Meissa, Mintaka, Rigel, Saiph

Ornament(al), Ornamentation Additament, Adorn, Aglet, Aiguillette, Anaglyph, Anthemion, Arabesque, Barbola, Baroque, Barrette, Bead, Bedeck, Billet, Blister, Boss, Bracelet, Broider, Brooch, Bugle, Bulla, Cartouche, Charm, Chase, Clock, Cockade, Conceit, Corbeil(le), Cornice, Coromandel work, Crocket, Cross-quarters, Curlicue, Decor, Decorate, Decoration, Diamanté, Die-work, Diglyph, Dog's-tooth, Doodad, Dreamcatcher, Egg and anchor, Egg and dart, Egg and tongue, Embellish, Emblem(a), Enrich, Epaulet(te), Epergne, Fallal, Fandangle, Festoon, Fiddlehead, Figuration, Figurine, Filagree, Filigrain, Filigree, Fillagree, Fleur de lis, Fleuret, Fleurette, Fleuron, Florid, Fret, Fretwork, Frill, Frounce, Furbelow, Furnish, Gadroon,

Gaud, Headwork, Helix, Hip-knob, Honeysuckle, Illustrate, Inlay, Knotwork, Labret, Leglet, Lotus, Lunette, Lunula, Macramé, Mantling, Millefleurs, Mordent, Moresque, Motif, Nail-head, Necklet, Netsuke, Nicknackery, Niello, Nose-ring, O, Ouch, Ovolo, Palmette, Parure, Patera, Paternoster, Pectoral, Pendant, Picot, Pipe, Piping, Pompom, Poppyhead, Pounce, Prettify, Prunt, Quatrefoil, Rel(l)ish, Rococo, Rosette, Scalework, Scrollwork, Shell, Shoulder-knot, Snowdome, Snowglobe, Spangle, Spar, Tassel, Tool, Torc, Torque, Torsade, Tracery, Trappings, Trill, Trimming, Trinket, Tsuba, Turn, Twiddle, Versal, Whim-wham

▷ **Ornate** *may indicate an anagram*

Orthodox Bien-pensant, Cocker, Conventional, Hardshell, Proper, Sound, Standard

Oscillate, Oscillation, Oscillator Fluctuate, Librate, Local, Relaxation, Ripple, Rock, Seesaw, Seiche, Squeg, Surge, Swing(swang), Vibrate, Waver

Osseous Bony, Hard, Skeletal, Spiny

Ostensibly Apparent, External, Seeming

Ostentation, Ostentatious Camp, Dash, Display, Dog, Éclat, Epideictical, Extravagant, Fantoosh, Fastuous, Flamboyant, Flash(y), Flaunt, Florid, Flourish, Garish, Gaudy, Ghetto fabulous, Highfalutin(g), Large, Parade, Pomp, Pretence, Puff, → SHOW(ING), Side, Splash, Swank, Tacky, Tulip

Osteoporosis Sudeck's atrophy

Ostler Stabler

Ostracise, Ostracism Banish, Blackball, Blacklist, Boycott, Cut, Exclude, Exile, Potsherd, Snub, Taboo

Other(s), Otherwise Additional, Aka, Alia, Alias, Allo-, Alternative, Besides, Different, Distinct, Else, Et al, Et alli, Etc, Excluding, Former, Further, It, Rest, Significant, Unlike

▷ **Otherwise** *may indicate an anagram*

Otologist Aurist

Ottawa Bytown

Ought All, Should

Ouija Board, Planchette

Our(selves) Us, We

▶ **Ousel** *see* OUZEL

Oust Depose, Dislodge, Eject, Evict, Expel, Fire, Supplant, Unseat

Out (of) Absent, Aglee, Agley, Al fresco, Asleep, Aus, Away, Begone, Bowl, Dated, En ville, Exposed, External, Forth, From, Furth, Haro, Harrow, Hence, Hors, Lent, Oust, Skittle, Striking, Stump, Taboo, Uit, Unfashionable, Up, York

▷ **Out** *may indicate an anagram*

Out and out Absolute, Arrant, Sheer, Stark, Teetotal, Thorough, Totally, Utter

Outbreak Ebullition, Epidemic, Eruption, Explosion, Plague, Putsch, Rash, Recrudescence

Outburst Access, Blurt, Bluster, Boutade, Evoe, Explosion, Fit, Flaw, Furore, Fusillade, Gale, Gush, Gust, Paroxysm, Passion, Salvo, Storm, Tantrum, Torrent, Tumult, Volley

Outcast Cagot, Discard, Exile, Exul, Ishmael, Leper, Mesel, Pariah, Robinson, Rogue

Outcome Aftermath, Consequence, Dénouement, Effect, Emergence, End, Event, Issue, → RESULT, Sequel, Upshot, Wash-up

Outcry Blue murder, Bray, Halloa, Howl, Hue, Humdudgeon, Protest, Racket, Steven, Uproar, Utas

Outdated, Out of date Archaic, Dinosaur, Effete, Feudal, Fossil, Horse and buggy, Obsolete, Old hat, Outmoded, Passé, Square

Outdoor(s) Alfresco, External, Garden, Open air, Outbye, Plein-air

Outer External, Extrogenous, Magpie, Top

Outfit(ter) Catsuit, Drawbar, Ensemble, Equipage, Fitout, Furnish, Get-up, Haberdasher, Habit, Kit, Rig, Samfoo, Samfu, Strip, Suit, Team, Trousseau, Turnout, Weed(s), Whites

Outflank Overlap

Outgoing Egression, Exiting, Extrovert, Migration, Open, Retiring

Outgrowth Ala(te), Aril, Bud, Caruncle, Enation, Epiphenomenon, Exostosis, Flagellum, Ligule, Offshoot, Osteophyte, Propagulum, Root-hair, Sequel, Strophiole, Trichome

Outhouse Lean to, Privy, Shed, Skilling, Skipper, Stable

Outing Excursion, Hike, Jaunt, Junket, Picnic, Sortie, Spin, Spree, Treat, Trip, Wayzgoose

Outlandish Barbarous, Bizarre, Exotic, Foreign, Peregrine, Rum

Outlaw Allan-a-Dale, Attaint, Badman, Ban, Bandit(ti), Banish, Broken man, Bushranger, Exile, Friar Tuck, Fugitive, Hereward, Horn, Jesse James, Klepht, Ned Kelly, Proscribe, Put to the horn, Robin Hood, Rob Roy, Ronin, Tory, Waive

Outlet Débouché, Egress, Estuary, Exit, Femerall, Market, Opening, Orifice, Outfall, Sluice, Socket, Tuyere, Tweer, Twier, Twire, Twyer(e), Vent

Outline Adumbration, Aperçu, Circumscribe, Configuration, Contorno, Contour, Delineate, Digest, → DRAFT, Draught, Footprint, Layout, Note, Perimeter, Plan, Profile, Projet, Relief, Scenario, Schematic, Shape, Silhouette, Skeletal, Skeleton, Sketch, Summary, Syllabus, Synopsis, T(h)alweg, Trace

Outlook Aspect, Casement, Perspective, Prospect, View(point), Vista

▷ **Out of** *may indicate* an anagram

▷ **Out of sorts** *may indicate* an anagram

Outpatient Externe

Output Data, Emanation, Get, Gross, Produce, Production, Turnout, Yield

▷ **Output** *may indicate* an anagram

Outrage(ous) Affront, Apoplectic, Atrocity, Desecrate, Disgust, Egregious, Enorm(ity), Flagitious, Flagrant, Insult, OTT, Rich, Sacrilege, Scandal, Shocking, Ungodly, Unholy, Violate

▷ **Outrageously** *may indicate* an anagram

Outright Clean, Complete, Entire, Point-blank, Utter

Outrun Spreadeagle

Outside Ab extra, Crust, Derma, Exterior, External, Extramural, Front, Furth, Hors, Periphery, Plein-air, Rim, Rind, Rine, Shell, Surface

Outsider Alien, Bolter, Bounder, Cad, Extern, Extremist, Foreigner, Incomer, Oustiti, Pariah, Ring-in, Roughie, Stranger, Stumer, Unseeded, Upstart

Outskirts Edge, Fringe, Periphery, Purlieu

Outspoken Bluff, Blunt, Broad, Candid, Explicit, Forthright, Frank, Plain, Rabelaisian, Round, Vocal, Vociferous

Outstand(ing) Ace, Beaut(y), Belter, Billowing, Bulge, Chief, Crackerjack, Debt, Eminent, Especial, Exceptional, Extant, Extraordinaire, Fugleman, Highlight, Humdinger, Impasto, Jut, Lulu, Marked, Matchless, Oner, Overdue, Owing, Paragon, Peerless, Phenom(enal), Prince, Prize, Prominent, Promontory, Prosilient, Protrude, Protuberant, Proud, Relief, Relievo, Salient, Signal, Special, Squarrose, Star, Stellar, Strout, Super(b), Tour de force, Unpaid, Unsettled, Vocal

Outward Efferent, Extern(e), External, Extrinsic, Extrorse, Extrovert, Posticous, Postliminary, Superficial

Outwit Baffle, Best, Circumvent, Crossbite, Dish, Euchre, Fox, Outthink, Over-reach, → THWART, Trick

Ouzel Merle, Ring, Water

Oval(s) Cartouche, Ellipse, Henge, Mandorla, Navette, Ooidal

Oven(-like) Aga®, Calcar, Combination, Convection, Cul-de-four, Dutch, Fan, Furnace, Hangi, Haybox, Horn(it)o, Kiln, Lear, Leer, Lehr, Lime kiln, Microwave, Muffle, Oast, Oon, Stove, Umu

Over Above, Across, Again, Atop, C, Clear, Done, Finished, Hexad, Left, Maiden, Of, On, Ore, Ort, Owre, Past, Sopra, Spare, Superior, Surplus, Through, Uber, Wicket maiden, Yon

Overbalance Outweigh

Overcast Cloudy, Lowering, Sew, Sombre

Overcharge Clip, Extort, Fleece, Gyp, OC, Rack-rent, Rook, Rush, Soak, Sting

Overcome Beat, Bested, Conquer, Convince, Dead-beat, Defeat, Expugn, Kill, Master, Mither, Moider, Moither, Prevail, Quell, Speechless, Stun, Subjugate, Surmount, Survive, Swampt, Underfong, Vanquish, Win

Overconfident, Overconfidence Besserwisser

▷ **Overdrawn** *may indicate* 'red' outside another word

Overdue Behindhand, Belated, Excessive, Late, Unpaid

Overflow(ing) Abrim, Lip, Nappe, Ooze, Outpour, Redound, Spillage, Surfeit, Teem

Overground Subaerial

Overhang(ing) Beetle, Bulge, →**JUT**, Loom, Project, Shelvy

Overhasty Rash

Overhaul Bump, Catch, Overtake, Recondition, Revision, Service, Strip

Overhead(s) Above, Aloft, Ceiling, Cost, Exes, Hair(s), Headgear, Oncost, Rafter, Upkeep, Zenith

Overhear Catch, Eavesdrop, Tap

Overheat Enrage

Overlap(ping) Correspond, Equitant, Imbricate, Incubous, Kern(e), Limbous, Obvolute, Tace, Tasse

Overlay Ceil, Smother, Stucco, Superimpose, Veneer

Overload Burden, Plaster, Strain, Surcharge, Tax

Overlook(ed) Condone, Disregard, Excuse, Forget, Miss, Neglect, Omit, Pretermit, Superintend, Unnoticed, Waive

Overpower(ing) Crush, Evince, Mighty, Onerous, Oppress, Overwhelm, Profound, Subdue, Surmount, Swelter, Whelm

Overprotective Nannyish

Override, Overrule Abrogate, Disallow, Outvote, Outweigh, Paramount, Preponderant, Reverse, Talk down, Veto

Overrun Exceed, Extra, Infest, Inundate, Invade, Lip, Swarm, Teem

Overseas Abroad, Colonial, Foreign, Outremer, Transmarine, Ultramarine

Oversee(r) Baas, Banksman, Boss, Captain, Care, Deputy, Direct, Eyebrow, Foreman, Grieve, Handle, Induna, Mediate, Periscope, Steward, Supercargo, Superintend, Survey(or)

Overshadow(ed) Cloud, Dominate, Dwarf, Eclipse, Obscure, Outclass, Umbraculate

Oversight Blunder, Care, Error, Gaffe, Inadvertence, Lapse, Neglect

Overstate(ment) Embroider, Exaggerate, Hyperbole

Overt Manifest, Patent, Plain, Public

Overtake Catch, For(e)hent, Lap, Leapfrog, Overget, Overhaul, →**PASS**, Supersede

Overthrow Dash, Defeat, Demolish, Depose, Dethrone, Down, Labefact(at)ion, Putsch, Ruin, Smite, Stonker, Subvert, Supplant, Unhorse, Vanquish, Whemmle, Whommle, Whummle, Worst

Overture Advance, Carnival, Egmont, Hebrides, Intro, Leonora, Offer, →**OPENING**, Prelude, Propose, Sinfonia, Toccata, Toccatella, Toccatina

Overturn(ing) Capsize, Catastrophe, Coup, Cowp, Engulf, Quash, Reverse, Tip, Topple, Up(set), Upend, Whemmle, Whomble, Whommle, Whummle

Overuse(d) Hackney(ed), RSI

Overwhelm(ed), Overwhelming Accablé, Assail, Banging, →**CRUSH**, Dearth, Deluge, Engulf, Flabbergast, Inundate, KO, Mind-boggling, Overcome, Plough under, Scupper, Smother, Snow, Submerge, Swamp

Overwork(ed) Fag, Hackneyed, Ornament, Slog, Stale, Supererogation, Tax, Tire, Toil, Travail

Overwritten Palimpsest

Owe(d), Owing Attribute, Due, OD

Owl(s) Barn, Barred, Blinker, Boobook, Brown, Bubo, Bunter, Eagle, Elegant, Fish, Glimmergowk, Grey, Hawk, Hoo(ter), Horned, Jenny, Little, Long-eared, Longhorn, Madge, Moper, Mopoke, Mopus, Night, Ogle, Parliament, Ruru, Saw-whet, Scops, Screech, Snowy, Spotted, Strich, Striges, Strigiformes, Tawny, Wood

Own(er), Owning, Ownership Admit, Agnise, Confess, Domain, Dominium, Fess, Have, Hold, Mortmain, Nain, Of, Personal, Possess, Proper, Proprietor, Recognise, Reputed, Title, Tod, Use

Own way More suo

Ox(en) Anoa, Aquinas, Aurochs, Banteng, Banting, Bison, Bonas(s)us, Buffalo, Bugle, Bullock, Cat(t)alo, Fee, Gaur, Gayal, Gyal, Kouprey, Mart, Musk, Musk-sheep, Neat, Ovibos, Rother, Saola, Sapi-utan, S(e)ladang, Steare, Steer, Taurus, Ure, Urus, Vu quang, Water buffalo, Yak, Yoke, Zebu

▷ **Oxtail** *may indicate* 'x'

Oxygen (and lack of) Anoxia, Epoxy, Liquid, Lox, Loxygen, O

Oyster (bed), Oyster disease, Oyster-eater Avicula, Bivalve, Bush, Cul(t)ch, Kentish, Lay, Mollusc, Native, Ostrea, Ostreophage, Pandore, Pearl, Plant, Prairie, Scallop, Scalp, Scaup, Seed(ling), Spat, Spondyl, Stew, Vegetable

Oz Amos, Australia

Ozone Air, Atmosphere, Oxygen

Pp

Pace, Pacemaker Canter, Clip, Cracking, Dog-trot, Easter, Footstep, Gait, Heel and toe, Jog-trot, Lope, Measure, Pari passu, Pioneer, Rack, → **RATE**, Single-foot, Snail's, Spank, Speed, Step, Stroll, Tempo, Tramp, Tread, Trot

Pacific, Pacify Appease, Bromide, Calm, Conciliate, Dove, Ease, Eirenic, Imperturbable, Irenic, Lull, Mild, Moderate, Ocean, Placid, Quiet, Serene, Soothe, Subdue, Sweeten, Tranquil

Pack(age), Packaging, Packed, Packing, Pack in Back, Bale, Blister, Bobbery, Box, Bubble(wrap), Bundle, Can, Cards, Cold, Compress, Congest, Cram, Crate, Crowd, Cry, Deck, Dense, Dunnage, Embox, Entity, Everest, Excelsior, Face, Fardel, Floe, Forswear, Gasket, Gaskin, Glut, Hamper, Hooker, Hunt, Ice, Jam, Kennel, Knapsack, Lies, Load, Matilda, Naughty, Pair, → **PARCEL**, Pikau, Power, Pun, Ram, Rat, Rout, Ruck, Rucksack, Set, Shiralee, Steeve, Stow, Suits, Sumpter, Tamp, Team, Tread, Troop, Truss, Wad, Wet, Wolf, Wrap

Packet Bindle, Boat, Bomb, Bundle, Liner, Mailboat, Mailer, Mint, Parcel, Roll, Sachet, Steamboat, Wage

Pact Agreement, Alliance, Bargain, Bilateral, Cartel, Contract, Covenant, Locarno, Stability, → **TREATY**, Warsaw

Pad(ding) Batting, Bombast, Brake, Bustle, Compress, Condo, Crash, Cushion, Dabber, Damper, Dossil, Enswathe, Expand, Falsies, Filler, Flat, Frog, Gumshield, Hard, Hassock, Horse, Ink, Jotter, Knee, Launch, Leg-guard, Lily, Nag, Note, Numnah, Patch, Paw, Ped, Pillow, Pincushion, Plastron, Pledget, Plumper, Porters' knot, Pouf(fe), Protract, Pudding, Puff, Pulvillus, Pulvinar, Scratch, Shoulder, Stamp, Stuff, Sunk, Swab, Tablet, Thief, Touch, Tournure, Tylopod, Tympan, Velour(s), Velure, Wad, Wase, Writing

Paddle, Paddle boat, Paddle-foot Canoe, Dabble, Doggy, Oar, Pinniped, Row, Seal, Side-wheel, Spank, Splash, Wade

Paediatrician Rett

Pagan(ism) Animist, Atheist, Gentile, Gentoo, Godless, Heathen, Idolater, Infidel, Lectisternium, Odinist, Paynim, Saracen, Sun cult

Page(s), Pageboy Back, Beep, Bellboy, Bellhop, Bleep, Boy, Buttons, Callboy, Centrefold, Flyleaf, Fold out, Folio, Foolscap, Front, Gate-fold, Groom, Haircut, Hairdo, Home, Hornbook, Leaf, Master, Messenger, Moth, Octavo, Op-ed, P, Pane, PP, Problem, Quarto, Ream, Recto, Ro, Servant, Sheet, Side, Splash, Squire, Tear sheet, Thirty-twomo, Tiger, Title, Varlet, Verso, Web, Yellow

Pageant Antic, Antique, Cavalcade, Pomp, Spectacle, Tattoo, Triumph

▶ **Paid** *see* **PAY(MASTER)**

▷ **Pain** *may indicate* bread French

Pain(ful), Pains Ache, Aggrieve, Agony, Ake, Angina, Anguish, A(a)rgh, Bad, Bale, Bitter, Bore, Bot(t), Bother, Causalgia, Colic, Cramp, Crick, CTS, Distress, Dole, Doleur, Dolour, Dool(e), Dysury, Excruciating, Fash, Felon, Gastralgia, Gip, Grief, Gripe, Gyp, Harrow, Heartburn, → **HURT**, Ill, Kink, Laborious, Lancination, Lumbago, Mal, Migraine, Misery, Molimen, Myalgia, Neuralgia, Pang, Persuant, Pest, Phantom, Prick, Pungent, Rack, Raw, Referred, Rick, Sair, Sciatica, Smart, Sore, Sorrow, Sten(d), Sternalgia, Sting, Stitch, Stung, Tarsalgia, Teen(e), Tene, Throe, Torment, Torture, Travail, Twinge, Wo(e), Wrench, Wring

Painkiller Aminobutene, Analgesic, Bute, Celecoxib, Cocaine, Coxib, Distalgesic, Endorphin, Enkephalin, Meperidine, Metopon, Morphine, Number, Pethidine

Paint(ed), Painting Abstract, Abstract expressionism, Acrylic, Action, Airbrush,

Aquarelle, Art autre, Art deco, Artificial, Art nouveau, Ash Can School, Baroque,
Battlepiece, Bice, Brushwork, Byzantine, Canvas, Cellulose, Cerograph, Chiaroscuro,
Clair-obscure, Clobber, Coat, Colour, Cubism, Dadaism, Daub, Dayglo, Decorate,
Depict, Describe, Diptych, Distemper, Eggshell, Emulsion, Enamel, Expressionist,
Fard, Finery, Finger, Flatting, Flemish, Fore-edge, Fresco, Genre, Gild, Gloss, Gothic,
Gouache, Graining, Gravure, Grease, Guernica, Hard-edge, Historical, Icon, Impasto,
Impressionism, Intumescent, Lead, Limn, Lithochromy, Luminous, Mannerist,
Maquillage, Matt, Mehndi, Miniate, Miniature, Modello, Mona Lisa, Monotint,
Mural, Naive, Neoclassical, Neo-expressionist, Neo-Impressionism, Neo-Plasticism,
Nightpiece, Nocturne, Non-drip, Oaker, Ochre, Oil, Old Master, Oleo(graph), Op art,
Orphism, Paysage, Pentimento, Pict, Picture, Pigment, Pinxit, Plein air, Pointillism(e),
Polyptych, Pop art, Portray, Poster, Post-Impressionism, Pre-Raphaelite, Primavera,
Primitive, Raddle, Rag-rolling, Realist, Renaissance, Rococo, Romantic, Rosemaling,
Roughstuff, Sand, Scenography, Scumble, Secco, Semi-gloss, Sfumato, Sien(n)ese,
Skyscape, Spray, Stencil, Stereochrome, Still life, Stipple, Surrealist, Tablature, Tag,
Tempera, Tondo, Townscape, Umber, Umbrian, Undercoat, Underglaze, War, Wax

Painter(s) Animalier, Aquarellist, →ARTIST, Ash Can School, Colourist, Cubist,
Decorator, Gilder, Illusionist, Impressionist, Limner, Little Master, Luminarist,
Miniaturist, Muralist, Old Master, Paysagist, Plein-airist, Primitive, Sien(n)ese,
Vedutista

Pair(ing) Brace, Couple(t), Doublet, Duad, Duo, Dyad(ic), Fellows, Geminate, Jugate,
Jumelle, King, Link, Lone, Match, Mate, Ocrea, Pigeon, Pr, Span, Spouses, Synapsis,
Syndyasmian, Syzygy, Tandem, Thummim, Twa(e), Tway, Two, Urim, Yoke

Pal Ally, Amigo, Bud(dy), China, Chum, Comrade, Crony, Cully, Friend, Mate,
Playmate, Wus(s)

Palace Alcazar, Alhambra, Basilica, Blenheim, Buckingham, Court, Crystal, Edo,
Élysée, Escorial, Escurial, Fontainebleau, Gin, Goslar, Hampton Court, Holyrood,
Hotel, Istana, Lambeth, Lateran, Louvre, Mansion, Nonsuch, Palatine, Pitti, Pushkin,
Quirinal, Sans Souci, Schloss, Seraglio, Serail, Shushan, Topkapi, Trianon, Tuileries,
Valhalla, Vatican, Versailles, Winter

Palatable, Palatalized, Palate Dainty, Relish, Roof, Sapid, Savoury, Soft, Taste,
Toothsome, Uranic, Uraniscus, Uvula, Velum

Pale, Paling Ashen, Blanch, Bleach, Cere, Dim, Etiolate(d), Fade, →FAINT, Fence,
Ghostly, Haggard, Insipid, Lily (white), Livid, Mealy, Ox-fence, Pastel, Pasty-faced,
Peaky, Peelie-wally, Picket, Sallow, Shilpit, Stang, Verge, Wan, Whey-faced, White,
Wishy-washy

Palestine, Palestinian Amorite, Fatah, Gadarene, Gaza, Hamas, Holy Land,
Intifada, Israel, Pal, Philistine, PLO, Samaria

Pall Bore, Cloy, Curtain, Damper, Glut, Hearse-cloth, Mantle, Satiate, Shroud

Pallet Bed, Cot, Couch, Mattress, Tick

Palm Accolade, Areca, Assai, Atap, Babassu, Betel, Buriti, Burrawang, Bussu,
Cabbage, Calamus, Carna(h)uba, Carpentaria, Chamaerops, Chiqui-chiqui, Coco,
Conceal, Coquito, Corozo, Corypha, Date (tree), Doom, Doum, Elaeis, Euterpe, Fan,
Feather, Fob, Foist, Gomuti, Gomuto, Groo-groo, Gru-gru, Hand, Hemp, Ita, Itching,
Ivory, Jip(p)i-Jap(p)a, Jipyapa, Jupati, Kentia, Laurels, Loof, Macahuba, Macaw,
Macoya, Miriti, Moriche, Nikau, Nipa, Oil, Palmyra, Paxiuba, Peach, Pupunha, Raffia,
Raphia, Rat(t)an, Royal, Sabal, Sago, Saw palmetto, Sugar, Talipat, Talipot, Thatch,
Thenar, Toddy, Triumph, Troelie, Troolie, Trooly, Trophy, Vola, Washingtonia, Wax,
Wine

Palm-oil Bribe, Payola

Paltry Bald, Cheap, Exiguous, Mean, Measly, Mere, Peanuts, Pelting, Petty, Pimping,
Poor, Puny, Scalled, Shabby, Shoestring, Sorry, Tin(-pot), Tinny, Trashy, Trifling,
Two-bit, Vile, Waff, Whiffet

Pamper(ed) Baby, Cocker, Coddle, Cosher, Cosset, Cuiter, Feather-bed, Gratify,
High-fed, →INDULGE, Mollycoddle, Pet, Pompey, Spoon-fed

Pamphlet Brochure, Catalogue, Leaflet, Notice, Sheet, Tract

Pan Agree, Auld Hornie, Bainmarie, Balit, Basin, Betel(-pepper), Braincase, Chafer, Dent, Dial, Drip, Dripping, Drub, Goat-god, Goblet, God, Hard, Ice-floe, Iron, Jelly, Karahi, Knee, Ladle, Lavatory, Muffin, Nature-god, Non-stick, Oil, Pancheon, Panchion, Patella, Patina, Peter, Poacher, Preserving, Prospect, Roast, Salt, Search, Skid, Skillet, Slag, Slate, Spider, Sweep, Tube, Vacuum, Vessel, Warming, Wo(c)k, Work

Panama Isthmus

Pancake Blin(i), Blintz(e), Burrito, Crêpe (suzette), Crumpet, Drop(ped)-scone, Flam(m), Flapjack, Flaune, Flawn, Fraise, Fritter, Froise, Latke, Pikelet, Poppadum, Potato, Quesadilla, Ro(e)sti, Slapjack, Suzette, Taco, Tortilla, Tostada, Waffle

Pane Glass, Light, Panel, Quarrel, Quarry, Sheet

Panel(ling) Array, Board, Cartouche, Console, Control, Dashboard, Fa(s)cia, Gore, Hatchment, Inset, Instrument, Jury, Mandorla, Mimic, Mola, Orb, Patch(board), Reredorse, Reredos(se), Rocker, Screen, Skreen, Solar, Stile, Stomacher, Table, Tablet, Valance, Volet, Wainscot

Pang Achage, Ache, Qualm, Spasm, Stab, Travail, Twinge, Wrench

Panic Alar(u)m, Amaze, Blue funk, Consternation, Fear, Flap, Flat-spin, Flip, Fright, Funk, Guinea-grass, Hysteria, Millet, Raggee, Raggy, Ragi, Scaremonger, Scarre, Stampede, Stampedo, State, Stew, Tailspin

Pannier Basket, Cacolet, Corbeil, Dosser, Skip, Whisket

Panorama, Panoramic Cyclorama, Range, Scenery, Veduta, View, Vista

Pant(s) Bags, Breeches, Capri, Cargo, Chaps, Chinos, Culottes, Deck, Dhoti, Drawers, Fatigues, Flaff, Gasp, Gaucho, Harem, Knickers, Long johns, Longs, Parachute, Pech, Pedal-pushers, Pegh, Puff, Rot, Slacks, Smalls, Stirrup, Stovepipe, Sweat, The pits, Throb, Toreador, Trews, Trousers, Trunks, Wheeze, Yearn

Panther Bagheera, Black, Cat, Cougar, Jaguar, Leopard, Pink

Pantomime, Pantomime character Charade, Cheironomy, Dumb-show, Farce, Galanty, Harlequinade, Play

Pantry Buttery, Closet, Larder, Spence, Stillroom

Papa Dad, Father, P

Papal, Papist, Papistry Catholic, Clementine, Concordat, Guelf, Guelph, Holy See, Legation, Pontifical, RC, Roman, Vatican

Paper(s), Paperwork, Papery Admin, Antiquarian, Art, Atlas, Ballot, Baryta, Bible, Blotting, Bond, Brief, Broadsheet, Broadside, Bromide, Brown, Building, Bumf, Bumph, Butter, Cap, Carbon, Cartridge, Cellophane®, Chad, Chinese, Chiyogami, Cigarette, Command, Commercial, Confetti, Corrugated, Cream-laid, Cream-wove, Credentials, Crêpe, Crown, Curl, Daily, Deckle-edge, Decorate, Demy, Document, Dossier, Eggshell, Elephant, Emery, Emperor, Essay, Exam, File, Filter, Final, Flock, Folio, Foolscap, Form(s), FT, Funny, Furnish, Galley, Garnet, Gazette, Gem, Glass(ine), Government, Grand eagle, Grand Jesus, Graph, Greaseproof, Green, Guardian, Hieratica, ID, Imperial, India, Japanese, Jesus, Journal, Kraft, Lace, Laid, Lavatory, Legal cap, Linen, Litmus, Loo-roll, Manifold, Manil(l)a, Marble, Mercantile, Mirror, MS, Music(-demy), Needle, News(print), →NEWSPAPER, Note, Notelet, Oil, Onion-skin, Order, Origami, Packing, Pad, Page, Papillote, Papyrus, Parchment, Pickwick, Plotting, Position, Post, Pot(t), Pravda, Press, Print, Printing, Quair, Quarto, Quire, Rag, Ramee, Rami(e), Ream, Red top, Retree, Rhea, Rice, Rolled, Rolling, Royal, Safety, Satin, Saxe, Scent, Scotsman, Scrip, Script, Scroll, Scrowl, Sheaf, Sheet, Ship's, Silver, Skin, Slipsheet, Spoilt, Stamp, Starch, State, Steamer, Sugar, Sun, Super-royal, Tabloid, Taffeta, Tar, Term, Ternion, TES, Test, Thesis, Thread, Tiger, Tissue, Today, Toilet, Torchon, Touch, Tracing, Trade, Transfer, Treatise, Treeware, Tri-chad, Turmeric, Two-name, Vellum, Velvet, Voucher, Walking, Wall, Waste, Watch, Wax(ed), Web, Whatman®, White, Willesden, Wirewove, Wood(chip), Woodfree, Worksheet, Wove, Wrapping, Writing

Paper-cutting, Paper-folding Decoupage, Kirigami, Origami, Psaligraphy

Paprika Spanish

Par Average, Equate, Equivalent, →NORMAL, Scratch

Parable Allegory, Fable, Proverb

Parachute, Parachutist Aeroshell, Aigrette, Drogue, Float, Freefall, Jump, Pack, Pappus, Para, Parabrake, Parapente, Red Devil, Silk, Skyman, Thistledown, Umbrella

Parade (ground) Air, Arcade, Catwalk, Cavalcade, Ceremony, Church, Display, Dress, Drill, Easter, Emu, Flaunt, Gala, Hit, Identification, Identity, Line-up, Maidan, March-past, Pageantry, Pomp, Prance, Procession, Prom(enade), Show, Sick, Sowarry, Stand-to, Ticker tape

Paradise Arcadia, Avalon, Bliss, Eden, Elysium, Garden, Happy-hunting-ground, Heaven, Lost, Malaguetta, Nirvana, Park, Regained, Shangri-la, Svarga, Swarga, Swerga, → UTOPIA

Paradox(ical) Absurdity, Cantor's, Contradiction, Dilemma, Electra, Epimenides, Gilbertian, Irony, Koan, Olber's, Puzzle, Russell's, Zeno's

Paraffin Earthwax, Kerosene, Kerosine, Liquid, Ozocerite, Ozokerite, Photogen(e), Propane

Paraguay PY

Parallel Analog, Arctic circle, Collateral, Collimate, Corresponding, Equal, Even, Forty-ninth, Like, Pattern

Paralysis, Paralyse Apoplexy, Cataplexy, Catatonia, Cramp, Curarise, Cycloplegia, Diplegia, Halt, Hemiplegia, Infantile, Monoplegia, Numbness, Ophthalmoplegia, Palsy, Paraplegia, Paresis, Polio, Quadriplegia, Scram, Shock, Shut, Spastic, Spina bifida, Stun, Torpefy, Transfix

Paranoid Tweak

Parapet (space) Bartisan, Bartizan, Battlement, Breastwork, Brisure, Bulwark, Crenel, Flèche, Machicolation, Merlon, Rampart, Redan, Surtout, Terreplein, Top, Wall

Parasite, Parasitic Ascarid, Autoecious, Aweto, Babesiasis, Beech-drops, Bilharzia, Biogenous, Biotroph, Bladder-worm, Bloodsucker, Bonamia, Bot, Candida, Chalcid, Coccus, Conk, Copepod, Cosher, Cryptosporidium, Cryptozoite, Dodder, Ectogenous, Ectophyte, Endamoeba, Endophyte, Entophyte, Entozoon, Epiphyte, Epizoon, Filarium, Flea, Freeloader, Giardia, Gregarinida, Haematozoon, Hair-eel, Heartworm, Heteroecious, Hook-worm, Ichneumon, Inquiline, Isopod, Kade, Ked, Lackey, Lamprey, Leech, Licktrencher, Liverfluke, Louse, Lungworm, Macdonald, Mallophagous, Measle, Mistletoe, Monogenean, Nematode, Nit, Orobanche, Phytosis, Pinworm, Plasmodium, Puccinia, Quandong, Rafflesia, Rhipidoptera, Rickettsia, Root, Roundworm, Schistosoma, Scrounger, Shark, Smut-fungus, Sponge(r), Sporozoa(n), Strangleweed, Strepsiptera, Strongyle, Strongyloid, Stylops, Sucker, Symphile, Tachinid, Tapeworm, Tick, Toady, Toxoplasma, Trematode, Trencher-friend, Trencher-knight, Trichina, Tryp(anosoma), Vampire, Viscum, Whipworm, Witchweed, Worms

Parcel Allocate, Allot, Aret, Bale, Bundle, Dak, Holding, Lot, Package, Packet, Plot, Sort, Wrap

Parch(ed), Parching Arid, Bake, Dry, Graddan, Hot coppers, Roast, Scorched, Sere, Thirsty, Torrefied, Torrid, Xerotes

Parchment Diploma, Forel, Mezuzah, Papyrus, Pell, Pergameneous, Roll, Roule, Scroll, Scrow, Sheepskin, Vellum

Pardon(able), Pardoner Absolution, Absolve, Amnesty, Anan, Assoil, Clear, Condone, Eh, Excuse, → FORGIVE, Grace, Mercy, Quaestuary, Qu(a)estor, Release, Remission, Remit, Reprieve, Venial, What

Parent(al) Ancestral, Father, Forebear, Generant, Genitor, Maternal, Mother, Paternal, Solo, Storge

Parish District, Flock, Kirkto(w)n, Parischan(e), Parishen, Parochin(e), Peculiar, Province, Title

Park(ing) Amusement, Business, Car, Caravan, Common, Country, Domain, Enclosure, Forest, Fun, Game, Garage, Grounds, Hardstand, Industrial, Lung, Motor, National, Off-street, P, Petrified Forest, Pitch, Preserve, Rec, Safari, Sanctuary,

Science, Siding, Stand, Stop, Technology, Terrain, Theme, Trailer, Valet, Water, Wildlife, Wind, Yard

Parka Atigi

Parliament Addled, Althing, Barebones, Black, Bundestag, Chamber, Commons, Congress, Cortes, Council, Cross-bench, Dail, Diet, Drunken, Eduskunta, Folketing, House, Imperial, Knesset, Lack-learning, Lagt(h)ing, Landst(h)ing, Lawless, Legislature, Lok Sabha, Long, Lords, Majlis, Merciless, Mongrel, Odelst(h)ing, Rajya Sabha, Reichstag, Riksdag, Rump, St Stephens, Sanhedrin, Seanad, Seanad Éireann, Sejm, Short, Stannary, Stirthing, Stormont, Stort(h)ing, The Beehive, Thing, Unicameral, Volkskammer, Westminster

Parliamentarian Cabinet, De Montfort, Fairfax, Ireton, Leveller, Member, MP, Politico, Roundhead, Whip

Parlour Beauty, Funeral, Ice-cream, Lounge, Massage, Salon, Snug, Spence

Parochial Insular, Narrow-minded

Parody Burlesque, Lampoon, Mock, Piss-take, Satire, Send-up, Skit, Spoof, Travesty

Parrot Amazon, Ape, Cockatoo, Conure, Copy, Echo, Flint, Green leek, Imitate, Kaka(po), Kea, Lorikeet, Lory, Lovebird, Macaw, Mimic, Nestor, Owl, Parakeet, Paroquet, Poll(y), Popinjay, Psittacine, Quarrion, Repeat, Rosella, Rote, Shell, Stri(n)gops, T(o)uraco

Parson Clergyman, Cleric, Holy Joe, Minister, Non juror, Pastor, Priest, Rector, Rev, Sky-pilot, Soul-curer, Yorick

Parsonage Glebe, Manse, Rectory, Vicarage

Part(s), Parting Accession, Aliquot, Antimere, Area, Aught, Bad, Behalf, Bit, Bulk, Bye, Cameo, Character, Chunk, Cog, Component, Constituent, Crack, Cue, Dislink, Diverge, Dole, Element, Episode, Escapement, Farewell, Fascicle, Fork, Fraction, Good, Goodbye, Great, Half, Ill, Imaginary, Ingredient, Instalment, Into, Lathe, Lead, Leave, Leg, Lill, Lilt, Lines, List, Livraison, Member, Meronym, Moiety, Organ, Parcel, Passus, →PIECE, Portion, Primo, Principal, Private, Proportion, Pt, Quit, Quota, Rape, Ratio, Real, Region, Rive, Role, Scena, Scene, Secondo, Section, Sector, Segment, Segregate, Separate, Serial, Sever, Shade, Share, Shed, Sleave, Sle(i)ded, Small, →SOME, Spare, Split, Stator, Sunder, Synthon, Tithe, Tranche, Twin(e), Unit, Vaunt, Voice, Walking, Walk on, Wrench

Partial(ity), Partially Biased, Ex-parte, Fan, Favour, Halflins, Imbalance, Incomplete, One-sided, Predilection, Prejudiced, Slightly, Unequal, Weakness

Particle(s) Alpha, Antielectron, Antineutron, Atom, Baryon, Beta, Bit, Boson, Charmonium, Corpuscle, Dander, Delta, Deuteron, Electron, Elementary, Episome, Exchange, Fleck, Floccule, Fragment, Fundamental, Gauge boson, Gemmule, Globule, Gluon, Grain, Granule, Heavy, Ion, J, Jot, J/psi, Lambda, Lepton, Lipoplast, Liposome, Meson, Mite, Molecule, Monopole, Mote, Muon, Negatron, Neutralino, Neutretto, Neutrino, Neutron, Nibs, Nucleon, Omega-minus, Parton, Pentaquark, Photon, Pion, Plastisol, Platelet, Positon, Positron, Preon, Proton, Psi(on), Quark, Radioactivity, Shives, Shower, Sigma, Singlet, Sinter, Smithereen, Spark, Speck, Strange, Submicron, Subnuclear, W, Whit, WIMP, XI, Z

Particular Choosy, Dainty, →DETAIL, Endemic, Especial, Essential, Express, Fiky, Fog, Fussy, Item, Itself, London fog, Minute, Nice, Niffy-naffy, Nipperty-tipperty, Nitpicker, Old-maidish, Own, Pea-souper, Peculiar, Pedant, Pernickety, Pet, Point, Prim, Proper, →RESPECT, Special, Specific, Stickler, Strict, Stripe

Partisan Adherent, Axe, Biased, Carlist, Champion, Devotee, Factional, Fan, Irregular, Partial, Provo, Queenite, Sider, Spear, Stalwart, Supporter, Tendentious, Yorkist, Zealot

Partition(ed) Abjoint, Bail, Barrier, Brattice, Bretasche, Bulkhead, Cloison, Cubicle, Diaphragm, Dissepiment, Divider, Division, Hallan, Mediastinum, Parpane, Parpen(d), Parpent, Parpoint, Perpend, Perpent, Replum, →SCREEN, Scriene, Septum, Skreen, Tabula, Wall, With

Partner(ship) Accomplice, Alliance, Ally, Associate, Butty, Cahoot(s), Coachfellow, Colleague, Comrade, Confederate, Consort, Couple, Date, Dutch, Escort, E-W, Firm, Gigolo, Husband, Limited, Mate, N-S, Offsider, Other half, Pair, Pal, Pard, Rival,

Sidekick, Significant other, Silent, Sleeping, SOP, Sparring, Spouse, Stablemate, Stand, Symbiosis, Wag, Wif(i)e

▷ **Part of** *may indicate* a hidden word

Party Acid house, Advance, Aftershow, Alliance, ANC, Assembly, At-home, Bake, Ball, Band, Barbecue, Bash, Beano, Bee, Bloc, Blowout, Body, Bottle, Buck's, Bunfight, Bust, Caboodle, Camp, Carousal, Carouse, Caucus, Celebration, Clambake, Coach, Cocktail, Colour, Commando, Communist, Concert, Congress, Conservative, Contingent, Cooperative, Coterie, Cult, Democratic, Detail, Ding, Dinner, Discotheque, Do, Drum, DUP, Faction, Fest, Fianna Fáil, Fiesta, Fine Gael, Firing, Foy, Function, Funfest, Gala, Galravage, Gang, Garden, Ghibel(l)ine, Green, Greenback, Grumbletonian, Guilty, Hen, Hoedown, Hooley, Hootenanny, House, Housewarming, Hurricane, Inkatha, Jana Sangh, Janata, Jol(lities), Junket, Junto, Knees-up, L, Labour, Launch, Lawn, Levee, Lib, Liberal, Lig, Love-in, Low heels, Mallemaroking, Movement, Musicale, National, Necking, Neck-tie, Octobrist, Opposition, Orgy, Peace, People's, Person, Petting, Plaid, Populist, Posse, Progressive, Prohibition, Pyjama, Radical, Rage, Rave, Rave-up, Razzle(-dazzle), Reception, Republican, Reunion, Revel(ry), Ridotto, Roast, Rocking, Roister, Rort, Rout, Scottish Nationalist, SDP, Search, Sect, Set, Shindig, Shindy, Shine, Shooting, Shower, Side, Sinn Fein, Slumber, Small and early, Smoker, SNP, Soc(ialist), Social, Social Credit, Social Democratic, Socialise, Soirée, Spree, Squad(rone), Squadrone volante, Stag, Symposium, Tea, Teafight, Third, Thrash, Tory, Treat, Unionist, United, Wake, Whig, Wine, Wingding, Working, Wrap

Pass(ed), Passing, Pass on, Past Absit, Aforetime, Ago, Agon, Annie Oakley, Aorist, Approve, Arise, Arlberg, Before, Behind, Beyond, Boarding, Botte, Brenner, Brief, Burgess, By (the by), Bygone, Caudine Forks, Centre, Cerro Gordo, Chine, Chit(ty), Cicilian Gates, Clear, Col, Cote, Cross, Cursory, Death, Dee, Defile, Delate, Demise, Die, Disappear, Double, Dummy, Dunno, Elapse, Emit, Enact, End, Ensue, Ephemeral, Exceed, Exeat, Flashback, Fleeting, Foist, Forby, Forgone, Former, Forward, Gap, Gate, Gha(u)t, Give, Glencoe, Glide, Go, Go by, Gorge, Great St Bernard, Gulch, Halse, Hand, Happen, Hause, Hospital, ID, Impart, Impermanent, Interrail, Interval, In transit, Jump, Khyber, Killiecrankie, La Cumbre, Lap, Late, Lead, Live, Migrate, Nek, Nine days' wonder, No bid, Nod through, Notch, Nutmeg, Occur, Oer, O grade, OK, Okay, Oke, Omit, One-time, Overhaul, Overshoot, Overtake, Pa, Palm, Parade, Participle, Perish, Permeate, Permit, Perpetuate, Poll, Poort, Predicament, Pretty, Proceed, Propagate, Pun(c)to, Qualify, Railcard, Reach, Reeve, Refer, Relay, Retro, Retroactive, Retrospect, Reverse, Run, Safe conduct, St Gotthard, San Bernardino, Sea-letter, Senile, Serve, Shangri-la, Simplon, Since, Skim, Skip, Skirt, Slap, Sling, Small and early, Snap, Spend, Stab, State, Temporal, Thermopylae, Thread, Through, Ticket, Time immemorial, Tip, Transient, Transilient, Transitory, Transmit, Transude, Travel, Troop, Uspallata, Veronica, Vet, Visa, Visé, Wall, Wayleave, Weather, While, Yesterday, Yesteryear

Passage(way) Abature, Adit, Airway, Aisle, Alley(way), Alure, Apostrophe, Arcade, Archway, Areaway, Arterial, Avenue, Bank, Breezeway, Bridge, Bylane, Cadenza, Career, Catwalk, Channel, Chute, Citation, Clarino, Clause, Close, Coda, Condie, Conduit, Corridor, Creep, Crossing, Crush, Dead-end, Defile, Drake, Drift, Duct, Eel-fare, Episode, Excerpt, Extract, Fare, Fat, Fauces, Flat, Flight, Flue, Fogou, Gallery, Gangway, Gap, Gat, Gate, Ghat, Gully-hole, Gut, Hall, Head, Inlet, Journey, Labyrinth, Lane, Lapse, Lick, Lientery, Loan, Lobby, Locus, Meatus, Meridian, Middle, Mona, Moto perpetuo, Movement, Northeast, Northwest, Para(graph), Parashah, Path, Pend, Phrase, Pore, Port, Portion, Prelude, Presto, Prose, Purple, Race, Retournelle, Ride, Ripieno, Rite, Road, Rough, Route, Sailing, Screed, Shaft, Shunt, Sinus, Skybridge, Skywalk, Slap, Snicket, Solus, Spillway, Strait, Street, Stretta, Stretto, Subway, Sump, Text, Thorough(fare), Throat, Tour, Trachea, Trance, Transe, Transit(ion), Travel, Tunnel, Tutti, Undercast, Unseen, Ureter, Voyage, Walkway, Way, Windpipe, Windway

▷ **Passage of arms** *may indicate* 'sleeve'

Passenger(s) Cad, Commuter, Fare, Parasite, Pax, Pillion, Rider, Slacker, Steerage, Straphanger, Traveller, Voyager, Wayfarer

Passible Patible

Passion(ate), Passionately Anger, Appetite, Ardour, Con calore, Con fuoco, Crush, Duende, Emotion, Fervour, Fire, Flame, Frampold, Fury, Gust, Heat, Hot, Hunger, Hwyl, Ileac, Iliac, Infatuation, Intense, Ire, Irish, Kama, Love, Lust, Mania, Messianic, Metromania, Obsession, Oestrus, Polemic, Rage, Sizzling, Stormy, Sultry, Torrid, Vehement, Violent, Warm, Wax, Wrath, Yen, Zeal, Zoolatria

Passive (stage) Apathetic, Dormant, Drifter, Inert, Pathic, Patient, Pupa, Stolid, Supine, Yielding

Passport Access, Clearance, Congé(e), E, Key, Laissez-passer, Nansen, Navicert, Sea-letter, Visa

Password Code, Countersign, Logon, Nayword, Parole, Sesame, Shibboleth, Tessera, Watchword

▶**Past** *see* **PASS(ED)**

Pasta Agnolotti, Anelli, Angel hair, Bucatini, Cannelloni, Cappelletti, Conchiglie, Durum, Eliche, Farfal, Farfalle, Farfel, Fedelini, Fettuc(c)ine, Fusilli, Lasagna, Lasagne, Linguini, Macaroni, Maccheroncini, Manicotti, Noodles, Orecchietti, Orzo, Pappardelle, Penne, Perciatelli, Ravioli, Rigatoni, Spaghetti, Spaghettina, Tagliarini, Tagliatelle, Tortelli(ni), Vermicelli, Ziti

Paste, Pasty Almond, Ashen, Batter, Beat, Botargo, Boule, Bridie, Cerate, Clobber, Cornish, Dentifrice, Dough, E, Electuary, Fake, Filler, Fondant, Frangipane, Gentleman's Relish®, Glue, Guarana, Harissa, Knish, Lute, Magma, Marchpane, Marzipan, Masala, Mastic, Meat, Miso, Mountant, Pale, Pallid, Panada, Pâté, Patty, Pearl-essence, Pie, Piroshki, Pirozhki, Poonac, Pulp, Punch, Putty, Rhinestone, Rillettes, Samosa, Sham, Slip, Slurry, Spread, Strass, Tahina, Tahini, Tapenade, Taramasalata, Trounce, Wan, Wasabi

Pastor(al) Arcadia, Bucolic, Curé, Eclogue, Endymion, Idyl(l), Minister, Priest, Rector, Rural, Shepherd, Simple

Pastry Baclava, Bakemeat, Baklava, Beignet, Bridie, Brik, Cannoli, Chausson, Cheese straw, Choux, Coquile, Creamhorn, Cream puff, Croustade, Cruller, Crust, Danish, Dariole, Dough, Eclair, Filo, Flaky, Flan, French, Millefeuille, Muffin, Phyllo, Pie, Pie-crust, Profiterole, Puff, Quiche, Raised, Rough-puff, Samosa, Shortcrust, Strudel, Tart, Turnover, Vol-au-vent

Pasture Alp, Eadish, Eddish, Feed, Fell, Fodder, Grassland, Graze, Herbage, Kar(r)oo, Lair, Lare, Lay, Lea, Lease, Leasow(e), Leaze, Lee, Ley, Machair, Mead(ow), Moose, Pannage, Pascual, Potrero, Raik, Rake, Sheal(ing), Shiel(ing), Soum, Sowm, Tie, Transhume, Tye

▶**Pasty** *see* **PASTE**

Patch(y) Bed, Bit, Blotchy, Cabbage, Chloasma, Clout, Coalsack, Cobble, Cooper, Court plaster, Cover, Friar, Fudge, →**MEND**, Mosaic, Mottled, Nicotine, Pasty, Piebald, Piece, Plage, Plaque, Plaster, Pot, Purple, Shinplaster, Shoulder, Solder, Sunspot, Tingle, Tinker, Transdermal, Turf, Vamp, Variegated

Path(way) Aisle, Allée, Alley, Arc, Berm, Berme, Boreen, Borstal(l), Bridle, Bridleway, Catwalk, Causeway, Causey, Clickstream, Corridor, Course, Downlink, Eclipse, Ecliptic, Eightfold, Flight, Gate, Ginnel, Glide, Lane, Ley, Lichwake, Lichway, Locus, Lykewake, Orbit, Packway, Pad, Parabola, Pavement, Peritrack, Primrose, Ride, Ridgeway, Route, Runway, Sidewalk, Slipway, Spurway, Stie, Sty(e), Swath(e), Taxiway, Track, Trail, Trajectory, Trod, Walkway, →**WAY**, Xystus

Pathetic(ally) Abysmal, Derisory, Doloroso, Drip, Forlorn, Piteous, Poignant, Sad, Saddo, Schlub, Touching

Pathogen Virus

Patience Calm, Endurance, Forbearance, Fortitude, Indulgence, Klondike, Klondyke, Monument, Solitaire, Stoicism, Virtue

Patient(s) Calm, Case, Clinic, Cot-case, Forbearing, Grisel(da), Grisilda, Invalid, Job, Long-suffering, Passive, Resigned, Stoic, Subject, Walking case, Ward

Patriot(ic), Patriotism Cavour, Chauvinist, DAR, Emmet, Flag-waving,

Flamingant, Garibaldi, Hereward, Irredentist, Jingoism, Loyalist, Maquis, Nationalist, Tell, Wallace, Zionist

Patrol Armilla, Beat, Guard, Outguard, Picket, Piquet, Prowl-car, Reconnaissance, Round, Scout, Sentinel, Sentry-go, Shark, Shore, Turm

Patron(age), Patroness, Patronise(d), Patronising Advowson, Aegis, Athena, Auspices, Backer, Benefactor, Business, Champion, Client, Customer, Donator, Egis, Fautor, Friend, Lady Bountiful, Maecenas, Nepotic, Protector, Protégé, Provider, Shopper, → **SPONSOR**, Stoop, Stoup

Pattern(ed) Agouti, Agouty, Aguti, Archetype, Argyle, Bird's eye, Blueprint, Branchwork, Candy stripe, Check, Chequer, Chiné, Clock, Crisscross, Design, Diaper, Diffraction, Dog's tooth, Draft, Epitome, Example, Exemplar, Faconné, Fiddle, Figuration, Format, Fret, Grain, Greek key, Greque, Herringbone, Holding, Hound's tooth, Ideal, Imprint, Intonation, Koru, Kowhaiwhai, Matrix, Meander, → **MODEL**, Moire, Moko, Mosaic, Norm, Paisley, Paradigm, Paragon, Pinstripe, Plan, Polka-dot, Pompadour, Precedent, Prototype, Queenstitch, Radiation, Raster, Rat-tail, Rhythm, Ribbing, Scansion, Shawl, Starburst, Stencil, Structure, Symmetry, Syndrome, Talea, Tangram, Tarsia, Template, Tessera, Test, Tracery, Traffic, Tread, Type, Veneration, Vol, Whorl, Willow

Pause Break, Breakpoint, Breather, Caesura, Cessation, Cesura, Comma, Desist, Er, Fermata, Hesitate, Hiatus, Interkinesis, Interval, Limma, Lull, Pitstop, Pregnant, Rest, Selah, Stop

Pave(d), Pavement, Paving Causeway, Causey, Clint, Cobble, Desert, Diaper, Flagging, Granolith, Limestone, Moving, Path, Plainstanes, Plainstones, Roadside, Set(t), Sidewalk, Travolator, Trottoir

Pawn(shop), Pawnbroker, Pawnee Agent, Betel, Chessman, Counter, Derby, Dip, Gage, Gallery, Hanging, Hock, Hockshop, Hostage, Leaving-shop, Lumber, Lumberer, Moneylender, Mont-de-piété, Monte di pietà, Nunky, Pan, Passed, Peacock, Piece, Pignerate, Pignorate, Pledge, Pop, Security, Sheeny, Siri, Spout, Stalking-horse, Three balls, Tiddleywink, Tool, Tribulation, Uncle, Usurer, Wadset, Weed

Pay(master), Payment, Paid, Pay off, Pay out Aby, Advertise, Amortise, Annat, Annuity, Ante, Arles, Atone, Balloon, Bank draft, Basic, Batta, Blench, Bonus, Bukshee, Cain, Cashier, Cheque, COD, Commute, Compensate, Consideration, Damage, Defray, Disburse, Discharge, Dividend, Down, Dub, E, Emolument, Endow, Equalisation, Eric, Escot, Farm, Fee, Feu-duty, Finance, Foot, Fork out, Fund, Gale, Gate, Give, Grave, Greenmail, Guarantee, Han(d)sel, Hazard, Hire, Honorarium, HP, Imburse, Intown multure, Kain, Kickback, Lump sum, Mail, Meet, Modus, Mortuary, Overtime, Payola, Pension, Pittance, Pony, Posho, Premium, Primage, Pro, Pro forma, Progress, Purser, Quit(-rent), Ransom, Reap-silver, Rebuttal, Redundancy, Refund, Remittance, Remuneration, Rent, Requite, Residual, Respects, Royalty, Salary, Satisfaction, Scot, Screw, Scutage, Settle, Severance, Shell, Shell out, Shot, Sick, Sink, SO, Sold(e), Soul-shot, → **SPEND**, Square, Stipend, Strike, Stump, Sub, Subscribe, Sweetener, Table, Take-home, Tar, Tender, Token, Tommy, Transfer, Treasure, Treat, Tribute, Truck, Veer, Wage

PC Constable, Right on

PE Aerobics, Gym

Pea(s) Carling, Chaparral, Chickling, D(h)al, Desert, Dholl, Garbanzo, Goober, Hastings, Legume, Mangetout, Marrowfat, Passiform, Pigeon, Pulse, Rounceval, Snow, Split, Sugar, Sugar snap

Peace(ful), Peaceable, Peace-keeper, Peace organisation, Peace symbol Ahimsa, Antiwar, Ataraxy, Calm, Ease, Frieda, Frith, Halcyon, Hush, Interceder, Irenic(on), King's, Lee, Lull, Nirvana, Olive, Pacific, Pax, Queen's, Quiet, Repose, Rest, Rose, Roskilde, Salem, Serene, Sh, Shalom, Siegfried, Siesta, Solomon, Soothing, Still, Tranquil, Truce, UN

Peach Blab, Cling, Clingstone, Dish, Dob, Freestone, Humdinger, Inform, Laetrile, Malakatoone, Melocoto(o)n, Nectarine, Oner, Quandang, Shop, Sing, Sneak, Split, Squeak, Stunner, Tattle, Tell, Victorine

Peacock Coxcomb, Dandy, Fop, Junonian, Muster, Paiock(e), Pajock(e), Pavo(ne), Pawn, Payock(e), Pown, Sashay

Peak(y) Acme, Aiguille, Alp, Ancohuma, Apex, Ben, Chimborazo, Comble, Communism, Cone, Crag, Crest, Darien, Drawn, Eiger, Flower, Gable, Gannett, Garmo, Harney, Horn, Ismail Samani, Kazbek, Matterhorn, Meridian, Mons, →MOUNTAIN, Nib, Nunatak, Optimum, Pale, Pin, Pinnacle, Rainier, Sallow, Snowcap, Snowdon, Spire, Top, Tor, Visor, Widow's, Zenith

Pear Aguacate, Alligator, Anchovy, Anjou, Asian, Asparagus, Avocado, Bartlett, Bergamot, Beurré, Blanquet, Carmelite, Catherine, Choke, Colmar, Comice, Conference, Cuisse-madame, Dutch admiral, Jargonelle, Muscadel, Muscatel, Musk, Nelis, Perry, Poperin, Poppering, Poprin, Prickly, Pyrus, Queez-maddam, Seckel, Seckle, Warden, William

Pearl(s), Pearly Barocco, Barock, Baroque, Cultured, False, Gem, Imitated, Jewel, Mabe, Margaret, Margaric, Nacrous, Olivet, Onion, Orient, Prize, Rope, Seed, Simulated, String, Sulphur, Unio(n)

Peasant Bogtrotter, Bonhomme, Boor, Bumpkin, Chouan, Churl, Clodhopper, Contadino, Cossack, Cottar, Cott(i)er, Fellah(s), Fellahin, Hick, Jungli, Kern(e), Kisan, Kulak, M(o)ujik, Muzhik, Raiyat, Roturier, Rustic, Ryot, Swain, Tyrolean, Whiteboy, Yokel

Pebble(s), Pebbly Banket, Calculus, Chuck, Cobblestone, Dreikanter, Gallet, Gooley, Gravel, Psephism, Pumie, Pumy, Scotch, Scree, Shingle

Peck Bill, Bushel, Dab, Forpet, Forpit, Gregory, Job, Kiss, Lip, Lippie, Nibble, Tap

▷ **Peculiar** *may indicate* an anagram

Peculiar(ity) Appropriate, Characteristic, Distinct, Eccentric, Especial, Exclusive, Ferly, Funny, Idiosyncratic, Kink, Kooky, Odd, Own, Proper, Queer, Quirk, Royal, Singular, →SPECIAL, Specific, Strange, Unusual

Pedal Accelerator, Bike, Brake, Chorus, Clutch, Cycle, Damper, Lever, P, Rat-trap, Soft, Sostenuto, Sustaining, Treadle, Treddle

Peddle, Pedlar Bodger, Boxwallah, Camelot, Chapman, Cheapjack, Colporteur, Crier, Drummer, Duffer, Hawk, Huckster, Jagger, Packman, Pedder, Pether, Sell, Smouch, Smouse(r), Sutler, Tallyman, Tink(er), Yagger

▷ **Peddling** *may indicate* an anagram

Pedestrian Banal, Commonplace, Dull, Ganger, Hack, Hike, Itinerant, Jaywalker, Laborious, Mediocre, Mundane, Trite, Walker

Pedigree(s) Ancestry, Blood, Breeding, Descent, Family tree, House, Lineage, Phylogeny, Stemma(ta), Stirp(s), Thoroughbred

Peel(er) Bark, Candied, Decorticate, Exfoliate, Flype, Grilse, Pare, PC, Rind, Rine, Rumbler, Scale, Sewen, Shell, Skin, →STRIP, Tirr, Zest

▷ **Peeled** *may indicate* outside letters to be removed from a word

Peep(er), Peephole Cheep, Cook, Glance, Gledge, Keek, Kook, Lamp, Nose, Peek, Pink, Pry, Snoop, Spy, Squeak, Squint, Stime, Styme, Voyeur

Peer(age), Peers Life, Representative, Spiritual, Temporal

Peevish(ness) Capernoited, Captious, Crabby, Cross, Doddy, Frabbit, Frampal, Frampold, Franzy, Fretful, Girner, Hipped, Lienal, Moody, Nattered, Pet, Petulant, Pindling, Protervity, Shirty, Sour, Teachie, Te(t)chy, Testy

Peg(gy) Cheville, Cleat, Clothespin, Die, Drift-pin, Fix, Freeze, Knag, Lee, Leg, Margaret, Nail, Nog, Odontoid, Pin(-leg), Piton, Shoe, Snort, Spigot, Spile, Square, Stengah, Stinger, Support, Tap, Tee, Thole, Tholepin, Thowel, Toggle, Tot, Woffington

Pegleg Timber-toes

Peking man Pithecanthropus, Sinanthropus

Pelican Alcatras, Bird, Crossing, Golden Hind, LA, Louisiana

Pellet Bolus, Buckshot, Bullet, Pill, Prill, Slug, Snow

Pelmet Valance

Pelt Assail, Clod, Fleece, Fur, Hail, Hide, Hie, Lam, Pepper, Random, Shower, Skin, Squail, Stone

Pen Author, Ballpoint, Bamboo, Bic®, Biro®, Cage, Calamus, Can, Cartridge, Catching, Confine, Coop, Corral, Crawl, Crib, Crow-quill, Cru(i)ve, Cub, Cyclostyle, Dabber, Data, Enclosure, Epi®, Fank, Farm, Felt(-tipped), Fold, Fountain, Gaol, Gladius, Hen, Highlighter, Hoosegow, J, →**JAIL**, Keddah, Kraal, Lair, Laser, Light, Magic marker, Marker, Mew, Mure, Music, Piggery, Poison, Pound, Quill(-nib), Rastrum, Ree, Reed, Ring, Rollerball, Scribe, Sheepfold, Stell, Stie, Stir, Sty(e), Stylet, Stylo, Stylograph, Stylus, Submarine, Swan, Sweatbox, Tank, Weir, Write, →**WRITER**

▷ **Pen** *may indicate* a writer

Penal(ize) Cost, Fine, Gate, Handicap, Huff, Mulct, Punitive, Servitude

Penalty Abye, Amende, Card, Cost, Endorsement, Eriach, Eric, Fine, Forfeit, Han(d)sel, Huff, Levy, Major, Pain, Price, Punishment, Rubicon, Sanction, Tap, Ticket, Wide

Pencil Beam, Ca(l)m, Caum, Charcoal, Chinagraph®, Crayon, Draft, Draw, Eyebrow, Fusain, Grease, Harmonic, Ink, Keelivine, Keelyvine, Lead, Outline, Propelling, Slate, Stump, Styptic, Tortillon

Pendant Albert, Chandelier, Drop, Earring, Girandole, Laval(l)ière, Medallion, Necklace, Poffle, Sautoir

Pending Imminent, In fieri, Unresolved, Until

Pendule Poffle

Penetrate, Penetrating, Penetration Acumen, Acuminate, Bite, Bore, Cut, Enpierce, Enter, Imbue, Impale, Incisive, Indent, Indepth, Infiltrate, Insight, Into, Intrant, Lance, Permeate, Pierce, Probe, Sagacious, Shear, Strike, Thrust, Touch, X-ray

Penguin Adélie, Aeroplane, Anana, Auk, Emperor, Fairy, Gentoo, King, Korora, Macaroni, Rock-hopper

Peninsula Arm, Neck, Promontory, Spit, Spur

Penny Bean, Cartwheel, Cent, Copper, D, Dreadful, New, P, Sen, Sou, Sterling, Stiver, Win(n), Wing

Penpusher Plumassier

Pension(er) Allowance, Ann(at), Annuitant, Board, Chelsea, Cod, Cor(r)ody, Gasthaus, Gratuity, Guest-house, Half-board, Hotel, Non-contributory, Occupational, Old-age, Payment, Personal, Retire(e), Serps, SIPP, Stakeholder, Stipend, Superannuation

Pentameter Elegiac, Iambic

Penultimate Y

People(s) Beings, Bods, Body, Chosen, Commonalty, Commons, Demos, Ecology, Electorate, Enchorial, Flower, Folk, Fraim, Gens, Grass roots, Guild, Human(kind), Inca, Indigenous, Inhabit, Janata, Kin, Land, Lapith, Lay, Man(kind), Masses, Men, Mob, Nair, Nation(s), Nayar, One, Peculiar, Personalities, Phalange, Populace, Proletariat(e), Public, Punters, Quorum, Rabble, Race, Raffle, September, Settle, Society, Souls, They, Tribe, Tuath, Tungus, Volk

Pepper(y) Alligator, All-spice, Ancho, Ava, Bird, Black, Caper, Capsicum, Cayenne, Cherry, Chilli, Chipotle, Condiment, Cubeb, Devil, Dittander, Dittany, Ethiopian, Green, Guinea, Habanero, Jalapeno, Jamaica, Kava, Malagueta, Matico, Negro, Paprika, Pelt, Pim(i)ento, Piper, Piperine, Piquillo, Red, Riddle, Sambal, Scotch bonnet, Spice, Sprinkle, Szechuan, Szechwan, Tabasco®, Techy, Water, Yaqona, Yellow

Peptide Cecropin, Substance P

Perceive, Perception, Perceptive Acumen, Alert, Anschauung, Apprehend, Astute, Clairvoyance, Clear-eyed, Cryptaesthetic, Descry, Dianoia, Discern, Divine, ESP, Extrasensory, Feel, Insight, Intelligence, Intuit(ion), Kinaesthesia, Noesis, Notice, Observe, Pan(a)esthesia, Remark, →**SEE**, Sense, Sensitive, Sentience, Shrewd, Sixth sense, Subliminal, Tact, Taste, Understanding

Percentage Agio, Commission, Contango, Cut, Proportion, Rake off, Royalty, Share, Vigorish

Perch(ing) Aerie, Alight, Anabis, Bass, Comber, Eyrie, Fish, Fogash, Gaper, Insessorial, Lug, Miserere, Ocean, Perca, Pole, Roost, Ruff(e), Seat, Serranid, → **SIT**, Zingel

Percussion (cap) Amorce, Battery, Gong, Idiophone, Impact, Knee, Knock, Spoons, Thump, Timbrel, Traps

Perennial Continual, Enduring, Flower, Livelong, Perpetual, Recurrent

Perfect(ly), Perfection(ist) Absolute, Accomplish, Accurate, Acme, Apple-pie, Bloom, Complete, Consummation, Cross-question, Dead, Develop, Edenic, Fare-thee-well, Finish, Flawless, Fulfil, Full, Holy, Hone, Ideal(ist), Impeccable, Intact, It, Matchless, Mature, Mint, Mr Right, Par, Paradisal, Paragon, Past, Pat, Peace, Pedant, Point-device, Practice, Present, Pure, Quintessential, Refine, Salome, Siddha, Soma, Sound, Spot-on, Stainless, Stickler, Sublime, The nines, Thorough, Three-pricker, To a t(ee), Unblemished, Unflawed, Unqualified, Utopian, Utter, Whole, Witeless

Perform(ed), Performer, Performing Achieve, Acrobat, Act(or), Action, Aerialist, Appear, Artist(e), Barnstorming, Basoche, Busk, Carry out, Chansonnier, Comedian, Contortionist, Discharge, Do, Duo, Enact, Entertainer, Execute, Exert, Exhibit, Fancy Dan, Fulfil, Function, Geek, Hand, Headliner, Hersall, Hot dog, Houdini, Implement, Interlocutor, Majorette, Make, Mime, Moke, Nonet, Octet, Officiate, On, Operant, Player, Praxis, Quartet(te), Quintet, Rap artist, Recite, Render, Ripieno, Scene-stealer, Septet, Sextet, Showstopper, Sword-swallower, Throw, Trio, Vaudevillian, Virtuoso, Wire-dancer

Performance Accomplishment, Achievement, Act(ion), Auto, Blinder, Bravura, Broadcast, Chevisance, Command, Concert, Dare, Deed, Demonstration, Discharge, Division, Double act, Enactment, Entr'acte, Execution, Floorshow, Gas, Gig, Hierurgy, Holdover, Hootenanny, House, Masque, Master-class, Masterstroke, Matinee, Mime, Monodrama, Monologue, One-night stand, Operation, Perpetration, Practice, Première, Production, Programme, Recital, Rehearsal, Rendering, Rendition, Repeat, Repertoire, Rigmarole, Scene, Show (stopper), Showing, Simul, Sketch, Sneak preview, Solo, Specific, Spectacle, Stunt, Theatricals, Track record, Turn, Unicycle

Perfume (box) Abir, Ambergris, Angel water, Aroma, Attar, Bergamot, Cassolette, Chypre, Civet, Cologne, Eau de cologne, Eau de toilette, Enfleurage, Essence, Fragrance, Frangipani, Incense, Ionone, Lavender (water), Linalool, Myrrh, Nose, Opopanax, Orris, Orrisroot, Otto, Patchouli, Patchouly, Pomander, Potpourri, Redolence, → **SCENT**, Smellies, Terpineol, Toilet water, Tonka bean

Perhaps A(i)blins, Belike, Haply, Happen, May(be), Peradventure, Percase, Perchance, Possibly, Relative, Say

▷ **Perhaps** *may indicate* an anagram

Perimeter Boundary, Circuit, Circumference, Limits

Period(ic) AD, Age, Alcher(ing)a, Andropause, Annual, Archaean, Base, Bi-weekly, Bout, Cal(l)ippic, Cambrian, Carboniferous, Chukka, Chukker, Climacteric, Comanchean, Cooling off, Cretaceous, Critical, Curse, Cycle, Day, Decad(e), Devonian, Diapause, Dot, Down, Dreamtime, → **DURATION**, Eocene, Epoch, Excerpt, Full-stop, Glacial, Grace, Great schism, Haute époque, Heyday, Incubation, Indiction, Innings, Interregnum, Jurassic, Kalpa, Latency, Latent, Lesson, Liassic, Limit, Meantime, Meanwhile, Menopause, Menses, Mesolithic, Mesozoic, Miocene, Mississippian, Monthly, Moratorium, Neocomian, Neolithic, Octave, Olde-worlde, Oligocene, Ordovician, Palaeogene, Paleolithic, Payback, Pennsylvanian, Phase, Phoenix, Pre-Cambrian, Proterozoic, QT, Quarter, Quaternary, Recurrent, Reformation, Refractory, Regency, Rent, Riss, Romantic, Saeculum, Safe, Saros, Season, Session, Sidereal, Span, Spasm, Spell, Stage, Stop, Stretch, Synodic, Teens, Term, Tertiary, Trecento, Triassic, Triduum, Trimester, Tri-weekly, Usance, Weekly, Window

Periodic(al) Bi-weekly, Comic, Digest, Economist, Etesian, Journal, Liassic, Listener, Mag, New Yorker, Organ, Paper, Phase, Publication, Punch, Rambler, Regency, Review, Scandal sheet, Spectator, Strand, Stretch, Tatter, Tract

Perish(able), Perished, Perishing Brittle, →DIE, End, Ephemeral, Expire, Fade, Forfair, Fungibles, Icy, Tine, Tint, Transitory, Tyne, Vanish

Perm(anent) Abiding, Durable, Eternal, Everlasting, Fixed, Full-time, Indelible, →LASTING, Marcel, Stable, Standing, Stative, Wave

Permeable, Permeability, Permeate Infiltrate, Leaven, Osmosis, Penetrate, Pervade, Poromeric, Porous, Seep, Transfuse

Permission, Permit(ted) Allow, Authorise, By-your-leave, Carnet, Chop, Clearance, Congé(e), Consent, Copyright, Enable, Give, Grant, Green light, Indult, Lacet, Laisser-passer, Latitude, Leave, Legal, Let, Liberty, Licence, License, Lief, Loan, Luit, Nihil obstat, Ok(e), Pace, Pass, Placet, Planning, Power, Pratique, Privilege, Remedy, Safe-conduct, Sanction, Stamp-note, Suffer, Ticket, Triptyque, Visa, Vouchsafe, Warrant, Way-leave, Wear

Perpendicular Aplomb, Apothem, Atrip, Cathetus, Erect, Normal, Orthogonal, Plumb, Sheer, Sine, →UPRIGHT, Vertical

Perplex(ed), Perplexity Anan, Baffle, Bamboozle, Bemuse, Beset, Bewilder, Bother, Buffalo, Bumbaze, Cap, Confound, Confuse, Embarrass, Feague, Floor, Flummox, Knotty, Meander, Mystify, Nonplus, Obfuscate, Out, Pother, Pudder, Puzzle, Quizzical, Stump, Tangle, Throw, Tickle, Tostication

Persecute, Persecution Afflict, Annoy, Badger, Bully, Crucify, Dragon(n)ades, Harass, Haze, Intolerant, McCarthyism, Oppress, Pogrom, Ride, Torture

Persevere, Perseverance Assiduity, Continue, Fortitude, Hold on, Insist, Jusqu'auboutisme, Patience, Persist, Plug, Soldier on, Stamina, Steadfastness, Stick, Stickability, Tenacity

Persia(n) Achaemenid, Babee, Babi, Bahai, Cyrus, Dari, Farsi, Iran(ian), Mazdean, Mede, Pahlavi, Parasang, Parsee, Pehlevi, Pushtu, Samanid, Sassanid, Sohrab, Xerxes, Zoroaster

Persist(ence), Persistent Adhere, Assiduity, Chronic, Constant, Continual, Diligent, Doggedness, Endure, Hang-on, Importunate, Incessant, Labour, Longeval, Lusting, Persevere, Press, Sedulous, Sneaking, Stick, Tenacity, Urgent

Person(s), Personal(ly) Alter, Artificial, Aymaran, Being, Bird, Bod(y), Chai, Chal, Chav, Chi, Cookie, Entity, Everyman, Figure, Fish, Flesh, Ga(u)dgie, Gadje, Gauje, Gut, Head, Human, Individual, Nabs, Natural, Nibs, One, Own, Party, Passer-by, Private, Quidam, Selfhood, Sod, Soul, Specimen, Tales, Wight

Personage, Personality Anima, Celeb(rity), Character, Charisma, Dignitary, Ego, Godhead, Grandee, Identity, Megastar, Noble, Notability, Panjandrum, Presence, Sama, Seity, Sel, Self, Sell, Somatotonia, Star, Temperament, Tycoon

Personified, Personification, Personify Embody, Incarnate, Prosopop(o)eia, Represent

Perspective Aerial, Atmosphere, Attitude, Distance, Point of view, Proportion, Scenography, Take, View, Vista

Persuade(d), Persuasion, Persuasive Cajole, Carrot and stick, Coax, Cogent, Conviction, Convince, Disarm, Eloquent, Faith, Feel, Forcible, Geed, Get, Induce, Inveigle, Move, Plausible, →PREVAIL, Religion, Rhetoric, Seduce, Smooth-talking, Soft sell, Suborn, Sweet-talk, Truckled, Wheedle, Winning

Pert(ness) Bold, Cocky, Dicacity, Flippant, Forward, Fresh, Impertinent, Insolent, Jackanapes, Minx, Quean, Saucy, Tossy

Pertinent Ad rem, Apropos, Apt, Fit, Germane, Relevant, Timely

Perturb(ation) Aerate, Confuse, Dismay, Disturb, Dither, Faze, Pheese, State, Trouble, Upset, Worry

Pervade, Pervasion, Pervasive(ness) Atmosphere, Diffuse, Drench, Immanence, Permeate, Saturate

Perverse, Perversion, Pervert(ed), Perversity Aberrant, Abnormal, Algolagnia, Awkward, Awry, Balky, Cam(stairy), Camsteary, Camsteerie, Cantankerous, →CONTRARY, Corrupt, Crabbed, Cussed, Decadent, Deviate, Distort, Donsie, False, Froward, Gee, Kam(me), Kinky, Licentious, Misinterpret, Misuse,

Nonce, Paraphilia, Protervity, Refractory, Sadist, Sicko, Stubborn, Thrawn, Traduce, Twist, Unnatural, Untoward, Uranism, Warp(ed), Wayward, Wilful, Wrest, Wry

▷ **Perverted** *may indicate* an anagram

Pessimism, Pessimist(ic) Alarmist, Bear, Cassandra, Crapehanger, Crepehanger, Cynic, Defeatist, Dismal Jimmy, Doom merchant, Doomwatch, Doomy, Doubter, Downbeat, Fatalist, Glumbum, Jeremiah, Killjoy, Negative

Pest(er) Aggravate, Badger, Bedbug, Beleaguer, Blight, Bot, →**BOTHER**, Brat, Breese, Bug, Dim, Disagreeable, Earbash, Fly, Fowl, Gapeworm, Greenfly, Harass, Hassle, Irritate, Microbe, Mither, Molest, Mouse, Nag, Nudnik, Nuisance, Nun, Pize, Plague, Rotter, Scourge, Tease, Terror, Thysanoptera, Vermin, Weevil

Pesticide Benomyl, Botanic(al), DDT, Derris, Dichlorvos, Endrin, Glucosinolate, Heptachlor, Mouser, Permethrin, Synergist, Warfarin

Pestilence, Pestilent Curse, Epidemic, Evil, Lues, Murrain, Murren, Noxious, Pernicious, Plague

Pet Aversion, Cade, Canoodle, Caress, Chou, Coax, Cosset, Cuddle, Dandle, Darling, Daut(ie), Dawt(ie), Dod, Dort, Ducky, Favourite, Fondle, Glumps, Hamster, Huff, Hump, Indulge, Ire, Jarta, Jo, Lallygag, Lapdog, Miff, Mouse, Neck, Pique, Rabbit, Smooch, Snog, Spat, Strum, Sulk(s), Tantrum, Teacher's, Temper, Tiff, Tout, Towt, Umbrage, Virtual, Yarta

Petition(er) Appeal, Beg, Boon, Crave, Entreaty, Litany, Millenary, Orison, Plaintiff, Postulant, Prayer, Representation, Request, Round robin, Solicit, Sue, Suit(or), Suppli(c)ant, Supplicat, Vesper

Petrify(ing) Fossilise, Frighten, Lapidescent, Niobe, Numb, Ossify, Scare, Terrify

Petrol(eum) Cetane, Diesel, Esso®, Ethyl, Fuel, Gas, High-octane, Leaded, Ligroin, Maz(o)ut, Octane, Olein, Platforming, Refinery, Rock oil, Rock-tar, STP, Unleaded

Petticoat Balmoral, Basquine, Crinoline, Female, Filabeg, Fil(l)ibeg, Jupon, Kilt, Kirtle, Phil(l)abeg, Phil(l)ibeg, Placket, Sarong, Shift, Underskirt, Wylie-coat

Petty, Pettiness Baubling, Bumbledom, Childish, Little, Mean, Minor, Narrow, Niggling, Nyaff, One-horse, Parvanimity, Picayunish, Piffling, Pimping, Puisne, Shoestring, Small, Small town, Stingy, Tin, Trivial, Two-bit

Petty officer Cox, CPO, PO

Petulance, Petulant Fretful, Huff, Mardy, Moody, Peevish, Perverse, Procacity, Sullen, Toutie, Waspish

Phaeton Spider

Phantom Apparition, Bogey, Bugbear, Eidolon, Feature, Idol, Incubus, Maya, Shade, Spectre, Tut, Wild hunt, Wraith

Pharmacist, Pharmacologist →**CHEMIST**, Dispenser, Druggist, Loewi, MPS, Officinal, Preparator

Phase Climacteric, Coacervate, Cycle, Form, Nematic, Period, Post-boost, Primary, REM, Schizont, Stage, State, Synchronise

Phenomenon Blip, Eclipse, Effect, Event, Flying saucer, Geohazard, Hormesis, Marvel, Meteor, Miracle, Mirage, Paranormal, Parascience, Phenology, Phi, Psi, Rankshift, Synergy

Philanthropist, Philanthropy Altruist, Barnardo, Benefactor, Carnegie, Charity, Chisholm, Coram, Donor, Freemason, Geldof, Guggenheim, Hammer, Lever, Mayer, Nobel, Nuffield, Peabody, Rockefeller, Rowntree, Samaritan, Shaftesbury, Tate, Wilberforce

Philistine, Philistinism Artless, Ashdod, Barbarian, Foe, Gath, Gaza, Gigman, Goliath, Goth, Lowbrow, Vandal

Philosopher, Philosophy Academist, Activism, Ahimsa, Analytical, Animism, Anthrosophy, Antinomianism, Antiochian, Atomic, Atomist, Attitude, Averr(h)oism, Cartesian, Casuist, Comtism, Conceptualism, Conservatism, Cracker-barrel, Critical, Cynic, Deipnosophist, Deontology, Eclectic, Eleatic, Empiricism, Enlightenment, Epistemology, Ethics, Existentialism, Fatalism, Gnostic, Gymnosophist, Hedonism, Hermeneutics, Hobbism, Holist, Humanism, I Ching, Idealism, Ideology, Instrumentalism, Ionic, -ism, Kaizen, Linguistic, Logical atomism, Logicism, Logos, Maieutic, Marxism, Materialism, Mechanism, Megarian, Metaphysician,

Metaphysics, Metempiricism, Monism, Moral(ist), Natural, Neoplatonism, Neoteric, Nihilism, Nominalism, Occamist, Occam's razor, Ockhamist, Opinion, Panhellenism, Peripatetic, Phenomenology, Platonism, Populism, Positivism, Rationalism, Realism, Rosminian, Sage, Sankhya, Sceptic, Schoolman, Scientology, Scotism, Secular-humanism, Sensist, Shankara(-charya), Solipsism, Sophist, Stoic, Synthetic, Taoism, Theism, Theosophy, Thomist, Thought, Transcendentalism, Ultraism, Utilitarianism, Utopianism, Vedanta, Voluntarism, Weltanschauung, Whitehead, Yoga, Yogi

Phon(e)y Bogus, Charlatan, Counterfeit, Faitor, Fake, Impostor, Poseur, Quack, →SHAM, Specious, Spurious

Phone Bell, Blower, Call, Cellular, Clamshell, Dial, Dual band, Flip, Intercom, Mob(i)e, Mobile, Picture, Ring, Roam, Satellite, Talkback, Tel, Text

Phonetic(s) Auditory, Interdental, Oral, Palaeotype, Palato-alveolar, Spoken, Symbol

▷ **Phonetically** *may indicate* a word sounding like another

▷ **Phony** *may indicate* an anagram

Photo(copy), Photograph(y), Photographic, Photo finish Anaglyph, Black and white, Blow-up, Cabinet, Close-up, Composite, Digicam, Duplicate, Dyeline, Exposure, Film, Flash, Half-tone, Headshot, Hologram, Karyogram, Microdot, Microprint, Montage, Mugshot, Negative, Nephogram, Panel, Picture, Polaroid®, Positive, Print, Rotogravure, Sepia, Shoot, Shot, Slide, Snap, Still, Take, Topo, Vignette, X-ray

Phrase Abject, Actant, Buzzword, Cadence, Catch(word), Catchcry, Cliché, Climacteric, Comma, Expression, Hapax legomenon, Heroic, Idiophone, Laconism, Leitmotiv, Lemma, Locution, Mantra, Motto, Phr, Prepositional, Refrain, Riff, Set, Slogan, Soundbite, Tag, Term, Trope, Verb

Physic(s) Cluster, Cryogenics, Culver's, Cure, Dose, Electrostatics, High-energy, Kinematics, Medicine, Nuclear, Nucleonics, Particle, Purge, Remedy, Rheology, Science, Sonics, Spintronics, Thermodynamics

Physician Addison, Allopath, Bach, Buteyko, Chagas, Doctor, Erastus, Eustachio, Galen, Gilbert, Graves, Guillotin, Hakim, Hansen, Harvey, Hippocrates, Internist, Jenner, Lamaze, Leech, Linacre, Lister, Medic(o), Menière, Mesmer, Mindererus, Paean, Paian, Paracelsus, Practitioner, Quack, Ranvier, Roget, Russell, Salk, Spiegel, Still, Therapist, Time, Vaidya, Wavell

Physicist →SCIENTIST

Pi, Pious Breast-beater, Devotional, Devout, Fraud, Gallio, God-fearing, Godly, Holy, Mid-Victorian, Sanctimonious, Savoury, Smug

Pi(ous) Orant, Reverent, Saintly

Piano Bechstein, Broadwood, Celesta, Celeste, Concert grand, Cottage, Dumb, Flugel, Forte, Grand, Hammerklavier, Honkytonk, Keyboard, Mbira, Overstrung, P, Player, Softly, Steinway, Stride, Thumb, Upright

Picaresque Roman à tiroirs

Pick(er), Pickaxe, Picking, Pick out, Pick up Break, Choice, Contract, Cream, Cull, Elite, Evulse, Flower, Gather, Glean, Hack, Holing, Hopper, Mattock, Nap, Nibble, Oakum, Plectrum, Pluck, Plum, Select, Single, Sort, Steal, Strum, Tong, Wale

▷ **Picked** *may indicate* an anagram

Pickle(r) Achar, Brine, Cabbage, Caper, Chow-chow, Chutney, Corn, Corner, Cucumber, Cure, Dilemma, Dill, Eisel, Esile, Gherkin, Girkin, Imp, Jam, Kimchi, Marinade, Marinate, Mess, Mull, Olive, Onion, Peculate, Peregrine, Piccalilli, Relish, Rod, Samp(h)ire, Scrape, Souse, Trouble, Vinegar, Wolly

Pickpocket(s) Adept, Bung, Cly-faker, Cutpurse, Dip, Diver, Fagin, File, Nipper, Swellmobsman, Whizzer, Wire

Picnic Alfresco, Braaivleis, Clambake, Fun, Junketing, Outing, Push-over, Spread, Tailgate, Valium, Wase-goose, Wayzgoose

Picture(s) Anaglyph, Art, B-movie, Canvas, Cinema, Cloudscape, Collage, Cutaway, Decoupage, Depict, Describe, Diptych, Drawing, Drypoint, Emblem, Envisage, Epitome, Etching, Film, Flick, Fresco, Gouache, Graphic, Histogram, Icon, Identikit®,

Imagery, Inset, Landscape, Lenticular, Likeness, Lithograph, Montage, Mosaic, Motion, Movie, Moving, Movy, Mugshot, Oil, Painture, Photo, Photofit®, Photogram, Photomontage, Pin-up, Pix, Plate, Portrait, Prent, Presentment, Print, Represent, Retrate, Rhyparography, Scene, Semble, Shadowgraph, Shot, Slide, Snapshot, Stereochrome, Stereogram, Stereograph, Stevengraph, Still-life, Table(au), Talkie, Thermogram, Tone, Topo, Transfer, Transparency, Vectograph, Vision, Votive, Word, Zincograph

▷ **Pie** *may indicate* an anagram

Pie(s) Anna, Banoffee, Battalia, Bird, Bridie, Camp, Chewet, Cinch, Cobbler, Cottage, Coulibiac, Curry puff, Custard, Deep-dish, Easy, Flan, Floater, Florentine, Hash, Humble, Koulibiaca, Madge, Meat, Mess, Mince(meat), Mud, Mystery bag, Pandowdy, Pastry, Pasty, Patty, Périgord, Pica, Piet, Pirog, Pizza, Printer's, Pyat, Pyet, Pyot, Quiche, Rappe, Resurrection, Shepherd's, Shoofly, Shred, Spoil, Squab, Stargaz(e)y, Star(ry)-gazy, Sugar, Tart, Tarte tatin, Torte, Tourtière, Turnover, Tyropitta, Umble, Vol-au-vent, Warden

Piece(s) Adagio, Add, Arioso, Bagatelle, Bishop, Bit, Blot, Cameo, Cannon, Cent, Charm, →**CHESSMAN**, Chip, Chunk, Coin, Companion, Component, Concerto, Conversation, Counter, Crumb, Domino, End, Episode, Extract, Firearm, Fit, Flake, Flitters, Fragment, Gat, Goring, →**GUN**, Haet, Hait, Hunk, Item, Join, Mammock, Médaillons, Mite, Money, Morsel, Museum, Nip, Novelette, Oddment, Off-cut, Ort, Part, Party, Pastiche, Patch, Pawn, Pce, Period, Peso, Pin, Pistareen, Pole, →**PORTION**, Recital, Scrap, Section, Sector, Set, Shard, Sherd, Slice, Slip, Sliver, Snatch, Sou, Spare part, Speck, String, Stub, Swatch, Tad, Tait, Tate, Tile, Toccata, Wedge, Wodge

Pier(s) Anta, Chain, Groyne, Jetty, Jutty, Landing, Mole, Plowman, Quay, Slipway, Swiss roll, Wharf, Wigan

Pierce(d), Piercer, Piercing Accloy, Awl, Bore, Broach, Cleave, Dart, Drill, Endart, Fenestrate(d), Fulminant, Gimlet, Gore, Gride, Gryde, Hull, Impale, Jag, Keen, Lance, Lancinate, Lobe, Move, Needle, Penetrate, Perforate, Pertusate, Pike, Pink, Poignant, Prince Albert, Punch, Puncture, Riddle, Rive, Shrill, Skewer, Slap, Sleeper, Spear, Spike, Spit, Stab, Steek, Stilet(to), Sting, Tap, Thirl, Thrill(ant)

Pig(s), Piggy, Pigmeat, Pigskin Anthony, Babe, Barrow, Bartholomew, Bland, Boar, Bush, Cutter, Doll, Elt, Farrow, Fastback, Football, Gadarene, Gilt, Gloucester Old Spot, Glutton, Grice, Gryce, Guinea, Gus, Gutzer, Ham, Hampshire, Hog, Ingot, Iron, Kentledge, Kintledge, Kunekune, Landrace, Land-shark, Large Black, Large White, Long, Napoleon, Peccary, Policeman, Porchetta, Pork(er), Raven, Razorback, Rosser, Runt, Saddleback, Shoat, Shot(e), Shott, Slip, Snowball, Sounder, Sow, Squealer, Suid(ae), Tamworth, Tithe, Toe, Truffle, Warthog, Yelt

Pigeon Archangel, Barb, Bird, Bronze-winged, Cape, Carrier, Clay, Cropper, Culver, Danzig, Dove, Fantail, Goura, Ground, Gull, Homer, Homing, Horseman, Jacobin, Kereru, Kuku, Manumea, Mourning dove, New Zealand, Nun, Owl, Passenger, Peristeronic, Piwakawaka, Pouter, Ringdove, Rock(er), Roller, Ront(e), Ruff, Runt, Scandaroon, Solitaire, Spot, Squab, Squealer, Stale, Stock-dove, Stool, Stork, Swift, Talkie-talkee, Tippler, Trumpeter, Tumbler, Turbit, Wonga(-wonga), Zoozoo

Pig-headed Self-willed

Pigment(s), Pigmentation Accessory, Anthoclore, Anthocyan(in), Argyria, Betacyanin, Bilirubin, Biliverdin, Bister, Bistre, Cappagh-brown, Carmine, Carotene, Carotenoid, Carotin, Carotinoid, Chlorophyll, Chrome, Chromogen, Cobalt, Colcothar, Colour, Curcumin, Dye, Etiolin, Eumelanin, Flavin(e), Fucoxanthin, Gamboge, Gossypol, Green earth, Haem, Hem(e), H(a)emocyanin, H(a)emoglobin, Iodopsin, King's yellow, Lake, Lamp-black, Lipochrome, Lithopone, Liverspot, Lutein, Luteolin, Lycopene, Madder, Madder lake, Melanin, Naevus, Naples yellow, Nigrosine, Ochre, Opsin, Orpiment, Paris-green, Phthalocyanine, Phycocyan, Phycoerythrin, Phycoxanthin, Phytochrome, Porphyrin, Porphyropsin, Pterin, Puccoon, Quercetin, Realgar, Retinene, Rhiboflavin, Rhodophane, Rhodopsin, Saffron, Sepia, Sienna, Sinopia, Sinopsis, Smalt, Tapetum, Tempera, Terre-verte, Tincture, Turacoverdin,

Umber, Urochrome, Verditer, Vermilion, Viridian, Xanthophyll, Xanthopterin(e), Yellow ochre

Pike Assegai, Crag, Dory, Fogash, Gar(fish), Ged, Gisarme, Glaive, Hie, Holostei, Javelin, Lance, Luce, Partisan, Pickerel, Ravensbill, Scafell, Snoek, Spear, Speed, Spontoon, Vouge, Walleyed

Pilchard Sardine

Pile(d), Piles, Piling Agger, Amass, Atomic, Bing, Bomb, Bubkes, Camp-sheathing, Camp-shedding, Camp-sheeting, Camp-shot, Clamp, Cock, Column, Crowd, Deal, Dolphin, Down, Emerods, Farmers, Fender, Fig, Floccus, Fortune, Galvanic, Hair, Haycock, Heap, Hept, Historic, Hoard, Load, Lot, Mansion, Marleys, Mass, Moquette, Nap, Pier, Post, Pyre, Raft, Reactor, Ream(s), Rouleau, Screw, Shag, Sheet, Slush, → **STACK**, Starling, Stilt, Toorie, Trichome, Upheap, Velvet, Voltaic, Wealth, Windrow, Wodge

Pilgrim(age) Aske, Childe Harold, Expedition, Fatima, Gaya, Hadj(i), Hajj(i), Kum, Loreto, Lourdes, Mathura, Mecca, Nasik, Nikko, Palmer, Pardoner, Qom, Questor, Qum, Reeve, Scallop-shell, Shrine, Umra(h), Voyage, Yatra

Pill(s) Abortion, Ball, Beverley, Bitter, Bolus, Cachou, Caplet, Capsule, Chill, Dex, Doll, Dose, Globule, Golfball, Goofball, Lob, Medication, Medicine, Number nine, Peace, Peel, Pellet, Pep, Pilula, Pilule, Placebo, Poison, Protoplasmal, Radio, Sleeping, Spansule, Tablet, Troche, Trochisk, Upper

Pillar(ed), Pillars Anta, Apostle, Atlantes, Baluster, Balustrade, Boaz, Canton, Caryatides, Chambers, Cippus, Columel, Column, Eustyle, Gendarme, Goal, Hercules, Herm, Impost, Islam, Jachin, Lat, Man, Modiolus, Monolith, Newel, Obelisk, Pedestal, Peristyle, Pier, Post, Respond, Saddle, Serac, Stack, Stalactite, Stalagmite, Stoop, Telamon, Trumeau

Pillow(case) Bear, Beer, Bere, Bolster, Cod, Cow, Cushion, Headrest, Hop, Lace, Pad, Pulvinar, Throw

Pilot Ace, Airman, Auto(matic), Aviator, Biggles, Branch, Bush, Captain, → **CONDUCT**, Experimental, Flier, George, Govern, Guide, Hobbler, Lead, Lodesman, Palinure, Palinurus, Pitt, Prune, Shipman, Steer, Test, Tiphys, Trial, Usher, Wingman

Pimpernel Bastard, Bog, Poor man's weatherglass, Scarlet, Water, Wincopipe, Wink-a-peep, Yellow

Pimple, Pimply Blackhead, Botch, Goosebump, Gooseflesh, Grog-blossom, Hickey, Horripilation, Milium, Papilla, Papula, Papule, Plook, Plouk, Pock, Pustule, Quat, Rumblossom, Rum-bud, Spot, Uredinial, Wen, Whelk, Whitehead, Zit

Pin Bayonet, Belaying, Bolt, Brooch, Candle, Cask, Corking, Cotter, Curling, Dowel, Drawing, Drift, End, Fasten, Fid, Firing, Fix, Gam, Gnomon, Gudgeon, Hair, Hairgrip, Hob, Hook, Joggle, Kevel, King, Leg, Nail, Needle, Nog, Panel, Peg, Pintle, Pivot, Preen, Rivet, Rolling, Saddle, Safety, Scarf, SCART, Scatter, Shear, Shirt, Skewer, Skittle, Skiver, Spike, Spindle, Split, Staple, Stick, Stump, Swivel, Taper, Tertial, Thole, Thumbtack, Tie, Tietac(k), Tre(e)nail, Trunnion, U-bolt, Woolder, Wrest, Wrist

Pinball Pachinko

Pinch(ed) Arrest, Bit, Bone, Chack, Constrict, Cramp, Crisis, Emergency, Gaunt, Misappropriate, Nab, Nick, Nim, Nip, Nirlit, Peculate, Peel, Pilfer, Pocket, Pook(it), Pouk, Prig, Pugil, Raft, Raw, Rob, Save, Scrimp, Scrounge, Skimp, Smatch, Snabble, Snaffle, Sneak, Sneap, Sneeshing, Snuff, Squeeze, → **STEAL**, Swipe, Tate, Trace, Tweak, Twinge

Pine(s), Pining Arolla, Bristlecone, Celery, Cembra, Chile, Cluster, Cone, Conifer, Cypress, Droop, Dwine, Earn, Erne, Fret, Green, Ground, Hone, Hoop, Huon, Jack, Japanese umbrella, Jeffrey, Kauri, Knotty, Languish, Languor, Loblolly, Lodgepole, Long, Longleaf, Lovesick, Monkey-puzzle, Monterey, Moon, Norfolk Island, Norway, Nut, Oregon, Parana, Picea, Pinaster, Pitch, Ponderosa, Radiata, Red, Scotch, Scots, Screw, Slash, Softwood, Spruce, Starve, Stone, Sugar, Tree, Umbrella, Urman, Waste, White, Yearn, Yellow

Pink Blush, Carnation, Carolina, Castory, Cheddar, Clove, Colour, Coral, Cyclamen, Dianthus, Dutch, Emperce, FT, Fuchsia, Gillyflower, Indian, Knock, Kook, Lake, Lily, Lychnis, Maiden, Moss, Mushroom, Old rose, Oyster, Peach-blow, Peak, Perce,

Pierce, Pompadour, Pounce, Rose(ate), Rose-hued, Ruddy, Salmon, Scallop, Sea, Shell, Shocking, Shrimp, Spigelia, Spit, Stab, Tiny

Pin-point Focus, Identify, Isolate, Localise

Pioneer Avant garde, Babbage, Baird, Bandeirante, Blaze, Boone, Colonist, Emigrant, Explore, Fargo, Fawkner, Fleming, Frontiersman, Harbinger, Herodotus, Innovator, Lead, Marconi, Oecist, Pathfinder, Rochdale, Sandgroper, Settler, Spearhead, Stopes, Trail-blazer, Trekker, Turing, Voortrekker, Wells, Yeager

▶ **Pious** *see* PI

Pipe(s), Piper, Pipeline, Piping Ait, Aorta, Aulos, Balance, Barrel, Blub, Boatswain's, Bong, Briar, Briarroot, Bronchus, Bubble, Calabash, Call, Calumet, Chanter, Cheep, Cherrywood, Chillum, Churchwarden, Clay, Cob, Conduit, Corncob, Crane, Cutty, Dip, Division, Down, Drain, Drill, Drillstring, Drone, Dry riser, Duct, Escape, Exhaust, Faucet, Feed, Fistula, Flue, Flute, Gage, Gas main, Hawse, Hod, Hogger, Hooka(h), Hose, Hubble-bubble, Hydrant, Indian, Injection string, Irish, Jet, Mains, Manifold, Meerschaum, Montre, Narghile, Nargile(h), Narg(h)il(l)y, Oat(en), Oboe, Organ, Ottavino, Outlet, Pan, Peace, Pepper, Pibroch, Piccolo, Pied, Pitch, Principal, Pule, Quill, Rainwater, Ree(d), Rise, Riser, Serpent, Service, Sewer, Sheesha, Shisha, Shoe, Sing, Siphon, Skirl, Sluice, Soil, Spout, Stack, Standpipe, Stopcock, Sucker, Tail, Tee, Throttle, Tibia, Tootle, Trachea, Tremie, Tube, Tweet, U-bend, Union, Uptake, U-trap, Vent, Ventiduct, Volcanic, Waste, Water(-spout), Watermain, Weasand, Whiss, Whistle, Woodcock's head, Woodnote, Worm

Pirate(s), Pirated, Piratical, Piracy Algerine, Barbarossa, Blackbeard, Boarder, Bootleg, Brigand, Buccaneer, Buccanier, Cateran, Condottier, Conrad, Corsair, Crib, Dampier, Fil(l)ibuster, Flint, Gunn, Hijack, Hook, Kidd, Lift, Loot, Morgan, Penzance, Picaro(on), Pickaroon, Plagiarise, Plunder, Rakish, Rover, Sallee-man, Sallee-rover, Sea-dog, Sea-king, Sea-rat, Sea-robber, Sea-wolf, Silver, Smee, Steal, Teach, Unauthorised, Viking, Water-rat, Water-thief

Pistol Air, Ancient, Automatic, Barker, Capture bolt, Colt®, Dag, Derringer, Gat, →GUN, Hackbut, Horse, Iron, Luger®, Pepperbox, Petronel, Pocket, Revolver, Rod, Shooter, Sidearm, Starter, Starting, Very, Water, Weapon, Zip gun

Pit(ted), Pitting Abyss, Alveolus, Antrum, Bed, Bottomless, Catch, Cave, Cesspool, Chasm, Cissing, Cloaca, Colliery, Crater, Den, Depression, Depth, Dungmere, Ensile, Fossa, Fougasse, Fovea, Foxhole, Gehenna, Hangi, Heapstead, Heartspoon, Hell, Hillhole, Hole, Hollow, Inferno, Inspection, Khud, Lacunose, Lime, Mark, Match, Measure, →MINE, Mosh, Orchestra, Parterre, Pip, Plague, Play, Pock-mark, Potato, Punctate, Putamen, Pyrene, Ravine, Rifle, Salt, Scrobicule, Silo, Slime, Soakaway, Solar plexus, Stone, Sump, Tar, Tear, Trap, Trous-de-loup, Underarm

Pitch(ed) Absolute, Asphalt, Atilt, Attune, Bitumen, Burgundy, Coal-tar, Concert, Crease, Diamond, Diesis, Dive, Ela, Elect, Elevator, Encamp, Erect, Establish, Fever, Fling, Fork(ball), French, Ground, Height, International, Intonation, Key, Knuckleball, Labour, Length, Level, Lurch, Maltha, Mineral, Nets, Neume, Outfield, Patter, Peck, Perfect, Philharmonic, Philosophical, Piceous, Pight, Pin, Plong(e), Plunge, Pop, Purl, Relative, Resin, Rock, Ruff(e), Sales, Scend, Seel, Send, Shape, Sling, Slope, Soprarino, Spiel, Spitball, Stoit, Tar, Tessitura, Tilt, Tone, Tonemic, Tonus, Tremolo, Tune, Unison, Vibrato, Wicket, Wild, Wood

Pitchstone Retinite

Pith(y) Ambatch, Aphorism, Apo(ph)thegm, Core, Down, Essence, Gnomic, Hat-plant, Heart, Laconic, Marrow, Meaty, Medulla, Moxa, Nucleus, Rag, Sententious, Succinct, Terse

Pitiless Flint-hearted, Hard, Hard-headed, Ruthless

Pity, Piteous, Pitiful, Pitiable Ah, Alack, Alas, Commiseration, →COMPASSION, Hapless, Mercy, Pathos, Pilgarlic, Poor, Quarter, Red-leg, Rue, Ruth(ful), Seely, Shame, Sin, Sympathy

Pivot(al) Ax(i)le, Central, Focal, Fulcrum, Gooseneck, Gudgeon, Kingbolt, Marker, Revolve, Rotate, Slue, →SWIVEL, Trunnion, Turn, Wheel

Place(ment) Aim, Allocate, Area, Arena, Assisted, Berth, Bro, Decimal, Deploy,

Deposit, Dispose, First, Fix, Habitat, Haunt, Hither, Howf, Identify, Impose, →IN
PLACE OF, Insert, Install, Job, Joint, Juxtapose, Lay, Lieu, Locality, Locate, Locus,
Parking, Pitch, Plat, Plaza, Point, Posit, →POSITION, Post, Product, Put, Realm,
Region, Repose, Room, Rowme, Scene, Second, Set, Sit, Site, Situate, Situation, Slot,
Spot, Stead, Sted(e), Stedd(e), Stratify, Third, Toponym, Town, Vendôme

Placebo Snake-oil

Plagiarise, Plagiarist Copy, Crib, Lift, Pirate, Steal

Plague (spot) Annoy, Bane, Bedevil, Black death, Boil, Bubonic, Burden, Curse,
Death, Dog, Dun, Frogs, Gay, Goodyear, Goujeers, Harry, Infestation, Locusts, Lues,
Molest, Murrain, Murran, Murrin, Murrion, Nag, Pest, Pester, Pox, Press, Scourge,
Tease, Token, Torment, Torture, Try, Vex

Plain(s) Abraham, Artless, Ascetic, Au naturel, Bald, Bare, Blatant, Broad, Campagna,
Campus Martius, Candid, Ceará, Clear, Dowdy, Downright, Dry, Esdraelon, Evident,
Explicit, Flat, Flood, Girondist, Gran Chaco, Great, Homely, Homespun, Inornate,
Jezreel, Liverpool, Llano, Lombardy, Lowland, Manifest, Marathon, Mare, Obvious,
Ocean of Storms, Olympia, →ORDINARY, Outspoken, Overt, Packstaff, Pampa(s),
Patent, Pikestaff, Plateau, Prairie, Prose, Sailing, Salisbury, Savanna(h), Secco,
Serengeti, Sharon, Simple, Sodom, Spoken, Staked, Steppe, Tableland, Thessaly,
Tundra, Unremarkable, Vanilla, Vega, Veldt, Visible, Walled

Plainchant Canto fermo

Plaint(ive) Complaint, Dirge, Lacrimoso, Lagrimoso, Lament, Melancholy, Sad,
Whiny

Plan(s), Planned, Planner, Planning Aim, American, Angle, Architect,
Arrange, Atlas, Battle, Blueprint, Brew, Budget, Care, Chart, Commission,
Contingency, Contrive, Dalton, Dart, Deep-laid, Deliberate, Delors, Design, Device,
Devise, Diagram, Draft, Drawing, Elevation, Engineer, European, Family, Figure
on, Five-Year, Flight, Floor, Format, Galveston, Game, Ground, Hang, Idea, Idée,
Instal(l)ment, Intent, Lay(out), Leicester, Leicestershire, Machinate, Map, Marshall,
Master, Mastermind, Mean, Meditate, Nominal, Open, Outline, Pattern, Pipe-dream,
Plot, Ploy, Policy, Premeditate, Procedure, Programme, Project, Projet, Proposal,
Prospectus, Rapacki, Road map, Scenario, Schedule, Scheme, Schlieffen, Shape,
Spec(ification), Stratagem, Strategy, Subterfuge, System, Tactician, Trace, View,
Wallchart, Wheeze

Plane(s) Aero(dyne), Air, →AIRCRAFT, Airliner, Airship, Axial, Bandit, Basal,
Boeing, Bomber, Bus, Buttock, Camel, Canard, Cartesian, Cessna, Chenar, Chinar,
Comet, Concorde, Crate, Dakota, Datum, Delta-wing, Even, Facet, Fault, Fillister, Flat,
Float, Glider, Gliding, Gotha, Hurricane, Icosahedron, Icosohedra, Jack, Jet, Jointer,
Jumbo, Level, London, MIG, Mirage, Mosquito, Moth, Octagon, Platan(us), Polygon,
Prop-jet, Rocket, Router, Shackleton, Shave, Smooth, Sole, Spitfire, Spokeshave,
STOL, Surface, Sycamore, Taube, Thrust, Trainer, Tree, Trident, Tropopause,
Two-seater, Viscount

Planet(s), Planetary Alphonsine, Ariel, Asteroid, Body, Cabiri, Ceres, Chiron,
Constellation, Dispositor, Earth, Eros, Extrasolar, Gas giant, Georgian, Giant, House,
Hyleg, Inferior, Inner, Jovian, Jupiter, Lucifer, Major, Mars, Mercury, Minor, Moon,
Neptune, Outer, Pallas, Pluto, Primary, Psyche, Quartile, Red, Satellitium, Saturn,
Sedna, Significator, Sphere, Starry, Sun, Superior, Terra, Terrestrial, Uranus, Venus,
Vista, Vulcan, World, Zog

Plank Board, Chess, Duckboard, Garboard, Plonk, Sarking, Slab, Spirketting, Straik,
Strake, Stringer, Wood

Plant(s), Plant part Amphidiploid, Anemochore, Annual, Anther, Aphotoic,
Autophyte, Bed, Biennial, Biota, Bloomer, Bonsai, Bryophyte, Chamaephyte,
Chomophyte, Cropper, Cultigen, Cultivar, Dayflower, Dibble, Ecad, Eccremocarpus,
Embed, Endogen, Enrace, Epilithic, Epiphyllous, Epiphyte, Establish, Factory, Fix,
Flora, Geophyte, Growth, Gymnosperm, Halosere, Herbage, Herbarium, Humicole,
Hydrastus, Hydrophyte, Hygrophyte, Hylophyte, Incross, Insert, Instil, Inter, Labiate,
Land, Lathe, Legume, Lithophyte, Livelong, Longday, Lurgi, Machinery, Mill,

Monocotyledon, Ornamental, Perennial, Phanerogam, Phloem, Pitcher, Protophyte, Psilophyte, Ramet, Resurrection, Root, Rosin, Saprophyte, Schizophyte, Sciophyte, Sclerophyll, Scrambler, Sere, Shortday, Shrub, Sow, Spermatophyte, Sponge, Steelworks, Stickseed, Sticktight, Strangler, Streptocarpus, Succulent, Superweed, Thalloplyte, Thickleaf, Trailer, →**TREE**, Trifolium, Trillium, Tropophyte, Twining, Vascular, Washery, Wilding, Works, Zoophyte

Plantation Arboretum, Bosket, Bosquet, Estate, Grove, Hacienda, Pen, Pinetum, Ranch, Tara, Tope, Veticetum, Vineyard

Plasm Germ

Plaster(ed), Plaster board Artex®, Bandage, Blister, Blotto, Butterfly clip, Cake, Cataplasm, Clam, Clatch, Compo, Court, Daub, Diachylon, Diachylum, Dressing, Drunk, Emplastrum, Fresco, Gesso, Grout, Gyprock®, Gypsum, Intonaco, Laying, Leep, Lit, Mud, Mustard, Parge(t), Polyfilla®, Porous, Poultice, Render, Roughcast, Scratch-coat, Screed, Secco, Shellac, Sinapism, Smalm, Smarm, Smear, Sowsed, Staff, Sticking, Stookie, Stucco, Teer, Wattle and daub

Plastic Bubblewrap, Ductile, Fibreglass, Fictile, Laminate, Loid, Mylar®, Pliant, Polythene, PVC, Vinyl, Wet-look, Xylonite, Yielding

▷ **Plastic** *may indicate* an anagram

Plasticine Morph

Plate(s), Plated, Platelet, Plating Acierage, Ailette, Anchor, Angle, Anode, Armadillo, Armour, Ashet, Baffle, Baleen, Base, Batten, Brass, Butt, Chape, Charger, Chrome, Coat, Communion, Copper, Ctene, Deadman, Denture, Diaphragm, Dinner, Disc, Dish, Echo, Electro, Electrotype, Elytron, Elytrum, Enamel, Equatorial, Escutcheon, Face, Fashion, Feet, Fine, Fish, Flatware, Foil, Frog, Gold, Graal, Gravure, Ground, Half, Hasp, Horseshoe, Hot, Hypoplastron, Illustration, Kick, L, Lame, Lamina, Lanx, Latten, Lead, Licence, Madreporic, Mascle, Mazarine, Nail, Nef, Neural, Nickel, Number, P, Paten, Patina, Petri, Phototype, Planometer, Plaque, Plastron, Platter, Poitrel, Print, Pygal, Quarter, Race, Registration, Roof, Rove, Salamander, Scale, Screw, Scrim, Scutcheon, Scute, Scutum, Selling, Sheffield, Shield, Shoe, Side, Sieve, Silver, Slab, Soup, Spacer, Spoiler, Stall, Steel, Stencil, Stereo(type), Sternite, Surface, Swash, T, Tablet, Tace, Tasse(l), Tea, Tectonic, Tergite, Terne, Thali, Theoretical, Tin(ware), Torsel, Touch, Trade, Tramp, Trencher, Trivet, Trophy, Tsuba, Vane, Vanity, Vassail, Vessel, Wall, Water, Web, Wet, Whirtle, Whole, Wobble, Workload, Wrap(a)round, Zincograph

Plateau Altiplano, Anatolian, Barkly Tableland, Central Karoo, Chota Nagpur, Darling Downs, Dartmoor, Deccan, Durango, Ellesworth Land, Fjeld, Fouta Djallon, Highland, Highveld, Horst, Kar(r)oo, Kimberleys, Kurdestan, Kurdistan, La Mancha, Lamington, Langres, Mat(t)o Grosso, Mesa Verde, Meseta, Najd, Nilgiris, Ozark, Paramo, Piedmont, Puna, Shire Highlands, Tableland, Ust Urt

Platform Accommodation, Balcony, Bandstand, Base, Bay, Bema, Bench, Bridge, Catwalk, Crane, Crow's nest, Dais, Deck, Dolly, Drilling, Estrade, Exedra, Exhedra, Fighting top, Flake, Footpace, Footplate, Foretop, Gangplank, Gantry, Gravity, Hustings, Landing stage, Launch-pad, Machan, Manifesto, Monkeyboard, Oil, Oil-rig, Pad, Paint-bridge, Pallet, Perron, Plank, Podium, Predella, Production, Programme, Pulpit, Quay, Raft, Rig, Rostrum, Round-top, Scaffold, Shoe, Skidway, Skylab, Soapbox, Space, Sponson, →**STAGE**, Stand, Stoep, Strandflat, Tee, Terminal, Ticket, Top, Tribunal, Tribune, Turntable, Wave-cut, Wharf

▷ **Play** *may indicate* an anagram

Play(s), Playing Accompany, Active, Amusement, Antic, Assist, Caper, Charm, Clearance, Closet, Coriolanus, Curtain-raiser, Dandle, Doodle, Drama, Echo, Endgame, Epitasis, Escapade, Everyman, Extended, Fair, Finesse, Freedom, Frisk, Frolic, Fun, Gamble, Gambol, Game, Grand Guignol, Harlequinade, History, Holiday, Inside, Interlude, Jam, Jape, Jest, Jeu, Lake, Lark, Latitude, Lear, Leeway, Licence, Long, Mask, Masque, May, Medal, Melodrama, Miracle, Morality, Mummers, Mysteries, Nativity, Noh, Nurse, Oberammergau, On, Parallel, Passion, Pastorale, Perform, Personate, Peter, Portray, Power, Prank, Pretend, Puppet, Recreation, Represent, Riff, Rollick, Romp, Room, Rope, RUR, Saw, Screen, Show, Shuffle, Sketch,

Sport, Squeeze, Stage, Strain, Stroke, Strum, Summerstock, Thrum, Tolerance, Tonguing, Touchback, Toy, Tragedy, Trifle, Triple, Twiddle, Vamp, Word

Player(s) Actor, Athlete, Back, Backstop, Black, Brass, Bugler, Busker, Cast, CD, Centre, Centre forward, Centre-half, Colt, Contestant, Cornerback, Cover point, Dealer, Disc, DVD, E, East, ENSA, Equity, Fetcher, Fiddle, Flanker, Fly-half, Flying wing, Fly-slip, Franchise, Fullback, Ghetto-blaster, Goalie, Gramophone, Grand master, Gridder, Half, Half-back, Half-forward, Hooker, Infielder, iPod®, It, Juke-box, Keg(e)ler, Kest, Kicker, Linebacker, Lineman, Lion, Lock, Long-leg, Longstop, Loose-head, Lutanist, Lutenist, Man, Marquee, Midfield, Mid-on, Mime, Muffin, Musician(er), N, Nickelback, Nightwatchman, North, Nose guard, Nose tackle, Ombre, Onside, Outfielder, Out(side)-half, Participant, Pianola®, Pitcher, Pocket, Pone, Pro, Prop, Quarterback, Receiver, Record, Red shirt, Reliever, Reserve, Rover, S, Safetyman, Scrape, Scratch, Scrum half, Seed, Shamateur, Short-leg, Shortstop, Side, South, Stand-off, Stand-off half, Stereo, Striker, Strings, Strolling, Substitute, Super, Sweeper, Tabrere, Target man, Team, Thesp(ian), Tight end, Troubador, Troupe, Upright, Utility, Virtuosi, W, Walker-on, Walkman®, West, White, Wide receiver, Wing(back), Winger, Wingman

Playful Arch, Coy, Frisky, Humorous, Impish, Jocose, Kittenish, Ludic, Merry, Piacevole, Scherzo, Skittish, Sportive, Wanton

Playwright Dramaturge, Dramaturgist, Scriptwriter

Plea(s) Alford, Appeal, Claim, Common, Defence, Entreaty, Essoin, Excuse, Exoration, Orison, Placit(um), Prayer, Rebuttal, Rebutter, Rogation, Suit

Plead(er), Pleading Answer, Argue, Beg, Entreat, Intercede, Litigate, Moot, Placitory, Special, Supplicant, Urge, Vakeel, Vakil

Please(d), Pleasant, Pleasing, Pleasure(-seeker), Pleasurable Affable, Aggrate, Agreeable, Alcina, Algolagnia, Amenable, Amene, Amiable, Amuse, Apolaustic, Arride, Benign, Bitte, Braw, Cheerful, Chuffed, Comely, Comfort, Content, Cordial, Cute, Delectation, Delice, Delight, Divine, Do, Euphonic, Eye candy, Fair, Felicitous, Fit, Flatter, Fun, Genial, Glad, Gladness, Gratify, Harmonious, Hedonism, Jammy, Joy, Kama, Kindly, Lekker, Lepid, List, Naomi, Oblige, Piacevole, Primrose path, Prithee, Prythee, Purr, Queme, Regale, Sapid, Satisfy, Sightly, Suit, Tasty, Thrill, Tickle, Tickle pink, Treat, Vanity, Voluptuary, Wally, Will, Winsome, Wrapped, Xanadu List

Pleat Accordion, Box, Crimp, Crystal, Fold, French, Frill, Goffer, Gusset, Kick, Kilt, Knife, Plait, Pranck(e), Prank, Ruff(le), Sunburst, Sunray

Pledge Affidavit, Arlene, Arles, Band, Betroth, Bond, Borrow, Bottomry, Collateral, Commitment, Dedicate, Deposit, Earnest(-penny), Engage, Fine, Frithborn, Gage, Gilbert, Giselle, Guarantee, Hand, Hock, Hypothecate, Impignorate, Mortgage, Oath, Pass, Pawn, Pignerate, Pignorate, Plight, Pop, Propine, Sacrament, Security, Sponsorship, Stake, Surety, Teetotal, Toast, Troth, Undertake, Vow, Wad, Wage(r), Wed

Plentiful, Plenty Abounding, Abundance, Abundant, Ample, Bags, Copious, Copy, Easy, Excess, Foison, Fouth, Ful(l)ness, Fushion, Galore, Goshen, Lashings, Loads, Lots, Oodles, Pleroma, Profusion, Quantity, Riches, Rife, Routh, Rowth, Scouth, Scowth, Slue, Sonce, Sonse, Teeming, Umpteen

▶**Pliers** see PLY

Plimsoll(s) Dap, Gutty, Gym-shoe, Line, Mutton-dummies, Sandshoe, Tacky

Plot(s) Allotment, Area, Babington, Bed, Brew, Carpet, Chart, Cliché, Collude, Connive, Conspiracy, Conspire, Covin, Covyne, Device, Engineer, Erf, Erven, Frame-up, Graph, Gunpowder, Imbroglio, Intrigue, Locus, Lot, Machination, Map, Meal-tub, Odograph, Pack, Parcel, Patch, Plan, Plat, Rye-house, Scenario, →**SCHEME**, Sect(ion), Shot, Site, Story, Storyline, Taluk, Terf, Turf, Web

Plough(man), Ploughed, Ploughing Arable, Ard, Arval, Big Dipper, Breaker, Bull tongue, Chamfer, Charles's Wain, Contour, Dipper, Disc, Drail, Drill, Ear, Earth-board, Ere, Fail, Fallow, Farmer, Feer, Flunk, Gadsman, Gang, Great bear, Harrow, Lister, Middlebreaker, Middlebuster, Mouldboard, Piers, Pip, Pleuch, Pleugh, Plodder, Push, Rafter, Rib, Ridger, Rive, Rotary, Rove, Sand, Scooter, Septentrion(e)s,

Sill, Sodbuster, Sow, Stump-jump, Swing, The Wagon, Till(er), Tractor, Trench, Triones, Wheel

Ploy Brinkmanship, Dodge, Finesse, Gambit, Manoeuvre, Stratagem, Strike, Tactic, Wile

Pluck(ing), Plucky Avulse, Bare, Carphology, Cock, Courage, Deplume, Epilate, Evulse, Floccillation, Gallus, Game, →**GRIT**, Guts, Loot, Mettle, Pick, Pinch, Pip, Pizzicato, Plectron, Plectrum, Ploat, Plot, Plumassier, Plunk, Pook(it), Pouk(it), Pull, Race, Scrappy, Snatch, Spin, Spirit, Spunk, Summon, Tug, Twang, Tweak, Tweeze, Vellicate, Yank

Plug Access eye, Ad, Advocate, Banana, Block, Bung, Caulk, Chaw, Chew, Commercial, Dam, DIN, Dook, Dossil, Dottle, Douk, Fipple, Fother, Gang, Glow, Go-devil, Heater, Hype, Jack, Lam, Operculum, Pessary, Phono, Prod, Promote, Publicity, Ram, Rawlplug®, Recommendation, Safety, Salt, Scart, Spark(ing), Spigot, Spile, Spiling, Stop(per), Stopple, Strobili, Suppository, Tampion, Tap, Tent, Tompion, Vent, Volcanic, Wage, Wall, Wander, Wedge

Plum Beach, Bullace, Cherry, Choice, Damson, Gage, Greengage, Ground, Jamaica, Japanese, Java, Kaki, Mammee-sapota, Marmalade, Maroon, Mirabelle, Musk, Mussel, Myrobalan, Naseberry, Neesberry, Peach, Persimmon, Proin(e), Pruin(e), Prune(llo), Quetsch, Raisin, Sapodilla, Sebesten, Victoria, Wodehouse

Plumage, Plume Aigrette, Crest, Egret, Feather, Hackle, Panache, Preen, Ptilosis, Quill

Plumb(er), Plumbing Bullet, Dredge, Fathom(eter), Lead(sman), Perpendicular, Plummet, Sheer, Sound, Test, True, U-trap, Vertical

Plump(er) Bold, Bonnie, Bonny, Buxom, Choose, Chopping, Chubbed, Chubby, Cubby, Cuddly, Dumpy, Embonpoint, Endomorph, Fat, Fleshy, Flop, Fubsy, Full, Lie, Matronly, Opt, Plank, Plonk, Plop, Podgy, Portly, Pudgy, Roll-about, Rolypoly, Rotund, Round(about), Rubenesque, Sonsie, Sonsy, Soss, Souse, Squab, Squat, Stout, Swap, Swop, Tidy, Well-covered, Well-fed, Well-padded, Well-upholstered, Zaftig, Zoftig

Plunder(er) Berob, Booty, Brigand, Depredate, Despoil, Devastate, Escheat, Fleece, Forage, Freebooter, Gut, Harry, Haul, Herriment, Herryment, Hership, Loot, Maraud, Peel, Pill(age), Predation, Prey, Privateer, →**RANSACK**, Rape, Rapparee, Ravine, Reave, Reif, Reive, Rieve, Rifle, Rob, Rummage, Sack, Scoff, Shave, Skoff, Spoil(s), Spoliate, Sprechery, Spuilzie, Spuly(i)e, Spulzie, Swag

Plunge(r) Demerge, Dive, Douse, Dowse, Duck, Enew, Immerge, Immerse, La(u)nch, Nose-dive, Plummet, Raker, Send, Sink, Souse, Swoop, Thrust

Ply, Plier(s) Bend, Birl, Cab, Exercise, Exert, Gondoliers, Importune, Layer, Practise, Run, Trade, Wield

▷**Plying** *may indicate* an anagram

Plymouth Brethren Darbyite

PM Addington, Afternoon, Attlee, Autopsy, Bute, Cabinet-maker, Callaghan, Chamberlain, Disraeli, Gladstone, Major, Melbourne, Peel, Pitt, Portland, Premier, →**PRIME MINISTER**, Salisbury, Taoiseach

Pocket Air, Appropriate, Bag, Bin, Breast, Cargo, Cavity, Cly, Cup, Enclave, Fob, Glom, Hideaway, Hip, Jenny, Misappropriate, Patch, Placket, Plaid-neuk, Pot, Pouch, Purloin, Purse, Sac, Sky, Slash, Sling, Slit, Steal, Take, Trouser, Vest, Watch, Whitechapel

Pocketbook Reader

Pod(s) Babul, Bean, Belly, Carob, Chilli, Dividivi, Gumbo, Lomentum, Neb-neb, Okra, Pipi, Pregnant, Pudding-pipe, Seed, Siliqua, Tamarind, Vanilla, Vine

Poem(s), Poetry Acmeism, Acrostic, Anthology, A Shropshire Lad, Ballad(e), Bucolic, Dit(t), Dithyramb, Doggerel, Dub, Elegy, Endymion, Epic(ede), Haiku, Heroic, Hokku, Idyl(l), Inferno, Kyrielle, Lay, Limerick, Madrigal, Mahabharata(m), Mahabharatum, Meliboean, Metre, Mock-heroic, Monostrophe, Ode, Odyssey, Pastoral, Pentameter, Performance, Poesy, Prelude, Prose, Punk, Quatorzain, Quatrain, Ramayana, Rhapsody, Rig-Veda, Rime, Rime riche, Rondeau, Sixain, Song, Sonnet, Sound, Stanza, Tetrastich, Thebaid, Title, Vers(e)

Poet(s), Poetic Amorist, Bard(ling), Beatnik, Cumberland, Cyclic, Elegist,

Georgian, Iambist, Idyllist, Imagist, Laureate, Layman, Liner, Lyrist, Makar, Maker, Meistersinger, Metaphysical, Metrist, Minnesinger, Minor, Minstrel, Mistral, Monodist, Odist, Parnassian, PL, Pleiad(e), Poetaster, Rhymer, Rhymester, Rhymist, Rymer, Scald, Scop, Skald, Smart, Sonneteer, Sound, Spasmodic, Spasmodic School, Thespis, Tragic, Trench, Troubadour, Trouvère, Trouveur, Verse-monger, Verse-smith, Versifier

▶ **Poetry** *see* POEM(S)

Po-faced Stolid

Point(ed), Pointer, Points Ace, Acnode, Aim, Angular, Antler, Apex, Apogee, Appui, Arrowhead, Ascendant, Bar, Barb, Base, Basis, Boiling, Break(ing), Brownie, Burble, Burbling, Cape, Cardinal, Cash, Catch, Centre, Choke, Clou, Clovis, Clue, Colon, Comma, Cone, Conic, Corner, Cover, Crag, Crisis, Crux, Curie, Cursor, Cusp, Cuss, Danger, Dead, Decimal, Deflater, Deflator, Degree, Descendant, Detail, Di(a)eresis, Direct, Dot, E, Épée, Extremity, Fang, Feature, Fescue, Fitch(e), Focal, Focus, Foreland, Freezing, Fulcrum, Germane, Gist, Gnomon, Hastate, Head, Hinge, Horn, Hour hand, Icicle, Index, Indicate, Indicator, Ippon, Jag, Jester, Jog, Juncture, Knub, Lance, Lanceolar, Lead, Limit, Lizard, Locate, Locus, Mark, Melting, Metacentre, Moot, Mull, Muricate, N, Nail, Neb, Needle, Ness, Nib, Node, Now, Nub, Obconic, Obelisk, Opinion, Ord, Organ, Oscillation, Particle, Peak, Periapsis, Periastron, Perigee, Pin, Pinnacle, Pixel, Place, Pour, Power, Pressure, Prong, Prow, Punchline, Punctilio, Punctual, Ras, S, Saturation, Scribe, Seg(h)ol, Selling, Set, Setter, Shaft, Sharpener, Show, Shy, Silly, Socket, Sore, Spearhead, Specie, Spicate, Spick, Spike, Stage, Sticking, Stiletto, Sting, Strong, Sum, Talking, Tang, Taper, Technicality, Tine, → TIP, Tongue, Trafficator, Trig, Triple, Turning, Use, Vane, Vantage, Verge, Verse, Vertex, Vowel, W, Zenith

Pointless Blunt, Curtana, Flat, Futile, Idle, Inane, Inutile, Muticous, Otiose, Stupid, Vain

Poison(er), Poisoning, Poisonous Bane, Botulism, Contact, Deleterious, Envenom, Ergotise, Food, Malevolent, Miasma, Noxious, Phalloidin, Plumbism, Rot, Sausage, Systemic, Taint, Toxic, Toxicology, Toxicosis, Toxin, Toxoid, Venom(ous), Viperous, Virose, Virous, Virulent

Poke, Poky Bonnet, Broddle, Dig, Garget, Itchweed, Jab, Meddle, Mock, Nousle, Nudge, Nuzzle, Ombu, Peg, Pick, Poach, Pote, Pouch, Powter, → PRISON, Prog, Proke, Punch, Root(le), Rout, Rowt, Stab, Thrust

Polar, Pole(s), Poler Animal, Anode, Antarctic, Arctic, Boathook, Boom, Bowsprit, Caber, Celestial, Clothes, Crossbar, Electret, Extremity, Fizgy, Flagstaff, Furlong, Gaff, Galactic, Geomagnetic, Icy, Lug, Magnetic, Mast, May, N, Nadir, Negative, Nib, North, Oar, Po, Polack, Positive, Punt, Quant, Quarterstaff, Range, Rood, Roost, S, Shaft, South, Spar, Spindle, Sprit, Staff, Stake, Stanchion, Starosta, Stilt, Sting, Telegraph, Terrestrial, Tongue, Topmast, Totem, Utility, Zenith

▷ **Polar** *may indicate* with a pole

Police(man), Policewoman Beria, Bill, Bluebottle, Blue heeler, Bobby, Boss, Boys in blue, Busy, Catchpole, CID, Constable, Cop(per), Darogha, Detective, DI, Dibble, Europol, Flatfoot, Flying Squad, Force, Fuzz, Garda, Garda Siochana, Gendarme, Gestapo, G-man, Guard, Inspector, Interpol, Jawan, Keystone, KGB, Kitchen, Lawman, Mata-mata, Met(ropolitan), Military, Mobile, Morse, Mountie, MP, Officer, Patrolman, PC, Peeler, Pointsman, Porn squad, Provincial, Provost, Redcap, Riot, Robert, Roundsman, Rozzer, RUC, Secret, Snatch squad, Special, Special Branch, State Trooper, Super, Superintendent, Sweeney, Texas Rangers, The Bill, The Law, Traffic, Vice squad, Vigilante, Yardie squad, Zabtieh

Police station Copshop, Lock-up, Watchhouse

Policy Assurance, Ballon d'essai, CAP, Comprehensive, Course, Demesne, Endowment, Expedience, First-loss, Gradualism, Insurance, Keystone, Knock for knock, Laisser-faire, Lend-lease, Line, Manifesto, Method, Open(-sky), Open door, Perestroika, Plank, Platform, Pork-barrel, Practice, Programme, Reaganomics, Revanchism, Scorched earth, Socred, Stop-go, Tack, Tactics, Ticket, White Australia

Polish(ed), Polisher Beeswax, Black(ing), Blacklead, Bob, Buff, Bull, Burnish,

Chamois, Complaisant, Edit, Elaborate, Elegant, Emery, Enamel, Finish, French, Furbish, Gentlemanly, Glass, Gloss, Heelball, Hone, Inland, Jeweller's rouge, Lap, Lustre, Nail, Perfect, Pewter-mill, Planish, Polite, Polverine, Refinement, Refurbish, Rottenstone, Rub, Sand, Sandblast, Sandpaper, Sheen, Shellac, Shine, Sleekstone, Slick, Sophistication, Supercalender, Svelte, Urbane, Veneer, Wax

Polite(ness) Cabinet, Civil, Courteous, Genteel, Grandisonian, Mannered, Suave, Urbane, Well-bred

Politic(al), Politics Apparat, Azapo, Body, Chartism, Civic, Diplomacy, Discreet, Dog-whistle, Expedient, Falange, Fascism, Gesture, Leftism, Neoliberalism, Party, Poujadism, Power, Practical, Public, Radicalism, Rightism, State, Statecraft, Tactful, Wise, Yuppie, Yuppy

Politician(s) Bright, Carpet-bagger, Catiline, Centrist, Chesterfield, Christian Democrat, Congressman, Coningsby, Delegate, Demagogue, Demo(crat), Diehard, Disraeli, DUP, Eden, Euro-MP, Eurosceptic, Evita, Gladstone, Green, Hardie, Hardliner, Incumbent, Independent, Ins, Isolationist, Laski, Left, Legislator, Liberal, Log-roller, MEP, Minister, Moderate, MP, Nationalist, Nazi, Obstructionist, Octobrist, Parliamentarian, Parnell, Politico, Pollie, Polly, Poujade, Powell, Puppet, Rad, Rep, Richelieu, Senator, Socialist, Statesman, Statist, Tadpole, Taper, TD, Thatcherite, Tory, Trotsky, Unionist, Veep, Warhorse, Whig, Whip, Wilberforce

▷ **Poll** *may indicate* a first letter

Poll(ing) Advance, Ballot, Bean, Canvass, Count, Cut, Deed, Dod, Election, Exit, Gallup, Head, Humlie, Hummel, MORI, Nestor, Not(t), Opinion, Parrot, Pineapple, Pow, Referendum, Scrutiny, Sondage, Straw, Votes

Pollen, Pollinate(d), Pollination Anemophilous, Beebread, Dust, Entomophilous, Errhine, Farina, Fertilised, Geitonogamy, Intine, Palynology, Sternotribe, Witch-meal, Xenia

Pollute(d), Pollutant, Pollution Acid rain, Adulterate, Atmosphere, Besmear, Contaminate, Defile, Dirty, Feculent, File, Foul, Impure, Infect, Light, Miasma, Nox, Rainout, Smog, Soil, Soilure, Stain, Sully, Taint, Thermal, Violate

Polyphemus Cyclops

Pome Apple

Pomp(ous) Big, Bloviate, Bombastic, Budge, Ceremonial, Display, Dogberry, Euphuistic, Fustian, Grandiloquent, Grandiose, Heavy, Highfalutin(g), High-flown, High-muck-a-muck, High-sounding, Hogen-mogen, Holier than thou, Inflated, Orotund, Ostentatious, Pageantry, Panjandrum, Parade, Pretentious, Self-important, Sententious, Solemn, Splendour, Starchy, State, Stilted, Stuffed shirt, Stuffy, Turgid

Pond(s) Curling, Dew, Dub, Flash, Hampstead, Lakelet, Oceanarium, Pool, Pound, Puddle, Shield(ing), Slough, Stank, Stew, Tank, Turlough, Vivarium, Viver

Ponder(ous) Brood, Cogitate, Contemplate, Deliberate, Heavy, Laboured, Mull, Muse, Perpend, Poise, Pore, Reflect, Ruminate, →**THINK**, Vise, Volve, Weigh, Weight(y), Wonder

Pontiff, Pontifical, Pontificate Aaron, Aaronic, Antipope, Dogmatise, Papal

Pontoon Blackjack, Bridge, Caisson, Chess, Game, Vingt-et-un

Pony Bidet, Canuck, Cayuse, Cow, Dales, Dartmoor, Eriskay, Exmoor, Fell, Garran, Garron, Gen(n)et, GG, Griffin, Griffon, Gryfon, Gryphon, Jennet, Jerusalem, Mustang, New Forest, One-trick, Pit, Polo, Pownie, Sable Island, Shanks', Sheltie, Shetland, Show, Tangun, Tat(too), Timor, Welsh, Welsh Mountain, Western Isles

Ponytail Queue

Pool Backwater, Bank, Bethesda, Billabong, Bogey hole, Cenote, Cess, Collect, Combine, Dub, Dump, Flash, Flow, Hag, Hot, Infinity, Jackpot, Kitty, Lasher, Lido, Lin(n), Malebo, Meer, Mere, Mickery, Mikvah, Mikveh, Moon, Natatorium, Paddling, Piscina, Piscine, Plash, Plesh, Plunge, →**POND**, Reserve, Snooker, Spa, Stank, Stanley, Sump, Tank, Tarn, Wading, Wave

▷ **Poor** *may indicate* an anagram

Poor(ly) Bad, Bare, Base, Bijwoner, Breadline, Buckeen, Bywoner, Catchpenny, Conch, Cronk, Destitute, Desuetude, Dirt, Gens de peu, Gritty, Half-pie, Hard-up, Have-nots, Hopeless, Humble, Hungry, Ill(-off), Impecunious, Indigent, Lazarus, Lean, Lo-fi,

Lousy, Low, Low-downer, Low-fi, Low-paid, Lumpen, Meagre, Mean, Needy, Obolary, One-horse, Pauper, Peaky, Poxy, Redleg, Roinish, Rop(e)y, Roynish, Sad, Scrub, Shabby, Shitty, Sober, Sorry, Sub, Tacky, Tatty, Thin, Third-rate, Tinpot, Trashy, Undeserving, Unwell

▷ **Pop** *may indicate* an anagram

Pop (off), Popper, Popping Bang, Brit, Burst, Cloop, Crease, Daddy, Die, →DRUG, Father, Fr, Ginger ale, Gingerbeer, Hip-hop, Hock, Iggy, Insert, Lemonade, Lumber, Mineral, Nip, Parent, Party, Pater, Pawn, Pledge, Population, Press-stud, Punk, Scoosh, Sherbet, Soda, Splutter, Sputter, Weasel

Pope(s) Adrian, Alexander, Atticus, Boniface, Borgia, Clement, Dunciad, Eminence, Fish, Great Schism, Gregory, Hildebrand, Holiness, Innocent, Joan, Leo, Papa, Pius, Pontiff, Ruff(e), Schism, Theocrat, Tiara, Urban, Vatican, Vicar-general of Christ, Vicar of Christ

Poppy Argemone, Bloodroot, California, Chicalote, Coquelicot, Corn, Diacodin, Eschscholtzia, Flanders, Horned, Iceland, Matilija, Mawseed, Opium, Papaver, Ponceau, Prickly, Puccoon, Rhoeadales, Shirley, Tall, Welsh

Popular(ity), Popularly Best-seller, Common, Crowd-pleaser, Democratic, Demotic, Fashionable, General, Heyday, Hit, Hot ticket, In, Laic, Lay, Mass, Plebeian, Prevalent, Public, Sell-out, Street cred, Successful, Tipped, Trendy, Vogue, Vulgo

Population, Populace Catchment, Census, Closed, Deme, Demography, Inhabitants, Malthusian, Mass, Mob, Optimum, →PEOPLE, Public, Universe

Porcelain Arita, Artificial, Bamboo, Celadon, Chantilly, Chelsea, China, Coalport, Crackle(ware), Crouch-ware, Crown Derby, Derby, Dresden, Eggshell, Famille, Famille jaune, Famille noir, Famille rose, Famille verte, Frit, Goss, Hard-paste, Hizen, Imari, Ivory, Jasp, Jasper(ware), Kakiemon, Limoges, Lithophane, Meissen, Minton, Parian, Petuntse, Petuntze, Sèvres, Softpaste, Spode, Sung, Yuan

Pore Browse, Hole, Hydrathode, Lenticel, Muse, Ostiole, Ostium, Outlet, Ponder, Stoma, Study

Pork(y) Bacon, Boar, Brawn, Chap, Char sui, Crackling, Cracknel, Flitch, Griskin, Ham, Lie, Pancetta, Scrapple, Spare-rib, Spek

Porridge Berry, Bird, Brochan, Brose, Busera, Crowdie, Drammach, Drammock, Gaol, Grits, Grouts, Gruel, Hominy, Kasha, Mahewu, Mealie pap, Mielie pap, Oaten, Oatmeal, Parritch, Pease-brose, Polenta, Pottage, Praiseach, Sadza, Samp, Sentence, Skilly, Stirabout, Stretch, Sup(p)awn, Time, Ugali

Port(s) Beeswing, Carry, Cinque, Entrepot, Free, Gate, Gateway, Geropiga, →HARBOUR, Haven, Hinterland, Larboard, Left, Manner, Mien, Outport, Parallel, Row, Ruby, Serial, Tawn(e)y, Treaty, USB, Wine

Porter Ale, Bearer, Bellboy, Bummaree, Caddie, Caddy, Cole, Concierge, Coolie, Door-keeper, Doorman, Dvornik, Entire, Gatekeeper, Ham(m)al, Hamaul, Humper, Janitor, October, Ostiary, Plain, Red-cap, Skycap, Stout, Ticket

Portion Ann(at), Bit, Deal, Distribute, Dole, Dose, Dotation, Fragment, Helping, Heritage, Hunk, Jointure, Lot, Lump, Meed, Modicum, Moiety, Nutlet, Ounce, Parcel, →PART, Piece, Ratio, Sample, Scantle, Scantling, Section, Segment, Serving, Share, Size, Slice, Something, Tait, Taste, Tate, Tittle, Tranche, Wodge

Portrait(ist) Composite, Depiction, Drawing, Eikon, Icon, Ikon, Image, Kit-cat, Lely, Likeness, Painting, Pin-up, Retraitt, Retrate, Sketch, Vignette

Portray(al) Caricature, Depict, Describe, Feature, Image, Limn, Notate, Paint, Personate, Render, Represent, →SHOW

Pose(r), Poseur Aesthete, Affect(ation), Arabesque, Asana, Ask, Contrapposto, Drape, Enigma, Lotus, Masquerade, Model, Place, Plastique, Posture, Pretend, Problem, Propound, Pseud, Puzzle, Sit, Stance, Sticker, Tableau vivant, Tickler

Position Arrange, Asana, Attitude, Bearing(s), Brace, Bridgehead, Case, Close, Codille, Delta, Ecarte, Emplacement, Enfilade, False, F(o)etal, Fixure, Foothold, Fowler's, Grade, Instal, Lay, Lie, Location, Locus, Lodg(e)ment, Lotus, Missionary, Mudra, Office, Open, Pass, Peak, Place, Plant, Point, Pole, Port, Possie, Post, Pozzy, Put, Rank, Recovery, Recumbent, Root, Seat, Set(ting), Sextile, Sims, Sinecure, Site,

Situ, Situs, Stance, Standing, Standpoint, Station, Status, Strategic, Syzygy, Tagmeme, Thesis, Tierce, Trendelenburg's, Tuck, Viewpoint

Positive, Positivist Absolute, Actual, Anode, Assertive, Categorical, →CERTAIN, Comte, Definite, Emphatic, Plus, Print, Rave, Sure, Thetic, Upbeat, Upside, Veritable, Yang, Yes

Possess(ed), Possession(s), Possessive Adverse, Apostrophe, Asset, Aver, Bedevil, Belonging(s), Demonic, Driven, Energumen, Estate, Ewe lamb, Have, Haveour, Haviour, Heirloom, His, Hogging, Know, Lares (et) penates, Mad, Obsessed, Occupation, →OWN, Proprietorial, Sasine, Seisin, Sprechery, Substance, Tenancy, Usucap(t)ion, Vacant, Worth

Possible, Possibility, Possibly Able, Contingency, Feasible, Imaginable, Likely, Maybe, Mayhap, On, Oyster, Peradventure, Perchance, Perhaps, Posse, Potential, Prospect, Resort, Viable, Well, Will

▷ **Possibly** *may indicate* an anagram

Post(s), Postage Affix, After, Assign, Bitt, Bollard, Command, Correspondence, Cossack, Delivery, Durn, Excess, Finger, First(-class), Flagpole, Fly, Goal, Graded, Gradient, Guardhose, Heel, Hitching, Hovel, Jamb, Joggle, Junk, King, Last, Laureate, Listening, Log, Mail, Mast, Newel, Observation, Outstation, Pale, Paling, Parcel, Pendant, Penny, Picket, Pigeon, Pile, Piling, Piquet, Placard, Place, Plant, Plum, Pole, Position, Puncheon, Pylon, Quoin, Registered, Remit, RM, Rubbing, Samson's, Seat, Send, Sheriff's, Snubbing, Sound, Staff, Staging, Stake, Stanchion, Starting, Station, Stud, Tana, Tee, Term(inal), Thanna(h), Tool, Totem pole, Trading, Upright, Vacancy, Waymark, Winning

Postman, Postmaster, Postwoman Carrier, Courier, Emily, Hill, Messenger, Nasby, Pat, Portionist, Sorter

Post-modern Po-mo

Postpone(ment), Postponed Adjourn, Backburner, Carryover, Contango, Defer, Delay, Frist, Hold over, Lay over, Long-finger, Moratorium, Mothball, Offput, On ice, Pigeon-hole, Postdate, Prorogue, Put over, Remanet, Reprieve, Respite, Roll back, Shelve, Spike, Stay, Suspend, Withhold

Posture(r), Posturing Affectation, Asana, Attitude, Counter-view, Decubitus, Deportment, Gesture, Mudra, Pose, Pretence, Site, Stance, Swank, Vorlage, Yoga

Post-war Post-bellum

Pot(s), Potting, Potty Ante, Bankroll, Basil, Belly, Billycan, Cafetière, Ca(u)ldron, Cannabis, Cannikin, Casserole, Ceramic, Chamber, Chanty, Chimney, Close-stool, Cocotte, Coil, Commode, Crewe, Crock(ery), Crucible, Cruse(t), Delf(t), Dixie, Ewer, Flesh, Gage, Grass, Hash(ish), Helmet, Hemp, Hooped, In off, Kaif, Kef, Kettle, Kitty, Lobster, Loco, Lota(h), Maiolica, Majolica, Marijuana, Marmite, Melting, Ming, Monkey, Olla, Olpe, Pan, Pat, Piñata, Pipkin, Planter, Pocket, Poot, →POTTERY, Pottle, Pout, Prize, Samovar, Shoot, Sink, Skeet, Skillet, Smudge, Steamer, Steane, Stomach, Tea, Test, Throw, Trivet, Tureen, Urn, Whitechapel

Potato(es) African, Aloo, Alu, Batata, Chat, Clean, Couch, Datura, Duchesse, Early, Fluke, Hashbrowns, Hog, Hole, Hot, Irish, Jacket, Jersey, Kidney, Kumara, Lyonnaise, Maris piper, Mash, Murphy, Parmentier, Peel-and-eat, Pratie, Praty, Roesti, Rumbledethump(s), Seed, Small, Solanum, Stovies, Sweet, Tatie, Tattie, Teddy, Tuber, Ware, White, Yam

Potential(ly) Action, Capability, Capacity, Chemical, Latent, Making(s), Manqué, Possible, Promise, Resting, Scope, Viable

▷ **Potentially** *may indicate* an anagram

Potter Cue, Dabbity, Dacker, Daidle, Daiker, Daker, Dibble, Dilly-dally, Dodder, Etruscan, Fettle, Fictor, Fiddle, Footer, Footle, Fouter, Gamesmanship, Idle, Mess, Minton, Muck, Niggle, One-upmanship, Plouter, Plowter, Poke, Spode, Thrower, Tiddle, Tink(er), Troke, Truck, Wedgwood

▷ **Potter** *may indicate* a snooker-player

Pottery Agatewear, Bank, Basalt, Bisque, Cameo ware, Celadon, Ceramet, Ceramic, China, Creamware, Crock, Crouch-ware, Dabbity, Delf(t), Earthenware, Encaustic, Etruria(n), Faience, Flatback, Gombroon, Granitewear, Hollowware, Ironstone, Jomon,

Lustreware, Maiolica, Majolica, Ming, Minton, Pebbleware, Raku, Red-figured, Satsuma, Scroddled, Sgraffito, Slab, Slipware, Smalto, Spode, Spongeware, Stoneware, Studio, Sung, Terra sigillata, Ware, Wedgwood®, Wemyss, Whieldon, Whiteware

Pouch(ed) Bag, Brood, Bum-bag, Bursa, Caecum, Cheek, Cisterna, Codpiece, Cyst, Diverticulum, Fanny pack, Gill, Jockstrap, Marsupial, Marsupium, Papoose, Poke, Posing, Purse, Sac, Scrip, Scrotum, Snood, Spleuchan, Sporran

Pouffe Humpty

Pound(er) Ache, As, Bar, Bash, Batter, Beat, Bombard, Bradbury, Bray, Broadpiece, Bruise, Clomp, Contund, Coop, Drub, Embale, Enclosure, Ezra, Fold, Green, Greenie, Greeny, Hammer, Hatter, Imagist, Intern, Iron man, Jail, Jimmy o'goblin, Kiddle, Kidel, Kin, Knevell, L, Lam, Lb, Lock, Mash, Nevel, Nicker, Oncer, One-er, Oner, Pale, Pen, Penfold, Pestle, Pin, Pindar, Pinfold, Pink, Powder, Pulverise, Pun, Quop, Rint, Scots, Smacker, Sov(ereign), Stamp, Sterling, Strum, Throb, Thump, Tower, Troy, Weight

Pour(ing) Affusion, Birl(e), Bucket, Cascade, Circumfuse, Decant, Diffuse, Disgorge, Flood, Flow, Jaw, Jirble, Libate, Rain, Seil, Shed, Sile, Skink, Spew, Stream, Teem, Trill, Turn, Vent, Weep, Well

Poverty Beggary, Dearth, Deprivation, Illth, Indigence, →**LACK**, Necessity, Need, Paucity, Penury, Poortith, Squalor, Tobacco Road, Want

Powder(ed), Powdery Allantoin, Alumina, Baking, Bleaching, Boracic, Calamine, Calomel, Chalk, Chilli, Colcothar, Cosmetic, Culm, Curry, Custard, Cuttlefish, Dentifrice, Dust, Dusting, Eupad, Explosive, Face, Flea, Floury, Fly, Fulminating, Giant, Gregory, Grind, Gun, Hair, Insect, Itching, Kohl, Litmus, Magnesia, Meal, Mepacrine, Mould-facing, Pearl, Percussion, Persian, Plaster of Paris, Plate, Polishing, Pollen, Pounce, Priming, Prismatic, Projecting, Pulver, Putty, Rachel, Rochelle, Rouge, Seidlitz, Sherbet, Sitosterol, Smokeless, Snuff, Soap, Talc(um), Talcose, Toner, Tooth, Tutty, Washing, Zedoary

Power(ful), Powers Ability, Able, Air, Almighty, Alpha, Arm, Arnold, Athletic, Atomic, Attorney, Audrey, Authority, Axis, Beef, Big, Capability, Cham, Charisma, Clairvoyance, Clout, Cogency, Colossus, Command, Corridor, Cube, Danger, Despotic, Diadem, Dominion, Effective, Electricity, Eminence, Éminence grise, Empathy, Energy, Eon, Exponent, Facility, Faculty, Fire, Flower, Force, Gaddi, Gas, Geothermal, Grey, Grip, Gutty, Hands, Hefty, Herculean, High, Horse, Hot, Hp, Hydroelectric, Influence, Kick, Kilowatt, Leccy, Log, Logarithm, Mandate, Mastery, Might, Mogul, Motive, Motor, Muscle, Natural, Nature, Nth, Nuclear, Od-force, Oligarch, Omnificent, Omnipotent, Option, P, Panjandrum, People, Pester, Plenary, Posse, Potency, Puissant, Punch, Purchasing, Regime, Resolving, Say-so, Sea, Sinew, Solar, Soup, Stamina, Staying, Steam, Steel, Stiff, Stopping, Stranglehold, Strength, →**STRONG**, Supercharge, Supreme, Teeth, Telling, Throne, Tidal, Tycoon, Tyranny, Ulric, Vertu(e), Vigour, Vis, Volt, Vroom, Water, Watt, Wattage, Wave, Weight, Welly, Wheel and axle, Whiphand, Wind, World, Yeast

Practical, Practicable, Practicalities Active, Applied, Brass tacks, Doable, Easy-care, Feasible, Hands on, Hard-boiled, Joker, Logistics, Nitty-gritty, No-nonsense, Nuts and bolts, On, Pragmatic, Realist(ic), Realpolitik, Rule of thumb, Sensible, Shrewd, Technical, Useful, Utilitarian, Viable, Virtual

Practice, Practise, Practitioner, Practised Abuse, Adept, Custom, Distributed, Do, Drill, Dry run, Enure, Exercise, Fire, General, Graft, Group, Habit, Inure, Ism, Keep, Knock-up, Massed, Meme, Mock, Nets, Operate, Order, Ordinance, Pipe opener, Ply, Policy, Praxis, Private, Prosecution, Pursuit, Rehearsal, Rehearse, Restrictive, Rite, Rule, Rut, Sadhana, Sharp, Sighter, Spanish, System, Target, Teaching, Test-run, Trade, Tradition, Train, Trial, Ure, Usage, Use, Wage

Prairie IL, Illinois, Llano, Plain, Savanna, Steppe, Tundra, Veldt

Praise(worthy) Acclaim, Adulation, Alleluia, Allow, Anthem, Applause, Beatify, Belaud, Bepuff, Bless, Blurb, Bouquet, Butter, Carol, Citation, CL, Commend(ation), Compliment, Congratulate, Cry up, Dulia, Ego boost, Encomium, Envy, Eulogise, Eulogium, Eulogy, Exalt, Exemplary, Extol, Gloria, Glory, Herry, Hery(e), Hosanna,

Hype, Incense, Laud, Lip service, Lo(o)s, Meritorious, Palmary, Panegyric, Rap, Rave, Roose, Talk-up, Tout, Tribute

Prance Brank, Canary, Caper, Cavort, Galumph, Gambol, Jaunce, Jaunse, Prank(le), Swagger, Tittup, Trounce

Prank(s) Attrap, Bedeck, Bedizen, Caper, Dido, Escapade, Fredaine, Frolic, Gaud, Jape, Lark, Mischief, Pliskie, Rag, Reak, Reik, Rex, Rig, Spoof, Trick, Vagary, Wedgie

Prattle Babble, Blat(her), Chatter, Gab(nash), Gas, Gibber, Gossip, Gup, Lalage, Patter, Yap

Pray(ing) Appeal, Bed, Beg, Beseech, Bid, Daven, →**ENTREAT**, Impetrate, Intone, Invoke, Kneel, Mantis, Patter, Solicit, Wrestle

▷ **Prayer** *may indicate* one who begs

Prayer(s), Prayer book Acoemeti, Act, Angelus, Ave (Maria), Bead, Beadswoman, Bede, Bene, Bidding, Breviary, Collect, Commination, Common, Cry, Devotion, Eleison, Entreaty, Evensong, Grace, Habdalah, Hail Mary, Intercession, Invocation, Kaddish, Khotbah, Kol Nidre, Kyrie, Kyrie eleison, Lauds, Litany, Lord's, Loulat-ul-qadr, Ma'ariv, Mantis, Mat(t)ins, Missal, Morning, Novena, Opus dei, Orant, Orarium, Orison, Our Father, Paternoster, Patter, Petition, Phylactery, Placebo, Plea, Preces, Requiem, Requiescat, Responses, Rogation, Rosary, Salat, Secret, Shema, State, Suffrage, Terce, Venite, Vesper, Vigils, Yajur-Veda

Preach(er) Ainger, Boanerges, Circuit rider, Dawah, Devil-dodger, Donne, Ecclesiastes, Evangelist, Exhort, Gospeller, Graham, Holy Roller, Itinerant, Kerygma, Knox, Lecture, Local, Mar-text, Minister, Patercove, Postillate, Predicant, Predicate, Predikant, Priest, Prophet, Pulpiteer, Rant, Revivalist, Sermonise, Soper, Spintext, Spurgeon, Teach, Televangelist

Prearrange(d) Book, Stitch up

Pre-Cambrian Torridonian

Precaution Care, Fail-safe, Guard, In case, Prophylaxis, Safeguard, Safety net

Precede(nce), Precedent Antedate, Example, Forego, Forerun, Herald, Pas, Predate, Preface, Prepotent, Priority, Protocol, Zeroth

Precinct(s) Ambit, Area, Banlieue, Close, Courtyard, District, Environs, Pedestrian, Peribolos, Region, Shopping, Temenos, Verge, Vihara

Precious Adored, Chary, Chichi, Costly, Dear, Dearbought, Ewe-lamb, La-di-da, Murr(h)a, Nice, Owre, Precise, Priceless, Prissy, Rare, Valuable

Precipitate, Precipitation, Precipitous, Precipitator Abrupt, Accelerate, Catalyst, Cause, Deposit, Hailstone, Hasty, Headlong, Impetuous, Launch, Lees, Pellmell, Pitchfork, Rash, Sca(u)r, Sheer, Shoot, Sleet, Snowflake, Start, →**STEEP**

Precise(ly), Precisian, Precision Absolute, Accurate, Dry, Exact, Explicit, Fine-drawn, Literal, Minute, Nice(ty), Niminy-piminy, Overnice, Particular, Perfect, Pernickety, Plumb, Point-device, Prig, Prim, Punctilious, Razor, Sharpness, Spang, Specific, Starchy, Stringent, Succinct, Surgical, Tight, Very

Predator(y) Carnivore, Eagle, Fox, Glede, Harpy-eagle, Honey badger, Jackal, Kestrel, Kite, Lycosa, Mantis, Marauder, Predacious, Prey, Puma, Skua, Tanrec, Tarantula, Tenrec, Trapper

Predecessor Ancestor, Forebear, Foregoer

Predetermine(d) Set

Predicament Box, Dilemma, Embroglio, Hobble, Hole, In chancery, Jam, Pass, Peril, Pickle, Plight, Quandary, Scrape, Spot

Predict(ion), Predictable, Predictor Astrologer, Augur, Belomancy, Bet, Damn, Divination, Doomsayer, Doomster, Doomwatch, Ex ante, Far-seeing, Forecast, Foreordain, Foreread, Foresay, Foresee, Foreshadow, Foreshow, Forespeak, Foretell, Formulaic, Forsay, Futurist, Geomancy, Horoscope, Jeremiah, Nap, Necromancy, Portend, Presage, Previse, Prognosis, Project, Prophecy, Prophesy, Quant, Regular, Second-guess, Soothsayer, Spae

Pre-eminence, Pre-eminent Arch, Foremost, Palm(ary), Paramount, Primacy, Supreme, Topnotch, Unique

Preface Avant-propos, Foreword, Herald, Intro, Preamble, Precede, Proem, Prolegomenon, Prolepsis, Usher

Prefer(ence), Preferred Advance, Better, Choose, Discriminate, Druthers, Elect, Faard, Faurd, Favour, Imperial, Incline, Lean, Liquidity, Predilect(ion), Prefard, Priority, Proclivity, Promote, Rather, Select, Sooner, Stocks, Taste, Will

Pregnancy, Pregnant Big, Clucky, Cyesis, Due (to), Ectopic, Enceinte, Extrauterine, Fertile, F(o)etation, Gestation, Gravid(a), Great, Great-bellied, Heavy, Hysterical, In foal, In pig, In pup, Knocked-up, Molar, Pseudocyesis, Retirement, Teem, Up the duff, Up the pole, Up the spout, Up the stick

Prehistoric Ancient, Azilian, Beaker Folk, Boskop, Brontosaurus, Cambrian, Clovis, Cro-Magnon, Eocene, Folsom, Primeval, Primitive, Pteranodon, Pterodactyl(e), Pterosaur, Saurian, Sinanthropus, Titanis, Titanosaurus, Trilith(on)

Prejudice(d) Ageism, Bias, Derry, Discrimination, Down, Illiberal, Impede, Inequity, Injure, Insular, Intolerance, Partiality, Parti pris, Preoccupy, Prepossession, Racism, Sexism, Slant, Unfair

Preliminary Curtain-raiser, Draft, Exploration, Heat, Initial, Introductory, Precursory, Preparatory, Previous, Prodrome, Proem, Prolusion, Propaedeutic, Rough, Title-sheet

Prelude Entrée, Forerunner, Intrada, Overture, Proem(ial), Ritornell(e), Ritornello, Verset

Premature Early, Precocious, Pre(e)mie, Premy, Pre term, Previous, Slink, Untimely, Untimeous

Premier Chief, Leader, Main, PM, →**PRIME MINISTER**, Tojo, Top (drawer)

Premise(s) Assumption, Datum, Epicheirema, Ground, Hypothesis, Inference, Lemma, Licensed, Major, Postulate, Property, Proposition, Reason, Syllogism, Unlicensed

Premium Ap, Bond, Bonus, Discount, Grassum, Pm, Reward, Scarce, Share

Preoccupation, Preoccupied, Preoccupy Absorb, Abstracted, Distrait, Engross, Hang-up, Intent, Obsess, Self-centred, Thing

Prepare(d), Preparation Address, À la, Arrange, Attire, Boun, Bowne, Brilliantine, Busk, Calver, Cock, Concoct, Cook, Cooper, Countdown, Decoct, Did, Do, Dress, Edit, Extract, Forearm, Game, Gear (up), Groom, Ground, Groundwork, Inspan, Key, Lay (out), Legwork, Lotion, Measure, Mobilise, Organise, Parasceve, Paste up, Pomade, Preliminary, Prime, Procinct, Prothesis, Provide, Psych, →**READY**, Redact, Rehearsal, Ripe, Set, Spadework, Stand-to, Suborn, Train, Trim, Truss, Type, Up to, Warm-up, Yare

▷ **Prepare(d)** *may indicate* an anagram

Preposterous Absurd, Chimeric, Foolish, Grotesque, Rich, Tall order, Unreasonable

▷ **Preposterous** *may indicate* a word reversed

Prerequisite Condition, Essential, Necessity, Sine qua non

Presbyter(ian) Berean, Blue, Cameronian, Classic, Classis, Covenanter, Elder, Knox, Macmillanite, Moderator, Sacrarium, Seceder, Secesher, Secession Church, Wee Free, Whig(gamore)

Prescribe, Prescription Appoint, Assign, Dictate, Enjoin, Impose, Negative, Ordain, Positive, Rule, Scrip, Set

Prescription Cipher, Decree, Direction, Formula, Medicine, Placebo, R, Rec, Receipt, Ritual, Specific

Presence Aspect, Bearing, Closeness, Company, Debut, Face, Hereness, Mien, Shechinah, Shekinah, Spirit

Present(ation), Presented, Presenter, Presently Advowson, Anchorman, Anon, Assists, Award, Befaba, Bestow, Bonsela, Boon, Bounty, Box, By and by, Cadeau, Congiary, Coram, Current, Debut, Dee-jay, Demo, Deodate, DJ, Donate, Dotal, Douceur, Dower, Endew, Endow, Endue, Enow, Étrenne, Exhibit, Existent, Exposition, Fairing, Feature, Format, Free-loader, Front-man, Gie, →**GIFT**, Give, Going, Grant, Gratuity, Hand, Here, Historical, Hodiernal, Host, Immediate, Inbuilt, Inst, Introduce, Jock(ey), Largess(e), Linkman, MC, Mod, Nonce, Now, Nuzzer, Offering, Porrect, Potlach, Pr, Produce, Proffer, Pro-tem, Put, Render, Serve-up,

Show, Slice, Stage, Study, Submit, The now, There, Tip, Today, Trojan horse, Vee-jay, Window dressing, Xenium, Yeven

Preserve(d), Preservative, Preserver Bottle, Burnettize, Can, Chill, Chow-chow, Cocoon, Confect, Corn, Creosote, Cure, Dehydrate, Dry, Eisel, Embalm, Enshield, Enshrine, Fixative, Formaldehyde, Formalin, Freeze, Guard, Hain, Hesperides, Index link, Jam, Jerk, Keep, Kinin, Kipper, Konfyt, Kyanise, Lay up, Lifebelt, →**MAINTAIN**, Marmalade, Mothball, Mummify, On ice, Paraben, Pectin, Peculiar, Piccalilli, Pickle, Pot, Powellise, Quince, Quinoline, Salt(petre), Salve, Saut, Season, Souse, Store, Stuff, Tanalized, Tar, Tin, Vinegar, Waterglass

Preshrunk Sanforized®

Preside(nt) Abe, Adams, Arthur, Ataturk, Banda, Botha, Buchanan, Bush, Carter, Chair, Chief Barker, Childers, Chirac, Cleveland, Clinton, Coolidge, Coty, Dean, Director, Eisenhower, Fillmore, Ford, Garfield, Grand Pensionary, Grant, Harding, Harrison, Hayes, Hoover, Ike, Jackson, Jefferson, Kennedy, Kruger, Lead, Lincoln, Madison, Mitterand, Moderator, Monroe, Mugabe, Nixon, P, Peron, Polk, Pr(a)eses, Prexy, Reagan, Roosevelt, Sa(a)dat, Speaker, Superintendent, Supervisor, Taft, Taylor, Tito, Truman, Tyler, Van Buren, Vasquez, Veep, Washington

Press(ed), Pressing, Pressure Acute, Atmospheric, Bar, Bench, Blackmail, Blood, Cabinet, Chivvy, Cider, Click, Closet, Clothes, Coerce, Compact, Compression, Copying, Cram, Crease, Crimp, Critical, Crowd, Crush, Cupboard, Cylinder, Dragoon, Drill, Dun, Durable, Duresse, Enforcement, Enslave, Exigent, Filter, Flat-bed, Fleet St, Fluid, Fly, Folding, Force, Fourth estate, Full-court, Goad, Gutter, Hasten, Head, Heat, Herd, Hie, High, Hug, Hurry, Hustle, Hydraulic, Hydrostatic, Impact, Important, Importune, Inarm, Intense, Iron, Jam, Jostle, Knead, Leverage, Lie, Lobby, Low, Mangle, Mill, Minerva, Newspapers, Obligate, Oil, Onus, PA, Partial, Pascal, Peer, Permanent, Persist, Ply, Printing, Private, Pump, →**PUSH**, Racket, Ram, Ratpack, Record, Recruit, Reportage, Reporter, Roll, Root, Rotary, Rub, Rush, Sandwich, Screw, Scrum, Serr(e), Sit, Speed, Spur, Squash, Squeeze, Stanhope, Static, Stop, Strain(t), Stress, Tension, Three-line-whip, Throng, Throttle, Thrutch, Tourniquet, Turgor, →**URGE**, Urgence, Urgency, Vanity, Vapour, Vice, Wardrobe, Weight, Wine, Wring, Yellow

Prestige, Prestigious Asma, Cachet, Credit, Distinguished, Fame, Influence, Izzat, Kudos, Mana, Notable, Status

Presume, Presumably, Presumption, Presumptuous Allege, Arrogant, Audacity, Believe, Bold, Brass, Cocksure, Cocky, Doubtless, →**EXPECT**, Familiar, Forward, Gall, Impertinent, Insolent, Liberty, Outrecuidance, Overweening, Pert, Probably, Put upon, Suppose, Uppish, Upstart, Whipper-snapper

Pretence, Pretend(er), Pretext Act, Affect(ation), Afflict, Assume, Blind, Bluff, Charade, Charlatan, Claim, Cover, Cram, Dauber(y), Dissemble, Dissimulate, Dive, Excuse, Feign, Feint, Gondolier, Guise, Hokum, Humbug, Hypocrisy, Impersonation, Impostor, Jactitation, Lambert Simnel, Let-on, Make-believe, Malinger, Masquerade, Obreption, Old, Parolles, Perkin Warbeck, Plea, Pose, Pretension, Profess, Pseud(o), Quack, Sham, Simulate, Stale, Stalking-horse, Subterfuge, Suppose, Swanking, Warbeck, Would-be, Young

Pretentious(ness), Pretension Arty, Bombast, Fantoosh, Fustian, Gaudy, Grandiose, High-falutin(g), Kitsch, La-di-da, Orotund, Ostentatious, Overblown, Paraf(f)le, Pompous, Ponc(e)y, Pseud(o), Sciolism, Showy, Snob, Snobbish, Squirt, Tat, Tinhorn, Uppity, Upstart, Vulgar

Pretty Attractive, Becoming, Bobby-dazzler, Chocolate-box, Comely, Cute, Dear, Decorate, Dish, Elegant, Fair(ish), Fairway, Inconie, Incony, Keepsaky, Looker, Moderately, Pass, Peach, Personable, Picturesque, Primp, Pulchritudinous, Purty, Quite, Sweet, Twee, Winsome

Prevail(ing) Dominate, Endure, Go, Induce, Outweigh, Persist, Persuade, Predominant, Preponderate, Reign, Ring, Triumph, Victor, Win

Prevalent Catholic, Common, Dominant, Endemic, Epidemic, Obtaining, Rife, Set in, Widespread

Prevent(ion), Prevent(at)ive Avert, Bar, Block, Daidzein, Debar, Deter, Disallow,

Dissuade, Embar, Estop, Foreclose, Forfend, Hamper, Help, Hinder, Hold back, Impound, Inhibit, Keep, Let, Nobble, Obstruct, Obturation, Obviate, Preclude, Prophylactic, Save, Sideline, Stop, Theriac, Thwart, Trammel

Previous(ly) Afore, Already, Before, Earlier, Ere(-now), Fore, Former, Hitherto, Once, Prior, Whilom

Prey Booty, Currie, Curry, Feed, Kill, Pelt, Plunder, Predate, Proul, Prowl, Quarry, Raven, Ravin(e), Soyle, Spreagh, Victim

Price(d), Pricing, Price-raising Appraise, Asking, Assess, Bride, Charge, Consequence, Contango, →**COST**, Cost-plus, Dearth, Due, Evens, Exercise, Expense, Factory-gate, Fee, Fiars, Hammer, Hire, Intervention, Issue, Limit, List, Lobola, Loco, Market, Mark up, Offer, Packet, Perverse, Predatory, Prestige, Quotation, Quote, Rack, Ransom, Rate, Regrate, Reserve, Sale, Selling, Shadow, Song, Spot, Starting, Street value, Striking, Subscription, Toll, Trade, Unit, Upset, Valorise, Value, Vincent, Weregild, Wergeld, Wergild, Worth, Yardage

Priceless Comic, Invaluable, Killing, Unique

Prick(ed), Prickle, Prickly Acanaceous, Acanthus, Accloy, Argemone, Arrect, Bearded, Brakier, Bramble, Brog, Bunya, Cactus, Cloy, Cnicus, Echinate, Goad, Gore, Gorse, Hedgehog, Hedgepig, Impel, Inject, Jab, Jag, Jaggy, Jook, Juk, Kali, Penis, Pierce, Prod, Prog, Puncture, Rubus, Ruellia, Seta, Setose, Smart, Spinate, Stab, Star-thistle, Stimulus, Sting, Tattoo, Tatu, Teasel, Thistle, Thorn, Tingle, Urge

Pride Bombast, Brag, Conceit, Elation, Esprit de corps, Glory, Hauteur, Hubris, Inordinate, Lions, London, Machismo, Plume, Preen, Purge, Triumphalism, Vainglory, Vanity

Priest(ess), Priests Abbot, Becket, Brahmin, Caiaphas, Cardinal, Celebrant, Clergyman, Cleric, Curé, Dalai Lama, Druid, Exorcist, Father, Flamen, High, H(o)ungan, John, Kohen, Lama, Lazarist, Mage, Mallet, Mass, Mess, Metropolitan, Minister, Missionary, Monsignor, Ordinand, P, Padre, Parish, Parson, Pastor, Père, Pontiff, Pope, Pope's knight, Preacher, Prelate, Presbyter, Prior(ess), Pujari, Pythoness, Rabbi, Rector, Rev, Salian, Seminarian, Sir John Lack-Latin, Sky pilot, Spoiled, Turbulent, Vicar, Zymite

Primacy, Primate Angwantibo, Ape, Australopithecus, Aye-aye, Bandar, Bigfoot, Biped, Bishop, Bush baby, Cardinal, Catar(r)hine, Colobus, Ebor, Gibbon, Hanuman, Hominid, Jackanapes, King Kong, Lemur, Loris, Macaque, Magot, Mammal, Marmoset, →**MONKEY**, Orang, Pongid, Potto, Prosimian, Quadruman, Ramapithecus, Rhesus, Sifaka, Slender loris, Wanderoo, Zinjanthropus

Prime(r), Primary, Priming Arm, Basic, Bloom, Cardinal, Charging, Chief, Choice, Claircolle, Clearcole, Clerecole, Closed, Detonator, Direct, Donat, Donet, Election, Enarm, Fang, First, Flower, Heyday, Mature, Open, Original, Paint, Paramount, Peak, Radical, Remex, Sell-by-date, Supreme, Thirteen, Tip-top, Totient, Totitive, Valuable, Windac, Windas, Ylem

Prime Minister Aberdeen, Asquith, Attlee, Baldwin, Balfour, Begin, Bute, Callaghan, Canning, Chamberlain, Chatham, Dewan, Diefenbaker, Disraeli, Diwan, Eden, Gladstone, Grafton, Grand Vizier, Grey, Home, Iron Duke, Leaderene, Liverpool, Lloyd George, Macdonald, Macmillan, Major, North, Number Ten, Palmerston, Peel, Perceval, Pitt, PM, Premier, Shastri, Tanaiste, Taoiseach, Thatcher, Trudeau, Walpole, Wilson, Winston

Primitive Aborigine, Amoeba, Antediluvian, Arabic, Archaic, Atavistic, Barbaric, Caveman, Crude, Early, Eozoon, Evolué, Fundamental, Hunter-gatherer, Medi(a)eval, Naive, Neanderthal, Neolithic, Oidia, Old, Persian, Prim(a)eval, Primordial, Pro, Prothyl(e), Protomorphic, Protyl(e), Radical, Rudimentary, Savage, Subman, Turkish, Uncivilised, Ur

Prince(ly) Albert, Amir, Arjuna, Black, Caliph, Charming, Crown, Donalbain, Elector, Emir, Florizel, Fortinbras, Ganymede, Gospodar, Hamlet, Highness, Igor, Jason, Ksar, Maharaja, Merchant, Noble, Orange, Pantagruel, Paris, Pirithous, Potentate, Rajah, Regal, Rudolph, Serene, Sherif, Student, Tereus

Princess Anastasia, Begum, Di(ana), Grace, Helle, Infanta, Isabella, Medea, Palatine, Philomela, Rani, Sadie, Sara(h), Yseult

Principal Arch, Capital, Central, →CHIEF, Decuman, Especial, First, Foremost, Grand, Head, Headmaster, Leading, Lion's share, Main(stay), Major, Mass, Mistress, Protagonist, Ringleader, Special, Staple, Star, Top banana

Principle(s), Principled Accelerator, Animistic, Anthropic, Archimedes, Aufbau, Axiom, Basis, Bernouilli, Brocard, Canon, Carnot, Code, Contradiction, Correspondence, Cosmological, Criterion, Cui bono, Cy pres, Doctrine, Dogma, Element, Equivalence, Essential, Estoppel, Exclusion, First, Fourier, Geist, Generale, Germ, Greatest happiness, Ground rule, Guideline, Hard line, Heisenberg uncertainty, Honourable, Ideal, Indeterminacy, Key, Law, Least time, Lights, Logos, Methodology, Modus, Object soul, Occam's razor, Organon, Peter, Plank, Platform, Pleasure, Precautionary, Precept, Prescript, Psyche, Purseyism, Rationale, Reality, Reason, Reciprocity, Relativity, Remonstrance, Right-thinking, Rudiment, Rule, Sanction, Scrupulous, Spirit, Tenet, Theorem, Ticket, Uncertainty, Uti possidetis, Verification, Vital, Weismannism, Word, Yang, Yin

Print(er), Printing A la poupée, Baskerville, Batik, Calotype, Caxton, Chain, Chapel, Chromo, Cicero, Collotype, Compositor, Contact, Copperplate, Counter, Creed, Cyclostyle, Dab, Dot matrix, Duotone, Electrostatic, Electrothermal, Electrotint, Electrotype, Elzevir, Engrave, Etching, Ferrotype, Film set, Fine, Font, Gravure, Half-tone, Hard copy, Hectograph, Heliotype, HMSO, Image, Impact, Impress, India, Ink-jet, Intaglio, Italic, Jobbing, Laser, Letterpress, Letterset, Line, Line-engraving, Lino-cut, Lithograph, Logotype, Lower-case, Matrix, Metallographer, Mezzotint, Mimeograph®, Monotype®, Moon, Non-impact, Off-line, Offset, Offset litho, Old-face, Oleo, Oleograph, Opaline, Perfector, Perfect proof, Phototype, Plate, Platinotype, Positive, Press, Process, Publish, Release, Remarque, Report, Reproduction, Retroussage, Reverse, Rotogravure, Screen, Ship, Shout, Silk-screen, Small, Splash, Spore, Stamp, Stereotype, Stonehand, Strike, Thermal, Three-colour, Thumb, Thumb mark, Trichromatic, Typesetter, Typewriter, Typography, Typothetae, Whorl, Woodburytype, Woodcut, Xylograph

Print out Hard copy

Prior(ity) Abbot, Afore, Antecedent, Earlier, Former, Grand, Hitherto, Monk, Overslaugh, Pre-, Precedence, Prefard, Preference, Previous, Privilege, Triage, Until

Prison Alcatraz, Bastille, Belmarsh, Big house, Bin, Bird, Boob, Bridewell, Brig, Brixton, Bullpen, Cage, Can, Carceral, Cell, Chok(e)y, Clink, Club, College, Confine, Cooler, Coop, Counter, Dartmoor, Dispersal, Dungeon, Durance, Encage, Fleet, Fotheringhay, Gaol, Glass-house, Gulag, Hokey, Holloway, Hulk(s), Internment, →JAIL, Jug, Kitty, Labour camp, Limbo, Little-ease, Lock-up, Marshalsea, Mattamore, Maze, Newgate, Nick, Oflag, On ice, Open, Parkhurst, Pen, Penitentiary, Pentonville, Pit, Pok(e)y, Porridge, Pound, Princetown, Quad, Quod, Reformatory, Roundhouse, Scrubs, Shop, Sing-Sing, Slammer, Spandau, Stalag, State, Stir, Strangeways, Supermax, Tol(l)booth, Tower, Wandsworth, Wormwood Scrubs

Prisoner Canary-bird, Captive, Collegian, Collegiate, Con(vict), Detainee, Detenu, Inmate, Internee, Lag, Lifer, Parolee, Passman, Political, POW, Rule 43, Trustee, Trusty, Yardbird, Zek

Private(ly) Ain, Apart, Aside, Atkins, Auricular, Buccaneer, Byroom, Clandestine, Close, Closet, Confidential, Enisle(d), Esoteric, Homefelt, Hush-hush, In camera, Individual, Inmost, Inner, Intimate, Inward, Non-com, Non-governmental, Own, Personal, Piou-piou, Poilu, Postern, Proprietary, Pte, Rank(er), Retired, Sanctum, Sapper, Secluded, Secret, Sequestered, Several, Single soldier, →SOLDIER, Sub rosa, Tommy, Under the rose

Privilege(d) Birthright, Blest, Charter, Curule, Enviable, Exempt, Favour, Franchise, Freedom, Indulgence, Liberty, Mozarab, Nomenklatura, Octroi, Palatine, Patent, Prerogative, Pryse, Regale, Regalia, Right, Sac, Sloane

Privy Apprised, Can, Closet, In on, Intimate, Jakes, John, Loo, Necessary, Reredorter, Secret, Sedge, Siege

Prize(s), Prizewinner, Prized Acquest, Apple, Archibald, Assess, Award, Best, Booby, Booker, Bravie, Bronze, Capture, Champion, Cherish, Consolation, Creach,

Cup, Dux, Efforce, →ESTEEM, Force, Garland, Gold, Goncourt, Grice, Honour, Jackpot, Jemmy, Lever, Lot, Man Booker, Money, Nobel, Palm, Pearl, Pewter, Pie, Plum, Plunder, Pot, Premium, Prix Goncourt, Pulitzer, Purse, Ram, Reprisal, →REWARD, Rollover, Rosette, Scalp, Ship, Silver, Spreaghery, Sprechery, Stakes, Sweepstake, Tern, Treasure, Trophy, Turner, Value, Win, Wooden spoon

Pro Aye, Coach, For, Harlot, Moll, Paid, Tramp, Yea, Yes

▶ **Pro** *see* PROSTITUTE

Probable, Probability Apparent, Belike, Classical, Ergodic, Feasible, Likely, Possible, Prior, Proball

Probe Antenna, Bore, Cassini, Delve, Dredge, Explore, Fathom, Feeler, Fossick, Gene(tic), Inquire, Investigate, Pelican, Poke, Pump, Ranger, →SEARCH, Seeker, Sound, Space, Stylet, Tent, Thrust, Tracer

Problem(s), Problematic Acrostic, Boyg, Brainteaser, Business, Can of worms, Catch, Crux, Difficulty, Dilemma, Egma, Enigma, Facer, Glitch, Handful, Hang-up, Headache, Hiccup, Hitch, How d'ye do, Hurdle, Indaba, Issue, Knot(ty), Koan, Mind-body, Miniature, Musive, Net, Nuisance, Obstacle, Pons asinorum, Poser, Predicament, Quandary, Question, Re, Rebus, Retractor, Riddle, Rider, Snag, Sorites, Sum, Teaser, Teething, Thing, Thorny, Tickler, Toughie, Trilemma, Tsuris, Weed, Yips

Proceed(s), Proceeding, Procedure Acta, Afoot, Algorithm, Assets, Continue, Course, Derive, Drill, Emanate, Fand, Flow, Fond, Goes, Haul, Issue, Machinery, March, Mechanics, Mine, MO, Modal, Move, On (course), Paracentesis, Pass, Point of order, Practice, Praxis, Process, Profit, Punctilio, Pursue, Put, Rake, Return, Rigmarole, Rite, Routine, Sap, Steps, Subroutine, System, Take, Tootle, Use, Yead(s), Yede, Yeed

Process(ing), Procession, Processor Acromion, Action, Ala, Ambarvalia, Anger, Axon, Ben Day, Bessemer, Calcination, Catalysis, Cibation, Coction, Concoction, Congelation, Conjunction, Corso, Cortège, Demo, Dissolution, Double, Exaltation, Fermentation, Frack(ing), Haber(-Bosch), Handle, Markov, Method, Moharram, Mond, Motorcade, Muharram, Multiple pounding, Multiplication, Open hearth, Pageant, Parade, Paseo, Photosynthesis, Pipeline, Pomp, Projection, Pterygoid, Puddling, Pultrusion, Purex, Putrefaction, Recycle, Ritual, Separation, Series, Single, Skimmington, Solvay, Speciation, Spinous, String, Sublimation, Tie and dye, Train, Transaction, Transverse, Treat, Trial, Vermiform

Proclaim, Proclamation Announce, Annunciate, Ban, Blaze, Blazon, Boast, Broadsheet, Cry, Edict, Enounce, Enunciate, Herald, Indiction, Kerygma, Oyez, Preconise, Profess, Publish, Ring, Shout, Trumpet, Ukase

Proconsul Ape, Hominid

Prodigious, Prodigy Abnormal, Amazing, Huge, Immense, Monster, Monument, Mozart, Phenomenal, Portentous, Tremendous, Wonder, Wonderwork, Wunderkind

Produce(r), Producing Afford, Bear, Beget, Breed, Cause, Create, Crop, Disney, D'oyly Carte, Dramaturg, Ean, Edit, Effect, Engender, Evoke, Exhibit, Extend, Fabricate, Fruit, Generate, Get, Giulini, Goldwyn, Grow, Impresario, Ingenerate, Issue, Kind, Make, Offspring, Onstream, Originate, Output, Propage, Propound, Puttnam, Raise, Roach, Selznick, Sloganeer, Son, Spielberg, Stage, Supply, Teem, Throw, Tree, Trot out, Upcome, Wares, Whelp, Yield, Ziegfeld

▷ **Produces** *may indicate* an anagram

Product(ion), Productive(ness), Productivity Actualities, Apport, Artefact, Ashtareth, Ashtaroth, Astarte, Autogeny, Bore, Cartesian, Coefficient, Commodity, Cross, Depside, Dot, Drama, Effectual, End, Factorial, Fecund, Fertile, Fruit, Genesis, Global, Handiwork, Harvest, Inner, Line, Net domestic, Net national, Output, Outturn, Pair, Partial, Power(house), Primary, Profilic, Result, Rich, Scalar, Secondary, Set, Show, Speiss, Substitution, Uberous, Uberty, Vector, Waste, Work, Yield

▷ **Production** *may indicate* an anagram

Profane, Profanation, Profanity Blaspheming, Coarse, Coprolalia, Desecrate, Impious, Irreverent, Sacrilege, Unholy, Violate

Profess(ed), Professor Absent-minded, Academic, Adjoint, Admit, Artist,

Aspro, Asset, Assistant, Associate, Challenger, Claim, Declare, Disney, Emeritus, Full, Higgins, Hodja, Kho(d)ja, Know-all, Ostensible, Own, Practise, Pundit, Regent, Regius, RP, STP

Profession(al) Admission, Assurance, Avowal, Buppy, Business, Career, Creed, Expert, Métier, Practice, Practitioner, Pretence, Pursuit, Regular, Salaried, Skilled, Trade, Vocation, Yuppie

Proficiency, Proficient Adept, Alert, Dan, Expert, Forte, Past master, Practised, Skill, Technique

Profile Analysis, Contour, Half-cheek, Half-face, High, Loral, Market, Outline, Silhouette, Sketch, Statant, T(h)alweg, Vignette

Profit(able), Profiteer, Profits Advantage, Arbitrage, Asset, Avail, Benefit, Bestead, Boon, Boot, Bunce, Cash cow, Cere, Clear, Divi(dend), Earn, Economic, Edge, Emblements, Emoluments, Exploit, Extortionist, Fat, Gain, Gelt, Graft, Gravy, Grist, Gross, Income, Increase, Increment, Issue, Jobbery, Juicy, Landshark, Leech, Lucrative, Makings, Margin, Melon, Mesne, Milch cow, Mileage, Moneymaker, Negative, Net, Overcharge, Pay(ing), Perk, Pickings, Preacquisition, Productive, Quids in, Rake-off, Return, Reward, Royalty, Scalp, Spoils, Tout, Use, Usufruct, Utile, Utility, Vail

Profuse, Profusion Abounding, Abundant, Copious, Excess, Free, Galore, Lavish, Liberal, Lush, Quantity, Rank, Rich, Two-a-penny

▶**Program(ming), Programming language, Programmer** *see* **COMPUTER PROGRAMS**

Programme(s) Agenda, Broadcast, Card, Chat show, Code, Community, Corrida, Countdown, Docudrama, Documentary, Docusoap, Docutainment, Double-header, Dramedy, Entitlement, Est, Event, Faction, Feature, Fly-on-the-wall, Format, Infotainment, Linear, Medicaid, Mockumentary, Neurolinguistic, Newscast, Newsreel, PDL, Phone-in, Pilot, Plan, Playbill, Prank, Race card, Radiothon, RECHAR, Regimen, Report, Schedule, Scheme, Sepmag, Serial, Shockumentary, Show, Simulcast, Sitcom, Sked, Soap, Software, Sportscast, Sustaining, Syllabus, System, Telecast, Teleplay, Telethon, Timetable, Twelve step, Webcast, YPO

Progress(ive), Progression →**ADVANCE**, Afoot, Arithmetic, Arpeggio, Avant garde, Course, Endosmometric, Fabian, Flow, Forge, Forward, Gain, Geometric, Get along, Go (ahead), Growth, Headway, Incede, Knight's, Left, Liberal, Move, Onwards, Paraphonia, Periegesis, Pilgrim's, Prosper, Rack, Radical, Rake's, Reformer, Roll, Run, Sequence, Series, Step, Stepping stone, Vaunce, Way, Yead, Yede, Yeed

Prohibit(ed), Prohibition(ist) Ban, Block, Debar, Dry, Embargo, Enjoin, Estop, Forbid, Hinder, Index, Injunct, Interdict, Noli-me-tangere, Off-limits, Prevent, Pussyfoot, Rahui, Suppress, Taboo, Tabu, Verboten, Veto

Project(ile), Projecting, Projection, Projector Aim, Ammo, Antitragus, Assignment, Astral, Astrut, Axonometric, Azimuthal, Ball, Ballistic, Beetle, Bullet, Butt, Buttress, Cam, Canopy, Carina, Cast, Catapult, Channel, Cinerama®, Cog, Conceive, Conical, Console, Cremaster, Dendron, Discus, Ear, Eaves, Enterprise, Episcope, Excrescence, Exsert, Extrapolate, Extrude, Fet(ter)lock, Flange, Gore, Guess, Halter(e), Hangover, Helicity, Hoe, Homolosine, Housing, Human genome, Hurtle, Inion, Jut, Kern, Kinetoscope, Knob, Ledge, Lobe, Lug, Magic lantern, Map, Mohole, Mucro, Nab, Nose, Oblique, Opaque, Orthogonal, Orthographic, Outcrop, Outjet, Outjut, Outrigger, Outshot, Overhang, Overhead, Oversail, Palmation, Peak, Peters', Pitch, Planetarium, Planisphere, Prickle, Promontory, Proud(er), Prow, Pseudopod, Quillon, Roach, Rocket, Sail, Salient, Sally, Sanson-Flamsteed, Scheme, Scrag, Screen, Shelf, Shot, Shrapnel, Sinusoidal, Skeg, Slide, Snag, Snout, Spur, Stand out, Stick out, Stud, Tang, Tappet, Tenon, Throw, Toe, Tongue, Tracer, Trimetric, Trippet, Turnkey, Turtleback, Tusk, Umbo, Underhung, Undertaking, Villiform, Whizzbang, Zenithal

Prolong(ed) Continue, Drag out, Extend, Lengthen, Protract, Sostenuto, Spin, Sustain

Prom(enade) Alameda, Boulevard, Cakewalk, Catwalk, Crush-room, Esplanade, Front, Mall, Parade, Paseo, Pier, Sea-front, Stroll, →**WALK**

Prominence, Prominent Antitragus, Blatant, Bold, Colliculus, Condyle,

Conspicuous, Egregious, Emphasis, Featured, Gonion, High profile, Important, Insistent, Luminary, Manifest, Marked, Mastoid, Obtrusive, Outstanding, Salient, Signal, Solar, Spotlight, Tall poppy, Teat, Toot, Tragus

Promise, Promising Accept, Assure, Augur, Auspicious, Avoure, Behest, Behight, Behote, Bode, Coming, Commit, Compact, Covenant, Earnest, Engagement, Foreshadow, Foretaste, Gratuitous, Guarantee, Hecht, Hest, Hete, Hight, IOU, Likely, Manifest, Oath, Parole, Pledge, Plight, Pollicitation, Potential, Pregnant, Recognisance, Recognizance, Rosy, Sign, Sponsor, Swear, Tile, Troth, Undertake, Upbeat, Vow, Warranty, Word

Promote(r), Promotion Ad, Adman, Advance, Advancement, →**ADVERTISE**, Advocate, Aggrandise, Aid, Assist, Back, Banner ad, Blurb, Boost, Breed, Buggin's turn, Campaign, Churn, Dog and pony show, Elevate, Encourage, Eulogy, Exponent, Foment, Foster, Further, Help, Hype, Incite, Increase, Kick upstairs, Leaflet, Lord of Misrule, Mailshot, Make, Market, Pracharak, Prefer, Prelation, Promulgate, Provoke, Push, Queen, Raise, Rear, Remove, Roadshow, Run, Salutary, Sell, Sponsor, Spruik, Stage, Step (up), Subserve, Tendencious, Tendentious, Tout, Upgrade, Uplead, Uprate

Prompt(er), Promptly, Promptness Actuate, Alacrity, Autocue®, Believe, Cause, Celerity, Chop-chop, Cue, Early, Egg, Expeditious, Feed, Frack, Idiot-board, Immediate, Incite, Inspire, Instigate, Move, Pernicious, Premove, Punctual, Quick, Ready, Sharp, Speed(y), Spur, Stage right, Stimulate, Sudden, Swift, Tight, Tit(e), Titely, Trigger, Tyte, Urgent

Prone Apt, Groof, Grouf, Grovel, Laid back, Liable, Lying, Prostrate, Recumbent, Subject, Susceptible

Pronounce(d), Pronouncement Adjudicate, Affirm, Agrapha, Articulate, Assert, Asseveration, Clear, Conspicuous, Declare, Definite, Dictum, Emphatic, Enunciate, Fatwa, Fiat, Indefinite, Marked, Opinion, Palatalise, Pontificate, Predication, Recite, Utter, Velarise, Vocal, Voice, Vote

Proof(s) Apagoge, Argument, Artist's, Assay, Bona fides, Confirmation, Direct, Evidence, Firm, Foundry, Galley, Godel's, India, Indirect, Justification, Lemma, Positive, Preif(e), Probate, Pull, Quality, Refutation, Remarque, Reproduction, Resistant, Revision, Secure, Slip, Smoking gun, Strength, Test, Tight, Token, Trial, Upmake, Validity

Prop Airscrew, Becket, Bolster, Buttress, Crutch, Dog-shore, Fulcrum, Leg, Loosehead, Misericord(e), Punch(eon), Rance, Rest, Scotch, Shore, Sprag, Spur, Staff, Stay, Stempel, Stemple, Stilt, Stoop, Stoup, Strut, Stull, →**SUPPORT**, Tighthead, Underpin

Propaganda, Propagandist Agitprop, Ballyhoo, Brainwashing, Chevalier, Doctrine, Promotion, Psyop, Psywar, Publicity, Slogan

Propel(ler) Airscrew, Ca', Drive, Fin, Launch, Leg, Lox, →**MOVE**, Oar(sman), Paddle, Pedal, Pole, Project, Push, Rotor, Row, Screw, Send, Tail rotor, Throw, Thruster, Tilt-rotor, Twin-screw, Vane

Proper(ly) Ain, Convenance, Correct, Decent, Decorous, Due, Eigen, En règle, Ethical, →**FIT**, Genteel, Governessy, Kosher, Legitimate, Nimity-pimity, Noun, Ought, Own, Pakka, Pathan, Prim, Pucka, Pukka, Puritanic, Real, Rightful, Seemly, Strait-laced, Suitable, Tao, Trew, True, Veritable, Well

Property, Properties Assets, Attribute, Aver, Belongings, Capacitance, Chattel, Chirality, Chose, Contenement, Dead-hand, Demesne, Des res, Dowry, Effects, Enclave, Enthalpy, Escheat, Escrow, Essence, Estate, Fee, Feu, Flavour, Fonds, Freehold, Goods, Haecceity, Hereditament, Heritable, Holding, Hot, Hotchpot, Immoveable, Inertia, In rem, Intellectual, Jointure, Land, Leasehold, Living, Means, Mortmain, Paraphernalia, Peculium, Personal, Personalty, Pertinent, Predicate, Premises, Private, Projective, Public, Quale, Quality, Real, Stock, Stolen, Theft, Thixotropy, Time-share, Timocracy, Trait, Usucapion, Usucaption

Prophesy, Prophecy, Prophet(s), Prophetess, Prophetic Amos, Augur, Bab, Balaam, Cassandra, Daniel, Deborah, Divine, Elias, Elijah, Elisha, Ezekiel, Ezra, Fatal, Forecast, Foretell, Hosea, Is, Isa, Is(a)iah, Jeremiah, Joel, Jonah, Mahdi, Major, Malachi, Mani, Mantic, Micah, Minor, Mohamet, Mohammed, Mormon, Moses,

Mother Shipton, Nahum, Nathan, Nostradamus, Obadiah, Ominous, Oracle, Portend, Predictor, Prognosticate, Pythoness, Samuel, Second sight, Seer, Sibyl, Zephaniah, Zoroaster

Proportion(ate) Commensurable, Cotangent, Dimension, Harmonic, Portion, Pro rata, Quantity, Quota, Ratio, Reason, Regulate, Relation, Sine, Size, Soum, Sowm, Symmetry, Tenor

Propose(r), Proposal Advance, Aim at, Ask, Bid, Bill, Eirenicon, Feeler, Fiancé, Idea, Irenicon, Mean, Motion, Move, Nominate, Offer, Overture, Plan, Pop, Premise, Proffer, Propound, Recommend, Resolution, Scheme, Slate, Submission, →SUGGEST, Table, Tender, Toast, Volunteer, Woot, Would

Proposition Axiom, Corollary, Deal, Disjunction, Ergo, Hypothesis, Implicature, Lemma, Overture, Pons asinorum, Porism, Premise, Premiss, Rider, Sorites, Spec, Superaltern, Theorem, Thesis

Proprietor, Propriety Bienséance, Convenance, Correctitude, Decorum, Etiquette, Grundy, Keeper, Lord, Master, Owner, Patron, Rectitude

Prose, Prosy Haikai, Polyphonic, Purple patch, Saga, Stich, Verbose, Version, Writing

Prosecute, Prosecutor, Prosecution Allege, Avvogadore, Charge, Crown, Do, Double jeopardy, Fiscal, Furtherance, Impeach, Indict, Lord Advocate, Practise, Public, Pursue, Sue, Wage

Prospect(or), Prospecting Costean, Dowser, Explore, Forty-niner, Fossick, Look-out, Mine, →OUTLOOK, Panorama, Perspective, Pleases, Reefer, Scenery, Search, Sourdough, Street, Sweep-washer, View, Vista, Visto, Wildcatter

Prosper(ity), Prospering, Prosperous Aisha, Ay(e)sha, Blessed, Blossom, Boom, Fair, Fat cat, Flourish, Get ahead, Heyday, Mérimée, Palmy, Sleek, →SUCCEED, Thee, Thrift, Thrive, Up, Warison, Wealth, Welfare, Well-heeled, Well-to-do, Well-to-live

Prosthetic Fals(i)e

Prostitute, Prostitution Brass, Broad, Catamite, Chippie, Cocotte, Comfort woman, Convertite, Debase, Dell, Dolly-mop, Doxy, Drab, Floozie, Floozy, Grande cocotte, Harlot, Hetaera, Hetaira, Hustler, Jailbait, Laced mutton, Lady of the night, Loon, Loose woman, Lowne, Madam, Magdalen(e), Moll, Mutton, Pict, Poule, Pro, Public woman, Pug, Rent-boy, Rough trade, Scrubber, Slap, Stale, Stew, Streetwalker, Strumpet, Tart, Tramp, Trull, Whore, Working girl

Protagonist Anti-hero

Protect(ed), Protection, Protector Adonise, Aegis, Aircover, Amulet, Antigropelo(e)s, Arm, Armour, Asylum, Auspice, Barbican, Bastion, Buckler, Bullet-proof, Cathodic, Chaffron, Chain mail, Chamfrain, Chamfron, Charm, Cherish, Cloche, Coat, Cocoon, Conserve, Copyright, Cosset, Cover, Covert, Cromwell, Curb, Cushion, Danegeld, Data, Defend, Defilade, Diaper, Egis, Enamel, Entrenchment, Escort, Fence, Firewall, Flank, Groundsheet, Guard(ian), Gumshield, Hedge, House, Hurter, Immune, Indemnify, Indusium, Insure, Integument, Keep, Kickback, Klendusic, Lee, Listed, Mac(k)intosh, Mail, Male, Mentor, Mollycoddle, Mother, Mothproof, Mouthpiece, Mudguard, Napkin, Nappy, Noddy suit, Noll, Nosey, Oliver, Ombrella, Overall, Palladium, Parados, Parapet, Patent, Patron, Pelta, Penthouse, Police, Polytunnel, Pomander, Preserve, Procrypsis, Rampart, Raymond, Reserve, Revetment, Ride shotgun, Safeguard, Sandbag, Save, Screen, Scug, Security, Shadow, Sheathing, Sheeting, Shelter, →SHIELD, Skug, Souteneur, Splashback, Splashboard, Splasher, Starling, Sunscreen, Supermax, Talisman, Telomere, Testa, Thimble, Thumbstall, Tribute, Tutelar, Twilled, Umbrella, Underlay, Underseal, Vaccine, Waist-cloth, Ward(ship), Weatherboard, Weatherstrip, Windbreaker, Windshield, Winterweight, Write

Protectorate Qatar

Protein Complement, Conjugated, Repressor, Simple

Protest(er) Abhor, Aver, Avouch, Boycott, Clamour, Come, Complaint, Démarche, Demo, Demonstrate, Demur, Deprecate, Dhurna, Dissent, Expostulate, Gripe, Hartal, Inveigh, I say, Lock-out, Luddite, March, Object, Outcry, Peenge, Picket, Plea, Rail,

Refus(e)nik, Remonstrate, Representation, Sit-in, Squawk, Squeak, Squeal, Stand, Work-to-rule

Protestant Amish, Anabaptist, Anglo, Arminian, Calvin, Congregationalism, Covenanter, Cranmer, Dissenter, Evangelic, Gospeller, Huguenot, Independent, Lady, Lutheran, Mennonite, Methodist, Moravian, Nonconformist, Oak-boy, Orangeman, Pentecostal, Pietism, Prod(die), Puritan, Reformed, Right-footer, Seventh Day Adventist, Stundist, Swaddler, Waldensian, Wesleyan

Protract(ed) Delay, →EXTEND, Lengthen, Livelong, Long, Prolong

Proud Arrogant, Boaster, Cocky, Conceited, Dic(k)ty, Egotistic, Elated, Flush, Haughty, Haut, Level, Lordly, Orgulous, Superb, Vain

Prove(d), Proving Apod(e)ictic, Argue, Ascertain, Assay, Attest, Attribution, Authenticate, Aver, Confirm, Convince, Establish, Evince, Justify, Probative, →PROOF, →SHOW, Substantiate, Test, Trie, Try

Proverb Adage, Axiom, Byword, Gnome, Maxim, Paroemia, Saw

▷ **Proverbial** *may refer to* the biblical Proverbs

Provide(d), Provident(ial) Afford, Allow, Arrange, Besee, Bring, Cater, Compare, Conditional, Endow, Endue, Equip, Far-seeing, Feed, Fend, Find, Furnish, Generate, Give, Grubstake, If, Lay on, Lend, Maintain, Offer, Plenish, Proviso, Purvey, Quote, Serve, So, Sobeit, →SUPPLY, Suttle

Province, Provincial(ism) Area, Circar, District, Exclave, Land, Nomarchy, Nomos, Regional, Sirkar, Small-town, Suburban, Territory

Provision(s), Provisional Acates, Ap(p)anage, Board, Entrenched, Fodder, Foresight, Insolvency, Jointure, Larder, Lend-lease, Proggins, Scran, Skran, Stock, Stuff, Supply, Suttle, Viands, Viaticum, Victuals

Proviso, Provisional Caution, Caveat, Clause, Condition, Interim, IRA, Makeshift, Nisi, On trial, Reservation, Salvo, Stipulation, Temporary, Tentative

Provocation, Provocative, Provoke Agacant, Aggro, Alluring, Challenge, Egg, Elicit, Erotic, Exacerbate, Excite, Flirty, Gar, Harass, Incense, Induce, Inflame, Instigate, Irk, Irritate, Kindle, Needle, Nettle, Occasion, Pique, Prompt, Raise, Red rag, Sedition, Sound, Spark, Stimulate, Stir, Tar, Tarty, Tease, Urge, Vex, Wind up

Prowl(er) Hunt, Lurch, Lurk, Mooch, Prog, Prole, Ramble, Roam, Rove, Snoke, Snook, Snowk, Tenebrio, Tom

Proxy Agent, Attorn, Deputy, PP, Regent, Sub, Surrogate, Vicar, Vice

Prude(nce), Prudent, Prudery Bluenose, Canny, Caution, Circumspect, Comstocker, Conservative, Discreet, Discretion, Far-sighted, Foresight, Frugal, Grundyism, Metis, Mrs Grundy, Politic, Prig, Prissy, Provident, Sage, Sensible, Sparing, Strait-laced, Strait-lacer, Thrifty, Vice-nelly, Victorian, Ware, Wary, Well-advised, Wise

Prune(r) Bill-hook, Clip, Dehorn, Lop, Plum, Proign, Proin(e), Reduce, Reform, Secateur, Slash, Sned, Snip, Thin, Trim

Pry Ferret, Force, Lever, Meddle, Nose, Paul, Peep, Question, Search, Snoop, Toot

Psalm Anthem, Cantate, Chant, Chorale, Hallel, Hymn, Introit, Jubilate, Metrical, Miserere, Neck-verse, Paean, Proper, Ps, Song, Tone, Tract, Tractus, Venite

Pseudonym Aka, Alias, Allonym, Anonym, Pen-name, Stage-name

Psychiatrist, Psychologist Adler, Alienist, Asperger, Clare, Coué, Ellis, Freud, Headshrinker, Jung, Kraft-Ebing, Laing, Müller-Lyer, Reich, Shrink, Skinner, Trick-cyclist

Psychic, Psychosis Clairvoyant, ESP, Fey, Lodge, Medium, Mind-reader, Seer, Telekinesis

Psychological, Psychology, Psychologist Analytical, Behaviourism, Clinical, Comparative, Constitutional, De Bono, Depth, Development, Dynamic, Educational, Experimental, Eysenck, Gestalt, Hedonics, Humanistic, Industrial, James, Latah, Occupational, Organisational, Piaget, Skinner, Social, Structural, Windt

Psychotherapist, Psychotherapy Coué, Laing, Rebirthing, Shen

Pub Bar, Boozer, Free-house, Gin-palace, Groggery, Houf(f), House, Howf(f), Inn, Joint, Local, Lush-house, Pothouse, Potshop, Shanty, Tavern, Tiddlywink, Tied house

Pubis Sharebone

Public (house) Apert, Bar, Brew, Civil, Common, Demos, Estate, General, Great unwashed, Hostelry, Inn, Janata, Lay, Limelight, National, Open, Out, Overt, PH, Populace, Roadhouse, State, Vulgar, World

Publican Ale-keeper, Bung, Host, Landlord, Licensee, Tapster, Taverner

Publication Announcement, Book, Booklet, Broadsheet, Edition, Exposé, Issue, →**JOURNAL**, Lady, Mag, Magazine, Organ, Pamphlet, Pictorial, Samizdat, Tabloid, Tatler, Tract, Tribune, Yearbook

Publicise, Publicist, Publicity Ad(vert), Airing, Announce, Ballyhoo, Billing, Build up, Coverage, Exposure, Flack, Glare, Headline, Hype, Leakage, Limelight, Notoriety, Plug, PR(O), Promo(te), Promotion, Promulgate, Propaganda, Réclame, Spin-doctor, Splash

Publish(er), Published, Publishing, Publicise Air, Blaze, Cape, Copyleft, Delator, Desktop, Disclose, Edit, Evulgate, Issue, Larousse, Noise, OUP, Out, Pirate, Plug, Post, Print(er), Proclaim, Propagate, Release, Ren, Run, Stationer, Vanity, Vent, Ventilate

Pudding Afters, Black, Blancmange, Bread (and butter), Brown Betty, Cabinet, Charlotte, Christmas, Clootie dumpling, College, Crumble, Custard, →**DESSERT**, Dog's body, Duff, Dumpling, Eve's, Flummery, Fritter, Fromenty, Frumenty, Furme(n)ty, Furmity, Haggis, Hasty, Ice-cream, Lokshen, Milk, Nesselrode, Panada, Pandowdy, Parfait, Pease, Plum, Plum-duff, Pockmanky, Pockmantic, Pock-pudding, Popover, Portmanteau, Queen's, Rice, Roly-poly, Savarin, Sowens, Sponge, Spotted dick, Spotted dog, Stickjaw, Stodge, Suet, Summer, Sundae, Sweet, Tansy, Tapioca, Umbles, White, White hass, White hause, White hawse, Yorkshire, Zabaglione

Pueblo Aldea, Zuni

Puff(ed), Puffer, Puffy Advertise, Blouse, Blow, Blowfish, Blurb, Bouffant, Breath, Chuff, Chug, Cream, Drag, Encomist, Eulogy, Exsufflicate, Fag, Flaff, Flatus, Fluffy, Fuff, Globe-fish, Grampus, Gust, Hype, Lunt, Pech, Pegh, Pluffy, Plug, Powder, Quilt, Recommend, Skiff, Slogan, Smoke, Steam, Swell, Toke, Twilt, Waff, Waft, Waif, Whiff, Whiffle

Pull (up), Pull out Adduce, Attraction, Charm, Crane, Cry off, Demand, Drag, Draw, Force, Haul, Heave, Heeze, Hook, →**INFLUENCE**, Lug, Mousle, Pluck, Pop-top, Rein, Ring, Rove, Rug, Saccade, Sally, Seduce, Sole, Sool(e), Sowl(e), Stop, Tit, Touse, Touze, Tow, Towse, Towze, Traction, Trice, Tug, Undertow, Wrest, Yank

Pulp Cellulose, Chyme, Chymify, Crush, Flong, Kenaf, Marrow, Mash, Mush, Pap, Paste, Pomace, Pound, Puree, Rot, Rubbish, Squeeze, Squidge

Pulpit Ambo(nes), Bully, Lectern, Mimbar, Minbar, Pew, Rostrum, Tent, Tub, Wood

Pulsar Geminga

Pulse Adsuki, Adzuki, Alfalfa, Beat, Calavance, Caravance, Chickpea, Daal, D(h)al, Dholl, Dicrotic, Fava (bean), Garbanzo, Gram, Groundnut, Ictus, Lentil, Lucerne, Pea, Rhythm, Sain(t)foin, Soy beans, Sphygmic, Sync, Systaltic, Systole, Throb

▷ **Pummelled** *may indicate* an anagram

Pump(ing) Aerator, Air, Bellows, Bicycle, Bilge, Bowser, Breast, Centrifugal, Chain, Compressor, Cross-examine, Cross-question, Diaphragm, Donkey, Drive, Electromagnetic, Elicit, Feed, Filter, Foot, Force, Fork, Geissler, Grease-gun, Grill, Heart, Heat, Hydropult, Inflate, Interrogate, Knee-swell, Lift, Monkey, Mud, Nodding-donkey, Optical, Parish, Petrol, Piston, Pulsometer, Question, Rotary, Scavenge, Shoe, Sodium, Stirrup, Stomach, Suction, Turbine, Vacuum, Water, Wind

Pumpernickel Rye (bread)

Pun Calembour, Clinch, Equivoque, Jeu de mots, Paragram, Paronomasia, Quibble, Quip, Ram

Punch(ed) Bell, Biff, Blow, Box, Bradawl, Card, Centre, Chad, Check, Chop, Clip, Cobbler's, Conk, Fist(ic), Fourpenny one, Gang, Haymaker, Hit, Hook, Horse, Jab, Key, Kidney, Knevell, Knobble, Knubble, KO, Lam, Lander, Milk, Nevel, One-er, One-two, Overhand, Perforate, Planter's, Plug, Poke, Polt, Pommel, Pounce, Prod, Pummel, Rabbit, Roundhouse, Rum, Sangria, Slosh, Sock, Steed, Sting(o), Stoush, Suffolk, Tape, Upper-cut, Wap, Wind, Zest

Punctuate, Punctuation (mark) Bracket, Colon, Comma, Emphasize, Interabang, Interrobang, Interrupt, Mark, Semicolon, Tittle

Puncture(d) Bore, Centesis, Criblé, Cribrate, Deflate, Drill, Flat, Hole, Lance, Lumbar, Pearse, Perforate, Pierce, Pounce, Prick, Thoracocentesis

Pungency, Pungent Acid, Acrid, Acrolein, Alum, Ammonia, Bite, Bitter, Caustic, Hot, Mordant, Nidorous, Piquant, Poignant, Point, Racy, Salt, Spice, Sting, Tangy, Witty

▷ **Punish** *may indicate* an anagram

Punish(ment), Punished, Punishing Algates, Amerce, Baculine, Baffle, Bastinado, Beat, Birch, Bum rap, Cane, Cang, Capital, Cart, Castigate, Chasten, Chastise, Come-uppance, Corporal, Correct, Dam(nation), Defrock, Desert(s), Detention, → **DISCIPLINE**, Fatigue, Fine, Flog, Gate, Gauntlet, Gruel, Hellfire, Hiding, High jump, Hot seat, Imposition, Impot, Interdict, Jankers, Kang, Keelhaul, Knee-capping, Knout, Lambast(e), Leathering, Lines, Necklace, Nemesis, Pack-drill, Padre Pio, Pay out, Peine forte et dure, Penalise, Penance, Pensum, Perdition, Picket, Pillory, Pine, Rap, Red card, Reprisal, Retribution, Scaffold, Scourge, Sentence, Serve out, Six of the best, Smack, Smite, Spank, Stocks, Strafe, Strap, Strappado, Tar and feather, Toco, Toko, Torture, Treadmill, Trim, Trounce, Vice anglais, What for, Whip, Whirligig, Wild mare

Punt(er), Punting Antepost, Back, Bet, Gamble, Kent, Kick, Pound, Quant, Turfite

Pupil Abiturient, Academical, Adie's, Apple, Apprentice, Boarder, Cadet, Catechumen, Daygirl, Disciple, Etonian, Eyeball, Fag, Follower, Greycoat, Gyte, Intake, Junior, L, Monitor, Prefect, Protégé(e), Scholar, Senior, Student, Tiro, Tutee, Ward, Wykehamist

▷ **Pupil** *may refer to* an eye

Puppet(s), Puppeteer Creature, Doll, Dummy, Fantoccini, Finger, Galanty show, Glove, Guignol, Judy, Marionette, Mawmet, Mommet, Motion generative, Pawn, Pinocchio, Punch(inello), Rod, Thunderbird, Tool

Purchase(r), Purchasing Acquisition, Bargain, Buy, Coff, Compulsory, Earn, Emption, Gadsden, Get, Grip, Halliard, Halyard, Hold, Layaway, → **LEVERAGE**, Louisiana, Money, Offshore, Oligopsony, Parbuckle, Perquisitor, Repeat, Secure, Shop, Toehold

Pure, Purist, Purity Absolute, Angelic, Cando(u)r, Cathy, Chaste, Chiarezza, Clean(ly), Cleanness, Cosher, Fine, Glenys, Good, Holy, Immaculate, Incorrupt, Innocent, Intemerate, Inviolate, Kathy, Kosher, Lily, Lilywhite, Maidenhood, Meer, Me(a)re, Net(t), Precisionist, Pristine, Quintessence, Sanctity, Sheer, Simon, Simple, Sincere, Snow-white, Stainless, True, Unalloyed, Unapplied, Undrossy, Vertue, Virgin, Virtue, White

Purgative, Purge Aloes, Aryanise, Cascara, Castor-oil, Catharsis, Comstockery, Delete, Drastic, Elaterium, Eliminate, Emetic, Erase, Evacuant, Expiate, Flux, Hydragogue, Ipecacuanha, Jalop, Laxative, Number nine, Physic, Pride's, Relaxant, Scur, Senna

Purgatory Cacatopia

Purification, Purifier, Purify(ing) Absolve, Bowdlerise, Catharsis, Clay, Clean(se), Depurate, Dialysis, Distil, Edulcorate, Eluent, Elution, Exalt, Expurgate, Filter, Fine, Gas-lime, Lustre, Lustrum, Osmosis, Refine, Retort, Reverse osmosis, Samskara, Sanctify, Sanitise, Scorify, Scrub, Smudging, Sublime, Try, Whiten

Puritan(ical) Ascetic, Bible belt, Bluenose, Browne, Cromwell, Digger(s), Ireton, Ironsides, Killjoy, Pi, Pilgrim, Precisian, Prig, Prude, Prynne, Roundhead, Seeker, Traskite, Waldenses, Wowser, Zealot

Purloin Abstract, Annex, Appropriate, Lift, Nab, Pilfer, Snaffle, Sneak, Steal

Purple Amaranthine, Amarantin(e), Amethyst, Aubergine, Burgundy, Cassius, Claret, Eminence, Fuchsia, Heather, Heliotrope, Hyacinthine, Indigo, Lavender, Lilac, Magenta, Mulberry, Pansy, Plum, Prune, Puce, Purpure, Royal, Violet

Purpose(ful) Advertent, Aim, Avail, Calculated, Cause, Cautel, Design, Errand, Ettle, Function, Goal, Here-to, Idea, → **INTENT**, Marrow, Mean(ing), Meant, Mint, Mission,

Motive, Object, Plan, Point, Raison d'être, →**REASON**, Resolution, Resolve, Sake, Telic, Telos, Tenor, Use, View

Purse Ad crumenam, Bag, Bung, Caba, Clutch, Contract, Crease, Crumenal, Egg, Embouchure, Fisc, Fisk, Long Melford, Pocket, Prim, Privy, Prize, Pucker, Spleuchan, Sporran, Wallet, Whistle

▷ **Pursed** *may indicate* one word within another

Purser Mud-clerk

Purslane Sea, Water

Pursue(r), Pursuit Alecto, Business, Chase, Chivvy, Course, Dog, Follow, Follow up, Harry, Hobby, Hot-trod, Hound, Hue and cry, Hunt, Line, Pastime, Practice, Practise, Proceed, Prosecute, Quest, Scouring, Stalk, Trivial

Pursuivant Blue Mantle

Push(er), Push in, Push out Astrut, Barge, Birr, Boost, Bunt, Ca', Detrude, Drive, Edge, Effort, Elbow, Fire, Horn, Hustle, Impulse, Invaginate, Jostle, Nose, Nudge, Nurdle, Obtrude, Onrush, Pitchfork, Plod, Ply, Press, Promote, Propel, Railroad, Ram, Rush, Sell, Shog, Shoulder, Snoozle, Subtrude, Thrust, Urge

Put (off; on; out; up) Accommodate, Add, Alienate, Bet, Board, Cup, Daff, Defer, Dish, Do, Don, Douse, Implant, Impose, Incommode, Inn, Lade, Launch, Lay, Locate, Lodge, Lump, Oust, Pit, Pitch, Place(d), Plonk, Set, Smore, Station, Stow, Temporise

Put down Abase, Degrade, Demean, Disparage, Floor, Humiliate, Land, Relegate, Repress, Reprime, Snuff, Write

▷ **Put off** *may indicate* an anagram

Putsch Revolution

Putty Glaziers', Jewellers', Painters', Plasterers', Polishers'

Puzzle(r) Acrostic, Baffle, Bemuse, Bewilder, Brainteaser, Chinese, Confound, Confuse, Conundrum, Crossword, Crux, Crux medicorum, Egma, Elude, Enigma, Fox, Get, Glaik, Gravel, Intrigue, Jigsaw, Kakuro, Kittle, Logogriph, Magic pyramid, Maze, Mind-bender, Monkey, Mystery, Mystify, Nonplus, Perplex, Ponder, Pose(r), Rebus, Riddle, Rubik's Cube®, Sorites, Sphinx, Stick(l)er, Stump, Sudoku, Tangram, Teaser, Thematic, Tickler, Wordsearch, Wordsquare

Pygmalion Centennial brown

Pyramid Cheops, Chephren, Frustum, Magic, Stack, Teocalli

Qq

Qatar Emirate

Q-boat Mystery ship

Quack Charlatan, Crocus, Dulcamara, Empiric, Fake, →**IMPOSTOR**, Katerfelto, Mountebank, Pretender, Saltimbanco

Quadrilateral Lambeth, Tetragon, Trapezium, Trapezoid

Quagmire Bog, Fen, Imbroglio, Marsh, Morass, Swamp, Wagmoire

Quahog Clam

Quail Asteria, Bevy, Bird, Blench, Bob-white, Button, Caille, Colin, Flinch, Harlot, Hen, Quake, Shrink, Tremble

Quaint Cute, Far(r)and, Farrant, Fie, Naive, Odd, Old-world, Picturesque, Strange, Twee, Wham, Whim(sy)

Quake(r), Quaking Aminadab, Broad-brim, Didder, Dither, Dodder, Fox, Friend, Fry, Hicksite, Obadiah, Penn, Quail, Seism, Shake(r), Shiver, →**TREMBLE**, Tremor, Trepid

Qualification, Qualified, Qualify Able, Adapt, Adverb, Capacitate, Caveat, Competent, Condition, Credential, Degree, Diplomatic, Eligible, Entitle, Fit, Graduate, Habilitate, Higher Still, Meet, Modifier, Nisi, Parenthetical, Pass, Past-master, Proviso, Quantify, Restrict, Temper, Versed

Quality Aroma, Attribute, Body, Calibre, Cast, Charisma, Esse, Essence, Fabric, Fame, First water, Five-star, Flavour, Grade, Inscape, Insight, It, Kite-mark, Letter, Long suit, Mystique, Nature, Phat, Pitch, Plus, Premium, Primary, Property, Q, Quale, Reception, Sanctitude, Savour, Sort, Standard, Stature, Style, Substance, Suchness, Terroir, Texture, Thew, Thisness, Timbre, Tone, Tophole, Top notch, Total, Up-market, Vein, Vinosity, Virgin, Virtu(e), Water, Worth

Quantity →**AMOUNT**, Analog(ue), Batch, Bundle, Capacity, Deal, Dose, Feck, Fother, Hank, Heaps, Hundredweight, Idempotent, Intake, Jag, Loads, Lock, Lot, Mass, Measure, Melder, Multitude, Myriad, Niblet, Nonillion, Number, Ocean(s), Omnium, Operand, Parameter, Parcel, Peck, Plenty, Posology, Pottle, Qs, Qt, Quire, Quota, Quotient, Radicand, Ream, Scalar, Slather, Slew, Slue, Sum, Surd, Tret, Unknown, Vector, Wad, Warp, Whips

Quarrel(some) Altercate, Argue, Barney, Bate, Bicker, Brawl, Bust-up, Cantankerous, Cat and dog, Clash, Contentious, Contretemps, Difference, Disagree, Dispute, Domestic, Dust-up, Fall out, Feisty, Feud, Fracas, Fray, Hassle, Loggerheads, Miff, Pugnacious, Ruction, Squabble, Tangle, Tiff, Tile, Tink, Vendetta, Vitilitigation, Wrangle

Quarry, Quarry face Chalkpit, Currie, Curry, Game, Mark, Mine, Pit, Prey, Scabble, Scent, Stone pit, Victim

Quarter(ing), Quarters Airt, Barrio, Billet, Camp, Canton(ment), Casbah, Casern(e), Chinatown, Chum, Clemency, Close, Coshery, District, Dorm, E, Empty, Enclave, Fardel, Farl, First, Fo'c'sle, Forecastle, Forpet, Forpit, Fourth, Ghetto, Ham(s), Harbour, Haunch, Last, Latin, Medina, →**MERCY**, N, Note, Oda, Pity, Point, Principium, Quadrant, Region, S, Season, Sector, Tail, Trimester, Two bits, W, Wardroom, Warp, Winter

▷ **Quarterdeck** *may indicate* a suit of cards

Quartermaster Seacunny

Quarto Crown, Demy, Foolscap, Imperial, Medium, Royal, Small

Quartz Adventurine, Agate, Amethyst, Bristol diamond, Buhrstone, Cacholong, Cairngorm, Chalcedony, Chert, Citrine, Flint, Granophyre, Granulite, Itacolumite,

Jasp(er), Morion, Onyx, Plasma, Prase, Rainbow, Rose, Rubasse, Sapphire, Silex, Silica, Smoky, Spanish topaz, Stishovite, Tiger-eye, Tonalite, Whin Sill

Quash Abrogate, Annul, Nullify, Quell, Rebut, Recant, Scotch, Subdue, Suppress, Terminate, Void

Quasimodo Bellringer, Gibbose, Hunchback

Quaver(ing) Shake, Trill, Vibrate, Warble

Quay Bund, Jetty, Landing, Levee, Staithe, Wharf

Queasy Delicate, Nauseous, Squeamish

Queen(ly) Adelaide, Alcestis, Alexandra, Anna, Anne, Artemesia, Atossa, Balkis, Beauty, Bee, Begum, Bess, Boadicea, Boudicca, Brun(n)hild(e), Camilla, Candace, Card, Caroline, Cat, Christina, Cleopatra, Dido, Drag, Eleanor(a), Ellery, Esther, Gertrude, Guinevere, Harvest, Hatshepset, Hatshepsut, Hecuba, Helen, Henrietta Maria, Hermione, Hippolyta, Isabel, Ishtar, Isolde, Jocasta, Juliana, Juno, Leda, Maam, Mab, Maeve, Margaret, Marie Antoinette, Mary (Tudor), Matilda, May, Monarch, Nefertiti, Omphale, Pansy, Pearly, Penelope, Persephone, Phaedra, Prom, Proserpina, Qu, R, Ranee, Regal, Regina(l), Semiramis, Sheba, Titania, Vashti, Victoria, Virgin

Queer(ness) Abnormal, Berdash, Bizarre, Crazy, Cure, Curious, Fey, Fie, Fifish, Fishy, Gay, Nance, Nancy, →**ODD**, Outlandish, Peculiar, Pervert, Poorly, Quaint, Rum, Spoil, Uranism, Vert

Quench Assuage, Cool, Extinguish, Satisfy, Slake, Slo(c)ken, Sta(u)nch, Yslake

▶**Query** *see* QUESTION(ING)

Quest Goal, Graal, Grail, Hunt, Pursuit, Search, Venture, Vision

Question(ing), Questionnaire Appose, Ask, Bi-lateral, Burning, Catechise, Chin, Consult, Contest, Conundrum, Cross-examine, Debrief, Dichotomous, Direct, Dispute, Dorothy Dixer, Doubt, Erotema, Eroteme, Erotesis, Examine, Fiscal, Good, Grill, Heckle, Homeric, Impeach, Impugn, Indirect, Information, Innit, Interpellation, Interrogate, Interview, Investigate, Issue, Koan, Leading, Loaded, Maieutic, Matter, Open, Oppugn, Peradventure, Point of order, Pop, Pose, Previous, Probe, Problem, Pump, Q, Qu, Quaere, Quiz, Rapid-fire, Refute, Rhetorical, Riddle, Socratic method, Sound, Speer, Speir, Survey, Suspect, Tag, Teaser, Tickler, Vexed, West Lothian, WH, What, Worksheet

Queue Braid, Breadline, Cercus, Crocodile, Cue, Dog, File, →**LINE**, Line up, Pigtail, Plait, Plat, Tail(back), Track

Quibble(r), Quibbling Balk, Carp, Carriwitchet, Casuist, Cavil, Chicaner, Dodge, Elenchus, Equivocate, Hairsplitting, Nitpick, Pedantry, Pettifoggery, Prevaricate, Pun, Quiddity, Quillet, Quirk, Sophist

Quick(en), Quickening, Quicker, Quickie, Quickly, Quickness Accelerate, Acumen, Adroit, Agile, Alive, Animate, Breakneck, Bright, Brisk, Celerity, Chop-chop, Cito, Deft, Enliven, Existent, Expeditious, Express, Fastness, Fleet, Hasten, Hie, Hotfoot, Impetuous, Impulsive, Intelligent, Jiffy, Keen, Living, Mercurial, Meteoric, Mistress, Mosso, Nailbed, Nimble, Nippy, Nooner, Pdq, Piercing, Post-haste, Prestissimo, Presto, Prompt, Pronto, Rapid, Ready, Sharp, Slippy, Smart, Snappy, Soon, Spry, Streamline, Stretta, Stretto, Sudden, Swift, Tout de suite, Trice, Up tempo, Veloce, Vital, Vite

Quid Chaw, Chew, L, Nicker, Plug, Pound, Quo, Sov, Tertium, Tobacco

Quiet(en), Quieter, Quietly Accoy, Allay, Appease, Barnacle, Calm, Clam, Compose, Decrescendo, Doggo, Ease, Easeful, Easy, Encalm, Entame, Gag, Grave, Kail, Laconic, Loun(d), Low, Lown(d), Low-profile, Lull, Meek, Mezzo voce, Muffle, Mute, Orderly, P, Pacify, Pastel, Pause, Peace, Piano, Pipe down, Plateau, QT, Reserved, Reticent, Sedate, Settle, Sh, Shtoom, Shtum, Silence, Sober, Soothe, Sotto voce, Still, Subact, Subdued, Tace, Taciturn, Tranquil, Whisht, Whist

Quilt(ed), Quilting Comfort(er), Counterpane, Cover, Doona®, Duvet, Echo, Eiderdown, Futon, Kantha, Matel(l)asse, Patch(work), Puff, Trapunto

Quip Carriwitchet, Crack, Epigram, Gibe, Jest, Jibe, Joke, Taunt, Zinger

Quirk Concert, Foible, Idiosyncrasy, Irony, Kink, Mannerism, Twist

Quit(s) Abandon, Absolve, Ap(p)ay, Cease, Desert, Desist, Even(s), Go, Leave, Meet, Part, Resign, Rid, Stash, →**STOP**, Vacate, Yield

Quite Actually, All, Ap(p)ay, Clean, Dead, Enough, Enow, Fairly, Fully, Mezzo, Precisely, Rather, Real(ly), Right, Sheer, Very, Yes

Quiver(ing) Aspen, Quake, Shake, Sheaf, Sheath, The yips, Tremble, Tremolo, Tremor, Tremulate, Trepid, Vibrant, Vibrate, Wobble

Quiz Bandalore, Banter, Catechism, Examine, Hoax, Interrogate, I-spy, Mastermind, Mockery, Oddity, Probe, Question, Smoke, Third degree, Trail, Yo-yo

Quota Proportion, Ration, Share

Quotation, Quote(d), Quote Adduce, Citation, Cite, Co(a)te, Duckfoot, Epigraph, Evens, Extract, Forward, Instance, Name, Price, Recite, Reference, Say, Scare, Soundbite, Tag, Verbatim, Wordbite

Quotient Intelligence, Kerma, Quaternion, Ratio, Respiratory

Rr

RA Academy, Argentina

Rabbit Angora, Astrex, Blather, Brer, Buck, Bun(ny), Chat, Chitchat, Con(e)y, Cottontail, Daman, Dassie, Doe, Duffer, Harp, Hyrax, Jack, Jaw, Klipdas, Marmot, Muff, Natter, Nest, Novice, Oarlap, Patzer, Prate, Rack, Rattle, Rex, Sage, Snowshoe, Tapeti, Terricole, Waffle, Yak, Yap, Yatter

Rabble, Rabble-rousing Canaille, Clamjamphrie, Clanjamfray, Colluvies, Crowd, Demagoguery, Doggery, Herd, Hoi-polloi, Horde, Legge, Meinie, Mein(e)y, Menyie, Mob, Raffle, Rag-tag, Rascaille, Rascal, Riff-raff, Rout, Scaff-raff, Shower, Tag, Tagrag

Race, Racing Alpine, Autocross, Autopoint, Bathtub, Boat, Bumping, Car rally, Caucus, Chantilly, Chase, Claiming, Classic, Comrades, Consolation, Country, Criterium, Cursus, Cyclo-cross, Dogs, Double sculls, Drag, Egg and spoon, F1, Flat, Formula One, Fun-run, Half-marathon, Handicap, Harness, Hialeah, High hurdles, Hurdles, Keiren, Keirin, Kentucky Derby, Leat, Leet, Marathon, Meets, Mile, Monza, Motocross, Nascar, National Hunt, Nursery, Nursery stakes, Obstacle, One-horse, Picnic, Plate, Point-to-point, Potato, Prep, Rallycross, Rallying, Rapids, Regatta, Relay, Rill, Road, Rod, Run-off, Sack, Scramble, Scratch, Selling(-plate), Sheep, Slalom, Slot-car, Smock, Speedway, Steeplechase, Supermoto, Sweepstake, Tail, Three-legged, Torch, Trotting, TT, Turf, Two-horse, Walking, Wetherby

Race Ancestry, Arms, Aztec, Belt, Breed, Career, Contest, Course, Current, Dash, Event, Fastnet, Flow, Generation, Ginger, Human(kind), Hurry, Inca, Kind, Lick, Lignage, Line(age), Man, Master, Mediterranean, Nation, →**NATIONAL**, Pre-Dravidian, Pursuit, Scud, Scurry, Seed, Slipstream, Sprint, Stakes, Stem, Stock, Strain, Streak, Tear, Tide, Torpids, Tribe, Walk-over, Waterway, Welter, White

Racehorse, Racer Arkle, Dragster, Eclipse, Filly, Hare, Maiden, Mudder, Neddy, Plater, Red Rum, Shergar, Snake, Steeplechaser, Trotter

Race meeting, Racetrack Aintree, Ascot, Cambridgeshire, Catterick, Cesarewitch, Derby, Doggett's Coat and Badge, Doncaster, Dromical, Epsom, Goodwood, Grand National, Grand Prix, Guineas, Imola, Indy, Kentucky Derby, Leger, Le Mans, Longchamps, Madison, National Hunt, Newmarket, Oaks, Racino, Redcar, St Leger, Super G, Thousand Guineas, Towcester, Two Thousand Guineas, Wincanton

Rack Bin, Cloud, Cratch, Drier, Flake, Frame, Hack, Hake, Heck, Pipe, Pulley, Roof, Stretcher, Toast, Torment, Torture, Touse, Towse

Racket(eer) Bassoon, →**BAT**, Battledore, Bloop, Blue murder, Brattle, Caterwaul, Chirm, Clamour, Con, Crime, Deen, Din, Discord, Earner, →**FIDDLE**, Gyp, Hubbub, Hullaballoo, Hustle, →**NOISE**, Noisiness, Protection, Ramp, Rattle, Rort, Sokaiya, Stridor, Swindle, Tirrivee, Tumult, Uproar, Utis

Radar Acronym, Angel, AWACS, Beacon, DEW line, Doppler, Gadget, Gee, Gull, Lidar, Loran, Monopulse, Navar, Rebecca-eureka, Shoran, Surveillance, Teleran®, Tracking

Radiance, Radiant Actinic, Aglow, Aureola, Beamish, Brilliant, Glory, Glow, Happy, Lustre, Refulgent, Sheen

Radiate, Radiating, Radiation, Radiator Actinal, Air-colour, Annihilation, Beam, Black body, Bremsstrahlung, Cavity, C(h)erenkov, Characteristic, Effulgence, Effuse, Emanate, Fluorescence, Glow, Heater, Infrared, Insolation, Isohel, Laser, Microwave, Millirem, Non-ionizing, Pentact, Photon, Picowave, Pulsar, Quasar, Rem(s), Rep, Roentgen, →**SHINE**, Sievert, Soft, Spherics, Spoke, Stellate, SU, Sun, Ultra violet, Van Allen

Radical Acetyl, Alkyl, Ammonium, Amyl, Aryl, Bolshevist, Bolshie, Butyl, Chartist, Dibutyl, Drastic, Elemental, Ester, Ethynyl, Extreme, Free, Fundamental, Hexyl,

Innate, Jacobin, Leftist, Methyl, Phenyl, Pink, Propyl, Red, Revolutionary, Root, Rudiment, Taliban, Taproot, Trot(sky), Vinyl, Vinylidene, Whig, Yippie, Yippy

Radio Beatbox, Blooper, Bluetooth, Boom-box, Cat's whisker, CB, Cellular, Citizen's band, Cognitive, Community, Crystal set, Digital, Ether, Gee, Ghetto-blaster, Ham, Local, Loudspeaker, Marconigraph, Pirate, Receiver, Receiving-set, Rediffusion®, Reflex, Rig, Set, Simplex, Sound, Steam, Talk, Talkback, Tranny, Transceiver, Transistor, Transmitter, Transponder, Walkie-talkie, Walkman®, Walky-talky, Wireless

Radioactive, Radioactivity Actinide, Americium, Astatine, Autinite, Bohrium, Cheralite, Cobalt 60, Curie, Emanation, Hot, Megacurie, Niton, Nucleonics, Steam, Thorianite, Thorite, Thorium, Torbernite, Uranite

Radiology Interventional

Raft(ing) Balsa, Carley float, Catamaran, Float, Kon-Tiki, Life, Log, Mohiki, Pontoon, Slew

Rafter Barge-couple, Beam, Chevron, Jack, Joist, Principal, Ridge, Spar, Timber

Rag(ged), Rags Bait, Bate, Clout, Coral, Deckle, Dud(s), Duddery, Duddie, Duster, Fent, Figleaf, Glad, Gutter press, Guyed, Haze, Kid, Lap(pie), Lapje, Mop, Moth-eaten, →NEWSPAPER, Paper, Red(top), Remnant, Revel, Rivlins, Roast, Rot, Scabrous, Scold, Scrap, S(c)hmatte, →SHRED, Slate, Slut, Splore, Tat(t), Tatter(demalion), Tatty, Taunt, →TEASE, Tiger, Tongue, Uneven

▷ **Rag(ged)** *may indicate* an anagram

Rage, Raging Amok, →ANGER, Ardour, Bait, Bate, Bayt, Boil, Chafe, Conniption, Explode, Fad, Fashion, Fierce, Fit, Fiz(z), Fume, Furibund, Furore, Fury, Gibber, Go, Irate, Ire, Mode, Paddy(-whack), Passion, Pelt, Pet, Rabid, Ramp, Rant, Road, 'roid, See red, Snit, Storm, Tear, Temper, Ton, Utis, Wax, Wrath

Raid(er) Assault, Attack, Bear, Bodrag, Bust, Camisado, Chappow, Commando, Do, Forage, For(r)ay, Imburst, Incursion, Inroad, Inrush, Invade, Jameson, Maraud, March-treason, Mosstrooper, Pict, Pillage, Plunder, Ransel, Razzia, Reive, Rob, Sack, Scrump, Skrimp, Skrump, Smash-and-grab, Sortie, Spreagh, Storm, Swoop, Viking

Rail(er), Railing Abuse, Arm(rest), Arris, Balustrade, Ban, Banister, →BAR, Barre, Barrier, Bird, Communion, Conductor, Coot, Corncrake, Crake, Criticise, Dado, Fender, Fiddle, Flanged, Flat-bottomed, Flite, Flow, Fulminate, Grab, Grinding, Guide, Gush, Insult, Inveigh, Light, Limpkin, Live, Metal, Monkey, Picture, Pin, Plate, Post, Pulpit, Pushpit, Rack, Rag, Rate, Rave, Rung, Scold, Slate, Slip, Sora, Soree, Spar, T, Taffrail, Takahe, Taunt, Third, Towel, Train

Railroad, Railway Aerial, Amtrak, BR, Bulldoze, Cable, Cash, Coerce, Cog, Crémaillère, Dragoon, El, Elevated, Funicular, Gantlet, GWR, Inclined, L, Light, Lines, LMS, LNER, Loop-line, Maglev, Marine, Metro, Monorail, Mountain, Narrow-gauge, Press, Rack, Rack and pinion, Rly, Road, Rollercoaster, Ropeway, ROSCO, Ry, Scenic, Ship, Siding, SR, Stockton-Darlington, Switchback, Telpher-line, Track, Train, Tramline, Tramway, Trans-Siberian, Tube, Underground

Rain(y), Rainstorm Acid, Blash, Deluge, Downpour, Drizzle, Flood, Hyad(e)s, Hyetal, Mistle, Mizzle, Oncome, Onding, Onfall, Pelt, Pelter, Piss, Plump, Pluviose, Pluvious, Pour, Precipitation, Right, Roke, Scat, Seil, Serein, Serene, Shell, Shower, Sile, Skiffle, Skit, Smir(r), Smur, Soft, Spat, Spet, Spit, Storm, Thunder-plump, Virga, Water, Weep, Wet

Raise(d), Raising Advance, Aggrade, Attollent, Boost, Bouse, Bowse, Build, Buoy up, Cat, Coaming, Cock, Collect, Elate, →ELEVATE, Emboss, Enhance, Ennoble, Erect, Escalate, Exalt, Fledge, Grow, Heave, Heezie, Heft, High(er), Hike, Hoick, Hoist, Increase, Jack, Key, Leaven, Lift, Mention, Overcall, Perk, Prise, Rear, Regrate, Repoussé, Revie, Rouse, Saleratus, Siege, Sky, Snarl, Sublimate, Take up, Up, Upgrade, Weigh

Rake, Raker, Rakish Bag of bones, Bed-hopper, Buckrake, Casanova, Comb, Corinthian, Dapper, Dissolute, Don Giovanni, Don Juan, Enfilade, Gay dog, Jaunty, Lecher, Libertine, Lothario, Raff, Reprobate, Rip, Roam, Roué, Scan, Scour, Scowerer, Scrape, Scratch, Strafe, Straff, Swash-buckler, Swinge-buckler, Wagons, Wolf, Womaniser

Rally, Rallying-point Autocross, Autopoint, Badinage, Banter, Demo, Gather, Jamboree, Meeting, Mobilise, Monte Carlo, Morcha, Muster, Oriflamme, Persiflage, Raise, Recover, Regroup, Rely, Rest, Reunion, Revive, Risorgimento, Roast, Rouse, Scramble, Spirit, Treasure hunt

Ram Aries, Battering, Buck, Bunt, Butt, Butter, Corvus, Crash, Drive, Hidder, Hydraulic, Mendes, Pound, Pun, Sheep, Stem, Tamp, Thrust, Tup, Wether

Ramble(r), Rambling Aberrant, Aimless, Digress, Incoherent, Liana, Liane, Maunder, Meander, Rabbit, Rigmarole, Roam, Rose, Rove, Skimble-skamble, Sprawl, Stray, Vagabond, Wander

Ramp Bank, Gradient, Helicline, Incline, Linkspan, Runway, Slipway, Slope, Speed, Vert

▷ **Rampant** *may indicate* an anagram or a reversed word

Rampart Abat(t)is, Brisure, Butt, Defence, Fortification, Parapet, Terreplein, Vallum, Wall

Ranch Bowery, Corral, Estancia, Farm, Fazenda, Hacienda, Spread, Stump

Rancid Frowy, Rafty, Reast(y), Reest(y), Reist(y), Sour, Turned

Rancour Bad blood, Gall, Hate, Malgré, Malice, Resentment, Spite

Random Accidental, Aleatoric, Arbitrary, →**AT RANDOM**, Blind, Casual, Desultory, Fitful, →**HAPHAZARD**, Harvest, Hit-or-miss, Indiscriminate, Lucky dip, Scattershot, Sporadic, Stochastic, Stray

▷ **Random(ly)** *may indicate* an anagram

Range(r), Rangy Admiralty, Aga, Align, Ambit, Andes, Atlas, AZ, Band, Bushwhack, Capsule, Carry, Cascade, Chain, Cheviot, Compass, Cotswolds, Course, Dandenong, Darling, Diapason, Dolomites, Dynamic, Err, →**EXTENT**, Eye-shot, Forest, Game warden, Gamme, Gamut, Grade, Great Dividing, Gunshot, Harmonic, Himalayas, Home, Interquartile, Kaikoura, Karakoram, Ken(ning), Kolyma, Limit, Line, Locus, Long, MacDonnell, Massif, →**MOUNT**, Musgrave, New England, Orbit, Otway, Oven, Owen Stanley, Palette, Pennine Hills, Point-blank, Prairie, Purview, Pyrenees, Radius, Rake, Reach, Register, Repertoire, Roam, Rocket, Rove, Ruivenzori, Run, Saga, Scale, Scope, Sc(o)ur, Selection, Serra, Shooting, Short, Sierra, Sloane, Spectrum, Sphere, Stanovoi, Stanovoy, Sweep, The Wolds, Urals, Wasatch, Waveband, Woomera

Range-finder Telemeter

Rank(s), Ranking Arrant, Assort, Begum, Brevet, Caste, Category, Cense, Classify, Cornet, Degree, Dignity, Downright, Earldom, Echelon, Estate, État(s), Flag, Grade, Gree, Gross, High, Malodorous, Olid, Petty Officer, Place, Rammish, Range, Rate, Reist, Rooty, Row, Sergeant, Serried, Sheer, Sort, Stance, →**STATION**, Status, Table, Taxi, Tier, →**TITLE**, Top drawer, Utter, Viscount

Ransack Fish, Loot, Pillage, Plunder, Rifle, Ripe, Rob, Rummage, Tot(ter)

Rant(er), Ranting Bluster, Bombast, Declaim, Fustian, Ham, Harangue, Rail, Rodomontade, Scold, Slang-whang, Spout, Spruik, Stump, Thunder, Tirade, Tub-thump

Rap(ped) Blame, Censure, Clour, Gangsta, Halfpenny, Knock, Ratatat, Shand, Strike, Swapt, Tack, Tap

Rape Abuse, Assault, Belinda, Cole-seed, Colza, Creach, Creagh, Date, Deflower, Despoil, Gangbang, Grass(line), Hundred, Lock, Lucretia, Navew, Oilseed, Plunder, Ravish, Stuprate, Thack, Violate, Vitiate

Rapid(ity), Rapidly Chute, Dalle, Express, Fast, Fleet, Meteoric, Mosso, Presto, Pronto, Quick-fire, Riffle, Sault, Shoot, Speedy, Stickle, Swift, Veloce, Vibrato, Whiz(zing), Wildfire

Rapport Accord, Affinity, Agreement, Harmony

Rapture, Rapturous Bliss, →**DELIGHT**, Ecstasy, Elation, Joy, Trance

Rare, Rarity Blue moon, Curio, Earth, Geason, Infrequent, Intemerate, Oddity, One-off, Rear, Recherché, Scarce, Seeld, Seld(om), Singular, Surpassing, Thin, →**UNCOMMON**, Uncooked, Underdone, Unusual

Rare earth Lu(tetium)

Rascal(ly) Arrant, Bad hat, Cad, Cullion, Cur, Devil, Gamin, Hallian, Hallion, Hallyon, Limner, Loon, Lorel, Low, Lozel(l), Rip, Rogue, Scallywag, Scamp, Scapegrace, Schelm, Skeesicks, Skellum, Skelm, Smaik, Spalpeen, Tinker, Toe-rag, Varlet, Varmint, Villain

Rash(ness), Rasher Acne, Bacon, Brash, Collop, Daredevil, Eczema, Eruption, Erysipelas, Fast, Foolhardy, Gum, Harum-scarum, →**HASTY**, Headlong, Heat, Hives, Hotspur, Impetigo, Impetuous, Imprudent, Impulsive, Indiscreet, Lichen, Madbrain, Madcap, Nettle, Outbreak, Overhasty, Pox, Precipitate, Reckless, Road, Roseola, Rubella, St Anthony's fire, Sapego, Serpigo, Spots, Temerity, Thoughtless, Unheeding, Unthinking, Unwise, Urticaria

Rat(s), Ratty Agouta, Bandicoot, Blackleg, Blackneb, Boodie, Brown, Bug-out, Cad, Camass, Cane, Cur, Cutting grass, Defect, Desert, Fink, Footra, Foutra, Geomyoid, Gym, Heck, Heel, Hood, Hydromys, Informer, Kangaroo, Malabar, Mall, Maori, Mole, Moon, Norway, Pack, Pig, Poppycock, Potoroo, Pouched, Pshaw, Pup(py), Renegade, Renegate, Rice, Rink, Rodent, Roland, Rot(ten), Scab, Sewer, Shirty, Squeal, Stinker, Tell, Turncoat, Vole, Water, Wharf, Whiskers, White, Wood

Rate(s), Rating A, Able, Able-bodied, Apgar, Appraise, Appreciate, Assess, Base, Basic, Birth, Bit, Carpet, Castigate, Cess, Cetane, Chide, Classify, Click, Conception, Conversion, Cost, Count, Credit, Deserve, Effective, ELO, Erk, Estimate, Evaluate, Exchange, Grade, Headline, Hearty, Horsepower, Hurdle, Incidence, Interest, ISO, Lapse, Leading, Mate's, Merit, Mortality, Mortgage, MPH, Mutation, Octane, Ordinary, OS, Pace, Penalty, Percentage, PG, Piece, Poor, Prime (lending), Rag, Rank, Rebuke, Red, Refresh, Reproof, Rocket, Row, Sailor, Scold, Sea-dog, Slew, →**SPEED**, Standing, Starting, Steerageway, Surtax, Take-up, TAM, Tariff, Tax, Tempo, Tog, U, Upbraid, Value, Water, Wig, World-scale, X

Rather Affirmative, Assez, Degree, Gay, Gey, Instead, Lief, Liever, Loor, More, Prefer, Pretty, Some(what), Somedele, Sooner

Ratio Advance, Albedo, Aspect, Bypass, Cash, Compound, Compression, Cosine, Distinctiveness, Duplicate, Focal, Fraction, Gear, Golden, Gyromagnetic, Inverse, Liquidity, Loss, Mark space, Mass, Neper, PE, Pi, Picture, Pogson, Poisson's, Position, Price-dividend, Prise-earnings, Proportion, Protection, Quotient, Reserve, Savings, Signal-to-noise, Sin(e), Slip, Space, Tensor, Trigonometric

Ration(s) Allocate, Allot, Apportion, Compo, Dole, Étape, Iron, K, Quota, Restrict, Scran, Share, Short commons, Size, Whack

Rational(ism), Rationalisation, Rationalize Descartes, Dianoetic, Dispassionate, Humanistic, Level-headed, Logical, Lucid, Matter-of-fact, Pragmatic, Reasonable, Sane, Sapient, Sensible, Sine, Sober, Tenable, Wice

Ratten Sabotage

Rattle (box), Rattling, Rattle on Alarm, Blather, Chatter, Clack, Clank, Clap, Clatter, Conductor, Death, Demoralise, Discombobulate, Discomfort, Disconcert, Gas-bag, Hurtle, Jabber, Jangle, Jar, Natter, Nonplus, Rale, Rap, Reel, Rhonchus, Ruckle, Shake, Sistrum, Tirl, Upset, Vuvuzela

Ravage Depredation, Desecrate, Despoil, Havoc, Pillage, Prey, Ruin, Sack, Waste

Raven(ous) Black, Corbel, Corbie, Corvine, Croaker, Daw, Grip, Hugin, Munin, Prey, Unkindness, Wolfish

Ravine Arroyo, Barranca, Barranco, Canada, Canyon, Chasm, Chine, Clough, Coulée, Couloir, Dip, Flume, Ghyll, Gorge, Goyle, Grike, Gulch, Gully, Kedron, Khor, Khud, Kidron, Kloof, Lin(n), Nal(l)a, Nallah, Nulla(h), Pit, Purgatory

Ravish Abduct, Constuprate, Debauch, Defile, Devour, Outrage, Rape, Stuprate, Transport, Violate

Raw Brut, Chill, Coarse, Crude, Crudy, Damp, Fresh, Green(horn), Natural, New, Recruit, Rude, Uncooked, Wersh

Ray(s), Rayed Actinic, Alpha, Beam, Beta, Bivium, Canal, Cathode, Cosmic, Cramp-fish, Delta, Devil, Devilfish, Diactine, Dun-cow, Eagle, Electric, Fish, Gamma, Grenz, Guitarfish, Homelyn, Manta, Medullary, Monactine, Polyact, R, Radius, Re,

Roentgen, Roker, Röntgen, Sawfish, Sea-devil, Sea-vampire, Sephen, Shaft, Skate, Stick, Sting, Stingaree, T, Tetract, Thornback, Torpedo

Reach(ed) Ar(rive), Attain, Boak, Boke, Carry, Come, Extend, Gain, Get at, Get out, Grasp, Hent, Hit, Key-bugle, Lode, Octave, Peak, Raught, Rax, Retch, Ryke, Seize, Stretch, Touch, Win

React(or), Reaction(ary) Addition, Allergy, Answer, Backlash, Backwash, Behave, Blimp, Blowback, Boiling water, Breeder, Bristle, Calendria, Cannizzaro, Catalysis, Chain, Convertor, Core, Counterblast, Dibasic, Dounreay, Emotion, Endergonic, Exoergic, Falange, Fast(-breeder), Feedback, Flehmen, Flinch, Friedel-Crafts, Furnace, Gut, Heavy-water, Incomplete, Interplay, Inulase, Kickback, Knee-jerk, Lightwater, Molten salt, Nuclear, Outcry, Pebble-bed, Pile, Polymerization, Pressure-tube, Pressurized water, Reciprocate, Recoil, Reflex, Repercussion, Respond, Reversible, Rigid, Sensitive, Sprocket, Stereotaxis, Thermal, Topochemistry, Ultraconservative

▷ **Reactionary** *may indicate* reversed or an anagram

Read(ing) Abomasum, Bearing, Browse, Decipher, Decode, Exegesis, First, Grind, Grounden, Haftarah, Haphtarah, Haphtorah, Interpret, Learn, Lection, Lesson, Lu, Maftir, Maw, Paired, Pericope, Peruse, Pore, Rad, Rennet-bag, Say, Scan, Second, See, Sight, Skim, Solve, Speed, Stomach, →**STUDY**, Third, Uni(versity), Vell, Version, Ycond

Reader(s) ABC, Academic, Alidad(e), Bookworm, Editor, Epistoler, Gentle, Lay, Lector, Microfilm, Primer, Silas Wegg, Softa, Taster

Readiest, Readily, Readiness, Ready Alacrity, Alamain, Alert, Amber, Amenability, Apt, Atrip, Available, Boun, Bound, Braced, Brass, Cash, Conditional, Dough, Eager, Early, Eftest, Fettle, Fit, Fiver, Forward, Game, Geared-up, Gelt, Go, Keyed, Latent, Lolly, Masterman, Money, On (call), Predy, Prepared, Present, Prest, Primed, Procinct, Prompt, Promptitude, Ransom, Reckoner, Ripe, Running costs, Set, Soon, Spot, Tenner, To hand, Turnkey, Unhesitant, Usable, Wherewithal, Willing, Yare, Yark

Readymade Bought, Precast, Prepared, Prêt-à-porter, Slops, Stock, Store

Real, Reality, Realities, Really Actual, Ah, Augmented, Bona-fide, Brass tacks, Coin, Deed, De facto, Dinkum, Dinky-di(e), Earnest, Echt, Ens, Entia, Entity, Essence, Fact(ion), →**GENUINE**, Hard, Honest, Indeed, Mackay, McCoy, McKoy, Naive, Ontic, Positive, Quite, Royal, Simon Pure, Sooth, Sterling, Straight up, Substantial, Tangible, Tennis, The case, Thing(li)ness, True, Verismo, Verity, Very, Virtual

Realise, Realisation, Realism, Realistic Achieve, Attain, Attuite, Cash (in), Dirty, Down-to-earth, Embody, Encash, Entelechy, Fetch, Fruition, Fulfil, Hard-edged, Learn, Lifelike, Magic, Naive, Naturalism, Practical, Pragmatism, See, Sell, Sense, Social, Socialist, Suss, Understand, Verisimilitude, Verismo, Verité

▶ **Realities, Reality** *see* **REAL**

Realm Dominion, Field, Kingdom, Land, Notogaea, Region, Special(i)ty, UK

Ream Bore, Foam, Froth, Paper, Rime, Screed

Reap(er) Binder, Crop, Death, Earn, Gather, Glean, Harvest, Scythe, Shear, Sickleman, Solitary, Stibbler

Rear(ing) Aft, Back(side), Baft, Behind, Bottom, Bring-up, Bunt, Butt, Cabré, Derrière, Empennage, Foster, Haunch, Hind, Loo, Nousell, Nurture, Podex, Poop, Prat(t), →**RAISE**, Retral, Rump, Serafile, Serrefile, Stern, Sternward, Tonneau

Reason(able), Reasoning A fortiori, Agenda, Analytical, Apagoge, A priori, Argue, Argument, Basis, Call, Casuistry, Cause, Colour, Consideration, Deduce, Economical, Expostulate, Fair, Ground(s), Ijtihad, Inductive, Intelligent, Ipso facto, Logic, Logical, Logistics, Metamathematics, Mind, Moderate, Motive, Noesis, Petitio principii, Plausible, Point, Pretext, Pro, Proof, Purpose, Rational(e), Sanity, Sense, Sensible, Settler, Somewhy, Sophism, Syllogism, Synthesis, Think, Viable, What for, Why, Wit

Rebate Diminish, Lessen, Refund, Repayment

Rebel(s), Rebellion, Rebellious Apostate, Beatnik, Blouson noir, Bolshy, Bounty, Boxer, Cade, Contra, Danton, Defiance, Diehard, Dissident, Drop out, Fifteen, Forty-five, Green Mountain Boys, Hippy, Iconoclast, Insubordinate, Insurgent,

Insurrection, IRA, Jacobite, Kick, Luddite, Maccabee, Malignant, Mutine(er), Mutiny, Oates, Pilgrimage of Grace, Putsch, Recalcitrant, Recusant, Resist, → **REVOLT**, Rise, Sedition, Straw, Tyler, Unruly, Warbeck, Wat Tyler, Young Turk, Zealot

▷ **Rebellious** *may indicate* a word reversed

Rebuff Check, Cold-shoulder, Noser, Quelch, Repulse, Retort, Rubber, Setdown, Sneb, Snib, Snub

Rebuild Haussmannize

Rebuke Admonish, Berate, Check, Chide, Earful, Lecture, Neb, Objurgate, Rap, Rate, Razz, Reprimand, Reproof, Reprove, Rollick, Scold, Slap, Slate, Snub, Strop, Threap, Threep, Tick off, Trim, Tut, Upbraid, Wig

Recall(ing) Annul, Echo, Eidetic, Encore, Evocative, Flashback, Go over, Memory, Reclaim, Recollect, Redolent, Remember, Remind, Reminisce, Repeal, Retrace, Revoke, Total, Withdraw

▷ **Recast** *may indicate* an anagram

Recede Decline, Ebb, Lessen, Regress, Retrograde, Shrink, Withdraw

Receipt(s) Acknowledge, Chit, Docket, Gate, Quittance, Recipe, Revenue, Take, Voucher

Receive(d), Receiver Accept, Accoil, Acquire, Admit, Antenna, Assignee, Bailee, Bleeper, Dipole, Dish, Donee, Ear, Earphone, Fence, Get, Grantee, Greet, Hydrophone, Inherit, Pernancy, Phone, Pocket, Radio, Radiopager, Remit, Reset, Roger, Set, Sounder, Take, Tap, Transistor, Transponder, Tuner, Wireless

Recent(ly) Alate, Current, Fresh, Hot, Just, Late, Low, Modern, New, New-found, Yesterday, Yestereve, Yesterweek

Receptacle Ash-tray, Basket, Bin, Bowl, Box, Chrismatory, Ciborium, Container, Cyst, Hell-box, Monstrance, Muffle, Reliquary, Relique, Sacculus, Spermatheca, Spittoon, Tank, Thalamus, Tidy, Tore, Torus

Reception, Receptive Accoil, At home, Bel-accoyle, Couchée, Court, Durbar, First-class, Ghost, Greeting, Infare, Kursaal, Levée, Open, Ovation, Ruelle, Saloon, Sensory, Soirée, Superheterodyne, Teleasthetic, Warm, Welcome

Receptor(s) Metabotropic, Steroid

▷ **Recess** *may indicate* 'reversed'

Recess(ion) Alcove, Apse, Bay, Break, Breaktime, Bunk, Corner, Cove, Dinette, Ebb, Embrasure, Fireplace, Grotto, Indent, Inglenook, Interval, → **NICHE**, Nook, Pigeonhole, Respite, Rest, Withdrawal

▷ **Recidivist** *may indicate* 'reversed'

Recipient Assignee, Beneficiary, Disponee, Donee, Grantee, Heir, Legatee, Receiver, Suscipient

Reciprocal, Reciprocate Corresponding, Elastance, Exchange, Inter(act), Mutual, Repay, Return, Two-way

Recite(r), Recital, Recitation(ist) Ave, Declaim, Diseuse, Enumerate, Litany, Monologue, Mystic, Parlando, Quote, Reading, Reel, Relate, Rhapsode, Say, Sing, Tell

▷ **Reckless** *may indicate* an anagram

Reckless(ness) Bayard, Blindfold, Careless, Catiline, Desperado, Desperate, Devil-may-care, Gadarene, Harum-scarum, Hasty, Headfirst, Headlong, Hell-bent, Irresponsible, Jaywalker, Madcap, Perdu(e), Ramstam, Rantipole, → **RASH**, Slapdash, Temerity, Ton-up, Wanton, Wildcat

Reckon(ed), Reckoning Assess, Bet, Calculate, Cast, Census, Computer, Consider, Count, Date, Doomsday, Estimate, Fancy, Figure, Guess, Impute, Number, Rate, Reputed, Settlement, Shot, Tab

Reclaim(ed), Reclamation Assart, Empolder, Impolder, Innings, Novalia, Polder, Recover, Redeem, Restore, Salvage, Swidden, Tame, Thwaite

Recognise(d), Recognition Accept, Accredit, Acknow(ledge), Admit, Anagnorisis, Appreciate, Ascetic, Character, Cit(ation), Discern, Exequatur, Gaydar, Identify, Isolated, Ken, → **KNOW**, Nod, Notice, Oust, Own, Perception, Resipiscence, Reward, Salute, Scent, Standard, Sung, Voice, Weet, Wot

Recoil Backlash, Bounce, Kick(back), Quail, Rebound, Redound, Repercussion, Resile, Reverberate, Shrink, Shy, Spring, Start, Whiplash

Recollect(ion) Anamnesis, Memory, Pelmanism, Recall, →**REMEMBER**, Reminisce

▷**Recollection** *may indicate an anagram*

Recommend(ation) Advise, Advocate, Counsel, Direct, Encourage, Endorse, Move, Nap, Praise, Precatory, Promote, Rider, Suggest, Testimonial, Tip, Tout, Urge

Recompense Cognisance, Deodand, Deserts, Eric, Expiate, Guerdon, Pay, Remunerate, Repayment, Requite, Restitution, Reward

Reconcile(d) Accord, Adapt, Adjust, Affrended, Atone, Harmonise, Henotic, Make up, Mend

Record(er), Recording (company) All-time, Book, Chart, Chronicle, Clock, Coat(e), Enter, Entry, Ever, Fact, File, Itemise, Log, Mark, Memorise, Notate, Note, Previous, Quote, Release, Remember, Set down, Sunshine, Take, Tally, Tallyman, Trace, Trip, Vote, Weigh, Write

Recover(y) Amend, Clawback, Comeback, Convalescence, Cure, Dead cat bounce, Lysis, Over, Perk, Rally, Rebound, Reclaim, Recoup, Redeem, Regain, Rehab, Repaint, Replevin, Replevy, Repo(ssess), Rescript, Rescue, Resile, →**RETRIEVE**, Revanche, Salvage, Salve, Upswing, Upturn

Recruit(s) Attestor, Bezonian, Choco, Conscript, Crimp, Draft, Employ, Engage, Enlist, Enrol, Headhunt, Intake, Muster, New blood, Nignog, Nozzer, Rookie, Sprog, Volunteer, Wart, Yardbird, Yobbo

Rectifier, Rectify Adjust, Amend, Dephlegmate, Redress, Regulate, →**REMEDY**, Right

Recumbent Prone

Recur(rent), Recurring Chronic, Quartan, Quintan, Recrudesce, Repeated, Repetend, Return

▷**Recurrent** *may indicate* 'reversed'

Recycle(r), Recycling Freegan, Pulp

▷**Red** *may indicate an anagram*

Red(den), Redness Admiral, Anarch(ist), Angry, Arun, Ashamed, Auburn, Bashful, Beet, Bloodshot, Blush, Bolshevik, Brick, Burgundy, C, Cain-coloured, Carmine, Carrot-top, Carroty, Cent, Cerise, Cherry, Chinese, Claret, Commie, Commo, Communist, Copper, Coral, Corallin(e), Crimson, Crocoite, Debit, Dubonnet, Duster, Embarrassed, Eosin, Eric, Erik, Erythema, Ffion, Flame, Flaming, Florid, Flush, Foxy, Garnet, Geranium, Ginger, Gory, Gule(s), Guly, Hat, Henna, Herring, Indian, Indigo, Inflamed, Infra, Inner, Iron, Judas-coloured, Lake, Left(y), Lenin, Letter, Magenta, Maoist, Maroon, Marxist, McIntosh, Medoc, Mulberry, Murrey, Neaten, Oxblood, Pillar-box, Pinko, Plum, Pompeian, Poppy, Raddle, Radical, Raspberry, Raw, Realgar, Rhodamine, Rhodopsin, Ridinghood, Roan, Rosaker, Rose, Rot, Rouge, Rubefaction, Rubefy, Rubella, Ruby, Ruddy, Rufus, Russ(e), Russet, Russian, Russky, Rust(y), Safranin(e), Sanguine, Santalin, Sard, Scarlet, Sea, Setter, Tape, Tidy, Tile, Titian, Trot, Trotsky, Turkey, Venetian, Vermilion, Vinaceous, Wax, Wine

Redeem(er), Redemption Cross, Liberate, Lowse, Mathurin, Ransom, Retrieve, Salvation, Save

Red-handed Bang to rights

▶**Red Indian** *see* **NORTH AMERICAN INDIAN**

▷**Rediscovered** *may indicate an anagram*

Redistil Cohobate

Reduce(d), Reducer, Reduction Abatement, Allay, Alleviate, Asyndeton, Attenuate, Bate, Beggar, Calcine, Clip, Commutation, Commute, Concession, Condense, Contract, Cull, Cut, Cutback, Damping, Debase, Decimate, Decrease, Decrement, De-escalate, Demote, Deplete, Detract, Devalue, Diminish, Diminuendo, Discount, Downgrade, Downscale, Downsize, Draw-down, Drop, Emasculate, Epitomise, Grate, Grind, Hatchet job, →**LESSEN**, Lite, Markdown, Miniature, Mitigate, Moderate, Palliate, Pot, Proclitic, Pulp, Put, Rarefaction, Regression, Remission, Retrench, Rundown, Scant, Shade, Shorten, Shrinkage, Slash, Strain, Supersaver, Taper, Telescope, Thin, Weaken, Whittle, Write-off

Redundancy, Redundant Frill, Futile, Lay-off, Needless, Otiose, Pink slip, Pleonasm, Retrenchment, Superfluous, Surplus

Reef Atoll, Barrier, Bombora, Bommie, Cay, Coral, Fringing, Great Barrier, Key, Knot, Lido, Motu, Sca(u)r, Skerry, Witwatersrand

Reel Bobbin, Dance, Eightsome, Hoolachan, Hoolican, Inertia, Lurch, Multiplier, Pirn, Spin, Spool, Stagger, Strathspey, Sway, Swift, Swim, Tirl, Totter, Wheel, Whirl, Wince, Wintle

Re-enlist Re-up

Reestablish Redintegrate, Transplant

Refer Advert, Allude, Assign, Cite, Direct, Mention, Pertain, Relate, Remit, Renvoi, Renvoy, See, Submit, Touch, Trade

Referee Arbiter, Commissaire, Linesman, Mediate, Oddsman, Ref, Umpire, Voucher, Whistler, Zebra

Reference, Reference room Allusion, Apropos, Autocue, Biaxal, Chapter and verse, Character, Coat, Grid, Guidebook, Index, Innuendo, Lexicon, Mention, Morgue, Passion, Promptuary, Quote, Regard, Renvoi, Respect, Retrospect, Testimonial, Thesaurus, Vide

Refine(d), Refinement, Refiner(y) Alembicated, Attic, Catcracker, Couth, Cultivate, Culture, Cupellation, Cut-glass, Distil, Distinction, Elaborate, Elegance, Ethereal, Exility, Exquisite, Genteel, Grace, Ladify, Nice, Nicety, Polish(ed), Polite, Précieuse, Preciosity, Pure, Rare(fy), Recherché, Saltern, Sift, Smelt, Spiritualize, Spirituel, Subtilise, Subtlety, Try, U, Urbane, Veneer

Reflect(ing), Reflection, Reflective, Reflector Albedo, Apotheosis, Blame, Cat's eye®, Chew, Cogitate, →CONSIDER, Echo, Glass, Glint, Glisten, Image, Meditate, Mirror, Muse, Ponder, Redound, Repercuss, Ruminate, Thought

Reflux Acid

▷**Reform(ed)** *may indicate* an anagram

Reform(er), Reforming, Reformist Agrarian, Amend, Apostle, Besant, Bloomer, Calvin, Chastise, Convert, Correct, Counter-Reformation, Enrage, Fourier, Fry, Gandhi, Howard, Improve, Knox, Lafayette, Lollard, Luther, Mend, Modify, Penn, Pietism, PR, Progressionist, Protestant, Puritan, Rad(ical), Recast, Reclaim, Reconstruction, Rectify, Regenerate, Ruskin, Simons, Stanton, Transmute, Wilberforce, Wilkes, Zinzendorf

Refrain Abstain, Alay, Avoid, Bob, Burden, Chorus, Desist, Epistrophe, Faburden, Fa-la, Forbear, Hemistich, Owreword, Repetend, Ritornello, Rumbelow, Rum(p)ti-iddity, Rum-ti-tum, Spare, Tag, Tirra-lirra, Tirra-lyra, Tra-la, Undersong, Waive, Wheel

Refresh(ment), Refresher Air, Bait, Be(a)vers, Buffet, Cheer, Coffee, Elevenses, Enliven, Exhilarate, Food, Four-hours, Milk shake, Nap, New, Nourishment, Purvey, Refection, Reflect, Refocillate, Reinvigorate, Renew, Repast, Restore, Revive, Seltzer, Shire, Slake, Tea, Water

Refrigerator Chill, Chiller, Cooler, Deep freeze, Esky®, Freezer, Freon, Fridge, Ice-box, Minibar, Reefer

Refuge Abri, Asylum, Bolthole, Bothie, Bothy, Caravanserai, Dive, Fastness, Funkhole, Girth, Grith, Harbour, Haven, Hideaway, Hole, Holt, Home, Hospice, Oasis, Port, Reefer, Resort, Retreat, Sanctuary, Sheet-anchor, →SHELTER, Soil, Stronghold

Refurbish New, Renew

▷**Refurbished** *may indicate* an anagram

Refusal, Refuse Bagasse, Ba(u)lk, Bilge, Bin, Black, Blackball, Boycott, Bran, Brash, Breeze, Brock, Bull, Bunkum, Cane-trash, Chaff, Cinder, Clap-trap, Contumacy, Crane, Crap, Debris, Decline, Deny, Disown, Draff, Drivel, Dross, Dunder, Dung, Fag-end, Fenks, Finks, First, Frass, Garbage, Guff, Hogwash, Hold-out, Husk, Interdict, Jews' houses, Jews' leavings, Jib, Junk, Knub, Lay-stall, Leavings, Litter, Lumber, Mahmal, Marc, Megass(e), Midden, Mother, Mush, Nay(-say), Nill, No (dice), Noser, Nould(e), Nub, Offal, Off-scum, Orts, Pigwash, Potale, Punk, Raffle, Rags, Rape(cake), Rat(s), Rebuff, Red(d), Redline, Reest, Regret, Reject, Reneg(u)e, Renig, Repudiate, Resist,

Rot, → **RUBBISH**, Ruderal, Scaff, Scrap, Scree, Screenings, Scum, Sewage, Shant, Shell heap, Slag, Spurn, Sullage, Sweepings, Swill, Tailings, Tinpot, Tip, Tosh, Trade, Trash, Tripe, Trumpery, Turndown, Twaddle, Unsay, Utter, Wash, Waste, Waste paper

▷ **Re-fused** *may indicate* an anagram

Regal Maeve, Organ

▶ **Regal** *see* **ROYAL(TY)**

Regard(ing) Anent, Apropos, As to, Attention, Care, Consider, → **ESTEEM**, Eye, Gaum, Look, Observe, Odour, Pace, Rate, Re, Repute, Respect, Revere, Sake, Steem, Value, Vis-à-vis

Regardless Anyway, Despite, Heedless, In any event, Irrespective, No matter, Notwithstanding, Rash, Though, Uncaring, Willy-nilly

Regiment Black Watch, Buffs, Colour(s), Discipline, Foot, Greys, Ironsides, Life Guards, Marching, Monstrous, Nutcrackers, Organise, RA, RE, REME, Rifle, Royals, Scots Greys, Tercio, Tertia

▷ **Regiment** *may indicate* an anagram

Region(s) → **AREA**, Belt, Central, Climate, Climature, Clime, District, Domain, End, Heaviside layer, Offing, Part, Province, Quart(er), Realm, Sector, Side, Territory, Thermosphere, Tract, Zone

Register(ing), Registration, Registry Actuarial, Almanac, Annal, Cadastral, Cadastre, Calendar, Cartulary, Cash, Census, Check-in, Child abuse, Dawn, Diptych, Docket, Enlist, Enrol, Enter, Flag out, Gross, Handicap, Index, Indicate, Inscribe, Inventory, Land, Ledger, List, Lloyd's, Log, Matricula, Menology, NAI, Net, Note, Notitia, Obituary, Parish, Park, Patent, Patent Rolls, Poll, Quotation, Read, Reception, Record, Reg(g)o, Rent-roll, Roll, Roule, Score, Shift(ing), Ship's, Sink in, Soprano, Terrier, Voice

Regret(ful), Regrettable Alack, Alas, Apologise, Bemoan, Deplore, Deprecate, Ewhow, Forthwink, Ichabod, Lackaday, Lament, Mourn, Otis, Penitent, Pity, Remorse, Repentance, Repine, Resent, Rew, Ruth, Sorrow, Tragic

Regular(ity), Regularly By turn, Clockwork, Constant, Custom, Daily, Episodic, Even, Giusto, Goer, Habitual, Habitude, Habitué, Hourly, Insider, Methodic, Nightly, Nine-to-five, Normal, Often, Orderly, Orthodox, Patron, Peloria, Periodic, Rhythmic, Routine, Set, Smooth, → **STANDARD**, Stated, Statutory, Steady, Strict, Symmetric, Uniform, Usual, Yearly

Regulate, Regulation, Regulator Adjust, Appestat, Ballcock, Bye-law, Code, Control, Correction, Curfew, Customary, Direct, Dispensation, Gibberellin, Governor, Guide, Logistics, Metrostyle, Order, Ordinance, Police, Prescriptive, Protocol, Rule, Snail, Square, Standard, Statute, Stickle, Sumptuary, Thermostat, Valve

Rehearsal, Rehearse Band-call, Dress, Drill, Dry-block, Dry-run, Dummy-run, Practice, Practise, Preview, Recite, Repeat, Run through, Technical, Trial, Walk through

Reign Era, Govern, Meiji, Prevail, Raine, Realm, Restoration, → **RULE**, Sway

Rein(s) Bearing, Caribou, Check, Control, Curb, Deer, Free, Long, Lumbar, Restrain, Ribbons, Safety, Stop, Tame, Tight, Walking

Reincarnation Palingenesis

Reinforce(ment) Aid, Augment, Beef up, Bolster, Boost, Brace, Buttress, Cleat, Counterfort, Line, Plash, Pleach, Positive, Re-bar, Recruit, Reserve, Ripieno, → **STRENGTHEN**, Support, Tenaiile, Tenaillon, Tetrapod, Underline, Welt

Reject(ion) Abhor, Abjure, Athetise, Bin, Blackball, Cast, Deny, Dice, Disallow, Discard, Disclaim, Disdain, Disown, Diss, Eliminate, Flout, Frass, Heave-ho, Jettison, Jilt, Kest, Kill, Knock-back, Ostracise, Oust, Outcast, Outtake, Pip, Plough, Quash, Rebuff, Recuse, Refuse, Reny, Reprobate, Repudiate, Repulse, Retree, Scout, Scrub, Spet, Spike, Spin, Spit, Sputum, Thumbs-down, Trash, Turndown, Veto

Rejoice, Rejoicing Celebrate, Exult, Festivity, Gaude, Glory, Joy, Maffick, Sing

Rejoin(der), Rejoined Answer, Comeback, Counter, Relide, Reply, Response, Retort, Reunite

Rekindle Relume

Relate(d), Relation(ship), Relations, Relative About, Account, Affair, Agnate, Akin, Allied, Appertain, Apposition, Associate, Blood, Blude, Bluid, Causality, Cognate, Commune, Concern, Connection, Connexion, Consanguinity, Cousin(-german), Coz, Dependent, Dispersion, Eme, Enate, Equation, Equivalence, External, False, Formula, German(e), Granny, Guanxi, Impart, In-law, Internal, International, Item, Kin, Kinsman, Labour, Liaison, Link, Love-hate, Mater, Material, Matrix, Nan(n)a, Narrative, Naunt, Nooky, Object, One-to-one, Pertain, Phratry, Pi, Platonic, Poor, Predation, → **PROPORTION**, Pro rata, Proxemics, Public, Race, Rapport, Ratio, Recite, Recount, Refer(ence), Relevant, Respect(s), Saga, Sib(b), Sibling, Sine, Symbiosis, Syntax, Tale, Tell, Truck, Who

Relax(ation), Relaxant, Relaxed Abate, Atony, Calm, Casual, Chill (óut), Com(m)odo, Dégagé, Délassement, Détente, Diversion, Downbeat, Ease, Easy-going, Flaccid, Informal, Laid-back, Laze, Leisured, Let-up, → **LOOSEN**, Mellow (out), Mitigate, Outspan, Peace, Relent, Relief, Remit, Rest, Settle, Sit down, Slacken, Sleep, Slump, Soma, Toneless, Unbend, Unknit, Untie, Unwind

▷ **Relaxed** *may indicate* an anagram

▷ **Relay(ing)** *may indicate* an anagram

Release Abreact, Abrogation, Announcement, Bail, Block, Cable, Catharsis, Clear, Day, Death, Deliver(y), Desorb, Disburden, Discharge, Disclose, Disengage, Disimprison, Dismiss, Disorb, Emancipate, Enfree, Excuse, Exeem, Exeme, Exonerate, Extricate, Exude, Free, Handout, Happy, → **LIBERATE**, Manumit, Merciful, Moksa, Nirvana, Outrush, Parole, Press, Quietus, Quitclaim, Quittance, Relinquish, Remission, Ripcord, Soft, Spring, Tre corde, Unconfine, Uncouple, Undo, Unhand, Unleash, Unlock, Unloose, Unpen, Unshackle, Unsnap, Unteam, Untie

Relevance, Relevant Ad rem, Applicable, Apposite, Apropos, Apt, Germane, Material, Pertinent, Point, Real world, Valid

▸ **Reliable, Reliance** *see* **RELY**

Relic Antique, Ark, Artefact, Fossil, Leftover, Memento, Neolith, Remains, Sangraal, Sangrail, Sangreal, Souvenir, Survival, Vestige

Relief, Relieve(d) Aid, Air-lift, Allay, Alleviate, Alms, Anodyne, Assistance, Assuage, Bas, Cameo, Catharsis, Cavo-relievo, Comfort, Cure, Détente, Ease(ment), Emboss, Emollient, Exempt, Free, Help, High, Indoor, Let-up, Lighten, Linocut, Low, Mafeking, MIRAS, On the parish, Outdoor, Palliate, Phew, Photo, Pog(e)y, Reassure, Redress, Refection, Remedy, Remission, Replacement, Repoussé, Reprieve, → **RESCUE**, Respite, Retirement, Rid, Spare, Spell, Stand-in, Succour, Taper, Tax, Thermoform, Whew, Woodcut

Religion, Religious (sect) Congregant, Creed, Cult, Denomination, Devout, Doctrine, Faith, God-squad, Hieratic, Hospital(l)er, Messeigneurs, Missionary, Missioner, Monastic, Monseigneur, Nun, Oblate, Opium, Pi, Russellite, Serious, Spiritual, State, Theology, Whore, Zealous

Relish(ing) Aspic, Botargo, Caponata, Catsup, Chow-chow, Condiment, Embellishment, Enjoy, Flavour, Gentleman's, Gout, Gust(o), Ketchup, Lap(-up), Lust, Opsonium, Palate, Pesto, Piccalilli, Sapid, Sar, Sauce, Savour, Seasoning, Tang, Tooth, Worcester sauce, Zest

Reluctant Averse, Backward, Chary, Circumspect, Cockshy, Grudging, Laith, Loath, Loth, Nolition, Renitent, Shy, Under protest, Unwilling

Rely, Reliance, Reliant, Reliable Addiction, Authentic, Bank, Brick, Confidence, Constant, Copper-bottomed, → **COUNT**, Dependent, Found, Honest, Hope, Inerrant, Jeeves, Leal, Lean, Loyal, Mensch, Presume, Pukka, Rest, Robin, Safe, Secure, Solid, Sound, Sponge, Stalwart, Stand-by, Staunch, Trade on, Trustworthy, Trusty, Unfailing

Remain(s), Remainder, Remaining Abide, Ash(es), Balance, Bide, Continue, Corse, Dreg(s), Dwell, Embers, Estate, Exuviae, Fag-end, Fossils, Kreng, Last, Late, Lave, Left, Lie, Locorestive, Manet, Nose, Oddment, Orts, Other, Outstand, Persist, Relic(ts), Reliquae, Residue, Rest, Ruins, Scourings, Scraps, Stay, Stick, Stub, Surplus, Survive, Tag-end, Talon, Tarry, Wait

Remark Aside, Barb, Bromide, Comment(ary), Descry, Dig, Generalise, Mention, Noise, →NOTE, Notice, Obiter dictum, Observe, Platitude, Reason, Sally, Shot, State

Remarkable, Remarkably A1, Amazing, A one, Arresting, Beauty, Bodacious, Come-on, Conspicuous, Dilly, Egregious, Eminent, Extraordinary, Heliozoan, Legendary, Lúlu, Mirable, Notable, Notandum, Noteworthy, Personal, Phenomenal, Rattling, →SIGNAL, Singular, Some, Striking, Tall, Unco, Uncommon, Visible

Remedial, Remedy Adaptogen, Aid, Antacid, Antibiotic, Antidote, Arnica, Bicarb, Boneset, Calomel, Corrective, Cortisone, →CURE, Decongestant, Drug, Elixir, Febrifuge, Feverfew, Fumitory, Ginseng, Heal, Ipecac, Medicate, Medicine, Nostrum, Palliative, Panacea, Paregoric, Poultice, Rectify, Redress, Repair, Salve, Simple, Specific, Therapeutic, Treatment

▷ **Remember** *may indicate* RE-member, viz. Sapper

Remember(ed), Remembering, Remembrance Bethink, Catchy, Commemorate, Con, Mem, Memorial, Memorise, Mention, Mneme, Poppy, Recall, Recollect, Remind, Reminisce, Retain, Rosemary, Souvenir

Remind(er) Aftertaste, Aide-memoire, Bell ringer, Bethought, Bookmark, Evocatory, Evoke, Jog, Keepsake, Mark, Memento, Memo, Mnemonic, Mnemotechnic, Monition, Nudge, Phylactery, Prod, Prompt, Shades of, Souvenir, Throwback, Token

Remission Abatement, Absolution, Acceptilation, Indulgence, Pardon, Pause

Remnant Butt, End, Fent, Heeltap, Leavings, Left-over, Odd-come-short, Offcut, Relic, Relict, →REMAINDER, Rump, Stub, Sweepings, Trace, Vestige, Witness

Remorse Angst, Ayenbite, Breast-beating, Compunction, Contrition, Had-i-wist, Pity, →REGRET, Repentance, Rue, Ruing, Ruth, Sorrow, Worm

Remote(ness) Aloof, Aphelion, Backveld, Backwater, Backwood, Boondocks, Bullamakanka, Bundu, Bush, →DISTANT, Forane, Foreign, Inapproachable, Insular, Irrelevant, Jericho, Lonely, Long(inquity), Mystique, Out(part), Outback, Out of the way, Reassert, Scrub, Secluded, Shut-out, Slightest, Surrealistic, Unlikely, Withdrawn, Wop-wops

Removal, Remove(d) Abduct, Abstract, Airbrush, Banish, Blot, Circumcision, Clear, Couch, Deaccession, Debridement, Declassify, Dele(te), Depilate, Depose, Detach, Dethrone, Detract, Dislodge, Dismiss, Dispel, Displace, Doff, Efface, Eject, Eliminate, Eloi(g)n, Emend, Eradicate, Erase, Esloin, Estrange, Evacuate, Evict, Exalt, Excise, Expunge, Extirpate, Far, Flit, Huff, Nick, Obviation, Ouster, Raise, Raze, Recuse, Rid, Scratch, Shift, Sideline, Spirit, Strip, Subtract, Supplant, Swipe, Transfer, Transport, Unbelt, Unload, Unseat, Unstep, Uproot

Render(ing) Construe, Deliver, Do, Gie, Give, Interpretation, Make, Melt, Pebble-dash, Plaster, Provide, Recite, Represent, Restore, Setting, Submit, Tallow, Try, Yeve, Yield

Rendezvous Date, Meeting, Philippi, Tryst, Venue

Rendition Account, Delivery, Interpretation, Translation, Version

Renegade, Renege, Renegue Apostate, Default, Defector, Deserter, Pike, Rat(ton), Recreant, Traitor, Turncoat, Weasel out

▷ **Renegade** *may indicate* a word reversal

Renew(al) Instauration, Neogenesis, Palingenesis, Refresh, Replace, Resumption, Retrace, Revival, Urban

Renounce, Renunciation Abandon, Abdicate, Abjure, Abnegate, Disclaim, Disown, Forfeit, For(e)go, Forisfamiliate, Forsake, For(e)say, Forswear, Kenosis, Pass up, Recede, Recuse, Relinquish, Renay, Retract, Sacrifice

Renovate(d), Renovation Duff, Face-lift, Instauration, Makeover, Refurbish, Renew, Repair, Restore, Revamp, Touch up, Translate

Rent(er), Rented, Renting Asunder, Broken, Charge, Cornage, Cost, Crack, Cranny, Cuddeehih, Cuddy, Division, Economic, Fair, Farm, Fee, Fissure, Gale, Gavel, Ground, →HIRE, Lease, Let, List, Mail, Market, Occupy, Pendicle, Penny(-mail), Peppercorn, Quit-rent, Rack, Rip, Rived, Riven, Screed, Seat, Slit, Split, Stallage, Subtenant, Tare, Tenant, Tithe, Tore, Torn, Tythe, White

▷ **Reorganised** *may indicate* an anagram

Repair(s), Repairer, Reparation Amend(s), Anaplasty, Botch, Cobble, Damages, Darn, DIY, Doctor, Expiation, Fettle, Fitter, Fix, Garage, Go, Haro, Harrow, Heel, →MEND, Neoplasty, Overhaul, Patch, Point, Recompense, Redress, Refit, Reheel, Remedy, Renew, Repoint, Resort, Restore, Retouch, Roadworks, Satisfaction, Service, Stitch, Tenorrhaphy, Ulling, Vamp, Volery

Repartee Backchat, Badinage, Banter, Persiflage, Rejoinder, Retort, Riposte, Wit, Wordplay

Repast Bever, Collection, Food, Meal, Tea, Treat

Repay(ment) Avenge, Compensate, Perseverate, Quit, Reassert, Refund, Requite, Retaliate, Revenge, Reward, Satisfaction

Repeat(ed), Repeatedly, Repetition, Repetitive Again, Alliteration, Belch, Bis, Burden, Burp, Copy, Cycle, Ditto(graphy), Do, Duplicate, →ECHO, Echolalia, Encore, Eruct, Facsimile, Habitual, Harp, Image, Imitate, Iterate, Leit-motiv, Parrot, Parrot-fashion, Passion, Perpetuate, Perseverate, Playback, Reassert, Recapitulate, Recite(r), Redo, Refrain, Regurgitate, Reiterate, Renew, Rep, Repetend, Rerun, Retail, Rote, Same(y), Screed, Tautology, Thrum, Trite

Repel(lent) Aversive, Camphor, Deet, Estrange, Harsh, Offensive, Rebarbative, Reject, Repulse, Revolt, Shoo, Squalid, Turn-off, Ug(h), Ward

▶ **Repetition** *see* REPEAT(ED)

Replace(ment), Replaceable, Replacing Change, Deputise, Diadochy, Euphorism, For, Instead, Novation, Pinch-hit, Pre-empt, Raincheck, Refill, Reinstate, Relief, Renew, Replenish, Restore, Spare part, Stand-in, Substitute, Supersede, Supplant, Surrogate, Taxis, Transform, Transliterate, Understudy, Usurp

Replete, Repletion Awash, Full, Gorged, Plenitude, Plethora, Sated, Satiation

Replica Clone, Copy, Duplicate, Facsimile, Image, Repetition, Spit

Reply Accept, Answer, Churlish, Duply, Echo, Rejoinder, Replication, Repost, Rescript, Response, Retort, Surrebut, Surrejoinder

Report(s), Reporter Account, Announce, Annual, Auricular, Bang, Beveridge, Blacksmith, Bruit, Bulletin, Cahier, Clap, Columnist, Comment, Commentator, Compte rendu, Correspondent, Court, Court circular, Cover, Crack, Crump, Cub, Debrief, Describe, Despatch, Disclose, Dispatch, Dissertation, Explosion, Fame, Fireman, Grapevine, Hansard, Hearsay, Informant, Item, Jenkins, Journalist, Legman, Libel, Narrative, News, Newsflash, Newshawk, Newshound, Newsman, Noise, Notify, Paper, Pop, Powwow, Pressman, Protocol, Rapporteur, Recount, Relate, Relay, Representation, Repute, Return, Roorback, Rumour, Sitrep, Sound(bite), Staffer, State(ment), Stringer, Tale, →TELL, Thesis, Transactions, Transcribe, Tripehound, Troop, Update, Weather, Whang, White paper, Wolfenden, Write up

▷ **Reported** *may indicate* the sound of a letter or word

Repossess(ion) Distringas

Represent(ation), Representative, Represented Agent, Ambassador, Archetypal, Caricature, Client, Commercial, Commissary, Commissioner, Cross-section, Delegate, Depict, Deputation, Describe, Display, Drawing, Drummer, Effigy, Elchee, Eltchi, Emblem, Embody, Emissary, Epitomise, Example, Histogram, Ikon, Image, Instantiate, John Bull, Legate, Limn, Lobby, Map, Mouthpiece, MP, Personate, Personify, Piechart, Portray, Proportional, Quintessence, Rep, Resemble, Salesman, Senator, Shop steward, Simulacrum, Spokesman, Stand-in, Statua, Status, Steward, Symbolic, Tableau, Tableau vivant, Transcription, Traveller, Typical, Vice-consul, Visitor-general

▷ **Represented** *may indicate* an anagram

Reprimand Blast, Bounce, Carpet, Castigate, →CENSURE, Chastise, Chide, Dressing-down, Earful, Jobe, Lace, Lecture, Rating, Rebuke, Reproof, Rocket, Rollicking, Scold, Slate, Strafe, Targe, Tick off, Tongue-lashing, Wig

Reproach Besom, Bisom, Blame, Braid, Byword, Cataian, Catayan, Chide, Discredit, Dispraise, Exprobate, Gib, Mispraise, Odium, Opprobrium, Rebuke, Ronyon, Runnion, Scold, Shend, Sloan, Stigma, Taunt, Truant, Twat, Twit, Upbraid, Upcast, Yshend

▷ **Reproduce** *may indicate* an anagram

Reproduce(r), Reproduction, Reproductive (organ) Arrhenotoky, Clone, Copy, Counterfeit, Depict, Edition, Etch, Eugenics, Loins, Megaspore, Mono, Monogenesis, Monogony, Multiply, Oogamy, Parthenogenesis, Phon(e)y, Pirate, Propagate, Refer, Replica, Roneo®, Seminal, Simulate, Stereo, Vegetative, Viviparism

Reproof, Reprove Admonish, Berate, Censure, Chide, Correction, Correption, Lecture, Rate, Rebuff, Rebuke, Reprehension, Scold, Sloan, Take to task, Tut, Upbraid

Reptile, Reptilian Agamid, Alligarta, Alligator, Base, Basilisk, Caiman, Cayman, Chameleon, Chelonian, Creeper, Crocodile, Cynodont, Diapsid, Dicynodont, Dinosaur, Goanna, Herpetology, Lacertine, Lizard, Mamba, Pelycosaur, Pit viper, Pteranodon, Pterodactyl, Rhynchocephalian, Sauroid, →**SNAKE**, Sphenodon, Squamata, Synapsid, Tegu(exin), Thecodont, Therapsid, Tortoise, Tuatara, Tuatera, Turtle, Worm

Republic(an) Antimonarchist, Belarussian, Democrat, Fenian, Fianna Fáil, Girondist, GOP, International Brigade, IRA, Iraqi, Leveller, Montagnard, Mugwump, Plato, Provisional, Provo, Red, Sansculotte, Sansculottic, Sinn Fein, Whig, Young Italy

Republic(s) Banana, Second, State, Weimar

Repudiate Abjure, Deny, Disaffirm, Discard, Disclaim, Disown, Ignore, Recant, Reject, Renounce, Repel

Repugnance, Repugnant Abhorrent, Alien, Disgust, Distaste, Fulsome, Horror, Loathing, Nastiness, Obscene, Odious, Revulsion

Reputable, Reputation, Repute(d) Bubble, Credit, Dit, Estimate, Fame, Good, Izzat, Loos, Los, Name, Note, Notoriety, Odour, Opinion, Prestige, Putative, Regard, Renown, Said, Sar, →**STANDING**, Stature, Status, Stink, Stock, Trustworthy

Request Adjure, Appeal, Apply, Ask, Beg, Desire, D-notice, Entreaty, Invite, Petition, Plea, Prayer, Precatory, Solicit, Supplication, Touch

Require(d), Requirement Charge, Crave, De rigueur, Desideratum, Desire, Enjoin, Essential, Exact, Expect, Incumbent, Lack, Mandatory, Necessity, Need, Prerequisite, Priority, Sine qua non, Stipulate, Then

Requisite, Requisition Commandeer, Due, Embargo, Essential, Indent, Necessary, Needful, Order, Press

Rescue(r) Aid, Air-sea, Deliver, Free, Liberate, Lifeline, Lifesave, Mountain, Ransom, Reclaim, Recover, Recower, Redeem, Regain, Relieve, Repatriate, Reprieve, Retrieve, Salvage, Salvation, →**SAVE**, White knight

Research(er) Audience, Boffin, Delve, Dig, Enquiry, Explore, Fieldwork, Indagator, Investigate, Legwork, Market, MORI, Near-market, Operational, Opposition, Pioneer, Post-doctoral, Psychical, Quest, Res, Scientist, Sus(s), Test

Resemblance, Resemble, Resembling Affinity, Apatetic, Approach, Assonant, Homophyly, Likeness, -oid, -opsis, Quasi, Replica, Similitude, Simulacrum, Simulate

Resent(ful), Resentment Anger, Bitter(ness), Bridle, Choler, Cross, Dudgeon, Embittered, Grudge, Indignation, Ire, Malign, Miff, Mind, Pique, Rancour, Rankle, Smart, Snarling, Spite, Umbrage

Reservation, Reserve(d), Reservist(s) Aloof, Arrière-pensée, Aside, Backlog, Bank, Bashful, Book, But, By, Capital, Caveat, Central, Cold, Condition, Coy, Demiss, Detachment, Distant, Earmark, Engage, Ersatz, Except, Fall-back, Federal, Fort Knox, Fund, General, Gold, Hold, Husband, Ice, Indian, Introvert, Landwehr, Layby, Locum, Median strip, Mental, Militiaman, Modesty, Nature, Nest-egg, Nineteenth man, Proviso, Qualification, Reddendum, Res, Rest, Restraint, Retain, Reticence, Retiring, Rez, Salvo, Sanctuary, Save, Scenic, Scruple, Serengeti, Set aside, Special, Spoken for, Stand-by, Stand-offishness, Starch, Stash, Stock(pile), Substitute, TA (men), Twelfth man, Uncommunicate, Understudy, Warren, Waves, Withhold

Reservoir Basin, Cistern, Font, G(h)ilgai, Gilgie, Oilcup, Repository, Stock, Sump, Tank, Well

Reside(nce), Resident(s), Residential Abode, Address, Amban, Chequers, Commorant, Consulate, Denizen, Domicile, Dwell, Embassy, Establishment, Expatriate, Exurb(anite), Gaff, Gremial, Guest, Home, Indweller, Inholder, Inmate, Intern, Ledger, Lei(d)ger, Lieger, Lodger, Masonry, Metic, Pad, Parietal, Resiant, Settle, Settlement, Sojourn, Squat, Stay, Tenant, Tenement, Uptown, Villager, Yamen

Residual, Residue Ash, Astatki, Calx, Caput, Chaff, Cinders, Crud, Draff, Dregs, Expellers, Greaves, Heeltap, Leavings, Mazout, Mortuum, Prefecture, Raffinate, Remainder, Remanent, Remnant, Scourings, Sediment, Slag, Slurry, Snuff, Vinasse

Resign(ed), Resignation Abandon, Abdicate, Demit, Fatalism, Heigh-ho, Leave, Meek, Philosophical, →**QUIT**, Reconcile, Step down, Stoic, Submit

Resin Acaroid, Amber, Amine, Amino, Arar, Asaf(o)etida, Bakelite®, Balsam, Benjamin, Benzoin, Burgundy pitch, Cachou, Cannabin, Caranna, Carauna, Catechu, Charas, Churrus, Colophony, Conima, Copai(ba), Copaiva, Copal(m), Courbaril, Cutch, Dam(m)ar, Dammer, Dragon's blood, Elemi, Epoxy, Frankincense, Galbanum, Galipot, Gambi(e)r, Gamboge, Glyptal, Guaiacum, Gum, Hasheesh, Hashish, Hing, Jalapic, Jalapin, Kino, Lac, Ladanum, Limonene, Lupulin, Mastic, Melamine, Myrrh, Natural, Olibanum, Opopanax, Phenolic, Podophyl(l)in, Polyester, Polymer, Polypropylene, Propolis, Retinite, Roset, Rosin, Rosit, Rozet, Rozit, Sagapenum, Sandarac(h), Saran®, Scammony, Shellac, Silicone, Storax, Styrene, Synthetic, Tacamahac, Tacmahack, Takamaka, Thus, Urea, Xylenol

Resist, Resistance, Resistant, Resistor All-weather, Anti, Antibiotic, Barretter, Bleeder, Bristle, Buck, Ceramal, Cermet, Chetnik, Coccidiostat, Combat, Consumer, Contest, Defiance, Defy, Drag, Element, Face, Fend, Friction, Gainstrive, Grapo, Hostile, Immunity, Impede, Impediment, Internal, Intifada, Invar, Klendusic, Klepht, Maquis, Maraging, Market, Megohm, Microhm, Negative, Obstacle, Ohm(age), Omega, Oppose, Partisan, Passive, Pull, R, Radiation, Redound, Reluct, Reluctance, Renitent, Resilient, Rheostat, Sales, Satyagraha, Shockproof, Soul-force, Specific, Stability, Stand (pat), Stonde, Stubborn, Tamil Tiger, Tough, Voltage divider

Resolute, Resolution Adamant, Analysis, Bold, Cast-iron, Closure, Courage, Decided, Decision, Denouement, Determined, Dogged, →**FIRM**, Fortitude, Granite, Grim, Grit, Hardiness, Insist, Motion, New Year, Pertinacity, Promotion, Rede, Reed(e), Resolve, Stable, Stalwart, Staunch, Stout(-hearted), Strength, Strong-willed, Sturdy, Tenacity, Unbending, Valiant, Willpower

Resolve(d), Resolver Analyse, Calculate, Conation, Decide, Declare, →**DETERMINE**, Deus ex machina, Factorise, Fix, Grit, Hellbent, Intent, Nerve, Pecker, →**PURPOSE**, Right, Settle, Sort out, Steadfast, Tenacity, Vow

▷ **Resolved** *may indicate* an anagram

Resort Acapulco, Aspen, Benidorm, Biarritz, Bognor, Cancun, Centre, Chamonix, Clacton, Copacabana, Davos, Dive, Étapes, Expedient, Frame, Frequent, Gstaad, Haunt, Health, Herne Bay, Hove, Hydro, Invoke, Klosters, Lair, Last, Las Vegas, Locarno, Malibu, Miami, Morecambe, Nassau, Nice, Palm Beach, Pau, Penzance, Pis aller, Poole, Rapallo, Recourse, Redcar, Repair, Riviera, St Ives, Seaside, Skegness, Southend, Spa(w), Thredbo, Torremolinos, Troon, Use, Utilise, Waikiki, Weston-super-Mare, Weymouth, Whitby, Worthing, Yalta

▷ **Resort(ing)** *may indicate* an anagram

Resource(s), Resourceful Assets, Beans, Bottom, Chevisance, Clever, Faculty, Funds, Gumption, Ingenious, Input, Inventive, Manpower, Means, Renewable, Shared, Sharp, Smeddum, Stock-in-trade, →**VERSATILE**, Wealth, Webliography

Respect(ed), Respectable, Respectful Admire, Ahimsa, Aspect, Behalf, Clean cut, Consecrate, Consider, Cred(it), Decent, Deference, Devoir, Doyen(ne), Duty, Eminent, Esteem, Fear, Genteel, Gigman, Homage, →**HONOUR**, Kempt, Kowtowing, Latria, Obeisant, Officious, Pace, Particular, Preppy, Prestige, Proper, Reference, Regard, Relation, Reputable, Revere, Sir, S(t)irrah, U, Venerate, Way, Wellborn, Well-thought-of, Wise, Worthy

Respirator, Respire, Respiration Artificial, Blow, Breathe, Exhale, External, Gasmask, Inhale, Iron lung, Mouth-to-mouth, Pant, Snorkel

Respond, Response, Responsive Amenable, Answer, Antiphon, Autoreply, Backlash, Bi, Comeback, Conditioned, Counteroffer, Duh, Echo, Feedback, Flechman, Grunt, Immune, Kneejerk, Kyrie, Litany, Nastic, Pavlovian, Photonasty, Plea, Prebuttal, Psychogalvanic, React(ion), Reagency, Rebutter, Reflex, Reply, Repost,

Retort, Rheotaxis, Rheotropism, Rise, Sensitive, Stayman, Synapte, Syntonic, Tender, Thigmotropic, Tic, Tropism, Unconditioned, Voice, Warm, Wilco

Responsibility, Responsible Accountable, Anchor, Answerable, Baby, Behind, Blame, Buck, Charge, Collective, Culpable, Dependable, Diminished, Duty, Frankpledge, Guilty, Hot seat, Incumbent, Instrumental, Liable, Mantle, Mea culpa, Millstone, Onus, Perpetrate, Pigeon, Sane, Solid, Stayman, Trust

Rest(ing), Rest day Anchor, Balance, Bed, Break, Breather, Calm, Catnap, Depend, Dwell, Ease, Easel, Etc, Feutre, Gallows, Gite, Halt, Inaction, Jigger, Lance, Lave, Lay to, Lean, Lie, Lie-in, Light, Lodge, Loll, Lound, Lull, Minim, Nap, Noah, Oasis, Others, Outspan, Pause, Quiescence, Quiet, Relâche, Relax, Rely, Remainder, Repose, Requiem, Reserve, Respite, Sabbath, Shut-eye, Sick leave, Siesta, Silence, →SLEEP, Slumber, Spell, Spider, Static, Stopover, Support, Surplus, Teabreak, Waypoint

Restaurant, Restaurateur Automat, Beanery, Bistro, Brasserie, British, Cabaret, Café, Canteen, Carvery, Chew'n'spew, Chinkie, Chinky, Chip-shop, Chophouse, Commissary, Cook shop, Creperie, Diner, Eatery, Eating-house, Estaminet, Gastropub, Greasy spoon, Grill, Grillroom, Grub shop, Luncheonette, Maxim's, Naafi, Noshery, Padrone, Pizzeria, Porter-house, Rathskeller, Ratskeller, Raw bar, Roadhouse, Rotisserie, Slap-bang, Steakhouse, Takeaway, Taqueria, Taverna, Tea garden, Teahouse, Tearoom, Teashop, Trat(toria)

Restive, Restless(ness) Agitato, Chafing, Chorea, Fidgety, Fikish, Free-arm, Itchy, Jactitation, Spring fever, Toey, Unsettled

▷ **Restless** *may indicate* an anagram

Restoration, Restorative, Restore(d) Bring to, Cure, Descramble, Heal, Mend, New, Pentimento, Pick-me-up, Postliminy, Rally, Recondition, Redeem, Redintegrate, Redux, Refresh, Refurbish, Regenerate, Rehabilitate, Reintegrate, Rejuvenate, Remedial, Renew, Renovate, Replenish, Replevy, Repone, Restitute, Resuscitate, Retouch, Revamp, Revive, Righten, Stet, Tonic, Undelete, Whole

Restrain(ed), Restraint Abstinence, Ban, Bate, Bit, Bottle, Branks, Bridle, Cage, Chain, Chasten, →CHECK, Checks and balances, Chokehold, Coerce, Cohibit, Compesce, Confinement, Contain, Control, Cramp, Curb, Dam, Decorum, Detent, Dry, Duress, Embargo, Enfetter, Fetter, Freeze, Gag-rein, Gyve, Halt, Hamshackle, Handcuffs, Harness, Heft, Hinder, Hopple, Immanacle, Impound, Inhibit, Jess, Leg-iron, Lid, Low-key, Manacle, Measure, Mince, Moderation, Muzzle, Patient, Quiet, Rein, Repress, Restrict, Ritenuto, Shackle, Sober, Sobriety, Squeeze, Stay, Stent, Stint, Straitjacket, Strait-waistcoat, Tabu, Temper, Tether, Tie, Tieback, Trash, Underplay

Restrict(ed), Restriction Band, Bar, Bind, Bit, Block, Burden, Cage, Catch, Censorship, Chain, Circumscribe, Closet, Condition, Cord, Corset, Cramp, Curb, Curfew, DORA, Fence, Fetter, Fold, Gate, Ground, Guard, Hamper, Hidebound, Hobble, Inhibit, Intern, Kennel, Let, →LIMIT, Localise, Lock, Mere, Narrow, Net, Nick, No-go, Oche, Pale, Parochial, Pen, Pent, Pier, Pin, Poky, Pot-bound, Private, Proscribed, Qualify, Regulate, Rein, Rent, Repression, Rope, Safety belt, Scant, Seal, Section, Selected, Shackle, Snare, Squeeze, Stenopaic, Stent, Stint, Stop, Straiten, Stunt, Swaddle, Tether, Tie

Result(s) After-effect, Aftermath, Ans(wer), Arise, Bring, Causal, Consequence, Effect, Emanate, End, End-product, Ensue, Entail, Event, Eventuate, Finding, Fruict, Fruition, Fruits, Issue, Karmic, Lattermath, →OUTCOME, Outturn, Pan, Pay off, Proceeds, Product, Quotient, Sequel, Side-effect, Sum, Therefore, Upshot, Verdict, Wale

Retain(er), Retains, Retention, Retentive Brief, Contain, Deposit, Fee, Hold, Keep, Long, Panter, Pantler, Reserve, Retinue, Servant, Ur(a)emia, Vassal

Retaliate, Retaliation Avenge, Carousel, Counter, Lex talionis, Pay back, Pay home, Quit(e), Redress, Repay, Reprisal, Requite, Retort, Revenge, Talion

Reticence, Reticent Clam, Cowardly, Coy, Dark, Guarded, Reserve, Restraint, Secretive, Shy, Taciturn

Retinue Comitatus, Company, Cortège, Equipage, Following, Meiney, Meinie, Meiny, Menyie, Sowarry, Suite

Retire(d), Retiree, Retirement, Retiring Abed, Aloof, Asocial, Baccare, Backare, Backpedal, Blate, Bowler-hat, Bow out, Cede, Coy, Demob, Demure, Depart, Ebb, Emeritus, Essene, Former, Leave, Lonely, Modest, Mothball, Nun, Outgoing, Pension, Private, Put out, Quit, Recede, Recluse, Reserved, Resign, Retract, Retreat, Retrocedent, Roost, Rusticate, Scratch, Sequester, Shy, Superannuate, Timid, Unassertive, Withdraw

▷ **Retirement** *may indicate* 'bed' around another word, or word reversed

Retort Alembic, Comeback, Courteous, Floorer, Quip, Repartee, → **REPLY**, Retaliate, Riposte, Still

Retract(ion) Disavow, Epanorthosis, Palinode, Recall, Recant, Renounce, Revoke

Retread Recap

Retreat Abbey, Arbour, Ashram(a), Asylum, Backwater, Berchtesgaden, Bower, Bug, Cell, Cloister, Convent, Dacha, Departure, Donjon, Funkhole, Girth, Grith, Hermitage, Hibernaculum, Hideaway, Hide-out, Hole, Ivory-tower, Lair, Lama(sery), Mew, Monastery, Nest, Nook, Pullback, Recede, Recoil, Redoubt, Reduit, Refuge, Retire, Retraite, Right-about, Rout, Shangri-La, Shelter, Skedaddle, Stronghold, Withdraw

Retribution Come-uppance, Deserts, Nemesis, Revenge, Reward, Utu, Vengeance

Retrieve(r), Retrieval Access, Bird-dog, Chesapeake Bay, Field, Gundog, Labrador, Read-out, Recall, Reclaim, Recoup, Recover, Redeem, Rescue, Salvage

Return(s) Agen, Answer, Bricole, Census, Comeback, Day, Diminishing, Dividend, Earnings, Elect, Er, Extradite, Gain, Homecoming, Nil, Pay, Payback, Proceeds, Profit, Rebate, Rebound, Recur, Redound, Regress, Reject, Rejoin, Render, Rent, Repair, Repay, Replace, Reply, Requital, Respond, Rest, Restitution, Restoration, Restore, Retort, Retour, Revenue, Reverse, Revert, Riposte, Takings, Tax, Tit for tat, Traffic, → **YIELD**

Reuse Cannibalise

Reveal(ing), Revelation Acute, Admit, Advertise, Air, Apocalyptic, Bar, Bare, Betray, Bewray, Confess, Descry, Disclose, Discover, Discure, → **DIVULGE**, Epiphany, Exhibit, Explain, Expose, Eye-opener, Giveaway, Hierophantic, Impart, Indicate, Indiscreet, Ingo, Kythe, Leak, Low-cut, Manifest, Open, Out, Parade, Pentimento, Satori, Scry, → **SHOW**, Skimpy, Spill, Tell-tale, Unclose, Uncover, Unfold, Unheal, Unmask, Unveil

Reveille Raise

Revel(ling), Revelry Ariot, Bacchanalia, Bend, Carnival, Carouse, Comus, Dionysian, Feast, Gloat, Glory, Joy, Maffick, Merriment, On the tiles, Orgy, Rant, Rejoice, Riot, Roister, Rollicks, Rout, Royst, Saturnalia, Splore, Swig, Upsee, Ups(e)y, Wallow, Wassail, Whoopee

Revenge(r), Revengeful Aftergame, Avenge, Commination, Goel, Grenville, Montezuma's, Nightrider, Payback, Reprise, Requite, Retaliation, Revanche, Settlement, Tit for tat, Ultion, Utu, Vigilante, Vindictive

Revere(nce) Admire, Adoration, Awe, Bostonian, Dread, Dulia, Esteem, Fear, Hallow, Hery, Homage, → **HONOUR**, Hyperdulia, Idolise, Latria, Obeisance, Paul, Respect, Venerate

Reversal, Reverse, Reversing, Reversion, Reversible Anatropy, Antithesis, Antonym, Arsy-versy, Atavism, Back(slide), B-side, Change-over, Chiasmus, Counter(mand), Escheat, Evaginate, Exergue, Flip, Flip side, Inversion, Mirror image, Misfortune, → **OPPOSITE**, Overturn, Palindrome, Pile, Regress, Repeal, Retrograde, Revoke, Rheotropic, Setback, Switchback, Tails, Throwback, Transit, Turn, Turnabout, Two-faced, Un-, Undo, Upend, U-turn, Verso, Vice versa, Volte-face, Woman

▷ **Review** *may indicate* an anagram or a reversed word

Review(er) Appeal, Censor, Credit, Critic, Critique, Editor, Feuilleton, Footlights, Glimpse, Inspect, Iso-, Judicial, Magazine, March-past, Notice, Pan, Peer, Recapitulate, Repeat, Revise, Rundown, Run over, Slate, Spithead, Summary, Summing-up, Survey, Write-up

▷ **Revise(d)** *may indicate* an anagram

Revise(r) | 352

Revise(r), Revision(ist) Alter, Amend, Change, Correct, Diaskeuast, Diorthosis, Edit, Emend, Heretic, Peruse, Reappraise, Reassess, Recense, Reform, Rev, Update

Revive, Revival, Revivify, Reviving Araise, Classical, Enliven, Gothic, Kiss of life, Rally, Reanimate, Reawake(n), Rebirth, Redintegrate, Redux, Refresh, Rekindle, Relive, Renaissance, Renascent, Renew, Renovate, Restore, Resurrect, Resuscitate, Risorgimento, Romantic, Romo, Rouse, Wake

Revolt(ing), Revolution(ary) Agitator, American, Anarchist, Apostasy, Barrel roll, Bloodless, Bolshevik, Boxer, Bukharin, Cade, Castro, Chartist, Che, Chinese, Circle, Coup d'état, Cultural, Cycle, Defection, Dervish, Desmoulins, De Valera, Disgust, Enragé, February, French, Girondin, Glorious, Green, Grody, Gyration, Ho Chi Minh, Icky, Industrial, →IN REVOLT, Insurgent, Insurrection, IRA, Lenin, Leninist, Mao, Marat, Marti, Marx, Marxist, Maximalist, Montagnard, Mutiny, Nauseating, October, Orbit, Paine, Palace, Paris Commune, Peasants, Putsch, →REBEL, Red Guard, Red Shirt, Reformation, Reign of terror, Riot, Robespierre, Roll, Rotation, Russian, Savimbi, Sedition, Septembrist, Sicilian Vespers, Spartacist, Syndicalism, Titanomachy, Trot(sky), Ugly, →UPRISING, Upryst, Velvet, Weatherman, Whirl

▷ **Revolutionary** *may indicate* 'reversed'

Revolve(r), Revolving Carrier, Catherine wheel, Centrifuge, Colt®, Gat, Girandole, Grindstone, →GUN, Gyrate, Iron, Klinostat, Lathe, Maelstrom, Peristrephic, Pistol, Pivot, Planet, Roller, Rotate, Rotifer, Rotor, Roundabout, Run, Spin, Swivel, Tone, Turn(stile), Turntable, Turret, Wheel, Whirl(igig), Whirlpool

Revulsion Abhorrence, Loathing, Repugnance, The creeps, Ugh

Reward(ing) Albricias, Bonus, Bounty, Compensate, Consideration, Desert, Emolument, Fee, Guerdon, Head money, Meed, Payment, Premium, Price, Prize, Profit, Purse, Push money, Reap, Recognise, Recompense, Reguerdon, Remuneration, Repay, Requital, Requite, S, Shilling, Tanti, Wage, War(r)ison

Rheostat Potentiometer

Rhetoric(al) Alliteration, Anaphora, Anastrophe, Antimetabole, Antithesis, Antostrophe, Apophasis, Aposiopesis, Assonance, Asteism, Asyndeton, Aureate, Bombast, Brachylogia, Cacophony, Catachresis, Chiasmus, Eloquence, Enantiosis, Epanadiplosis, Epanados, Epanalepsis, Epanorthosis, Epexegesis, Epistrophe, Epizeuxis, Erotema, Eroteme, Erotesis, Euphemism, Hendiadys, Litotes, Metonymy, Oratory, Oxymoron, Paradox, Paral(e)ipsis, Periphrasis, Peroration, Pleonasm, Scesisonomaton, Speechcraft, Syllepsis, Trivial, Trivium, Zeugma

Rhomboid Fusil

Rhyme(s), Rhymer, Rhyming Assonance, Clerihew, Closed couplet, Counting out, Couplet, Crambo, Cynghanedd, Doggerel, Double, Eye, Feminine, Head, Internal, Jingle, Macaronic, Masculine, Measure, Mother Goose, Nursery, Perfect, Poetry, Poulter's measure, Rondel, Runic, Sight, Slang, Slant, Tercet, Terza-rima, Thomas, Triple, →VERSE, Virelay

Rhythm(ic) Agoge, Alpha, Asynartete, Backbeat, Beat, Beta, Bo Diddley beat, Breakbeat, Cadence, Circadian, Clave, Dolichurus, Dotted, Duple, Euouae, Evovae, Four-four, Ictic, In-step, Meter, Movement, Oompah, Ostinato, Prosody, Pyrrhic, Rising, Rubato, Sdrucciola, Sesquialtera, Singsong, Sprung, Stride piano, Swing, Syncopation, Tala, Talea, Theta, Three-four, Time, Two-four, Voltinism

Rib(bed), Ribbing, Rib-joint Bar, Chaff, Cod, Cord, Costa, Cross-springer, Dutch, Eve, False, Floating, Futtock, Groin, Intercostal, Lierne, Nervate, Nervular, Nervure, Ogive, Persiflage, Rally, Spare, Springer, Subcosta, Tease, Tierceron, Tracery, True, Wife

Ribbon Band, Bandeau, Blue, Bow, Braid, Caddis, Caddyss, Cordon, Fattrels, Ferret, Fillet, Grosgrain, Hatband, Infula, Pad, Petersham, Radina, Red, Rein, Riband, Rosette, Rouleau, Soutache, Taenia, Tape, Teniate, Tie, Topknot, Torsade

Rice (cake) Arborio, Basmati, Brown, Elmer, Entertainer, Golden, Idli, Indian, Kedgeree, Patna, Pilaf, Pilau, Pilaw, Reis, Risotto, Sushi, Twigs, Vialone nano, Wild, Zizania

Rich(es) Abounding, Abundant, Affluent, Amusing, Bonanza, Buttery, Comic,

Copious, Croesus, Dives, Edmund, Edwin, Fat, Feast, Fertile, Filthy, Flamboyant, Flush, Fruity, Full, Golconda, Haves, Heeled, High, Loaded, Luscious, Lush, Luxurious, Mammon, Moneybags, Moneyed, Nabob, New, Oberous, Oofy, Plenteous, Plush, Plutocrat, Rolling, Silvertail, Sumptuous, Toff, Treasure, Vulgarian, →**WEALTHY**, Well-heeled, Well off, Well-to-do

▷ **Rickety** *may indicate* an anagram

Riddle(r) Boulter, Charade, Colander, Dilemma, Enigma, Koan, Logogriph, Pepper, Perforate, Permeate, Puzzle, Screen, Searce, Search, Seil, Sieve, Sift, Sile, Siler, Sorites, Sphinx, Strain, Tems(e), Trommel

Ride, Riding Annoy, Bareback, Bestride, Bruise, Burn, Canter, Coast, Cycle, District, Division, Draisene, Draisine, Drive, Equitation, Field, Free, Hack, Harass, Haute école, Hitchhike, Lift, Merry-go-round, Mount, Pick(-a-)back, Piggyback, Postil(l)ion, Rape, Revere's, Roadstead, Rollercoaster, Rural, Sit, Spin, Stang, Surf, Switchback, Third, Trot, Weather, Welter, Wheelie, White-knuckle

Rider(s) Addendum, Adjunct, Appendage, Attachment, Boundary, Bucket, Cavalier, Charioteer, Circuit, Clause, Codicil, Condition, Corollary, Dispatch, Equestrian, Eventer, Freedom, Gaucho, Godiva, Guidon, Haggard, Horseman, Jockey, Lochinvar, Messenger, Peloton, Postil(l)ion, Proviso, PS, Revere, Scrub, Spurrer, Transport, Walkyrie

Ridge(pole) Arête, As(ar), Aseismic, Bank, Baulk, Chine, Coteau, Crease, Crest, Culmen, Dune, Eskar, Esker, Hoe, Hog's back, Kaim, Kame, Ledge, List(er), Middleback, Moraine, Offset, Promontory, Riblet, Roof-tree, Wale, Weal, Whorl, Witwatersrand

Ridicule, Ridiculous Absurd, Badinage, Bathos, Chaff, Cockamamie, Deride, Derisory, Egregious, Foolish, Gibe, Gird, Goad, Guy, Haze, Jibe, Josh, Lampoon, Laughable, Ludicrous, Mimic, Mock, Paradox, Pasquin, Pillory, Pish, Pooh-pooh, Rag, Raillery, Rally, Rib, Rich, Risible, Roast, Satire, Scoff, Scout, Screwy, Send up, Sight, Silly, Skimmington, Taunt, Travesty

Rifle Air, Armalite®, Assault, Bone, Browning, Bundook, Burgle, Carbine, Chassepot, Enfield, Enfield musket, Escopette, Express, Garand, →**GUN**, Kalashnikov, Loot, Magazine, Martini®, Mauser®, Minié, Pick, Pilfer, Pillage, Raid, Ransack, Reave, Reive, Repeater, Rieve, Rob, Saloon, Springfield, Winchester®

Rig(ging), Rigger Accoutre, Attire, Bermuda, Drilling, Equip, Feer, Frolic, Gaff, Get-up, Gunter, Hoax, Jack-up, Manipulate, Marconi, Martingale, Outfit, Panoply, Platform, Ratline, Ropes, Roughneck, Schooner, Sport, Stack, Swindle, Tackle, Togs, Top hamper, Trull

▷ **Rigged** *may indicate* an anagram

Right(s), Righten, Rightness Affirmative, Ancient lights, Animal, Appropriate, Ay, Bang, Befit, Blue-pencil, Cabotage, Civil, Claim, Competence, Conjugal, Conservative, →**CORRECT**, Cuddy, Cure, Dead on, Direct, Divine, Droit, Due, Entitlement, Equity, Ethical, Exactly, Fascist, Fitting, Forestage, Franchise, Freedom, Gay, Germane, Hedge-bote, Human, Interest, Jure, Jus (mariti), Legal, Liberty, Lien, Maternity, Meet, Merit, Miner's, Miranda, Moral, New, Offside, OK, Okay, Option, Pannage, Pasturage, Patent, Paternity, Performing, Pit and gallows, Pre-emption, Prerogative, Priority, Privilege, Proper, Property, Pukka, R, Rain, Reason, Rectify, Redress, Remedy, Repair, Ripe, Rt, Serial, Slap, So, Spot-on, Stage, Substantive, Suo jure, Suo loco, Tenants', Tickety-boo, Tory, Trover, True, Water, Women's

Rigid(ity) Acierated, Catalepsy, Craton, Extreme, Fixed, Formal, Hidebound, Inflexible, Lignin, Renitent, Set, Slavish, Starch(y), Stern, Stiff, Stretchless, Strict, Stringent, Tense, Turgor

Rigorous, Rigour Accurate, Austere, Cruel, Exact, Firm, Hard, Inclement, Iron-bound, Stern, Strait, Strict, Stringent, Thorough

▷ **Rile(y)** *may indicate* an anagram

Rim Atlantic, Border, Chimb, Chime, Edge, Felloe, Felly, Flange, Girdle, →**LIP**, Margin, Strake, Verge

Ring(ed), Ringer, Ringing, Rings Anchor, Angelus, Annual, Annulus, Arena, Band, Bangle, Bayreuth, Bell, Benzine, Betrothal, Boom-iron, Call, Cambridge,

Carabiner, Cartel, Change, Chime, Circle, Circlet, Circlip, Circus, Clang, Clink, Coil, Cordon, Cornice, Corona, Corral, Cramp, Cycle, Dead, Death's head, Dial, Diffraction, Ding, Disc, Dong, Donut, D(o)uar, Echo, Encircle, Enclosure, Encompass, Engagement, Enhalo, Enlace, Envelop, Environ, Enzone, Eternity, Extension, Eyelet, Fairy, Ferrule, Gas, Gimmer, Gird(le), Girr, Gloriole, Grom(m)et, Growth, Halo, Hank, Hob, →**HOOP**, Hoop-la, Hula-hoop, Ideal, Image, Inner, Inorb, Keeper, Key, Knell, Knock-out, Kraal, Lactam, Laer, Lifebelt, Link, Loop, Lute, Magpie, Manacle, Mourning, Napkin, Nimbus, Nose, O, Oil-control, Orb, Outer, Parral, Parrel, Peal, Pen, Phone, Ping, Piston, Potato, Price, Prize, Quoit, Re-echo, Resonant, Resound, Retaining, Reverberate, Round, Rove, Rowel, Runner, Rush, Sale, Scarf, Scraper, Seal, Signet, Slinger, Slip, Snap-link, Solomon, Sound, Spell, Split, Stonehenge, Surround, Swivel, Syndicate, Tang, Tattersall, Teething, Thimble, Thumb, Timbre, Ting, Tingle, Tink(le), Tintinnabulate, Toe, Token, Toll, Tore, Torquate, Torques, Torret, Torus, Trochus, Troth, Vice, Vortex, Wagnerian, Washer, Wedding, Woggle, Zero

Rink Ice, Roller, Skating

Riot(er), Riotous(ly), Riots Anarchy, Brawl, Clamour, Demo, Deray, Gordon, Hilarious, Hubbub, Luddite, Medley, Mêlée, Orgy, Pandemonium, Peterloo, Porteous, Profusion, Quorum, Rag, Ragmatical, Rebecca, Rebel, Roister, Rout, Rowdy, Ruffianly, Swing, Tumult

▷ **Rioters, Riotous** *may indicate* an anagram

Rip(per), Ripping, Rip off Avulse, Basket, Buller, Cur, Dilacerate, Fleece, Grand, Handful, Horse, Jack, Lacerate, Rent, Rep, Roué, Splendid, Tear, Tide, Topnotch, To-rend, Unseam

Ripe, Ripen(ing) Auspicious, Full, Geocarpy, Mature, Mellow, Rathe, Ready

▷ **Rippling** *may indicate* an anagram

Rise(r), Rising Advance, Appreciate, Ascend, Aspire, Assurgent, Bull, Butte, Cause, Dry, Easter, Eger, Elevation, Emerge, Émeute, Eminence, Erect, Escalate, Get up, Hance, Hauriant, Haurient, Heave, Hike, Hill, Hummock, Hunt's up, Improve, Increase, Incremental, Insurgent, Intifada, Intumesce, Jibe, Knap, Knoll, Lark, Levee, Levitate, Lift, Molehill, Motte, Mount, Mutiny, Orient, Origin, Peripety, Point, Putsch, Rear, Resurgent, Resurrection, →**REVOLT**, Rocket, Saleratus, Scarp, Sky-rocket, Soar, Spiral, Stand, Stie, Sty, Stye, Surface, Surge, Tor, Tower, Transcend, Up, Upbrast, Upburst, Upcurl, Upgo, Uprest, Upshoot, Upspear, Upsurge, Upswarm, Upturn, Well

Risk(y) Actuarial, Adventure, Apperil, Back, Calculated, Chance, Compromise, Counterparty, →**DANGER**, Daring, Dice, Dicy, Emprise, Endanger, Fear, Gamble, Game, Hairy, Hazard, High-wire, Imperil, Impetuous, Jeopardy, Liability, Morass, Nap, Peril(ous), Precarious, Security, Spec, Stake, Throw, Unsafe, Venture

Rite(s) Asperges, Bora, Ceremony, Eastern, Exequies, Initiation, Last offices, Liturgy, Mystery, Nagmaal, Obsequies, Powwow, Ritual, Sacrament, Sarum use, Superstition, York

Ritual Agadah, Arti, Ceremony, Chanoyu, Cultus, Customary, Formality, Haggada, Lavabo, Liturgy, Rite, Sacring, Seder, Social, Tantric, Telestic, Use

Rival(ry), Rivals Absolute, Acres, Aemule, Compete, Contender, Emulate, Emule, Envy, Fo(n)e, →**MATCH**, Needle, Opponent, Touch, Vie

River(s) Bayou, Creek, Dalles, Ea, Eau, Estuary, Flood, Flower, Fluvial, Potamic, Potamology, R, Riverain, Runner, Stream, Tide(-way), Tributary, Waterway

RMA The Shop

Road(s), Roadside, Road surface A, A1, Access, Anchorage, Arterial, Asphalt, Autobahn, Autopista, Autostrada, Ave(nue), B, Beltway, Blacktop, Boulevard, Burma, Bypass, Carriageway, Causeway, Clay, Clearway, Close, Cloverleaf, Coach, Concession, Corduroy, Corniche, Course, Crossover, Cul-de-sac, Dirt, Drift-way, Driveway, Drove, Dunstable, Escape, Exit, Expressway, Fairway, Feeder, Fly-over, Fly-under, Foss(e) Way, Freeway, Frontage, Grid, Hampton, Hard, Highway, Horseway, Interstate, Kerb, Lane, Loan, Loke, M1, Mall, Metal, Motorway, Off-ramp, Orbital, Overpass, Parkway, Path, Pike, Post, Private, Rat-run, Rd, Relief, Ride, Ridgeway, Ring, Royal, Service, Shoulder, Shunpike, Side, Silk, Skid, Slip, Speedway, Spur(way), St(reet), Superhighway, Switchback, Tarmac, Tar-seal, Terrace, Thoroughfare, Throughway,

Tobacco, Toby, Tollway, Track(way), Trunk, Turning, Turnpike, Unadopted, Underpass, Unmade, Verge, Via, Viaduct, Way

Roadstead La Hogue

Roam Enrange, Extravagate, Peregrinate, Rake, Ramble, Rove, Stray, Wander, Wheel

Roar(ing) Bawl, Bell(ow), Bluster, Boom, Boys, Cry, Forties, Guffaw, Laugh, Leonine, Roin, Rote, Rout, Royne, Thunder, Tumult, Vroom, Wuther, Zoom

Roast Bake, Barbecue, Baste, Birsle, Brent, Cabob, Cook, Crab, Crown, Decrepitate, Excoriate, Grill, Kabob, Pan, Pot, Ridicule, Scald, Scathe, Sear, Slate, Spit, Tan, Torrefy

Rob(bed), Robber(y) Abactor, Abduct, Bandit, Bereave, Bonnie, Brigand, Burgle, Bust, Cateran, Clyde, Dacoit, Daylight, Depredation, Do, Fake, Filch, Fleece, Footpad, Heist, Highjack, High toby, Highwayman, Hijack, Hold-up, Hustle, Job, Kondo, Ladrone, Land-pirate, Larceny, Latron, Loot, Moskonfyt, Pad, Pillage, Pinch, Piracy, Pluck, Plunder, Ramraid, Rapine, Reave, Reft, Reive, Rieve, Rifle, Robertsman, Roll, Roy, Rustler, Sack, Score, Screw, Sheppard, Short change, Sirup, Skinner, Smash and grab, Spoiler, Spring-heeled Jack, → STEAL, Steaming, Stick-up, Sting, Swindle, Syrup, Thief, Thug(gee), Toby, Turn-over, Turpin

Robe(s) Alb, Amice, Amis, Attrap, Buffalo, Camis, Camus, Canonicals, Cassock, Chimer, Chrisom(-cloth), Christom, Dalmatic, Dolman, → DRESS, Gown, Habit, Ihram, Kanga, Kanzu, Khalat, Khilat, Kill(a)ut, Kimono, Mantle, Night, Parament, Parliament, Pedro, Peplos, Pontificals, Purple, Regalia, Rochet, Saccos, Sanbenito, Soutane, Sticharion, Stola, Stole, Talar, Tire, Vestment, Yukata

Robot Android, Automaton, Cyborg, Dalek, Golem, Nanobot, Puppet, RUR, Telechir

Rock(s), Rocker, Rocking, Rocky Acid, Ages, Agitate, Astound, Ayers, Cap, Cock, Country, Cradle, Destabilise, Edinburgh, Erratic, Extrusive, Garage, Gem, Gib(raltar), Goth, Heavy metal, Jounce, Jow, Lithology, Mantle, Marciano, Marlstone, Matrix, Native, Nunatak(kr), Permafrost, Petrology, Petrous, Platform, Plymouth, Progressive, Punk, Quake, Reggae, Reservoir, Rimrock, Rip-rap, Sally, Scare, Scaur, Sclate, → SHAKE, Shoogle, Showd, Soft, Stonehenge, Stun, Sway, Swee, Swing, Ted, Teeter, Totter, Tremble, Ultrabasic, Ultramafic, Uluru, Unstable, Unsteady, Wall, Weeping, Whin, Wind, Windsor

Rocket Arugula, Blue, Booster, Capsule, Carpet, Carrier, Congreve, Delta, Drake, Dressing down, Earful, Engine, Flare, Jato, Life, Missile, Onion, Payload, Posigrade, Reprimand, Reproof, Retro, Rucola, SAM, Skylark, Soar, Sounding, Space probe, Stephenson, Thruster, Tourbillion, Upshoot, V1, Vernier, Warhead, Weld

▷ **Rocky** *may indicate* an anagram

Rod(-shaped), Rodlike, Rods Aaron's, Angler, Axle, Bar, Barbel(l), Barre, Birch, Caduceus, Caim, Can, Cane, Cue, Cuisenaire®, Dipstick, Divining, Dopper, Dowser, Drain, Firearm, Fisher, Fly, Fuel, Gauging, Gold stick, Gun, Handspike, Laver, Linchpin, Lug, Mapstick, Mopstick, Moses, Newel, Perch, Pin, Pistol, Piston, Pitman, Pointer, Poker, Poking-stick, Pole, Pontie, Pontil, Ponty, Puntee, Punty, Push, Raddle, Range, Riding, Rood, Shaft, Spindle, Spit, Stair, Staple, Stave, Stay-bolt, Stick, Sticker, Switch, Tie, Twig, Verge, Virgate, Virgulate, Wand, Withe

Rodent Acouchi, Acouchy, Agouty, Ag(o)uti, Bandicoot, Bangsring, Banxring, Beaver, Biscacha, Bizcacha, Bobac, Bobak, Boomer, Capybara, Cavy, Chickaree, Chincha, Chinchilla, Chipmunk, Civet, Coypu, Cricetus, Dassie, Deer-mouse, Degu, Delundung, Dormouse, Fieldmouse, Gerbil(le), Glires, Glutton, Gnawer, Gopher, Groundhog, Guinea pig, Ham(p)ster, Hedgehog, Hog-rat, Hutia, Hyrax, Hystricomorph, Jerboa, Jird, Lemming, Loir, Mara, Marmot, Mole rat, Mouse, Murid, Mus, Musk-rat, Musquash, Nutria, Ochotona, Ondatra, Paca, Porcupine, Potoroo, Prairie dog, Rat, Ratel, Ratton, Renegade, Runagate, Sciurine, Sewellel, Shrew, Simplicidentate, Spermophile, Springhaas, Springhase, Squirrel, S(o)uslik, Taguan, Taira, Tuco-tuco, Tucu-tuco, Vermin, Viscacha, Vole, Woodchuck, Woodmouse

Rogue, Roguish(ness) Aberrant, Arch, Bounder, Charlatan, Chiseller, Drole, Dummerer, Elephant, Espiègle(rie), Ganef, Ganev, Ganof, Gonif, Gonof, Greek, Gypsy, Hedge-creeper, Heel, Hempy, Herries, Imp, Knave, Latin, Limmer, Monkey, Palliard, Panurge, Picaresque, Picaroon, Pollard, Poniard, Rapparee, Ra(p)scal(l)ion, Reprobate,

Riderhood, Rotter, Savage, Scallywag, Scamp, Schellum, Schelm, Scoundrel, Skellum, Sleeveen, Slip-string, Sly, Swindler, Terror, Varlet, Villain, Wrong 'un

Roin Roar

Roll(ed), Roller, Roll-call, Rolling, Rolls Absence, Bagel, Bap, Birmingham, Bolt, Bridge, Brioche, Bun, Calender, Cambridge, Comber, Cop, Couch, Court, Croissant, Cylinder, Dandy, Drum, Dutch, Electoral, Enwallow, Eskimo, Even, Finger, Forward, Furl, Go, Goggle, Holy, Hotdog, Labour, List, Loaded, Mangle, Marver, Morning, Moving, Music, Muster, Opulent, Pain au chocolat, Patent, Pay, Petit-pain, Piano, Pigeon, Pipe, Platen, Porteous, Ragman, Record, Reef, Reel, Register, Ren, Rent, Revolute, Revolve, Rich, Ring, Road, Rob, Rolag, Roster, Rota, Rotate, Roul(e), Roulade, Row, RR, Rumble, Run, Sausage, Skin up, Snap, Somersault, Souter's clod, Spool, Spring, Summar, Sway, Swell, Swiss, Table, Tandem, Taxi, Temple, Tent, Terrier, Thread, Toilet, Tommy, Toss, Trill, Trindle, Trundle, Upfurl, Valuation, Victory, Volume, Wad, Wallow, Wave, Weather, Western, Yaw, Zorbing

▷ **Rollicking** *may indicate* an anagram

Roman Agricola, Agrippa, Aurelius, Calpurnia, Candle, Catholic, Cato, Consul, CR, Crassus, Dago, Decemviri, Decurion, Empire, Flavian, Galba, Holiday, Italian, Jebusite, Latin, Maecenas, Papist, Patrician, PR, Quirites, Raetic, RC, Retarius, Rhaetia, Road, Scipio, Seneca, Sulla, Tarquin, Tiberius, Trebonius, Type, Uriconian, Veneti

Romance, Romantic (talk) Affair, Amoroso, Amorous, Byronic, Casanova, Catalan, Dreamy, Fancy, Fantasise, Fib, Fiction, Gest(e), Gothic, Invention, Ladin(o), Ladinity, Langue d'oc(ian), Langue d'oil, Langue d'oui, Liaison, Lie, Neo-Latin, New, Novelette, Poetic, Quixotic, R(o)uman, Ruritania, Stardust, Sweet nothings, Tale, Tear-jerker

▶ **Romany** *see* GYPSY

Rome Holy See, Imperial City

Ronnie Biggs

Roof (edge), Roofing Belfast, Bell, Broach, Ceil, Cl(e)ithral, Cover, Curb, Divot, Dome, Drip, Eaves, French, Gable, Gambrel, Hardtop, Hip(ped), Home, Housetop, Hypostyle, Imperial, Jerkin-head, Leads, M, Mansard, Monopitch, Onion dome, Palate, Pavilion, Pop-top, Porte-cochère, Rag top, Rigging, Saddle, Shingle, Skirt, Targa top, Tectiform, Tectum, Tegula, Thatch, Thetch, Tiling, Top, Uraniscus, Vaulting

Room(y) Capacity, Ceiling, Clearance, Commodious, Elbow, Family, Latitude, Leeway, Margin, Place, Scope, Smoke-filled, →SPACE, Spacious, Standing, Wiggle

Root(s), Rooted, Rooting Aruhe, Asarum, Calamus, Cassava, Cheer, Cocco, Couscous, Cube, Cuscus, Delve, Derivation, Dig, Eddo, Eradicate, Etymon, Fern, Foundation, Ginseng, Grass, Grub, Heritage, Horseradish, Hurrah, Immobile, Incorrigible, Insane, Khuskhus, Knee, Mandrake, Navew, Nuzzle, Pleurisy, Poke, Pry, Radish, Rhizome, Skirret, Snuzzle, Source, Spur, Square, Stilt, Strike, Tap, Taro, Tuber, Tulip, Turnip, Turpeth, Ventral, Zedoary

Rope(s) Backstay, Ba(u)lk, Bind, Bobstay, Boltrope, Bracer, Brail, Breeching, Bunt-line, Cable, Cablet, Cord, Cordage, Cordon, Cringle, Downhaul, Drag, Earing, Fall, Flake, Flemish coil, Foot, Fore-brace, Foresheet, Forestay, Futtock-shroud, Gantline, Garland, Grass line, Guest, Guide, Guy, Halliard, Halser, Halter, Halyard, Hawser, Hawser-laid, Headfast, Inhaul, Jack-stay, Jeff, Jib-sheet, Jump, Kernmantel, Kickling, Ladder, Lanyard, Lasher, Lasso, Lazo, Leg, Lifeline, Line, Longe, Lunge, Mainbrace, Mainsheet, Manil(l)a, Marlin(e), Match-cord, Monkey, Mooring, Nip, Noose, Outhaul, Painter, Pastern, Prolonge, Prusik, Pudding, Rawhide, Reef point, Riata, Ridge, Ringstopper, Roband, Robbin, Rode, Runner, St Johnston's ribbon, St Johnston's tippet, Sally, Salt-eel, Seal, Selvagee, Sennit, Sheet, Shroud, Sinnet, Span, Spun-yarn, Stay, Sternfast, Stirrup, String, Strop, Sugan, Swifter, Tackle, Tail, Tether, Tie, Timenoguy, Tow(line), Trace, Trail, Triatic, Triatic stay, Vang, Wanty, Widdy, Wire, Yarn

Rose(-red), Rosie, Rosy Albertine, Alexandra, Avens, Blooming, Bourbon, Briar, Brier, Burnet, Cabbage, Canker, China, Christmas, Compass, Crampbark, Damask,

Dog, Eglantine, England, English, Floribunda, G(u)elder, Geum, Hybrid, Lancaster, Lee, Monthling, Moss, Multiflora, Musk, Noisette, Peace, Pink, Promising, Rambler, Red(dish), Rhoda, Rugosa, Scotch, Snowball, Sprinkler, Standard, Tea, Tokyo, Tudor, York

Roseland SE

Rosemary Rosmarine

Rot(ten), Rotting Addle, Baloney, Boo, Bosh, Botrytis, Brown, Bull, Caries, Carious, Corrode, Corrupt, Daddock, Decadent, → **DECAY**, Decompose, Degradable, Dotage, Dricksie, Druxy, Dry, Eat, Erode, Fester, Foul, Gangrene, Kibosh, Manky, Mildew, Noble, Nonsense, Off, Poppycock, Poxy, Punk, Putid, Putrefy, Putrescent, Putrid, Rail, Rancid, Rank, Rat, Red, Ret, Rhubarb, Rust, Sapropel, Septic, Sour, Squish, Twaddle, Vrot, Wet

Rotate, Rotating, Rotation, Rotator Backspin, Crankshaft, Crop, Gyrate, Laevorotation, Pivot, Pronate, Rabat(te), Reamer, Revolve, Roll, Selsyn, Succession, Teres, Topspin, Trochilic, Trundle, Turn, Vortex, Wheel, Windmill

▶ **Rotten** see ROT(TEN)

▷ **Rotten** may indicate an anagram

Rough(en), Roughly, Roughness About, Abrasive, Approximate, Asper(ate), Broad, Broad brush, Burr, C, Ca, Choppy, Circa, Coarse, Craggy, Craig, Crude, Frampler, Grained, Gross, Gruff, Guestimate, Gurly, Gusty, Hard, Harsh, Hispid, Hoarse, Hoodlum, Hooligan, Ill, Impolite, Imprecise, Incondite, Inexact, Irregular, Jagged, Karst, Keelie, Kokobeh, Muricate, Obstreperous, Of sorts, Or so, Push, Ragged, Ramgunshoch, Raspy, Raucle, Rip, Risp, Robust, Row, Rude, Rugged, Rusticate, Rusty, Scabrid, Scabrous, Scratchy, Sea, Shaggy, Sketchy, Some, Spray, Spreathe, Squarrose, Stab, Strong-arm, Stubbly, Swab, Tartar, Tearaway, Ted, Textured, Tiger country, Tousy, Touzy, Towsy, Towzy, Uncut, Violent, Yahoo

▷ **Roughly** may indicate an anagram

▷ **Round** may indicate a word reversed

Round(ed), Roundness About, Ammo, Ball, Beat, Bout, Cartridge, Catch, Circle, Complete, Cycle, Dome, Doorstep, Fat, Figure, Full, Geoidal, Global, Hand, Heat, Jump-off, Lap, Leg, Milk, O, Oblate, Orb, Orbit, Orby, Patrol, Peri-, Pirouette, Plump, Pudsy, Qualifying, Quarter, Rev, Ring, Robin, Roly-poly, Rota, Rotund, Route, Routine, Rung, Salvo, Sandwich, Sarnie, Semi-final, Shot, Skirt, Slice, Sphere, Step, Table, Tour, Tubby, Tune, U-turn, Walk

Roundabout Ambages, Approximately, Bypass, Carousel, Circuit, Circumambient, Circumbendibus, Circus, Devious, Eddy, → **INDIRECT**, Peripheral, Rotary, Tortuous, Traffic circle, Turntable, Waltzer, Whirligig, Windlass

▷ **Roundabout** may indicate an anagram

Routine Automatic, Day-to-day, Drill, Everyday, Grind, Groove, Habitual, Heigh-ho, Helch-how, Ho-hum, Jogtrot, Journeywork, Monotony, Pattern, Perfunctory, Pipe-clay, Red tape, Rota, Rote, Round, Run-of-the-mill, Rut, Schtik, S(c)htick, SOP, Treadmill, Workaday

Rove(r), Roving Car, Errant, Freebooter

Row(er) Align, Altercation, Arew, Argue, Argument, Bank, Barney, Bedlam, Bow, Cannery, Colonnade, Death, Debate, Din, Dispute, Dust-up, Feud, File, Fireworks, Food, Hoo-ha, Hullabaloo, Leander, Line(-up), Noise, Oar, Octastich, Orthostichy, Paddle, Parade, Pluriserial, Ply, Pull, Quarrel, Range, Rank, Reproach, Rew, Rotten, Ruction, Rumpus, Savile, Scene, Scrap, Scull, Series, Set, Shindig, Shindy, Shine, Skid, Spat, Stern, Stound, Street, Stroke, Sweep, Terrace, Tier, Tiff, Torpid, Twelve-tone, Wetbob, Wherryman

Rowdy, Rowdiness Bovver, Hoo, Hooligan, Loud, Noisy, Rorty, Rough, Roughhouse, Ruffian, Scourer, Skinhead, Stroppy, Unruly, Uproarious

Royal(ty), Royalist Academy, Angevin, Basilical, Battle, Bourbon, Crowned, Emigré, Exchange, Fee, Hanoverian, HR(H), Imperial, Imposing, Inca, Kingly, Majestic, Malignant, Palatine, Payment, Pharaoh, Plantagenet, Prince, Purple, Queenly, Real, Regal, Regis, Regius, Regnal, Sail, Sceptred, Society, Tsarista

Rub(bing), Rubber(y), Rub out Abrade, Buff, Bungie, Bungy, Calk, Caoutchouc,

Chafe, Cold, Condom, Corrode, Cow gum®, Crepe, Delete, Destroy, Ebonite, Efface, Elastic, Elaterite, Embrocate, Emery, Eradicator, Erase, Factis, Fawn, Foam, Fray, Fret, Friction, Frottage, Frotteur, Grate, Graze, Grind, Gum elastic, Gutta-percha, Hard, High-hysteresis, Hule, India, Irritate, Jelutong, Johnnie, Latex, Masseur, Obstacle, Polish, Root, Safe, Sandpaper, Scour, Scrub, Scuff, Seringa, Smoked, Sorbo®, Sponge, Synthetic, Towel, Trace, Ule, Wipe

▷ **Rubbed** *may indicate* an anagram

Rubbish Bad mouth, Balls, Bilge, Brash, Brock, Bull, Bunkum, Cack, Clap-trap, Cobblers, Codswallop, Culch, Debris, Detritus, Dirt, Discredit, Dre(c)k, Drivel, Dross, Eyewash, Fiddlesticks, Garbage, Grot, Grunge, Guff, Hogwash, Kack, Kak, Landfill, Leavings, Litter, Mullock, Nonsense, Phooey, Piffle, Pish, Raff, Raffle, Red(d), →REFUSE, Riff-raff, Scrap, Sewage, Spam, Stuff, Tinpot, Tinware, Tip, Tom(fool), Tosh, Totting, Trade, Tripe, Trouch, Truck, Trumpery, Twaddle, Urethra

Rude(ness) Abusive, Barbaric, Bear, Bestial, Bumpkin, Callow, Carlish, Churlish, Coarse, Discourteous, Disrespect, Elemental, Goustrous, Green, Ill-bred, Impolite, Indecorous, Indelicate, Inficete, Ingram, Ingrum, Insolent, Ocker, Offensive, Peasant, Profane, Raw, Ribald, Risqué, Rough, Simple, Surly, Unbred, Uncivil, Uncomplimentary, Uncourtly, Unlettered, Unmannered, Vulgar, Yobbish

▷ **Ruffle** *may indicate* an anagram

Rug Afghan, Bearskin, Bergama, Buffalo-robe, Carpet, Drugget, Ensi, Flokati, Gabbeh, Hearth, Herez, Heriz, Kelim, K(h)ilim, Kirman, Lap robe, Mat, Maud, Numdah, Oriental, Pilch, Prayer, Rag, Runner, Rya, Scatter, Steamer, Tatami, Throw, Travelling, Wig

Ruin(ed), Ruins, Ruinous Annihilate, Banjax, Bankrupt, Blast, Blight, Blue, Butcher, Carcase, Collapse, Corrupt, Crash, Crock, Damn, Decay, Defeat, Demolish, Despoil, Destroy, Devastate, Dilapidation, Disaster, Disfigure, Dish, Disrepair, Dogs, Do in, Doom, Downcome, Downfall, End, Fine, Fordo, Hamstring, Heap, Hell, Insolvent, Inure, Kaput(t), Kibosh, Loss, Mar, Mocers, Mockers, Mother's, Overthrow, Perdition, Perish, Petra, Pigs and whistles, Pot, Puckerood, Ravage, Reck, Relic, Scotch, Screw, Scupper, Scuttle, Shatter, Sink, Smash, Spill, →SPOIL, Stramash, Subvert, Undo, Unmade, Ur, Violate, Vitiate, Whelm, Write off, Woe, Wrack

▷ **Ruined** *may indicate* an anagram

Rule(r), Rules, Ruling Advantage, Align, Bosman, Bylaw, Calliper, Canon, Chain, Club-law, Code, Condominium, Constitution, Control, Criterion, Decree, Domineer, Dominion, Em, Empire, En, Establishment, Etiquette, Fatwa, Feint, Fetwa, Formation, Formula, Gag, Global, Golden, Govern, Ground, Gynocracy, Home, In, Institutes, Jackboot, Law, Leibniz's, Lex, Lindley, Liner, Majority, Markownikoff's, Mastery, Maxim, Measure, Mede, Method, Mobocracy, Motto, Norm(a), Ordinal, Organon, Organum, Pantocrator, Parallel, Parallelogram, Phase, Phrase-structure, Placitum, Plumb, Precedent, Precept, Prevail, Principle, Protocol, Ptochocracy, Rafferty's, Realm, Reciprocity, Rector, Regal, Regnant, Reign, Rewrite, Ring, Routine, Rubric, Selection, Setting, Slide, Standard, Statute, Straight edge, Stylebook, Sway, System, Ten-minute, Ten-yard, Theorem, Three, Thumb, Transformation(al), Trapezoid, T-square, Tycoon, Tyrant, Uti possidetis, Wield

Rumble, Rumbling Borborygmus, Brool, Curmurring, Drum-roll, Groan, Growl, Guess, Lumber, Mutter, Roll, Rumour, Thunder, Tonneau, Twig

Rumour Breeze, Bruit, Buzz, Canard, Cry, Fame, Furphy, →GOSSIP, Grapevine, Hearsay, Kite, Noise, On-dit, Pig's-whisper, Report, Repute, Say-so, Smear, Talk, Underbreath, Unfounded, Vine, Voice, Whisper, Word

Run(ning), Run away, Run into, Run off, Runny, Runs Admin(ister), Arpeggio, Black, Bleed, Blue, Bolt, Break, Bunk, Bye, Canter, Career, Chase, Chicken, Clip, Coop, Corso, Course, Cresta, Cross-country, Current, Cursive, Cursorial, Cut, Dart, Dash, Decamp, Diarrhoea, Dinger, Direct, Double, Dribble, Drive, Dry, Dummy, Enter, Escape, Execute, Extra, Fartlek, Flee, Flit, Flow, Fly, Follow, Fun, Fuse, Gad, Gallop, Gauntlet, Go, Green, Ground, Hare, Haste(n), Hennery, Hie, Hightail, Home, Idle, Jog, Jump bail, Ladder, Lam, Lauf, Leg(work), Leg bye, Lienteric, Liquid, Lope, Manage, Marathon, Melt, Milk, Mizzle, Mole, Molt, Monkey, Neume, Now, On,

On-line, Operate, Pace, Pacific, Paper chase, Parkour, Pelt, Pilot, Ply, Pour, Print, Purulent, R, Race, Range, Rear end, Red, Renne, Rin, Roadwork, Romp, Root, Roulade, Rounder, Ruck, Scamper, Scapa, Scarpa, Scarper, School, Schuss, Scud, Scuddle, Scutter, Scuttle, See, Sequence, Shoot, Single, Skate, Skedaddle, Ski, Skid, Skirr, Skitter, Slalom, Slide, Smuggle, Spew, Split, Spread, Sprint, Sprue, Squitters, Stampede, Straight, Streak, Stream, Taxi, Tear, Tenor, Tick over, Tie-breaker, Tirade, Trial, Trickle, Trill, Trot, Well

Runner(s) Atalanta, Bean, Blade, Bow Street, Carpet, Coe, Courser, Dak, Deserter, Drug, Emu, Field, Geat, Gentleman, Harrier, Internuncio, Leg bye, Legman, Messenger, Miler, Milk, Oribi, Ovett, Owler, Policeman, Racehorse, Rhea, → **RIVER**, Rum, → **RUN(NING)**, Scarlet, Scud, Series, Slipe, Smuggler, Stolon, Stream, Tailskid, Trial

▷ **Running, Runny** *may indicate* an anagram

Run of the mill Mediocre

Rural Agrarian, Agrestic, Backwoodsman, Boo(h)ai, Booay, Boondocks, Bucolic, Country, Forane, Georgic, Mofussil, Platteland, Praedial, Predial, Redneck, Rustic, Sticks, The Shires, Ulu, Upland, Wop-wops

Rush(ed) Accelerate, Barge, Bolt, Bustle, Career, Charge, Dart, Dash, Dutch, Expedite, Fall, Feese, Fly, Forty-nine, Gold, Hare, Hasten, High-tail, Horsetail, → **HURRY**, Hurry and Scurry, Hurtle, Jet, Lance, Leap, Odd-man, Onset, Pellmell, Phase, Plunge, Pochard, Precipitate, Railroad, Rampa(u)ge, Rash, Reed, Rip, Scamp(er), Scour(ing), Scramble, Scud, Scurry, Sedge, Shave-grass, Spate, Speed, Stampede, Star(r), Streak, Streek, Surge, Swoop, Swoosh, Tantivy, Tear, Thrash, Thresh, Tilt, Torrent, Tule, Whoosh, Zap, Zoom

Russia(n), Russian headman, Russian villagers Apparatchik, Ataman, Bashkir, Belorussian, Beria, Bolshevik, Boris, Boyar, Buryat, Byelorussian, Cesarevitch, Chechen, Circassian, Cossack, Dressing, D(o)ukhobor, Esth, Evenki, Ewenki, Igor, Ivan, Kabardian, Kalmuk, Kalmyck, Leather, Leonid, Lett, Mari, Menshevik, Minimalist, Mir, Misha, Muscovy, Octobrist, Osset(e), Red, Romanov, Rus, Russ(niak), Russki, Ruthene, Salad, Serge, Sergei, Slav, Stakhanovite, SU, Tatar, The Bear, Thistle, Udmurt, Uzbeg, Uzbek, Vladimir, Vogul, Yuri, Zyrian

Rust(y) Aeci(di)um, Brown, Corrode, Cor(ro)sive, Eat, Erode, Etch, Ferrugo, Goethite, Iron-stick, Laterite, Maderise, Oxidise, Rubiginous, Soare, Stem, Teleutospore, Telium, Uredine, Uredo, Verdigris, Wheat

Rustic Arcady, Bacon, Bor(r)el(l), Bucolic, Bumpkin, Carl, Carlot, Chawbacon, Churl, Clodhopper, Clown, Corydon, Crackle, Damon, Doric, Forest, Georgic, Hayseed, Hick, Hillbilly, Hind, Hob, Hobbinoll, Hodge, Homespun, Idyl(l), Pastorale, Peasant, Pr(a)edial, Put(t), Rube, Rural, Silk, Strephon, Swain, Uplandish, Villager, Villatic, Yokel

▷ **Rustic** *may indicate* an anagram

Rustle(r), Rustling Abactor, Crackle, Crinkle, Duff, Fissle, Frou-frou, Gully-raker, Poach, Silk, Speagh(ery), Sprechery, Steal, Stir, Susurration, Swish, Thief, Whig

Rut Channel, Furrow, Groove, Heat, Routine, Track

Ruthless Brutal, Cruel, Dog eat dog, Fell, Hard, Hardball, Hard-bitten, Indomitable

Ss

S Ogee, Saint, Second, Sierra, Society, South, Square

SA It, Lure

Sabotage, Saboteur Cripple, Destroy, Frame-breaker, Hacktivism, Ratten, Spoil, Worm, Wrecker

Sack(cloth), Sacking Axe, Bag, Bed, Boot, Bounce, Budget, Burlap, Can, Cashier, Chasse, Coal, Compression, Congé, Congee, Dash, Depose, Depredate, Despoil, Discharge, Dismissal, Doss, Fire, Growbag, Gunny, Havoc, Hessian, Jute, Knap, Loot, Mailbag, Maraud, Marching orders, Mat, Mitten, Pillage, Plunder, Poke, Postbag, Push, Raid, Rapine, Ravage, Reave, Rieve, Road, Rob, Sad, Sanbenito, Sherris, Sherry, Spoliate, Vandalise, Walking papers

▷ **Sacks** *may indicate* an anagram

Sacrifice Corban, Cost, Forego, Gambit, Gehenna, Immolate, Lay down, Molochize, Oblation, →**OFFERING**, Relinquish, Suttee

Sad(den), Sadly, Sadness Alas, Attrist, Blue, Con dolore, Dejected, Depressed, Desolate, Disconsolate, Dismal, Doleful, Dolour, Downcast, Drear, Dull, Dumpy, Fadeur, Forlorn, Heartache, Lovelorn, Low, Lugubrious, Mesto, Mournful, Niobe, Oh, Plaintive, Plangent, Poignancy, Proplastid, Sorrowful, Sorry, Tabanca, Tearful, Tear-jerker, Threnody, Tragic, Triste, Tristesse, Unhappy, Wan, Weltschmerz, Wo(e)begone

Saddle (bag, cloth, flap, girth, pad), Saddled Alforja, Aparejo, Arson, Bicycle, Burden, Cantle, Cinch, Col, Crupper, Demipique, Kajawah, Lumber, Numnah, Oppress, Pack, Panel, Pigskin, Pilch, Pillion, Seat, Sell(e), Shabrack, Side, Skirt, Stock, Tree, Unicycle, Western

▷ **Sadly** *may indicate* an anagram

Safe(ty) Active, Awmrie, Copper-bottomed, Deposit, Harmless, Hunk, Immunity, Impunity, Inviolate, Meat, Night, Passive, Peter, Proof, Reliable, Roadworthy, Sanctuary, Secure, Sheltered, Sound, Strong-box, Strongroom, Sure, Whole-skinned, Worthy

Safebreaker Yegg

Safeguard Bulwark, Caution, Ensure, Fail-safe, Frithborh, Fuse, Hedge, Palladium, Protection, Register, Ward

Saga Aga, Chronicle, Edda, Epic, Forsyte, Icelandic, Legend

Sago Portland

Saharan Hassaniya, Sahrawi

Sahelian Chad, Mali, Mauritinia, Niger

▷ **Said** *may indicate* 'sounding like'

Sail(s), Sailing Balloon, Bunt, Canvas, Cloth, Coast, Course, Cruise, Fan, Gaff(-topsail), Gennaker, Genoa, Head, Jib, Jut, Land, Lateen, Leech, Luff, Lug, Moonraker, Muslin, Navigate, Orthodromy, Peak, Ply, Rag, Reef, Rig, Ring-tail, Royal, Sheet, Shoulder-of-mutton, Smoke, Solar, Spanker, Spencer, Spinnaker, Spritsail, Square, Staysail, Steer, Storm-jib, Studding, Stuns'l, Top(-gallant), Yard

Sailor(s) AB, Admiral, Argonaut, Blue-jacket, Boatman, Boatswain, Bos'n, Bos(u)n, Budd, Canvas-climber, Commodore, Crew, Deckhand, Drake, Evans, Foremastman, Freshwater, Gob, Greenhand, Hand, Hat, Hearties, Helmsman, Hornblower, Hydronaut, Jack, Jaunty, Lascar, Leadsman, Liberty man, Limey, Lt, Lubber, Mariner, Matelot, Matlo(w), Middy, MN, Nelson, Noah, NUS, Oceaner, Oldster, OS, Petty Officer, Polliwog, Pollywog, Popeye, Privateer, Rating, Reefer, RN, Salt, Seabee,

Seacunny, Sea-dog, Seafarer, Sea-lord, →**SEAMAN**, Serang, Sin(d)bad, Steward, Submariner, Swabber, Swabby, Tar, Topman, Wandering, Wave, Wren, Yachtsman

Saint(ly) Canonise, Canonize, Hagiology, Hallowed, Holy, Latterday, Leger, Patron, Pillar, Plaster, St, Templar, Thaumaturgus

Sake Account, Behalf, Cause, Drink, Mirin

Salad Beetroot, Caesar, Chef's, Coleslaw, Cos, Cress, Cucumber, Days, Endive, Fennel, Finoc(c)hio, Frisée, Fruit, Greek, Guacamole, Horiatiki, Lettuce, Lovage, Mache, Mixture, Mizuna, Niçoise, Purslane, Radicchio, Radish, Rampion, Rocket, Russian, Slaw, Tabbouli, Tomato, Waldorf, Watercress

▷**Salad** *may indicate* an anagram

Salary Emolument, Fee, Hire, Pay, Prebend, Screw, Stipend, →**WAGE**

Sale(s) Attic, Auction, Boot, Breeze up, Cant, Car-boot, Clearance, Farm-gate, Fire, Garage, Jumble, Market, Outroop, Outrope, Pitch, Raffle, Retail, Roup, Rummage, Subhastation, Trade, Turnover, Upmarket, Venal, Vend, Vendue, Vent, Voetstoets, Voetstoots, Warrant, Wash, White, Wholesale, Yard

Salisbury Cecil, Sarum

Salmon Atlantic, Chinook, Chum, Cock, Coho(e), Grav(ad)lax, Grayling, Grilse, Kelt, Keta, Par(r), Pink, Redfish, Rock, Silver, Smelt, Smolt, Smowt, Sockeye, Springer, Umber

Salt(s), Salty AB, Acid, Alginate, Aluminate, Andalusite, Antimonite, Arseniate, Arsenite, Aspartite, Attic, Aurate, Azide, Base, Bath, Benzoate, Bicarbonate, Bichromate, Borate, Borax, Brackish, Brine, Bromate, Bromide, Capr(o)ate, Caprylate, Carbamate, Carbonate, Carboxylate, Celery, Cerusite, Chlorate, Chlorite, Chromate, Citrate, Columbate, Complex, Corn, Cure(d), Cyanate, Cyclamate, Datolite, Deer lick, Diazonium, Dichromate, Dioptase, Dithionate, Double, Enos, Eosin, Epsom, Ferricyanide, Formate, Glauber, Glutamate, Halite, Halo-, Health, Hydrochloride, Hygroscopic, Iodide, Ioduret, Isocyanide, Kosher, Lactate, Lake-basin, Linoleate, Lithate, Liver, Magnesium, Malate, Malonate, Manganate, Mariner, Matelot, Mersalyl, Microcosmic, Monohydrate, Mucate, Muriate, NaCl, Niobate, Nitrate, Nitrite, Oleate, Orthoborate, Orthosilicate, Osm(i)ate, Oxalate, Palmitate, Pandermite, Perborate, Perchlorate, Periodate, Phosphate, Phosphite, Phthalate, Picrate, Piquancy, Plumbate, Plumbite, Potassium, Powder, Propionate, Pyruvate, Rating, Reh, Resinate, Rochelle, Rock, Rosinate, Sailor, Sal ammoniac, Salicylate, Salify, Sal volatile, Saut, Sea-dog, Seafarer, Seasoned, Sebate, Selenate, Smelling, Soap, Sodium, Solar, Sorbate, Sorrel, Stannate, Stearate, Suberate, Succinate, Sulfite, Sulphate, Sulphite, Sulphonate, Table, Tannate, Tantalate, Tartrate, Tellurate, Tellurite, Thiocyanate, Thiosulphate, Titanate, Tungstate, Uranin, Urao, Urate, Vanadate, Volatile, Water-dog, White, Wit(ty), Xanthate

Salutation, Salute Address, Asalam-wa-leikum, Australian, Ave, Banzai, Barcoo, Bid, Cap, Cheer, Command, Coupé(e), Curtsey, Embrace, Feu de joie, Fly-past, Genuflect, Greet, Hail, Hallo, Halse, Homage, Honour, Jambo, Kiss, Middle finger, Namas kar, Namaste, Present, Salaam, Salvo, Sieg Heil, Toast, Tribute, Wassail

Salvage Dredge, Lagan, Ligan, Reclaim, Recover, Recycle, Rescue, Retrieve, Tot

Salve Anele, Anoint, Assuage, Ave, Lanolin(e), Lotion, Ointment, Remedy, Saw, Tolu, Unguent

Same(ness) Ae, Agnatic, Congruent, Contemporaneous, Do, Egal, Equal, Equivalent, Ib(id), Ibidem, Id, Idem, Identical, Identity, Ilk, Iq, Like, One, Thick(y), Thilk, Uniform, Ylke

Sample, Sampling Amniocentesis, Biopsy, Blad, Browse, Example, Foretaste, Handout, Muster, Pattern, Pree, Prospect, Quadrat, Random, Scantling, Smear, Snip, Specimen, Swatch, Switch, →**TASTE**, Taster, Transect, Try

▷**Sam Weller** *may indicate* the use of 'v' for 'w' or vice versa

Sanction(s), Sanctioned Allow, Appro, Approbate, Approof, Approve, Assent, Authorise, Bar, Countenance, Economic, Endorse, Fatwa(h), Fetwa, Fiat, Green light, Homologate, Imprimatur, Legitimate, Mandate, OK, Pass, Pragmatic, Ratify, Smart, Sustain, Upstay, Warrant

Sanctuary, Sanctum Adytum, Ark, Asylum, By-room, Cella, Ch, Church, Delubrum, Frithsoken, Frithstool, Girth, Grith, Holy, JCR, Lair, Naos, Oracle, Penetralia, Preserve, Refuge, Sacellum, Sacrarium, Salvation, SCR, →**SHELTER**, Shrine, Temple

Sandgroper Pioneer

Sandhopper Amphipod

Sandwich(es) Bruschetta, Butty, Club, Clubhouse, Croque-monsieur, Cuban, Doorstep, Earl, Hamburger, Hoagie, Island, Open, Panini, Roti, Round, Sanger, Sango, Sarmie, Sarney, Sarnie, Smørbrød, Smörgåsbord, Smørrebrød, Sub, Submarine, Tartine, Thumber, Toastie, Toebie, Triple-decker, Twitcher, Victoria, Western, Zak(o)uski

▷ **Sandwich(es)** *may indicate* a hidden word

Sane, Sanity Compos mentis, Formal, Healthy, Judgement, Rational, Reason, Right-minded, Sensible, Wice

Sanguine Confident, Haemic, Hopeful, Optimistic, Roseate, Ruddy

Sap Benzoin, Bleed, Cremor, Drain, Enervate, Entrench, Ichor, Juice, Laser, Latex, Lymph, Mine, Mug, Nuclear, Pulque, Ratten, Resin, Roset, Rosin, Rozet, Rozit, Secretion, Soma, Sura, Swot, Undermine, Weaken

Sarcasm, Sarcastic Acidity, Biting, Cutting, Cynical, Derision, Irony, Mordacious, Mordant, Pungent, Quip, Sarky, Satire, Sharp, Sharp-tongued, Snide, Sting, Wisecrack

Sardonic Cutting, Cynical, Ironical, Scornful

Sash Baldric(k), Band, Belt, Burdash, Cummerbund, Fillister, Lungi, Obi, Scarf, Window

Saskatchewan .sk

Satan Adversary, Apollyon, Arch-enemy, Arch-foe, Cram, →**DEVIL**, Eblis, Lucifer, Prince of darkness, Shaitan, The old serpent

Satellite Adrastea, Ananke, Ariel, Artificial, Astra, Atlas, Attendant, Aussat, Belinda, Bianca, Bird, Callisto, Calypso, Camenae, Carme, Charon, Communications, Comsat®, Cordelia, Cosmos, Cressida, Deimos, Desdemona, Despina, Dione, Disciple, Early bird, Earth, Echo, Elara, Enceladus, Europa, Explorer, Fixed, Follower, Galatea, Galilean, Ganymede, Geostationary, Helene, Henchman, Himalia, Hipparchus, Hyperion, Iapetus, Intelsat, Io, Janus, Lackey, Larissa, Leda, Lysithea, Meteorological, Metis, Mimas, Miranda, Moon, Mouse, Naiad, Navigation, Nereid, Oberon, Ophelia, Orbiter, Pan, Pandora, Pasiphae, Phobos, Phoebe, Planet, Portia, Prometheus, Puck, Rhea, Rosalind, Sinope, Smallset, Space probe, SPOT, Sputnik, Syncom, Telesto, Telstar, Tethys, Thalassa, Thebe, Tiros, Titan, Titania, Triton, Umbriel, Weather

▶ **Satin** *see* **SILK(Y)**

Satisfaction, Satisfactory, Satisfy(ing), Satisfied, Satisfactorily Adequate, Agree, Ah, Ap(p)ay, Appease, Assuage, Atone, Change, Compensation, Complacent, →**CONTENT**, Defrayment, Enough, Feed, Fill, Fulfil, Glut, Gratify, Happy camper, Indulge, Jake, Job, Liking, Meet, Nice, OK, Okey-dokey, Pacation, Palatable, Pay, Please, Pride, Propitiate, Qualify, Redress, Relish, Repay, Replete, Revenge, Sate, Satiate, Sensual, Serve, Settlement, Slake, Smug, Square, Suffice, Supply, Tickety-boo, Well

Saturate(d) Drench, Glut, Imbue, Impregnate, Infuse, Permeate, →**SOAK**, Sodden, Steep, Surcharge, Waterlog

Sauce, Saucy Agrodolce, Alfredo, Allemanse, Apple, Arch, Baggage, Barbecue, Béarnaise, Béchamel, Bigarade, Bold(-faced), Bolognese, Bordelaise, Bourguignonne, Bread, Brown, Caper, Carbonara, Catchup, Catsup, Chasseur, Chaudfroid, Cheek, Chilli, Chutney, Condiment, Coulis, Cranberry, Cream, Creme anglaise, Cumberland, Custard, Dapper, Dip, Dressing, Enchilada, Espagnole, Fenberry, Fondue, Fricassee, Fudge, Fu yong, Fu yung, Gall, Garum, Gravy, Hard, Hoisin, Hollandaise, Horseradish, HP®, Impudence, Jus, Ketchup, Lip, Malapert, Marinade, Marinara, Matelote, Mayo(nnaise), Melba, Meunière, Mint, Mirepoix, Mole, Monkeygland, Mornay, Mousseline, Mouth, Nam pla, Nerve, Newburg, Nuoc mam, Oxymal, Oyster, Panada,

Parsley, Passata, Peart, Peking, Pert, Pesto, Piert, Piri-piri, Pistou, Pizzaiola, Ponzu, Portugaise, Puttanesca, Ragu, Ravigote, Relish, Remoulade, Rouille, Roux, Sabayon, Sal, Salad cream, Salpicon, Salsa, Salsa verde, Sambal, Sass, Satay, Shoyu, Soja, Soubise, Soy, Soya, Stroganoff, Sue, Sugo, Supreme, Sweet and sour, Tabasco®, Tamari, Tartar(e), Tomato, Topping, Tossy, Trimmings, Velouté, Vinaigrette, Vindaloo, White, Wine, Worcester, Worcestershire, Yakitori

Sausage(s) Andouille, Andouillette, Banger, Black pudding, Boerewors, Bologna, Bratwurst, Cervelat, Cheerio, Chipolata, Chorizo, Corn dog, Cumberland, Devon, Drisheen, Frankfurter, Garlic, Kielbasa, Knackwurst, Knockwurst, Liver(wurst), Lorne, Mortadella, Pep(p)eroni, Polony, Pudding, Salami, Sav(eloy), Snag(s), Snarler, Square, String, Vienna, Weenie, Weeny, White pudding, Wiener(wurst), Wienie, Wurst, Zampone

Sauté Fry

Savage Barbarian, Boor, Brute, Cruel, Fierce, Frightful, Grim, Immane, Inhuman, Maul, Sadistic, Truculent, Vitriolic, Wild

Save, Saving(s) Bank, Bar, Besides, But, Capital, Conserve, Cut-rate, Deposit, Economy, Except, Hain, Hoard, Husband, ISA, Keep, Layby, Nest egg, Nirlie, Nirly, Not, PEPS, Post office, Preserve, Put by, Reclaim, Recycle, Redeem, Relieve, Reprieve, →**RESCUE**, Reskew, Sa', Salt (away), Salvage, SAYE, Scrape, Scrimp, Shortcut, Slate club, Soak away, Sock away, Sou-sou, Spare, Stokvel, Succour, Susu, TESSA, Unless

Savvy Sense

Saw Adage, Aphorism, Apothegm, Azebiki, Back, Band, Beheld, Bucksaw, Buzz, Chain, Circular, Cliché, Compass, Coping, Cross-cut, Crown, Cut, Dictum, Double-ender, Dovetail, Dozuki, Flooring, Frame, Fret, Gang, Glimpsed, Gnome, Grooving, Hack, Hand, Jig, Keyhole, Legend, Log, Maxim, Met, Motto, Pad, Panel, Paroemia, Pitsaw, Proverb, Pruning, Quarter, Rabbeting, Rack, Ribbon, Rip, Ryoba, Sash, Saying, Scroll, Serra, Skil®, Skip-tooth, Slasher, Slogan, Span, Spied, Stadda, Stone, Sweep, Tenon, Trepan, Trephine, Whip, Witnessed

Sawbill Merganser

Sawyer Logger, Tom

Saxophone Axe

Say, Saying(s) Adage, Agrapha, Allege, Aphorism, Apophthegm, Apostrophise, Articulate, Axiom, Beatitude, Bon mot, Bromide, Byword, Cant, Catchphrase, Cliché, Declare, Dict(um), Eg, Enunciate, Epigram, Expatiate, Express, Fadaise, For instance, Gnome, Impute, Input, Logia, Logion, Mean, Mot, Mouth, Observe, Predicate, Pronounce, Proverb, Put, Quip, Recite, Rede, Relate, Remark, Report, Saine, Saw, Sc, Sententia, →**SPEAK**, Suppose, Sutra, Talk, Utter, Voice, Word

▷ **Say, Saying(s)** *may indicate* a word sounding like another

▷ **Scale(d)** *may indicate* a fish

Scale(s), Scaly API gravity, Ascend, Balance, Beaufort, Brix, Bud, Burnham, Celsius, Centigrade, Chromatic, →**CLIMB**, Cottony-cushion, Dander, Dandruff, Diagonal, Diatonic, Enharmonic(al), Escalade, Fahrenheit, Flake, Fujita, Full, Gamme, Gamut, Gapped, Gauge, Gravity, Gray, Heptatonic, Hexachord, Humidex, Indusium, Interval, Kelvin, Krab, Ladder, Lamina, Layer, Leaf, Lepid, Libra, Ligule, Magnitude, Major, Mercalli, Mesel, Minor, Mohs, Natural, Nominal, Ordinal, Oyster shell, Palet, Peel, Pentatonic, Plate, Platform, Proportion, →**RANGE**, Rankine, Ratio, Réau(mur), Regulo, Richter, San Jose, Scalade, Scan, Scent, Scurf, Shin, Sliding, Spring, Submediant, Tegula, Tonal, Tron(e), Unified, Vernier, Wage, Weighbridge, Wentworth, Whole-tome, Wind

Scallion Leek

Scan(ning), Scanner Barcode, CAT, CT, EEG, Examine, Flat-bed, Helical, Inspect, Iris, OCR, Oversee, Peruse, PET, Rake, Raster, Scrutinise, SEM, SPET, Study, Survey, Tomography, Ultrasound, Vet

Scandal(ous), Scandalise Belie, Canard, Commesse, Disgrace, Gamy, -gate, Hearsay, Muck-raking, Opprobrium, Outrage, Shame, Slander, Stigma, Watergate

Scandalmonger Muckraker

Scant(y), Scantness Bare, Brief, Exiguous, Jejune, Jimp, Low, Meagre, Oligotrophy, Poor, Scrimpy, Short, Shy, Slender, Spare, Sparse, Stingy

Scapegoat, Scapegrace Butt, Fall-guy, Hazazel, Joe Soap, Patsy, Skainesmate, Stooge, Target, Victim, Whipping-boy

Scarce(ly), Scarcity Barely, Dear, Dearth, Famine, Few, Hardly, Ill, Lack, Paucity, Rare, Scanty, Seldom, Short, Strap, Uncommon, Want

Scarecrow Bogle, Bugaboo, Dudder, Dudsman, Gallibagger, Gallibeggar, Gallicrow, Gallybagger, Gallybeggar, Gallycrow, Malkin, Mawkin, Potato-bogle, Ragman, S(h)ewel, Tattie-bogle

Scarf Babushka, Belcher, Cataract, Comforter, Cravat, Curch, Doek, Dupatta, Fascinator, Fichu, Hai(c)k, Haique, Hyke, Lambrequin, Madras, Mantilla, Muffettee, Muffler, Neckatee, Neckcloth, Neckerchief, Neckgear, Neckpiece, Necktie, Neckwear, Nightingale, Orarium, Pagri, Palatine, Patka, Rail, Rebozo, Sash, Screen, Shash, Stock, Stole, Tallith, Tippet, Trot-cosy, Trot-cozy, Vexillum

Scatter(ed), Scattering Bestrew, Broadcast, Diaspora, Disgregation, Disject, Dispel, Dissipate, Flurr, Inelastic, Litter, Rayleigh, Rout, Scail, Skail, Sow, Sparge, Sparse, Splutter, Sporadic, Sprad, Spread, Sprinkle, Squander, Straw, Strew, Strinkle

Scavenge(r) Ant, Dieb, Forage, Hunt, Hy(a)ena, Jackal, Rake, Ratton, Rotten, Scaffie, Sweeper, Totter

Scene(ry) Arena, Boscage, Cameo, Coulisse, Decor, Flat(s), Landscape, Locale, Periaktos, Phantasmagoria, Prop, Prospect, Riverscape, Set, Sight, Site, Sketch, Stage, Tableau, Take, Tormenter, Tormentor, Venue, View, Wing

Scent Aroma, Attar, Chypre, Civet, Cologne, Essence, Fragrance, Frangipani, Fumet(te), Gale, Moschatel, Musk, Nose, Odour, Orris, Ottar, Otto, Perfume, Sachet, Smell, Spoor, Vent, Waft, Wind

Sceptic, Sceptical(ly), Scepticism Askant, Cynic, Doubter, Europhobe, Incredulous, Infidel, Jaundiced, Nihilistic, Nullifidian, Pyrrho(nic), Sadducee, Thomas

Schedule Agenda, Calendar, Classification, Itinerary, Prioritise, Programme, Register, Slot, Table, Timetable

Scheme, Schemer, Scheming Angle, CATS, Colour, Concoct, Conspire, Crafty, Cunning, Dare, Darien, Dart, Decoct, Design, Devisal, Diagram, Dodge, Draft, Gin, Honeytrap, Housing, Intrigue, Jezebel, Machiavellian, Machinate, Manoeuvre, Master plan, Nostrum, Pilot, →**PLAN**, Plat, Plot, Ponzi, Project, Proposition, Purpose, Put-up job, Racket, Rhyme, Ruse, Scam, Set-aside, Stratagem, System, Table, Top-hat, Wangle, Wheeler-dealer, Wheeze

Schmook Drip

Scholar, Scholiast Abelard, Academic, Alcuin, Alumni, BA, Bookman, Classicist, Clergy, Clerk, Commoner, Demy, Disciple, Don, Erasmus, Erudite, Etonian, Exhibitioner, Extern(e), Faculty, Graduate, Hebraist, Literate, MA, Maulana, Ollamh, Ollav, Pauline, Plutarch, Polymath, Pupil, Rhodes, Sap, Savant, Saxonist, Schoolboy, Soph, →**STUDENT**, Tom Brown, Varro

School Business, Discipline, Drill, Educate, Exercise, Feeder, Institute, Integrated, Madrasa, Peripatetic, Teach, →**TRAIN**, Tutor

Science Anatomy, Anthropology, Applied, Art, Astrodynamics, Astrophysics, Atmology, Avionics, Axiology, Behavioural, Biology, Biotech, Botany, Chemistry, Christian, Cognitive, Computer, Crystallography, Cybernetics, Dismal, Domestic, Earth, Ekistics, Electrodynamics, Entomology, Eth(n)ology, Euphenics, Exact, Forensic, Gay, Geodesy, Geology, Hard, Information, Life, Lithology, Macrobiotics, Materia medica, Mechanics, Metallurgy, Military, Mineralogy, Natural, Noble, Nomology, Noology, Nosology, Occult, Ology, Ontology, Optics, Optometry, Pedagogy, Penology, Phrenology, Physical, Physics, Policy, Political, Psychics, Pure, Rocket, Rural, Semiology, Serology, Skill, Social, Soft, Soil, Sonics, Stinks, Stylistics, Tactics, Technics, Technology, Tectonics, Telematics, Thremmatology, Toxicology, Tribology, Typhlology, Zootechnics

Scoff Belittle, Boo, Chaff, Deride, Dor, Eat, Feast, Flout, Food, Gall, Geck, Gibe, Gird,

Gobble, →**JEER**, Jest, Mock, Rail, Rib, Ridicule, Roast, Scaff, Scorn, Send up, Sneer, Taunt

Scold(ing) Admonish, Berate, Callet, Catamaran, Chastise, Chide, Clapperclaw, Do, Earful, Earwig, Flite, Flyte, Fuss, Jaw(bation), Jobation, Lecture, Nag, Objurgate, Philippic, Rag, Rant, Rate, →**REBUKE**, Reprimand, Reprove, Revile, Rollick, Rollock, Rouse on, Row, Sas(s)arara, Sis(s)erary, Slang, Slate, Termagant, Tick-off, Tongue-lash, Trimmer, Upbraid, Virago, Wig, Xant(h)ippe, Yaff, Yankie, Yap

Scooter Vespa®

Scope Ambit, Bargaining, Breadth, Compass, Diapason, Domain, Elbow-room, Extent, Freedom, Gamut, Indulgence, Ken, Latitude, Leeway, Purview, Range, Remit, Room, Rope, South, Scowth, Size, Sphere

Scorch(er) Adust, Birsle, Blister, Brasero, →**BURN**, Char, Destroy, Frizzle, Fry, Parch, Scouther, Scowder, Scowther, Sear, Singe, Soar, Speed, Swale, Swayl, Sweal, Sweel, Torrefy, Torrid, Wither

Score(s), Scoring Apgar, Behind, Bill, Birdie, Bradford, Bye, Capot, Chalk up, Chase, Clock up, Conversion, Count, Crena, Debt, Dunk, Eagle, Etch, Full, Gash, Groove, Hail, Honours, Incise, Ingroove, Ippon, Koka, Law, Leaderboard, Lots, Magpie, Make, Mark, Music, Net, Nick, Notation, Notch, Nurdle, Open, Orchestrate, Partitur(a), Peg(board), Pique, Point, Record, Repique, Rit(t), Rouge, Run, Rut, Scotch, Scrat, Scratch, Scribe, Scrive, Set, Sheet music, Single, Spare, Stableford, Stria, String, Sum, Tablature, →**TALLY**, TE, Try, Twenty, Vocal, Waza-ari, Win, Yuko

▷ **Scorer** *may indicate* a composer

▷ **Scoring** *may indicate* an anagram

Scorn(ful) Arrogant, Bah, Contemn, Contempt, Contumely, Deride, Despise, Dis(s), Disdain, Dislike, Disparagement, Flout, Geck, Haughty, Insult, Meprise, Mock, Opprobrium, Phooey, Putdown, Rebuff, Ridicule, Sarcastic, Sardonic, Sarky, Scoff, Scout, Sdaine, Sdeigne, Sneer, Sniffy, Spurn, Wither

Scot(sman), Scots(woman), Scottish Alistair, Blue-bonnet, Fingal, Kelvinside, Morningside, Shetlander, Tartan, Tax

Scotland Alban(y), Albion, Caledonia, Lallans, Lothian, NB, Norland, Scotia

Scoundrel Cad, Cur, Dog, Heel, Hound, Knave, Miscreant, Rat, Reprobate, Scab, Smaik, Varlet, →**VILLAIN**, Wretch

▷ **Scour** *may indicate* an anagram

Scouse Liver bird, Wacker

Scout Akela, Beaver, Bedmaker, Bird dog, Colony, Disdain, Emissary, Explorer, Flout, Guide, Outrider, Pathfinder, Pickeer, Pioneer, Reconnoitre, Rover, Runner, Scoff, Scorn, Scourer, Scurrier, Sixer, Talent, Tenderfoot, Tonto, Venture

Scrap(s), Scrappy Abandon, Abolish, Abrogate, Bin, →**BIT**, Brock, Cancel, Conflict, Discard, Dump, →**FIGHT**, Fisticuffs, Fragment, Fray, Iota, Jot, Junk, Mêlée, Mellay, Morceau, Morsel, Odd, Off-cut, Ort, Ounce, Patch, Piece, Pig's-wash, Rag, Rase, Raze, Remnant, Rescind, Scarmoge, Scissel, Scissil, Scroddled, Scrub, Set-to, Shard, Sherd, Shred, Skerrick, Skirmish, Snap, Snippet, Spall, Stoush, Tait, Tate, Tatter, Titbit, Trash, Truculent, Tussle, Whit

Scrape(r) Abrade, Agar, Bark, Clat, Claw, Comb, Curette, D and C, Escapade, Grate, Graze, Gride, Harl, Hoe, Hole, Jar, Kowtow, Lesion, Lute, Pick, Predicament, Racloir, Rake, Rasorial, Rasp, Rasure, Raze, Razure, Saw, Scalp, Scart, Scrat(ch), Scroop, Scuff, Shave, Skimp, Skin, Skive, Squeegee, Strake, Strigil, Xyster

▷ **Scratch(ed)** *may indicate* an anagram

Scratch(es), Scratched, Scratching Cracked heels, Etch, Grabble, Key, Mar, Pork, Ritt, Score, Scrawp, Scrooch, Scrorp, Streak, Striation, Withdraw

Scream(er) Bellow, Cariama, Caterwaul, Comedian, Comic, Cry, Eek, Headline, Hern, Hoot, Kamichi, Laugh, Priceless, Primal, Riot, Scare-line, Screech, Seriema, Shriek, Skirl, Squall, Sutch, Yell

Screen(s), Screening Air, Arras, Back projection, Backstop, Blind(age), Block, Blue, Boss, Camouflage, Cervical, Chancel, Check, Chick, Cinerama®, Cloak, Cornea, Cover, Curtain, Divider, Dodger, Eyelid, Fight, Fire, Flat, Fluorescent, Glib, Grid,

Grille, Hallan, Help, Hide, Hoard, Hoarding, Intensifying, Lattice, Long-persistence, Mantelet, Mask, Monitor, Net, Nintendo®, Nonny, Obscure, Organ, Overhead, Parclose, Partition, Pella, Plasma, Pulpitum, Purdah, Radar, Radarscope, Reardos, Reredorse, Reredos(se), Retable, Riddle, Rood, Scog, Sconce, Scope, → **SHADE**, Shelter, Shield, Show, Sift, Sight, Silver, Skug, Small, Smoke, Split, Sunblock, Televise, Tems, Test, Testudo, TFT, Touch, Traverse, Umbrella, VDU, Vet, Wide, Windbreak, Window, Windshield

Screw Adam, Allen, Archimedes, Blot, Butterfly, Cap, Cheat, Coach, Coitus, Countersunk, Double-threaded, Dungeon, Extort, Female, Fleece, Grub, Guard, Gyp, Ice, Interrupted, Jailer, Jailor, Lag, Lead, Levelling, Lug, Machine, Male, Mar, Micrometer, Miser, Monkey-wrench, Niggard, Pay, Perpetual, Phillips®, Prop(ellor), Pucker, Raised head, Robertson, Rotate, Ruin, Salary, Screweye, Scrunch, Skinflint, Spiral, Squinch, Swiz(zle), Thumb(i)kins, Twin, Twist, Vice, Wages, Whitworth, Worm, Wreck

Script (reader) Book, Demotist, Devanagari, Gurmukhi, Hand, Hieratic, Hiragana, Italic, Jawi, Kana, Kufic, Libretto, Linear A, Linear B, Lines, Lombardic, Longhand, Miniscule, Nagari, Nastalik, Nastaliq, Og(h)am, Prompt book, Ronde, Scenario, Screenplay, Writing

Scripture(s), Scriptural version Adi Granth, Agadah, Alcoran, Antilegomena, Avesta, Bible, Gemara, Gematria, Gospel, Granth (Sahib), Guru Granth, Haggada(h), Hermeneutics, Hexapla, Holy book, Holy writ, Koran, K'thibh, Lesson, Lotus Sutra, Mishna(h), OT, Rig-veda, Smriti, Tantra, Targum, Testament, Upanishad, Veda, Vedic, Verse, Vulgate

Scrivener Tabellion

Scrotum Oscheal

Scrounge(r) Beg, Blag, Bludge(r), Borrow, Bot, Cadge, Forage, Freeload, Layabout, Ligger, Scunge, Sponge

▷ **Scrub** *may indicate* 'delete'

Scrub(ber), Scrubland, Scrubs Abandon, Cancel, Chaparral, Cleanse, Dele(te), Exfoliate, Facial, Fynbos, Gar(r)igue, Horizontal, Loofa(h), Luffa, Masseur, Negate, Pro, Rescind, Rub, Scour, Sticks, Strim, Tart, Wormwood

Scrutinize, Scrutiny Check, Docimasy, Examine, Inspect, Observe, Peruse, Pore, Pry, → **SCAN**, Size up, Study

▷ **Scuffle** *may indicate* an anagram

Sculpt(ure) Bas-relief, Bronze, Bust, Carve, Della-robbia, Figure, Glyptics, High-relief, Kouros, Mezzo-relievo, Mezzo-rilievo, Mobile, Nude, Pietà, Relievo, Shape, → **STATUARY**, Topiary

Scum, Scumbag Dregs, Dross, Epistasis, Film, Louse, Pellicle, Pond, Rat, Scorious, Scruff, Slag, Slime, Spume, Sullage, Vermin

Scurf, Scurvy Dander, Dandriff, Dandruff, Furfur, Horson, Lepidote, Lepra, Leprose, Scabrous, Scall, Scorbutic, Whoreson, Yaws, Yaw(e)y

Sea(s), Seawards Billow, Brine, Briny, Cortes, Ditch, Drink, Electron, Euxine, Foam, Herring-pond, Main, Mare, Mare clausum, Mare liberum, Molten, → **OCEAN**, Offing, Offshore, Open, Out, Quantity, Strand, Tide, Water

Seaman, Seamen AB, Crew, Jack, Lascar, Lubber, Mariner, OD, Ordinary, PO, Rating, RN, → **SAILOR**, Salt, Swabby, Tar

Sear Brand, Burn, Catch, Cauterise, Char, Frizzle, Parch, Scath(e), Scorch, Singe, Wither

Search(ing) Beat, Body, Comb, Delve, Dragnet, Examine, Ferret, Fish, → **FORAGE**, Fossick, Frisk, Google(-whack), Grope, Home, Hunt, Indagate, Inquire, Jerk, Jerque, Kemb, Manhunt, Perscrutation, Probe, Proll, Prospect, Proul, Prowl, Pursue, Quest, Rake, Rancel, Ransack, Ransel, Ranzel, Ravel, Ripe, Root, Rootle, Rummage, Scan, Scavenge, Scour, Scout, Scur, Sker, Skirr, Snoop, Strip, Surf, Sweep, Thumb, Trace, Trawl, Zotetic

Season(able), Seasonal, Seasoned, Seasoning Accustom, Age, Aggrace, Autumn, Betimes, Christmas, Close, Condiment, Devil, Dress, Duxelles, Easter, Enure, Etesian, Fall, Fennel, Festive, Fines herbes, Flavour, Garlic, G(h)omasco,

Growing, Heat, Hiems, High, In, Inure, Lent, Marjoram, Master, Mature, Noel,
Nutmeg, Open, Paprika, Peak, Pepper, Powellise, Practised, Ripen, Salt, Sar, Seal,
Seel, Sele, Silly, Solstice, Spice, Spring, Summer(y), Tahini, Ticket, Tide, Time,
Timeous, Weather-beaten, Whit, Winter

Seat(ing) Barstool, Beanbag, Behind, Bosun's chair, Bunker, Catbird, Country,
Judgement, Sagbag, Sedile, Selle, Siege Perilous, Window

Seaweed Agar, Alga(e), Arame, Badderlock, Bladderwort, Bladderwrack,
Carrag(h)een, Ceylon moss, Chondrus, Conferva, Coralline, Cystocarp, Desmid,
Diatom, Dulse, Enteromorpha, Florideae, Fucus, Gulfweed, Heterocontae, Karengo,
Kelp, Kilp, Kombu, Laminaria, Laver, Maerl, Nori, Nullipore, Oarweed, Ore, Peacock's
tail, Porphyra, Redware, Rockweed, Sargasso, Seabottle, Sea-furbelow, Sea-girdle,
Sea-lace, Sea-lettuce, Sea-mat, Sea-moss, Sea-tangle, Seaware, Sea-whistle,
Sea-wrack, Tang(le), Ulva, Varec(h), Vraic, Wakame, Ware, Wrack

Seclude(d), Seclusion Cloister, Incommunicado, Isolate, Ivory tower, Maroon,
Nook, Pleasance, Poke(y), Privacy, Purdah, Quarantine, Retiracy, Retreat, Secret,
Sequester, Shyness, Solitude

Second(ary), Seconds Abet, Alternative, Another (guess), Appurtenance, Assist,
Atomic, Back(er), Beta, Byplay, Chaser, Collateral, Coming, Comprimario, Congener,
Cornerman, Deuteragonist, Fiddle, Flash, Friend, Handler, Imperfect, Indirect,
Inferior, Instant, Jiffy, Latter, Lesser, Minor, Mo(ment), Nature, Other, Pig's-whisper,
Red ribbon, Runner-up, Saybolt-Universal, Sec, Shake, Share, Side(r), Sideline, Sight,
Silver, Split, Subsidiary, Subtype, Support, Tick, Tone, Trice, Twinkling, Universal,
Wind

Second-hand Hearsay, Reach-me-down, Used

Secrecy, Secret(s), Secretive Apocrypha, Arcana, Arcane, Backstairs, Cabbalistic,
Cagey, Clam, Clandestine, Classified, Closet, Code, Conference, Confidence, Couvert,
Covert, Cranny, Cryptic, Dark, Deep, Deep-laid, Devious, Esoteric, Hidden, Hole and
corner, Hush-hush, Inly, Inmost, Inner, In pectore, In petto, Know-nothing, Latent,
Mysterious, Mystical, Mystique, Open, Oyster, Password, Penetralia, **→ PRIVATE**,
Privy, QT, Rune, Seal, Sensitive, Shelta, Silent, Slee, Sly, State, Stealth, Sub rosa,
Tight-lipped, Top, Trade, Unbeknown, Underboard, Undercover, Underhand,
Unknown, Unre(a)d, Unrevealed, Untold

Secretary Aide, Amanuensis, Chancellor, Chronicler, CIS, Desk, Desse, Famulus,
Minuteman, Moonshee, Munshi, Notary, Permanent, Prot(h)onotary, Scrive, Social,
Stenotyper, Temp

Sect(arian), Secret society Ahmadiy(y)ah, Albigenses, Campbellite, Covenantes,
Cynic, Disciples of Christ, Encratite, Familist, Fifth monarchy, Gabar, Glassite, Hassid,
Hemerobaptist, Hesychast, Holy Roller, Hutterite, Ismaili, Jehovah's Witness, Jodo,
Mendaites, Nasorean, Noetian, Ophites, Patripassian, Paulician, Perfectation, Pietist,
Plymouth Brethren, Pure Land, Ranter, Russellite, Saktas, Sandeman, Schwenkfelder,
Seventh Day Adventist, Shafiite, Shembe, Soka Gakkai, Sons of Freedom, Taliban,
Utraquist, Vaishnava, Zealot

Section, Sector Area, Balkanize, Caesarian, Chapter, Classify, Conic, Cross, Cut,
Department, Division, Ellipse, Empennage, Episode, Eyalet, Gan, Golden, Gore,
Hyperbola, Length, Lith, Lune, Meridian, Metamere, Mortice, Movement, Octant,
Outlier, Panel, Passus, **→ PIECE**, Platoon, Private, Public, Pull-out, Quarter, Rhythm,
Rib, S, Segment, Severy, Shard, Sherd, Slice, Stage, Ungula, Unit, Wing, Zone

Secure(d), Security Anchor, Assurance, Bag, Bail, Band, Bar, **→ BASIC**, Batten,
Belay, Bellwether, Belt and braces, Bolt, Bond, Buck Rogers, Calm, Cash ratio, Catch,
Cement, Chain, Cinch, Clamp, Clasp, Clench, Clinch, Close, Cocoon, Collateral,
Collective, Come by, Consolidate, Consols, Cosy, Counterseal, Cushy, Debenture,
Deposit, Disreputable, Doorman, Earthwork, Engage, Enlock, Ensure, Equity,
Establishment, Fasten, Fastness, Firm, Fortify, Fungibles, Gain, Gilt, Gilt-edged,
Guarantee, Guy, Heritable, Immune, Impregnable, Indemnity, Inlock, Invest(ment),
Knot, Lace, Land, Lash, Latch, Lien, Listed, Lock, Lockaway, Lockdown, Lockfast,
Longs, Mortgage, Nail, National, Obtain, Padlock, Patte, Pin, Pledge, Pot, Pre-empt,
Preference, Procure, Protect, Quad, Rope, Rug, **→ SAFE**, Safety, Screw, Seal, Settle,

Shutter, Snell, Snug, Social, Sound, Stable, Staple, Stock, Strap, Sure(ty), Tack, Take, Tie, Tight, Trap, Tyde, Vest, Warrant, Watertight, Wedge, Win

Sedative Amytal®, Anodyne, Aspirin, Barbitone, Bromal, Bromide, Chloral, Depressant, Deserpidine, Hypnic, Lenitive, Lupulin(e), Meprobamate, Metopryl, Miltown, Morphia, Narcotic, Nembutal®, Opiate, Paraldehyde, Pethidine, Phenobarbitone, Premed(ication), Rohypnol®, Roofie, Scopolamine, Seconal®, Soothing, Temazepam, Thridace, Veronal®

Sediment Alluvium, Chalk, Deposit, Dregs, F(a)eces, Fecula, Flysch, Foots, Graded, Grounds, Incrustation, Lees, Molasse, Placer, Residue, Salt, Sapropel, Silt, Sludge, Terrigenous, Till, Varve, Warp

▷ **Seduce** *may indicate* one word inside another

Seduce(r), Seduction, Seductive Bed, Beguilement, Bewitch, Come-hither, Debauch, Dishonour, Honeyed, Honied, Jape, Lothario, Luring, Mislead, Siren, Tempt, Vamp

See(ing) Behold, Bishopric, Carlisle, Consider, Date, Descry, Diocesan, Discern, Ebor, Episcopal, Exeter, Eye, Get, Glimpse, Holy, In as much as, Lo, Notice, Observe, Papal, Perceive, Realise, Rochester, Rubberneck, St David's, Salisbury, Sight, Spot, Spy, Twig, Understand, Vatican, Vid(e), View, Vision, Voilà, Witness

Seed(s), Seedy Achene, Apiol, Argan, Arilli, Arillode, Ash-key, Bean, Ben, Best, Blue, Bonduc, Cacoon, Caraway, Cardamom, Carvy, Cebadilla, Cevadilla, Chickpea, Coriander, Corn, Cum(m)in, Dragon's teeth, Embryo, Endosperm, Ergot, Favourite, Germ, Grain, Gritty, Inseminate, Issue, Ivory-nut, Kernel, Lentil, Lomentum, Mangy, Mawseed, Miliary, Mote, Nickar, Nicker, Nucellous, Nut, Oat, Offspring, Ovule, Pea, Pinon, Pip, Poorly, Poppy, Pyxis, Sabadilla, Samariform, Scuzz, Semen, Seminal, Senvy, Sesame, Shabby, Silique, Sorus, Sow, Sperm, Spore, Stane, Stone, Thistledown, Zoosperm

Seek(er), Seeking Ask, Beg, Busk, Cap-in-hand, Chase, Court, Endeavour, Fish, Gun for, Pursue, Quest, Scur, Search, Skirr, Solicit, Suitor, Try

Seem(ing), Seemingly Apparent, Appear, As if, Look, Ostensible, Purport, Quasi, Think

Seemly Apt, Comely, Decent, Decorous, Fit, Suitable

Seer Balaam, Eye, Nahum, Observer, Onlooker, Oracle, Prescience, Prophet, Sage, Sibyl, Soothsayer, Witness, Zoroaster

Segment(ation) Antimere, Arthromere, Cut, Division, Gironny, Gyronny, Intron, Lacinate, Lith, Lobe, Merogenesis, Merome, Merosome, Metamere, Metathorax, Piece, Pig, Proglottis, Prothorax, Scliff, Section, Share, Shie, Skliff, Somite, Split, Sternite, Syllable, Tagma, Telson, Urite, Uromere

Segregate, Segregation Apartheid, Exile, Insulate, Intern, →**ISOLATE**, Jim Crow, Seclude, Separate

Seize, Seizure Angary, Apprehend, Appropriate, Areach, Arrest, Attach(ment), Bag, Bone, Capture, Catch, Claw, Cleek, Cly, Collar, Commandeer, Confiscate, Distrain, Distress, For(e)hent, →**GRAB**, Grip, Hend, Ictus, Impound, Impress, Maverick, Nab, Na(a)m, Nap, Nim, Poind, Possess, Pot, Raid, Ravin, Replevy, Rifle, Sease, Sequestrate, Smug, Snag, Snatch, Tackle, Wingding, Wrest

Select(ion), Selecting, Selector Adopt, Artificial, Assortment, Bla(u)d, Cap, Casting, Choice, Choose, Classy, Clonal, Cull, Darwinism, Discriminate, Draft, Draw, Eclectic, Edit, Elite, Excerpt, Exclusive, Extract, Favour, Garble, Inside, K, Nap, Natural, Pericope, →**PICK**, Pot-pourri, Prefer, Recherché, Redline, Sample, Seed, Single, Sort, Stream, Tipster, Triage, UCCA, Vote

Self Atman, Auto, Character, Ego, Person, Psyche, Seity, Sel, Soul

Self-concern Dog-eat-dog

Self-conscious Guilty

▶ **Self-defence** *see* **MARTIAL ARTS**

Self-destructive Lemming

Self-esteem Amour-propre, Conceit, Confidence, Egoism, Pride, Vainglory

Self-important, Self-indulgent, Self-interested Aristippus, Arrogant, Bumptious, Conceited, Egocentric, Immoderate, Jack-in-office, Licentious,

Narcissistic, Pompous, Pooterish, Pragmatic, Primadonna, Profligate, Solipsist, Sybarite

Selfish(ness) Avaricious, Egocentric, Egoist, Greedy, Hedonist, Mean, Solipsism

Self-possession Aplomb, Assurance, Composure, Cool, Nonchalant, Phlegm

Self-satisfied, Self-satisfaction Complacent, Narcissism, Smug, Tranquil

Self-styled Soi-disant

Sell(er), Selling Apprize, Auction, Barter, Bear, Betray, Blackmail, Blockbuster, Cant, Catch, Chant, Chaunt, Cold-call, Cope, Costermonger, Direct, Dispose, Divest, Do, Eggler, Fancier, Fellmonger, Flog, Go, Hard, Have, Hawk, Huckster, Hustle, Inertia, Knock down, Market, Marketeer, Ménage, Merchant, Missionary, Oligopoly, Pardoner, Party, Peddle, Peddler, Pick-your-own, Purvey, Push, Pyramid, Rabbito(h), Realise, Rep, Retail, Ruse, Scalp, Short, Simony, Soft, Stall-man, Sugging, Switch, Tout, →TRADE, Trick, Vend, Vent

Semblance Appearance, Aspect, Guise, Likeness, Sign, Verisimilitude

Semi-circular D, Hemicycle

Semolina Couscous

Senator Antiani, Cicero, Concept father, Elder, Legislator, Patrician, Shadow, Solon

Send, Sent Consign, →DESPATCH, Disperse, Emanate, Emit, Entrance, Extradite, Issue, Launch, Order, Post, Rapt, Remit, Ship, Transmit, Transport

Send up Chal(l)an, Lampoon, Promote

Senile, Senility Caducity, Dementia, Disoriented, Doddery, Doited, Doitit, Dotage, Eild, Eld, Gaga, Nostology, Twichild

Senior(ity) Aîné, Doyen, Elder, Father, Grecian, Major, Majorat, Old(er), Oubaas, Père, Primus, Superior, Upper

Sensation(al) Acolouthite, Anoesis, Aura, Blood, Blood and thunder, Commotion, Drop-dead, Emotion, Empfindung, Feeling, Gas, Lurid, Melodrama, Organic, Phosphene, Photism, Pyrotechnic, Rush, Shocker, Shock-horror, Splash, Stir, Styre, Synaesthesia, Thrill, Tingle, Vibes, Wow, Yellow

Sense, Sensual(ist), Sensing Acumen, Attuite, Aura, Carnal, Coherence, Common, Dress, Ear, ESP, Faculty, Feel, Gaydar, Gross, Gumption, Gustation, Hearing, Horse, Idea, Import, Instinct, Intelligence, Intuition, Lewd, Loaf, Logic, Marbles, Meaning, Moral, Nous, Olfactory, Palate, Perceptual, Proprioceptive, Rational, Receptor, Remote, Rumble-gumption, Rum(m)el-gumption, Rumgumption, Rum(m)le-gumption, Sanity, Satyr, Sight, Sixth, Slinky, Smell, Spirituality, Sybarite, Synesis, Taste, Taste bud, Touch, Voluptuary, Voluptuous, Wisdom, Wit

Senseless Absurd, Anosmia, Asinine, Illogical, Lean-witted, Mad, Numb, Stupid, Stupor, Unconscious, Unwise, Vegetal

Sensible Aware, Clear-headed, Dianoetic, No-nonsense, Prudent, Raisonné, Rational, Realistic, Sane, Solid, Together, Well-balanced

Sensitive, Sensitivity Aesthete, Alive, Allergic, Dainty, Delicate, Discreet, Keen, Passible, Quick, Radiesthesia, Sympathetic, Tactful, Tender, Thin-skinned, Ticklish, Touchy(-feely), Vulnerable

Sentence(s) Antiphon, Assize, Bird, Carpet, Clause, Commit, Condemn, Custodial, Death, Decree(t), Deferred, Doom, Fatwah, Indeterminate, Judgement, Life, Matrix, Paragraph, Period(ic), Porridge, Predicate, Punish, Rap, Rheme, Rune, Send up, Stretch, Suspended, Swy, Tagmene, Verdict, Versicle

Sentiment(al), Sentimentality Byronism, Corn, Cornball, Drip, Feeling, Goo, Govey, Gucky, Gush, Lovey-dovey, Maudlin, Mawkish, Mind, Mush, Nationalism, Opinion, Posy, Romantic, Rose-pink, Rosewater, Saccharin, Schmaltzy, Sloppy, Slushy, Smoochy, Soppy, Spoony, Swoony, Syrupy, Tear-jerker, Too-too, Traveller, Treacly, Twee, View, Weepy, Wertherian, Yucky

Sentry Cordon sanitaire, Look-out, Picket, Sentinel, Vedette, Vidette, Watch

Separate(d), Separation, Separately, Separatist Abscise, Abstract, Apart, Asunder, Bust up, Comma, Compartmentalise, Cull, Cut, Decollate, Decompose, Decouple, Deduct, Demarcate, Demerge, Detach, Dialyse, Disaggregate, Disally, Disconnect, Disjunction, Dissociate, Distance, Distinct, Disunite, Divide, Division, Divorce, Eloi(g)n, Elute, Elutriate, Esloin, Estrange, ETA, Filter, Grade, Gulf, Heckle,

Hive, Hyphenate, Insulate, Intervene, Isolate, Judicial, Laminate, Lease, Legal, Part, Particle, Partition, Partitive, Peel off, Piece, Prescind, Prism, Red(d), Rift, Sashing, Scatter, Screen, Segregate, Sequester, Sever, Several, Shear, Shed, Shore, Shorn, Sift, Sleave, Sle(i)ded, Solitary, Sort, →**SPLIT**, Spread, Stream, Sunder, Sundry, Tems(e), Tmesis, Try, Twin(e), Unclasp, Unhitch, Unravel, Winnow, Wrench

Sepulchral, Sepulchre Bier, Cenotaph, Charnel, Crypt, Easter, Funeral, Monument, Pyramid, Tomb, Vault, Whited

Sequence, Sequential Agoge, Algorithm, Byte, Cadence, Chronological, Consecution, Consensus, Continuity, Continuum, Fibonacci, Gene, Intron, Line, Linear, Montage, Order, Program(me), Run, Seriatim, Series, Shot, Sonnet, Storyboard, String, Succession, Suit, Suite, Train, Vector

Serene, Serenity Calm, Composed, Placid, Quietude, Repose, Sangfroid, Sedate, Seraphic, Smooth, →**TRANQUIL**

Serf(dom) Adscript, Bondman, Ceorl, Churl, Helot, Manred, →**SLAVE**, Thete, Thrall, Vassal, Velle(i)nage, Villein

Sergeant Buzfuz, Chippy, Chips, Cuff, Drill, Flight, Halberdier, Havildar, Kite, Master, Pepper, Platoon, RSM, Sarge, SL, SM, Staff, Technical, Troy

Series Actinide, Actinium, Arithmetical, Battery, Chain, Concatenation, Consecution, Continuum, Course, Cycle, Cyclus, Docusoap, Electromotive, Enfilade, En suite, Episode, Epos, Ethylene, Exponential, Geometric, Gradation, Harmonic, Homologous, Lanthanide, Line, Loop, Methane, Molasse, Neptunium, Partwork, Pedigree, Power, Process, →**PROGRESSION**, Radioactive, Rally, Random walk, Ranks, Rest, Rosalia, Rosary, Routine, Rubber, Run, Sequence, Ser, Set, Sitcom, String, Succession, Suit, Thorium, Time, Tone, Tournament, Train, Uranium, World

Serious(ly) Critical, Earnest, For real, Grave, Gravitas, Harsh, Important, In earnest, Intense, Major, Momentous, Pensive, Radical, Real, Sad, Serpentine, Sober, Solemn, Sombre, Staid, Straight(-faced), Very

Sermon Address, Discourse, Gatha, Homily, Khutbah, Lecture, Preachment, Prone, Ser, Spital

Serpent(ine) Adder, Anguine, Asp, Aspic(k), Basilisk, Boa, Cockatrice, Dipsas, Firedrake, Nagas, Pharaoh's, Sea-snake, →**SNAKE**, Traitor, Verd-antique, Verde-antico, Viper

Serum Albumin, Antiglobulin, Antilymphocyte, Antitoxin, ATS, Fluid, Globulin, Humoral, Opsonin, Senega

Servant, Server Aid(e), Attendant, Ayah, Batman, Bearer, Bedder, Bedmaker, Between-maid, Boot-catcher, Boots, Boy, Busboy, Butler, Caddie, Chokra, Civil, Columbine, Cook, Cook-general, Daily, Dogsbody, Domestic, Dromio, Drudge, Employee, Factotum, File, Flunkey, Footboy, Footman, Friday, General, G(h)illie, Gip, Gully, Gyp, Handmaid, Helot, Henchman, Hind, Hireling, Jack, Jack-slave, Kitchen-knave, Kitchen-maid, Knave, Lackey, Lady's maid, Leroy, Maid, Major-domo, Man, Man Friday, Menial, Minion, Mixologist, Muchacha, Muchacho, Myrmidon, Obedient, Page, Pantler, Parlourmaid, Pistol, Public, Pug, Retainer, Retinue, Scout, Scullion, Servitor, Slavey, Soldier, Soubrette, Steward, Tablespoon, Tiger, Trotter, Turnspit, Tweeny, Underling, Valet, Valkyrie, Varlet, Vassal, Waiter

Serve(r), Service(s) Acas, Ace, Act, Active, All-up, Amenity, Answer, Army, Assist, Attendance, Avail, Baptism, Barista, Barman, Barperson, Benediction, Breakfast, Campaign, Candlemas, Cannonball, China, Christingle, Civil, Communion, Community, Complin(e), Conscription, Credo, Devotional, Dien, Dinnerset, Diplomatic, Divine, Dollop, Drumhead, Dry, Duty, Ecosystem, Emergency, Employ, Evensong, Facility, Fault, Fee, Feudal, Fish, Foreign, Forensic, Forward, →**FUNCTION**, Funeral, Help, Helpline, Ibadat, Jury, Kol Nidre, Ladle, Lip, Litany, Liturgy, Ma'ariv, Marriage, Mass, Mat(t)ins, Memorial, Mincha, Minister, Ministration, Ministry, Missa, National, Navy, Nocturn, Nones, Oblige, Offertory, Office, Oracle, Overarm, Overhaul, Pass, Pay, Personal, Pit stop, Possum, Pottery, Pour, Prime, Proper, Public, Radio, RAF, Regular, Requiem, Rite, Sacrament, SAS, Satisfy, SBS, Secret, Selective, Senior, Sext, Shacharis, Shaharith, Shuttle, Silver, Skeleton, Social,

Sue, Tableware, Tea, Tierce, Vespers, Wait, Waitron, Waitstaff, Watch-night, Wild, Worship, Yeoman('s)

▷ **Serviceman** *may indicate* a churchman

Servile, Servility Abasement, Base, Crawling, Knee, Kowtowing, Lickspittle, Menial, Minion, Obsequious, Slavish, Slimy, Submissive, Suck-hole, Sycophantic, Tintookie, Truckle

Session(s) All-nighter, Bout, Executive, Galah, Hearing, Jam, Kirk, Meeting, Nightshift, Petty, Poster, Quarter, Rap, Round, Séance, Sederunt, Settle, Sitting, Special, Term

Set(ting) (about; aside; down; in; off; out; up) Activate, Apply, Array, Assiege, Brooch, Cabal, Coagulate, Codomain, Cyclorama, Data, Dead, Detonate, Direct, Duchesse, Earmark, Enchase, Ensky, Explode, Film, Firm, Flash, Gelatinise, Hairdo, Heliacal, Inchase, Incrowd, Infinite, Inlay, Jet, Julia, Knit, Mental, Miserere, Nail, Open, Ordain, Ordered, Ouch, Pair, Pavé, Permanent, Point, Power, Rate, Rig, Rouse, Saw, Settle(d), Slate, Smart, Solution, Stud, Subscriber, Televisor, The four hundred, Theme, Tiffany, Toilet, Trannie, Transistor, Truth, TV, Union, Universal

Setback Checkmate, Downturn, Glitch, Hiccough, Hiccup, Jolt, Knock, Relapse, Retard, Retreat, Reversal, Scarcement, Sickener, Tes, Vicissitude, Whammy

Settle(d), Settlement, Settler Adjust, Agree, Alight, Ante, Appoint, Arrange, Ascertain, Avenge, Balance, Bed, Bench, Boer, Borghetto, Botany Bay, Camp, Clear, Clench, Clinch, Colonial, Colonise, Colony, Compose, Compound, Compromise, Decide, Defray, Determine, Discharge, Dispose, Dowry, Encamp, Endow, Ensconce, Entail, Establish, Expat, Faze, Finalise, Fix, Foot, Foreclose, Gravitate, Guilder, Habitant, Hama, Hyannis, Illegitimate, Informal, Jamestown, Jointure, Kibbutz, Land, Ledge, Light, Lull, Manyat(t)a, Meet, Merino, Mise, Mission, Moreton Bay, Nest, Nestle, New Amsterdam, Opt, Outpost, Over, Pa(h), Pale, Patroon, Pay, Payment, Penal, People, Perch, Pilgrim, Pioneer, Placate, Planter, Populate, Port Arthur, Port Nicholson, Pueblo, Readjust, Reduction, Reimburse, Remit, Reside, Resolve, Rest, Roofie, Roost, Sate, Satisfaction, Seal, Seat, Secure, Sedimentary, Set fair, Shtetl, Silt, Snuggle, Sofa, Soldier, Solve, Soweto, Square, Square up, State, Still, Straits, Subside, Township, Undertaker, Vest(ed), Viatical, Voortrekker, Wrap up

▷ **Settlement** *may indicate* an anagram

▷ **Settler** *may indicate* a coin

Seven(th), Seven-sided Ages, Days, Dials, Great Bear, Hebdomad, Hepta-, Hills, Nones, Pleiad(es), S, Sages, Seas, Septenary, Septilateral, Septimal, Sins, Sisters, Sleepers, Stars, Wonders, Zeta

Seven-week Omer

Several Divers, Many, Multiple, Plural, Some, Sundry, Various

Severe(ly), Severity Acute, Astringent, Austere, Bad, Chronic, Cruel, Dour, Draconian, Drastic, Eager, Extreme, Grave, Grievous, Gruel(ling), Hard, →HARSH, Ill, Inclement, Morose, Penal, Rhadamanthine, Rigo(u)r, Roundly, Ruthless, Serious, Sharp, Snell(y), Sore, Spartan, Stark, Stern, Strict

Sew(ing), Sew up Baste, Cope, Darn, Embroider, Fell, Fine-draw, Machine, Mitre, Overlock, Run up, Seam, Seel, Stitch, Tack, Whip

Sewage, Sewer Cesspool, Cloaca, Culvert, Dorcas, →DRAIN, Effluence, Jaw-box, Jaw-hole, Mimi, Needle, Privy, Seamster, Shore, Soil, Sough, Soughing-tile, Sure, Waste

Sex(ist), Sexual, Sexy Bed-hopping, Carnal, Congress, Cottaging, Coupling, Cybersex, Erotic, Favours, Female, Gam(ic), Gender, Greek love, Hump, Incest, Intercourse, Intimacy, Jailbait, Kind, Knee-trembler, Libidinous, Libido, Lingam, Lumber, Male, Mate, Non-penetrative, Nookie, Oomph, Oral, Outercourse, Paedophilia, Paraphilia, Pederasty, Phallocratic, Phat, Phone, Priapean, Prurient, Race, Randy, Raunchy, Rough trade, Rut(ish), Salacious, Screw, Sect, Six, Slinky, SM, Steamy, Sultry, Tantric, Teledildonics, Unsafe, Venereal, Venery, VI, Voluptuous

Shabby Base, Buckeen, Dog-eared, Down-at-heel, Fusc(ous), Grotty, Grungy, Low-lived, Mean, Moth-eaten, Old hat, Oobit, Oorie, Oubit, Ourie, Outworn, Owrie,

Raunch, Scaly, Scarecrow, Scruffy, Seedy, Shoddy, Squalid, Tatty, Tawdry, Threadbare, Unkempt, Worn, Woubit

Shackle(s) Bind, Bracelet, Chain, Darbies, Entrammel, Fetter(lock), Hamper, Irons, Manacle, Restrict, Tie, Trammel, Yoke

Shade(d), Shades, Shading, Shadow, Shady Adumbrate, Arbour, Awning, Blend, Blind, Bongrace, Bowery, Brocken spectre, Buff, Cast, Chiaroscuro, Chroma, Cloche, Cloud, Cross-hatch, Degree, Demirep, Dis, Dog, Dubious, Eclipse, Eye, Five o'clock, Galanty, Gamp, Ghost, Gnomon, Gradate, Gray, Hachure, Hatch, Hell, Herbar, Hint, Hue, Inumbrate, Larva, Lee, Magnolia, Mezzotint, Modena, Nuance, Opaque, Overtone, Parasol, Pastel, Phantom, Presence, Ray-Bans®, Satellite, Screen, Shroud, Sienna, Silhouette, Silvan, Skia-, Soften, Sound, Spectre, Spirit, Stag, Sunglasses, Swale, Swaly, Tail, Tenebrious, Tinge, Tint, Titian, Tone, Track, Trail, Ugly, Umbra(tile), Umbrage(ous), Underhand, Velamen, Velar(ium), Velum, Visitant, Visor

Shaft(ed), Shafting Arbor, Arrow, Barb, Barrow-train, Beam, Befool, Capstan, Cardan, Chimney, Collet, Column, Crank, Cue, Disselboom, Dolly, Downcast, Drive, Escape, Fil(l), Fust, Gleam, Incline, Journal, Lay, Limber, Loom, Mandrel, Mandril, Moulin, Parthian, Passage, Pile, Pit, Pitbrow, Pitch, Pole, Propeller, Ray, Rib, Rise, Scape, Scapus, Shank, Snead, Spindle, Staff, Stale, Steal(e), Steel, Steen, Stele, Stulm, Sunbeam, Telescopic, Thill, Tige, Tomo, Trave, Truncheon, Upcast, Winning, Winze

Shaggy Ainu, Beetle-browed, Bushy, Comate, Hairy, Hearie, Hirsute, Horrid, Horror, Maned, Rough, Rugged, Shock, Shough, Tatty, Tousy, Touzy, Towsy, Towzy, Untidy

▷ **Shake** *may indicate an anagram*

Shake(n), Shake off, Shakes, Shaky Agitate, Ague(-fit), Astonish, Bebung, Brandish, Coggle, Concuss, Dabble, Dick(e)y, Didder, Diddle, Disconcert, Dither, Dodder, Feeble, Groggy, Hod, Hotch, Ictal, Jar, Jiggle, Joggle, Jolt, Jounce, Judder, Jumble, Lose, Milk, Mo, Nid-nod, Press flesh, Quake, Quiver, Quooke, Rattle, Rickety, Rickle, **→ ROCK**, Rouse, Shimmer, Shiver, Shock, Shog, Shoogle, Shudder, Succuss(ation), Sweat, Swish, Tremble, Tremolo, Tremor, Tremulous, Trill(o), Tumbledown, Undulate, Unsteady, Vibrate, Vibrato, Wag, Waggle, Wind, Wobble, Wonky

Shallow(s) Ebb, Flat, Fleet, Flew, Flue, Justice, Neritic, Rattlebrain, Riffle, Sandbank, Sandbar, Shoal, Slight, Superficial

Sham Apocryphal, Bluff, Bogus, Braide, Charade, Counterfeit, Deceit, Fake, **→ FALSE**, Hoax, Idol, Impostor, Mimic, Mock, Phony, Pinchbeck, Pretence, Pseudo, Repro, Snide, Spurious, Straw man

Shaman Angek(k)ok, Sorcerer

Shame(ful), Shame-faced Abash, Aidos, Atimy, Confusion, Contempt, Crying, Degrade, Discredit, Disgrace, Dishonour, Disrepute, Embarrass, Fie, Gross, Hangdog, Honi, Humiliate, Ignominy, Infamy, Inglorious, Modesty, Mortify, Ohone, Pity, Pudor, Pugh, Sad, Shend, Sin, Slander, Stain, Stigma, Yshend

Shape(d), Shapely, Shaping Blancmange, Boast, Cast, Contour, Cuneiform, Die-cast, Face, Fashion, Figure, Form, Format, Fractal, Geoid, Geometrical, Gnomon, Headquarters, Hew, Jello, Model, Morphology, **→ MOULD**, Polyomine, Ream, Rhomb(us), Roughcast, Scabble, Sculpt, Step-cut, Voluptuous, Wrought

Share(d), Shares, Sharing Allocation, Allotment, Angels' cost, Apportion, Blue-chip, Chop, Co, Cohabit, Coho(e), Common, Communal, Contango, Co-portion, Co-tenant, Culter, Cut, Deferred, Divi(dend), Divide, Divvy (up), Dole, Dutch, Equity, Finger, Flatmate, Founders, Golden, Grubstake, Impart, Interest, Job, Kaffer, Kaf(f)ir, Kangaroo, Law, Lion's, Market, Moiety, Mutual, Odd lot, OFEX, Ordinary, **→ PART**, Partake, Participate, Penny, PIBS, Plough, Plough-iron, Portfolio, Portion, Prebend, Pref(erred), Preference, Pro rata, Prorate, Quarter, Quota, Rake off, Ration, Rug, Scrip, Security, Shr, Slice, Snack, Snap, Sock, Split, Stock, Taurus, Time, Tranche, Two-way, Whack

Shark Angel, Basking, Beagle, Blue, Bonnethead, Bull, Carpet, Cestracion, Cow, Demoiselle, Dog(fish), Great white, Hammerhead, Houndfish, Huss, Lemonfish, Leopard catshark, Loan, Mackerel, Mako, Noah, Nurse, Penny-dog, Plagiostomi, Porbeagle, Requiem, Reremai, Rhin(e)odon, Rigg, Rook, Sail-fish, Sand, Sea-ape,

Sea-fox, Sevengill, Sharp, Shortfin mako, Shovelhead, Smoothhound, Spotted ragged-tooth, Squaloid, Swindler, Thrasher, Thresher, Tiger, Tope, Usurer, Whale, Whaler, Wobbegong, Zygaena

Sharp(er), Sharpen(er), Sharpness Abrupt, Accidental, Acerose, Acidulous, Acrid, Aculeus, Acumen, Acuminate, Acute, Alert, Angular, Arris, Astringent, Bateless, Becky, Bitter, Brisk, Cacuminous, Cheat, Clear, Coticular, Cutting, Dital, Edge(r), Fine, Gleg, Grind, Hone, Hot, Keen, Kurtosis, Massé, Mordant, Oilstone, Peracute, Piquant, Poignant, Pronto, Pungent, Quick-witted, Razor, Rogue, Rook, Saw doctor, Set, Shrewd, Snap, Snell, Sour, Spicate, Strop, Swindler, Tart, Tomium, Varment, Vivid, Volable, Vorpal, Whet

Sharp-sighted Lynx-eyed

Shawl Afghan, Buibui, Cashmere, Chuddah, Chuddar, Dopatta, Dupatta, Fichu, India, Kaffiyeh, Kashmir, Manta, Mantilla, Maud, Paisley, Partlet, Pashmina, Prayer, Serape, Sha(h)toosh, Stole, Tallis, Tallit(ot), Tallith, Tonnag, Tozie, Tribon, Whittle, Wrap(per), Zephyr

Shed(ding), Shedder Autotomy, Barn, Byre, Cast, Cho(u)ltry, Coducity, Cootch, Cwtch, Depot, Discard, Doff, Downsize, Drop, Effuse, Exuviate, Hangar, Hovel, Hut, Infuse, Lair, Lean-to, Linhay, Linn(e)y, Mew, Moult, Pent, Potting, Salmon, Shippen, Shippon, Shuck, Skeo, Skillion, Skio, Slough, Sow, Spend, Spent, Spill, Spit, Tilt, Tool

Sheep(ish) Ammon, Ancon(es), Aoudad, Argali, Ashamed, Barbary, Bell(wether), Bharal, Bident, Bighorn, Black, Blackface, Blate, Border Leicester, Broadtail, Burhel, Burrel(l), Caracul, Charollais, Cheviots, Coopworth, Corriedale, Cotswold, Cotswold lion, Coy, Crone, Dall('s, Dinmont, Domestic, Dorset Down, Dorset Horn, Down, Drysdale, Embarrassed, Ewe, Exmoor, Fank, Fat-tailed, Flock, Fold, Hair, Hampshire, Hampshire Down, Hangdog, Herdwick, Hidder, Hirsel, Hog(g), Hogget, Jacob, Jemmy, Jumbuck, Karakul, Kent, Kerry Hill, Lamb, Lanigerous, Leicester, Lincoln, Lo(a)ghtan, Loghtyn, Long, Lonk, Marco Polo, Masham, Merino, Mor(t)ling, Mouf(f)lon, Mountain, Muflon, Mug, Mus(i)mon, Mutton, Oorial, Ovine, Oxford Down, Perendale, Portland, Ram, Rambouillet, Romeldale, Romney Marsh, Rosella, Ryeland, Scottish Blackface, Shearling, Shetland, Shidder, Short, Shorthorn, →SHY, Soay, Southdown, Spanish, Stone('s, Suffolk, Sumph, Swaledale, Teeswater, Teg(g), Texel, Theave, Trip, Tup, Twinter, Two-tooth, Udad, Urial, Vegetable, Welsh Mountain, Wensleydale, Wether, Wiltshire Horn, Woollyback, Yow(e), Yowie

Sheet(ing), Sheets Balance, Cel, Cere-cloth, Cerement, Charge, Chart, Crime, Cutch, Dope, Expanse, Film, Folio, Foolscap, Heft, Intrusive, Lasagne, Leaf, Membrane, Nappe, Out-hauler, Page, Pane, Pot(t), Pour, Proof, Prospectus, Rap, Ream, Rope, Sail, Scandal, Shroud, Stern, Stratus, Taggers, Tarpaulin(g), Tear, Tentorium, Terne, Thunder, Time, Web, Winding

Shell(ed), Shellfish, Shellwork Abalone, Acorn-shell, Admiral, Ambulacrum, Ammo, Argonaut, Balamnite, Balanus, Balmain bug, Belemnite, Bivalve, Blitz, Boat, Bodywork, Bombard, Buckie, Camera, Capiz, Capsid, Carapace, Cartridge, Casing, Chank, Chelonia, Chitin, Clam, Cleidoic, Clio, Coat-of-mail, Cochlea, Cockle, Cohog, Conch, Cone, Copepoda, Cover, Cowrie, Cowry, Crab, Cracked, Crustacea, Cuttlebone, Dariole, Deerhorn, Dentalium, Dop, Drill, Electron, Escallop, Eugarie, Foraminifer, Framework, Frustule, Gas, Geoduck, Globigerina, Haliotis, Hull, Husk, Hyoplastron, Isopoda, Kernel, Lamp, Langouste, Limacel, Limpet, Live, Lobster, Lorica, Lyre, Malacostraca, Midas's ear, Mitre, Mollusc, Money, Monocoque, Moon, Moreton Bay bug, Mother-of-pearl, Murex, Music, Mussel, Nacre, Nautilus, Olive, Ormer, Ostracod, Ostrea, Otter, Oyster, Paua, Pawa, Pea(s)cod, Peag, Peak, Pecten, Peel, Pereia, Periostracum, Periwinkle, Pilgrim's, Pipi, Pipsqueak, Plastron, Pod, Prawn, Projectile, Purple, Putamen, Quahaug, Quahog, Razor, Rocaille, Sal, Scalarium, Scallop, Scollop, Sea-ear, Sea-pen, Shale, Shard, Sheal, Sheel, Shiel, Shill, Shock, Shot, Shrapnel, Shrimp, Shuck, Sial, Smoke-ball, Spat, Spend, Spindle, Star, Stomatopod, Stonk, Straddle, Strafe, Stromb(us), Swan-mussel, Tear, Tellen, Tellin, Test(a), Thermidor, Toheroa, Tooth, Top, Torpedo, Tracer, Trivalve, Trough, Trumpet, Turbo, Turritella, Tusk, Univalve, Valency, Venus, Wakiki, Wampum, Whelk, Whiz(z)bang, Winkle, Xenophya, Yabbie, Yabby, Zimbi

▷ **Shelled** *may indicate* an anagram

Shelter(ed) Abri, A l'abri, Anderson, Arbour, Asylum, Awn, Awning, Barn, Bay, · Belee, Bender, Bield, Billet, Blind, Blockhouse, Booth, Bunker, Burladero, Butt, Cab, Carport, Casemate, Coop, Cot(e), Cove, Covert, Coverture, Defence, Dodger, Donga, Dovecote, Dripstone, Dug-out, Fall-out, Garage, Gunhouse, Gunyah, Harbour, Haven, Hithe, Hospice, Hostel, House, Hovel, Humpy, Hut, Hutchie, Igloo, Imbosom, Kipsie, Lee, Lee-gage, Loun, Lound, Lown, Lownd, Mai mai, Mission, Morrison, Nissen, Nodehouse, Palapa, Pilothouse, → **REFUGE**, Retreat, Roadstead, Roof, Sanctuary, Scog, Sconce, Scoog, Scoug, Screen, Scug, Secluded, Shed, Shiel(ing), Shroud, Skug, Snowhole, Snowshed, Stell, Storm-cellar, Succah, Sukkah, Summerhouse, Suntrap, Tax, Tent, Te(e)pee, Testudo, Tortoise, Tupik, Twigloo, Umbrage, Weather, Wheelhouse, Wickyup, Wi(c)kiup, Wil(t)ja, Windbreak, Windscreen, Windshield

Shepherd(ess) Abel, Acis, Amaryllis, Amos, Bergère, Bo-peep, Bucolic, Chloe, Clorin, Conduct, Corin, Corydon, Cuddy, Daphnis, Dorcas, Drover, Endymion, Escort, Ettrick, Feeder, Flock-master, German, Grubbinol, Gyges, Herdsman, Hobbinol, Lindor, Marshal, Menalcas, Padre, Pastor(al), Pastorella, Phebe, Pilot, Sheepo, Strephon, Tar-box, Thenot, Thyrsis, Tityrus

Sherbet Beer, Soda

Sherry Amoroso, Cobbler, Cream, Cyprus, Doctor, Dry, Fino, Gladstone, Jerez, Manzanilla, Oloroso, Sack, Solera, Sweet, Whitewash, Xeres

Shiah Ismaili

Shield(s), Shield-shaped Ablator, Achievement, Aegis, Ancile, Armour, Arms, Baltic, Biological, Bodyguard, Box, Brolly, Buckler, Canadian, Cartouche, Clypeus, Defend, Dress, Escutcheon, Fence, Gobo, Guard, Gumshield, Gyron, Hatchment, Heat, Hielaman, Human, Inescutcheon, Insulate, Laurentian, Lozenge, Mant(e)let, Mask, Pavis(e), Pelta, Plastron, Protect, Randolph, Ranfurly, Riot, Rondache, Scandinavian, Screen, Scute, Scutum, Sheffield, Splashboard, Sternite, Targe(t), Thyroid, Toecap, Vair, Visor, Water

Shift(er), Shifty Amove, Astatic, Blue, Budge, Change, Chemise, Core, Cymar, Devious, Displace, Doppler, Dress, Dying, Evasive, Expedient, Fend, Graveyard, Hedging, Landslide, Lateral, Linen, Meve, Move, Night, Nighty, Red, Relay, Remove, Ruse, Scorch, Shirt, Shovel, Shunt, Simar(re), Slicker, Slip(pery), Spell, Stagehand, Steal, Stint, Switch, Tergiversate, Tour, Transfer, Tunic, Turn, Turnabout, Vary, Veer, Warp

▷ **Shift(ing)** *may indicate* an anagram

▷ **Shimmering** *may indicate* an anagram

Shin Clamber, Climb, Cnemial, Leg, Shank, Skink, Swarm

Shine(r), Shining, Shiny Aglitter, Aglow, Beam, Buff, Burnish, Deneb, Effulge, Excel, Flash, Gleam, Glisten, Gloss, → **GLOW**, Irradiant, Japan, → **LAMP**, Leam, Leme, Lucent, Luminous, Lustre, Mouse, Nitid, Nugget, Phoebe, Phosphoresce, Polish, Radiant, Radiator, Relucent, Resplend, Rutilant, Shimmer, Skyre, Sleek, Twinkle, Varnish

▷ **Shiny** *may indicate* a star

Ship(ping), Ships Boat, Container, Convoy, → **DISPATCH**, Embark, Export, Flota, Her, Hulk, Jolly, Keel, Man, MV, Nautical, Post, Privateer, Prize, Prow, Raft, Ram, Sail, Saique, She, SS, Tall, Tub, Vessel, Weather

Shipment Cargo

Shipshape Apple-pie, Neat, Orderly, Tidy, Trim

Shirt Aloha, Boiled, Brown, Calypso, Camese, Camise, Chemise, Choli, Cilice, Dasheki, Dashiki, Dick(e)y, Dress, Fiesta, Garibaldi, Grandad, Hair, Hawaiian, Jacky Howe, Kaftan, Kaross, K(h)urta, Muscle, Nessus, Non-iron, Parka, Partlet, Polo, Rash, Red, Rugby, Safari, Sark, Serk, Set, Shift, Smock, Stuffed, Subucula, T

▷ **Shiver(ed)** *may indicate* an anagram

Shiver(ing), Shivers, Shivery Aguish, Atingle, Break, Brrr, Chitter, Crumble, Dash, Dither, Fragile, Frisson, Gooseflesh, Grew, Grue, Malaria, Matchwood, Oorie,

Ourie, Owrie, Quake, Quiver, →SHAKE, Shatter, Shrug, Shudder, Smash, Smither, Smithereens, Splinter, Timbers, Tremble

Shock(ed), Shocker, Shocking Acoustic, Aghast, Agitate, Amaze, Anaphylactic, Appal, Astone, Astony, Astound, Awful, Bombshell, Bunch, Criminal, Culture, Defibrillate, Disgust, Dreadful, Drop, Dumbfound, Earthquake, ECT, Egregious, Electric, Electrocute, EST, Eye-opener, Fleg, Floccus, Galvanism, Gobsmack, Hair, Haycock, Haystack, Horrify, Horror, Impact, Infamous, Insulin, Isoseismic, Jar, Jolt, Knock cold, Live, Mane, Mop, Numb, Obscene, Outrage, Poleaxe, Putrid, Recoil, Return, Revolt, Rick(er), Rigor, Scandal(ise), Seismic, Septic, Shake, Sheaf, Shell, Shog, Stagger, Start(le), Stun, Surgical, Tangle, Thermal, Trauma, Turn

▷ **Shocked** may indicate an anagram

Shoe(s) Accessory, Arctic, Athletic, Ballet, Balmoral, Bauchle, Birkenstock, Blocked, Boat, Boot, Bootee, Brake, Brogan, Brogue, Brothel creepers, Buskin, Calceate, Calk(er), Calkin, Carpet slipper, Casuals, Caulker, Cawker, Charlier, Chaussures, Chopin(e), Clodhopper, Clog, Co-respondent, Court, Creeper, Dap, Deck, Espadrille, Flattie, Flip-flops, Galoche, Galosh, Gatty, Geta, Ghillie, Golosh, Gumboot, Gumshoe, Gym, High-low, High tops, Hot, Hush-puppies®, Jandal®, Jellies, Kletterschue, Kurdaitcha, Lace up, Launch(ing), Loafer, Mary-Janes®, Mocassin, Moccasin, Muil, Mule, Open-toe, Oxford, Oxonian, Panton, Patten, Peeptoe, Pennyloafer, Pile, Plate, Plimsole, Plimsoll, Poulaine, Pump, Rivlin, Rope-soled, Rubbers, Rullion, Runner, Sabaton, Sabot, Saddle, Safety, Sandal, Sandshoe, Sannie, Scarpetto, Shauchle, Skid, Skimmer, Slingback, Slip-on, Slipper, Slip-slop, Sneaker, Snow, Sock, Soft, Solleret, Spike, Stoga, Stogy, Suede, Tackies, Takkies, Tennis, Tie, Topboot, Track, Trainer, T-strap, Upper, Vamp(er), Veld-schoen, Veldskoen, Velskoen, Vibram®, Vibs, Wagon lock, Wedgie, Welt, Winkle-picker, Zori

Shoemaker Blacksmith, Clogger, Cobbler, Cordiner, Cordwainer, Cosier, Cozier, Crispi(a)n, Farrier, Leprechaun, Sachs, Smith, Snob, Soutar, Souter, Sowter, Sutor

Shoot(er), Shooting Ack-ack, Airgun, Arrow, Bine, Bostryx, Braird, Breer, Bud, Bulbil, Camera, Catapult, Chit, Cion, Cyme, Dart(le), Delope, Discharge, Drib, Elance, Enate, Eradiate, Film, Fire, Germ, Germain(e), Germen, Germin(ate), Glorious twelfth, →GUN, Gunsel, Head-reach, Hurl, Imp, Jet, Lateral, Layer, Lens, Limb, Loose, Marksmanship, Offset, Osier, Photograph, Pip, Plink, Pluff, Plug, Poot, Pop, Pot, Pout, Ramulus, Rapids, Ratoon, Riddle, Rod, Rough, Rove, Runner, Scion, Septembriser, Sien(t), Skeet, Snipe, Spire, Spirt, Spout, Spray, Sprout, Spurt, Spyre, Start, Stole, Stolon, Strafe, Sucker, Syen, Tellar, Teller, Tendril, Tendron, Tiller, Turion, Twelfth, Twig, Udo, Vimen, Wand, Weapon, Whiz(z), Wildfowler

Shop(per), Shopping, Shops Agency, Arcade, Assembly, Atelier, Automat, Bag, Betray, Body, Boutique, Bucket, Buy, Chain, Charity, Chippy, Chop, Closed, Coffee, Commissary, Cook, Co-op, Cop, Corner, Cut-price, Dairy, Delicatessen, Denounce, Dobbin, Dolly, Duddery, Duka, Duty-free, Emporium, Factory, Five and dime, Food court, Galleria, Gift, Grass, In bond, Inform, Junk, Luckenbooth, Machine, Mall, Mall crawl, Mall-rat, Market, Megastore, Mercat, Messages, Minimart, Muffler, Office, Officinal, Off-licence, Off-sales, Op(portunity), Open, Outlet, Parlour, Patisserie, Personal, Pharmacy, Precinct, Print, PX, Rat on, Report, Retail, RMA, Salon, Sex, Shambles, Share, Shebang, Spaza, Squat, →STORE, Strip mall, Studio, Sundry, Superette, Supermarket, Superstore, Swap, Talking, Tally, Tea (room), Thrift, Tick, Tommy, Trade, Truck, Tuck, Union, Vintry, Warehouse, Whistle-blow, Works

Shopkeeper British, Butcher, Chemist, Gombeen-man, Greengrocer, Grocer, Haberdasher, Hosier, Ironmonger, Merchant, Newsagent, Provisioner, Retailer, Stationer

Shore Bank, Beach, Buttress, Coast, Coste, Landfall, Lee, Littoral, Machair, Offing, Prop, Rivage, Seaboard, Strand, Strandline

Short(en), Shortly Abbreviate, Abridge, Abrupt, Anon, Brief, Brusque, Close-in, Commons, Concise, Contract, Crisp, Cross, Curt, Curtail, Curtal, Cutty, Digest, Diminish, Drink, Epitomise, Ere-long, Flying, Impolite, Inadequate, In a while, Lacking, Laconical, Light, Limited, Low, Mini, Near, Nip, Nutshell, Offing, Pithy,

Punch, Reduce, Reef, Scantle, Scanty, Scarce, Shrift, Shy, Soon, Sparse, Spirit, Squab, Staccato, Stint, Stocky, Strapped, Stubby, Succinct, Taciturn, Teen(s)y, Telescope, Temporal, Terse, Tight, Tot, Wee

Shortage Brevity, Dearth, Deficiency, Deficit, Drought, Famine, Lack, Need, Paucity, Scarcity, Sparsity, Ullage, Wantage

Shortfall Deficit

Shorts Bermuda, Board, Boxer, Briefs, Culottes, Hot pants, Kaccha, Lederhosen, Plus-fours, Skort, Stubbies®, Trunks

Shot(s) Ammo, Approach, Attempt, Backhand, Ball, Bank, Barrage, Blank, Blast, Bull, Bullet, Burl, Canna, Cannonball, Cartridge, Case, Chain, Chip, Close up, Corner, Cover, Crab, Crack, Daisy cutter, Dink, Dolly, Dram, Draw, Drop, Duckhook, Dum dum, Dunk, Elt, Essay, Exhausted, Explosion, Flew, Forehand, Fusillade, Gesse, Get, Glance, Go, Grape, Guess, Hazard, Hook, In-off, Iridescent, Jump, Kill, Lay-up, Marksman, Maroon, Massé, Matte, Mitraille, Money, Moon-ball, Mulligan, Musket, Noddy, Pack, Parthian, Parting, Passing, Pellet, Penalty, Photo, Pitch, Plant, Pop, Pot, Puff, Push, Rake, Rid, Round, Safety, Salvo, Scratch, Shy, Silk, Six, Slam-dunk, Slap, Slice, Slug, Slung, Snap, Snifter, Sped, Spell, Spent, Square cut, Stab, Still, Streaked, Tap in, Tee, Throw, Toepoke, Tonic, Tot, Tracking, Trial, Try, Turn, Volley, Warning, Wrist, Yahoo

Shout(er), Shouting Alley-oop, Barrack, Bawl, Bellow, Boanerges, Call, Claim, Clamour, Conclamation, Cry, Din, Exclaim, Heckle, Hey, Hoi(cks), Holla, Holla-ho(a), Holler, Hollo, Holloa, Hooch, Hosanna, Howzat, Hue, Oi, Oy, Rah, Rant, Roar, Root, Round, Sa sa, Treat, Trumpet, Vociferate, Whoop, Yammer, Yell(och), Yippee, Yodel, Yoohoo

Shovel Backhoe, Dustpan, Hat, Loy, Main, Peel, Power, Scoop, Shool, Spade, Steam, Trowel, Van

Show(ing), Shown, Showy Appearance, Aquacade, Bad, Bench, Betray, Branky, Broadcast, Burlesque, Cabaret, Cattle, Chat, Circus, Come, Con, Cruft's, Demo(nstrate), Depict, Describe, Dime museum, Diorama, Display, Do, Dramedy, Dressy, Dumb, Effere, Entertainment, Establish, Evince, →**EXHIBIT**, Expo, Express, Extravaganza, Exude, Facade, Fair, Fangled, Farce, Flamboyant, Flash, Flaunt, Floor, Folies Bergere, Game, Garish, Gaudy, Gay, Gig, Give, Glitter, Glitz(y), Gloss, Good, Horse, Indicate, Jazzy, Light, Loud, Manifest, Matinée, Minstrel, Moon, Musical, One-man, Ostentatious, Pageant, Panel game, Panto(mime), Parade, Patience, Peacock, Performance, Phen(o), Phone-in, Point, Pomp, Portray, Presentation, Pretence, Pride, Procession, Prog(ramme), Project, Prominence, Prove, Pseudery, Puff, Puppet, Quiz, Raree, Razzmatazz, Reality, Register, Represent, Reveal, Revue, Road, Rodeo, Ruddigore, Rushes, Screen, Shaw, Sight, Singspiel, Sitcom, Slang, Soap, Son et lumière, Specious, Spectacle, Splash, Splay, Stage, Stunt, Talk, Tattoo, Tawdry, Telecast, Telethon, Theatrical, Three-man, Tinhorn, Tinsel(ly), Tulip, Unbare, Uncover, Usher, Vain, Variety, Vaudeville, Veneer, Viewy, Wear, Wild west

Shower Douche, Exhibitor, Flurry, Hail, Indicant, Indicator, Lavish, Lot, Meteor, Party, Pelt, Pepper, Precipitation, Rain, Scat, Scouther, Scowther, Scud, Skit, Snow, Spat, Spet, Spit, Splatter, Spray, Sprinkle, Ticker tape, Volley

▷ **Showing, Shown in** *may indicate* a hidden word

Shred Clout, Filament, Grate, Mammock, Mince, Rag, Screed, Swarf, Tag, Tatter, Tear up, Thread, Wisp

Shrewd(ness) Acumen, Acute, Arch, Argute, Artful, Astucious, Astute, Callid, Canny, Clued-up, Cute, Far-sighted, File, Gnostic, Gumptious, Judicious, Knowing, Pawky, Politic, Prudent(ial), Sagacious, Sapient(al), Savvy, Sharp-sighted, Wide boy, Wily, Wise

Shriek Cry, Scream, Shright, Shrike, Shrill, Shritch, Skirl, Yell

Shrine Adytum, Altar, Dagaba, Dagoba, Dargah, Delphi, Fatima, Feretory, Harem, Holy, Joss house, Kaaba, Lourdes, Marabout, Memorial, Naos, Pagoda, Pilgrimage, Reliquary, Scrine, Scryne, Stupa, Tabernacle, Temple, Tope, Vimana, Walsingham

Shrink(age), Shrink from, Shrinking, Shrunk Abhor, Alienist, Blanch, Blench, Cling, Compress, Contract, Cour, Cower, Creep, Crine, Cringe, Dare, Decrew,

Depreciate, Dread, Dwindle, Flinch, Funk, Less, Nirl, →**PSYCHIATRIST**, Quail, Recoil, Reduce, Retract, Sanforised, Shrivel, Shy, Violet, Waste, Wince, Wizened

Shrove Tuesday Fastens, J'ouvert, Pancake

Shrub(bery) →**BUSH**, Petty whin, Plant, Undergrowth, Wintergreen

Shuck Peel

▷**Shuffle(d)** *may indicate* an anagram

Shuttle Alternate, Challenger, Commute, Drawer, Flute, Go-between, Navette, Shoot, Shunt, Space, Tat(t), Weave

Shy Bashful, Blate, Blench, Cast, Catapult, Chary, Coconut, Coy, Deficient, Demure, Farouche, Flinch, Funk, Heave, Introvert, Jerk, Jib, Laithfu', Lob, Mim, Modest, Mousy, Rear, Recoil, Reserved, Sheepish, Shrinking violet, Skeigh, Start, Throw, Timid, Tongue-tied, Toss, Try, Wallflower, Withdrawn

Shyster Ambulance chaser

Sick(en), Sickening, Sickliness, Sickly, Sickness Affection, Ague, Ail, Altitude, Anaemic, Bad, Bends, Bilious, Cat, Chunder, Colic, Crapulence, Cringeworthy, Crook, Decompression, Delicate, Disorder, Emetin(e), Gag, Green, Hacked off, Hangover, Icky, Ill, Infection, Leisure, Mal, Mawkish, Milk, Morbid, Morning, Motion, Mountain, Nauseous, Pale, Peaky, Peelie-wallie, Peely-wally, Pestilent, Pindling, Plague, Poorly, Queasy, Radiation, Regorge, Repulsive, Retch, Serum, Sleeping, Sleepy, Spue, Squeamish, Sweating, Travel, Twee, Valetudinarian, Virus, Vomit, Wan

Side, Sidepiece Abeam, Airs, B, Beam, Border, Camp, Distaff, Division, Edge, Effect, Eleven, English, Epistle, Facet, Flank, Flip, Gunnel, Hand, Heavy, Hypotenuse, Iliac, Lateral, Lee(ward), Left, Long, Lore, Obverse, Off, On, OP, Pane, Part, Partisan, Party, Pleura, Port, Pretension, Profile, Prompt, Rave, Reveal, Reverse, Right, Rink, Short, Silver, Slip, Spear, Spindle, Starboard, Swank, →**TEAM**, Tight, West, Windward, Wing, XI

Sidekick Right-hand man, Satellite

Sidepost Cheek

Sienese Tuscan

Sienna Burnt, Raw

Sierra Range, S

Sierra Leone Mende

Sight(ed) Aim, Barleycorn, Bead, Conspectuity, Eye(ful), Eyesore, Glimpse, Ken, Long, Oculated, Prospect, Range, Riflescope, Scene, Scotopia, Second, See, Short, Spectacle, Taish, Telescopic, Vane, →**VIEW**, Visie, Vision, Vista, Vizy, Vizzie

Sign(ing), Signpost, Signs Accidental, Addition, Air, Ale-pole, Ampersand, Aquarius, Archer, Aries, Arrow, Auspice, Autograph, Badge, Balance, Beck, Beckon, Birth, Board, Brand, Bull, Bush, Call, Cancer, Capricorn, Caract, Caret, Character, Chevron, Clue, Crab, Cross, Cue, Dele, Denote, Di(a)eresis, Division, Dollar, DS, Earmark, Earth, Emblem, Endorse, Endoss, Enlist, Enrol(l), Evidence, Exit, Fascia, Fire, Fish, Gemini, Gesture, Goat, Hallmark, Harbinger, Harvey Smith, Hash, Hex, Hieroglyphic, Hint, Ideogram, Indian, Indicate, Indication, Initial, INRI, Inscribe, Ivy-bush, Leo, Libra, Local, Logogram, Milepost, Milestone, Minus, Motion, Mudra, Multiplication, Negative, Nod, Notice, Obelisk, Obelus, Omen, Peace, Pisces, Plus, Positive, Pound, Presage, Prodrome, Radical, Ram, Ratify, Red lattice, Rest, Rune, Sacrament, Sagittarius, Sain, Scorpio, Segno, Semeion, Semiotics, Shingle, Show, Sigil, Sigla, Signal, Star, Subscribe, Subtraction, Superscribe, Symbol, Symptom, Syndrome, Tag, Taurus, Tic(k)tac(k), Tilde, Titulus, Token, Trace, Twins, Umlaut, V, Vestige, Virgo, Vital, Warison, Warning, Water, Waymark, Word, Zodiac

Signal(ler) Alarm, Alert, Amber, Assemble, Beacon, Beckon, Bell, Bleep, Bugle, Busy, Buzz, Call, Code, Cone, Cue, Detonator, Distant, Distress, Duplex, Earcon, Emit, Flag, Flagman, Flare, Flash, Fog, Gantry, Gesticulate, Gong, Griffin, Gun, Harmonic, Heliograph, Heliostat, Herald, Heterodyne, High sign, Hooter, Icon, Important, Indicator, Interrupt, Interval, Knell, Luminance, Mark, Message, Modem, Morse, NICAM, Notation, Noted, Output, Password, Peter, Pheromone, Pinger, Pip,

Pollice verso, Prod, Radio, Renowned, Reveille, Robot, Salient, Semaphore, Simplex, Singular, Smoke, Sonogram, SOS, Spoiler, Squawk, Taps, Target, Tattoo, Telegraph, Thumb, Tic(k)-tac(k), Time, Token, Traffic, Transmit, Troop, Vehicle-actuated, Very, Video, V-sign, Waff, Waft, Wave, Word, Yeoman

Signature Alla breve, Allograph, Autograph, By-line, Digital, Hand, John Hancock, John Henry, Key, Mark, Onomastic, Per pro, Sheet, Specimen, Subscription, Thermal, Time

Significance, Significant Cardinal, Consequence, Cosmic, Emblem, Ethos, Impact, Important, Indicative, Key, Landmark, Magnitude, Major, Matter, M(a)cGuffin, Meaningful, Moment(ous), Notable, Noted, Noteworthy, Operative, Paramount, Pith, Pregnant, Salient, Special, Telling

Silage Haylage

Silence(r), Silent Choke-pear, Clam, Clamour, Creepmouse, Dead air, Dumbstruck, Earplug, Gag, Hist, Hush, Hushkit, Mim(budget), Muffler, Mum(p), Mute, Omertà, Quench, Quiesce, →QUIET, Reticence, Shtoom, Shtum, Shush, Speechless, Squelch, Still, Sulky, Tace(t), Tacit(urn), Throttle, Tight-lipped, Tongue-tied, Unvoiced, Wheesh(t)

Silk(y), Silk screen Alamode, Artificial, Atlas, Barathea, Blonde-lace, Brocade, Bur(r), Charmeuse®, Chenille, Chiffon, Cocoon, Corn, Crape, Crepe, Duchesse, Dupion, Faille, Filoselle, Florence, Florentine, Flosh, Floss, Flox, Foulard, Gazar, Georgette, Glossy, Grosgrain, Honan, Kente, Kincob, Lustrine, Lustring, Lutestring, Madras, Makimono, Marabou(t), Matelasse, Milanese, Near, Ninon, Organza, Ottoman, Paduasoy, Parachute, Peau de soie, Pongee, Prunella, Prunelle, Prunello, Pulu, QC, Raw, Samite, Sars(e)net, Satin, Schappe, Sendal, Seric, Sericeous, Serigraph, Shalli, Shantung, Sien-tsan, Sleave, Sleek, Smooth, Soft, Spun, Surah, Tabaret, Tabby, Taffeta, Tasar, Thistledown, Thrown, Tiffany, Tram, Tulle, Tussah, Tusseh, Tusser, Tussore, Velvet

Silly, Silliness Absurd, Apish, Brainless, Childish, Crass, Cuckoo, Daffy, Daft, Ditsy, Divvy, Dotish, Drippy, Dumb(o), Dunce, Fatuous, Fluffy, Folly, Fool, Foolery, Footling, Frivolous, Goopy, Goosey, Gormless, Idiotic, Imbecile, Inane, Inept, Infield(er), Mid-off, Mid-on, Mopoke, Prune, Puerile, Season, Simple, Soft(y), Spoony, →STUPID, Tomfoolery, Tripe, Wacky

▷**Silver** *may indicate* a coin

Similar(ity) Akin, Analog(ue), Analogical, Corresponding, Equivalent, Etc, Homoeoneric, Homogeneous, Homoiousian, Homologous, Homonym, Isomorphism, Kindred, →LIKE, Likeness, Parallel, Resemblance, Samey

Simile Epic, Homeric

Simple(r), Simplicity, Simplify, Simply Arcadian, Artless, Austere, Bald, Bare, Basic, Bog-standard, Breeze, Crude, Daw, Doddle, Doric, →EASY, Eath(e), Elegant, Elemental, ESN, Ethe, Facile, Fee, Folksy, Gotham, Green, Gullish, Herb(alist), Homespun, Idyllic, Incomposite, Inornate, Mere, Naive(té), Naked, Niaiserie, No brainer, One-fold, Open and shut, Ordinary, Paraphrase, Pastoral, Peter, Plain, Pleon, Provincial, Pure, Reduce, Renormalise, Rustic, Sapid, Semplice, Sheer, Silly, Simon, Spartan, Straight, Stupid, Suave, Uncluttered, Understated, Unicellular, Unsophisticated, Woollen

Sin(ful) Aberrant, Anger, Avarice, Besetting, Bigamy, Capital, Cardinal, Covetousness, Crime, Deadly, Debt, Envy, Err, Evil, Folly, Gluttony, Hamartiology, Harm, Hate, Impious, Impure, Lapse, Lust, Misdeed, Misdoing, Mortal, →OFFENCE, Original, Peccadillo, Piacular, Pride, Scape, Scarlet, Sine, Sloth, Transgress, Trespass, Unrighteous, Venial, Vice, Wicked, Wrath, Wrong

Sincere(ly), Sincerity Bona-fide, Candour, Earnest, Entire, Frank, Genuine, Heartfelt, Heartwhole, Honest, Open, Real(ly), Realtie, Simple-hearted, True, Verity, Whole-hearted

▶**Sinful** *see* SIN(FUL)

Sing(ing) Antiphony, Barbershop, Bel canto, Belt out, Carol, Chant, Cheep, Chorus, Coloratura, Community, Cough, Croon, Crow, Diaphony, Diddle, Glee club, Gregorian, Hum, Incant, Inform, Intone, Karaoke, La-la, Lilt, Lyricism, Melic, Parlando, Peach,

Pen(n)illion, Pipe, Plainchant, Rand, Rant, Rap, Record, Render, Scat, Second(o), Serenade, Squeal, Tell, Thrum, Trill, Troll, Vocalese, Warble, Woodshedding, Yodel

Singapore .sg

Singer(s) Alto, Baillie, Baker, Bard, Baritone, Bass, Beatle, Bing, →**BIRD**, Bono, Brel, Buffo, Canary, Cantatrice, Cantor, Car, Castrato, Chanteur, Chanteuse, Chantor, Chauntress, Chazan, Cher, Chorister, Coloratura, Countertenor, Crooner, Diva, Falsetto, Gigli, Glee club, Gleeman, Griot, Hammond, Kettle, Lark, Lauder, Lay clerk, Lorelei, Melba, Melodist, Mezzo, Minstrel, Opera, Orbison, Piaf, Rapper, Semi-chorus, Shrike, Siren, Songman, Songstress, Soprano, Soubrette, Succentor, Tenor, Tenure, Torch, Treble, Troubador, Vocalist, Voice, Warbler

Single, Singly Ace, Aefa(u)ld, Aefawld, Alone, Azygous, Bachelor, Celibate, Discriminate, EP, Exclusive, Feme sole, Haplo-, Individual, Lone, Matchless, Monact, Mono, Odd, One-off, One-shot, Only, Pick, Run, Seriatim, Sole, Solitary, Solo, Spinster, Unary, Unattached, Uncoupled, Uniparous, Unique, Unwed, Versal, Yin

Singular(ity) Curious, Especial, Exceptional, Extraordinary, Ferly, Odd, Once, One, Peculiar, Queer(er), Rare, S, →**UNIQUE**, Unusual

Sink(ing), Sunken Abandon, Basin, Bidet, Bog, Cadence, Carbon, Cower, Delapse, Depress, Descend, Devall, Dip, Down, Drain, Draught-house, Drink, Drop, Drown, Ebb, Embog, Flag, Founder, Gravitate, Heat, Hole, Immerse, Invest, Jarbox, Kitchen, Lagan, Laigh, Lapse, Ligan, Merger, Pad, Poach, Pot, Prolapse, Put(t), Relapse, Sag, Scupper, Scuttle, Set, Settle, Shipwreck, Slump, Steep-to, Stoop, Sty, Submerge, Subside, Swag, Swamp

Sioux Sitting Bull

Siren Alarm, Alert, Charmer, Delilah, Hooter, Houri, Ligea, Lorelei, Mermaid, Oceanides, Parthenope, Salamander, Shark, Teaser, Temptress, Vamp

Sirius Sothic

Sister(s) Anne, Beguine, Carmelite, Fatal, Minim, →**NUN**, Nurse, Religeuse, Sib, Sibling, Sis, Sob, Soul, Swallow, Titty, Ugly, Ursuline, Verse, Ward, Weak, Weird

Sistine Chapel, Sextus

Sit(ter), Sitting Bestride, Clutch, Dharna, Duck, Gaper, Gimme, Incubate, Lime, Model, Perch, Pose, Reign, Roost, Séance, Sederunt, Sesh, Session, Squat

Site, Siting Area, Arpa, Brochure, Camp, Caravan, Chat room, Cobweb, Feng shui, Gap, Greenfield, Home-page, Location, Lot, Mirror, Orphan, Pad, Place, Plot, Ramsar, Rogue, Silo, Spot, Stance, World Heritage

Situation Affair, Ballpark, Berth, Cart, Case, Catch, Catch-22, Chicken and egg, Cliff-hanger, Contretemps, Cow, Dilemma, Drama, Galère, Hole, Hornet's nest, Hot seat, Job, Knife-edge, Lie, Location, Lurch, Matrix, Mire, Nail-biter, Niche, No-win, Office, Place, Plight, Position, Post, Scenario, Scene, Schmear, Schmeer, Set-up, Shebang, Showdown, State of play, Status quo, Sticky wicket, Strait, Stringalong, Where, Worst case

Size(able) Amplitude, Area, Bulk, Calibre, Clearcole, Countess, Demy, →**EXTENT**, Format, Girth, Glair, Glue, Guar, Gum, Imperial, Measure, Particle, Party, Physique, Pot(t), Princess, Proportion, Tempera, Tidy

Skate(r), Skateboard(er), Skateboarding, Skating Blade, Fakie, Figure, Fish, Half-pipe, Hot dog, In-line, Maid, Mohawk, Ollie, Overacid, Rink, Rock(er), Roller, Rollerblade®, Runner, Short-track, Sit spin, Torvill

Skeleton, Skeletal Anatomy, Atomy, Axial, Bones, Cadaverous, Cadre, Cage, Coenosteum, Coral, Corallum, Framework, Hydrostatic, Key, Ossify, Outline, Scenario, Sclere

Sketch(y) Bozzetto, Cameo, Character, Charade, Croquis, Delineate, Diagram, Draft, →**DRAW**, Ébauche, Esquisse, Illustration, Limn, Line, Maquette, Modello, Outline, Pencilling, Playlet, Pochade, Précis, Profile, Rough, Skit, Summary, Thumbnail, Trick, Vignette, Visual

Ski(er), Skiing Aquaplane, Carving, Free ride, Glide, Glissade, Hot-dog, Langlauf, Nordic, Schuss, Schussboomer, Super G, Telemark, Vorlage, Wedeln

Skilful, Skill(ed) Ability, Able, Accomplished, Ace, Address, Adept, Adroit, Art, Bravura, Canny, Chic, Competence, Craft, Deacon, Deft, Demon, Dextrous, Enoch,

Expertise, Facility, Feat, Finesse, Flair, Gleg, Habile, Hand, Handicraft, Handy, Hend, Hot, Ingenious, Keepy-uppy, Knack, Know-how, Knowing, Lear(e), Leir, Lere, Masterly, Masterpiece, Mastery, Mean, Métier, Mistery, Mystery, Mystique, Practised, Proficient, Prowess, Quant, Resource, Savvy, Science, Skeely, Sleight, Soft, Speciality, Tactics, Talent, Technic, Technique, Touch, Trade, Transferable, Trick, Versed, Virtuoso, Wise, Workmanship

Skin(s) Ablate, Agnail, Armour, Bark, Basan, Basil, Bingo wing, Box-calf, Bronzed, Calf, Callus, Case, Cere, Chevrette, Coat, Cortex, Crackling, Cutaneous, Cuticle, Cutis, Deacon, Deer, Derm(a), Dermis, Dewlap, Disbark, Ectoderm, Enderon, Epicarp, Eschar, Excoriate, Exterior, Fell, Film, Flaught, Flay, Flench, Flense, Flinch, Fourchette, Goldbeater's, Hangnail, Hide, Integra®, Jacket, Kip, Leather, Membrane, Muktuk, Nympha, Pachyderm, Patagium, Peau, Peel, Pell, Pellicle, Pelt, Plew, Prepuce, Rack, Rape, Rind, Scalp, Scarfskin, Serosa, Shagreen, Shell, Spetch, Strip, Swindle, Tegument, Veneer, Wattle, Woolfell

Skin disease, Skin problem, Skin trouble Boba, Boil, Buba, Chloasma, Chloracne, Cowpox, Cyanosis, Dartre, Dermatitis, Dermatosis, Dyschroa, Ecthyma, Eczema, Erysipelas, Exanthem(a), Favus, Framboesia, Herpes, Hives, Ichthyosis, Impetigo, Leishmaniasis, Leucodermia, Livedo, Lupus vulgaris, Maidism, Mal del pinto, Mange, Miliaria, Morula, Pellagra, Pemphigus, Pinta, Pityriasis, Prurigo, Pseudofolliculitis, Psoriasis, Pyoderma, Rash, Ringworm, Rosacea, Rose-rash, Sapego, Scabies, Sclerodermia, Scurvy, Seborrhoea, Serpigo, Strophulus, Tetter, Tinea, Vaccinia, Verruca, Verruga, Vitiligo, Xanthoma, Xerosis, Yaws

Skinless Ecorché

Skip(ped), Skipper Boss, Caper, Captain, Cavort, Drakestone, Elater, Frisk, Hesperian, Jump, Jumping-mouse, Lamb, Luppen, Miss, Omit, Patroon, Ricochet, Saury, Scombresox, Spring, Tittup, Trip, Trounce(r)

Skirt(ing) Bypass, Fil(l)ibeg, Grass, Petticoat, Philibeg, Pinafore, Stringboard, Tube, Valance, Washboard, Wrapover

Skua Boatswain, Bos'n

Skull Brainpan, Bregma(ta), Calvaria, Cranium, Death's head, Harnpan, Head, Malar, Obelion, Occiput, Pannikell, Phrenology, Scalp, Sinciput, Vault, Yorick

Sky(-high), Sky-tinctured, Skywards Air, Azure, Blue, Canopy, Carry, El Al, E-layer, Element, Empyrean, Ether, Firmament, Heaven, Lift, Lob, Loft, Mackerel, Occident, Octa, Okta, Raise, Rangi, Welkin

Slab(s) Briquette, Cake, Cap(e)stone, Chunk, Dalle, Hawk, Ledger, Metope, Mihrab, Mud, Paver, Plank, Slice, Stela, Tab, Tablet, Tile, Wood-wool

Slack(en), Slacker, Slackness Abate, Careless, Crank, Dilatory, Dross, Ease (off), Easy-going, Idle, Lax(ity), Lazybones, Loose, Malinger, Nerveless, Off-peak, Off-season, Relax, Release, Remiss, Shirk, Skive, Slatch, Slow, Surge, Unscrew, Unwind, Veer

Slander(ous) Asperse, Backbite, Calumny, Defame, Derogatory, Disparage, Insult, Libel, Malediction, Malign, Missay, Mud, Mudslinging, Obloquy, Sclaunder, Smear, Traduce, Vilify, Vilipend

Slang Abuse, Argot, Back, Berate, Blinglish, Cant, Colloquial, Ebonics, Flash, Jargon, Lingo, Nadsat, Rhyming, Slate, Vernacular, Zowie

Slant(ed), Slanting Angle, Asklent, Atilt, Bevel, Bias, Brae, Cant, Careen, Chamfer, Clinamen, Diagonal, Escarp, Oblique, Prejudice, Slew, →**SLOPE**, Splay, Talus, Tilt, Virgule

Slash(ed) Chive, Cut, Diagonal, Gash, Jag, Laciniate, Leak, Oblique, Rash, Rast, Reduce, Scorch, Scotch, Separatrix, Slice, Slit, Solidus, Stroke, Virgule, Wee

Slaughter(house), Slaughterer Abattoir, Bleed, Bloodshed, Butcher, Carnage, Decimate, Hal(l)al, Holocaust, Immolation, Jhatka, Kill, Mactation, →**MASSACRE**, Scupper, Shambles, S(c)hechita(h), Shochet, Smite

Slave(ry), Slaves, Slavish Addict, Aesop, Aida, Androcles, Barracoon, Blackbird, Bond, Bond(s)man, Bondwoman, Boy, Caliban, Contraband, Dogsbody, Drudge, Drug, Dulosis, Esne, Galley, Helot, Jack, Mameluke, Mamluk, Marmaluke, Maroon, Minion, Nativity, Odali(s)que, Odalisk, Peasant, Pr(a)edial, Rhodope, Serf, Servitude,

Spartacus, Terence, Theow, Thersites, Thete, Thrall, Toil, Topsy, Vassal, Villein, Wage, Wendic, White, Yoke

Slay(er), Slaying Destroy, Execute, Ghazi, →**KILL**, Mactation, Murder, Quell, Saul, Slaughter, Transport

Sled(ge), Sleigh(-ride) Bob, Dog train, Dray, Hurdle, Hurley-hacket, Kibitka, Komatic, Komatik, Lauf, Luge, Mush, Polack, Pulk(h)(a), Pung, Rocket, Skeleton bob(sleigh), Skidoo®, Slipe, Stoneboat, Tarboggin, Toboggan, Travois

Sleep, Sleeper(s), Sleepiness, Sleeping, Sleepy Beauty, Bed, Bivouac, Blet, Bundle, Bye-byes, Car, Catnap, Coma, Couchette, Crash, Cross-sill, Cross-tie, Dormant, Dormient, Dormouse, Doss, Doze, Drop off, Drowse, Flop, Gowl, Gum, Hibernate, Hypnology, Hypnos, Kip, Land of Nod, Lassitude, Lethargic, Lie, Morpheus, Nap, Narcolepsy, Narcosis, Nod, Oscitation, Over, Paradoxical, Petal, Pop off, REM, Repast, Repose, Rest, Rip Van Winkle, Sandman, Shuteye, Siesta, Skipper, Sleepover, Sloom, Slumber, Snooz(l)e, Somnolent, Sopor(ose), Sownd, Spine bashing, Tie, Torpid, Twilight, Wink, Zeds, Zizz

Sleeping sickness Trypanosomiasis

Sleeve (opening) Arm(hole), Balloon, Batwing, Bishop's, Bush, Cap, Collet, Cover, Dolman, Gatefold, Gigot, Gland, Kimono, Lawn, Leg-o'-mutton, Liner, Magyar, Manche, Pagoda, Pudding, Querpo, Raglan, Record, Sabot, Scye, Slashed, Trunk, Turnbuckle, Wind

Sleeveless Exomis

▶**Sleigh** *see* **SLED(GE)**

Slender(ness) Asthenic, Ectomorph, Elongate, Exiguity, Exility, Fine, Flagelliform, Flimsy, Gracile, Jimp, Leptosome, Loris, Narrow, Rangy, Skinny, Slight, Slim, Small, Spindly, Stalky, Styloid, Svelte, Swank, Sylph, Tenuous, Trim, Waif

Slice Cantle, Chip, Collop, Cut, Doorstep, Fade, Frustrum, Lop, Piece, Rasure, Round, Sector, Segment, Share, Sheave, Shive, Slab, Sliver, Spoon, Tranche, Wafer, Whang

Slide Barrette, Chute, Cursor, Diapositive, Drift, Fader, Glissando, Helter-skelter, Hirsle, Hollow-ground, Ice-run, Illapse, Lantern, Mount, Pulka, Schuss, Scoop, Ski, Skid, Skite, Slip, Slither, Snowboard, Telescope, Transparency, Volplane

Slight(ly) Affront, Belittle, Cold shoulder, Cut, Detract, Disparage, Disregard, Disrespect, Facer, Flimsy, Halfway, Insult, Minor, Misprise, Neglect, Nominal, Pet, Petty, Puny, Rebuff, Remote, →**SLENDER**, Slim, Slimsy, Slur, Small, Smattering, Sneaking, Snub, Sparse, Stent, Subtle, Superficial, Sylphine, Tenuous, Thin, Tiny, Trivial, Wee, Wispy

Slime, Slimy Glair, Glareous, Glit, Gorydew, Guck, Gunk, Mother, Muc(o)us, Oily, Ooze, Sapropel, Slabbery, Slake, Sludge, Uliginous

Sling Balista, Catapult, Drink, Fling, Hang, Parbuckle, Prusik, Shy, Singapore, Support, Toss, Trebuchet

Slip(ped), Slipping, Slips Avalanche, Boner, Come home, Coupon, Cutting, Disc, Docket, Drift, EE, Elapse, Elt, Error, Escape, Faux pas, Fielder, Form, Freudian, Glide, Glissade, Infielder, Label, Landslide, Lapse, Lath, Leash, Lingerie, Lingual, Mistake, Muff, Nod, Oversight, Peccadillo, Petticoat, Plant, Prolapse, Quickset, Rejection, Relapse, Run, Scape, Sc(h)edule, Scoot, Set, Shim, Sin, Ski, Skid, Skin, Skite, Slade, Slidder, Slide, Slither, Slive, Spellican, Spillican, Stumble, Surge, Ticket, Trip, Tunicle, Underskirt, Unleash

Slipper(s) Baboosh, Babouche, Babuche, Calceolate, Carpet, Eel, Errorist, Mocassin, Moccasin, Moyl, Muil, Mule, Pabouche, Pampootie, Pantable, Pantof(f)le, Panton, Pantoufle, Pump, Rullion, Runner, Ski, Sledge, Sneaker, Sock

Slippery Eely, Elusive, Errorist, Foxy, Glid, Icy, Lubric, Shady, Shifty, Skidpan, Slick, Slimy

▷**Slipshod** *may indicate* an anagram

Slit Cranny, Cut, Fent, Fissure, Fitchet, Gash, Loop, Pertus(at)e, Placket, Race, Rit, Scissure, Spare, Speld(er), Vent

Sloan Snib, Snub

Slogan Amandla, Byword, Catchword, Chant, Jai Hind, Jingle, Masakhane, Mot(to),

Murdabad, Nayword, Phrase, Rallying-cry, Slughorn(e), Splash, Street cry, Warcry, Watchword

Slop(pily), Slops, Sloppy Lagrimoso, Lowse, Madid, Mushy, Remiss, Schmaltzy, Shower, Slapdash, Slipshod, Sloven, Slushy, Sozzly, Untidy, Weepie

Slope(s), Sloping Acclivity, Angle, Anticline, Bahada, Bajada, Bank, Batter, Bevel, Borrow, Borstal(l), Brae, Breast, Camber, Chamfer, Cle(e)ve, Cuesta, Declivity, Delve, Diagonal, Dip, Dry, Escarp, Escarpment, Fastigiate, Fla(u)nch, Foothill, Geanticline, Glacis, Grade, Gradient, Heel, Hill, Hipped, Incline, Isoclinical, Kant, Lean, Natural, Nursery, Oblique, Pediment, Pent, Periclinal, Pitch, Rake, Ramp, Rollway, Scarp, Schuss, Scrae, Scree, Shelve, Sideling, Skewback, Slade, Slant, Slippery, Slipway, Splay, Steep, Stoss, Talus, Tilt, Verge, Versant, Weather

▷ **Sloppy** *may indicate* an anagram

Sloth(ful) Accidie, Acedia, Ai, Bradypus, Edentate, Ground, Idle, Inaction, Indolent, Inertia, Lazy, Lie-abed, Megatherium, Sweer(t), Sweir(t), Three-toed, Torpor

Slough(ing) Cast, Despond, Ecdysis, Eschar, Exfoliate, Exuviae, Lerna, Marsh, Mire, Morass, Paludine, Shed, Shuck, Swamp

Slovakia .sk

Sloven(ly) Careless, Dag(gy), D(r)aggle-tail, Dishevelled, Down-at-heel, Frowsy, Grobian, Jack-hasty, Mawkin, Slattern, Sleazy, Slipshod, Slummock, Slut, Untidy

Slow(er), Slowing, Slowly, Slow-witted Adagio, Allargando, Andante, Andantino, Brady, Brake, Broad, Calando, Calf, Crawl, Dawdle, Decelerate, Deliberate, Dilatory, Draggy, Dull, Dumka, ESN, Flag, Gradual, Halting, Inchmeal, Lag, Langram, Larghetto, Largo, Lash, Lassu, Late, Leisurely, Lentamente, Lentando, Lento, Lifeless, Loiter, Losing, Meno mosso, Obtuse, Pedetentous, Rall(entando), Rein, Reluctant, Retard, Ribattuta, Rit, Ritardando, Ritenuto, Roll-out, Slack, Slug, Sluggish, Snail's pace, Snaily, Solid, Stem, Tardigrade, Tardive, Tardy, Tardy-gaited, Thick

Slowcoach Slowpoke, Slug

Slug(s) Ammo, Bêche-de-mer, Blow, Brain, Bullet, Cosh, Drink, Grapeshot, Knuckle sandwich, Limaces, Limax, Mollusc, Nerita, Pellet, Shot, Snail, Trepang

Sluggish Dilatory, Drumble, Idler, Inert, Jacent, Lacklustre, Laesie, Languid, Lazy, Lentor, Lethargic, Lug, Phlegmatic, Saturnine, Sleepy, → **SLOW**, Stagnant, Tardy, Torpid, Unalive

Slumber Doze, Drowse, Nap, Nod, Sleep, Sloom, Snooze

Slump Decrease, Depression, Deteriorate, Dip, Flop, Recession, Sag, Sink, Slouch, Sprawl

Slur(ring) Defame, Drawl, Innuendo, Opprobrium, Slight, Smear, Synaeresis, Tie

Sly Christopher, Clandestine, Coon, Covert, Cunning, Foxy, Leery, Peery, Reynard, Secretive, Shifty, Slee, Sleeveen, Sneaky, Stallone, Stealthy, Subtle, Surreptitious, Tinker, Tod, Tricky, Weasel, Wily

▷ **Slyly** *may indicate* an anagram

Smack(er) Aftertaste, Buss, Cuff, Flavour, Foretaste, Fragrance, Hooker, Kiss, Klap, Lander, Lips, Pra(h)u, Relish, Salt, Saut, Skelp, Slap, Slat, Smatch, Smell, Smouch, Soupçon, Spank, Spice, Splat, Tack, Taste, Thwack, Tincture, Trace, Twang, X, Yawl

Small (thing), Smallest amount Atom, Bantam, Beer, Bijou, Bittie, Bitty, Chickenfeed, Chotta, Denier, Diddy, Diminutive, Dinky, Dreg, Drib, Driblet, Elfin, Elfish, Few, Fry, Grain, Haet, Ha'it, Half-pint, Handful, Hint, Hobbit, Holding, Hole-in-the-wall, Hyperosmia, Insect, Ion, Itsy-bitsy, Knurl, Leet, Leetle, Lepton, Lilliputian, Limited, Lite, → **LITTLE**, Lock, Low, Meagre, Mean, Measly, Microscopic, Midget, Mignon, Miniature, Minikin, Minority, Minute, Mite, Modest, Modicum, Neap, Nurl, Peerie, Peewee, Petit(e), Petty, Pickle, Pigmy, Pink(ie), Pinky, Pint-size, Pittance, Pocket, Poky, Puckle, Rap, Reduction, Runt, S, Scantling, Scattering, Scrump, Scrunt, Scruple, Scut, Shoebox, Shortarse, Shrimp, Single, Slight, Slim, Smattering, Smidge(o)n, Smidgin, Smithereen, Smout, Snippet, Soupçon, Sprinkling, Spud, Squirt, Stim, Stunted, Tad, Teenty, Thin, Tidd(l)y, Tiny, Titch(y), Tittle, Tot(tie), Totty, Trace, Trivial, Wee, Weedy, Whit

Smart(en), Smartest, Smartness Ache, Acute, Alec, Astute, Best, Bite, Burn, Chic, Classy, Clever, Cute, Dandy, Dapper, Dressy, Elegant, Flash, Flip, Fly, Groom,

Jemmy, Kookie, Kooky, Larnery, Natty, Neat, New pin, Nifty, Nip, Nobby, Pac(e)y, Pacy, Posh, Preen, Primp, Prink, Pusser, Raffish, Rattling, Ritzy, Saucy, Slick, Sly, Smoke, Smug, Snappy, Snazzy, Soigné(e), Spiff, Sprauncy, Sprightly, Spruce, Sprush, Spry, Sting, Street cred, Stylish, Swagger, Sweat, Swish, Tiddley, Tippy, Titivate, Toff, Trendy, U, Zippy

Smash(ed), Smasher, Smashing Atom, Brain, Break, Cannon, Corker, Crush, Demolish, Devastate, Dish, Drunk, High, Kaput, Kill, Lulu, Shatter, Shiver, Slam, Stave, Super, Terrific, Tight, →**WRECK**

▷ **Smash(ed)** *may indicate an anagram*

Smear Anoint, Assoil, Besmirch, Blur, Calumniate, Cervical, Clam, Daub, Defile, Denigrate, Discredit, Drabble, Enarm, Gaum, Gorm, Lick, Mud, Oil, Oint, Pay, Plaster, Slairg, Slaister, Slander, Slather, Slime, Slubber, Slur, Smalm, Smarm, Smudge, Spredd, Sully, Swipe, Teer, Traduce, Wax

Smell(ing), Smelly Aroma, BO, Cacodyl, Effluvium, Exhale, F(o)etid, Fetor, Fug, Gale, Gamy, Graveolent, Guff, Hing, Honk, Hum, Ionone, Mephitis, Miasm(a), Ming, Musk, Niff, Nose, Odour, Olent, Olfact(ory), Osmatic, Osmic, Perfume, Pong, Ponk, Pooh, Rank, Redolent, Reech, Reek, Sar, Savour, →**SCENT**, Sensory, Sniff, Snifty, Snook, Snuff, Steam, Stench, Stifle, Stink, Tang, Whiff

Smile(s), Smiling, Smily Agrin, Beam, Cheese, Emoticon, Favour, Gioconda, Grin, Rictus, Self-help, Simper, Smirk, Watch the birdie

Smog Electronic, Photochemical

Smoke(r), Smoking, Smoky Blast, Bloat, Censer, Chain, Chillum, →**CIGAR(ETTE)**, Cure, Drag, Exhaust, Fog, Fuliginous, Fume, Fumigate, Funk, Gasper, Hemp, Incense, Indian hemp, Inhale, Kipper, Latakia, London ivy, Lum, Lunt, Manil(l)a, Nicotian, Peaty, Pother, Pudder, Puff, Reech, Reek, Reest, Roke, Secondary, Sidestream, Smeech, Smeek, Smirting, Smoor, Smother, Smoulder, Smudge, Snout, Tear, Tobacconalian, Toke, Vapour, Viper, Whiff, Wreath

Smooth(e), Smoother, Smoothly Alabaster, Bald, Bland, Brent, Buff, Cantabile, Chamfer, Clean, Clockwork, Dress, Dub, Easy, Even, Fettle, File, Flat, Fluent, Fretless, Glabrous, Glare, Glassy, Glib, Goose, Iron, Legato, Level, Levigate, Linish, Mellifluous, Mellow, Millpond, Oil, Plane, Planish, Plaster, Pumice, Rake, Roll, Rub, Sad-iron, Sand(er), Satiny, Scrape, Shiny, Sleek, Slick, Slickenslide, Slithery, Slur, Smug, Snod, Sostenuto, Straighten, Streamlined, Suave, Swimmingly, Terete, Terse, Trim, Unwrinkled, Urbane

Smother Burke, Choke, Dampen, Muffle, Oppress, Overlie, Smoor, Smore, Stifle, Suppress

Smug Complacent, Conceited, Goody-goody, Goody-two-shoes, Neat, Oily, Pi, Self-satisfied, Trim

Smuggle(d), Smuggler, Smuggling Bootleg, Contraband, Coyote, Donkey, Fair trade, Free trader, Gunrunning, Moonshine, Mule, Owler, Rum-runner, Run, Secrete, Steal, Traffic

Smut(ty) Bawdy, Blight, Blue, Brand, Burnt-ear, Coom, Crock, Filth, Grime, Racy, Soot, Speck

Snack Bever, Bhelpuri, Bite, Blintz, Bombay mix, Breadstick, Breakfast bar, Brunch, Burger, Butty, Canapé, Chack, Churro, Crisps, Croque monsieur, Crudités, Doner kebab, Elevenses, Entremets, Four-by-two, Gorp, Hoagie, Hors (d'oeuvres), Hot dog, Knish, Meze, Munchies, Nacho, Nacket, Nibble, Nigiri, Nocket, Nooning, Nuncheon, Padkos, Pie, Piece, Ploughman's lunch, Popcorn, Rarebit, Refreshment, Samo(o)sa, Sandwich, Sarnie, Savoury, Scroggin, Sloppy joe, Small chop, Spring roll, Tapa, Taste, Toast(y), Trail mix, Vada, Voidee, Wada, Wrap, Zakuska

Snag Aggro, Anoint, Contretemps, Drawback, Hindrance, Hitch, Impediment, Knob, Nog, Obstacle, Remora, Rub, Tear

Snail(s) Brian, Cowrie, Cowry, Dodman, Escargot, Gasteropod, Heliculture, Helix, Hodmandod, Limnaea, Lymnaea, Nautilus, Nerite, Roman, Slow, Slug, Strombus, Unicorn-shell, Univalve, Wallfish, Whelk

Snake, Snaking Drag, Meander, →**SERPENT**, Slither, Wind

Snap(per), Snappy, Snap up Abrupt, Alligator, Autolycus, Bite, Break, Brittle,

Camera, Click, Cold, Cold wave, Crack, Crocodile, Cross, Curt, Edgy, Fillip, Girnie, Glitch, Glom, Gnash, Grab, Hanch, Knacker, Knap, Livery, Mugshot, Photo, Photogene, Scotch, Snack, Snatch, Spell, Still, Tetchy, Vigour

Snare Bait, Benet, Engine, Entrap, Gin, Grin, Honeytrap, Hook, Illaqueate, Inveigle, Mantrap, Net, Noose, Rat-trap, Springe, Toil, →**TRAP**, Trapen, Trepan, Web, Weel, Wire

Snarl(ing) Chide, Complicate, Cynic, Enmesh, Gnar(l), Gnarr, Growl, Grumble, Knar, Knot, Snap, Tangle, Yirr

Sneak(y) Area, Carry-tale, Clipe, Clype, Creep, Furtive, Infiltrate, Inform, Lurk, Mumblenews, Nim, Peak, Scunge, Skulk, Slip, Slyboots, Snitch, Snoop, Split, Steal, Stoolie, Tell(-tale)

Sneeze (at), Sneezing Atishoo, Errhine, Sternutation

Sniff Inhale, Nose, Nursle, Nuzzle, Scent, Smell, Snivel, Snort, Snuffle, Vent, Whiff

Snob(bery), Snobbish Cobbler, Crachach, Crispin, Dic(k)ty, High-hat, Prudish, Pseud, Scab, Side, Sloane, Snooty, Snow, Soutar, Souter, Sowter, Toffee-nose, Vain, Vamp

Snore, Snoring Rhonchus, Rout, Snort, Snuffle, Stertorous, Zz

Snort(er) Dram, Drink, Grunt, Nare, Nasal, Roncador, Snore, Toot

Snout Bill, Boko, Cigar, Informer, Muzzle, Nose, Nozzle, Proboscis, Schnozzle, Tinker, Tobacco, Wall

Snow(y), Snowdrift, Snowstorm Marine, Nivose, Noise, Powder, Red, Sleet, Spotless, Virga, Yellow

Snub Cut, Diss, Go-by, Lop, Pug, Quelch, Rebuff, Reproof, Retroussé, Short, Slap, Slight, Sloan, Sneap, Snool, Wither

Snuff(le) Asarabacca, Douse, Dout, Errhine, Extinguish, Maccaboy, Ptarmic, Pulvil, Rappee, Smother, Snaste, Sneesh(an), Sniff, Snift, Snotter, Snush, Tobacco, Vent

Snuffbox Mill, Mull, Ram's horn

Snug(gery), Snuggle Burrow, Comfy, Cose, →**COSY**, Couthie, Couthy, Croodle, Cubby(hole), Cuddle, Embrace, Intime, Lion, Neat, Nestle, Nuzzle, Rug, Snod, Tight, Trim

So Ergo, Hence, Sic(h), Sol, Such, Therefore, Thus, True, Very, Yes

Soak(ed) Bate, Bath(e), Beath, Bewet, Bloat, Blot, Buck, Cree, Deluge, Drench, Drent, Drink, Drook, Drouk, Drown, Drunk, Duck, Dunk, Embay, Embrue, Fleece, Grog, Imbrue, Impregnate, Infuse, Lush, Macerate, Marinate, Mop, Oncome, Permeate, Plastered, Rait, Rate, Ret(t), Rob, Saturate, Seep, Sipe, Sog, Sop, Sorb, Souce, Souse, Sows(s)e, Steep, Sype, Thwaite, Toper, Waterlog, Wet, Wino

Soap(y), Soap opera Cake, Carbolic, Coronation St, Eluate, Flake, Flannel, Flattery, Glass, Green, Hard, Joe, Lather, Lux®, Marine, Metallic, Moody, Mountain, Pinguid, Saddle, Safrole, Saponaceous, Saponin, Sawder, Shaving, Slime, Soft, Spanish, Suds, Sudser, Sugar, Tablet, Tallow, The Bill, Toilet(ry), Washball, Yellow

Soar(ing) Ascend, Essorant, Fly, Glide, Plane, Rise, Tower, Zoom

Soccer Footer, Footie

Sociable, Sociability Affable, Cameraderie, Chummy, Clubby, Cosy, Couthie, Extravert, Folksy, Friendly, Genial, Gregarious, Mixer, Phatic

Socialism, Socialist Champagne, Chartist, Dergue, Fabian, Fourierism, Hardie, ILP, International, Karmathian, Lansbury, Left(y), Marxism, Nihilism, Owen(ist), Owenite, Parlour pink, Pasok, Pinko, Red, Revisionist, Sandinista, Second international, Spartacist, Utopian, Webb

Society Affluent, Alternative, Association, Band of Hope, Benefit, Black Hand, Body, Boxer, Brahma, Brahmo, Building, Camorra, Casino, Choral, Class, Club, College, Company, Consumer, Co-op, Cooperative, Culture, Debating, Dorcas, Duddieweans, Elite, Elks, Fabian, Fashion, Fellowship, Foresters, Freemans, Freemasons, Friendly, Friends, Glee club, Grand monde, Group, Guarantee, Guilds, Haut monde, High, High life, Humane, Institute, Invincibles, John Birch, Ku-Klux-Klan, Law, Linnean, Lodge, Mafia, Masonic, Mass, Mau-Mau, Ménage, Molly Maguire, National, Oddfellows, Open, Oral, Orangemen, Oratory, Order, Permissive, Plural, Pop, Provident, Repertory, Risk, Rotary, Royal, S, Samaj, School, Secret, Soc, Sodality, Somaj, Soroptomist,

Sorority, Stakeholder, Surveillance, Tammany, Theosophical, Toc H, Ton, Tong, Triad, U, Whiteboy

Socket Acetabulum, Alveole, Budget, Eyepit, Gudgeon, Hollow, Hosel, Hot shoe, Jack, Keeper, Lampholder, Nave, Nozzle, Orbit, Ouch, Outlet, Plug, Pod, Port, Power-point, Serial port, Strike

Socle Tube, Zocco(lo)

Sod Clump, Delf, Delph, Divot, Fail, Gazo(o)n, Mool, Mould, Mouls, Scraw, Sward, Turf

Sodomy Vice anglais

Sofa Canapé, Chaise longue, Chesterfield, Couch, Daybed, Divan, Dos-à-dos, Dosi-do, Lounge, Ottoman, Settee, Squab, Tête-à-tête

Soft(en), Softener, Softening, Softly Amalgam, Anneal, Assuage, B, BB, Blet, Boodle, Cedilla, Cottony, Cree, Cushion, Dim, Doughy, Emolliate, Emollient, Flabby, Furry, Gentle, Hooly, Humanise, Lash, Lax, Lenient, Limp, Low, Mease, Mellow, Melt, Mild, Milksop, Mitigate, Modulate, Mollify, Morendo, Mulch, Mush(y), Mute, Neale, Nesh, Option, P, Palliate, Pastel, Piano, Plushy, Porous, Propitiate, Rait, Rate, Relent, Sentimental, Silly, Slack, Spongy, Squashy, Squidgy, Squishy, Temper, →TENDER, Tone, Velvet, Weak

Soil(ed), Soily Acid, Adscript, Agrology, Agronomy, Alkali(ne), Alluvium, Azonal, Backfill, Bedraggle, Bemire, Beray, Besmirch, Chernozem, Clay, Cohesive, Contaminate, Defile, Desecrate, Desert, Dinge, Dirt(y), Discolour, Earth, Edaphic, Edaphology, Frictional, Gault, Glebe, Grey, Grimy, Ground, Gumbo, Hotbed, Humus, Illuvium, Intrazonal, Lair, Land, Latosol, Lithosol, Loam, Loess, Lome, Loss, Marl, Mire, Mo(u)ld, Mool, Mud, Mulch, Mull, Night, Ordure, Peat, Ped, Pedogenic, Pedology, Phreatic, Planosol, Podsol, Podzol, Prairie, Pure, Regar, Regolith, Regosol, Regur, Rendzina, Rhizosphere, Root-ball, Sal, Sedentary, Smudge, Smut, Solonchak, Solonetz, Solum, Soot, Stain, Stonebrash, Sub, Sully, Tarnish, Tash, Terrain, Terricolous, Tilth, Top, Udal, Umber, Virgin, Zonal

Soldier(s) Ant, Chocolate, Detachment, Fighter, Gyrene, Insect, Old Bill, Regular, Unknown

▷ **Soldiers** *may indicate* bread for boiled eggs

Sole, Solitaire, Solitary Alone, Anchoret, Anchorite, Antisocial, Asocial, Clump, Corporation, Eremite, Fish, Friendless, Incommunicado, Inner, Lemon, Lonesome, Megrim, Merl, Meunière, Monkish, On ice, Only, Pad, Palm, Patience, Pelma, Planta(r), Plantigrade, Platform, Recluse, Sand, Scaldfish, Single(ton), Skate, Slip, Smear-dab, Tap, Thenar, Unique, Vibram®, Vola

Solemn Austere, Devout, Earnest, Grave, Gravitas, Owlish, Po-faced, Sacred, Sedate, Serious, Sober, Sobersides, Sombre

Solicit Accost, Approach, Ask, Attract, Bash, →BEG, Canvass, Cottage, Drum up, Importun(at)e, Plead, Ply, Speer, Speir, Touch, Tout, Woo

Solid(arity), Solidify, Solidity Cake, Chunky, Clot, Clunky, Compact, Comradeship, Concrete, Cone, Congeal, Consolidate, Cube, Cylinder, Dense, Dilitancy, Enneahedron, Esprit de corps, Ethal, Firm, Foursquare, Freeze, Frustrum, Fuchsin(e), Gel, Hard, Holosteric, Impervious, Kotahitanga, Merbromin, Octahedron, Pakka, Parallelepiped, Petrarchan, Platonic, Polyhedron, Prism, Pucka, Pukka, Purin(e), Robust, Set, Square, Squatly, Stilbene, Sturdy, Sublimate, Substantial, Tetrahedron, Thick, Trusty, Unanimous

▶ **Solitary** *see* SOLE

Solo Aria, Cadenza, Cavatine, Concertante, Lone, Monodrama, Monody, Ombre, One-man, Recit, Scena, Unaided, Variation

Solution Amrit, Colloidal, Electrolyte, Final, Hairspray, Normal, Oleum, Reducer, Remedy, Rubber, Soup, Standard, Tone, Viscose

▷ **Solution** *may indicate* an anagram

Solve(d), Solver Absolve, Assoil, Calculate, Casuist, Clear, Crack, Decode, Loast, Loose, Read(er), Troubleshoot, Unclew, Unriddle, Work

Solvent Above water, Acetaldehyde, Acetone, Alcahest, Aldol, Alkahest, Anisole, Aqua-regia, Banana oil, Benzene, Chloroform, Cleanser, Cymene, Decalin,

Denaturant, Diluent, Dioxan(e), Eleunt, Eluant, Ether, Funded, Furan, Heptane, Hexane, Ligroin, Megilp, Menstruum, Methanol, Methylal, Naphtha, Paraldehyde, Picoline, Protomic, Pyridine, Sound, Stripper, Terebene, Terpineol, Terts, Tetrachloromethane, Thiophen, Toluene, Toluol, Trike, Trilene, Turpentine, White spirit

Somalia .so

Sombre Dark, Drab, Drear, Dull, Funereal, Gloomy, Grave, Morne, Morose, Subfusc, Subfusk, Sullen, Triste

Some Any, Arrow, Ary, Certain, Divers, Few, One, Part, Portion, Quota, Sundry, These, They, Wheen

▷ **Some** *may indicate* a hidden word

▷ **Somehow** *may indicate* an anagram

Somerset Protector

Sometime(s) Erstwhile, Ex, Former, Occasional, Off and on, Otherwhiles, Quondam

Somnolence Drowsiness

Son Boy, Disciple, Epigon(e), Fils, Fitz, Lad, Lewis, M(a)c, Native, Offspring, Prodigal, Progeny, Scion

Sonata Moonlight

Song Air, Amoret, Anthem, Aria, Ariette, Art, Aubade, Ballad, Barcarol(l)e, Berceuse, Blues, Burden, Cabaletta, Calypso, Cante hondo, Cante joudo, Canticle, Cantion, Carol, Catch, Chanson, Cha(u)nt, Chantey, Conductus, Corroboree, Cycle, Descant, Dirge, Ditty, Elegy, Fitt, Flamenco, Folk, Gaudeamus, Gita, Glee, Hillbilly, Hymn, Internationale, Lament, Lay, Lied(er), Lilt, Lullaby, Lyric, Madrigal, Marseillaise, Melody, Minnesang, Negro spiritual, Number, Nunc dimittis, Paean, Part, Plain, Plantation, Pop, Psalm, Rap, Red Flag, Rhapsody, Roulade, Roundelay, Rune, Scat, Scolion, Sea-shanty, Serenade, Shanty, Shosholoza, Siren, Sososholoza, Spiritual, Stave, Stomper, Strain, Strophe, Swan, Taps, Theme, Torch, Trill, Tune, Tyrolienne, Villanella, Waiata, War, Warble, Yodel

Sonnet Amoret, Italian, Petrarch(i)an, Shakespearean, Shakespearian, Spenserian

Soon(er) Anon, Directly, Enow, Erelong, Imminent, OK, Oklahoma, Presently, Shortly, Tight, Timely, Tit(ely), Tite, Tyte

Soothe(r), Soothing Accoy, Allay, Anetic, Appease, Assuage, Bucku, Calm, Compose, Demulcent, Ease, Emollient, Irenic, Lenitive, Lull, Mellifluous, Mollify, Obtundent, Pacific, Paregoric, Poultice, Quell, Rock, Stroke

Sophisticate(d) Blasé, Boulevardier, City slicker, Civilised, Classy, Cosmopolitan, Couth, Doctor, High-end, Hitec, Patrician, Polished, Sative, Slicker, Suave, Svelte, Urbane, Worldly

▷ **Sophoclean** *may indicate* Greek alphabet, etc

Sorbet Glacé, Water ice

Sorcerer, Sorceress, Sorcery Angek(k)ok, Ashipu, Circe, Conjury, Diablerie, Diabolist, Hoodoo, Kadaitcha, Kurdaitcha, Lamia, Mage, Magic(ian), Magus, Medea, Merlin, Morgan le Fay, Mother Shipton, Necromancer, Obi, Pishogue, Shaman, Sortilege, Voodoo, Warlock, Witch, Witch knot, Wizard

Sore(ly), Sores Abrasion, Bitter, Blain, Boil, Canker, Chancre, Chap, Chilblain, Cold, Dearnly, Felon, Gall, Impost(h)ume, Ireful, Kibe, Nasty, Pressure, Quitter, Quittor, Raw, Rupia(s), Saddle, Sair, Sensitive, Shiver, Sitfast, Soft, Surbate, Tassell, Tercel, Ulcer(s), Whitlow, Wound

Sorrow(ful) Affliction, Attrition, Deplore, Distress, Dole, Doloroso, Dolour, →GRIEF, Lament, Misery, Nepenthe, Ochone, Penance, Pietà, Remorse, Rue, Triste, Wae, Waugh, Wirra, Woe, Yoop

Sorry Apologetic, Ashamed, Contrite, Miserable, Oops, Penitent, Pitiful, Poor, Regretful, Relent, Rueful, Simple, Wan, Wretched

▷ **Sorry** *may indicate* an anagram

▶ **Sorts** *see* OUT OF SORTS

▷ **So to speak** *may indicate* 'sound of'

Soul(ful) Alma, Ame, Anima, Animist, Atman, Ba, Brevity, Deep, Eschatology,

Essence, Expressive, Heart, Inscape, Ka, Larvae, Manes, Motown, Person, Psyche, Saul, Shade, Spirit, Traducian

Sound(ed), Sounding, Soundness, Sound system Accurate, Ach-laut, Acoustic, Albemarle, Allophone, All there, Alveolar, Audio, Bleep, Blip, Bloop, Blow, Bong, Bray, Breathed, Cacophony, Chime, Chirl, Chirr(e), Chord, Chug, Clam, Clang, Clank, Clink, Cloop, Clop, Clunk, Compos, Consistent, Copper-bottomed, Dah, Dental, Diphthong, Dit, Dive, Dream, Dusky, Echo, Eek, Fast, Fathom, Fettle, Fit, Flow, Foley, Glide, Good, Hale, Harmonics, Healthy, Hearty, Hi-fi, Inlet, Islay, Jura, Kalmar, Knell, Lo-fi, Long Island, Low, Lucid, Mach, Madrilene, Mersey, Milford, Monophthong, Murmur, Musak, Music, Muzak®, Narrow, Nicam, →**NOISE**, Off-glide, Onomatopaeia, Oompah, Optical, Orate, Orinasal, Orthodox, Palatal, Paragog(u)e, Peal, Phone(me), Phonetic, Phonic, Phonology, Pitter(-patter), Plap, Plink, Plonk, Plop, Plosion, Plosive, Plumb, Plummet, Plunk, Plymouth, Probe, Pronounce, Put-put, Quadraphonic(s), Rale, Rational, Rat-tat, Real, Reasonable, Reliable, Ring, Robust, Rumble, Rustle, Safe, Sandhi, Sane, Sensurround®, S(c)hwa, Skirl, Solid, Sondage, Sone, Souffle, Sough, Speech, Splat, Stereo, Stereophony, Strait, Surround, Swish, Tannoy®, Tchick, Tenable, Thorough, Timbre, Ting, Tone, Toneme, Trig, Trill, Triphthong, Trumpet, Twang, Ultrasonic(s), Unharmed, Uvular, Valid, Viable, Voice, Vowel, Watertight, Well, Whine, Whinny, Whistle, Whole(some), Whoosh, Wolf

Sounding board Abat-voix

Soup Alphabet, Bird's nest, Bisque, Borsch, Bouillabaisse, Bouillon, Broth, Cal(l)aloo, Chowder, Cioppino, Cock-a-leekie, Cockieleekie, Cockyleeky, Consommé, Crab chowder, Gazpacho, Gumbo, Lokshen, Minestrone, Mock turtle, Mulligatawny, Oxtail, Pho, Pot(t)age, Pot-au-feu, Primordial, Puree, Ramen, Rice, Rubaboo, Sancoche, Scoosh, Scotch broth, Skink, Stock, Turtle, Vichyssoise

▷ **Soup** *may indicate* an anagram

Sour(puss) Acerb, Acescent, Acid, Acidulate, Aigre-deux, Alegar, Bitter, Citric, Crab, Eager, Esile, Ferment, Moody, Stingy, Turn, Unamiable, Verjuice, Vinegarish

Source Authority, Basis, Bottom, Centre, Closed, Database, Derivation, Egg, Fons, Font, Fount, Fountain-head, Germ, Head-stream, Leak, Literary, Mine, Mother, Neutron, Origin, Parent, Pi, Pion, Point, Principle, Prot(h)yle, Provenance, Quarry, Reference, Rise, Root, Seat, Seed, Spring, Springhead, Stock, Supply, Urn, Well, Wellhead, Wellspring, Ylem

South(ern), Southerner Austral, Confederacy, Dago, Decanal, Decani, Dixieland, Meridian, S, Scal(l)awag, Scallywag

South Africa(n) Bantu, Caper, Grikwa, Griqua, Hottentot, Kaf(f)ir, Lebowa, SA, Soutie, Soutpiel, Springbok, Swahili, Xhosa, ZA, Zulu

South-east Roseland, SE

Souvenir Goss, Keepsake, Memento, Relic, Remembrance, Scalp, Token, Trophy

Sou'wester Cornishman

Sovereign(ty), Sovereign remedy Anne, Autocrat, Bar, Condominium, Couter, Dominant, Emperor, ER, Goblin, Haemony, Harlequin, Imperial, Imperium, James, King, L, Liege, Napoleon, Nizam, Pound, Quid, Rangatiratanga, Royalty, Ruler, Shiner, Supreme, Swaraj, Synarchy

Sow(ing) Catchcrop, Elt, Foment, Gilt, Inseminate, Plant, Scatter, Seed, Sprue, Strew, Yelt

Spa Aachen, Baden, Baden-Baden, Bath, Evian, Fat farm, Harrogate, Hydro, Kurhaus, Kursaal, Leamington, Malvern, Vichy

Space, Spaced (out), Spaceman, Spacing, Spacious, Spatial Abyss, Acre, Alley, Area, Areola, Bay, Bolthole, Bracket, Breathing, Bronchus, Cellule, Cislunar, Clearing, C(o)elom(e), Cofferdam, Concourse, Crawl, Cubbyhole, Daylight, Deducted, Deep, Distal, Distance, Elbow-room, Elliptic, Em, En, Esplanade, Ether, Exergue, Expanse, Extent, Flies, Footprint, Freeband, Gagarin, Gap, Glade, Glenn, Goaf, Gob, Gutter, Hair, Hash(mark), Headroom, Hell, Indention, Inner, Intergalactic, Interim, Interlinear, Interplanetary, Interstellar, Interstice, Invader, Kneehole, Lacuna, Lair, Leading, Legroom, Life, Lobby, Logie, Lumen, Lunar, Lung, Maidan, Manifold,

Manorial, Metope, Minkowski, Mosh pit, MUD, Muset, Musit, Orbit, Outer, Palatial, Parking, Parvis(e), Personal, Polemics, Proportional, Proxemics, Quad, Retrochoir, Riemannian, →ROOM, Ruelle, Sample, Sheets, Shelf room, Slot, Spandrel, Spandril, Sparse, Step, Steric, Storage, Third, Topological, Tympanum, Ullage, Uncluttered, Vacua, Vacuole, Vacuum, Vast, Vector, Virtual, Void, Volume, Well

Spacecraft, Space agency, Space object, Spaceship, Space station Apollo, Capsule, Columbia, Columbus, Deep Space, Explorer, Galileo, Gemini, Genesis, Giotto, Lander, LEM, Luna, Lunik, Mariner, Mercury, MIR, Module, NASA, Orbiter, Pioneer, Probe, Quasar, Ranger, Salyut, Shuttle, Skylab, Soyuz, Space lab, Sputnik, Starship, Tardis, Viking, Voskhod, Vostok, Voyager, Zond

Spacer (plate) Bead(s)

Spade Breastplough, Caschrom, Cas crom, Castrato, Detective, Graft, Loy, Negro, Paddle, Paddle staff, Pattle, Peat, Pettle, Pick, S, Shovel, Slane, Spit, Suit, Tus(h)kar, Tus(h)ker, Twiscar

Span Age, Arch, Attention, Bestride, Bridge, Chip, Ctesiphon, Extent, Life, Range, Timescale

Spaniard, Spanish Alguacil, Alguazil, Asturian, Balearic, Barrio, Basque, Cab, Caballero, Carlist, Castilian, Catalan, Chicano, Dago, Diego, Don, Fly, Grandee, Hidalgo, Hispanic, José, Main, Mestizo, Mozarab, Pablo, Señor, Spic(k), Spik

Spaniel Cavalier, Field, Irish water, King Charles, Toady, Toy, Water, Welsh springer

Spar Barite, Barytes, Blue John, Boom, Bowsprit, Box, Cauk, Cawk, Derbyshire, Fight, Gaff, Heavy, Iceland, Icestone, Jib-boom, Mainyard, Martingale, Mast, Nail-head, Outrigger, Rafter, Rail, Ricker, Satin, Shearleg, Sheerleg, Snotter, Spathic, Sprit, Steeve, Stile, Triatic, Yard

Spare, Sparing(ly) Angular, Cast-off, Dup(licate), Economical, Fifth wheel, Free, Frugal, Galore, Gash, Gaunt, Hain, Lean, Lenten, Narrow, Other, Pardon, Reserve, Rib, Save, Scant, Skinny, Slender, Stint, Subsecive, Tape, Thin

Spark Animate, Arc, Beau, Blade, Bluette, Dandy, Flash, Flicker, Flint, Funk, Ignescent, Ignite, Kindle, Life, Quenched, Scintilla, Smoulder, Spunk, Trigger, Zest

Sparkle(r), Sparkling Aerated, Bling, Burnish, Coruscate, Crémant, Diamanté, Effervesce, Élan, Emicate, Fire, Fizz, Flicker, Frizzante, Gem, Glint, Glisten, Glitter, Pétillant, Scintillate, Seltzer, Seltzogene, Spangle, Spritzig, Spumante, Twinkle, Verve, Witty, Zap

Spartan(s) Ascetic, Austere, Basic, Enomoty, Hardy, Helot, Laconian, Lysander, Menelaus, Severe, Valiant

Spasm(s), Spasmodic Ataxic, Blepharism, Chorea, Clonus, Convulsive, Cramp, Crick, Fit(ful), Hiccup, Hippus, Intermittent, Irregular, →JERK, Kink, Laryngismus, Nystagmus, Paroxysm, Periodical, Start, Strangury, Tetany, Throe, Tonic, Tonus, Trismus, Twinge, Twitch, Vaginismus

▷ **Spasmodic** *may indicate* an anagram

▶ **Spatial** *see* SPACE

Spatula Applicator, Tongue depressor

Speak(er), Speaking Address, Articulate, Bang on, Broach, Chat, Cicero, Collocuter, Communicate, Converse, Coo, Declaim, Diction, Dilate, Discourse, Diseur, Dwell, Effable, Elocution, Eloquent, Expatiate, Express, Extemporise, Filibuster, Intercom, Intone, Inveigh, Jabber, Jaw, Lip, Loq, Loquitur, Management, Mang, Mention, Mike, Mina, Mouth, Mouthpiece, Nark, Native, Open, Orate, Orator, Palaver, Parlance, Parley, Perorate, Pontificate, Prate, Preach, Prelector, Public, Rhetor, →SAY, Sayne, Soliloquize, Spout, Spruik, Stump, Talk, Tannoy®, Tongue, Trap, Tweeter, Utter, Voice, Waffle, Wibble, Witter, Word

Spear Ash, Asparagus, Assagai, Assegai, Barry, Dart, Demi-lance, Engore, Fishgig, Fizgig, Gad, Gavelock, Gig, Glaive, Gleave, Gum digger's, Gungnir, Hastate, Impale, Javelin, Lance(gay), Launcegaye, Leister, Morris-pike, Partisan, Pierce, Pike, Pilum, Prong, Skewer, Spike, Trident, Trisul(a), Waster

Spearhead Lead

Special(ly) Ad hoc, Constable, Designer, Disparate, Distinctive, Extra, Important, Notable, Notanda, Particular, Peculiar, Red-letter, Specific, Strong suit, Vestigial

Specialise, Specialist(s) Allergist, Authority, Concentrate, Connoisseur, Consultant, ENT, Esoteric, Expert, Illuminati, Internist, Maestro, Major, Quant, Recondite, Technician

Specific(ally), Specification, Specified, Specify Adduce, As, Ascribe, Assign, Cure, Define, Detail, Explicit, Formula, Itemise, Medicine, Namely, Precise, Quantify, Remedy, Sp, Special, Spell out, Stipulate, Stylesheet, The, To wit, Trivial, Vide licit

Speck, Speckle(d) Atom, Bit, Dot, Fleck, Floater, Freckle, Mealy, Muscae volitantes, Particle, Peep(e), Pip, Spreckle, Stud

Spectacle(s), Spectacled, Spectacular Bifocals, Blinks, Colourful, Epic, Escolar, →GLASSES, Goggles, Horn-rims, Lorgnette, Lorgnon, Meteoric, Optical, Pageant, Pebble glasses, Pince-nez, Pomp, Preserves, Scene, Show, Sight, Son et lumière, Staggering, Sunglasses, Tattoo, Trifocal, Varifocals

Spectate, Spectator(s) Audience, Bystander, Dedans, Etagère, Eyer, Gallery, Gate, Groundling, Kibitzer, Observer, Onlooker, Ringsider, Standerby, Wallflower, Witness

Spectral, Spectre Apparition, Bogle, Bogy, Eidolon, Empusa, Ghost, Idola, Iridal, Larva, Malmag, Phantasm, Phantom, Phasma, Spirit, Spook, Tarsier, Walking-straw, Wraith

Speculate, Speculative, Speculator, Speculation Arb(itrage), Bear, Better, Boursier, Bull, Conjecture, Flier, Flyer, Gamble, Guess, Ideology, If, Imagine, Meditate, Notional, Operate, Pinhooker, Raider, Shark, Stag, Theoretical, Theorise, Theory, Thought, Trade, Wonder

Speech, Speech element Accents, Address, Argot, Articulation, Bunkum, Burr, Curtain, Delivery, Dialect, Diatribe, Diction, Direct, Discourse, Dithyramb, Drawl, Éloge, English, Epilogue, Eulogy, Filibuster, Free, Gab, Glossolalia, Grandiloquence, Guttural, Harangue, Helium, Idiolect, Idiom, Inaugural, Indirect, Jargon, Keynote, King's, Lallation, →LANGUAGE, Lingua franca, Litany, Logopaedics, Maiden, Monologue, Morph(eme), Musar, Oblique, Occlusive, Oral, Oration, Parabasis, Parle, Peroration, Phasis, Philippic, Phonetics, Prolog(ue), Queen's, Reported, Rhetoric, RP, Sandhi, Scanning, Screed, Sermon, Set, Side, Slang, Soliloquy, Stemwinder, Stump, Tagmeme, Talk, Taxeme, Tirade, Tongue, Uptalk, Vach, Verbal, Visible, Voice, Wawa, Whaikorero, Whistle-stop, Xenoglossia

Speech-writer Logographer

Speed(ily), Speedy Accelerate, Alacrity, Amain, Amphetamine, ANSI, Apace, ASA, Average, Bat, Belive, Belt, Benzedrine, Breakneck, Burn, Cast, Celerity, Clip, Dart, Despatch, DIN, Dispatch, Expedite, Fang, Fast, Film, Fleet, Further, Gait, Gallop, Goer, Group, Gun, Hare, Haste, Hie, Hotfoot, Hypersonic, Induce, Instantaneous, Knot, Landing, Lick, Mach, Merchant, MPH, →PACE, Pelt, Phase, Pike, Post-haste, Prompt, Pronto, Race, Rapidity, Rate, RPS, Rush, Scorch, Scud, Scurr, Skirr, Soon, Spank, Split, Stringendo, Supersonic, Swift, Tach, Tear, Tempo, Teraflop, Ton up, V, Velocity, Ventre à terre, Vroom, Wave, Whid, Wing, Zoom

Spell(ing) Abracadabra, Bewitch, Bout, Cantrip, Charm, Conjuration, Do, Elf-shoot, Enchantment, Entrance, Fit, Go, Gri(s)-gri(s), Hex, Incantation, Innings, Jettatura, Juju, Knock, Knur, →MAGIC, Mojo, Need-fire, Nomic, Orthography, Period, Phase, Philter, Philtre, Pinyin, Relieve, Ride, Romaji, Run, Rune, Scat, Shift, Shot, Signify, Sitting, Snap, Snatch, Sorcery, Sp, Spasm, Splinter, Stint, Stretch, Tack, Time, Tour, Trick, Turn, Weird, Whammy, Wicca, Witchcraft

Spend(er), Spending Anticipate, Birl, Blow, Blue, Boondoggling, Consume, Deficit, Deplete, Disburse, Exhaust, Fritter, Lay out, Live, Outlay, Pass, Pay, Splash, Splurge, Squander, Squandermania, Ware

Spendthrift Prodigal, Profligate, Profuser, Wastrel

Sphere, Spherical Armillary, Attraction, Ball, Benthoscope, Celestial, Discipline, Earth, Element, Field, Firmament, Globe, Magic, Mound, Orb(it), Planet, Primum mobile, Prolate, Province, Realm, Theatre, Wheel

Sphincter Pylorus

Spice, Spicy Anise, Aniseed, Baltic, Caraway, Cardamom, Cayenne, Chili powder,

Cinnamon, Clove, Clow, Coriander, Cough drop, Cum(m)in, Dash, Devil, Garam masala, Ginger, Green ginger, Mace, Marjoram, Masala, Myrrh, Nutmeg, Oregano, Paprika, Peppercorn, Picante, Pimento, Piquant, Root ginger, Saffron, Season, Sexed up, Tansy, Tarragon, Taste, Turmeric, Vanilla, Variety, Za'atar

Spider(s) Arachnid, Aranea, Araneida, Attercop, Bird, Black widow, Bobbejaan, Bolas, Cardinal, Cheesemite, Citigrade, Diadem, Epeira, Ethercap, Ettercap, Funnel-web, Harvest(er), Harvestman, House, Hunting, Huntsman, Jumping, Katipo, Lycosa, Mite, Money, Mygale, Orb-weaver, Pan, Phalangid, Podogona, Program, Pycnogonid, Red, Redback, Rest, Ricinulei, Saltigrade, Scorpion, Solpuga, Spinner, Strap, Tarantula, Telary, Trapdoor, Violin, Water, Wolf, Zebra

Spike(d) Barb, Brod, Calk, Calt(h)rop, Chape, Cloy, Crampon, Doctor, Ear, Fid, Filopodium, Foil, Gad, Gadling, Goad, Grama, Herissé, Impale, Kebab, Lace, Locusta, Marlin(e), Nail, Needle, →PIERCE, Piton, Point, Pricket, Prong, Puseyite, Rod, Sharp, Shod, Skewer, Spadix, Spear, Spicate, Spicule, Stroboloid, Tang, Thorn, Tine

Spill(age) Divulge, Drop, Fidibus, Jackstraw, Lamplighter, Leakage, Let, Overflow, Overset, Scail, Scale, Shed, Skail, Slart, Slop, Stillicide, Taper, Tumble

Spin(ner), Spinning (wheel) Aeroplane, Arabian, Arachne, Aswirl, Bielmann, Birl, Camel, Centrifuge, Chark(h)a, Cribellum, Cut, Dance, Day trip, Dextrorse, DJ, Flat, Flip, Gimp, Googly, Gymp, Gyrate, Gyre, Gyroscope, Hurl, Isobaric, Isotopic, Jenny, Lachesis, Mole, Nun, Peg-top, Piecener, Piecer, Pirouette, Pivot, PR, Precess, Prolong, Purl, Reel, Rev(olve), Ride, Rotate, Royal, Screw, Side, Sinistrorse, Slant, Slide, Somersault, Spider, Stator, Strobic, Swirl, Swivel, Throstle, Tirl, Toss, Trill, Trundle, Turntable, Twirl, Twist, Wheel, Whirl, Whirligig, Work

Spinal (chord), Spine(d), Spiny Acanthoid, Acerose, Acicular, Acromion, Aculeus, Areole, Arête, Backbone, Barb, Chine, Coccyx, Column, Doorn, Epidural, Muricate, Myelon, Notochord, Ocotillo, Prickle, Quill, Rachial, R(h)achis, Ray, Ridge bone, Thorn, Torso, Tragacanth

▶**Spine** *see* SPINAL

Spin-off By-product

Spirit, Spirited Animal, Animation, Animus, Ardent, Blithe, Dash, →DRINK, Élan, Element(al), Emit, Entrain, Essence, Etheric, Ethos, Fettle, Fight, Free, Geist, Ginger, Gism, Go, Grit, Gumption, Heart, Holy, Hugh, Kindred, →LIQUOR, Lively, Mettle, Morale, Mystique, Nobody, Panache, Pecker, Pep, Presence, Pride, Racy, Scientology, Soul, Spunk, Steam, Stomach, Team, Ton, Verve, Vigour, Vim, Zing

Spiritual(ism), Spiritualist, Spirituality Aerie, Aery, Channelling, Coon-song, Ecclesiastic, Ethereous, Eyrie, Eyry, Incorporeal, Inwardness, Mystic, Negro, Planchette, Slate-writing, Swedenborg, Yogi

Spit(ting), Spittle Bar, Barbecue, Broach, Brochette, Chersonese, Dead ringer, Dribble, Drool, Emptysis, Eructate, Expectorate, Fuff, Gob, Golly, Gooby, Grill, Hawk, Impale, Jack, Lookalike, Peninsula, Phlegm, Ras, Ringer, Rotisserie, Saliva, Skewer, Slag, Spade(ful), Spawl, Sputter, Sputum, Tombolo, →TONGUE, Yesk, Yex

Spite(ful) Backbite, Bitchy, Catty, Grimalkin, Harridan, Irrespective, Malevolent, Malgré, Malice, Mean, Nasty, Petty, Pique, Rancour, Spleen, Venom, Viperish, Waspish

Splash Befoam, Blash, Blue, Dabble, Dash, Dog, Drip, Feature, Flouse, Fl(o)ush, Gardyloo, Jabble, Ja(u)p, Jirble, Paddle, Plap, Plop, Plowter, Sket, Slosh, Soda, Soss, Sozzle, Spairge, Spat(ter), Spectacle, Splat(ch), Splatter, Splodge, Splosh, Splotch, Spray, Spree, Squatter, Swash, Swatter, Water, Wet

▷**Splash** *may indicate* an anagram

Splendid, Splendour Braw, Brilliant, Bully, Capital, Champion, Clinker, Dandy, Divine, Éclat, Effulgent, Excellent, Fine, Finery, Fulgor, Gallant, Garish, Glittering, Glorious, Glory, Gorgeous, Grand(eur), Grandiose, Heroic, Hunky-dory, Lustrous, Majestic, Noble, Palatial, Panache, Pomp, Proud, Radiant, Rich, Ripping, Royal, Stunning, Super(b), Superduper, Wally, Zia

▷**Spliced** *may indicate* an anagram

Splinter(s) Flinder, Fragment, Matchwood, Shatter, Shiver, Skelf, Sliver, Spale, Spicula, Spill

Split(ting) Areolate, Axe, Banana, Bifid, Bifurcate, Bisect, Breach, Break, Broach, Burst, Chasm, Chine, Chop, Chorism, Cleave, Clint, Clove(n), Crack, Crevasse, Cut, Decamp, Disjoin, Distrix, → **DIVIDE**, Division, Divorce, End, Fissile, Fissure, Flake, Fork(ed), Fragment, Grass, Lacerate, Left, Partition, Red(d), Rift(e), Rip, Rive, Rupture, Russian, Ryve, Schism, Scissor, Segment, Segregate, Separate, Sever, Share, Skive, Slit, Sliver, Spall, Spalt, Speld, Spring, Tattle, Tmesis, Told, Trifurcate, Wedge

▷ **Split** *may indicate* a word to become two; one word inside another; or a connection with Croatia (or the former Yugoslavia)

Spode Roderick

▷ **Spoil(ed), Spoilt** *may indicate* an anagram

Spoil(s), Spoiler, Spoilt Addle, Air dam, Blight, Booty, Botch, Bribe, Coddle, Corrupt, → **DAMAGE**, Dampen, Deface, Defect, Deform, Disfigure, Dish, Fairing, Foul, Gum, Hames, Harm, Impair(ed), Impoverish, Indulge, Loot, Maltreat, Mar, Mollycoddle, Muck, Mutilate, Mux, Pamper, Party pooper, Pet, Pickings, Pie, Plunder, Prejudicate, Prize, Queer, Rait, Rate, Ravage, Ret, Rot, Ruin, Screw up, Scupper, Swag, Taint, Tarnish, Vitiate, Winnings, Wreck

▷ **Spoken** *may indicate* the sound of a word or letter

Sponge(r), Spongy Battenburg, Bum, Cadge, → **CAKE**, Diact, Free-loader, Lig, Loofa(h), Madeira, Madeleine, Mooch, Mop, Parasite, Scrounge, Shule, Sop, Sucker, Swab, Sweetbriar, Sycophant, Tectratine, Tetract, Tetraxon, Tiramisu, Wangle, Wipe, Zoophyte

Sponsor(ship) Aegis, Angel, Backer, Bankroll, Egis, Finance, Godfather, Godparent, Gossip, Guarantor, Lyceum, Patron, Surety, Undertaker

Spontaneous Autonomic, Exergonic, Free, Gratuitous, Immediate, Impromptu, Improvised, Impulsive, Instant, Intuitive, Natural, Off-the-cuff, Unrehearsed, Untaught

Spoof Chouse, Cozenage, Deception, Delusion, Fallacy, → **HOAX**, Imposture, Ramp, Swindle, Trick

Spoon(ful), Spoon-shaped Apostle, Canoodle, Cochlear, Dollop, Dose, Eucharistic, Gibby, Horn, Labis, Ladle, Mote, Neck, Rat-tail, Runcible, Salt, Scoop, Scud, Server, Spatula, Sucket, Trout, Woo, Wooden

Sport(ing), Sportive, Sports, Sporty Amusement, Bet, Blood, Breakaway, Brick, By-form, Contact, Daff, Dalliance, Dally, Demonstration, Deviant, Extreme, Field, Freak, Frisky, Frolic, Fun, → **GAME**, Gent, In, Joke, Laik, Lake, Lark, Merimake, Merry, Morph, Mutagen, Pal, Pastime, Recreate, Rogue, Rules, Spectator, Tournament, Tourney, Toy, Wear, Winter

▷ **Sport(s)** *may indicate* an anagram

Sportsground Rec

Sportswear Gie, Wet suit

Spot(s), Spotted, Spotting, Spotty Ace, Acne, Area, Areola, Areole, Bead, Beauty, Befoul, Bespatter, Blackhead, Blain, Blemish, Blind, Blip, Blister, Blob, Blot, Blotch(ed), Blur, Brind(l)ed, Café-au-lait, Carbuncle, Caruncle, Cash, Check, Cloud, Colon, Comedo, Corner, Cyst, Dance, Dapple(-bay), Defect, Descry, Detect, Dick, Dilemma, Discern, Discover, Dot, Drop, Eruption, Espy, Eye, Flat, Flaw, Fleck, Floater, Flyspeck, Foxed, Freak, Freckle, Furuncle, G, Gay, Glimpse, Gout, High, Hot, Identify, Jam, Leaf, Lentago, Light, Little, Liver, Locale, Location, Loran, Mackle, Macle, Macul(at)e, Mail, Meal, Measly, Microdot, Moil, Mole, Mote, Motty, Naevoid, Naevus, Note, Notice, Ocellar, Ocellus, Paca, Papule, Parhelion, Patch, Peep(e), Penalty, Perceive, Performance, Pied, Pimple, Pin, Pip, Place, Plague, Plight, Plot, Pock, Point, Poxy, Predicament, Punctuate, Pupil, Pustule, Quat, Radar, Rash, Recognise, Red, Scene, Situation, Skewbald, Smut, Soft, Speck(le), Speculum, Splodge, Spoil, Spy, Stigma, Sully, Sun, Sweet, Taint, Tar, Tight, Touch, Trace, Trouble, Venue, Weak, Whelk, Whitehead, Witness, X, Yellow, Zit

Spouse Companion, Consort, Dutch, Feare, Feer, F(i)ere, Hubby, Husband, Mate, Oppo, Partner, Pheer, Pirrauru, Wife, Xant(h)ippe

Spout(er) Adjutage, Erupt, Gargoyle, Geyser, Grampus, Gush, Impawn, Jet, Mouth, Nozzle, Orate, Pawn, Pourer, Raile, Rote, Spurt, Stream, Stroup, Talk, Tap, Vent

Sprain(ed) Crick, Reckan, Rick, Stave, Strain, Wrench, Wrick

Spray Aerosol, Aigrette, Airbrush, Antiperspirant, Atomiser, Bespatter, Blanket, Buttonhole, Corsage, Egret, Hair, Nebuliser, Pesticide, Posy, Rose, Rosula, Scatter, Shower, Sparge, Spindrift, Splash, Sprent, Sprig, Sprinkle, Spritz, Strinkle, Syringe, Twig, Wet

▷ **Spray** *may indicate* an anagram

▷ **Spread** *may indicate* an anagram

Spread(ing), Spreader Air, Apply, Banquet, Bestrew, Beurre, Bid offer, Blow-out, Branch, Bush, Butter, Carpet, Centre, Circumfuse, Contagious, Couch, Coverlet, Coverlid, Deploy, Diffract, Diffuse, Dilate, Disperse, Dissemination, Distribute, Divulge, Double, Double-page, Drape, Dripping, Elongate, Emanate, Engarland, Expand, Extend, Fan, Feast, Flare, Guac(h)amole, Honeycomb, Jam, Lay, Mantle, Marge, Marmite®, Meal, Metastasis, Middle-age(d), Multiply, Mushroom, Nutter, Oleo, Open, Overgrow, Paste, Pâté, Patent, Patté, Patulous, Perfuse, Pervade, Picnic, Pour, Proliferate, Propagate, Radiant, Radiate, Rampant, Ran, Ranch, Run, Scale, Scatter, Sea-floor, Set, Sheet, Slather, Smear, Smörgåsbord, Sow, Span, Speld, Spelder, Spillover, Splay, Sprawl, Spray, Straddle, Straw, Stretch, Strew, Strow, Suffuse, Systemic; Tath, Teer, Unfold, Unfurl, Unguent, Unroll, Vegemite®, Widen, Wildfire

Spring(s), Springtime, Springy Air, Arise, Black smoker, Bolt, Bounce, Bound, Box, Bunt, Cabriole, Caper, Capriole, Cavort, Cee, Coil, Dance, Elastic, Eye, Fount(ain), Free, Gambado, Germinate, Geyser, Grass, Hair, Helix, Hop, Hot, Jeté, Jump, Leaf, Leap, Lent, May, Mineral, Originate, Persephone, Pierian, Pounce, Prance, Primavera, Prime, Resilient, Ribbon, Rise, Saddle, Season, Skip, Snap, Source, Spa, Spang, Spaw, Start, Stem, Stot, Submarine, Sulphur, Summer, Suspension, Teal, Thermae, Thermal, Valve, Vault, Vernal, Ware, Watch, Waterhole, Weeping, Well(-head), Whip

▷ **Spring(y)** *may indicate* an anagram

Sprinkle(r), Sprinkling Asperge, Aspergill(um), Bedash, Bedew, Bedrop, Bescatter, Caster, Disponge, Dispunge, Dredge, Dust, Hyssop, Lard, Pouncet, Rose, Scatter, Shower, Sow, Spa(i)rge, Spatter, Splash, Spray, Spritz, Strinkle

Sprocket Whelp

Sprout Braird, Breer, Bud, Burgeon, Chit, Crop, Eye, Germ(inate), Grow, Pullulate, Shoot, Spire, Tendron, Vegetate

Spruce Balsam, Dapper, Engelmann, Hemlock, Natty, Neat, Norway, Picea, Pitch-tree, Prink, Shipshape, Sitka, Smart, Spiff, Tidy, Tree, Trim, Tsuga

Spur(s) Accourage, Activate, Aphrodisiac, Calcar(ate), Encourage, Fame, Fire, Fuel, Gee, Gilded, Goad, Groyne, Heel, Incite, Limb, Lye, Needle, Prick, Prong, Rippon, Rowel, Shoot, Spica, Stimulus, Strut, Stud, Tar, Urge

▷ **Spurious** *may indicate* an anagram

Spurrey Yarr

Spy(ing), Spies Agent, Beagle, Blunt, Burgess, Caleb, CIA, Descry, Dicker, Double agent, Eavesdrop, Emissary, Fink, Infiltrate, Informer, Keeker, Maclean, Mata Hari, MI, Mole, Mossad, Mouchard, Nark, Ninja, Nose, Operative, Pickeer, Pimp, Plant, Pry, Recce, Scout, See, Setter, Shadow, Sinon, Sleeper, Snoop, Spetsnaz, Spook, Tachometer, Tout, Wait

Squalid, Squalor Abject, Colluvies, Dinge, Dingy, Filth, Frowsy, Grungy, Mean, Poverty, Scuzzy, Seedy, Skid Row, Sleazy, Slum(my), Slurb, Sordid

Squall Blast, Blow, Commotion, Cry, Drow, Flaw, Flurry, Gust, Rainstorm, Sumatra, Wail, Williwaw, Yell, Yowl

Squander Blow, Blue, Dissipate, Fritter, Frivol, Mucker, Slather, Splash, Splurge, Ware, →**WASTE**

Square(d), Squares Agree, Anta, Arrière, Ashlar, Ashler, Bang, Barrack, Belgrave, Berkeley, Bevel, Block, Bribe, Chequer, Compone, Compony, Corny, Deal, Dinkum, Even(s), Fair, Fog(e)y, Forty-nine, Fossil, Four, Gobony, Grey, Grosvenor, Latin, Least, Leicester, Level, Magic, Market, Meal, Mean, Mitre, Nasik, Neandert(h)aler, Nine,

Norma, Old-fashioned, Out, Palm, Passé, Pay, Perfect, Piazza, Place, Platz, Plaza, Quad(rangle), Quadrate, Quarry, Quits, Red, Rhomboid, Rood, S, Set(t), Sloane, Solid, Squier, Squire, Stick-in-the-mud, Straight, T, Tee, Tiananmen, Times, Traditionalist, Trafalgar, Try, Unhip

Squash(y) Adpress, Butternut, Conglomerate, Crush, Flatten, Gourd, Kia-ora®, Knead, Marrow, Mash, Obcompress, Oblate, Pattypan, Press, Pulp, Pumpkin, Shoehorn, Silence, Slay, Slew, Slue, Soft, Squeeze, Squidge, Squidgy, Summer, Suppress, Torpedo, Winter

Squeeze(r) Bleed, Chirt, Coll, Compress, Concertina, Constrict, Cram, Cramp, Crowd, Crush, Dispunge, Exact, Express, Extort, Extrude, Hug, Jam, Mangle, Milk, Pack, Preace, Press, Reamer, Sandwich, Sap, Scrooge, Scrouge, Scrowdge, Scruze, Shoehorn, Squash, Squish, Sweat, Thrutch, Vice, Wring

Squid Calamari, Calamary, Cephalopod, Cuttlefish, Ink-fish, Loligo, Mortar, Nautilus, Octopus

▷ **Squiggle** *may indicate* an anagram

Squill Sea, Spring

Squint(ing) Boss-eyed, Cast, Cock-eye, Cross-eye, Glance, Gledge, Glee, Gley, Heterophoria, Louche, Opening, Proptosis, Skellie, Skelly, Sken, Squin(n)y, Strabism, Swivel-eye, Vergence, Wall-eye

Squire Armiger(o), Beau, Donzel, Escort, Hardcastle, Headlong, Land-owner, Sancho Panza, Scutiger, Swain, Western

Squirm(ing) Fidget, Reptation, Twist, Worm, Wriggle, Writhe

Squirt(er) Chirt, Cockalorum, Douche, Jet, Scoosh, Scoot, Skoosh, Spirt, Spout, Spritz, Urochorda, Wet, Whiffet, Whippersnapper

Stab Bayonet, Chib, Chiv, Crease, Creese, Dag, Effort, Go, Gore, Guess, Jab, Knife, Kreese, Kris, Lancinate, Pang, Pierce, Pink, Poniard, Prick, Prong, Punch, Stick, Stiletto, Turk, Wound

Stabilise(r), Stability Aileron, Balance, Balloonet, Emulsifier, Even, Fin, Fixure, Gyroscope, Maintain, Peg, Permanence, Plateau, Poise, Steady

Stable(s) Augean, Balanced, Barn, Byre, Certain, Consistent, Constant, Durable, Equerry, Equilibrium, Firm, Livery, Loose box, Manger, Mews, Permanent, Poise, Secure, Solid, Sound, Stall, Static(al), Steadfast, Steady, Stud, Sure, Together, Well-adjusted

Stack(s) Accumulate, Chimney, Clamp, Cock, End, Funnel, Heap, Lum, → **PILE**, Reckan, Rick, Shock, Sight, Smoke, Staddle

Stadium Arena, Astrodome, Ballpark, Bowl, Circus, Circus Maximus, Coliseum, Headingley, Hippodrome, Murrayfield, Velodrome, Wembley

Staff Aesculapius, Alpenstock, Ash-plant, Bato(o)n, Bouche, Bourdon, Burden, Caduceus, Cane, Crew, Crook, Crosier, Cross(e), Crozier, Crutch, Cudgel, Entourage, Equerry, Establishment, État-major, Faculty, Ferula, Ferule, Flagpole, General, Ground, Jacob's, Jeddart, Linstock, Lituus, Mace, Man, Office, Omlah, Pastoral, Personnel, Pike, Pole, Ragged, Rod, Rung, Runic, Sceptre, Seniority, Skeleton, Stave, Stick, Supernumerary, Taiaha, Tapsmen, Tau, Thyrsus, Token, Truncheon, Verge, Wand, Workers, Workforce, Wring

Stage Act, Anaphase, Apron, Arena, Ashrama, Bandstand, Bema, Boards, Catasta, Chrysalis, Committee, Diligence, Dog-leg, Estrade, Fargo, Fit-up, Grade, Hop, Imago, Instar, Juncture, Key, Landing, Leg, Level, Metaphase, Milestone, Moment, Mount, Napron, Oidium, Orbital, Perform, Phase, Phasis, Pier, Pin, Platform, Podium, Point, Postscenium, Prophase, PS, Puberty, Report, Resting, Rostrum, Scene, Sensorimotor, Sound, Stadium, Step, Stepping stone, Stor(e)y, Subimago, Theatre, Theatrical, Thrust, Transition, Trek, Wells Fargo, Yuga, Zoea

Stagger(ed) Alternate, Amaze, Astichous, Astonish, Astound, Dodder, Falter, Floor, Lurch, Recoil, Reel, Rock, Shock, Stoiter, Stot(ter), Stumble, Sway, Teeter, Thunderstruck, Titubate, Tolter, Totter

▷ **Staggered** *may indicate* an anagram

Stain(er) Aniline, Bedye, Besmirch, Blemish, Blob, Blot, Blotch, Chica, Discolour, Dishonour, Dye, Embrue, Ensanguine, Eosin, Fox, Gram-negative, Gram-positive,

Gram's, Grime, Imbrue, Inkspot, Iodophile, Keel, Maculate, Mail, Meal, Mote, Portwine, Slur, Smirch, Smit, Soil, Splodge, Splotch, Stigma, Sully, Taint, Tarnish, Tinge, Tint, Vital, Woad

Stair(case), Stairs Apples, Apples and pears, Caracol(e), Cochlea, Companionway, Escalator, Flight, Moving, Perron, Rung, Scale (and platt), Spiral, Step, Tread, Turnpike, Vice, Wapping

Stake(s) Ante, Bet, Claim, Deposit, Extracade, Gage, Go, Holding, Impale, Impone, Interest, Lay, Loggat, Mark, Mise, Nursery, Paal, Pale, Paling, Palisade, Peel, Peg, Pele, Picket, Pile, Play, Post, Pot, Punt, Rest, Revie, Risk, Set, Spike, Spile, Stang, Stob, Sweep, Tether, Vie, Wager, Weir

Stalagmite Onyx marble

Stale Aged, Banal, Flat, Fozy, Frowsty, Hackneyed, Handle, Hoary, Mouldy, Musty, Old, Pretext, Rancid, Urine, Worn

▷ **Stale** *may indicate* an obsolete word

Stalemate Deadlock, Dilemma, Draw, Hindrance, Impasse, Mexican standoff, Saw-off, Standoff, Tie, Zugswang

Stalinist Kirov

Stalk(er), Stalks Bennet, Bun, Cane, Follow, Funicle, Ha(u)lm, Pedicel, Pedicle, Peduncle, Petiole, Petiolule, Phyllode, Prowler, Pursue, Reed, Scape, Seta, Shaw, Spear, Spire, Stem, Still-hunter, Stipe(s), Strae, Straw, Stride, Strig, Strut, Stubble, Stump, Trail, Yolk

Stall(s) Arrest, Bay, Booth, Box, Bulk, Crib, → **DELAY**, Floor, Flypitch, Hedge, Horse-box, Kiosk, Loose-box, Orchestra, Pen, Pew, Prebendal, Seat, Shamble, Sideshow, Stable, Stand, Stasidion, Sty, Sutlery, Temporise, Trap, Traverse, Travis, Trevis(s), Whipstall

Stamina Endurance, Fibre, Fortitude, Guts, Last, Stay, Steel, Vigour

Stammer(ing) Hesitate, Hum, Stumble, Waffle

Stamp(s), Stamped Albino, Appel, Cast, Character, Coin, Date(r), Die, Dry print, Enface, Enseal, Fiscal, Frank, Gutter-pair, Health, Imperforate, Impress, Imprint, Incuse, Kind, Label, Matchmark, Mint, Mintage, Obsign, Pane, Penny black, Perfin, Philately, Pintadera, Postage, Press(ion), Rubber, Seal, Seebeck, Se-tenant, Signet, Spif, Strike, Swage, Tête-bêche, Touch, Touchmark, Trading, Trample, Tread, Tromp, Type

Stand(ing), Stand for, Stand up Apron, Arraign, Attitude, Base, Bay, Be, Bear, Bide, Bier, Binnacle, Bipod, Bristle, Brook, Caste, Cradle, Crease, Dais, Degree, Desk, Dock, Dree, Dumb-waiter, Easel, Epergne, Étagère, Face, Foothold, Freeze, Gantry, Gueridon, Hard, Hob, Importance, Insulator, Last, Lazy Susan, Lectern, Leg, Lime, Music, Nef, Odour, One-night, Ovation, Pedestal, Place, Plant, Podium, Pose, Position, Predella, Prestige, Promenade, Protest, Qua, Rack, Rank, Regent, Remain, Represent, Repute, Rise, Rouse, Stall, Statant, Station, Stay, Stillage, Stock, Stomach, Stool, Straddle, Striddle, Stroddle, Strut, Table, Tantalus, Taxi, Teapoy, Terrace, Toe, → **TREAT**, Tree, Tripod, Trivet, Umbrella, Upright, Whatnot, Witness

Standard(s) Banner, Base, Baseline, Basic, Benchmark, Bog, Bogey, British, Canon, CAT, Classic(al), Cocker, Code, Colour(s), Copybook, Criterion, Double, Eagle, English, Ethics, Etiquette, Examplar, Example, Exemplar, Fiducial, Flag, Ga(u)ge, Gold, Gonfalon, Grade, Guidon, Horsetail, Ideal, Jolly Roger, Kite-marker, Labarum, Level, Living, Model, Netiquette, Norm(a), Normal, Numeraire, Old Glory, Oriflamme, Par, Parker Morris, Pennon, Principle, Rate, Regular, Rod, Rose, Routine, Royal, → **RULE**, Scruples, Silver, Spec(ification), Staple, Sterling, Stock, Time, Touchstone, Tricolour, Troy, Two-power, Usual, Valuta, Vexillum, Yardstick

Stanza Antistrophe, Ballad, Elegiac, Envoi, Envoy, Matoke, Ottava rima, Quatrain, Spasm, Tantum ergo, Troparion

Star(s) Adept, Aster(isk), Binary, Body, Celebrity, Champ, Companion, Constant, Constellation, Cushion, Cynosure, Dark, Death, Double, Esther, Exploding, Falling, Fate, Feather, Feature, Film, Fixed, Flare, Giant, Headline, Hero, Hester, Hexagram, Idol, Late type, Lead, Lion, Main sequence, Mogen David, Movie, Mullet, Multiple, Pentacle, Personality, Phad, Pip, Plerion, Pointer, Principal, Pulsating, Seven, Shell,

Shine, Shooting, Sidereal, Solomon's seal, Spangle, Starn(ie), Stellar, Stern, Swart, (The) Pointers, Top banana, Top-liner, Ultraviolet, Valentine, Variable, Vedette

Stare Eyeball, Fisheye, Gape, Gapeseed, Gawp, Gaze, Glare, Goggle, Gorp, Look, Ogle, Outface, Peer, Rubberneck, Scowl

Stark Apparent, Austere, Bald, Bare, Gaunt, Harsh, Naked, Nude, Sheer, Stiff, Utterly

▷ **Start** *may indicate* an anagram or first letters

Start(ed), Starter, Starting-point Abrade, Abraid, Abray, Activate, Actuate, Begin, Bhajee, Boggle, Boot-up, Bot, Broach, Bug, Bully off, Bump, Chance, Commence, Consommé, Course, Crank, Create, Crudités, Dart, Debut, Ean, Embryo, Entrée, Face-off, False, Fire, Flinch, Float, Flush, Flying, Found, Gambit, Gan, Generate, Genesis, Getaway, Gun, Handicap, Head, Hors-d'oeuvres, Hot-wire, Impetus, Imprimis, Incept(ion), Initiate, Instigate, Institute, Intro(duce), Jar, Jerk, Judder, Jump, Jump lead, Jump-off, Kick-off, L, Lag, Launch, Lead, Melon, Nidus, Novice, Off, Offset, Onset, Ope(n), Ord, Origin, Outset, Poppadom, Potage, Preliminary, Prelude, Push, Put-up, Reboot, Resume, Roll, Roul, Rouse, Scare, Set off, Shy, Slip, Snail, Soup, Spark, Spring, Springboard, Spud, String, Tee-off, Terminus a quo, Toehold, Wince

Starvation, Starve(d), Starving Anorexia, Anoxic, Cold, Diet, Famish, Foodless, Perish, Pine, Undernourished

▷ **Starving** *may indicate* an 'o' in the middle of a word

Stash Hide, Hoard, Secrete

State(s), Stateside Affirm, Alle(d)ge, Aread, Arrede, Assert, Assever, Attest, Aver, Avow, Buffer, Case, Circar, Cite, Client, Commonwealth, Condition, Confederate, Construct, Country, Critical, Cutch, Declare, Dependency, Dirigisme, Emirate, Empire, État, Express, Federal, Fettle, Flap, Formulate, Free, Going, Habitus, Humour, Kingdom, Land, Lesh, Limbo, Mess, Metastable, Mode, Name, Nanny, Nation, Native, Palatinate, Para, Plateau, Plight, Police, Posit, Power, Predicament, Predicate, Premise, Profess, Pronounce, Protectorate, Puppet, Quantum, Realm, Republic, Rogue, Samadhi, Sanctitude, Satellite, Say, Sircar, Sirkar, Slave, Sorry, Standard, Standing, Steady, Succession, Threeness, Thusness, Uncle Sam, Union, Welfare, Yap

▷ **Stated** *may indicate* a similar sounding word

Stately, Stately home August, Dome, Grand, Imposing, Junoesque, Majestic, Mansion, Noble, Regal, Solemn

Statement Accompt, Account, Affidavit, Aphorism, Assertion, Asseveration, Attestation, Avowal, Axiom, Bill, Bulletin, Case, Communiqué, Deposition, Dictum, Diktat, Encyclical, Enigma, Evidence, Expose, Factoid, Grand Remonstrance, Impact, Invoice, Jurat, Manifesto, Mission, Non sequitur, Outline, Pleading, Press release, Profession, Pronouncement, Pronunciamento, Proposition, Quotation, Release, Report, Sentence, Shema, Shout out, Soundbite, Sweeping, Testament, Testimony, Theologoumenon, Truism, Utterance, Verbal

Station(s) Action, Aid, Air, Base, Berth, Birth, Camp, Caste, CCS, Coaling, Comfort, Crewe, Deploy, Depot, Docking, Dressing, Earth, Euston, Filling, Fire, Garrison, Gas, Generation, Halt, Head, Hill, Hilversum, Ice, Lay, Location, Marylebone, Meridian, Mir, Nick, Outpost, Paddington, Panic, Pay, Petrol, Pitch, Place, Plant, Point, Police, Polling, Post, Power, Powerhouse, Quarter, Radio, Rank, Relay, Rowme, Seat, Service, Sheep, Sit, Space, Stance, Stand, Star, Status, Stond, Subscriber, Tana, Tanna(h), Terminus, Testing, Thana(h), Thanna(h), Tracking, Transfer, Triangulation, Vauxhall, Victoria, Waterloo, Waverley, Way, Weather, Whistlestop, Wind farm, Wireless, Work

Statuary, Statue(tte) Acrolith, Bronze, Bust, Discobolus, Effigy, Figure, Figurine, Galatea, Idol, Image, Kore, Kouros, Liberty, Memnon, Monolith, Monument, Oscar, Palladium, Pietà, Sculpture, Sphinx, Stonework, Stookie, Tanagra, Torso, Xoanon

Staunch Amadou, Leal, Resolute, Steady, Stem, Stout, Styptic, Watertight

Stay(ing), Stays Abide, Alt, Avast, Bide, Bolster, Cohab(it), Corselet, Corset, Embar, Endure, Fulcrum, Gest, Guy, Hawser, Hold, Indwell, Jump, Lie, Lig, Linger, Moratorium, Pause, Postpone, Prop, → **REMAIN**, Reprieve, Restrain, Settle, Sist, Sleepover, Sojourn, Stamina, Strut, Sustain, Tarry

Steadfast Abiding, Constance, Constant, Dilwyn, Firm, Implacable, Perseverant, Resolute, Sad, Stable

Steadier, Steady Andantino, Ballast, Beau, Boyfriend, Composer, Consistent, Constant, Even, Faithful, Firm, Girlfriend, Level-headed, Malstick, Measured, Regular, Rock-solid, Stabilise, Stable, Unswerving

Steak Chateaubriand, Chuck, Diane, Entrecote, Fillet, Flitch, Garni, Mignon, Minute, Pepper, Pope's eye, Porterhouse, Ribeye, Rump, Slice, Tartare, T-bone, Tenderloin, Tournedos, Vienna

Steal(ing), Steal away Abstract, Bag, Bandicoot, Bone, Boost, Cabbage, Cly, Convey, Creep, Crib, Duff, Edge, Elope, Embezzle, Filch, Glom, Grab, Half-inch, Heist, Joyride, Kidnap, Knap, Knock down, Knock off, Lag, Liberate, Lift, Loot, Mag(g), Mahu, Mill, Misappropriate, Naam, Nam, Nap, Nick, Nim, Nip, Nobble, Nym, Peculate, Phone-jack, Pilfer, Pillage, Pinch, Piracy, Plagiarise, Plunder, Poach, Pocket, Prig, Proll, Purloin, Purse, Ram-raid, Remove, Rifle, Rip-off, Rob, Rustle, Scrump, Skrimp, Smug, Snaffle, Snatch, Sneak, Snitch, Souvenir, Swipe, Take, Theft, Thieve, Tiptoe, TWOC, Whip

Steam(ed), Steaming, Steamy Boil, Condensation, Cushion, Dry, Fume, Gaseous, Het, Humid, Live, Livid, Mist, Porn, Radio, Roke, Sauna, Spout, Vapor, Vapour, Wet

Steel(y) Bainite, Cast, Chrome, Chromium, Cold, Concrete, Damascus, Damask, High-carbon, High-speed, Low-carbon, Magnet, Manganese, Mild, Pedal, Shear, Silver, Spray, Taggers, Terne plate

Steep(ening) Abrupt, Arduous, Bold, Brent, Buck, Cliff-face, Embay, Expensive, Hilly, Immerse, Krans, Krantz, Kranz, Macerate, Marinade, Marinate, Mask, Monocline, Plo(a)t, Precipice, Precipitous, Rait, Rapid, Rate, Ret, Saturate, Scarp, Soak, Sog, Sop, Souse, Stey, Stickle

Steer(er), Steering Ackerman, Airt, Buffalo, Bullock, Bum, Cann, Castor, Con(n), Cox, Direct, →**GUIDE**, Helm, Navaid, Navigate, Ox, Pilot, Ply, Rudder, Stot, Whipstaff, Zebu

Stem Alexanders, Arrow, Axial, Bind, Bine, Bole, Caudex, Caulicle, Caulome, Check, Cladode, Cladophyll, Confront, Corm, Culm, Dam, Eddo, Epicotyl, Floricane, Ha(u)lm, Kex, Pedicle, Peduncle, Pin, Rachis, Rhizome, Rise, Sarment, Scapus, Seta, Shaft, Shank, Spring, Stalk, Staunch, Stipe, Stolon, Sympodium, Tail, Tamp, Terete

Step(s) Act, Apples and pears, Balancé, Chassé, Choctaw, Corbel, Corbie, Curtail, Dance, Degree, Démarche, Echelon, Escalate, False, Flight, Fouetté, Gain, Gait, Glissade, Goose, Grade, Grapevine, Grecian, Greece, Grees(e), Greesing, Grese, Gressing, Grice, Griece, Grise, Grize, Halfpace, Increment, Lavolt, Lock, Measure, Move, Notch, Pace, Pas, Pas de souris, Phase, Pigeon('s) wing, Quantal, Raiser, Ratlin(e), Rattlin(e), Rattling, Roundel, Roundle, Rung, Sashay, Shuffle, Slip, Stage, Stair, Stalk, Stile, Stope, Stride, Sugarfoot, Toddle, Trap, Tread, Trip, Unison, Waddle, Walk, Whole, Winder

Stereoscope Pseudoscope

Stereotype(d) Hackney, Ritual, Spammy

Sterile, Sterilise(r), Sterilisation, Sterility Barren, Clean, Dead, Fruitless, Impotent, Infertile, Neuter, Pasteurise, Spay, Tubal ligation, Vasectomy

Stern Aft, Austere, Back, Counter, Dour, Flinty, Grim, Hard, Implacable, Iron, Isaac, Nates, Poop, Rear, Relentless, Rugged, Stark, Strict, Tailpiece

Stew(ed), Stews Bath, Blanquette, Boil, Bouillabaisse, Bouilli, Bourguignon, Braise, Bredie, Brothel, Burgoo, Carbonade, Casserole, Cassoulet, Chowder, Coddle, Colcannon, Compot(e), Daube, Flap, Fume, Fuss, Goulash, Haricot, Hash, Hell, Hot(ch)pot(ch), Irish, Jug, Lobscouse, Matelote, Mulligan, Navarin, Olla podrida, Osso bucco, Oyster, Paddy, Paella, Pepperpot, Pot-au-feu, Pot-pourri, Ragout, Ratatouille, Salmi, Sass, Scouse, Seethe, Simmer, Squiffy, Stie, Stove, Stovies, Sty, Succotash, Sweat, Swelter

Steward(ess) Chiltern Hundreds, Flight attendant, Keeper, Major domo, Sewer, Smallboy

▷ **Stewed** *may indicate* an anagram

St Francis Seraphic Father

Stick(ing) (out), Sticks, Stuck, Sticky Adhere, Affix, Aground, Ash, Ashplant, Attach, Bamboo, Bastinado, Bat, Baton, Bauble, Bayonet, Beanpole, Blackthorn, Bludgeon, Bond, Boondocks, Broadside, Cambrel, Cane, Celery, Cement, Chalk, Chapman, Clag, Clam(my), Clarty, Clave, Cleave, Cleft, Cling, Clog, Club, Cocktail, Cohere, Coinhere, Composing, Control, Crab, Crayon, Crosier, Cross(e), Crotch, Crozier, Cue, Distaff, Divining-rod, Dog, Dure, Endure, Execration, Exsert, Fag(g)ot, Firewood, Fix, Flak, Founder, Fuse, Gad(e), Gambrel, Gelatine, Glair, Glit, Gloopy, Glue, Goad, Gold, Goo, Gore, Ground-ash, Gum, Gunge, Gunk, Harpoon, Hob, Hold on, Hurley, Immobile, Impale, Inhere, Isinglass, Jab, Jam, Joss, Jut, Kebbie, Kid, Kindling, Kip, Kiri, Knife, Knitch, Knobkerrie, Lance, Lath(i), Lug, Mallet, Message, Minder, Needle, Orange, Parasitic, Paste, Penang-lawyer, Persist, Pierce, Plaster, Pogo, Pole, Posser, Pot, Protrude, Protuberant, Q-tip, Quarterstaff, Rash, Ratten, Rhubarb, Rhythm, Rod, Ropy, Rural, Scouring, Seat, Shillela(g)h, Shooting, Size, Ski, Smeary, Smudge, Spanish windlass, Spear, Spillikin, Spurtle, Stab, Staff, Stand, Stang, Stob, Stodgy, Stubborn, Swagger, Switch, Swizzle, Swordstick, Tack(y), Tally, Tar, Thick, Throwing, Toddy, Tokotoko, Truncheon, Twig, Viscid, Viscose, Viscous, Waddy, Wait, Walking, Wand, Wedge, White, Woomera(ng), Yardward

Sticker Barnacle, Bumper, Bur, Burr, Flash, Gaum, Glue, Label, Limpet, Pin, Poster, Post-it®, Viscose

Stickybeak Nosy Parker, Paul Pry

Stiff, Stiffen(er), Stiffening, Stiffness Anchylosis, Angular, Ankylosis, Baleen, Bandoline, Body, Brace, Buckram, Budge, Cadaver, Corpse, Corpus, Dear, Defunct, Dilate, Expensive, Fibrositis, Formal, Frore(n), Goner, Gromet, Grummet, Gut, Hard, Inelastic, Mort, Petrify, Pokerish, Prim, Ramrod, Rheumatic(ky), Rigid, Rigor, Rigor mortis, Sad, Set, Size, Solid, Starch, Stark, Stay, Steeve, Stieve, Stilted, Stoor, Stour, Stowre, Sture, Tensive, Unbending, Unyielding, Upper lip, Whalebone, Wigan, Wooden

Still Accoy, Airless, Alembic, Assuage, At rest, Becalm, Breathless, Calm, Check, Current, Doggo, Ene, Even(ness), Howbe, However, Hush, Illicit, Inactive, Inert, Kill, Languid, Limbec(k), Lull, Motionless, Nevertheless, Nonetheless, Patent, Peaceful, Photograph, Placate, Placid, Polaroid, Posé, Quiescent, Quiet, Resting, Silent, Snapshot, Soothe, Stagnant, Static, Stationary, Stock, Stone, Though, Tranquil, Windless, Yet

Stimulate, Stimulus, Stimulant, Stimulation Activate, Adrenaline, Anilingus, Ankus, Antigen, Aperitif, Aphrodisiac, Arak, Arouse, Benny, Brace, Caffeine, Cardiac, Cinder, Coca, Conditioned, Cue, Dart, Dex(edrine)®, Digitalin, Digoxin, Doxapram, Egg, Energise, Erotogenic, Evoke, Excitant, Fillip, Foreplay, Fuel, Galvanize, Ginger, Goad, Grains of Paradise, G-spot, Guinea grains, Hop up, Hormone, Incentive, Incitant, Incite, Innerve, Inspire, Irritate, Jog, K(h)at, Key, Kick, Mneme, Motivate, Oestrus, Pa(a)n, Paratonic, Pep, Pep pill, Peyote, Philtre, Pick-me-up, Piquant, Potentiate, Prod, Promote, Provoke, Psych, Qat, Rim, Ritalin®, Roborant, Rowel, Rub, Sassafras, Sensuous, Somatosensory, Spark, Spur, Sting, Stir, Suggestive, Tannin, Tar, Theine, Tickle, Tik-tik, Titillate, Tone, Tonic, Tropism, Unconditioned, Upper, Urge, Whet(stone), Winter's bark

Sting(er), Stinging Aculeate, Barb, Bite, Cheat, Cnida, Con, Goad, Nematocyst, Nettle(tree), Overcharge, Perceant, Piercer, Poignant, Prick, Provoke, Pungent, Rile, Scorcher, Scorpion, Sea anemone, Sephen, Smart, Spice, Stang, Stimulus, Surcharge, Tang, Tingle, Trichocyst, Urent, Urtica, Venom

Stingy Cheeseparing, Chintzy, Close, Costive, Hard, Illiberal, Mean, Miserly, Narrow, Near, Nippy, Parsimonious, Save-all, Snippy, Snudge, Tight(wad), Tight-arse

▷ **Stingy** *may indicate* something that stings

Stipulate, Stipulation Clause, Condition, Covenant, Insist, Provision, Proviso, Rider, Specify

Stir(red), Stirrer, Stirring Accite, Admix, Ado, Afoot, Agitate, Amo(o)ve,

Animate, Annoy, Araise, Arouse, Awaken, Bother, Bustle, Buzz, Can, Churn, Cooler, Evocative, Excite, Foment, Furore, Fuss, Gaol, Hectic, Impassion, Incense, Incite, Inflame, Insurrection, Intermix, Jee, Jog, Jug, Kitty, Limbo, Live, Makebate, →**MIX**, Molinet, Move, Newgate, Nick, Noy, Poach, Poss, Pother, →**PRISON**, Prod, Provoke, Quad, Quatch, Quetch, Qui(t)ch, Quinche, Quod, Rabble, Rear, Roil, Rouse, Roust, Rummage, Rustle, Sod, Steer, Styre, Swizzle, To-do, Touch, Upset, Upstart, Wake

▷ **Stir(red), Stirring** *may indicate an anagram*

Stitch(ing), Stitch up Bargello, Bar tack, Basket, Baste, Blanket, Blind, Box, Buttonhole, Cable, Chain, Couching, Crewel, Crochet, Cross, Daisy, Embroider, Fancy, Feather, Fell, Flemish, Florentine, Garter, Gathering, Grospoint, Hem, Herringbone, Honeycomb, Insertion, Kettle, Knit, Lazy daisy, Lock, Middle, Monk's seam, Moss, Needle, Open, Overlock, Pearl, Petit point, Pinwork, Plain, Purl, Queen, Rag, Railway, Rib, Rope, Running, Saddle, Satin, Screw, Sew, Slip, Smocking, Spider, Split, Stab, Stay, Steek, Stem, Stockinette, Stocking, Straight, Sutile, Suture, Tack, Tailor's tack, Tent, Topstitch, Wheat-ear, Whip, Whole, Zigzag

Stock(ed), Stocks, Stocky Aerie, Aery, Alpha, Ambulance, Arsenal, Barometer, Blue-chip, Bouillon, Bree, Breech, Buffer, But(t), Capital, Cards, Carry, Cattle, Choker, Cippus, Common, Congee, Court-bouillon, Cravat, Dashi, Debenture, Delta, Die, Endomorph, Equip, Evening, Fumet, Fund, Gamma, Gear(e), Government, Graft, Growth, Gun, Hackneyed, Handpiece, He(a)rd, Hilt, Hoosh, Industrial, Intervention, Inventory, Joint, Just-in-time, Kin, Larder, Laughing, Line, Little-ease, Log, Night-scented, Omnium, Pigeonhole, Preferred, Pycnic, Race, Ranch, Recovery, Rep(ertory), Replenish, Reserve, Resource, Rolling, Root, Scrip, Seed, Shorts, Soup, Squat, Staple, Stash, Steale, Steelbow, Stirp(e)s, →**STORE**, Strain, Stubby, Supply, Surplus, Talon, Tap, Taurus, Team, Tie, Trite, Trust(ee), Utility, Virginian, Water

Stock Exchange Big Board

Stocking(s) Body, Fishnet, Hogger, Hose, Leather, Legwear, Moggan, Netherlings, Netherstocking, Nylons, Popsock, Seamless, Sheer, Silk, Sock, Spattee, Surgical, Tights

Stole(n) Bent, Boa, Epitrachelion, Hot, Maino(u)r, Manner, Manor, Nam, Orarion, Orarium, Reft, Scarf, Screen, Soup, Staw, Tippet, Waif, Wrap

Stomach(ic) Abdomen, Abomasum, Accept, Alvine, Appetite, Belly, Bible, Bingy, Bonnet, Bread-basket, Brook, C(o)eliac, Corporation, Craw, Epiploon, Face, Gaster, Gizzard, Gut, Heart, Inner man, Jejunum, King's-hood, Kite, Kyte, Little Mary, Manyplies, Mary, Maw, Mesaraic, Midriff, Omasum, Opisthosoma, Paunch, Potbelly, Psalterium, Puku, Pylorus, Rennet, Reticulum, Rumen, Stand, Stick, Swagbelly, →**SWALLOW**, Tripe, Tum, Tun-belly, Urite, Vell, Venter, Wame, Washboard, Wem

Stoneware Crouch-ware

Stool Bar, Buffet, Coppy, Cracket, Creepie, Cricket, Cucking, Curule, Cutty, Faeces, Foot, Hassock, Litany, Milking, Piano, Pouf(fe), Ruckseat, Seat, Sir-reverence, Step, Stercoral, Sunkie, Taboret, Tripod, Turd

Stop(page), Stopcock, Stopper, Stopping Abort, Adeem, Anchor, Aperture, Arrest, Aspirate, Avast, Bait, Ba(u)lk, Belay, Bide, Block, Brake, Buffer, Bung, Carillon, →**CEASE**, Cessation, Chapter, Check, Checkpoint, Cheese, Clarabella, Clarino, Clarion, Clog, Close, Cog, Colon, Comfort, Comma, Conclude, Conversation, Cork, Coupler, Cremo(r)na, Cut, Cut out, Deactivate, Debar, Demurral, Desist, Deter, Devall, Diapason, Diaphone, Discontinue, Discourage, Dit, Dock, Dolce, Dot, Echo, Embargo, End, Enough, Expression, Extinguish, F, Fagotto, Fare stage, Field, Fifteenth, Flag, Flue, Flute, Forbid, Foreclose, Forestall, Foundation, Freeze, Frustrate, Full, Full point, Gag, Gamba, Gemshorn, Glottal, Gong, Halt, Hartal, Heave to, Hinder, Hitch, Ho, Hoa, Hoh, Hold, Hoy, Inhibit, Intermit, Jam, Kibosh, Lay to, Let-up, Lill, Lin, Lute, Media, Mutation, Nasard, Oboe, Obstruent, Obturate, Occlude, Oppilate, Organ, Outage, Outspan, Pack in, Pause, Period, Piccolo, Pit, Plug, Point, Poop, Preclude, Prevent, Principal, Prop, Prorogue, Pull-in, Pull over, Pull-up, Punctuate, Pyramidon, Quash, Quint, Quit, Racket, Red, Reed, Refrain, Register, Rein, Remain, Request, Rest, Salicional, Scotch, Screw-top, Semi-colon, Sext, Sist, Sneb, Snub, Snuff out, Sojourn, Solo, Spigot, Stall, Stanch, Standstill, Stap, Stash, Stasis, Station, Staunch, Stay, Stent, Stive, Strike, Subbase, Suction, Supersede, Suppress, Suspend, T, Tab,

Tamp(ion), Tap, Tea break, Tenuis, Terminate, Thwart, Toby, Truck, Trumpet,
Twelfth, Voix celeste, Waypoint, When, Whistle, Whoa

Stopwatch Chronograph

Storage, Store(house) Accumulate, Archive, Armoury, Arsenal, Associative,
Backing, Barn, Big box, Bin, Bottle, Bottom drawer, Boxroom, Buffer, Bunker,
Buttery, Byte, Cache, Capacitance, Catacomb, Cell, Cellar(et), Chain, Cheek pouch,
Clamp, Clipboard, Coffer, Convenience, Co-op(erative), Co-operative, Core,
Corn-crib, Cupboard, Cutch, Database, Deep freeze, Deli, Dene-hole, Dépanneur,
Department(al), Depository, Depot, Dime, Discount, Dolly-shop, Elevator, Emporium,
Ensile, Entrepot, Étape, External, Freezer, Fridge, Fund, Galleria, Garner, Gasholder,
Girnal, Glory hole, Go-down, Granary, Hive, →**HOARD**, Hog, Hold, Honeycomb,
Hope chest, House, Houseroom, Humidor, Husband, Hypermarket, Larder, Lastage,
Liquor, Locker, Lumber room, Magazine, Main, Mart, Meat safe, Memory, Mine,
Minimart, Morgue, Mothball, Mow, Multiple, Nest-egg, Off-licence, One-step,
Package, Pantechnicon, Pantry, Pithos, Provision, Pumped, Rack(ing), RAM, Reel,
Repertory, Reposit, ROM, Root house, Save, Sector, Shed, →**SHOP**, Silage, Silo,
Spence, Springhouse, Squirrel, Stack, Stash, Stock, Stockpile, Stockroom, Stow,
Superbaza(a)r, Superette, Supermarket, Supply, Tack-room, Tank, Thesaurus,
Tithe-barn, Tommy-shop, Trading post, Vestiary, Vestry, Virtual, Warehouse,
Woodshed, Woodyard, Wool (shed), WORM

▶**Storey** see **STORY**

Storm(y) Ablow, Adad, Assail, Assault, Attack, Baguio, Blizzard, Bluster, Brouhaha,
Buran, Charge, Cockeye(d) bob, Cyclone, Devil, Dirty, Dust, Electric, Enlil, Expugn,
Furore, Gale, Gusty, Haboob, Hurricane, Ice, Line, Magnetic, Monsoon, Onset, Pelter,
Rage(ful), Raid, Rain, Rampage, Rant, Rate, Rave, Red spot, Rugged, Rush, Shaitan,
Snorter, Squall, Tea-cup, Tempest, Tornade, Tornado, Tropical, Unruly, Violent,
Weather, White squall, Willy-willy, Zu

▷**Stormy** may indicate an anagram

Story, Storyline, Stories Account, Allegory, Anecdote, Apocrypha, Attic, Bar,
Basement, Baur, Biog, Blood and thunder, Chestnut, Clearstory, Clerestory, Cock and
bull, Conte, Cover, Decameron, Edda, Epic, Episode, Etage, Exclusive, Fable, Fabliau,
Falsehood, Feature, Fib, Fiction, Flat, Floor, Folk-lore, Folk-tale, Gag, Geste, Ghost,
Glurge, Hair-raiser, Hard-luck, Heptameron, Horror, Idyll, Iliad, Jataka, Lee, Legend,
Lie, Märchen, Mezzanine, Myth(os), Mythus, Narrative, Nouvelle, Novel(la), Oratorio,
Parable, Passus, Pentameron, Photo, Plot, Rede, Report, Roman a clef, Romance,
Rumour, Saga, Scoop, Script, Serial, SF, Shaggy dog, Shocker, Short, Smoke-room,
Sob, Spiel, Spine-chiller, Splash, Spoiler, Stage, Success, Tale, Tall, Thread, Thriller,
Tier, Triforium, Upper, Version, Whodun(n)it, Yarn

Storyteller Aesop, Fibber, Griot, Liar, Miller, Munchausen, Narrator, Raconteur,
Sagaman, Shannachie, Tusitala, Uncle Remus

Stout(ness) Ale, Burly, Chopping, Chubby, Cobby, Corpulent, Doughty, Embonpoint,
Endomorph, Entire, Fat, Fubsy, Hardy, Humpty-dumpty, Lusty, Manful, Milk, Obese,
Overweight, Porter, Portly, Potbelly, Robust, Stalwart, Stalworth, Sta(u)nch, Strong,
Stuggy, Sturdy, Substantial, Tall

Stove Aga, Baseburner, Break, Calefactor, Chauf(f)er, Chiminea, Cockle, Cooker,
Cooktop, Furnace, Gasfire, Oven, Potbelly, Primus®, Range, Salamander

Straggle(r), Straggly Estray, Gad, Meander, Ramble, Rat-tail, Spidery, Sprawl,
Stray, Wander

Straight(en), Straightness Align, Bald, Beeline, Boning, Correct, Die, Direct,
Downright, Dress, Frank, Gain, Het(ero), Honest, Lank, Legit, Level, Line, Normal,
Ortho-, Rectilineal, Rectitude, Righten, Sheer, Slap, Tidy, True, Unbowed, Unlay,
Upright, Veracious, Virgate

Straightfaced Agelast

Straightforward Candid, Direct, Downright, Easy, Even, Forthright, Honest,
Jannock, Level, Plain sailing, Pointblank, Simple, Uncomplicated

Strain(ed), Strainer, Straining Agonistic, Ancestry, Aria, Breed, Bulk, Carol,
Charleyhorse, Clarify, Colander, Distend, Drawn, Effort, Exert, Filter, Filtrate, Fit,

Fitt(e), Force, Fray, Fytt(e), Intense, Kind, Melody, Milsey, Minus, Molimen, Music, Nervy, Note, Overstretch, Overtask, Passus, Percolate, Pressure, Pull, Rack, Raring, Reck(an), Repetitive, Retch, Rick, Seep, Seil(e), Set, Shear, Sieve, Sift, Sile, Stape, Start, Stirps, Stock, Streak, Stress, Stretch, Sye, Tamis, Tammy, Tax, Tems(e), Tenesmus, Tense, Tension, Threnody, Try, Vein, Vice, Work, Wrick

Strait(s) Bab el Mandeb, Basilan, Desperate, Dover, Drake Passage, East River, Florida, Golden Gate, Great Belt, Hainan, Kerch, Mackinac, Mona Passage, North Channel, Oresund, Soenda, Sumba, Tatar, Tiran, Tsugaru, Windward Passage

▷ **Strange** *may indicate* an anagram

Strange(ness), Stranger Alien, Aloof, Amphitryon, Bizarre, Curious, Dougal, Eccentric, Eerie, Exotic, Ferly, Foreign, Fraim, Freaky, Frem(d), Fremit, Frenne, Funny, Guest, Jimmy, Malihini, New, Novel, Odd(ball), Outlandish, Outsider, Quare, Quark, Queer, Rum, S, Screwy, Selcouth, Singular, Surreal, Tea-leaf, Uncanny, Unco, Uncommon, Unfamiliar, Unked, Unket, Unkid, Unused, Unusual, Wacky, Weird, Weyard, Wondrous

Strap(ping) Able-bodied, Band, Barber, Beat, Bowyangs, Braces, Brail, Braw, Breeching, Browband, Cheekpiece, Crownpiece, Crupper, Cuir-bouilli, Curb, Deckle, Girth, Halter, Harness, Holdback, Jess, Jock(ey), Kicking, Larrup, Lash, Leather, Ligule, Lorate, Lore, Manly, Martingale, Nicky-tam, Octopus, Overcheck, Palmie, Pandy, Rand, Rein, Robust, Shoulder, Sling, Spaghetti, Spider, Strop, Surcingle, Suspender, T, Tab, Taws(e), T-bar, Thong, Thoroughbrace, Throatlash, Throatlatch, Trace, Tump-line, Wallop, Watch, Watchband

Stratagem, Strategist, Strategy Artifice, Clausewitz, Contrivance, Coup, Deceit, Device, Dodge, Exit, Fetch, Finesse, Fraud, Game plan, Guile, Heresthetic, Kaupapa, Lady Macbeth, Manoeuvre, Maskirovka, Masterstroke, Maximum, Minimax, Plan, Realpolitik, Rope-a-dope, Salami, Scheme, Scorched earth, Sleight, Subterfuge, Tack, Tactic(s), Tactician, Trick, Wheeze, Wile

Straw(s), Strawy Balibuntal, Boater, Buntal, Chaff, Cheese, Crosswort, Halm, Hat, Haulm, Hay, Insubstantial, Kemple, Last, Leghorn, Nugae, Oaten, Panama, Parabuntal, Pedal, Rush, Stalk, Strae, Stramineous, Strammel, Strummel, Stubble, Trifles, Truss, Wisp, Ye(a)lm

Stray(ing) Abandoned, Aberrant, Alleycat, Chance, Depart, Deviate, Digress, Err, Forwarder, Foundling, Maverick, Meander, Misgo, Pye-dog, Ramble, Roam, Sin, Straggle, Streel, Traik, Unowned, Waff, Waif, Wander, Wilder

Streak(ed), Streaker, Streaky Bended, Blue, Brindle, Comet, Flambé, Flaser, Flash, Fleck, Freak, Hawked, Hawkit, Highlights, Lace, Layer, Leonid, Lowlight, Marble, Mark, Merle, Mottle, Primitive, Race, Ra(t)ch, Run, Schlieren, Seam, Shot, Striate, Striga, Strip(e), Vein, Venose, Vibex, Waif, Wake, Wale, Yellow

Stream Acheron, Beam, Beck, Blast, Bourne, Brook, Burn, Consequent, Course, Current, Driblet, Fast, Flow, Flower, Freshet, Ghyll, Gill, Gulf, Gush, Headwater, Influent, Jet, Kill, Lade, Lane, Leet, Logan, Meteor, Nala, Nalla(h), Nulla(h), Obsequent, Pokelogan, Pour, Pow, Riffle, Rill, River, Rivulet, Rubicon, Run, Runnel, Sike, Slough, Spill, Spruit, Squirt, Star, Strand, Streel, Subsequent, Syke, The Fleet, Third, Thrutch, Tide-race, Torrent, Tributary, Trickle, Trout, Watercourse, Water-splash, Winterbourne

Streamer Banner(all), Ribbon, Tape, Tippet

Street Alley, Ave(nue), Bay, Boulevard, Bowery, Broad, Carey, Carnaby, Cato, Causey, Cheapside, Civvy, Close, Corso, Court, Crescent, Downing, Drive, Easy, Ermine, Fleet, Gate, Grub, Harley, High(way), Lane, Main drag, Meuse, Mews, One-way, Parade, Paseo, Poultry, Queer, Road, Side, Sinister, St, Strand, Terrace, Thoroughfare, Threadneedle, Throgmorton, Wall, Wardour, Watling, Way, Whitehall

Strength(en), Strengthened, Strengthening Afforce, Anneal, Arm, Asset, Augment, Bant, Beef, Brace, Brawn, Build, Confirm, Consolidate, Edify, Embattle, Enable, Energy, Fish, Foison, Force, Force majeure, Forte, Fortify, Fortitude, Freshen, Fus(h)ion, Grit, Herculean, Horn, Intensity, Invigorate, Iron, Lace, Line, Main, Man, Might, Munite, Muscle, Neal, Nerve, **→ POWER**, Prepotence, Pre-stress, Proof,

Reinforce, Roborant, Shear, Sinew, Spike, Spine, Stamina, Steel, Sthenia, Stoutness, →**STRONG**, Tensile, Thews, Titration, Unity, Vim, Willpower

Stress(ed), Stressful Actuate, Careworn, Creep, Drive home, Oxidative, Paroxytone, Post-traumatic, Primary, Proclitic, Rhythm, Secondary, Sentence, Shear, Testing, Thetic, Tonic, Wind shear, Word, Yield (point)

Stretch(able), Stretched, Stretcher, Stretching Alength, Belt, Brick, Crane, Distend, Doolie, Draw, Ectasis, Eke, Elastic, Elongate, Exaggerate, Expanse, Extend, Extensile, Farthingale, Fib, Frame, Give, Gurney, Home, Lengthen, Lie, Limo, Litter, Narrows, Outreach, Pallet, Porrect, Procrustes, Prolong, Pretend, Pull, Rack, Rax, →**REACH**, Sentence, Shiner, Spell, Spread, Strain, Streak, Taut, Tend, Tense, Tensile, Tenter, Term, Time, Tract, Tractile, Traction, Tree, Trolley

Stretcher-bearer Fuzzy-wuzzy angel

Strict(ly) De rigueur, Dour, Exacting, Harsh, Literal, Orthodox, Penal, Puritanical, Religious, Rigid, Rigorous, Severe, Spartan, Stern, Strait(-laced)

Stride(s) Gal(l)umph, Jeans, Leg, Lope, March, Pace, Piano, Stalk, Sten, Stend, Straddle, Stroam, Strut, Stump

Strident Brassy, Discordant, Grinding, Harsh, Raucous, Screech, Shrill

Strife Bargain, Barrat, Bate(-breeding), Brigue, Conflict, Contest, Discord, Disharmony, Dissension, Feud, Food, Friction, Ignoble, Scrap(ping)

Strike(r), Striker, Striking, Strike out Air, Alight, Annul, Arresting, Astonishing, Attitude, Backhander, Baff, Band, Bang, Bash, Bat, Baton, Batsman, Batter, Beat, Belabour, Better, Biff, Black, Bla(u)d, Bonanza, Bop, British disease, Buff, Buffet, Butt, Cane, Catch, Chime, Chip, Clap, Clash, Clatch, Clip, Clock, Clout, Club, Cob, Collide, Conk, Constitutional, Coup, Cue, Cuff, Dad, Dent, Dev(v)el, Ding, Dint, Dismantle, Douse, Dowse, Dramatic, Drive, Dush, Éclat, Effective, Emphatic, Especial, Fat, Fet(ch), Fillip, Firk, Fist, Flail, Flog, Frap, General, Get, Gnash, Go-slow, Gowf, Hail, Handsome, Hartal, Head-butt, →**HIT**, Horn, Hour, Hunger, Ictus, Illision, Impact, Impinge, Impress, Jarp, Jaup, Jole, Joll, Joule, Jowl, Knock, Lam, Lambast, Laser, Lay(-off), Lightning, Match, Middle, Mint, Notable, Noticeable, Official, Out, Pash, Pat(ter), Pat, Peen, Percuss, Picket, Plectrum, Pronounced, Pummel, Punch, Quarter-jack, Rag-out, Ram, Rap, Remarkable, Rolling, Salient, Scrub, Scutch, Shank, Sick out, Sideswipe, Signal, Sitdown, Sit-in, Sizzling, Slam, Slap, Slat, Slog, Slosh, Smack, Smash, Smite, Sock, Souse, Spank, Stayaway, Stop(page), Stub, Swap, Swat, Swinge, Swipe, Swop, Sympathy, Tan, Tangent, Tat, Thump, Thwack, Tip, Token, Tripper, Twat, Unconstitutional, Unofficial, Walk-out, Wallop, Wap, Whack, Whale, Whang, Whap, Wherret, Who does what, Wildcat, Wipe, Wondrous, Zap

String(s), Stringy Anchor, Band, Bant, Beads, Bootlace, Bow, Cello, Chalaza, Chanterelle, Cord, Cosmic, Drill, Enfilade, Fiddle, First, G, Glass, Gut, Henequin, Hypate, Idiot, Injection, Keyed, Kill, Lace, Lag, Leading, Lichanos, Macramé, Mese, Necklace, Nete, Nicky-tam, Oil, Paranete, Production, Proviso, Purse, Quint, Ripcord, Rope, Rosary, Rough, Second, Series, Shoe(-tie), Silly®, Sinewy, Snare, Spit, Stable, Straggle, Strand, Sultana, Sympathetic, Team, Tendon, Thairm, Tie, Tough, Train, Trite, Twiddling-line, Viola, Violin, Worry-beads, Wreathed

Strip(ped), Stripper, Striptease Airfield, Armband, Band, Bare, Bark, Batten, Belt, Bereave, Bimetallic, Blowtorch, Caprivi, Chippendale, Comic, Cote, Defoliate, Denude, Deprive, Derobe, Despoil, Devest, Disbark, Dismantle, Dismask, Disrobe, Divest, Doab, Dosing, Drag, Écorché, Fannel(l), Fiche, Film, Flashing, Flaught, Flay, Fleece, Flench, Flense, Flight, Flinch, Flounce, Flype, Furring, Gaza, Goujon, Hatband, Infula, Jib, Label, Landing, Lap-dancer, Lardon, Lath, Ledge, Linter, List, Littoral, Loading, Locust, Magnetic, Mail-rod, Maniple, Median, Möbius, Paint, Panhandle, Parting, Peel, Pillage, Pluck, Pull, Puttee, Puttie, Rand, Raunch, Raw, Reglet, Reservation, Riband, Ribbon, Roon, Royne, Rumble, Rund, Runway, Scent, Screed, Scrow, Shear, Shed, Shim, Shred, Shuck, Skin, Slat, Slit, Sliver, Spellican, Spilikin, Spill(ikin), Splat, Splent, Spline, Splint, Splinter, Spoil, Straik, Strake, Strap, Streak, Strop, Sugar soap, Swath(e), Sweatband, Tack, Tear, Tear-off, Tee, Thong, Tirl, Tirr, Tombolo, Tongue, Trash, Unbark, Uncase, Unclothe, Undeck, Undress, Unfrock, Unrig, Unrip, Unrobe, Valance, Weather, Zona, Zone

Stripling Lad

Strive, Striving Aim, Aspire, →ATTEMPT, Contend, Endeavour, Enter, Kemp, Labour, Nisus, Persevere, Pingle, Press, Strain, Struggle, Toil, Try, Vie

Stroke Apoplex(y), Backhander, Bat, Bisque, Blow, Boast, Breast, Butterfly, Caress, Carom, Chip, Chop, Counterbuff, Coup, Coy, Crawl, Dab, Dash, Dint, Dog(gy)-paddle, Down-bow, Drear(e), Dropshot, Effleurage, Exhaust, Feat, Flick, Fondle, Forehand, Glance, Ground, Hairline, Hand(er), Ictus, Jenny, Jole, Joll, Joule, Jowl, Knell, Knock, Lash, Lightning, Like, Line, Loft, Long jenny, Loser, Oarsman, Oblique, Odd, Off-drive, Outlash, Palp, Paw, Pot-hook, Pull, Punto reverso, Put(t), Reverso, Ridding straik, Roquet, Rub, Scart, Scavenge, Sclaff, Scoop, Seizure, Sheffer's, Short Jenny, Sider, Sixte, Slash, Smooth, Solidus, Spot, Strike, Stripe, Sweep, Swipe, Tact, Tittle, Touch, Touk, Trait, Trudgen, Trudgeon, Tuck, Upbow, Virgule, Wale, Whang, Wrist shot

Strong(est) Able, Boofy, Brawny, Buff, Cast-iron, Doughty, Durable, F, Fat, Fierce, Fit, Forceful, Forcible, Forte, Hale, Hercules, High-powered, Humming, Husky, Intense, Ironside, Marrowy, Mighty, Nappy, Ox, Pithy, Pollent, Potent, Powerful, Pronounced, Pungent, Racy, Rank, Robust, Samson, Solid, Sour, Stale, Stalwart, Stark, Steely, Sthenic, Stiff, Stout, Str, Strapping, →STRENGTH, Sturdy, Substantial, Suit, Tarzan, Theory, Thesis, Thewy, Thickset, Tough, Trusty, Valid, Vegete, Vehement, Vigorous, Violent, Well-set, Wight, Ya(u)ld

Stronghold Acropolis, Aerie, Bastion, Castle, Citadel, Eyrie, Fastness, Fortalice, Fortress, Keep, Kremlin, Redoubt, Tower

Strongroom Genizah, Safe

Structural, Structure Acrosome, Analysis, Anatomy, Armature, Atomic, Building, Centriole, Chromosome, Conus, Database, Edifice, Erection, Fabric, Fairing, Flaser, Format(ion), Frame, Gantry, Hut, Ice-apron, Idant, Lantern, Lattice, Malpighian, Manubrium, Mole, Organic, Ossature, Parawalker, Pediment, Pergola, Physique, Shape, Shell, Shoring, Skeleton, Squinch, Staging, Stand, Starling, Syntax, System, Texas, Texture, Thylakoid, Trabecula, Trilithon, Trochlea, Undercarriage

Struggle, Struggling Agon(ise), Agonistes, Amelia, Buckle, Camp, Chore, Class, Conflict, Contend, Contest, Cope, Debatement, Duel, Effort, Encounter, Endeavour, Fight, Flounder, Grabble, Grapple, Hassle, Jockey, Kampf, Labour, Luctation, Maul, Mill, Pingle, Rat-race, Reluct, Resist, Scrabble, Scramble, Scrape, Scrimmage, Scrum, Scrummage, Scuffle, Slugfest, Sprangle, Strain, →STRIVE, Toil, Tug, Tuilyie, Tussle, Up a tree, Uphill, Vie, War(sle), Warfare, Work, Wrestle

▷ **Struggle** *may indicate* an anagram

Stubborn(ness) Adamant, Bigoted, Bull-headed, Contumacious, Cross-grained, Cussed, Diehard, Entêté, Hard(-nosed), Hidebound, Intransigent, Inveterate, Moyl(e), Mulish, Mumpsimus, Obdurate, Obstinate, Opinionated, Ornery, Ortus, Pertinacious, Perverse, Recalcitrant, Reesty, Refractory, Rigwiddie, Rigwoodie, Self-willed, Stiff, Stoor, Tenacious, Thrawn, Tough, Wrong-headed

Stucco Cement

Stud(ded) Doornail, Entire, Farm, Frost, Press, Shear, Shirt, Stop

Student(s) Abiturient, Alumnus, Apprentice, Bajan, Bejant, Bursar, Cadet, Candle-waiter, Class, Coed, Commoner, Dan, Dig, Disciple, Dresser, Dux, Exchange, Exhibitioner, External, Form, Fresher, Freshman, Gownsman, Graduand, Green welly, Gyte, Hafiz, Ikey, Internal, Junior, →LEARNER, Magistrand, Matie, Mature, Medical, NUS, Opsimath, Ordinand, Oxonian, Plebe, Poll, Postgraduate, Preppy, Pupil, Reader, Rushee, Sap, →SCHOLAR, Self-taught, Semi, Seminar, Senior, Shark, Sixth former, Sizar, Sizer, Smug, Softa, Soph(omore), Sophister, Spod, Subsizar, Swot, Talibe, Templar, Tiro, Tosher, Trainee, Tuft, Tukkie, Tutee, Underclassman, Undergraduate, Welly, Witsie, Wooden spoon, Wooden wedge, Wrangler, Year

Study, Studies, Studied, Studious, Studying Analyse, Bionics, Bone, Brown, Carol, Case, Classics, Comparability, Con(ne), Conscious, Consider, Course, Cram, Den, Dig, Étude, Examine, Eye, Feasibility, Field, Gen up, Intramural, Isagogics, Lair, Learn, Liberal, Media, Motion, Mug up, Mull, Muse, Nature, Perusal, Peruse, Pilot, Pore, Post-doctoral, Prep(aration), Probe, Read, Recce, Reconnoitre, Research, Revise,

Sanctum, Sap, Scan, Science, Scrutinise, Shiur, Sketch, Swat, Swot, Take, Time and motion, Trade-off, Train, Tutorial, Typto, Voulu, Work

Stuff(iness), Stuffing, Stuffy Airless, Bloat, Canvas, Close, Cloth, Codswallop, Cram, Crap, Dimity, Farce, Feast, Fiddlesticks, Fill, Force, Forcemeat, Frows(t)y, Frowzy, Fug, Gear, Glut, Gobble, Gorge, Guff, Hair, Havers, Hooey, Horsehair, Inlay, Kapok, Lard, Line, Linen, →**MATERIAL**, Matter, No-meaning, Nonsense, Overeat, Pad, Pang, Panne, Pompous, Ram, Replete, Rot, Sate, Scrap, Sob, Stap, Steeve, Stew, Taxidermy, Trig, Upholster, Wad, Youth

Stumble Blunder, Daddle, Err, Falter, Flounder, Founder, Lurch, Peck, Snapper, Stoit, Titubate, Trip

Stun(ned), Stunning Astonish, Astound, Awhape, Bludgeon, Concuss, Cosh, Daze, Dazzle, Deafen, Dove(r), Drop-dead, Eclectic, Glam, Gobsmack, KO, Numb, Poleaxe, Shell-shocked, Shock, Stoun, Stupefy

Stunt(ed) Aerobatics, Confine, Droichy, Dwarf, Exploit, Feat, Gimmick, Hot-dog, Hype, Jehad, Jihad, Loop, Nirl, Puny, Ront(e), Runt, Ruse, Scroggy, Scrub(by), Scrunt(y), Stub, Trick, Wanthriven

Stupid, Stupid person Anserine, Asinine, Besotted, Blithering, Blockish, Braindead, Clay-brained, Crass, Daft, Datal, Dense, Desipient, Dim(wit), Donner(e)d, Dozy, Dull(ard), Fatuous, Flat, Gross, Half-arsed, Half-baked, Hammerheaded, Hare-brained, Hen-witted, Inane, Insensate, Insipient, Lamming, Mindless, Natural, Obtuse, Senseless, Silly, Thick, Thick-witted, Torpid, Wooden(head)

Sturdy Burly, Dunt, Gid, Hardy, Hefty, Lusty, Robust, Rugged, Solid, Stalwart, Staunch, Steeve, Strapping, Strong, Thickset, Turnsick, Vigorous

Style(s), Stylish, Stylist Adam, À la, A-line, Anime, Band, Barocco, Barock, Baroque, Blocked, Blow-dry, Brachylogy, Burin, Call, Chic, Chippendale, Class, Cultism, Cursive, Cut, Dapper, Dash, Decor, Decorated, Demotic, Diction, Dress sense, Dub, Élan, Elegance, Empire, Entitle, Execution, Face, Farand, →**FASHION**, Fetching, Finesse, Flamboyant, Flava, Flossy, Fly, Font, Form(at), Free, Friseur, Galant, Genre, Ghetto fabulous, Gnomon, Gothic, Grace, Grand, Gr(a)ecism, Groovy, Hair-do, Hand, Hepplewhite, Heuristic, Hip, Homeric, House, International (Gothic), Katharev(o)usa, Locution, Manner, Metrosexual, Mod(e), Modernism, Modish, Natty, New, New Look, Nib, Nifty, Novelese, Old, Panache, Pattern, Pen, Perm, Perpendicular, Personal, Phrase, Picturesque, Pistil, Plateresque, Pointel, Port, Posh, Post-modernism, Preponderant, Probe, Prose, Queen Anne, Rakish, Rank, Regency, Retro, Ritzy, Rococo, Romanesque, Rudie, Sheraton, Silk, Slap-up, Smart, Snappy, Snazzy, Soigné, Spiffy, Sporty, Street, Surname, Swish, Taste, Term, Title, Ton, Tone, Tony, Touch, Traditional, Tuscan, Uncial, Vain, Va-va-voom, Verismo, Vogue, Way

Subaltern Lt

Subarea Talooka

Subconscious Inner, Instinctive, Not-I, Subliminal, Suppressed

Subcontract Outsource

Subdue(d) Abate, Allay, Chasten, Conquer, Cow, Dominate, Lick, Low-key, Master, Mate, Mute, Overbear, Quail, Quieten, Reduce, Refrain, Repress, Slow, Sober, Soft pedal, Suppress, Tame, Under

Subheading Strapline

Subject(ed), Subjection, Subjects, Subject to Amenable, Art, Bethrall, Caitive, Case, Citizen, Core, Cow, Dhimmi, Enthrall, Gist, Hobby, Hobby-horse, Inflict, Liable, Liege(man), Matter, Metic, National, On, Oppress, Overpower, PE, People, Poser, RE, RI, Serf, Servient, Servitude, Sitter, Slavery, Snool, Submit, Suit, Syllabus, →**THEME**, Thirl, Thrall, Topic, Under, Undergo, Vassal, Villein

Sub-lieutenant Cornet

Sublime Ali, Alice, August, Empyreal, Grand, Great, Holy, Lofty, Majestic, Outstanding, Perfect, Porte, Splendid

▷**Submarine** *may indicate* a fish

Submarine Boomer, Diver, Nautilus, Polaris, Sub, U-boat, Undersea

Submerge(d) Dip, Dive, Drown, Embathe, Engulf, Imbathe, Impinge, Lemuria, Overwhelm, Ria, Sink, Take, Whelm

Submissive, Submission, Submit Acquiesce, Bow, Capitulate, Comply, Defer, Docile, Folio, Gimp, Knuckle, Lapdog, Meek, Obedient, Passive, Pathetic, Refer, Render, Resign, Snool, Stepford, Stoop, Succumb, Truckle, → **YIELD**

Subordinate Adjunct, Dependent, Flunky, Inferior, Junior, Minion, Myrmidon, Offsider, Postpone, Secondary, Servient, Stooge, Subject, Subservient, Surrender, Under(ling), Underman, Under-strapper, Vassal

Subscribe(r), Subscription Approve, Assent, Conform, Due, Pay, Pay TV, Sign(atory), Signature, Undersign, Underwrite

Subsequent(ly) Anon, Consequential, Future, Later, Next, Postliminary, Since, Then

Subside, Subsidence, Subsidy Abate, Adaw, Aid, Assuage, Bonus, Cauldron, Diminish, Ebb, Grant, Headage, Sink, Sit, Swag

Substance, Substantial Ambergris, Antitoxin, Apiol, Blanco, Body, Castoreum, Cermet, Chalone, Chitin, Cofactor, Colloid, Considerable, Content, Creatine, Cytochalasin, Ectoplasm, Elemi, Endorphin, Enzyme, Essential, Ethambutol, Exudate, Fabric, Fixative, Flavanone, Getter, Gist, Gluten, Gossypol, Gravamen, Gutta-percha, Hearty, Hefty, Hirudin, Imine, Indol, Inhibitor, Isatin(e), Isomer, Kryptonite, Lase, Lectin, Linin, Material, Matter, Meaning, Meat(y), Metabolite, Mineral, Misoprostol, Mitogen, Mole, Morphactin, Myelin, Neotoxin, Noselite, Nutrient, Orgone, P, Particulate, Pepsinogen, Perforine, Phosphor, Pith, Polymer, Proinsulin, Promoter, Prostaglandin, Protyl(e), Quid, Reality, Resin, Salacin(e), Secretagogue, Sense, Sequestrant, Smeclic, Solid, Sorbitol, Stramonium, Stuff, Suint, Sum, Sunblock, Synergist, Syntonin, Taeniafuge, Tangible, Terra alba, Thermoplastic, Thiouracil, Thiourea, Tocopherol, Weighty, Ylem

▶**Substantial** *see* **SUBSTANCE**

Substitute, Substitution Acting, Change, Changeling, Commute, Creamer, Deputy, Emergency, Ersatz, -ette, Euphemism, Exchange, Fill-in, Imitation, Improvise, Instead, Lieu(tenant), Locum, Makeshift, Nominee, Novation, Pinch-hit, Proxy, Regent, Relieve, Replace, Represent, Reserve, Resolution, Ringer, Sentence, Soya, Stalking-horse, Stand-in, Stead, Step in, Stopgap, Supernumerary, Supply, Surrogate, Switch, Swop, Twelfth man, Twentieth man, Understudy, Vicarious

Subterfuge Artifice, Chicane, Evasion, Hole, Manoeuvre, Off-come, Ruse, Strategy, Trick

Subtle(ty) Abstruse, Alchemist, Crafty, Fine(spun), Finesse, Ingenious, Nice(ty), Nuance, Overtone, Refinement, Sly, Suttle, Thin, Wily

Subtract(ion) Deduct, Discount, Take, Tithe, Withdraw

Suburb(s) Dormitory, Environs, Exurbia, Metroland, Outskirts, Purlieu

Subverse, Subversion, Subversive, Subvert Agitprop, Fifth column, Overthrow, Reverse, Sabotage, Sedition, Treasonous, Undermine, Upset

Succeed, Success(ful) Accomplish, Achieve, Answer, Arrive, Big-hitter, Bingo, Blockbuster, Boffo, Breakthrough, Chartbuster, Coast, Contrive, Coup, Do well, Éclat, Effective, Efficacious, Ensue, Fadge, Fare, Felicity, Flourish, Follow, Fortune, Gangbuster, Get, Go, Hit, Hotshot, Inherit, Killing, Landslide, Luck, Made, Make good, Make it, Manage, Masterstroke, Mega, Midas touch, Offcome, Parlay, Pass, Prevail, Procure, Prosper, Purple patch, Pyrrhic, Reach, Replace, Result, Riot, Score, Seal, Seel, Sele, Sell out, Soaraway, Socko, Speed, Stardom, Superstar, Sure thing, Take, Tanistry, The bitch goddess, Thumbs up, Triumph, Up, Up and coming, Upstart, Vault, Victory, Weather, Win, Winnitude, W(h)iz(z)kid, Wow, Wunderkind

Successor Co(m)arb, Deluge, Descendant, Ensuite, Epigon(e), Heir, Incomer, Inheritor, Khalifa, Next, Syen

Succulent Aloe, Cactus, Echeveria, Hoodia, Juicy, Lush, Rich, Saguaro, Sappy, Spekboom, Tender, Toothy

Suck(er), Sucking Absorb, Aspirator, Ass, Dracula, Drink, Dupe, Fawn, Felch, Gnat, Gobstopper, Graff, Graft, Gull, Hoove, Lamia, Lamprey, Leech, Liquorice, Lollipop, Mammal, Mouth, Mug, Patsy, Plunger, Shoot, Siphon, Slurp, Smarm, Sweetmeat, Swig, Sycophant, Toad-eater, Vampire

Sudden(ly) Abrupt, Astart, Astert, Extempore, Ferly, Flash, Fleeting, Foudroyant,

Hasty, Headlong, Impulsive, Overnight, Precipitate, Rapid, Slap, Sodain, Subitaneous, Swap, Swop, Unexpected

Sue Apply, Ask, Beseech, Dun, Entreat, Implead, Implore, Petition, Pray, Process, Prosecute, Woo

Suffer(er), Suffering Abide, Aby(e), Ache, Affliction, Agonise, Auto, → BEAR, Brook, Calvary, Cop, Die, Distress, Dree, Endurance, Endure, Feel, Gethsemane, Golgotha, Grief, Hardship, Have, Hell, Incur, Languish, Let, Luit, Mafted, Martyr, Pain, Passible, Passion, Passive, Patible, Patience, Pay, Pellagrin, Permit, Pine, Plague, Purgatory, Stand, Stomach, Stress, Sustain, Thole, Tolerate, Toll, Torment, Torture, Trial, Tribulation, Undergo, Use, Victim

Suffice, Sufficient Adequate, Ample, Basta, Do, Due, Enough, Enow, Nuff, Satisfy, Serve

Suffocate Asphyxiate, Choke, Smother, Stifle, Stive, Strangle, Throttle

Sugar(y), Sugar cane Aldohexose, Aldose, Amygdalin, Arabinose, Barley, Beet, Blood, Brown, Candy, Cane, Caramel, Cassonade, Caster, Cellobiose, Cellose, Confectioner's, Cube, Daddy, Demerara, Deoxyribose, Dextrose, Disaccharide, Flattery, Fructose, Fucose, Furanose, Galactose, Gallise, Glucose, Glucosoric, Glycosuria, Goo(r), Granulated, Granulose, Grape, Gur, Heptose, Heroin, Hexose, Honeydew, Hundreds and thousands, Iced, Icing, Inulin, Invert, Jaggary, Jaggery, Jagghery, Ketose, Lactose, Laevulose, Loaf, Lump, Maltose, Manna, Mannose, Maple, Milk, Money, Monosaccharide, Muscovado, Nectar, Nucleoside, Palm, Panocha, Pentose, Penuche, Pyranose, Raffinose, Rhamnose, Ribose, Saccharine, Saccharoid, Simple, Sis, Sorbose, Sorghum, Sorg(h)o, Sparrow, Spun, Sweet, Tetrose, Trehalose, Triose, White, Wood, Xylose

Suggest(ion), Suggestive Advance, Advice, Advise, Breath, Connote, Cue, Float, Hint, Hypnotic, Idea, Imply, Innuendo, Insinuate, Intimate, Kite, Mention, Modicum, Moot, Nominate, Posit, Posthypnotic, Postulate, Prompt, Proposal, Propound, Provocative, Racy, Raise, Recommend, Redolent, Reminiscent, Risqué, Savour, Scenario, Smacks, Soft core, Suspicion, Threat, Touch, Trace, Twang, Vote

Suicide Felo-de-se, Hara-kiri, Hari-kari, Kamikaze, Lemming, Lethal, Sati, Seppuku, Suttee

Suit Action, Adapt, Adjust, Agree, Answer, Anti-G, Apply, Appropriate, Become, Befit, Beho(o)ve, Bequest, Besit, Birthday, Cards, Case, Cat, Clubs, Conform, Courtship, Demob, Diamonds, Dittos, Diving, Do, Dress, Dry, Etons, Exec(utive), Fashion, Fit, G, Garb, Gee, Gree, Hearts, Hit, Jump, Lis pendens, Long, Lounge, Major, Mao, Match, Minor, Monkey, NBC, Noddy, Orison, Outcome, Paternity, Penguin, Petition, Plaint, Play, Plea, Please, Point, Prayer, Pressure, Process, Pyjama, Quarterdeck, Queme, Romper(s), Safari, Sailor, Salopettes, Satisfy, Serve, Shell, Siren, Skeleton, Slack, Space, Spades, Strong, Sun, Sunday, Supplicat, Sweat, Swim, Swords, Tailleur, Three-piece, Track, Trouser, Trumps, Tsotsi, Tweeds, Twin, Two-piece, Uniform, Union, Wet, Wingsuit, Zoot

Suitable Apposite, Appropriate, Apt, Becoming, Capable, Competent, Congenial, Consonant, Convenance, Convenient, Decorous, Due, Expedient, → FIT, Habile, Keeping, Meet, Opportune, Relevant, Seemly, Sittlichkeit, Worthy

Suite Allemande, Apartment, Chambers, Court, Dolly, Edit, Ensemble, Entourage, Hospitality, Lounge, Nutcracker, Partita, Retinue, Rooms, Serenade, Set, Tail, Three-piece, Train, Two-piece

Suitor Beau, Gallant, Lover, Petitioner, Pretendant, Pretender, Swain

Sulk(y), Sulkiness B(r)oody, Disgruntled, Dod, Dort, Gee, Glout(s), Glower, Glum, Grouchy, Grouty, Grumps, Gumple-foisted, Huff, Hump, Jinker, Mope, Mump, Pet, Petulant, Pique, Pout, Snit, Spider, Strunt, Sullen

Sullen Black, Brooding, Dorty, Dour, Farouche, Glum(pish), Grim, Grumpy, Moody, Mumpish, Peevish, Stunkard, Sulky, Sumph, Surly

Sully Assoil, Bedye, Besmirch, Blot, Deface, Defile, Glaur(y), Smear, Smirch, Soil(ure), Tarnish, Tar-wash

Sultry Houri, Humid, Sexy, Smouldering, Steamy, Tropical

Sum(s), Sum up Add(end), Aggregate, All (told), Amount, Bomb, Encapsulate,

Foot, Logical, Lump, Number, Perorate, →**QUANTITY**, Re-cap, Refund, Remittance, Reversion, Slump, Solidum, Total, Vector

Summarize, Summary Abridge, Abstract, Aperçu, Bird's eye, Breviate, Brief, Coda, Compendium, Condense, Conspectus, Digest, Docket, Epanodos, Epitome, Gist, Instant, Minute, Offhand, Outline, Overview, Pirlicue, Précis, Purlicue, Recap(itulate), Resume, Résumé, Round-up, Rundown, Short (shrift), Sitrep, Syllabus, Synopsis, Tabloid, Tabulate, Tabulation, Wrap-up

Summer(time) Aestival, August, BST, Computer, Estival, Heyday, Indian, Lintel, Luke, Prime, St Luke's, St Martin's, Season, Solstice, Totter

Summit Acme, Acro-, Apex, Brow, Climax, Conference, →**CREST**, Crown, Eminence, Height, Hillcrest, Jole, Mont Blanc, Peak, Pike, Pinnacle, Spire, Vertex, Vertical, Yalta

Summon(s) Accite, Arraign, Arrière-ban, Azan, Beck(on), Bleep, Call, Call in, Cist, Cital, Citation, Command, Convene, Drum, Evoke, Garnishment, Gong, Hail, Invocation, Muster, Order, Originating, Page, Post, Preconise, Rechate, Recheat, Reveille, Signal, Sist, Subpoena, Ticket, Warn, Warrant, What-ho, Whoop, Writ

Sun(-god), Sunlight, Sunny, Sunshine Amen-Ra, Amon-Ra, Apollo, Aten, Bright, Cheer, Day(star), Dry, Earthshine, Eye of the day, Glory, Heater, Helio(s), Helius, Horus, Mean, Midnight, Mock, New Mexico, Nova, Orb, Paper, Parhelion, Phoebean, Photosphere, Ra, Radiant, Rays, Re, Rising, Shamash, Sol(ar), Soleil, Sonne, Surya, Svastika, Swastika, Tabloid, Tan, Titan, UV

Sunblock Parasol

Sunder Divide, Divorce, Part, Separate, Sever, Split

▶**Sun-god** *see* SUN(-GOD)

▶**Sunken** *see* SINK(ING)

Sunshade Awning, Bongrace, Canopy, Parasol, Umbrella

Sup Dine, Eat, Feast, Sample, Sip, Swallow

Super A1, Actor, Arch, Extra, Fab(ulous), Great, Grouse, Ideal, Lulu, Paramount, Superb, Terrific, Tip-top, Top-notch, Tops, Walker-on, Wizard

Superb A1, Fine, Gorgeous, Grand, Majestic, Splendid, Top-notch

Supercilious Aloof, Arrogant, Bashaw, Cavalier, Haughty, Lordly, Snide, Sniffy, Snooty, Snotty, Snouty, Superior, Withering

Supercontinent Pangaea

Superficial Cosmetic, Cursenary, Cursory, Exterior, Facile, Glib, Outside, Outward, Overlying, Perfunctory, Shallow, Sketchy, Skindeep, Smattering, Veneer

▷**Superficial(ly)** *may indicate* a word outside another

Superfluous, Superfluity De trop, Extra, Lake, Mountain, Needless, Otiose, Redundant, Spare, Unnecessary

Superhuman Bionic, Herculean, Heroic, Supernatural

Superintend(ent) Boss, Curator, Director, Foreman, Guide, Janitor, Oversee(r), Preside, Provost, Sewer, Surveillant, Warden, Zanjero

Superior(ity) Abbess, Abbot, Abeigh, Above, Advantage, Ahead, Aloof, Ascendant, Atop, Better, Brahmin, Choice, Condescending, Custos, De luxe, Dinger, Elite, Eminent, Excellent, Exceptional, Feuar, Finer, Forinsec, Gree, Herrenvolk, High-class, High-grade, Jethro, Lake, Liege, Master race, Mastery, Morgue, Mother, Nob, Outstanding, Over, Overlord, Paramount, Pooh-Bah, Posh, Predominance, Premium, Prestige, Pretentious, Prevalent, Prior, Smug, Snooty, Speciesism, Superordinate, Supremacy, Swell, Top(-loftical), Transcendent(al), U, Udal, Upmarket, Upper(most), Upper crust, Uppish, Upstage

Superlative Best, Exaggerated, Peerless, Supreme, Utmost

Supernatural Divine, Eerie, Endemon, Fay, Fey, Fie, Fly, Gothic, Mana, Manito(u), Paranormal, Selky, Sharp, Siddhi, Tokoloshe, Unearthly, Wargod

Supernumerary Additional, Corollary, Extra, Mute, Orra

Supersede Replace, Stellenbosch, Supplant

Supervise(d), Supervision, Supervisor Administer, Chaperone, Check, Direct, Engineer, Foreman, Gaffer, Grieve, Handle, Honcho, Invigilate, Key grip, Manager,

Monitor, Officiate, Organise, Overman, Oversee(r), Probation, Proctor, Regulate, Seneschal, Shopwalker, Steward, Symposiarch, Targe, Tool pusher, Under, Walla(h)

Supper Bar, Burns, Dinner, →**DRINK(ER)**, Fork, Hawkey, Hockey, Horkey, Last, Meal, Nagmaal, Repast, Soirée

Supplant Displace, Exchange, Overthrow, Pre-empt, Replace, Substitute, Supersede

Supple Compliant, Leish, Limber, Lissom(e), Loose, Loose-limbed, Lythe, Pliable, Sinuous, Souple, Wan(d)le, Wannel, Whippy

Supplement(ary), Supplementing Addend(um), Addition, Adjunct, And, Annex(e), Appendix, As well as, Auxiliary, Bolt-on, Colour, Eche, Eik, Eke, Extra, Glucosamine, Inset, Paralipomena, Postscript, Practicum, PS, Relay, Ripienist, Ripieno, Rutin, Sports, TES, Weighting

Supply, Supplies, Supplier Accommodate, Advance, Afford, Amount, Cache, Cater, Commissariat, Contribute, Crop, Deal, Endue, Equip, Excess, Exempt, Feed, Fill, Find, Fit, Foison, Fund, Furnish, Give, Grist, Grubstake, Heel, Holp(en), Indew, Indue, Issue, Lay on, Lend, Lithely, Mains, Matériel, Pipeline, Plenish, Ply, →**PROVIDE**, Provision, Purvey, Push, RASC, Replenishment, Reservoir, Resource, Retailer, Serve, Source, Stake, Stock, →**STORE**, Viands, Vintner, Water, Widow's cruse, Yield

Support(er), Supporting Abet, Adherent, Advocate, Aegis, Affirm, Aficionado, Aftercare, Aid, Aide, Ally, Ancillary, Andiron, Anta, Arch, Arm, Assistant, Athletic, Axle, Back(bone), Back-up, Baluster, Banister, Bankroll, Barrack, Barre, Base, Basis, Batten, Beam, Bear, Befriend, Behind, Belt, Benefactor, Bier, Bolster, Boom, Bra, Brace, Bracket, Brassiere, Breadwinner, Bridge, Buttress, Carlist, Chair, Champion, Cherish, Circumstantiate, Clientele, Clipboard, Colonnade, Column, Confirm, Console, Cornerstone, Countenance, Cradle, Cripple, Cross-beam, Cruck, Crutch, C(ee)-spring, Dado, Doula, Easel, Encourage, Endorse, Endoss, Endow, Engager, Enlist, Enthusiast, Espouse, Family, Fan, Favour, Fid, Finance, Flying buttress, Fly-rail, Footrest, Footstool, For, Friend, Gamb, Gantry, Garter, Girder, Groundswell, Handrail, Hanger, Headrest, Help, Henchman, Hold with, Home help, I-beam, Impost, Income, Indorse, Jack, Jackstay, Jockstrap, Joist, Keep, Kingpost, Knee, Knife rest, Lath, Learning, Lectern, Leg, Lifebelt, Lifebuoy, Lobby, Loyalist, Mainbrace, Mainstay, Maintain, Makefast, Mill-rind, Miserere, Misericord(e), Moral, Mount, Neck, -nik, Nourish, Pack, Pack-frame, Packstaff, Partisan, Partners, Patronage, Pedestal, Peronist, Phalanx, Pier, Pile(-cap), Pillar, Pin, Plinth, Poppet, Post, Potent, Price, Prop, Proponent, PTA, Pull-for, Puncheon, Pylon, Raft, Rally round, Rebato, Regular, Reinforce, Relieve, Respond, Rest, Rind, Rod, Root, Royalist, Samaritan, Sanction, Sarking, Sawhorse, Scaffolding, Second, Shoetree, Shore, Skeg, Skeleton, Skid, Sleeper, Sling, Socle, Solidarity, Spectator, Splat, Splint, Sponson, Sponsor, Sprag, Spud, Squinch, Staddle, Staddlestone, Staff, Staging, Stake, Stalwart, Stanchion, Stand(-by), Stay, Steady, Step, Stick, Stirrup, Stool, Stringer, Strut, Stull, Subscribe, Subsidy, Succour, Summer, Suspender, Sustain, Sustentacular, Sustentaculum, Sustentation, Tartan army, Technical, Tee, Tendril, Third, Tie, Tige, Torsel, Trestle, Tripod, Trivet, Truss, Tumpline, Underlay, Underpin, Understand, Uphold, Upkeep, Verify, Viva, Walker, Waterwings, Welfare, Well-wisher, Yorkist, Zealot

Suppose(d), Supposition An, Assume, Believe, Conjecture, Daresay, Expect, Guess, Hypothetical, Idea, If, Imagine, Imply, Infer, Opine, Presume, Putative, Sepad, Theory, What if

Suppository Pessary

Suppress(ion), Suppressed Abolish, Adaw, Burke, Cancel, Censor, Check, Clampdown, Conditioned, Crackdown, Crush, Ecthlipsis, Elide, Elision, Epistasis, Gag, Gleichschaltung, Hide, Mob(b)le, Quash, Quell, Quench, Restrain, Silence, Sit on, Smother, Squash, Squelch, Stifle, Strangle, Submerge, Subreption, Under

Supreme, Supremacy, Supremo Baaskap, Best, Caudillo, Consummate, Dominant, Kronos, Leader, Napoleon, Overlord, Paramount, Peerless, Pre-eminent, Regnant, Sovereign, Sublime, Sudder, Top, Utmost

Sure(ly) Assured, Ay, Bound, Cert(ain), Certes, Confident, Definite, Doubtless, Firm,

Indeed, Know, Pardi(e), Pardy, Perdie, Positive, Poz, Safe, Secure, Shoo-in, Sicker, Syker, Uh-huh, Unerring, Yeah, Yes

Surety Bail, Guarantee, Mainprise, Security, Sponsional

Surface Aerofoil, Appear, Area, Arise, Astroturf®, Brane, Camber, Carpet, Caustic, Control, Crust, Cutis, Day, Dermal, Dermis, Emerge, Epigene, Exterior, External, Face, Facet, Finish, Flock, Interface, Linish, Macadam, Meniscus, Nanograss, Notaeum, Out, Outcrop, Outward, Overglaze, Paintwork, Patina, Pave, Plane, Reveal, Rise, Salband, Scarfskin, Side, Skim, Skin, Soffit, Spandrel, Superficial, Superficies, Tarmac®, Tar-seal, Texture, Top, Topping, Toroid, Veneer, Wearing course, Worktop

Surfeit(ed) Blasé, Cloy, Excess, Glut, Overcloy, Plethora, Satiate, Stall, Staw

Surge Billow, Boom, Drive, Gush, Onrush, Seethe, Sway, Swell, Wind

Surgeon Abernethy, Barber, BCh, BS, CHB, CM, Doctor, DS, Dupuytren, Hunter, Lister, Medic, Operator, Orthopod, Plastic, Sawbones, Tang, Vet(erinary)

Surgery Anaplasty, Bypass, Cordotomy, Cosmetic, Facelift, Hobday, Keyhole, Knife, Laparotomy, Laser, LASIK, Mammoplasty, Medicine, Nip and tuck, Nose job, Op, Open-heart, Orthop(a)edics, Osteoplasty, Plastic, Prosthetics, Spare-part, Stereotaxis, Thoracoplasty, Tuboplasty, Zolatrics

Surly Bluff, Cantankerous, Chough, Chuffy, Churl(ish), Crusty, Cynic, Glum, Gruff, Grum, Grumpy, Rough, Snarling, Sullen, Truculent

Surpass(ing) Bang, Beat, Best, Cap, Ding, Eclipse, Efface, Exceed, Excel, Frabjous, Outdo, Outgo, Outgun, Out-Herod, Outman, Outshine, Outstrip, Overshadow, Overtop, Transcend, Trump

Surplus De trop, Excess, Extra, Glut, Lake, Mountain, Offcut, Out-over, Over, Overabundance, Overcome, Remainder, Residue, Rest, Spare, Superplus, Surfeit

Surprise(d), Surprising Ag, Alert, Amaze, Ambush, Astonish, Aykhona wena, Bewilder, Blimey, Bombshell, By Jove, Caramba, Catch, Confound, Coo, Cor, Crikey, Criminé, Cripes, Crumbs, Dear, Eye-opener, Gadso, Gee, Geewhiz, Gemini, Gobsmacked, Godsend, Golly, Good-lack, Gorblimey, Gordon Bennett, Gosh, Great Scott, Ha, Hah, Hallo, Heavens, Hech, Heck, Heh, Hello, Hey, Hit for six, Ho, Holy cow, Hullo, Jeepers, Jeepers creepers, Jeez(e), Jinne, Jirre, Law, Lawks, Lor, Lordy, Lumme, Lummy, Man alive, Marry, Musha, My, Nooit, Och, Odso, Omigod, Oops, Open-mouthed, Overtake, Phew, Pop-eyed, Really, Sheesh, Shock, Singular, Sjoe, Spot, Stagger, Startle, Strewth, Stun, Sudden, Treat, Turn-up, Uh, Whew, Whoops, Whoops-a-daisy, Wide-eyed, Wonderment, Wow, Wrongfoot, Yikes, Yipes, Yow, Zart, Zowie

Surrender Capitulate, Cave-in, Cessio honorum, Cession, Enfeoff, Extradite, Fall, Forego, Forfeit, Handover, Hulled, Recreant, Release, Relinquish, Roll over, Strike, Submit, Succumb, Waive, →**YIELD**, Yorktown

Surround(ed), Surrounding(s) Ambient, Amid, Architrave, Background, Bathe, Bego, Beset, Bundwall, Cinct, Circumvallate, Circumvent, Compass, Doughnutting, Ecology, Embail, Encase, →**ENCIRCLE**, Enclave, Enclose, Encompass, Enfold, Entomb, Environ, Enwrap, Fence, Gherao, Gird, Girt, Hedge, Impale, Inorb, Invest, Mid, Orb, Orle, Outflank, Outside, Perimeter, Setting, Wall

Surveillance, Survey(ing), Surveyor Behold, Browse, Cadastre, Case, Census, Chartered, Conspectus, Domesday, Doomwatch, Espial, Examination, Eye, Geodesy, Geological, Groma, Look-see, Map, Once-over, Ordnance, Overeye, Poll, Prospect, Recce, Reconnaissance, Regard, Review, Rodman, Scan, Scrutiny, Staffman, Stakeout, Straw poll, Supervision, Terrier, Theodolite, Triangulate, Vigil, Watch

Survival, Survive, Surviving, Survivor Castaway, Cope, Die hard, Endure, Exist(ence), Extant, Finalist, Hibakusha, Last (out), Leftover, Live, Outlast, Outlive, Overlive, Persist, Pull through, Relic(t), Ride (out), Weather

Suspect, Suspicion, Suspicious Askance, Assume, Breath, Cagey, Dodgy, Doubt, Dubious, Equivocal, Fishy, Grain, Grey list, Guess, Hinky, Hint, Hunch, Hunky, Imagine, Inkling, Jalouse, Jealous, Leery, Misdeem, Misdoubt, Misgiving, Mistrust, Modicum, Notion, Paranoia, Queer, Scent, Sense, Smatch, Soupçon, Thought, Tinge, Whiff

▷ **Suspect, Suspicious** *may indicate* an anagram

Suspend(ed), Suspender, Suspense, Suspension Abate, Abeyance, Adjourn, Anti-shock, Cliffhanger, Colloid, Dangle, Defer, Delay, Dormant, Freeze,

Garter, Ground, → HANG, Hydraulic, Independent, Intermit, Lay off, Mist, Moratorium, Nailbiter, Pensile, Poise, Prorogue, Put on ice, Reprieve, Respite, Rub out, Rusticate, Sideline, Sol, Stand off, Stay, Swing, Tension, Tenterhooks, Truce, Underslung, Withhold

▷ **Suspended** *may indicate* 'ice' on ice at the end of a down light

Sustain(ed), Sustaining, Sustenance Abide, Aliment, Bear, Constant, Depend, Endure, Food, Keep, Last, Maintain, Nourish, Nutriment, Nutrition, Pedal, Prolong, Sostenuto, Succour, Support

Suture Coronal, Lambda, Pterion, Sagittal, Stitch

Swab Dossil, Dry, Mop, Pledget, Scour, Sponge, Squeegee, Stupe, Tampon, Tompon, Wipe

Swagger(er), Swaggering Birkie, Bluster, Boast, Brag, Bragadisme, Bravado, Bucko, Cock, Cockiness, Crow, Jaunty, Matamore, Nounce, Panache, Pra(u)nce, Roist, Roll, Rollick, Roul, Royster, Ruffle, Sashay, Side, Strive, Swagman, Swank, Swash(-buckler)

Swallow(able), Swallowing Absorb, Accept, Barn, Bird, Bolt, Bredit, Consume, Credit, Devour, Down(flow), Drink, Eat, Endue, Engulf, Esculent, Glug, Gobble, Gulch, Gulp, Incept, Ingest, Ingulf, Ingurgitate, Itys, Lap, Martin, Martlet, Neck, Progne, Quaff, Shift, Sister, Slug, Stomach, Swig, Take

Swamp(y) Bog, Bunyip, Cowal, Deluge, Dismal, Drown, Engulf, Everglade, Flood, Inundate, Lentic, Lerna, Lerne, Loblolly, Mar(i)sh, Morass, Muskeg, Overrun, Overwhelm, Pakihi, Paludal, Poles'ye, Pripet Marshes, Purgatory, Quagmire, Slash, Slough, Sudd, Vlei, Vly

▷ **Swap(ped)** *may indicate* an anagram

Swarm(ing) Abound, Alive, Bike, Bink, Byke, Cast, Clamber, Cloud, Crowd, Flood, Geminid, Host, Hotch, Hotter, Infest, Pullulate, Rife, Shin, Shoal, Teem, Throng

Sway(ing) Careen, Carry, Command, Diadrom, Domain, Dominion, Flap, Fluctuate, Govern, Hegemony, Influence, Lilt, Oscillate, Prevail, Reel, Reign, Rock, Roll, Rule, Sally, Shog, Shoogie, Shoogle, Swag, Swale, Swee, Swing(e), Teeter, Titter, Totter, Vacillate

Swear(ing), Swear word Attest, Avow, Billingsgate, Coprolalia, Curse, Cuss, Depose, Execrate, Jurant, Juratory, Oath, Objure, Pledge, Plight, Rail, Sessa, Tarnal, Tarnation, Verify, Vow

Sweat(ing), Sweaty Apocrine, Clammy, Dank, Diaphoresis, Eccrine, Egest, English, Excrete, Exude, Forswatt, Glow, Hidrosis, Lather, Muck, Ooze, Osmidrosis, Secretion, Slave, Stew, Sudament, Sudamina, Sudate, Suint, Swelter, Toil

Sweater Aran, Argyle, Circassian, Circassienne, Cowichan, Fair Isle, Gansey, Guernsey, Indian, Jersey, Polo, Pullover, Roll-neck, Siwash, Skinny-rib, Skivvy, Slip-on, Slop-pouch, Sloppy Joe, Turtleneck, Woolly

Sweep(er), Sweeping(s) Besom, Broad, Broom, Brush, Chimney, Chummy, Clean, Curve, Debris, Detritus, Expanse, Extensive, Generalisation, Lash, Lottery, Net, Oars, Pan, Phasing, Range, Scavenger, Scud, Sling, Snowball, Soop, Street, Stroke, Surge, Swathe, Sway, Vacuum, Waft, Well, Wide, Widespread

Sweet, Sweeten(er), Sweetmeat, Sweetness Afters, Baclava, Baklava, Bonus, Bribe, Bung, Cachou, Charity, Charming, Cherubic, Cloying, Confect(ion), Conserve, Crème, Cute, Douce(t), Drop, Dulcet, Dulcie, Dulcitude, Edulcorate, Flummery, Fool, Fragrant, Fresh, Glycerin, Goody, Honey(ed), Kiss, Lavender, Liqueur, Luscious, Melodious, Nectared, Nonpareil, Nothing, Pea, Pet, Pie, Pontefract cake, Pud(ding), Redolent, Seventeen, Sillabub, Sixteen, Soot(e), Sop, Sorbet, Spice, Split, Sucrose, Sugar, Sugary, Syllabub, Syrupy, Tart(let), Torte, Trifle, Twee, Uses, William, Winsome, Zabaglione

Sweetheart Amoret, Amour, Beau, Boyfriend, Darling, Dona(h), Dowsabel(l), Doxy, Dulcinea, Flame, Follower, Girlfriend, Honey(bunch), Honeybun, Jarta, Jo(e), Lass, Leman, Lover, Masher, Neaera, Peat, Romeo, Steady, Toots(y), True-love, Valentine, Yarta, Yarto

Sweet talk Taffy

Swell(ing) Adenomata, Ague-cake, Anasarca, Aneurysm, Apophysis, Bag, Balloon, Bellying, Berry, Billow, Blab, Blister, Bloat, Blow, Boil, Boll, Bolster, Botch, Braw, Bubo,

Bulb, Bulge, Bump, Bunion, Burgeon, Capellet, Cat, Chancre, Chilblain, Cratches, Cyst, Dandy, Diapason, Dilate, Dom, Don, Eger, Elephantiasis, Encanthis, Enhance, Entasis, Epulis, Excellent, Farcy-bud, Frog, Gall, Gathering, Gent, Goiter, Goitre, Gout, Grandee, Ground, Heave, Heighten, H(a)ematoma, Hove, Hydrocele, Increase, Inflate, Intumesce, Kibe, L, Lampas(se), Lampers, Lump, Macaroni, Milk leg, Mouse, Nodule, Odontoma, Oedema, OK, Onco-, Ox-warble, Parotitis, Plim, Plump, Protrude, Proud, Pulvinus, Rise, Roil, Scirrhus, Scleriasis, Sea, Strout, Struma, Stye, Stylopodium, Sudamina, Surge, Teratoma, Toff, Tuber(cle), Tumefaction, Tumour, Tympanites, Tympany, Upsurge, Varicose, Venter, Vesicle, Vulvitis, Vulvovaginitis, Warble, Wen, Whelk, Windgall, Xanthoma
▷ **Swelling** *may indicate* a word reversed
Swerve, Swerving Bias, Broach, Careen, Deflect, Deviate, Lean, Sheer, Shy, Stray, Sway, Swing, Veer, Warp, Wheel
Swift(ly) Apace, Bird, Dean, Dromond, Fleet, Flock, Hasty, Martlet, Newt, Nimble, Presto, Prompt, Quick, → **RAPID**, Slick, Spanking, Velocipede, Wight
▷ **Swilling** *may indicate* an anagram
▷ **Swim** *may indicate* an anagram
Swim(ming) Bathe, Bogey, Bogie, Crawl, Dip, Float, Freestyle, Naiant, Natant, Natatorial, Paddle, Reel, Run, Skinny-dip, Soom, Synchro(nized), Trudgen, Whim, Whirl
▷ **Swimmer** *may indicate* a fish
Swindle(r) Beat, Bunco, Cajole, Champerty, → **CHEAT**, Chiz(z), Con, Concoct, Defraud, Diddle, Do, Escroc, Fake, Fiddle, Finagle, Fleece, Fraud, Gazump, Gip, Gold brick, Graft, Grifter, Gyp, Hocus, Hustler, Leg, Leger, Mulct, Nobble, Peter Funk, Plant, Ponzi scheme, Racket, Ramp, Rig, Rogue, Scam, Sell, Shaft, Shakedown, Shark, Sharper, Shicer, Shyster, Skin, Slicker, Sting, Stitch-up, Suck, Swiz(z), Take, Trick, Tweedle, Twist, Two-time
Swing(er), Swinging Colt, Dangle, Flail, Gate, Hang, Hep, Hip, Kip(p), Lilt, Metronome, Mod, Music, Oscillate, Pendulate, Pendulum, Reverse, Rock, Rope, Shog, Shoogie, Shuggy, Slew, Swale, Sway, Swee, Swerve, Swey, Swipe, Trapeze, Vibratile, Voop, Wave, Western, Wheel, Whirl, Yaw
▷ **Swirling** *may indicate* an anagram
Switch(ed), Switches, Switching Birch, Change, Churn, Convert, Crossbar, Cryotron, Dead man's handle, Dimmer, Dip, Dolly, Exchange, Gang, Hairpiece, Knife, Legerdemain, Master, Mercury, Mercury tilt, Message, Pear, Point, Relay, Replace, Retama, Rocker, Rod, Scutch, Thyristor, Time, Toggle, Tress, Trip, Tumbler, Twig, Wave, Zap
Switchback Rollercoaster
▷ **Switched** *may indicate* an anagram
Swivel Caster, Pivot, Root, Rotate, Spin, Terret, Territ, Torret, Turret, Wedein
Swollen Blown, Bollen, Bulbous, Full, Gourdy, Gouty, Incrassate, Nodose, Puffy, Tumid, Turgescent, Turgid, Varicose, Ventricose, Vesiculate
Swoon Blackout, Collapse, Dwa(l)m, Dwaum, Faint, Swarf, Swerf
Sword(-like), Swordplay Andrew Ferrara, Anelace, Angurvadel, Anlace, Arondight, Assegai, Balisarda, Balmunc, Balmung, Bilbo, Blade, Brand, Brandiron, Broad(sword), Brondyron, Cemitare, Claymore, Cold steel, Court, Curtal-ax, Curtana, Curtax, Cutlass, Damascene, Damocles, Dance, Dirk, Ensate, Ensiform, Epée, Espada, Estoc, Excalibur, Falchion, Faulchi(o)n, Foil, Gladius, Glaive, Glamdring, Gleave, Glorious, Hanger, Iai-do, Jacob's staff, Joyeuse, Katana, Kendo, Khanda, Kirpan, Kreese, Kris, Kukri, Machete, Morglay, Parang, Rapier, Reverso, Sabre, Samurai, Schiavone, Schläger, Scimitar, Semita(u)r, Shabble, Shamshir, Sharp, Sigh, Simi, Skene-dhu, Smallsword, Spadroon, Spirtle, Spit, Spurtle(blade), Steel, Toledo, Tulwar, Two-edged, Whinger, Whiniard, Whinyard, White-arm, Yatag(h)an
Sycophant(ic) Brown-nose, Claqueur, Crawler, Creeper, Fawner, Groveller, Hanger-on, Lickspittle, Parasite, Servile, Toad-eater, Toady, Yesman
Syllable(s) Acatalectic, Anacrusis, Aretinian, Om, Outride, Thesis, Tonic, Ultima
Syllabus Program(me), Prospectus, Résumé, Summary, Table, Timetable
Symbiotic Adnascent

Symbol(ic), Symbolism, Symbolist Allegory, Character, Charactery, Decadent, Del, Diesis, Iconography, Metaphor, Minus, Moral, Mystical, Nominal, Notation, Operator, Placeholder, Plus, Quantifier, Semicolon, Sex, Shadowy, Shamrock, Slur, Status, Syllabary, Synthetism, Type, Weather

Symmetric(al), Symmetry Balance, Bilateral, Digonal, Diphycercal, Even, Harmony, Isobilateral, Radial, Regular

Sympathetic, Sympathise(r), Sympathy Affinity, Approval, Commiserate, Compassion, Condole(nce), Condone, Congenial, Crypto, Dear-dear, Empathy, Fellow-traveller, Humane, Kind, Mediagenic, Par, Pathos, Pity, Rapport, Ruth, Side, Understanding, Vicarious, Well-disposed

Symphony Alpine, Antar, Babi Yar, Bear, Clock, Concert, Drum-roll, Echo, Eroica, Farewell, Feuer, Fifth, Haffner, Horn-signal, Hunt, Ilya Murometz, Jupiter, Laudon, London, Manfred, Matin, Midi, Miracle, Music, New World, Ninth, Opus, Oxford, Pastoral, Queen, Resurrection, Rhenish, Sinfonia, Surprise, Tragic, Unfinished

Symptom(s) Epiphenomenon, Feature, Indicia, Merycism, Mimesis, Prodrome, Semiotic, Sign, Syndrome, Token, Trait, Withdrawal

Synclinal Basin

Syncopated, Syncopation, Syncope Abridged, Breakbeat, Revamp, Zoppa, Zoppo

Syndrome Adams-Stokes, Alport's, Asperger's, Carpal tunnel, Cerebellar, Characteristic, China, Chinese restaurant, Chronic fatigue, Compartment, Couvade, Cri du chat, Crush, Cushing's, De Clerambault's, Down's, Economy-class, Empty nest, Erotomania, False memory, Fetal alcohol, Fragile X, Goldenhar's, Gorlin, Guillain-Barré, Gulf War, Hughes, Hutchinson-Gilford, Irritable-bowel, Jerusalem, Klinefelter's, Korsakoff's, Locked-in, Long QT, Marfan, ME, Menières, Metabolic, Munch(h)ausen's, Nonne's, Overuse, Parkinson's, Pattern, POS, Postviral, Prader-Willi, Premenstrual, Proteus, Reiter's, Rett's, Revolving door, Reye's, SADS, SARS, Savant, Sezary, Shaken baby, Sick building, SIDS, Sjogren's, Stevens-Johnson, Stockholm, Stokes-Adams, Sturge-Weber, Tall-poppy, Temperomandibular, TMJ, Total allergy, Tourette's, Toxic shock, Turner's, Wag the dog, Wernicke-Korsakoff, Williams, Wobbler, XYY

Synopsis Abstract, Blurb, Conspectus, Digest, Outline, Résumé, Schema, →**SUMMARY**

Synthetic Ersatz, Fake, False, Mock, Neoprene, Polyamide, Spencerian, Urea

Syringe(s) Douche, Flutes, Harpoon, Hypo, Needle, Reeds, Spray, Squirt, Wash

Syrup(y) Cassareep, Cassis, Coquito, Corn, Flattery, Glycerol, Goo, Grenadine, Linctus, Maple, Molasses, Orgeat, Rob, Starch, Sugar, Treacle, Viscous

System(s), Systematic ABO, Alpha, An mo, Apartheid, Auditory, BACS, Beam, Binary, Black, Bordereau, Braille, Brunonian, Carboniferous, Ceefax, Centauri, Circulatory, Closed loop, Code, Colloidal, Colonial, Compander, Complexus, Continental, Cosmos, Course, Crystal, Cybernetics, Decimal, Dewey (Decimal), Dianetics, Distributed, Dolby®, Early warning, Economy, Eocene, Establishment, Expert, Feng Shui, Feudal, Fixed, Folksonomy, Formal, Fourierism, Froebel, Front-end, Grading, Harvard, Haversian, Hexagonal, HLA, Holist, Honour, Hub and spoke, I Ching, Immune, Imperial, Imprest, Imputation, Induction loop, Inertial, ISA, Ism, Kalamazoo, Kanban, Life-support, Limbic, Lobby, Long wall, Loop, Lymphatic, Madras, Mercantile, Mereology, Merit, →**METHOD**, Metric, Midi, Minitel, MKSA, Movable, Muschelkalk, Natural, Navigational, Neat, Nervous, Network, Nicam, Notation, Number, Octal, Operating, Order, Organon, Orphism, Orrery, Panel, Periodic, Plenum, Points, Portal, Process, Public address, Purchase, Quota, Quote-driven, Raisonné, Regime, Regular, Reproductive, Respiratory, Root, Run-time, Scheme, Schmitt, Scientific, Selsyn, Servo, Sexual, SI, Sofar, Solar, Solmisation, Sonar, Sound, Spoils, Sprinkler, Squish lip, Stack(ing), Staff, Stakhanovism, Stand-alone, Star, STOL, Structure, Studio, Support, Sweating, Tactic, Talk-down, Tally, Ternary, Theory, Third-rail, Tommy, Totalitarianism, Touch, Truck, Turnkey, Tutorial, Two-party, Universe, Unix, Urogenital, Vestibular, VOIP, Warehousing, Water, Water vascular, Weapon, Windows

Tt

Tabernacle Niche
Table(-like) Altar, Board, Bradshaw, Breakfast, Calendar, Capstan, →**CHART**,
Coffee, Communion, Console, Corbel, Counter, Cricket, Decision, Desk, Diagram,
Dinner, Dissecting, Draw-leaf, Draw-top, Dressing, Drop-leaf, Drum, Experience,
Food, Gateleg, Gate-legged, Glacier, Graph, Green-cloth, High, Imposing, Index,
Key, Ladder, League, Life, Light, →**LIST**, Log, Lord's, Lowboy, Mahogany, Matrix,
Mensa(l), Mesa, Mortality, Multiplication, Occasional, Operating, Orientation,
Pembroke, Periodic, Piecrust, Pier, Plane, Plateau, Platen, Pool, Pythagoras,
Ready-reckoner, Reckoner, Refectory, Roll, Round, Sand, Schedule, Scheme, Slab,
Sofa, Spoon, Stall, Statistical, Stone, Suggest, Tariff, Tea, Te(a)poy, Throwing, Tide,
Times, Toilet, Toning, Top, Tray(mobile), Trestle, Trolley, Truth, Twelve, Washstand,
Water, Whirling, Wool, Workbench, Writing
Tablet Abacus, Album, Aspirin, Caplet, Cartouche, E, Eugebine, Medallion,
Opisthograph, Osculatory, Ostracon, Ostrakon, →**PAD**, →**PILL**, Plaque, Slate, Stele,
Stone, Tabula, Tombstone, Torah, Triglyph, Triptych, Troche, Trochisk, Ugarit, Wax
Taboo, Tabu Ban(ned), Bar, Blackball, Forbidden, No-no, Tapu
Tachograph Spy-in-the-cab
Tack(y) Bar, Baste, Beat, Boxhaul, Brass, Cinch, Clubhaul, Cobble, Gybe, Leg,
Martingale, Nail, Saddlery, Salt-horse, →**SEW**, Sprig, Stirrup, Tasteless, Veer,
White-seam, Yaw, Zigzag
Tackle Accost, Approach, Attempt, Beard, Bobstay, Burton, Cat, Chin, Claucht,
Claught, Clevis, Collar, Dead-eye, Garnet, Gear, Haliard, Halyard, Harness, Jury-rig,
Ledger, Nose, Rig, Rigging, Sack, Scrag, Spear, Stick, Undertake
Tact, Tactful Delicacy, Diplomacy, Diplomatic, Discreet, Discretion, Kidglove,
Politic, Savoir-faire
Tactic(s) Audible, Carrot and stick, Crossruff, Hardball, Manoeuvre, Masterstroke,
Plan, Ploy, Salami, Scare, Shock, Smear, →**STRATEGY**, Strong-arm
Tactless(ness) Blundering, Brash, Crass, Gaffe, Gauche, Indelicate, Indiscreet, Loud
mouth
Tail, Tailpiece, Tailboard All-flying, Amentum, →**APPENDAGE**, Bob, Brush,
Bun, Caudal, Coda, Colophon, Cue, Dock, Endgate, Fan, Fee, →**FOLLOW**, Fud,
Liripoop, Parson's nose, Point, Pole, Pope's nose, PS, Queue, Scut, Seat, Shirt, Stag,
Stern, Telson, →**TIP**, Train, Uropod, Women
▷ **Tailor** *may indicate* an anagram
Tailor(ed) Bespoke, Bushel, Cabbager, Couturier, Cutter, Darzi, Draper, Durzi,
Epicene, Feeble, Form, Nine, Outfitter, Pick-the-louse, Pricklouse, Sartor, Seamster,
Snip, Starveling, Style, Whipcat, Whipstitch
Taint(ed) Besmirch, Blemish, Fly-blown, Foughty, High, Infect, Leper, Off, Poison,
→**SPOIL**, Stain, Stale, Stigma, Trace, Unwholesome
Take(n), Take in, Taking(s), Take over, Takeover Absorb, →**ACCEPT**,
Adopt, Appropriate, Assume, Attract, Bag, Beg, Bewitch, Bite, Bone, Borrow, Bottle,
→**CAPTURE**, Catch, Charming, Claim, Cop, Coup (d'etat), Detract, Dishy, Eat,
Entr(y)ism, Epris, Exact, Expropriate, Film, Get, Grab, Greenmail, Handle, Haul,
Hent, House, Howe, Huff, Incept, Ingest, Leveraged buy out, Mess, Misappropriate,
Nationalise, Nick, Occupy, On, Pocket, Poison pill, Quote, R, Rec, Receipt, Receive,
Recipe, Reverse, Rob, Seise, Sequester, Ship, Smitten, Snaffle, Snatch, Sneak,
→**STEAL**, Stomach, Subsume, Swallow, Sweet, Swipe, Toll, Trump, Turnover, Usher,
Usurp, Wan, Winsome, Wrest

Take down, Take up Appropriate, Cap, Choose, Osmose, Shot, Snaffle, Unhook
▷ **Taken up** *may indicate reversed*
Tale(s) Aga-saga, Allegory, Anecdote, Blood, Cautionary, Conte, Decameron, Edda, Fable, Fabliau, Fairy, Fiction, Gag, Geste, Hadith, Iliad, Jataka, Jeremiad, Legend, Lie, Mabinogion, Maise, Märchen, Ma(i)ze, Narrative, Odyssey, Rede, Saga, Score, Sinbad, Spiel, → STORY, Tradition, Traveller's, Weird, Yarn
Talent(ed) Accomplishment, Aptitude, Beefcake, Bent, Budding, Dower, Endowment, Faculty, Flair, Genius, Gift, Idiot savant, Knack, Nous, Obol, Prodigy, Schtick, Strong point, Versatile, Virtuoso, Whiz-kid, W(h)iz(z)
Talk(ing), Talking point, Talker, Talks Address, Ana, Articulate, Babble, Blab, Blat, Blather, Blether-skate, Cant, Chalk, Chat, Chew the fat, Chinwag, Chirp, Commune, Confer, Converse, Coo, Cross, Descant, Dialog(ue), Diatribe, Dilate, Discourse, Diseur, Dissert, Double, Earbash, Earful, Expatiate, Express, Fast, Froth, Gab, Gabble, Gabnash, Gas, Gibber, Gossip, Guff, Harp, High-level, Hobnob, Hot air, Imparl, Jabber, Jargon, Jaw, Jazz, Lalage, Lalla, Lip, Mang, Maunder, Mince, Monologue, Nashgab, Natter, Noise, Palaver, Parlance, Parley, Patter, Pawaw, Pep, Pidgin, Pillow, Pitch, Potter, Powwow, Prate, Prattle, Presentation, Prose, Proximity, Ramble, Rap, Rigmarole, Rote, Sales, SALT, Shop, Slang(-whang), Small, Soliloquy, → SPEAK, Spiel, Spout, Straight, Sweet, Table, Tachylogia, Topic, Turkey, Twaddle, Twitter, Up(s), Utter, Vocal, Waffle, Wibble, Witter, Wrangle, Yabber, Yack, Yad(d)a-yad(d)a-yad(d)a, Yak, Yalta, Yammer, Yap, Yatter
Talkative Chatty, Expansive, Fluent, Gabby, Garrulous, Gash, Glib, Loquacious, Vocular, Voluble, Windbag
Tall Etiolated, Exaggerated, Far-fetched, Hie, High, Hye, Lanky, Lathy, Leggy, Lofty, Long, Order, Procerity, Randle-tree, Tangle, Taunt, Tower, Towery
Tally Accord, → AGREE, Census, Correspond, Count, Match, Nickstick, Notch, Record, → SCORE, Stick, Stock, Tab, Tag
Tame Amenage, Break, Docile, Domesticate, Mail, Mansuete, Meek, Mild, Safe, Snool, Subdue
Tamper(ing) Bishop, Cook, Doctor, Fake, Fiddle, Meddle, Medicate, Monkey, Nobble, Phreaking
Tan(ned), Tanned skin, Tanning Adust, Bablah, Babul, Bark, Basil, Beige, Bisque, Bronze, → BROWN, Catechu, Insolate, Lambast, Leather, Neb-neb, Paste, Pipi, Puer, Pure, Spank, Sun, Tenné, Umber, Valonea, Val(l)onia, Ybet
Tangle Alga, Badderlock, Burble, Driftweed, Dulse, Embroil, Enmesh, Entwine, Fank, Fankle, Heap, Hole, Implication, Ket, → KNOT, Labyrinth, Laminaria, Lutin, Mat, Mess, Mix, Nest, Oarweed, Ore, Perplex, Pleach, Raffle, Sea-girdle, Seaweed, Skean, Skein, Snarl, Taigle, Taut(it), Tawt, Thicket, Tousle, Varec
▷ **Tangled** *may indicate an anagram*
Tango Dance, T
Tank(ed) Abrams, Alligator, Amphibian, Aquarium, Back boiler, Belly, Bosh, Casspir, Centurion, Cesspool, Challenger, Chieftain, Cistern, Crusader, Dracone, Drop, Drunk, Fail, Feedhead, Float, Flotation, Fuel, Gasholder, Gasometer, Header, Keir, Kier, Panzer, Pod, Quiescent, → RESERVOIR, Ripple, Sedimentation, Septic, Sherman, Shield pond, Sponson, Sump, Surge, Think, Tiger, Vat, Venter, Ventral, Vivarium
Tantalise Entice, Tease, Tempt, Torture
Tantrum Paddy, Pet, Rage, Scene, Snit, Tirrivee, Tirrivie, Wobbly
Tap(ping), Taps Accolade, Ague, Blip, Bob, Broach, Bug, Cock, Dip into, Drum, Eavesdrop, Faucet, Fever, Fillip, Flick, Hack, H and C, Listen, Mixer, Paracentesis, Pat, Patter, Percuss, Petcock, → RAP, Screw, Spigot, Stopcock, Tack, Tat, Tit
Tape Chrome, DAT, Demo, → DRINK, Duct, Ferret, Finish, Friction, Gaffer, Grip, Idiot, Incle, Inkle, Insulating, Magnetic, Masking, Measure, Metal, Narrowcast, Paper, Passe-partout, Perforated, Punched, Record, Red, Reel to reel, Scotch, Sellotape®, Shape, Stay, Sticky, Ticker, Tit, Video, Welding
Taper(ed), Tapering Candle, Diminish, Fastigiate, Featheredge, Flagelliform, Fusiform, Lanceolate, Narrow, Nose, Subulate, Tail

Tapestry Alentous, Arras(ene), Bayeux, Bergamot, Crewel-work, Dosser, Gobelin, Hanging, Mural, Oudenarde, Sewing, Tapet, Weaving

Target Admass, →AIM, Attainment, Blank, Butt, Clay, Clout, Cockshy, Dart, Drogue, End, Ettle, Hit, Home, Hub, Inner, Magpie, Mark, Mark-white, Motty, Nick, →OBJECT, Object ball, Outer, Peg, Pelta, Pin, Popinjay, Prey, Prick, Quintain, Sitter, Sitting (duck), Tee, Victim, Wand, Zero in, Zero on

Tarry Bide, Dally, Leng, →LINGER, Stay, Sticky

Tartar Argal, Argol, Beeswing, Crust, Hell, Plaque, Rough, Scale, Tam(b)erlane, Zenocrate

Tarzan Greystoke

Task Assignment, Aufgabe, Clat, Duty, Emprise, Errand, Exercise, Fag, Imposition, Legwork, Mission, Onus, Ordeal, Stint, Thankless, Vulgus

Taste(ful), Taster, Tasty Acquired, Aesthetic, Appetite, Assay, Degust, Delibate, Delicious, Discrimination, →EAT, Elegant, Excerpt, Fad, Fashion, Flavour, Form, Gout, Gust, Gustatory, Hint, Lekker, Lick, Liking, Palate, Penchant, Pica, Pree, Refinement, Relish, →SAMPLE, Sapor, Sar, Savour, Seemly, Sensation, S(c)hme(c)k, Sip, Smack, Smatch, Smattering, Snack, Soupçon, Stomach, Succulent, Tang, Titbit, Toothsome, →TRY, Umami, Vertu, Virtu, Waft, Wine

Tasteless Appal, Fade, Flat, Indelicate, Insipid, Insulse, Kitsch, Stale, Vapid, Vulgar, Watery, Wearish, Wersh

Tattle(r) Blab, Chatter, →GOSSIP, Prate, Rumour, Sneak, Snitch, Totanus, Willet

Taunt Dig, Fling, Gibe, Gird, →JEER, Jest, Rag, Ridicule, Twight, Twit

Tavern Bar, Bodega, Bousing-ken, Bush, Fonda, →INN, Kiddleywink, Kneipe, Mermaid, Mitre, Mughouse, Night-house, Pothouse, Shebeen, Taphouse

Tawdry Brash, Catchpenny, →CHEAP, Flashy, Gaudy, Gingerbread, Sleazy, Tatty

Tax(ation), Taxing ACT, Agist, Aid, Alms-fee, Arduous, Assess, Capital gains, Capitation, Carbon, Cense, Cess, →CHARGE, Corporation, Council, CRT, Custom, Danegeld, Death duty, Deferred, Direct, Duty, Energy, EPT, Escot, Escuage, Eurotax, Exact, Excise, Exercise, EZT, Fat, Geld, Gelt, Gift, Green, Head, Head money, Hearth money, Hidden, Impose, Imposition, Impost, Impute, Indirect, Inheritance, IR, Keelage, Land, Levy, Lot, Negative, Octroi, Operose, Overtask, Overwork, PAYE, Poll, Poundage, Precept, Primage, Property, Proportional, PT, Punish, Purchase, Rate, Regressive, Road, Sales, Scat(t), Scot (and lot), Scutage, Sess, SET, Ship money, Sin, Single, Skat, Stealth, Stent, Stretch, Stumpage, Super, Tariff, Tartan, Task, Teind, Tithe, Tobin, Toilsome, Toll, Tonnage, Tribute, Try, Turnover, Unitary, Value-added, VAT, Wattle, Wealth, Weary, White rent, Windfall, Window, Withholding

Tax-collector, Taxman Amildar, Cheater, Exciseman, Farmer, Gabeller, Ghostbuster, Inspector, IR(S), Publican, Stento(u)r, Tidesman, Tithe-proctor, Tollman, Undertaker, Vatman, Zemindar

Taxiway Peritrack

Tea Afternoon, Assam, Beef, Black, Bohea, Brew, Brew-up, Brick, Bubble, Bush, Cambric, Camomile, Caper, Ceylon, Cha, Chai, Chamomile, Chanoyu, Char, China, Chirping-cup, Congo(u), Cream, Cuppa, Darjeeling, Earl Grey, Grass, Green, Gunfire, Gunpowder, Herb(al), High, Hyson, Ice(d), Indian, Jasmine, K(h)at, Kitchen, Labrador, Lapsang, Lapsang Souchong, Leaves, Ledum, Lemon, Malt, Manuka, Marijuana, Maté, Mexican, Mint, Morning, Mountain, New Jersey, Oolong, Orange pekoe, Oulong, Paraguay, Pekoe, Post and rail, Pot, Qat, Red-root, Rooibos, Rosie Lee, Russian, Sage, Senna, Souchong, Stroupach, Stroupan, Switchel, Tay, Thea, Theophylline, Tousy, Twankay, White, Yerba (de Maté)

Teach(er), Teaching (material), Teachings Adjoint, Advisory, Agrege, Anthroposophy, Apostle, Aristotle, AUT, Beale, BEd, Buss, Chalk and talk, →COACH, Con(ne), Didactic, Doctrine, Dogma, Dominie, Dressage, Edify, →EDUCATE, Educationalist, Edutainment, Explain, Faculty, Froebel, Gospel, Governess, Guru, Head, Inculcate, Indoctrinate, Inform, Instil, Instruct, Ism, Kindergart(e)ner, Kumon (Method), Lair, Lear(e), Lecturer, Leir, Lere, Maam, Magister, Marker, Marm, Master, Mentor, Message, Miss, Mistress, Molla(h), Monitor, Mufti, Mullah, Munshi,

Mwalimu, Nuffield, NUT, PAT, Pedagogue, Pedant, Peripetatic, Phonic method, Posture-master, Preceptor, Pr(a)efect, Proctor, Prof, Prog, PT, Pupil, Rabbetzin, Rabbi, Rav, Rebbe, Remedial, Rhetor, Scholastic, Schoolie, Schoolman, Scribe, Show, Sir, Socrates, Sophist, Specialist, Staff, Stinks, Substitute, Sunna, Supply, Swami, Tantra, Team, Tonic sol-fa, Train(er), Tuition, Tutelage, Tutor, Tutress, Tutrix, Usher

Teal Spring

Team Argyll, Colts, Crew, Dream, Écurie, Eleven, Équipe, Fifteen, Hearts, Nine, Outfit, Oxen, Panel, Possibles, Proto, Relay, Scrub, Set, →SIDE, Span, Spurs, Squad, Squadron, Staff, Syndicate, Troupe, Turnout, Unicorn, Unit, United, XI

Tear(s), Tearable, Tearful, Tearing Beano, Claw, Crocodile, Drop(let), Eye-drop, Eye-water, Greeting, Hurry, Lacerate, Lachrymose, Laniary, Mammock, Pelt, Ranch, Rash, Reave, Rheum, Rip, Rive, Rume, Screed, Shred, Snag, Split, Spree, Tire, Vale, Wet, Worry, Wrench, Wrest

Tease, Teaser, Teasing Arch, Backcomb, Badinage, Bait, Ballyrag, Banter, Chap, Chiack, Chip, Cod, Coquet, Enigma, Grig, Guy, Hank, Imp, Ironic, Itch, Josh, Kemb, Kid, Mag, Nark, Persiflage, →RAG, Raillery, Rally, Razz, Rib, Rip on, Rot, Strip, →TANTALISE, Torment(or), Touse, Touze, Towse, Towze, Twit

Teat Dug, Dummy, Mamilla, Mastoid, Nipple, Pap, Soother, Tit

Technical, Technician, Technique Adept, Alexander, Artisan, Brushwork, Campimetry, College, Cusum, Delphi, Execution, Foley artist, Footsteps editor, Harmolodics, Honey-trap, Junior, Kiwi, Know-how, Layback, Manner, Metamorphic, →METHOD, Operative, Phasing, Pixil(l)ation, Reflectography, Salami, Sandwich, Science, Senior, Serial, Split-screen, Stop-motion, Toe and heel, Touch, Western blotting, Work around

Tedium, Tedious Boring, Chore, Deadly, Drag, Dreariness, Dreich, Dull, Ennui, Foozle, Heaviness, Ho-hum, Langueur, Long, Longspun, Monotony, Operose, Prosy, Soul-destroying, Tiresome, →TIRING, Wearisome, Yawn

Teem(ing) Abound, Bustling, Empty, Great, Heaving, Pullulate, Swarm

Teenager Adolescent, Bobbysoxer, Junior, Juvenile, Minor, Mod, Rocker, Sharpie

▶ **Teeth** see TOOTH(ED)

Teetotal(ler) Abdar, Abstainer, Blue Ribbon, Nephalist, Rechabite, Sober, Temperate, TT, Water-drinker, Wowser

Telegram, Telegraph Bush, Cable, Ems, Facsimile, Fax, Grapevine, Greetings, Marconi, Message, Moccasin, Overseas, Quadruplex, Radiogram, Telautograph®, Telex, Wire

Telephone Ameche, ATLAS, Bell, Blackberry, Blower, BT, Call, Cellphone, Centrex, Cordless, Detectophone, Dial, Freephone®, GRACE, Handset, Horn, Hotline, Intercom, Line, Mercury, Noki, Patchboard, Payphone, Pdq, Ring, Snitch line, Speakerphone, STD, Telebridge, Tie line, Touch-tone, Utility, Vodafone®, Wire

Telescope Altazimuth, Astronomical, Binocle, Cassegrain(ian), Collimator, Comet finder, Coronagraph, Coronograph, Coudé, Electron, Equatorial, Finder, Galilean, Gemini, Glass, Gregorian, Heliometer, Hubble, Interferometer, Intussuscept, Meniscus, Newtonian, Night-glass, Optical, Palomar, Perspective, Prospect(ive)-glass, Radio, Reading, Reflecting, Reflector, Refractor, Schmidt, Shorten, Sniperscope, Snooperscope, Speculum, Spyglass, Stadia, Terrestrial, Tube, X-ray, Zenith

Television, Telly Appointment, Box, Breakfast, Closed-circuit, Confessional, Digibox®, Digital, Diorama, Docu-soap, Flatscreen, Goggle box, Iconoscope, Interactive, ITV, MAC, Narrowcast, PAL, RTE, Set, Small screen, Tube, →TV, Video

Tell(ing), Teller, Telltale Acquaint, Announce, Apprise, Beads, Blab, Cashier, Clipe, Clype, Confess, Direct, →DISCLOSE, Divulge, Effective, Fess, Give, Grass, Impart, Influential, Inform(er), →NARRATE, Noise, Nose, Notify, Number, Rat, Recite, Recount, Relate, Report, Retail, Rumour, Scunge, Sneak, Snitch, Spin, Teach, Unbosom, William

Temper, Temperate Abstinent, Allay, Alloy, Anneal, Assuage, Attune, Balmy, Bate, Bile, Blood, Calm, Cantankerous, Choler, Continent, Dander, Delay, Ease, Fireworks, Flaky, Inure, Irish, Leaven, →MILD, Mitigate, Moderate, Modify, →MOOD, Neal,

Paddy, Pet, Rage, Season, Sober, Soften, Spitfire, Spleen, Strop, Tantrum, Techy, Teen, Teetotal, Tetchy, Tiff, Tone, Trim, Tune, Wax

Temperament(al) Bent, Blood, Choleric, Crasis, Cyclothymia, Disposition, Equal, Just, Kidney, Mean-tone, Melancholy, Mettle, Moody, →**NATURE**, Neel, Over-sensitive, Phlegmatic, Prima donna, Sanguine, Unstable, Up and down, Viscerotonia

Temperature Absolute, Black body, Celsius, Centigrade, Chambré, Core, Curie, Eutectic, Fahrenheit, Fever, Flashpoint, Heat, Heterothermal, Hyperthermia, Ignition, Kelvin, Melting, Néel, Permissive, Regulo, Room, Supercritical, T, Transition, Weed, Weid

Template Stencil

Temple, Temple gate Abu Simbel, Abydos, Capitol, Chapel, Church, Delphi, Delubrum, Ephesus, Erechtheum, Erechthion, Fane, Gurdwara, Heroon, Inner, Josshouse, Masjid, Middle, Mosque, Museum, Naos, Pagod(a), Pantheon, Parthenon, Sacellum, Serapeum, →**SHRINE**, Shul(n), Teocalli, Teopan, Torii, Vihara, Wat

Temporal Petrosal, Petrous

Temporary Acting, Caretaker, Casual, Cutcha, Ephemeral, Fleeting, Hobjob, Impermanent, Interim, Jury-rigged, Kutcha, Lash-up, Locum, Makeshift, Pro tem, Provisional, Quick-fix, Short-term, Stopgap, Temp, Transient, Transitional

Tempt(ation), Tempting, Tempter, Temptress Allure, Apple, Bait, Beguile, Beset, Dalilah, Dangle, Decoy, Delilah, →**ENTICE**, Eve, Femme fatale, Groundbait, Impulse, Lure, Mephistopheles, Peccable, Providence, Satan, Seduce, Serpent, Sexy, Siren, Snare, Tantalise, Test, Tice, Trial

Ten Commandments, Decad, Iota, Long, Tera-, Tribes, X

Tenacious, Tenacity Clayey, Determined, Dogged, Fast, Guts, Hold, Intransigent, Persevering, Persistent, Resolute, Retentive, Sticky

Tenancy, Tenant(s) Boarder, Censuarius, Cosherer, Cottager, Cottar, Cotter, Cottier, Dreng, Feuar, Feudatory, Homage, Ingo, Inhabit, Kindly, Leaseholder, Lessee, Liege, →**LODGER**, Mailer, Metayer, Occupier, Pendicler, Regulated, Rentaller, Renter, Shorthold, Sitting, Socager, Socman, Sokeman, Suckener, Tacksman, Valvassor, Vassal, Vavasour, Villein, Visit

Tend(ing) Apt, Care, Dress, Herd, Incline, Keep, Lean, Liable, Mind, Nurse, Prone, Run, Shepherd, Verge

Tendency Apt, Bent, Bias, Conatus, Disposition, Drift, Import, Inclination, Leaning, Militant, Orientation, Penchant, Proclivity, Propensity, Trend

Tender(iser), Tenderly, Tenderness Affettuoso, Amoroso, Bid, Bill, Coin, Con amore, Crank, Dingey, Ding(h)y, Fond, Frail, Gentle, Green, Humane, Jolly-boat, Legal, Nesh, Nurse, →**OFFER**, Papain, Pinnace, Pra(a)m, Prefer, Present, Proffer, Proposal, Quotation, Red Cross, Sair, Shepherd, →**SOFT**, Sore, SRN, Submit, Sweet, Swineherd, Sympathy, Tendre

Tendon Achilles, Aponeurosis, Hamstring, Leader, Paxwax, Sinew, String, Vinculum, Whiteleather

Tenor Caruso, Course, Direction, →**DRIFT**, Effect, Gigli, Gist, Heldentenor, Purport, Sense, Singer, T, Timbre, Trial, Vein

Tense Agitato, Aor, Aorist, Case, Clench, Cliffhanger, Conditional, Drawn, Edgy, Electric, Essive, Flex, Fraught, Imperfect, Keyed up, Knife-edge, Laconic, Mood(y), Nervy, Overstrung, Past, Perfect, Pluperfect, Preterite, Rigid, Stiff, Stressed(-out), Strict, T, Tighten, Uptight

Tension Creative, Dialectic, High, Isometrics, Isotonic, Meniscus, Nail-biting, Nerviness, Premenstrual, →**STRAIN**, Stress, Stretch, Surface, Tone, Tonicity, Tonus, Yips

Tent Bell, Bivvy, Cabana, Douar, Duar, Ger, Gur, Kedar, Kibitka, Marquee, Oxygen, Pavilion, Probe, Ridge, Shamiana(h), Shamiyanah, Shelter, Tabernacle, Teepee, Tepee, Tipi, Top, Topek, Trailer, Tupek, Tupik, Wigwam, Y(o)urt

Term(s), Terminal, Termly Air, Anode, Boundary, Buffer, Buzzword, Cathode, Coast, Container, Coste, Designate, Desinent(ial), Distal, Distributed, Dub, Dumb, Easy, Euphemism, Expression, Final, Gnomon, Goal, Half, Hilary, Inkhorn, Intelligent,

Law, Lent, Major, Michaelmas, Middle, Minor, Misnomer, →**PERIOD**, Point-of-sale, Rail(head), Real, Removal, Sabbatical, School, Semester, Session, Smart, Stint, Stretch, Trimester, Trimestrial, Trinity, Verb, Waterloo, →**WORD**, Work station

Terminate, Termination, Terminus Abolish, Abort, Axe, Cease, Conclude, Depot, Desinent, Earth, →**END**, Expiry, →**FINISH**, Goal, Liquidate, Naricorn, Railhead, Suffix

Terminology Jargon

Terpene Squalene

Terrace Barbette, Beach, Bench, Crescent, Kop, Linch, Lynchet, Patio, Perron, River, Row house, Shelf, Stoep, Tarras, Undercliff, Veranda(h)

Terrible, Terribly Atrocity, Awful, Deadly, Dire, Fearsome, Fell, Fiendish, Frightful, Ghastly, Hellacious, Horrible, Humgruffi(a)n, Ivan, Much, Odious, Very

Terrier Australian silky, Bedlington, Cesky, Dandie Dinmont, Fox, Glen of Imaal, Irish, Jack Russell, Schauzer, Scotch, Scottish, Soft-coated wheaten, Staffordshire bull, Sydney silky, West Highland white, Westie, Wheaten, Wire-haired

Terrific, Terrified, Terrify(ing) Affright, Aghast, Agrise, Agrize, Agryze, Appal, Awe, Enorm, Fear, Fine, Fley, Gast, Helluva, Huge, Mega, Overawe, →**PETRIFY**, Scare, Superb, Unman, Yippee

Territory, Territorialist Abthane, Ap(p)anage, Area, Colony, Coral Sea Islands, Doab, Domain, Dominion, Duchy, Emirate, Enclave, Exclave, Goa, Irredentist, Lebensraum, Mandated, Manor, Margravate, No-man's-land, Northern, Nunavut, Panhandle, Patch, Princedom, Principality, Principate, Protectorate, Province, Realm, →**REGION**, Rupert's Land, Sphere, Stamping ground, Sultanate, Swazi, Ter(r), Trieste, Trust, Tuath, Yukon

Test(er), Testing Achievement, Acid, Alpha, Ames, Analyse, Appro, Aptitude, Assay, Audition, Barany, Bench, Bender, Benedict, Beta, Bioassay, Blood, Breath, Breathalyser®, Burn-in, Candle, Canopy, Check, Chi-square, Cis-trans, Cloze, Conn(er), Coomb's, Crash, Criterion, Cross-match, Crucial, Crucible, Crunch, Dick, Driving, Drop, Dummy-run, Esda, Essay, Exacting, Examine, Exercise, Experiment, Fehling's, Field, Finals, Flame, Frog, Hagberg, Ink-blot, Intelligence, International, Litmus, Lydian stone, Match, Mazzin, Means, Medical, Mom, MOT, Mug, Neckverse, Needs, Objective, Oral, →**ORDEAL**, Pale, Pap, Paraffin, Patch, Paternity, Performance, Personality, PH, Pilot, Pons asinorum, Pree, Preeve, Preve, Prieve, Probative, Probe, Projective, Proof, Prove, PSA, Pyx, Q-sort, Qualification, Quiz, Rally, Reagent, Reliability, Road, Rorschach, SAT, Scan, Schutz-Charlton, Scientise, Scratch, Screen, Shadow, Shibboleth, Showdown, Shroff, Sign, Signed-ranks, Significance, Sixpence, Skin, Slump, Smear, Smoke, Snellen, Soap, Sound, Sounding, Spinal, Stress, Task, Tempt, Tensile, Thematic apperception, Tongue-twister, Touch, Touchstone, Trial, Trier, Trior, Try, Turing, Ultrasonic, Viva, Weigh, Zohar

Testament Bible, Heptateuch, Hexateuch, New, Old, Pentateuch, Scripture, Septuagint, Tanach, Targum, Will

Test-drive Trial run

Testicle(s) Ballocks, Balls, Bollix, Bollocks, Bush oyster, Cojones, Cruet, Doucets, Dowsets, Family jewels, Goolie, Gool(e)y, Knackers, Monorchid, Nuts, Orchis, Pills, Prairie oyster, Ridgel, Ridgil, Rig(gald), Rocks, Stone

Testify(ing), Testimonial, Testimony Attestation, Character, Chit, Declare, Depone, Deposition, →**EVIDENCE**, Hard, Rap, Reference, Scroll, Viva voce, Vouch, Witness

Tether Cord, Endurance, Knot, Lariat, Leash, Noose, Picket, Seal, Stringhalt, →**TIE**

Text(s), Textbook, Texting ABC, Apocrypha, Body, Brahmana, Church, Codex, Copy, Corpus, Donat, Ennage, Greeked, Harmony, Letterpress, Libretto, Mandaean, Mantra(m), Masoretic, Mezuzah, Minitel, Nynorsk, Octapla, Op-cit, Philology, Plain, Proof, Purana, Pyramid, Quran, Responsa, Rubric, S(h)astra, Script, Shema, SMS, →**SUBJECT**, Sura, Sutra, Tao Te Ching, Tefillin, Tephillin, Tetrapla, Thesis, Topic, Tripitaka, Typography, Upanis(h)ad, Urtext, Variorum, Viewdata, Vulgate, Writing, Zohar

Thank(s), Thankful, Thanksgiving Appreciate, Collins, Deo gratias, Gloria, Grace, Gramercy, Grateful, Gratitude, Kaddish, Mercy, Roofer

Thatch(er), Thatching At(t)ap, Hair, Heard, Hear(i)e, Hele, Hell, Lath, Mane, PM, Reed, Straw, Sway, Thack, Theek, Wig, Ye(a)lm

▷ **Thaw** *may indicate* 'ice' to be removed from a word

Theatre(s), Theatrical(ity) Abbey, Absurd, Adelphi, Aldwych, Arena, Auditorium, Balcony, Broadway, Camp, Cinema, Circle, Coliseum, Criterion, Crucible, Drama, Drury Lane, Epic, Event, Everyman, Field, Folies Bergere, Fourth-wall, Fringe, Gaff, Gaiety, Globe, Grand Guignol, Great White Way, Hall, Haymarket, Hippodrome, Histrionic, House, Kabuki, La Scala, Legitimate, Little, Living, Lyceum, Melodramatic, Mermaid, Music-hall, National, News, Nickelodeon, Noh, Odeon, Odeum, Off-Broadway, Off-off-Broadway, Old Vic, Operating, OUDS, Palladium, Panache, Pennygaff, Pit, Playhouse, Political, Rep(ertory), Sadler's Wells, Shaftesbury, Sheldonian, Shop, Stage, Stalls, Stoll, Straw-hat, Street, Summer stock, Tivoli, Total, Touring, Vic, Windmill, Zarzuela

Theft, Thieving Appropriation, Bluesnarfing, Burglary, Heist, Identity, Kinchinlay, Larceny, Maino(u)r, Manner, Petty larceny, Pilfery, Pillage, Plagiarism, Plunder, Pugging, Ram-raid, Rip off, Robbery, Shrinkage, Stealth, Stouth(rief), → **THIEF**, Touch, TWOC, Walk-in

Theme Crab canon, Donnée, Fugue, Idea, Leitmotiv, Lemma, Lemmata, → **MELODY**, Motif, Mythos, Mythus, Peg, Question, → **SUBJECT**, Subtext, Text, Topic, Topos

Theologian, Theologist, Theology Abelard, Ambrose, Aquinas, Arminius, Baur, Calvin, Christology, Colet, DD, Divine, Eckhart, Erastus, Eschatology, Eusebius, Exegetics, Faustus, Fideism, Harnack, Hase, Irenics, Isidore, Jansen, Kierkegaard, Knox, Laelius, Luther, Mullah, Newman, Niebuhr, Origen, Paley, Pastoral, Patristics, Pelagius, Peritus, Pusey, Rabbi, Religious, Schoolman, Schwenkfeld, Socinus, Softa, STP, Swedenborg, Tertullian, Thomas à Kempis, Tirso de Molina, Ulema

Theory, Theorem, Theoretical, Theorist Abstract, Academic, Atomic, Attachment, Attribution, Auteur, Automata, Band, Big bang, Binomial, Boo-hurrah, Boolean, Calorific, Catastrophe, Chaos, Communications, Complexity, Connectionism, Conspiracy, Corpuscular, Cosmogony, Creationism, Decision, Deduction, Dependency, Dictum, Doctrinaire, Domino, Double aspect, Dow, Einstein, Emboîtement, Empiricism, Euhemerism, Exponential, Fermat's (last), Fortuitism, Gaia, Galois, Game, Gauge, Germ, Grand Unified, Grotian, Group, Guess, Holism, Hormic, Hypothesis, Ideal, Identity, Ideology, Information, Ism(y), Jordan curve, Kinetic, Kock's, Lemma, Lunar, MAD, Metaphysical, Milankovitch, Model, Mythical, Nebular, Neo-Lamarckism, Neovitalism, Nernst heat, Notion, Number, Object relations, Pancosmism, Pantologism, Perturbation, Petrinism, Pluralism, Positivism, Probability, Proof, Pure, Pythagoras, Quantity, Quantum, Quantum field, Queueing, Random walk, Rational choice, Reception, Relativism, Relativity, Satisfaction, Set, Solipsism, Steady state, String, Superdense, Superstring, Supersymmetry, System, Traducianism, Trickle-down, Twistor, Tychism, Unified Field, Utilitarianism, Voluntarism, Vortex, Wages fund, Wave

Therapy, Therapeutic, Therapist Analyst, Family, Fever, Insight, Non directive, Past life, → **TREATMENT**

Thermodynamic Enthalpy, Entropy

Thermometer Aethrioscope, Centesimal, Cryometer, Glass, Katathermometer, Pyrometer, Wet and dry bulb

Thick(en), Thickening, Thickener, Thickness, Thickset Abundant, Algin, Burly, Bushy, Callosity, Callus, Clavate, Cloddy, Cruddle, Curdle, Dense, Dextrin(e), Dumb, Dumose, Engross, Fat, Grist, Grume, Guar, Gum, Hyperostosis, In cahoots, Incrassate, Inspissate, Kuzu, Liaison, Luxuriant, Pally, Panada, Ply, Reduce, Roux, Sclerosis, → **SOLID**, Soupy, Spissitude, Squat, Stocky, Stumpy, → **STUPID**, Thieves, This, Thixotropic, Turbid, Viscous, Waulk, Wooden, Xantham

Thicket Bosk, Brake, Brush, Cane-brake, Chamisal, Chap(arral), Coppice, Copse,

Covert, Dead-finish, Fernshaw, Greve, Grove, Macchia, Maquis, Queach, Reedrand, Reedrond, Salicetum, Shola

Thief, Thieves, Thievish Area sneak, Autolycus, Blood, Bulker, Chummy, Coon, Corsair, Cracksman, Cutpurse, Dip, Filcher, Flood, Footpad, Freebooter, Gully-raker, Heist, Hotter, Ice-man, Jackdaw, Joyrider, Kiddy, Larcener, Lifter, Light-fingered, Looter, Mag, Magpie, Nip(per), Pad, Pickpocket, Pilferer, Pirate, Plagiarist, Poacher, Prig, Raffles, → ROBBER, Rustler, Safeblower, Safebreaker, Safecracker, Scrump, Shark, Shop-lifter, Sneak, Snowdropper, Taffy, Taker, Tarry-fingered, Tea-leaf, Thick, Twoccer

Thin(ner), Thinness Acetone, Atomy, Bald, Beanpole, Bony, Cadaverous, Cornstalk, Cull, Diluent, Dilute, Emaciated, Enseam, Fine, Fine-drawn, Flimsy, Gaunt, Hair('s-)breadth, Inseam, Lanky, Lean, Puny, Rangy, Rare, Rarefied, Reedy, Scant, Scraggy, Scrawny, Sheer, Sieve, Skeletal, Skelf, Skimpy, Skinking, Slender, Slim, Slimline, Slink, → SPARE, Sparse, Spindly, Stilty, Stringy, Subtle, Taper, Tenuous, Threadbare, Turpentine, Turps, Wafer, Washy, Waste, Watch, Water(y), → WEAK, Weedy, Wiry, Wispy, Wraith

Thing(s) Alia, Article, Chattel, Chose, Craze, Doodah, Doofer, Entia, Fetish, First, Fixation, It, Item, Jingbang, Job, Last, Material, Matter, Near, Noumenon, → OBJECT, Obsession, Paraphernalia, Phobia, Res, Tool, Vision, Whatnot

Thingumabob, Thingummy Dingbat, Dinges, Dingus, Doodad, Doodah, Doofer, Doohickey, Gubbins, Hootenanny, Hoot(a)nanny, Jigamaree, Oojamaflip, Whatsit, Yoke

Think(er), Thinking Associate, Audile, Believe, Brain, Brainstorm, Brood, Casuistry, Chew over, Cogitate, Cognition, Conjecture, Consider, Contemplant, Deem, Deliberate, Descartes, Devise, Dianoetic, Divergent, Esteem, Fancy, Fear, Feel, Fogramite, Ghesse, Gnostic, Guess, Hegel, Hold, → IMAGINE, Judge, Lateral, Meditate, Mentation, Mindset, Mull, Muse, Opine, Pensive, Philosopher, Phrontistery, Ponder, Pore, Presume, Ratiocinate, Rational, Reckon, Reflect, Reminisce, Ruminate, Speculate, Synectics, Trow, Vertical, Ween, Wishful

Third, Third rate Bronze, C, Eroica, Gamma, Gooseberry, Interval, Major, Mediant, Minor, Picardy, Quartan, Tertius, Tierce, Trisect

Thirst(y) → CRAVE, Dives, Drought, Drouth, Dry, Hydropic, Nadors, Pant, Polydipsia, Thrist

Thirteen Baker's dozen, Long dozen, Riddle, Unlucky

Thistle Canada, Carduus, Carline, Cnicus, Creeping, Echinops, Musk, Rauriki, Safflower, Sow, Star, Thrissel, Thristle

Thomas Aquinas, Arnold, Christadelphian, De Quincey, Didymus, Doubting, Dylan, Erastus, Hardy, Loco, Parr, Rhymer, Tompion, True, Turbulent

Thomas Aquinas Angelic Doctor

Thorn(y) Acantha, Aculeus, Bael, Bel, Bhel, Bramble, Briar, Coyotillo, Doom, Edh, Eth, Irritation, Jerusalem, Jew's, Mahonia, Mayflower, Nabk, Nar(r)as, Nebbuk, Nebe(c)k, → NEEDLE, Paloverde, Prickle, Slae, Spine, Spinescent, Spinulate, Trial, Wagn'bietjie, Ye, Zare(e)ba, Zariba, Zeriba

Thorough(ly) À fond, Complete, Even-down, Firm, Fully, In depth, Ingrained, Inly, Intensive, Not half, Out, Out and out, Painstaking, Pakka, Pucka, Pukka, Radical, Rigorous, Ripe, Sound, Strict, Total, Tout à fait, Up

Thought(s), Thoughtful(ness) Avisandum, Broody, Censed, Cerebration, Charitable, Cogitation, Concept, Considerate, Contemplation, Dianoetic, Felt, Idea, Imagination, Indrawn, Innate, Kind, Maieutic, Mind, Musing, Notion, Opinion, Pansy, Pensée, Pensive, Philosophy, Reason, Reflection, Rumination, Second

Thoughtless Blindfold, Careless, Goop, Heedless, Inconsiderate, Pillock, → RASH, Reckless, Reflexive, Remiss, Scatter-brained, Stupid, Unintentional, Unkind, Vacant

Thousand(s) Chiliad, G, Gorilla, Grand, K, Lac, Lakh, M, Millenary, Millennium, Octillion, Plum, Sextillion, Toman

Thrash(ing) → BEAT, Belabour, Belt, Bepelt, Binge, Bless, Cane, Dress, Drub, Flail, Flog, Jole, Joll, Joule, Jowl, Lace, Laidie, Laidy, Lambast, Larrup, Lather, Leather, Lick,

Marmelise, Onceover, Paste, Ploat, Quilt, Slog, Smoke, Strap-oil, Swaddle, Swat, Targe, Towel, Trim, Trounce, Whale, Whap, Work over

Thread(ed), Threadlike Acme screw, Addenda, Ariadne, Bar, Bottom, Bride, Buttress, Chalaza, Chromosome, Clew, Clue, Cord, Coventry blue, Eel-worm, End, Female, Fibre, Filament, File, Filiform, Filose, Float, Floss, Flourishing, Gist, Gold, Gossamer, Heddle, Ixtle, Lace, Lap, Lingel, Lingle, Link, Lisle, Lurex®, Male, Meander, Microfibre, Needle, Organzine, Pack, Pearlin(g), Pick, Ravel, Reeve, Roon, Rope-yarn, Rove, Sacred, Screw, Sellers screw, Seton, Shoot, Silver, Single, Spider line, Spireme, Sporangiophore, Stamen, Stroma, Suture, Tassel, Tendril, Theme, Thrid, Thrum, Trace, Tram, Trundle, Tussore, Twine, Twist, Two-start, Warp, Wax(ed) end, Weft, Wick, →**WIND**, Wisp, Worm, Zari

Threat(en), Threatened, Threatening Baleful, Black(en), Blackmail, Bluster, Brew, Brutum fulmen, Bully, Coerce, Comminate, Discovered check, Duress, Extort, Face, Fatwa, Fraught, Greenmail, Greymail, Hazard, Impend, Imperil, Intimidate, Jeopardise, Loom, →**MENACE**, Minacious, Minatory, Mint, Omen, Ominous, Or else, Overcast, Overhang, Parlous, Peril, Portent, Ramp, Shore, Strongarm, Ugly, Veiled, Warning, Yellow peril

Three, Threefold, Three-wheeler, Thrice Cheers, Graces, Har, Harpies, Jafenhar, Leash, Muses, Musketeers, Pairial, Pair-royal, Parial, Prial, Ter, Tercet, Tern, Terzetta, Thridi, Tid, T.i.d, Tierce, Tray, Trey, Triad, Trial, Tricar, Triennial, Trifid, Trigon, Trilogy, Trinal, Trine, Trinity, Trio, Triple, Triptote, Troika

Three-quarter Wing

Threshold Absolute, Brink, Cill, Difference, Doorstep, Limen, Liminal, Nuclear, Sill, Tax, Verge

▶**Thrice** see **THREE**

Thrift(y) Economy, Frugal, Husbandry, Oeconomy, Scrimping, Sea-grass, Sea-pink, Virtue, Wary

Thrill(er), Thrilling Atingle, Buzz, Charge, Delight, Dindle, Dinnle, Dirl, Dread, Dynamite, Electric, Emotive, →**ENCHANT**, Enliven, Excite, Film noir, Frisson, Gas, Jag, Kick, Page-turner, Perceant, Plangent, Pulsate, Pulse, Quiver, Sensation, Thirl, Tinglish, Tremor, Vibrant, Whodunit, Wow(-factor)

Thrive Batten, Blossom, Boom, Do, Fl, →**FLOURISH**, Flower, Grow, Mushroom, →**PROSPER**, Succeed, Thee

Throat(y) Craw, Crop, Deep, Dewlap, Fauces, Gorge, Gular, Gullet, Guttural, Jugular, Laryngeal, Maw, Oropharynx, Pereion, Pharynx, Prunella, Quailpipe, Roopit, Roopy, Strep, Swallet, Thrapple, Thropple, Throttle, Weasand, Wesand, Whistle, Windpipe

Throb(bing) Beat, Palpitate, Pant, Pit-a-pat, Pound, Pulsate, Quop, Stang, Tingle, Vibrato

▷**Throbbing** *may indicate* an anagram

Throne Bed-of-justice, Cathedra, Episcopal, Gadi, →**LAVATORY**, Rule, Seat, See, Siege, Stool, Tribune

Throttle →**CHOKE**, Gar(r)otte, Gun, Mug, Scrag, Silence, Stifle, Strangle, Strangulate, We(a)sand

Through, Throughout Along, Ana, By, Dia-, During, Everywhere, Over, Passim, Per, Pr, Sempre, Sic passim, To, Trans, Via, Yont

▶**Throw(n)** see **TOSS(ING)**

Throw (up), Thrower, Throw-out Bin, Cast-off, Chunder, Egesta, Eject, Estrapade, Floor, Flummox, Flying mare, Go, Jettison, Mangonel, Pash, Puke, Reject, Slam-drunk, Spatter, Spew, Squirt, Squit, →**TOSS**, Ventriloquism

Thrust(er) Abdominal, Aventre, Bear, Boost, Botte, Burn, Burpee, Detrude, Dig, Drive, Elbow, Engine, Exert, Extrude, Foin, →**FORCE**, Gist, Hay, Hustle, Impulse, Jet, Job, Lift-off, Lunge, Muscle, Obtrude, Oust, Pass, Passado, Peg, Perk, Pitchfork, Poach, Poke, Potch(e), Pote, Probe, Prog, Propel, Pun, Punto, →**PUSH**, Put, Ram, Remise, Repost, Run, Shoulder, Shove, Sock, Sorn, Squat, Stap, Stick, Stoccado, Stoccata, Stock, Stuck, Thrutch, Tilt, Tuck, Venue

Thug(s) Brute, Gangster, Goon(da), Gorilla, Gurrier, Hood(lum), Keelie, Loord, Ninja, Ockers, Phansigar, Rough(neck), SS, Strangler, Ted, Tityre-tu, Tsotsi, Yahoo

Thump(ing) Blow, Bonk, Cob, Crump, Dawd, Ding, Dod, Drub, Dub, Hammer, Knevell, Knock, Lamp, Nevel, Oner, Paik, Percuss, → **POUND**, Pummel, Ribroast, Slam, Slosh, Swat, Swingeing, Thud, Tund, Whump

Thunder(ing), Thunderstorm Astrophobia, Bolt, Boom, Clap, Donnerwetter, Foudroyant, Foulder, Fulminate, Intonate, Lei-king, Microburst, Pil(l)an, Raiden, → **ROAR**, Rumble, Summanus, Tempest, Thor, Tonant

Thunderbolt Ward

Thwart Baffle, Balk, → **CROSS**, Dish, Foil, Frustrate, Hamstring, Hogtie, Obstruct, Outwit, Pip, Prevent, Scotch, Scupper, Snooker, Spike, Spite, Stonker, Stymie, Transverse

Tick, Tick off Acarida, Acarus, Beat, Click, Cr, → **CREDIT**, Deer, HP, Idle, Instant, Jar, Ked, Mattress, Mile, Mo, Moment, Ricinulei, Second, Seed, Sheep, Soft, Strap, Worm

Ticket(s) Billet, Bone, Brief, Carnet, Commutation, Complimentary, Coupon, Day, Docket, Dream, E(lectronic), Excursion, Hot, Kangaroo, Label, Meal, One-day, One-way, Open-jaw, Parking, Pass, Pass-out, Pasteboard, Pawn, Platform, Raffle, Raincheck, Return, Round-trip, Rover, Saver, Scratchcard, Season, Single, Soup, Split, Straight, Stub, Supersaver, Tempest, Tessera(l), Through, Tix, Transfer, Tyburn, Unity, Voucher, Walking, Zone

Tickle, Ticklish Amuse, Delicate, Divert, Excite, Gratify, Gump, → **ITCH**, Kittle, Queasy, Thrill, Titillate

Tide, Tidal Current, Drift, Eagre, Easter, Eger, Estuary, Flood, High, Low, Marigram, Neap, River, Roost, Sea, Seiche, Slack water, Spring, Trend, Wave

Tidy Big, Comb, Considerable, Curry, Fair, Fettle, Kempt, Large, Neat, Neaten, → **ORDER**, Pachyderm, Predy, Preen, Primp, Red(d), Slick, Snug, Sort, Spruce, Trim

Tie, Tied, Tying Ascot, Attach, Barcelona, Berth, Bind, Black, Bolo, → **BOND**, Bootlace, Bow, Bowyang, Cable, Clip-on, Cope, Cord, Cravat, Cup, Dead-heat, Drag, Draw, Fetter, Four-in-hand, Frap, Halter, Handicap, Harness, Hitch, Holdfast, Kipper, → **KNOT**, Lace, Lash, Level, Ligament, Ligate, Ligature, Link, Marry, Match, Moor, Neck and neck, Oblige, Obstriction, Old School, Oop, Oup, Overlay, Raffia, Restrain, Rod, Rope, Scarf, School, Score draw, Scrunchie, Semifinal, Shackle, Sheave, Shoelace, Shoestring, Sleeper, Slur, Solitaire, Soubise, Splice, Stake, Standoff, Strap, String, Tawdry-lace, Tether, Together, Trice, Truss, Unite, White, Windsor

Tiff Bicker, Contretemps, Difference, Dispute, Exchange, Feed, Feud, Huff, Miff, Skirmish, Spat, Squabble

Tiger Bengal, → **CAT**, Clemenceau, Demoiselle, Lily, Machairodont, Machairodus, Man-eater, Margay, Paper, Sabre-tooth, Shere Khan, Smilodon, Stripes, Tasmanian, Woods

Tight(en), Tightness, Tights Boozy, Bosky, Brace, Canny, Cinch, Close(-hauled), Constriction, Cote-hardie, Fishnet, Fleshings, High, Hose, Jam, Leggings, Leotards, Lit, Loaded, Maillot, Mean, Merry, Niggardly, Oiled, Pang, Pantihose, Phimosis, Pickled, Pinch(penny), Plastered, Prompt, Proof, Rigour, Snug, Squiffy, Stenosis, → **STINGY**, Stinko, Strict, Stringent, Swift, Swig, Taut, Tense, Tipsy, Trig, Woozy

Tight-lipped Shtum

Tile(s), Tiled Antefix, Arris, Azulejo, Dalle, Derby, Encaustic, → **HAT**, Hung, Imbrex, Imbricate, Lid, Mahjong(g), Ostracon, Ostrakon, Peever, Quarrel, Quarry, Rag(g), Ridge, Rooftop, Sclate, Shingle, Slat, Tegular, Tessella, Tessera, Titfer, Topper, Wall, Wally

Till Cashbox, Checkout, Coffer, Ear, Eulenspiegel, Farm, Hasta, Hoe, Husband, Lob, Peter, → **PLOUGH**, Rotavate, Set, Unto, Up to

Tilt(ed) Awning, Bank, Camber, Cant, Careen, Cock, Dip, Heel, Hut, Joust, Just, → **LIST**, Quintain, Rock, Tip, Trip, Unbalance, Version

Timber Apron, Ashlaring, Balk, Batten, Beam, Bolster, Bond, Bowsprit, Bridging, Cant-rail, Cedarwood, Chess, Clapboard, Compass, Cross-tree, Cruck, Dogshores, Driftwood, Druxy, Elmwood, Flitch, Float, Four-by-two, Greenheart, Groundsell, Hardwood, Harewood, Intertie, Iroko, Ironwood, Joist, Knee, Ligger, Lignum,

Lintel, Log, Lumber, Nogging, Purlin(e), Putlock, Putlog, Rib, Ridgepole, Roseweed, Roundwood, Rung, Sandalwood, Sapele, Sapodilla, Satinwood, Scantling, Shook, Shorts, Skeg, Sneezewood, Softwood, Souari, Stemson, Stere, Sternpost, Sternson, Straddle, Stud, Stull, Summer, Swing-stock, Tilting fillet, Towing-bitts, Transom, Two-by-four, Wale, Wall plate, Weatherboard, Whitewood, **→ WOOD**, Yang

Time(s), Timer Access, African, Agoge, Apparent, Assymetric, Astronomical, Atlantic, Atomic, Autumn, Awhile, Bird, BST, By, Central, Chronaxy, Chronic, Chronometer, Chronon, Clock, Closing, Common, Compound, Connect, Core, Counter, Cryptozoic, Date, Day, Dead, Decade, Dimension, Double, Duple, Duration, Early, Eastern, Eastern Standard, Egg-glass, Enemy, Eon, Ephemeris, Epoch, Epocha, Equinox, Era, EST, European, Eve(ning), Extra, Father, Flexitime, Fold, Forelock, Four-four, Fourth dimension, Free, Full, Geological, Gest, Glide, Half, Healer, High, Hour, Hourglass, Hr, Idle, Imprisonment, Injury, Innings, Instant, Interim, Interlude, Jiff, Juncture, Kalpa, Killing, Latent, Lead, Lean, Leisure, Life, Lighting-up, Lilac, Local, Lowsing, Man-day, Mean, Menopause, Metronome, Multiple, Needle, Nonce, Nones, Normal, Occasion, Oft, Opening, Pacific, Paralysis, Part, Peak, Period, Phanerozoic, Pinger, Porridge, Post, Precambrian, Prime, Proper, Quadruple, Quality, Question, Quick, Reaction, Real, Reaper, Recovery, Released, Response, Responsum, Reverberation, Rhythm, Run(ning), Sandglass, Sands, Schedule, Seal, **→ SEASON**, Seel, Seil, Serial, Session, Shelf-life, Sidereal, Sight, Simple, Sith(e), Slow, Solar, Solstice, Space, Spacious, Span, Spare, Spell, Spin, Split, Spring, Squeaky-bum, Standard, Stoppage, Stopwatch, Stound, Stownd, Stretch, Summer, Sundial, Sundown, Sythe, T, Tem, Tempo, Tempore, Tense, Thief, Three-four, Thunderer, Tick, Tid, Tide, Trice, Triple, True, Two-four, Universal, Usance, Whet, While, Winter, X, Yonks, Yukon, Zero

Time-keeper, Timepiece Ben, Clock, Hourglass, Ref, Sand-glass, Sundial, Ticker, Tompion, Watch

Timely Appropriate, Apropos, Happy, Heaven-sent, Opportune, Pat, Prompt, Punctual

Timeshare Box and cox

Timetable ABC(ee), Absee, Bradshaw, **→ CHART**, Schedule

Timid, Timorous Afraid, Aspen, Bashful, Blate, Chicken, Cowardly, Eerie, Eery, Faint-hearted, Fearful, Hare, Hen-hearted, Meticulous, Milquetoast, Mouse, Mous(e)y, Pavid, Pigeon-hearted, Pusillanimous, Pussy, Quaking, Shrinking, **→ SHY**, Skeary, Sook, Tremulous, Wuss, Yellow

Tin(ned), Tinfoil, Tinny Argentine, Britannia metal, Can, Cash, Debe, Dixie, Maconochie, **→ MONEY**, Moola(h), Ochre, Plate, Rhino, Sn, Stannary, Stannic, Tain, Tole

Tincture Arnica, Brown, Bufo, Chroma, Elixir, Fur, Infusion, Laudanum, Metal, Or, Sericon, Sol, Spice, Taint, Tenné, Vert

Tinder Amadou, Faggot, Fuel, Funk, Punk, Spark, Spunk, Touchwood

Tingle, Tingling Dinnle, Dirl, Paraesthesia, Pins and needles, Prickle, Thrill, Throb, Tinkle

Tinker Bell, Caird, Coster, Didicoy, Didikoi, **→ FIDDLE**, Gypsy, Meddle, Mender, Pedlar, Potter, Prig, Putter, Repair, Sly, Smouse, Snout, Tamper, Tramp, Traveller, Tweak

Tiny Atto-, Baby, Diddy, Dwarf, Ha'it, Infinitesimal, Itsy-bitsy, Lilliputian, Midget, Minikin, Minim, Mite, Negligible, Petite, Pint-sized, Pitiful, Pittance, Small, Smidge(o)n, Smidgin, Stime, Teeny, Tim, Tine, Toy, Wee(ny)

Tip (off), Tipping Apex, Arrowhead, Asparagus, Backshish, Baksheesh, Batta, Beer-money, Cant, Cert, Chape, Counsel, Coup, Cowp, Crown, Cue, Cumshaw, Douceur, Dump, Extremity, Fee, Felt, Ferrule, Filter, Forecast, Glans, Gratuity, Heel, **→ HINT**, Hunch, Inkle, Iridise, Largess(e), List, Mag(g), Mess, Nap, Nib, Noop, Ord, Perk, Perquisite, Point, Pointer, Pour, Previse, Suggestion, Summit, Tag, Tail, Tilt, Toom, Touch, Tronc, Upset, Vail, Vales, Warn, Whisper, Wrinkle

Tipper Ale

Tipsy Bleary, Boozy, Bosky, Elevated, Merry, Moony, Nappy, Oiled, On, Rocky, Screwed, Slewed, Slued, Squiffy, Tight, Wet

▷ **Tipsy** *may indicate* an anagram

Tirade Diatribe, Invective, Jobation, Laisse, Philippic, Rand, Rant, Screed, Slang

Tire(d), Tiredness, Tiring All-in, Aweary, Beat, Bejade, Bleary-eyed, Bore, Brain fag, Bushed, Caparison, Cooked, Dress, Drowsy, → **EXHAUST**, Fag, Fatigue, Flag, Footsore, Fordid, Fordod, Forjeskit, Frazzle, Gruel, Irk, Jack, Jade, Languor, Lassitude, Limp, ME, Poop, Puggled, → **ROBE**, Rubber, Sap, Shagged, Sicken, Sleepry, Sleepy, Snoozy, Swinkt, Tax, Tedious, Trying, Tucker, Wabbit, Wappend, Weary, World-weary, Wrecked

▶ **Tiro** *see* **TYRO**

Tissue Adenoid, Adhesion, Adipose, Aerenchyma, Aponeurosis, Archesporium, Bast, Callus, Carbon, Cartilage, C(o)elom, Cementum, Chalaza, Cheloid, Chlorenchyma, Coenosarc, Collagen, Collenchyma, Commissure, Conducting, Connective, Corpus luteum, Corpus Striatum, Cortex, Dentine, Diploe, Elastic, Elastin, Endarch, Endosperm, Endosteum, Epigenesis, Epimysium, Epineurium, Epithelium, Eschar, Evocator, Fabric, Fascia, Fibroid, Filament, Flesh, Gamgee, Gauze, Gleba, Glia, Granulation, Granuloma, Gum, Handkerchief, Hankie, Heteroplasia, Histogen, Histoid, Hypoderm(is), Infarct, Interlay, Junk, Keloid, Kleenex®, Lamina, Liber, Lies, Ligament, Luteal, Lymphate, Lymphoid, Macroglia, Marrow, Matrix, Mechanical, Medulla, → **MEMBRANE**, Meristem, Mesenchyme, Mesophyll, Mestom(e), Mole, Muscle, Myelin(e), Myocardium, Neoplasia, Neoplasm, Neuroglia, Nucellus, Olivary, Pack, Palisade, Pannus, Paper, Papilla, Parenchyma, Periblem, Perichylous, Pericycle, Peridesmium, Perimysium, Perinephrium, Perineurium, Perisperm, Phellogen, Phloem, Pith, Placenta, Plerome, Polyarch, Pons, Primordium, Procambium, Prosenchyma, Prothallis, Pterygium, Pulp, Radula, Retina, Sarcenet, Sars(e)net, Scar, Sclerenchyma, Scleroma, Sequestrum, Sinew, Siphonostele, Siphuncle, Soft, Somatopleure, Stereome, Stroma, Submucosa, Suet, Tarsus, Tela, Tendon, Toilet, Tonsil, Trace, Tunica, Vascular, Velum, Web, Wound, Xylem, Zoograft

Tit, Tit-bit(s) Analecta, Currie, Curry, Delicacy, Dug, Nag, Nipple, Pap, Quarry, Sample, Scrap, Snack, Teat, Tug, Twitch, Zakuska

Titan(ic), Titaness Atlas, Colossus, Cronos, Enormous, Giant, Ginormous, Huge, Hyperion, Kronos, Large, Leviathan, Liner, Oceanus, Phoebe, Prometheus, Rhea, Superman, Themis, Vast

Title Abbé, → **ADDRESS**, Ag(h)a, Agname, Appellative, Bab, Baroness, Baronet, Bart, Bastard, Bhai, Burra sahib, Calif, Caliph, Caption, Charta, Chogyal, Claim, Conveyance, Count(ess), Courtesy, Credit, Dan, Datin, Dauphin, Dayan, Deeds, Denominative, Devi, Dom, Don, Don(n)a, Dowager, Dub, Duchess, Duke, Earl, Effendi, Eminence, Epithet, Esquire, Excellency, Fra, Frau(lein), Ghazi, Grand Master, Great Mogul, Handle, Header, Heading, Headline, Highness, Hojatoleslam, Hon, Honour, Imperator, Interest, Kabaka, Kalif, Kaliph, Khan, King, Kumari, Lady, Lala, Lemma, Lord, Mal(l)am, Marchesa, Marchese, Marquess, Marquis, Master, Masthead, Memsahib, Meneer, Miladi, Milady, Milord, Mr(s), Name, Native, Negus, Nemn, Nizam, Nomen, Padishah, Pasha, Peerage, Pir, Polemarch, Prefix, Prince(ss), Queen, → **RANK**, Reb, Reverence, Reverend, → **RIGHT**, Rubric, Running, Sahib, Sama, San, Sardar, Sayid, Senhor(a), Señor(a), Shri, Singh, Sir, Sirdar, Son, Sowbhagyawati, Sri, Stratum, Tannie, Tenno, Titule, Torrens, Tuanku, Tycoon, U, Voivode, Worship

To(wards) At, Beside, Inby, Intil, Oncoming, Onto, Shet, Shut, Till, Until

Toad(y) Bootlicker, Bufo, Bumsucker, Cane, Clawback, Crawler, Fawn, Frog, Hanger-on, Horned, Jackal, Jenkins, Knot, Lackey, Lickspittle, Midwife, Minion, Natterjack, Nototrema, Paddock, Parasite, Pipa, Placebo, Platanna, Poodle, Puddock, Sook, Spade-foot, Squit, Surinam, Sycophant, Tuft-hunter, Warty, Xenopus, Yesman

Toadstone Lava

Toadstool Amanita, Death-cap, Death-cup, → **FUNGUS**, Grisette, Marasmus, Paddock-stool, Parrot, Saffron milk cap, Sickener, Sulphur tuft

Toast(er) Bacchus, Bell, Birsle, Brindisi, → **BROWN**, Bruschetta, Bumper, Cheers,

Chin-chin, Crostini, Crouton, Drink-hail, French, Gesundheit, Grace-cup, Grill, Health, Heat, Iechyd da, Immortal memory, Kia-ora, L'chaim, Lechayim, Loyal, Melba, Pledge, Propose, Prosit, Round, Salute, Scouther, Scowder, Scowther, Sentiment, Sippet, Skoal, Slainte, Soldier, Sunbathe, Zwieback

Tobacco, Tobacco-field Alfalfa, Bacchi, Baccy, Bird's eye, Broadleaf, Burley, Burn, Canaster, Capa, Caporal, Cavendish, Chew, Dottle, Honeydew, Indian, Killikinnick, Kinnikinick, Latakia, Mundungus, Nailrod, Navy-cut, Negro-head, Nicotine, Niggerhead, Perique, Pigtail, Pipe, Plug, Quid, Régie, Returns, Shag, Sneesh, Snout, Snuff, Stripleaf, Turkish, Twist, Vega, Virginia, Weed, Wrapper

To be arranged TBA

To boot Furthermore

Today Hodiernal, Now, Present

Toddle(r) Baim, Gangrel, Mite, Tot, Totter, Trot, Waddle

Toe(s) Dactyl, Digit, Hallux, Hammer, Piggy, Pinky, Pointe, Poulaine, Prehallux, Tootsie

Toffee Butterscotch, Caramel, Cracknel, Gundy, Hard-bake, Hokey-pokey, Humbug, Tom-trot

Together Among, At-one, Atone, Attone, Col, Gathered, Hand-in-glove, Hand-in-hand, In concert, Infere, →**JOINT**, Pari-passu, Sam, Simultaneous, Unison, Wed, Y, Yfere, Ysame

Toil(s) Drudge, Fag, Industry, →**LABOUR**, Mesh, Net, Seine, Sisyphus, Slog, Sweat, Swink, Tela, Tew, Trap, Travail, Tug, Web, →**WORK**, Wrest, Yacker, Yakka, Yakker

Toilet Can, Chemical, Coiffure, Garderobe, Head(s), John, Lat(rine), Lavabo, →**LAVATORY**, Loo, Necessary house, Necessary place, Pot, Powder room, Toot, WC

Token Abbey-piece, Buck, Chip, Counter, Coupon, Disc, Double-axe, Emblem, Gift, Indication, Mark, →**MEMENTO**, Monument, Nominal, Omen, Portend, Seal, Sign, Signal, Slug, Symbol, Symptom, Tessella, Tessera, Valentine, Voucher

Tolerable Acceptable, Bearable, Mediocre, Passable, So-so

Tolerance, Tolerant, Tolerate(d) Abear, Abide, Accept, →**ALLOW**, Bear, Broadminded, Brook, Countenance, Endure, Enlightened, Good-natured, Hack, Had, Immunological, Latitude, →**LENIENT**, Liberal, Lump, Mercy, Permit, Stand (for), Stick, Stomach, Studden, Suffer, Support, Thole, Wear, Zero

Toll Chime, Chok(e)y, Customs, Due, Duty, Excise, Jole, Joll, Joule, Jow, Octroi, Pierage, Pike, Pontage, Rates, →**RING**, Scavage, Streetage, Tariff, Tax

Toll-breaker Rebecca

Tom(my) Atkins, Bell, Bowling, Bread, Brown, →**CAT**, Collins, Edgar, Gib, Grub, Gun, He-cat, Jerry, Jones, Mog(gy), Nosh, Peeping, Private, Pro(stitute), Pte, Puss, Ram-cat, Sawyer, Snout, Soldier, Stout, Thos, Thumb, Tiddler, Tucker

Tomato Beef(steak), Cherry, Husk, Love-apple, Plum, Strawberry, Tamarillo, Wolf's peach

Tomb(stone) Burial, Catacomb, Catafalque, Cenotaph, Cist, Coffin, Dargah, Durgah, Grave, Hypogeum, Inurn, Kistvaen, Marmoreal, Mastaba, Mausoleum, Megalithic, Monument, Pyramid, Repository, →**SEPULCHRE**, Sepulture, Serdab, Shrine, Speos, Tholos, Tholus, Through-stane, Through-stone, Treasury, Vault

Tomboy Gamine, Gilpey, Gilpy, Hoyden, Ladette, Ramp, Romp

Tomorrow Future, Manana, Morrow, The morn

Ton(nage) C, Century, Chic, Displacement, Freight, Gross, Hundred, Long, Measurement, Metric, Net register, Register, Shipping, Short, T

Tone, Tonality Aeolian, Brace, Combination, Compound, Difference, Differential, Fifth, Gregorian, Harmonic, Hypate, Inflection, Key, Klang, Mediant, Minor, Ninth, Partial, Passing, Pure, Qualify, Real, Ring, →**SOUND**, Strain, Summational, Temper, Tenor, Timbre, Trite, Whole

Tongue, Tonguing Brogue, Burr, Chape, Clack, Clapper, Doab, Final, Flutter, Forked, Glossa, Glossolalia, Glottal, Isthmus, Jinglet, →**LANGUAGE**, Languet(te), Lap, Ligula, Lill, Lingo, Lingual, Lingulate, Lytta, Mother, Organ, Radula, Ranine, Rasp, Red rag, Spit, Tab, Voice

Tonic Booster, Bracer, C(h)amomile, Cascara, Doh, Elixir, Key, Keynote, Mease,

Medicinal, Mishmee, Mishmi, Oporice, Pick-me-up, Quassia, Refresher, Roborant, Sarsaparilla, Solfa

▷ **Tonic** *may indicate* a musical note

Too Als(o), Besides, Eke, Excessive, Item, Likewise, Moreover, Oer, Over, Overly, Plus, Troppo

Tool(s) Flatter, →**IMPLEMENT**, →**INSTRUMENT**, Maker, Penis, Percussion, Power, Property, Utensil

Tooth(ed), Toothy, Teeth Baby, Bicuspid, Bit, Buck, Bunodont, Cadmean, Canine, Carnassial, Chactodon, Cheek tooth, Chisel, Choppers, Cog, Comb, Comer, Cott's, Crena(te), Ctenoid, Cusp, Deciduous, Denticle, Dentin(e), Dentures, Egg, Eye, False, Fang, Gam, Gap, Gat, Gnashers, Grinder, Heterodont, Impacted, Incisor, Ivory, Joggle, Laniary, Milk, Mill, Molar, Nipper, Odontoid, Orthodontics, Overbite, Pawl, Pearly gates, Pectinate, Periodontics, Peristome, Permanent, Phang, Plate, Poison-fang, Pre-molar, Prong, Radula, Ratch, Ratchet, Scissor, Secodont, Sectorial, Selenodont, Serration, Set, Snaggle, Sprocket, Stomach, Store, Sweet, Trophi, Tush, Tusk, Uncinus, Upper, Wallies, Wang, Wiper, Wisdom, Wolf, Zalambdodont, Zygodont

▷ **Top** *may indicate* first letter

Top (drawer; hole; line; notcher), Topmost, Topper 1st, A1, Ace, Acme, Altissimo, Apex, Apical, Behead, Best, Better, Big, Blouse, Blouson, Boob tube, Brow, Bustier, Cap, Capstone, Ceiling, Coma, Cop, Coping, Corking, Cream, →**CREST**, Crista, Crop, Crown, Culmen, De capo, Decollate, Diabolo, Dog, Dome, Double, Drawer, Dux, Elite, Execute, Fighting, Finial, Flip, Gentry, Gyroscope, Halterneck, Hard, Hat, →**HEAD**, Height, Hummer, Humming, Imperial, Impost, Jumper, Lid, Maillot, Nun, One-er, Optimate, Orb, Parish, →**PEAK**, Peerie, Peery, Peg, Peplos, Peplus, Pinnacle, Pitch, Quark, Replenish, Ridge, Roof, Sawyer, Screw, Secret, Shaw, Shirt, Skim, Sky, Slay, Soft, Spinning, Star, Summit, Superb, Supreme, Supremo, Surface, Sweater, Table, Tambour, Targa, Teetotum, Texas, Tile, Trash, Trump, T-shirt, Up(most), Uppermost, V, Vertex, Whipping, Whirligig, Winner

Topic(al) Head, Item, Local, Motion, Place, Subject, Text, →**THEME**

Topping Grand, Icing, Meringue, Pepperoni, Piecrust, Streusel

Topple Dethrone, Oust, Overbalance, Overturn, Tip, Upend, →**UPSET**

Topsy-turvy Careen, Cockeyed, Inverted, Summerset, Tapsalteerie, Tapsleteerie

Torah Maftir

Torch Blow, Brand, Cresset, Fire, Flambeau, Lamp, Lampad, Link, Penlight, Plasma, Tead(e), Weld, Wisp

Toreador Escamillo, Matador, Picador, Torero

Torment(ed), Tormentor Agony, Anguish, Bait, Ballyrag, Bedevil, Butt, Cruciate, Crucify, Curse, Distress, Excruciate, Frab, Grill, Hag-ridden, Harass, Harry, Hell, Martyrdom, Molest, Nag, Nettle, Pang, Pine, Plague, →**RACK**, Sadist, Tantalise, Wrack

Torpedo Bangalore, Bomb, Missile, Ray, Weapon

Torpid, Torpor Comatose, Dormant, Gouch, Languid, Lethargic, Sluggish, Slumbering

Torrid Amphiscian, Fiery, Hot, Sultry, Tropical

Torso Body, Midriff, Trunk

Tortoise Chelonia, Emydes, Emys, Galapagos, Hic(c)atee, Kurma, Pancake, Snapping-turtle, Terrapin, Testudo, Timothy, Turtle

Tortoiseshell Epiplastra, Hawksbill, Testudo

▷ **Tortuous** *may indicate* an anagram

Torture, Torture chamber, Torture instrument Agonise, Auto-da-fé, Bastinade, Bastinado, Boot, Bootikin, Catasta, Chinese burn, Chinese water, Crucify, Devil-on-the-neck, Engine, Excruciate, Flageolet, Fry, Gadge, Gauntlet, Gyp, Hell, Iron maiden, Knee-cap, Naraka, Peine forte et dur, Persecute, Pilliwinks, Pine, Pinniewinkle, Pinnywinkle, →**RACK**, Sadism, Scaphism, Scarpines, Scavenger, Scavenger's daughter, Scourge, Skeffington's daughter, Skevington's daughter, Strappado, Tantalise, Third degree, Thumb(i)kins, Thumbscrew, Torment, Treadmill, Triphook, Tumbrel, Tumbril, Water, Wheel, Wrack

▷ **Tortured** *may indicate* an anagram

Tosh Old bean

Toss(ing), Throw(n) Abject, Bandy, Birl, Bounce, Buck, Bung, Buttock, Cant, Canvass, Cast, Catapult, Crabs, Crap, Cross-buttock, Dad, Daud, Dawd, Deal, Dink, Discomfit, Disconcert, Dod, Elance, Estrapade, Falcade, Faze, →**FLING**, Flip, Floor, Flump, Flutter, Flying (head)-mare, Gollum, Hanch, Haunch, Heave, Hipt, Hoy, →**HURL**, Jact(it)ation, Jaculation, Jeff, Jump, Lance, Launch, Lob, Loft, Nick, Pash, Pick, Pitch, Purl, Round-arm, Salad, Seamer, Shy, Slat, Sling, Squail, Unhorse, Unseat, Upcast, Wheech, Yuko

Tot Add, Babe, Bairn, →**CHILD**, Dop, Dram, Infant, Mite, Moppet, Nightcap, Nip(per), Nipperkin, Slug, Snifter, Snort, Tad

Total(ity), Toto Absolute, Aggregate, All(-out), All told, Amount, Balance, Be-all, →**COMPLETE**, Entire, Gross, Lot, Mass, Ouroborus, Overall, Sum(mate), Tale, Tally, Unqualified, Uroborus, Utter, Whole

To the point Ad rem

Totter Abacus, Daddle, Daidle, Didakai, Didakei, Didicoi, Did(d)icoy, Halt, Lurch, Ragman, Reel, Rock, Shamble, →**STAGGER**, Swag, Sway, Topple, Waver

Toucan Ariel, Ramphastos

Touch(ed), Touching, Touchy Abut, Accolade, Adjoin, Affect, Against, Anent, Apropos, Badass, Barmy, Cadge, Captious, Carambole, Caress, Carom, Common, Concern, Connivent, Contact, Contiguous, Dash, Easy, Emove, →**FEEL**, Feisty, Finger, Finishing, Flick, Fondle, Haptic, Heart-warming, Huffish, Huffy, Iracund, Irascible, Irritable, J'adoube, Liaison, Libant, Loan, Loco, Meet, Midas, Miffy, Near, Nie, Nigh, Nudge, Palp, Pathetic, Paw, Potty, Re, Sense, Shade, Skiff, Soft, Sore, Spice, →**SPOT**, Tactile, Tactual, Tag, Tangible, Tap, Taste, Tat, Tetchy, Tickle, Tig, Tinderbox, Tinge, Titivate, Trace, Trait, Trifle, Tuck, Vestige

Touchdown Rouge

Touchstone Basanite, Criterion, Norm, Standard

Touch wood Unberufen

Tough(en) Adamantine, Anneal, Apache, Arduous, Ballsy, Bruiser, Burly, Chewy, →**HARD**, Hardball, Hard-boiled, Hard nut, Hardy, Heavy duty, He-man, Hood, Husky, Indurate, Keelie, Knotty, Leathern, Leathery, Nut, Pesky, Rambo, Resilient, Rigwiddie, Rigwoodie, Robust, Roughneck, Sinewy, Skinhead, Spartan, Steely, Stiff, Strict, String, Sturdy, Teuch, Thewed, Tityre-tu, Virile, Withy, Yob

Tour(er), Tourism, Tourist Adventure, Barnstorm, Benefit, Circuit, Conducted, Cook's, Emmet, Excursion, Gig, Grand, Grockle, GT, Holiday-maker, Itinerate, →**JOURNEY**, Lionise, Mystery, Outing, Package, Posting, Pub crawl, Reality, Roadie, Road show, Rubberneck, Safari, Sightsee, Spin, →**TRAVEL**, Trip(per), Viator, Weather, Whistle-stop

Tournament Basho, Bridge drive, Carousel, Drive, Event, Joust, Just, Plate, Pro-am, Pro-celebrity, Round robin, Royal, Spear-running, Tilt, Tourney, Whist drive, Wimbledon

Tow(ing), Towpath Button, Fibre, →**HAUL**, Pull, →**ROPE**, Skijoring, Stupe, Track road

▶ **Towards** *see* **TO(WARDS)**

Towel Dry, Jack, Nappy, Pantyliner, Roller, Rub, Sanitary, Tea, Tea-cloth, Terry, Turkish

Tower AA, Aspire, Atalaya, Babel, Barbican, Bastille, Bastion, Belfry, Bell, Bloody, Brattice, Brettice, Brogh, Campanile, Clock, Conning, Control, Cooling, Donjon, Dungeon, Edifice, Eiffel, Fly, Fortress, Gantry, Garret, Gate, Hawser, Horologium, Husky, Ivory, Keep, Leaning, Loom, Maiden, Martello, Minar(et), Monument, Mooring, Mouse, Nurhag, Overtop, Peel, Pinnacle, Pisa, Pound, Pylon, Rear, Rise, Rood, Round, Sail, Sears, Shot, Signal, Silo, Ski-lift, Spire, Stealth, Steeple, Swiss Re, Tête-de-pont, Texas, Tractor, Tugboat, →**TURRET**, Victoria, Watch, Water, Ziggurat

Town, Township Boom, Borgo, Borough, Bourg, Burg(h), City, Company, Conurbation, County, Deme, Dormitory, Dorp, Favella, Five, Ghost, Ham(let), Market,

Municipal, Nasik, One-horse, Open, Place, Podunk, Pueblo, Satellite, Shanty, Shire, Soweto, Tp, Twin, Urban, Whistle stop, Wick

Townee, Townsman Cad, Cit(izen), Dude, Freeman, Oppidan, Philister, Resident, Snob

Toxic(ity), Toxin Abrin, Aflatoxin, Antigen, Botox®, Botulin, Cadmium, Chlorin(e), Coumarin, Curare, Deadly, Dioxan, Dioxin, Eclampsia, Lethal, Melittin, Muscarine, Nicotine, Phenol, Phenothiazine, Pre-eclampsia, Psoralen, Sepsis, Serology, Venin, Venomous, Yellow rain

Toy Babyhouse, Bauble, Bottle-imp, Bull-roarer, Cartesian devil, Cockhorse, Coral, Cyberpet, Dally, Dandle, Dinky®, Doll, Doll's house, Dreid(e)l, Executive, Faddle, Finger, Flirt, Frisbee®, Gewgaw, Golly, Gonk, Jack-in-the-box, Jumping-jack, Kaleidoscope, Kickshaw, Knack, Lego®, Meccano®, Newton's cradle, Noah's ark, Novelty, Paddle, Pantine, Peashooter, Pinwheel, Plaything, Pogo stick, Popgun, Praxinoscope, Quiz, Rattle, Russian doll, Scooter, Shoofly, Skipjack, Stroboscope, Tantalus-cup, Taste, Teddy, Thaumatrope, Top, → **TRIFLE**, Trinket, Tu(r)ndun, Wheel of life, Whirligig, Windmill, Yoyo, Zoetrope

Trace Atom, Cast, Derive, Describe, Draft, Draw, Dreg, Echo, Footprint, Ghost, Gleam, → **HINT**, Mark, Outline, Relic, Relict, Remnant, Scan, Scintilla, Semblance, Sign, Smack, Soupçon, Strap, Tinge, → **TOUCH**, Track, Vestige, Whit

Track(s), Tracker, Tracking, Trackman Aintree, Aisle, Band, B-road, Caterpillar®, Cinder, Circuit, Course, Crawler, Cycleway, Dirt, Dog, DOVAP, Drag strip, Drift, Ecliptic, El, Fast, Fettler, Flap(ping), Footing, Gandy dancer, Green road, Greenway, Groove, Hunt, Ichnite, Ichnolite, Icknield Way, Inside, Lane, Ley, Line, Loipe, Loopline, Mommy, Monitor, Monza, Pad, → **PATH**, Persue, Piste, Pitlane, Pug, Pursue, Race, Raceway, Rail, Railway, Rake, Ridgeway, Riding, Route, Run, Rut, Scent, Siding, Sign, Skidway, Sleuth, Slot, Sonar, Speedway, Spoor, Tan, Tan-ride, Taxiway, Tenure, Tideway, Title, Trace, → **TRAIL**, Trajectory, Tram, Tramline, Tramroad, Tramway, Tread, Trode, Tug(boat), Twin, Wake, Wallaby, Way, Y

Tract(able), Tracts Area, Belt, Bench, Clime, Common, Dene, Digestive, Enclave, Enteral, Flysheet, Lande, Leaflet, Monte, Moor, → **PAMPHLET**, Park, Prairie, Province, Purlieu, Pusey, Pyramidal, Region, Scabland, Taluk, Tawie, Terrain, Wold

Tracy Dick, Spencer

Trade(r), Tradesman, Trading Arb(itrageur), Art, Banian, Banyan, Bargain, Barter, Bear, Bilateral, Bricks and clicks, Bull, Burgher, Business, Cabotage, Calling, Carriage, Chaffer, Chandler, Chapman, Cheapjack, Cheesemonger, Clicks and mortar, Coaster, → **COMMERCE**, Coster, Costermonger, Crare, Crayer, Deal(er), Dicker, Errand, Exchange, Exporter, Factor, Fair, Floor, Free, Galleon, Handle, Horse, Hosier, Hot, Importer, Indiaman, Industry, Insider, Ironmonger, Jobber, Kidder, Line, Matrix, Mercantile, Mercer, Merchant, Mercosur, Métier, Middleman, Mister, Monger, Mystery, Occupy, Outfitter, Paralleling, Pitchman, Ply, Program(me), Rag, Retailer, Roaring, Rough, Roundtripping, Salesman, Scalp, Screen, Sell, Shrivijaya, Simony, Slave, Stallholder, Stationer, Sutler, Suttle, → **SWAP**, Traffic, Transit, Trant, Truck, Union, Vaisya, Vend, Wholesaler, Wind

Trademark, Trade name Brand, Chop, Idiograph, Label, Logo, TN

Tradition(s), Traditional(ist) Ancestral, Classical, Convention, Custom(ary), Eastern, Folksy, Folkway, Hadith, Heritage, Legend, Lore, Mahayana, Misoneist, Old guard, Old-line, Old-school, Orthodox, Pharisee, Pompier, Practice, Purist, Square, Suburban, Time-honoured, Trad, Tralaticious, Tralatitious, Unwritten

Traffic(ker), Traffic pattern Air, Barter, Broke, Cabotage, Clover-leaf, Commerce, Contraflow, Coyote, Deal, Export, Negotiate, Passage, Run, Slave trade, Smuggle, Tailback, Trade, Truck, Vehicular, Way

Tragedian, Tragedy, Tragic Aeschylus, Antigone, Buskin, Calamity, Cenci, Corneille, Dire, → **DRAMA**, Euripides, Lear, Macready, Melpomene, Oedipean, Oresteia, Otway, Pathetic, Seneca, Sophoclean, Thespian, Thespis

Trail(er), Trailing Abature, Advert, Appalachian, Bedraggle, Caravan, Creep, Dissipation, Drag, Draggle, Fire, Follow, Horsebox, Ipomaea, Ivy, Lag, Liana, Liane, Nature, Oregon, Paper, Path, Persue, Preview, Prevue, Promo(tion), Pursue, Repent,

Runway, Scent, Shadow, Sickle-cell, Sign, Sleuth, Slot, Spoor, Straggle, Stream, Streel, Tow, Trace, →**TRACK**, Trade, Traipse, Trape, Trauchle, Trayne, Troad, Vapour, Vine, Virga, Wake

▷ **Train(ed)** *may indicate* an anagram

Train(er), Training Accommodation, Advanced, APT, Autogenic, Baggage, Boot camp, BR, Breed, Brighton Belle, Bullet, Caravan, Cat, Cavalcade, Choo-choo, Circuit, Coach, Commuter, Condition, Cortège, Day release, Diesel, Direct, Discipline, Dog, Double-header, Dressage, Drill, Drive, Educate, Entourage, Enure, Eurostar®, Excursion, Exercise, Express, Fartlek, Field, Flier, Flight simulator, Freightliner®, Fuse, Gear, Ghan, Ghost, Gravy, Grounding, GWR, Handle(r), HST, →**INSET**, Instruct, Intercity®, Interval, Journey, Liner, Link, LMS, LNER, Loco, Lunge, Maglev, Mailcar, Manège, Manrider, Mentor, Milk, Mixed, Multiple unit, Nopo, Nurture, Nuzzle, Omnibus, Orient Express, Outward Bound®, Owl, Pack, Paddy, Parliamentary, PE, Pendolino, Personal, Potty, Power, Practise, →**PREPARE**, Procession, PT, Puffer, Puff-puff, Push-pull, Q, Queue, Rattler, Rehearse, Retinue, Road, Roadwork, Rocket, Roughrider, Royal Scot, Ry, Sack, Sacque, →**SCHOOL**, Series, Shoe, Shuttle service, Siege, Simulator, Skill centre, Sloid, Sloyd, Sowarry, Special, Square-bashing, SR, Steer, String, Suite, Tail, Tame, →**TEACH**, Through, Tire, Track shoe, Trail, Trellis, Tube, Twin bill, Wage, Wagon, Wave, Way, Whale oil

Traipse Gad

Traitor Betrayer, Casement, Dobber-in, Fifth column, Joyce, Judas, Nid(d)ering, Nid(d)erling, Nithing, Proditor, Quisling, Renegade, Reptile, Snake, Tarpeian, Traditor, Treachetour, Turncoat, Viper, Wallydraigle, Weasel

Tram, Tramcar Tip, Trolley

▷ **Trammel** *may indicate* an anagram

Tramp, Trample Bog-trotter, Bum, Caird, Clochard, Clump, Deadbeat, Derelict, Derro, Dingbat, Dosser, Down and out, Estragon, Footslog, Freighter, Gadling, Gangrel, Gook, Hike, Hobo, Knight of the road, Lumber, Override, Overrun, Pad, Piepowder, Piker, Plod, Poach, Potch(e), Prostitute, Rover, Scorn, Ship, Slut, Splodge, Sundowner, Swagman, →**TINKER**, Toe-rag(ger), Tom, Track, Traipse, Tread, Trek, Trog, Tromp, Truant, Trudge, Tub, Vagabond, Vagrant, Weary Willie, Whore

Trance Aisling, Catalepsy, Cataplexy, Goa, Narcolepsy, Somnambulism

Tranquil(lity) Ataraxy, Calm, Compose, Composure, Halcyon, Lee, Peace(ful), Placid, Quietude, Restful, Sedate, →**SERENE**, Still

Tranquillise(r) Appease, Ataractic, Ataraxic, →**CALM**, Diazepam, Downer, Hypnone, Hypnotic, Largactil®, Librium®, Nervine, Nitrazepam, Oxazepam, Placate, Satisfy, Soothe, Still, Valium®

Transcend(ent), Transcendental(ist), Transcendentalism Emerson, Excel, Mystic, Overtop, Surpass, Thoreau

Transfer(ence), Transference Alien, Alienate, →**ASSIGN**, Attorn, Bosman, Calk, Calque, Carryover, Cede, Chargeable, Communize, Consign, Convey(ance), Credit, Crosstalk, Cutover, Dabbity, Decal(comania), Deed, Demise, Devolve, Download, Embryo, Exchange, Explant, Extradite, Flit, Gene, Hive off, Letraset®, Make over, Mancipation, Metathesis, Mortmain, Nuclear, On-lend, Pass, Photomechanical, Print through, Provection, Reassign, Redeploy, Remit, Remove, Render, Repot, Second, Settlement, Slam, Spool, Thought, Transcribe, Transduction, Transfection, Transhume, Translocation, Uproot, Vire, Virement

▷ **Transferred** *may indicate* an anagram

Transform(ation), Transformer Affine, Alchemist, Alter, Balun, Change, Linear, Lorentz, Metamorphism, Metamorphose, Metamorphosis, Metaplasia, Metastasis, Morphallaxis, Morphing, Permute, Rectifier, Sea change, Sepalody, Tinct, Toroid, Toupee, Transfigure, Transmogrify, Variation, Wig

▷ **Transform(ed)** *may indicate* an anagram

Transgress(ion) Encroach, Err, Infraction, Infringe, Offend, Overstep, Peccancy, →**SIN**, Violate

Transient, Transit(ion), Transitory Brief, Caducity, Ecotone, Ephemeral,

Evanescent, Fleeting, Fly-by-night, Fugacious, Hobo, Metabasis, Passage, Passing, Provisional, Rapid, Seque, Sfumato, T, Temporary

Translate, Translation, Translator Calque, Construe, Convert, Coverdale, Crib, Decode, Decrypt, Encode, Explain, Free, Horse, Interpret, In vitro, Jerome, Key, Linguist, Loan, Machine, Metaphrase, Nick, Paraphrase, Pinyin, Polyglot, Pony, Reduce, Render, Rendition, Rhemist, Septuagint, Simultaneous, Targum, Tr, Transcribe, Transform, Trot, Tyndale, Unseen, Version(al), Vulgate, Wycliffe

▷ **Translate(d)** *may indicate* an anagram

Transmit(ter), Transmitted, Transmission Aerial, Air, Aldis lamp, Analogue, Band, Baseband, Beacon, →**BROADCAST**, Carry, CB, Communicate, Compander, Compandor, Consign, Contagion, Convection, Convey, Digital, Diplex, Forward, Gearbox, Gene, Heredity, Impart, Intelsat, Localizer, Manual, Mast, Mic(rophone), Modem, Nicol, Permittivity, Pipe, Propagate, Racon, Radiate, Radio, Receiver, Responser, Send, Simulcast, Sonabuoy, Spark, Tappet, Telautograph®, Telecast, Telegony, Telematics, Telemetry, Telepathy, Teleprinter, Teletex, Televise, Telex, Tiptronic®, Tiros, Traduce, Traject, Tralaticious, Tralatitious, UART, Ultrawideband, Uplink, Upload, Walkie-talkie, WAP, Webcam, Wi-Fi®

Transparent, Transparency Adularia, Clarity, Clear, Crystal(line), Diaphanous, Dioptric, Glassy, Glazed, Hyaloid, Iolite, Leno, Limpid, Lucid, Luminous, Patent, Pellucid, Porcelain, Sheer, Slide, Tiffany, Transpicuous

Transport(ed), Transporter, Transportation Aerotrain, Air-lift, Ar(a)ba, Argo, Bathorse, Bear, Bike, Broomstick, BRS, Buggy, Bus, Cargo, Carract, →**CARRY**, Cart, Casevac, Cat-train, Charabanc, Charm, Conductor, Convey, Cycle, Delight, Deliver, Ecstasy, Elation, Eloin, Enrapt, Enravish, Entrain, Esloin, Estro, Exalt, Ferriage, Ferry, Fishyback, Freight (train), Haul(age), Hearse, Helicopter, Jerrican, Joy, Kart, Kurvey, Lift, Maglev, Matatu, Medevac, Minicab, Monorail, Overjoy, Pack animal, Palanquin, Pantechnicon, Park and ride, Paytrain, Public, Put, Rape, Rapine, Rapture, Roadster, Ship, Shorthaul, Shuttle, Skateboard, Sledge, Sno-Cat, Snowmobile, Supersonic, Tandem, Tape, Tardis, Tote, Train, Tramway, Trap, Troopship, Tuktuk, Ubiquinone, Waft, Waterbus, Wheels, Wireway

Transpose, Transposition Anagram, Commute, Convert, Invert, Metathesis, Shift, Spoonerism, Switch, Tr

▷ **Transposed** *may indicate* an anagram

Trap(s), Trapdoor, Trapped, Trappings Ambush, →**BAGGAGE**, Bags, Belongings, Birdlime, Booby, Buckboard, Bunker, Carriage, Catch, Catch-pit, Clapnet, Cobweb, Corner, Cru(i)ve, Deadfall, Death, Decoy, Dip, Dogcart, Downfall, Drain, Eelset, Emergent, Ensnare, Entoil, Entrain, Fall, Fit-up, Fly, Flypaper, Frame-up, Fyke, Geel, Gig, Gin, Gob, Gravel, Grin, Hatch, Housings, Ice-bound, Illaqueate, Jinri(c)ksha(w), Keddah, Kettle, Kheda, Kiddle, Kidel, Kipe, Kisser, Knur(r), Light, Lime, Live, Lobster pot, →**LUGGAGE**, Lure, Mesh, Mouth, Net, Nur(r), Oil, Paraphernalia, Pitfall, Plant, Polaron, Police, Pot, Poverty, Putcheon, Putcher, Quicksand, Radar, Regalia, Sand, Scruto, Scuttle, →**SNARE**, Speed, Spell, Spider, Springe, Stake-net, Star, Steam, Stench, Sting, Stink, Sun, Tangle, Tank, Teagle, Toil, Tonga, Tourist, Trapfall, Tripwire, Trojan horse, Trou-de-loup, Two-wheeler, U, U-bend, Vampire, Waterseal, Web, Weel, Weir, Wire

Trash(y) Bosh, Deface, Desecrate, Dre(c)k, Garbage, Junk, Kitsch, Pulp, →**RUBBISH**, Schlock, Scum, Tinpot, Trailer, Vandalise, Worthless

Travel(ler), Travelling Aeneas, Backpack, Bagman, Columbus, Commercial, Commute, Crustie, Crusty, Drive, Drummer, Explorer, Fare, Fellow, Fly, Fogg, Geoffrey, Gipsen, Gipsy, Gitano, Globe-trotter, Go, Gulliver, Gypsy, Hike, Hitchhiker, Interrail, Itinerant, Jet-setter, Journey, Locomotion, Long-haul, Marco Polo, Meve, Migrant, Motor, Move, Mush, Nomad, Odysseus, Passepartout, Peregrination, Peripatetic, Pilgrim, Ply, Polo, Range, Rep, Ride, Road, Roam, Rom(any), Rove, Safari, Sail, Salesman, Samaritan, Sinbad, Teleport, Tool, →**TOUR**, Tourist, Trek, Tripper, Tsigane, Viator, Voyage, Wayfarer, Wend, Wildfire, Zigan

Travesty Burlesque, Charade, Distortion, Parody, Show, Skit

Tray Antler, Carrier, Case, Charger, Coaster, Gallery, In, Joe, Lazy Susan, Mould, Out, Plateau, Tea, Trencher, Typecase, Voider

Treacherous, Treachery Bad faith, Betrayal, Deceit, Delilah, Fickle, Ganelon, Guile, Insidious, Knife, Medism, Perfidious, Punic, Punic faith, Quicksands, Sedition, Serpentine, Sleeky, Snaky, Sneaky, Trahison, Traitor, Trappy, →**TREASON**, Two-faced, Viper, Weasel

Tread Clamp, Clump, Dance, Pad, Step, Stramp, Track, Trample

Treadle Footboard

Treason Betrayal, Constructive, High, Insurrection, Lèse-majesté, Lese-majesty, Perduellion, Sedition, →**TREACHERY**

Treasure(r), Treasury Banker, Bursar, Cache, Camera, Camerlengo, Camerlingo, Cherish, Chest, Cimelia, Coffer, Ewe-lamb, Exchequer, Fisc(al), Fisk, Godolphin, Golden, Heritage, Hoard, Hon(ey), Montana, Palgrave, →**PRIZE**, Procurator, Purser, Quaestor, Relic, Riches, Steward, Thesaurus, Trove

Treat, Treatment Actinotherapy, Action, Acupressure, Acupuncture, Allopathy, Antidote, Apitherapy, Aromatherapy, Beano, Beneficiate, Besee, Body wrap, Botox®, Capitulate, Care, Chemotherapy, Condition, Course, Coverage, Crymotherapy, Cupping, Cure, Deal, Detox(ification), Dialysis, Do, →**DOCTOR**, Dose, Dress, Dutch, Electrotherapy, Entertain, EST, Facial, Faith-healing, Fango, Faradism, Figuration, Foment, Frawzey, Handle, Heliotherapy, Hellerwork, Holistic, Homeopathy, HRT, Hydrotherapy, Hypnotherapy, Intermediate, Kenny, Laser, Manage, Massotherapy, Mechanotherapy, Medicament, Medicate, Mercerise, Mesotherapy, Narcotherapy, Naturopathy, Negotiate, Organotherapy, Orthoptics, Osteopathy, →**OUTING**, Pasteur, Pedicure, Pelotherapy, Phototherapy, Physiatrics, Physic, Physiotherapy, Pie, Poultice, Process, Psychoanalysis, Psychodrama, Psychotherapy, Radiotherapy, Regale, Rehab(ilitation), Rest cure, Root, Secretage, Serotherapy, Setter, Shout, Shrift, Sironise, Smile, Softener, Speleotherapy, →**STAND**, Tablet, TENS, →**THERAPY**, Thermotherapy, Titbit, Traction, Turkish bath, Twelve-step, UHT, Usance, Use, Vet

▷ **Treated** *may indicate an anagram*

Treatise Almagest, Bestiary, Commentary, Cybele, Didache, Discourse, Monograph, Pandect, Profound, Summa, Tract(ate), Upanishad, Vedanta

Treaty Agreement, Alliance, Assiento, Concordat, Covenant, Entente, GATT, Lateran, Locarno, Lunéville, Maastricht, Nijmegen, →**PACT**, Paris, Protocol, Rapallo, Ryswick, San Stefano, Sovetsk, Test-ban, Utrecht

Treble Castrato, Choirboy, Chorist(er), Pairial, Soprano, →**TRIPLE**, Triune

Tree(s) Actor, →**ANCESTRY**, Axle, Beam, Bluff, Boom, Bosk, Conifer, Corner, Cross, Daddock, Deciduous, Decision, Dendrology, Descent, Family, Fault, Fringe, Gallows, Grove, Hang, Hardwood, Jesse, Nurse, Pedigree, Phanerophyte, Pole, Sawyer, Shoe, Silviculture, Softwood, Staddle, Stemma, Summer, Thicket, Timber, Tyburn, Ulmaceous, Wicopy, →**WOOD**

Tremble, Trembling, Tremor Aftershock, Butterfly, Dither, Dodder, Hotter, Judder, Marsquake, Milk sickness, Palpitate, Quail, Quake, Quaver, Quiver, Seismal, →**SHAKE**, Shiver, Shock, Shudder, Stound, Temblor, Titubation, Trepid, Twitchy, Vibrate, Vibration, Vibratiuncle, Vibrato, Wobble, Wuther, Yips

Tremendous Big, Enormous, Howling, Immense, Marvellous, Thundering

▶ **Tremor** *see* **TREMBLE**

Trench(er) Boyau, Cunette, Cuvette, Delf, Delph, Dike(r), →**DITCH**, Dyke(r), Encroach, Fleet, Foss(e), Foxhole, Fur(r), Furrow, Grip, Gullet, Gutter, Leat, Line, Mariana, Moat, Oceanic, Outwork, Rill, Rille, Ring-dyke, Salient, Sap, Shott, Slidder, Slit, Sod, Sondage

Trend(y), Trendsetter Bellwether, Bent, Bias, Chic, Climate, Drift, Fashion, Hep, Hip, Hipster, In, Mainstream, Newfangled, Pacemaker, Pop, Poserish, Posey, Rage, Smart, Style, Swim, Tendency, Tendenz, Tenor, Tide, Tonnish

Trepidation Butterflies

Trespass, Trespasser, Trespass(ing) Encroach, Errant, Hack, Impinge, Infringe, Offend, Peccancy, Sin, Trench, Wrong(doer)

Trial Acid test, Adversity, Affliction, Appro, Approbation, Approval, Assize, Attempt, Bane, Bernoulli, Bout, Burden, Case, Compurgation, Corsned, Court-martial, Cow, Cross, Dock, Drumhead, Empirical, Essay, → **EXPERIMENT**, Field, Fitting, Go, Hearing, Jeddart justice, Jethart justice, Lydford law, Nuremberg, Ordeal, Pest, Pilot, Pree, Probation, Proof, Race, Rehearsal, Salem, Scramble, State, Taste, Test, Test bed

Triangle(d), Triangular Acute, Bermuda, Cosec, Deltoid, Equilateral, Eternal, Gair, Golden, Gore, Gyronny, Isosceles, Obtuse, Pascal's, Pedimental, Pyramid, Rack, Right-angled, Scalene, Similar, Trigon, Triquetral, Tromino, Warning

Tribe(s), Tribal, Tribesman Cimmerii, Clan(nish), Cree, Crow, D(a)yak, Dynasty, Ephraim, Family, Gond, Guarani, Issachar, Iwi, Judah, Levite, Longobardi, Lost, Manasseh, Nation, Ordovices, Picts, → **RACE**, Schedule, Strandloper, Ute, Zebulun

Tribune, Tribunal Aeropagus, Bema, Bench, → **COURT**, Divan, Forum, Hague, Industrial, Leader, Platform, Rienzi, Rota, Star-chamber

Tributary Affluent, Bogan, Branch, Creek, Fork

Tribute Cain, Citation, Commemoration, Compliment, Crants, Deodate, → **DUE**, Encomium, Epitaph, Festschrift, Floral, Gavel, Heriot, Homage, Kain, Memento, Ode, Panegyric, Peter's pence, → **PRAISE**, Rome-penny, Rome-scot, Scat(t), Tax, Testimonial, Toast, Toll, Wreath, Wroth

▷ **Trick** *may indicate* an anagram

Trick(ed), Trickery, Tricks(ter), Tricky Antic, Art, Artifice, Attrap, Awkward, Bamboozle, Begunk, Book, Bunco, Bunko, Cantrip, Capot, Catch, Charley pitcher, Cheat, Chicane(ry), Chouse, Claptrap, Cod(-act), Cog, Con(fidence), Coyote, Crook, Davenport, Deck, Delicate, Delude, Device, Dirty, → **DO**, → **DODGE**, Double, Dupe, Elf, Elfin, Elvan, Elven, Fard, Feat, Fetch, Fiddle, Finesse, Finicky, Flam, Flim-flam, Fob, Fox, Fraud, Fun, Gambit, Game, Gammon, Gaud, Gimmick, Gleek, Glike, Gowk, Guile, Had, Hanky-panky, Hey presto, Hoax, Hocus(-pocus), Hoodwink, Hot potato, Hum, Illude, Illusion, Imposture, Jape, Jockey, John, Kittle, Knack, Lark, Leg pull, Magsman, Mislead, Monkey, Monkey-shine, Murphy's game, Nap, Palter, Parlour, Pass, Pawk, Phish, Pleasantry, Prank, Prestige, Put-on, Quick, Ramp, Raven, Reak, Reik, Rex, Rig, Rope, Ropery, Ruse, Scam, Sell, Set-up, Shanghai, Shenanigan, Shifty, Shill, Skite, Skul(l)duggery, Skylark, Skyte, Slam, Sleight, Slight, Sophism, Spoof, Stall, Stealth, Stint, Stunt, Subterfuge, Three-card, Ticklish, Tip, Trait, Trap, Trump, Turn, Underplot, Vole, Wangle, Wheeze, Wile, Wrinkle

Tricycle Pedicab

Trifle(s), Trifling Bagatelle, Banal, Bauble, Bibelot, Birdseed, Bit, Bric-a-brac, Bubkes, Cent, Chickenfeed, Coquette, Dabble, Dalliance, Denier, Dessert, Do, Doit, Faddle, Falderal, Falderol, Fallal, Feather, Fewtril, Fiddle, Fiddle-faddle, Fig, Fizgig, Flamfew, Fleabite, Flirt, Folderol, Fool, Footle, Fribble, Frippery, Fritter, Frivol, Gewgaw, Idle, Insignificant, Iota, Kickshaw, Knick-knack, Mess, Mite, Nothing, Old song, Palter, Paltry, Peanuts, Peddle, Peppercorn, Petty, Philander, Piddle, Piffle, Pin, Pingle, Pittance, Play, Potty, Quelquechose, Quiddity, Quiddle, Slight, Small beer, Small wares, Smatter, Song, Sport, Stiver, Strae, Straw, Sundry, Tiddle, Tom, Toy, Trinket, Trivia, Whit

Trigger Detent, Hair, Instigate, Pawl, Precipitate, Set off, Spark, Start, Switch on, Tripwire

Trill(ed), Triller, Trilling Burr, Churr, Hirrient, Quaver, Ribattuta, Roll, Staphyle, Trim, Twitter, Warble

Trim(med), Trimmer, Trimming Abridge, Ballast, Barb, Bleed, Braid, Bray, Chipper, Clip, Dapper, Defat, Dinky, Dress, Ermine, Face, Fettle, File, Froufrou, Garnish, Garniture, Gimp, Guimpe, Hog, Macramé, Macrami, Marabou, Neat, Net(t), Ornament, Pare, Pipe, Plight, Posh, Preen, Pruin(e), Prune, Roach, Robin, Ruche, Sax, Sett, Shear, Shipshape, Smirk, Smug, Sned, Snod, Soutache, → **SPRUCE**, Straddle, Stroddle, Stylist, Svelte, → **TIDY**, Time-server, Top, Torsade, Trick, Wig

Trinket(s) Bauble, Bibelot, Bijou(terie), Charm, Falderal, Fallal, Folderol, Nicknack, Toy, Trankum

▷ **Trip** *may indicate* an anagram

Trip(per) Awayday, Cruise, Dance, Day, Druggie, Ego, Errand, Expedition, →**FALL**, Field, Flight, Flip, Guilt, Head, High, Joint, Jolly, Journey, Junket, Kilt, Link, Outing, Passage, Pleasure, Ply, Power, Ride, Round, Run, Sail, Sashay, Spin, Spurn, →**STUMBLE**, Tootle, Tour, Trek, Trial, Voyage

Triple, Triplet Codon, Hemiol(i)a, Perfect, Sdrucciola, Ternal, Tiercet, Treble, Trifecta, Trilling, Trin(e), Tripling

Trite Banal, Boilerplate, Corny, Hackneyed, Hoary, Mickey Mouse, Novelettish, Pabulum, Rinky-dink, Stale, Stock, Time-worn, Worn

Triumph(ant) Cock-a-hoop, Codille, Cowabunga, Crow, Exult, Glory, Impostor, Killing, Oho, Olé, Ovation, Palm, Prevail, Victorious, →**WIN**

Trivia(l), Triviality Adiaphoron, Bagatelle, Balaam, Bald, →**BANAL**, Bathos, Footling, Frippery, Frothy, Futile, Idle, Inconsequential, Light, Minutiae, Nitpicking, No-brainer, Nothingism, Paltry, Pap, Peppercorn, Pettifoggery, Petty, Picayune, Piddling, Piffling, Puerile, Shallow, Small, Small beer, Small fry, Snippety, Squirt, Squit, Toy(s), Twaddle, Vegie

Trixie Bea

Trolley Brute, Cart, Crane, Dinner-wagon, Dolly, Gurney, Shopping, Tea, Teacart, Truck, Trundler

▶**Trollop** *see* **LOOSE(N)**

Trompe l'oeil Quadratura, Quadrature

Troop(s), Trooper Alpini, Anzac, Band, BEF, Brigade, Cohort, Company, Depot, Detachment, Garrison, Guard, Horde, Household, Logistics, Midianite, Militia, Monkeys, Pultan, Pulton, Pultoon, Pultun, SAS, School, Shock, →**SOLDIER**, Sowar, State, Storm, Subsidiary, Tp, Turm(e), Velites

Trope Euouae, Evovae

Trophy Adward, Ashes, →**AWARD**, Bag, Belt, Cup, Emmy, Memento, Palm, Plate, →**PRIZE**, Scalp, Schneider, Shield, Silverware, Spoils, Tourist, Triple crown, TT

Trot(ter), Trot out Air, Clip, Crib, Crubeen, Hag, Job, Jog, Passage, Pettitoes, Piaffe, Pony, Ranke, Red(-shirt), Rising, Tootsie, Trotskyist

Trouble(s), Troublemaker, Troublesome Ache, Ado, Affliction, Aggro, Agitate, Ail, Alarm, Annoy, Bale, Barrat, Bedevil, Beset, →**BOTHER**, Bovver, Brickle, Burden, Care, Coil, Concern, Debate, Disaster, Dismay, Disquiet, Distress, Disturb, Dog, Dolour, Eat, Exercise, Fash, Finger, Firebrand, Frondeur, Gram(e), Grief, Harass, Harry, Hassle, Hatter, Heat, Heist, Hellion, Hot water, Howdyedo, Incommode, Inconvenience, Infest, →**IN TROUBLE**, Irk, Jam, Kaugh, Malcontent, Mayhem, Mess, Mixer, Moil, Molest, Noy, Onerous, Perturb, Pester, Pestiferous, Picnic, Plague, Play up, Poke, Reck, Rub, Scamp, Scrape, Shake, Shtook, Soup, Spiny, Stir, Stirrer, Storm, Sturt, Tartar, Teen, Teething, Thorny, Tine, Toil, Trial, Turn-up, Tyne, Typhoid Mary, Unpleasant, Unrest, Unsettle, Vex, →**WORRY**

▷**Troublesome** *may indicate* an anagram

Trough Back, Backet, Bed, Buddle, Channel, Chute, Culvert, Graben, Gutter, Hod, Hutch, Manger, Stock, Straik, Strake, Syncline, Troffer, Tundish, Tye

Trouser(s) Bags, Bell-bottoms, Bloomers, Breeches, Bumsters, Capri pants, Cargo pants, Chinos, Churidars, Clam-diggers, Combat, Continuations, Cords, Corduroys, Cossacks, Culottes, Daks, Denims, Drainpipe, Drawers, Ducks, Dungarees, Eel-skins, Flannels, Flares, Galligaskins, Gaskins, Gauchos, Hip-huggers, Hipsters, Indescribables, Inexpressibles, Innominables, Jazzpants, Jeans, Jodhpurs, Jog-pants, Kaccha, Ke(c)ks, Knee cords, Lederhosen, Levis, Longs, Loon-pants, Loons, Moleskins, Overalls, Oxford bags, Palazzo (pants), Palazzos, Pantalet(te)s, Pantaloons, Pants, Pedal pushers, Pegtops, Plus-fours, Plus-twos, Pyjamas, Rammies, Reach-me-downs, Salopettes, Shalwar, Ski pants, Slacks, Stirrup pants, Stovepipes, Strides, Strossers, Sweatpants, Thornproofs, Trews, Trouse, Trunk-breeches, Unmentionables, Unutterables, Utterless

Trout Aurora, Brook, Brown, Bull, Coral, Cutthroat, Finnac(k), Finnock, Fish, Gillaroo, Herling, Hirling, Peal, Peel, Phinnock, Pogies, Quintet, Rainbow, Sewen, Sewin, Speckled, Splake, Steelhead, Togue, Whitling

Truant Absentee, AWOL, Bunk off, Dodge, Hooky, Idler, Kip, Mich(e), Mitch, Mooch, Mouch, Wag

Truce Armistice, Barley, Ceasefire, Fainites, Fains, Hudna, Interlude, Keys, Pax, Stillstand, Treague, Treaty

Truck Bakkie, Bogie, Breakdown, Business, Cabover, Cattle, Cocopan, Dealings, Dolly, Dumper, Flatbed, Forklift, Haul, Hopper, Journey, → **LORRY**, Low-loader, Monster, Pallet, Panel, Pick-up, Road-train, Semi, Sound, Stacking, Tipper, Tommy, Tow(ie), Traffic, Tram, Trolley, Trundle, Ute, Utility, Van, Wrecker

Trudge Footslog, Jog, Lumber, Pad, Plod, Stodge, Stramp, Taigle, Traipse, Trash, Trog, Vamp

True Accurate, Actual, Apodictic, Axiomatic, Constant, Correct, Exact, Factual, Faithful, Genuine, Honest, Indubitable, Leal, Literal, Loyal, Platitude, Plumb, Pure, Real, Realistic, Sooth, Vera, Very

Truly Certainly, Certes, Fegs, Forsooth, Honestly, Indeed, Insooth, Surely, Verily, Yea

Trump(s), Trumpet(er) Agami, Alchemy, Alchymy, Bach, Blare, Blast, Bray, Buccina, Bugle(r), Call, Card, Clang, Clarion, Conch, Cornet, Corona, Crossruff, Crow, Daffodil, Elephant, Extol, Fanfare, Hallali, Honours, → **HORN**, Invent, Jew's, Last, Lituus, Lur(e), Lurist, Manille, Marine, Megaphone, Overruff, Pedro, Proclaim, Ram's-horn, Resurrect, Ruff, Salpingian, Salpinx, Sancho, Satchmo, Sennet, Shell, Shofar, Shophar, Slug-horn, Splash, Surpass, Tantara, Tantarara, Tar(at)antara, Theodomas, Tiddy, Triton, Triumph

Trunk(s) Aorta(l), A-road, Body, Bole, Box, Bulk, But(t), Caber, Carcase, Chest, Coffer, Hose, Imperial, Log, Nerve, Peduncle, Pollard, Portmanteau, Portmantle, Proboscis, Puncheon, Ricker, Road, Saratoga, Shorts, STD, Steamer, Stock, Stud, Synangium, Togs, Torso, Valise, Wardrobe

Trust(y), Trusting, Trustworthy Affy, Apex, Authentic, Belief, Bet on, Blind, Box, Camaraderie, Care, Cartel, Charge, Combine, Confide, Count on, Credit, Dependable, Dewy-eyed, Discretionary, → **FAITH**, Fidelity, Fiduciary, Foundation, Gullible, Honest, Hope, Hospital, Investment, Leal, Lippen, Loyal, Naif, National, NT, Reliable, Reliance, Rely, Repose, Reputable, Responsible, Staunch, Tick, Trojan, Trow, True, Trump, Unit

Truth(ful), Truism Accuracy, Alethic, Axiom, Bromide, Cliché, Cold turkey, Dharma, Dialectic, → **FACT**, Facticity, Forsooth, Gospel, Griff, Home, Honesty, Idea(l), Logical, Maxim, Naked, Necessary, Pravda, Principle, Reality, Sooth, Soothfast, Strength, Troggs, Veracity, Veridical, Verisimilitude, Verity, Vraisemblance

Try(ing) Aim, Approof, Assay, Attempt, Audition, Bash, Bate, Bid, Birl, Burden, Burl, Conative, Contend, Court martial, Crack, Effort, Empiric(utic), → **ENDEAVOUR**, Essay, Examine, Experiment, Fand, Fish, Fling, Foretaste, Go, Gun for, Harass, Hard, Hear, Importunate, Irk, Noy, Offer, Ordalium, Penalty, Pop, Practise, Pree, Prieve, Prove, → **SAMPLE**, Seek, Shot, Sip, Stab, Strain, Strive, Taste, Tax, Tempt, Test, Touchdown, → **TRIAL**, Whirl

Tub(by), Tubbiness, Tubman, Tub-thumper Ash-leach, Back, Bath, Boanerges, Bran, Bucket, Cooper, Corf, Cowl, Dan, Diogenes, Endomorph, Firkin, Hip bath, Keeve, Kid, Kieve, Kit, Pin, Podge, Powdering, Pudge, Pulpit, Rolypoly, Seasoning, Tun, Vat, Wash, Whey

Tube, Tubing, Tubular Acorn, Arteriole, Artery, Barrel, Blowpipe, Bronchus, Buckyball, Buckytube, Burette, Calamus, Camera, Can(n)ula, Capillary, Casing, Catheter, Cathode-ray, Cave, Conduit, Crookes, Digitron, Diode, Discharge, Drain, Draw, Drift, Dropper, Duct, Electron, Endiometer, Eustachian, Extension, Fallopian, Fistula, Flash, Fluorescent, Germ, Glowstick, Grommet, Hawsepipe, Hose, Idiot box, Inner, Kinescope, Macaroni, Matrass, Metro, Morris, Nasogastric, Neural, Nixie, Optic, Orthicon, Oval, Oviduct, Pastille, Peashooter, Pentode, Picture, → **PIPE**, Pipette, Piping, Pneumatic, Pollen, Postal, Promethean, Salpinx, Saticon®, Saucisse, Saucisson, Schnorkel, Shock, Sieve, Siphon(al), Siphonet, Sleeve, Slide, Snorkel, Spaghetti, Speaking, Spout, Staple, Static, Stent, Stone canal, Storage, Strae, Straw, Strip light, Subway, Sucker, Swallet, Syringe, Tele, Telescope, Teletron, Television,

Telly, Terete, Test, Tetrode, Thermionic, Tile, Torpedo, Torricellian, Trachea, Travelling-wave, Trocar, Trochotron, Trunk, Tunnel, Tuppenny, TV, U, Underground, Ureter, Urethra, Vacuum, Vas, VDU, Vein, Vena, Venturi, Video, Vidicon®, Worm, X-ray

Tuber(s) Arnut, Arracacha, Bulb, Chufa, Coc(c)o, Dasheen, Earth-nut, Eddoes, Ginseng, Jicama, Mashua, Oca, Pignut, Potato, Salep, Taproot, Taro, Tuckahoe, Yam, Yautia

Tuberculosis Consumption, Crewels, Cruel(l)s, Decline, Lupus, Lupus vulgaris, Phthisis, Scrofula

Tuck Dart, Friar, Gather, Grub, Hospital corner, Kilt, Pin, Pleat, Scran

Tudor Stockbrokers'

Tuff Schalstein

Tuft(ed) Aigrette, Amentum, Beard, Candlewick, Catkin, C(a)espitose, Cluster, Coma, Comb, Cowlick, Crest, Dollop, Ear, Flaught, Floccus, Goatee, Hank, Hassock, Pappus, Penicillate, Pledget, Quiff, Scopate, Shola, Tait, Tassel, Toorie, Topknot, Toupee, Tourie, Tussock, Tuzz, Whisk

Tug Chain, Drag, Haul, Jerk, Lug, Pug, → PULL, Rive, Rug, Ship, Sole, Soole, Sowl(e), Tit, Tow, Towboat, Yank

Tumble, Tumbler Acrobat, Cartwheel, Drier, Fall, → GLASS, Jack, Jill, Lock, Pitch, Popple, Purl, Realise, Spill, Stumble, Topple, Touser, Towser, Trip, Twig, Voltigeur, Welter

▷ **Tumble** *may indicate* an anagram

Tumour Adenoma, Anbury, Angioma, Angiosarcoma, Astrocytoma, Burkitt('s) lymphoma, Cancer, Carcinoid, Carcinoma, Carcinosarcoma, Chondroma, Condyloma, Crab(-yaws), Craniopharyngioma, Dermoid, Encanthis, Encephaloma, Enchondroma, Endothelioma, Epulis, Exostosis, Fibroid, Fibroma, Ganglion, Gioblastoma, Glioma, Granuloma, Grape, → GROWTH, Gumma, Haemangioma, Haematoma, Hepatoma, Lipoma, Lymphoma, Medulloblastoma, Melanoma, Meningioma, Mesothelioma, Metastasis, Mole, Myeloma, Myoma, Myxoma, Neoplasm, Neuroblastoma, Neurofibroma, Neuroma, -oma, Oncogenesis, Oncology, Osteoclastoma, Osteoma, Osteosarcoma, Papilloma, Polypus, Retinoblastoma, Rous sarcoma, Sarcoma, Scirrhous, Seminoma, Steatoma, Struma, Talpa, Teratocarcinoma, Teratoma, Thymoma, Wart, Wen, Wilms', Windgall, Wolf, Xanthoma, Yaw

Tumult Brattle, Brawl, Coil, Deray, Ferment, Fracas, Hirdy-girdy, Hubbub, Reird, Riot, → ROAR, Romage, Rore, Stoor, Stour, Stowre, Stramash, Tew, Tristan, Tristram, → UPROAR

Tuna Ahi, Pear, Skipjack, Yellowfin

Tune(s), Tuneful, Tuner, Tuning Adjust, Air, Aria, Ayre, Canorous, Carillon, Catch, Choral(e), Dump, Étude, Fork, Gingle, Harmony, Hornpipe, Hunt's up, Jingle, Key, Maggot, Measure, Melisma, → MELODY, Morrice, Morris, Old Hundred, Peg, Planxty, Port, Potpourri, Raga, Rant, Ranz-des-vaches, Reel, Signature, Snatch, Song, Spring, Strain, Sweet, Syntonise, Syntony, Temper, Theme, Tone, Toy, Tweak

Tungstate, Tungsten Scheelite, W, Wolfram

Tunic Ao dai, Caftan, Chiton, Choroid, Cote-hardie, Dalmatic, Dashiki, Gymslip, Hauberk, Kabaya, Kaftan, Kameez, K(h)urta, Tabard, Toga

Tunnel(ler) Bore, Channel, Condie, Countermine, Culvert, Cundy, Gallery, Head, Mine, Mole, Qanat, Sewer, Simplon, Stope, Subway, Sure, Syrinx, Transmanche, Tube, Underpass, Wind, Wormhole

Turban Bandanna, Hat, Mitral, Pagri, Puggaree, Puggery, Puggree, Sash, Scarf

Turbulence, Turbulent Atmospheric, Becket, Bellicose, Buller, Factious, Fierce, Overfall, Rapids, Roil, Stormy

▷ **Turbulent, Turbulence** *may indicate* an anagram

Tureen Terreen

Turf Caespitose, Clod, Divot, Earth, Fail, Feal, Flaught, Gazo(o)n, → GRASS, Greensward, Kerf, Peat, Racing, Scraw, → SOD, Sward

Turk(ish) Anatolian, Bashaw, Bashkir, Bey, Bimbashi, Bostangi, Byzantine, Caimac(am), Crescent, Effendi, Gregory, Horse(tail), Irade, Kaimakam, Kazak(h), Kurd,

Mameluke, Mutessarif(at), Omar, Osman(li), Ottamite, Ottoman, Ottomite, Rayah, Scanderbeg, Selim, Seljuk(ian), Seraskier, Spahi, Tatar, Timariot, Usak, Uzbeg, Uzbek, Yakut

Turkey, Turkey-like Anatolia, Antioch, Brush, Bubbly(-jock), Curassow, Eyalet, Flop, Gobbler, Lame brain, Norfolk, Sultanate, Talegalla, TR, Trabzon, Vulturn

Turkish delight Rahat lacoum, Trehala

Turmoil Ariot, Chaos, Confusion, Din, Dust, Ferment, Mess, Pother, Pudder, Stoor, Stour, Tornado, Tracasserie, Tumult, →**UPROAR**, Welter

▷ **Turn(ing)** *may indicate* an anagram

Turn(ing), Turn(ed) away, Turn(ed) up, Turns Act, Adapt, Addle, Advert, Antrorse, Avert, Bad, Bank, Become, Bend, Blow in, Bump, Careen, Cartwheel, Cast, Change, Char(e), Chore, Christiana, Christie, Christy, Churn, Cock, Coil, Corotate, Crank(le), Cuff, Curd(le), Curve, Defect, Deflect, Detour, Deviate, Dig, Digress, Divert, Ear, Earn, Elbow, Evert, Fadge, Ferment, Flip, Forfend, Go, Good, Gyrate, Hairpin, Handbrake, Head-off, Hie, High, Hinge, Hup, Influence, Innings, Invert, Jar, Jink, Jump, Keel, Kick, Lodging, Lot, Luff, Mohawk, Nip, Number, Obvert, Parallel, Parry, Penchant, Pivot, Plough, Pronate, Prove, PTO, Quarter, Rebut, Refer, Refract, Retroflex, Retroussé, Retrovert, Rev, Revolt, Ride, Riffle, Rocker, Roll, Root, →**ROTATE**, Rote, Roulade, Rout, Routine, Screw, Sheer, →**SHOT**, Shout, Sicken, Skit, Slew, Slue, Solstice, Sour, →**SPELL**, Spin, Spot, Sprain, Star, Start, Stem, Step, Stunt, Swash, Swerve, Swing, Swivel, Telemark, Thigmotropism, Three-point, Throw, Tiptilt, Tirl, T-junction, Transpose, Trend, Trick, Trie, Turtle, Twiddle, Twist, Twizzle, U, Uey, U-ie, Up, Veer, Versed, Version, Vertigo, Volta, Volte-face, Volutation, Wap, Warp, Wend, Went, →**WHEEL**, Whelm, Whirl, Whorl, Wimple, Wind, Wrast, Wrest, Wriggle, Zigzag

Turn-coat Apostate, Cato, Defector, Quisling, Rat, Renegade, Tergiversate, Traitor

Turner Axle, Capstan, Lana, Lathe, Painter, Pivot, Rose-engine, Spanner, Tina, Worm, Wrench

Turning point Crisis, Crossroads, Landmark, Watershed

Turnip(-shaped) Baggy, Bagie, Hunter, Indian, Napiform, Navew, Neep, Rutabaga, Shaw, →**STUPID PERSON**, Swede, Tumshie

Turn on Boot

Turn over Capsize, Careen, Flip, Inversion, Mull, Production, PTO, Somersault, TO, Up-end

Turret(ed) Barmkin, Bartisan, Garret, Louver, Louvre, Mirador, Pepperbox, Sponson, Tank top, →**TOWER**, Turriculate

Turtle, Turtle head Bale, Box, Calipash, Calipee, Chelone, Cooter, Diamondback, Emys, Floor, Green, Hawk(s)bill, Inverted, Leatherback, Loggerhead, Matamata, Mossback, Mud, Musk, Painted, Ridley, Screen, Snapper, Snapping, Soft-shelled, Stinkpot, Terrapin, Thalassian

Tuscany Chiantishire

Tusk Gam, Horn, Ivory, Tooth, Tush

Tussle Giust, Joust, Mêlée, Scrimmage, Scrum, Scuffle, Skirmish, Touse, Touze, Towse, Towze, Tuilyie, Wrestle

Tutor Abbé, Aristotle, Ascham, Bear, →**COACH**, Crammer, Don, Edify, Instruct, Leader, Preceptor, Répétiteur, Supervisor, Teacher, Train

TV Baird, Box, Breakfast, Cable, Digibox®, Digital, Docudrama, Docusoap, Flat screen, Idiot-box, Lime Grove, Monitor, NICAM, PAL, SECAM, Sitcom, Sky, Tele, Telly, Tie-in, Triniscope, Tube, Video

Twaddle Blether, Drivel, Fadaise, Rot, Slipslop, Tripe

Tweak Pinch, Pluck, Primp, Twiddle, Twist, Twitch

Twelfth, Twelve Apostles, Dozen, Epiphany, Glorious, Grouse, Midday, Midnight, N, Night, Noon(tide), Ternion, Twal

▶ **Twice** *see* **TWO(SOME)**

Twig(s) Besom, Birch, Brushwood, Cotton, Cow, Dig, Grasp, Kow, Osier, Realise, Reis, Rice, Rod, Rumble, Sarment, See, Sprig, Sticklac, Switch, Understand, Wand, Wattle, Whip, Wicker, Withe

Twilight Astronomical, Civil, Cockshut, Crepuscular, Demi-jour, Dimpsy, Dusk, Gloam(ing), Götterdämmerung, Nautical, Ragnarok, Summerdim

Twin(s) Asvins, Castor, Coetaneous, Couplet, Didymous, Dioscuri, Ditokous, Dizygotic, Double, Fraternal, Gemel, Geminate, Gemini, Identical, Isogeny, Juxtaposition, Kindred, Kray, Look-alike, Macle, Monozygotic, Parabiotic, Pigeon-pair, Pollux, Siamese, Thomas, Tweedledee, Tweedledum

Twine Binder, Braid, Coil, Cord, Inosculate, Packthread, Sisal, Snake, String, Twist, Wreathe

Twinkle, Twinkling Glimmer, Glint, Mo(ment), →**SPARKLE**, Starnie, Trice

▷ **Twirling** *may indicate* an anagram

Twist(ed), Twister, Twisting, Twisty Askant, Askew, Baccy, Becurl, Bought, Braid, Buckle, Card-sharper, Chisel, Coil, Contort, Convolution, Corkscrew, Crinkle, Crisp, Cue, Curl(icue), Curliewurlie, Cyclone, Deform, Detort, Dishonest, Distort, →**DODGE**, Eddy, Embraid, Entrail, Entwine, Garrot, Helix, Kink, Lemon peel, Loop, Mangulate, Mat, Oliver, Plait, Quirk, Raddle, Ravel, Rick, Rogue, Rotate, Rove, Serpent, Skew, Slew, Slub(b), Slue, Snake, Snarl, Spin, Spiral, Sprain, Squiggle, Squirm, Strand, Swivel, Tendril, Thraw(n), Torc, Tornado, Torque, Torsade, Torsion, Tortile, Turn, Tweak, Twiddle, Twine, Twirl, Twizzle, Typhoon, Wamble, Warp, Wind, Wreathe, Wrench, Wrest, Wriggle, Wring, Writhe, Wry, Zigzag

▷ **Twisted, Twisting** *may indicate* an anagram

Twit, Twitter Birdbrain, Chaff, Cherup, Chirrup, Dotterel, Gear(e), Giber, →**JEER**, Rag, Stupid, Taunt, Warble

Twitch(ing), Twitchy Athetosis, Clonic, Fibrillation, Grass, Jerk, Life-blood, Saccadic, Sneer, Spasm, Start, Subsultive, Tic, Tig, Tippet, Tit, Tweak, Twinge, Vellicate, Yips

Two(some), Twofold, Twice Bice, Bis, Bisp, Both, Brace, Couple(t), Deuce, Double, Duad, Dual, Duet, Duo, Duple, Dyad, Item, →**PAIR**, Swy, Tête-à-tête, Twain, Twins, Twister

Two-pronged Bidental

Two-tone Shot

Tycoon Baron, Fat cat, Magnate, Murdoch, Nabob, Onassis, Plutocrat, Shogun

Tyke Geit, RC

Tympany Castanets, Cymbal, Drum, Kitchen, Triangle, Xylophone

Type(s), Typing A, Agate, Aldine, Antimony, Antique, B, Balaam, Baskerville, Bastard, Batter, Beard, Black-letter, Block, Blood, Body, Bold face, Bourgeois, Braille, Brand, Brevier, Brilliant, Canon, Caslon, Category, Character, Chase, Cicero, Clarendon, Class, Columbian, Condensed, Cut, Egyptian, Elite, Elzevir, Em, Emblem, Emerald, En(nage), English, Face, Font, Footer, Form(e), Founder's, Fount, Fraktur, Fudge, Garamond, Gem, Genre, Gent, Gothic, Great primer, Hair, Hot metal, Ilk, Image, Key, Keyboard, Kidney, Kind, Late-star, Ligature, Light-faced, Logotype, Longprimer, Ludlow, Make, Mating, Melanochroi, Minion, Modern, Monospaced, Moon, Mould, Non-pareil, Norm, Old English, Old-face, Old Style, Paragon, Pattern, Pearl, Peculiar, Personality, Pi, Pica, Pie, Plantin, Point, Primer, Print, Quad(rat), Roman, Ronde, Ruby, Sanserif, Secretary, Semibold, Serif, Serological, Slug, Sp, Species, Spectral, Stanhope, Style, Times, Tissue, Touch, Version

▷ **Type of** *may indicate* an anagram

Typesetting Hot metal

Typical Average, Characteristic, Classic, Everyman, Normal, Representative, Standard, Symbolic, True-bred, Usual

Tyrant, Tyranny, Tyrannical Absolutism, Autocrat, Caligula, Czar, Despot, Dictator, Drawcansir, Gelon, Herod, Ivan the Terrible, Lordly, Nero, Oppressor, Pharaoh, Pisistratus, Sardanapalus, Satrap, Stalin, Totalitarian, Tsar, Yoke

Tyre(s) Balloon, Cross-ply, Cushion, Earthing, Flat, Michelin®, Pericles, Pneumatic, Radial(-ply), Recap, Remould, Retread, Shoe, Sidewall, Slick, Snow, Spare, Stepney, Toe in, Tread, Tubeless, Whitewall

Tyro Beginner, Ham, →**NOVICE**, Rabbit, Rookie, Rooky, Starter

Uu

U-bend Airtrap
UFO Roswell
Ugly Butters, Cow, Crow, Customer, Eyesore, Faceache, Foul, Gorgon, Gruesome, Hideous, Homely, Huckery, Jolie laide, Loath, Loth, Mean, Ominous, Plain, Sight
Ulcer(ous) Abscess, Aphtha, Canker, Chancre, Chancroid, Decubitus, Duodenal, Enanthema, Gastric, Helcoid, Imposthume, Mouth, Noma, Peptic, Phagedaena, Plague-sore, Rodent, Rupia, Sore, Wolf
Ulster NI, Overcoat, Raincoat, Ulad
Ultimate(ly) Absolute, Basic, Deterrent, Eventual, Final, Furthest, Last, Maximum, Mostest, Omega, So, Supreme, Thule, Ult
Ultimatum Threat
Ultrasound Lithotripsy
Ululate Wail
Umbrage Offence, Pique, Resentment, Shade
Umbrella(-shaped) Bumbershoot, Chatta, Gamp, Gingham, Gloria, Mush(room), Parasol, Sunshade, Tee
Umpire Arb(iter), Byrlawman, Daysman, Decider, Judge, Mediate, Oddjobman, Odd(s)man, Overseer, Referee, Rule, Stickler, Thirdsman
Unable Can't, Downa-do, Incapable
Unacceptable Beyond the pale, Non-U, Not on, Out, Repugnant, Stigmatic, Taboo
Unaccompanied A cappella, Alone, High-lone, Secco, Single, Solo, Solus
Unacknowledged Covert
Unaffected Artless, Genuine, Homely, Insusceptible, Natural, Plain, Sincere, Unattached
Unanswerable Erotema, Irrefragable, Irrefutable
Unappealing Distasteful, Grim, Offensive, Rank
Unappreciated, Unappreciative Ingrate, Thankless
Unapproachable Remote
Unassisted Naked eye
Unattached Fancy free, Freelance, Loose
Unattractive Demagnetised, Drac(k), Hideous, Lemon, Munter, Plain, Plug-ugly, Rebarbative, Scungy, Seamy, Skanky, Ugly
▷ **Unauthentic** *may indicate* an anagram
Unavail(able), Unavailing Bootless, Futile, Ineluctable, Lost, NA, No use, Off, Vain
Unaware(ness) Blind-side, Cloistered, Coma, Heedless, Ignorant, Incognisant, Innocent, Oblivious, Stupor
Unbalanced Asymmetric, Deranged, Doolalli, Doolally, Loco, Lopsided, Nutty, Out to lunch, Twisted, Uneven
Unbecoming, Unbefitting Improper, Indecent, Infra dig, Shabby, Unfitting, Unseemly, Unsuitable, Unworthy
Unbelievable, Unbeliever Agnostic, Atheist, Cassandra, Doubter, Giaour, Heathen, Heretic, Incredible, Infidel, Pagan, Painim, Paynim, Sceptic, Tall, Zendik
Unbend(ing) Relent, Strict
Unbiased Fair, Impartial, Just, Neutral, Objective, Unattainted
Unblock(ing) Free, Recanalization
Unbounded Infinite
Unbranded Cleanskin

Unbreakable Infrangible, Inviolate

Unbridled Fancy free, Footloose, Lawless, Uncurbed, Unrestricted, Unshackled, Untramelled

Uncanny Eerie, Eldritch, Extraordinary, Geason, Rum, Spooky, Wanchancie, Wanchancy, Weird

Unceasing Continuous

▷ **Uncertain** *may indicate* an anagram

Uncertain(ty) Acatalepsy, Agnostic, Blate, Broken, Chancy, Chary, Contingent, Delicate, Dicey, Dither, Dodgy, Doubtful, Dubiety, Hesitant, Iffy, Indeterminate, Indistinct, Irresolute, Obscure, Parlous, Peradventure, Precarious, Queasy, Risky, Slippery, Suspense, Tentative, Vor, Wide open

Unchangeable, Unchanged, Unchanging As is, Enduring, Eternal, Idempotent, Immutable, Monotonous, Perennial, Read only, Stable, Timeless

Unchaste Corrupt, Immodest, Immoral, Impure, Lewd, Light-heeled, Wanton

Uncivil(ised) Barbaric, Benighted, Boondocks, Brutish, Discourteous, Disrespectful, Giant-rude, Heathen, Impolite, Liberty, Military, Rude, Rudesby, Short, Unmannerly

Uncle Abbas, Afrikaner, Arly, Bob, Dutch, Eme, Nunky, Oom, Pawnbroker, Pledgee, Pop-shop, Remus, Sam, Silas, Tio, Tom, U, Usurer, Vanya

Unclean Defiled, Dirty, Impure, Obscene, Ordure, Squalid, Tabu, T(e)refa(h)

Unclear Ambitty, Blurred, Cloudy, Grey area, Hazy, Nebulous, Obscure, Opaque, Sketchy, Slurred

Uncoded En clair

Uncomfortable Awkward, Mean, Uneasy

Uncommon Rara avis, Rare, Sparse, Strange, Unusual

▷ **Uncommon(ly)** *may indicate* an anagram

Uncompromising Cutthroat, Hardline, Hardshell, Intransigent, Relentless, Rigid, Strict, Ultra

Unconcerned Bland, Careless, Casual, Cold, Indifferent, Insouciant, Nonchalant, Strange

Unconditional Absolute, Free, No strings, Pure

Uncongenial Icy

Unconnected Asyndetic, Detached, Disjointed, Enodal, Off-line

Unconscionable Ordinate, Ungodly

Unconscious(ness) Asleep, Catalepsy, Cold, Comatose, Instinctive, Non-ego, Subliminal, Syncope, Trance, Unaware, Under, Zonked out

Unconsummated Mariage blanc

Uncontrolled Adrift, Anarchic, Atactic, Free, Incontinent, Intemperate, Loose, Rampant, Wild

Uncontroversial Anodyne

Unconventional Anti-hero, Avant garde, Beatnik, Bohemian, Divergent, Drop-out, Eccentric, Far-out, Freeform, Gonzo, Heretic, Heterodox, Hippy, Informal, Irregular, Offbeat, Off-the-wall, Original, Outlandish, Outré, Out there, Raffish, Rebel, Screwball, Spac(e)y, Swinger, Unorthodox, Way-out, Wild

▷ **Unconventional** *may indicate* an anagram

Uncooked Rare, Raw

Uncooperative Bolshie, Recalcitrant

Uncouth(ness) Backwoodsman, Bear, Boorish, Churlish, Crude, Gothic, Inelegant, Rube, Rude, Rugged, Slob, Sloven, Uncivil

Uncover(ed) Bare, Denude, Disclose, Expose, Inoperculate, Open, Peel, Reveal, Shave, Shill, Shuck, Uncap

Uncritical Indiscriminate

Unction, Unctuous(ness) Anele, Balm, Chrism, Extreme, Ointment, Oleaginous, Ooze, Smarm, Soapy

Uncultivated, Uncultured Artless, Bundu, Fallow, Ignorant, Incult, Philistine, Rude, Tramontane, Wild, Wildland, Wildwood

Undecided Aboulia, Double-minded, Doubtful, Moot, Non-committal, Open-ended, Pending, Pendulous, Torn, Uncertain, Wavering

Under(neath) Aneath, Below, Beneath, Hypnotized, Hypo-, Infra, Sotto, Sub-, Unconscious, Unneath

Undercoat Base, Primer

Undercover Espionage, Secret, Veiled

▶**Undergarment** *see* UNDERWEAR

Undergo Bear, Dree, Endure, Sustain

Undergraduate Commoner, Fresher, L, Pup, Questionist, Sizar, Sophomore, Student, Subsizar

Underground (group) Basement, Catacomb, Cellar, Clandestine, Fogou, Hell, Hypogaeous, Infernal, Irgun, Kiva, Macchie, Maquis, Mattamore, Metro, Phreatic, Pict, Plutonia, Pothole, Secret, Souterrain, Subsoil, Subterranean, Subway, Tube

Undergrowth Brush, Chaparral, Firth, Frith, Scrub

Underhand Backstair, Dirty, Haunch, Insidious, Lob, Oblique, Sculduggery, Secret, Shady, Sinister, Sly, Sneaky, Surreptitious

Underline Emphasise, Insist, Sublineation

Underling Bottle-washer, Cog, Inferior, Jack, Menial, Minion, Munchkin, Subordinate

Undermine Destabilise, Erode, Fossick, Handbag, Sap, Subvert, Tunnel, Weaken

Underpaid Rat

Understand(able), Understanding, Understood Accept, Acumen, Agreement, Apprehend, Capeesh, Clear, Cognisable, Comprehend, Conceive, Concept, Connivance, Cotton-on, Deal, Dig, Digest, Empathy, Enlighten, Entente, Exoteric, Fathom, Follow, Gather, Gauge, Gaum, Geddit, Get it, Gorm, Grasp, Grok, Have, Head, Heels, Hindsight, Implicit, Insight, Intelligible, Intuit, Ken, Kind, Knowhow, Learn, Light(s), Lucid, OK, Omniscient, Pact, Perspicuous, Plumb, Prajna, Rapport, Rapprochement, Realise, Roger, Savey, Savvy, See, Sense, Sole, Subintelligitur, Substance, Tacit, Take, Tolerance, Treaty, Tumble, Twig, Unspoken, Unstated, Uptak(e), Wisdom, Wit

Understate(d), Understatement Litotes, Minify, M(e)iosis

Understood *see* UNDERSTAND(ABLE)

Understudy Deputy, Double, Stand-in, Sub

Undertake, Undertaking Attempt, Commitment, Contract, Covenant, Emprise, Endeavour, Enterprise, Essay, Guarantee, Misere, Pledge, Promise, Scheme, Shoulder, Task, Warranty

Undertaker Editor, Entrepreneur, Mortician, Obligor, Sponsor, Upholder

Underwear Alb, Balbriggan, Balconette, Bloomers, Bodice, Body, Bodyshaper, Body stocking, Body suit, Bra(ssiere), Briefs, Broekies, Butt bra, Camiknickers, Camisole, Chemise, Chemisette, Chuddies, Combinations, Combs, Corselet, Corset, Dainties, Drawers, (French) knickers, Frillies, Girdle, Grundies, G-string, Hosiery, Innerwear, Jump, Linen, Lingerie, Linings, Long johns, Pantalets, Pantaloons, Panties, Pantihose, Panty girdle, Petticoat, Scanties, Semmit, Shift, Shimmy, Shorts, Singlet, Skivvy, Slip, Smalls, Stammel, Stays, Step-ins, Subucula, Suspender-belt, Suspenders, Tanga, Teddy, Thermal, Trunks, Underdaks, Undergarments, Underlinen, Underpants, Underset, Undershirt, Underthings, Undies, Unmentionables, Vest, Wyliecoat, Y-fronts®

Underworld All-fired, Avernus, Chthonic, Criminal, Hell, Lowlife, Mafia, Pluto, Shades, Tartar(e), Tartarus, Tartary

Underwrite, Underwritten Assure, Endorse, Guarantee, Insure, Lloyds, PS

Undeveloped Ament, Backward, Depauperate, Green, Inchoate, Latent, Ridgel, Ridgil, Ridgling, Rig, Riggald, Riglin(g), Rudimentary, Seminal

Undiluted Neat, Pure, Sheer, Straight

Undisturbed Halcyon

Undivided Aseptate, Complete, Entire, Indiscrete, One

Undo(ing) Annul, Defeat, Destroy, Downfall, Dup, Poop, Poupe, Release, Rescind, Ruin, Unravel

Undone Arrears, Left, Postponed, Ran, Ruined, Unlast

Undoubtedly Ay, Certes, Positively, Sure, To be sure

Undress(ed) Bare, Disarray, Disrobe, En cuerpo, Expose, Négligé, Nude, Nue, Peel, Querpo, Raw, Rough, Self-faced, Spar, Strip, Unapparelled

Undue Premature

Undulate, Undulating Billow, Nebule, Ripple, Roll, Swell, Wave

▷ **Unduly** *may indicate* an anagram

Unearth(ly) Astral, Dig, Discover, Disentomb, Exhumate, Indagate

Unease, Uneasiness, Uneasy Angst, Anxious, Creeps, Inquietude, Itchy, Malaise, Queasy, Restive, Shy, Tense, The willies, Trepidation, Uptight, Windy, Womble-cropped

Unemployed, Unemployment Drone, Idle, Jobless, Laik, Lake, Latent, Lay-off, Redundant

Unending Chronic, Eternal, Lasting, Sempiternal

Unequal(led) Aniso-, Disparate, Non(e)such, Scalene, Unjust

Unerring Dead, Exact, Precise

Uneven(ness) Accident, Blotchy, Bumpy, Erratic, Irregular, Jaggy, Patchy, Ragged, Rough, Scratchy, Streaky

▷ **Unevenly** *may indicate* an anagram

Unexceptional Ordinary, Run of the mill, Workaday

Unexciting Flat, Mundane, Staid, Tame

Unexpected(ly) Abrupt, Accidental, Adventitious, Fortuitous, Infra dig, Inopinate, Ironic, Snap, Sodain(e), Sudden, Turn-up, Unawares, Unforeseen, Untoward, Unware, Unwary, Windfall

Unexploded Live

Unfair Bias(s)ed, Crook, Dirty, Discriminatory, Inclement, Iniquitous, Invidious, Mean, Partial, Raw deal, Thick, Unsportsmanlike

Unfaithful Disloyal, Godless, Infidel, Traitor

Unfashionable Cube, Daggy, Demode, Dowdy, Lame, Mumsy, Passé, Square, Vieux jeu

▷ **Unfashionable** *may indicate* 'in' to be removed

Unfasten Undo, Untie, Untruss

Unfathomable Abysmal, Bottomless, Deep

Unfavourable Adverse, Ill, Poor, Untoward

Unfeeling Adamant, Callous, Cold, Cruel, Dead, Hard, Inhuman(e), Insensate, Iron-witted, Robotic, Stony-hearted

Unfinished, Unfinishable Crude, Inchoate, Incondite, Raw, Scabble, Scapple, Sisyphean, Stickit

▷ **Unfit** *may indicate* an anagram

Unfit(ting) Disabled, Faulty, Ill, Impair, Inept, Outré, Stiffie, Unable

Unflappable Stoic

Unfocused Glazed

Unfold Deploy, Display, Divulge, Evolve, Interpret, Open, Relate, Spread

Unfortunate(ly) Accursed, Alack, Alas, Catastrophic, Devil, Hapless, Ill-starred, Indecorous, Luckless, Shameless, Sorry, Star-crossed, Unlucky, Worse luck

Unfrequented Lonely

Unfriendly Aloof, Antagonistic, Asocial, Chill(y), Cold, Cold fish, Fraim, Fremd, Fremit, Hostile, Icy, Inhospitable, Remote, Standoffish, Surly, Wintry

Unfruitful Abortive, Barren, Sterile

Ungainly Awkward, Gawkish, Uncouth, Weedy

Ungracious Cold, Mesquin(e), Offhand, Rough, Rude

Unguent Nard, Pomade, Salve

Ungulate Anta, Antelope, Dinoceras, Eland, Equidae, Hoofed, Moose, Pachydermata, Rhino, Ruminantia, Takin, Tapir, Tylopoda

Unhappily, Unhappy, Unhappiness Blue, Depressed, Disconsolate, Dismal, Doleful, Downcast, Down-hearted, Dysphoria, Glumpish, Love-lorn, Lovesick, Miserable, Sad, Sore, Tearful, Unlief, Upset

▷ **Unhappily** *may indicate* an anagram

Unhealthy Bad, Clinic, Diseased, Epinosic, Insalubrious, Morbid, Noxious, Peaky, Poxy, Prurient, Sickly, Twisted

Unhurt Whole-skinned

Unhygienic Grubby

Uniform Abolla, Alike, Battledress, Consistent, Doublet, Dress, Equable, Equal, Even, Flat, Forage-cap, Homogeneous, Identical, Khaki, Kit, Level, Livery, Monkey suit, Regimentals, Regular, Rig, Robe, Same, Sole, Standard, Steady, Strip, Suit, U, Unvaried

Unimaginative Banausic, Literalistic, Meagre, Pedestrian, Pooter, Short-sighted, Slavish

Unimportant Academic, Cog, Down-the-line, Fiddling, Folderol, Footling, Frivolous, Hot air, Idle, Immaterial, Inconsequent, Inconsiderable, Insignificant, Junior, MacGuffin, Makeweight, Miniscule, Minnow, Minutiae, Negligible, Nonentity, Nugatory, Peddling, Peripheral, Petty, Piddling, Small beer, Small-time, Trifling, Trivia(l)

Uninhabited Bundu, Deserted, Lonely

Uninjured Inviolate

Uninspired, Uninspiring Barren, Bored, Flat, Humdrum, Pedestrian, Pompier, Stereotyped, Tame

Uninterested, Uninteresting Apathetic, Bland, Drab, Dreary, Dry, Dull, Grey, Incurious, Nondescript

Uninterrupted Constant, Continuous, Incessant, Running, Steady

Union(ist) Affiance, African, Agreement, Allegiance, Alliance, Art, Association, Bed, Benelux, Bond, Brotherhood, Civil, Close, Combination, Company, Concert, Confederacy, Craft, Credit, Customs, Diphthong, Economic, Enosis, Ensemble, Equity, EU, European, Federal, Federation, French, Frithgild, Fusion, Group, Guild, Heterogamy, Horizontal, Industrial, Integration, Isogamy, Latin, Liaison, Liberal, Link-up, Management, Marriage, Match, Merger, NUM, Nuptials, NUR, NUS, NUT, OILC, Pan-American, Pearl, Postal, Print, RU, Rugby, Samiti, Sex, Sherman, Solidarity, Soviet, Splice, Sponsal, Student, Synthesis, Syssarcosis, Teamsters, Tenorrhaphy, TU, U, UNISON, USDAW, Uxorial, Vertical, Vienna, Wedding, Wedlock, Western European, Wield, Yoke, ZANU

Unique(ness) Alone, A-per-se, Farid, Hacceity, Inimitable, Lone, Matchless, Nonesuch, Nonpareil, Nonsuch, One-off, One(-to)-one, Onliest, Only, Peerless, Rare, Singular, Sole, Sui generis

Unit(s) Bargaining, Board of Trade, Brigade, Cadre, Cell, Cohort, Commune, Control, Corps, Derived, Detachment, Division, Ecosystem, Element, Ensuite, Feedlot, Flight, Fundamental, Home, Hub, Income, Item, Last, Measure, Message, Module, Monetary, Panzer, Peninsular, Period, Peripheral, Practical, Sealed, Secure, Shed, Squad, Stock, Syllable, Team, Terminal, Theme, Timocracy, Tower

Unite(d), Uniting Accrete, Bind, Cement, Coalesce, Combine, Concordant, Connate, Connect, Consolidate, Consubstantiate, Covalent, Ecumenical, Fay, Federal, Federate, Fuse, Gene, Graft, Injoint, Join, Joinder, Kingdom, Knit, Lap, Link, Marry, Meint, Meng, Ment, Merge, Meynt, Ming, Nations, Oop, Oup, Piece, Siamese, Solid, States, Tie, Tightknit, Unify, → **WED**, Weld, Yoke

Unity Cohesion, Harmony, One, Solidarity, Sympathy, Togetherness

Universal, Universe All, Catholic, Cosmogony, Cosmos, Creation, Ecumenic(al), Emma, General, Global, Infinite, Macrocosm, Mandala, Microcosm, Omnify, Oscillating, Sphere, U, World(wide)

University Academe, Academy, Alma mater, Aston, Bath, Berkeley, Bonn, Brown, Campus, Civic, College, Columbia, Cornell, Dartmouth, Exeter, Gown, Harvard, Heidelberg, Ivy League, Keele, Open, OU, Oxbridge, Pennsylvania, Princeton,

Reading, Redbrick, St Andrews, Sorbonne, Stamford, Syracuse, Varsity, Wittenberg, Witwatersrand, Yale

Unjust(ified) Groundless, Inequitable, Inequity, Iniquitous, Invalid, Tyrannical

Unknot Burl

Unknown, Unknowable Acamprosate, Agnostic, Anon, A.N. Other, Hidden, Ign, Incog(nito), Inconnu, N, Nobody, Noumenon, Occult, Quantity, Secret, Soldier, Strange, Symbolic, Tertium quid, Unchartered, Untold, Warrior, X, Y

Unlawful Illegal, Non-licit

Unless Nisi, Save, Without

Unlike(ly) As if, Difform, Disparate, Dubious, Far-fetched, Implausible, Improbable, Inauspicious, Last, Long shot, Outsider, Remote, Tall, Unlich

Unlimited Almighty, Boundless, Indefinite, Measureless, Nth, Open-ended, Pure, Universal, Vast

Unload Disburden, Discharge, Drop, Dump, Jettison, Land, Unship

Unlucky Donsie, Hapless, Ill(-starred), Ill-omened, Inauspicious, Infaust, Jonah, Misfallen, S(c)hlimazel, Sinister, Stiff, Thirteen, Untoward, Wanchancie, Wanchancy, Wanion

Unmarried Bachelor, Celibate, Common-law, Single, Spinster

Unmentionable(s) Bra, Foul, No-no, → **UNDERWEAR**, Undies

Unmindful Heedless, Oblivious

Unmistakable Clear, Manifest, Plain

Unnatural Abnormal, Absonant, Affected, Artificial, Cataphysical, Contrived, Eerie, Far-fetched, Flat, Geep, Irregular, Man-made, Strange, Studied, Transuranian

▷ **Unnaturally** *may indicate* an anagram

Unnecessary De trop, Extra, Gash, Gratuitous, Needless, Otiose, Redundant, Superfluous

Unobserved Backstage, Sly, Unseen

Unobtainable Nemesis

Unoccupied Désouvré, Empty, Idle, Inactive, Otiose, Vacant, Void

Unopened Sealed

Unoriginal Banal, Copy, Derivative, Imitation, Plagiarised, Slavish, Trite

Unorthodox Heretic, Heterodox, Maverick, Off-beat, Off-the-wall, Outré, Stagyrite, Unconventional

▷ **Unorthodox** *may indicate* an anagram

Unpaid Amateur, Brevet, Hon(orary), Voluntary

Unperturbed Bland, Calm, Serene

Unpigmented Albino

Unplanned Disorganised, Impromptu, Improvised, Spontaneous

Unpleasant, Unpleasant person Creep, Drastic, Foul, God-awful, Grim, Grotty, Gruesome, Hoor, Horrible, Icky, Insalubrious, Invidious, Nasty, Obnoxious, Odious, Offensive, Painful, Pejorative, Poxy, Rebarbative, Reptile, Scrote, Shady, Shitty, Shocker, Skanky, Snot, Sour, Sticky, Thorny, Toerag, Wart

Unpredictable Aleatory, Capricious, Dicy, Erratic, Maverick, Scatty, Vagary, Wayward, Wild card

Unprepared Ad lib, Cold, Extempore, Impromptu, Raw, Unready

Unprincipled Amoral, Dishonest, Irregular, Opportunist, Reprobate

Unproductive Arid, Atokal, Atokous, Barren, Dead-head, Eild, Fallow, Futile, Infertile, Lean, Poor, Shy, Sterile, Yeld, Yell

Unprofessional Laic, Malpractice

Unprofitable Bootless, Fruitless, Lean, Thankless, Wasted

Unproportionate Incommensurate

Unprotected Exposed, Nude, Vulnerable

Unqualified Absolute, Arrant, Categoric, Entire, Outright, Profound, Pure, Quack, Sheer, Straight, Thorough, Total, Tout court, Utter

Unquestionably, Unquestioning, Unquestioned Absolute, Axiomatic, Certain, Doubtless, Implicit

Unravel(ling) Construe, Denouement, Disentangle, Feaze, Fray, Solve

Unreadable Poker-faced

Unreal(istic) Alice-in-Wonderland, Cockamamie, Eidetic, En l'air, Escapist, Fake, Fancied, Illusory, Mirage, Oneiric, Phantom, Phon(e)y, Pseudo, Romantic, Sham, Spurious, Virtual

Unreasonable, Unreasoning Absurd, Bigot, Exorbitant, Extreme, Illogical, Irrational, Misguided, Perverse, Rabid, Tall order

Unrecognised Incognito, Inconnu, Invalid, Thankless, Unsung

Unrefined Bestial, Coarse, Common, Crude, Earthy, Gur, Natural, Rude, Slob, Vul(g), Vulgar

Unreformed Impenitent

Unregistered Flapping

Unrelenting Implacable, Remorseless, Severe, Stern

Unreliable Broken reed, Chequered, Dodgy, Erratic, Fickle, Flibbertigibbet, Flighty, Fly-by-night, Insincere, Kludge, Shonky, Skitter, Unstable, Wankle, Weak sister, Wonky

Unreserved Implicit

Unresponsive Aloof, Blank, Catatonic, Cold, Frigid, Nastic, Rigor

Unrest Discontent, Ferment, The Troubles

Unrestrained Ariot, Free, Freewheeling, Hearty, Homeric, Immoderate, Incontinent, Lax, Lowsit, Rampant, Wanton, Wild

Unruly Anarchic, Bodgie, Buckie, Camstairy, Camsteary, Camsteerie, Coltish, Disruptive, Exception, Fractious, Lawless, Obstreperous, Obstropalous, Ragd(e), Raged, Ragged, Rambunctious, Rampageous, Rattlebag, Refractory, Riotous, Tartar, Torn-down, Turbulent, Turk, Wanton, Wayward, Zoo

▷ **Unruly** *may indicate* an anagram

Unsafe Deathtrap, Fishy, Insecure, Perilous, Precarious, Unsound, Vulnerable

Unsatisfactory, Unsatisfying Bad, Lame, Lemon, Lousy, Meagre, Rocky, Thin, Wanting

Unseasonable, Unseasoned Green, Hors de saison, Murken, Raw, Untimely

Unseemly Coarse, Improper, Indecent, Indecorous, Indign, Risque, Untoward

Unseen Masked

Unselfish Altruist, Generous

Unsentimental Gradgrindery, Hard-nosed

Unsettle(d) Homeless, Hunky, Indecisive, Nervous, Open, Outstanding, Overdue, Queasy, Restive, Restless

▷ **Unsettled** *may indicate* an anagram

Unsight(ed), Unsightly Hideous, Repulsive, Ugly

Unskilled, Unskilful Awkward, Dilutee, Gauche, Green, Hunky, Inexpert, Menial, Raw, Rude, Stumblebum, Talentless, Whitechapel

Unsolicited Sponte sua

Unsophisticated Alf, Boondocks, Boonies, Bushie, Cornball, Corny, Cracker-barrel, Direct, Down-home, Faux-naïf, Hick, Hillbilly, Homebred, Homespun, Inurbane, Jaap, Jay, Naive, Natural, Primitive, Provincial, Rube, Rustic, Verdant

Unsound Barmy, Infirm, Invalid, Shaky, Wildcat, Wonky

▷ **Unsound** *may indicate* an anagram

Unspeakable Dreadful, Ineffable, Nefandous

Unspoiled, Unspoilt Innocent, Natural, Perfect, Pristine, Pure, Virgin

Unspotted Innocent

Unstable, Unsteady Anomic, Astatic, Bockedy, Casual, Crank(y), Dicky, Erratic, Fitful, Flexuose, Flexuous, Flit(ting), Fluidal, Giddy, Groggy, Infirm, Insecure, Labile, Minute-jack, Quicksand, Rickety, Shifty, Skittish, Slippy, Tickle, Top-heavy, Tottery, Totty, Variable, Walty, Wambling, Wankle, Warby, Wobbly, Wonky

▶ **Unsteady** *see* UNSTABLE

▷ **Unstuck** *may indicate* an anagram

Unsubstantial Aeriform, Airy, Flimsy, Paltry, Shadowy, Slight, Thin, Yeasty

Unsubtle Overt, Sledgehammer

Unsuccessful Abortive, Disastrous, Duff, Futile, Joyless, Manqué, Vain

Unsuitable Amiss, Ill-timed, Impair, Improper, Inapt, Incongruous, Inexpedient, Malapropos, Misbecoming, Unfit

Unsystematic Piecemeal

Untidy Daggy, Dishevelled, Dog's breakfast, Dog's dinner, Dowd(y), Frowzy, Frump, Guddle, Litterbug, Ragged, Ragtag, Scruff(y), Slipshod, Slovenly, Slut, Straggly, Tatty

▷ **Untidy** *may indicate* an anagram

Untie Free, Undo, Unlace

Unto Intil, Until

Untold Secret, Umpteen, Unread, Unred, Vast

Untouchable Burakumin, Dalit, Harijan, Immune, Sealed

▷ **Untrained** *may indicate* 'BR' to be removed

Untreated Raw

Untroubled Carefree, Insouciant

Untrue, Untruth Apocryphal, Eccentric, Fable, Faithless, False(hood), Lie, Prefabrication, Unleal

Untrustworthy Dishonest, Eel, Fickle, Shifty, Sleeky, Slippery, Tricky

Unused, Unusable Impracticable, New, Over, Wasted

▷ **Unusual** *may indicate* an anagram

Unusual(ly) Aberration, Abnormal, Atypical, Departure, Different, Exceptional, Extra(ordinary), Eye-popping, Freak, Gonzo, Kinky, New, Novel, Odd, Offbeat, Out-of-the-way, Outré, Particular, Quaint, Queer, Rare (bird), Remarkable, Singular, Special, →**STRANGE**, Unco, Unique, Untypical, Unwonted, Variant, Wacko

Unvarying Constant, Eternal, Monotonous, Repetitive, Stable, Static, Uniform

Unwanted De trop, Exile, Gooseberry, Nimby, Outcast, Pidog, Sorn

Unwashed Grubby

Unwelcome, Unwelcoming Frosty, Hostile, Icy, Lulu, Obtrusive, (Persona) Non grata

Unwell Ailing, Crook, Dicky, Ill, Impure, Indisposed, Poorly, Rop(e)y, Rough, Seedy, Toxic

Unwholesome Insalutary, Miasmous, Morbid, Noxious, Stinkpot

Unwilling(ness) Averse, Disinclined, Intestate, Laith, Loath, Loth, Nolition, Nolo, Perforce, Reluctant, Tarrow

Unwind Relax, Straighten, Unclew, Undo, Unreave, Unreeve

▷ **Unwind** *may indicate* an anagram

Unwise(ly) Foolish, Ill-advised, Ill-judged, Impolitic, Imprudent, Inexpedient, Injudicious, Insipient, Rash

Unworldly Naif, Naive

Unworthy Below, Beneath, Golden calf, Indign, Inferior, Infra dig, Substandard, Undeserving

Unyielding Adamant, Eild, Firm, Granite, Inexorable, Intransigent, Obdurate, Relentless, Rigid, Steely, Stern, Stolid, Stubborn, Tough

Up(on), Upturned, Upper, Uppish, Uppity A, Afoot, Ahead, Antidepressant, Arrogant, Astir, Astray, Astride, Cloud-kissing, Erect, Euphoric, Heavenward, Hep, Horsed, Incitant, Off, On, Overhead, Primo, Quark, Range, Ride, Riding, Senior, Skyward, Speed, →**UPPER CLASS**, Vamp, Ventral, Wart

Upbraid Abuse, Rebuke, Reproach, Reprove, Scold, Twit

Update Brief, Refresh, Renew, Report, Sitrep

Upfront Open

Upheaval Cataclysm, Eruption, Seismic, Shake out, Stir, Upturn, Volcano

▷ **Upheld** *may indicate* 'up' in another word

Uphill Arduous, Borstal, Sisyphean

Upholster(ed), Upholstery Fleshy, Lampas, Moquette, Tabaret, Trim

Uplift Boost, Edify, Elate, Elevation, Exalt, Hoist, Levitation, Sky

Upmarket Smart

Upper class, Upper crust Aristocrat, County, Crachach, Nobility, Patrician, Posh, Sial, Top-hat, Tweedy, U

Upright(s), Uprightness Aclinic, Anend, Apeak, Apeek, Aplomb, Arrect, Erect, Goalpost, Honest, Jamb, Joanna, Merlon, Mr Clean, Mullion, Orthograde, Perpendicular, Piano, Pilaster(s), Post, Probity, Rectitude, Roman, Splat, Stanchion, Stares, Stile, Stud, Vertical, Virtuous, White

Uprising Incline, Insurrection, Intifada, Meerut, Naxalbari, Rebellion, Revolt, Tumulus

Uproar(ious) Ballyhoo, Bedlam, Blatancy, Brouhaha, Charivari, Clamour, Collieshangie, Commotion, Cry, Din, Dirdam, Dirdum, Durdum, Emeute, Ferment, Flaw, Fracas, Furore, Garboil, Hell, Hooha, Hoopla, Hubbub(oo), Hullabaloo, Hurly(-burly), Imbroglio, Katzenjammer, Noise, Noyes, Outcry, Pandemonium, Racket, Raird, Randan, Razzmatazz, Reird, Riotous, Roister, Romage, Rough music, Rowdedow, Rowdydow(dy), Ruckus, Ruction, Rumpus, Shemozzle, Stramash, Tumult, Turmoil, Utis, Whoobub

Uproot Averruncate, Dislodge, Eradicate, Evict, Outweed, Supplant, Weed

▷ **Upset** *may indicate* an anagram; a word upside down; or 'tes'

Upset(ting) Aerate, Aggrieve, Alarm, Applecart, Ate, Bother, Capsize, Catastrophe, Choked, Coup, Cowp, Crank, Derail, Derange, Dip, Discomboberate, Discombobulate, Discomfit, Discomfort, Discommode, Disconcert, Dismay, Disquiet, Distraught, Disturb, Dod, Eat, Fuss, Gutted, Heart-rending, Inversion, Keel, Miff, Nauseative, Offend, Overthrow, Overtip, Overturn, Peeve, Perturb, Pip, Pother, Purl, Rattle, Renverse, Rile, Ruffle, Rumple, Sad(den), Seel, Shake, Shatter, Shook up, Sore, Spill, Tapsalteerie, Teary, Tip, Topple, Trauma, Undo

Upshot Outcome, Result, Sequel

Upside down Inverted, Resupinate, Tapsie-teerie, Topsy-turvy

Upsilon Hyoid

▷ **Upstart** *may indicate* 'u'

Up to Till, Until

Up-to-date Abreast, Advanced, Contemporary, Current, Hip, Mod, New-fashioned, Rad, Right-on, State-of-the-art, Swinging, Topical, Trendy

Upwards Acclivious, Aloft, Antrorse, Cabré

Urban Civic, Megalopolis, Municipal, Town

Urbane, Urbanity Civil, Debonair, Eutrapelia, Smooth, Townly

Urchin Arab, Asterias, Brat, Crinoid, Crossfish, Cystoid, Echinoidea, Echinus, Gamin, Gutty, Heart, Mudlark, Nipper, Pedicellaria, Ragamuffin, Sand-dollar, Sea-egg, Spatangoidea, Spatangus, Street-arab, Townskip

Urge, Urgency, Urgent Acute, Admonish, Ca, Coax, Coerce, Constrain, Crying, Dire, Drive, Egg, Enjoin, Exhort, Exigent, Goad, Hard, Haste, Hie, Hoick, Hunger, Hurry, Id, Immediate, Impel, Imperative, Impulse, Incense, Incite, Insist(ent), Instance, Instigate, Itch, Kick, Libido, Nag, Orexis, Peremptory, Persuade, Press(ing), Prod, Push, Scrub, Set on, Sore, Spur, Stat, Strenuous, Strident, Strong, Vehement, Wanderlust, Whig, Whim, Yen

▷ **Urgent** *may indicate* 'Ur-gent', viz. Iraqi

Urinal Bog, John, Jordan, → **LAVATORY**, Loo, Pissoir

Urinate(d), Urine Chamber-lye, Emiction, Enuresis, Lant, Leak, Micturition, Number one, Pee, Piddle, Piss, Slash, Stale, Strangury, Tiddle, Uresis, Whiz(z), Widdle

Urn(s), Urn-shaped Canopic, Cinerarium, Ewer, Grecian, Lachrymal, Olla, Ossuary, Samovar, Storied, Vase

Us 's, UK, Uns, We

Usage, Use(r), Used, Utilise Accustomed, Application, Apply, Avail, Boot, Consume, Custom, Deploy, Dow, → **EMPLOY**, Enure, Ex, Exercise, Exert, Exploit, Flesh, Function, Habit, Hand-me-down, Inured, Manner, Milk, Ply, Practice, Sarum, Snorter, Spent, Sport, Stock, Tradition, Treat, Try, Ure, Utilisation, Wield, With, Wont

Useful Asset, Availing, Commodity, Dow, Expedient, Invaluable, Practical

Useless Appendix, Base, Bung, Cumber, Cumber-ground, Dead duck, Dead-wood, Dud, Empty, Futile, Gewgaw, Ground, Idle, Inane, Incapable, Ineffective, Inutile, Lame, Lemon, Nugatory, Otiose, Plug, Pointless, Sculpin, Sterile, Swap, US, Vain, Void, Wet

Usher Black Rod, Blue Rod, Chobdar, Commissionaire, Conduct(or), Doorman, Escort, Gentleman, Guide, Herald, Huissier, Macer, Rod, Show, Steward

Usual Common, Customary, Habit(ual), Most, Natural, Normal, Ordinary, Routine, Rule, Solito, Standard, Stock, Tipple, Typical, Vanilla, Wont

Usurer, Usury Gombeen, Gripe, Lender, Loanshark, Moneylender, Note-shaver, Shark, Uncle

Utensil(s) Batterie, Battery, Ca(u)ldron, Canteen, Chopsticks, Colander, Cookware, Corer, Double boiler, Egg-slice, Fish-kettle, Fork, Funnel, Gadget, Grater, Gridiron, Holloware, Implement, Instrument, Jagger, Knife, Mandolin(e), Ricer, Scoop, Sieve, Skillet, Spatula, Spoon, Things, Tool, Whisk, Zester

▶**Utilise** *see* **USAGE**

Utilitarian Benthamite, Mill, Practical, Useful

Utility Elec(tricity), Gas, Water

Utmost Best, Extreme, Farthest, Maximum

Utopia(n) Adland, Cloud-cuckoo-land, Ideal, More, Pantisocracy, Paradise, Perfect, Shangri-la

Utter(ance), Uttered, Utterly Absolute, Accent, Agrapha, Agraphon, Arrant, Cry, Dead, Deliver, Dictum, Dog, Downright, Ejaculate, Enunciate, Express, Extreme, Glossolalia, Issue, Judgement, Lenes, Lenis, Locution, Most, Oracle, Pass, Phonate, Pronounce, Pure, Quo(th), Rank, Rattle, Remark, Saw, → **SAY**, Sheer, Speak, Spout, Stark, State, Syllable, Tell, Thorough, Tongue, Unmitigated, Vend, Vent, Very, Voice

Vv

V Anti, Bomb, Del, Five, Nabla, See, Sign, Verb, Verse, Versus, Victor(y), Volt, Volume

Vacancy, Vacant Blank, Empty, Glassy, Goaf, Hole, Hollow, Inane, Place, Space, Vacuum

Vacation Holiday, Leave, Long, Outing, Recess, Trip, Voidance, Volunteer

Vaccination, Vaccine Antigen, Antiserum, Attenuated, Booster, Cure, HIB, Jenner, Sabin, Salk, Serum, Subunit

Vacuum Blank, Cleaner, Dewar, Emptiness, Magnetron, Nothing, Nothingness, Plenum, Thermos®, Void

Vagabond Bergie, Gadling, →GYPSY, Hobo, Landlo(u)per, Outcast, Picaresque, Rapparee, Romany, Rover, Runagate, Tramp

Vagina Box, Crack

Vague(ness) Amorphous, Bleary, Blur, Confused, Dim, Dreamy, Equivocal, General, Hazy, Ill-defined, Ill-headed, Imprecise, Indecisive, Indefinite, Indeterminate, Indistinct, Loose, Mist, Nebulous, Obscure, Shadowy, Woolly-minded

▷ **Vaguely** *may indicate* an anagram

Vain Bootless, Conceited, Coxcomb, Coxcomical, Dandyish, Egoistic, Empty, Fruitless, →FUTILE, Hollow, Idle, Pompous, Proud, Strutting, Unuseful, Useless, Vogie

Valet Aid, Andrew, Jeames, Jeeves, Man, Passepartout, Servant, Skip-kennel

Valiant Brave, Doughty, Heroic, Redoubtable, Resolute, Stalwart, Stouthearted, Wight

Valid(ity), Validate Confirm, Establish, Just, Legal, Legitimate, Probate, Right, Sound

Valley Argolis, Beqaa, Cleavage, Cleugh, Clough, Comb(e), Coomb, Cwm, Dale, Dean, Death, Defile, Dell, Den, Dene, Dingle, Dip, Drowned, Dry, Emmental, Ghyll, Glen, Glencoe, Gleneagles, Glyn, Gorge, Griff(e), Grindelwald, Gulch, Hollow, Imperial, Indus, Monument, Napa, Po, Ravine, Ria, Rift, Ruhr, Seaton, Silicon, Sonoma, Strathmore, Tempe, U-shaped, Vale, Vallis Alpes, Water gap, Yosemite

Valour Bravery, Courage, Gallantry, Heroism, Merit, Prowess

Valuable, Valuation, Value(s) Absolute, Acid, Appraise, Appreciate, Apprize, Assess(ment), Asset, Attention, Bargain, Book, Break up, Calibrate, Calorific, Carbon, Checksum, Cherish, CIF, Cop, Cost, Crossover, Datum, Dear, Denomination, Entry, Equity, Esteem, Estimate, Exit, Expected, Face, Feck, Hagberg, Intrinsic, Jew's eye, Limit, Market, Merit, Modulus, Museum piece, Net present, Net realizable, Nominal, Nuisance, Omnium, Par, PH, Place, Prairie, Precious, Premium, Present, Price, Prize, Prys, Q, Quartile, Rarity, Rate, Rateable, Rating, Regard, Residual, Respect, Rogue, Salt, Sentimental, Set, Snob, Steem, Stent, Store, Street, Surplus, Surrender, Taonga, Time, Treasure, Tristimulus, Truth, Valuta, →WORTH

Valve Air, Ball, Bicuspid, Bleed, Blow, Butterfly, Check, Clack, Cock, Diode, Dynatron, Eustachian, Flip-flop, Gate, Inlet, Magnetron, Mitral, Non-return, Outlet, Pentode, Petcock, Piston, Poppet, Puppet, Resnatron, Safety, Seacock, Semilunar, Shut-off, Side, Sleeve, Sluice, Stopcock, Tap, Tetrode, Thermionic, Throttle, Thyratron, Tricuspid, Triode, Ventil, Vibrotron

Vampire Bat, Dracula, False, Ghoul, Lamia, Lilith, Nosferatu, Pontianak

Van(guard) Advance, Box-car, Brake, Breakdown, Camper, Cart, Cube, Dormobile®, Forefront, Foremost, Freight-car, Front, Head, Kombi®, Lead, Leader(s), Lorry, Loudspeaker, Panel, Pantechnicon, Removal, Spearhead, Tartana, Truck, Ute, Wagon

Vandal(ise), Vandalism Desecrate, Freebooter, Hooligan, Hun, Loot, Pillage, Ravage, Rough, Sab(oteur), Sack, Saracen, Skinhead, Slash, Smash, Trash, Wrecker

Vanish(ed), Vanishing Cease, Disappear, Disperse, Dissolve, Evanesce(nt), Evaporate, Extinct, Faint(ed), Mizzle, Slope, Transitory, Unbe

Vanity Amour-propre, Arrogance, Ego, Ego-trip, Esteem, Futility, Pomp, Pretension, Pride, Self-esteem

Vaporise, Vapour Boil, Cloud, Contrail, Fog, Fume, Halitus, Inhalant, Iodine, Miasma, Mist, Reek, Roke, Skywriting, →STEAM, Steme, Water

▶**Variable, Variance, Variant, Variation** see VARY(ING)

▶**Varied, Variety** see VARY(ING)

▷**Varied** may indicate an anagram

Variegate(d) Dappled, Flecked, Fretted, Harlequin, Motley, Mottle, Pied, Rainbow, Skewbald, Tissue

▷**Variety of** may indicate an anagram

Various Divers(e), Manifold, Multifarious, Several, Sundry

Varnish(ing) Arar, Bee-glue, Copal, Cowdie-gum, Dam(m)ar, Desert, Dope, Dragon's-blood, French polish, Glair, Japan, Lacquer, Lentisk, Mastic, Nail, Nibs, Resin, Shellac, Spirit, Tung-oil, Tung-tree, Vernis martin, Vernissage

Vary(ing), Variable, Variance, Variant, Variation, Varied, Variety Ablaut, Alter, Amphoteric, Assorted, Assortment, Breed, Brew, Cepheid, Change, Chequered, Colour, Contrapuntal, Counterpoint, Dependent, Differ, Discrepancy, Diverse, Diversity, Dummy, Eclectic, Eclipsing, Enigma, Fickle, Fluctuating, Form, Grid, Heterodox, Iid, Inconsistent, Inconstant, Independent, Intervening, Isotopy, Line, Local, Medley, Mix, Morph, Multifarious, Multiplicity, Music hall, Mutable, Nimrod, Nuance, Nutation, Olio, Omniform, Parametric, Protean, Random, Remedy, Response, Smörgåsbord, Sort, Species, Spice, Sport, Stirps, Stochastic, Strain, String, Timeserver, Tolerance, Twistor, Var, Varicellar-zoster, Vaudeville, Versatile, Versiform, Version, Vicissitude, Vl, Wane, Wax, X, Y, Z

Vase Bronteum, Canopus, Diota, Hydria, Jardinière, Kalpis, Lachrymal, Lecythus, Lekythos, Lustre, Murr(h)a, Portland, Pot, Potiche, Stamnos, Urn, Vessel

Vasectomy Desexing

Vast(ness) Big, Cosmic, Enormous, Epic, Extensive, Googol, Huge(ous), Immeasurable, Immense, Mighty, Ocean, Prodigious

Vat Back, Barrel, Bath, Blunger, Chessel, Copper, Cowl, Cuvée, Fat, Girnel, Keir, Kier, Tank, Tub, Tun

▷**Vault** may indicate an anagram

Vault(ed), Vaulting Arch, Barrel, Cavern, Cellar, Chamber, Charnel house, Clear, Cross, Crypt, Cul-de-four, Cupola, Dome, Dungeon, Fan, Firmament, Fornicate, Groin, Hypogeum, Jump, Kiva, Leap(frog), Lierne, Mausoleum, Palm, Pend, Pendentive, Pole, Rib, Safe, Sepulchre, Serdab, Severy, Shade, Souterrain, Tomb, Undercroft, Vaut, Wagon, Weem

Veda Yajurveda

Veer Bag, Boxhaul, Broach, Clubhaul, Deviate, Gybe, Swerve, Tack, Turn, Wear, Yaw

Veg(etate), Vegetator, Vegetation Alga, Biome, Flora, Fynbos, Greenery, Herb, Laze, Lemna, Maquis, Quadrat, Scrub, Stagnate

Vegan Parev(e), Parve

Vegetable(s) Flora, Hastings, Inert, Jardinière, Plant, Root, Salad, Sauce, Truck

Vegetarian Herbivore, Lactarian, Meatless, Vegan, Veggie

Vehemence, Vehement(ly) Amain, Ardent, Fervid, Frenzy, Heat, Hot, Intense, Violent

Vehicle Agent, Artic, Articulated, Base, Commercial, Conveyance, Half-track, High occupancy, Hybrid, Machine, Means, Medium, Multipurpose, Offroad, Oil, Recovery, Recreational, Re-entry, Space, Superload, Tempera, Tracked, Ute, Utility, Wheels, Wrecker

Veil Burk(h)a, Calyptra, Chad(d)ar, Chador, Chuddah, Chuddar, Cloud, Cover, Curtain, Envelop, Eucharistic, Hejab, Hijab, Humeral, Kalyptra, Kiss-me, Lambrequin, Mantilla, Mist, Niqab, Obscure, Purdah, Scene, Veale, Volet, Weeper, Wimple, Yashmak

Vein Artery, Basilic, Brachiocephalic, Coronary, Costa, Epithermal, Fahlband, Gate, H(a)emorrhoid, Innominate, Jugular, Ledge, Lode, Mainline, Media, Midrib, Mood, Nervure, Outcrop, Percurrent, Pipe, Portal, Postcava, Precava, Pulmonary, Radius, Rake, Rib, Saphena, Sectorial, Stockwork, Stringer, Style, Varicose, Varix, Vena, Venule

Velocity Circular, Muzzle, Parabolic, Radial, Rate, Speed, Terminal, V

Veneer Facade, Gloss, Varnish

Venerable Aged, August, Augustus, Bede, Guru, Hoary, Iconic, Sacred, Sage, Vintage

Venerate, Veneration Adore, Awe, Douleia, Dulia, Filiopietistic, GOM, Hallow, Homage, Honour, Hyperdulia, Idolise, Latria, Respect, Revere, Worship

Vengeance, Vengeful Erinyes, Reprisal, Ultion, Vindictive, Wan(n)ion, Wrack, Wreak

Venial Base, Excusable

Venom(ous) Poison, Rancour, Spite, Toxic, Virus, Zootoxin

Vent Aperture, Belch, Chimney, Emit, Express, Fumarole, Hornito, Issue, Louver, Louvre, Ostiole, Outlet, Solfatara, Spiracle, Undercast, Wreak

Ventilate, Ventilator Air, Air-brick, Air-hole, Discuss, Draught, Express, Louvre, Plenum, Shaft, Voice, Winze

Venture(d) Ante, Assay, Bet, Callet, Chance, Dare, Daur, Durst, Enterprise, Flutter, Foray, Handsel, Hazard, Opine, Presume, Promotion, Prostitute, Risk, Spec, Strive, Throw

Venue Bout, Locale, Place, Showground, Stadium, Stateroom, Tryst, Visne

Venus Clam, Cohog, Cytherean, Hesper(us), Love, Lucifer, Morning-star, Primavera, Quahaug, Quahog, Rokeby, Vesper

Veracity, Veracious Accurate, Factual, Sincere, Truth(ful)

Veranda(h) Balcony, Gallery, Lanai, Patio, Porch, Sleep-out, Stoep, Stoop, Terrace

Verb(al), Verbs Active, Auxiliary, Conative, Copula, Factitive, Finite, Infinitive, Intransitive, Irregular, Passive, Perfective, Performative, Phrasal, Preterite, Stative, Transitive, Vb, Word-of-mouth

Verbose, Verbosity Gassy, Padding, Prolix, Talkative, Wordy

Verdict Decision, Fatwah, Judg(e)ment, Narrative, Open, Opinion, Pronouncement, Resolution, Ruling

Verge Border, Brink, →**EDGE**, Hard shoulder, Incline, Rim, Threshold

Verify, Verification Affirm, Ascertain, Check, Constatation, Control, Crosscheck, Prove, Validate

Vermin(ous) Lice, Mice, Pest, Ratty, →**RODENT**, Scum

Vernacular Common, Dialect, Idiom, Jargon, Lingo, Native, Patois, Slang, Vulgate

Versatile Adaptable, All-rounder, Flexible, Handy, Many-sided, Multipurpose, Protean, Resourceful

Verse(s), Versed Dactyl, Free, Linked, Logaoedic, Passus, Poetry, Political, Reported, →**RHYME**, System

▷ **Versed** *may indicate* reversed

Version Account, Authorised, Cephalic, Cover, Edition, Form, Paraphrase, Rede, Remake, Rendering, Rendition, Revised, Revision, Rhemish, Standard, Summary, Translation, Urtext, Variorum

Vertical Apeak, Apeek, Atrip, Erect, Lapse, Muntin(g), Ordinate, Perpendicular, Plumb, Sheer, Standing, Stemmed, Stile, Upright

Vertigo Dinic, Dizziness, Fainting, Giddiness, Megrim, Nausea, Staggers, Whirling

Vertue Visne

Very (good, well) A1, Ae, Assai, Awfully, Bonzer, Boshta, Boshter, Dashed, Dead, Def, Ever, Extreme(ly), Fell, Frightfully, Full, Gey, Grouse, Heap, Hellova, Helluva, Highly, Hugely, Jolly, Keen, Light, Mighty, Molto, Much, OK, Opt, Precious, Precise, Purler, Real(ly), Self same, So, Sore, Stinking, Très, Unco, Utter, V, VG, Way

Vessel →**BOAT**, Capillary, Container, Craft, Dish, Lacteal, Logistics, Motor, Pressure, Receptacle, Seed, →**SHIP**, Tomentum, Utensil, Vascular, Weaker

Vest Beset, Confer, Crop top, Gilet, Modesty, Rash, Semmit, Singlet, Skivvy, Spencer, Sticharion, String, Undercoat, Waistcoat

Vestibule Anteroom, Atrium, Entry, Exedra, Foyer, Hall, Lobby, Narthex, Porch, Portico, Pronaos, Tambour

Vestment Alb, Breastplate, Chasuble, Cotta, Dalmatic, Ephod, Fannel, Fanon, Garb, **→ GARMENT**, Mantelletta, Omophorion, Pallium, Parament, Ph(a)elonian, Pontificals, Raiment, Rational, Rochet, Rocquet, Sakkos, Sticharion, Stole, Superhumeral, Surplice, Tunic(le)

Vet(ting), Veterinary, Vets Censor, Check, Doc(tor), Examine, Herriot, Horse-doctor, Inspect, OK, Positive, Screen, Veteran, Zoiatria, Zootherapy

Veteran BL, Expert, GAR, Master, Old-stager, Oldster, Old sweat, Old-timer, Old 'un, Retread, Seasoned, Soldier, Stager, Stalwart, Stalworth, Vet, War-horse, Warrior

▷ **Veteran** *may indicate* 'obsolete'

Veto Ban, Bar, Blackball, Debar, Item, Line-item, Local, Negative, Pocket, Reject, Taboo, Tabu

Vex(ing), Vexatious, Vexed Ail, Anger, Annoy, Bepester, Bother, Chagrin, Debate, Fret, Gall, Grieve, Harass, Haze, Irritate, Mortify, Noy, Peeve, Pester, Rankle, Rile, Sore, Spite, Tease, Torment, Trouble

Via By, Per, Through

Viable Economic, Going, Healthy, Possible

Vibrate, Vibration(s), Vibrant Atmosphere, Diadrom, Dinnle, Dirl, Flutter, Free, Fremitus, Hotter, Jar, Judder, Oscillate, Pulse, Purr, Quake, Resonance, Seiche, Shimmy, Shudder, Thrill, Throb, Tingle, Tremble, Tremor, Trill, Trillo, Twinkle, Wag, Whir(r)

Vicar Bray, Elton, Incumbent, Pastoral, Plenarty, Primrose, Rector, Rev(erend), Trimmer

Vice Clamp, Cramp, Crime, Deputy, Eale, Evil, Foible, Greed, Iniquity, Instead, Jaws, Regent, Second (in command), **→ SIN**, Stair

Viceroy Khedive, Nawab, Provost, Satrap, Willingdon

Vicinity Area, Environs, Locality, Neighbourhood, Region, Round about

Victim(s) Abel, Butt, Casualty, Currie, Curry, Dupe, Easy meat, Fall guy, Frame, Hitlist, Host, Lay-down, Mark, Martyr, Nebbich, Neb(b)ish, Pathic, Patsy, Prey, Quarry, Sacrifice, Scapegoat, Sitting duck, Target

Victor(y) Bangster, Banzai, Beater, Cadmean, Cannae, Captor, Champ(ion), Conqueror, Conquest, Epinicion, Epinikion, Eunice, Flagship, Fool's mate, Gree, Gris, Hugo, Jai, Jai Hind, Kobe, Landslide, Lepanto, Ludorum, Mature, Nike, Palm, Philippi, Pyrrhic, Romper, Runaway, Scalp, Shut-out, Signal, Squeaker, Triumph, V, VE (day), Vee, Vic, Walkover, Win(ner)

Vie Compete, Contend, Emulate, Strive

Vietcong Charley, Charlie

View(er) Aim, Angle, Aspect, Attitude, Behold, Belief, Bird's eye, Cineaste, Consensus, Consider, Cosmorama, Cutaway, Dekko, Dogma, Doxy, Endoscope, Eye, Facet, Gander, Glimpse, Grandstand, Heresy, Idea, Introspect, Kaleidoscope, Landscape, Notion, Observe, Opinion, Optic, Outlook, Pan, Panorama, Parallax, Perspective, Point, Private, Profile, **→ PROSPECT**, Scan, Scape, Scene(ry), Scope, See, Sight, Sightlined, Slant, Snapshot, Specular, Spyglass, Standpoint, Stereoscope, Survey, Synop(sis), Tenet, Thanatopsis, Theory, Veduta, Vista, Visto, Watch, Witness, Worm's eye

Viewpoint Angle, Attitude, Belvedere, Conspectus, Eyeshot, Grandstand, Instance, Observatory, Perspective, Sight, Sightline, Tendentious, Voxpop, Watch tower

Vigil, Vigilant(e) Awake, Aware, Baseej, Basij, Deathwatch, Eve, Lyke-wake, Wake, Wake-rife, Wary, Watch, Waukrife

Vigorous(ly), Vigour Aggressive, Athletic, Bant, Bellona, Billy-o, Billy-oh, Birr, Blooming, Bouncing, Brio, Brisk, Con brio, Cracking, Drastic, Élan, Emphatic, Energetic, Flame, Forceful, Full-blooded, Furioso, Go, Green, Heart(y), Heterosis, Hybrid, Lush, Lustihood, Lustique, Lusty, Moxie, P, Pep, Pith, Potency, Punchy,

Pzazz, Racy, Rank, Raucle, Robust, Round, Rude, Smeddum, Spirit, Sprack, Sprag, Steam, Sthenic, Stingo, Strength, Strenuous, Strong, Thews, Tireless, Tone, Tooth and nail, Trenchant, Two-fisted, Up, Vegete, Vim, Vinegar, Vitality, Vivid, Vivo, Voema, Zip

▷ **Vigorously** *may indicate* an anagram

Vile(ness) Base, Corrupt, Depraved, Dregs, Durance, Earthly, Infamy, Mean, Offensive, Scurvy, Vicious

Villa Bastide, Chalet, Dacha, House

Village Aldea, Auburn, Borghetto, Burg, Clachan, Dorp, Endship, Global, Gram, Greenwich, Hamlet, Kainga, Kampong, Kirkton, Kraal, Legoland, Mir, Outlet, Outpost, Pit, Pueblo, Rancheria, Rancherie, Shtetl, Thorp(e), Vill, Wick

Villain(y) Baddy, Bluebeard, Bravo, Crim(inal), Crime, Dastard, Dog, Fagin, Heavy, Iago, Knave, Lawbreaker, Macaire, Miscreant, Mohock, Nefarious, Ogre, Rogue, Scelerat, Scoundrel, Tearaway, Traitor

Vim Go, Vigour, Vitality, Zing

Vindicate, Vindication Absolve, Acquit, Apologia, Avenge, Clear, Compurgation, Darraign(e), Darrain(e), Darrayn, Defend, Deraign, Exculpate, Justify

Vindictive Bunny-boiler, Hostile, Malevolent, Repay(ing), Spiteful

Vinegar Acetic, Alegar, Balsam, Balsamic, Eisel(l), Esile, Oxymel, Tarragon, Wine

Vintage Classic, Crack, Cru, Old, Quality

Viol(a), Violet African, Alto, Amethyst, Archil, Dame's, Dog, Dog's tooth, Gamba, Gentian, Gridelin, Heart's ease, Ianthine, Indole, Ionone, Kiss-me, Lyra, Mauve, Orchil, Pansy, Parma, Prater, Quint(e), Rock, Saintpaulia, Shrinking, Tenor

Violate, Violating, Violation Abuse, Breach, Contravene, Defile, Desecrate, Fract, Infraction, March-treason, Outrage, Peccant, Rape, Ravish, Solecism, Stuprate, Transgress, Trespass

Violence, Violent(ly) Acquaintance, Amain, Attentat, Bangster, Berserk, Bloody, Brutal, Brute force, Cataclysmic, Crude, Drastic, Droog, Extreme, Fierce, Flagrant, Force, Frenzied, Furious, Heady, Het, High, Hot, Inbreak, Mighty, Onset, Rage, Rampage, Rampant, Riot, Rough, Rude, Rumbustious, Savage, Severe, Slap, Stormy, Strongarm, Ta(r)tar, Tearaway, Thuggery, Tinderbox, Tub-thumping, Vehement, Vie

Violet Crystal, Ianthine, Iodine, Lilac, Shrinking, → **VIOLA**

Violin(ist), Violin-maker, Violin-shaped Alto, Amati, Cremona, Fiddle, Griddle, Guarneri(us), Guarnieri, Kit, Leader, Luthier, Nero, Paganini, Rebeck, Rote, Stradivarius

VIP Bashaw, Bigshot, Bigwig, Brass, Cheese, Cob, Effendi, Envoy, Imago, Kingpin, Magnate, Magnifico, Mugwump, Nabob, Nib, Nob, Pot, Snob, Someone, Swell, Tuft, Tycoon, Worthy

Virago Amazon, Battle-axe, Beldam(e), Harpy, Randy, Shrew, Termagant

Virgin(al), Virginity, Virgin Mary Celibate, Chaste, Cherry, Intact, Ladykin, Madonna, Maiden, Maidenhead, Maidenhood, Marian, May, New, Our lady, Pan(h)agia, Pietà, Pucel(l)age, Pucelle, Pure, Queen, Snood, Tarpeia, Theotokos, Vestal, Zodiacal

Virile, Virility Energetic, Machismo, Macho, Male, Manly, Red-blooded

Virtue(s), Virtuous, Virtual Angelic, Aret(h)a, Assay-piece, Attribute, Cardinal, Caritas, Charity, Chastity, Continent, Cyber, Dharma, Efficacy, Ethical, Excellent, Faith, Foison, Fortitude, Fus(h)ion, Good, Grace, Hope, Justice, Moral(ity), Natural, Patience, Plaster-saint, Practical, Principal, Prudence, Pure, Qua, Say-piece, Squeaky-clean, Straight and narrow, Temperance, Theological, Upright, Worth

Virulent Acrimonious, Deadly, Hostile, Malign, Noxious, Toxic, Vitriolic, Waspish

Viscera Bowels, Entrails, Giblets, Guts, Harigal(d)s, Haslet, Innards, Omentum, Umbles, Vitals

Viscous (liquid), Viscosity Absolute, Glaireous, Gleety, Gluey, Gummy, Kinematic, Slab, Specific, Sticky, Stoke, Tacky, Tar, Thick

Visible, Visibility Clear, Conspicuous, Evident, Explicit, In sight, Obvious, Zero-zero

Vision(ary) Abstraction, Aery, Aisling, Apparition, Awareness, Binocular,

Bourignian, Day-dreamer, Double, Dream(er), Emmetropia, Fancy, Fantast, Fey, Foresight, Idealist, Ideologist, Illusionist, Image, Kef, Moonshine, Mouse-sight, Mystic, Ocular, Phantasm(a), Phantom, Pholism, Photism, Photopia, Romantic, Seeing, Seer, Sight, Sightline, Stereo, Stereopsis, Tunnel, Twenty-twenty, Viewy

Visit(or) Affliction, Alien, Caller, Day-tripper, Domiciliary, ET, Event, First-foot, Guest, Habitué, Haunt, Hit, Inflict, Kursaal, Look up, Pop in, See, Sightseer, Sojourn, State, Stay, Stranger, Take, Wait upon

Visor, Vizor Eyeshade, Face-saver, Mesail, Mezail, Umbrel, Umbr(i)ere, Umbril, Vent(ayle)

Vital(ity) Alive, Bounce, Central, Critical, Crucial, Energy, Esprit, Essential, Existent, Foison, Gusto, Indispensable, Juice, Key, Kick, Life-blood, Linchpin, Lung, Mites, Momentous, Necessary, Oomph, Organ, Pizzazz, Pulse, Salvation, Sap, Verve, Viable, Vigour, Zing, Zoetic

Vitriol(ic) Acid, Acrimonious, Biting, Caustic, Mordant

Vituperate Abuse, Berate, Castigate, Censure, Defame, Inveigh, Lash, Rail, Scold

Vivid Bright, Brilliant, Colourful, Dramatic, Eidetic, Fresh, Graphic, Keen, Live, Pictorial, Picturesque, Sharp, Violent

Vivien Leigh

▶**Vizor** *see* **VISOR**

Vocabulary Idiolect, Idioticon, Jargon, (Kata)kana, Lexicon, Lexis, Meta-language, Nomenclator, Wordbook

Vocation Call, Career, Métier, Mission, Priesthood, Profession, Pursuit, Shop

Vogue Chic, Day, →**FASHION**, Groovy, Mode, Rage, Style, Ton, Trend

Voice(d) Active, Air, Alto, Ancestral, Bass, Chest, Contralto, Countertenor, Descant, Edh, Emit, Eth, Express, Falsetto, Glottis, Harp, Head, Inner, Intonate, Lyric, Mastersinger, Meistersinger, Mezzo-soprano, Middle, Mouth, Opinion, Passive, Phonic, Pipe, Presa, Quill, Say, Sonant, Soprano, Speak, Spinto, Sprechstimme, Steven, Syrinx, Tais(c)h, Tenor, Throat, Tone, →**TONGUE**, Treble, Utter, White

Voiceless Aphonia, Aphony, Dumb, Edh, Eth, Mute, Silent, Tacit

Void Abyss, Annul, Belch, Blank, Chasm, Counter, Defeasance, Defecate, Diriment, Empty, Evacuate, Gap, Hollow, Inane, Inoperative, Invalid, Irritate, Lapse, Negate, Nullify, Quash, Space, Vacuum

Volatile Excitable, Explosive, Inconsistent, Latin, Live(ly), Mercurial, Skittish, Tear gas, Temperamental, Terpene, Tinderbox

Volcano(es), Volcanic Agglomerate, Black smoker, Burning mountain, Composite, Cone, Conic, Fumarole, Greystone, Hornito, Ice, Idocrase, Igneous, Ignimbrite, Monticule, Mud, Obsidian, Pele, Pelée, Plinian, Pozz(u)olana, Pumice, Puzzolana, Sandblow, Shield, Soffioni, Solfatara, Stratovolcano, Tephra, Trass, Tuff

Volley Barrage, Boom, Broadside, Platoon, Salvo, Tirade, Tire

Volume Atomic, Band, Bande, Barrel, Book, Bushel, Capacity, CC, Code(x), Content, Cubage, Gallon, Hin, Loudness, Mass, Ml, Omnibus, Peck, Pint, Quart(o), Roll, Roul(e), Size, Space, Stere, Tom, Tome, Ullage, Vol

Voluntary, Volunteer Docent, Enlist, Fencible, Free, Honorary, Offer, Postlude, Reformado, Spontaneous, Tender, Tennessee, Terrier, TN, Ultroneous, Yeoman

Voluptuary, Voluptuous Carnal, Hedonist, Luscious, Sensuist, Sensuous, Sybarite

Vomit(ing) Barf, Black, Boak, Boke, Cascade, Cat, Chuck up, Chunder, Disgorge, Egest, Egurgitate, Emesis, Honk, Keck, Kotch, Posset, Puke, Ralph, Regorge, Retch, Rolf, Spew, Technicolour yawn, Upchuck

Voracious, Voracity Bulimia, Edacity, Gluttony, Greed, Ravenous, Serrasalmo

Vote(r), Votes, Voting Alternative, Assentor, Aye, Ballot, Ballotee, Block, Card, Casting, Choose, Colonist, Constituent, Coopt, Cross, Crossover, Cumulative, Division, Donkey, Fag(g)ot, Floating, Franchise, Free, Grey, Informal, Mandate, Nay, Negative, No, Opt, People, Placet, Plebiscite, Plump, Plural, Poll, Postal, PR, Preferential, Proportional representation, Protest, Qualified majority, Referendum, Return, Scrutin de liste, Scrutiny, Show of hands, Side, Single transferable,

Straw(-poll), Suffrage, Swinging, Sympathy, Tactical, The stump, Theta, Ticket, Token, Transferable, Voice, X, Yea, Yes

Vouch(er), Vouchsafe Accredit, Assure, Attest, Beteem(e), Chit, Coupon, Endorse, Gift, Guarantee, Luncheon, Meal-ticket, Promise, Receipt, Slip, Ticket, Token, Warrant

Vow Affirm, Baptismal, Behight, Behot(e), Earnest, Ex voto, Hecht, Hest, I do, Nuncupate, →**OATH**, Obedience, Pledge, Plight, Promise, Simple, Solemn, Swear, Troth

Vowel(s) Ablaut, Anaptyxis, Aphesis, Breve, Cardinal, Diphthong, Indeterminate, Monophthong, Murmur, Seg(h)ol, S(c)hwa, Svarabhakti, Triphthong

Voyage(r) Anson, Columbus, Course, Cruise, Launch, Passage, Peregrinate, Sinbad, Travel

Vulgar(ian) Base, Filthy, Gorblim(e)y, Gross, Kitsch, Lavatorial, Plebby, Ribald, Rude, Scurrilous, Slag, Snob, Tarty

Vulnerable Defenceless, Exposed, Open, Pregnable, Susceptible, Unguarded, Weak, Wide-open

Vulture Aasvogel, Bearded, Bird, Buzzard, California (condor), Condor, Culture, Falcon, Gallinazo, Gier, Griffon, Gripe, Grype, King, Lammergeier, Lammergeyer, Ossifrage, Predator, Turkey, Urubu, Zopilote

Ww

Wad(ding) Batt(ing), Lump, Pad, Pledget, Roll, Swab, Wodge

Wade(r), Wading Antigropelo(e)s, Ardea, Crane, Curlew, Dikkop, Egret, Flamingo, Ford, Gallae, Grallatorial, Greenshank, Gumboot, Heron, Ibis, Jacksnipe, Lapwing, Limpkin, Paddle, Phalarope, Plodge, Plover, Ree, Sandpiper, Sarus, Seriema, Shoebill, Snipe, Splodge, Stilt(bird), Terek, Virginia

Wafer Biscuit, Cracker, Crisp, Gaufer, Gaufre, Gofer, Gopher, Host, Papad, Seal

Waffle Adlib, Blather, Cake, Equivocate, Fudge, Gas, Gaufer, Gaufre, Gofer, Gopher, Hedge, Poppycock, Prate, Rabbit, Wibble

Wag(gish), Waggle Arch, Card, Comedian, Joker, Lick, Nod, Rogue, Shake, Sway, Wit(snapper), Wobble

Wage(s) Ante, Award, Fee, Hire, Income, Living, Meed, Minimum, Nominal, Pay, Portage, Practise, Prosecute, Rate, Salary, Screw, Subsistence

Wage-earner Breadwinner, Employee, Proletariat(e)

Wager Ante, Back, →BET, Gamble, Lay, Pascal's, Stake, Wed

Wagon(er) Ar(a)ba, Aroba, Boötes, Boxcar, Brake, Break, Buck, Buckboard, Buggy, Caisson, Carriage, Cart, Cattle truck, Chuck, Coachman, Cocopan, Conestoga, Corf, Covered, Democrat, Drag, Dray, Flatcar, Fourgon, Freight-car, Gambo, Go-cart, Hopper, Hutch, Low-loader, Mammy, Paddy, Palabra, Patrol, Plaustral, Police, Prairie schooner, Rave, Reefer, Rubberneck, Shandry, Stage, Station, Tank, Tartana, Telega, Tender, Trap, Trekker, Truck, Van, Victoria, Wain, Water

Wail(er) Banshee, Bawl, Blubber, Howl, Keen, Lament, Moan, Skirl, Threnody, Threnos, Ululate, Vagitus, Wah-wah, Yammer

Waist(band) Belt, Cummerbund, Girdlestead, Hour-glass, Middle, Midship, Obi, Sash, Shash, Wasp, Zoster

Waistcoat Gilet, Jerkin, Lorica, MB, Sayon, Sleeve(d), Stabvest, Vest, Weskit

Wait(er), Waiting Abid(e), Ambush, Attend, Barista, Bide, Busboy, Butler, Buttle, Carhop, Commis, Cupbearer, Dally, Delay, Estragon, Expect, Flunkey, Frist, Garçon, Hang on, Hesitate, Hover, Interval, Khidmutgar, Lead time, Lime, Linger, Lurch, Maître d', Maître d'hôtel, Minority, Omnibus, Pannier, Pause, Penelope, Pozzo, Queue, Remain, Serve(r), Sommelier, Stacking, Stay, Steward, Suspense, Taihoa, Tarry, Tend(ance), Tray, Vladimir, Wine, Won

Waitress Bunny girl, Hebe, Miss, Mousme(e), Nippy, Server

Waive Abandon, Defer, Forgo, Overlook, Postpone, Relinquish, Renounce, Suspend

Wake(n) Abrade, Abraid, Abray, Aftermath, Alert, Animate, Arouse, Astern, Deathwatch, Excite, Hereward, Keen, Prod, Rear, Surface, Trail, Train, Wash

Walk(er), Walking, Walkabout, Walkway Alameda, Alley, Alure, Amble, Ambulate, Arcade, Birdcage, Charity, Cloister, Clump, Constitutional, Daddle, Dander, Emu, Esplanade, EVA, Festination, Flânerie, Gait, Gallery, Ghost, Go, Gradient, Hike, Hookey, Hump, Lambeth, Leg, Lumber, Mall, March, Mince, Mosey, Nordic, Pace, Pad, Paddle, Pasear, Paseo, Passage, Passerby, Path, Pavement, Ped(estrianism), Perambulate, Pergola, Perp, Piaffe, Piazza, Pole, Pound, Power, Prance, Prom(enade), Rack, Ramble, Rampart, Random, Ring, Routemarch, Sashay, Scamble, Schlep, Shamble, Sidle, Slommock, Space, Spanish, Sponsored, Stalk, Step, Stoa, Stride, Stroll, Strut, Stump, Taligrade, Terrace, Toddle, Tramp, Trash, Travolator, Tread, Trog, Truck, Trudge, Turn, Wade, Wander, Wayfare

Wall Bail, Bailey, Barrier, Berm, Cavity, Cell, Chinese, Climbing, Crib, Curtain, Dado, Dam, Dike, Dry-stone, Fail-dike, Fourth, Frustule, Gable, Great, Groyne, Hadrian's, Hanging, Hangman, Head, Immure, Mutual, Non-bearing, Parapet,

Parpane, Parpen(d), Parpent, Partition, Party, Peribolos, Perpend, Perpent, Podium, Puteal, Retaining, Reveal, Revet(ment), Ring, River, Roman, Roughcast, Screen, Sea, Septum, Side, Street, Studding, Tambour, Tariff, Vallation, Video, Wa', Wailing, Western, Withe

Wallaby Brusher, Dama, Kangaroo, Pademelon, Pad(d)ymelon, Quokka, Tammar

Wall-covering, Wallpaper Anaglypta®, Arras, Burlap, Lincrusta, Paper, Tapestry, Tapet

Wallet Billfold, Case, Flybook, Folder, Notecase, Pochette, Purse, Scrip

Wallop Bash, Baste, Batter, Beat, Biff, Clout, Cob, Gigantic, →**HIT**, Lam, Lounder, Oner, Polt, Pound, Slog, Strap, Swinge, Tan, Tat, Thud, Trounce

Wallow(ing) Bask, Flounder, Luxuriate, Revel, Roll, Slubber, Splash, Swelter, Tolter, Volutation, Welter

Wallpaper →**WALL-COVERING**, Woodchip

Walrus Morse, Moustache, Pinniped, Rosmarine, Sea-horse, Tash

Wan Lurid, Pale, Pallid, Pasty, Sanguine, Sorry

Wander(er), Wandering Bedouin, Berber, Bum, Caird, Daiker, Delirious, Deviate, Digress, Drift, Errant, Estray, Excursive, Expatiate, Gad(about), Grope, Hobo, Itinerant, Jew, Landloper, Maunder, Meander, Mill, Mither, Moider, Moither, Moon, Nomad(e), Odysseus, Peregrine, Peripatetic, Prodigal, Ramble, Range, Romany, Room, Rove, Stooge, Straggle, Stray, Stroam, Stroll, Swan, Ta(i)ver, Tramp, Troll, Truant, Vagabond, Vagile, Vagrant, Vague, Waif, Wend, Wheel, Wilder

▷ **Wandering** *may indicate* an anagram

Want(ing), Wants Absence, Conative, Covet, Crave, Dearth, Defect, Deficient, Derth, Desiderata, →**DESIRE**, Destitution, Envy, For, Hardship, Indigent, Itch, Lack, Like, Long, Mental, Moldwarp, Mole, Need, Penury, Require, Scarceness, Scarcity, Shortfall, Shy, Void, Wish, Yen

Wanton(ness) Bona-roba, Cadgy, Chamber, Cocotte, Deliberate, Demirep, Filly, Flirt-gill, Gammerstang, Giglet, Giglot, Gillflirt, Hussy, Jay, Jezebel, Jillflirt, Lewd, Licentious, Light o' love, Loose, Nice, Protervity, Roué, Slut, Smicker, Sportive, Sybarite, Toyish, Twigger, Unchaste, Wayward

War(fare), Wars American Civil, American Independence, Ares, Armageddon, Arms, Asymmetrical, Attrition, Bacteriological, Bate, Battle, Biological, Chemical, Civil, Clash, Class, Cod, Cold, Combat, Conflict, Crimean, Crusade, Culture, Electronic, Emergency, Feud, →**FIGHT**, Flagrante bello, Flame, Food, Franco-Prussian, Fray, Germ, Great, Guer(r)illa, Gulf, Holy, Hostilities, Hot, Hundred Years', Information, Internecine, Jenkins' ear, Jihad, Korean, Limited, Mars, Mexican, Napoleonic, Nuclear, Opium, Peasants', Peloponnesian, Peninsular, Phony, Price, Private, Propaganda, Psychological, Punic, Push-button, Queen Anne's, Rebellion, Revolutionary, Roses, Russo-Japanese, Secession, Seven against Thebes, Seven Years', Shooting, Six Day, Social, Spanish-American, Spanish Civil, Star, Sword, Theomachy, Thirty Years', Total, Trench, Trojan, Turf, Vietnam, Winter, World, Yom Kippur

Warble(r) Carol, Cetti's, Chiff-chaff, Chirl, Fauvette, Peggy, Rel(l)ish, Trill, Vibrate, Yodel, Yodle

Ward (off) Artemus, Averruncate, Avert, Care, Casual, Casualty, Charge, Defend, District, Fend, Guard, Inner, Marginal, Maternity, Minor, Nightingale, Oppose, Outer, Parry, Protégé, Pupil, Soc, Soken, Thunderbolt, Vintry, Wear, Weir

Warden Caretaker, Church, Concierge, Constable, Curator, Custodian, Game, Guardian, Keeper, Meter maid, Pear, Provost, Ranger, Septimus, Sidesman, Spooner, Steward, Traffic

Ware(s) Arretine, Basalt, Beware, Biscuit, Cameo, Canton, Chelsea, China, Etruria, Fabergé, Faience, Goods, Hollow(w)are, Jasper, Lapis lazuli, Lustre, Merchandise, Palissy, Plate(d), Queen's, Samian, Sanitary, Satsuma, Shippo, Truck, Wemyss

Warehouse Bonded, Data, Depository, Entrepôt, Freight-shed, Go-down, Hong, Store

▶ **Warfare** *see* **WAR(FARE)**

Wariness, Wary Ca'canny, Cagey, Careful, Cautel, Caution, Chary, Discreet,

Distrust, Gingerly, Guarded, Leery, Mealy-mouthed, Prudent, Sceptical, Suspicious, Vigilant

Warlike Battailous, Bellicose, Gung-ho, Lachlan, Martial, Militant

Warm(er), Warming, Warmth Abask, Admonish, Air, Ardour, Atingle, Balmy, Bonhomie, British, Calefacient, Calid(ity), Cardigan, Chambré, Cordial, Eager, El Nino, Empressement, Enchafe, Fervour, Flame, Foment, Genial, Global, Glow, →HEAT, Hot, Incalescent, Kang, Kindly, Lew, Logic, Loving, Muff, Muggy, Mull, Nuke, Radiator, Tepid, Thermal, Toast, Toasty

Warn(ing) Admonish, Alar(u)m, Alert, Amber, Apprise, Beacon, Bell, Beware, Bleep, Buoy, Caution, Cave, Caveat, Caveat emptor, Cone, Counsel, Cowbell, Detector, DEW, Document, Early, En garde, Example, Foghorn, Fore, Foretoken, Gardyloo, Garnishment, Griffin, Harbinger, Hazchem, Heads up, Hoot, Horn, Illocution, Klaxon, Knell, Larum, Lesson, Light, Maroon, Minatory, Nix, Noli-me-tangere, Nota bene, Notice, Notification, Omen, Pi-jaw, Portent, Premonish, Premonitory, Presage, Profit, Protevangelium, Red alert, Red flag, Red light, Remind, Riot Act, Rumble strip, Scaldings, Signal, Spindle, Storm, Tattler, Threat, Timber, Tip-off, Token, Toot, Yellow card

Warp(ed) Bent, Bias, Buckle, Cast, Contort, Distort, Hog, Kam, Kedge, Pandation, Spring, Time, Twist, Weft, Zag

▷ **Warped** *may indicate* an anagram

Warrant(y), Warrant officer Able, Authorise, Behight, Behote, Bosun, Capias, Caption, Certificate, Deserve, Detainer, Distress, Dividend, Fiat, Fiaunt, Fugle, Guarantee, Justify, Merit, Mittimus, Peace, Permit, Precept, Reprieve, Royal, Search, Sepad, Swear, Transire, Vouch, Warn, Writ

Warrior Achilles, Agamemnon, Ajax, Amazon, Anzac, Attila, Brave, Cold, Crusader, Eorl, Fighter, Finlay, Finley, Geronimo, Haiduk, Heyduck, Impi, Jihadi, Lewis, Louis, Myrmidon, Nestor, Roger, Samurai, Soldier, Tatar, Unknown, Wardog, Warhorse, Warwolf, Zulu

Warship Battleship, Blockship, Castle, Cog, Corvette, Cruiser, Destroyer, Drake, Dromon(d), Galleass, Galliass, Invincible, Man-o-war, Mine-layer, Monitor, Privateer, Ram, Repulse

▶ **Wary** *see* **WARINESS**

Wash(ed), Washer, Washing (up), Wash out Ablution, Affusion, Alluvion, Bath, Bay(e), Bidet, Bur(r), Calcimine, Circlip, Clean(se), Cradle, D, Dashwheel, Dele(te), Dip, Edulcorate, Elute, Enema, Erode, Fen, Flush, Freshen, Front-loader, Gargle, Grom(m)et, Grummet, Hose, Hush, Irrigate, Kalsomine, Lap, →LAUNDER, Lavabo, Lave, Leather, Lip, Lotion, Marsh, Maundy, Mop, Nipter, Pan, Pigswill, Poss, Purify, Rinse, Sapple, Scrub, Shampoo, Shim, Sind, Sloosh, Sluice, Soogee, Soojee, Soojey, Squeegie, Sujee, Swab, Synd, Syne, Tie, Twin tub, Tye, Wake

▷ **Wasp** *may indicate* a rugby player

Wasp(ish) Bembex, Bink, Bite, Chalcid, Cuckoo-fly, Cynipidae, Cynips, Digger, Fig, Fretful, Gall(-fly), Hornet, Horntail, Hoverfly, Irritable, Marabunta, Mason, Miffy, Muddauber, Paper, Peevish, Pompilid, Potter, Seed, Solitary, Spider, Syrphus, Vespa, Yellow jacket

Wastage, Waste(d), Wasting, Wasteful, Wasteland, Waster, Wastrel Amyotrophy, Atrophy, Blow, Blue, Bluer, Boondoggle(r), Cesspit, Cirrhosis, Colliquative, Consume, Coom(b), Cotton, Crud, Culm, Decay, Desert, Detritus, Devastate, Dilapidate, Dissipate, Dross, Dung, Dwindle, Dwine, Dystrophy, Effluent, Egesta, Emaciate, Erode, Excrement, Exhaust, Expend, Faeces, Flue, Fribble, Fritter, Garbage, Gash, Gob, Grog, Gunge, Haggard, Half-cut, Havoc, Hazardous, High-level, Hi(r)stie, Husk, Knub, Landfill, Lavish, Lean, Loose, Lose, Loss, Low-level, Merino, Misspent, Moor, Muir, Mungo, Natural, Nub, Nuclear, Offal, Offcut, Oller, Ordure, Pellagra, Perish, Pigswill, Pine, Prodigalise, Rack and manger, Radioactive, Rammel, Ravage, Red mud, Red tape, →REFUSE, Rubble, Ruderal, Ruin, Scant o' grace, Scissel, Scoria, Scrap, Scum, Sewage, Slag, Slurry, Spend, Spill, Spoil(age), Squander, Sullage, Swarf, Tailing, Thin, Thwaite, Ureal, Urine, Vast, Wear, Wilderness

▷ **Wasted** *may indicate* an anagram

Watch(er) Accutron®, Analog(ue), Argus, Await, Bark, Behold, Big brother, Bird-dog, Black, Case, Chronograph, Clock, Coastguard, Digital, Dog, Eryl, Espy, Eyeball, Fob, Gregory, Guard, Half-hunter, Huer, Hunter, Lever, Lo, Look, Look-out, Middle, Monitor, Morning, Nark, Neighbourhood, Night, Nit, Note, Observe, Overeye, Patrol, Posse, Quartz, Regard, Repeater, Rolex®, Scout, Sentinel, Sentry, Shadow, Snoop, Spectate, Spie, Spotter, Spy, Stemwinder, Suicide, Surveillance, Tend, Ticker, Timekeeper, Timepiece, Timer, Tompion, Tout, Turnip, Vedette, →**VIGIL**, Voyeur, Wait, Wake, Weather eye, Wrist(let)

Watchman Argus, Bellman, Charley, Charlie, Cho(w)kidar, Chok(e)y, Guard, Huer, Sentinel, Sentry, Speculator, Tompion, Viewer

Watch-tower Atalaya, Barbican, Beacon, Garret, Mirador, Sentry-go, Turret

Water(ed), Waters, Watery Adam's ale, Adam's wine, Aerated, Apollinaris, Aq(ua), Aquatic, Aqueous, Ascites, Barley, Bayou, Bedabble, Bilge, Bound, Branch, Brine, Broads, Brook, Burn, Canal, Cancer, Chuck, Cold, Cologne, Compensation, Conductivity, Connate, Dead, Deg, Dew, Dill, Dilute, Dribble, Drinking, Eau, Ebb, Element, Evian®, First, Flood, Ford, Fossil, Functional, Grey, Gripe, Ground, Hard, Heavy, Hellespont, High, Holy, Hot, Irrigate, Javel(le), Kyle, Lagoon, Lagune, Lake, Laurel, Lavender, Leachate, Light, Lime, Loch(an), Lode, Lough, Low, Lubricated, Lymph, Melt, Meteoric, Mineral, Miner's inch, Moiré, Mother, Nappe, North, Oasis®, Oedema, Orange-flower, Overfall, Pani, Pawnee, Pee, Perrier®, Pisces, Polly, Poppy, Potash, Potass, Pump, Purest, Quarry, Quick, Quinine, Rain, Rapids, Rate, Reach, Rheumy, Rice, Rip, Riverine, Rose, Running, Runny, Rydal, Saltchuck, Scorpio, Sea, Seltzer, Sera, Serous, Serum, Shoal, Shower, Skinkling, Slack, Slick, Sluice, Soda, Sodden, Soft, Sound, Souse, Southampton, Sprinkle, Steam, Stream, Surface, Tabby, Table, Tap, Tar, Temper, Territorial, Thermocline, Thin, Tide, Toilet, Tonic, Urine, Utility, Vichy, Viscous, Wai, Wake, Wash(y), Weak, Wee, Whey, White, White coal, Wild, Wishy-washy

Waterbuck Kob

Water-carrier Aqueduct, Bheestie, Bheesty, Bhistee, Bhisti, Bucket, Carafe, Chatty, Drain, Furphy, Hose, Hydra, Hydria, Kirbeh, Pail, Pitcher, Rigol

Water-course Arroyo, Billabong, Canal, Ditch, Dyke, Falaj, Furrow, Gutter, Khor, Lead, Leat, Nala, Nala(h), Nulla, Nullah, Rean, Rhine, Rill, River(et), Serpentine, Shott, Spruit, Wadi

Watercress Nasturtium

Waterfall Angel (Falls), Cataract, Churchill, Chute, Cuquenan, Espelands, →**FALL(S)**, Force, Foss, Kahiwa, Kile, Lasher, Lin(n), Lower Mar Valley, Mardel, Montmorency, Mtarazi, Niagara, Overfall, Rapid, Salmon leap, Sault, Sutherland, Takakkaw, Tugela, Tyssestrengene, Utigord, Yosemite

Waterman Aquarius, Bargee, Ferryman, Oarsman

Water-plant Alisma, Aquatic, Cress, Crowfoot, Elodea, Gulfweed, Lace-leaf, Lattice-leaf, Nelumbo, Nenuphar, Nuphar, Ouvirandra, Pontederia, Quillwort, Reate, Sea-mat, Sedge, Seg, Stratiotes, Urtricularia, Vallisneria

Waterproof, Water-tight Caisson, Camlet, Caulk, Cerecloth, Cofferdam, Corfam®, Curry, Dampcourse, Dubbin(g), Groundsheet, Loden, Mac, Mino, Oilers, Oilskin, Pay, Sealant, Seaworthy, Sta(u)nch, Stank, Suberin, Tar-paper, Tarpaulin, Waders

Water pump Ee, Eye

Water-sprite Kelpie, Kelpy, Nix(ie), Nixy, Tangie, Undine, Water-nymph

Waterway Aqueduct, Canal, Channel, Creek, Culvert, Ditch, Igarapé, Illinois, Intracoastal, Lode, River, St Lawrence Seaway, Sny(e), Sound, Straight, Suez

Water-wheel Noria, Pelton, Sakia, Saki(y)eh, Tympanum

Wave(s), Waved, Waveform, Wavelength, Wavy Alpha, Beachcomber, Beam, Beck, Beta, Billow, Bore, Bow, Brain, Brandish, Breaker, Carrier, Cold, Comber, Complex, Continuous, Crest, Crime, Crimp, Crispate, Delta, Dominant, Dumper, Electromagnetic, Feather, Finger, Flap, Flaunt, Float, Flote, Flourish, Fourier series, Gesticulate, Gravitational, Gravity, Graybeard, Ground, Groundswell, Harmonic,

Haystack, Head sea, Heat, Internal, Ionospheric, Lee, Long, Longitudinal, Marcel, Matter, Medium, Mexican, New, Perm(anent), Plunger, Primary, Pulse, Radar, Radiation, Radio, Rip, Ripple, Roller, Rooster, Sea, Secondary, Seiche, Seismic, Shake, Shock, Short, Sine, Sinuate, Skipper's daughter, Sky, Skyrmion, Snaky, Sound, Spiller, Square, Squiggle, Standing, Stationary, Stern, Stream, Supplementary, Surf, Surge, Sway, Tabby, Theta, Third, Thought, Tidal, Tidal bore, Tide, Train, Transverse, Travelling, Tsunami, Ultrasonic, Undate, Unde, Undulate, Waffle, Waft, Wag, Waive, Wash, Waw, Wawe, Whelm, Whitecap, White-horse, Wigwag

▷ **Wave(s)** *may indicate* an anagram

Waver(ing), Waverer Dither, Double-minded, Falter, Flag, Gutter, Hesitate, Indecision, Oscillate, Reel, Stagger, Sway, Swither, Teeter, Vacillate, Waffle, Wet, Wow

Wax(ed), Waxing, Waxy Ambergris, Appal, Bate, Bees, Bone, Brazilian, Cere, Ceresin, Cerumen, Chinese, Cobbler's, Cutin, Earth, Effuse, Enseam, Ethal, Geraldton, Grave, Greaves, Grow, Heelball, Honeycomb, Increase, Increscent, Inseam, Ire, Japan, Kiss, Livid, Lost, Lyrical, Mineral, Mummy, Myrtle, Paraffin, Pela, Petroleum, Rage, Seal, Sealing, Spermaceti, Tallow, Tantrum, Temper, Toxaphene, Vegetable, White, Yielding

Way(s), Wayside Access, Agate, Appian, Autobahn, Avenue, Borstal(l), Budo, Bypass, Companion, Course, Crescent, Defile, Direction, Door, Draw, E, Each, Entrance, Family, Fashion, Flaminian, Foss(e), Four-foot, Gate, Habit, Hatch, Hedge, High, Hither, How, Icknield, Lane, Manner, Means, Method, Milky, MO, Mode, N, Pass, Path, Permanent, Pilgrim's, Procedure, Railroad, Regimen, Ridge, →ROAD, Route, S, Sallypost, St(reet), Style, System, Technique, Thoroughfare, Thus, Trace, Trail, Troade, Turnpike, Underpass, Untrodden, Via, W, Wise

Way-out Advanced, Bizarre, Egress, Esoteric, Exit, Exotic, Extreme, Offbeat, Trendy

Wayward Capricious, Disobedient, Errant, Erratic, Loup-the-dyke, Obstreperous, Perverse, Scapegrace, Stray, Unruly, Wilful

WC Gents, Ladies, Lav, Loo

Weak(er), Weaken(ing), Weakest, Weakness Achilles' heel, Adynamia, Appair, Appal, Arsis, Attenuate, Blot, Brittle, Chink, Cissy, Cripple(d), Debile, Debilitate, Decrease, Delay, Delicate, Deplete, Dilling, Dilute, Disable, Effete, Emasculate, Embrittle, Enervate, Enfeeble, Entender, Fade, Faible, Failing, Faint, Fatigue, Feeble, Fissile, Flag, Flaw, Flimsy, Foible, Fragile, Frailty, Give, Glass chin, Gone, Groggy, Ham, Helpless, Honeycomb, Impair, Impotence, Infirm, Knock-kneed, Lame, Lassitude, Loophole, Low, Low ebb, Meagre, Mild, Milk and water, Namby-pamby, Pale, Pall, Paresis, Penchant, Puny, Push-over, Pusillanimous, Reduce, Simp, Slack, Soft spot, Spineless, Tenuous, Thesis, Thin, Thready, Tottery, Unable, Underdog, Undermine, Unman, Unnerve, Unstable, Vapid, Vessel, Vulnerability, W, Washy, Water(y), Wish(y)-wash(y)

Wealth(y) Abundance, Affluence, Bullion, Capital, Croesus, Digerati, Ease, Fat-cat, Fortune, Golconda, Jet-set, Klondike, Klondyke, Loaded, Loadsamoney, Lolly, Magnate, Mammon, Means, Mine, Mint, Moneyed, Nabob, Opulence, Ore, Pelf, Plutocrat, Reich, Rich, Ritzy, Solid, Substance, Treasure, Trustafarian, Untold, Well-heeled, Well-off, Well-to-do

Weapon(s) Ammo, Antitank, Arm, Arsenal, Assault, Binary, Cultural, Deterrent, Greek fire, →GUN, Hoplology, Long-range, Missile, Munition, Nuclear, Nuke, Ordnance, Piece, →PISTOL, →SWORD, Theatre, Tool, Traditional

▷ **Wear** *may indicate* the NE eg Sunderland

Wear(ing), Wear Out Abate, Ablative, Abrade, Attrition, Chafe, Corrade, Corrode, Deteriorate, Detrition, Efface, Erode, Erosion, Fashion, For(e)spend, Fray, Frazzle, Fret, Garb, Impair, In, Mush, Pack, Sap, Scuff, Sport, Stand, Tedy, Tolerate

Weariness, Wearisome, Weary(ing) Beat, Bejade, Blethered, Bore, Cloy, Dog-tired, Ennui, Ennuyé, Exhaust, Fag, Fatigate, Fatigue, Flag(ging), Harass, Hech, Heigh-ho, Irk, Jade, Lacklustre, Lassitude, Pall, Puny, Ramfeezle, Sick, Sleepy, Spent, Tire, Tiresome, Trash, Try, Tucker, Wabbit, Worn

Weasel Beech-marten, Cane, Delundung, Ermine, Ferret, Glutton, Grison, Kolinsky,

Marten, Mink, Mustela, Pekan, Pine-marten, Polecat, Stoat, Taira, Tayra, Vermin, Whit(t)ret, Whitterick, Whittrick, Wolverine, Woodshock

Weather, Weather forecast Atmosphere, Cyclone, Discolour, Ecoclimate, Elements, Endure, Hail, La Nina, Met, Monkey's wedding, Rain, Sky, Snow, Stand, Survive, Tiros, Undergo, Withstand

Weatherboard Rusticating

Weave(r), Weaves, Weaving Arachne, Basket, Broché, Cane, Complect, Contexture, Entwine, Finch, Heald, Heddle, Interlace, Jacquard, Lace, Lease, Leno, Lion, Loom, Marner, Osiery, Penelope, Plain, Plait, Raddle, Ripstop, Rya, Shuttle, Sparrow, Spider, Splice, Stevengraph, Taha, Textorial, Texture, Throstle, Throwster, Tissue, Tweel, Twill, Twine, Wabster, Waggle, Webster, Zigzag

Web(bed), Webbing, Web-footed, Web-site Aranea, Food, Fourchette, Hit, Infomediary, Internet, Mat, Maze, Mesh(work), Network, Offset, Palama, Palmate, Palmiped, Patagium, Pinnatiped, Portal, Skein, Snare, Tela, Tissue, Toil, Totipalmate, Vane, World Wide

Wed(ding), Wedlock Alliance, Bet, Diamond, Espousal, Golden, Hymen, Join, Knobstick, Liaison, Link, Marriage, Marry, Mate, Meng(e), Me(i)nt, Meynt, Ming, Nuptials, Pair, Penny, Ruby, Shotgun, Silver, Spousal, → UNION, Unite, White, Y

Wedge(d) Chock, Chunk, Cleat, Cotter, Cuneal, Doorstop, Feather, Forelock, Gad, Gagger, Gib, Jack, Jam, Key, Niblick, Prop, Quoin, Scotch, Shim, Spaceband, Sphenic, Stick, Texas, Trig, Vomerine, Whipstock

Wee Leak, Little, Pee, Slash, Sma(ll), Tinkle, Tiny, → URINATE, Widdle

▷ **Weed** *may indicate* 'urinated'

Weed(y) Adderwort, Agrestal, Alga, Allseed, Anacharis, Arenaria, Bedstraw, Bell-bind, Blinks, Burdock, Buttercup, Carpetweed, Catch, Charlock, Chickweed, Chlorella, Cigar(ette), Cissy, Clotbur, Clover, Cobbler's pegs, Cockle, Cocklebur, Colonist, Coltsfoot, Corncockle, Couch, Daisy, Dallop, Dandelion, Darnel, Dock, Dollop, Dulse, Elder, Elodea, Ers, Fag, Fat hen, Femitar, Fenitar, Fluellen, Fluellin, Fork, Fucoid, Fumitory, Gangly, Goutweed, Goutwort, Ground elder, Groundsel, Helodea, Hoe, Indian, Joe-pye, Knapweed, Knawel, Knot-grass, Lanky, Lemna, Mare's-tail, Marijuana, Matfelon, Mayweed, Nard, Nettle, Nipplewort, Nostoc, Onion, Oxygen, Paterson's curse, Pearlwort, Pilewort, Pineapple, Piri-piri, Plantain, Potamogeton, Purslane, Ragi, Ragwort, Reate, Rest-harrow, Ribbon, Rib-grass, Ribworth, Ruderal, Runch, Sagittaria, Sargasso, Scal(l)awag, Scallywag, Senecio, Softy, Sorrel, Speedwell, Spurge, Spurrey, Sudd, Sun-spurge, Swine's-cress, Tab, Tansy, Tare, Thistle, Tine, Tobacco, Tormentil, Twitch, Ulotrichale, Ulva, Vetch, Viper's bugloss, Wartcress, Widow's, Winnow, Yarr

Weedkiller Arsenic, Atrazine, Dalapon, Diquat, Diuron, Herbicide, Paraquat®, Simazine

Week(s), Weekly Ember, Expectation, Great, Hebdomadary, Holy, Omer, Orientation, Ouk, Oulk, Passion, Periodical, Prophetic, Rag, Rogation, Schoolies, Sennight, Working

Weep(er), Weeping, Weepy, Wept Bawl, Blubber, Cry, Grat, Greet, Lachrymose, Lament, Loser, Maudlin, Niobe, Ooze, Pipe, Sob, Wail, Waterworks

Weigh(ing), Weigh down, Weight(y) All-up, Atomic, Avoirdupois, Balance, Bantam, Bob, Bow, Bulk, Burden, Clout, Consider, Count, Counterpoise, Cruiser, Dead, Deliberate, Drail, Dumbbell, Emphasis, Equivalent, Feather, Formula, Great, Handicap, Heft, Import, Importance, Impost, Incumbent, Journey, Kerb, Live, Load, Mark, Massive, Matter, Metage, Metrology, Minimum, Molecular, Moment, Mouse, Onerous, One-sided, Oppress, Overpoise, Perpend, Plumb-bob, Plummet, Poise, Preponderance, Prey, Rate, Sinker, Slang, Stress, Tare, Throw, Ton(nage), Tophamper, Tron(e), Troy, Unmoor, Welter, Wey

Weir Cauld, Dam, Garth, Kiddle, Kidel, Lasher, Pen, Watergate

Weird Bizarre, Curious, Dree, Eerie, Eery, Eldritch, Far out, Kookie, Offbeat, Spectral, Strange, Supernatural, Taisch, Uncanny, Zany

Welch, Welsh Abscond, Cheat, Default, Embezzle, Levant, Rat, Reneg(u)e, Renig, Skedaddle, Weasel

Welcome, Welcoming Aloha, Ave, Bel-accoyle, Ciao, Embrace, Entertain, Glad-hand, Greet, Haeremai, Hallo, Halse, Hello, Hospitable, How, Hullo, Open house, Receive, Reception, Salute, Ticker-tape

Welfare Advantage, Alms, Benison, Common weal, Ha(y)le, Heal, Health, Sarvodaya, Weal

Well (done) Artesian, Atweel, Ave, Aweel, Bien, Bore(hole), Bravo, Carbon, Casinghead, Cenote, Chipper, Development, Discovery, Downhole, Dry hole, Easily, Euge, Famously, Fine, Fit, Foot, Gasser, Good, Gosh, Gusher, Hale, →**HEALTHY**, Hot, Inkpot, Ka pai, Law, Mickery, My, Namma hole, Odso, Oh, Oil(er), Phreatic, Potential, Pour, So, Source, Spa, Spouter, Spring, Sump, Surge, Teek, Tube, Um, Upflow, Wildcat, Worthily, Zemzem

Wellbeing Atweel, Bien-être, Comfort, Euphoria, Euphory, Good, Health, Welfare

Well-born Eugene

Well-known Famous, Illustrious, Notorious, Notour, Prominent

Well-off Affluent, Far, Rich, Wealthy

▶ **Welsh** *see* **WELCH**

Welsh(man), Welshwoman Aled, Briton, Brittonic, Brython, Cake, Cambrian, Celtic, Cog, Crachach, Cym(ric), Cymry, Dafydd, Dai, Emlyn, Evan, Fluellen, Gareth, Harp, Idris, Ifor, Ivor, Keltic, Megan, P-Celtic, P-Keltic, Rabbit, Rarebit, Rees, Rhys, Sion, Taff(y), Tudor, W, Walian

West(ern), Westerly Ang mo, Favonian, Hesperian, Mae, Movie, Oater, Occidental, Ponent, Spaghetti, Sunset, W, Westlin, Wild

▷ **West end** *may indicate* 't' or 'W1'

Wet(ting), Wetland Bedabble, Bedraggled, Clammy, Daggle, Damp, Dank, Dew, Dip, Douse, Dowse, Drench, Drip(ping), Drook, Drouk, Embrue, Enuresis, Feeble, Humect, Humid, Hyetal, Imbrue, Imbue, Irrigate, Irriguous, Madefy, Madid, Marshy, Moil, Moist(en), Molly, Namby-pamby, Pee, Piddle, Pouring, Rainy, Ramsar site, Ret(t), Rheumy, Roral, Roric, Runny, Saturate, Shower, Simp(leton), Sipe, Sissy, Sluice, →**SOAK**, Sodden, Sopping, Sour, Steep, Tiddle, Tipsy, Urinate, Wat, Wee, Widdle, Wimpy, Wringing

Wetsuit Steamer

▷ **Whale** *may indicate* an anagram

Whale(meat), Whaling Baleen, Beaked, Beluga, Blower, Blubber, Blue, Bottlehead, Bottlenose, Bowhead, Cachalot, Calf, Cetacea(n), Cete, Cetology, Dolphin, Fall, Fin(back), Finner, Gam, Glutton, Grampus, Greenland (right), Grey, Humpback, Ishmael, Killer, Kreng, Leviathan, Manatee, Minke, Monodon, Mysticeti, Orc(a), Paste, Pilot, Pod, Porpoise, Right, River dolphin, Rorqual, School, Scrag, Sei, Sperm, Thrasher, Toothed, Toothless, White, Ziphius

What, Whatever Anan, Eh, How, Pardon, Que, Regardless, Siccan, That, Which

Whatnot, What's-its-name Dinges, Dingus, Doings, Doobrey, Doobrie, Étagère, Gismo, Jigamaree, Jiggumbob, Thingamy, Thingumajig, Thingumbob, Thingummy, Timenoguy

Wheat Allergen, Amber, Amelcorn, Bald, Beard(ed), Beardless, Blé, Bulg(h)ur, Cracked, Durum, Einkorn, Emmer, Federation, Fromenty, Frumenty, Furme(n)ty, Furmity, Grain, Hard, Mummy, Red, Rivet, Sarrasin, Sarrazin, Seiten, Semolina, Sharps, Spelt, Summer, Triticum, White

Wheedle Banter, Barney, Blandish, Cajole, Coax, Cog, Cuiter, Cuittle, Flatter, Inveigle, Tweedle, Whilly(whaw)

Wheel(er) Balance, Bedel, Bevel, Bicycle, Big, Bogy, Breast, Bucket, Buff(ing), Cart's tail, Caster, Castor, Catherine, Chain, Chark(h)a, Circle, Cistern, Count, Crown, Cycle, Daisy, Diamond, Disc, Driving, Emery, Epicycloidal, Escape, Fan, Felloe, Felly, Ferris, Fifth, Fortune, Gear, Grinding, Gyrate, Helm, Hurl, Idle(r), Jagger, Jigger, Jolley, Joy, Kick, Lantern, Magnate, Master, Medicine, Mitre, Monkey, Nabob, Nave, Nose, Paddle, Pattern, Pedal, Pelton, Perambulator, Persian, Pin, Pinion, Pitch, Pivot, Planet, Potter's, Prayer, Pulley, Rag, Ratchet, Roll, Roller, Rotate, Roulette, Rowel, Sheave, Snail, Spare, Spider, Spinning, Sprocket, Spur, Star, Steering, Stitch, Swing,

Tail, Throwing-table, Training, Tread, Treadmill, Trindle, Trolley, Truckle, Trundle, →TURN, Water, Web, Whirling-table, Wire, Worm

Wheelwright Spokesman

Wheeze Asthma, Breathe, Jape, Joke, Pant, Pech, Ploy, Rale, Reak, Reik, Rhonchus, Ruse, Stridor, Trick, Whaisle, Whaizle

Where(abouts) Location, Neighbourhood, Place, Site, Vicinity, Whaur, Whither

Wherewithal Finance, Means, Money, Needful, Resources

Whet(stone) Coticular, Excite, Hone, Oilstone, Rubstone, Sharpen, Stimulate, Stroke

Whether Conditional, If

Which(ever), Which is Anyway, As, QE, Whatna, Whilk, Who

While Although, As, Interim, Since, Space, Span, Spell, Though, Throw, Time, When, Whenas, Whereas, Yet

Whim(s), Whimsical, Whimsy Bizarre, Caprice, Conceit, Crotchet, Fad, Fancy, Fay, Fey, Fie, Flisk, Kicksy-wicksy, Kink, Maggot, Notion, Quaint, Quirk, Tick, Toy, Vagary

Whine, Whinge(r) Cant, Carp, Complain, Cry, Grumble, Kvetch, Mewl, Miaow, Moan, Peenge, Pule, Snivel, Sword, Whimper, Yammer

Whip(ped), Whip out, Whipping Beat, Braid, Bullwhip, Cat, Cat o' nine tails, Chastise, Chief, Colt, Crop, Drive, Firk, Five-line, Flagellate, Flay, Gad, Hide, Jambok, Knout, Larrup, →LASH, Leather, Limber, Lunge, Quirt, Rawhide, Riem, Scourge, Sjambok, Slash, Steal, Stock, Swinge, Swish, Switch, Taw, Thong, Three-line, Thresh, Trounce, Welt, West Country, Whap

Whippoorwill Wishtonwish

Whirl(er), Whirling Circumgyrate, Dervish, Eddy, Gyrate, →IN A WHIRL, Maelstrom, Pivot, Reel, Spin, Swing, Swirl, Vortex, Vortical, Whirry

Whirlpool Eddy, Gulf, Gurge, Maelstrom, Moulin, Swelchie, Vorago, Vortex, Weel, Wiel

Whirlwind Cyclone, Dust devil, Eddy, Tornado, Tourbillion, Typho(o)n, Vortex, Willy-willy

Whirr Birr

Whisk(e)y Alcohol, Bond, Bourbon, Canadian, Cape smoke, Corn, Creature, Fife, Fire-water, Grain, Hard stuff, Hoo(t)ch, Irish, Malt, Moonshine, Morning, Mountain dew, Nip, Peat-reek, Pot(h)een, Red eye, Rye, Scotch, Southern Comfort®, Tun, Usquebaugh, W

Whisker(s) Beard, Beater, Bristles, Burnsides, Cat's, Dundreary, Excrement, Face fungus, Hackle, Hair, Moustache, Mutton-chop, Samuel, Side(-boards), Side-burns, Sidelevers, Stibble, Stubble, Vibrissa

▷**Whisky** *may indicate* an anagram

Whisper Breath(e), Bur(r), Hark, Hint, Innuendo, Murmur, Pig's, Round, Rumour, Rustle, Sigh, Stage, Susurrus, Tittle, Undertone, Whittie-whattie

Whistle(r) Blow, Calliope, Catcall, Feedback, Flute, Hewgh, Hiss, Marmot, Pedro, Penny, Phew, Ping, Pipe, Quail-pipe, Ref, Siffle(ur), Sowf(f), Sowth, Steam, Stop, Stridor, Swab(ber), Swanee, Tin, Toot, Tweedle, Tweet, Warbler, Wheeple, Wheugh, Whew, Wolf

Whistle-blower Informer, Nark, Ref

White(n), Whitener, Whiteness, White-faced Agene, Agenise, Alabaster, Albedo, Albescent, Albino, Albumen, Argent, Ashen, Au lit, Blameless, Blanch, Blanche, Blanco, Bleach, Buckra, Cabbage, Calm, Cam, Camstone, Candid, Candida, Candour, Canescent, Canities, Caucasian, Chalk(y), Chardonnay, Chaste, China, Chinese, Christmas, Cliffs, Collar, Company, Cream, Cue ball, Egg, Elephant, Ermine, European, Fang, Fard, Feather, Flag, Flake, French, Glair, Gwen(da), Gwendolen, Gwyn, Hawked, Hoar(y), Hock, Honorary, Hore, House, Innocent, Ivory, Large, Leucoma, Lie, Lily, Livid, Man, Marbled, Mealy, Opal, Oyster, Pale(face), Pallor, Paper, Paris, Pearl(y), Poor, Pure, Redleg, Russian, Sclerotic, Sheep, Silver, Small, Snow(y), Spanish, Taw, Wan, Wedding, Wyn, Zinc

White man Ba(c)kra, Buckra, Caucasian, Corn-cracker, Cracka, Gora, Gub(bah),

Haole, Honkie, Honky, Larney, Mzungu, Norteno, Occidental, Ofay, Pakeha, Paleface, Redleg, Redneck, WASP, Wigga, Wigger

Who knows Quien sabe

Whole, Wholehearted, Wholeness, Wholly All, Cosmos, Eager, Entire(ty), Entity, Every inch, Fully, Hale, Intact, Integer, Integrity, Largely, Lot, Shebang, Sum, Systemic, Thoroughly, Total, Tout à fait, Unbroken, Uncut

Wholesale(r) Cutprice, En bloc, Engrosser, Ingross, Jobber, Stockjobber, Sweeping

Whoop(er), Whooping cough Alew, Celebrate, Chincough, Crane, Cry, Excite, Kink(cough), Kink-host, Pertussis, Swan

Whopper, Whopping Barn, Crammer, Huge, Immense, Jumbo, Lie, Lig, Oner, Out and outer, Plumper, Scrouger, Slapper, Slockdolager, Soc(k)dalager, Soc(k)dolager, Soc(k)doliger, Soc(k)dologer, Sogdolager, Sogdoliger, Sogdologer, Tale, Taradiddle

Whore Drab, Harlot, Loose woman, Pinnace, Pro, Prostitute, Quail, Road, Strumpet, Tart

▷ **Wicked** *may indicate* containing a wick

Wicked(ness) Atrocity, →**BAD**, Candle, Criminal, Cru(i)sie, Crusy, Depravity, Devilish, Evil, Goaty, Godless, Heinous, Immoral, Impious, Improbity, Iniquity, Lantern, Miscreant, Naughty, Nefarious, Night-light, Pernicious, Perverse, Pravity, Rush, Satanic, Scelerate, Sin(ful), Taper, Turpitude, Unholy, Vile

Wicket Gate, Hatch, Maiden, Pitch, Square, Sticky, Stool, Stump, W, Yate

Wide, Widen(ing), Width Abroad, Ample, Bay, Braid, Broad, Comprehensive, Dilate, Drib, Eclectic, Expand, Extend, Far, Flanch, Flange, Flare, Flaunch, Ga(u)ge, General, Miss, Prevalent, Roomy, Set, Spacious, Span, Spread, Sundry, Sweeping, Vast

Widespread Diffuse, Epidemic, Extensive, General, Pandemic, Panoramic, Pervasive, Prevalent, Prolate, Routh(ie), Sweeping, Universal

Widow(ed) Black, Dame, Discovert, Dowager, Golf, Grass, Jointress, Relict, Sati, Sneerwell, Suttee, Vidual, Viduous, Whydah-bird, Widdy

Wife, Wives Ball and chain, Better half, Bride, Concubine, Consort, Devi, Dutch, Enid, Evadne, Feme, Feme covert, Frau, Goody, Haram, Harem, Harim, Helpmate, Helpmeet, Hen, Her indoors, Kali, Little woman, Mate, Memsahib, Missis, Missus, Mrs, Partner, Penelope, Potiphar's, Rib, Seraglio, Spouse, Squaw, Stepford, Trophy, Trouble and strife, Umfazi, Ux(or), Vrou, W, Wag

Wig Bagwig, Bob(wig), Brutus, Buzz-wig, Campaign, Carpet, Cauliflower, Caxon, Chevelure, Chide, Cockernony, Dalmahoy, Full-bottomed, Gizz, Gregorian, Hair(piece), Heare, Jas(e)y, Jizz, Major, Periwig, Peruke, Postiche, Ramil(l)ie(s), Rate, Reprimand, Rug, Scold, Scratch, Sheitel, Spencer, Syrup, Targe, Tie, Toupee, Toupet, Tour

Wild(er) Aberrant, Agitato, Agrestal, Amok, Angry, Barbarous, Berserk, Bundu, Bush, Chimeric, Crazy, Demented, Earl, Enthusiastic, Errant, Erratic, Extravagant, Farouche, Feral, Frantic, Frenetic, Gene, Haggard, Hectic, Lawless, Mad(cap), Manic, Meshugge, Myall, Natural, Outlaw, Rampant, Raver, Riotous, Romantic, →**SAVAGE**, Skimble-skamble, Tearaway, Unmanageable, Unruly, Violent, Warrigal, West, Woolly

▷ **Wild(ly)** *may indicate* an anagram

Wilde Marty, Oscar

Wile, Wily Art, Artful, Artifice, Astute, Braide, →**CUNNING**, Deceit, Foxy, Peery, Ruse, Shifty, Shrewd, Slee, →**SLY**, Spider, Stratagem, Streetwise, Subtle, Trick, Versute, Wide

Wilful Deliberate, Headstrong, Heady, Obstinate, Recalcitrant, Wayward

Will, Willing(ly) Alsoon, Amenable, Bard, Bequeath, Bewildered, Biddable, Bill(y), Can do, Complaisant, Compliant, Conation, Content, Desire, Devise, Fain, Force, Free, Game, General, Hay, Holographic, Leave, Legator, Leve, Lief, Lieve, Living, Mind, Nerve, Noncupative, Obedient, On, Open, Pacable, Please, Prone, Purpose, Raring, Rather, Ready, Receptive, Resolution, Scarlet, Soon, Spirit, Swan, Testament, Testate, Thelma, Volens, Volition, Voluntary, Volunteer, Way, Wimble, Woot

▷ **Will** *may indicate* an anagram

William(s) Bill(y), Conqueror, Occam, Orange, Pear, Rufus, Silent, Sweet, Tell, Tennessee

Willow(ing), Willowy Arctic, Crack, Lissom(e), Lithe, Osier, Poplar, Pussy, Sale, Salix, Sallow, Sauch, Saugh, Seal, Supple, Twilly, Weeping, Withy

▶ **Wily** *see* **WILE**

Wimp(ish) Drip, Mouse, Namby-pamby, Pantywaist, Saddo, Weed

▷ **Wimple** *may indicate* an anagram

Win(ner), Winning Achieve, Acquire, Adorable, Ahead, Appealing, Backgammon, Bangster, Banker, →**BEAT**, Capot, Carry off, Cert, Champion, Conciliate, Conquer, Cup, Cute, Decider, Disarming, Dividend, Dormie, Dormy, Earn, Effect, Endearing, Engaging, First, Gain, Gammon, Grand slam, Hit, Jackpot, Land, Laureate, Lead, Luck out, Medallist, Motser, Motza, Nap hand, Nice, On a roll, Pile, Pot, Prevail, Profit, Purler, Reap, Repique, Result, Rubicon, Scoop, Shoo-in, Slam, Snip, Success, Sweet, Take, Top dog, →**TRIUMPH**, Up, Vellet, Velvet, Victor(y), Vole, Walk over, Wrest, Yellow jersey, Yokozuna

Wind(er), Winding(s), Windy Air, Airstream, Anfractuous, Backing, Bend, Blow, Bottom, Brass, Burp, Capstan, Chill, Coil, Colic, Crank, Creeky, Curl, Curve, Draught, Draw, Entwist, Evagation, Fearful, Flatulence, Flatus, Flaw, Gas, Gust, Meander, Nervous, Periodic, Ponent, Poop, Prevailing, Purl, Quarter, Quill, Reeds, Reel, Roll, Screw, Sea, Second, Series, Serpentine, Serpentize, Sinuous, Slant, Snake, Spiral, Spool, Surface, Swirl, Tail, Thread, Throw, Tortuous, Trade, Trend, Turn, Twaddle, Twine, Twisty, Veer, Veering, Ventose, Waffle, Weave, Wiggle, Winch, Windle, Winnle, Wrap, Wreathe, Wrest

Window(s) Atmosphere, Bay, Bow, Casement, Catherine-wheel, Companion, Compass, Day, Deadlight, Dormer, Double-hung, Dream-hole, Entry, Eye, Eyelids, Fanlight, Fenestella, Fenestra, French, Gable, Garret, Glaze, Guichet, Jalousie, Jesse, Judas, Jut, Lancet, Lattice, Launch, Loop-light, Louver, Louvre, Lozen, Lucarne, Lunette, Luthern, Lychnoscope, Marigold, Mezzanine, Mirador, Monial, Mullion, Oculus, Oeil-de-boeuf, Ogive, Opportunity, Orb, Oriel, Ox-eye, Pane, Pede, Picture, Pop-under, Pop-up, Porthole, Program, Quarterlight, Radio, Re-entry, Rosace, Rose, Round, Sash, Sexfoil, Shed dormer, Shop, Shot, Spyhole, Storm, Transom, Trellis, Ventana, Weather, Wheel, Wicket, Windock, Windore, Winnock

Window-bar, Window-fastening Astragal, Espagnolette

Windsor Castle, Knot

Wine Bin, Blush, Cabinet, Case, Cup, Cuvée, Doc, Espumoso, Essence, Fortified, Grand cru, Low, Must, Piece, Pigment, Premier cru, Prisage, Rotgut, Rouge, Semi-dry, Sparkling, Steen, Tannin, Terroir, The grape, Tirage, Unoaked, Varietal, Vat, Vintage, Zymurgy

Wing(s), Winged, Winger, Wing-like Aerofoil, Ala(r), Alula, Annexe, Appendage, Arm, Bastard, →**BIRD**, Branch, Buffalo, Canard, Cellar, Corium, Coulisse, Delta, Dipteral, El(l), Elevon, Elytral, Elytriform, Elytron, Elytrum, Fan, Fender, Flap, Flew, Flipper, Forward, Halteres, Hurt, Left, Limb, Offstage, Parascenia, Parascenium, Patagium, Pennate, Pennon, Pinero, Pinion, Pip, Pterygoid, Putto, Right, Rogallo, Sail, Satyrid, Scent-scale, Segreant, Seraphim, Sweepback, Sweptback, Sweptwing, Swift, Swingwing, Tailplane, Tectrix, Tegmen, Tormentor, Transept, Van, Vol(et), Water, Wound(ed)

▷ **Winger** *may indicate* a bird

Wink (at) Bat, Condone, Connive, Flicker, Ignore, Instant, Nap, Nictitate, Pink, Twinkle

Winnow Fan, Riddle, Separate, Sift, Van, Wecht

Winter, Wintry Bleak, Brumal, Cold, Dec, Fimbul, Frigid, Frore, Hibernate, Hiemal, Hiems, Hodiernal, Jasmine, Nuclear, Shrovetide, Snowy, Subniveal

Wipe (out), Wiping Abolish, Abrogate, Absterge, Amortise, Cancel, Cleanse, Demolish, Destroy, Deterge, Dicht, Dight, Efface, Erase, Expunge, Forget, Hanky, Mop, Nose-rag, Null, Purge, Raze, Sponge, Tersion, Tissue

Wire(s), Wiry Aerial, Barb(ed), Cable, Cat's whiskers, Chicken, Coil, Earth, Element,

Fencing, Filament, Filar, File, Heald, Heddle, High, In on, Kirschner, Lead, Lean, Lecher, Live, Marconigram, Messenger, Mil, Nichrome®, Nipper, Number eight, Piano, Pickpocket, Razor, Sevice, Shroud, Sinewy, Snake, Solenoid, Spit, Staple, Stilet, Strand, String, Stylet, Telegram, Telegraph, Thoth, Thread, Trace, Trip

Wise(acre), Wisdom Advisedly, Athena, Athene, Canny, Conventional, Cracker barrel, Depth, Ernie, Gothamite, Gudrun, Hep, Hindsight, Judgement, Learned, Long-headed, Lore, Manner, Mimir, Minerva, Norman, Oracle, Owl, Pearl, Philosopher, Philosophy, Politic, Polymath, Prajna, Profound, Prudence, Sagacity, Sage, Salomonic, Sapience, Savvy, Shrewd, Smartie, Solon, Sophia, Tooth, Wice

Wise man Balthazar, Caspar, Gaspar, Hakam, Heptad, Melchior, Nestor, Pandit, Sage, Sapient, Seer, Solomon, Swami, Thales, Worldly

Wish(es), Wishing Ache, Ake, Covet, Crave, Death, Desiderate, → DESIRE, Envy, For, Hope, Itch, List, Long, Nill, Pleasure, Pray, Precatory, Regards, RIP, Velleity, Want, Yearn

Wistful Elegiac

Wit(s), Witticism, Witty Acumen, Attic, Badinage, Banter, Bon mot, Brevity, Commonsense, Concetto, Cunning, Dry, Epigram, Esprit, Estimation, Eutrapelia, Eutrapely, Facetious, Fantasy, Gnome, Hartford, Horse sense, Humour, Imagination, Intelligence, Irony, Jest, Jeu d'esprit, Joke, Marbles, Marinism, Memory, Mind, Mot, Mother, Native, Nous, Oscar Wilde, Pawky, Pun, Quipster, Repartee, Rogue, Sally, Salt, Saut, Sconce, → SENSE, Shaft, Smart, Sparkle, Videlicet, Viz, Wag, Weet, Wisecrack, Word-play

Witch(craft) Beldam(e), Besom-rider, Broomstick, Cantrip, Carline, Circe, Coven, Craigfluke, Crone, Cutty Sark, Diabolism, Ensorcell, Galdragon, Glamour, Goety, Gramary(e), Gyre-carlin, Hag, Hecat(e), Hex, Lamia, Magic, Medea, Myal(ism), Night-hag, Obeahism, Obia, Obiism, Pishogue, Pythoness, Salem, Selim, Sibyl, Sieve, Sorceress, Speller, Sycorax, Trout, Valkyrie, Vaudoo, Vilia, Voodoo, Water, Weird, Wicca, Wise woman

With And, By, Con, Cum, Hereby, In, Mit, Of, W

Withdraw(al), Withdrawn Abdicate, Alienate, Aloof, Back out, Breakaway, Cloistered, Cold turkey, Cry off, Detach, Disengage, Distrait, Enshell, Evacuate, Hive off, Inshell, Introvert, Leave, Offish, Palinode, Phantom, Precede, Preserve, Recant, Recoil, Repair, Rescind, Resile, Reticent, Retire, Retract(ion), Retreat, Revoke, Revulsion, Scratch, Secede, Secesh, Sequester, Shrink, Shy, Stand down, Subduce, Subduct, Unreeve, Unsay

Wither(ed), Withering, Withers Arefy, Atrophy, Burn, Corky, Die, Droop, Dry, Evanish, Fade, Forpine, Gizzen, Googie, Languish, Marcescent, Miff, Nose, Scram, Sere, Shrink, Shrivel, Welk, Welt

▷ **With gaucherie** *may indicate* an anagram

Withhold(ing), Withheld Abstain, Conceal, Curt, Deny, Detain, Detinue, Hide, Keep, → RESERVE, Ritenuto, Trover

Within Enclosed, Endo-, Immanent, Indoors, Inside, Interior, Intra

Without Bar, Beyond, Ex, Lack(ing), Less, Minus, Orb, Outdoors, Outside, Sans, Save, Sen, Senza, Sine, X

▷ **Without** *may indicate* one word surrounding another

▷ **Without restraint** *may indicate* an anagram

Witless Crass, → STUPID PERSON

Witness Attend, Attest, Bystander, Catch, Character, Confirm, Deponent, Depose, Endorse, Evidence, Experience, Expert, Eye, Glimpse, Hostile, Jehovah's, Mark, Martyr, Material, Muggletonian, Note, Notice, Observe, Obtest, Onlooker, Perceive, Proof, → SEE, Show, Sight, Sign, Spy, Stander-by, Survey, Testament, Teste, Testify, Testimony, View, Vouchee, Watch

▶ **Witticism** *see* WIT(S)

Wizard (priest) Archimage, Awesome, Carpathian, Conjuror, Demon, Expert, Gandalf, Hex, Mage, Magician, Merlin, Obiman, Oz, Prospero, Shaman, Sorcerer, Super, Warlock

Wobble, Wobbling, Wobbly Chandler's, Coggle, Hissy fit, Precess, Quaver, Rock, Shimmy, Shoggle, Shoogle, Teeter, Totter, Tremble, Trillo, Wag, Waggle, Walty, Waver

Woe(ful), Woebegone Agony, Alack, Alas, Bale, Bane, Distress, Dool(e), Dule, Ewhow, Execrable, Gram, Grief, Hurt, Jeremiad, Lack-a-day, Misery, Pain, Plague, →**SORROW**, Tribulation, Triste, Wailful

Wolds Lincoln(shire), Yorkshire

Wolf(ish), Wolf-like Akela, Assyrian, Bolt, Cancer, Carcajou, Casanova, Coyote, Cram, Dangler, Dasyure, Dire, Earth, Engorge, Fenrir, Fenris, Gorge, Grey, Ise(n)grim, Lobo, Lone, Lothario, Lupine, Luster, Lycanthrope, MI, Michigan, Pack, Prairie, Rake, Ravenous, Red, Rip, Roué, Rout, Rudolph, Rye, Scoff, Sea, Seducer, Strand, Tasmanian, Thylacine, Tiger, Timber, Wanderer, Were, Whistler

Woman(hood), Women Aguna(h), Anile, Beldam(e), Besom, Biddy, Bimbo, Bint, Bit, Boiler, Broad, Callet, Chai, Chap(p)ess, Chook, Cotquean, Crone, Crumpet, Cummer, Dame, Daughter, Distaff, Doe, Dona(h), Dorcas, Doris, Drab, Duenna, Eve, F, Fair, Fair sex, →**FEMALE**, Feme, Femme fatale, Flapper, Floozy, Frail, Frow, Gammer(stang), Gin, Girl, Gyno-, -gyny, Harpy, Harridan, Hausfrau, Hen, Her, Ho, Housewife, Inner, It, Jade, Jane, Kloo(t)chman, Lady, Liberated, Lilith, Lorette, Madam(e), Mademoiselle, Mary, Miladi, Milady, Millie, Minge, Mob, Mort, Ms, Painted, Pandora, Peat, Pict, Piece, Piece of goods, Placket, Point, Popsy, Puna(a)ni, Puna(a)ny, Pussy, Quean, Queen, Ramp, Rib, Ribibe, Rudas, Runnion, Sabine, Scarlet, Shawlay, Shawlie, She, Skirt, Sloane Ranger, Sort, Squaw, Tail, Tib, Tiring, Tit, Tottie, Totty, Trot, Wahine, Weaker sex, Wifie, Zena

Wonder(s) Admire, Agape, Amazement, AR, Arkansas, Arrah, Awe, Chinless, Colossus, Ferly, Grape-seed, Hanging Gardens, Marle, →**MARVEL**, Mausoleum, Meteor, Mirabilia, Miracle, Muse, Nine-day, Pharos, Phenomenon, Prodigy, Pyramids, Speculate, Statue of Zeus, Stupor, Suppose, Surprise, Temple of Artemis, Thaumatrope, Wheugh, Whew, Wow(ee)

Wonderful(ly) Amazing, Bees' knees, Bitchin(g), Chinless, Divine, Épatant, Fantastic, Far-out, Ferly, Geason, Gee-whiz, Glorious, Gramercy, Great, Heavenly, Lal(l)apalooza, Magic, Mirable, Must-see, Old, Purely, Ripping, Smashing, Stellar, Sublime, Wicked

▷ **Wood** *may indicate* an anagram in sense of mad

Wood(s), Wooden, Woodland, Woody Arboretum, Batten, Beam, Birken, Board, Boord(e), Bough, Brake, Cask, Channel, Chipboard, Chuck, Chump, Clapboard, Conductor, Dead, Deadpan, Expressionless, Fardage, Fathom, Fire, Fish, Funk, Furious, Gantry, Gauntree, Guthrie, Hanger, Hard, Hyle, Kindling, Knee, Krummholz, Late, Lath, Lumber, Mad, Magnetic, Miombo, Nemoral, Nemorous, Offcut, Pallet, Pulp(wood), Punk, Silvan, Slat, Spinney, Splat, Spline, Splint, Stolid, Sylvan, Tenon, Three-ply, Timber, Tinder, Touch, Treen, Trees, Twiggy, Vert, Xylem, Xyloid

Woodpecker Bird, Flicker, Hairy, Hickwall, Picalet, Picarian, Pileated, Rainbird, Sapsucker, Saurognathae, Witwall, Woodspite, Woodwale, Woody, Yaffle

Woodwind Bassoon, Clarinet, Cornet, Flute, Oboe, Piccolo, Pipe, Recorder, Reed

Wool(len), Woolly (haired) Alpaca, Angora, Aran, Beige, Berlin, Botany, Bouclé, Cardi(gan), Cashmere, Clean, Clip, Combings, Cotton, Dog, Doily, Down, Doyley, Drugget, Duffel, Fadge, Fingering, Fleece, Flock, Fuzz, Glass, Guernsey, Hank, Heather mixture, Jaeger, Jersey, Kashmir, Ket, Lanate, Lock, Merino, Mineral, Noil(s), Offsorts, Oo, Paco, Pashm, Pelage, Persian, Pine, Rock, Say, Shetland, Shoddy, Skein, Skin, Slag, Slipe, Slip-on, Slub, Smart, Spencer, Staple, Steel, Stuff, Swansdown, Tammy, Telltale, Three-ply, Tod, Tricot, Tweed, Ulotrichous, Vicuña, Virgin, Wire, Yarn

Word(s), Wording, Wordy Al(l)-to, Aside, Buzz, Cataphor(a), Catch, Cheville, Claptrap, Clipped, Clitic, Code, Comment, Content, Dick, Dit(t), Echoic, Effable, Embolalia, Epitaph, Epithet, Epos, Etymon, Faith, Four-letter, Function, Functor, Ghost, Grace, Hapax legomenon, Hard, Heteronym, Hint, Holophrase, Homograph, Homonym, Horseman's, Household, →**IN A WORD**, →**IN TWO WORDS**, Janus, Jonah, Key, Last, Lexeme, Lexicon, Lexis, Loan, Logia, Logos, Long-winded, Lyrics, Mantra, Meronym, Message, Mot, Neologism, News, Nonce, Nonsense, Noun, Om,

Operative, Oracle, Order, Palabra, Paragram, Paranym, Parenthesis, Parlance, Parole, Paronym, Particle, Peristomenon, Phrase, Piano, Pledge, Pleonasm, Polysemen, Portmanteau, Preposition, Prolix, Promise, Pronoun, Reserved, Rhyme, Rumbelow, Rumour, Saying, Semantics, Signal, Soundbite, Subtitle, Surtitle, Syntagma, Talkative, Tatpurusha, Term, Tetragram, Text, Trigger, Trope, Typewriter, Verb, Verbiage, Verbose, Vocab(ulary), Vogue, Warcry, Weasel, Winged, Written

Wordsmith Logodaedalus

▷ **Work** *may indicate* a book or play, etc

Workaholic, Work(er), Working(-class), Workmen, Works, Workman(ship) Act(ivate), Aga saga, Ant, Application, Appliqué, Apronman, Artefact, Artel, Artifact, Artificer, Artisan, At it, At task, Barmaid, Beamer, Beaver, Bee, Blue-collar, Blue-singlet, Bohunk, Boon(er), Brief, Bull, Business, Busy, Careerist, Casual, Char, Chare, Chargehand, Chigga, Chippy, Chore, Claim, Clock, Colon, Community, Contingent, Coolie, Cooly, Corvée, Craftsman, Crew, Cultivate, Dig, Do, Dog, Dogsbody, Donkey, Draft-mule, Drudge, Drug, Earn, Effect, Effort, Em, Ergon, Ergonomics, Eta, Everything, Evince, Exercise, Exergy, Exploit, Factotum, Facture, Fast, Fat, Fettler, Field, Flex(i)time, Fret, Fuller, →**FUNCTION**, Gae, Gel, Girl Friday, Go, Graft, Grass, Grind, Grunt, Guest, Hand, Harness, Hat, Hobo, Horse, Hot-desking, Hunky, Indian, Industry, Innards, Jackal, Job, Journeyman, Key, Knead, Knowledge, Labour, Laid, Leave, Luddite, Lump, Machinist, Maid, Man, Manipulate, Manpower, McJob, Mechanic(ian), Menge, Menial, Midinette, Mine, Ming, MO, Moil, Moonlight, Movement, Navvy, Neuter, Number, Oeuvre, On, Op, Opera(tion), Operative, Operator, Opus, Outreach, Outside, Ouvrier, Ox, Part, Passage, Peasant, Peg, Pensum, Peon, Pink-collar, Plasterer, Ply, Poker, Portfolio, Postlude, Potboiler, Practicum, Practise, Production, Prole(tariat), Public, Pursuit, Red-neck, Reduction, Rep, Ride, Robot, Rotovate, Roughneck, Round, Rouseabout, Roustabout, Run, Salaryman, Sandhog, Satisfactory, Scabble, Serve, Service, Servile, Seven, Sewage, Shift, Shop (floor), Situation, Skanger, Slogger, Smithy, Social, Soldier, Spiderman, Staff, Stagehand, Stevedore, Stint, Strap, Straw, Strive, Support, Surface, Swaggie, Swagman, Sweat, Swink, Take, Tamper, Task, Team, Technician, Telecommuter, Temp, Tenail(le), Termite, Tew, Text, Tick, Till, Toccata, Toil, Travail, Treatise, Trojan, TU, TUC, Turk, Tut, Tutman, Uphill, Walla(h), Welfare, White-collar, Yarco

▷ **Working** *may indicate* an anagram

Works, Workplace, Workshop Atelier, Engine, Factory, Forge, Foundry, Garage, Hacienda, Hangar, Innards, Lab, Mill, Passage, Plant, Public, Shed, Sheltered, Shipyard, Shop, Skylab, Smithy, Studio, Study, Sweatshop, Telecottage, Time, Tin, Turnery, Upper

World(ly), Worldwide Adland, Carnal, Chthonic, Cosmopolitan, Cosmos, Cyberspace, Dream, Earth, First, Fleshly, Fourth, Free, Ge, Global village, Globe, Kingdom, Lay, Lower, Mappemond, Meatspace, Microcosm, Midgard, Mondaine, Mondial, Mould, Mundane, Natural, Nether, New, Old, Orb, Other, Oyster, Planet, Possible, Second, Secular, Sensual, Small, Society, Sphere, Spirit, Temporal, Terra, Terrene, Terrestrial, Third, Universe, Vale, Web, Welt, Whole

Worm(-like), Worms, Wormy Acorn, Angle, Anguillula, Annelid, Annulata, Apod(e), Apodous, Army, Arrow, Articulata, Ascarid, Bilharzia, Bladder, Blind, Blood, Bob, Bootlace, Brandling, Bristle, Caddis, Capeworm, Caseworm, Catworm, Cercaria, Cestode, Cestoid, Chaetopod, Clamworm, Copper, Dew, Diet, Diplozoon, Dracunculus, Edge, Enteropneust, Fan, Filander, Filaria, Flag, Flat, Flesh, Fluke, Galley, Gape, Gilt-tail, Gordius, Gourd, Gru-gru, Guinea, Hair, Hair-eel, Hairworm, Heartworm, Helminth, Hemichordata, Hookworm, Horsehair, Idle, Inchworm, Leech, Liver-fluke, Lob, Lumbricus, Lytta, Maw, Measuring, Merosome, Miner's, Mopani, Muck, Nemathelminthes, Nematoda, Nematode, Nematodirus, Nematomorpha, Nemertean, Nemertina, Nereid, Night-crawler, Oligochaete, Onychophoran, Paddle, Palmer, Palolo, Paste-eel, Peripatus, Phoronid, Pile, Pin, Piper, Planarian, Platyhelminth, Polychaete, Ragworm, Redia, Ribbon, Rootworm, Roundworm, Sabella, Sand mason, Schistosome, Scoleciform, Scolex, Screw, Seamouse, Serpula, Servile, Ship, Sipunculacea, Sipunculoidea, Spiny-headed, Stomach,

Strawworm, Strongyl(e), Taenia, Tag-tail, Taint, Tapeworm, Tenioid, Teredo, Termite, Threadworm, Tiger, Tiger tail, Tongue, Toxocara, Trematode, Trichin(ell)a, Trichinosed, Triclad, Tube, Tubifex, Turbellaria, Vermiform, Vinegar, Vinegar eel, Wheat-eel, Wheatworm, Whipworm

Worn (out) Attrite, Bare, Decrepit, Detrition, Effete, Épuisé, Exhausted, Forfairn, Forfoughten, Forjaskit, Forjeskit, Frazzled, Gnawn, Old, On, Passé, Raddled, Rag, Seedy, Shabby, Shopsoiled, Shot, Spent, Stale, Tatty, Threadbare, Tired, Traikit, Trite, Used, Weathered, Whacked

Worried, Worrier, Worry Agonise, Annoy, Anxiety, Badger, Bait, Beset, Bother, Brood, Burden, Care(worn), Cark, Chafe, Concern, Consternate, Deave, Deeve, Distress, Disturb, Dog, Eat, Exercise, Faze, Feeze, Frab, Fret, Fuss, Gnaw, Harass, Harry, Hyp, Inquietude, Knag, Nag, Niggle, Perturb, Pester, Pheese, Pheeze, Phese, Pingle, Pium, Rattle, Rile, Sool, Stew, Tew, Touse, Towse, Trouble, Vex, Wherrit, Worn

▷ **Worried** *may indicate* an anagram

Worse(n) Adversely, Compound, Degenerate, Deteriorate, Exacerbate, Impair, Inflame, Pejorate, Regress, Relapse, War(re), Waur, Well away

Worship(per) Adore, Adulation, Ancestor, Angelolatry, Aniconism, Animist, Autolatry, Bardolatry, Bless, Churchgoer, Cosmolatry, Cult, Deify, Devotion, Dote, Douleia, Doxology, Dulia, Epeolatry, Exalt, Exercise, Fetish, Glorify, Gurdwara, Happy-clappy, Henotheism, Hero, Ibadah, Iconology, Idolatry, Idolise, Latria, Lauds, Lionise, Liturgics, Lordolatry, Mariolatry, Meeting-house, Monolatry, Oncer, Orant, Praise, Puja, Revere, Sabaism, Sakta, Service, Shacharis, Shakta, Sun, Synaxis, Thiasus, Vaishnava, Venerate, Votary, Wodenism

Worst Beat, Best, Defeat, Get, Less, Nadir, Outdo, Overpower, Pessimum, Rock-bottom, Scum, Severest, Throw, Trounce

Worsted Caddis, Caddyss, Challis, Coburg, Crewel, Genappe, Lea, Ley, Serge, Shalli, Tamin(e), Whipcord

▷ **Worsted** *may indicate* an anagram

Worth(while), Worthy, Worthies Admirable, Asset, Be, Cop, Cost effective, Deserving, Eligible, Estimable, Face value, Feck, →**MERIT**, Notable, Substance, Tanti, Use, Value, Vertu, Virtu(e), Virtuous, Wealth

Worthless (person) Average, Base, Beggarly, Bilge, Blown, Bodger, Bootless, Bum, Candy floss, Catchpenny, Cheapjack, Crumb, Cypher, Damn, Despicable, Doit, Dreck, Dross, Duff, Ephemeron, Fallal, Frippery, Gimcrack, Gingerbread, Gubbins, Hilding, Jimcrack, Knick-knack, Left, Light, Mauvais sujet, Mud, Nugatory, Nyaff, Obol, Ornery, Orra, Otiose, Pabulum, Paltry, Pin, Poxy, Punk, Raca, Rag, Rap, Razoo, Riffraff, Rubbishy, Scabby, Scrote, Scum, Shotten, Siwash, Sorry, Straw, Tawdry, Tinhorn, Tinpot, Tinsel, Tittle, Toerag, Trangam, Trashy, Tripy, Trumpery, Tuppenny, Twat, Two-bit, Twopenny, Useless, Vain, Vile, Zero

Wound(ed) Battery, Bite, Bless, Blighty, Bruise, Chagrin, Coiled, Crepance, Cut, Dere, Dunt, Engore, Entry, Exit, Ganch, Gash, Gaunch, Gore, Harm, Hurt, Injury, Knee, Lacerate, Lesion, Maim, Maul, Molest, Mortify, Offend, Pip, Sabre-cut, Scab, Scar, Scath, Scotch, Scratch, Shoot, Snaked, Snub, Sore, Stab, Sting, Trauma, Twined, Umbrage, Vuln, Vulnerary, Walking, Wing, Wint

Woundwort Clown's, Marsh

Wrangle(r), Wrangling Altercate, Argie-bargie, →**ARGUE**, Bandy, Bicker, Brangle, Broil, Cample, Controvert, Dispute, Haggle, Horse, Mathematical, Rag, Vitilitigation

Wrap(per), Wrapped, Wrapping, Wraparound, Wrap up Amice, Amis, Bag, Bathrobe, Bind, Boa, Bubble, Bundle, Carton(age), Cellophane®, Cere, Clingfilm, Cloak, Clothe, Cocoon, Conclude, Cover-up, Drape, Emboss, Enfold, Enrol(l), Ensheath(e), Envelop(e), Enwind, Foil, Folio, Furl, Gladwrap®, Hap, Hem, Infold, Kimono, Kraft, Lag, Lap, Mail, Muffle, Negligee, Outsert, Package, Parcel, Plastic, Roll, Rug, Shawl, Sheath(e), Sheet, Shrink, Shroud, Stole, Swaddle, Swathe, Tinfoil, Tsutsumu, Velamen, Wap, Wimple

Wreath(e) Adorn, Anadem, Chaplet, Civic crown, Coronal, Crown, Entwine, Festoon, Garland, Laurel, Lei, Steven, Torse, Tortile, Twist

Wreck(age), Wrecked, Wrecker Banjax, Blight, Crab, Debris, Demolish, Devastate, Flotsam, Founder, Goner, Hesperus, Hulk, Lagan, Ligan, Luddite, Mutilate, Ruin(ate), Sabotage, Saboteur, Shambles, Shatter, Sink, Smash, Spif(f)licate, Stramash, Subvert, Torpedo, Trash, Vandalise, Wrack

▷ **Wrecked** *may indicate* an anagram

Wrench Allen, Fit, Jerk, Lug, Mole, Monkey, Nut, Pin, Pull, Screw, Socket, Spanner, Sprain, Stillson®, Strain, Tear, Twist, Windlass, Wrest

Wrestle(r), Wrestling All-in, Arm, Backbreaker, Basho, Bearhug, Bodycheck, Boston crab, Catchweight, Clinch, Clothes line, Cross buttock, Cross press, Featherweight, Flying mare, Forearm smash, Freestyle, Full-nelson, Grapple, Gr(a)eco-Roman, Grovet, Half-nelson, Hammerlock, Haystacks, Headlock, Hip-lock, →**HOLD**, Indian, Judo, Knee-drop, Milo, Monkey climb, Mud, Nelson, Niramiai, Pinfall, Posting, Sambo, Stable, Straight arm lift, Stranglehold, Struggle, Sumo, Suplex, Tag (team), Toehold, Tussle, Whip, Wristlock, Writhe

Wretch(ed) Abject, Blackguard, Blue, Caitiff, Chap-fallen, Crumb, Cullion, Cur, Darned, Forlorn, Git, Goddamned, Hapless, Ignoble, Lorn, Measly, Miscreant, Miser, Miserable, Peelgarlic, Pilgarlick, Pipsqueak, Poltroon, Poor, Punk, Rakeshame, Rascal, Rat, Scoundrel, Scroyle, Seely, Snake, Sorry, Toerag, Unblest, Waeful, Wo(e)

▷ **Wretched** *may indicate* an anagram

Wrinkle(d), Wrinkly Clue, Cockle, Corrugate, Crankle, Crease, Crepy, Crimple, Crimpy, Crinkle, Crow's-foot, Crumple, Fold, Frounce, Frown, Frumple, Furrow, Gen, Groove, Headline, Hint, Idea, Knit, Line, Lirk, Plissé, Plough, Pucker, Purse, Ridge, Rimple, Rivel, Rop(e)y, Ruck(le), Rugose, Rumple, Runkle, Seamy, Shrivel, Sulcus, Time-worn, Tip, Whelk, Wizened, Wrizled

Writ(s) Attachment, Capias, Certiorari, Cursitor, Dedimus, Devastatit, Distringas, Elegit, Fieri facias, Filacer, Habeas corpus, Holy, Injunction, Latitat, Law-burrows, Mandamus, Mittimus, Noverint, Praemunire, Process, Quare impedit, Replevin, Scirefacias, Significat, Subpoena, Summons, Supersedeas, Tolt, Venire, Warrant

Write(r), Writing Amphigory, Apocrypha, →**AUTHOR**, Automatic, Ballpoint, Bellet(t)rist, BIC®, Biographer, Biro®, Blog, Bloomsbury Group, Book-hand, Calligraphy, Causerie, Cento, Charactery, Clerk, Clinquant, Columnist, Continuity, Copperplate, Creative, Cursive, Diarist, Dissertation, Dite, Draft, Endorse, Endoss, Engross, Enrol, Epigrammatise, Epistle, →**ESSAYIST**, Expatiate, Farceur, Feudist, Fist, Form, Formulary, Freelance, Ghost, Graffiti, Graphite, Hack, Hairline, Hand, Haplography, Hieratic, Hieroglyphics, Hierology, Hiragana, Homiletics, Indite, Ink, Inkhorn-mate, Ink-jerker, Inkslinger, Inscribe, Join-hand, Jot(tings), Journalese, Journalist, Journo, Kaleyard School, Kana, Leader, Leetspeak, Lexigraphy, Lexis, Linear A, Lipogram, Littérateur, Longhand, Lucubrate, Memoirist, Mimographer, Mirror, Miscellany, Monodist, Ms(s), Nib, Notary, Notate, Novelese, →**NOVELIST**, Palaeography, Pamphleteer, Pen, Pencil, Penmanship, Penny-a-liner, Pentel®, Phrasemonger, Picture, Planchette, →**POET**, Polemic, Polygraphy, Pot-hook, Prosaist, Proser, Psychogram, Psychography, Purana, Purple patch, Quill, Rhymer, Roundhand, Sanskrit, Scenarist, Sci-fi, Score, Scratch, Scrawl, Screed, Screeve, Scribble, Scribe, Script(t), Scripture, Scrivener, Secretary, Sign, Sing, Sling-ink, Small-hand, Space, Spirit, Stichometry, Style, Stylography, Subscript, Superscribe, Sutra, Syllabary, Syllabic, Syllabism, Tantra, Text, Tractarian, Transcribe, Treatise, Type, Uncial, Varityper®, Wisdom, Wordsmith, Zend-Avesta

▷ **Writhing** *may indicate* an anagram

▷ **Wrong** *may indicate* an anagram

Wrong(ful), Wrongdoer, Wrongdoing Aggrieve, Agley, Amiss, Astray, Awry, Bad, Chout, Delict, Disservice, Err, Fallacious, False, Harm, Ill, Immoral, Improper, Incorrect, Injury, Mischief, Misconduct, Misfaring, Misintelligence, Misled, Mistake(n), Misuse, Nocent, Offbase, Offend, Pear-shaped, Peccadillo, Perpetrator, Perverse, Sin(ful), Sinner, Tort, Tortious, Transgress, Unethical, Unright, Unsuitable, Withershins, Wryly, X

Wry Askew, Contrary, Devious, Distort, Droll, Grimace, Ironic

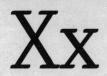

Xx

X(-shaped) Buss, By, Chi, Christ, Cross, Decussate, Drawn, Generation, Kiss, Ten, Times, Unknown, X-ray

Xenophobia Insularism

▶ **Xmas** *see* **CHRISTMAS(TIME)**

X-ray Angiogram, Arthrogram, Characteristic, Cholangiography, Emi-Scanner, Encephalogram, Encephalograph, Fermi, Grenz, Mammogram, Plate, Pyelogram, Radiogram, Radioscopy, Rem, Roentgen, Sciagram, Screening, Skiagram, Tomography, Venogram, X

Xylophone Marimba, Semantra, Sticcado, Sticcato

Yy

Yacht Britannia, Dragon, Ice, Keelboat, Ketch, Land, Maxi, Sailboat, Sand, Yngling

Yachtsman, Yachtsmen Chichester, Heath, RYS

▷ **Yank** *may indicate* an anagram

Yank(ee) Bet, Carpetbagger, Hitch, Jerk, Jonathan, Lug, Northerner, Pluck, Pull, Rug, Schlep(p), So(o)le, Sowl(e), → **TUG**, Tweak, Twitch, Wrench, Wrest, Y

Yard(s) Area, CID, Close, Court, Farm-toun, Garden, Hard, Haw, Hof, Junk, Kail, Knacker's, Main, Marshalling, Mast, Measure, Met, Navy, Patio, Poultry, Prison, Ree(d), Sail, Scotland, Show, Spar, Sprit, Steel, Stick, Stockyard, Stride, Switch, Tilt, Timber, Victualling, Y, Yd

Yarn(s) Abb, Berlin, Bouclé, Caddice, Caddis, Chenille, Clew, Clue, Cop, Cord, Crewel, Fib, Fibroline, Fingering, Genappe, Gimp, Gingham, Guimp(e), Gymp, Homespun, Jaw, Knittle, Knot, Lay, Lea, Ley, Line, Lisle, Lurex®, Marl, Merino, Nylon, Organzine, Orlon®, Ply, Rigmarole, Ripping, Saxony, Sennit, Sinnet, Skein, Small stuff, Story, Strand, Tale, Taradiddle, Thread, Thrid, Thrum(my), Tram, Twice-laid, Warp, Water twist, Weft, Woof, Wool, Worsted, Zephyr

Yawn(ing) Boredom, Chasmy, Fissure, Gant, Gape, Gaunt, Greys, Hiant, Oscitation, Pandiculation, Rictus

Year(ly), Years A, Age, Anno, Annual, Anomalistic, Astronomical, AUC, Autumn, Calendar, Canicular, Civil, Common, Cosmic, Decennium, Donkey's, Dot, Ecclesiastical, Egyptian, Embolismic, Equinoctial, Financial, Fiscal, Gap, Grade, Great, Hebrew, Holy, Indiction, Julian, Leap, Legal, Light, Locust, Lunar, Lunisolar, Natural, PA, Perfect, Platonic, Prophetic week, Riper, Sabbatical, School, Sidereal, Solar, Sothic, Spring, Summer, Sun, Tax, Theban, Time, Towmon(d), Towmont, Tropical, Twelvemonth, Vintage, Wanderjahr), Winter, Zodiac

Yearn(ing) Ache, Ake, Aspire, Brame, Burn, Covet, Crave, Curdle, Desire, Erne, Greed, Green, Grein, Hanker, Hone, → **LONG**, Lust, Nostalgia, Pant, Pine, Sigh

▷ **Yearning** *may indicate* an anagram

Yeast Barm, Bees, Brewer's, Ferment, Flor, Leaven, Saccharomycete, Torula, Vegemite®

Yellow(ish) Amber, Auburn, Back, Beige, Bisque, Bistre, Buff, Butternut, Canary, Chartreuse, Chicken, Chrome, Citrine, Clay-bank, Cowardly, Craven, Daffadowndilly, Daffodil, Eggshell, Etiolin, Fallow, Fever, Filemot, Flavin(e), Flaxen, Gamboge, Gold, Icteric, Isabel(le), Isabella, Jack, Jaundiced, King's, Lemon(y), Lurid, Luteous, Maize, Mustard, Nankeen, Naples, Oaker, Ochroid, Or(eide), Pages, Peach, Peril, Pink, Primrose, Queen's, River, Saffron, Sallow, Sand, Sear, Sherry, Spineless, Strae, Straw, Sulfur, Sulphur, Tawny, Topaz, Tow, Weld, Yolk

Yerd Inter

Yes Agreed, Ay(e), Da, I, Indeed, Ja, Jokol, Nod, OK, Oke, Quite, Sure, Truly, Uh-huh, Whoopee, Wilco, Yah, Yea, Yokul, Yup

Yesterday Démodé, Eve, Hesternal, Pridian

Yield(ing), Yielded Abandon, Afford, Bear, Bend, Bow, Breed, Capitulate, Catch, Cede, Come, Comply, Concede, Crack, Crop, Defer, Dividend, Docile, Ductile, Easy, Elastic, Facile, Flaccid, Flexible, Give, Harvest, Interest, Knock under, Knuckle, Meek, Meltith, Mess, Obtemper, Output, Pan, Pay, Pliant, Produce, Quantum, Relent, Render, Return, Sag, Soft, Squashy, → **SUBMIT**, Succumb, Supple, Surrender, Susceptible, Sustained, Temporise, Truckle, Yold

Yob Lager lout, Lout, Oaf, Ted

Yoke Bow, Cang(ue), Collar, Couple, Harness, Inspan, Jugal, Pair, Span

Yokel Boor, Bumpkin, Chaw(-bacon), Clumperton, Culchie, Hayseed, Hick, Jake, Jock, Peasant, Rustic

Yon(der) Distant, Further, O'erby, Thae, There, Thether, Thither

York(shire), Yorkshireman Batter, Bowl, Dales, Ebor, Pudding, Ridings, See, Tyke, White rose

You One, Sie, Thee, Thou, Usted, Wena, Ye

Young (person), Youngster, Youth(ful) Adolescent, Ageless, Bairn, Bev(an), Bit, Boy, Boyhood, Bub, Buckeen, Buppie, Calf-time, Ch, Charver, Chick, Chicken, Chiel, Child, Chile, Cion, Cock(erel), Cockle, Colt, Cub, Day-old, Dell, Dilling, DJ, Early, Ephebe, Ephebus, Esquire, Flapper, Fledgling, Foetus, Fox, Fry, Gigolo, Gilded, Gillet, Girl, Hebe, Hobbledehoy, Immature, Imp, Infant, Issue, Jeunesse d'orée, Junior, Juvenal, Juvenesce, Juvenile, Kid, Kiddo, Kiddy, Kipper, Lad, Lamb, Latter-day, Leaping-time, Less, Litter, Little, Middle, Minor, Misspent, Mod, Mormon, Mot, Muchacha, Nance, Narcissus, Ned(ette), Nestling, New, New Romantic, Nipper, Nurs(e)ling, Nymph, Plant, Popsy, Progeny, Protégé(e), Punk, Pup, Rude boy, Salad days, Sapling, Scent, Scion, Screenager, Shaveling, Shaver, Sien(t), Skinhead, Slip, Small, Son, Spark, Spawn, Spide, Sprig, Stripling, Subteen, Swain, Ted, Teenager, Teens, Teenybopper, Tir na n'Og, Tit, Toyboy, Waif, Well-preserved, Whelp, Whippersnapper, Widge, Wigga, Wigger, Wimp

Younger, Youngest Baby, Benjamin, Cadet, Last born, Less, Minimus, Seneca, Wallydrag, Wallydraigle, Yr

▶**Youth** *see* YOUNG PERSON

Zz

Z Izzard, Izzet, Zambia, Zebra
Zambia .zm
Zanzibar Swahili
Zap Nuke
Zeal(ous) Ardour, Bigotry, Devotion, Eager, Earnest, Enthusiasm, Evangelic, Fanatical, Fanaticism, Fervour, Fire, Hamas, Perfervid, Rabid, Study, Zest
Zealot Bigot, Crusader, Devotee, Essene, Fan(atic), St Simon, Votary
Zebu Brahmin bull, Brahmin cow
Zenith Acme, Apogee, Height, Pole, Summit, Vertex
Zephyr Breeze, Wind
Zeppelin Airship, Balloon, Dirigible
Zero Absolute, Blob, Cipher, Circle, Double, Ground, Nil, None, Nothing, Nought, O, Year, Z
Zest Condiment, Crave, Élan, Enthusiasm, Gusto, Peel, Pep, Piquancy, Relish, Spark, Spice, Tang, Taste, Zap, Zing
Zigzag Crémaillère, Crinkle-crankle, Dancette, Feather-stitch, Indent, Ric-rac, Slalom, Stagger, Tack, Traverse, Vandyke, Yaw
Zimbabwe -.zw
Zinc Blende, Gahnite, Mossy, Sherardise, Spelter, Sphalerite, Tutenag, Tutty, Willemite, Wurtzite, Zn
Zip(per) Dart, Dash, Energy, Fastener, Fly, Go, Nada, O, Oomph, Presto, Slide fastener, Stingo, Verve, Vim, Vivacity, Whirry, Zero
Zodiac(al) Aquarius, Archer, Aries, Bull, Cancer, Capricorn, Counter-glow, Crab, Fish, Gegenschein, Gemini, Goat, Horoscope, Leo, Libra, Lion, Ophiuchus, Pisces, Ram, Sagittarius, Scales, Scorpio(n), Taurus, Twins, Virgin, Virgo, Watercarrier
Zone(s) Abyssal, Anacoustic, Area, Arid, Auroral, Band, Bathyal, Belt, Benioff, Buffer, Canal, Climate, Collision, Comfort, Convergence, Crumple, Dead, Demilitarized, District, Drop, Economic, Ecotone, End, Enterprise, Erogenous, Eruv, Euro, Exclusion, Exclusive, F layer, Fracture, Free(-fire), Fresnel, Frigid, Hadal, Home, Hot, Impact, Ionopause, Krumhole, Low velocity, Mix, Neutral, No-fly, Nuclear-free, Precinct, → REGION, Rift, Ring, Russian, Sahel, Saturation, Schlieren, Sector, Shear, Skip, Smokeless, Soviet, Stratopause, Strike, Subduction, T, Temperate, Time, Tolerance, Torrid, Tundra, Twilight, Vadose, Z
Zygote Oospore